Stewart C. Myers Richard A. Brealey

Welcome to the 7th edition of *Principles of Corporate Finance.* We are proud of the success of previous editions, and we have done our best to make this edition better.

This book may be your first view of the world of modern finance. If so, you will read first for new ideas, for an understanding of how finance theory translates to practice, and occasionally, we hope, for entertainment. But eventually you will be in a position to make financial decisions, not just study them. At that point you can turn to this book as a reference and guide.

Of course finance will not stand still. Basic concepts will not change, but markets, institutions, and applications will. At some point you will want something more up-to-date on your bookshelf. We suggest the 8th and subsequent editions of this book.

McGraw-Hill / Irwin has agreed to sell the next edition of this book at half price to purchasers of this Career Edition. The only requirement is that you buy a new copy of the book and send in the enclosed card to register in the Brealey / Myers *Principles of Corporate Finance* database. You will be informed when the next edition appears and can then trade in your book for the new model.

Many purchasers of *Principles of Corporate Finance* are not new students of finance, but practicing financial managers. They too can register and receive the next edition at half price. Regardless of the reader's experience and responsibilities in finance, we are confident that this book will be a positive-NPV investment.

SOME COMMONLY USED SYMBOLS

APV	Adjusted present value
BV	Book value
C_t	Cash flow at time t
CEQ$_t$	Certainty-equivalent cash flow at time t
DIV$_t$	Dividend payment at time t
D	Market value of firm's debt
DEP$_t$	Depreciation in year t
DF$_t$	Discount factor for cash flow in period t
e	2.718 (base for natural logarithms)
E	Market value of firm's equity
EPS$_t$	Earnings per share in year t
EX	Exercise price of option
f_t	Expected return on a one-period forward loan maturing at time t
$f_{\$/£}$	Forward rate of exchange between dollars and pounds
g	Growth rate
i_t	Expected inflation in year t
IRR	Internal rate of return
LCF$_t$	Lease's cash outflow in year t
NPV	Net present value
P_t	Price at time t
PV	Present value
PVGO	Present value of growth opportunities
r_t	Expected rate of return (or cost of capital) in period t. We omit the subscript where the expected return is identical in each period. Sometimes we use a *second* subscript to define the date at which the investment is made. Thus, ${}_{t-1}r_t$ is the (spot) rate of return on an investment made at $t-1$ and paying off at time t.
$\tilde{r}_t$	Uncertain actual rate of return in period t
r_D	Expected rate of return on firm's debt
r_E	Expected rate of return on firm's equity
r_f	Risk-free interest rate
r_m	Expected rate of return on the market portfolio
$r_\$$	Dollar rate of interest
$s_{\text{SFr/\$}}$	Spot rate of exchange between Swiss francs and dollars
t	Time
$\mathbf{T}_c$	Rate of corporate income tax
$\mathbf{T}_p$	Rate of personal income tax
V	Market value of firm: $V = D + E$
y	Yield to maturity
β	Beta: A measure of market risk
δ	Delta: Hedge ratio
ρ_{12}	Rho: Correlation coefficient between investments 1 and 2
σ	Sigma: Standard deviation
σ_{12}	Covariance of investment 1 with investment 2
σ^2	Sigma squared: Variance
Σ	Capital sigma: "The sum of"

To Our Parents

ABOUT THE AUTHORS

RICHARD A. BREALEY

Emeritus Professor of Finance at the London Business School. He is the former president of the European Finance Association and a former director of the American Finance Association. He is a fellow of the British Academy and has served as a special advisor to the Governor of the Bank of England and director of a number of financial institutions. Other books written by Professor Brealey include *Introduction to Risk and Return from Common Stocks.*

STEWART C. MYERS

Gordon Y Billard Professor of Finance at MIT's Sloan School of Management. He is past president of the American Finance Association and a research associate of the National Bureau of Economic Research. His research has focused on financing decisions, valuation methods, the cost of capital, and financial aspects of government regulation of business. Dr. Myers is a director of The Brattle Group, Inc., and is active as a financial consultant.

"FINANCE IN THE NEWS" BOXES

Timely, relevant news articles from financial publications appear in several chapters throughout the text. Aimed at bringing real life to the classroom, these boxes provide insight into the business world today.

FINANCE IN THE NEWS

THE DIVIDEND CUT HEARD 'ROUND THE WORLD

On May 9, 1994, FPL Group, the parent company of Florida Power & Light Company, announced a 32 percent reduction in its quarterly dividend payout, from 62 cents per share to 42 cents. In its announcement, FPL did its best to spell out to investors why it had taken such an unusual step. It stressed that it had studied the situation carefully and that, given the prospect of increased competition in the electric utility industry, the company's

FPL's substitution of stock repurchases for dividends was also designed to increase the company's financial flexibility in preparation for a new era of heightened competition among utilities. Although much of the cash savings from the dividend cut would be returned to shareholders in the form of stock repurchases, the rest would be used to retire debt and so reduce the company's leverage ratio. This deleveraging was intended to pre-

NEW AND ENHANCED PEDAGOGY

In this edition of *Principles of Corporate Finance,* we've included several more features to help students succeed in learning the fundamental concepts of financial management.

PART INTRODUCTIONS

New introductions have been added to each part explaining links between different concepts. They include real-world examples that provide motivation for the chapters that follow.

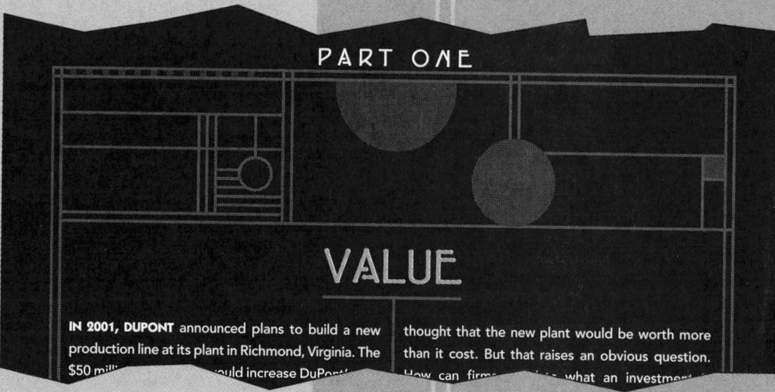
PART ONE

VALUE

IN 2001, DUPONT announced plans to build a new production line at its plant in Richmond, Virginia. The

thought that the new plant would be worth more than it cost. But that raises an obvious question.

STANDARD & POOR'S INTEGRATION

Now included in the end-of-chapter material are problems directly incorporating the Educational Version of Market Insight, a service based on Standard & Poor's renowned Compustat database. These problems provide you with an easy method of including current real-world data into your course.

STANDARD & POOR'S

16. Look up Hawaiian Electric Co. (HI) on the Standard & Poor's Market Insight website (**www.mhhe.com/edumarketinsight**). Hawaiian Electric was one of the companies in Table 4.2. That table was constructed in 2001.
    a. What is the company's dividend yield? How has it changed since 2001?
    b. Table 4.2 projected growth of 2.6 percent. How fast have the company's dividends and EPS actually grown since 2001?
    c. Calculate a sustainable growth rate for the company based on its five-year average return on equity (ROE) and plowback ratio.
    d. Given this updated information, would you modify the cost-of-equity estimate given in Table 4.2? Explain.

STANDARD & POOR'S

17. Browse through the companies in the Standard & Poor's Market Insight website (**www.mhhe.com/edumarketinsight**). Find three or four companies for which the earnings-price ratio reported on the website drastically *under*states the market capi-

EXCEL SPREADSHEET EXERCISES

New to this edition, each chapter includes several problems, noted by an icon EXCEL, that are tied to a financial analysis spreadsheet found on the Student CD that is packaged with the text. This feature allows students to enhance their knowledge and use of spreadsheets.

13. Borghia Pharmaceuticals has $1 million allocated for capital expenditures. Which of the following projects should the company accept to stay within the $1 million budget? How much does the budget limit cost the company in terms of its market value? The opportunity cost of capital for each project is 11 percent.

Project	Investment ($ thousands)	NPV ($ thousands)	IRR (%)
1	300	66	17.2
2	200	−4	10.7
3	250	43	16.6
4	100	14	12.1
5	100	7	11.8
6	350	63	18.0

MINI-CASES

To enhance the concepts discussed within a chapter, several mini-cases are included so students can apply their knowledge to typical real-world scenarios.

MINI-CASE

Vegetron's CFO Calls Again

(The first episode of this story was presented in Section 5.1.)

Later that afternoon, Vegetron's CFO bursts into your office in a state of anxious confusion. The problem, he explains, is a last-minute proposal for a change in the design of the fermentation tanks that Vegetron will build to extract hydrated zirconium from a stockpile of powdered ore. The CFO has brought a printout (Table 5.1) of the forecasted revenues, costs, income, and book rates of return for the standard, low-temperature design. Vegetron's engineers have just proposed an alternative high-temperature design that will extract most of the hydrated zirconium over a shorter period, five instead of seven years. The forecasts for the high-temperature method are given in Table 5.2.[16]

www.mhhe.com/bm7e

TABLE 5.1

Income statement and book rates of return for high-temperature ext...

	Year 1	2	3	4	5
1. Revenue	180	180	180	180	180

PART WEBSITES

In today's world the Internet provides students and instructors with a useful and powerful tool. Relevant websites are provided at the end of each part for ease in referencing the best sites for financial data and information.

PART SIX RELATED WEBSITES

The Chicago Board site contains explanations of options markets and lots of data:

www.cboe.com

There are a number of good options sites, many of which provide data and calculators for Black–Scholes values and implied standard deviations:

www.cfo.com

www.fintools.net/options/optcalc.html (very good calculators)

www.numa.com

...scentral.com

www.schaffersresearch.com/stock/calculator.asp

Two sites devoted to real options are:

www.real-options.com

www.puc-rio.br/marco.ind

Examples of journals specializing in options and other derivatives include:

www.appliederivatives.com

www.erivativesreview.com

www.futuresmag.com

GLOBAL INDEX

Because many concepts in financial management are relevant around the world, the international coverage in the text has been enhanced and updated. To make this information easier to access, a Global Index was created for this edition.

GLOBAL INDEX

PREFACE

This book describes the theory and practice of corporate finance. We hardly need to explain why financial managers should master the practical aspects of their job, but we should spell out why down-to-earth, red-blooded managers need to bother with theory.

Managers learn from experience how to cope with routine problems. But the best managers are also able to respond to change. To do this you need more than time-honored rules of thumb; you must understand *why* companies and financial markets behave the way they do. In other words, you need a *theory* of finance.

Does that sound intimidating? It shouldn't. Good theory helps you grasp what is going on in the world around you. It helps you to ask the right questions when times change and new problems must be analyzed. It also tells you what things you do *not* need to worry about. Throughout this book we show how managers use financial theory to solve practical problems.

Of course, the theory presented in this book is not perfect and complete—no theory is. There are some famous controversies in which financial economists cannot agree on what firms ought to do. We have not glossed over these controversies. We set out the main arguments for each side and tell you where we stand.

Once understood, good theory is common sense. Therefore we have tried to present it at a common-sense level, and we have avoided proofs and heavy mathematics. There are no ironclad prerequisites for reading this book except algebra and the English language. An elementary knowledge of accounting, statistics, and microeconomics is helpful, however.

CHANGES IN THE SEVENTH EDITION

This book is written for students of financial management. For many readers, it is their first look at the world of finance. Therefore in each edition we strive to make the book simpler, clearer, and more fun to read. But the book is also used as a reference and guide by practicing managers around the world. Therefore we also strive to make each new edition more comprehensive and authoritative.

We believe this edition is better for both the student and the practicing manager. Here are some of the major changes:

We have streamlined and simplified the exposition of major concepts, with special attention to Chapters 1 through 12, where the fundamental concepts of valuation, risk and return, and capital budgeting are introduced. In these chapters we cover only the most basic institutional material. At the same time we have rewritten Chapter 14 as a free-standing introduction to the nature of the corporation, to the major sources of corporate financing, and to financial markets and institutions. Some readers will turn first to Chapter 14 to see the contexts in which financial decisions are made.

We have also expanded coverage of important topics. For example, real options are now introduced in Chapter 10—you don't have to master option-pricing theory in order to grasp what real options are and why they are important. Later in the book, after Chapter 20 (Understanding Options) and Chapter 21 (Valuing Options), there is a brand-new Chapter 22 on real options, which covers valuation methods and a range of practical applications.

Other examples of expanded coverage include behavioral finance (Chapter 13) and new international evidence on the market-risk premium (Chapter 7). We have also reorganized the chapters on financial planning and working capital management. In fact we have revised and updated every chapter in the book.

This edition's international coverage is expanded and woven into the rest of the text. For example, international investment decisions are now introduced in Chapter 6, right alongside domestic investment decisions. Likewise the cost of capital for international investments is discussed in Chapter 9, and international differences in security issue procedures are reviewed in Chapter 15. Chapter 34 looks at some of the international differences in financial architecture and ownership. There is, however, a separate chapter on international risk management, which covers foreign exchange rates and markets, political risk, and the valuation of capital investments in different currencies. There is also a new international index.

The seventh edition is much more Web-friendly than the sixth. Web references are highlighted in the text, and an annotated list of useful websites has been added to each part of the book.

Of course, as every first-grader knows, it is easier to add than to subtract, but we have pruned judiciously. Some readers of the sixth edition may miss a favorite example or special topic. But new readers should find that the main themes of corporate finance come through with less clutter.

MAKING LEARNING EASIER

Each chapter of the book includes an introductory preview, a summary, and an annotated list of suggestions for further reading. There is a quick and easy quiz, a number of practice questions, and a few challenge questions. Many questions use financial data on actual companies accessible by the reader through Standard & Poor's Educational Version of Market Insight. In total there are now over a thousand end-of-chapter questions. All the questions refer to material in the same order as it occurs in the chapter. Answers to the quiz questions may be found at the end of the book, along with a glossary and tables for calculating present values and pricing options.

We have expanded and revised the mini-cases and added specific questions for each mini-case to guide the case analysis. Answers to the mini-cases are available to instructors on this book's website (**www.mhhe.com/bm7e**).

Parts 1 to 3 of the book are concerned with valuation and the investment decision, Parts 4 to 8 with long-term financing and risk management. Part 9 focuses on financial planning and short-term financial decisions. Part 10 looks at mergers and corporate control and Part 11 concludes. We realize that many teachers will prefer a different sequence of topics. Therefore, we have ensured that the text is modular, so that topics can be introduced in a variety of orders. For example, there will be no difficulty in reading the material on financial statement analysis and short-term decisions before the chapters on valuation and capital investment.

We should mention two matters of style now to prevent confusion later. First, the most important financial terms are set out in boldface type the first time they appear; less important but useful terms are given in italics. Second, most algebraic symbols representing dollar values are shown as capital letters. Other symbols are generally lowercase letters. Thus the symbol for a dividend payment is "DIV," and the symbol for a percentage rate of return is "*r*."

SUPPLEMENTS

In this edition, we have gone to great lengths to ensure that our supplements are equal in quality and authority to the text itself.

Instructor's Manual

ISBN 0072467886

The Instructor's Manual was extensively revised and updated by C. R. Krishnaswamy of Western Michigan University. It contains an overview of each chapter, teaching tips, learning objectives, challenge areas, key terms, and an annotated outline that provides references to the PowerPoint slides.

Test Bank

ISBN 0072468025

The Test Bank was also updated by C. R. Krishnaswamy, who included well over 1,000 new multiple-choice and short answer/discussion questions based on the revisions of the authors. The level of difficulty is varied throughout, using a label of easy, medium, or difficult.

PowerPoint Presentation System

Matt Will of the University of Indianapolis prepared the PowerPoint Presentation System, which contains exhibits, outlines, key points, and summaries in a visually stimulating collection of slides. Found on the Student CD-ROM, the Instructor's CD-ROM, and our website, the slides can be edited, printed, or rearranged in any way to fit the needs of your course.

Financial Analysis Spreadsheet Templates (F.A.S.T.)

Mike Griffin of KMT Software created the templates in Excel. They correlate with specific concepts in the text and allow students to work through financial problems and gain experience using spreadsheets. Each template is tied to a specific problem in the text.

Solutions Manual

ISBN 0072468009

The Solutions Manual, prepared by Bruce Swensen, Adelphi University, contains solutions to all practice questions and challenge questions found at the end of each chapter. Thoroughly checked for accuracy, this supplement is available to be purchased by your students.

Study Guide

ISBN 0072468017

The new Study Guide was carefully revised by V. Sivarama Krishnan of Cameron University and contains useful and interesting keys to learning. It includes an introduction to each chapter, key concepts, examples, exercises and solutions, and a complete chapter summary.

Videos

ISBN 0072467967

The McGraw-Hill/Irwin Finance Video Series is a complete video library designed to bring added points of discussion to your class. Within this professionally developed series, you will find examples of how real businesses face today's hottest topics, like mergers and acquisitions, going public, and careers in finance.

Student CD-ROM

Packaged with each text is a CD-ROM for students that contains many features designed to enhance the classroom experience. Three learning modules from the new Finance Tutor Series are included on the CD: Time Value of Money Tutor, Stock and Bond Valuation

Tutor, and Capital Budgeting Tutor. In each module, students answer questions and solve problems that not only assess their general understanding of the subject but also their ability to apply that understanding in real-world business contexts. In "Practice Mode," students learn as they go by receiving in-depth feedback on each response before proceeding to the next question. Even better, the program anticipates common misunderstandings, such as incorrect calculations or assumptions, and then provides feedback only to the student making that specific mistake. Students who want to assess their current knowledge may select "Test Mode," where they read an extensive evaluation report after they have completed the test.

Also included are the PowerPoint presentation system, Financial Analysis Spreadsheet Templates (F.A.S.T.), video clips from our Finance Video Series, and many useful Web links.

Instructor's CD-ROM

ISBN 0072467959

We have compiled many of our instructor supplements in electronic format on a CD-ROM designed to assist with class preparation. The CD-ROM includes the Instructor's Manual, the Solutions Manual, a computerized Test Bank, PowerPoint slides, video clips, and Web links.

Online Learning Center

(www.mhhe.com/bm7e)

This site contains information about the book and the authors, as well as teaching and learning materials for the instructor and the student, including:

PageOut: The Course Website Development Center and PageOut Lite

www.pageout.net

This Web page generation software, free to adopters, is designed for professors just beginning to explore website options. In just a few minutes, even the most novice computer user can have a course website.

Simply type your material into the template provided and PageOut Lite instantly converts it to HTML—a universal Web language. Next, choose your favorite of three easy-to-navigate designs and your Web home page is created, complete with online syllabus, lecture notes, and bookmarks. You can even include a separate instructor page and an assignment page.

PageOut offers enhanced point-and-click features including a Syllabus Page that applies real-world links to original text material, an automated grade book, and a discussion board where instructors and their students can exchange questions and post announcements.

ACKNOWLEDGMENTS

We have a long list of people to thank for their helpful criticism of earlier editions and for assistance in preparing this one. They include Aleijda de Cazenove Balsan, John Cox, Kedrum Garrison, Robert Pindyck, and Gretchen Slemmons at MIT; Stefania Uccheddu at London Business School; Lynda Borucki, Marjorie Fischer, Larry Kolbe, James A. Read, Jr., and Bente Villadsen at The Brattle Group, Inc.; John Stonier at Airbus Industries; and Alex Triantis at the University of Maryland. We would also like to thank all those at McGraw-Hill/Irwin who worked on the book, including Steve Patterson, Publisher; Rhonda Seelinger, Executive Marketing Manager; Sarah Ebel, Senior Developmental Editor; Jean Lou Hess, Senior Project Manager; Keith McPherson, Design Director; Joyce Chappetto, Supplement Coordinator; and Michael McCormick, Senior Production Supervisor.

We want to express our appreciation to those instructors whose insightful comments and suggestions were invaluable to us during this revision:

Noyan Arsen *Koc University*
Penny Belk *Loughborough University*
Eric Benrud *University of Baltimore*
Peter Berman *University of New Haven*
Jean Canil *University of Adelaide*
Robert Everett *Johns Hopkins University*

Winfried Hallerbach *Erasmus University, Rotterdam*
Milton Harris *University of Chicago*
Mark Griffiths *Thunderbird, American School of International Management*
Jarl Kallberg *NYU, Stern School of Business*
Steve Kaplan *University of Chicago*
Ken Kim *University of Wisconsin—Milwaukee*
C. R. Krishnaswamy *Western Michigan University*
Ravi Jaganathan *Northwestern University*
David Lovatt *University of East Anglia*
Joe Messina *San Francisco State University*
Dag Michalson *Bl, Oslo*
Peter Moles *University of Edinburgh*
Claus Parum *Copenhagen Business School*
Narendar V. Rao *Northeastern University*
Tom Rietz *University of Iowa*
Robert Ritchey *Texas Tech University*
Mo Rodriguez *Texas Christian University*
John Rozycki *Drake University*
Brad Scott *Webster University*
Bernell Stone *Brigham Young University*
Shrinivasan Sundaram *Ball State University*
Avanidhar Subrahmanyam *UCLA*
Stephen Todd *Loyola University—Chicago*
David Vang *St. Thomas University*
John Wald *Rutgers University*
Jill Wetmore *Saginaw Valley State University*
Matt Will *Johns Hopkins University*
Art Wilson *George Washington University*

This list is almost surely incomplete. We know how much we owe to our colleagues at the London Business School and MIT's Sloan School of Management. In many cases, the ideas that appear in this book are as much their ideas as ours. Finally, we record the continuing thanks due to our wives, Diana and Maureen, who were unaware when they married us that they were also marrying *The Principles of Corporate Finance.*

Richard A. Brealey
Stewart C. Myers

BRIEF CONTENTS

CONTENTS

Chapter 11

WHERE POSITIVE NET PRESENT VALUES COME FROM 286

Chapter 12

MAKING SURE MANAGERS MAXIMIZE NPV 310

Part Four

FINANCING DECISIONS AND MARKET EFFICIENCY 343

Chapter 13

CORPORATE FINANCING AND THE SIX LESSONS OF MARKET EFFICIENCY 344

Chapter 14

AN OVERVIEW OF CORPORATE FINANCING 376

PART ONE

VALUE

IN 2001, DUPONT announced plans to build a new production line at its plant in Richmond, Virginia. The $50 million investment would increase DuPont's output of Kevlar high-strength fiber by 15 percent. Meanwhile, in New Orleans Procter & Gamble had started work on a 100,000 square foot facility to produce Folger's coffee. This was expected to open in 2002 at a cost of $100 million.

What was special about these two developments? The answer is "nothing." We cite them because they are typical of the investments in new products and equipment that U.S. companies are making every day.

Presumably, DuPont and Procter & Gamble decided to undertake the investments because they thought that the new plant would be worth more than it cost. But that raises an obvious question. How can firms calculate what an investment is worth when its returns may stretch 10, 20, or more years into the future?

This is the topic of Part One. Chapter 1 sets the scene by showing how businesses are organized and the role that the financial manager plays in evaluating investments and finding money to pay for them. Chapter 2 starts to build a theory of value. By the end of Chapter 6, you should be able to tackle a standard investment decision such as those faced by DuPont or Procter & Gamble.

CHAPTER ONE

FINANCE AND THE FINANCIAL MANAGER

THIS BOOK IS about financial decisions made by corporations. We should start by saying what these decisions are and why they are important.

Corporations face two broad financial questions: What investments should the firm make? and How should it pay for those investments? The first question involves spending money; the second involves raising it.

The secret of success in financial management is to increase value. That is a simple statement, but not very helpful. It is like advising an investor in the stock market to "Buy low, sell high." The problem is how to do it.

There may be a few activities in which one can read a textbook and then do it, but financial management is not one of them. That is why finance is worth studying. Who wants to work in a field where there is no room for judgment, experience, creativity, and a pinch of luck? Although this book cannot supply any of these items, it does present the concepts and information on which good financial decisions are based, and it shows you how to use the tools of the trade of finance.

We start in this chapter by explaining what a corporation is and introducing you to the responsibilities of its financial managers. We will distinguish *real assets* from *financial assets* and *capital investment decisions* from *financing decisions.* We stress the importance of financial markets, both national and international, to the financial manager.

Finance is about money and markets, but it is also about people. The success of a corporation depends on how well it harnesses everyone to work to a common end. The financial manager must appreciate the conflicting objectives often encountered in financial management. Resolving conflicts is particularly difficult when people have different information. This is an important theme which runs through to the last chapter of this book. In this chapter we will start with some definitions and examples.

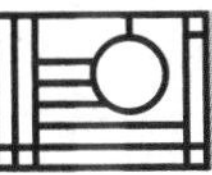

1.1 WHAT IS A CORPORATION?

Not all businesses are corporations. Small ventures can be owned and managed by a single individual. These are called *sole proprietorships.* In other cases several people may join to own and manage a *partnership.*[1] However, this book is about *corporate* finance. So we need to explain what a **corporation** is.

Almost all large and medium-sized businesses are organized as corporations. For example, General Motors, Bank of America, Microsoft, and General Electric are corporations. So are overseas businesses, such as British Petroleum, Unilever, Nestlé, Volkswagen, and Sony. In each case the firm is owned by stockholders who hold shares in the business.

When a corporation is first established, its shares may all be held by a small group of investors, perhaps the company's managers and a few backers. In this case the shares are not publicly traded and the company is *closely held.* Eventually, when the firm grows and new shares are issued to raise additional capital, its shares will be widely traded. Such corporations are known as *public companies.*

[1]Many professional businesses, such as accounting and legal firms, are partnerships. Most large investment banks started as partnerships, but eventually these companies and their financing needs grew too large for them to continue in this form. Goldman Sachs, the last of the leading investment-bank partnerships, issued shares and became a public corporation in 1998.

Most well-known corporations in the United States are public companies. In many other countries, it's common for large companies to remain in private hands.

By organizing as a corporation, a business can attract a wide variety of investors. Some may hold only a single share worth a few dollars, cast only a single vote, and receive a tiny proportion of profits and dividends. Shareholders may also include giant pension funds and insurance companies whose investment may run to millions of shares and hundreds of millions of dollars, and who are entitled to a correspondingly large number of votes and proportion of profits and dividends.

Although the stockholders own the corporation, they do not manage it. Instead, they vote to elect a *board of directors.* Some of these directors may be drawn from top management, but others are non-executive directors, who are not employed by the firm. The board of directors represents the shareholders. It appoints top management and is supposed to ensure that managers act in the shareholders' best interests.

This *separation of ownership and management* gives corporations permanence.[2] Even if managers quit or are dismissed and replaced, the corporation can survive, and today's stockholders can sell all their shares to new investors without disrupting the operations of the business.

Unlike partnerships and sole proprietorships, corporations have **limited liability,** which means that stockholders cannot be held personally responsible for the firm's debts. If, say, General Motors were to fail, no one could demand that its shareholders put up more money to pay off its debts. The most a stockholder can lose is the amount he or she has invested.

Although a corporation is owned by its stockholders, it is legally distinct from them. It is based on *articles of incorporation* that set out the purpose of the business, how many shares can be issued, the number of directors to be appointed, and so on. These articles must conform to the laws of the state in which the business is incorporated.[3] For many legal purposes, the corporation is considered as a resident of its state. As a legal "person," it can borrow or lend money, and it can sue or be sued. It pays its own taxes (but it cannot vote!).

Because the corporation is distinct from its shareholders, it can do things that partnerships and sole proprietorships cannot. For example, it can raise money by selling new shares to investors and it can buy those shares back. One corporation can make a takeover bid for another and then merge the two businesses.

There are also some *disadvantages* to organizing as a corporation. Managing a corporation's legal machinery and communicating with shareholders can be time-consuming and costly. Furthermore, in the United States there is an important tax drawback. Because the corporation is a separate legal entity, it is taxed separately. So corporations pay tax on their profits, and, in addition, shareholders pay tax on any dividends that they receive from the company. The United States is unusual in this respect. To avoid taxing the same income twice, most other countries give shareholders at least some credit for the tax that the company has already paid.[4]

[2]Corporations can be immortal but the law requires partnerships to have a definite end. A partnership agreement must specify an ending date or a procedure for wrapping up the partnership's affairs. A sole proprietorship also will have an end because the proprietor is mortal.

[3]Delaware has a well-developed and supportive system of corporate law. Even though they may do little business in that state, a high proportion of United States corporations are incorporated in Delaware.

[4]Or companies may pay a lower rate of tax on profits paid out as dividends.

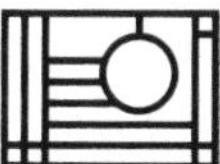

1.2 THE ROLE OF THE FINANCIAL MANAGER

To carry on business, corporations need an almost endless variety of **real assets.** Many of these assets are tangible, such as machinery, factories, and offices; others are intangible, such as technical expertise, trademarks, and patents. All of them need to be paid for. To obtain the necessary money, the corporation sells claims on its real assets and on the cash those assets will generate. These claims are called **financial assets** or **securities.** For example, if the company borrows money from the bank, the bank gets a written promise that the money will be repaid with interest. Thus the bank trades cash for a financial asset. Financial assets include not only bank loans but also shares of stock, bonds, and a dizzying variety of specialized securities.[5]

The financial manager stands between the firm's operations and the **financial** (or **capital) markets,** where investors hold the financial assets issued by the firm.[6] The financial manager's role is illustrated in Figure 1.1, which traces the flow of cash from investors to the firm and back to investors again. The flow starts when the firm sells securities to raise cash (arrow 1 in the figure). The cash is used to purchase real assets used in the firm's operations (arrow 2). Later, if the firm does well, the real assets generate cash inflows which more than repay the initial investment (arrow 3). Finally, the cash is either reinvested (arrow 4*a*) or returned to the investors who purchased the original security issue (arrow 4*b*). Of course, the choice between arrows 4*a* and 4*b* is not completely free. For example, if a bank lends money at stage 1, the bank has to be repaid the money plus interest at stage 4*b*.

Our diagram takes us back to the financial manager's two basic questions. First, what real assets should the firm invest in? Second, how should the cash for the investment be raised? The answer to the first question is the firm's **investment,** or **capital budgeting, decision.** The answer to the second is the firm's **financing decision.**

Capital investment and financing decisions are typically *separated,* that is, analyzed independently. When an investment opportunity or "project" is identified, the financial manager first asks whether the project is worth more than the capital required to undertake it. If the answer is yes, he or she then considers how the project should be financed.

But the separation of investment and financing decisions does *not* mean that the financial manager can forget about investors and financial markets when analyzing capital investment projects. As we will see in the next chapter, the fundamental financial objective of the firm is to maximize the value of the cash invested in the firm by its stockholders. Look again at Figure 1.1. Stockholders are happy to contribute cash at arrow 1 only if the decisions made at arrow 2 generate at least adequate returns at arrow 3. "Adequate" means returns at least equal to the returns available to investors outside the firm in financial markets. If your firm's projects consistently generate *in*adequate returns, your shareholders will want their money back.

Financial managers of large corporations also need to be men and women of the world. They must decide not only *which* assets their firm should invest in but also *where* those assets should be located. Take Nestlé, for example. It is a Swiss company, but only a small proportion of its production takes place in Switzerland. Its 520 or so

[5]We review these securities in Chapters 14 and 25.

[6]You will hear financial managers use the terms *financial markets* and *capital markets* almost synonymously. But *capital markets* are, strictly speaking, the source of long-term financing only. Short-term financing comes from the *money market.* "Short-term" means less than one year. We use the term *financial markets* to refer to all sources of financing.

FIGURE 1.1

Flow of cash between financial markets and the firm's operations. Key: (1) Cash raised by selling financial assets to investors; (2) cash invested in the firm's operations and used to purchase real assets; (3) cash generated by the firm's operations; (4*a*) cash reinvested; (4*b*) cash returned to investors.

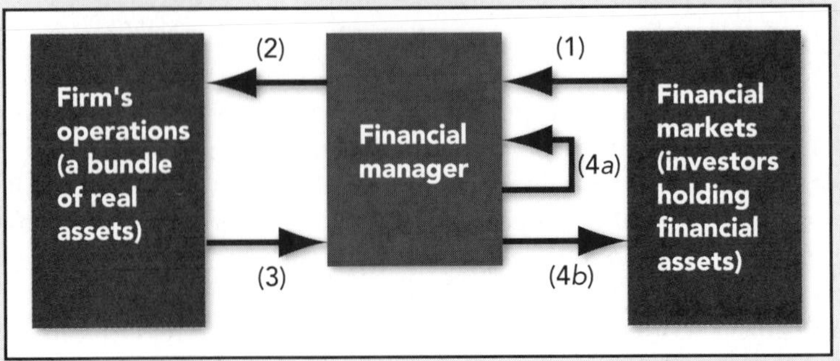

factories are located in 82 countries. Nestlé's managers must therefore know how to evaluate investments in countries with different currencies, interest rates, inflation rates, and tax systems.

The financial markets in which the firm raises money are likewise international. The stockholders of large corporations are scattered around the globe. Shares are traded around the clock in New York, London, Tokyo, and other financial centers. Bonds and bank loans move easily across national borders. A corporation that needs to raise cash doesn't have to borrow from its hometown bank. Day-to-day cash management also becomes a complex task for firms that produce or sell in different countries. For example, think of the problems that Nestlé's financial managers face in keeping track of the cash receipts and payments in 82 countries.

We admit that Nestlé is unusual, but few financial managers can close their eyes to international financial issues. So throughout the book we will pay attention to differences in financial systems and examine the problems of investing and raising money internationally.

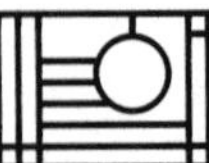

1.3 WHO IS THE FINANCIAL MANAGER?

In this book we will use the term *financial manager* to refer to anyone responsible for a significant investment or financing decision. But only in the smallest firms is a single person responsible for all the decisions discussed in this book. In most cases, responsibility is dispersed. Top management is of course continuously involved in financial decisions. But the engineer who designs a new production facility is also involved: The design determines the kind of real assets the firm will hold. The marketing manager who commits to a major advertising campaign is also making an important investment decision. The campaign is an investment in an intangible asset that is expected to pay off in future sales and earnings.

Nevertheless there are some managers who specialize in finance. Their roles are summarized in Figure 1.2. The **treasurer** is responsible for looking after the firm's cash, raising new capital, and maintaining relationships with banks, stockholders, and other investors who hold the firm's securities.

For small firms, the treasurer is likely to be the only financial executive. Larger corporations also have a **controller,** who prepares the financial statements, manages the firm's internal accounting, and looks after its tax obligations. You can see that the treasurer and controller have different functions: The treasurer's main responsibility is to obtain and manage the firm's capital, whereas the controller ensures that the money is used efficiently.

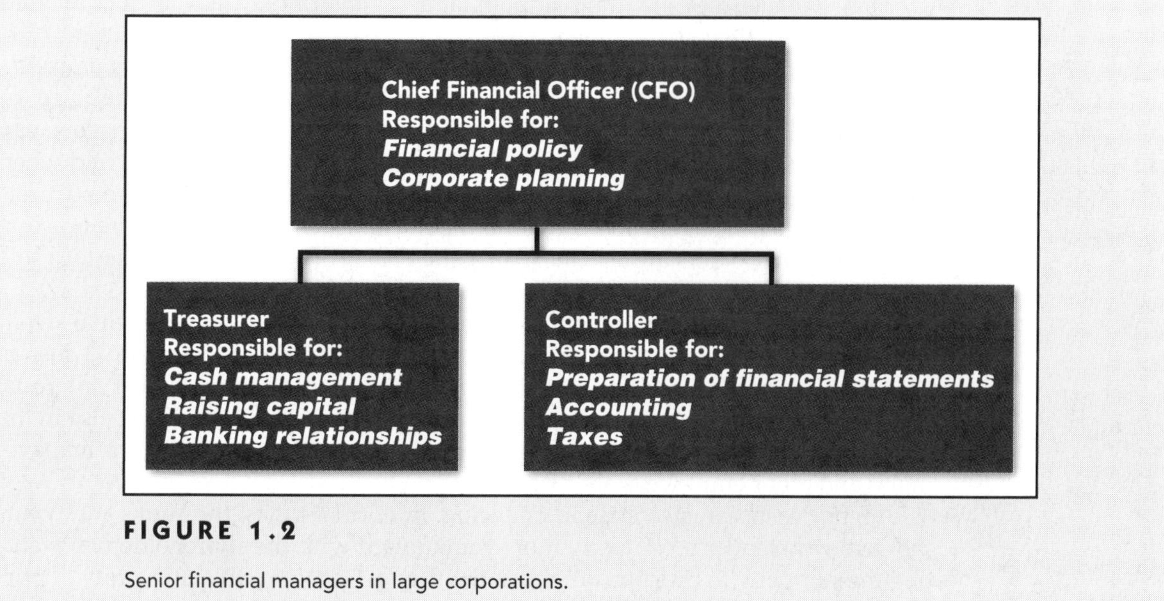

FIGURE 1.2

Senior financial managers in large corporations.

Still larger firms usually appoint a **chief financial officer (CFO)** to oversee both the treasurer's and the controller's work. The CFO is deeply involved in financial policy and corporate planning. Often he or she will have general managerial responsibilities beyond strictly financial issues and may also be a member of the board of directors.

The controller or CFO is responsible for organizing and supervising the capital budgeting process. However, major capital investment projects are so closely tied to plans for product development, production, and marketing that managers from these areas are inevitably drawn into planning and analyzing the projects. If the firm has staff members specializing in corporate planning, they too are naturally involved in capital budgeting.

Because of the importance of many financial issues, ultimate decisions often rest by law or by custom with the board of directors. For example, only the board has the legal power to declare a dividend or to sanction a public issue of securities. Boards usually delegate decisions for small or medium-sized investment outlays, but the authority to approve large investments is almost never delegated.

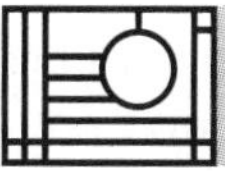

1.4 SEPARATION OF OWNERSHIP AND MANAGEMENT

In large businesses separation of ownership and management is a practical necessity. Major corporations may have hundreds of thousands of shareholders. There is no way for all of them to be actively involved in management: It would be like running New York City through a series of town meetings for all its citizens. Authority has to be delegated to managers.

The separation of ownership and management has clear advantages. It allows share ownership to change without interfering with the operation of the business. It allows the firm to hire professional managers. But it also brings problems if the managers' and owners' objectives differ. You can see the danger: Rather than attending to the wishes of shareholders, managers may seek a more leisurely or luxurious working lifestyle; they may shun unpopular decisions, or they may attempt to build an empire with their shareholders' money.

Such conflicts between shareholders' and managers' objectives create *principal–agent problems.* The shareholders are the principals; the managers are their agents. Shareholders want management to increase the value of the firm, but managers may have their own axes to grind or nests to feather. **Agency costs** are incurred when (1) managers do not attempt to maximize firm value and (2) shareholders incur costs to monitor the managers and influence their actions. Of course, there are no costs when the shareholders are also the managers. That is one of the advantages of a sole proprietorship. Owner–managers have no conflicts of interest.

Conflicts between shareholders and managers are not the only principal–agent problems that the financial manager is likely to encounter. For example, just as shareholders need to encourage managers to work for the shareholders' interests, so senior management needs to think about how to motivate everyone else in the company. In this case senior management are the principals and junior management and other employees are their agents.

Agency costs can also arise in financing. In normal times, the banks and bondholders who lend the company money are united with the shareholders in wanting the company to prosper, but when the firm gets into trouble, this unity of purpose can break down. At such times decisive action may be necessary to rescue the firm, but lenders are concerned to get their money back and are reluctant to see the firm making risky changes that could imperil the safety of their loans. Squabbles may even break out between different lenders as they see the company heading for possible bankruptcy and jostle for a better place in the queue of creditors.

Think of the company's overall value as a pie that is divided among a number of claimants. These include the management and the shareholders, as well as the company's workforce and the banks and investors who have bought the company's debt. The government is a claimant too, since it gets to tax corporate profits.

All these claimants are bound together in a complex web of contracts and understandings. For example, when banks lend money to the firm, they insist on a formal contract stating the rate of interest and repayment dates, perhaps placing restrictions on dividends or additional borrowing. But you can't devise written rules to cover every possible future event. So written contracts are incomplete and need to be supplemented by understandings and by arrangements that help to align the interests of the various parties.

Principal–agent problems would be easier to resolve if everyone had the same information. That is rarely the case in finance. Managers, shareholders, and lenders may all have different information about the value of a real or financial asset, and it may be many years before all the information is revealed. Financial managers need to recognize these *information asymmetries* and find ways to reassure investors that there are no nasty surprises on the way.

Here is one example. Suppose you are the financial manager of a company that has been newly formed to develop and bring to market a drug for the cure of toetitis. At a meeting with potential investors you present the results of clinical trials, show upbeat reports by an independent market research company, and forecast profits amply sufficient to justify further investment. But the potential investors are still worried that you may know more than they do. What can you do to convince them that you are telling the truth? Just saying "Trust me" won't do the trick. Perhaps you need to *signal* your integrity by putting your money where your mouth is. For example, investors are likely to have more confidence in your plans if they see that you and the other managers have large personal stakes in the new

Differences in information	Different objectives
Stock prices and returns (13)	Managers vs. stockholders (2, 12, 33, 34)
Issues of shares and other securities (15, 18, 23)	Top management vs. operating management (12)
Dividends (16)	Stockholders vs. banks and other lenders (18)
Financing (18)	

FIGURE 1.3

Differences in objectives and information can complicate financial decisions. We address these issues at several points in this book (chapter numbers in parentheses).

enterprise. Therefore your decision to invest your own money can provide information to investors about the true prospects of the firm.

In later chapters we will look more carefully at how corporations tackle the problems created by differences in objectives and information. Figure 1.3 summarizes the main issues and signposts the chapters where they receive most attention.

1.5 TOPICS COVERED IN THIS BOOK

We have mentioned how financial managers separate investment and financing decisions: Investment decisions typically precede financing decisions. That is also how we have organized this book. Parts 1 through 3 are almost entirely devoted to different aspects of the investment decision. The first topic is how to value assets, the second is the link between risk and value, and the third is the management of the capital investment process. Our discussion of these topics occupies Chapters 2 through 12.

As you work through these chapters, you may have some basic questions about financing. For example, What does it mean to say that a corporation has "issued shares"? How much of the cash contributed at arrow 1 in Figure 1.1 comes from shareholders and how much from borrowing? What types of debt securities do firms actually issue? Who actually buys the firm's shares and debt—individual investors or financial institutions? What are those institutions and what role do they play in corporate finance and the broader economy? Chapter 14, "An Overview of Corporate Financing," covers these and a variety of similar questions. This chapter stands on its own bottom—it does not rest on previous chapters. You can read it any time the fancy strikes. You may wish to read it now.

Chapter 14 is one of three in Part 4, which begins the analysis of corporate financing decisions. Chapter 13 reviews the evidence on the *efficient markets* hypothesis, which states that security prices observed in financial markets accurately reflect underlying values and the information available to investors. Chapter 15 describes how debt and equity securities are issued.

Part 5 continues the analysis of the financing decision, covering dividend policy and the mix of debt and equity financing. We will describe what happens when firms land in financial distress because of poor operating performance or excessive borrowing. We will also consider how financing decisions may affect decisions about the firm's investment projects.

Part 6 introduces options. Options are too advanced for Chapter 1, but by Chapter 20 you'll have no difficulty. Investors can trade options on stocks, bonds, currencies, and commodities. Financial managers find options lurking in *real* assets—that is, *real options*—and in the securities the firms may issue. Having mastered options, we proceed in Part 7 to a much closer look at the many varieties of long-term debt financing.

An important part of the financial manager's job is to judge which risks the firm should take on and which can be eliminated. Part 8 looks at risk management, both domestically and internationally.

Part 9 covers financial planning and short-term financial management. We address a variety of practical topics, including short- and longer-term forecasting, channels for short-term borrowing or investment, management of cash and marketable securities, and management of accounts receivable (money lent by the firm to its customers).

Part 10 looks at mergers and acquisitions and, more generally, at the control and governance of the firm. We also discuss how companies in different countries are structured to provide the right incentives for management and the right degree of control by outside investors.

Part 11 is our conclusion. It also discusses some of the things that we *don't* know about finance. If you can be the first to solve any of these puzzles, you will be justifiably famous.

In Chapter 2 we will begin with the most basic concepts of asset valuation. However, we should first sum up the principal points made in this introductory chapter.

Large businesses are usually organized as corporations. Corporations have three important features. First, they are legally distinct from their owners and pay their own taxes. Second, corporations provide limited liability, which means that the stockholders who own the corporation cannot be held responsible for the firm's debts. Third, the owners of a corporation are not usually the managers.

The overall task of the financial manager can be broken down into (1) the investment, or capital budgeting, decision and (2) the financing decision. In other words, the firm has to decide (1) what real assets to buy and (2) how to raise the necessary cash.

In small companies there is often only one financial executive, the treasurer. However, most companies have both a treasurer and a controller. The treasurer's job is to obtain and manage the company's financing, while the controller's job is to confirm that the money is used correctly. In large firms there is also a chief financial officer or CFO.

Shareholders want managers to increase the value of the company's stock. Managers may have different objectives. This potential conflict of interest is termed a principal–agent problem. Any loss of value that results from such conflicts is termed an agency cost. Of course there may be other conflicts of interest. For example, the interests of the shareholders may sometimes conflict with those of the firm's banks and bondholders. These and other agency problems become more complicated when agents have more or better information than the principals.

The financial manager plays on an international stage and must understand how international financial markets operate and how to evaluate overseas investments. We discuss international corporate finance at many different points in the chapters that follow.

FURTHER READING

Financial managers read *The Wall Street Journal (WSJ), The Financial Times (FT)*, or both daily. You should too. *The Financial Times* is published in Britain, but there is a North American edition. *The New York Times* and a few other big-city newspapers have good business and financial sections, but they are no substitute for the *WSJ* or *FT*. The business and financial sections of most United States dailies are, except for local news, nearly worthless for the financial manager.

The Economist, Business Week, Forbes, and *Fortune* contain useful financial sections, and there are several magazines that specialize in finance. These include *Euromoney, Corporate Finance, Journal of Applied Corporate Finance, Risk,* and *CFO Magazine.* This list does not include research journals such as the *Journal of Finance, Journal of Financial Economics, Review of Financial Studies,* and *Financial Management.* In the following chapters we give specific references to pertinent research.

QUIZ

1. Read the following passage: "Companies usually buy (*a*) assets. These include both tangible assets such as (*b*) and intangible assets such as (*c*). In order to pay for these assets, they sell (*d*) assets such as (*e*). The decision about which assets to buy is usually termed the (*f*) or (*g*) decision. The decision about how to raise the money is usually termed the (*h*) decision." Now fit each of the following terms into the most appropriate space: *financing, real, bonds, investment, executive airplanes, financial, capital budgeting, brand names.*
2. Vocabulary test. Explain the differences between:
   a. Real and financial assets.
   b. Capital budgeting and financing decisions.
   c. Closely held and public corporations.
   d. Limited and unlimited liability.
   e. Corporation and partnership.
3. Which of the following are real assets, and which are financial?
   a. A share of stock.
   b. A personal IOU.
   c. A trademark.
   d. A factory.
   e. Undeveloped land.
   f. The balance in the firm's checking account.
   g. An experienced and hardworking sales force.
   h. A corporate bond.
4. What are the main *disadvantages* of the corporate form of organization?
5. Which of the following statements more accurately describe the treasurer than the controller?
   a. Likely to be the only financial executive in small firms.
   b. Monitors capital expenditures to make sure that they are not misappropriated.
   c. Responsible for investing the firm's spare cash.
   d. Responsible for arranging any issue of common stock.
   e. Responsible for the company's tax affairs.
6. Which of the following statements always apply to corporations?
   a. Unlimited liability.
   b. Limited life.
   c. Ownership can be transferred without affecting operations.
   d. Managers can be fired with no effect on ownership.
   e. Shares must be widely traded.
7. In most large corporations, ownership and management are separated. What are the main implications of this separation?
8. What are agency costs and what causes them?

CHAPTER TWO

PRESENT VALUE AND THE OPPORTUNITY COST OF CAPITAL

COMPANIES INVEST IN a variety of real assets. These include tangible assets such as plant and machinery and intangible assets such as management contracts and patents. The object of the investment, or capital budgeting, decision is to find real assets that are worth more than they cost. In this chapter we will take the first, most basic steps toward understanding how assets are valued.

There are a few cases in which it is not that difficult to estimate asset values. In real estate, for example, you can hire a professional appraiser to do it for you. Suppose you own a warehouse. The odds are that your appraiser's estimate of its value will be within a few percent of what the building would actually sell for.[1] After all, there is continuous activity in the real estate market, and the appraiser's stock-in-trade is knowledge of the prices at which similar properties have recently changed hands. Thus the problem of valuing real estate is simplified by the existence of an active market in which all kinds of properties are bought and sold. For many purposes no formal theory of value is needed. We can take the market's word for it.

But we need to go deeper than that. First, it is important to know how asset values are reached in an active market. Even if you can take the appraiser's word for it, it is important to understand *why* that warehouse is worth, say, $250,000 and not a higher or lower figure. Second, the market for most corporate assets is pretty thin. Look in the classified advertisements in *The Wall Street Journal:* It is not often that you see a blast furnace for sale.

Companies are always searching for assets that are worth more to them than to others. That warehouse is worth more to you if you can manage it better than others. But in that case, looking at the price of similar buildings will not tell you what the warehouse is worth under your management. You need to know how asset values are determined. In other words, you need a theory of value.

This chapter takes the first, most basic steps to develop that theory. We lead off with a simple numerical example: Should you invest to build a new office building in the hope of selling it at a profit next year? Finance theory endorses investment if net present value is positive, that is, if the new building's value *today* exceeds the required investment. It turns out that net present value is positive in this example, because the rate of return on investment exceeds the opportunity cost of capital.

So this chapter's first task is to define and explain net present value, rate of return, and opportunity cost of capital. The second task is to explain why financial managers search so assiduously for investments with positive net present values. Is increased value today the *only* possible financial objective? And what does "value" mean for a corporation?

Here we will come to the fundamental objective of corporate finance: maximizing the current market value of the firm's outstanding shares. We will explain why *all* shareholders should endorse this objective, and why the objective overrides other plausible goals, such as "maximizing profits."

Finally, we turn to the *managers'* objectives and discuss some of the mechanisms that help to align the managers' and stockholders' interests. We ask whether attempts to increase shareholder value need be at the expense of workers, customers, or the community at large.

In this chapter, we will stick to the simplest problems to make basic ideas clear. Readers with a taste for more complication will find plenty to satisfy them in later chapters.

[1]Needless to say, there are some properties that appraisers find nearly impossible to value—for example, nobody knows the potential selling price of the Taj Mahal or the Parthenon or Windsor Castle.

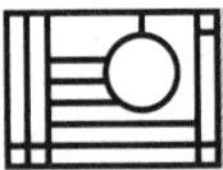

2.1 INTRODUCTION TO PRESENT VALUE

Your warehouse has burned down, fortunately without injury to you or your employees, leaving you with a vacant lot worth \$50,000 and a check for \$200,000 from the fire insurance company. You consider rebuilding, but your real estate adviser suggests putting up an office building instead. The construction cost would be \$300,000, and there would also be the cost of the land, which might otherwise be sold for \$50,000. On the other hand, your adviser foresees a shortage of office space and predicts that a year from now the new building would fetch \$400,000 if you sold it. Thus you would be investing \$350,000 now in the expectation of realizing \$400,000 a year hence. You should go ahead if the **present value (PV)** of the expected \$400,000 payoff is greater than the investment of \$350,000. Therefore, you need to ask, What is the value today of \$400,000 to be received one year from now, and is that present value greater than \$350,000?

Calculating Present Value

The present value of \$400,000 one year from now must be less than \$400,000. After all, *a dollar today is worth more than a dollar tomorrow,* because the dollar today can be invested to start earning interest immediately. This is the first basic principle of finance. Thus, the present value of a delayed payoff may be found by multiplying the payoff by a **discount factor** which is less than 1. (If the discount factor were more than 1, a dollar today would be worth *less* than a dollar tomorrow.) If C_1 denotes the expected payoff at period 1 (one year hence), then

$$\text{Present value (PV)} = \text{discount factor} \times C_1$$

This discount factor is the value today of \$1 received in the future. It is usually expressed as the reciprocal of 1 plus a *rate of return:*

$$\text{Discount factor} = \frac{1}{1 + r}$$

The rate of return r is the reward that investors demand for accepting delayed payment.

Now we can value the real estate investment, assuming for the moment that the \$400,000 payoff is a sure thing. The office building is not the only way to obtain \$400,000 a year from now. You could invest in United States government securities maturing in a year. Suppose these securities offer 7 percent interest. How much would you have to invest in them in order to receive \$400,000 at the end of the year? That's easy: You would have to invest \$400,000/1.07, which is \$373,832.[2] Therefore, at an interest rate of 7 percent, the present value of \$400,000 one year from now is \$373,832.

Let's assume that, as soon as you've committed the land and begun construction on the building, you decide to sell your project. How much could you sell it for? That's another easy question. Since the property will be worth \$400,000 in a year, investors would be willing to pay \$373,832 for it today. That's what it would

[2] Let's check this. If you invest \$373,832 at 7 percent, at the end of the year you get back your initial investment plus interest of .07 × 373,832 = \$26,168. The total sum you receive is 373,832 + 26,168 = \$400,000. Note that 373,832 × 1.07 = \$400,000.

cost them to get a $400,000 payoff from investing in government securities. Of course, you could always sell your property for less, but why sell for less than the market will bear? The $373,832 present value is the only feasible price that satisfies both buyer and seller. Therefore, the present value of the property is also its market price.

To calculate present value, we discount expected payoffs by the rate of return offered by equivalent investment alternatives in the capital market. This rate of return is often referred to as the **discount rate, hurdle rate,** or **opportunity cost of capital.** It is called the *opportunity cost* because it is the return foregone by investing in the project rather than investing in securities. In our example the opportunity cost was 7 percent. Present value was obtained by dividing $400,000 by 1.07:

$$\text{PV} = \text{discount factor} \times C_1 = \frac{1}{1+r} \times C_1 = \frac{400{,}000}{1.07} = \$373{,}832$$

Net Present Value

The building is worth $373,832, but this does not mean that you are $373,832 better off. You committed $350,000, and therefore your **net present value (NPV)** is $23,832. Net present value is found by subtracting the required investment:

$$\text{NPV} = \text{PV} - \text{required investment} = 373{,}832 - 350{,}000 = \$23{,}832$$

In other words, your office development is worth more than it costs—it makes a *net* contribution to value. The formula for calculating NPV can be written as

$$\text{NPV} = C_0 + \frac{C_1}{1+r}$$

remembering that C_0, the cash flow at time 0 (that is, today), will usually be a negative number. In other words, C_0 is an investment and therefore a cash *outflow*. In our example, $C_0 = -\$350{,}000$.

A Comment on Risk and Present Value

We made one unrealistic assumption in our discussion of the office development: Your real estate adviser cannot be *certain* about future values of office buildings. The $400,000 represents the best *forecast*, but it is not a sure thing.

If the future value of the building is risky, our calculation of NPV is wrong. Investors could achieve $400,000 with certainty by buying $373,832 worth of United States government securities, so they would not buy your building for that amount. You would have to cut your asking price to attract investors' interest.

Here we can invoke a second basic financial principle: *A safe dollar is worth more than a risky one.* Most investors avoid risk when they can do so without sacrificing return. However, the concepts of present value and the opportunity cost of capital still make sense for risky investments. It is still proper to discount the payoff by the rate of return offered by an equivalent investment. But we have to think of *expected* payoffs and the *expected* rates of return on other investments.[3]

[3]We define "expected" more carefully in Chapter 9. For now think of expected payoff as a realistic forecast, neither optimistic nor pessimistic. Forecasts of expected payoffs are correct on average.

Not all investments are equally risky. The office development is more risky than a government security but less risky than a start-up biotech venture. Suppose you believe the project is as risky as investment in the stock market and that stock market investments are forecasted to return 12 percent. Then 12 percent becomes the appropriate opportunity cost of capital. That is what you are giving up by not investing in equally risky securities. Now recompute NPV:

$$\text{PV} = \frac{400{,}000}{1.12} = \$357{,}143$$

$$\text{NPV} = \text{PV} - 350{,}000 = \$7{,}143$$

If other investors agree with your forecast of a $400,000 payoff and your assessment of its risk, then your property ought to be worth $357,143 once construction is underway. If you tried to sell it for more, there would be no takers, because the property would then offer an expected rate of return lower than the 12 percent available in the stock market. The office building still makes a net contribution to value, but it is much smaller than our earlier calculations indicated.

The value of the office building depends on the timing of the cash flows and their uncertainty. The $400,000 payoff would be worth exactly that if it could be realized instantaneously. If the office building is as risk-free as government securities, the one-year delay reduces value to $373,832. If the building is as risky as investment in the stock market, then uncertainty further reduces value by $16,689 to $357,143.

Unfortunately, adjusting asset values for time and uncertainty is often more complicated than our example suggests. Therefore, we will take the two effects separately. For the most part, we will dodge the problem of risk in Chapters 2 through 6, either by treating all cash flows as if they were known with certainty or by talking about expected cash flows and expected rates of return without worrying how risk is defined or measured. Then in Chapter 7 we will turn to the problem of understanding how financial markets cope with risk.

Present Values and Rates of Return

We have decided that construction of the office building is a smart thing to do, since it is worth more than it costs—it has a positive net present value. To calculate how much it is worth, we worked out how much one would need to pay to achieve the same payoff by investing directly in securities. The project's present value is equal to its future income discounted at the rate of return offered by these securities.

We can say this in another way: Our property venture is worth undertaking because its rate of return exceeds the cost of capital. The rate of return on the investment in the office building is simply the profit as a proportion of the initial outlay:

$$\text{Return} = \frac{\text{profit}}{\text{investment}} = \frac{400{,}000 - 350{,}000}{350{,}000} = .143, \text{ about } 14\%$$

The cost of capital is once again the return foregone by *not* investing in securities. If the office building is as risky as investing in the stock market, the return foregone is 12 percent. Since the 14 percent return on the office building exceeds the 12 percent opportunity cost, you should go ahead with the project.

Here then we have two equivalent decision rules for capital investment:[4]

- *Net present value rule.* Accept investments that have positive net present values.
- *Rate-of-return rule.* Accept investments that offer rates of return in excess of their opportunity costs of capital.[5]

The Opportunity Cost of Capital

The opportunity cost of capital is such an important concept that we will give one more example. You are offered the following opportunity: Invest $100,000 today, and, depending on the state of the economy at the end of the year, you will receive one of the following payoffs:

Slump	Normal	Boom
$80,000	$110,000	$140,000

You reject the optimistic (boom) and the pessimistic (slump) forecasts. That gives an expected payoff of $C_1 = 110{,}000$,[6] a 10 percent return on the $100,000 investment. But what's the right discount rate?

You search for a common stock with the same risk as the investment. Stock X turns out to be a perfect match. X's price next year, given a normal economy, is forecasted at $110. The stock price will be higher in a boom and lower in a slump, but to the same degrees as your investment ($140 in a boom and $80 in a slump). You conclude that the risks of stock X and your investment are identical.

Stock X's current price is $95.65. It offers an expected rate of return of 15 percent:

$$\text{Expected return} = \frac{\text{expected profit}}{\text{investment}} = \frac{110 - 95.65}{95.65} = .15, \text{ or } 15\%$$

This is the expected return that you are giving up by investing in the project rather than the stock market. In other words, it is the project's opportunity cost of capital.

To value the project, discount the expected cash flow by the opportunity cost of capital:

$$\text{PV} = \frac{110{,}000}{1.15} = \$95{,}650$$

This is the amount it would cost investors in the stock market to buy an expected cash flow of $110,000. (They could do so by buying 1,000 shares of stock X.) It is, therefore, also the sum that investors would be prepared to pay you for your project.

To calculate net present value, deduct the initial investment:

$$\text{NPV} = 95{,}650 - 100{,}000 = -\$4{,}350$$

[4]You might check for yourself that these are equivalent rules. In other words, if the return $50{,}000/350{,}000$ is greater than r, then the net present value $-350{,}000 + [400{,}000/(1 + r)]$ *must* be greater than 0.

[5]The two rules can conflict when there are cash flows in more than two periods. We address this problem in Chapter 5.

[6]We are assuming that the probabilities of slump and boom are equal, so that the expected (average) outcome is $110,000. For example, suppose the slump, normal, and boom probabilities are all 1/3. Then the expected payoff $C_1 = (80{,}000 + 110{,}000 + 140{,}000)/3 = \$110.000$.

The project is worth $4,350 less than it costs. It is *not* worth undertaking.

Notice that you come to the same conclusion if you compare the expected project return with the cost of capital:

$$\text{Expected return on project} = \frac{\text{expected profit}}{\text{investment}}$$
$$= \frac{110{,}000 - 100{,}000}{100{,}000} = .10, \text{ or } 10\%$$

The 10 percent expected return on the project is less than the 15 percent return investors could expect to earn by investing in the stock market, so the project is not worthwhile.

Of course in real life it's impossible to restrict the future states of the economy to just "slump," "normal," and "boom." We have also simplified by assuming a perfect match between the payoffs of 1,000 shares of stock X and the payoffs to the investment project. The main point of the example does carry through to real life, however. Remember this: The opportunity cost of capital for an investment project is the expected rate of return demanded by investors in common stocks or other securities subject to the same risks as the project. When you discount the project's expected cash flow at its opportunity cost of capital, the resulting present value is the amount investors (including your own company's shareholders) would be willing to pay for the project. Any time you find and launch a positive-NPV project (a project with present value exceeding its required cash outlay) you have made your company's stockholders better off.

A Source of Confusion

Here is a possible source of confusion. Suppose a banker approaches. "Your company is a fine and safe business with few debts," she says. "My bank will lend you the $100,000 that you need for the project at 8 percent." Does that mean that the cost of capital for the project is 8 percent? If so, the project would be above water, with PV at 8 percent = 110,000/1.08 = $101,852 and NPV = 101,852 − 100,000 = +$1,852.

That can't be right. First, the interest rate on the loan has nothing to do with the risk of the project: It reflects the good health of your existing business. Second, whether you take the loan or not, you still face the choice between the project, which offers an expected return of only 10 percent, or the equally risky stock, which gives an expected return of 15 percent. A financial manager who borrows at 8 percent and invests at 10 percent is not smart, but stupid, if the company or its shareholders can borrow at 8 percent and buy an equally risky investment offering 15 percent. That is why the 15 percent expected return on the stock is the opportunity cost of capital for the project.

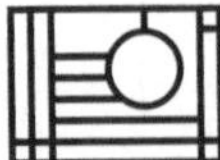

2.2 FOUNDATIONS OF THE NET PRESENT VALUE RULE

So far our discussion of net present value has been rather casual. Increasing value *sounds* like a sensible objective for a company, but it is more than just a rule of thumb. You need to understand why the NPV rule makes sense and why managers look to the bond and stock markets to find the opportunity cost of capital.

In the previous example there was just one person (you) making 100 percent of the investment and receiving 100 percent of the payoffs from the new office building. In corporations, investments are made on behalf of thousands of shareholders with varying risk tolerances and preferences for present versus future income. Could a positive-NPV project for Ms. Smith be a negative-NPV proposition for Mr. Jones? Could they find it impossible to agree on the objective of maximizing the market value of the firm?

The answer to both questions is no; Smith and Jones will always agree if both have access to capital markets. We will demonstrate this result with a simple example.

How Capital Markets Reconcile Preferences for Current vs. Future Consumption

Suppose that you can look forward to a stream of income from your job. Unless you have some way of storing or anticipating this income, you will be compelled to consume it as it arrives. This could be inconvenient or worse. If the bulk of your income comes late in life, the result could be hunger now and gluttony later. This is where the capital market comes in. The capital market allows trade between dollars today and dollars in the future. You can therefore eat moderately both now and in the future.

We will now illustrate how the existence of a well-functioning capital market allows investors with different time patterns of income and desired consumption to agree on whether investment projects should be undertaken. Suppose that there are two investors with different preferences. *A* is an ant, who wishes to save for the future; *G* is a grasshopper, who would prefer to spend all his wealth on some ephemeral frolic, taking no heed of tomorrow. Now suppose that each is confronted with an identical opportunity—to buy a share in a $350,000 office building that will produce a sure-fire $400,000 at the end of the year, a return of about 14 percent. The interest rate is 7 percent. *A* and *G* can borrow or lend in the capital market at this rate.

A would clearly be happy to invest in the office building. Every hundred dollars that she invests in the office building allows her to spend $114 at the end of the year, while a hundred dollars invested in the capital market would enable her to spend only $107.

But what about *G*, who wants money now, not in one year's time? Would he prefer to forego the investment opportunity and spend today the cash that he has in hand? Not as long as the capital market allows individuals to borrow as well as to lend. Every hundred dollars that *G* invests in the office building brings in $114 at the end of the year. Any bank, knowing that *G* could look forward to this sure-fire income, would be prepared to lend him $114/1.07 = $106.54 today. Thus, instead of spending $100 today, *G* can spend $106.54 if he invests in the office building and then borrows against his future income.

This is illustrated in Figure 2.1. The horizontal axis shows the number of dollars that can be spent today; the vertical axis shows spending next year. Suppose that the ant and the grasshopper both start with an initial sum of $100. If they invest the entire $100 in the capital market, they will be able to spend $100 \times 1.07 = \$107$ at the end of the year. The straight line joining these two points (the innermost line in the figure) shows the combinations of current and future consumption that can be achieved by investing none, part, or all of the cash at the 7 percent rate offered in the capital market. (The interest rate determines the slope of this line.) Any other point along the line could be achieved by spending

FIGURE 2.1

The grasshopper (*G*) wants consumption now. The ant (*A*) wants to wait. But each is happy to invest. *A* prefers to invest at 14 percent, moving up the burgundy arrow, rather than at the 7 percent interest rate. *G* invests and then borrows at 7 percent, thereby transforming $100 into $106.54 of immediate consumption. Because of the investment, *G* has $114 next year to pay off the loan. The investment's NPV is 106.54 − 100 = +6.54.

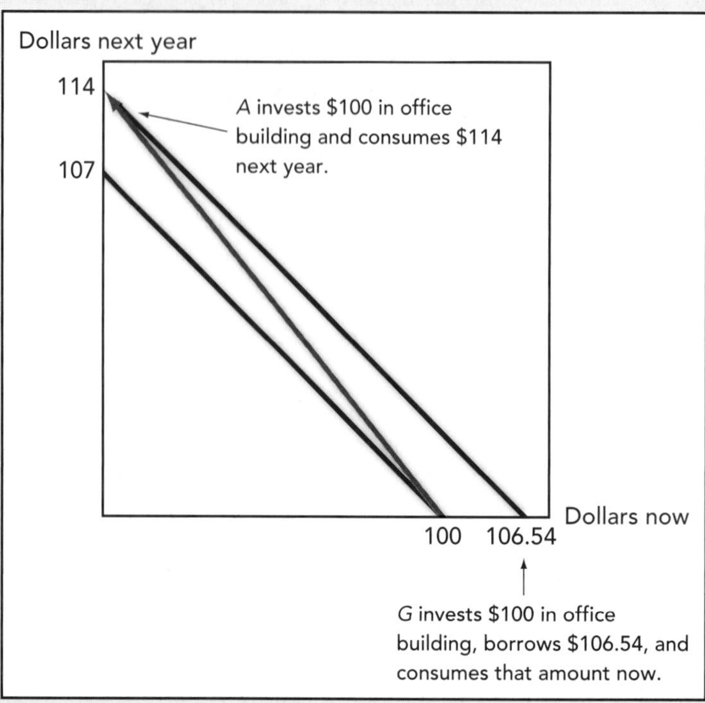

part of the $100 today and investing the balance.[7] For example, one could choose to spend $50 today and $53.50 next year. However, *A* and *G* would each reject such a balanced consumption schedule.

The burgundy arrow in Figure 2.1 shows the payoff to investing $100 in a share of your office project. The rate of return is 14 percent, so $100 today transmutes to $114 next year.

The sloping line on the right in Figure 2.1 (the outermost line in the figure) shows how *A*'s and *G*'s spending plans are enhanced if they can choose to invest their $100 in the office building. *A*, who is content to spend nothing today, can invest $100 in the building and spend $114 at the end of the year. *G*, the spendthrift, also invests $100 in the office building but borrows 114/1.07 = $106.54 against the future income. Of course, neither is limited to these spending plans. In fact, the right-hand sloping line shows all the combinations of current and future expenditure that an investor could achieve from investing $100 in the office building and borrowing against some fraction of the future income.

You can see from Figure 2.1 that the present value of *A*'s and *G*'s share in the office building is $106.54. The *net* present value is $6.54. This is the distance be-

[7]The exact balance between present and future consumption that each individual will choose depends on personal preferences. Readers who are familiar with economic theory will recognize that the choice can be represented by superimposing an indifference map for each individual. The preferred combination is the point of tangency between the interest-rate line and the individual's indifference curve. In other words, each individual will borrow or lend until 1 plus the interest rate equals the marginal rate of time preference (i.e., the slope of the indifference curve). A more formal graphical analysis of investment and the choice between present and future consumption is on the Brealey–Myers website at **www://mhhe.com/bm/7e.**

tween the \$106.54 present value and the \$100 initial investment. Despite their different tastes, both *A* and *G* are better off by investing in the office block and then using the capital markets to achieve the desired balance between consumption today and consumption at the end of the year. In fact, in coming to their investment decision, both would be happy to follow the two equivalent rules that we proposed so casually at the end of Section 2.1. The two rules can be restated as follows:

- *Net present value rule.* Invest in any project with a positive net present value. This is the difference between the discounted, or present, value of the future cash flow and the amount of the initial investment.
- *Rate-of-return rule.* Invest as long as the return on the investment exceeds the rate of return on equivalent investments in the capital market.

What happens if the interest rate is not 7 percent but 14.3 percent? In this case the office building would have zero NPV:

$$\text{NPV} = 400{,}000/1.143 - 350{,}000 = \$0$$

Also, the return on the project would be $400{,}000/350{,}000 - 1 = .143$, or 14.3 percent, exactly equal to the rate of interest in the capital market. In this case our two rules would say that the project is on a knife edge. Investors should not care whether the firm undertakes it or not.

It is easy to see that with a 14.3 percent interest rate neither *A* nor *G* would gain anything by investing in the office building. *A* could spend exactly the same amount at the end of the year, regardless of whether she invests her money in the office building or in the capital market. Equally, there is no advantage in *G* investing in an office block to earn 14.3 percent and at the same time borrowing at 14.3 percent. He might just as well spend whatever cash he has on hand.

In our example the ant and the grasshopper placed an identical value on the office building and were happy to share in its construction. They agreed because they faced identical borrowing and lending opportunities. Whenever firms discount cash flows at capital market rates, they are implicitly assuming that their shareholders have free and equal access to competitive capital markets.

It is easy to see how our net present value rule would be damaged if we did not have such a well-functioning capital market. For example, suppose that *G* could not borrow against future income or that it was prohibitively costly for him to do so. In that case he might well prefer to spend his cash today rather than invest it in an office building and have to wait until the end of the year before he could start spending. If *A* and *G* were shareholders in the same enterprise, there would be no simple way for the manager to reconcile their different objectives.

No one believes unreservedly that capital markets are perfectly competitive. Later in this book we will discuss several cases in which differences in taxation, transaction costs, and other imperfections must be taken into account in financial decision making. However, we will also discuss research which indicates that, in general, capital markets function fairly well. That is one good reason for relying on net present value as a corporate objective. Another good reason is that net present value makes common sense; we will see that it gives obviously silly answers less frequently than its major competitors. But for now, having glimpsed the problems of imperfect markets, we shall, like an economist in a shipwreck, simply *assume* our life jacket and swim safely to shore.

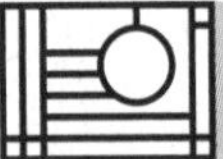

2.3 A FUNDAMENTAL RESULT

Our justification of the present value rule was restricted to two periods and to a certain cash flow. However, the rule also makes sense for uncertain cash flows that extend far into the future. The argument goes like this:

1. A financial manager should act in the interests of the firm's owners, its stockholders. Each stockholder wants three things:
   a. To be as rich as possible, that is, to maximize current wealth.
   b. To transform that wealth into whatever time pattern of consumption he or she desires.
   c. To choose the risk characteristics of that consumption plan.
2. But stockholders do not need the financial manager's help to achieve the best time pattern of consumption. They can do that on their own, providing they have free access to competitive capital markets. They can also choose the risk characteristics of their consumption plan by investing in more or less risky securities.
3. How then can the financial manager help the firm's stockholders? There is only one way: by increasing the market value of each stockholder's stake in the firm. The way to do that is to seize all investment opportunities that have a positive net present value.

Despite the fact that shareholders have different preferences, they are unanimous in the amount that they want to invest in real assets. This means that they can cooperate in the same enterprise and can safely delegate operation of that enterprise to professional managers. These managers do not need to know anything about the tastes of their shareholders and should not consult their own tastes. Their task is to maximize net present value. If they succeed, they can rest assured that they have acted in the best interest of their shareholders.

This gives us the fundamental condition for successful operation of a modern capitalist economy. Separation of ownership and control is essential for most corporations, so authority to manage has to be delegated. It is good to know that managers can all be given one simple instruction: Maximize net present value.

Other Corporate Goals

Sometimes you hear managers speak as if the corporation has other goals. For example, they may say that their job is to maximize profits. That sounds reasonable. After all, don't shareholders prefer to own a profitable company rather than an unprofitable one? But taken literally, profit maximization doesn't make sense as a corporate objective. Here are three reasons:

1. "Maximizing profits" leaves open the question, Which year's profits? Shareholders might not want a manager to increase next year's profits at the expense of profits in later years.
2. A company may be able to increase future profits by cutting its dividend and investing the cash. That is not in the shareholders' interest if the company earns only a low return on the investment.
3. Different accountants may calculate profits in different ways. So you may find that a decision which improves profits in one accountant's eyes will reduce them in the eyes of another.

2.4 DO MANAGERS REALLY LOOK AFTER THE INTERESTS OF SHAREHOLDERS?

We have explained that managers can best serve the interests of shareholders by investing in projects with a positive net present value. But this takes us back to the principal–agent problem highlighted in the first chapter. How can shareholders (the principals) ensure that management (their agents) don't simply look after their own interests? Shareholders can't spend their lives watching managers to check that they are not shirking or maximizing the value of their *own* wealth. However, there are several institutional arrangements that help to ensure that the shareholders' pockets are close to the managers' heart.

A company's board of directors is elected by the shareholders and is supposed to represent them. Boards of directors are sometimes portrayed as passive stooges who always champion the incumbent management. But when company performance starts to slide and managers do not offer a credible recovery plan, boards do act. In recent years the chief executives of Eastman Kodak, General Motors, Xerox, Lucent, Ford Motor, Sunbeam, and Lands End were all forced to step aside when each company's profitability deteriorated and the need for new strategies became clear.

If shareholders believe that the corporation is underperforming and that the board of directors is not sufficiently aggressive in holding the managers to task, they can try to replace the board in the next election. If they succeed, the new board will appoint a new management team. But these attempts to vote in a new board are expensive and rarely successful. Thus dissidents do not usually stand and fight but sell their shares instead.

Selling, however, can send a powerful message. If enough shareholders bail out, the stock price tumbles. This damages top management's reputation and compensation. Part of the top managers' paychecks comes from bonuses tied to the company's earnings or from stock options, which pay off if the stock price rises but are worthless if the price falls below a stated threshold. This should motivate managers to increase earnings and the stock price.

If managers and directors do not maximize value, there is always the threat of a hostile takeover. The further a company's stock price falls, due to lax management or wrong-headed policies, the easier it is for another company or group of investors to buy up a majority of the shares. The old management team is then likely to find themselves out on the street and their place is taken by a fresh team prepared to make the changes needed to realize the company's value.

These arrangements ensure that few managers at the top of major United States corporations are lazy or inattentive to stockholders' interests. On the contrary, the pressure to perform can be intense.

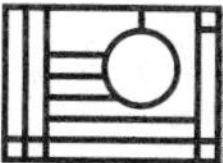

2.5 *SHOULD* MANAGERS LOOK AFTER THE INTERESTS OF SHAREHOLDERS?

We have described managers as the agents of the shareholders. But perhaps this begs the question, Is it *desirable* for managers to act in the selfish interests of their shareholders? Does a focus on enriching the shareholders mean that managers must act as greedy mercenaries riding roughshod over the weak and helpless? Do they not have wider obligations to their employees, customers, suppliers, and the communities in which the firm is located?[8]

Most of this book is devoted to financial policies that increase a firm's value. None of these policies requires gallops over the weak and helpless. In most instances there is little conflict between doing well (maximizing value) and doing good. Profitable firms are those with satisfied customers and loyal employees; firms with dissatisfied customers and a disgruntled workforce are more likely to have declining profits and a low share price.

Of course, ethical issues do arise in business as in other walks of life, and therefore when we say that the objective of the firm is to maximize shareholder wealth, we do not mean that anything goes. In part, the law deters managers from making blatantly dishonest decisions, but most managers are not simply concerned with observing the letter of the law or with keeping to written contracts. In business and finance, as in other day-to-day affairs, there are unwritten, implicit rules of behavior. To work efficiently together, we need to trust each other. Thus huge financial deals are regularly completed on a handshake, and each side knows that the other will not renege later if things turn sour.[9] Whenever anything happens to weaken this trust, we are all a little worse off.[10]

In many financial transactions, one party has more information than the other. It can be difficult to be sure of the quality of the asset or service that you are buying. This opens up plenty of opportunities for financial sharp practice and outright fraud, and, because the activities of scoundrels are more entertaining than those of honest people, airport bookstores are packed with accounts of financial fraudsters.

The response of honest firms is to distinguish themselves by building long-term relationships with their customers and establishing a name for fair dealing and financial integrity. Major banks and securities firms know that their most valuable asset is their reputation. They emphasize their long history and responsible behavior. When something happens to undermine that reputation, the costs can be enormous.

Consider the Salomon Brothers bidding scandal in 1991.[11] A Salomon trader tried to evade rules limiting the firm's participation in auctions of U.S. Treasury bonds by submitting bids in the names of the company's customers without the customers' knowledge. When this was discovered, Salomon settled the case by paying almost $200 million in fines and establishing a $100 million fund for payments of claims from civil lawsuits. Yet the value of Salomon Brothers stock fell by

[8]Some managers, anxious not to offend any group of stakeholders, have denied that they are maximizing profits or value. We are reminded of a survey of businesspeople that inquired whether they attempted to maximize profits. They indignantly rejected the notion, objecting that their responsibilities went far beyond the narrow, selfish profit motive. But when the question was reformulated and they were asked whether they could increase profits by raising or lowering their selling price, they replied that neither change would do so. The survey is cited in G. J. Stigler, *The Theory of Price,* 3rd ed. (New York: Macmillan Company, 1966).

[9]In U.S. law, a contract can be valid even if it is not written down. Of course documentation is prudent, but contracts are enforced if it can be shown that the parties reached a clear understanding and agreement. For example, in 1984, the top management of Getty Oil gave verbal agreement to a merger offer with Pennzoil. Then Texaco arrived with a higher bid and won the prize. Pennzoil sued—and won—arguing that Texaco had broken up a valid contract.

[10]For a discussion of this issue, see A. Schleifer and L. H. Summers, "Breach of Trust in Corporate Takeovers," *Corporate Takeovers: Causes and Consequences* (Chicago: University of Chicago Press, 1988).

[11]This discussion is based on Clifford W. Smith, Jr., "Economics and Ethics: The Case of Salomon Brothers," *Journal of Applied Corporate Finance* 5 (Summer 1992), pp. 23–28.

far more than $300 million. In fact the price dropped by about a third, representing a $1.5 billion decline in the company's market value.

Why did the value of Salomon Brothers drop so dramatically? Largely because investors were worried that Salomon would lose business from customers that now distrusted the company. The damage to Salomon's reputation was far greater than the explicit costs of the scandal and was hundreds or thousands of times more costly than the potential gains Salomon could have reaped from the illegal trades.

SUMMARY

In this chapter we have introduced the concept of present value as a way of valuing assets. Calculating present value is easy. Just discount future cash flow by an appropriate rate r, usually called the *opportunity cost of capital,* or hurdle rate:

$$\text{Present value (PV)} = \frac{C_1}{1 + r}$$

Net present value is present value plus any immediate cash flow:

$$\text{Net present value (NPV)} = C_0 + \frac{C_1}{1 + r}$$

Remember that C_0 is negative if the immediate cash flow is an investment, that is, if it is a cash outflow.

The discount rate is determined by rates of return prevailing in capital markets. If the future cash flow is absolutely safe, then the discount rate is the interest rate on safe securities such as United States government debt. If the size of the future cash flow is uncertain, then the expected cash flow should be discounted at the expected rate of return offered by equivalent-risk securities. We will talk more about risk and the cost of capital in Chapters 7 through 9.

Cash flows are discounted for two simple reasons: first, because a dollar today is worth more than a dollar tomorrow, and second, because a safe dollar is worth more than a risky one. Formulas for PV and NPV are numerical expressions of these ideas. The capital market is the market where safe and risky future cash flows are traded. That is why we look to rates of return prevailing in the capital markets to determine how much to discount for time and risk. By calculating the present value of an asset, we are in effect estimating how much people will pay for it if they have the alternative of investing in the capital markets.

The concept of net present value allows efficient separation of ownership and management of the corporation. A manager who invests only in assets with positive net present values serves the best interests of each one of the firm's owners, regardless of differences in their wealth and tastes. This is made possible by the existence of the capital market which allows each shareholder to construct a personal investment plan that is custom tailored to his or her own requirements. For example, there is no need for the firm to arrange its investment policy to obtain a sequence of cash flows that matches its shareholders' preferred time patterns of consumption. The shareholders can shift funds forward or back over time perfectly well on their own, provided they have free access to competitive capital markets. In fact, their plan for consumption over time is limited by only two things: their personal wealth (or lack of it) and the interest rate at which they can borrow or lend. The financial manager cannot affect the interest rate but can increase stockholders' wealth. The way to do so is to invest in assets having positive net present values.

There are several institutional arrangements which help to ensure that managers pay close attention to the value of the firm:

- Managers' actions are subject to the scrutiny of the board of directors.
- Shirkers are likely to find that they are ousted by more energetic managers. This competition may arise within the firm, but poorly performing companies are also more likely to be taken over. That sort of takeover typically brings in a fresh management team.
- Managers are spurred on by incentive schemes, such as stock options, which pay off big if shareholders gain but are valueless if they do not.

Managers who focus on shareholder value need not neglect their wider obligations to the community. Managers play fair by employees, customers, and suppliers partly because they know that it is for the common good, but partly because they know that their firm's most valuable asset is its reputation. Of course, ethical issues do arise in financial management and, whenever unscrupulous managers abuse their position, we all trust each other a little less.

FURTHER READING

The pioneering works on the net present value rule are:

I. Fisher: *The Theory of Interest,* Augustus M. Kelley, Publishers. New York, 1965. Reprinted from the 1930 edition.

J. Hirshleifer: "On the Theory of Optimal Investment Decision," *Journal of Political Economy,* 66:329–352 (August 1958).

For a more rigorous textbook treatment of the subject, we suggest:

E. F. Fama and M. H. Miller: *The Theory of Finance,* Holt, Rinehart and Winston. New York, 1972.

If you would like to dig deeper into the question of how managers can be motivated to maximize shareholder wealth, we suggest:

M. C. Jensen and W. H. Meckling: "Theory of the Firm: Managerial Behavior, Agency Costs, and Ownership Structure," *Journal of Financial Economics,* 3:305–360 (October 1976).

E. F. Fama: "Agency Problems and the Theory of the Firm," *Journal of Political Economy,* 88:288–307 (April 1980).

QUIZ

1. C_0 is the initial cash flow on an investment, and C_1 is the cash flow at the end of one year. The symbol r is the discount rate.
   a. Is C_0 usually positive or negative?
   b. What is the formula for the present value of the investment?
   c. What is the formula for the net present value?
   d. The symbol r is often termed the *opportunity cost of capital.* Why?
   e. If the investment is risk-free, what is the appropriate measure of r?

2. If the present value of $150 paid at the end of one year is $130, what is the one-year discount factor? What is the discount rate?

3. Calculate the one-year discount factor DF_1 for discount rates of (a) 10 percent, (b) 20 percent, and (c) 30 percent.

4. A merchant pays $100,000 for a load of grain and is certain that it can be resold at the end of one year for $132,000.
   a. What is the return on this investment?
   b. If this return is *lower* than the rate of interest, does the investment have a positive or a negative NPV?
   c. If the rate of interest is 10 percent, what is the PV of the investment?
   d. What is the NPV?
5. What is the net present value rule? What is the rate of return rule? Do the two rules give the same answer?
6. Define the opportunity cost of capital. How in principle would you find the opportunity cost of capital for a risk-free asset? For a risky asset?
7. Look back to the numerical example graphed in Figure 2.1. Suppose the interest rate is 20 percent. What would the ant (*A*) and grasshopper (*G*) do? Would they invest in the office building? Would they borrow or lend? Suppose each starts with $100. How much and when would each consume?
8. We can imagine the financial manager doing several things on behalf of the firm's stockholders. For example, the manager might:
   a. Make shareholders as wealthy as possible by investing in real assets with positive NPVs.
   b. Modify the firm's investment plan to help shareholders achieve a particular time pattern of consumption.
   c. Choose high- or low-risk assets to match shareholders' risk preferences.
   d. Help balance shareholders' checkbooks.

   But in well-functioning capital markets, shareholders will vote for *only one* of these goals. Which one? Why?
9. Why would one expect managers to act in shareholders' interests? Give some reasons.
10. After the Salomon Brothers bidding scandal, the aggregate value of the company's stock dropped by far more than it paid in fines and settlements of lawsuits. Why?

1. Write down the formulas for an investment's NPV and rate of return. Prove that NPV is positive *only* if the rate of return exceeds the opportunity cost of capital.
2. What is the net present value of a *firm's* investment in a U.S. Treasury security yielding 5 percent and maturing in one year? *Hint:* What is the opportunity cost of capital? Ignore taxes.
3. A parcel of land costs $500,000. For an additional $800,000 you can build a motel on the property. The land and motel should be worth $1,500,000 next year. Suppose that common stocks with the same risk as this investment offer a 10 percent expected return. Would you construct the motel? Why or why not?
4. Calculate the NPV and rate of return for each of the following investments. The opportunity cost of capital is 20 percent for all four investments.

Investment	Initial Cash Flow, C_0	Cash Flow in Year 1, C_1
1	−10,000	+18,000
2	−5,000	+9,000
3	−5,000	+5,700
4	−2,000	+4,000

a. Which investment is most valuable?
b. Suppose each investment would require use of the same parcel of land. Therefore you can take only one. Which one? *Hint:* What is the firm's objective: to earn a high rate of return or to increase firm value?

5. In Section 2.1, we analyzed the possible construction of an office building on a plot of land appraised at $50,000. We concluded that this investment had a positive NPV of $7,143 at a discount rate of 12 percent.

   Suppose E. Coli Associates, a firm of genetic engineers, offers to purchase the land for $60,000, $30,000 paid immediately and $30,000 after one year. United States government securities maturing in one year yield 7 percent.
   a. Assume E. Coli is sure to pay the second $30,000 installment. Should you take its offer or start on the office building? Explain.
   b. Suppose you are *not* sure E. Coli will pay. You observe that other investors demand a 10 percent return on their loans to E. Coli. Assume that the other investors have correctly assessed the risks that E. Coli will not be able to pay. Should you accept E. Coli's offer?

6. Explain why the discount rate equals the *opportunity* cost of capital.

7. Norman Gerrymander has just received a $2 million bequest. How should he invest it? There are four immediate alternatives.
   a. Investment in one-year U.S. government securities yielding 5 percent.
   b. A loan to Norman's nephew Gerald, who has for years aspired to open a big Cajun restaurant in Duluth. Gerald had arranged a one-year bank loan for $900,000, at 10 percent, but asks for a loan from Norman at 7 percent.
   c. Investment in the stock market. The expected rate of return is 12 percent.
   d. Investment in local real estate, which Norman judges is about as risky as the stock market. The opportunity at hand would cost $1 million and is forecasted to be worth $1.1 million after one year.

   Which of these investments have positive NPVs? Which would you advise Norman to take?

8. Show that your answers to Practice Question 7 are consistent with the rate of return rule for investment decisions.

9. Take another look at investment opportunity (d) in Practice Question 7. Suppose a bank offers Norman a $600,000 personal loan at 8 percent. (Norman is a long-time customer of the bank and has an excellent credit history.) Suppose Norman borrows the money, invests $1 million in real estate opportunity (d) and puts the rest of his money in opportunity (c), the stock market. Is this a smart move? Explain.

10. Respond to the following comments.
    a. "My company's cost of capital is the rate we pay to the bank when we borrow money."
    b. "Net present value is just theory. It has no practical relevance. We maximize profits. That's what shareholders really want."
    c. "It's no good just telling me to maximize my stock price. I can easily take a short view and maximize today's price. What I would prefer is to keep it on a gently rising trend."

11. Ms. Smith is retired and depends on her investments for retirement income. Mr. Jones is a young executive who wants to save for the future. They are both stockholders in Airbus, which is investing over $12 billion to develop the A380, a new super-jumbo airliner. This investment's payoff is many years in the future. Assume the investment is positive-NPV for Mr. Jones. Explain why it should also be positive-NPV for Ms. Smith.

12. Answer this question by drawing graphs like Figure 2.1. Casper Milktoast has $200,000 available to support consumption in periods 0 (now) and 1 (next year). He

wants to consume *exactly* the same amount in each period. The interest rate is 8 percent. There is no risk.

a. How much should he invest, and how much can he consume in each period?
b. Suppose Casper is given an opportunity to invest up to $200,000 at 10 percent risk-free. The interest rate stays at 8 percent. What should he do, and how much can he consume in each period?
c. What is the NPV of the opportunity in (b)?

13. We said that maximizing value makes sense only if we assume well-functioning capital markets. What does "well-functioning" mean? Can you think of circumstances in which maximizing value would not be in all shareholders' interests?

14. Why is a reputation for honesty and fair business practice important to the financial value of the corporation?

CHALLENGE QUESTIONS

1. It is sometimes argued that the NPV criterion is appropriate for corporations but not for governments. First, governments must consider the time preferences of the community as a whole rather than those of a few wealthy investors. Second, governments must have a longer horizon than individuals, for governments are the guardians of future generations. What do you think?

2. In Figure 2.2, the sloping line represents the opportunities for investment in the capital market and the solid curved line represents the opportunities for investment in plant and machinery. The company's only asset at present is $2.6 million in cash.
   a. What is the interest rate?
   b. How much should the company invest in plant and machinery?
   c. How much will this investment be worth next year?
   d. What is the average rate of return on the investment?
   e. What is the marginal rate of return?
   f. What is the PV of this investment?
   g. What is the NPV of this investment?
   h. What is the total PV of the company?
   i. How much will the individual consume today?
   j. How much will he or she consume tomorrow?

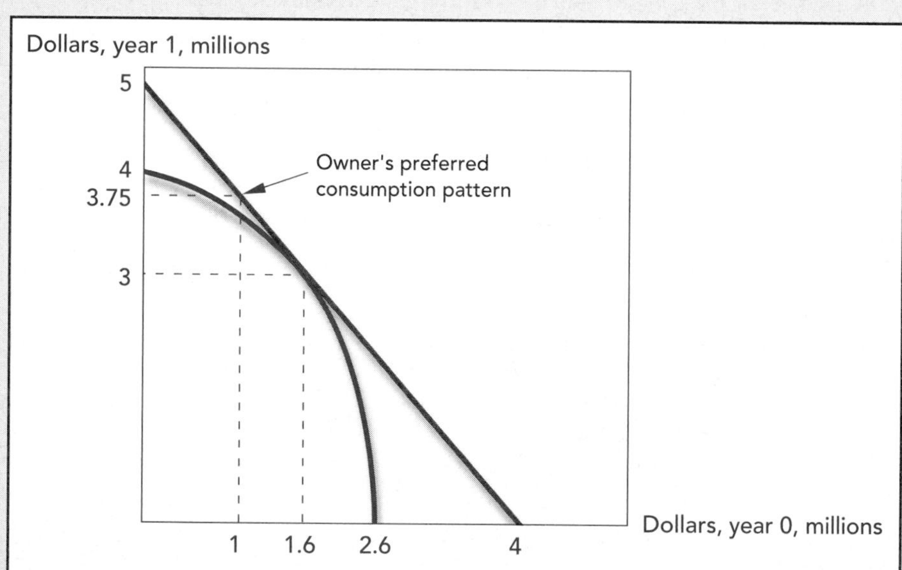

FIGURE 2.2

See Challenge Question 2.

3. Draw a figure like Figure 2.1 to represent the following situation.
   a. A firm starts out with $10 million in cash.
   b. The rate of interest r is 10 percent.
   c. To maximize NPV the firm invests today $6 million in real assets. This leaves $4 million which can be paid out to the shareholders.
   d. The NPV of the investment is $2 million.

   When you have finished, answer the following questions:

   e. How much cash is the firm going to receive in year 1 from its investment?
   f. What is the marginal return from the firm's investment?
   g. What is the PV of the shareholders' investment after the firm has announced its investment plan?
   h. Suppose shareholders want to spend $6 million today. How can they do this?
   i. How much will they then have to spend next year? Show this on your drawing.

4. For an outlay of $8 million you can purchase a tanker load of bucolic acid delivered in Rotterdam one year hence. Unfortunately the net cash flow from selling the tanker load will be very sensitive to the growth rate of the world economy:

Slump	Normal	Boom
$8 million	$12 million	$16 million

   a. What is the expected cash flow? Assume the three outcomes for the economy are equally likely.
   b. What is the expected rate of return on the investment in the project?
   c. One share of stock Z is selling for $10. The stock has the following payoffs after one year:

Slump	Normal	Boom
$8	$12	$16

   Calculate the expected rate of return offered by stock Z. Explain why this is the opportunity cost of capital for your bucolic acid project.
   d. Calculate the project's NPV. Is the project a good investment? Explain why.

5. In real life the future health of the economy cannot be reduced to three equally probable states like slump, normal, and boom. But we'll keep that simplification for one more example.

   Your company has identified two more projects, B and C. Each will require a $5 million outlay immediately. The possible payoffs at year 1 are, in millions:

	Slump	Normal	Boom
B	4	6	8
C	5	5.5	6

   You have identified the possible payoffs to investors in three stocks, X, Y, and Z:

	Current Price per Share	Payoff at Year 1		
		Slump	Normal	Boom
X	95.65	80	110	140
Y	40	40	44	48
Z	10	8	12	16

a. What are the expected cash inflows of projects B and C?
b. What are the expected rates of return offered by stocks X, Y, and Z?
c. What are the opportunity costs of capital for projects B and C? *Hint:* Calculate the percentage differences, slump versus normal and boom versus normal, for stocks X, Y, and Z. Match up to the percentage differences in B's and C's payoffs.
d. What are the NPVs of projects B and C?
e. Suppose B and C are launched and $5 million is invested in each. How much will they add to the total market value of your company's shares?

CHAPTER THREE

HOW TO CALCULATE PRESENT VALUES

IN CHAPTER 2 we learned how to work out the value of an asset that produces cash exactly one year from now. But we did not explain how to value assets that produce cash two years from now or in several future years. That is the first task for this chapter. We will then have a look at some shortcut methods for calculating present values and at some specialized present value formulas. In particular we will show how to value an investment that makes a steady stream of payments forever (a *perpetuity*) and one that produces a steady stream for a limited period (an *annuity*). We will also look at investments that produce a steadily growing stream of payments.

The term *interest rate* sounds straightforward enough, but we will see that it can be defined in various ways. We will first explain the distinction between *compound interest* and *simple interest.* Then we will discuss the difference between the nominal interest rate and the real interest rate. This difference arises because the purchasing power of interest income is reduced by inflation.

By then you will deserve some payoff for the mental investment you have made in learning about present values. Therefore, we will try out the concept on bonds. In Chapter 4 we will look at the valuation of common stocks, and after that we will tackle the firm's capital investment decisions at a practical level of detail.

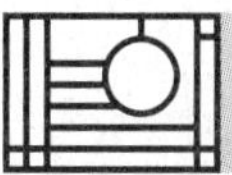

3.1 VALUING LONG-LIVED ASSETS

Do you remember how to calculate the present value (PV) of an asset that produces a cash flow (C_1) one year from now?

$$\text{PV} = \text{DF}_1 \times C_1 = \frac{C_1}{1 + r_1}$$

The discount factor for the year-1 cash flow is DF_1, and r_1 is the opportunity cost of investing your money for one year. Suppose you will receive a certain cash inflow of \$100 next year ($C_1 = 100$) and the rate of interest on one-year U.S. Treasury notes is 7 percent ($r_1 = .07$). Then present value equals

$$\text{PV} = \frac{C_1}{1 + r_1} = \frac{100}{1.07} = \$93.46$$

The present value of a cash flow two years hence can be written in a similar way as

$$\text{PV} = \text{DF}_2 \times C_2 = \frac{C_2}{(1 + r_2)^2}$$

C_2 is the year-2 cash flow, DF_2 is the discount factor for the year-2 cash flow, and r_2 is the annual rate of interest on money invested for two years. Suppose you get another cash flow of \$100 in year 2 ($C_2 = 100$). The rate of interest on two-year Treasury notes is 7.7 percent per year ($r_2 = .077$); this means that a dollar invested in two-year notes will grow to $1.077^2 = \$1.16$ by the end of two years. The present value of your year-2 cash flow equals

$$\text{PV} = \frac{C_2}{(1 + r_2)^2} = \frac{100}{(1.077)^2} = \$86.21$$

Valuing Cash Flows in Several Periods

One of the nice things about present values is that they are all expressed in current dollars—so that you can add them up. In other words, the present value of cash flow $A + B$ is equal to the present value of cash flow A plus the present value of cash flow B. This happy result has important implications for investments that produce cash flows in several periods.

We calculated above the value of an asset that produces a cash flow of C_1 in year 1, and we calculated the value of another asset that produces a cash flow of C_2 in year 2. Following our additivity rule, we can write down the value of an asset that produces cash flows in *each* year. It is simply

$$PV = \frac{C_1}{1 + r_1} + \frac{C_2}{(1 + r_2)^2}$$

We can obviously continue in this way to find the present value of an extended stream of cash flows:

$$PV = \frac{C_1}{1 + r_1} + \frac{C_2}{(1 + r_2)^2} + \frac{C_3}{(1 + r_3)^3} + \cdots$$

This is called the **discounted cash flow** (or **DCF**) formula. A shorthand way to write it is

$$PV = \sum \frac{C_t}{(1 + r_t)^t}$$

where Σ refers to the sum of the series. To find the *net* present value (NPV) we add the (usually negative) initial cash flow, just as in Chapter 2:

$$NPV = C_0 + PV = C_0 + \sum \frac{C_t}{(1 + r_t)^t}$$

Why the Discount Factor Declines as Futurity Increases—And a Digression on Money Machines

If a dollar tomorrow is worth less than a dollar today, one might suspect that a dollar the day after tomorrow should be worth even less. In other words, the discount factor DF_2 should be less than the discount factor DF_1. But is this *necessarily* so, when there is a different interest rate r_t for each period?

Suppose r_1 is 20 percent and r_2 is 7 percent. Then

$$DF_1 = \frac{1}{1.20} = .83$$

$$DF_2 = \frac{1}{(1.07)^2} = .87$$

Apparently the dollar received the day after tomorrow is *not* necessarily worth less than the dollar received tomorrow.

But there is something wrong with this example. Anyone who could borrow and lend at these interest rates could become a millionaire overnight. Let us see how such a "money machine" would work. Suppose the first person to spot the opportunity is Hermione Kraft. Ms. Kraft first lends $1,000 for one year at 20 percent. That is an attractive enough return, but she notices that there is a way to earn an *immediate* profit on her investment and be ready to play the game again. She reasons as follows. Next year she will have \$1,200 which can be reinvested for a further year. Although she does not know what interest rates will be at that time, she does know that she can always put the money in a checking account and be sure of having \$1,200 at the end of year 2. Her next step, therefore, is to go to her bank and borrow the present value of this \$1,200. At 7 percent interest this present value is

$$PV = \frac{1200}{(1.07)^2} = \$1,048$$

Thus Ms. Kraft invests \$1,000, borrows back \$1,048, and walks away with a profit of \$48. If that does not sound like very much, remember that the game can be played again immediately, this time with \$1,048. In fact it would take Ms. Kraft only 147 plays to become a millionaire (before taxes).[1]

Of course this story is completely fanciful. Such an opportunity would not last long in capital markets like ours. Any bank that would allow you to lend for one year at 20 percent and borrow for two years at 7 percent would soon be wiped out by a rush of small investors hoping to become millionaires and a rush of millionaires hoping to become billionaires. There are, however, two lessons to our story. The first is that a dollar tomorrow *cannot* be worth less than a dollar the day after tomorrow. In other words, the value of a dollar received at the end of one year (DF_1) must be greater than the value of a dollar received at the end of two years (DF_2). There must be some extra gain[2] from lending for two periods rather than one: $(1 + r_2)^2$ must be greater than $1 + r_1$.

Our second lesson is a more general one and can be summed up by the precept "There is no such thing as a money machine."[3] In well-functioning capital markets, any potential money machine will be eliminated almost instantaneously by investors who try to take advantage of it. Therefore, beware of self-styled experts who offer you a chance to participate in a sure thing.

Later in the book we will invoke the *absence* of money machines to prove several useful properties about security prices. That is, we will make statements like "The prices of securities X and Y must be in the following relationship—otherwise there would be a money machine and capital markets would not be in equilibrium."

Ruling out money machines does not require that interest rates be the same for each future period. This relationship between the interest rate and the maturity of the cash flow is called the **term structure of interest rates.** We are going to look at term structure in Chapter 24, but for now we will finesse the issue by assuming that the term structure is "flat"—in other words, the interest rate is the same regardless of the date of the cash flow. This means that we can replace the series of interest rates $r_1, r_2, \ldots, r_t$, etc., with a single rate r and that we can write the present value formula as

$$PV = \frac{C_1}{1 + r} + \frac{C_2}{(1 + r)^2} + \cdots$$

[1]That is, $1,000 \times (1.04813)^{147} = \$1,002,000$.

[2]The extra return for lending two years rather than one is often referred to as a *forward rate of return*. Our rule says that the forward rate cannot be negative.

[3]The technical term for money machine is *arbitrage*. There are no opportunities for arbitrage in well-functioning capital markets.

Calculating PVs and NPVs

You have some bad news about your office building venture (the one described at the start of Chapter 2). The contractor says that construction will take two years instead of one and requests payment on the following schedule:

1. A $100,000 down payment now. (Note that the land, worth $50,000, must also be committed now.)
2. A $100,000 progress payment after one year.
3. A final payment of $100,000 when the building is ready for occupancy at the end of the second year.

Your real estate adviser maintains that despite the delay the building will be worth $400,000 when completed.

All this yields a new set of cash-flow forecasts:

Period	t = 0	t = 1	t = 2
Land	−50,000		
Construction	−100,000	−100,000	−100,000
Payoff			+400,000
Total	$C_0 = -150{,}000$	$C_1 = -100{,}000$	$C_2 = +300{,}000$

If the interest rate is 7 percent, then NPV is

$$\begin{aligned} NPV &= C_0 + \frac{C_1}{1+r} + \frac{C_2}{(1+r)^2} \\ &= -150{,}000 - \frac{100{,}000}{1.07} + \frac{300{,}000}{(1.07)^2} \end{aligned}$$

Table 3.1 calculates NPV step by step. The calculations require just a few keystrokes on an electronic calculator. Real problems can be much more complicated, however, so financial managers usually turn to calculators especially programmed for present value calculations or to spreadsheet programs on personal computers. In some cases it can be convenient to look up discount factors in present value tables like Appendix Table 1 at the end of this book.

Fortunately the news about your office venture is not all bad. The contractor is willing to accept a delayed payment; this means that the present value of the contractor's fee is less than before. This partly offsets the delay in the payoff. As Table 3.1 shows,

TABLE 3.1

Present value worksheet.

Period	Discount Factor	Cash Flow	Present Value
0	1.0	−150,000	−150,000
1	$\frac{1}{1.07} = .935$	−100,000	−93,500
2	$\frac{1}{(1.07)^2} = .873$	+300,000	+261,900
			Total = NPV = $18,400

the net present value is \$18,400—not a substantial decrease from the \$23,800 calculated in Chapter 2. Since the net present value is positive, you should still go ahead.[4]

3.2 LOOKING FOR SHORTCUTS—PERPETUITIES AND ANNUITIES

Sometimes there are shortcuts that make it easy to calculate present values. Let us look at some examples.

Among the securities that have been issued by the British government are so-called **perpetuities.** These are bonds that the government is under no obligation to repay but that offer a fixed income for each year to perpetuity. The annual rate of return on a perpetuity is equal to the promised annual payment divided by the present value:

$$\text{Return} = \frac{\text{cash flow}}{\text{present value}}$$

$$r = \frac{C}{\text{PV}}$$

We can obviously twist this around and find the present value of a perpetuity given the discount rate r and the cash payment C. For example, suppose that some worthy person wishes to endow a chair in finance at a business school with the initial payment occurring at the end of the first year. If the rate of interest is 10 percent and if the aim is to provide \$100,000 a year in perpetuity, the amount that must be set aside today is[5]

$$\text{Present value of perpetuity} = \frac{C}{r} = \frac{100{,}000}{.10} = \$1{,}000{,}000$$

How to Value Growing Perpetuities

Suppose now that our benefactor suddenly recollects that no allowance has been made for growth in salaries, which will probably average about 4 percent a year starting in year 1. Therefore, instead of providing \$100,000 a year in perpetuity, the benefactor must provide \$100,000 in year 1, 1.04 × \$100,000 in year 2, and so on. If

---

[4]We assume the cash flows are safe. If they are risky forecasts, the opportunity cost of capital could be higher, say 12 percent. NPV at 12 percent is just about zero.

[5]You can check this by writing down the present value formula

$$\text{PV} = \frac{C}{1+r} + \frac{C}{(1+r)^2} + \frac{C}{(1+r)^3} + \cdots$$

Now let $C/(1+r) = a$ and $1/(1+r) = x$. Then we have (1) $\text{PV} = a(1 + x + x^2 + \cdots)$.

Multiplying both sides by x, we have (2) $\text{PV}x = a(x + x^2 + \cdots)$.

Subtracting (2) from (1) gives us $\text{PV}(1 - x) = a$. Therefore, substituting for a and x,

$$\text{PV}\left(1 - \frac{1}{1+r}\right) = \frac{C}{1+r}$$

Multiplying both sides by $(1 + r)$ and rearranging gives

$$\text{PV} = \frac{C}{r}$$

we call the growth rate in salaries g, we can write down the present value of this stream of cash flows as follows:

$$\begin{aligned} PV &= \frac{C_1}{1+r} + \frac{C_2}{(1+r)^2} + \frac{C_3}{(1+r)^3} + \cdots \\ &= \frac{C_1}{1+r} + \frac{C_1(1+g)}{(1+r)^2} + \frac{C_1(1+g)^2}{(1+r)^3} + \cdots \end{aligned}$$

Fortunately, there is a simple formula for the sum of this geometric series.[6] If we assume that r is greater than g, our clumsy-looking calculation simplifies to

$$\text{Present value of growing perpetuity} = \frac{C_1}{r-g}$$

Therefore, if our benefactor wants to provide perpetually an annual sum that keeps pace with the growth rate in salaries, the amount that must be set aside today is

$$PV = \frac{C_1}{r-g} = \frac{100{,}000}{.10 - .04} = \$1{,}666{,}667$$

How to Value Annuities

An **annuity** is an asset that pays a fixed sum each year for a specified number of years. The equal-payment house mortgage or installment credit agreement are common examples of annuities.

Figure 3.1 illustrates a simple trick for valuing annuities. The first row represents a perpetuity that produces a cash flow of C in each year beginning in year 1. It has a present value of

$$PV = \frac{C}{r}$$

FIGURE 3.1

An annuity that makes payments in each of years 1 to t is equal to the difference between two perpetuities.

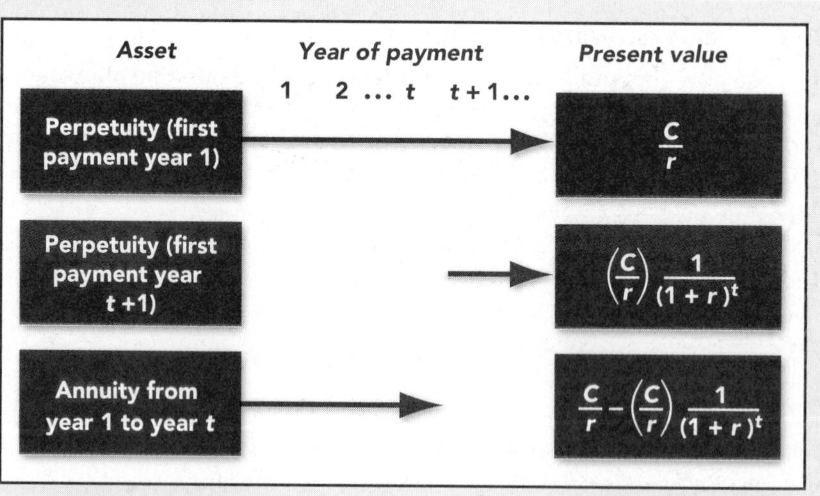

[6] We need to calculate the sum of an infinite geometric series $PV = a(1 + x + x^2 + \cdots)$ where $a = C_1/(1 + r)$ and $x = (1 + g)/(1 + r)$. In footnote 5 we showed that the sum of such a series is $a/(1 - x)$. Substituting for a and x in this formula,

$$PV = \frac{C_1}{r-g}$$

The second row represents a second *perpetuity* that produces a cash flow of C in each year *beginning in year* $t+1$. It *will* have a present value of C/r in year t and it therefore has a present value today of

$$\text{PV} = \frac{C}{r(1+r)^t}$$

Both perpetuities provide a cash flow from year $t+1$ onward. The only difference between the two perpetuities is that the first one *also* provides a cash flow in each of the years 1 through t. In other words, the difference between the two perpetuities is an annuity of C for t years. The present value of this annuity is, therefore, the difference between the values of the two perpetuities:

$$\text{Present value of annuity} = C\left[\frac{1}{r} - \frac{1}{r(1+r)^t}\right]$$

The expression in brackets is the *annuity factor,* which is the present value at discount rate r of an annuity of \$1 paid at the end of each of t periods.[7]

Suppose, for example, that our benefactor begins to vacillate and wonders what it would cost to endow a chair providing \$100,000 a year for only 20 years. The answer calculated from our formula is

$$\text{PV} = 100{,}000\left[\frac{1}{.10} - \frac{1}{.10(1.10)^{20}}\right] = 100{,}000 \times 8.514 = \$851{,}400$$

Alternatively, we can simply look up the answer in the annuity table in the Appendix at the end of the book (Appendix Table 3). This table gives the present value of a dollar to be received in each of t periods. In our example $t = 20$ and the interest rate $r = .10$, and therefore we look at the twentieth number from the top in the *10 percent* column. It is 8.514. Multiply 8.514 by \$100,000, and we have our answer, \$851,400.

Remember that the annuity formula assumes that the first payment occurs one period hence. If the first cash payment occurs immediately, we would need to discount each cash flow by one less year. So the present value would be increased by the multiple $(1 + r)$. For example, if our benefactor were prepared to make 20 annual payments *starting immediately,* the value would be \$851,400 × 1.10 = \$936,540. An annuity offering an immediate payment is known as an *annuity due.*

[7]Again we can work this out from first principles. We need to calculate the sum of the finite geometric series (1) $\text{PV} = a(1 + x + x^2 + \cdots + x^{t-1})$,

where $a = C/(1+r)$ and $x = 1/(1+r)$.

Multiplying both sides by x, we have (2) $\text{PV}x = a(x + x^2 + \cdots + x^t)$.

Subtracting (2) from (1) gives us $\text{PV}(1 - x) = a(1 - x^t)$.

Therefore, substituting for a and x,

$$\text{PV}\left(1 - \frac{1}{1+r}\right) = C\left[\frac{1}{1+r} - \frac{1}{(1+r)^{t+1}}\right]$$

Multiplying both sides by $(1 + r)$ and rearranging gives

$$\text{PV} = C\left[\frac{1}{r} - \frac{1}{r(1+r)^t}\right]$$

You should always be on the lookout for ways in which you can use these formulas to make life easier. For example, we sometimes need to calculate how much a series of annual payments earning a fixed annual interest rate would amass to by the end of t periods. In this case it is easiest to calculate the *present* value, and then multiply it by $(1 + r)^t$ to find the future value.[8] Thus suppose our benefactor wished to know how much wealth $100,000 would produce if it were invested each year instead of being given to those no-good academics. The answer would be

$$\text{Future value} = \text{PV} \times 1.10^{20} = \$851{,}400 \times 6.727 = \$5.73 \text{ million}$$

How did we know that 1.10^{20} was 6.727? Easy—we just looked it up in Appendix Table 2 at the end of the book: "Future Value of $1 at the End of t Periods."

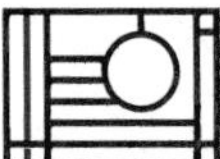

3.3 COMPOUND INTEREST AND PRESENT VALUES

There is an important distinction between **compound interest** and **simple interest.** When money is invested at compound interest, each interest payment is reinvested to earn more interest in subsequent periods. In contrast, the opportunity to earn interest on interest is not provided by an investment that pays only simple interest.

Table 3.2 compares the growth of $100 invested at compound versus simple interest. Notice that in the simple interest case, *the interest is paid only on the initial in-*

	Simple Interest					Compound Interest				
Year	**Starting Balance**	+	**Interest**	=	**Ending Balance**	**Starting Balance**	+	**Ending Interest**	=	**Balance**
1	100	+	10	=	110	100	+	10	=	110
2	110	+	10	=	120	110	+	11	=	121
3	120	+	10	=	130	121	+	12.1	=	133.1
4	130	+	10	=	140	133.1	+	13.3	=	146.4
10	190	+	10	=	200	236	+	24	=	259
20	290	+	10	=	300	612	+	61	=	673
50	590	+	10	=	600	10,672	+	1,067	=	11,739
100	1,090	+	10	=	1,100	1,252,783	+	125,278	=	1,378,061
200	2,090	+	10	=	2,100	17,264,116,042	+	1,726,411,604	=	18,990,527,646
226	2,350	+	10	=	2,360	205,756,782,755	+	20,575,678,275	=	226,332,461,030

TABLE 3.2

Value of $100 invested at 10 percent simple and compound interest.

[8]For example, suppose you receive a cash flow of C in year 6. If you invest this cash flow at an interest rate of r, you will have by year 10 an investment worth $C(1 + r)^4$. You can get the same answer by calculating the *present value* of the cash flow $\text{PV} = C/(1 + r)^6$ and then working out how much you would have by year 10 if you invested this sum today:

$$\text{Future value} = \text{PV}(1 + r)^{10} = \frac{C}{(1 + r)^6} \times (1 + r)^{10} = C(1 + r)^4$$

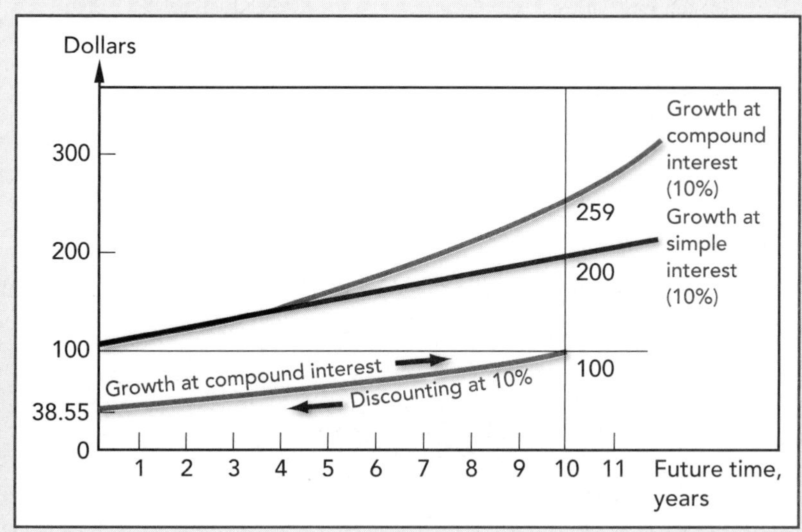

FIGURE 3.2

Compound interest versus simple interest. The top two ascending lines show the growth of $100 invested at simple and compound interest. The longer the funds are invested, the greater the advantage with compound interest. The bottom line shows that $38.55 must be invested now to obtain $100 after 10 periods. Conversely, the present value of $100 to be received after 10 years is $38.55.

vestment of $100. Your wealth therefore increases by just $10 a year. In the compound interest case, you earn 10 percent on your initial investment in the first year, which gives you a balance at the end of the year of $100 \times 1.10 = \$110$. Then in the second year you earn 10 percent on this $110, which gives you a balance at the end of the second year of $100 \times 1.10^2 = \$121$.

Table 3.2 shows that the difference between simple and compound interest is nil for a one-period investment, trivial for a two-period investment, but overwhelming for an investment of 20 years or more. A sum of $100 invested during the American Revolution and earning compound interest of 10 percent a year would now be worth over $226 billion. If only your ancestors could have put away a few cents.

The two top lines in Figure 3.2 compare the results of investing $100 at 10 percent simple interest and at 10 percent compound interest. It looks as if the rate of growth is constant under simple interest and accelerates under compound interest. However, this is an optical illusion. We know that under compound interest our wealth grows at a *constant* rate of 10 percent. Figure 3.3 is in fact a more useful presentation. Here the numbers are plotted on a semilogarithmic scale and the constant compound growth rates show up as straight lines.

Problems in finance almost always involve compound interest rather than simple interest, and therefore financial people always assume that you are talking about compound interest unless you specify otherwise. Discounting is a process of compound interest. Some people find it intuitively helpful to replace the question, What is the present value of $100 to be received 10 years from now, if the opportunity cost of capital is 10 percent? with the question, How much would I have to invest now in order to receive $100 after 10 years, given an interest rate of 10 percent? The answer to the first question is

$$\text{PV} = \frac{100}{(1.10)^{10}} = \$38.55$$

FIGURE 3.3

The same story as Figure 3.2, except that the vertical scale is logarithmic. A constant compound rate of growth means a straight ascending line. This graph makes clear that the growth rate of funds invested at simple interest actually *declines* as time passes.

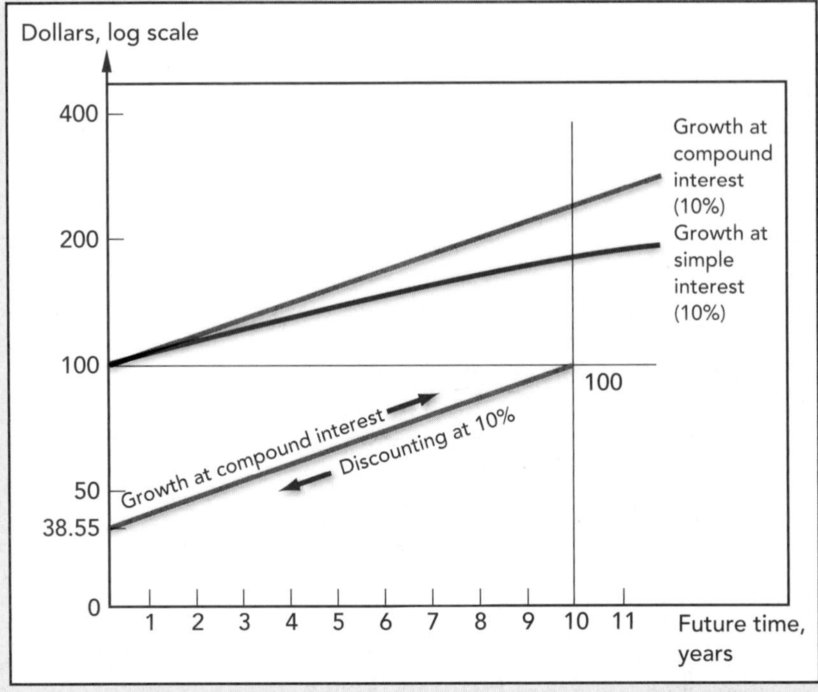

And the answer to the second question is

$$\text{Investment} \times (1.10)^{10} = \$100$$

$$\text{Investment} = \frac{100}{(1.10)^{10}} = \$38.55$$

The bottom lines in Figures 3.2 and 3.3 show the growth path of an initial investment of \$38.55 to its terminal value of \$100. One can think of discounting as traveling *back* along the bottom line, from future value to present value.

A Note on Compounding Intervals

So far we have implicitly assumed that each cash flow occurs at the end of the year. This is sometimes the case. For example, in France and Germany most corporations pay interest on their bonds annually. However, in the United States and Britain most pay interest semiannually. In these countries, the investor can earn an additional six months' interest on the first payment, so that an investment of \$100 in a bond that paid interest of 10 percent per annum compounded semiannually would amount to \$105 after the first six months, and by the end of the year it would amount to $1.05^2 \times 100 = \$110.25$. In other words, 10 percent compounded semiannually is equivalent to 10.25 percent compounded annually.

Let's take another example. Suppose a bank makes automobile loans requiring monthly payments at an *annual percentage rate (APR)* of 6 percent per year. What does that mean, and what is the true rate of interest on the loans?

With monthly payments, the bank charges one-twelfth of the APR in each month, that is, $6/12 = .5$ percent. Because the monthly return is compounded, the bank actually earns more than 6 percent per year. Suppose that the bank starts with \$10 million of automobile loans outstanding. This investment grows to $\$10 \times 1.005 = \$10.05$ million after month 1, to $\$10 \times 1.005^2 = \$10.10025$ million after month 2, and to $\$10 \times 1.005^{12} = \$10.61678$ million after 12 months.[9] Thus the bank is quoting a 6 percent APR but actually earns 6.1678 percent if interest payments are made monthly.[10]

In general, an investment of \$1 at a rate of r per annum compounded m times a year amounts by the end of the year to $[1 + (r/m)]^m$, and the equivalent annually compounded rate of interest is $[1 + (r/m)]^m - 1$.

Continuous Compounding The attractions to the investor of more frequent payments did not escape the attention of the savings and loan companies in the 1960s and 1970s. Their rate of interest on deposits was traditionally stated as an annually compounded rate. The government used to stipulate a maximum annual rate of interest that could be paid but made no mention of the compounding interval. When interest ceilings began to pinch, savings and loan companies changed progressively to semiannual and then to monthly compounding. Therefore the equivalent annually compounded rate of interest increased first to $[1 + (r/2)]^2 - 1$ and then to $[1 + (r/12)]^{12} - 1$.

Eventually one company quoted a **continuously compounded rate,** so that payments were assumed to be spread evenly and continuously throughout the year. In terms of our formula, this is equivalent to letting m approach infinity.[11] This might seem like a lot of calculations for the savings and loan companies. Fortunately, however, someone remembered high school algebra and pointed out that as m approaches infinity $[1 + (r/m)]^m$ approaches $(2.718)^r$. The figure 2.718—or e, as it is called—is simply the base for natural logarithms.

One dollar invested at a continuously compounded rate of r will, therefore, grow to $e^r = (2.718)^r$ by the end of the first year. By the end of t years it will grow to $e^{rt} = (2.718)^{rt}$. Appendix Table 4 at the end of the book is a table of values of e^{rt}. Let us practice using it.

Example 1 Suppose you invest \$1 at a continuously compounded rate of 11 percent ($r = .11$) for one year ($t = 1$). The end-year value is $e^{.11}$, which you can see from the second row of Appendix Table 4 is \$1.116. In other words, investing at 11 percent a year *continuously* compounded is exactly the same as investing at 11.6 percent a year *annually* compounded.

Example 2 Suppose you invest \$1 at a continuously compounded rate of 11 percent ($r = .11$) for two years ($t = 2$). The final value of the investment is $e^{rt} = e^{.22}$. You can see from the third row of Appendix Table 4 that $e^{.22}$ is \$1.246.

[9]Individual borrowers gradually pay off their loans. We are assuming that the aggregate amount loaned by the bank to all its customers stays constant at \$10 million.

[10]Unfortunately, U.S. truth-in-lending laws require lenders to quote interest rates for most types of consumer loans as APRs rather than true annual rates.

[11]When we talk about *continuous* payments, we are pretending that money can be dispensed in a continuous stream like water out of a faucet. One can never quite do this. For example, instead of paying out \$100,000 every year, our benefactor could pay out \$100 every 8¾ hours or \$1 every 5¼ minutes or 1 cent every 3⅛ seconds but could not pay it out *continuously.* Financial managers *pretend* that payments are continuous rather than hourly, daily, or weekly because (1) it simplifies the calculations, and (2) it gives a *very* close approximation to the NPV of frequent payments.

There is a particular value to continuous compounding in capital budgeting, where it may often be more reasonable to assume that a cash flow is spread evenly over the year than that it occurs at the year's end. It is easy to adapt our previous formulas to handle this. For example, suppose that we wish to compute the present value of a perpetuity of C dollars a year. We already know that if the payment is made at the end of the year, we divide the payment by the *annually* compounded rate of r:

$$\text{PV} = \frac{C}{r}$$

If the same total payment is made in an even stream throughout the year, we use the same formula but substitute the *continuously* compounded rate.

Example 3 Suppose the annually compounded rate is 18.5 percent. The present value of a \$100 perpetuity, with each cash flow received at the end of the year, is $100/.185 = \$540.54$. If the cash flow is received continuously, we must divide \$100 by 17 percent, because 17 percent continuously compounded is equivalent to 18.5 percent annually compounded ($e^{.17} = 1.185$). The present value of the continuous cash flow stream is $100/.17 = \$588.24$.

For any other continuous payments, we can always use our formula for valuing annuities. For instance, suppose that our philanthropist has thought more seriously and decided to found a home for elderly donkeys, which will cost \$100,000 a year, starting immediately, and spread evenly over 20 years. Previously, we used the annually compounded rate of 10 percent; now we must use the continuously compounded rate of $r = 9.53$ percent ($e^{.0953} = 1.10$). To cover such an expenditure, then, our philanthropist needs to set aside the following sum:[12]

$$\text{PV} = C\left(\frac{1}{r} - \frac{1}{r} \times \frac{1}{e^{rt}}\right)$$

$$= 100{,}000\left(\frac{1}{.0953} - \frac{1}{.0953} \times \frac{1}{6.727}\right) = 100{,}000 \times 8.932 = \$893{,}200$$

Alternatively, we could have cut these calculations short by using Appendix Table 5. This shows that, if the annually compounded return is 10 percent, then \$1 a year spread over 20 years is worth \$8.932.

If you look back at our earlier discussion of annuities, you will notice that the present value of \$100,000 paid at the *end* of each of the 20 years was \$851,400.

[12]Remember that an annuity is simply the difference between a perpetuity received today and a perpetuity received in year t. A continuous stream of C dollars a year in perpetuity is worth C/r, where r is the continuously compounded rate. Our annuity, then, is worth

$$\text{PV} = \frac{C}{r} - \text{present value of } \frac{C}{r} \text{ received in year } t$$

Since r is the continuously compounded rate, C/r received in year t is worth $(C/r) \times (1/e^{rt})$ today. Our annuity formula is therefore

$$\text{PV} = \frac{C}{r} - \frac{C}{r} \times \frac{1}{e^{rt}}$$

sometimes written as

$$\frac{C}{r}(1 - e^{-rt})$$

Therefore, it costs the philanthropist $41,800—or 5 percent—more to provide a continuous payment stream.

Often in finance we need only a ballpark estimate of present value. An error of 5 percent in a present value calculation may be perfectly acceptable. In such cases it doesn't usually matter whether we assume that cash flows occur at the end of the year or in a continuous stream. At other times precision matters, and we do need to worry about the exact frequency of the cash flows.

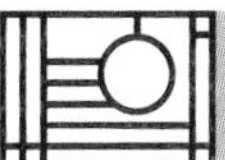

3.4 NOMINAL AND REAL RATES OF INTEREST

If you invest $1,000 in a bank deposit offering an interest rate of 10 percent, the bank promises to pay you $1,100 at the end of the year. But it makes no promises about what the $1,100 will buy. That will depend on the rate of inflation over the year. If the prices of goods and services increase by more than 10 percent, you have lost ground in terms of the goods that you can buy.

Several indexes are used to track the general level of prices. The best known is the Consumer Price Index, or CPI, which measures the number of dollars that it takes to pay for a typical family's purchases. The change in the CPI from one year to the next measures the rate of inflation. Figure 3.4 shows the rate of inflation in the United

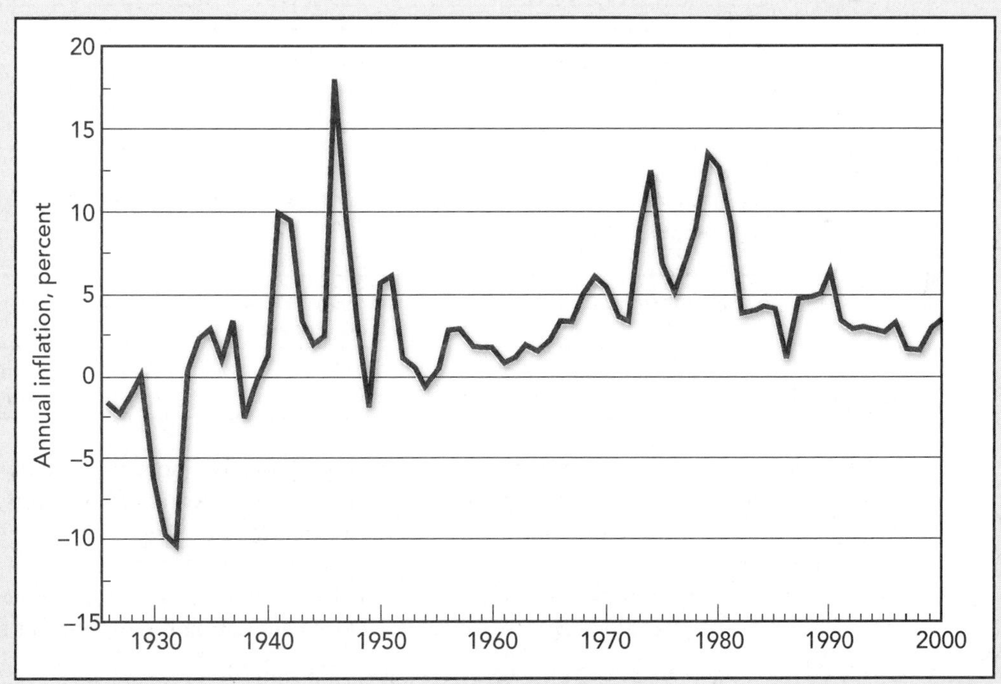

FIGURE 3.4

Annual rates of inflation in the United States from 1926 to 2000.

Source: Ibbotson Associates, Inc., *Stocks, Bonds, Bills, and Inflation,* 2001 Yearbook, Chicago, 2001.

States since 1926. During the Great Depression there was actual *de*flation; prices of goods on average fell. Inflation touched a peak just after World War II, when it reached 18 percent. This figure, however, pales into insignificance compared with inflation in Yugoslavia in 1993, which at its peak was almost 60 percent *a day.*

Economists sometimes talk about current, or nominal, dollars versus constant, or real, dollars. For example, the *nominal* cash flow from your one-year bank deposit is $1,100. But suppose prices of goods rise over the year by 6 percent; then each dollar will buy you 6 percent less goods next year than it does today. So at the end of the year $1,100 will buy the same quantity of goods as 1,100/1.06 = $1,037.74 today. The nominal payoff on the deposit is $1,100, but the *real* payoff is only $1,037.74.

The general formula for converting nominal cash flows at a future period t to real cash flows is

$$\text{Real cash flow} = \frac{\text{nominal cash flow}}{(1 + \text{inflation rate})^t}$$

For example, if you were to invest that $1,000 for 20 years at 10 percent, your future nominal payoff would be $1{,}000 \times 1.1^{20} = \$6{,}727.50$, but with an inflation rate of 6 percent a year, the real value of that payoff would be $6{,}727.50/1.06^{20} = \$2{,}097.67$. In other words, you will have roughly six times as many dollars as you have today, but you will be able to buy only twice as many goods.

When the bank quotes you a 10 percent interest rate, it is quoting a nominal interest rate. The rate tells you how rapidly your money will grow:

Invest Current Dollars		Receive Period-1 Dollars	Result
1,000	→	1,100	10% *nominal* rate of return

However, with an inflation rate of 6 percent you are only 3.774 percent better off at the end of the year than at the start:

Invest Current Dollars		Expected Real Value of Period-1 Receipts	Result
1,000	→	1,037.74	3.774% expected *real* rate of return

Thus, we could say, "The bank account offers a 10 percent nominal rate of return," or "It offers a 3.774 percent expected real rate of return." Note that the nominal rate is certain but the real rate is only expected. The actual real rate cannot be calculated until the end of the year arrives and the inflation rate is known.

The 10 percent nominal rate of return, with 6 percent inflation, translates into a 3.774 percent real rate of return. The formula for calculating the real rate of return is

$$\begin{aligned} 1 + r_{\text{nominal}} &= (1 + r_{\text{real}})(1 + \text{inflation rate}) \\ &= 1 + r_{\text{real}} + \text{inflation rate} + (r_{\text{real}})(\text{inflation rate}) \end{aligned}$$

In our example,

$$1.10 = 1.03774 \times 1.06$$

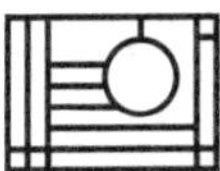

3.5 USING PRESENT VALUE FORMULAS TO VALUE BONDS

When governments or companies borrow money, they often do so by issuing bonds. A bond is simply a long-term debt. If you own a bond, you receive a fixed set of cash payoffs: Each year until the bond matures, you collect an interest payment; then at maturity, you also get back the face value of the bond. The face value of the bond is known as the *principal.* Therefore, when the bond matures, the government pays you principal and interest.

If you want to buy or sell a bond, you simply contact a bond dealer, who will quote a price at which he or she is prepared to buy or sell. Suppose, for example, that in June 2001 you invested in a 7 percent 2006 U.S. Treasury bond. The bond has a coupon rate of 7 percent and a face value of $1,000. This means that each year until 2006 you will receive an interest payment of .07 × 1,000 = $70. The bond matures in May 2006. At that time the Treasury pays you the final $70 interest, plus the $1,000 face value. So the cash flows from owning the bond are as follows:

Cash Flows ($)				
2002	**2003**	**2004**	**2005**	**2006**
70	70	70	70	1,070

What is the present value of these payoffs? To determine that, we need to look at the return provided by similar securities. Other medium-term U.S. Treasury bonds in the summer of 2001 offered a return of about 4.8 percent. That is what investors were giving up when they bought the 7 percent Treasury bonds. Therefore to value the 7 percent bonds, we need to discount the cash flows at 4.8 percent:

$$\text{PV} = \frac{70}{1.048} + \frac{70}{(1.048)^2} + \frac{70}{(1.048)^3} + \frac{70}{(1.048)^4} + \frac{1070}{(1.048)^5} = 1{,}095.78$$

Bond prices are usually expressed as a percentage of the face value. Thus, we can say that our 7 percent Treasury bond is worth $1,095.78, or 109.578 percent.

You may have noticed a shortcut way to value the Treasury bond. The bond is like a package of two investments: The first investment consists of five annual coupon payments of $70 each, and the second investment is the payment of the $1,000 face value at maturity. Therefore, you can use the annuity formula to value the coupon payments and add on the present value of the final payment:

$$\begin{aligned} \text{PV(bond)} &= \text{PV(coupon payments)} + \text{PV(final payment)} \\ &= (\text{coupon} \times \text{five-year annuity factor}) + \\ &\quad (\text{final payment} \times \text{discount factor}) \\ &= 70\left[\frac{1}{.048} - \frac{1}{.048(1.048)^5}\right] + \frac{1000}{1.048^5} = 304.75 + 791.03 = 1095.78 \end{aligned}$$

Any Treasury bond can be valued as a package of an annuity (the coupon payments) and a single payment (the repayment of the face value).

Rather than asking the value of the bond, we could have phrased our question the other way around: If the price of the bond is $1,095.78, what return do investors expect? In that case, we need to find the value of r that solves the following equation:

$$1095.78 = \frac{70}{1 + r} + \frac{70}{(1 + r)^2} + \frac{70}{(1 + r)^3} + \frac{70}{(1 + r)^4} + \frac{1070}{(1 + r)^5}$$

The rate r is often called the bond's **yield to maturity.** In our case r is 4.8 percent. If you discount the cash flows at 4.8 percent, you arrive at the bond's price of $1,095.78. The only *general* procedure for calculating the yield to maturity is trial and error, but spreadsheet programs or specially programmed electronic calculators will usually do the trick.

You may have noticed that the formula that we used for calculating the present value of 7 percent Treasury bonds was slightly different from the general present value formula that we developed in Section 3.1, where we allowed r_1, the rate of return offered by the capital market on one-year investments, to differ from r_2, the rate of return offered on two-year investments. Then we finessed this problem by assuming that r_1 was the same as r_2. In valuing our Treasury bond, we again assume that investors use the same rate to discount cash flows occurring in different years. That does not matter as long as the term structure is flat, with short-term rates approximately the same as long-term rates. But when the term structure is not flat, professional bond investors discount each cash flow at a different rate. There will be more about that in Chapter 24.

What Happens When Interest Rates Change?

Interest rates fluctuate. In 1945 United States government bonds were yielding less than 2 percent, but by 1981 yields were a touch under 15 percent. International differences in interest rates can be even more dramatic. As we write this in the summer of 2001, short-term interest rates in Japan are less than .2 percent, while in Turkey they are over 60 percent.[13]

How do changes in interest rates affect bond prices? If bond yields in the United States fell to 2 percent, the price of our 7 percent Treasuries would rise to

$$PV = \frac{70}{1.02} + \frac{70}{(1.02)^2} + \frac{70}{(1.02)^3} + \frac{70}{(1.02)^4} + \frac{1070}{(1.02)^5} = \$1,235.67$$

If yields jumped to 10 percent, the price would fall to

$$PV = \frac{70}{1.10} + \frac{70}{(1.10)^2} + \frac{70}{(1.10)^3} + \frac{70}{(1.10)^4} + \frac{1070}{(1.10)^5} = \$886.28$$

Not surprisingly, the higher the interest rate that investors demand, the less that they will be prepared to pay for the bond.

Some bonds are more affected than others by a change in the interest rate. The effect is greatest when the cash flows on the bond last for many years. The effect is trivial if the bond matures tomorrow.

Compounding Intervals and Bond Prices

In calculating the value of the 7 percent Treasury bonds, we made two approximations. First, we assumed that interest payments occurred annually. In practice,

[13]Early in 2001 the Turkish overnight rate exceeded 20,000 percent.

most U.S. bonds make coupon payments *semiannually*, so that instead of receiving \$70 every year, an investor holding 7 percent bonds would receive \$35 every *half* year. Second, yields on U.S. bonds are usually quoted as semiannually compounded yields. In other words, if the semiannually compounded yield is quoted as 4.8 percent, the yield over six months is 4.8/2 = 2.4 percent.

Now we can recalculate the value of the 7 percent Treasury bonds, recognizing that there are 10 six-month coupon payments of \$35 and a final payment of the \$1,000 face value:

$$PV = \frac{35}{1.024} + \frac{35}{(1.024)^2} + \cdots + \frac{35}{(1.024)^9} + \frac{1035}{(1.024)^{10}} = \$1,096.77$$

SUMMARY

The difficult thing in any present value exercise is to set up the problem correctly. Once you have done that, you must be able to do the calculations, but they are not difficult. Now that you have worked through this chapter, all you should need is a little practice.

The basic present value formula for an asset that pays off in several periods is the following obvious extension of our one-period formula:

$$PV = \frac{C_1}{1 + r_1} + \frac{C_2}{(1 + r_2)^2} + \cdots$$

You can always work out any present value using this formula, but when the interest rates are the same for each maturity, there may be some shortcuts that can reduce the tedium. We looked at three such cases. The first is an asset that pays C dollars a year in perpetuity. Its present value is simply

$$PV = \frac{C}{r}$$

The second is an asset whose payments increase at a steady rate g in perpetuity. Its present value is

$$PV = \frac{C_1}{r - g}$$

The third is an annuity that pays C dollars a year for t years. To find its present value we take the difference between the values of two perpetuities:

$$PV = C\left[\frac{1}{r} - \frac{1}{r(1 + r)^t}\right]$$

Our next step was to show that discounting is a process of compound interest. Present value is the amount that we would have to invest now at compound interest r in order to produce the cash flows C_1, C_2, etc. When someone offers to lend us a dollar at an annual rate of r, we should always check how frequently the interest is to be compounded. If the compounding interval is annual, we will have to repay $(1 + r)^t$ dollars; on the other hand, if the compounding period is continuous, we will have to repay 2.718^{rt} (or, as it is usually expressed, e^{rt}) dollars. In capital budgeting we often assume that the cash flows occur at the end of each year, and therefore we discount them at an annually compounded rate of interest.

Sometimes, however, it may be better to assume that they are spread evenly over the year; in this case we must make use of continuous compounding.

It is important to distinguish between *nominal* cash flows (the actual number of dollars that you will pay or receive) and *real* cash flows, which are adjusted for inflation. Similarly, an investment may promise a high *nominal* interest rate, but, if inflation is also high, the *real* interest rate may be low or even negative.

We concluded the chapter by applying discounted cash flow techniques to value United States government bonds with fixed annual coupons.

We introduced in this chapter two very important ideas which we will come across several times again. The first is that you can add present values: If your formula for the present value of $A + B$ is not the same as your formula for the present value of A plus the present value of B, you have made a mistake. The second is the notion that there is no such thing as a money machine: If you think you have found one, go back and check your calculations.

FURTHER READING

The material in this chapter should cover all you need to know about the mathematics of discounting; but if you wish to dig deeper, there are a number of books on the subject. Try, for example:

R. Cissell, H. Cissell, and D. C. Flaspohler: *The Mathematics of Finance,* 8th ed., Houghton Mifflin Company, Boston, 1990.

QUIZ

1. At an interest rate of 12 percent, the six-year discount factor is .507. How many dollars is $.507 worth in six years if invested at 12 percent?
2. If the PV of $139 is $125, what is the discount factor?
3. If the eight-year discount factor is .285, what is the PV of $596 received in eight years?
4. If the cost of capital is 9 percent, what is the PV of $374 paid in year 9?
5. A project produces the following cash flows:

Year	Flow
1	432
2	137
3	797

   If the cost of capital is 15 percent, what is the project's PV?
6. If you invest $100 at an interest rate of 15 percent, how much will you have at the end of eight years?
7. An investment costs $1,548 and pays $138 in perpetuity. If the interest rate is 9 percent, what is the NPV?
8. A common stock will pay a cash dividend of $4 next year. After that, the dividends are expected to increase indefinitely at 4 percent per year. If the discount rate is 14 percent, what is the PV of the stream of dividend payments?
9. You win a lottery with a prize of $1.5 million. Unfortunately the prize is paid in 10 annual installments. The first payment is next year. How much is the prize really worth? The discount rate is 8 percent.

10. Do not use the Appendix tables for these questions. The interest rate is 10 percent.
   a. What is the PV of an asset that pays $1 a year in perpetuity?
   b. The value of an asset that appreciates at 10 percent per annum approximately doubles in seven years. What is the approximate PV of an asset that pays $1 a year in perpetuity beginning in year 8?
   c. What is the approximate PV of an asset that pays $1 a year for each of the next seven years?
   d. A piece of land produces an income that grows by 5 percent per annum. If the first year's flow is $10,000, what is the value of the land?
11. Use the Appendix tables at the end of the book for each of the following calculations:
   a. The cost of a new automobile is $10,000. If the interest rate is 5 percent, how much would you have to set aside now to provide this sum in five years?
   b. You have to pay $12,000 a year in school fees at the end of each of the next six years. If the interest rate is 8 percent, how much do you need to set aside today to cover these bills?
   c. You have invested $60,476 at 8 percent. After paying the above school fees, how much would remain at the end of the six years?
12. You have the opportunity to invest in the Belgravian Republic at 25 percent interest. The inflation rate is 21 percent. What is the real rate of interest?
13. The continuously compounded interest rate is 12 percent.
   a. You invest $1,000 at this rate. What is the investment worth after five years?
   b. What is the PV of $5 million to be received in eight years?
   c. What is the PV of a continuous stream of cash flows, amounting to $2,000 per year, starting immediately and continuing for 15 years?
14. You are quoted an interest rate of 6 percent on an investment of $10 million. What is the value of your investment after four years if the interest rate is compounded: **a.** Annually, **b.** monthly, or **c.** continuously?
15. Suppose the interest rate on five-year U.S. government bonds falls to 4.0 percent. Recalculate the value of the 7 percent bond maturing in 2006. (See Section 3.5.)
16. What is meant by a bond's yield to maturity and how is it calculated?

Visit us at www.mhhe.com/bm7e

PRACTICE QUESTIONS

1. Use the *discount factors* shown in Appendix Table 1 at the end of the book to calculate the PV of $100 received in:
   a. Year 10 (at a discount rate of 1 percent).
   b. Year 10 (at a discount rate of 13 percent).
   c. Year 15 (at a discount rate of 25 percent).
   d. Each of years 1 through 3 (at a discount rate of 12 percent).
2. Use the *annuity factors* shown in Appendix Table 3 to calculate the PV of $100 in each of:
   a. Years 1 through 20 (at a discount rate of 23 percent).
   b. Years 1 through 5 (at a discount rate of 3 percent).
   c. Years 3 through 12 (at a discount rate of 9 percent).
3. a. If the one-year discount factor is .88, what is the one-year interest rate?
   b. If the two-year interest rate is 10.5 percent, what is the two-year discount factor?
   c. Given these one- and two-year discount factors, calculate the two-year annuity factor.
   d. If the PV of $10 a year for three years is $24.49, what is the three-year annuity factor?
   e. From your answers to (c) and (d), calculate the three-year discount factor.

4. A factory costs $800,000. You reckon that it will produce an inflow after operating costs of $170,000 a year for 10 years. If the opportunity cost of capital is 14 percent, what is the net present value of the factory? What will the factory be worth at the end of five years?

5. Harold Filbert is 30 years of age and his salary next year will be $20,000. Harold forecasts that his salary will increase at a steady rate of 5 percent per annum until his retirement at age 60.
   a. If the discount rate is 8 percent, what is the PV of these future salary payments?
   b. If Harold saves 5 percent of his salary each year and invests these savings at an interest rate of 8 percent, how much will he have saved by age 60?
   c. If Harold plans to spend these savings in even amounts over the subsequent 20 years, how much can he spend each year?

6. A factory costs $400,000. You reckon that it will produce an inflow after operating costs of $100,000 in year 1, $200,000 in year 2, and $300,000 in year 3. The opportunity cost of capital is 12 percent. Draw up a worksheet like that shown in Table 3.1 and use tables to calculate the NPV.

7. Halcyon Lines is considering the purchase of a new bulk carrier for $8 million. The forecasted revenues are $5 million a year and operating costs are $4 million. A major refit costing $2 million will be required after both the fifth and tenth years. After 15 years, the ship is expected to be sold for scrap at $1.5 million. If the discount rate is 8 percent, what is the ship's NPV?

8. As winner of a breakfast cereal competition, you can choose one of the following prizes:
   a. $100,000 now.
   b. $180,000 at the end of five years.
   c. $11,400 a year forever.
   d. $19,000 for each of 10 years.
   e. $6,500 next year and increasing thereafter by 5 percent a year forever.

   If the interest rate is 12 percent, which is the most valuable prize?

9. Refer back to the story of Ms. Kraft in Section 3.1.
   a. If the one-year interest rate were 25 percent, how many plays would Ms. Kraft require to become a millionaire? (*Hint:* You may find it easier to use a calculator and a little trial and error.)
   b. What does the story of Ms. Kraft imply about the relationship between the one-year discount factor, DF_1, and the two-year discount factor, DF_2?

10. Siegfried Basset is 65 years of age and has a life expectancy of 12 more years. He wishes to invest $20,000 in an annuity that will make a level payment at the end of each year until his death. If the interest rate is 8 percent, what income can Mr. Basset expect to receive each year?

11. James and Helen Turnip are saving to buy a boat at the end of five years. If the boat costs $20,000 and they can earn 10 percent a year on their savings, how much do they need to put aside at the end of years 1 through 5?

12. Kangaroo Autos is offering free credit on a new $10,000 car. You pay $1,000 down and then $300 a month for the next 30 months. Turtle Motors next door does not offer free credit but will give you $1,000 off the list price. If the rate of interest is 10 percent a year, which company is offering the better deal?

13. Recalculate the NPV of the office building venture in Section 3.1 at interest rates of 5, 10, and 15 percent. Plot the points on a graph with NPV on the vertical axis and the discount rates on the horizontal axis. At what discount rate (approximately) would the project have zero NPV? Check your answer.

14. a. How much will an investment of $100 be worth at the end of 10 years if invested at 15 percent a year simple interest?
    b. How much will it be worth if invested at 15 percent a year compound interest?
    c. How long will it take your investment to double its value at 15 percent compound interest?

15. You own an oil pipeline which will generate a $2 million cash return over the coming year. The pipeline's operating costs are negligible, and it is expected to last for a very long time. Unfortunately, the volume of oil shipped is declining, and cash flows are expected to decline by 4 percent per year. The discount rate is 10 percent.
    a. What is the PV of the pipeline's cash flows if its cash flows are assumed to last forever?
    b. What is the PV of the cash flows if the pipeline is scrapped after 20 years?

    [*Hint for part (b):* Start with your answer to part (a), then subtract the present value of a declining perpetuity starting in year 21. Note that the forecasted cash flow for year 21 will be much less than the cash flow for year 1.]

16. If the interest rate is 7 percent, what is the value of the following three investments?
    a. An investment that offers you $100 a year in perpetuity with the payment at the *end* of each year.
    b. A similar investment with the payment at the *beginning* of each year.
    c. A similar investment with the payment spread evenly over each year.

17. Refer back to Section 3.2. If the rate of interest is 8 percent rather than 10 percent, how much would our benefactor need to set aside to provide each of the following?
    a. $100,000 at the end of each year in perpetuity.
    b. A perpetuity that pays $100,000 at the end of the first year and that grows at 4 percent a year.
    c. $100,000 at the end of each year for 20 years.
    d. $100,000 a year spread evenly over 20 years.

18. For an investment of $1,000 today, the Tiburon Finance Company is offering to pay you $1,600 at the end of 8 years. What is the annually compounded rate of interest? What is the continuously compounded rate of interest?

19. How much will you have at the end of 20 years if you invest $100 today at 15 percent *annually* compounded? How much will you have if you invest at 15 percent *continuously* compounded?

20. You have just read an advertisement stating, "Pay us $100 a year for 10 years and we will pay you $100 a year thereafter in perpetuity." If this is a fair deal, what is the rate of interest?

21. Which would you prefer?
    a. An investment paying interest of 12 percent compounded annually.
    b. An investment paying interest of 11.7 percent compounded semiannually.
    c. An investment paying 11.5 percent compounded continuously.

    Work out the value of each of these investments after 1, 5, and 20 years.

22. Fill in the blanks in the following table:

Nominal Interest Rate (%)	Inflation Rate (%)	Real Interest Rate (%)
6	1	—
—	10	12
9	—	3

23. Sometimes real rates of return are calculated by *subtracting* the rate of inflation from the nominal rate. This rule of thumb is a good approximation if the inflation rate is low. How big is the error from using this rule of thumb to calculate real rates of return in the following cases?

Nominal Rate (%)	Inflation Rate (%)
6	2
9	5
21	10
70	50

24. In 1880 five aboriginal trackers were each promised the equivalent of 100 Australian dollars for helping to capture the notorious outlaw Ned Kelley. In 1993 the granddaughters of two of the trackers claimed that this reward had not been paid. The prime minister of Victoria stated that, if this was true, the government would be happy to pay the $100. However, the granddaughters also claimed that they were entitled to compound interest. How much was each entitled to if the interest rate was 5 percent? What if it was 10 percent?

25. A leasing contract calls for an immediate payment of $100,000 and nine subsequent $100,000 semiannual payments at six-month intervals. What is the PV of these payments if the *annual* discount rate is 8 percent?

26. A famous quarterback just signed a $15 million contract providing $3 million a year for five years. A less famous receiver signed a $14 million five-year contract providing $4 million now and $2 million a year for five years. Who is better paid? The interest rate is 10 percent.

27. In August 1994 *The Wall Street Journal* reported that the winner of the Massachusetts State Lottery prize had the misfortune to be both bankrupt and in prison for fraud. The prize was $9,420,713, to be paid in 19 equal annual installments. (There were 20 installments, but the winner had already received the first payment.) The bankruptcy court judge ruled that the prize should be sold off to the highest bidder and the proceeds used to pay off the creditors. **a.** If the interest rate was 8 percent, how much would you have been prepared to bid for the prize? **b.** Enhance Reinsurance Company was reported to have offered $4.2 million. Use Appendix Table 3 to find (approximately) the return that the company was looking for.

28. You estimate that by the time you retire in 35 years, you will have accumulated savings of $2 million. If the interest rate is 8 percent and you live 15 years after retirement, what annual level of expenditure will those savings support?

    Unfortunately, inflation will eat into the value of your retirement income. Assume a 4 percent inflation rate and work out a spending program for your retirement that will allow you to maintain a level *real* expenditure during retirement.

29. You are considering the purchase of an apartment complex that will generate a net cash flow of $400,000 per year. You normally demand a 10 percent rate of return on such investments. Future cash flows are expected to grow with inflation at 4 percent per year. How much would you be willing to pay for the complex if it:
    a. Will produce cash flows forever?
    b. Will have to be torn down in 20 years? Assume that the site will be worth $5 million at that time net of demolition costs. (The $5 million includes 20 years' inflation.)

    Now calculate the real discount rate corresponding to the 10 percent nominal rate. Redo the calculations for parts (a) and (b) using real cash flows. (Your answers should not change.)

Visit us at www.mhhe.com/bm7e

30. Vernal Pool, a self-employed herpetologist, wants to put aside a fixed fraction of her annual income as savings for retirement. Ms. Pool is now 40 years old and makes $40,000 a year. She expects her income to increase by 2 percentage points over inflation (e.g., 4 percent inflation means a 6 percent increase in income). She wants to accumulate $500,000 in real terms to retire at age 70. What fraction of her income does she need to set aside? Assume her retirement funds are conservatively invested at an expected real rate of return of 5 percent a year. Ignore taxes.

31. At the end of June 2001, the yield to maturity on U.S. government bonds maturing in 2006 was about 4.8 percent. Value a bond with a 6 percent coupon maturing in June 2006. The bond's face value is $10,000. Assume annual coupon payments and annual compounding. How does your answer change with semiannual coupons and a semiannual discount rate of 2.4 percent?

32. Refer again to Practice Question 31. How would the bond's value change if interest rates fell to 3.5 percent per year?

33. A two-year bond pays a coupon rate of 10 percent and a face value of $1,000. (In other words, the bond pays interest of $100 per year, and its principal of $1,000 is paid off in year 2.) If the bond sells for $960, what is its approximate yield to maturity? *Hint:* This requires some trial-and-error calculations.

1. Here are two useful rules of thumb. The "Rule of 72" says that with discrete compounding the time it takes for an investment to double in value is roughly 72/interest rate (in percent). The "Rule of 69" says that with continuous compounding the time that it takes to double is *exactly* 69.3/interest rate (in percent).
   a. If the annually compounded interest rate is 12 percent, use the Rule of 72 to calculate roughly how long it takes before your money doubles. Now work it out exactly.
   b. Can you prove the Rule of 69?

2. Use a spreadsheet program to construct your own set of annuity tables.

3. An oil well now produces 100,000 barrels per year. The well will produce for 18 years more, but production will decline by 4 percent per year. Oil prices, however, will increase by 2 percent per year. The discount rate is 8 percent. What is the PV of the well's production if today's price is $14 per barrel?

4. Derive the formula for a growing (or declining) annuity.

5. Calculate the real cash flows on the 7 percent U.S. Treasury bond (see Section 3.5) assuming annual interest payments and an inflation rate of 2 percent. Now show that by discounting these real cash flows at the real interest rate you get the same PV that you get when you discount the nominal cash flows at the nominal interest rate.

6. Use a spreadsheet program to construct a set of bond tables that shows the present value of a bond given the coupon rate, maturity, and yield to maturity. Assume that coupon payments are semiannual and yields are compounded semiannually.

MINI-CASE

The Jones Family, Incorporated

The Scene: Early evening in an ordinary family room in Manhattan. Modern furniture, with old copies of *The Wall Street Journal* and the *Financial Times* scattered around. Autographed photos of Alan Greenspan and George Soros are prominently displayed. A picture window reveals a distant view of lights on the Hudson River. John Jones sits at a computer terminal, glumly sipping a glass of chardonnay and trading Japanese yen over the Internet. His wife Marsha enters.

Marsha: Hi, honey. Glad to be home. Lousy day on the trading floor, though. Dullsville. No volume. But I did manage to hedge next year's production from our copper mine. I couldn't get a good quote on the right package of futures contracts, so I arranged a commodity swap.

John doesn't reply.

Marsha: John, what's wrong? Have you been buying yen again? That's been a losing trade for weeks.

John: Well, yes. I shouldn't have gone to Goldman Sachs's foreign exchange brunch. But I've got to get out of the house somehow. I'm cooped up here all day calculating covariances and efficient risk-return tradeoffs while you're out trading commodity futures. You get all the glamour and excitement.

Marsha: Don't worry dear, it will be over soon. We only recalculate our most efficient common stock portfolio once a quarter. Then you can go back to leveraged leases.

John: You trade, and I do all the worrying. Now there's a rumor that our leasing company is going to get a hostile takeover bid. I knew the debt ratio was too low, and you forgot to put on the poison pill. And now you've made a negative-NPV investment!

Marsha: What investment?

John: Two more oil wells in that old field in Ohio. You spent $500,000! The wells only produce 20 barrels of crude oil per day.

Marsha: That's 20 barrels day in, day out. There are 365 days in a year, dear.

John and Marsha's teenage son Johnny bursts into the room.

Johnny: Hi, Dad! Hi, Mom! Guess what? I've made the junior varsity derivatives team! That means I can go on the field trip to the Chicago Board Options Exchange. *(Pauses.)* What's wrong?

John: Your mother has made another negative-NPV investment. More oil wells.

Johnny: That's OK, Dad. Mom told me about it. I was going to do an NPV calculation yesterday, but my corporate finance teacher asked me to calculate default probabilities for a sample of junk bonds for Friday's class.

(Grabs a financial calculator from his backpack.) Let's see: 20 barrels per day times $15 per barrel times 365 days per year . . . that's $109,500 per year.

John: That's $109,500 *this* year. Production's been declining at 5 percent every year.

Marsha: On the other hand, our energy consultants project increasing oil prices. If they increase with inflation, price per barrel should climb by roughly 2.5 percent per year. The wells cost next to nothing to operate, and they should keep pumping for 10 more years at least.

Johnny: I'll calculate NPV after I finish with the default probabilities. Is a 9 percent nominal cost of capital OK?

Marsha: Sure, Johnny.

John: *(Takes a deep breath and stands up.)* Anyway, how about a nice family dinner? I've reserved our usual table at the Four Seasons.

Everyone exits.

Announcer: Were the oil wells really negative-NPV? Will John and Marsha have to fight a hostile takeover? Will Johnny's derivatives team use Black-Scholes or the binomial method? Find out in the next episode of The Jones Family, Incorporated.

You may not aspire to the Jones family's way of life, but you will learn about all their activities, from futures contracts to binomial option pricing, later in this book. Meanwhile, you may wish to replicate Johnny's NPV analysis.

Questions

1. Forecast future cash flows, taking account of the decline in production and the (partially) offsetting forecasted increase in oil prices. How long does production have to continue for the oil wells to be a positive-NPV investment? You can ignore taxes and other possible complications.

CHAPTER FOUR

THE VALUE OF COMMON STOCKS

WE SHOULD WARN you that being a financial expert has its occupational hazards. One is being cornered at cocktail parties by people who are eager to explain their system for making creamy profits by investing in common stocks. Fortunately, these bores go into temporary hibernation whenever the market goes down.

We may exaggerate the perils of the trade. The point is that there is no easy way to ensure superior investment performance. Later in the book we will show that changes in security prices are fundamentally unpredictable and that this result is a natural consequence of well-functioning capital markets. Therefore, in this chapter, when we propose to use the concept of present value to price common stocks, we are not promising you a key to investment success; we simply believe that the idea can help you to understand why some investments are priced higher than others.

Why should you care? If you want to know the value of a firm's stock, why can't you look up the stock price in the newspaper? Unfortunately, that is not always possible. For example, you may be the founder of a successful business. You currently own all the shares but are thinking of going public by selling off shares to other investors. You and your advisers need to estimate the price at which those shares can be sold. Or suppose that Establishment Industries is proposing to sell its concatenator division to another company. It needs to figure out the market value of this division.

There is also another, deeper reason why managers need to understand how shares are valued. We have stated that a firm which acts in its shareholders' interest should accept those investments which increase the value of their stake in the firm. But in order to do this, it is necessary to understand what determines the shares' value.

We start the chapter with a brief look at how shares are traded. Then we explain the basic principles of share valuation. We look at the fundamental difference between growth stocks and income stocks and the significance of earnings per share and price–earnings multiples. Finally, we discuss some of the special problems managers and investors encounter when they calculate the present values of entire businesses.

A word of caution before we proceed. Everybody knows that common stocks are risky and that some are more risky than others. Therefore, investors will not commit funds to stocks unless the expected rates of return are commensurate with the risks. But we say next to nothing in this chapter about the linkages between risk and expected return. A more careful treatment of risk starts in Chapter 7.

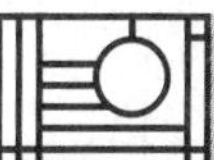

4.1 HOW COMMON STOCKS ARE TRADED

There are 9.9 billion shares of General Electric (GE), and at last count these shares were owned by about 2.1 million shareholders. They included large pension funds and insurance companies that each own several million shares, as well as individuals who own a handful of shares. If you owned one GE share, you would own .000002 percent of the company and have a claim on the same tiny fraction of GE's profits. Of course, the more shares you own, the larger your "share" of the company.

If GE wishes to raise additional capital, it may do so by either borrowing or selling new shares to investors. Sales of new shares to raise new capital are said to occur in the *primary market.* But most trades in GE shares take place in existing shares, which investors buy from each other. These trades do not raise new capital for the firm. This market for secondhand shares is known as the *secondary market.* The principal secondary marketplace for GE shares is the New York Stock Exchange

(NYSE).[1] This is the largest stock exchange in the world and trades, on an average day, 1 billion shares in some 2,900 companies.

Suppose that you are the head trader for a pension fund that wishes to buy 100,000 GE shares. You contact your broker, who then relays the order to the floor of the NYSE. Trading in each stock is the responsibility of a *specialist,* who keeps a record of orders to buy and sell. When your order arrives, the specialist will check this record to see if an investor is prepared to sell at your price. Alternatively, the specialist may be able to get you a better deal from one of the brokers who is gathered around or may sell you some of his or her own stock. If no one is prepared to sell at your price, the specialist will make a note of your order and execute it as soon as possible.

The NYSE is not the only stock market in the United States. For example, many stocks are traded *over the counter* by a network of dealers, who display the prices at which they are prepared to trade on a system of computer terminals known as NASDAQ (National Association of Securities Dealers Automated Quotations System). If you like the price that you see on the NASDAQ screen, you simply call the dealer and strike a bargain.

The prices at which stocks trade are summarized in the daily press. Here, for example, is how *The Wall Street Journal* recorded the day's trading in GE on July 2, 2001:

YTD	52 Weeks								
% Chg	**Hi**	**Lo**	**Stock (SYM)**	**Div**	**Yld %**	**PE**	**Vol 100s**	**Last**	**Net Chg**
+4.7	60.50	36.42	General Electric (GE)	.64	1.3	38	215287	50.20	+1.45

You can see that on this day investors traded a total of 215,287 × 100 = 21,528,700 shares of GE stock. By the close of the day the stock traded at $50.20 a share, up $1.45 from the day before. The stock had increased by 4.7 percent from the start of 2001. Since there were about 9.9 billion shares of GE outstanding, investors were placing a total value on the stock of $497 billion.

Buying stocks is a risky occupation. Over the previous year, GE stock traded as high as $60.50, but at one point dropped to $36.42. An unfortunate investor who bought at the 52-week high and sold at the low would have lost 40 percent of his or her investment. Of course, you don't come across such people at cocktail parties; they either keep quiet or aren't invited.

The Wall Street Journal also provides three other facts about GE's stock. GE pays an annual dividend of $.64 a share, the dividend yield on the stock is 1.3 percent, and the ratio of the stock price to earnings (P/E ratio) is 38. We will explain shortly why investors pay attention to these figures.

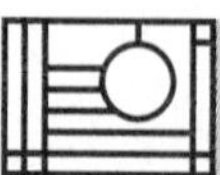

4.2 HOW COMMON STOCKS ARE VALUED

Think back to the last chapter, where we described how to value future cash flows. The discounted-cash-flow (DCF) formula for the present value of a stock is just the same as it is for the present value of any other asset. We just discount the cash flows

[1]GE shares are also traded on a number of overseas exchanges.

by the return that can be earned in the capital market on securities of comparable risk. Shareholders receive cash from the company in the form of a stream of dividends. So

$$\text{PV(stock)} = \text{PV(expected future dividends)}$$

At first sight this statement may seem surprising. When investors buy stocks, they usually expect to receive a dividend, but they also hope to make a capital gain. Why does our formula for present value say nothing about capital gains? As we now explain, there is no inconsistency.

Today's Price

The cash payoff to owners of common stocks comes in two forms: (1) cash dividends and (2) capital gains or losses. Suppose that the current price of a share is P_0, that the expected price at the end of a year is P_1, and that the expected dividend per share is DIV_1. The rate of return that investors expect from this share over the next year is defined as the expected dividend per share DIV_1 plus the expected price appreciation per share $P_1 - P_0$, all divided by the price at the start of the year P_0:

$$\text{Expected return} = r = \frac{\text{DIV}_1 + P_1 - P_0}{P_0}$$

This expected return is often called the **market capitalization rate.**

Suppose Fledgling Electronics stock is selling for $100 a share ($P_0 = 100$). Investors expect a $5 cash dividend over the next year ($\text{DIV}_1 = 5$). They also expect the stock to sell for $110 a year hence ($P_1 = 110$). Then the expected return to the stockholders is 15 percent:

$$r = \frac{5 + 110 - 100}{100} = .15, \text{ or } 15\%$$

On the other hand, if you are given investors' forecasts of dividend and price and the expected return offered by other equally risky stocks, you can predict today's price:

$$\text{Price} = P_0 = \frac{\text{DIV}_1 + P_1}{1 + r}$$

For Fledgling Electronics $\text{DIV}_1 = 5$ and $P_1 = 110$. If r, the expected return on securities in the same risk class as Fledgling, is 15 percent, then today's price should be $100:

$$P_0 = \frac{5 + 110}{1.15} = \$100$$

How do we know that $100 is the right price? Because no other price could survive in competitive capital markets. What if P_0 were above $100? Then Fledgling stock would offer an expected rate of return that was *lower* than other securities of equivalent risk. Investors would shift their capital to the other securities and in the process would force down the price of Fledgling stock. If P_0 were less than $100, the process would reverse. Fledgling's stock would offer a higher rate of return than comparable securities. In that case, investors would rush to buy, forcing the price up to $100.

The general conclusion is that at each point in time *all securities in an equivalent risk class are priced to offer the same expected return.* This is a condition for equilibrium in well-functioning capital markets. It is also common sense.

But What Determines Next Year's Price?

We have managed to explain today's stock price P_0 in terms of the dividend DIV_1 and the expected price next year P_1. Future stock prices are not easy things to forecast directly. But think about what determines next year's price. If our price formula holds now, it ought to hold then as well:

$$P_1 = \frac{\text{DIV}_2 + P_2}{1 + r}$$

That is, a year from now investors will be looking out at dividends in year 2 and price at the end of year 2. Thus we can forecast P_1 by forecasting DIV_2 and P_2, and we can express P_0 in terms of DIV_1, DIV_2, and P_2:

$$P_0 = \frac{1}{1 + r}(\text{DIV}_1 + P_1) = \frac{1}{1 + r}\left(\text{DIV}_1 + \frac{\text{DIV}_2 + P_2}{1 + r}\right) = \frac{\text{DIV}_1}{1 + r} + \frac{\text{DIV}_2 + P_2}{(1 + r)^2}$$

Take Fledgling Electronics. A plausible explanation why investors expect its stock price to rise by the end of the first year is that they expect higher dividends and still more capital gains in the second. For example, suppose that they are looking today for dividends of \$5.50 in year 2 and a subsequent price of \$121. That would imply a price at the end of year 1 of

$$P_1 = \frac{5.50 + 121}{1.15} = \$110$$

Today's price can then be computed either from our original formula

$$P_0 = \frac{\text{DIV}_1 + P_1}{1 + r} = \frac{5.00 + 110}{1.15} = \$100$$

or from our expanded formula

$$P_0 = \frac{\text{DIV}_1}{1 + r} + \frac{\text{DIV}_2 + P_2}{(1 + r)^2} = \frac{5.00}{1.15} + \frac{5.50 + 121}{(1.15)^2} = \$100$$

We have succeeded in relating today's price to the forecasted dividends for two years (DIV_1 and DIV_2) plus the forecasted price at the end of the *second* year (P_2). You will probably not be surprised to learn that we could go on to replace P_2 by $(\text{DIV}_3 + P_3)/(1 + r)$ and relate today's price to the forecasted dividends for three years (DIV_1, DIV_2, and DIV_3) plus the forecasted price at the end of the *third* year (P_3). In fact we can look as far out into the future as we like, removing P's as we go. Let us call this final period H. This gives us a general stock price formula:

$$\begin{aligned} P_0 &= \frac{\text{DIV}_1}{1 + r} + \frac{\text{DIV}_2}{(1 + r)^2} + \dots + \frac{\text{DIV}_H + P_H}{(1 + r)^H} \\ &= \sum_{t=1}^{H} \frac{\text{DIV}_t}{(1 + r)^t} + \frac{P_H}{(1 + r)^H} \end{aligned}$$

The expression $\sum_{t=1}^{H}$ simply means the sum of the discounted dividends from year 1 to year H.

TABLE 4.1

Applying the stock valuation formula to fledgling electronics.

Assumptions:
1. Dividends increase at 10 percent per year, compounded.
2. Capitalization rate is 15 percent.

	Expected Future Values		Present Values		
Horizon Period (H)	**Dividend (DIV_t)**	**Price (P_t)**	**Cumulative Dividends**	**Future Price**	**Total**
0	—	100	—	—	100
1	5.00	110	4.35	95.65	100
2	5.50	121	8.51	91.49	100
3	6.05	133.10	12.48	87.52	100
4	6.66	146.41	16.29	83.71	100
10	11.79	259.37	35.89	64.11	100
20	30.58	672.75	58.89	41.11	100
50	533.59	11,739.09	89.17	10.83	100
100	62,639.15	1,378,061.23	98.83	1.17	100

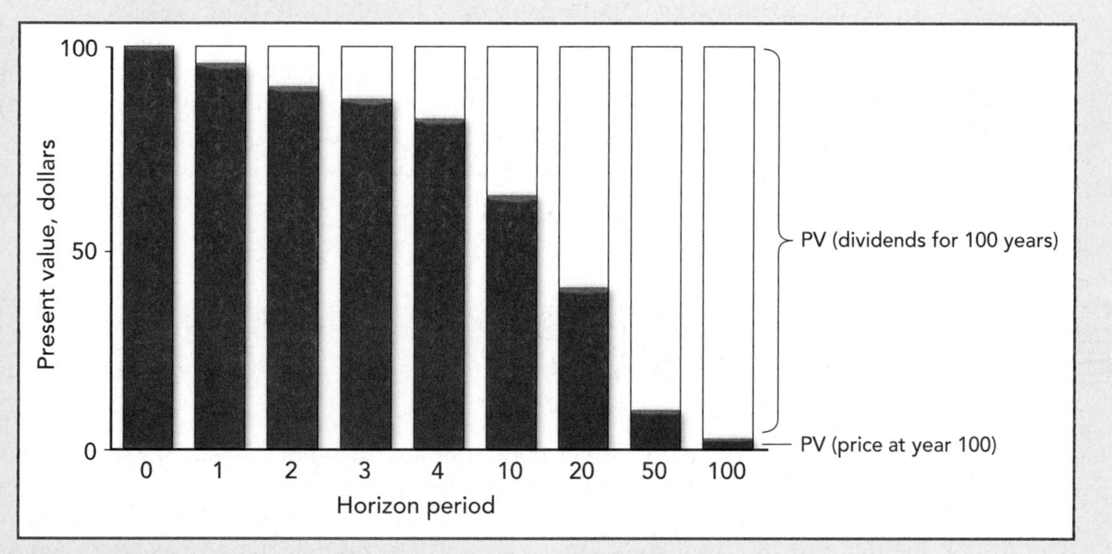

FIGURE 4.1

As your horizon recedes, the present value of the future price (shaded area) declines but the present value of the stream of dividends (unshaded area) increases. The *total* present value (future price and dividends) remains the same.

Table 4.1 continues the Fledgling Electronics example for various time horizons, assuming that the dividends are expected to increase at a steady 10 percent compound rate. The expected price P_t increases at the same rate each year. Each line in the table represents an application of our general formula for a different value of H. Figure 4.1 provides a graphical representation of the table. Each column shows the present value of the dividends up to the time horizon and the present value of the price at the horizon. As the horizon recedes, the dividend stream accounts for an increasing proportion of present value, but the *total* present value of dividends plus terminal price always equals $100.

How far out could we look? In principle the horizon period H could be infinitely distant. Common stocks do not expire of old age. Barring such corporate hazards as bankruptcy or acquisition, they are immortal. As H approaches infinity, the present value of the terminal price ought to approach zero, as it does in the final column of Figure 4.1. We can, therefore, forget about the terminal price entirely and express today's price as the present value of a perpetual stream of cash dividends. This is usually written as

$$P_0 = \sum_{t=1}^{\infty} \frac{\text{DIV}_t}{(1 + r)^t}$$

where ∞ indicates infinity.

This discounted-cash-flow (DCF) formula for the present value of a stock is just the same as it is for the present value of any other asset. We just discount the cash flows—in this case the dividend stream—by the return that can be earned in the capital market on securities of comparable risk. Some find the DCF formula implausible because it seems to ignore capital gains. But we know that the formula was *derived* from the assumption that price in any period is determined by expected dividends *and* capital gains over the next period.

Notice that it is *not* correct to say that the value of a share is equal to the sum of the discounted stream of earnings per share. Earnings are generally larger than dividends because part of those earnings is reinvested in new plant, equipment, and working capital. Discounting earnings would recognize the rewards of that investment (a higher *future* dividend) but not the sacrifice (a lower dividend *today*). The correct formulation states that share value is equal to the discounted stream of dividends per share.

4.3 A SIMPLE WAY TO ESTIMATE THE CAPITALIZATION RATE

In Chapter 3 we encountered some simplified versions of the basic present value formula. Let us see whether they offer any insights into stock values. Suppose, for example, that we forecast a constant growth rate for a company's dividends. This does not preclude year-to-year deviations from the trend: It means only that *expected* dividends grow at a constant rate. Such an investment would be just another example of the growing perpetuity that we helped our fickle philanthropist to evaluate in the last chapter. To find its present value we must divide the annual cash payment by the difference between the discount rate and the growth rate:

$$P_0 = \frac{\text{DIV}_1}{r - g}$$

Remember that we can use this formula only when g, the anticipated growth rate, is less than r, the discount rate. As g approaches r, the stock price becomes infinite. Obviously r must be greater than g if growth really is perpetual.

Our growing perpetuity formula explains P_0 in terms of next year's expected dividend DIV_1, the projected growth trend g, and the expected rate of return on other securities of comparable risk r. Alternatively, the formula can be used to obtain an estimate of r from DIV_1, P_0, and g:

$$r = \frac{\text{DIV}_1}{P_0} + g$$

The market capitalization rate equals the **dividend yield** (DIV_1/P_0) plus the expected rate of growth in dividends (g).

These two formulas are much easier to work with than the general statement that "price equals the present value of expected future dividends."[2] Here is a practical example.

Using the DCF Model to Set Gas and Electricity Prices

The prices charged by local electric and gas utilities are regulated by state commissions. The regulators try to keep consumer prices down but are supposed to allow the utilities to earn a fair rate of return. But what is fair? It is usually interpreted as r, the market capitalization rate for the firm's common stock. That is, the fair rate of return on equity for a public utility ought to be the rate offered by securities that have the same risk as the utility's common stock.[3]

Small variations in estimates of this return can have a substantial effect on the prices charged to the customers and on the firm's profits. So both utilities and regulators devote considerable resources to estimating r. They call r the **cost of equity capital.** Utilities are mature, stable companies which ought to offer tailor-made cases for application of the constant-growth DCF formula.[4]

Suppose you wished to estimate the cost of equity for Pinnacle West Corp. in May 2001, when its stock was selling for about $49 per share. Dividend payments for the next year were expected to be $1.60 a share. Thus it was a simple matter to calculate the first half of the DCF formula:

$$\text{Dividend yield} = \frac{\text{DIV}_1}{P_0} = \frac{1.60}{49} = .033, \text{ or } 3.3\%$$

The hard part was estimating g, the expected rate of dividend growth. One option was to consult the views of security analysts who study the prospects for each company. Analysts are rarely prepared to stick their necks out by forecasting dividends to kingdom come, but they often forecast growth rates over the next five years, and these estimates may provide an indication of the expected long-run growth path. In the case of Pinnacle West, analysts in 2001 were forecasting an

[2]These formulas were first developed in 1938 by Williams and were rediscovered by Gordon and Shapiro. See J. B. Williams, *The Theory of Investment Value* (Cambridge, Mass.: Harvard University Press, 1938); and M. J. Gordon and E. Shapiro, "Capital Equipment Analysis: The Required Rate of Profit," *Management Science* 3 (October 1956), pp. 102–110.

[3]This is the accepted interpretation of the U.S. Supreme Court's directive in 1944 that "the returns to the equity owner [of a regulated business] should be commensurate with returns on investments in other enterprises having corresponding risks." *Federal Power Commission v. Hope Natural Gas Company,* 302 U.S. 591 at 603.

[4]There are many exceptions to this statement. For example, Pacific Gas & Electric (PG&E), which serves northern California, used to be a mature, stable company until the California energy crisis of 2000 sent wholesale electric prices sky-high. PG&E was not allowed to pass these price increases on to retail customers. The company lost more than $3.5 billion in 2000 and was forced to declare bankruptcy in 2001. PG&E is no longer a suitable subject for the constant-growth DCF formula.

annual growth of 6.6 percent.[5] This, together with the dividend yield, gave an estimate of the cost of equity capital:

$$r = \frac{\text{DIV}_1}{P_0} + g = .033 + .066 = .099, \text{ or } 9.9\%$$

An alternative approach to estimating long-run growth starts with the **payout ratio,** the ratio of dividends to earnings per share (EPS). For Pinnacle, this was forecasted at 43 percent. In other words, each year the company was plowing back into the business about 57 percent of earnings per share:

$$\text{Plowback ratio} = 1 - \text{payout ratio} = 1 - \frac{\text{DIV}}{\text{EPS}} = 1 - .43 = .57$$

Also, Pinnacle's ratio of earnings per share to book equity per share was about 11 percent. This is its **return on equity,** or **ROE:**

$$\text{Return on equity} = \text{ROE} = \frac{\text{EPS}}{\text{book equity per share}} = .11$$

If Pinnacle earns 11 percent of book equity and reinvests 57 percent of that, then book equity will increase by $.57 \times .11 = .063$, or 6.3 percent. Earnings and dividends per share will also increase by 6.3 percent:

$$\text{Dividend growth rate} = g = \text{plowback ratio} \times \text{ROE} = .57 \times .11 = .063$$

That gives a second estimate of the market capitalization rate:

$$r = \frac{\text{DIV}_1}{P_0} + g = .033 + .063 = .096, \text{ or } 9.6\%$$

Although this estimate of the market capitalization rate for Pinnacle stock seems reasonable enough, there are obvious dangers in analyzing any single firm's stock with the constant-growth DCF formula. First, the underlying assumption of regular future growth is at best an approximation. Second, even if it is an acceptable approximation, errors inevitably creep into the estimate of g. Thus our two methods for calculating the cost of equity give similar answers. That was a lucky chance; different methods can sometimes give very different answers.

Remember, Pinnacle's cost of equity is not its personal property. In well-functioning capital markets investors capitalize the dividends of all securities in Pinnacle's risk class at exactly the same rate. But any estimate of r for a single common stock is "noisy" and subject to error. Good practice does not put too much weight on single-company cost-of-equity estimates. It collects samples of similar companies, estimates r for each, and takes an average. The average gives a more reliable benchmark for decision making.

Table 4.2 shows DCF cost-of-equity estimates for Pinnacle West and 10 other electric utilities in May 2001. These utilities are all stable, mature companies for which the constant-growth DCF formula *ought* to work. Notice the variation in the cost-of-equity estimates. Some of the variation may reflect differences in the risk, but some is just noise. The average estimate is 10.7 percent.

---

[5]In this calculation we're assuming that earnings and dividends are forecasted to grow forever at the same rate g. We'll show how to relax this assumption later in this chapter. The growth rate was based on the average earnings growth forecasted by Value Line and IBES. IBES compiles and averages forecasts made by security analysts. Value Line publishes its own analysts' forecasts

	Stock Price, P_0	Dividend, DIV_1	Dividend Yield, DIV_1/P_0	Growth Rate, g	Cost of Equity, $r = DIV_1/P_0 + g$
American Corp.	$41.71	$2.64	6.3%	3.8%	10.1%
CH Energy Corp.	43.85	2.20	5.0	2.0	7.0
CLECO Corp.	46.00	.92	2.0	8.8	10.8
DPL, Inc.	30.27	1.03	3.4	9.6	13.0
Hawaiian Electric	36.69	2.54	6.9	2.6	9.5
Idacorp	39.42	1.97	5.0	5.7	10.7
Pinnacle West	49.16	1.60	3.3	6.6	9.9
Potomac Electric	22.00	1.75	8.0	5.7	13.7
Puget Energy	23.49	1.93	8.2	4.8	13.0
TECO Energy	31.38	1.44	4.6	7.7	12.3
UIL Holdings	48.21	2.93	6.1	1.9	8.0
				Average	10.7%

TABLE 4.2

DCF cost-of-equity estimates for electric utilities in 2001.

Source: The Brattle Group, Inc.

Figure 4.2 shows DCF costs of equity estimated at six-month intervals for a sample of electric utilities over a seven-year period. The burgundy line indicates the median cost-of-equity estimates, which seem to lie about 3 percentage points above the 10-year Treasury bond yield. The dots show the scatter of individual estimates. Again, most of this scatter is probably noise.

Some Warnings about Constant-Growth Formulas

The simple constant-growth DCF formula is an extremely useful rule of thumb, but no more than that. Naive trust in the formula has led many financial analysts to silly conclusions.

We have stressed the difficulty of estimating r by analysis of one stock only. Try to use a large sample of equivalent-risk securities. Even that may not work, but at least it gives the analyst a fighting chance, because the inevitable errors in estimating r for a single security tend to balance out across a broad sample.

In addition, resist the temptation to apply the formula to firms having high current rates of growth. Such growth can rarely be sustained indefinitely, but the constant-growth DCF formula assumes it can. This erroneous assumption leads to an overestimate of r.

Consider Growth-Tech, Inc., a firm with $DIV_1 = \$.50$ and $P_0 = \$50$. The firm has plowed back 80 percent of earnings and has had a return on equity (ROE) of 25 percent. This means that *in the past*

$$\text{Dividend growth rate} = \text{plowback ratio} \times \text{ROE} = .80 \times .25 = .20$$

The temptation is to assume that the future long-term growth rate g also equals .20. This would imply

$$r = \frac{.50}{50.00} + .20 = .21$$

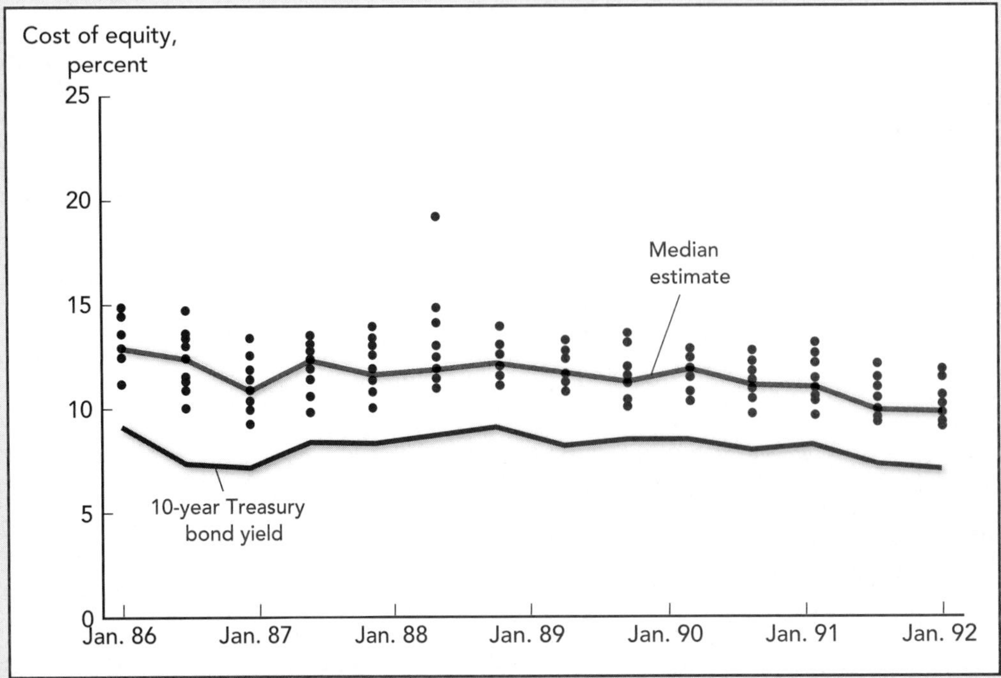

FIGURE 4.2

DCF cost-of-equity estimates for a sample of 17 utilities. The median estimates (burgundy line) track long-term interest rates fairly well. (The blue line is the 10-year Treasury yield.) The dots show the scatter of the cost-of-equity estimates for individual companies.

Source: S. C. Myers and L. S. Borucki, "Discounted Cash Flow Estimates of the Cost of Equity Capital—A Case Study," *Financial Markets, Institutions and Instruments* 3 (August 1994), pp. 9–45.

But this is silly. No firm can continue growing at 20 percent per year forever, except possibly under extreme inflationary conditions. Eventually, profitability will fall and the firm will respond by investing less.

In real life the return on equity will decline gradually over time, but for simplicity let's assume it suddenly drops to 16 percent at year 3 and the firm responds by plowing back only 50 percent of earnings. Then g drops to $.50(.16) = .08$.

Table 4.3 shows what's going on. Growth-Tech starts year 1 with assets of $10.00. It earns $2.50, pays out 50 cents as dividends, and plows back $2. Thus it starts year 2 with assets of $10 + 2 = $12. After another year at the same ROE and payout, it starts year 3 with assets of $14.40. However, ROE drops to .16, and the firm earns only $2.30. Dividends go up to $1.15, because the payout ratio increases, but the firm has only $1.15 to plow back. Therefore subsequent growth in earnings and dividends drops to 8 percent.

Now we can use our general DCF formula to find the capitalization rate r:

$$P_0 = \frac{\text{DIV}_1}{1 + r} + \frac{\text{DIV}_2}{(1 + r)^2} + \frac{\text{DIV}_3 + P_3}{(1 + r)^3}$$

Investors in year 3 will view Growth-Tech as offering 8 percent per year dividend growth. We will apply the constant-growth formula:

	Year			
	1	2	3	4
Book equity	10.00	12.00	14.40	15.55
Earnings per share, EPS	2.50	3.00	2.30	2.49
Return on equity, ROE	.25	.25	.16	.16
Payout ratio	.20	.20	.50	.50
Dividends per share, DIV	.50	.60	1.15	1.24
Growth rate of dividends (%)	—	20	92	8

TABLE 4.3

Forecasted earnings and dividends for Growth-Tech. Note the changes in year 3: ROE and earnings drop, but payout ratio increases, causing a big jump in dividends. However, subsequent growth in earnings and dividends falls to 8 percent per year. Note that the increase in equity equals the earnings not paid out as dividends.

$$P_3 = \frac{\text{DIV}_4}{r - .08}$$

$$P_0 = \frac{\text{DIV}_1}{1 + r} + \frac{\text{DIV}_2}{(1 + r)^2} + \frac{\text{DIV}_3}{(1 + r)^3} + \frac{1}{(1 + r)^3}\frac{\text{DIV}_4}{r - .08}$$

$$= \frac{.50}{1 + r} + \frac{.60}{(1 + r)^2} + \frac{1.15}{(1 + r)^3} + \frac{1}{(1 + r)^3}\frac{1.24}{r - .08}$$

We have to use trial and error to find the value of r that makes P_0 equal \$50. It turns out that the r implicit in these more realistic forecasts is approximately .099, quite a difference from our "constant-growth" estimate of .21.

DCF Valuation with Varying Growth Rates

Our present value calculations for Growth-Tech used a *two-stage* DCF valuation model. In the first stage (years 1 and 2), Growth-Tech is highly profitable (ROE = 25 percent), and it plows back 80 percent of earnings. Book equity, earnings, and dividends increase by 20 percent per year. In the second stage, starting in year 3, profitability and plowback decline, and earnings settle into long-term growth at 8 percent. Dividends jump up to \$1.15 in year 3, and then also grow at 8 percent.

Growth rates can vary for many reasons. Sometimes growth is high in the short run not because the firm is unusually profitable, but because it is recovering from an episode of *low* profitability. Table 4.4 displays projected earnings and dividends for Phoenix.com, which is gradually regaining financial health after a near meltdown. The company's equity is growing at a moderate 4 percent. ROE in year 1 is only 4 percent, however, so Phoenix has to reinvest all its earnings, leaving no cash for dividends. As profitability increases in years 2 and 3, an increasing dividend can be paid. Finally, starting in year 4, Phoenix settles into steady-state growth, with equity, earnings, and dividends all increasing at 4 percent per year.

Assume the cost of equity is 10 percent. Then Phoenix shares should be worth \$9.13 per share:

$$P_0 = \underbrace{\frac{0}{1.1} + \frac{.31}{(1.1)^2} + \frac{.65}{(1.1)^3}}_{\text{PV (first-stage dividends)}} + \underbrace{\frac{1}{(1.1)^3}\frac{.67}{(.10 - .04)}}_{\text{PV (second-stage dividends)}} = \$9.13$$

We could go on to three- or even four-stage valuation models—but you get the idea. Two warnings, however. First, it's almost always worthwhile to lay out a simple

TABLE 4.4

Forecasted earnings and dividends for Phoenix.com. The company can initiate and increase dividends as profitability (ROE) recovers. Note that the increase in book equity equals the earnings not paid out as dividends.

	Year			
	1	2	3	4
Book equity	10.00	10.40	10.82	11.25
Earnings per share, EPS	.40	.73	1.08	1.12
Return on equity, ROE	.04	.07	.10	.10
Dividends per share, DIV	0	.31	.65	.67
Growth rate of dividends (%)	—	—	110	4

spreadsheet, like Table 4.3 or 4.4, to assure that your dividend projections are consistent with the company's earnings and the investments required to grow. Second, do not use DCF valuation formulas to test whether the market is correct in its assessment of a stock's value. If your estimate of the value is different from that of the market, it is probably because you have used poor dividend forecasts. Remember what we said at the beginning of this chapter about simple ways of making money on the stock market: There aren't any.

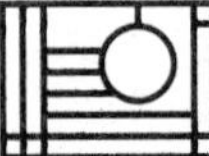

4.4 THE LINK BETWEEN STOCK PRICE AND EARNINGS PER SHARE

Investors often use the terms *growth stocks* and *income stocks.* They buy growth stocks primarily for the expectation of capital gains, and they are interested in the future growth of earnings rather than in next year's dividends. On the other hand, they buy income stocks primarily for the cash dividends. Let us see whether these distinctions make sense.

Imagine first the case of a company that does not grow at all. It does not plow back any earnings and simply produces a constant stream of dividends. Its stock would resemble the perpetual bond described in the last chapter. Remember that the return on a perpetuity is equal to the yearly cash flow divided by the present value. The expected return on our share would thus be equal to the yearly dividend divided by the share price (i.e., the dividend yield). Since all the earnings are paid out as dividends, the expected return is also equal to the earnings per share divided by the share price (i.e., the earnings–price ratio). For example, if the dividend is \$10 a share and the stock price is \$100, we have

$$\begin{aligned}\text{Expected return} &= \text{dividend yield} = \text{earnings–price ratio}\\ &= \frac{\text{DIV}_1}{P_0} \qquad\qquad = \frac{\text{EPS}_1}{P_0}\\ &= \frac{10.00}{100} \qquad\qquad = .10\end{aligned}$$

The price equals

$$P_0 = \frac{\text{DIV}_1}{r} = \frac{\text{EPS}_1}{r} = \frac{10.00}{.10} = 100$$

The expected return for *growing* firms can *also* equal the earnings–price ratio. The key is whether earnings are reinvested to provide a return equal to the market capitalization rate. For example, suppose our monotonous company suddenly hears of an opportunity to invest $10 a share next year. This would mean no dividend at $t = 1$. However, the company expects that in each subsequent year the project would earn $1 per share, so that the dividend could be increased to $11 a share.

Let us assume that this investment opportunity has about the same risk as the existing business. Then we can discount its cash flow at the 10 percent rate to find its net present value at year 1:

$$\text{Net present value per share at year 1} = -10 + \frac{1}{.10} = 0$$

Thus the investment opportunity will make no contribution to the company's value. Its prospective return is equal to the opportunity cost of capital.

What effect will the decision to undertake the project have on the company's share price? Clearly none. The reduction in value caused by the nil dividend in year 1 is exactly offset by the increase in value caused by the extra dividends in later years. Therefore, once again the market capitalization rate equals the earnings–price ratio:

$$r = \frac{\text{EPS}_1}{P_0} = \frac{10}{100} = .10$$

Table 4.5 repeats our example for different assumptions about the cash flow generated by the new project. Note that the earnings–price ratio, measured in terms of EPS_1, next year's expected earnings, equals the market capitalization rate (r) *only* when the new project's NPV = 0. This is an extremely important point—managers frequently make poor financial decisions because they confuse earnings–price ratios with the market capitalization rate.

In general, we can think of stock price as the capitalized value of average earnings under a no-growth policy, plus **PVGO,** the **present value of growth opportunities:**

$$P_0 = \frac{\text{EPS}_1}{r} + \text{PVGO}$$

Project Rate of Return	Incremental Cash Flow, C	Project NPV in Year 1*	Project's Impact on Share Price in Year 0†	Share Price in Year 0, P_0	$\frac{\text{EPS}_1}{P_0}$	r
.05	$ .50	−$ 5.00	−$ 4.55	$ 95.45	.105	.10
.10	1.00	0	0	100.00	.10	.10
.15	1.50	+ 5.00	+ 4.55	104.55	.096	.10
.20	2.00	+ 10.00	+ 9.09	109.09	.092	.10
.25	2.50	+ 15.00	+ 13.64	113.64	.088	.10

TABLE 4.5

Effect on stock price of investing an additional $10 in year 1 at different rates of return. Notice that the earnings–price ratio overestimates r when the project has negative NPV and underestimates it when the project has positive NPV.

*Project costs $10.00 ($\text{EPS}_1$). NPV = $-10 + C/r$, where $r = .10$.

†NPV is calculated at year 1. To find the impact on P_0, discount for one year at $r = .10$.

The earnings–price ratio, therefore, equals

$$\frac{\text{EPS}}{P_0} = r\left(1 - \frac{\text{PVGO}}{P_0}\right)$$

It will underestimate r if PVGO is positive and overestimate it if PVGO is negative. The latter case is less likely, since firms are rarely *forced* to take projects with negative net present values.

Calculating the Present Value of Growth Opportunities for Fledgling Electronics

In our last example both dividends and earnings were expected to grow, but this growth made no net contribution to the stock price. The stock was in this sense an "income stock." Be careful not to equate firm performance with the growth in earnings per share. A company that reinvests earnings at below the market capitalization rate may increase earnings but will certainly reduce the share value.

Now let us turn to that well-known *growth stock,* Fledgling Electronics. You may remember that Fledgling's market capitalization rate, r, is 15 percent. The company is expected to pay a dividend of $5 in the first year, and thereafter the dividend is predicted to increase indefinitely by 10 percent a year. We can, therefore, use the simplified constant-growth formula to work out Fledgling's price:

$$P_0 = \frac{\text{DIV}_1}{r - g} = \frac{5}{.15 - .10} = \$100$$

Suppose that Fledgling has earnings per share of $8.33. Its payout ratio is then

$$\text{Payout ratio} = \frac{\text{DIV}_1}{\text{EPS}_1} = \frac{5.00}{8.33} = .6$$

In other words, the company is plowing back 1 − .6, or 40 percent of earnings. Suppose also that Fledgling's ratio of earnings to book equity is ROE = .25. This explains the growth rate of 10 percent:

$$\text{Growth rate} = g = \text{plowback ratio} \times \text{ROE} = .4 \times .25 = .10$$

The capitalized value of Fledgling's earnings per share if it had a no-growth policy would be

$$\frac{\text{EPS}_1}{r} = \frac{8.33}{.15} = \$55.56$$

But we know that the value of Fledgling stock is $100. The difference of $44.44 must be the amount that investors are paying for growth opportunities. Let's see if we can explain that figure.

Each year Fledgling plows back 40 percent of its earnings into new assets. In the first year Fledgling invests $3.33 at a permanent 25 percent return on equity. Thus the cash generated by this investment is .25 × 3.33 = $.83 per year starting at t = 2. The net present value of the investment as of t = 1 is

$$\text{NPV}_1 = -3.33 + \frac{.83}{.15} = \$2.22$$

Everything is the same in year 2 except that Fledgling will invest \$3.67, 10 percent more than in year 1 (remember $g = .10$). Therefore at $t = 2$ an investment is made with a net present value of

$$\text{NPV}_2 = -3.33 \times 1.10 + \frac{.83 \times 1.10}{.15} = \$2.44$$

Thus the payoff to the owners of Fledgling Electronics stock can be represented as the sum of (1) a level stream of earnings, which could be paid out as cash dividends if the firm did not grow, and (2) a set of tickets, one for each future year, representing the opportunity to make investments having positive NPVs. We know that the first component of the value of the share is

$$\text{Present value of level stream of earnings} = \frac{\text{EPS}_1}{r} = \frac{8.33}{.15} = \$55.56$$

The first ticket is worth \$2.22 in $t = 1$, the second is worth \$2.22 × 1.10 = \$2.44 in $t = 2$, the third is worth \$2.44 × 1.10 = \$2.69 in $t = 3$. These are the forecasted cash values of the tickets. We know how to value a stream of future cash values that grows at 10 percent per year: Use the constant-growth DCF formula, replacing the forecasted dividends with forecasted ticket values:

$$\text{Present value of growth opportunities} = \text{PVGO} = \frac{\text{NPV}_1}{r - g} = \frac{2.22}{.15 - .10} = \$44.44$$

Now everything checks:

$$\begin{aligned}\text{Share price} &= \text{present value of level stream of earnings} \\ &\quad + \text{present value of growth opportunities} \\ &= \frac{\text{EPS}_1}{r} + \text{PVGO} \\ &= \$55.56 + \$44.44 \\ &= \$100\end{aligned}$$

Why is Fledgling Electronics a growth stock? Not because it is expanding at 10 percent per year. It is a growth stock because the net present value of its future investments accounts for a significant fraction (about 44 percent) of the stock's price.

Stock prices today reflect investors' expectations of future operating *and investment* performance. Growth stocks sell at high price–earnings ratios because investors are willing to pay now for expected superior returns on investments that have not yet been made.[6]

Some Examples of Growth Opportunities?

Stocks like Microsoft, Dell Computer, and Wal-Mart are often described as growth stocks, while those of mature firms like Kellogg, Weyerhaeuser, and Exxon Mobil are regarded as income stocks. Let us check it out. The first column of Table 4.6

[6]Michael Eisner, the chairman of Walt Disney Productions, made the point this way: "In school you had to take the test and then be graded. Now we're getting graded, and we haven't taken the test." This was in late 1985, when Disney stock was selling at nearly 20 times earnings. See Kathleen K. Wiegner, "The Tinker Bell Principle," *Forbes* (December 2, 1985), p. 102.

Stock	Stock Price, P_0 (October 2001)	EPS*	Cost of Equity, $r^{\dagger}$	PVGO $= P_0 - \text{EPS}/r$	PVGO, percent of Stock Price
Income stocks:					
Chubb	$77.35	$4.90	.088	$21.67	28
Exxon Mobil	42.29	2.13	.072	12.71	30
Kellogg	29.00	1.42	.056	3.64	13
Weyerhaeuser	50.45	3.21	.128	25.37	50
Growth stocks:					
Amazon.com	8.88	−.30	.24	10.13	114
Dell Computer	23.66	.76	.22	20.20	85
Microsoft	56.38	1.88	.184	46.16	82
Wal-Mart	52.90	1.70	.112	37.72	71

TABLE 4.6

Estimated PVGOs.

*EPS is defined as the average earnings under a no-growth policy. As an estimate of EPS, we used the forecasted earnings per share for 2002. Source: MSN Money (moneycentral.msn.com).

†The market capitalization rate was estimated using the capital asset pricing model. We describe this model and how to use it in Sections 8.2 and 9.2. For this example, we used a market risk premium of 8 percent and a risk-free interest rate of 4 percent.

shows the stock price for each of these companies in October 2001. The remaining columns estimate PVGO as a proportion of the stock price.

Remember, if there are no growth opportunities, present value equals the average future earnings from existing assets discounted at the market capitalization rate. We used analysts' forecasts for 2002 as a measure of the earning power of existing assets. You can see that most of the value of the growth stocks comes from PVGO, that is, from investors' expectations that the companies will be able to earn more than the cost of capital on their future investments. However, Weyerhaeuser, though usually regarded as an income stock, does pretty well on the PVGO scale. But the most striking growth stock is Amazon.com. Its earnings have been consistently negative, so its PVGO accounts for *more than 100 percent* of its stock price. None of the company's value can be based on its current earnings. The value comes entirely from future earnings and the NPV of its future investments.[7]

Some companies have such extensive growth opportunities that they prefer to pay no dividends for long periods of time. For example, up to the time that we wrote this chapter, "glamour stocks" such as Microsoft and Dell Computer had never paid a dividend, because any cash paid out to investors would have meant either slower growth or raising capital by some other means. Investors were happy to forgo immediate cash dividends in exchange for increasing earnings and the expectation of high dividends some time in the future.

[7]However, Amazon's reported earnings probably understate its earnings potential. Amazon is growing very rapidly, and some of the investments necessary to finance that growth are written off as expenses, thus reducing current income. Absent these "investment expenses," Amazon's current income would probably be positive. We discuss the problems encountered in measuring earnings and profitability in Chapter 12.

What Do Price–Earnings Ratios Mean?

The **price–earnings ratio** is part of the everyday vocabulary of investors in the stock market. People casually refer to a stock as "selling at a high P/E." You can look up P/Es in stock quotations given in the newspaper. (However, the newspaper gives the ratio of current price to the most recent earnings. Investors are more concerned with price relative to *future* earnings.) Unfortunately, some financial analysts are confused about what price–earnings ratios really signify and often use the ratios in odd ways.

Should the financial manager celebrate if the firm's stock sells at a high P/E? The answer is usually yes. The high P/E shows that investors think that the firm has good growth opportunities (high PVGO), that its earnings are relatively safe and deserve a low capitalization rate (low r), or both. However, firms can have high price–earnings ratios not because price is high but because earnings are low. A firm which earns *nothing* (EPS = 0) in a particular period will have an *infinite* P/E as long as its shares retain any value at all.

Are relative P/Es helpful in evaluating stocks? Sometimes. Suppose you own stock in a family corporation whose shares are not actively traded. What are those shares worth? A decent estimate is possible if you can find traded firms that have roughly the same profitability, risks, and growth opportunities as your firm. Multiply your firm's earnings per share by the P/E of the counterpart firms.

Does a high P/E indicate a low market capitalization rate? No. There is *no* reliable association between a stock's price–earnings ratio and the capitalization rate r. The ratio of EPS to P_0 measures r only if PVGO = 0 and only if reported EPS is the average future earnings the firm could generate under a no-growth policy. Another reason P/Es are hard to interpret is that the figure for earnings depends on the accounting procedures for calculating revenues and costs. We will discuss the potential biases in accounting earnings in Chapter 12.

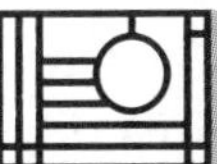

4.5 VALUING A BUSINESS BY DISCOUNTED CASH FLOW

Investors routinely buy and sell shares of common stock. Companies frequently buy and sell entire businesses. In 2001, for example, when Diageo sold its Pillsbury operation to General Mills for $10.4 billion, you can be sure that both companies burned a lot of midnight oil to make sure that the deal was fairly priced.

Do the discounted-cash-flow formulas we presented in this chapter work for entire businesses as well as for shares of common stock? Sure: It doesn't matter whether you forecast dividends per share or the total free cash flow of a business. Value today always equals future cash flow discounted at the opportunity cost of capital.

Valuing the Concatenator Business

Rumor has it that Establishment Industries is interested in buying your company's concatenator manufacturing operation. Your company is willing to sell if it can get the full value of this rapidly growing business. The problem is to figure out what its true present value is.

Table 4.7 gives a forecast of **free cash flow** (FCF) for the concatenator business. Free cash flow is the amount of cash that a firm can pay out to investors after paying for

	Year									
	1	2	3	4	5	6	7	8	9	10
Asset value	10.00	12.00	14.40	17.28	20.74	23.43	26.47	28.05	29.73	31.51
Earnings	1.20	1.44	1.73	2.07	2.49	2.81	3.18	3.36	3.57	3.78
Investment	2.00	2.40	2.88	3.46	2.69	3.04	1.59	1.68	1.78	1.89
Free cash flow	−.80	−.96	−1.15	−1.39	−.20	−.23	1.59	1.68	1.79	1.89
Earnings growth from previous period (%)	20	20	20	20	20	13	13	6	6	6

TABLE 4.7

Forecasts of free cash flow, in $ millions, for the Concatenator Manufacturing Division. Rapid expansion in years 1–6 means that free cash flow is negative, because required additional investment outstrips earnings. Free cash flow turns positive when growth slows down after year 6.

Notes:

1. Starting asset value is $10 million. Assets required for the business grow at 20 percent per year to year 4, at 13 percent in years 5 and 6, and at 6 percent afterward.
2. Profitability (earnings/asset values) is constant at 12 percent.
3. Free cash flow equals earnings minus net investment. Net investment equals total capital expenditures less depreciation. Note that earnings are also calculated net of depreciation.

all investments necessary for growth. As we will see, free cash flow can be negative for rapidly growing businesses.

Table 4.7 is similar to Table 4.3, which forecasted earnings and dividends per share for Growth-Tech, based on assumptions about Growth-Tech's equity per share, return on equity, and the growth of its business. For the concatenator business, we also have assumptions about assets, profitability—in this case, after-tax operating earnings relative to assets—and growth. Growth starts out at a rapid 20 percent per year, then falls in two steps to a moderate 6 percent rate for the long run. The growth rate determines the net additional investment required to expand assets, and the profitability rate determines the earnings thrown off by the business.[8]

Free cash flow, the next to last line in Table 4.7, is negative in years 1 through 6. The concatenator business is paying a negative dividend to the parent company; it is absorbing more cash than it is throwing off.

Is that a bad sign? Not really: The business is running a cash deficit not because it is unprofitable, but because it is growing so fast. Rapid growth is good news, not bad, so long as the business is earning more than the opportunity cost of capital. Your company, or Establishment Industries, will be happy to invest an extra $800,000 in the concatenator business next year, so long as the business offers a superior rate of return.

Valuation Format

The value of a business is usually computed as the discounted value of free cash flows out to a *valuation horizon (H)*, plus the forecasted value of the business at the horizon, also discounted back to present value. That is,

[8]Table 4.7 shows *net* investment, which is total investment less depreciation. We are assuming that investment for replacement of existing assets is covered by depreciation and that net investment is devoted to growth.

$$PV = \underbrace{\frac{FCF_1}{1+r} + \frac{FCF_2}{(1+r)^2} + \dots + \frac{FCF_H}{(1+r)^H}}_{\text{PV(free cash flow)}} + \underbrace{\frac{PV_H}{(1+r)^H}}_{\text{PV(horizon value)}}$$

Of course, the concatenator business will continue after the horizon, but it's not practical to forecast free cash flow year by year to infinity. PV_H stands in for free cash flow in periods $H + 1, H + 2$, etc.

Valuation horizons are often chosen arbitrarily. Sometimes the boss tells everybody to use 10 years because that's a round number. We will try year 6, because growth of the concatenator business seems to settle down to a long-run trend after year 7.

Estimating Horizon Value

There are several common formulas or rules of thumb for estimating horizon value. First, let us try the constant-growth DCF formula. This requires free cash flow for year 7, which we have from Table 4.7, a long-run growth rate, which appears to be 6 percent, and a discount rate, which some high-priced consultant has told us is 10 percent. Therefore,

$$\text{PV(horizon value)} = \frac{1}{(1.1)^6}\left(\frac{1.59}{.10 - .06}\right) = 22.4$$

The present value of the near-term free cash flows is

$$\begin{aligned}\text{PV(cash flows)} &= -\frac{.80}{1.1} - \frac{.96}{(1.1)^2} - \frac{1.15}{(1.1)^3} - \frac{1.39}{(1.1)^4} - \frac{.20}{(1.1)^5} - \frac{.23}{(1.1)^6} \\ &= -3.6\end{aligned}$$

and, therefore, the present value of the business is

$$\begin{aligned}\text{PV(business)} &= \text{PV(free cash flow)} + \text{PV(horizon value)} \\ &= -3.6 \qquad\qquad + 22.4 \\ &= \$18.8 \text{ million}\end{aligned}$$

Now, are we done? Well, the mechanics of this calculation are perfect. But doesn't it make you just a little nervous to find that 119 percent of the value of the business rests on the horizon value? Moreover, a little checking shows that the horizon value can change dramatically in response to apparently minor changes in assumptions. For example, if the long-run growth rate is 8 percent rather than 6 percent, the value of the business increases from $18.8 to $26.3 million.[9]

In other words, it's easy for a discounted-cash-flow business valuation to be mechanically perfect and practically wrong. Smart financial managers try to check their results by calculating horizon value in several different ways.

Horizon Value Based on P/E Ratios Suppose you can observe stock prices for mature manufacturing companies whose scale, risk, and growth prospects today

[9]If long-run growth is 8 rather than 6 percent, an extra 2 percent of period-7 assets will have to be plowed back into the concatenator business. This reduces free cash flow by $.53 to $1.06 million. So,

$$\text{PV(horizon value)} = \frac{1}{(1.1)^6}\left(\frac{1.06}{.10 - .08}\right) = \$29.9$$

$$\text{PV(business)} = -3.6 + 29.9 = \$26.3 \text{ million}$$

roughly match those projected for the concatenator business in year 6. Suppose further that these companies tend to sell at price–earnings ratios of about 11. Then you could reasonably guess that the price–earnings ratio of a mature concatenator operation will likewise be 11. That implies:

$$\text{PV(horizon value)} = \frac{1}{(1.1)^6}(11 \times 3.18) = 19.7$$

$$\text{PV(business)} = -3.6 + 19.7 = \$16.1 \text{ million}$$

Horizon Value Based on Market–Book Ratios Suppose also that the market–book ratios of the sample of mature manufacturing companies tend to cluster around 1.4. (The market–book ratio is just the ratio of stock price to book value per share.) If the concatenator business market–book ratio is 1.4 in year 6,

$$\text{PV(horizon value)} = \frac{1}{(1.1)^6}(1.4 \times 23.43) = 18.5$$

$$\text{PV(business)} = -3.6 + 18.5 = \$14.9 \text{ million}$$

It's easy to poke holes in these last two calculations. Book value, for example, often is a poor measure of the true value of a company's assets. It can fall far behind actual asset values when there is rapid inflation, and it often entirely misses important intangible assets, such as your patents for concatenator design. Earnings may also be biased by inflation and a long list of arbitrary accounting choices. Finally, you never know when you have found a sample of truly similar companies.

But remember, the purpose of discounted cash flow is to estimate market value—to estimate what investors would pay for a stock or business. When you can *observe* what they actually pay for similar companies, that's valuable evidence. Try to figure out a way to use it. One way to use it is through valuation rules of thumb, based on price–earnings or market–book ratios. A rule of thumb, artfully employed, sometimes beats a complex discounted-cash-flow calculation hands down.

A Further Reality Check

Here is another approach to valuing a business. It is based on what you have learned about price–earnings ratios and the present value of growth opportunities.

Suppose the valuation horizon is set not by looking for the first year of stable growth, but by asking when the industry is likely to settle into competitive equilibrium. You might go to the operating manager most familiar with the concatenator business and ask:

> Sooner or later you and your competitors will be on an equal footing when it comes to major new investments. You may still be earning a superior return on your core business, but you will find that introductions of new products or attempts to expand sales of existing products trigger intense resistance from competitors who are just about as smart and efficient as you are. Give a realistic assessment of when that time will come.

"That time" is the horizon after which PVGO, the net present value of subsequent growth opportunities, is zero. After all, PVGO is positive only when investments can be expected to earn more than the cost of capital. When your competition catches up, that happy prospect disappears.[10]

[10]We cover this point in more detail in Chapter 11.

We know that present value in any period equals the capitalized value of next period's earnings, plus PVGO:

$$PV_t = \frac{\text{earnings}_{t+1}}{r} + \text{PVGO}$$

But what if PVGO = 0? At the horizon period H, then,

$$PV_H = \frac{\text{earnings}_{H+1}}{r}$$

In other words, when the competition catches up, the price–earnings ratio equals $1/r$, because PVGO disappears.

Suppose competition is expected to catch up by period 8. We can recalculate the value of the concatenator business as follows:[11]

$$\begin{aligned} \text{PV(horizon value)} &= \frac{1}{(1+r)^8}\left(\frac{\text{earnings in period 9}}{r}\right) \\ &= \frac{1}{(1.1)^8}\left(\frac{3.57}{.10}\right) \\ &= \$16.7 \text{ million} \\ \text{PV(business)} &= -2.0 + 16.7 = \$14.7 \text{ million} \end{aligned}$$

We now have four estimates of what Establishment Industries ought to pay for the concatenator business. The estimates reflect four different methods of estimating horizon value. There is no best method, although in many cases we put most weight on the last method, which sets the horizon date at the point when management expects PVGO to disappear. The last method forces managers to remember that sooner or later competition catches up.

Our calculated values for the concatenator business range from \$14.7 to \$18.8 million, a difference of about \$4 million. The width of the range may be disquieting, but it is not unusual. Discounted-cash-flow formulas only estimate market value, and the estimates change as forecasts and assumptions change. Managers cannot know market value for sure until an actual transaction takes place.

How Much Is the Concatenator Business Worth per Share?

Suppose the concatenator division is spun off from its parent as an independent company, Concatco, with one million outstanding shares. What would each share sell for?

We have already calculated the value of Concatco's free cash flow as \$18.8 million, using the constant-growth DCF formula to calculate horizon value. If this value is right, and there are one million shares, each share should be worth \$18.80. This amount should also be the present value of Concatco's *dividends* per share—although here we must slow down and be careful. Note from Table 4.7 that free cash flow is negative from years 1 to 6. Dividends can't be negative, so Concatco will have to raise outside financing. Suppose it issues additional shares. Then Concatco's one million *existing* shares will not receive all of Concatco's dividend payments when the company starts paying out cash in year 7.

[11]The PV of free cash flow before the horizon improves to −\$2.0 million because inflows in years 7 and 8 are now included.

There are two approaches to valuing a company's existing shares when new shares will be issued. The first approach discounts the net cash flow to existing shareholders if they buy *all* the new shares issued. In this case the existing shareholders would pay out cash to Concatco in years 1 to 6, and then receive all subsequent dividends; they would pay for or receive all free cash flow from year 1 to year 8 and beyond. The value of a share therefore equals free cash flow for the company as a whole, taking account of negative as well as positive amounts, divided by the number of existing shares. We have already done this calculation: If the value of the company is $18.8 million, the value of each of the one million existing shares should be $18.80.

The second approach discounts the dividends that will be paid when free cash flow turns positive. But you must discount *only* the dividends paid on *existing* shares. The new shares issued to finance the negative free cash flows in years 1 to 6 will claim a portion of the dividends paid out later.

Let's check that the second method gives the same answer as the first. Note that the present value of Concatco's free cash flow from years 1 to 6 is −$3.6 million. Concatco decides to raise this amount now and put it in the bank to take care of the future cash outlays through year 6. To do this, the company has to issue 191,500 shares at a price of $18.80:

$$\begin{aligned}\text{Cash raised} &= \text{price per share} \times \text{number of new shares}\\ &= 18.80 \times 191{,}500 = \$3{,}600{,}000\end{aligned}$$

If the existing stockholders buy none of the new issue, their ownership of the company shrinks to

$$\frac{\text{Existing shares}}{\text{Existing} + \text{new shares}} = \frac{1{,}000{,}000}{1{,}191{,}500} = .839, \text{ or } 83.9\%$$

The value of the existing shares should be 83.9 percent of the present value of each dividend paid after year 6. In other words, they are worth 83.9 percent of PV(horizon value), which we calculated as $22.4 million from the constant-growth DCF formula.

$$\begin{aligned}\text{PV to existing stockholders} &= .839 \times \text{PV(horizon value)}\\ &= .839 \times 22.4 = \$18.8 \text{ million}\end{aligned}$$

Since there are one million existing shares, each is worth $18.80.

Finally, let's check whether the new stockholders are getting a fair deal. They end up with 100 − 83.9 = 16.1 percent of the shares in exchange for an investment of $3.6 million. The NPV of this investment is

$$\begin{aligned}\text{NPV to new stockholders} &= -3.6 + .161 \times \text{PV(horizon value)}\\ &= -3.6 + .161 \times 22.4 = -3.6 + 3.6 = 0\end{aligned}$$

On reflection, you will see that our two valuation methods must give the same answer. The first assumes that the existing shareholders provide all the cash whenever the firm needs cash. If so, they will also receive every dollar the firm pays out. The second method assumes that *new* investors put up the cash, relieving existing shareholders of this burden. But the new investors then receive a share of future payouts. If investment by new investors is a zero-NPV transaction, then it doesn't make existing stockholders any better or worse off than if they had invested themselves. The key assumption, of course, is that new shares are issued on fair terms, that is, at zero NPV.[12]

[12]The same two methods work when the company will use free cash flow to repurchase and retire outstanding shares. We discuss share repurchases in Chapter 16.

SUMMARY

In this chapter we have used our newfound knowledge of present values to examine the market price of common stocks. The value of a stock is equal to the stream of cash payments discounted at the rate of return that investors expect to receive on other securities with equivalent risks.

Common stocks do not have a fixed maturity; their cash payments consist of an indefinite stream of dividends. Therefore, the present value of a common stock is

$$\text{PV} = \sum_{t=1}^{\infty} \frac{\text{DIV}_t}{(1 + r)^t}$$

However, we did not just *assume* that investors purchase common stocks solely for dividends. In fact, we began with the assumption that investors have relatively short horizons and invest for both dividends and capital gains. Our fundamental valuation formula is, therefore,

$$P_0 = \frac{\text{DIV}_1 + P_1}{1 + r}$$

This is a condition of market equilibrium. If it did not hold, the share would be overpriced or underpriced, and investors would rush to sell or buy it. The flood of sellers or buyers would force the price to adjust so that the fundamental valuation formula holds.

This formula will hold in each future period as well as the present. That allowed us to express next year's forecasted price in terms of the subsequent stream of dividends $\text{DIV}_2, \text{DIV}_3, \ldots$.

We also made use of the formula for a growing perpetuity presented in Chapter 3. If dividends are expected to grow forever at a constant rate of g, then

$$P_0 = \frac{\text{DIV}_1}{r - g}$$

It is often helpful to twist this formula around and use it to estimate the market capitalization rate r, given P_0 and estimates of DIV_1 and g:

$$r = \frac{\text{DIV}_1}{P_0} + g$$

Remember, however, that this formula rests on a *very* strict assumption: constant dividend growth in perpetuity. This may be an acceptable assumption for mature, low-risk firms, but for many firms, near-term growth is unsustainably high. In that case, you may wish to use a *two-stage* DCF formula, where near-term dividends are forecasted and valued, and the constant-growth DCF formula is used to forecast the value of the shares at the start of the long run. The near-term dividends and the future share value are then discounted to present value.

The general DCF formula can be transformed into a statement about earnings and growth opportunities:

$$P_0 = \frac{\text{EPS}_1}{r} + \text{PVGO}$$

The ratio EPS_1/r is the capitalized value of the earnings per share that the firm would generate under a no-growth policy. PVGO is the net present value of the investments

Visit us at www.mhhe.com/bm7e

that the firm will make in order to grow. A growth stock is one for which PVGO is large relative to the capitalized value of EPS. Most growth stocks are stocks of rapidly expanding firms, but expansion alone does not create a high PVGO. What matters is the profitability of the new investments.

The same formulas that are used to value a single share can also be applied to value the total package of shares that a company has issued. In other words, we can use them to value an entire business. In this case we discount the free cash flow thrown off by the business. Here again a two-stage DCF model is deployed. Free cash flows are forecasted and discounted year by year out to a horizon, at which point a horizon value is estimated and discounted.

Valuing a business by discounted cash flow is easy in principle but messy in practice. We concluded this chapter with a detailed numerical example to show you what practice is really like. We extended this example to show how to value a company's existing shares when new shares will be issued to finance growth.

In earlier chapters you should have acquired—we hope painlessly—a knowledge of the basic principles of valuing assets and a facility with the mechanics of discounting. Now you know something of how common stocks are valued and market capitalization rates estimated. In Chapter 5 we can begin to apply all this knowledge in a more specific analysis of capital budgeting decisions.

FURTHER READING

There are a number of discussions of the valuation of common stocks in investment texts. We suggest:

Z. Bodie, A. Kane, and A. J. Marcus: *Investments*, 5th ed., Irwin/McGraw-Hill, 2002.

W. F. Sharpe, G. J. Alexander, and J. V. Bailey: *Investments*, 6th ed., Prentice-Hall, Inc., Englewood Cliffs, N.J., 1999.

J. B. Williams's original work remains very readable. See particularly Chapter V of:

J. B. Williams: *The Theory of Investment Value*, Harvard University Press, Cambridge, Mass., 1938.

The following articles provide important developments of Williams's early work. We suggest, however, that you leave the third article until you have read Chapter 16:

D. Durand: "Growth Stocks and the Petersburg Paradox," *Journal of Finance*, 12:348–363 (September 1957).

M. J. Gordon and E. Shapiro: "Capital Equipment Analysis: The Required Rate of Profit," *Management Science*, 3:102–110 (October 1956).

M. H. Miller and F. Modigliani: "Dividend Policy, Growth and the Valuation of Shares," *Journal of Business*, 34:411–433 (October 1961).

Leibowitz and Kogelman call PVGO the "franchise factor." They analyze it in detail in:

M. L. Leibowitz and S. Kogelman: "Inside the P/E Ratio: The Franchise Factor," *Financial Analysts Journal*, 46:17–35 (November–December 1990).

Myers and Borucki cover the practical problems encountered in estimating DCF costs of equity for regulated companies; Harris and Marston report DCF estimates of rates of return for the stock market as a whole:

S. C. Myers and L. S. Borucki: "Discounted Cash Flow Estimates of the Cost of Equity Capital—A Case Study," *Financial Markets, Institutions and Instruments*, 3:9–45 (August 1994).

R. S. Harris and F. C. Marston: "Estimating Shareholder Risk Premia Using Analysts' Growth Forecasts," *Financial Management,* 21:63–70 (Summer 1992).

The following book covers valuation of businesses in great detail:

T. Copeland, T. Koller, and J. Murrin: *Valuation: Measuring and Managing the Value of Companies,* John Wiley & Sons, Inc., New York, 1994.

QUIZ

1. True or false?
   a. All stocks in an equivalent-risk class are priced to offer the same expected rate of return.
   b. The value of a share equals the PV of future dividends per share.
2. Respond briefly to the following statement.

   "You say stock price equals the present value of future dividends? That's crazy! All the investors I know are looking for capital gains."
3. Company X is expected to pay an end-of-year dividend of $10 a share. After the dividend its stock is expected to sell at $110. If the market capitalization rate is 10 percent, what is the current stock price?
4. Company Y does not plow back any earnings and is expected to produce a level dividend stream of $5 a share. If the current stock price is $40, what is the market capitalization rate?
5. Company Z's earnings and dividends per share are expected to grow indefinitely by 5 percent a year. If next year's dividend is $10 and the market capitalization rate is 8 percent, what is the current stock price?
6. Company Z-prime is like Z in all respects save one: Its growth will stop after year 4. In year 5 and afterward, it will pay out all earnings as dividends. What is Z-prime's stock price? Assume next year's EPS is $15.
7. If company Z (see question 5) were to distribute all its earnings, it could maintain a level dividend stream of $15 a share. How much is the market actually paying per share for growth opportunities?
8. Consider three investors:
   a. Mr. Single invests for one year.
   b. Ms. Double invests for two years.
   c. Mrs. Triple invests for three years.

   Assume each invests in company Z (see question 5). Show that each expects to earn an expected rate of return of 8 percent per year.
9. True or false?
   a. The value of a share equals the discounted stream of future earnings per share.
   b. The value of a share equals the PV of earnings per share assuming the firm does not grow, plus the NPV of future growth opportunities.
10. Under what conditions does r, a stock's market capitalization rate, equal its earnings–price ratio EPS_1/P_0?
11. What do financial managers mean by "free cash flow"? How is free cash flow related to dividends paid out? Briefly explain.
12. What is meant by a two-stage DCF valuation model? Briefly describe two cases where such a model could be used.
13. What is meant by the *horizon value* of a business? How is it estimated?
14. Suppose the horizon date is set at a time when the firm will run out of positive-NPV investment opportunities. How would you calculate the horizon value?

Visit us at www.mhhe.com/bm7e

PRACTICE QUESTIONS

1. Look in a recent issue of *The Wall Street Journal* at "NYSE-Composite Transactions."
   a. What is the latest price of IBM stock?
   b. What are the annual dividend payment and the dividend yield on IBM stock?
   c. What would the yield be if IBM changed its yearly dividend to $1.50?
   d. What is the P/E on IBM stock?
   e. Use the P/E to calculate IBM's earnings per share.
   f. Is IBM's P/E higher or lower than that of Exxon Mobil?
   g. What are the possible reasons for the difference in P/E?
2. The present value of investing in a stock should not depend on how long the investor plans to hold it. Explain why.
3. Define the market capitalization rate for a stock. Does it equal the opportunity cost of capital of investing in the stock?

EXCEL

4. Rework Table 4.1 under the assumption that the dividend on Fledgling Electronics is $10 next year and that it is expected to grow by 5 percent a year. The capitalization rate is 15 percent.

EXCEL

5. In March 2001, Fly Paper's stock sold for about $73. Security analysts were forecasting a long-term earnings growth rate of 8.5 percent. The company was paying dividends of $1.68 per share.
   a. Assume dividends are expected to grow along with earnings at $g = 8.5$ percent per year in perpetuity. What rate of return r were investors expecting?
   b. Fly Paper was expected to earn about 12 percent on book equity and to pay out about 50 percent of earnings as dividends. What do these forecasts imply for g? For r? Use the perpetual-growth DCF formula.
6. You believe that next year the Superannuation Company will pay a dividend of $2 on its common stock. Thereafter you expect dividends to grow at a rate of 4 percent a year in perpetuity. If you require a return of 12 percent on your investment, how much should you be prepared to pay for the stock?

7. Consider the following three stocks:
   a. Stock A is expected to provide a dividend of $10 a share forever.
   b. Stock B is expected to pay a dividend of $5 next year. Thereafter, dividend growth is expected to be 4 percent a year forever.
   c. Stock C is expected to pay a dividend of $5 next year. Thereafter, dividend growth is expected to be 20 percent a year for 5 years (i.e., until year 6) and zero thereafter.

   If the market capitalization rate for each stock is 10 percent, which stock is the most valuable? What if the capitalization rate is 7 percent?
8. Crecimiento S.A. currently plows back 40 percent of its earnings and earns a return of 20 percent on this investment. The dividend yield on the stock is 4 percent.
   a. Assuming that Crecimiento can continue to plow back this proportion of earnings and earn a 20 percent return on the investment, how rapidly will earnings and dividends grow? What is the expected return on Crecimiento stock?
   b. Suppose that management suddenly announces that future investment opportunities have dried up. Now Crecimiento intends to pay out all its earnings. How will the stock price change?
   c. Suppose that management simply announces that the expected return on new investment would in the future be the same as the market capitalization rate. Now what is Crecimiento's stock price?

STANDARD & POOR'S

9. Look up General Mills, Inc., and Kellogg Co. on the Standard & Poor's Market Insight website (**www.mhhe.com/edumarketinsight**). The companies' ticker symbols are GIS and K.
   a. What are the current dividend yield and price–earnings ratio (P/E) for each company? How do the yields and P/Es compare to the average for the food

industry and for the stock market as a whole? (The stock market is represented by the S & P 500 index.)

b. What are the growth rates of earnings per share (EPS) and dividends for each company over the last five years? Do these growth rates appear to reflect a steady trend that could be projected for the long-run future?

c. Would you be confident in applying the constant-growth DCF valuation model to these companies' stocks? Why or why not?

10. Look up the following companies on the Standard & Poor's Market Insight website (**www.mhhe.com/edumarketinsight**): Citigroup (C), Dell Computer (DELL), Dow Chemical (DOW), Harley Davidson (HDI), and Pfizer, Inc. (PFE). Look at "Financial Highlights" and "Company Profile" for each company. You will note wide differences in these companies' price–earnings ratios. What are the possible explanations for these differences? Which would you classify as growth (high-PVGO) stocks and which as income stocks?

STANDARD &POOR'S

11. Vega Motor Corporation has pulled off a miraculous recovery. Four years ago, it was near bankruptcy. Now its charismatic leader, a corporate folk hero, may run for president.

Vega has just announced a $1 per share dividend, the first since the crisis hit. Analysts expect an increase to a "normal" $3 as the company completes its recovery over the next three years. After that, dividend growth is expected to settle down to a moderate long-term growth rate of 6 percent.

Vega stock is selling at $50 per share. What is the expected long-run rate of return from buying the stock at this price? Assume dividends of $1, $2, and $3 for years 1, 2, 3. A little trial and error will be necessary to find *r*.

12. P/E ratios reported in *The Wall Street Journal* use the latest closing prices and the last 12 months' reported earnings per share. Explain why the corresponding earnings–price ratios (the reciprocals of reported P/Es) are *not* accurate measures of the expected rates of return demanded by investors.

13. Each of the following formulas for determining shareholders' required rate of return can be right or wrong depending on the circumstances:

a. $r = \dfrac{\text{DIV}_1}{P_0} + g$

b. $r = \dfrac{\text{EPS}_1}{P_0}$

For each formula construct a *simple* numerical example showing that the formula can give wrong answers and explain why the error occurs. Then construct another simple numerical example for which the formula gives the right answer.

14. Alpha Corp's earnings and dividends are growing at 15 percent per year. Beta Corp's earnings and dividends are growing at 8 percent per year. The companies' assets, earnings, and dividends per share are now (at date 0) exactly the same. Yet PVGO accounts for a greater fraction of Beta Corp's stock price. How is this possible? *Hint:* There is more than one possible explanation.

15. Look again at the financial forecasts for Growth-Tech given in Table 4.3. This time assume you *know* that the opportunity cost of capital is $r = .12$ (discard the .099 figure calculated in the text). Assume you do *not* know Growth-Tech's stock value. Otherwise follow the assumptions given in the text.

a. Calculate the value of Growth-Tech stock.

b. What part of that value reflects the discounted value of P_3, the price forecasted for year 3?

c. What part of P_3 reflects the present value of growth opportunities (PVGO) after year 3?

Visit us at www.mhhe.com/bm7e

d. Suppose that competition will catch up with Growth-Tech by year 4, so that it can earn only its cost of capital on any investments made in year 4 or subsequently. What is Growth-Tech stock worth now under this assumption? (Make additional assumptions if necessary.)

STANDARD &POOR'S

16. Look up Hawaiian Electric Co. (HI) on the Standard & Poor's Market Insight website (**www.mhhe.com/edumarketinsight**). Hawaiian Electric was one of the companies in Table 4.2. That table was constructed in 2001.

a. What is the company's dividend yield? How has it changed since 2001?

b. Table 4.2 projected growth of 2.6 percent. How fast have the company's dividends and EPS actually grown since 2001?

c. Calculate a sustainable growth rate for the company based on its five-year average return on equity (ROE) and plowback ratio.

d. Given this updated information, would you modify the cost-of-equity estimate given in Table 4.2? Explain.

STANDARD &POOR'S

17. Browse through the companies in the Standard & Poor's Market Insight website (**www.mhhe.com/edumarketinsight**). Find three or four companies for which the earnings-price ratio reported on the website drastically *under*states the market capitalization rate r for the company. (*Hint:* you don't have to estimate r to answer this question. You know that r must be higher than current interest rates on U.S. government notes and bonds.)

STANDARD &POOR'S

18. The Standard & Poor's Market Insight website (**www.mhhe.com/edumarketinsight**) contains information all of the companies in Table 4.6 except for Chubb and Weyerhaeuser. Update the calculations of PVGO as a percentage of stock price. For simplicity use the costs of equity given in Table 4.6. You will need to track down an updated forecast of EPS, for example from MSN money (**www.moneycentral.msn.com**) of Yahoo (**http://finance.yahoo.com**).

19. Compost Science, Inc. (CSI), is in the business of converting Boston's sewage sludge into fertilizer. The business is not in itself very profitable. However, to induce CSI to remain in business, the Metropolitan District Commission (MDC) has agreed to pay whatever amount is necessary to yield CSI a 10 percent book return on equity. At the end of the year CSI is expected to pay a $4 dividend. It has been reinvesting 40 percent of earnings and growing at 4 percent a year.

a. Suppose CSI continues on this growth trend. What is the expected long-run rate of return from purchasing the stock at $100? What part of the $100 price is attributable to the present value of growth opportunities?

b. Now the MDC announces a plan for CSI to treat Cambridge sewage. CSI's plant will, therefore, be expanded gradually over five years. This means that CSI will have to reinvest 80 percent of its earnings for five years. Starting in year 6, however, it will again be able to pay out 60 percent of earnings. What will be CSI's stock price once this announcement is made and its consequences for CSI are known?

20. List at least four different formulas for calculating PV(horizon value) in a two-stage DCF valuation of a business. For each formula, describe a situation where that formula would be the best choice.

21. Look again at Table 4.7.

a. How do free cash flow and present value change if asset growth rate is only 15 percent in years 1 to 5? If value declines, explain why.

b. Suppose the business is a publicly traded company with one million shares outstanding. Then the company issues new stock to cover the present value of negative free cash flow for years 1 to 6. How many shares will be issued and at what price?

c. Value the company's one million existing shares by the two methods described in Section 4.5.

22. Icarus Air has one million shares outstanding and expects to earn a constant $10 million per year on its existing assets. All earnings will be paid out as dividends. Suppose that next year Icarus plans to double in size by issuing an additional one million shares at \$100 a share. Everything will be the same as before but twice as big. Thus from year 2 onward the company earns a constant \$20 million, all of which is paid out as dividends on the 20 million shares. What is the value of the company? What is the value of each existing Icarus Air share?

23. Look one more time at Table 4.1, which applies the DCF stock valuation formula to Fledgling Electronics. The CEO, having just learned that stock value is the present value of future dividends, proposes that Fledgling pay a bumper dividend of \$15 a share in period 1. The extra cash would have to be raised by an issue of new shares. Recalculate Table 4.1 assuming that profits and payout ratios in all subsequent years are unchanged. You should find that the total present value of dividends *per existing share* is unchanged at \$100. Why?

CHALLENGE QUESTIONS

1. Look again at Tables 4.3 (Growth-Tech) and 4.7 (Concatenator Manufacturing). Note the discontinuous increases in dividends and free cash flow when asset growth slows down. Now look at your answer to Practice Question 11: Dividends are expected to grow smoothly, although at a lower rate after year 3. Is there an error or hidden inconsistency in Practice Question 11? Write down a general rule or procedure for deciding how to forecast dividends or free cash flow.

2. The constant-growth DCF formula

$$P_0 = \frac{\text{DIV}_1}{r - g}$$

is sometimes written as

$$P_0 = \frac{\text{ROE}(1 - b)\text{BVPS}}{r - b\text{ROE}}$$

where BVPS is book equity value per share, b is the plowback ratio, and ROE is the ratio of earnings per share to BVPS. Use this equation to show how the price-to-book ratio varies as ROE changes. What is price-to-book when ROE $= r$?

3. Portfolio managers are frequently paid a proportion of the funds under management. Suppose you manage a \$100 million equity portfolio offering a dividend yield (DIV_1/P_0) of 5 percent. Dividends and portfolio value are expected to grow at a constant rate. Your annual fee for managing this portfolio is .5 percent of portfolio value and is calculated at the end of each year. Assuming that you will continue to manage the portfolio from now to eternity, what is the present value of the management contract?

Visit us at www.mhhe.com/bm7e

MINI-CASE

Reeby Sports

Ten years ago, in 1993, George Reeby founded a small mail-order company selling high-quality sports equipment. Reeby Sports has grown steadily and been consistently profitable (see Table 4.8). The company has no debt and the equity is valued in the company's books at nearly \$41 million (Table 4.9). It is still wholly owned by George Reeby.

George is now proposing to take the company public by the sale of 90,000 of his existing shares. The issue would not raise any additional cash for the company, but it would allow

TABLE 4.8

Summary income data (figures in $ millions).

Note: Reeby Sports has never paid a dividend and all the earnings have been retained in the business.

	1999	2000	2001	2002	2003
Cash flow	5.84	6.40	7.41	8.74	9.39
Depreciation	1.45	1.60	1.75	1.97	2.22
Pretax profits	4.38	4.80	5.66	6.77	7.17
Tax	1.53	1.68	1.98	2.37	2.51
Aftertax profits	2.85	3.12	3.68	4.40	4.66

TABLE 4.9

Summary balance sheet for year ending December 31st (figures in $ millions).

Note: Reeby Sports has 200,000 common shares outstanding, wholly owned by George Reeby.

Assets			Liabilities and Equity		
	2002	2003		2002	2003
Cash & securities	3.12	3.61	Current liabilities	2.90	3.20
Other current assets	15.08	16.93			
Net fixed assets	20.75	23.38	Equity	36.05	40.71
Total	38.95	43.91	Total	38.95	43.91

George to cash in on part of his investment. It would also make it easier to raise the substantial capital sums that the firm would later need to finance expansion.

George's business has been mainly on the East Coast of the United States, but he plans to expand into the Midwest in 2005. This will require a substantial investment in new warehouse space and inventory. George is aware that it will take time to build up a new customer base, and in the meantime there is likely to be a temporary dip in profits. However, if the venture is successful, the company should be back to its current 12 percent return on book equity by 2010.

George settled down to estimate what his shares are worth. First he estimated the profits and investment through 2010 (Tables 4.10 and 4.11). The company's net working capital includes a growing proportion of cash and marketable securities which would help to meet the cost of the expansion into the Midwest. Nevertheless, it seemed likely that the company would need to raise about $4.3 million in 2005 by the sale of new shares. (George distrusted banks and was not prepared to borrow to finance the expansion.)

Until the new venture reached full profitability, dividend payments would have to be restricted to conserve cash, but from 2010 onward George expected the company to pay out about 40 percent of its net profits. As a first stab at valuing the company, George assumed that after 2010 it would earn 12 percent on book equity indefinitely and that the cost of capital for the firm was about 10 percent. But he also computed a more conservative valuation, which recognized that the mail-order sports business was likely to get intensely competitive by 2010. He also looked at the market valuation of a comparable business on the West Coast, Molly Sports. Molly's shares were currently priced at 50 percent above book value and were selling at a prospective price–earnings ratio of 12 and a dividend yield of 3 percent.

George realized that a second issue of shares in 2005 would dilute his holdings. He set about calculating the price at which these shares could be issued and the number of shares that would need to be sold. That allowed him to work out the dividends *per share* and to check his earlier valuation by calculating the present value of the stream of per-share dividends.

	2004	2005	2006	2007	2008	2009	2010
Cash flow	10.47	11.87	7.74	8.40	9.95	12.67	15.38
Depreciation	2.40	3.10	3.12	3.17	3.26	3.44	3.68
Pretax profits	8.08	8.77	4.62	5.23	6.69	9.23	11.69
Tax	2.83	3.07	1.62	1.83	2.34	3.23	4.09
Aftertax profits	5.25	5.70	3.00	3.40	4.35	6.00	7.60
Dividends	2.00	2.00	2.50	2.50	2.50	2.50	3.00
Retained profits	3.25	3.70	.50	.90	1.85	3.50	4.60

TABLE 4.10

Forecasted profits and dividends (figures in $ millions).

	2004	2005	2006	2007	2008	2009	2010
Gross investment in fixed assets	4.26	10.50	3.34	3.65	4.18	5.37	6.28
Investments in net working capital	1.39	.60	.28	.42	.93	1.57	2.00
Total	5.65	11.10	3.62	4.07	5.11	6.94	8.28

TABLE 4.11

Forecasted investment expenditures (figures in $ millions).

Questions

1. Use Tables 4.10 and 4.11 to forecast free cash flow for Reeby Sports from 2004 to 2010. What is the present value of these cash flows in 2003, including PV(horizon value) in 2010?
2. Use the information given for Molly Sports to check your forecast of horizon value. What would you recommend as a reasonable range for the present value of Reeby Sports?
3. What is the present value of a share of stock in the company? Give a reasonable range.
4. Reeby Sports will have to raise $4.3 million in 2005. Does this prospective share issue affect the per-share value of Reeby Sports in 2003? Explain.

CHAPTER FIVE

WHY NET PRESENT VALUE LEADS TO BETTER INVESTMENT DECISIONS THAN OTHER CRITERIA

IN THE FIRST four chapters we introduced, at times surreptitiously, most of the basic principles of the investment decision. In this chapter we begin by consolidating that knowledge. We then take a look at three other measures that companies sometimes use when making investment decisions. These are the project's payback period, its book rate of return, and its internal rate of return. The first two of these measures have little to do with whether the project will increase shareholders' wealth. The project's internal rate of return—if used correctly—should always identify projects that increase shareholder wealth. However, we shall see that the internal rate of return sets several traps for the unwary.

We conclude the chapter by showing how to cope with situations when the firm has only limited capital. This raises two problems. One is computational. In simple cases we just choose those projects that give the highest NPV per dollar of investment. But capital constraints and project interactions often create problems of such complexity that linear programming is needed to sort through the possible alternatives. The other problem is to decide whether capital rationing really exists and whether it invalidates net present value as a criterion for capital budgeting. Guess what? NPV, properly interpreted, wins out in the end.

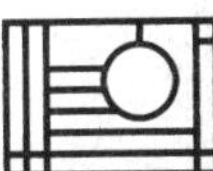

5.1 A REVIEW OF THE BASICS

Vegetron's chief financial officer (CFO) is wondering how to analyze a proposed $1 million investment in a new venture called project X. He asks what you think.

Your response should be as follows: "First, forecast the cash flows generated by project X over its economic life. Second, determine the appropriate opportunity cost of capital. This should reflect both the time value of money and the risk involved in project X. Third, use this opportunity cost of capital to discount the future cash flows of project X. The sum of the discounted cash flows is called present value (PV). Fourth, calculate *net* present value (NPV) by subtracting the $1 million investment from PV. Invest in project X if its NPV is greater than zero."

However, Vegetron's CFO is unmoved by your sagacity. He asks why NPV is so important.

Your reply: "Let us look at what is best for Vegetron stockholders. They want you to make their Vegetron shares as valuable as possible."

"Right now Vegetron's total market value (price per share times the number of shares outstanding) is $10 million. That includes $1 million cash we can invest in project X. The value of Vegetron's other assets and opportunities must therefore be $9 million. We have to decide whether it is better to keep the $1 million cash and reject project X or to spend the cash and accept project X. Let us call the value of the new project PV. Then the choice is as follows:

	Market Value ($ millions)	
Asset	**Reject Project X**	**Accept Project X**
Cash	1	0
Other assets	9	9
Project X	0	PV
	10	9 + PV

FIGURE 5.1

The firm can either keep and reinvest cash or return it to investors. (Arrows represent possible cash flows or transfers.) If cash is reinvested, the opportunity cost is the expected rate of return that shareholders could have obtained by investing in financial assets.

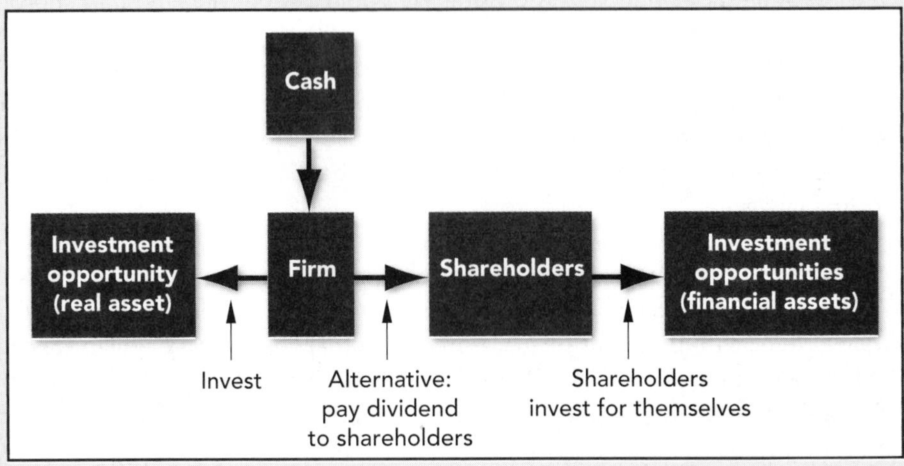

"Clearly project X is worthwhile if its present value, PV, is greater than $1 million, that is, if net present value is positive."

CFO: "How do I know that the PV of project X will actually show up in Vegetron's market value?"

Your reply: "Suppose we set up a new, independent firm X, whose only asset is project X. What would be the market value of firm X?

"Investors would forecast the dividends firm X would pay and discount those dividends by the expected rate of return of securities having risks comparable to firm X. We know that stock prices are equal to the present value of forecasted dividends.

"Since project X is firm X's only asset, the dividend payments we would expect firm X to pay are exactly the cash flows we have forecasted for project X. Moreover, the rate investors would use to discount firm X's dividends is exactly the rate we should use to discount project X's cash flows.

"I agree that firm X is entirely hypothetical. But if project X is accepted, investors holding Vegetron stock will really hold a portfolio of project X and the firm's other assets. We know the other assets are worth $9 million considered as a separate venture. Since asset values add up, we can easily figure out the portfolio value once we calculate the value of project X as a separate venture.

"By calculating the present value of project X, we are replicating the process by which the common stock of firm X would be valued in capital markets."

CFO: "The one thing I don't understand is where the discount rate comes from."

Your reply: "I agree that the discount rate is difficult to measure precisely. But it is easy to see what we are *trying* to measure. The discount rate is the opportunity cost of investing in the project rather than in the capital market. In other words, instead of accepting a project, the firm can always give the cash to the shareholders and let them invest it in financial assets.

"You can see the trade-off (Figure 5.1). The opportunity cost of taking the project is the return shareholders could have earned had they invested the funds on their own. When we discount the project's cash flows by the expected rate of return on comparable financial assets, we are measuring how much investors would be prepared to pay for your project."

"But which financial assets?" Vegetron's CFO queries. "The fact that investors expect only 12 percent on IBM stock does not mean that we should purchase Fly-by-Night Electronics if it offers 13 percent."

Your reply: "The opportunity-cost concept makes sense only if assets of equivalent risk are compared. In general, you should identify financial assets with risks equivalent to the project under consideration, estimate the expected rate of return on these assets, and use this rate as the opportunity cost."

Net Present Value's Competitors

Let us hope that the CFO is by now convinced of the correctness of the net present value rule. But it is possible that the CFO has also heard of some alternative investment criteria and would like to know why you do not recommend any of them. Just so that you are prepared, we will now look at three of the alternatives. They are:

1. The book rate of return.
2. The payback period.
3. The internal rate of return.

Later in the chapter we shall come across one further investment criterion, the profitability index. There are circumstances in which this measure has some special advantages.

Three Points to Remember about NPV

As we look at these alternative criteria, it is worth keeping in mind the following key features of the net present value rule. First, the NPV rule recognizes that *a dollar today is worth more than a dollar tomorrow,* because the dollar today can be invested to start earning interest immediately. Any investment rule which does not recognize the *time value of money* cannot be sensible. Second, net present value depends solely on the *forecasted cash flows* from the project and the *opportunity cost of capital.* Any investment rule which is affected by the manager's tastes, the company's choice of accounting method, the profitability of the company's existing business, or the profitability of other independent projects will lead to inferior decisions. Third, *because present values are all measured in today's dollars, you can add them up.* Therefore, if you have two projects A and B, the net present value of the combined investment is

$$\text{NPV}(A + B) = \text{NPV}(A) + \text{NPV}(B)$$

This additivity property has important implications. Suppose project B has a negative NPV. If you tack it onto project A, the joint project (A + B) will have a lower NPV than A on its own. Therefore, you are unlikely to be misled into accepting a poor project (B) just because it is packaged with a good one (A). As we shall see, the alternative measures do not have this additivity property. If you are not careful, you may be tricked into deciding that a package of a good and a bad project is better than the good project on its own.

NPV Depends on Cash Flow, Not Accounting Income

Net present value depends only on the project's cash flows and the opportunity cost of capital. But when companies report to shareholders, they do not simply show the cash flows. They also report book—that is, accounting—income and book assets; book income gets most of the immediate attention.

Financial managers sometimes use these numbers to calculate a book rate of return on a proposed investment. In other words, they look at the prospective book income as a proportion of the book value of the assets that the firm is proposing to acquire:

$$\text{Book rate of return} = \frac{\text{book income}}{\text{book assets}}$$

Cash flows and book income are often very different. For example, the accountant labels some cash outflows as *capital investments* and others as *operating expenses.* The operating expenses are, of course, deducted immediately from each year's income. The capital expenditures are put on the firm's balance sheet and then depreciated according to an arbitrary schedule chosen by the accountant. The annual depreciation charge is deducted from each year's income. Thus the book rate of return depends on which items the accountant chooses to treat as capital investments and how rapidly they are depreciated.[1]

Now the merits of an investment project do not depend on how accountants classify the cash flows[2] and few companies these days make investment decisions just on the basis of the book rate of return. But managers know that the company's shareholders pay considerable attention to book measures of profitability and naturally, therefore, they think (and worry) about how major projects would affect the company's book return. Those projects that will reduce the company's book return may be scrutinized more carefully by senior management.

You can see the dangers here. The book rate of return may not be a good measure of true profitability. It is also an *average* across all of the firm's activities. The average profitability of past investments is not usually the right hurdle for new investments. Think of a firm that has been exceptionally lucky and successful. Say its average book return is 24 percent, double shareholders' 12 percent opportunity cost of capital. Should it demand that all *new* investments offer 24 percent or better? Clearly not: That would mean passing up many positive-NPV opportunities with rates of return between 12 and 24 percent.

We will come back to the book rate of return in Chapter 12, when we look more closely at accounting measures of financial performance.

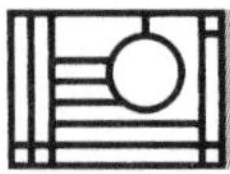

5.2 PAYBACK

Some companies require that the initial outlay on any project should be recoverable within a specified period. The **payback** period of a project is found by counting the number of years it takes before the cumulative forecasted cash flow equals the initial investment.

[1]This chapter's mini-case contains simple illustrations of how book rates of return are calculated and of the difference between accounting income and project cash flow. Read the case if you wish to refresh your understanding of these topics. Better still, do the case calculations.

[2]Of course, the depreciation method used for tax purposes does have cash consequences which should be taken into account in calculating NPV. We cover depreciation and taxes in the next chapter.

Consider the following three projects:

Project	Cash Flows ($) C_0	C_1	C_2	C_3	Payback Period (years)	NPV at 10%
A	–2,000	500	500	5,000	3	+2,624
B	–2,000	500	1,800	0	2	–58
C	–2,000	1,800	500	0	2	+50

Project A involves an initial investment of $2,000 ($C_0 = -2{,}000$) followed by cash inflows during the next three years. Suppose the opportunity cost of capital is 10 percent. Then project A has an NPV of +$2,624:

$$\text{NPV(A)} = -2{,}000 + \frac{500}{1.10} + \frac{500}{1.10^2} + \frac{5{,}000}{1.10^3} = +\$2{,}624$$

Project B also requires an initial investment of $2,000 but produces a cash inflow of $500 in year 1 and $1,800 in year 2. At a 10 percent opportunity cost of capital project B has an NPV of –$58:

$$\text{NPV(B)} = -2{,}000 + \frac{500}{1.10} + \frac{1{,}800}{1.10^2} = -\$58$$

The third project, C, involves the same initial outlay as the other two projects but its first-period cash flow is larger. It has an NPV of +$50.

$$\text{NPV(C)} = -2{,}000 + \frac{1{,}800}{1.10} + \frac{500}{1.10^2} = +\$50$$

The net present value rule tells us to accept projects A and C but to reject project B.

The Payback Rule

Now look at how rapidly each project pays back its initial investment. With project A you take three years to recover the $2,000 investment; with projects B and C you take only two years. If the firm used the payback *rule* with a cutoff period of two years, it would accept only projects B and C; if it used the payback rule with a cutoff period of three or more years, it would accept all three projects. Therefore, regardless of the choice of cutoff period, the payback rule gives answers different from the net present value rule.

You can see why payback can give misleading answers:

1. *The payback rule ignores all cash flows after the cutoff date.* If the cutoff date is two years, the payback rule rejects project A regardless of the size of the cash inflow in year 3.
2. *The payback rule gives equal weight to all cash flows before the cutoff date.* The payback rule says that projects B and C are equally attractive, but, because C's cash inflows occur earlier, C has the higher net present value at any discount rate.

In order to use the payback rule, a firm has to decide on an appropriate cutoff date. If it uses the same cutoff regardless of project life, it will tend to accept many poor short-lived projects and reject many good long-lived ones.

Some companies discount the cash flows before they compute the payback period. The **discounted-payback rule** asks, How many periods does the project have to last in order to make sense in terms of net present value? This modification to the payback rule surmounts the objection that equal weight is given to all flows before the cutoff date. However, the discounted-payback rule still takes no account of any cash flows after the cutoff date.

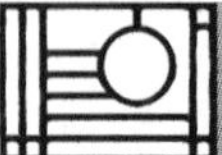

5.3 INTERNAL (OR DISCOUNTED-CASH-FLOW) RATE OF RETURN

Whereas payback and return on book are ad hoc measures, internal rate of return has a much more respectable ancestry and is recommended in many finance texts. If, therefore, we dwell more on its deficiencies, it is not because they are more numerous but because they are less obvious.

In Chapter 2 we noted that net present value could also be expressed in terms of rate of return, which would lead to the following rule: "Accept investment opportunities offering rates of return in excess of their opportunity costs of capital." That statement, properly interpreted, is absolutely correct. However, interpretation is not always easy for long-lived investment projects.

There is no ambiguity in defining the true rate of return of an investment that generates a single payoff after one period:

$$\text{Rate of return} = \frac{\text{payoff}}{\text{investment}} - 1$$

Alternatively, we could write down the NPV of the investment and find that discount rate which makes NPV = 0.

$$\text{NPV} = C_0 + \frac{C_1}{1 + \text{discount rate}} = 0$$

implies

$$\text{Discount rate} = \frac{C_1}{-C_0} - 1$$

Of course C_1 is the payoff and $-C_0$ is the required investment, and so our two equations say exactly the same thing. *The discount rate that makes NPV = 0 is also the rate of return.*

Unfortunately, there is no wholly satisfactory way of defining the true rate of return of a long-lived asset. The best available concept is the so-called **discounted-cash-flow (DCF) rate of return** or **internal rate of return (IRR).** The internal rate of return is used frequently in finance. It can be a handy measure, but, as we shall see, it can also be a misleading measure. You should, therefore, know how to calculate it and how to use it properly.

The internal rate of return is defined as the rate of discount which makes NPV = 0. This means that to find the IRR for an investment project lasting T years, we must solve for IRR in the following expression:

$$\text{NPV} = C_0 + \frac{C_1}{1 + \text{IRR}} + \frac{C_2}{(1 + \text{IRR})^2} + \cdots + \frac{C_T}{(1 + \text{IRR})^T} = 0$$

Actual calculation of IRR usually involves trial and error. For example, consider a project that produces the following flows:

Cash Flows ($)		
C_0	C_1	C_2
–4,000	+2,000	+4,000

The internal rate of return is IRR in the equation

$$\text{NPV} = -4{,}000 + \frac{2{,}000}{1 + \text{IRR}} + \frac{4{,}000}{(1 + \text{IRR})^2} = 0$$

Let us arbitrarily try a zero discount rate. In this case NPV is not zero but +$2,000:

$$\text{NPV} = -4{,}000 + \frac{2{,}000}{1.0} + \frac{4{,}000}{(1.0)^2} = +\$2{,}000$$

The NPV is positive; therefore, the IRR must be greater than zero. The next step might be to try a discount rate of 50 percent. In this case net present value is –$889:

$$\text{NPV} = -4{,}000 + \frac{2{,}000}{1.50} + \frac{4{,}000}{(1.50)^2} = -\$889$$

The NPV is negative; therefore, the IRR must be less than 50 percent. In Figure 5.2 we have plotted the net present values implied by a range of discount rates. From this we can see that a discount rate of 28 percent gives the desired net present value of zero. Therefore IRR is 28 percent.

The easiest way to calculate IRR, if you have to do it by hand, is to plot three or four combinations of NPV and discount rate on a graph like Figure 5.2, connect the

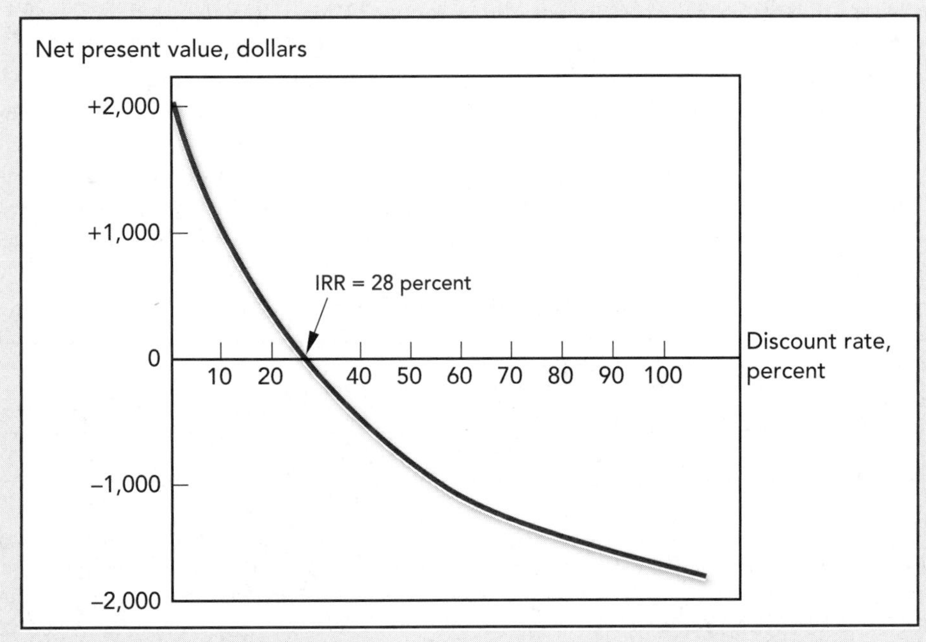

FIGURE 5.2

This project costs $4,000 and then produces cash inflows of $2,000 in year 1 and $4,000 in year 2. Its internal rate of return (IRR) is 28 percent, the rate of discount at which NPV is zero.

points with a smooth line, and read off the discount rate at which NPV = 0. It is of course quicker and more accurate to use a computer or a specially programmed calculator, and this is what most financial managers do.

Now, the *internal rate of return rule* is to accept an investment project if the opportunity cost of capital is less than the internal rate of return. You can see the reasoning behind this idea if you look again at Figure 5.2. If the opportunity cost of capital is less than the 28 percent IRR, then the project has a *positive* NPV when discounted at the opportunity cost of capital. If it is equal to the IRR, the project has a *zero* NPV. And if it is greater than the IRR, the project has a *negative* NPV. Therefore, when we compare the opportunity cost of capital with the IRR on our project, we are effectively asking whether our project has a positive NPV. This is true not only for our example. The rule will give the same answer as the net present value rule *whenever the NPV of a project is a smoothly declining function of the discount rate.*[3]

Many firms use internal rate of return as a criterion in preference to net present value. We think that this is a pity. Although, properly stated, the two criteria are formally equivalent, the internal rate of return rule contains several pitfalls.

Pitfall 1—Lending or Borrowing?

Not all cash-flow streams have NPVs that decline as the discount rate increases. Consider the following projects A and B:

	Cash Flows ($)			
Project	C_0	C_1	IRR	NPV at 10%
A	−1,000	+1,500	+50%	+364
B	+1,000	−1,500	+50%	−364

Each project has an IRR of 50 percent. (In other words, −1,000 + 1,500/1.50 = 0 *and* + 1,000 − 1,500/1.50 = 0.)

Does this mean that they are equally attractive? Clearly not, for in the case of A, where we are initially paying out $1,000, we are *lending* money at 50 percent; in the case of B, where we are initially receiving $1,000, we are *borrowing* money at 50 percent. When we lend money, we want a *high* rate of return; when we borrow money, we want a *low* rate of return.

If you plot a graph like Figure 5.2 for project B, you will find that NPV increases as the discount rate increases. Obviously the internal rate of return rule, as we stated it above, won't work in this case; we have to look for an IRR *less* than the opportunity cost of capital.

This is straightforward enough, but now look at project C:

	Cash Flows ($)					
Project	C_0	C_1	C_2	C_3	IRR	NPV at 10%
C	+1,000	−3,600	+4,320	−1,728	+20%	−.75

[3]Here is a word of caution: Some people confuse the internal rate of return and the opportunity cost of capital because both appear as discount rates in the NPV formula. The internal rate of return is a *profitability measure* that depends solely on the amount and timing of the project cash flows. The opportunity cost of capital is a *standard of profitability* for the project which we use to calculate how much the project is worth. The opportunity cost of capital is established in capital markets. It is the expected rate of return offered by other assets equivalent in risk to the project being evaluated.

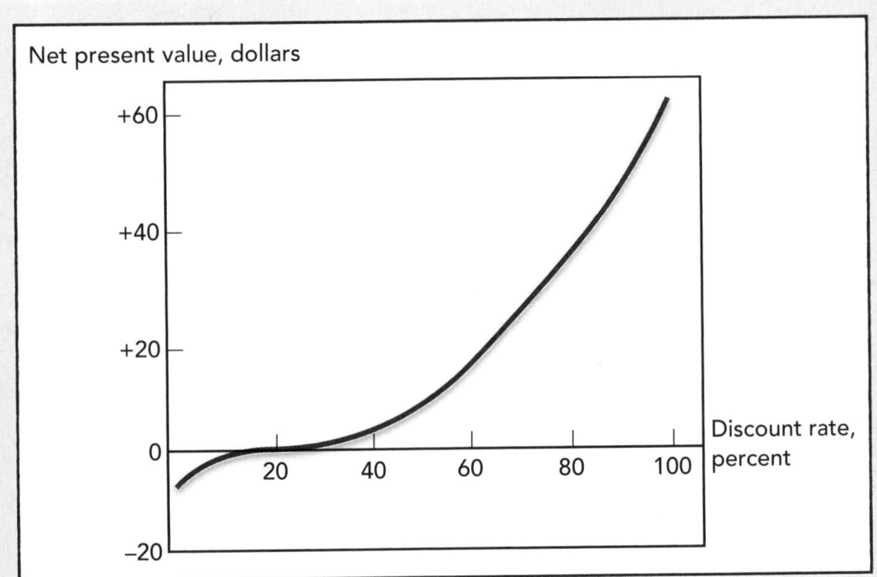

FIGURE 5.3

The NPV of project C increases as the discount rate increases.

It turns out that project C has zero NPV at a 20 percent discount rate. If the opportunity cost of capital is 10 percent, that means the project is a good one. Or does it? In part, project C is like borrowing money, because we receive money now and pay it out in the first period; it is also partly like lending money because we pay out money in period 1 and recover it in period 2. Should we accept or reject? The only way to find the answer is to look at the net present value. Figure 5.3 shows that the NPV of our project *increases* as the discount rate increases. If the opportunity cost of capital is 10 percent (i.e., less than the IRR), the project has a very small negative NPV and we should reject.

Pitfall 2—Multiple Rates of Return

In most countries there is usually a short delay between the time when a company receives income and the time it pays tax on the income. Consider the case of Albert Vore, who needs to assess a proposed advertising campaign by the vegetable canning company of which he is financial manager. The campaign involves an initial outlay of $1 million but is expected to increase pretax profits by $300,000 in each of the next five periods. The tax rate is 50 percent, and taxes are paid with a delay of one period. Thus the expected cash flows from the investment are as follows:

Cash Flows ($ thousands)							
	Period						
	0	1	2	3	4	5	6
Pretax flow	–1,000	+300	+300	+300	+300	+300	
Tax		+500	–150	–150	–150	–150	–150
Net flow	–1,000	+800	+150	+150	+150	+150	–150

Note: The $1 million outlay in period 0 *reduces* the company's taxes in period 1 by $500,000; thus we enter +500 in year 1.

FIGURE 5.4

The advertising campaign has two internal rates of return. NPV = 0 when the discount rate is −50 percent and when it is +15.2 percent.

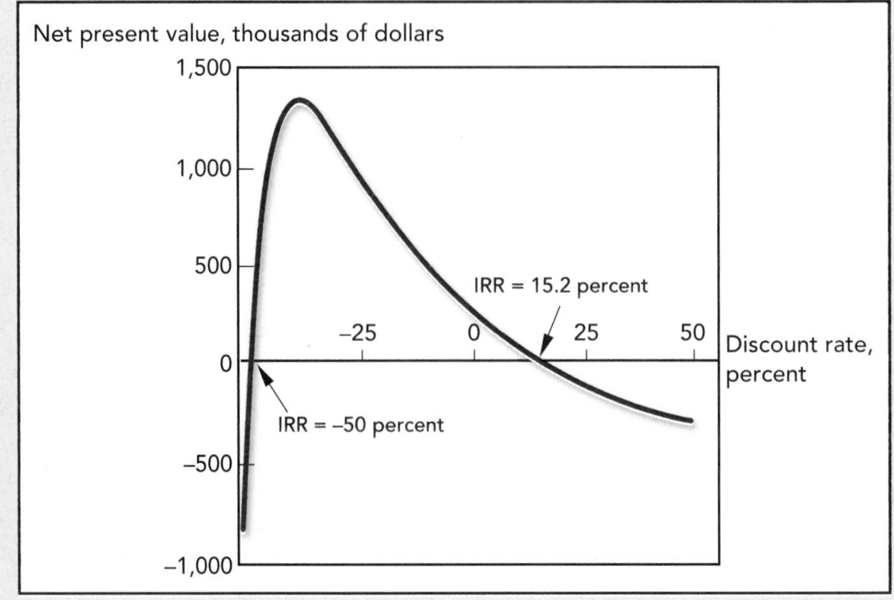

Mr. Vore calculates the project's IRR and its NPV as follows:

IRR (%)	NPV at 10%
−50 *and* 15.2	74.9 or $74,900

Note that there are *two* discount rates that make NPV = 0. That is, *each* of the following statements holds:

$$\text{NPV} = -1{,}000 + \frac{800}{.50} + \frac{150}{(.50)^2} + \frac{150}{(.50)^3} + \frac{150}{(.50)^4} + \frac{150}{(.50)^5} - \frac{150}{(.50)^6} = 0$$

and

$$\text{NPV} = -1{,}000 + \frac{800}{1.152} + \frac{150}{(1.152)^2} + \frac{150}{(1.152)^3} + \frac{150}{(1.152)^4} + \frac{150}{(1.152)^5} - \frac{150}{(1.152)^6} = 0$$

In other words, the investment has an IRR of both –50 *and* 15.2 percent. Figure 5.4 shows how this comes about. As the discount rate increases, NPV initially rises and then declines. The reason for this is the double change in the sign of the cash-flow stream. There can be as many different internal rates of return for a project as there are changes in the sign of the cash flows.[4]

[4]By Descartes's "rule of signs" there can be as many different solutions to a polynomial as there are changes of sign. For a discussion of the problem of multiple rates of return, see J. H. Lorie and L. J. Savage, "Three Problems in Rationing Capital," *Journal of Business* 28 (October 1955), pp. 229–239; and E. Solomon, "The Arithmetic of Capital Budgeting," *Journal of Business* 29 (April 1956), pp. 124–129.

In our example the double change in sign was caused by a lag in tax payments, but this is not the only way that it can occur. For example, many projects involve substantial decommissioning costs. If you strip-mine coal, you may have to invest large sums to reclaim the land after the coal is mined. Thus a new mine creates an initial investment (negative cash flow up front), a series of positive cash flows, and an ending cash outflow for reclamation. The cash-flow stream changes sign twice, and mining companies typically see two IRRs.

As if this is not difficult enough, there are also cases in which *no* internal rate of return exists. For example, project D has a positive net present value at all discount rates:

	Cash Flows ($)				
Project	C_0	C_1	C_2	**IRR (%)**	**NPV at 10%**
D	+1,000	–3,000	+2,500	None	+339

A number of adaptations of the IRR rule have been devised for such cases. Not only are they inadequate, but they also are unnecessary, for the simple solution is to use net present value.[5]

Pitfall 3—Mutually Exclusive Projects

Firms often have to choose from among several alternative ways of doing the same job or using the same facility. In other words, they need to choose from among **mutually exclusive projects.** Here too the IRR rule can be misleading.

Consider projects E and F:

	Cash Flows ($)			
Project	C_0	C_1	**IRR (%)**	**NPV at 10%**
E	–10,000	+20,000	100	+ 8,182
F	–20,000	+35,000	75	+11,818

[5]Companies sometimes get around the problem of multiple rates of return by discounting the later cash flows back at the cost of capital until there remains only one change in the sign of the cash flows. A *modified internal rate of return* can then be calculated on this revised series. In our example, the modified IRR is calculated as follows:

1. Calculate the present value of the year 6 cash flow in year 5:

$$\text{PV in year 5} = -150/1.10 = -136.36$$

2. Add to the year 5 cash flow the present value of subsequent cash flows:

$$C_5 + \text{PV(subsequent cash flows)} = 150 - 136.36 = 13.64$$

3. Since there is now only one change in the sign of the cash flows, the revised series has a unique rate of return, which is 15 percent:

$$\text{NPV} = -1{,}000 + \frac{800}{1.15} + \frac{150}{1.15^2} + \frac{150}{1.15^3} + \frac{150}{1.15^4} + \frac{13.64}{1.15^5} = 0$$

Since the modified IRR of 15 percent is greater than the cost of capital (and the initial cash flow is negative), the project has a positive NPV when valued at the cost of capital.

Of course, it would be much easier in such cases to abandon the IRR rule and just calculate project NPV.

Perhaps project E is a manually controlled machine tool and project F is the same tool with the addition of computer control. Both are good investments, but F has the higher NPV and is, therefore, better. However, the IRR rule seems to indicate that if you have to choose, you should go for E since it has the higher IRR. If you follow the IRR rule, you have the satisfaction of earning a 100 percent rate of return; if you follow the NPV rule, you are $11,818 richer.

You can salvage the IRR rule in these cases by looking at the internal rate of return on the incremental flows. Here is how to do it: First, consider the smaller project (E in our example). It has an IRR of 100 percent, which is well in excess of the 10 percent opportunity cost of capital. You know, therefore, that E is acceptable. You now ask yourself whether it is worth making the additional $10,000 investment in F. The incremental flows from undertaking F rather than E are as follows:

	Cash Flows ($)			
Project	C_0	C_1	**IRR (%)**	**NPV at 10%**
F–E	−10,000	+15,000	50	+3,636

The IRR on the incremental investment is 50 percent, which is also well in excess of the 10 percent opportunity cost of capital. So you should prefer project F to project E.[6]

Unless you look at the incremental expenditure, IRR is unreliable in ranking projects of different scale. It is also unreliable in ranking projects which offer different patterns of cash flow over time. For example, suppose the firm can take project G *or* project H but not both (ignore I for the moment):

	Cash Flows ($)								
Project	C_0	C_1	C_2	C_3	C_4	C_5	**Etc.**	**IRR (%)**	**NPV at 10%**
G	−9,000	+6,000	+5,000	+4,000	0	0	. . .	33	3,592
H	−9,000	+1,800	+1,800	+1,800	+1,800	+1,800	. . .	20	9,000
I		−6,000	+1,200	+1,200	+1,200	+1,200	. . .	20	6,000

Project G has a higher IRR, but project H has the higher NPV. Figure 5.5 shows why the two rules give different answers. The blue line gives the net present value of project G at different rates of discount. Since a discount rate of 33 percent produces a net present value of zero, this is the internal rate of return for project G. Similarly, the burgundy line shows the net present value of project H at different discount rates. The IRR of project H is 20 percent. (We assume project H's cash flows continue indefinitely.) Note that project H has a higher NPV so long as the opportunity cost of capital is less than 15.6 percent.

The reason that IRR is misleading is that the total cash inflow of project H is larger but tends to occur later. Therefore, when the discount rate is low, H has the higher NPV; when the discount rate is high, G has the higher NPV. (You can see from Figure 5.5 that the two projects have the *same* NPV when the discount rate is 15.6 percent.) The internal rates of return on the two projects tell us that at a discount rate of 20 percent H has a zero NPV (IRR = 20 percent) and G has a positive

[6] You may, however, find that you have jumped out of the frying pan into the fire. The series of incremental cash flows may involve several changes in sign. In this case there are likely to be multiple IRRs and you will be forced to use the NPV rule after all.

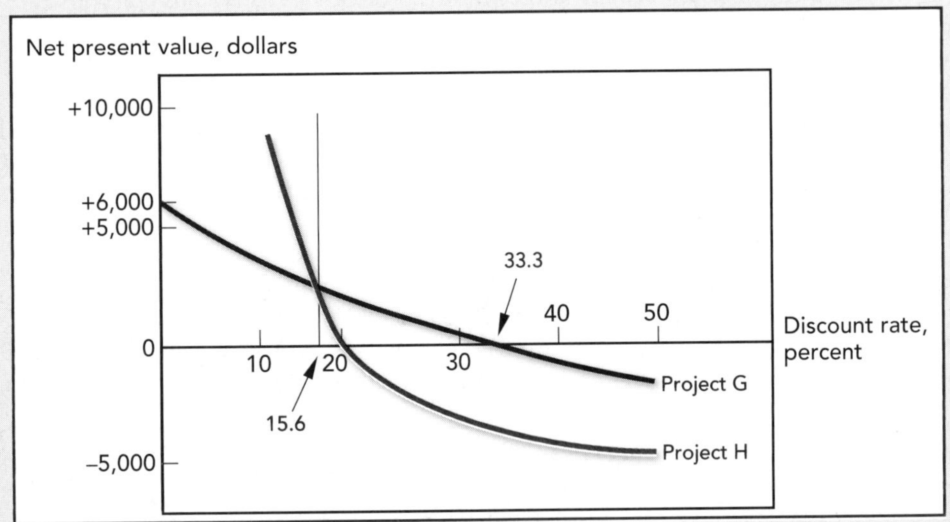

FIGURE 5.5

The IRR of project G exceeds that of project H, but the NPV of project G is higher *only* if the discount rate is greater than 15.6 percent.

NPV. Thus if the opportunity cost of capital were 20 percent, investors would place a higher value on the shorter-lived project G. But in our example the opportunity cost of capital is not 20 percent but 10 percent. Investors are prepared to pay relatively high prices for longer-lived securities, and so they will pay a relatively high price for the longer-lived project. At a 10 percent cost of capital, an investment in H has an NPV of $9,000 and an investment in G has an NPV of only $3,592.[7]

This is a favorite example of ours. We have gotten many businesspeople's reaction to it. When asked to choose between G and H, many choose G. The reason seems to be the rapid payback generated by project G. In other words, they believe that if they take G, they will also be able to take a later project like I (note that I can be financed using the cash flows from G), whereas if they take H, they won't have money enough for I. In other words they implicitly assume that it is a *shortage of capital* which forces the choice between G and H. When this implicit assumption is brought out, they usually admit that H is better if there is no capital shortage.

But the introduction of capital constraints raises two further questions. The first stems from the fact that most of the executives preferring G to H work for firms that would have no difficulty raising more capital. Why would a manager at IBM, say, choose G on the grounds of limited capital? IBM can raise plenty of capital and can take project I regardless of whether G or H is chosen; therefore I should not affect the choice between G and H. The answer seems to be that large firms usually impose capital budgets on divisions and subdivisions as a part of the firm's planning and control system. Since the system is complicated and cumbersome, the

[7]It is often suggested that the choice between the net present value rule and the internal rate of return rule should depend on the probable reinvestment rate. This is wrong. The prospective return on another *independent* investment should *never* be allowed to influence the investment decision. For a discussion of the reinvestment assumption see A. A. Alchian, "The Rate of Interest, Fisher's Rate of Return over Cost and Keynes' Internal Rate of Return," *American Economic Review* 45 (December 1955), pp. 938–942.

budgets are not easily altered, and so they are perceived as real constraints by middle management.

The second question is this. If there is a capital constraint, either real or self-imposed, should IRR be used to rank projects? The answer is no. The problem in this case is to find that package of investment projects which satisfies the capital constraint and has the largest net present value. The IRR rule will not identify this package. As we will show in the next section, the only practical and general way to do so is to use the technique of linear programming.

When we have to choose between projects G and H, it is easiest to compare the net present values. But if your heart is set on the IRR rule, you can use it as long as you look at the internal rate of return on the incremental flows. The procedure is exactly the same as we showed above. First, you check that project G has a satisfactory IRR. Then you look at the return on the additional investment in H.

	Cash Flows ($)								
Project	C_0	C_1	C_2	C_3	C_4	C_5	Etc.	IRR (%)	NPV at 10%
H–G	0	−4,200	−3,200	−2,200	+1,800	+1,800	...	15.6	+5,408

The IRR on the incremental investment in H is 15.6 percent. Since this is greater than the opportunity cost of capital, you should undertake H rather than G.

Pitfall 4—What Happens When We Can't Finesse the Term Structure of Interest Rates?

We have simplified our discussion of capital budgeting by assuming that the opportunity cost of capital is the same for all the cash flows, C_1, C_2, C_3, etc. This is not the right place to discuss the term structure of interest rates, but we must point out certain problems with the IRR rule that crop up when short-term interest rates are different from long-term rates.

Remember our most general formula for calculating net present value:

$$\text{NPV} = C_0 + \frac{C_1}{1 + r_1} + \frac{C_2}{(1 + r_2)^2} + \frac{C_3}{(1 + r_3)^3} + \cdots$$

In other words, we discount C_1 at the opportunity cost of capital for one year, C_2 at the opportunity cost of capital for two years, and so on. The IRR rule tells us to accept a project if the IRR is greater than the opportunity cost of capital. But what do we do when we have several opportunity costs? Do we compare IRR with $r_1, r_2, r_3, \ldots$? Actually we would have to compute a complex weighted average of these rates to obtain a number comparable to IRR.

What does this mean for capital budgeting? It means trouble for the IRR rule whenever the term structure of interest rates becomes important.[8] In a situation where it is important, we have to compare the project IRR with the expected IRR (yield to maturity) offered by a traded security that (1) is equivalent in risk to the project and (2) offers the same time pattern of cash flows as the project. Such a comparison is easier said than done. It is much better to forget about IRR and just calculate NPV.

[8]The source of the difficulty is that the IRR is a derived figure without any simple economic interpretation. If we wish to define it, we can do no more than say that it is the discount rate which applied to all cash flows makes NPV = 0. The problem here is not that the IRR is a nuisance to calculate but that it is not a useful number to have.

Many firms use the IRR, thereby implicitly assuming that there is no difference between short-term and long-term rates of interest. They do this for the same reason that we have so far finessed the term structure: simplicity.[9]

The Verdict on IRR

We have given four examples of things that can go wrong with IRR. We spent much less space on payback or return on book. Does this mean that IRR is worse than the other two measures? Quite the contrary. There is little point in dwelling on the deficiencies of payback or return on book. They are clearly ad hoc measures which often lead to silly conclusions. The IRR rule has a much more respectable ancestry. It is a less easy rule to use than NPV, but, used properly, it gives the same answer.

Nowadays few large corporations use the payback period or return on book as their primary measure of project attractiveness. Most use discounted cash flow or "DCF," and for many companies DCF means IRR, not NPV. We find this puzzling, but it seems that IRR is easier to explain to nonfinancial managers, who think they know what it means to say that "Project G has a 33 percent return." But can these managers use IRR properly? We worry particularly about Pitfall 3. The financial manager never sees all possible projects. Most projects are proposed by operating managers. Will the operating managers' proposals have the highest NPVs or the highest IRRs?

A company that instructs nonfinancial managers to look first at projects' IRRs prompts a search for high-IRR projects. It also encourages the managers to *modify* projects so that their IRRs are higher. Where do you typically find the highest IRRs? In short-lived projects requiring relatively little up-front investment. Such projects may not add much to the value of the firm.

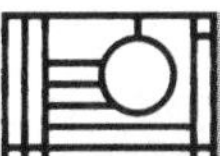

5.4 CHOOSING CAPITAL INVESTMENTS WHEN RESOURCES ARE LIMITED

Our entire discussion of methods of capital budgeting has rested on the proposition that the wealth of a firm's shareholders is highest if the firm accepts *every* project that has a positive net present value. Suppose, however, that there are limitations on the investment program that prevent the company from undertaking all such projects. Economists call this *capital rationing.* When capital is rationed, we need a method of selecting the package of projects that is within the company's resources yet gives the highest possible net present value.

An Easy Problem in Capital Rationing

Let us start with a simple example. The opportunity cost of capital is 10 percent, and our company has the following opportunities:

	Cash Flows ($ millions)			
Project	C_0	C_1	C_2	NPV at 10%
A	–10	+30	+5	21
B	–5	+5	+20	16
C	–5	+5	+15	12

[9]In Chapter 9 we will look at some other cases in which it would be misleading to use the same discount rate for both short-term and long-term cash flows.

All three projects are attractive, but suppose that the firm is limited to spending \$10 million. In that case, it can invest *either* in project A *or* in projects B and C, but it cannot invest in all three. Although individually B and C have lower net present values than project A, when taken together they have the higher net present value. Here we cannot choose between projects solely on the basis of net present values. When funds are limited, we need to concentrate on getting the biggest bang for our buck. In other words, we must pick the projects that offer the highest net present value per dollar of initial outlay. This ratio is known as the **profitability index:**[10]

$$\text{Profitability index} = \frac{\text{net present value}}{\text{investment}}$$

For our three projects the profitability index is calculated as follows:[11]

Project	Investment (\$ millions)	NPV (\$ millions)	Profitability Index
A	10	21	2.1
B	5	16	3.2
C	5	12	2.4

Project B has the highest profitability index and C has the next highest. Therefore, if our budget limit is \$10 million, we should accept these two projects.[12]

Unfortunately, there are some limitations to this simple ranking method. One of the most serious is that it breaks down whenever more than one resource is rationed. For example, suppose that the firm can raise only \$10 million for investment in *each* of years 0 and 1 and that the menu of possible projects is expanded to include an investment next year in project D:

	Cash Flows (\$ millions)				
Project	C_0	C_1	C_2	NPV at 10%	Profitability Index
A	–10	+30	+5	21	2.1
B	–5	+5	+20	16	3.2
C	–5	+5	+15	12	2.4
D	0	–40	+60	13	0.4

One strategy is to accept projects B and C; however, if we do this, we cannot also accept D, which costs more than our budget limit for period 1. An alternative is to

[10]If a project requires outlays in two or more periods, the denominator should be the present value of the outlays. (A few companies do not discount the benefits or costs before calculating the profitability index. The less said about these companies the better.)

[11]Sometimes the profitability index is defined as the ratio of the present value to initial outlay, that is, as PV/investment. This measure is also known as the *benefit–cost ratio.* To calculate the benefit–cost ratio, simply add 1.0 to each profitability index. Project rankings are unchanged.

[12]If a project has a positive profitability index, it must also have a positive NPV. Therefore, firms sometimes use the profitability index to select projects when capital is *not* limited. However, like the IRR, the profitability index can be misleading when used to choose between mutually exclusive projects. For example, suppose you were forced to choose between (1) investing \$100 in a project whose payoffs have a present value of \$200 or (2) investing \$1 million in a project whose payoffs have a present value of \$1.5 million. The first investment has the higher profitability index; the second makes you richer.

accept project A in period 0. Although this has a lower net present value than the combination of B and C, it provides a $30 million positive cash flow in period 1. When this is added to the $10 million budget, we can also afford to undertake D next year. A and D have *lower* profitability indexes than B and C, but they have a *higher* total net present value.

The reason that ranking on the profitability index fails in this example is that resources are constrained in each of two periods. In fact, this ranking method is inadequate whenever there is *any* other constraint on the choice of projects. This means that it cannot cope with cases in which two projects are mutually exclusive or in which one project is dependent on another.

Some More Elaborate Capital Rationing Models

The simplicity of the profitability-index method may sometimes outweigh its limitations. For example, it may not pay to worry about expenditures in subsequent years if you have only a hazy notion of future capital availability or investment opportunities. But there are also circumstances in which the limitations of the profitability-index method are intolerable. For such occasions we need a more general method for solving the capital rationing problem.

We begin by restating the problem just described. Suppose that we were to accept proportion x_A of project A in our example. Then the net present value of our investment in the project would be $21x_A$. Similarly, the net present value of our investment in project B can be expressed as $16x_B$, and so on. Our objective is to select the set of projects with the highest *total* net present value. In other words we wish to find the values of x that maximize

$$\text{NPV} = 21x_A + 16x_B + 12x_C + 13x_D$$

Our choice of projects is subject to several constraints. First, total cash outflow in period 0 must not be greater than $10 million. In other words,

$$10x_A + 5x_B + 5x_C + 0x_D \leq 10$$

Similarly, total outflow in period 1 must not be greater than $10 million:

$$-30x_A - 5x_B - 5x_C + 40x_D \leq 10$$

Finally, we cannot invest a negative amount in a project, and we cannot purchase more than one of each. Therefore we have

$$0 \leq x_A \leq 1, \qquad 0 \leq x_B \leq 1, \ldots$$

Collecting all these conditions, we can summarize the problem as follows:

Maximize $21x_A + 16x_B + 12x_C + 13x_D$
Subject to

$$\begin{aligned} &10x_A + 5x_B + 5x_C + 0x_D \leq 10 \\ &-30x_A - 5x_B - 5x_C + 40x_D \leq 10 \\ &0 \leq x_A \leq 1, \qquad 0 \leq x_B \leq 1, \ldots \end{aligned}$$

One way to tackle such a problem is to keep selecting different values for the x's, noting which combination both satisfies the constraints and gives the highest net present value. But it's smarter to recognize that the equations above constitute a linear programming (LP) problem. It can be handed to a computer equipped to solve LPs.

The answer given by the LP method is somewhat different from the one we obtained earlier. Instead of investing in one unit of project A and one of project D, we are told to take half of project A, all of project B, and three-quarters of D. The reason is simple. The computer is a dumb, but obedient, pet, and since we did not tell it that the x's had to be whole numbers, it saw no reason to make them so. By accepting "fractional" projects, it is possible to increase NPV by $2.25 million. For many purposes this is quite appropriate. If project A represents an investment in 1,000 square feet of warehouse space or in 1,000 tons of steel plate, it might be feasible to accept 500 square feet or 500 tons and quite reasonable to assume that cash flow would be reduced proportionately. If, however, project A is a single crane or oil well, such fractional investments make little sense.

When fractional projects are not feasible, we can use a form of linear programming known as *integer* (or *zero-one*) *programming,* which limits all the x's to integers.

Uses of Capital Rationing Models

Linear programming models seem tailor-made for solving capital budgeting problems when resources are limited. Why then are they not universally accepted either in theory or in practice? One reason is that these models can turn out to be very complex. Second, as with any sophisticated long-range planning tool, there is the general problem of getting good data. It is just not worth applying costly, sophisticated methods to poor data. Furthermore, these models are based on the assumption that all future investment opportunities are known. In reality, the discovery of investment ideas is an unfolding process.

Our most serious misgivings center on the basic assumption that capital is limited. When we come to discuss company financing, we shall see that most large corporations do not face capital rationing and can raise large sums of money on fair terms. Why then do many company presidents tell their subordinates that capital is limited? If they are right, the capital market is seriously imperfect. What then are they doing maximizing NPV?[13] We might be tempted to suppose that if capital is not rationed, they do not *need* to use linear programming and, if it is rationed, then surely they *ought* not to use it. But that would be too quick a judgment. Let us look at this problem more deliberately.

Soft Rationing Many firms' capital constraints are "soft." They reflect no imperfections in capital markets. Instead they are provisional limits adopted by management as an aid to financial control.

Some ambitious divisional managers habitually overstate their investment opportunities. Rather than trying to distinguish which projects really are worthwhile, headquarters may find it simpler to impose an upper limit on divisional expenditures and thereby force the divisions to set their own priorities. In such instances budget limits are a rough but effective way of dealing with biased cash-flow forecasts. In other cases management may believe that very rapid corporate growth could impose intolerable strains on management and the organization. Since it is difficult to quantify such constraints explicitly, the budget limit may be used as a proxy.

Because such budget limits have nothing to do with any inefficiency in the capital market, there is no contradiction in using an LP model in the division to maximize net present value subject to the budget constraint. On the other hand, there

[13]Don't forget that in Chapter 2 we had to assume perfect capital markets to derive the NPV rule.

is not much point in elaborate selection procedures if the cash-flow forecasts of the division are seriously biased.

Even if capital is not rationed, other resources may be. The availability of management time, skilled labor, or even other capital equipment often constitutes an important constraint on a company's growth.

Hard Rationing Soft rationing should never cost the firm anything. If capital constraints become tight enough to hurt—in the sense that projects with significant positive NPVs are passed up—then the firm raises more money and loosens the constraint. But what if it *can't* raise more money—what if it faces *hard* rationing?

Hard rationing implies market imperfections, but that does not necessarily mean we have to throw away net present value as a criterion for capital budgeting. It depends on the nature of the imperfection.

Arizona Aquaculture, Inc. (AAI), borrows as much as the banks will lend it, yet it still has good investment opportunities. This is not hard rationing so long as AAI can issue stock. But perhaps it can't. Perhaps the founder and majority shareholder vetoes the idea from fear of losing control of the firm. Perhaps a stock issue would bring costly red tape or legal complications.[14]

This does not invalidate the NPV rule. AAI's *shareholders* can borrow or lend, sell their shares, or buy more. They have free access to security markets. The type of portfolio they hold is independent of AAI's financing or investment decisions. The only way AAI can help its shareholders is to make them richer. Thus AAI should invest its available cash in the package of projects having the largest aggregate net present value.

A barrier between the firm and capital markets does not undermine net present value so long as the barrier is the *only* market imperfection. The important thing is that the firm's *shareholders* have free access to well-functioning capital markets.

The net present value rule *is* undermined when imperfections restrict shareholders' portfolio choice. Suppose that Nevada Aquaculture, Inc. (NAI), is solely owned by its founder, Alexander Turbot. Mr. Turbot has no cash or credit remaining, but he is convinced that expansion of his operation is a high-NPV investment. He has tried to sell stock but has found that prospective investors, skeptical of prospects for fish farming in the desert, offer him much less than he thinks his firm is worth. For Mr. Turbot capital markets hardly exist. It makes little sense for him to discount prospective cash flows at a market opportunity cost of capital.

[14]A majority owner who is "locked in" and has much personal wealth tied up in AAI may be effectively cut off from capital markets. The NPV rule may not make sense to such an owner, though it will to the other shareholders.

SUMMARY

If you are going to persuade your company to use the net present value rule, you must be prepared to explain why other rules may *not* lead to correct decisions. That is why we have examined three alternative investment criteria in this chapter.

Some firms look at the book rate of return on the project. In this case the company decides which cash payments are capital expenditures and picks the appropriate rate to depreciate these expenditures. It then calculates the ratio of book income to the book value of the investment. Few companies nowadays base their investment decision simply on the book rate of return, but shareholders pay attention to book measures of firm profitability and some managers therefore look with a jaundiced eye on projects that would damage the company's book rate of return.

Some companies use the payback method to make investment decisions. In other words, they accept only those projects that recover their initial investment within some specified period. Payback is an ad hoc rule. It ignores the order in which cash flows come within the payback period, and it ignores subsequent cash flows entirely. It therefore takes no account of the opportunity cost of capital.

The simplicity of payback makes it an easy device for *describing* investment projects. Managers talk casually about quick-payback projects in the same way that investors talk about high-P/E common stocks. The fact that managers talk about the payback periods of projects does not mean that the payback rule governs their decisions. Some managers *do* use payback in judging capital investments. Why they rely on such a grossly oversimplified concept is a puzzle.

The internal rate of return (IRR) is defined as the rate of discount at which a project would have zero NPV. It is a handy measure and widely used in finance; you should therefore know how to calculate it. The IRR rule states that companies should accept any investment offering an IRR in excess of the opportunity cost of capital. The IRR rule is, like net present value, a technique based on discounted cash flows. It will, therefore, give the correct answer if properly used. The problem is that it is easily misapplied. There are four things to look out for:

1. *Lending or borrowing?* If a project offers positive cash flows followed by negative flows, NPV can *rise* as the discount rate is increased. You should accept such projects if their IRR is *less* than the opportunity cost of capital.
2. *Multiple rates of return.* If there is more than one change in the sign of the cash flows, the project may have several IRRs or no IRR at all.
3. *Mutually exclusive projects.* The IRR rule may give the wrong ranking of mutually exclusive projects that differ in economic life or in scale of required investment. If you insist on using IRR to rank mutually exclusive projects, you must examine the IRR on each incremental investment.
4. *Short-term interest rates may be different from long-term rates.* The IRR rule requires you to compare the project's IRR with the opportunity cost of capital. But sometimes there is an opportunity cost of capital for one-year cash flows, a different cost of capital for two-year cash flows, and so on. In these cases there is no simple yardstick for evaluating the IRR of a project.

If you are going to the expense of collecting cash-flow forecasts, you might as well use them properly. Ad hoc criteria should therefore have no role in the firm's decisions, and the net present value rule should be employed in preference to other techniques. Having said that, we must be careful not to exaggerate the payoff of proper technique. Technique is important, but it is by no means the only determinant of the success of a capital expenditure program. If the forecasts of cash flows are biased, even the most careful application of the net present value rule may fail.

In developing the NPV rule, we assumed that the company can maximize shareholder wealth by accepting every project that is worth more than it costs. But, if capital is strictly limited, then it may not be possible to take every project with a positive NPV. If capital is rationed in only one period, then the firm should follow a simple rule: Calculate each project's profitability index, which is the project's net present value per dollar of investment. Then pick the projects with the highest profitability indexes until you run out of capital. Unfortunately, this procedure fails when capital is rationed in more than one period or when there are other constraints on project choice. The only general solution is linear or integer programming.

Hard capital rationing always reflects a market imperfection—a barrier between the firm and capital markets. If that barrier also implies that the firm's shareholders lack free access to a well-functioning capital market, the very foundations of net present value crumble. Fortunately, hard rationing is rare for corporations in the United States. Many firms do use soft capital rationing, however. That is, they set up self-imposed limits as a means of financial planning and control.

FURTHER READING

Classic articles on the internal rate of return rule include:

J. H. Lorie and L. J. Savage: "Three Problems in Rationing Capital," *Journal of Business,* 28:229–239 (October 1955).

E. Solomon: "The Arithmetic of Capital Budgeting Decisions," *Journal of Business,* 29:124–129 (April 1956).

A. A. Alchian: "The Rate of Interest, Fisher's Rate of Return over Cost and Keynes' Internal Rate of Return," *American Economic Review,* 45:938–942 (December 1955).

The classic treatment of linear programming applied to capital budgeting is:

H. M. Weingartner: *Mathematical Programming and the Analysis of Capital Budgeting Problems,* Prentice-Hall, Inc., Englewood Cliffs, N.J., 1963.

There is a long scholarly controversy on whether capital constraints invalidate the NPV rule. Weingartner has reviewed this literature:

H. M. Weingartner: "Capital Rationing: *n* Authors in Search of a Plot," *Journal of Finance,* 32:1403–1432 (December 1977).

QUIZ

1. What is the opportunity cost of capital supposed to represent? Give a concise definition.

2. a. What is the payback period on each of the following projects?

	Cash Flows ($)				
Project	C_0	C_1	C_2	C_3	C_4
A	–5,000	+1,000	+1,000	+3,000	0
B	–1,000	0	+1,000	+2,000	+3,000
C	–5,000	+1,000	+1,000	+3,000	+5,000

b. *Given* that you wish to use the payback rule with a cutoff period of two years, which projects would you accept?

c. If you use a cutoff period of three years, which projects would you accept?

d. If the opportunity cost of capital is 10 percent, which projects have positive NPVs?

e. "Payback gives too much weight to cash flows that occur after the cutoff date." True or false?

f. "If a firm uses a single cutoff period for all projects, it is likely to accept too many short-lived projects." True or false?

g. If the firm uses the discounted-payback rule, will it accept any negative-NPV projects? Will it turn down positive-NPV projects? Explain.

3. What is the book rate of return? Why is it *not* an accurate measure of the value of a capital investment project?

4. Write down the equation defining a project's internal rate of return (IRR). In practice how is IRR calculated?

5. a. Calculate the net present value of the following project for discount rates of 0, 50, and 100 percent:

Cash Flows ($)		
C_0	C_1	C_2
−6,750	+4,500	+18,000

b. What is the IRR of the project?

6. You have the chance to participate in a project that produces the following cash flows:

Cash Flows ($)		
C_0	C_1	C_2
+5,000	+4,000	−11,000

The internal rate of return is 13 percent. If the opportunity cost of capital is 10 percent, would you accept the offer?

7. Consider a project with the following cash flows:

C_0	C_1	C_2
−100	+200	−75

a. How many internal rates of return does this project have?
b. The opportunity cost of capital is 20 percent. Is this an attractive project? Briefly explain.

8. Consider projects Alpha and Beta:

	Cash Flows ($)			
Project	C_0	C_1	C_2	IRR (%)
Alpha	−400,000	+241,000	+293,000	21
Beta	−200,000	+131,000	+172,000	31

The opportunity cost of capital is 8 percent.

Suppose you can undertake Alpha or Beta, but not both. Use the IRR rule to make the choice. *Hint:* What's the incremental investment in Alpha?

9. Suppose you have the following investment opportunities, but only $90,000 available for investment. Which projects should you take?

Project	NPV	Investment
1	5,000	10,000
2	5,000	5,000
3	10,000	90,000
4	15,000	60,000
5	15,000	75,000
6	3,000	15,000

10. What is the difference between hard and soft capital rationing? Does soft rationing mean the manager should stop trying to maximize NPV? How about hard rationing?

PRACTICE QUESTIONS

1. Consider the following projects:

	Cash Flows ($)					
Project	C_0	C_1	C_2	C_3	C_4	C_5
A	−1,000	+1,000	0	0	0	0
B	−2,000	+1,000	+1,000	+4,000	+1,000	+1,000
C	−3,000	+1,000	+1,000	0	+1,000	+1,000

a. If the opportunity cost of capital is 10 percent, which projects have a positive NPV?
b. Calculate the payback period for each project.
c. Which project(s) would a firm using the payback rule accept if the cutoff period were three years?

2. How is the discounted payback period calculated? Does discounted payback solve the deficiencies of the payback rule? Explain.

3. Does the following manifesto make sense? Explain briefly.

We're a darn successful company. Our book rate of return has exceeded 20 percent for five years running. We're determined that new capital investments won't drag down that average.

4. Respond to the following comments:
a. "I like the IRR rule. I can use it to rank projects without having to specify a discount rate."
b. "I like the payback rule. As long as the minimum payback period is short, the rule makes sure that the company takes no borderline projects. That reduces risk."

5. Unfortunately, your chief executive officer refuses to accept any investments in plant expansion that do not return their original investment in four years or less. That is, he insists on a *payback rule* with a *cutoff period* of four years. As a result, attractive long-lived projects are being turned down.

The CEO is willing to switch to a *discounted payback* rule with the same four-year cutoff period. Would this be an improvement? Explain.

6. Calculate the IRR (or IRRs) for the following project:

C_0	C_1	C_2	C_3
−3,000	+3,500	+4,000	−4,000

For what range of discount rates does the project have positive-NPV?

7. Consider the following two mutually exclusive projects:

	Cash Flows ($)			
Project	C_0	C_1	C_2	C_3
A	−100	+60	+60	0
B	−100	0	0	+140

a. Calculate the NPV of each project for discount rates of 0, 10, and 20 percent. Plot these on a graph with NPV on the vertical axis and discount rate on the horizontal axis.
b. What is the approximate IRR for each project?

Visit us at www.mhhe.com/bm7e

c. In what circumstances should the company accept project A?
d. Calculate the NPV of the incremental investment (B – A) for discount rates of 0, 10, and 20 percent. Plot these on your graph. Show that the circumstances in which you would accept A are also those in which the IRR on the incremental investment is less than the opportunity cost of capital.

8. Mr. Cyrus Clops, the president of Giant Enterprises, has to make a choice between two possible investments:

	Cash Flows ($ thousands)			
Project	C_0	C_1	C_2	**IRR (%)**
A	–400	+250	+300	23
B	–200	+140	+179	36

The opportunity cost of capital is 9 percent. Mr. Clops is tempted to take B, which has the higher IRR.
a. Explain to Mr. Clops why this is not the correct procedure.
b. Show him how to adapt the IRR rule to choose the best project.
c. Show him that this project also has the higher NPV.

9. The Titanic Shipbuilding Company has a noncancelable contract to build a small cargo vessel. Construction involves a cash outlay of $250,000 at the end of each of the next two years. At the end of the third year the company will receive payment of $650,000. The company can speed up construction by working an extra shift. In this case there will be a cash outlay of $550,000 at the end of the first year followed by a cash payment of $650,000 at the end of the second year. Use the IRR rule to show the (approximate) range of opportunity costs of capital at which the company should work the extra shift.

10. "A company that ranks projects on IRR will encourage managers to propose projects with quick paybacks and low up-front investment." Is that statement correct? Explain.

11. Look again at projects E and F in Section 5.3. Assume that the projects are mutually exclusive and that the opportunity cost of capital is 10 percent.
a. Calculate the profitability index for each project.
b. Show how the profitability-index rule can be used to select the superior project.

12. In 1983 wealthy investors were offered a scheme that would allow them to postpone taxes. The scheme involved a debt-financed purchase of a fleet of beer delivery trucks, which were then leased to a local distributor. The cash flows were as follows:

Year	Cash Flow	
0	–21,750	Tax savings
1	+7,861	
2	+8,317	
3	+7,188	
4	+6,736	
5	+6,231	
6	–5,340	Additional taxes paid later
7	–5,972	
8	–6,678	
9	–7,468	
10	+12,578	Salvage value

Calculate the approximate IRRs. Is the project attractive at a 14 percent opportunity cost of capital?

13. Borghia Pharmaceuticals has $1 million allocated for capital expenditures. Which of the following projects should the company accept to stay within the $1 million budget? How much does the budget limit cost the company in terms of its market value? The opportunity cost of capital for each project is 11 percent.

Project	Investment ($ thousands)	NPV ($ thousands)	IRR (%)
1	300	66	17.2
2	200	–4	10.7
3	250	43	16.6
4	100	14	12.1
5	100	7	11.8
6	350	63	18.0
7	400	48	13.5

14. Consider the following capital rationing problem:

Project	C_0	C_1	C_2	NPV
W	–10,000	–10,000	0	+6,700
X	0	–20,000	+5,000	+9,000
Y	–10,000	+5,000	+5,000	+0
Z	–15,000	+5,000	+4,000	–1,500
Financing available	20,000	20,000	20,000	

Set up this problem as a linear program.

1. Some people believe firmly, even passionately, that ranking projects on IRR is OK if each project's cash flows can be reinvested at the project's IRR. They also say that the NPV rule "assumes that cash flows are reinvested at the opportunity cost of capital." Think carefully about these statements. Are they true? Are they helpful?
2. Look again at the project cash flows in Practice Question 6. Calculate the modified IRR as defined in footnote 5 in Section 5.3. Assume the cost of capital is 12 percent.

   Now try the following variation on the modified IRR concept. Figure out the fraction x such that x times C_1 and C_2 has the same present value as (minus) C_3.

$$xC_1 + \frac{xC_2}{1.12} = \frac{C_3}{1.12^2}$$

   Define the modified project IRR as the solution of

$$C_0 + \frac{(1 - x)C_1}{1 + \text{IRR}} + \frac{(1 - x)C_2}{(1 + \text{IRR})^2} = 0$$

   Now you have two modified IRRs. Which is more meaningful? If you can't decide, what do you conclude about the usefulness of modified IRRs?
3. Construct a series of cash flows with *no* IRR.
4. Solve the linear programming problem in Practice Question 14. You can allow partial investments, that is, $0 \le x \le 1$. Calculate and interpret the shadow prices[15] on the capital constraints.

[15] A shadow price is the marginal change in the objective for a marginal change in the constraint.

5. Look again at projects A, B, C, and D in Section 5.4. How would the linear programming setup change if:
   a. Cash not invested at date 0 could be invested at an interest rate r and used at date 1.
   b. Cash is not the only scarce resource. For example, there may not be enough people in the engineering department to complete necessary design work for all four projects.

MINI-CASE

Vegetron's CFO Calls Again

(The first episode of this story was presented in Section 5.1.)

Later that afternoon, Vegetron's CFO bursts into your office in a state of anxious confusion. The problem, he explains, is a last-minute proposal for a change in the design of the fermentation tanks that Vegetron will build to extract hydrated zirconium from a stockpile of powdered ore. The CFO has brought a printout (Table 5.1) of the forecasted revenues, costs, income, and book rates of return for the standard, low-temperature design. Vegetron's engineers have just proposed an alternative high-temperature design that will extract most of the hydrated zirconium over a shorter period, five instead of seven years. The forecasts for the high-temperature method are given in Table 5.2.[16]

TABLE 5.1

Income statement and book rates of return for high-temperature extraction of hydrated zirconium ($ thousands).

	Year				
	1	2	3	4	5
1. Revenue	180	180	180	180	180
2. Operating costs	70	70	70	70	70
3. Depreciation*	80	80	80	80	80
4. Net income	30	30	30	30	30
5. Start-of-year book value†	400	320	240	160	80
6. Book rate of return (4 ÷ 5)	7.5%	9.4%	12.5%	18.75%	37.5%

*Straight-line depreciation over five years is 400/5 = 80, or $80,000 per year.
†Capital investment is $400,000 in year 0.

TABLE 5.2

Income statement and book rates of return for low-temperature extraction of hydrated zirconium ($ thousands).

	Year						
	1	2	3	4	5	6	7
1. Revenue	140	140	140	140	140	140	140
2. Operating costs	55	55	55	55	55	55	55
3. Depreciation*	57	57	57	57	57	57	57
4. Net income	28	28	28	28	28	28	28
5. Start-of-year book value†	400	343	286	229	171	114	57
6. Book rate of return (4 ÷ 5)	7%	8.2%	9.8%	12.2%	16.4%	24.6%	49.1%

*Rounded. Straight-line depreciation over seven years is 400/7 = 57.14, or $57,140 per year.
†Capital investment is $400,000 in year 0.

[16]For simplicity we have ignored taxes. There will be plenty about taxes in Chapter 6.

CFO: Why do these engineers always have a bright idea at the last minute? But you've got to admit the high-temperature process looks good. We'll get a faster payback, and the rate of return beats Vegetron's 9 percent cost of capital in every year except the first. Let's see, income is $30,000 per year. Average investment is half the $400,000 capital outlay, or $200,000, so the average rate of return is 30,000/200,000, or 15 percent—a lot better than the 9 percent hurdle rate. The average rate of return for the low-temperature process is not that good, only 28,000/200,000, or 14 percent. Of course we might get a higher rate of return for the low-temperature proposal if we depreciated the investment faster—do you think we should try that?

You: Let's not fixate on book accounting numbers. Book income is not the same as cash flow to Vegetron or its investors. Book rates of return don't measure the true rate of return.

CFO: But people use accounting numbers all the time. We have to publish them in our annual report to investors.

You: Accounting numbers have many valid uses, but they're not a sound basis for capital investment decisions. Accounting changes can have big effects on book income or rate of return, even when cash flows are unchanged.

Here's an example. Suppose the accountant depreciates the capital investment for the low-temperature process over six years rather than seven. Then income for years 1 to 6 goes down, because depreciation is higher. Income for year 7 goes up because the depreciation for that year becomes zero. But there is no effect on year-to-year cash flows, because depreciation is not a cash outlay. It is simply the accountant's device for spreading out the "recovery" of the up-front capital outlay over the life of the project.

CFO: So how do we get cash flows?

You: In these cases it's easy. Depreciation is the only noncash entry in your spreadsheets (Tables 5.1 and 5.2), so we can just leave it out of the calculation. Cash flow equals revenue minus operating costs. For the high-temperature process, annual cash flow is:

$$\text{Cash flow} = \text{revenue} - \text{operating cost} = 180 - 70 = 110, \text{ or } \$110{,}000.$$

CFO: In effect you're adding back depreciation, because depreciation is a noncash accounting expense.

You: Right. You could also do it that way:

$$\text{Cash flow} = \text{net income} + \text{depreciation} = 30 + 80 = 110, \text{ or } \$110{,}000.$$

CFO: Of course. I remember all this now, but book returns seem important when someone shoves them in front of your nose.

You: It's not clear which project is better. The high-temperature process appears to be less efficient. It has higher operating costs and generates less total revenue over the life of the project, but of course it generates more cash flow in years 1 to 5.

CFO: Maybe the processes are equally good from a financial point of view. If so we'll stick with the low-temperature process rather than switching at the last minute.

You: We'll have to lay out the cash flows and calculate NPV for each process.

CFO: OK, do that. I'll be back in a half hour—and I also want to see each project's true, DCF rate of return.

Questions

1. Are the book rates of return reported in Table 5.1 useful inputs for the capital investment decision?
2. Calculate NPV and IRR for each process. What is your recommendation? Be ready to explain to the CFO.

CHAPTER SIX

MAKING INVESTMENT DECISIONS WITH THE NET PRESENT VALUE RULE

WE HOPE THAT by now you are convinced that wise investment decisions are based on the net present value rule. In this chapter we can think about how to apply the rule to practical capital investment decisions. Our task is threefold. First, what should be discounted? We know the answer in principle: discount cash flows. But useful forecasts of cash flows do not arrive on a silver platter. Often the financial manager has to make do with raw data supplied by specialists in product design, production, marketing, and so on.

This information has to be checked for completeness, consistency, and accuracy. The financial manager has to ferret out hidden cash flows and take care to reject accounting entries that look like cash flows but truly are not.

Second, how does the financial manager pull everything together into a forecast of overall, "bottom-line" cash flows? This requires careful tracking of taxes; changes in working capital; inflation; and the end-of-project "salvage values" of plant, property, and equipment. We will work through a realistic example.

Third, how should a financial manager apply the net present value rule when choosing between investments in plant or equipment with different economic lives? For example, suppose you must decide between machine Y, with a 5-year useful life, and machine Z, with a 10-year useful life. The present value of Y's lifetime investment and operating costs is naturally less than Z's, because Z will last twice as long. Does that necessarily make Y the better choice? Of course not.

We will show you how to transform the present value of an asset's investment and operating costs into an *equivalent annual cost,* that is, the total cost per year of buying and operating the asset. We will also show how to use equivalent annual costs to decide when to replace aging plant or equipment.

Choices between short- and long-lived production facilities, or between new and existing facilities, almost always involve *project interactions,* because a decision about one project cannot be separated from a decision about another, or from future decisions. We close this chapter with further examples of project interactions, for example, the choice between investing now and waiting to invest later.

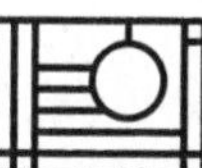

6.1 WHAT TO DISCOUNT

Up to this point we have been concerned mainly with the mechanics of discounting and with the net present value rule for project appraisal. We have glossed over the problem of deciding *what* to discount. When you are faced with this problem, you should always stick to three general rules:

1. Only cash flow is relevant.
2. Always estimate cash flows on an incremental basis.
3. Be consistent in your treatment of inflation.

We will discuss each of these rules in turn.

Only Cash Flow Is Relevant

The first and most important point: Net present value depends on future cash flows. Cash flow is the simplest possible concept; it is just the difference between dollars received and dollars paid out. Many people nevertheless confuse cash flow with accounting profits.

Accountants *start* with "dollars in" and "dollars out," but to obtain accounting income they adjust these inputs in two important ways. First, they try to show profit as it is *earned* rather than when the company and the customer get around to paying their bills. Second, they sort cash outflows into two categories: current expenses and capital expenses. They deduct current expenses when calculating profit but do *not* deduct capital expenses. Instead they depreciate capital expenses over a number of years and deduct the annual depreciation charge from profits. As a result of these procedures, profits include some cash flows and exclude others, and they are reduced by depreciation charges, which are not cash flows at all.

It is not always easy to translate the customary accounting data back into actual dollars—dollars you can buy beer with. If you are in doubt about what is a cash flow, simply count the dollars coming in and take away the dollars going out. Don't assume without checking that you can find cash flow by routine manipulations of accounting data.

Always estimate cash flows on an after-tax basis. Some firms do not deduct tax payments. They try to offset this mistake by discounting the cash flows before taxes at a rate higher than the opportunity cost of capital. Unfortunately, there is no reliable formula for making such adjustments to the discount rate.

You should also make sure that cash flows are recorded *only when they occur* and not when work is undertaken or a liability is incurred. For example, taxes should be discounted from their actual payment date, not from the time when the tax liability is recorded in the firm's books.

Estimate Cash Flows on an Incremental Basis

The value of a project depends on *all* the additional cash flows that follow from project acceptance. Here are some things to watch for when you are deciding which cash flows should be included:

Do Not Confuse Average with Incremental Payoffs Most managers naturally hesitate to throw good money after bad. For example, they are reluctant to invest more money in a losing division. But occasionally you will encounter turnaround opportunities in which the *incremental* NPV on investment in a loser is strongly positive.

Conversely, it does not always make sense to throw good money after good. A division with an outstanding past profitability record may have run out of good opportunities. You would not pay a large sum for a 20-year-old horse, sentiment aside, regardless of how many races that horse had won or how many champions it had sired.

Here is another example illustrating the difference between average and incremental returns: Suppose that a railroad bridge is in urgent need of repair. With the bridge the railroad can continue to operate; without the bridge it can't. In this case the payoff from the repair work consists of all the benefits of operating the railroad. The incremental NPV of such an investment may be enormous. Of course, these benefits should be net of all other costs and all subsequent repairs; otherwise the company may be misled into rebuilding an unprofitable railroad piece by piece.

Include All Incidental Effects It is important to include all incidental effects on the remainder of the business. For example, a branch line for a railroad may have a negative NPV when considered in isolation, but still be a worthwhile investment when one allows for the additional traffic that it brings to the main line.

These incidental effects can extend into the far future. When GE, Pratt & Whitney, or Rolls Royce commits to the design and production of a new jet engine, cash inflows are not limited to revenues from engine sales. Once sold, an engine may be in service for 20 years or more, and during that time there is a steady demand for replacement parts. Some engine manufacturers also run profitable service and overhaul facilities. Finally, once an engine is proven in service, there are opportunities to offer modified or improved versions for other uses. All these "downstream" activities generate significant incremental cash inflows.

Do Not Forget Working Capital Requirements **Net working capital** (often referred to simply as *working capital*) is the difference between a company's short-term assets and liabilities. The principal short-term assets are cash, accounts receivable (customers' unpaid bills), and inventories of raw materials and finished goods. The principal short-term liabilities are accounts payable (bills that *you* have not paid). Most projects entail an additional investment in working capital. This investment should, therefore, be recognized in your cash-flow forecasts. By the same token, when the project comes to an end, you can usually recover some of the investment. This is treated as a cash inflow.

Include Opportunity Costs The cost of a resource may be relevant to the investment decision even when no cash changes hands. For example, suppose a new manufacturing operation uses land which could otherwise be sold for $100,000. This resource is not free: It has an opportunity cost, which is the cash it could generate for the company if the project were rejected and the resource were sold or put to some other productive use.

This example prompts us to warn you against judging projects on the basis of "before versus after." The proper comparison is "with or without." A manager comparing before versus after might not assign any value to the land because the firm owns it both before and after:

Before	Take Project	After	Cash Flow, Before versus After
Firm owns land	→	Firm still owns land	0

The proper comparison, with or without, is as follows:

With	Take Project	After	Cash Flow, with Project
Firm owns land	→	Firm still owns land	0

Without	Do Not Take Project	After	Cash Flow, without Project
	→	Firm sells land for $100,000	$100,000

Comparing the two possible "afters," we see that the firm gives up $100,000 by undertaking the project. This reasoning still holds if the land will not be sold but is worth $100,000 to the firm in some other use.

Sometimes opportunity costs may be very difficult to estimate; however, where the resource can be freely traded, its opportunity cost is simply equal to the market price. Why? It cannot be otherwise. If the value of a parcel of land to the firm is less than its market price, the firm will sell it. On the other hand, the opportunity cost of using land in a particular project cannot exceed the cost of buying an equivalent parcel to replace it.

Forget Sunk Costs Sunk costs are like spilled milk: They are past and irreversible outflows. Because sunk costs are bygones, they cannot be affected by the decision to accept or reject the project, and so they should be ignored.

This fact is often forgotten. For example, in 1971 Lockheed sought a federal guarantee for a bank loan to continue development of the TriStar airplane. Lockheed and its supporters argued it would be foolish to abandon a project on which nearly $1 billion had already been spent. Some of Lockheed's critics countered that it would be equally foolish to continue with a project that offered no prospect of a satisfactory return on that $1 billion. Both groups were guilty of the *sunk-cost fallacy;* the $1 billion was irrecoverable and, therefore, irrelevant.[1]

Beware of Allocated Overhead Costs We have already mentioned that the accountant's objective is not always the same as the investment analyst's. A case in point is the allocation of overhead costs. Overheads include such items as supervisory salaries, rent, heat, and light. These overheads may not be related to any particular project, but they have to be paid for somehow. Therefore, when the accountant assigns costs to the firm's projects, a charge for overhead is usually made. Now our principle of incremental cash flows says that in investment appraisal we should include only the *extra* expenses that would result from the project. A project may generate extra overhead expenses; then again, it may not. We should be cautious about assuming that the accountant's allocation of overheads represents the true extra expenses that would be incurred.

Treat Inflation Consistently

As we pointed out in Chapter 3, interest rates are usually quoted in *nominal* rather than *real* terms. For example, if you buy a one-year 8 percent Treasury bond, the government promises to pay you $1,080 at the end of the year, but it makes no promise what that $1,080 will buy. Investors take inflation into account when they decide what is a fair rate of interest.

Suppose that the yield on the Treasury bond is 8 percent and that next year's inflation is expected to be 6 percent. If you buy the bond, you get back $1,080 in year-1 dollars, which are worth 6 percent less than current dollars. The nominal payoff is $1,080, but the expected *real* value of your payoff is 1,080/1.06 = $1,019. Thus we could say, "The *nominal* rate of interest on the bond is 8 percent," *or* "The expected *real* rate of interest is 1.9 percent." Remember that the formula linking the nominal interest rate and the real rate is

$$1 + r_{\text{nominal}} = (1 + r_{\text{real}})(1 + \text{inflation rate})$$

If the discount rate is stated in nominal terms, then consistency requires that cash flows be estimated in nominal terms, taking account of trends in selling price, labor and materials cost, etc. This calls for more than simply applying a single assumed inflation rate to all components of cash flow. Labor cost per hour of work, for example, normally increases at a faster rate than the consumer price index because of improvements in productivity and increasing real wages throughout the economy. Tax savings from depreciation do not increase with inflation; they are

[1]See U. E. Reinhardt, "Break-Even Analysis for Lockheed's TriStar: An Application of Financial Theory," *Journal of Finance,* 28 (September 1973), pp. 821–838.

constant in nominal terms because tax law in the United States allows only the original cost of assets to be depreciated.

Of course, there is nothing wrong with discounting real cash flows at a real discount rate, although this is not commonly done. Here is a simple example showing the equivalence of the two methods.

Suppose your firm usually forecasts cash flows in nominal terms and discounts at a 15 percent nominal rate. In this particular case, however, you are given project cash flows estimated in real terms, that is, current dollars:

Real Cash Flows ($ thousands)			
C_0	C_1	C_2	C_3
−100	+35	+50	+30

It would be inconsistent to discount these real cash flows at 15 percent. You have two alternatives: Either restate the cash flows in nominal terms and discount at 15 percent, or restate the discount rate in real terms and use it to discount the real cash flows. We will now show you that both methods produce the same answer.

Assume that inflation is projected at 10 percent a year. Then the cash flow for year 1, which is $35,000 in current dollars, will be 35,000 × 1.10 = $38,500 in year-1 dollars. Similarly the cash flow for year 2 will be 50,000 × $(1.10)^2$ = $60,500 in year-2 dollars, and so on. If we discount these nominal cash flows at the 15 percent nominal discount rate, we have

$$\text{NPV} = -100 + \frac{38.5}{1.15} + \frac{60.5}{(1.15)^2} + \frac{39.9}{(1.15)^3} = 5.5, \text{ or } \$5{,}500$$

Instead of converting the cash-flow forecasts into nominal terms, we could convert the discount rate into real terms by using the following relationship:

$$\text{Real discount rate} = \frac{1 + \text{nominal discount rate}}{1 + \text{inflation rate}} - 1$$

In our example this gives

$$\text{Real discount rate} = \frac{1.15}{1.10} - 1 = .045, \text{ or } 4.5\%$$

If we now discount the real cash flows by the real discount rate, we have an NPV of $5,500, just as before:

$$\text{NPV} = -100 + \frac{35}{1.045} + \frac{50}{(1.045)^2} + \frac{30}{(1.045)^3} = 5.5, \text{ or } \$5{,}500$$

Note that the real discount rate is approximately equal to the *difference* between the nominal discount rate of 15 percent and the inflation rate of 10 percent. Discounting at 15 − 10 = 5 percent would give NPV = $4,600—not exactly right, but close.

The message of all this is quite simple. Discount nominal cash flows at a nominal discount rate. Discount real cash flows at a real rate. Obvious as this rule is, it is sometimes violated. For example, in the 1970s there was a political storm in Ireland over the government's acquisition of a stake in Bula Mines. The price paid by the government reflected an assessment of £40 million as the value of Bula Mines; however, one group of consultants thought that the company's value was only £8 million and others thought that it was as high as £104 million. Although these valuations used different cash-flow projections, a significant part of the difference in views seemed to reflect confusion about real and nominal discount rates.[2]

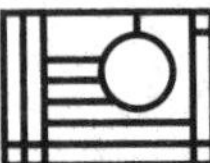

6.2 EXAMPLE—IM&C'S FERTILIZER PROJECT

As the newly appointed financial manager of International Mulch and Compost Company (IM&C), you are about to analyze a proposal for marketing guano as a garden fertilizer. (IM&C's planned advertising campaign features a rustic gentleman who steps out of a vegetable patch singing, "All my troubles have guano way.")[3]

You are given the forecasts shown in Table 6.1. The project requires an investment of $10 million in plant and machinery (line 1). This machinery can be dismantled and sold for net proceeds estimated at $1.949 million in year 7 (line 1, column 7). This amount is your forecast of the plant's *salvage value*.

	Period							
	0	1	2	3	4	5	6	7
1. Capital investment	10,000							−1,949*
2. Accumulated depreciation		1,583	3,167	4,750	6,333	7,917	9,500	0
3. Year-end book value	10,000	8,417	6,833	5,250	3,667	2,083	500	0
4. Working capital		550	1,289	3,261	4,890	3,583	2,002	0
5. Total book value (3+4)	10,000	8,967	8,122	8,511	8,557	5,666	2,502	0
6. Sales		523	12,887	32,610	48,901	35,834	19,717	
7. Cost of goods sold†		837	7,729	19,552	29,345	21,492	11,830	
8. Other costs‡	4,000	2,200	1,210	1,331	1,464	1,611	1,772	
9. Depreciation		1,583	1,583	1,583	1,583	1,583	1,583	
10. Pretax profit (6 − 7 − 8 − 9)	−4,000	−4,097	2,365	10,144	16,509	11,148	4,532	1,449§
11. Tax at 35%	−1,400	−1,434	828	3,550	5,778	3,902	1,586	507
12. Profit after tax (10 − 11)	−2,600	−2,663	1,537	6,594	10,731	7,246	2,946	942

TABLE 6.1

IM&C's guano project—projections ($ thousands) reflecting inflation.

*Salvage value.
†We have departed from the usual income-statement format by *not* including depreciation in cost of goods sold. Instead, we break out depreciation separately (see line 9).
‡Start-up costs in years 0 and 1, and general and administrative costs in years 1 to 6.
§The difference between the salvage value and the ending book value of $500 is a taxable profit.

[2]In some cases it is unclear what procedure was used. At least one expert seems to have discounted nominal cash flows at a real rate. For a review of the Bula Mines controversy see E. Dimson and P. R. Marsh, *Cases in Corporate Finance* (London: Wiley International, 1987).

[3]Sorry.

	Period							
	0	1	2	3	4	5	6	7
1. Sales		523	12,887	32,610	48,901	35,834	19,717	
2. Cost of goods sold		837	7,729	19,552	29,345	21,492	11,830	
3. Other costs	4,000	2,200	1,210	1,331	1,464	1,611	1,772	
4. Tax on operations	−1,400	−1,434	828	3,550	5,778	3,902	1,586	
5. Cash flow from operations (1 − 2 − 3 − 4)	−2,600	−1,080	3,120	8,177	12,314	8,829	4,529	
6. Change in working capital		−550	−739	−1,972	−1,629	1,307	1,581	2,002
7. Capital investment and disposal	−10,000							1,442*
8. Net cash flow (5 + 6 + 7)	−12,600	−1,630	2,381	6,205	10,685	10,136	6,110	3,444
9. Present value at 20%	−12,600	−1,358	1,654	3,591	5,153	4,074	2,046	961
Net present value = +3,519 (sum of 9)								

TABLE 6.2

IM&C's guano project—cash-flow analysis ($ thousands).

*Salvage value of $1,949 less tax of $507 on the difference between salvage value and ending book value.

Whoever prepared Table 6.1 depreciated the capital investment over six years to an arbitrary salvage value of $500,000, which is less than your forecast of salvage value. *Straight-line depreciation* was assumed. Under this method annual depreciation equals a constant proportion of the initial investment less salvage value ($9.5 million). If we call the depreciable life T, then the straight-line depreciation in year t is

$$\text{Depreciation in year } t = 1/T \times \text{depreciable amount} = 1/6 \times 9.5 = \$1.583 \text{ million}$$

Lines 6 through 12 in Table 6.1 show a simplified income statement for the guano project.[4] This will be our starting point for estimating cash flow. In preparing this table IM&C's managers recognized the effect of inflation on prices and costs. Not all cash flows are equally affected by inflation. For example, wages generally rise faster than the inflation rate. So labor costs per ton of guano will rise in real terms unless technological advances allow more efficient use of labor. On the other hand, inflation has no effect on the tax savings provided by the depreciation deduction, since the Internal Revenue Service allows you to depreciate only the original cost of the equipment, regardless of what happens to prices after the investment is made.

Table 6.2 derives cash-flow forecasts from the investment and income data given in Table 6.1. Cash flow from operations is defined as sales less cost of goods sold, other costs, and taxes. The remaining cash flows include the changes in working capital, the initial capital investment, and the recovery of your estimated salvage value. If, as you expect, the salvage value turns out higher than the depreciated value of the machinery, you will have to pay tax on the difference. So you must also include this figure in your cash-flow forecast.

[4]We have departed from the usual income-statement format by separating depreciation from costs of goods sold.

IM&C estimates the nominal opportunity cost of capital for projects of this type as 20 percent. When all cash flows are added up and discounted, the guano project is seen to offer a net present value of about $3.5 million:

$$\text{NPV} = -12{,}600 - \frac{1{,}630}{1.20} + \frac{2{,}381}{(1.20)^2} + \frac{6{,}205}{(1.20)^3} + \frac{10{,}685}{(1.20)^4} + \frac{10{,}136}{(1.20)^5} + \frac{6{,}110}{(1.20)^6} + \frac{3{,}444}{(1.20)^7} = +3{,}519, \text{ or } \$3{,}519{,}000$$

Separating Investment and Financing Decisions

Our analysis of the guano project takes no notice of how that project is financed. It may be that IM&C will decide to finance partly by debt, but if it does we will not subtract the debt proceeds from the required investment, nor will we recognize interest and principal payments as cash outflows. We analyze the project as if it were all equity-financed, treating all cash outflows as coming from stockholders and all cash inflows as going to them.

We approach the problem in this way so that we can separate the analysis of the investment decision from the financing decision. Then, when we have calculated NPV, we can undertake a separate analysis of financing. Financing decisions and their possible interactions with investment decisions are covered later in the book.

A Further Note on Estimating Cash Flow

Now here is an important point. You can see from line 6 of Table 6.2 that working capital increases in the early and middle years of the project. What is working capital? you may ask, and why does it increase?

Working capital summarizes the net investment in short-term assets associated with a firm, business, or project. Its most important components are *inventory, accounts receivable,* and *accounts payable.* The guano project's requirements for working capital in year 2 might be as follows:

$$\begin{array}{ccccccc} \text{Working capital} & = & \text{inventory} & + & \text{accounts receivable} & - & \text{accounts payable} \\ \$1{,}289 & = & 635 & + & 1{,}030 & - & 376 \end{array}$$

Why does working capital increase? There are several possibilities:

1. Sales recorded on the income statement overstate actual cash receipts from guano shipments because sales are increasing and customers are slow to pay their bills. Therefore, accounts receivable increase.
2. It takes several months for processed guano to age properly. Thus, as projected sales increase, larger inventories have to be held in the aging sheds.
3. An offsetting effect occurs if payments for materials and services used in guano production are delayed. In this case accounts payable will increase.

The additional investment in working capital from year 2 to 3 might be

$$\begin{array}{ccccccc} \begin{array}{c}\text{Additional}\\ \text{investment in}\\ \text{working capital}\end{array} & = & \begin{array}{c}\text{increase in}\\ \text{inventory}\end{array} & + & \begin{array}{c}\text{increase in}\\ \text{accounts}\\ \text{receivable}\end{array} & - & \begin{array}{c}\text{increase in}\\ \text{accounts}\\ \text{payable}\end{array} \\ \$1{,}972 & = & 972 & + & 1{,}500 & - & 500 \end{array}$$

A more detailed cash-flow forecast for year 3 would look like Table 6.3.

Cash Flows		Data from Forecasted Income Statement		Working-Capital Changes
Cash inflow	=	Sales	−	Increase in accounts receivable
\$31,110	=	32,610	−	1,500
Cash outflow	=	Cost of goods sold, other costs, and taxes	+	Increase in inventory net of increase in accounts payable
\$24,905	=	(19,552 + 1,331 + 3,550)	+	(972 − 500)
		Net cash flow = cash inflow − cash outflow		
		\$6,205 = 31,110 − 24,905		

TABLE 6.3

Details of cash-flow forecast for IM&C's guano project in year 3 (\$ thousands).

Instead of worrying about changes in working capital, you could estimate cash flow directly by counting the dollars coming in and taking away the dollars going out. In other words,

1. If you replace each year's sales with that year's cash payments received from customers, you don't have to worry about accounts receivable.
2. If you replace cost of goods sold with cash payments for labor, materials, and other costs of production, you don't have to keep track of inventory or accounts payable.

However, you would still have to construct a projected income statement to estimate taxes.

We discuss the links between cash flow and working capital in much greater detail in Chapter 30.

A Further Note on Depreciation

Depreciation is a noncash expense; it is important only because it reduces taxable income. It provides an annual *tax shield* equal to the product of depreciation and the marginal tax rate:

$$\text{Tax shield} = \text{depreciation} \times \text{tax rate}$$
$$= 1{,}583 \times .35 = 554, \text{ or } \$554{,}000$$

The present value of the tax shields (\$554,000 for six years) is \$1,842,000 at a 20 percent discount rate.[5]

Now if IM&C could just get those tax shields sooner, they would be worth more, right? Fortunately tax law allows corporations to do just that: It allows *accelerated depreciation.*

The current rules for tax depreciation in the United States were set by the Tax Reform Act of 1986, which established a modified accelerated cost recovery system

[5] By discounting the depreciation tax shields at 20 percent, we assume that they are as risky as the other cash flows. Since they depend only on tax rates, depreciation method, and IM&C's ability to generate taxable income, they are probably less risky. In some contexts (the analysis of financial leases, for example) depreciation tax shields are treated as safe, nominal cash flows and are discounted at an after-tax borrowing or lending rate. See Chapter 26.

TABLE 6.4

Tax depreciation allowed under the modified accelerated cost recovery system (MACRS) (figures in percent of depreciable investment).

Notes:

1. Tax depreciation is lower in the first year because assets are assumed to be in service for only six months.
2. Real property is depreciated straight-line over 27.5 years for residential property and 31.5 years for nonresidential property.

	Tax Depreciation Schedules by Recovery-Period Class					
Year(s)	3-Year	5-Year	7-Year	10-Year	15-Year	20-Year
1	33.33	20.00	14.29	10.00	5.00	3.75
2	44.45	32.00	24.49	18.00	9.50	7.22
3	14.81	19.20	17.49	14.40	8.55	6.68
4	7.41	11.52	12.49	11.52	7.70	6.18
5		11.52	8.93	9.22	6.93	5.71
6		5.76	8.93	7.37	6.23	5.28
7			8.93	6.55	5.90	4.89
8			4.45	6.55	5.90	4.52
9				6.55	5.90	4.46
10				6.55	5.90	4.46
11				3.29	5.90	4.46
12					5.90	4.46
13					5.90	4.46
14					5.90	4.46
15					5.90	4.46
16					2.99	4.46
17–20						4.46
21						2.25

(MACRS). Table 6.4 summarizes the tax depreciation schedules. Note that there are six schedules, one for each recovery period class. Most industrial equipment falls into the five- and seven-year classes. To keep things simple, we will assume that all the guano project's investment goes into five-year assets. Thus, IM&C can write off 20 percent of its depreciable investment in year 1, as soon as the assets are placed in service, then 32 percent of depreciable investment in year 2, and so on. Here are the tax shields for the guano project:

	Year					
	1	2	3	4	5	6
Tax depreciation (MACRS percentage × depreciable investment)	2,000	3,200	1,920	1,152	1,152	576
Tax shield (tax depreciation × tax rate, T = .35)	700	1,120	672	403	403	202

The present value of these tax shields is $2,174,000, about $331,000 higher than under the straight-line method.

Table 6.5 recalculates the guano project's impact on IM&C's future tax bills, and Table 6.6 shows revised after-tax cash flows and present value. This time we have incorporated realistic assumptions about taxes as well as inflation. We of course arrive at a higher NPV than in Table 6.2, because that table ignored the additional present value of accelerated depreciation.

There is one possible additional problem lurking in the woodwork behind Table 6.5: It is the *alternative minimum tax,* which can limit or defer the tax shields of accelerated depreciation or other *tax preference* items. Because the alternative mini-

	Period							
	0	1	2	3	4	5	6	7
1. Sales*		523	12,887	32,610	48,901	35,834	19,717	
2. Cost of goods sold*		837	7,729	19,552	29,345	21,492	11,830	
3. Other costs*	4,000	2,200	1,210	1,331	1,464	1,611	1,772	
4. Tax depreciation		2,000	3,200	1,920	1,152	1,152	576	
5. Pretax profit (1 − 2 − 3 − 4)	−4,000	−4,514	748	9,807	16,940	11,579	5,539	1,949†
6. Taxes at 35%‡	−1,400	−1,580	262	3,432	5,929	4,053	1,939	682

TABLE 6.5

Tax payments on IM&C's guano project ($ thousands).

*From Table 6.1.

†Salvage value is zero, for tax purposes, after all tax depreciation has been taken. Thus, IM&C will have to pay tax on the full salvage value of $1,949.

‡A negative tax payment means a cash *inflow*, assuming IM&C can use the tax loss on its guano project to shield income from other projects.

	Period							
	0	1	2	3	4	5	6	7
1. Sales*		523	12,887	32,610	48,901	35,834	19,717	
2. Cost of goods sold*		837	7,729	19,552	29,345	21,492	11,830	
3. Other costs*	4,000	2,200	1,210	1,331	1,464	1,611	1,772	
4. Tax†	−1,400	−1,580	262	3,432	5,929	4,053	1,939	682
5. Cash flow from operations (1 − 2 − 3 − 4)	−2,600	−934	3,686	8,295	12,163	8,678	4,176	−682
6. Change in working capital		−550	−739	−1,972	−1,629	1,307	1,581	2,002
7. Capital investment and disposal	−10,000							1,949*
8. Net cash flow (5 + 6 + 7)	−12,600	−1,484	2,947	6,323	10,534	9,985	5,757	3,269
9. Present value at 20%	−12,600	−1,237	2,047	3,659	5,080	4,013	1,928	912
Net present value = +3,802 (sum of 9)								

TABLE 6.6

IM&C's guano project—revised cash-flow analysis ($ thousands).

*From Table 6.1.

†From Table 6.5.

mum tax can be a motive for leasing, we discuss it in Chapter 26, rather than here. But make a mental note not to sign off on a capital budgeting analysis without checking whether your company is subject to the alternative minimum tax.

A Final Comment on Taxes

All large U.S. corporations keep two separate sets of books, one for stockholders and one for the Internal Revenue Service. It is common to use straight-line depreciation on the stockholder books and accelerated depreciation on the tax books. The IRS doesn't object to this, and it makes the firm's reported earnings higher than if accelerated depreciation were used everywhere. There are many other differences between tax books and shareholder books.[6]

The financial analyst must be careful to remember which set of books he or she is looking at. In capital budgeting only the tax books are relevant, but to an outside analyst only the shareholder books are available.

Project Analysis

Let's review. Several pages ago, you embarked on an analysis of IM&C's guano project. You started with a simplified statement of assets and income for the project that you used to develop a series of cash-flow forecasts. Then you remembered accelerated depreciation and had to recalculate cash flows and NPV.

You were lucky to get away with just two NPV calculations. In real situations, it often takes several tries to purge all inconsistencies and mistakes. Then there are "what if" questions. For example: What if inflation rages at 15 percent per year, rather than 10? What if technical problems delay start-up to year 2? What if gardeners prefer chemical fertilizers to your natural product?

You won't truly understand the guano project until all relevant what-if questions are answered. *Project analysis* is more than one or two NPV calculations, as we will see in Chapter 10.

Calculating NPV in Other Countries and Currencies

Before you become too deeply immersed in guano, we should take a quick look at another company that is facing a capital investment decision. This time it is the French firm, Flanel s.a., which is contemplating investment in a facility to produce a new range of fragrances. The basic principles are the same: Flanel needs to determine whether the present value of the future cash flows exceeds the initial investment. But there are a few differences that arise from the change in project location:

1. Flanel must produce a set of cash-flow forecasts like those that we developed for the guano project, but in this case the project cash flows are stated in euros, the European currency.
2. In developing these cash-flow forecasts, the company needs to recognize that prices and costs will be influenced by the French inflation rate.
3. When they calculate taxable income, French companies cannot use accelerated depreciation. (Remember that companies in the United States can use the MACRS depreciation rates which allow larger deductions in the early years of the project's life.)
4. Profits from Flanel's project are liable to the French rate of corporate tax. This is currently about 37 percent, a trifle higher than the rate in the United States.[7]
5. Just as IM&C calculated the net present value of its investment in the United States by discounting the expected *dollar* cash flows at the *dollar* cost

[6]This separation of tax accounts from shareholder accounts is not found worldwide. In Japan, for example, taxes reported to shareholders must equal taxes paid to the government; ditto for France and many other European countries.

[7]The French tax rate is made up of a basic corporate tax rate of 33.3 percent plus a surtax of 3.33 percent.

> of capital, so Flanel can evaluate an investment in France by discounting the expected *euro* cash flows at the *euro* cost of capital. To calculate the opportunity cost of capital for the fragrances project, Flanel needs to ask what return its shareholders are giving up by investing their euros in the project rather than investing them in the capital market. If the project were risk-free, the opportunity cost of investing in the project would be the interest rate on safe euro investments, for example euro bonds issued by the French government.[8] As we write this, the 10-year euro interest rate is about 4.75 percent, compared with 4.5 percent on U.S. Treasury securities. But since the project is undoubtedly not risk-free, Flanel needs to ask how much risk it is asking its shareholders to bear and what extra return they demand for taking on this risk. A similar company in the United States might come up with a different answer to this question. We will discuss risk and the cost of capital in Chapters 7 through 9.

You can see from this example that the principles of valuation of capital investments are the same worldwide. A spreadsheet table for Flanel's project could have exactly the same format as Table 6.6.[9] But inputs and assumptions have to conform to local conditions.

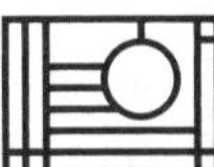

6.3 EQUIVALENT ANNUAL COSTS

When you calculate NPV, you transform future, year-by-year cash flows into a lump-sum value expressed in today's dollars (or euros, or other relevant currency). But sometimes it's helpful to reverse the calculation, transforming a lump sum of investment today into an equivalent stream of future cash flows. Consider the following example.

Investing to Produce Reformulated Gasoline at California Refineries

In the early 1990s, the California Air Resources Board (CARB) started planning its "Phase 2" requirements for reformulated gasoline (RFG). RFG is gasoline blended to tight specifications designed to reduce pollution from motor vehicles. CARB consulted with refiners, environmentalists, and other interested parties to design these specifications.

As the outline for the Phase 2 requirements emerged, refiners realized that substantial capital investments would be required to upgrade California refineries. What might these investments mean for the retail price of gasoline? A refiner might ask: "Suppose my company invests $400 million to upgrade our refinery to meet Phase 2. How many cents per gallon extra would we have to charge to recover that cost?" Let's see if we can help the refiner out.

Assume $400 million of capital investment and a real (inflation-adjusted) cost of capital of 7 percent. The new equipment lasts for 25 years, and the refinery's total

[8]It is interesting to note that, while the United States Treasury can always print the money needed to repay its debts, national governments in Europe do not have the right to print euros. Thus there is always some possibility that the French government will not be able to raise sufficient taxes to repay its bonds, though most observers would regard the probability as negligible.

[9]You can tackle Flanel's project in Practice Question 13.

production of RFG will be 900 million gallons per year. Assume for simplicity that the new equipment does not change raw-material and operating costs.

How much additional revenue would the refinery have to receive each year, for 25 years, to cover the $400 million investment? The answer is simple: Just find the 25-year annuity with a present value equal to $400 million.

$$\text{PV of annuity} = \text{annuity payment} \times \text{25-year annuity factor}$$

At a 7 percent cost of capital, the 25-year annuity factor is 11.65.

$$\$400 \text{ million} = \text{annuity payment} \times 11.65$$
$$\text{Annuity payment} = \$34.3 \text{ million per year}$$[10]

This amounts to 3.8 cents per gallon:

$$\frac{\$34.3 \text{ million}}{900 \text{ million gallons}} = \$.038 \text{ per gallon}$$

These annuities are called **equivalent annual costs.** Equivalent annual cost is the annual cash flow sufficient to recover a capital investment, including the cost of capital for that investment, over the investment's economic life.

Equivalent annual costs are handy—and sometimes essential—tools of finance. Here is a further example.

Choosing between Long- and Short-Lived Equipment

Suppose the firm is forced to choose between two machines, A and B. The two machines are designed differently but have identical capacity and do exactly the same job. Machine A costs $15,000 and will last three years. It costs $5,000 per year to run. Machine B is an economy model costing only $10,000, but it will last only two years and costs $6,000 per year to run. These are real cash flows: The costs are forecasted in dollars of constant purchasing power.

Because the two machines produce exactly the same product, the only way to choose between them is on the basis of cost. Suppose we compute the present value of cost:

	Costs ($ thousands)				
Machine	C_0	C_1	C_2	C_3	**PV at 6% ($ thousands)**
A	+15	+5	+5	+5	28.37
B	+10	+6	+6		21.00

Should we take machine B, the one with the lower present value of costs? Not necessarily, because B will have to be replaced a year earlier than A. In other

[10]For simplicity we have ignored taxes. Taxes would enter this calculation in two ways. First, the $400 million investment would generate depreciation tax shields. The easiest way to handle these tax shields is to calculate their PV and subtract it from the initial outlay. For example, if the PV of depreciation tax shields is $83 million, equivalent annual cost would be calculated on an after-tax investment base of $400 − 83 = $317 million. Second, our cents-per-gallon calculation is after-tax. To actually earn 3.8 cents after tax, the refiner would have to charge the customer more. If the tax rate is 35 percent, the required extra pretax charge is:

$$\text{Pretax charge} \times (1 - .35) = \$.038$$
$$\text{Pretax charge} = \$.0585$$

words, the timing of a future investment decision is contingent on today's choice of A or B.

So, a machine with total PV(costs) of $21,000 spread over three years (0, 1, and 2) is not necessarily better than a competing machine with PV(costs) of $28,370 spread over four years (0 through 3). We have to convert total PV(costs) to a cost per year, that is, to an equivalent annual cost. For machine A, the annual cost turns out to be 10.61, or $10,610 per year:

	Costs ($ thousands)				
Machine	C_0	C_1	C_2	C_3	**PV at 6% ($ thousands)**
Machine A	+15	+5	+5	+5	28.37
Equivalent annual cost		+10.61	+10.61	+10.61	28.37

We calculated the equivalent annual cost by finding the three-year annuity with the same present value as A's lifetime costs.

$$\text{PV of annuity} = \text{PV of A's costs} = 28.37$$
$$= \text{annuity payment} \times \text{three-year annuity factor}$$

The annuity factor is 2.673 for three years and a 6 percent real cost of capital, so

$$\text{Annuity payment} = \frac{28.37}{2.673} = 10.61$$

A similar calculation for machine B gives:

	Costs ($ thousands)			
	C_0	C_1	C_2	**PV at 6% ($ thousands)**
Machine B	+10	+6	+6	21.00
Equivalent annual cost		+11.45	+11.45	21.00

Machine A is better, because its equivalent annual cost is less ($10,610 versus $11,450 for machine B).

You can think of the equivalent annual cost of machine A or B as an annual rental charge. Suppose the financial manager is asked to *rent* machine A to the plant manager actually in charge of production. There will be three equal rental payments starting in year 1. The three payments must recover both the original cost of machine A in year 0 and the cost of running it in years 1 to 3. Therefore the financial manager has to make sure that the rental payments are worth $28,370, the total PV(costs) of machine A. You can see that the financial manager would calculate a fair rental payment equal to machine A's equivalent annual cost.

Our rule for choosing between plant and equipment with different economic lines is, therefore, to select the asset with the lowest fair rental charge, that is, the lowest equivalent annual cost.

Equivalent Annual Cost and Inflation The equivalent annual costs we just calculated are *real* annuities based on forecasted *real* costs and a 6 percent *real* discount rate. We could, of course, restate the annuities in nominal terms. Suppose the expected inflation rate is 5 percent; we multiply the first cash flow of the annuity by 1.05, the second by $(1.05)^2 = 1.105$, and so on.

		C_0	C_1	C_2	C_3
A	Real annuity		10.61	10.61	10.61
	Nominal cash flow		11.14	11.70	12.28
B	Real annuity		11.45	11.45	
	Nominal cash flow		12.02	12.62	

Note that B is still inferior to A. Of course the present values of the nominal and real cash flows are identical. Just remember to discount the real annuity at the real rate and the equivalent nominal cash flows at the consistent nominal rate.[11]

When you use equivalent annual costs simply for comparison of costs per period, as we did for machines A and B, we strongly recommend doing the calculations in real terms.[12] But if you actually rent out the machine to the plant manager, or anyone else, be careful to specify that the rental payments be "indexed" to inflation. If inflation runs on at 5 percent per year and rental payments do not increase proportionally, then the real value of the rental payments must decline and will not cover the full cost of buying and operating the machine.

Equivalent Annual Cost and Technological Change So far we have the following simple rule: Two or more streams of cash outflows with different lengths or time patterns can be compared by converting their present values to equivalent annual costs. Just remember to do the calculations in real terms.

Now any rule this simple cannot be completely general. For example, when we evaluated machine A versus machine B, we implicitly assumed that their fair rental charges would *continue* at \$10,610 versus \$11,450. This will be so only if the *real* costs of buying and operating the machines stay the same.

Suppose that this is not the case. Suppose that thanks to technological improvements new machines each year cost 20 percent less in real terms to buy and operate. In this case future owners of brand-new, lower-cost machines will be able to cut their rental cost by 20 percent, and owners of old machines will be forced to match this reduction. Thus, we now need to ask: If the real level of rents declines by 20 percent a year, how much will it cost to rent each machine?

If the rent for year 1 is rent_1, rent for year 2 is $\text{rent}_2 = .8 \times \text{rent}_1$. Rent_3 is $.8 \times \text{rent}_2$, or $.64 \times \text{rent}_1$. The owner of each machine must set the rents sufficiently high to recover the present value of the costs. In the case of machine A,

$$\text{PV of renting machine A} = \frac{\text{rent}_1}{1.06} + \frac{\text{rent}_2}{(1.06)^2} + \frac{\text{rent}_3}{(1.06)^3} = 28.37$$

$$= \frac{\text{rent}_1}{1.06} + \frac{.8(\text{rent}_1)}{(1.06)^2} + \frac{.64(\text{rent}_1)}{(1.06)^3} = 28.37$$

$$\text{rent}_1 = 12.94, \text{ or } \$12{,}940$$

[11]The nominal discount rate is

$$r_{\text{nominal}} = (1 + r_{\text{real}})(1 + \text{inflation rate}) - 1$$
$$= (1.06)(1.05) - 1 = .113, \text{ or } 11.3\%$$

Discounting the nominal annuities at this rate gives the same present values as discounting the real annuities at 6 percent.

[12]Do *not* calculate equivalent annual costs as level *nominal* annuities. This procedure can give incorrect rankings of true equivalent annual costs at high inflation rates. See Challenge Question 2 at the end of this chapter for an example.

and for machine B,

$$\frac{\text{rent}_1}{1.06} + \frac{.8(\text{rent}_1)}{(1.06)^2} = 21.00$$
$$\text{rent}_1 = 12.69, \text{ or } \$12{,}690$$

The merits of the two machines are now reversed. Once we recognize that technology is expected to reduce the real costs of new machines, then it pays to buy the shorter-lived machine B rather than become locked into an aging technology with machine A in year 3.

You can imagine other complications. Perhaps machine C will arrive in year 1 with an even lower equivalent annual cost. You would then need to consider scrapping or selling machine B at year 1 (more on this decision below). The financial manager could not choose between machines A and B in year 0 without taking a detailed look at what each machine could be replaced with.

Our point is a general one: Comparing equivalent annual costs should never be a mechanical exercise; always think about the assumptions that are implicit in the comparison. Finally, remember why equivalent annual costs are necessary in the first place. The reason is that A and B will be replaced at different future dates. The choice between them therefore affects future investment decisions. If subsequent decisions are not affected by the initial choice (for example, because neither machine will be replaced) then we do *not need to take future decisions into account.*[13]

Equivalent Annual Cost and Taxes We have not mentioned taxes. But you surely realized that machine A and B's lifetime costs should be calculated after-tax, recognizing that operating costs are tax-deductible and that capital investment generates depreciation tax shields.

Deciding When to Replace an Existing Machine

The previous example took the life of each machine as fixed. In practice the point at which equipment is replaced reflects economic considerations rather than total physical collapse. *We* must decide when to replace. The machine will rarely decide for us.

Here is a common problem. You are operating an elderly machine that is expected to produce a net cash *inflow* of $4,000 in the coming year and $4,000 next year. After that it will give up the ghost. You can replace it now with a new machine, which costs $15,000 but is much more efficient and will provide a cash inflow of $8,000 a year for three years. You want to know whether you should replace your equipment now or wait a year.

We can calculate the NPV of the new machine and also its *equivalent annual cash flow*, that is, the three-year annuity that has the same net present value:

	Cash Flows ($ thousands)				
	C_0	C_1	C_2	C_3	NPV at 6% ($ thousands)
New machine	−15	+8	+8	+8	6.38
Equivalent annual cash flow		+2.387	+2.387	+2.387	6.38

[13]However, if neither machine will be replaced, then we have to consider the extra revenue generated by machine A in its third year, when it will be operating but B will not.

In other words, the cash flows of the new machine are equivalent to an annuity of \$2,387 per year. So we can equally well ask at what point we would want to replace our old machine with a new one producing \$2,387 a year. When the question is put this way, the answer is obvious. As long as your old machine can generate a cash flow of \$4,000 a year, who wants to put in its place a new one that generates only \$2,387 a year?

It is a simple matter to incorporate salvage values into this calculation. Suppose that the current salvage value is \$8,000 and next year's value is \$7,000. Let's see where you come out next year if you wait and then sell. On one hand, you gain \$7,000, but you lose today's salvage value *plus* a year's return on that money. That is, $8{,}000 \times 1.06 = \$8{,}480$. Your net loss is $8{,}480 - 7{,}000 = \$1{,}480$, which only partly offsets the operating gain. You should not replace yet.

Remember that the logic of such comparisons requires that the new machine be the best of the available alternatives and that it in turn be replaced at the optimal point.

Cost of Excess Capacity

Any firm with a centralized information system (computer servers, storage, software, and telecommunication links) encounters many proposals for using it. Recently installed systems tend to have excess capacity, and since the immediate marginal costs of using them seem to be negligible, management often encourages new uses. Sooner or later, however, the load on a system increases to the point at which management must either terminate the uses it originally encouraged or invest in another system several years earlier than it had planned. Such problems can be avoided if a proper charge is made for the use of spare capacity.

Suppose we have a new investment project that requires heavy use of an existing information system. The effect of adopting the project is to bring the purchase date of a new, more capable system forward from year 4 to year 3. This new system has a life of five years, and at a discount rate of 6 percent the present value of the cost of buying and operating it is \$500,000.

We begin by converting the \$500,000 present value of cost of the new system to an equivalent annual cost of \$118,700 for each of five years.[14] Of course, when the new system in turn wears out, we will replace it with another. So we face the prospect of future information-system expenses of \$118,700 a year. If we undertake the new project, the series of expenses begins in year 4; if we do not undertake it, the series begins in year 5. The new project, therefore, results in an *additional* cost of \$118,700 in year 4. This has a present value of $118{,}700/(1.06)^4$, or about \$94,000. This cost is properly charged against the new project. When we recognize it, the NPV of the project may prove to be negative. If so, we still need to check whether it is worthwhile undertaking the project now and abandoning it later, when the excess capacity of the present system disappears.

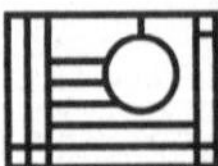

6.4 PROJECT INTERACTIONS

Almost all decisions about capital expenditure involve either–or choices. The firm can build either a 90,000-square-foot warehouse in northern South Dakota or a 100,000-square-foot warehouse in southern North Dakota. It can heat it either by

[14]The present value of \$118,700 for five years discounted at 6 percent is \$500,000.

oil or natural gas, and so on. These mutually exclusive options are simple examples of *project interactions.*

All of the examples in the last section involved project interactions. Think back to the first example, the choice between machine A, with a three-year life, and machine B, with a two-year life. A and B interact because they are mutually exclusive, and also because the choice of A or B ripples forward to affect future machine purchases.

Project interactions can arise in countless ways. The literature of operations research and industrial engineering sometimes addresses cases of extreme complexity and difficulty. We will be content with two more simple but important examples.

Case 1: Optimal Timing of Investment

The fact that a project has a positive NPV does not mean that it is best undertaken now. It might be even more valuable if undertaken in the future. Similarly, a project with a currently negative NPV might become a valuable opportunity if we wait a bit. Thus *any* project has two mutually exclusive alternatives: Do it now, or wait and invest later.

The question of optimal timing of investment is not difficult under conditions of certainty. We first examine alternative dates (t) for making the investment and calculate its net *future* value as of each date. Then, in order to find which of the alternatives would add most to the firm's *current* value, we must work out

$$\frac{\text{Net future value as of date } t}{(1 + r)^t}$$

For example, suppose you own a large tract of inaccessible timber. In order to harvest it, you have to invest a substantial amount in access roads and other facilities. The longer you wait, the higher the investment required. On the other hand, lumber prices will rise as you wait, and the trees will keep growing, although at a gradually decreasing rate.

Let us suppose that the net present value of the harvest at different *future* dates is as follows:

	Year of Harvest					
	0	**1**	**2**	**3**	**4**	**5**
Net *future* value ($ thousands)	50	64.4	77.5	89.4	100	109.4
Change in value from previous year (%)		+28.8	+20.3	+15.4	+11.9	+9.4

As you can see, the longer you defer cutting the timber, the more money you will make. However, your concern is with the date that maximizes the net *present* value of your investment, that is, its contribution to the value of your firm *today.* You therefore need to discount the net future value of the harvest back to the present. Suppose the appropriate discount rate is 10 percent. Then if you harvest the timber in year 1, it has a net *present* value of $58,500:

$$\text{NPV if harvested in year 1} = \frac{64.4}{1.10} = 58.5, \text{ or } \$58{,}500$$

The net present value (at $t = 0$) for other harvest dates is as follows:

	Year of Harvest					
	0	1	2	3	4	5
Net present value ($ thousands)	50	58.5	64.0	67.2	68.3	67.9

The optimal point to harvest the timber is year 4 because this is the point that maximizes NPV.

Notice that before year 4 the net future value of the timber increases by more than 10 percent a year: The gain in value is greater than the cost of the capital that is tied up in the project. After year 4 the gain in value is still positive but less than the cost of capital. You maximize the net present value of your investment if you harvest your timber as soon as the rate of increase in value drops below the cost of capital.[15]

The problem of optimal timing of investment under uncertainty is, of course, much more complicated. An opportunity not taken at $t = 0$ might be either more or less attractive at $t = 1$; there is rarely any way of knowing for sure. Perhaps it is better to strike while the iron is hot even if there is a chance it will become hotter. On the other hand, if you wait a bit you might obtain more information and avoid a bad mistake.[16]

Case 2: Fluctuating Load Factors

Although a $10 million warehouse may have a positive net present value, it should be built only if it has a higher NPV than a $9 million alternative. In other words, the NPV of the $1 million *marginal* investment required to buy the more expensive warehouse must be positive.

One case in which this is easily forgotten is when equipment is needed to meet fluctuating demand. Consider the following problem: A widget manufacturer operates two machines, each of which has a capacity of 1,000 units a year. They have an indefinite life and no salvage value, and so the only costs are the operating expenses of $2 per widget. Widget manufacture, as everyone knows, is a seasonal business, and widgets are perishable. During the fall and winter, when demand is high, each machine produces at capacity. During the spring and summer, each machine works at 50 percent of capacity. If the discount rate is 10 percent and the machines are kept indefinitely, the present value of the costs is $30,000:

---

[15]Our timber-cutting example conveys the right idea about investment timing, but it misses an important practical point: The sooner you cut the first crop of trees, the sooner the second crop can start growing. Thus, the value of the second crop depends on when you cut the first. This more complex and realistic problem might be solved in one of two ways:

1. Find the cutting dates that maximize the present value of a series of harvests, taking account of the different growth rates of young and old trees.
2. Repeat our calculations, counting the future market value of cut-over land as part of the payoff to the first harvest. The value of cut-over land includes the present value of all subsequent harvests.

The second solution is far simpler if you can figure out what cut-over land will be worth.

[16]We return to optimal investment timing under uncertainty in Chapters 10 and 22.

	Two Old Machines
Annual output per machine	750 units
Operating cost per machine	2 × 750 = $1,500
PV operating cost per machine	1,500/.10 = $15,000
PV operating cost of two machines	2 × 15,000 = $30,000

The company is considering whether to replace these machines with newer equipment. The new machines have a similar capacity, and so two would still be needed to meet peak demand. Each new machine costs $6,000 and lasts indefinitely. Operating expenses are only $1 per unit. On this basis the company calculates that the present value of the costs of two new machines would be $27,000:

	Two New Machines
Annual output per machine	750 units
Capital cost per machine	$6,000
Operating cost per machine	1 × 750 = $750
PV total cost per machine	6,000 + 750/.10 = $13,500
PV total cost of two machines	2 × 13,500 = $27,000

Therefore, it scraps both old machines and buys two new ones.

The company was quite right in thinking that two new machines are better than two old ones, but unfortunately it forgot to investigate a third alternative: to replace just one of the old machines. Since the new machine has low operating costs, it would pay to operate it at capacity all year. The remaining old machine could then be kept simply to meet peak demand. The present value of the costs under this strategy is $26,000:

	One Old Machine	One New Machine
Annual output per machine	500 units	1,000 units
Capital cost per machine	0	$6,000
Operating cost per machine	2 × 500 = $1,000	1 × 1,000 = $1,000
PV total cost per machine	1,000/.10 = $10,000	6,000 + 1,000/.10 = $16,000
PV total cost of both machines	$26,000	

Replacing one machine saves $4,000; replacing two machines saves only $3,000. The net present value of the *marginal* investment in the second machine is −$1,000.

SUMMARY

By now present value calculations should be a matter of routine. However, forecasting cash flows will never be routine. It will always be a skilled, hazardous occupation. Mistakes can be minimized by following three rules:

1. Concentrate on cash flows after taxes. Be wary of accounting data masquerading as cash-flow data.
2. Always judge investments on an incremental basis. Tirelessly track down all cash-flow consequences of your decision.
3. Treat inflation consistently. Discount nominal cash-flow forecasts at nominal rates and real forecasts at real rates.

We worked through a detailed numerical example (IM&C's guano project), showing the basic steps in calculating project NPV. Remember to track changes in working capital, and stay alert for differences between tax depreciation and the depreciation used in reports to shareholders.

The principles of valuing capital investment projects are the same worldwide, but inputs and assumptions vary by country and currency. For example, cash flows from a project undertaken in France would be in euros, not dollars, and would be forecasted after French taxes.

We might add still another rule: Recognize project interactions. Decisions involving only a choice of accepting or rejecting a project rarely exist, since capital projects can rarely be isolated from other projects or alternatives. The simplest decision normally encountered is to accept or reject or delay. A project having a positive NPV if undertaken today may have a still higher NPV if undertaken tomorrow.

Projects also interact because they are mutually exclusive. You can install machine A or B, for example, but not both. When mutually exclusive choices involve different lengths or time patterns of cash outflows, comparison is difficult unless you convert present values to equivalent annual costs. Think of the equivalent annual cost as the period-by-period rental payment necessary to cover all the cash outflows. Choose A over B, other things equal, if A has the lower equivalent annual cost. Remember, though, to calculate equivalent annual costs in real terms and adjust for technological change if necessary.

This chapter is concerned with the mechanics of applying the net present value rule in practical situations. All our analysis boils down to two simple themes. First, be careful about the definition of alternative projects. Make sure you are comparing like with like. Second, make sure that your calculations include all incremental cash flows.

FURTHER READING

There are several good general texts on capital budgeting that cover project interactions. Two examples are:

E. L. Grant, W. G. Ireson, and R. S. Leavenworth: *Principles of Engineering Economy,* 8th ed., John Wiley & Sons, New York, 1990.

H. Bierman and S. Smidt: *The Capital Budgeting Decision,* 8th ed., Prentice-Hall, Inc., Englewood Cliffs, N.J., 1992.

Reinhardt provides an interesting case study of a capital investment decision in:

U. E. Reinhardt: "Break-Even Analysis for Lockheed's TriStar: An Application of Financial Theory," *Journal of Finance,* 32:821–838 (September 1973).

QUIZ

1. Which of the following should be treated as incremental cash flows when deciding whether to invest in a new manufacturing plant? The site is already owned by the company, but existing buildings would need to be demolished.

- **a.** The market value of the site and existing buildings.
- **b.** Demolition costs and site clearance.
- **c.** The cost of a new access road put in last year.
- **d.** Lost earnings on other products due to executive time spent on the new facility.
- **e.** A proportion of the cost of leasing the president's jet airplane.
- **f.** Future depreciation of the new plant.
- **g.** The reduction in the corporation's tax bill resulting from tax depreciation of the new plant.

h. The initial investment in inventories of raw materials.
i. Money already spent on engineering design of the new plant.

2. M. Loup Garou will be paid 100,000 euros one year hence. This is a nominal flow, which he discounts at an 8 percent nominal discount rate:

$$PV = \frac{100{,}000}{1.08} = €92{,}593$$

The inflation rate is 4 percent.

Calculate the PV of M. Garou's payment using the equivalent *real* cash flow and *real* discount rate. (You should get exactly the same answer as he did.)

3. True or false?
a. A project's depreciation tax shields depend on the actual future rate of inflation.
b. Project cash flows should take account of interest paid on any borrowing undertaken to finance the project.
c. In the U.S., income reported to the tax authorities must equal income reported to shareholders.
d. Accelerated depreciation reduces near-term project cash flows and therefore reduces project NPV.

4. How does the PV of depreciation tax shields vary across the recovery-period classes shown in Table 6.4? Give a general answer; then check it by calculating the PVs of depreciation tax shields in the five-year and seven-year classes. The tax rate is 35 percent. Use any reasonable discount rate.

5. The following table tracks the main components of working capital over the life of a four-year project.

	2000	2001	2002	2003	2004
Accounts receivable	0	150,000	225,000	190,000	0
Inventory	75,000	130,000	130,000	95,000	0
Accounts payable	25,000	50,000	50,000	35,000	0

Calculate net working capital and the cash inflows and outflows due to investment in working capital.

6. Suppose the guano project were undertaken in France by a French company. What inputs and assumptions would have to change? Make a checklist.

7. When appraising mutually exclusive investments in plant and equipment, many companies calculate the investments' equivalent annual costs and rank the investments on this basis. Why is this necessary? Why not just compare the investments' NPVs? Explain briefly.

8. Think back to the timber-cutting example in Section 6.4. State the rule for deciding *when* to undertake a project.

9. Air conditioning for a college dormitory will cost $1.5 million to install and $200,000 per year to operate. The system should last 25 years. The real cost of capital is 5 percent, and the college pays no taxes. What is the equivalent annual cost?

10. Machines A and B are mutually exclusive and are expected to produce the following cash flows:

	Cash Flows ($ thousands)			
Machine	C_0	C_1	C_2	C_3
A	−100	+110	+121	
B	−120	+110	+121	+133

The real opportunity cost of capital is 10 percent.

a. Calculate the NPV of each machine.
b. Calculate the equivalent annual cash flow from each machine.
c. Which machine should you buy?

11. Machine C was purchased five years ago for $200,000 and produces an annual cash flow of $80,000. It has no salvage value but is expected to last another five years. The company can replace machine C with machine B (see question 10 above) *either* now *or* at the end of five years. Which should it do?

PRACTICE QUESTIONS

1. Restate the net cash flows in Table 6.6 in real terms. Discount the restated cash flows at a real discount rate. Assume a 20 percent *nominal* rate and 10 percent expected inflation. NPV should be unchanged at +3,802, or $3,802,000.

2. In 1898 Simon North announced plans to construct a funeral home on land he owned and rented out as a storage area for railway carts. (A local newspaper commended Mr. North for not putting the cart before the hearse.) Rental income from the site barely covered real estate taxes, but the site was valued at $45,000. However, Mr. North had refused several offers for the land and planned to continue renting it out if for some reason the funeral home was not built. Therefore he did not include the value of the land as an outlay in his NPV analysis of the funeral home. Was this the correct procedure? Explain.

3. Discuss the following statement: "We don't want individual plant managers to get involved in the firm's tax position. So instead of telling them to discount after-tax cash flows at 10 percent, we just tell them to take the pretax cash flows and discount at 15 percent. With a 35 percent tax rate, 15 percent pretax generates approximately 10 percent after tax."

4. Consider the following statement: "We like to do all our capital budgeting calculations in real terms. It saves making any forecasts of the inflation rate." Discuss briefly.

5. Each of the following statements is true. Explain why they are consistent.
   a. When a company introduces a new product, or expands production of an existing product, investment in net working capital is usually an important cash outflow.
   b. Forecasting changes in net working capital is not necessary if the timing of *all* cash inflows and outflows is carefully specified.

6. Mrs. T. Potts, the treasurer of Ideal China, has a problem. The company has just ordered a new kiln for $400,000. Of this sum, $50,000 is described by the supplier as an installation cost. Mrs. Potts does not know whether the Internal Revenue Service (IRS) will permit the company to treat this cost as a tax-deductible current expense or as a capital investment. In the latter case, the company could depreciate the $50,000 using the five-year MACRS tax depreciation schedule. How will the IRS's decision affect the after-tax cost of the kiln? The tax rate is 35 percent and the opportunity cost of capital is 5 percent.

7. A project requires an initial investment of $100,000 and is expected to produce a cash inflow before tax of $26,000 per year for five years. Company A has substantial accumulated tax losses and is unlikely to pay taxes in the foreseeable future. Company B pays corporate taxes at a rate of 35 percent and can depreciate the investment for tax purposes using the five-year MACRS tax depreciation schedule.

   Suppose the opportunity cost of capital is 8 percent. Ignore inflation.
   a. Calculate project NPV for each company.
   b. What is the IRR of the after-tax cash flows for each company? What does comparison of the IRRs suggest is the effective corporate tax rate?

8. A widget manufacturer currently produces 200,000 units a year. It buys widget lids from an outside supplier at a price of $2 a lid. The plant manager believes that it

	2003	2004	2005	2006–2013
1. Capital expenditure	−10,400			
2. Research and development	−2,000			
3. Working capital	−4,000			
4. Revenue		8,000	16,000	40,000
5. Operating costs		−4,000	−8,000	−20,000
6. Overhead		−800	−1,600	−4,000
7. Depreciation		−1,040	−1,040	−1,040
8. Interest		−2,160	−2,160	−2,160
9. Income	−2,000	0	3,200	12,800
10. Tax	0	0	420	4,480
11. Net cash flow	−16,400	0	2,780	8,320
12. Net present value = +13,932				

TABLE 6.7

Cash flows and present value of Reliable Electric's proposed investment ($ thousands). See Practice Question 9.

Notes:

1. *Capital expenditure:* $8 million for new machinery and $2.4 million for a warehouse extension. The full cost of the extension has been charged to this project, although only about half of the space is currently needed. Since the new machinery will be housed in an existing factory building, no charge has been made for land and building.
2. *Research and development:* $1.82 million spent in 2002. This figure was corrected for 10 percent inflation from the time of expenditure to date. Thus 1.82 × 1.1 = $2 million.
3. *Working capital:* Initial investment in inventories.
4. *Revenue:* These figures assume sales of 2,000 motors in 2004, 4,000 in 2005, and 10,000 per year from 2006 through 2013. The initial unit price of $4,000 is forecasted to remain constant in real terms.
5. *Operating costs:* These include all direct and indirect costs. Indirect costs (heat, light, power, fringe benefits, etc.) are assumed to be 200 percent of direct labor costs. Operating costs per unit are forecasted to remain constant in real terms at $2,000.
6. *Overhead:* Marketing and administrative costs, assumed equal to 10 percent of revenue.
7. *Depreciation:* Straight-line for 10 years.
8. *Interest:* Charged on capital expenditure and working capital at Reliable's current borrowing rate of 15 percent.
9. *Income:* Revenue less the sum of research and development, operating costs, overhead, depreciation, and interest.
10. *Tax:* 35 percent of income. However, income is negative in 2003. This loss is carried forward and deducted from taxable income in 2005.
11. *Net cash flow:* Assumed equal to income less tax.
12. *Net present value:* NPV of net cash flow at a 15 percent discount rate.

would be cheaper to make these lids rather than buy them. Direct production costs are estimated to be only $1.50 a lid. The necessary machinery would cost $150,000. This investment could be written off for tax purposes using the seven-year tax depreciation schedule. The plant manager estimates that the operation would require additional working capital of $30,000 but argues that this sum can be ignored since it is recoverable at the end of the 10 years. If the company pays tax at a rate of 35 percent and the opportunity cost of capital is 15 percent, would you support the plant manager's proposal? State clearly any additional assumptions that you need to make.

9. Reliable Electric is considering a proposal to manufacture a new type of industrial electric motor which would replace most of its existing product line. A research breakthrough has given Reliable a two-year lead on its competitors. The project proposal is summarized in Table 6.7.
   a. Read the notes to the table carefully. Which entries make sense? Which do not? Why or why not?
   b. What additional information would you need to construct a version of Table 6.7 that makes sense?
   c. Construct such a table and recalculate NPV. Make additional assumptions as necessary.

10. Marsha Jones, whom you met in the Chapter 3 Mini-case, has bought a used Mercedes horse transporter for her Connecticut estate. It cost $35,000. The object is to save on horse transporter rentals.

Marsha had been renting a transporter every other week for $200 per day plus $1.00 per mile. Most of the trips are 40 or 50 miles one-way. Marsha usually gives the driver a $40 tip. With the new transporter she will only have to pay for diesel fuel and maintenance, at about $.45 per mile. Insurance costs for Marsha's transporter are $1,200 per year.

The transporter will probably be worth $15,000 (in real terms) after eight years, when Marsha's horse Nike will be ready to retire.

Is the transporter a positive-NPV investment? Assume a nominal discount rate of 9 percent and a 3 percent forecasted inflation rate. Marsha's transporter is a personal outlay, not a business or financial investment, so taxes can be ignored.

11. United Pigpen is considering a proposal to manufacture high-protein hog feed. The project would make use of an existing warehouse, which is currently rented out to a neighboring firm. The next year's rental charge on the warehouse is $100,000, and thereafter the rent is expected to grow in line with inflation at 4 percent a year. In addition to using the warehouse, the proposal envisages an investment in plant and equipment of $1.2 million. This could be depreciated for tax purposes straight-line over 10 years. However, Pigpen expects to terminate the project at the end of eight years and to resell the plant and equipment in year 8 for $400,000. Finally, the project requires an initial investment in working capital of $350,000. Thereafter, working capital is forecasted to be 10 percent of sales in each of years 1 through 7.

Year 1 sales of hog feed are expected to be $4.2 million, and thereafter sales are forecast to grow by 5 percent a year, slightly faster than the inflation rate. Manufacturing costs are expected to be 90 percent of sales, and profits are subject to tax at 35 percent. The cost of capital is 12 percent.

What is the NPV of Pigpen's project?

12. In the International Mulch and Compost example (Section 6.2), we assumed that losses on the project could be used to offset taxable profits elswhere in the corporation. Suppose that the losses had to be carried forward and offset against future taxable profits from the project. How would the project NPV change? What is the value of the company's ability to use the tax deductions immediately?

13. Table 6.8 shows investment and projected income in euros for Flanel's new perfume factory. Forecast cash flows and calculate NPV. The nominal cost of capital in euros is 11 percent.

14. As a result of improvements in product engineering, United Automation is able to sell one of its two milling machines. Both machines perform the same function but differ in age. The newer machine could be sold today for $50,000. Its operating costs are $20,000 a year, but in five years the machine will require a $20,000 overhaul. Thereafter operating costs will be $30,000 until the machine is finally sold in year 10 for $5,000.

The older machine could be sold today for $25,000. If it is kept, it will need an immediate $20,000 overhaul. Thereafter operating costs will be $30,000 a year until the machine is finally sold in year 5 for $5,000.

Both machines are fully depreciated for tax purposes. The company pays tax at 35 percent. Cash flows have been forecasted in real terms. The real cost of capital is 12 percent.

Which machine should United Automation sell? Explain the assumptions underlying your answer.

15. Hayden Inc. has a number of copiers that were bought four years ago for $20,000. Currently maintenance costs $2,000 a year, but the maintenance agreement expires at the end of two years and thereafter the annual maintenance charge will rise to $8,000. The machines have a current resale value of $8,000, but at the end of year 2 their value will have fallen to $3,500. By the end of year 6 the machines will be valueless and would be scrapped.

	0	1	2	3	4	5	6	7	8
1. Capital investment	83.5								−12.0
2. Accumulated depreciation		11.9	23.9	35.8	47.7	59.6	71.6	83.5	
3. Year-end book value		71.6	59.6	47.7	35.8	23.9	11.9	0.0	
4. Working capital	2.3	4.4	7.6	6.9	5.3	3.2	2.5	0.0	
5. Total book value (3 + 4)	85.8	76.0	67.2	54.6	41.1	27.1	14.4	0.0	
6. Sales		27.0	51.3	89.1	81.0	62.1	37.8	29.7	
7. Cost of goods sold		9.2	17.4	30.3	27.5	21.1	12.9	10.1	
8. Other costs		15.5	15.5	5.2	5.2	5.2	5.2	5.2	
9. Depreciation		11.9	11.9	11.9	11.9	11.9	11.9	11.9	
10. Pretax profit (6 − 7 − 8 − 9)		−9.6	6.4	41.7	36.3	23.9	7.8	2.5	
11. Tax at 40%		−3.8	2.6	16.7	14.5	9.5	3.1	1.0	4.8
12. Profit after tax (10 – 11)		−5.8	3.9	25.0	21.8	14.3	4.7	1.5	7.2

TABLE 6.8

Projected investment and income for Flanel's new perfume factory. Figures in millions of euros.

Note: The format of this table matches Table 6.1. Cost of goods sold excludes depreciation.

Hayden is considering replacing the copiers with new machines that would do essentially the same job. These machines cost $25,000, and the company can take out an eight-year maintenance contract for $1,000 a year. The machines have no value by the end of the eight years and would be scrapped.

Both machines are depreciated by using seven-year MACRS, and the tax rate is 35 percent. Assume for simplicity that the inflation rate is zero. The real cost of capital is 7 percent.

When should Hayden replace its copiers?

16. Return to the start of Section 6.3, where we calculated the equivalent annual cost, in cents per gallon, of producing reformulated gasoline in California. Capital investment was $400 million. Suppose this amount can be depreciated for tax purposes on the 10-year MACRS schedule from Table 6.4. The marginal tax rate, including California taxes, is 39 percent, and the cost of capital is 7 percent. The refinery improvements have an economic life of 25 years.

a. Calculate the after-tax equivalent annual cost. *Hint:* It's easiest to use the PV of depreciation tax shields as an offset to the initial investment.

b. How much extra would retail gasoline customers have to pay to cover this equivalent annual cost? *Note:* Extra income from higher retail prices would be taxed.

17. You own 500 acres of timberland, with young timber worth $40,000 if logged now. This represents 1,000 cords of wood worth $40 per cord net of costs of cutting and hauling. A paper company has offered to purchase your tract for $140,000. Should you accept the offer? You have the following information:

Years	Yearly Growth Rate of Cords per Acre
1–4	16%
5–8	11
9–13	4
14 and subsequent years	1

- You expect price per cord to increase at 4 percent per year indefinitely.
- The cost of capital is 9 percent. Ignore taxes.

- The market value of your land would be $100 per acre if you cut and removed the timber this year. The value of cut-over land is also expected to grow at 4 percent per year indefinitely.

18. The Borstal Company has to choose between two machines that do the same job but have different lives. The two machines have the following costs:

Year	Machine A	Machine B
0	$40,000	$50,000
1	10,000	8,000
2	10,000	8,000
3	10,000 + replace	8,000
4		8,000 + replace

These costs are expressed in real terms.

a. Suppose you are Borstal's financial manager. If you had to buy one or the other machine and rent it to the production manager for that machine's economic life, what annual rental payment would you have to charge? Assume a 6 percent real discount rate and ignore taxes.

b. Which machine should Borstal buy?

c. Usually the rental payments you derived in part (a) are just hypothetical—a way of calculating and interpreting equivalent annual cost. Suppose you actually do buy one of the machines and rent it to the production manager. How much would you actually have to charge in each future year if there is steady 8 percent per year inflation? (*Note:* The rental payments calculated in part (a) are real cash flows. You would have to mark up those payments to cover inflation.)

19. Look again at your calculations for question 18 above. Suppose that technological change is expected to reduce costs by 10 percent per year. There will be new machines in year 1 that cost 10 percent less to buy and operate than A and B. In year 2 there will be a second crop of new machines incorporating a further 10 percent reduction, and so on. How does this change the equivalent annual costs of machines A and B?

20. The president's executive jet is not fully utilized. You judge that its use by other officers would increase direct operating costs by only $20,000 a year and would save $100,000 a year in airline bills. On the other hand, you believe that with the increased use the company will need to replace the jet at the end of three years rather than four. A new jet costs $1.1 million and (at its current low rate of use) has a life of six years. Assume that the company does not pay taxes. All cash flows are forecasted in real terms. The real opportunity cost of capital is 8 percent. Should you try to persuade the president to allow other officers to use the plane?

CHALLENGE QUESTIONS

1. One measure of the effective tax rate is the difference between the IRRs of pretax and after-tax cash flows, divided by the pretax IRR. Consider, for example, an investment I generating a perpetual stream of pretax cash flows C. The pretax IRR is C/I, and the after-tax IRR is $C(1 - T_c)/I$, where T_c is the statutory tax rate. The effective rate, call it T_E, is

$$T_E = \frac{C/I - C(1 - T_c)/I}{C/I} = T_c$$

In this case the effective rate equals the statutory rate.

a. Calculate T_E for the guano project in Section 6.2.

b. How does the effective rate depend on the tax depreciation schedule? On the inflation rate?

c. Consider a project where all of the up-front investment is treated as an expense for tax purposes. For example, R&D and marketing outlays are always expensed in the U.S. They create no tax depreciation. What is the effective tax rate for such a project?

2. We warned that equivalent annual costs should be calculated in real terms. We did not fully explain why. This problem will show you.

Look back to the cash flows for machines A and B (in "Choosing between Long- and Short-Lived Equipment"). The present values of purchase and operating costs are 28.37 (over three years for A) and 21.00 (over two years for B). The real discount rate is 6 percent, and the inflation rate is 5 percent.

a. Calculate the three- and two-year *level nominal* annuities which have present values of 28.37 and 21.00. Explain why these annuities are *not* realistic estimates of equivalent annual costs. (*Hint:* In real life machinery rentals increase with inflation.)

b. Suppose the inflation rate increases to 25 percent. The real interest rate stays at 6 percent. Recalculate the level nominal annuities. Note that the *ranking* of machines A and B appears to change. Why?

3. Suppose that *after-tax* investment is defined as the investment outlay minus the present value of future depreciation tax shields. In the guano project, for example, after-tax investment would be $10,000,000 – 2,174,000 = $7,826,000. This figure would be entered as the investment outlay, then future cash flows would be calculated ignoring depreciation.

a. Does this change in format affect bottom-line NPV? Does the format have any advantages or disadvantages?

b. This format requires discounting depreciation tax shields separately. What should the discount rate be? Note that depreciation tax shields are safe if the company will be consistently profitable.

c. If depreciation tax shields are not discounted at the ordinary cost of capital, should the discount rate for the other cash flows change? Why or why not?

MINI-CASE

New Economy Transport

The New Economy Transport Company (NETCO) was formed in 1952 to carry cargo and passengers between ports in the Pacific Northwest. By 2002 its fleet had grown to four vessels, one of which was a small dry-cargo vessel, the *Vital Spark*.

The *Vital Spark* is badly in need of an overhaul. Peter Handy, the finance director, has just been presented with a proposal, which would require the following expenditures:

Install new engine and associated equipment	$185,000
Replace radar and other electronic equipment	50,000
Repairs to hull and superstructure	130,000
Painting and other maintenance	35,000
	$400,000

NETCO's chief engineer, McPhail, estimates the postoverhaul operating costs as follows:[17]

Fuel	$ 450,000
Labor and benefits	480,000
Maintenance	141,000
Other	110,000
	$1,181,000

[17]All estimates of costs and revenues ignore inflation. Mr. Handy's bankers have suggested that inflation will average 3 percent a year.

The *Vital Spark* is carried on NETCO's books at a net value of only $30,000, but could probably be sold "as is," along with an extensive inventory of spare parts, for $100,000. The book value of the spare parts inventory is $40,000.

The chief engineer has also suggested installation of a more modern navigation and control system, which would cost an extra $200,000.[18] This additional equipment would not substantially affect the *Vital Spark's* performance, but it would result in the following reduced annual fuel, labor, and maintenance costs:

Fuel	$420,000
Labor and benefits	405,000
Maintenance	70,000
Other	90,000
	$985,000

There is no question that the *Vital Spark* needs a new engine and general overhaul soon. However, Mr. Handy feels it unwise to proceed without also considering the purchase of a new boat. Cohn and Doyle, Inc., a Wisconsin shipyard, has approached NETCO with a new design incorporating a Kort nozzle, extensively automated navigation and power control systems, and much more comfortable accommodations for the crew. Estimated annual operating costs of the new boat are

Fuel	$370,000
Labor and benefits	330,000
Maintenance	70,000
Other	74,000
	$844,000

The crew would require additional training to handle the new boat's more complex and sophisticated equipment and this would probably require an expenditure of $50,000 to $100,000.

The estimated operating costs for the new boat assume that it would be operated in the same way as the *Vital Spark*. However, the new boat should be able to handle a larger load on some routes, and this might generate additional revenues, net of additional out-of-pocket costs, of as much as $100,000 per year. Moreover, a new boat would have a useful service life of 20 years or more. The *Vital Spark*, even if rehabilitated, could not last that long—probably only 15 years. At that point it would be worth only its scrap value of about $40,000.

Cohn and Doyle offered the new boat for a fixed price of $2,000,000, payable half immediately and half on delivery in nine months. Of this amount $600,000 was for the engine and associated equipment and $510,000 was for navigation, control, and other electronic equipment.

NETCO was a private company, soundly financed and consistently profitable. Cash on hand was sufficient to rehabilitate or improve the *Vital Spark* but not to buy the new boat. However, Mr. Handy was confident that the new boat could be financed with medium-term debt, privately placed with an insurance company. NETCO had borrowed via a private placement once before when it negotiated a fixed rate of 12.5 percent on a seven-year loan. Preliminary discussions with NETCO's bankers led Mr. Handy to believe that the firm could arrange an 8 percent fixed-rate medium-term loan.

NETCO had traditionally estimated its opportunity cost of capital for major business investments by adding a risk premium of 10 percentage points to yields on newly issued

[18]All investments qualify for the seven-year MACRS class.

Treasury bonds.[19] Mr. Handy thought this was a reasonable rule of thumb for the dry-cargo business.

Questions

1. Calculate equivalent annual costs of the three alternatives—overhaul, overhaul with improved navigation and control, or a brand-new boat. To do the calculation, you will have to prepare a spreadsheet table showing all costs after taxes over each investment's economic life. Take special care with your assumptions about depreciation tax shields and inflation.

[19]In 2002 Treasury bonds were yielding 5 percent.

PART 1 RELATED WEBSITES

Chapter 1 described the role of the financial manager. More information on careers in finance can be found at:

www.careers-in-finance.com

The following websites, which are concerned largely with personal finance, provide discussions of the time value of money and calculators:

www.bankrate.com

www.financenter.com

www.financialplayerscenter.com

www.invest-faq.com

www.money.cnn.com

www.unb.ca/web/transpo/mynet/mtw21b.htm *(how to use Excel for compound interest calculations)*

One of the few sites with material on capital investment decisions is:

www.asbdc.ualr.edu/fod/1518.htm

Chapter 3 explained how bonds are valued. Helpful material and data on bond markets are available on:

www.bondsonline.com *(good bond data)*

http://bonds.yahoo.com

www.finpipe.com *(good explanations of bond markets)*

www.fintools.net *(contains a bond calculator)*

www.ganesha.org *(explanation of bond markets and calculator)*

www.hsh.com *(good bond data)*

www.investinginbonds.com *(also contains links to related sites)*

www.investorguide.com/university.html *(good explanations of bond and equity markets)*

http://money.cnn.com/markets/bondcenter

Chapter 4 was concerned with stock markets and equity valuation. Most major stock exchanges have good websites. See, for example:

www.nyse.com *(New York Exchange)*

www.nasdaq.com *(NASDAQ)*

www.londonstockexchange.com *(London Exchange)*

www.tse.or.jp *(Tokyo Exchange)*

www.123world.com/stockexchanges *(links to exchanges)*

www.fibv.com *(The World Federation of Exchanges publishes useful comparative statistics)*

Data on stock market indexes can be found on:

www.djindexes.com *(Dow Jones index)*

www.spglobal.com *(Standard & Poor's indexes)*

www.barra.com *(market indices with information on dividend yields, P/Es etc.)*

www.wilshire.com

There is a large number of sites with market commentary and data on individual firms and stocks. We find Finance.Yahoo particularly useful.

http://finance.yahoo.com

www.bloomberg.com

http://hoovers.com

www.cbs.marketwatch.com

www.finance.lycos.com

http://money.cnn.com

http://moneycentral.msn.com

www.wsrn.com

http://my.zacks.com *(includes earnings forecasts)*

The following sites provide useful software and data for calculating company values:

http://financialplayerscenter.com

www.valuepro.net

PART TWO

RISK

AMAZON.COM STOCK STARTED trading in May 1997 at a price of $1.73. By December 1999, the stock price had risen by over 6,000 percent. Within little more than a year it had slumped by 90 percent. These gyrations in Amazon's stock price were unusually large, but they remind us how risky investment in common stocks can be.

Most investors are not adrenaline junkies; they don't *enjoy* taking risks. Therefore they require a higher expected return from risky investments. Companies recognize this in their capital budgeting decisions. An investment in a risky new project adds value only if the expected return is higher than investors could expect from an equally risky investment in the capital market.

But that raises two questions. How should risk be measured? And what is the relationship between risk and expected return? We tackle these two questions in Part Two.

CHAPTER SEVEN

INTRODUCTION TO RISK, RETURN, AND THE OPPORTUNITY COST OF CAPITAL

WE HAVE MANAGED to go through six chapters without directly addressing the problem of risk, but now the jig is up. We can no longer be satisfied with vague statements like "The opportunity cost of capital depends on the risk of the project." We need to know how risk is defined, what the links are between risk and the opportunity cost of capital, and how the financial manager can cope with risk in practical situations.

In this chapter we concentrate on the first of these issues and leave the other two to Chapters 8 and 9. We start by summarizing 75 years of evidence on rates of return in capital markets. Then we take a first look at investment risks and show how they can be reduced by portfolio diversification. We introduce you to beta, the standard risk measure for individual securities.

The themes of this chapter, then, are portfolio risk, security risk, and diversification. For the most part, we take the view of the individual investor. But at the end of the chapter we turn the problem around and ask whether diversification makes sense as a *corporate* objective.

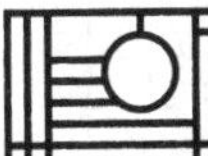

7.1 SEVENTY-FIVE YEARS OF CAPITAL MARKET HISTORY IN ONE EASY LESSON

Financial analysts are blessed with an enormous quantity of data on security prices and returns. For example, the University of Chicago's Center for Research in Security Prices (CRSP) has developed a file of prices and dividends for each month since 1926 for every stock that has been listed on the New York Stock Exchange (NYSE). Other files give data for stocks that are traded on the American Stock Exchange and the over-the-counter market, data for bonds, for options, and so on. But this is supposed to be one easy lesson. We, therefore, concentrate on a study by Ibbotson Associates that measures the historical performance of five portfolios of securities:

1. A portfolio of Treasury bills, i.e., United States government debt securities maturing in less than one year.
2. A portfolio of long-term United States government bonds.
3. A portfolio of long-term corporate bonds.[1]
4. Standard and Poor's Composite Index (S&P 500), which represents a portfolio of common stocks of 500 large firms. (Although only a small proportion of the 7,000 or so publicly traded companies are included in the S&P 500, these companies account for over 70 percent of the *value* of stocks traded.)
5. A portfolio of the common stocks of small firms.

These investments offer different degrees of risk. Treasury bills are about as safe an investment as you can make. There is no risk of default, and their short maturity means that the prices of Treasury bills are relatively stable. In fact, an investor who wishes to lend money for, say, three months can achieve a perfectly certain payoff by purchasing a Treasury bill maturing in three months. However, the investor cannot lock in a *real* rate of return: There is still some uncertainty about inflation.

By switching to long-term government bonds, the investor acquires an asset whose price fluctuates as interest rates vary. (Bond prices fall when interest rates rise and rise when interest rates fall.) An investor who shifts from government to

[1]The two bond portfolios were revised each year to maintain a constant maturity.

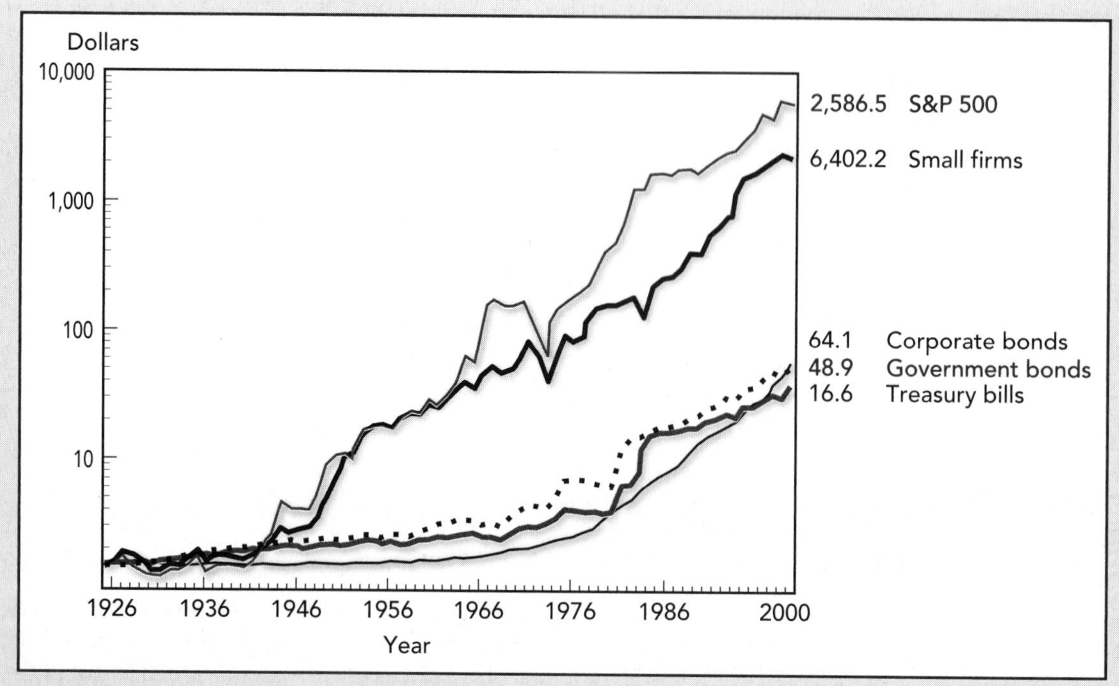

FIGURE 7.1

How an investment of $1 at the start of 1926 would have grown, assuming reinvestment of all dividend and interest payments.

Source: Ibbotson Associates, Inc., *Stocks, Bonds, Bills, and Inflation, 2001 Yearbook*, Chicago, 2001; cited hereafter in this chapter as the *2001 Yearbook*. © 2001 Ibbotson Associates, Inc.

corporate bonds accepts an additional *default* risk. An investor who shifts from corporate bonds to common stocks has a direct share in the risks of the enterprise.

Figure 7.1 shows how your money would have grown if you had invested $1 at the start of 1926 and reinvested all dividend or interest income in each of the five portfolios.[2] Figure 7.2 is identical except that it depicts the growth in the *real* value of the portfolio. We will focus here on nominal values.

Portfolio performance coincides with our intuitive risk ranking. A dollar invested in the safest investment, Treasury bills, would have grown to just over $16 by 2000, barely enough to keep up with inflation. An investment in long-term Treasury bonds would have produced $49, and corporate bonds a pinch more. Common stocks were in a class by themselves. An investor who placed a dollar in the stocks of large U.S. firms would have received $2,587. The jackpot, however, went to investors in stocks of small firms, who walked away with $6,402 for each dollar invested.

Ibbotson Associates also calculated the rate of return from these portfolios for each year from 1926 to 2000. This rate of return reflects both cash receipts—dividends or interest—and the capital gains or losses realized during the year. Averages of the 75 annual rates of return for each portfolio are shown in Table 7.1.

[2]Portfolio values are plotted on a log scale. If they were not, the ending values for the two common stock portfolios would run off the top of the page.

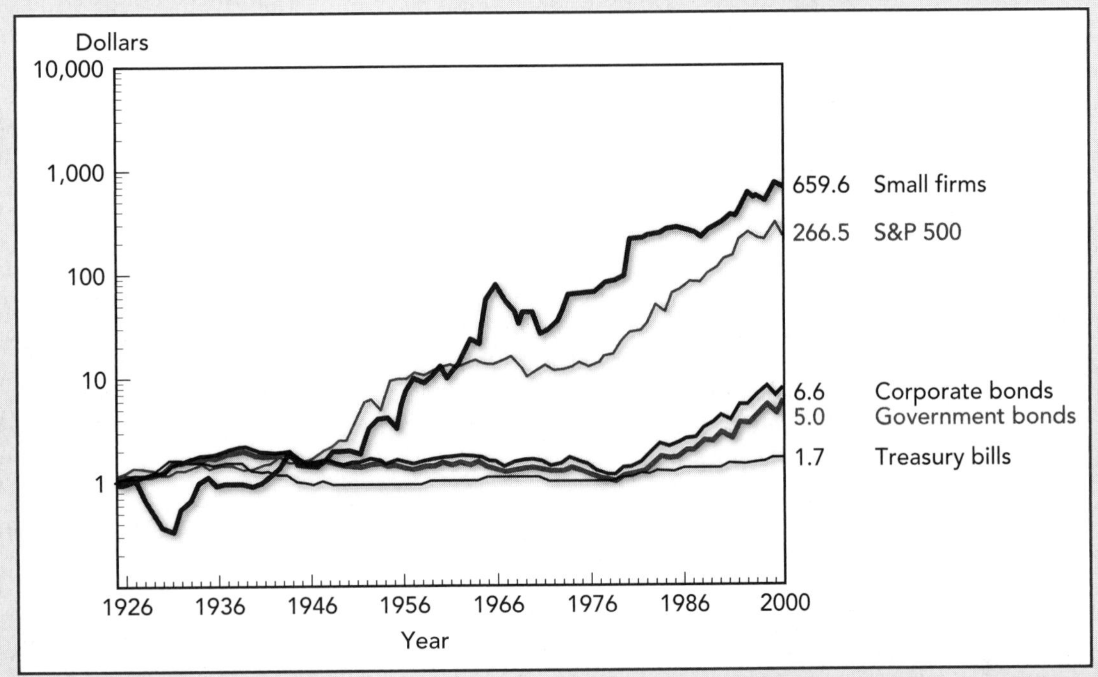

FIGURE 7.2

How an investment of $1 at the start of 1926 would have grown in real terms, assuming reinvestment of all dividend and interest payments. Compare this plot to Figure 7.1, and note how inflation has eroded the purchasing power of returns to investors.

Source: Ibbotson Associates, Inc., *2001 Yearbook*. © Ibbotson Associates, Inc.

Portfolio	Average Annual Rate of Return: Nominal	Average Annual Rate of Return: Real	Average Risk Premium (Extra Return Versus Treasury Bills)
Treasury bills	3.9	.8	0
Government bonds	5.7	2.7	1.8
Corporate bonds	6.0	3.0	2.1
Common stocks (S&P 500)	13.0	9.7	9.1
Small-firm common stocks	17.3	13.8	13.4

TABLE 7.1

Average rates of return on Treasury bills, government bonds, corporate bonds, and common stocks, 1926–2000 (figures in percent per year).

Source: Ibbotson Associates, Inc., *2001 Yearbook*.

Since 1926 Treasury bills have provided the lowest average return—3.9 percent per year in *nominal* terms and .8 percent in *real* terms. In other words, the average rate of inflation over this period was just over 3 percent per year. Common stocks were again the winners. Stocks of major corporations provided on average a *risk premium* of 9.1 percent a year over the return on Treasury bills. Stocks of small firms offered an even higher premium.

You may ask why we look back over such a long period to measure average rates of return. The reason is that annual rates of return for common stocks fluctuate so much that averages taken over short periods are meaningless. Our only hope of gaining insights from historical rates of return is to look at a very long period.[3]

Arithmetic Averages and Compound Annual Returns

Notice that the average returns shown in Table 7.1 are arithmetic averages. In other words, Ibbotson Associates simply added the 75 annual returns and divided by 75. The arithmetic average is higher than the compound annual return over the period. The 75-year compound annual return for the S&P index was 11.0 percent.[4]

The proper uses of arithmetic and compound rates of return from past investments are often misunderstood. Therefore, we call a brief time-out for a clarifying example.

Suppose that the price of Big Oil's common stock is \$100. There is an equal chance that at the end of the year the stock will be worth \$90, \$110, or \$130. Therefore, the return could be −10 percent, +10 percent, or +30 percent (we assume that Big Oil does not pay a dividend). The *expected* return is ⅓(−10 +10 +30) = +10 percent.

If we run the process in reverse and discount the expected cash flow by the expected rate of return, we obtain the value of Big Oil's stock:

$$\text{PV} = \frac{110}{1.10} = \$100$$

The expected return of 10 percent is therefore the correct rate at which to discount the expected cash flow from Big Oil's stock. It is also the opportunity cost of capital for investments that have the same degree of risk as Big Oil.

Now suppose that we observe the returns on Big Oil stock over a large number of years. If the odds are unchanged, the return will be −10 percent in a third of the years, +10 percent in a further third, and +30 percent in the remaining years. The arithmetic average of these yearly returns is

$$\frac{-10 + 10 + 30}{3} = +10\%$$

Thus the arithmetic average of the returns correctly measures the opportunity cost of capital for investments of similar risk to Big Oil stock.

The average compound annual return on Big Oil stock would be

$$(.9 \times 1.1 \times 1.3)^{1/3} - 1 = .088, \text{ or } 8.8\%,$$

[3]We cannot be sure that this period is truly representative and that the average is not distorted by a few unusually high or low returns. The reliability of an estimate of the average is usually measured by its *standard error.* For example, the standard error of our estimate of the average risk premium on common stocks is 2.3 percent. There is a 95 percent chance that the *true* average is within plus or minus 2 standard errors of the 9.1 percent estimate. In other words, if you said that the true average was between 4.5 and 13.7 percent, you would have a 95 percent chance of being right. (*Technical note*: The standard error of the average is equal to the standard deviation divided by the square root of the number of observations. In our case the standard deviation is 20.2 percent, and therefore the standard error is $20.2/\sqrt{75} = 2.3$.)

[4]This was calculated from $(1 + r)^{75} = 2{,}586.5$, which implies $r = .11$. *Technical note:* For lognormally distributed returns the annual compound return is equal to the arithmetic average return minus half the variance. For example, the annual standard deviation of returns on the U.S. market was about .20, or 20 percent. Variance was therefore $.20^2$, or .04. The compound annual return is $.04/2 = .02$, or 2 percentage points less than the arithmetic average.

less than the opportunity cost of capital. Investors would not be willing to invest in a project that offered an 8.8 percent expected return if they could get an expected return of 10 percent in the capital markets. The net present value of such a project would be

$$\text{NPV} = -100 + \frac{108.8}{1.1} = -1.1$$

Moral: If the cost of capital is estimated from historical returns or risk premiums, use arithmetic averages, not compound annual rates of return.

Using Historical Evidence to Evaluate Today's Cost of Capital

Suppose there is an investment project which you *know*—don't ask how—has the same risk as Standard and Poor's Composite Index. We will say that it has the same degree of risk as the *market portfolio,* although this is speaking somewhat loosely, because the index does not include all risky securities. What rate should you use to discount this project's forecasted cash flows?

Clearly you should use the currently expected rate of return on the market portfolio; that is the return investors would forgo by investing in the proposed project. Let us call this market return r_m. One way to estimate r_m is to assume that the future will be like the past and that today's investors expect to receive the same "normal" rates of return revealed by the averages shown in Table 7.1. In this case, you would set r_m at 13 percent, the average of past market returns.

Unfortunately, this is *not* the way to do it; r_m is not likely to be stable over time. Remember that it is the sum of the risk-free interest rate r_f and a premium for risk. We know that r_f varies. For example, in 1981 the interest rate on Treasury bills was about 15 percent. It is difficult to believe that investors in that year were content to hold common stocks offering an expected return of only 13 percent.

If you need to estimate the return that investors expect to receive, a more sensible procedure is to take the interest rate on Treasury bills and add 9.1 percent, the average *risk premium* shown in Table 7.1. For example, as we write this in mid-2001 the interest rate on Treasury bills is about 3.5 percent. Adding on the average risk premium, therefore, gives

$$\begin{aligned} r_m(2001) &= r_f(2001) + \text{normal risk premium} \\ &= .035 + .091 = .126, \text{ or about } 12.5\% \end{aligned}$$

The crucial assumption here is that there is a normal, stable risk premium on the market portfolio, so that the expected *future* risk premium can be measured by the average past risk premium.

Even with 75 years of data, we can't estimate the market risk premium exactly; nor can we be sure that investors today are demanding the same reward for risk that they were 60 or 70 years ago. All this leaves plenty of room for argument about what the risk premium *really* is.[5]

Many financial managers and economists believe that long-run historical returns are the best measure available. Others have a gut instinct that investors

[5]Some of the disagreements simply reflect the fact that the risk premium is sometimes defined in different ways. Some measure the average difference between stock returns and the returns (or yields) on long-term bonds. Others measure the difference between the compound rate of growth on stocks and the interest rate. As we explained above, this is not an appropriate measure of the cost of capital.

don't need such a large risk premium to persuade them to hold common stocks.[6] In a recent survey of financial economists, more than a quarter of those polled believed that the expected risk premium was about 8 percent, but most of the remainder opted for a figure between 4 and 7 percent. The average estimate was just over 6 percent.[7]

If you believe that the expected market risk premium is a lot less than the historical averages, you probably also believe that history has been unexpectedly kind to investors in the United States and that their good luck is unlikely to be repeated. Here are three reasons why history *may* overstate the risk premium that investors demand today.

Reason 1 Over the past 75 years stock prices in the United States have outpaced dividend payments. In other words, there has been a long-term decline in the dividend yield. Between 1926 and 2000 this decline in yield added about 2 percent a year to the return on common stocks. Was this yield change anticipated? If not, it would be more reasonable to take the long-term growth in dividends as a measure of the capital appreciation that investors were expecting. This would point to a risk premium of about 7 percent.

Reason 2 Since 1926 the United States has been among the world's most prosperous countries. Other economies have languished or been wracked by war or civil unrest. By focusing on equity returns in the United States, we may obtain a biased view of what investors expected. Perhaps the historical averages miss the possibility that the United States could have turned out to be one of those less-fortunate countries.[8]

Figure 7.3 sheds some light on this issue. It is taken from a comprehensive study by Dimson, Marsh, and Staunton of market returns in 15 countries and shows the average risk premium in each country between 1900 and 2000.[9] Two points are worth making. Notice first that in the United States the risk premium over 101 years has averaged 7.5 percent, somewhat less than the figure that we cited earlier for the period 1926–2000. The period of the First World War and its aftermath was in many ways not typical, so it is hard to say whether we get a more or less representative picture of investor expectations by adding in the extra years. But the ef-

[6]There is some theory behind this instinct. The high risk premium earned in the market seems to imply that investors are extremely risk-averse. If that is true, investors ought to cut back their consumption when stock prices fall and wealth decreases. But the evidence suggests that when stock prices fall, investors spend at nearly the same rate. This is difficult to reconcile with high risk aversion and a high market risk premium. See R. Mehra and E. Prescott, "The Equity Premium: A Puzzle," *Journal of Monetary Economics* 15 (1985), pp. 145–161.

[7]I. Welch, "Views of Financial Economists on the Equity Premium and Other Issues," *Journal of Business* 73 (October 2000), pp. 501–537. In a later unpublished survey undertaken by Ivo Welch the average estimate for the equity risk premium was slightly lower at 5.5 percent. See I. Welch, "The Equity Premium Consensus Forecast Revisited," Yale School of Management, September 2001.

[8]This possibility was suggested in P. Jorion and W. N. Goetzmann, "Global Stock Markets in the Twentieth Century," *Journal of Finance* 54 (June 1999), pp. 953–980.

[9]See E. Dimson, P. R. Marsh, and M. Staunton, *Millenium Book II: 101 Years of Investment Returns*, ABN-Amro and London Business School, London, 2001.

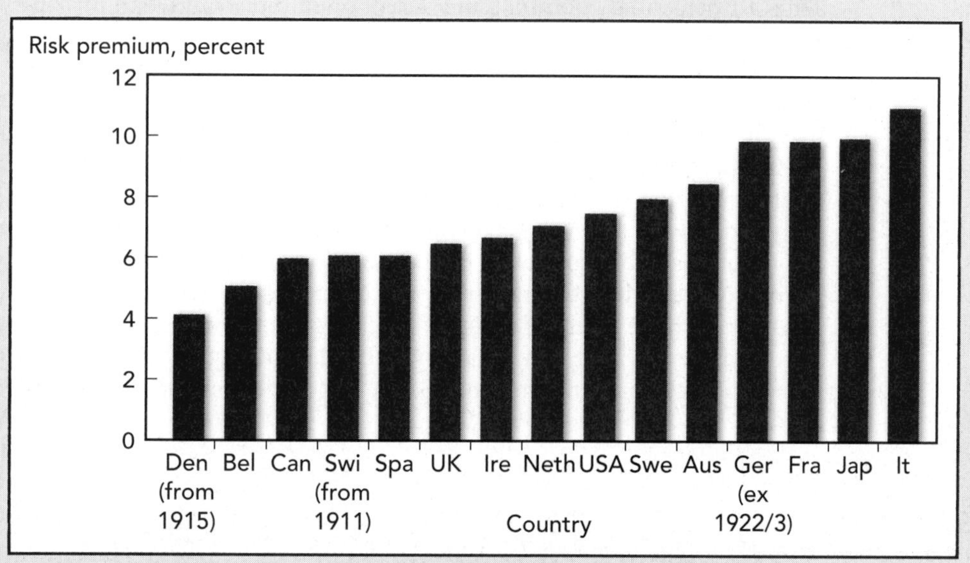

FIGURE 7.3

Average market risk premia, 1900–2000.

Source: E. Dimson, P. R. Marsh, and M. Staunton, *Millenium Book II: 101 Years of Investment Returns,* ABN-Amro and London Business School, London, 2001.

fect of doing so is an important reminder of how difficult it is to obtain an accurate measure of the risk premium.

Now compare the returns in the United States with those in the other countries. There is no evidence here that U.S. investors have been particularly fortunate; the USA was exactly average in terms of the risk premium. Danish common stocks came bottom of the league; the average risk premium in Denmark was only 4.3 percent. Top of the form was Italy with a premium of 11.1 percent. Some of these variations between countries may reflect differences in risk. For example, Italian stocks have been particularly variable and investors may have required a higher return to compensate. But remember how difficult it is to make precise estimates of what investors expected. You probably would not be too far out if you concluded that the *expected* risk premium was the same in each country.

Reason 3 During the second half of the 1990s U.S. equity prices experienced a remarkable boom, with the annual return averaging nearly 25 percent more than the return on Treasury bills. Some argued that this price rise reflected optimism that the new economy would lead to a golden age of prosperity and surging profits, but others attributed the rise to a reduction in the market risk premium.

To see how a rise in stock prices can stem from a fall in the risk premium, suppose that investors in common stocks initially look for a return of 13 percent, made up of a 3 percent dividend yield and 10 percent long-term growth in dividends. If they now decide that they are prepared to hold equities on a prospective return of 12 percent, then other things being equal the dividend yield must fall to 2 percent.

Thus a 1 percentage point fall in the risk premium would lead to a 50 percent rise in equity prices. If we include this price adjustment in our measures of past returns, we will be doubly wrong in our estimate of the risk premium. First, we will overestimate the return that investors required in the past. Second, we will not recognize that the return that investors require in the future is lower than in the past.

As stock prices began to slide back from their highs of March 2000, this belief in a falling market risk premium began to wane. It seems that if the risk premium truly did fall in the 1990s, then it also rose again as the new century dawned.[10]

Out of this debate only one firm conclusion emerges: Do not trust anyone who claims to *know* what returns investors expect. History contains some clues, but ultimately we have to judge whether investors on average have received what they expected. Brealey and Myers have no official position on the market risk premium, but we believe that a range of 6 to 8.5 percent is reasonable for the United States.[11]

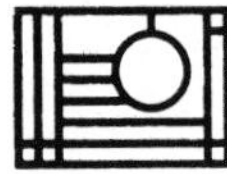

7.2 MEASURING PORTFOLIO RISK

You now have a couple of benchmarks. You know the discount rate for safe projects, and you have an estimate of the rate for average-risk projects. But you *don't* know yet how to estimate discount rates for assets that do not fit these simple cases. To do that, you have to learn (1) how to measure risk and (2) the relationship between risks borne and risk premiums demanded.

Figure 7.4 shows the 75 annual rates of return calculated by Ibbotson Associates for Standard and Poor's Composite Index. The fluctuations in year-to-year returns are remarkably wide. The highest annual return was 54.0 percent in 1933—a partial rebound from the stock market crash of 1929–1932. However, there were losses exceeding 25 percent in four years, the worst being the −43.3 percent return in 1931.

Another way of presenting these data is by a histogram or frequency distribution. This is done in Figure 7.5, where the variability of year-to-year returns shows up in the wide "spread" of outcomes.

Variance and Standard Deviation

The standard statistical measures of spread are **variance** and **standard deviation.** The variance of the market return is the expected squared deviation from the expected return. In other words,

$$\text{Variance}\,(\tilde{r}_m) = \text{the expected value of}\,(\tilde{r}_m - r_m)^2$$

[10]The decline in the stock market in 2001 also reduces the long-term average risk premium. The average premium from 1926 to September 2001 is 8.7 percent, .4 percentage points lower than the figure quoted in Table 7.1.

[11]This range seems to be consistent with company practice. For example, Kaplan and Ruback, in an analysis of valuations in 51 takeovers between 1983 and 1998, found that acquiring companies appeared to base their discount rates on a market risk premium of about 7.5 percent over average returns on long-term Treasury bonds. The risk premium over Treasury bills would have been about a percentage point higher. See S. Kaplan and R. S. Ruback, "The Valuation of Cash Flow Forecasts: An Empirical Analysis," *Journal of Finance* 50 (September 1995), pp. 1059–1093.

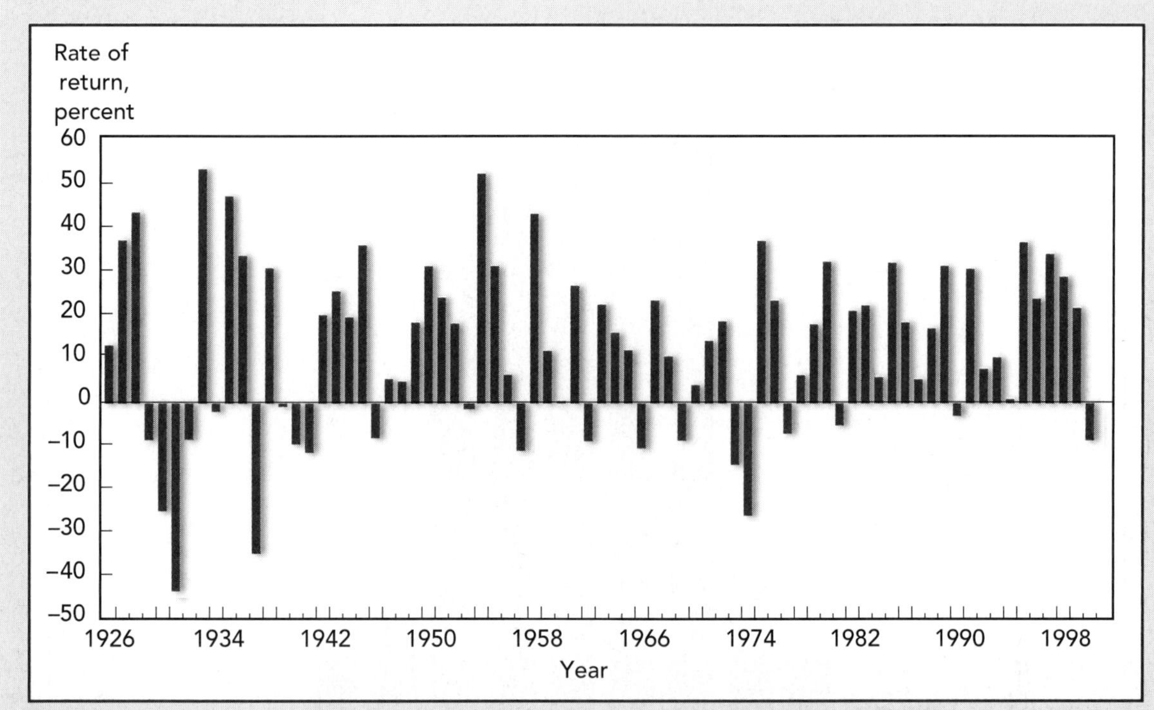

FIGURE 7.4

The stock market has been a profitable but extremely variable investment.

Source: Ibbotson Associates, Inc., *2001 Yearbook*, © 2001 Ibbotson Associates, Inc.

where $\tilde{r}_m$ is the actual return and r_m is the expected return.[12] The standard deviation is simply the square root of the variance:

$$\text{Standard deviation of } \tilde{r}_m = \sqrt{\text{variance } (\tilde{r}_m)}$$

Standard deviation is often denoted by σ and variance by σ^2.

Here is a very simple example showing how variance and standard deviation are calculated. Suppose that you are offered the chance to play the following game. You start by investing $100. Then two coins are flipped. For each head that comes up you get back your starting balance *plus* 20 percent, and for each tail that comes up you get back your starting balance *less* 10 percent. Clearly there are four equally likely outcomes:

- Head + head: You gain 40 percent.
- Head + tail: You gain 10 percent.

[12]One more technical point: When variance is estimated from a sample of *observed* returns, we add the squared deviations and divide by $N - 1$, where N is the number of observations. We divide by $N - 1$ rather than N to correct for what is called *the loss of a degree of freedom.* The formula is

$$\text{Variance } (\tilde{r}_m) = \frac{1}{N-1}\sum_{t=1}^{N}(\tilde{r}_{mt} - r_m)^2$$

where $\tilde{r}_{mt}$ is the market return in period t and r_m is the mean of the values of $\tilde{r}_{mt}$.

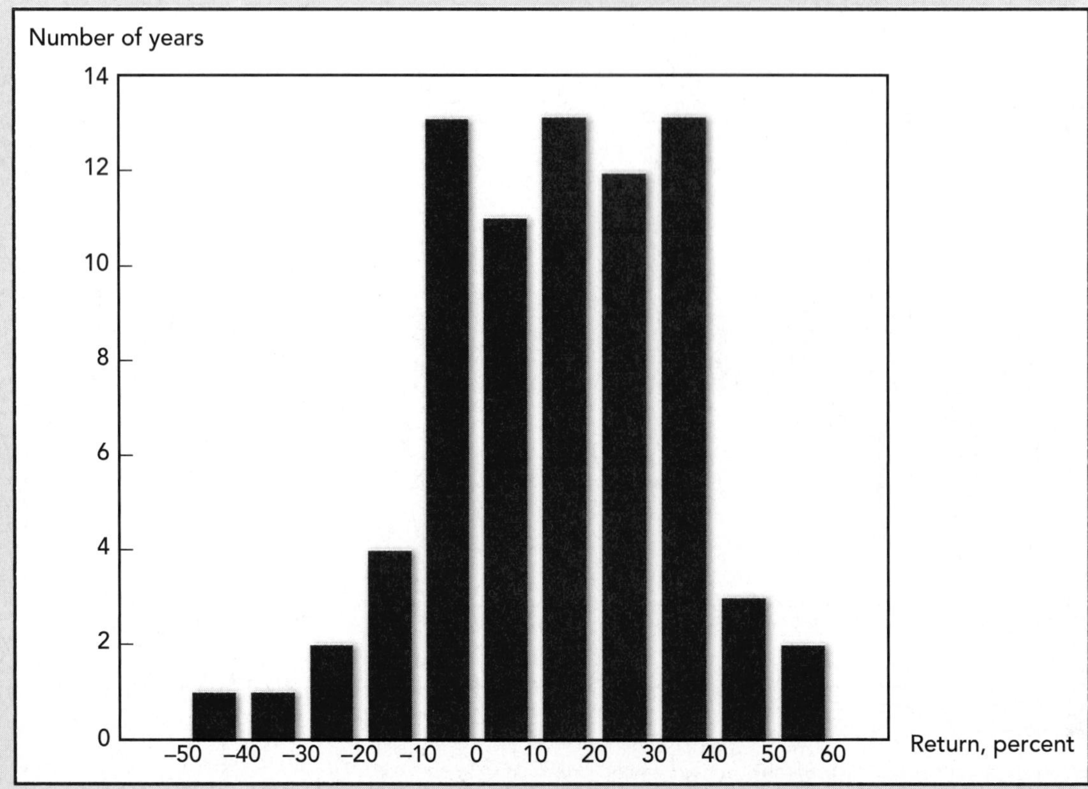

FIGURE 7.5

Histogram of the annual rates of return from the stock market in the United States, 1926–2000, showing the wide spread of returns from investment in common stocks.

Source: Ibbotson Associates, Inc., *2001 Yearbook.*

- Tail + head: You gain 10 percent.
- Tail + tail: You lose 20 percent.

There is a chance of 1 in 4, or .25, that you will make 40 percent; a chance of 2 in 4, or .5, that you will make 10 percent; and a chance of 1 in 4, or .25, that you will lose 20 percent. The game's expected return is, therefore, a weighted average of the possible outcomes:

$$\text{Expected return} = (.25 \times 40) + (.5 \times 10) + (.25 \times -20) = +10\%$$

Table 7.2 shows that the variance of the percentage returns is 450. Standard deviation is the square root of 450, or 21. This figure is in the same units as the rate of return, so we can say that the game's variability is 21 percent.

One way of defining uncertainty is to say that more things can happen than will happen. The risk of an asset can be completely expressed, as we did for the coin-tossing game, by writing all possible outcomes and the probability of each. In prac-

(1) Percent Rate of Return ($\tilde{r}$)	(2) Deviation from Expected Return ($\tilde{r} - r$)	(3) Squared Deviation $(\tilde{r} - r)^2$	(4) Probability	(5) Probability × Squared Deviation
+40	+30	900	.25	225
+10	0	0	.5	0
−20	−30	900	.25	225
		Variance = expected value of $(\tilde{r} - r)^2$ = 450		
		Standard deviation = $\sqrt{\text{variance}} = \sqrt{450} = 21$		

TABLE 7.2

The coin-tossing game: Calculating variance and standard deviation.

tice this is cumbersome and often impossible. Therefore we use variance or standard deviation to summarize the spread of possible outcomes.[13]

These measures are natural indexes of risk.[14] If the outcome of the coin-tossing game had been certain, the standard deviation would have been zero. The actual standard deviation is positive because we *don't* know what will happen.

Or think of a second game, the same as the first except that each head means a 35 percent gain and each tail means a 25 percent loss. Again, there are four equally likely outcomes:

- Head + head: You gain 70 percent.
- Head + tail: You gain 10 percent.
- Tail + head: You gain 10 percent.
- Tail + tail: You lose 50 percent.

For this game the expected return is 10 percent, the same as that of the first game. But its standard deviation is double that of the first game, 42 versus 21 percent. By this measure the second game is twice as risky as the first.

Measuring Variability

In principle, you could estimate the variability of any portfolio of stocks or bonds by the procedure just described. You would identify the possible outcomes, assign a probability to each outcome, and grind through the calculations. But where do the probabilities come from? You can't look them up in the newspaper; newspapers seem to go out of their way to avoid definite statements about prospects for securities. We once saw an article headlined "Bond Prices Possibly Set to Move Sharply Either Way." Stockbrokers are much the same. Yours may respond to your query about possible market outcomes with a statement like this:

> The market currently appears to be undergoing a period of consolidation. For the intermediate term, we would take a constructive view, provided economic recovery

[13]Which of the two we use is solely a matter of convenience. Since standard deviation is in the same units as the rate of return, it is generally more convenient to use standard deviation. However, when we are talking about the *proportion* of risk that is due to some factor, it is usually less confusing to work in terms of the variance.

[14]As we explain in Chapter 8, standard deviation and variance are the correct measures of risk if the returns are normally distributed.

continues. The market could be up 20 percent a year from now, perhaps more if inflation continues low. On the other hand, . . .

The Delphic oracle gave advice, but no probabilities.

Most financial analysts start by observing past variability. Of course, there is no risk in hindsight, but it is reasonable to assume that portfolios with histories of high variability also have the least predictable future performance.

The annual standard deviations and variances observed for our five portfolios over the period 1926–2000 were:[15]

Portfolio	Standard Deviation (σ)	Variance (σ^2)
Treasury bills	3.2	10.1
Government bonds	9.4	88.7
Corporate bonds	8.7	75.5
Common stocks (S&P 500)	20.2	406.9
Small-firm common stocks	33.4	1118.4

As expected, Treasury bills were the least variable security, and small-firm stocks were the most variable. Government and corporate bonds hold the middle ground.[16]

You may find it interesting to compare the coin-tossing game and the stock market as alternative investments. The stock market generated an average annual return of 13.0 percent with a standard deviation of 20.2 percent. The game offers 10 and 21 percent, respectively—slightly lower return and about the same variability. Your gambling friends may have come up with a crude representation of the stock market.

Of course, there is no reason to believe that the market's variability should stay the same over more than 70 years. For example, it is clearly less now than in the Great Depression of the 1930s. Here are standard deviations of the returns on the S&P index for successive periods starting in 1926.[17]

---

[15] Ibbotson Associates, Inc., *2001 Yearbook.* In discussing the riskiness of *bonds,* be careful to specify the time period and whether you are speaking in real or nominal terms. The *nominal* return on a long-term government bond is absolutely certain to an investor who holds on until maturity; in other words, it is risk-free if you forget about inflation. After all, the government can always print money to pay off its debts. However, the real return on Treasury securities is uncertain because no one knows how much each future dollar will buy.

The bond returns reported by Ibbotson Associates were measured annually. The returns reflect year-to-year changes in bond prices as well as interest received. The *one-year* returns on long-term bonds are risky in *both* real and nominal terms.

[16] You may have noticed that corporate bonds come in just ahead of government bonds in terms of low variability. You shouldn't get excited about this. The problem is that it is difficult to get two sets of bonds that are alike in all other respects. For example, many corporate bonds are *callable* (i.e., the company has an option to repurchase them for their face value). Government bonds are not callable. Also interest payments are higher on corporate bonds. Therefore, investors in corporate bonds get their money sooner. As we will see in Chapter 24, this also reduces the bond's variability.

[17] These estimates are derived from *monthly* rates of return. Annual observations are insufficient for estimating variability decade by decade. The monthly variance is converted to an annual variance by multiplying by 12. That is, the variance of the monthly return is one-twelfth of the annual variance. The longer you hold a security or portfolio, the more risk you have to bear.

This conversion assumes that successive monthly returns are statistically independent. This is, in fact, a good assumption, as we will show in Chapter 13.

Because variance is approximately proportional to the length of time interval over which a security or portfolio return is measured, *standard deviation* is proportional to the square root of the interval.

Period	Market Standard Deviation (σ_m)
1926–1930	21.7
1931–1940	37.8
1941–1950	14.0
1951–1960	12.1
1961–1970	13.0
1971–1980	15.8
1981–1990	16.5
1991–2000	13.4

These figures do not support the widespread impression of especially volatile stock prices during the 1980s and 1990s. These years were below average on the volatility front.

However, there were brief episodes of extremely high volatility. On Black Monday, October 19, 1987, the market index fell by 23 percent *on a single day.* The standard deviation of the index for the week surrounding Black Monday was equivalent to 89 percent per year. Fortunately, volatility dropped back to normal levels within a few weeks after the crash.

How Diversification Reduces Risk

We can calculate our measures of variability equally well for individual securities and portfolios of securities. Of course, the level of variability over 75 years is less interesting for specific companies than for the market portfolio—it is a rare company that faces the same business risks today as it did in 1926.

Table 7.3 presents estimated standard deviations for 10 well-known common stocks for a recent five-year period.[18] Do these standard deviations look high to you? They should. Remember that the market portfolio's standard deviation was about 13 percent in the 1990s. Of our individual stocks only Exxon Mobil came close to this figure. Amazon.com was about eight times more variable than the market portfolio.

Take a look also at Table 7.4, which shows the standard deviations of some well-known stocks from different countries and of the markets in which they trade. Some of these stocks are much more variable than others, but you can see that once again the individual stocks are more variable than the market indexes.

This raises an important question: The market portfolio is made up of individual stocks, so why doesn't its variability reflect the average variability of its components? The answer is that *diversification reduces variability.*

Stock	Standard Deviation (σ)	Stock	Standard Deviation (σ)
Amazon.com*	110.6	General Electric	26.8
Boeing	30.9	General Motors	33.4
Coca-Cola	31.5	McDonald's	27.4
Dell Computer	62.7	Pfizer	29.3
Exxon Mobil	17.4	Reebok	58.5

TABLE 7.3

Standard deviations for selected U.S. common stocks, August 1996–July 2001 (figures in percent per year).

*June 1997–July 2001.

[18]These standard deviations are also calculated from monthly data.

Stock	Standard Deviation (σ)	Market	Standard Deviation (σ)	Stock	Standard Deviation (σ)	Market	Standard Deviation (σ)
Alcan	31.0	Canada	20.7	LVMH	41.9	France	21.5
BP Amoco	24.8	UK	14.5	Nestlé	19.7	Switzerland	19.0
Deutsche Bank	37.5	Germany	24.1	Nokia	57.6	Finland	43.2
Fiat	38.1	Italy	26.7	Sony	46.3	Japan	18.2
KLM	39.6	Netherlands	20.6	Telefonica de Argentina	45.4	Argentina	34.3

TABLE 7.4

Standard deviation for selected foreign stocks and market indexes, September 1996–August 2001 (figures in percent per year).

FIGURE 7.6

The risk (standard deviation) of randomly selected portfolios containing different numbers of New York Stock Exchange stocks. Notice that diversification reduces risk rapidly at first, then more slowly.

Source: M. Statman, "How Many Stocks Make a Diversified Portfolio?" *Journal of Financial and Quantitative Analysis* 22 (September 1987), pp. 353–363.

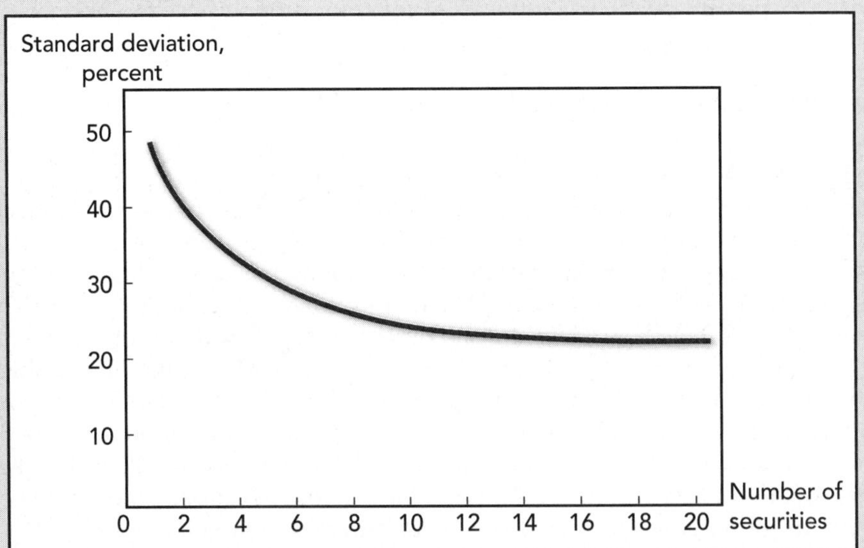

Even a little diversification can provide a substantial reduction in variability. Suppose you calculate and compare the standard deviations of randomly chosen one-stock portfolios, two-stock portfolios, five-stock portfolios, etc. A high proportion of the investments would be in the stocks of small companies and individually very risky. However, you can see from Figure 7.6 that diversification can cut the variability of returns about in half. Notice also that you can get most of this benefit with relatively few stocks: The improvement is slight when the number of securities is increased beyond, say, 20 or 30.

Diversification works because prices of different stocks do not move exactly together. Statisticians make the same point when they say that stock price changes are less than perfectly correlated. Look, for example, at Figure 7.7. The top panel shows returns for Dell Computer. We chose Dell because its stock has

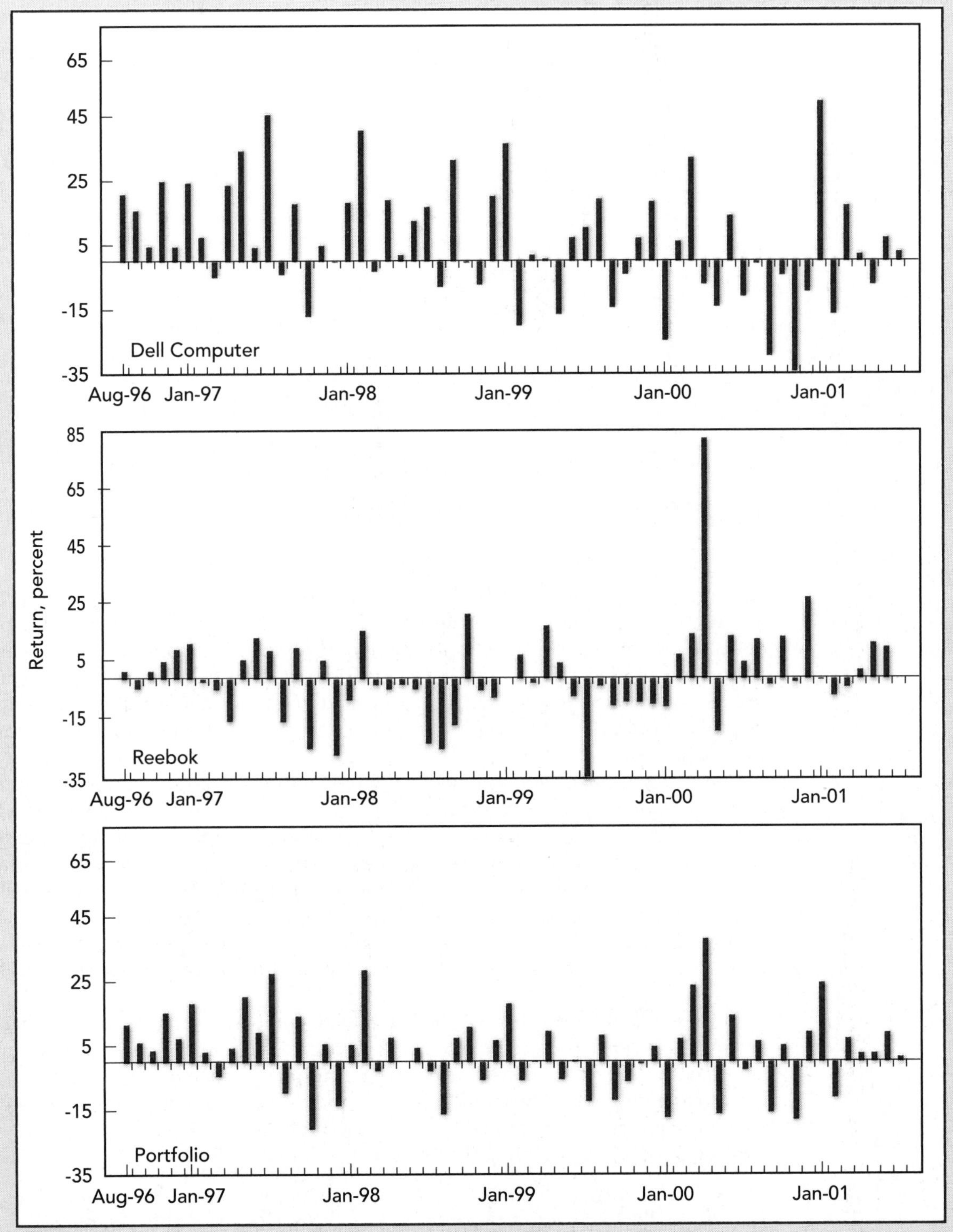

FIGURE 7.7

The variability of a portfolio with equal holdings in Dell Computer and Reebok would have been less than the average variability of the individual stocks. These returns run from August 1996 to July 2001.

FIGURE 7.8

Diversification eliminates unique risk. But there is some risk that diversification *cannot* eliminate. This is called *market risk.*

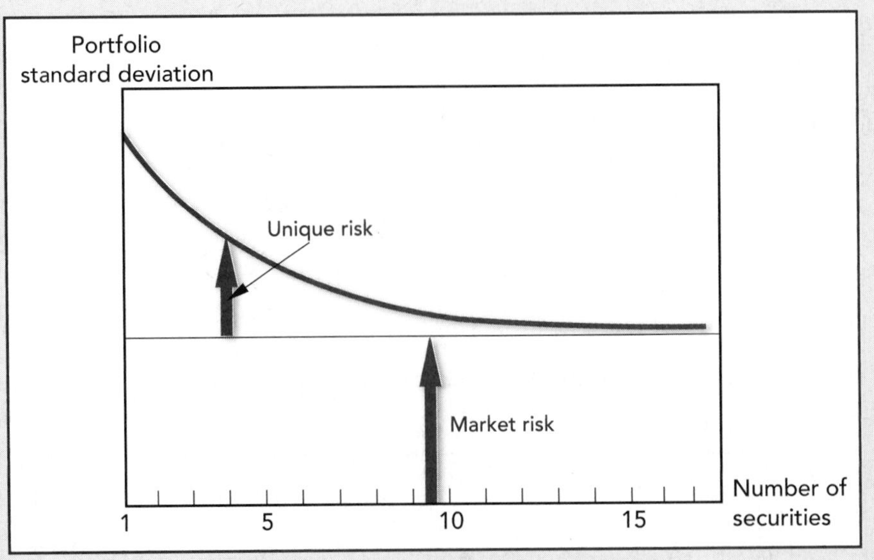

been unusually volatile. The middle panel shows returns for Reebok stock, which has also had its ups and downs. But on many occasions a decline in the value of one stock was offset by a rise in the price of the other.[19] Therefore there was an opportunity to reduce your risk by diversification. Figure 7.7 shows that if you had divided your funds evenly between the two stocks, the variability of your portfolio would have been substantially less than the average variability of the two stocks.[20]

The risk that potentially can be eliminated by diversification is called **unique risk.**[21] Unique risk stems from the fact that many of the perils that surround an individual company are peculiar to that company and perhaps its immediate competitors. But there is also some risk that you can't avoid, regardless of how much you diversify. This risk is generally known as **market risk.**[22] Market risk stems from the fact that there are other economywide perils that threaten all businesses. That is why stocks have a tendency to move together. And that is why investors are exposed to market uncertainties, no matter how many stocks they hold.

In Figure 7.8 we have divided the risk into its two parts—unique risk and market risk. If you have only a single stock, unique risk is very important; but once you have a portfolio of 20 or more stocks, diversification has done the bulk of its work. For a reasonably well-diversified portfolio, only market risk matters. Therefore, the predominant source of uncertainty for a diversified investor is that the market will rise or plummet, carrying the investor's portfolio with it.

[19]Over this period the correlation between the returns on the two stocks was approximately zero.

[20]The standard deviations of Dell Computer and Reebok were 62.7 and 58.5 percent, respectively. The standard deviation of a portfolio with half invested in each was 43.3 percent.

[21]Unique risk may be called *unsystematic risk, residual risk, specific risk,* or *diversifiable risk.*

[22]Market risk may be called *systematic risk* or *undiversifiable risk.*

7.3 CALCULATING PORTFOLIO RISK

We have given you an intuitive idea of how diversification reduces risk, but to understand fully the effect of diversification, you need to know how the risk of a portfolio depends on the risk of the individual shares.

Suppose that 65 percent of your portfolio is invested in the shares of Coca-Cola and the remainder is invested in Reebok. You expect that over the coming year Coca-Cola will give a return of 10 percent and Reebok, 20 percent. The expected return on your portfolio is simply a weighted average of the expected returns on the individual stocks:[23]

$$\text{Expected portfolio return} = (0.65 \times 10) + (0.35 \times 20) = 13.5\%$$

Calculating the expected portfolio return is easy. The hard part is to work out the risk of your portfolio. In the past the standard deviation of returns was 31.5 percent for Coca-Cola and 58.5 percent for Reebok. You believe that these figures are a good forecast of the spread of possible *future* outcomes. At first you may be inclined to assume that the standard deviation of your portfolio is a weighted average of the standard deviations of the two stocks, that is $(.65 \times 31.5) + (.35 \times 58.5) = 41.0$ percent. That would be correct *only* if the prices of the two stocks moved in perfect lockstep. In any other case, diversification reduces the risk below this figure.

The exact procedure for calculating the risk of a two-stock portfolio is given in Figure 7.9. You need to fill in four boxes. To complete the top left box, you weight the variance of the returns on stock 1 (σ_1^2) by the *square* of the proportion invested in it (x_1^2). Similarly, to complete the bottom right box, you weight the variance of the returns on stock 2 (σ_2^2) by the *square* of the proportion invested in stock 2 (x_2^2).

The entries in these diagonal boxes depend on the variances of stocks 1 and 2; the entries in the other two boxes depend on their **covariance.** As you might guess, the covariance is a measure of the degree to which the two stocks "covary." The covariance can be expressed as the product of the correlation coefficient ρ_{12} and the two standard deviations:[24]

$$\text{Covariance between stocks 1 and 2} = \sigma_{12} = \rho_{12}\sigma_1\sigma_2$$

For the most part stocks tend to move together. In this case the correlation coefficient ρ_{12} is positive, and therefore the covariance σ_{12} is also positive. If the prospects of the stocks were wholly unrelated, both the correlation coefficient and the covariance would be zero; and if the stocks tended to move in opposite directions, the correlation coefficient and the covariance would be negative. Just as you

[23]Let's check this. Suppose you invest \$65 in Coca-Cola and \$35 in Reebok. The expected dollar return on your Coca-Cola holding is $.10 \times 65 = \$6.50$, and on Reebok it is $.20 \times 35 = \$7.00$. The expected dollar return on your portfolio is $6.50 + 7.00 = \$13.50$. The portfolio *rate* of return is $13.50/100 = 0.135$, or 13.5 percent.

[24]Another way to define the covariance is as follows:

$$\text{Covariance between stocks 1 and 2} = \sigma_{12} = \text{expected value of } (\tilde{r}_1 - r_1) \times (\tilde{r}_2 - r_2)$$

Note that any security's covariance with itself is just its variance:

$$\begin{aligned}\sigma_{11} &= \text{expected value of } (\tilde{r}_1 - r_1) \times (\tilde{r}_1 - r_1)\\ &= \text{expected value of } (\tilde{r}_1 - r_1)^2 = \text{variance of stock 1} = \sigma_1^2.\end{aligned}$$

FIGURE 7.9

The variance of a two-stock portfolio is the sum of these four boxes. x_1, x_2 = proportions invested in stocks 1 and 2; σ_1, σ_2, = variances of stock returns; σ_{12} = covariance of returns ($\rho_{12}\,\sigma_1\,\sigma_2$); ρ_{12} = correlation between returns on stocks 1 and 2.

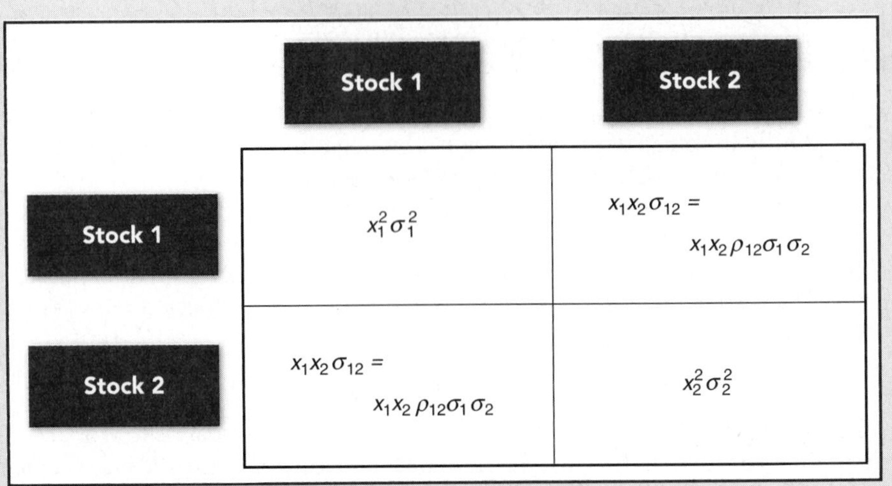

weighted the variances by the square of the proportion invested, so you must weight the covariance by the *product* of the two proportionate holdings x_1 and x_2.

Once you have completed these four boxes, you simply add the entries to obtain the portfolio variance:

$$\text{Portfolio variance} = x_1^2\sigma_1^2 + x_2^2\sigma_2^2 + 2(x_1x_2\rho_{12}\sigma_1\sigma_2)$$

The portfolio standard deviation is, of course, the square root of the variance.

Now you can try putting in some figures for Coca-Cola and Reebok. We said earlier that if the two stocks were perfectly correlated, the standard deviation of the portfolio would lie 45 percent of the way between the standard deviations of the two stocks. Let us check this out by filling in the boxes with $\rho_{12} = +1$.

	Coca-Cola	Reebok
Coca-Cola	$x_1^2\sigma_1^2 = (.65)^2 \times (31.5)^2$	$x_1x_2\rho_{12}\sigma_1\sigma_2$ $= (.65) \times (.35) \times 1 \times (31.5) \times (58.5)$
Reebok	$x_1x_2\rho_{12}\sigma_1\sigma_2$ $= .65 \times .35 \times 1 \times 31.5 \times 58.5$	$x_2^2\sigma_2^2 = (.35)^2 \times (58.5)^2$

The variance of your portfolio is the sum of these entries:

$$\text{Portfolio variance} = [(.65)^2 \times (31.5)^2] + [(.35)^2 \times (58.5)^2] + 2(.65 \times .35 \times 1 \times 31.5 \times 58.5) = 1{,}676.9$$

The standard deviation is $\sqrt{1{,}676.9} = 41.0$ percent or 35 percent of the way between 31.5 and 58.5.

Coca-Cola and Reebok do not move in perfect lockstep. If past experience is any guide, the correlation between the two stocks is about .2. If we go through the same exercise again with $\rho_{12} = +.2$, we find

$$\text{Portfolio variance} = [(.65)^2 \times (31.5)^2] + [(.35)^2 \times (58.5)^2] + 2(.65 \times .35 \times .2 \times 31.5 \times 58.5) = 1{,}006.1$$

The standard deviation is $\sqrt{1{,}006.1} = 31.7$ percent. The risk is now *less* than 35 percent of the way between 31.5 and 58.5; in fact, it is little more than the risk of investing in Coca-Cola alone.

The greatest payoff to diversification comes when the two stocks are negatively correlated. Unfortunately, this almost never occurs with real stocks, but just for illustration, let us assume it for Coca-Cola and Reebok. And as long as we are being unrealistic, we might as well go whole hog and assume perfect negative correlation ($\rho_{12} = -1$). In this case,

$$\text{Portfolio variance} = [(.65)^2 \times (31.5)^2] + [(.35)^2 \times (58.5)^2] + 2[.65 \times .35 \times (-1) \times 31.5 \times 58.5] = 0$$

When there is perfect negative correlation, there is always a portfolio strategy (represented by a particular set of portfolio weights) which will completely eliminate risk.[25] It's too bad perfect negative correlation doesn't really occur between common stocks.

General Formula for Computing Portfolio Risk

The method for calculating portfolio risk can easily be extended to portfolios of three or more securities. We just have to fill in a larger number of boxes. Each of those down the diagonal—the shaded boxes in Figure 7.10—contains the variance weighted by the square of the proportion invested. Each of the other boxes contains the covariance between that pair of securities, weighted by the product of the proportions invested.[26]

Limits to Diversification

Did you notice in Figure 7.10 how much more important the covariances become as we add more securities to the portfolio? When there are just two securities, there are equal numbers of variance boxes and of covariance boxes. When there are many securities, the number of covariances is much larger than the number of variances. Thus the variability of a well-diversified portfolio reflects mainly the covariances.

Suppose we are dealing with portfolios in which equal investments are made in each of N stocks. The proportion invested in each stock is, therefore, $1/N$. So in each variance box we have $(1/N)^2$ times the variance, and in each covariance box we have $(1/N)^2$ times the covariance. There are N variance boxes and $N^2 - N$ covariance boxes. Therefore,

$$\begin{aligned}\text{Portfolio variance} &= N\left(\frac{1}{N}\right)^2 \times \text{average variance} \\ &\quad + (N^2 - N)\left(\frac{1}{N}\right)^2 \times \text{average covariance} \\ &= \frac{1}{N} \times \text{average variance} + \left(1 - \frac{1}{N}\right) \times \text{average covariance}\end{aligned}$$

[25] Since the standard deviation of Reebok is 1.86 times that of Coca-Cola, you need to invest 1.86 times more in Coca-Cola to eliminate risk in this two-stock portfolio.

[26] The formal equivalent to "add up all the boxes" is

$$\text{Portfolio variance} = \sum_{i=1}^{N}\sum_{j=1}^{N} x_i x_j \sigma_{ij}$$

Notice that when $i = j$, σ_{ij} is just the variance of stock i.

FIGURE 7.10

To find the variance of an *N*-stock portfolio, we must add the entries in a matrix like this. The diagonal cells contain variance terms ($x_i^2\sigma_i^2$), and the off-diagonal cells contain covariance terms ($x_i x_j \sigma_{ij}$).

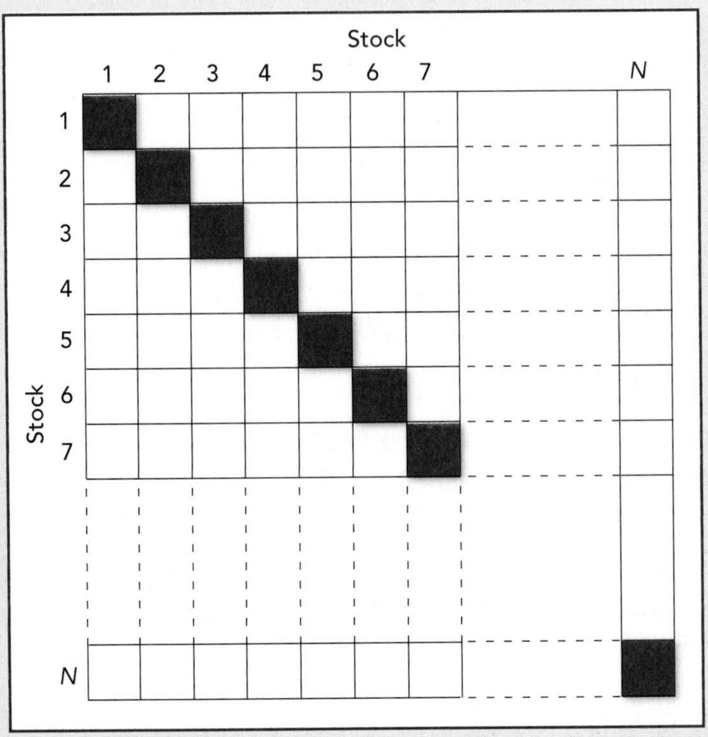

Notice that as *N* increases, the portfolio variance steadily approaches the average covariance. If the average covariance were zero, it would be possible to eliminate *all* risk by holding a sufficient number of securities. Unfortunately common stocks move together, not independently. Thus most of the stocks that the investor can actually buy are tied together in a web of positive covariances which set the limit to the benefits of diversification. Now we can understand the precise meaning of the market risk portrayed in Figure 7.8. It is the average covariance which constitutes the bedrock of risk remaining after diversification has done its work.

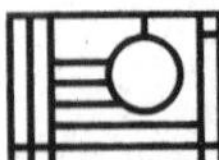

7.4 HOW INDIVIDUAL SECURITIES AFFECT PORTFOLIO RISK

We presented earlier some data on the variability of 10 individual U.S. securities. Amazon.com had the highest standard deviation and Exxon Mobil had the lowest. If you had held Amazon on its own, the spread of possible returns would have been six times greater than if you had held Exxon Mobil on its own. But that is not a very interesting fact. Wise investors don't put all their eggs into just one basket: They reduce their risk by diversification. They are therefore interested in the effect that each stock will have on the risk of their portfolio.

This brings us to one of the principal themes of this chapter. *The risk of a well-diversified portfolio depends on the market risk of the securities included in the portfolio.* Tattoo that statement on your forehead if you can't remember it any other way. It is one of the most important ideas in this book.

Stock	Beta (β)	Stock	Beta (β)
Amazon.com*	3.25	General Electric	1.18
Boeing	.56	General Motors	.91
Coca-Cola	.74	McDonald's	.68
Dell Computer	2.21	Pfizer	.71
Exxon Mobil	.40	Reebok	.69

TABLE 7.5

Betas for selected U.S. common stocks, August 1996–July 2001.

*June 1997–July 2001.

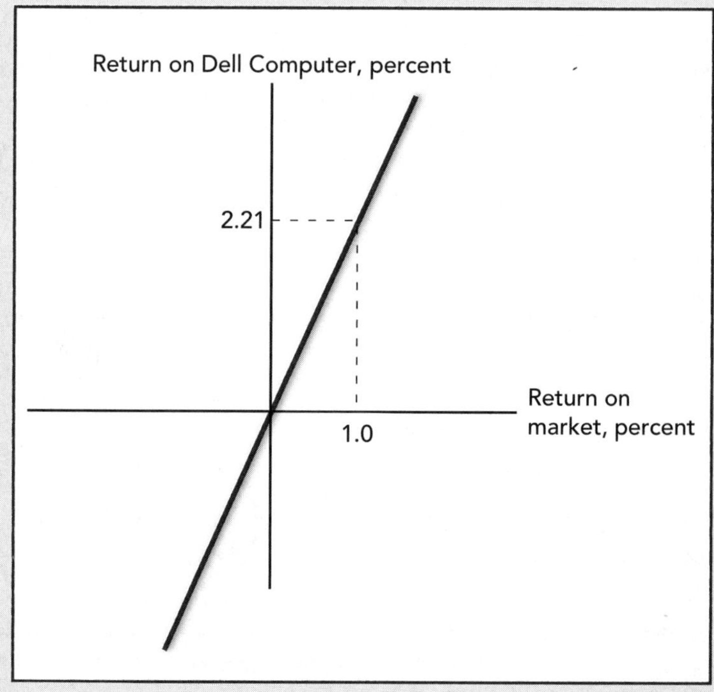

FIGURE 7.11

The return on Dell Computer stock changes on average by 2.21 percent for each additional 1 percent change in the market return. Beta is therefore 2.21.

Market Risk Is Measured by Beta

If you want to know the contribution of an individual security to the risk of a well-diversified portfolio, it is no good thinking about how risky that security is if held in isolation—you need to measure its *market* risk, and that boils down to measuring how sensitive it is to market movements. This sensitivity is called **beta** (β).

Stocks with betas greater than 1.0 tend to amplify the overall movements of the market. Stocks with betas between 0 and 1.0 tend to move in the same direction as the market, but not as far. Of course, the market is the portfolio of all stocks, so the "average" stock has a beta of 1.0. Table 7.5 reports betas for the 10 well-known common stocks we referred to earlier.

Over the five years from mid-1996 to mid-2001, Dell Computer had a beta of 2.21. If the future resembles the past, this means that *on average* when the market rises an extra 1 percent, Dell's stock price will rise by an extra 2.21 percent. When the market falls an extra 2 percent, Dell's stock prices will fall an extra $2 \times 2.21 = 4.42$ percent. Thus a line fitted to a plot of Dell's returns versus market returns has a slope of 2.21. See Figure 7.11.

TABLE 7.6

Betas for foreign stocks, September 1996–August 2001 (betas are measured relative to the stock's home market).

Stock	Beta	Stock	Beta
Alcan	.66	LVMH	1.42
BP Amoco	.82	Nestlé	.64
Deutsche Bank	1.18	Nokia	1.29
Fiat	1.03	Sony	1.38
KLM	.82	Telefonica de Argentina	1.06

Of course Dell's stock returns are not perfectly correlated with market returns. The company is also subject to unique risk, so the actual returns will be scattered about the line in Figure 7.11. Sometimes Dell will head south while the market goes north, and vice versa.

Of the 10 stocks in Table 7.5 Dell has one of the highest betas. Exxon Mobil is at the other extreme. A line fitted to a plot of Exxon Mobil's returns versus market returns would be less steep: Its slope would be only .40.

Just as we can measure how the returns of a U.S. stock are affected by fluctuations in the U.S. market, so we can measure how stocks in other countries are affected by movements in *their* markets. Table 7.6 shows the betas for the sample of foreign stocks.

Why Security Betas Determine Portfolio Risk

Let's review the two crucial points about security risk and portfolio risk:

- Market risk accounts for most of the risk of a well-diversified portfolio.
- The beta of an individual security measures its sensitivity to market movements.

It's easy to see where we are headed: In a portfolio context, a security's risk is measured by beta. Perhaps we could just jump to that conclusion, but we'd rather explain it. In fact, we'll offer two explanations.

Explanation 1: Where's Bedrock? Look back to Figure 7.8, which shows how the standard deviation of portfolio return depends on the number of securities in the portfolio. With more securities, and therefore better diversification, portfolio risk declines until all unique risk is eliminated and only the bedrock of market risk remains.

Where's bedrock? It depends on the average beta of the securities selected.

Suppose we constructed a portfolio containing a large number of stocks—500, say—drawn randomly from the whole market. What would we get? The market itself, or a portfolio *very* close to it. The portfolio beta would be 1.0, and the correlation with the market would be 1.0. If the standard deviation of the market were 20 percent (roughly its average for 1926–2000), then the portfolio standard deviation would also be 20 percent.

But suppose we constructed the portfolio from a large group of stocks with an average beta of 1.5. Again we would end up with a 500-stock portfolio with virtually no unique risk—a portfolio that moves almost in lockstep with the market. However, *this* portfolio's standard deviation would be 30 percent, 1.5 times that of the market.[27] A well-diversified portfolio with a beta of 1.5 will amplify every market move by 50 percent and end up with 150 percent of the market's risk.

Of course, we could repeat the same experiment with stocks with a beta of .5 and end up with a well-diversified portfolio half as risky as the market. Figure 7.12 shows these three cases.

The general point is this: The risk of a well-diversified portfolio is proportional to the portfolio beta, which equals the average beta of the securities included in the portfolio. This shows you how portfolio risk is driven by security betas.

Explanation 2: Betas and Covariances. A statistician would define the beta of stock *i* as

$$\beta_i = \frac{\sigma_{im}}{\sigma_m^2}$$

where σ_{im} is the covariance between stock *i*'s return and the market return, and σ_m^2 is the variance of the market return.

It turns out that this ratio of covariance to variance measures a stock's contribution to portfolio risk. You can see this by looking back at our calculations for the risk of the portfolio of Coca-Cola and Reebok.

Remember that the risk of this portfolio was the sum of the following cells:

	Coca-Cola	Reebok
Coca-Cola	$(.65)^2 \times (31.5)^2$	$.65 \times .35 \times .2 \times 31.5 \times 58.5$
Reebok	$.65 \times .35 \times .2 \times 31.5 \times 58.5$	$(.35)^2 \times (58.5)^2$

If we add each *row* of cells, we can see how much of the portfolio's risk comes from Coca-Cola and how much comes from Reebok:

Stock	Contribution to Risk	
Coca-Cola	$.65 \times \{[.65 \times (31.5)^2] + [.35 \times .2 \times 31.5 \times 58.5]\} =$	$.65 \times 774.0$
Reebok	$.35 \times \{[.65 \times .2 \times 31.5 \times 58.5] + [.35 \times (58.5)^2]\} =$	$.35 \times 1{,}437.3$
	Total portfolio	1,006.1

Coca-Cola's contribution to portfolio risk depends on its relative importance in the portfolio (.65) and its average covariance with the stocks in the portfolio (774.0). (Notice that the average covariance of Coca-Cola with the portfolio includes its covariance with itself, i.e., its variance.) The *proportion* of the risk that comes from the Coca-Cola holding is

$$\text{Relative market value} \times \frac{\text{average covariance}}{\text{portfolio variance}} = .65 \times \frac{774.0}{1{,}006.1} = .65 \times .77 = .5$$

Similarly, Reebok's contribution to portfolio risk depends on its relative importance in the portfolio (.35) and its average covariance with the stocks in the

[27] A 500-stock portfolio with $\beta = 1.5$ would still have some unique risk because it would be unduly concentrated in high-beta industries. Its actual standard deviation would be a bit higher than 30 percent. If that worries you, relax; we will show you in Chapter 8 how you can construct a fully diversified portfolio with a beta of 1.5 by borrowing and investing in the market portfolio.

FIGURE 7.12

(*a*) A randomly selected 500-stock portfolio ends up with $\beta = 1$ and a standard deviation equal to the market's—in this case 20 percent. (*b*) A 500-stock portfolio constructed with stocks with average $\beta = 1.5$ has a standard deviation of about 30 percent—150 percent of the market's. (*c*) A 500-stock portfolio constructed with stocks with average $\beta = .5$ has a standard deviation of about 10 percent—half the market's.

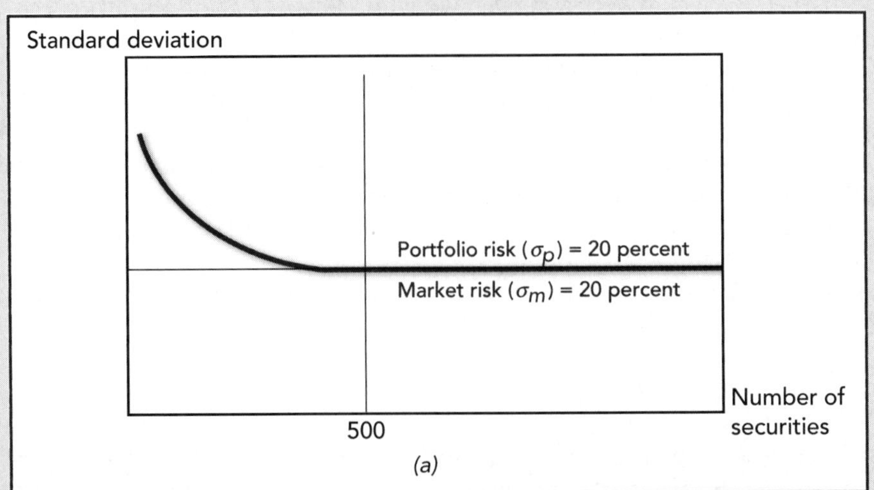

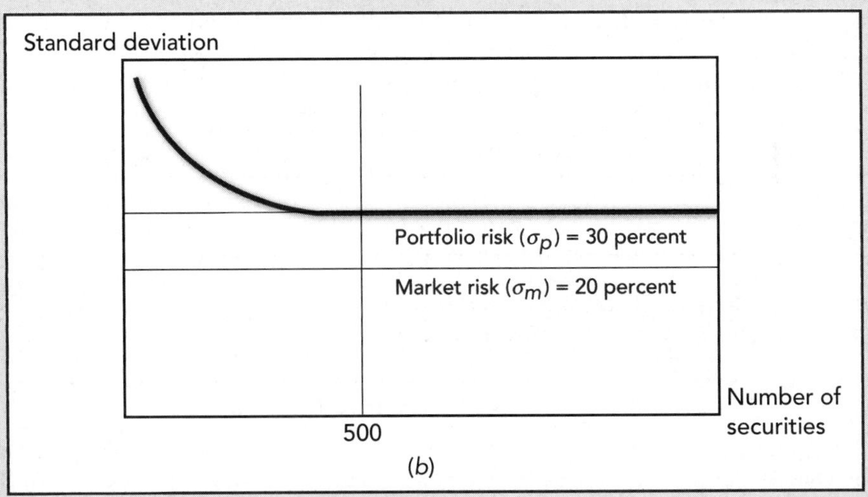

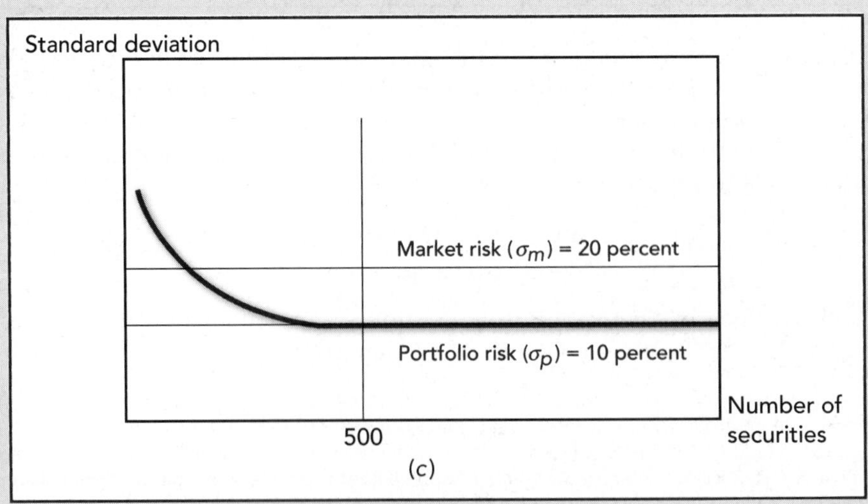

portfolio (1,437.3). The *proportion* of the risk that comes from the Reebok holding is also .5:

$$.35 \times \frac{1{,}437.3}{1{,}006.1} = .35 \times 1.43 = .5$$

In each case the proportion depends on two numbers: the relative size of the holding (.65 or .35) and a measure of the effect of that holding on portfolio risk (.77 or 1.43). The latter values are the betas of Coca-Cola and Reebok *relative to that portfolio.* On average, an extra 1 percent change in the value of the portfolio would be associated with an extra .77 percent change in the value of Coca-Cola and a 1.43 percent change in the value of Reebok.

To calculate Coca-Cola's beta relative to the portfolio, we simply take the covariance of Coca-Cola with the portfolio and divide by the portfolio variance. The idea is exactly the same if we wish to calculate the beta of Coca-Cola *relative to the market portfolio.* We just calculate its covariance with the market portfolio and divide by the variance of the market:

$$\begin{array}{c}\text{Beta relative to market portfolio}\\ \text{(or, more simply, beta)}\end{array} = \frac{\text{covariance with market}}{\text{variance of market}} = \frac{\sigma_{im}}{\sigma_m^2}$$

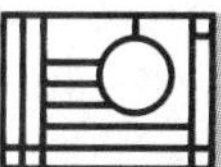

7.5 DIVERSIFICATION AND VALUE ADDITIVITY

We have seen that diversification reduces risk and, therefore, makes sense for investors. But does it also make sense for the firm? Is a diversified firm more attractive to investors than an undiversified one? If it is, we have an *extremely* disturbing result. If diversification is an appropriate corporate objective, each project has to be analyzed as a potential addition to the firm's portfolio of assets. The value of the diversified package would be greater than the sum of the parts. So present values would no longer add.

Diversification is undoubtedly a good thing, but that does not mean that firms should practice it. If investors were *not* able to hold a large number of securities, then they might want firms to diversify for them. But investors *can* diversify.[28] In many ways they can do so more easily than firms. Individuals can invest in the steel industry this week and pull out next week. A firm cannot do that. To be sure, the individual would have to pay brokerage fees on the purchase and sale of steel company shares, but think of the time and expense for a firm to acquire a steel company or to start up a new steel-making operation.

You can probably see where we are heading. If investors can diversify on their own account, they will not pay any *extra* for firms that diversify. And if they have a sufficiently wide choice of securities, they will not pay any *less* because they are unable to invest separately in each factory. Therefore, in countries like the United States, which have large and competitive capital markets, diversification does not add to a firm's value or subtract from it. The total value is the sum of its parts.

This conclusion is important for corporate finance, because it justifies adding present values. The concept of *value additivity* is so important that we will give a

[28]One of the simplest ways for an individual to diversify is to buy shares in a mutual fund that holds a diversified portfolio.

formal definition of it. If the capital market establishes a value PV(A) for asset A and PV(B) for B, the market value of a firm that holds only these two assets is

$$PV(AB) = PV(A) + PV(B)$$

A three-asset firm combining assets A, B, and C would be worth PV(ABC) = PV(A) + PV(B) + PV(C), and so on for any number of assets.

We have relied on intuitive arguments for value additivity. But the concept is a general one that can be proved formally by several different routes.[29] The concept of value additivity seems to be widely accepted, for thousands of managers add thousands of present values daily, usually without thinking about it.

[29]You may wish to refer to the Appendix to Chapter 33, which discusses diversification and value additivity in the context of mergers.

SUMMARY

Our review of capital market history showed that the returns to investors have varied according to the risks they have borne. At one extreme, very safe securities like U.S. Treasury bills have provided an average return over 75 years of only 3.9 percent a year. The riskiest securities that we looked at were common stocks. The stock market provided an average return of 13.0 percent, a premium of more than 9 percent over the safe rate of interest.

This gives us two benchmarks for the opportunity cost of capital. If we are evaluating a safe project, we discount at the current risk-free rate of interest. If we are evaluating a project of average risk, we discount at the expected return on the average common stock. Historical evidence suggests that this return is about 9 percent above the risk-free rate, but many financial managers and economists opt for a lower figure. That still leaves us with a lot of assets that don't fit these simple cases. Before we can deal with them, we need to learn how to measure risk.

Risk is best judged in a portfolio context. Most investors do not put all their eggs into one basket: They diversify. Thus the effective risk of any security cannot be judged by an examination of that security alone. Part of the uncertainty about the security's return is diversified away when the security is grouped with others in a portfolio.

Risk in investment means that future returns are unpredictable. This spread of possible outcomes is usually measured by standard deviation. The standard deviation of the *market portfolio,* generally represented by the Standard and Poor's Composite Index, is around 20 percent a year.

Most individual stocks have higher standard deviations than this, but much of their variability represents *unique* risk that can be eliminated by diversification. Diversification cannot eliminate *market* risk. Diversified portfolios are exposed to variation in the general level of the market.

A security's contribution to the risk of a well-diversified portfolio depends on how the security is liable to be affected by a general market decline. This sensitivity to market movements is known as *beta* (β). Beta measures the amount that investors expect the stock price to change for each additional 1 percent change in the market. The average beta of all stocks is 1.0. A stock with a beta greater than 1 is unusually sensitive to market movements; a stock with a beta below 1 is unusually insensitive to market movements. The standard deviation of a well-diversified portfolio is proportional to its beta. Thus a diversified portfolio invested in stocks with a beta of 2.0 will have twice the risk of a diversified portfolio with a beta of 1.0.

One theme of this chapter is that diversification is a good thing *for the investor.* This does not imply that *firms* should diversify. Corporate diversification is redundant if investors can diversify on their own account. Since diversification does not affect the firm value, present values add even when risk is explicitly considered. Thanks to *value additivity,* the net present value rule for capital budgeting works even under uncertainty.

FURTHER READING

A very valuable record of the performance of United States securities since 1926 is:

Ibbotson Associates, Inc.: *Stocks, Bonds, Bills, and Inflation, 2001 Yearbook,* Ibbotson Associates, Chicago, 2001.

Dimson, Marsh, and Staunton compare market returns in 15 countries over the years 1900–2000 in:

E. Dimson, P. R. Marsh, and M. Staunton: *Millenium Book II: 101 Years of Investment Returns,* ABN-Amro and London Business School, London, 2001.

Fama and French derive measures of expected dividend growth to argue that historical data on the market risk premium overstate the expected premium. See:

E. F. Fama and K. R. French: "The Equity Premium," *Journal of Finance,* forthcoming.

Merton discusses the problems encountered in measuring average returns from historical data:

R. C. Merton: "On Estimating the Expected Return on the Market: An Exploratory Investigation," *Journal of Financial Economics,* 8:323–361 (December 1980).

The classic analysis of the degree to which stocks move together is:

B. F. King: "Market and Industry Factors in Stock Price Behavior," *Journal of Business, Security Prices: A Supplement,* 39:179–190 (January 1966).

There have been several studies of the way that standard deviation is reduced by diversification, including:

M. Statman: "How Many Stocks Make a Diversified Portfolio?" *Journal of Financial and Quantitative Analysis,* 22:353–364 (September 1987).

Formal proofs of the value additivity principle can be found in:

S. C. Myers: "Procedures for Capital Budgeting under Uncertainty," *Industrial Management Review,* 9:1–20 (Spring 1968).

L. D. Schall: "Asset Valuation, Firm Investment and Firm Diversification," *Journal of Business,* 45:11–28 (January 1972).

QUIZ

1. **a.** What was the average annual return on United States common stocks from 1926 to 2000 (approximately)?
   b. What was the average difference between this return and the return on Treasury bills?
   c. What was the average return on Treasury bills in real terms?
   d. What was the standard deviation of returns on the market index?
   e. Was this standard deviation more or less than on most individual stocks?
2. A game of chance offers the following odds and payoffs. Each play of the game costs $100, so the net profit per play is the payoff less $100.

Probability	Payoff	Net Profit
.10	\$500	\$400
.50	100	0
.40	0	−100

What are the expected cash payoff and expected rate of return? Calculate the variance and standard deviation of this rate of return.

3. The following table shows the nominal returns on the Mexican stock market and the Mexican rate of inflation.
   a. What was the standard deviation of the market returns?
   b. Calculate the average real return.

Year	Nominal Return (%)	Inflation (%)
1995	16.5	52.0
1996	21.9	27.7
1997	53.4	15.7
1998	−20.8	18.6
1999	84.3	12.3

4. Fill in the missing words:

   Risk is usually measured by the variance of returns or the _____, which is simply the square root of the variance. As long as the stock price changes are not perfectly _____, the risk of a diversified portfolio is _____ than the average risk of the individual stocks. The risk that can be eliminated by diversification is known as _____ risk. But diversification cannot remove all risk; the risk that it cannot eliminate is known as _____ risk.

5. Lawrence Interchange, ace mutual fund manager, produced the following percentage rates of return from 1996 to 2000. Rates of return on the S&P 500 are given for comparison.

	1996	1997	1998	1999	2000
Mr. Interchange	+16.1	+28.4	+25.1	+14.3	−6.0
S&P 500	+23.1	+33.4	+28.6	+21.0	−9.1

   Calculate the average return and standard deviation of Mr. Interchange's mutual fund. Did he do better or worse than the S&P by these measures?

6. True or false?
   a. Investors prefer diversified companies because they are less risky.
   b. If stocks were perfectly positively correlated, diversification would not reduce risk.
   c. The contribution of a stock to the risk of a well-diversified portfolio depends on its market risk.
   d. A well-diversified portfolio with a beta of 2.0 is twice as risky as the market portfolio.
   e. An undiversified portfolio with a beta of 2.0 is less than twice as risky as the market portfolio.

7. In which of the following situations would you get the largest reduction in risk by spreading your investment across two stocks?
   a. The two shares are perfectly correlated.
   b. There is no correlation.
   c. There is modest negative correlation.
   d. There is perfect negative correlation.

TABLE 7.7

See Quiz Question 11.

	Expected Stock Return if Market Return Is:	
Stock	**−10%**	**+10%**
A	0	+20
B	−20	+20
C	−30	0
D	+15	+15
E	+10	−10

8. To calculate the variance of a three-stock portfolio, you need to add nine boxes:

Use the same symbols that we used in this chapter; for example, x_1 = proportion invested in stock 1 and σ_{12} = covariance between stocks 1 and 2. Now complete the nine boxes.

9. Suppose the standard deviation of the market return is 20 percent.
   a. What is the standard deviation of returns on a well-diversified portfolio with a beta of 1.3?
   b. What is the standard deviation of returns on a well-diversified portfolio with a beta of 0?
   c. A well-diversified portfolio has a standard deviation of 15 percent. What is its beta?
   d. A poorly diversified portfolio has a standard deviation of 20 percent. What can you say about its beta?
10. A portfolio contains equal investments in 10 stocks. Five have a beta of 1.2; the remainder have a beta of 1.4. What is the portfolio beta?
    a. 1.3.
    b. Greater than 1.3 because the portfolio is not completely diversified.
    c. Less than 1.3 because diversification reduces beta.
11. What is the beta of each of the stocks shown in Table 7.7?
12. True or false? Why? "Diversification reduces risk. Therefore corporations ought to favor capital investments with low correlations with their existing lines of business."

PRACTICE QUESTIONS

1. Here are inflation rates and stock market and Treasury bill returns between 1996 and 2000:

Year	Inflation	S&P 500 Return	T-Bill Return
1996	3.3	23.1	5.2
1997	1.7	33.4	5.3
1998	1.6	28.6	4.9
1999	2.7	21.0	4.7
2000	3.4	−9.1	5.9

   a. What was the real return on the S&P 500 in each year?
   b. What was the average real return?

Visit us at www.mhhe.com/bm7e

c. What was the risk premium in each year?
d. What was the average risk premium?
e. What was the standard deviation of the risk premium?

STANDARD & POOR'S

2. Most of the companies in Tables 7.3 are covered in the Standard & Poor's Market Insight website (**www.mhhe.com/edumarketinsight**). Pick at least three companies. For each company, download "Monthly Adjusted Prices" as an Excel spreadsheet. Calculate each company's variance and standard deviation from the monthly returns given on the spreadsheet. The Excel functions are VAR and STDEV. Convert the standard deviations from monthly to annual units by multiplying by the square root of 12. How has the stand-alone risk of these stocks changed, compared to the figures reported in Table 7.3?
3. Each of the following statements is dangerous or misleading. Explain why.
   a. A long-term United States government bond is always absolutely safe.
   b. All investors should prefer stocks to bonds because stocks offer higher long-run rates of return.
   c. The best practical forecast of future rates of return on the stock market is a 5- or 10-year average of historical returns.
4. "There's upside risk and downside risk. Standard deviation doesn't distinguish between them." Do you think the speaker has a fair point?
5. Hippique s.a., which owns a stable of racehorses, has just invested in a mysterious black stallion with great form but disputed bloodlines. Some experts in horseflesh predict the horse will win the coveted Prix de Bidet; others argue that it should be put out to grass. Is this a risky investment for Hippique shareholders? Explain.
6. Lonesome Gulch Mines has a standard deviation of 42 percent per year and a beta of +.10. Amalgamated Copper has a standard deviation of 31 percent a year and a beta of +.66. Explain why Lonesome Gulch is the safer investment for a diversified investor.
7. Respond to the following comments:
   a. "Risk is not variability. If I know a stock is going to fluctuate between $10 and $20, I can make myself a bundle."
   b. "There are all sorts of risk in addition to beta risk. There's the risk that we'll have a downturn in demand, there's the risk that my best plant manager will drop dead, there's the risk of a hike in steel prices. You've got to take all these things into consideration."
   c. "Risk to me is the probability of loss."
   d. "Those guys who suggest beta is a measure of risk make the big assumption that betas don't change."
8. Lambeth Walk invests 60 percent of his funds in stock I and the balance in stock J. The standard deviation of returns on I is 10 percent, and on J it is 20 percent. Calculate the variance of portfolio returns, assuming
   a. The correlation between the returns is 1.0.
   b. The correlation is .5.
   c. The correlation is 0.
9. a. How many variance terms and how many covariance terms do you need to calculate the risk of a 100-share portfolio?
   b. Suppose all stocks had a standard deviation of 30 percent and a correlation with each other of .4. What is the standard deviation of the returns on a portfolio that has equal holdings in 50 stocks?
   c. What is the standard deviation of a fully diversified portfolio of such stocks?
10. Suppose that the standard deviation of returns from a typical share is about .40 (or 40 percent) a year. The correlation between the returns of each pair of shares is about .3.
    a. Calculate the variance and standard deviation of the returns on a portfolio that has equal investments in two shares, three shares, and so on, up to 10 shares.

	Correlation Coefficients							
	Alcan	BP	Deutsche Bank	KLM	LVMH	Nestlé	Sony	Standard Deviation
Alcan	1.0	.48	.40	.32	.43	.26	.27	31.0%
BP		1.0	.05	.20	.08	.23	.15	24.8
Deutsche Bank			1.0	.45	.50	.37	.42	37.5
KLM				1.0	.31	.32	.01	39.6
LVMH					1.0	.16	.36	41.9
Nestlé						1.0	.14	19.7
Sony							1.0	46.3

TABLE 7.8

Standard deviations and correlation coefficients for a sample of seven stocks.

Note: Correlations and standard deviations are calculated using returns in each country's own currency; in other words, they assume that the investor is hedged against exchange risk.

- **b.** Use your estimates to draw a graph like Figure 7.8. How large is the underlying market risk that cannot be diversified away?
- **c.** Now repeat the problem, assuming that the correlation between each pair of stocks is zero.

11. Download the "Monthly Adjusted Prices" spreadsheets for Coca-Cola, Citigroup, and Pfizer from the Standard & Poor's Market Insight website (**www.mhhe.com/edumarketinsight**).

STANDARD &POOR'S

- **a.** Calculate the annual standard deviation for each company, using the most recent three years of monthly returns. Use the Excel function STDEV. Multiply by the square root of 12 to convert to annual units.
- **b.** Use the Excel function CORREL to calculate the correlation coefficient between the monthly returns for each pair of stocks.
- **c.** Calculate the standard deviation of a portfolio with equal investments in each of the three stocks.

12. Table 7.8 shows standard deviations and correlation coefficients for seven stocks from different countries. Calculate the variance of a portfolio 40 percent invested in BP, 40 percent invested in KLM, and 20 percent invested in Nestlé.

13. Most of the companies in Tables 7.5 are covered in the Standard & Poor's Market Insight website (**www.mhhe.com/edumarketinsight**). For those that are covered, you can easily calculate beta. Download the "Monthly Adjusted Prices" spreadsheet, and note the columns for returns on the stock and the S&P 500 index. Beta is calculated by the Excel function SLOPE, where the "y" range refers to the company's return (the dependent variable) and the "x" range refers to the market returns (the independent variable). Calculate the betas. How have they changed from the betas reported in Table 7.5?

14. Your eccentric Aunt Claudia has left you $50,000 in Alcan shares plus $50,000 cash. Unfortunately her will requires that the Alcan stock not be sold for one year and the $50,000 cash must be entirely invested in one of the stocks shown in Table 7.8. What is the safest attainable portfolio under these restrictions?

15. There are few, if any, real companies with negative betas. But suppose you found one with $\beta = -.25$.

- **a.** How would you expect this stock's rate of return to change if the overall market rose by an extra 5 percent? What if the market fell by an extra 5 percent?

b. You have $1 million invested in a well-diversified portfolio of stocks. Now you receive an additional $20,000 bequest. Which of the following actions will yield the safest overall portfolio return?

i. Invest $20,000 in Treasury bills (which have $\beta = 0$).

ii. Invest $20,000 in stocks with $\beta = 1$.

iii. Invest $20,000 in the stock with $\beta = -.25$.

Explain your answer.

STANDARD &POOR'S

16. Download "Monthly Adjusted Prices" for General Motors (GM) and Harley Davidson (HDI) from the Standard & Poor's Market Insight website (**www.mhhe.com/edumarketinsight**).

a. Calculate each company's beta, following the procedure described in Practice Question 13.

b. Calculate the annual standard deviation of the market from the monthly returns for the S&P 500. Use the Excel function STDEV, and multiply by the square root of 12 to convert to annual units. Also calculate the annual standard deviations for GM and HDI.

c. Let's assume that your answers to (a) and (b) are good forecasts. What would be the standard deviation of a well-diversified portfolio of stocks with betas equal to Harley Davidson's beta? How about a well-diversified portfolio of stocks with GM's beta?

d. How much of the total risk of GM was unique risk? How much of HDI's?

17. Diversification has enormous value to investors, yet opportunities for diversification should not sway capital investment decisions by corporations. How would you explain this apparent paradox?

CHALLENGE QUESTIONS

1. Here are some historical data on the risk characteristics of Dell and Microsoft:

	Dell	Microsoft
β (beta)	2.21	1.81
Yearly standard deviation of return (%)	62.7	50.7

Assume the standard deviation of the return on the market was 15 percent.

a. The correlation coefficient of Dell's return versus Microsoft's is .66. What is the standard deviation of a portfolio invested half in Dell and half in Microsoft?

b. What is the standard deviation of a portfolio invested one-third in Dell, one-third in Microsoft, and one-third in Treasury bills?

c. What is the standard deviation if the portfolio is split evenly between Dell and Microsoft and is financed at 50 percent margin, i.e., the investor puts up only 50 percent of the total amount and borrows the balance from the broker?

d. What is the *approximate* standard deviation of a portfolio composed of 100 stocks with betas of 2.21 like Dell? How about 100 stocks like Microsoft? *Hint:* Part (d) should not require anything but the simplest arithmetic to answer.

2. Suppose that Treasury bills offer a return of about 6 percent and the expected market risk premium is 8.5 percent. The standard deviation of Treasury-bill returns is zero and the standard deviation of market returns is 20 percent. Use the formula for portfolio risk to calculate the standard deviation of portfolios with different proportions in Treasury bills and the market. (Note that the covariance of two rates of return must be zero when the standard deviation of one return is zero.) Graph the expected returns and standard deviations.

3. It is often useful to know how well your portfolio is diversified. Two measures have been suggested:
   a. The variance of the returns on a fully diversified portfolio as a proportion of the variance of returns on *your* portfolio.
   b. The number of shares in a portfolio that (*i*) has the same risk as yours, (*ii*) is invested in "typical" shares, and (*iii*) has equal amounts invested in each share.

   Suppose that you hold eight stocks. All are fairly typical; they have a standard deviation of 40 percent a year and the correlation between each pair is .3. Of your fund, 20 percent is invested in one stock, 20 percent is invested in a second stock, and the remaining 60 percent is spread evenly over a further six stocks. Calculate each measure of portfolio diversification. What are the advantages and disadvantages of each?
4. Some stocks have high standard deviations and relatively low betas. Sometimes it is the other way around. Why do you think this is so? Illustrate your answer by calculating some standard deviations and betas using data for 60 recent months. (Monthly stock price and index data can be found on **finance.yahoo.com**.)
5. Select two bank stocks and two oil stocks and then calculate the returns for 60 recent months. (Monthly stock price and index data can be obtained from **finance.yahoo.com**.) Now
   a. Calculate the standard deviation of monthly returns for each of these stocks and the correlation between each pair of stocks.
   b. Use your results to find the standard deviation of a portfolio that is evenly divided between different pairs of stocks. Do you reduce risk more by diversifying across stocks in the same industry or those in different industries?

CHAPTER EIGHT

RISK AND RETURN

IN CHAPTER 7 we began to come to grips with the problem of measuring risk. Here is the story so far.

The stock market is risky because there is a spread of possible outcomes. The usual measure of this spread is the standard deviation or variance. The risk of any stock can be broken down into two parts. There is the *unique risk* that is peculiar to that stock, and there is the *market risk* that is associated with marketwide variations. Investors can eliminate unique risk by holding a well-diversified portfolio, but they cannot eliminate market risk. *All* the risk of a fully diversified portfolio is market risk.

A stock's contribution to the risk of a fully diversified portfolio depends on its sensitivity to market changes. This sensitivity is generally known as *beta.* A security with a beta of 1.0 has average market risk—a well-diversified portfolio of such securities has the same standard deviation as the market index. A security with a beta of .5 has below-average market risk—a well-diversified portfolio of these securities tends to move half as far as the market moves and has half the market's standard deviation.

In this chapter we build on this newfound knowledge. We present leading theories linking risk and return in a competitive economy, and we show how these theories can be used to estimate the returns required by investors in different stock market investments. We start with the most widely used theory, the capital asset pricing model, which builds directly on the ideas developed in the last chapter. We will also look at another class of models, known as arbitrage pricing or factor models. Then in Chapter 9 we show how these ideas can help the financial manager cope with risk in practical capital budgeting situations.

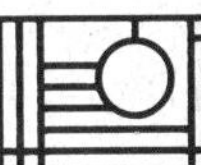

8.1 HARRY MARKOWITZ AND THE BIRTH OF PORTFOLIO THEORY

Most of the ideas in Chapter 7 date back to an article written in 1952 by Harry Markowitz.[1] Markowitz drew attention to the common practice of portfolio diversification and showed exactly how an investor can reduce the standard deviation of portfolio returns by choosing stocks that do not move exactly together. But Markowitz did not stop there; he went on to work out the basic principles of portfolio construction. These principles are the foundation for much of what has been written about the relationship between risk and return.

We begin with Figure 8.1, which shows a histogram of the daily returns on Microsoft stock from 1990 to 2001. On this histogram we have superimposed a bell-shaped normal distribution. The result is typical: When measured over some fairly short interval, the past rates of return on any stock conform closely to a normal distribution.[2]

Normal distributions can be completely defined by two numbers. One is the average or expected return; the other is the variance or standard deviation. Now you can see why in Chapter 7 we discussed the calculation of expected return and standard deviation. They are not just arbitrary measures: If returns are normally distributed, they are the *only* two measures that an investor need consider.

---

[1] H. M. Markowitz, "Portfolio Selection," *Journal of Finance* 7 (March 1952), pp. 77–91.

[2] If you were to measure returns over *long* intervals, the distribution would be skewed. For example, you would encounter returns greater than 100 percent but none less than −100 percent. The distribution of returns over periods of, say, one year would be better approximated by a *lognormal* distribution. The lognormal distribution, like the normal, is completely specified by its mean and standard deviation.

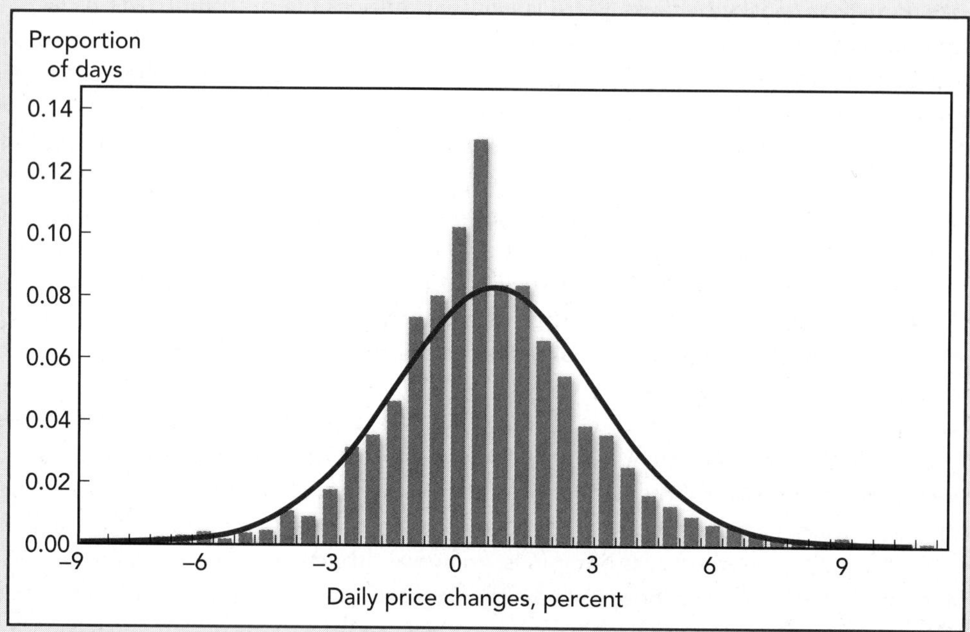

FIGURE 8.1

Daily price changes for Microsoft are approximately normally distributed. This plot spans 1990 to 2001.

Figure 8.2 pictures the distribution of possible returns from two investments. Both offer an expected return of 10 percent, but A has much the wider spread of possible outcomes. Its standard deviation is 15 percent; the standard deviation of B is 7.5 percent. Most investors dislike uncertainty and would therefore prefer B to A.

Figure 8.3 pictures the distribution of returns from two other investments. This time both have the *same* standard deviation, but the expected return is 20 percent from stock C and only 10 percent from stock D. Most investors like high expected return and would therefore prefer C to D.

Combining Stocks into Portfolios

Suppose that you are wondering whether to invest in shares of Coca-Cola or Reebok. You decide that Reebok offers an expected return of 20 percent and Coca-Cola offers an expected return of 10 percent. After looking back at the past variability of the two stocks, you also decide that the standard deviation of returns is 31.5 percent for Coca-Cola and 58.5 percent for Reebok. Reebok offers the higher expected return, but it is considerably more risky.

Now there is no reason to restrict yourself to holding only one stock. For example, in Section 7.3 we analyzed what would happen if you invested 65 percent of your money in Coca-Cola and 35 percent in Reebok. The expected return on this portfolio is 13.5 percent, which is simply a weighted average of the expected returns on the two holdings. What about the risk of such a portfolio? We know that thanks to diversification the portfolio risk is less than the average of the risks of the

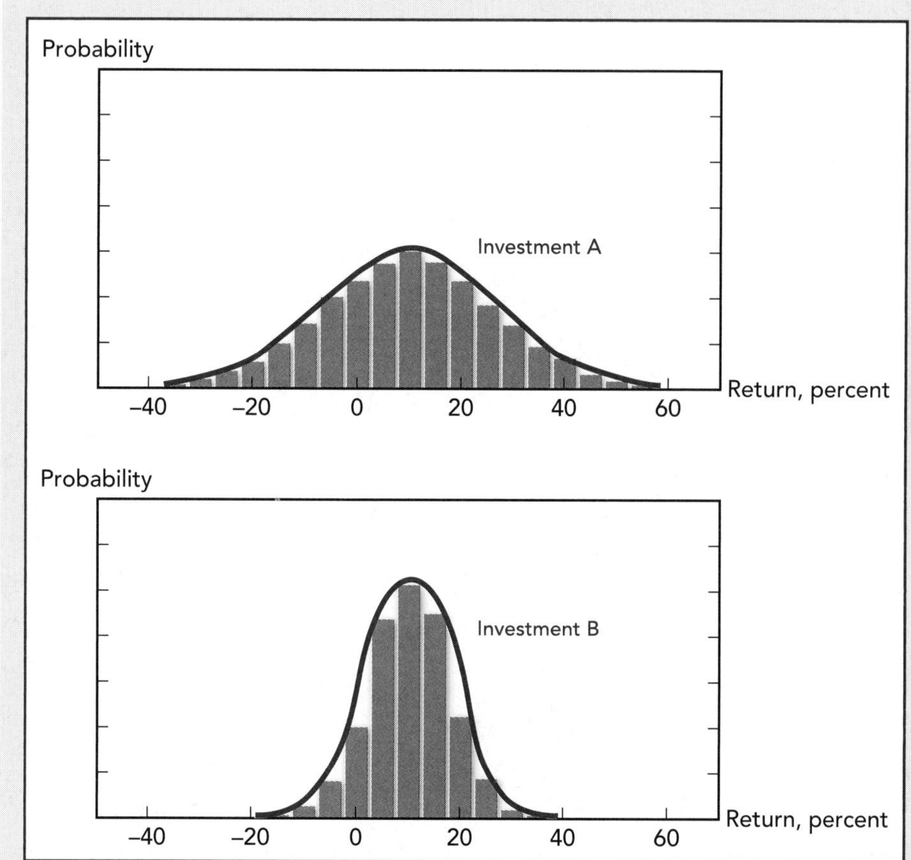

FIGURE 8.2

These two investments both have an *expected* return of 10 percent but because investment A has the greater spread of *possible* returns, it is more risky than B. We can measure this spread by the standard deviation. Investment A has a standard deviation of 15 percent; B, 7.5 percent. Most investors would prefer B to A.

separate stocks. In fact, on the basis of past experience the standard deviation of this portfolio is 31.7 percent.[3]

In Figure 8.4 we have plotted the expected return and risk that you could achieve by different combinations of the two stocks. Which of these combinations is best? That depends on your stomach. If you want to stake all on getting rich quickly, you will do best to put all your money in Reebok. If you want a more peaceful life, you should invest most of your money in Coca-Cola; to minimize risk you should keep a small investment in Reebok.[4]

In practice, you are not limited to investing in only two stocks. Our next task, therefore, is to find a way to identify the best portfolios of 10, 100, or 1,000 stocks.

---

[3]We pointed out in Section 7.3 that the correlation between the returns of Coca-Cola and Reebok has been about .2. The variance of a portfolio which is invested 65 percent in Coca-Cola and 35 percent in Reebok is

$$\begin{aligned}\text{Variance} &= x_1^2\sigma_1^2 + x_2^2\sigma_2^2 + 2x_1x_2\rho_{12}\sigma_1\sigma_2 \\ &= [(.65)^2 \times (31.5)^2] + [(.35)^2 \times (58.5)^2] + 2(.65 \times .35 \times .2 \times 31.5 \times 58.5) \\ &= 1006.1\end{aligned}$$

The portfolio standard deviation is $\sqrt{1006.1} = 31.7$ percent.

[4]The portfolio with the minimum risk has 21.4 percent in Reebok. We assume in Figure 8.4 that you may not take negative positions in either stock, i.e., we rule out short sales.

FIGURE 8.3

The standard deviation of possible returns is 15 percent for both these investments, but the expected return from C is 20 percent compared with an expected return from D of only 10 percent. Most investors would prefer C to D.

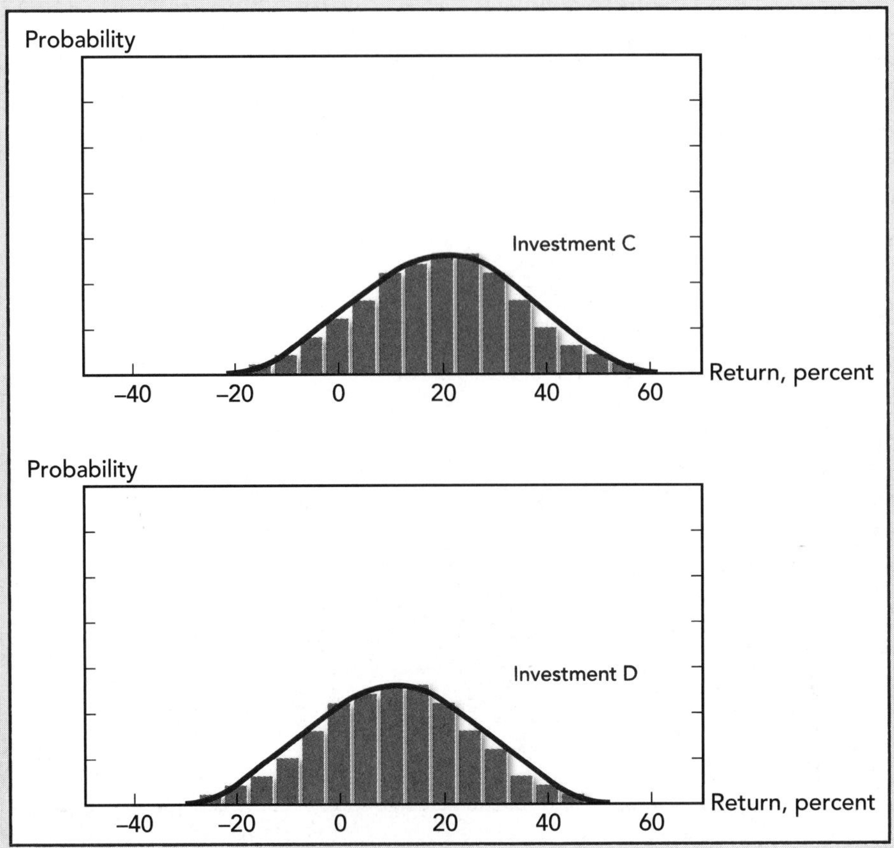

FIGURE 8.4

The curved line illustrates how expected return and standard deviation change as you hold different combinations of two stocks. For example, if you invest 35 percent of your money in Reebok and the remainder in Coca-Cola, your expected return is 13.5 percent, which is 35 percent of the way between the expected returns on the two stocks. The standard deviation is 31.7 percent, which is *less* than 35 percent of the way between the standard deviations on the two stocks. This is because diversification reduces risk.

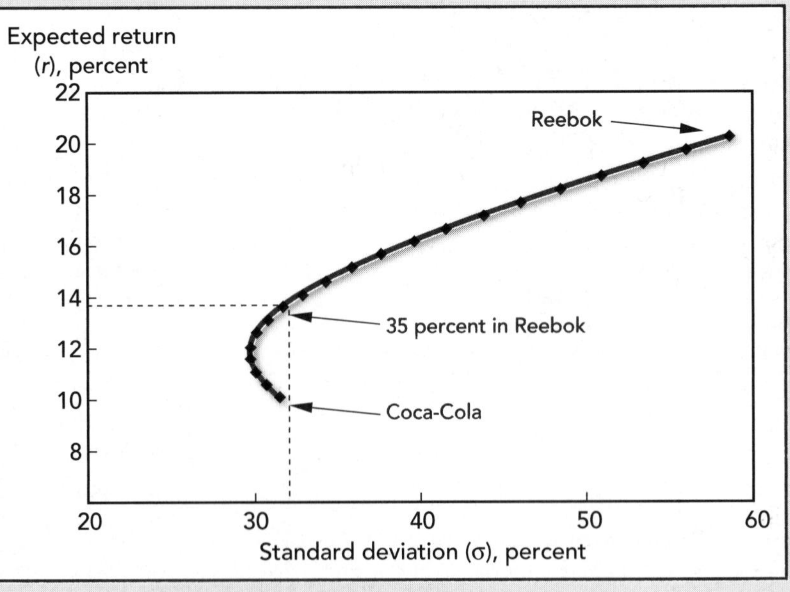

	Expected Return	Standard Deviation	Efficient Portfolios—Percentages Allocated to Each Stock			
			A	B	C	D
Amazon.com	34.6%	110.6%	100	9.3	4.5	
Boeing	13.0	30.9		2.1	9.6	0.6
Coca-Cola	10.0	31.5				0.4
Dell Computer	26.2	62.7		21.1	14.4	
Exxon Mobil	11.8	17.4			3.6	56.3
General Electric	18.0	26.8		46.8	39.7	10.2
General Motors	15.8	33.4				9
McDonald's	14.0	27.4			5.4	10
Pfizer	14.8	29.3			9.8	13.3
Reebok	20.0	58.5		20.7	13.0	
Expected portfolio return			34.6	21.6	19.0	13.4
Portfolio standard deviation			110.6	30.8	23.7	14.6

TABLE 8.1

Examples of efficient portfolios chosen from 10 stocks.

Note: Standard deviations and the correlations between stock returns were estimated from monthly stock returns, August 1996–July 2001. Efficient portfolios are calculated assuming that short sales are prohibited.

We'll start with 10. Suppose that you can choose a portfolio from any of the stocks listed in the first column of Table 8.1. After analyzing the prospects for each firm, you come up with the return forecasts shown in the second column of the table. You use data for the past five years to estimate the risk of each stock (column 3) and the correlation between the returns on each pair of stocks.[5]

Now turn to Figure 8.5. Each diamond marks the combination of risk and return offered by a different individual security. For example, Amazon.com has the highest standard deviation; it also offers the highest expected return. It is represented by the diamond at the upper right of Figure 8.5.

By mixing investment in individual securities, you can obtain an even wider selection of risk and return: in fact, *anywhere* in the shaded area in Figure 8.5. But where in the shaded area is best? Well, what is your goal? Which direction do you want to go? The answer should be obvious: You want to go up (to increase expected return) and to the left (to reduce risk). Go as far as you can, and you will end up with one of the portfolios that lies along the heavy solid line. Markowitz called them **efficient portfolios.** These portfolios are clearly better than any in the interior of the shaded area.

We will not calculate this set of efficient portfolios here, but you may be interested in how to do it. Think back to the capital rationing problem in Section 5.4. There we wanted to deploy a limited amount of capital investment in a mixture of projects to give the highest total NPV. Here we want to deploy an investor's funds to give the highest expected return for a given standard deviation. In principle, both problems can be solved by hunting and pecking—but only in principle. To solve the capital

[5]There are 90 correlation coefficients, so we have not listed them in Table 8.1.

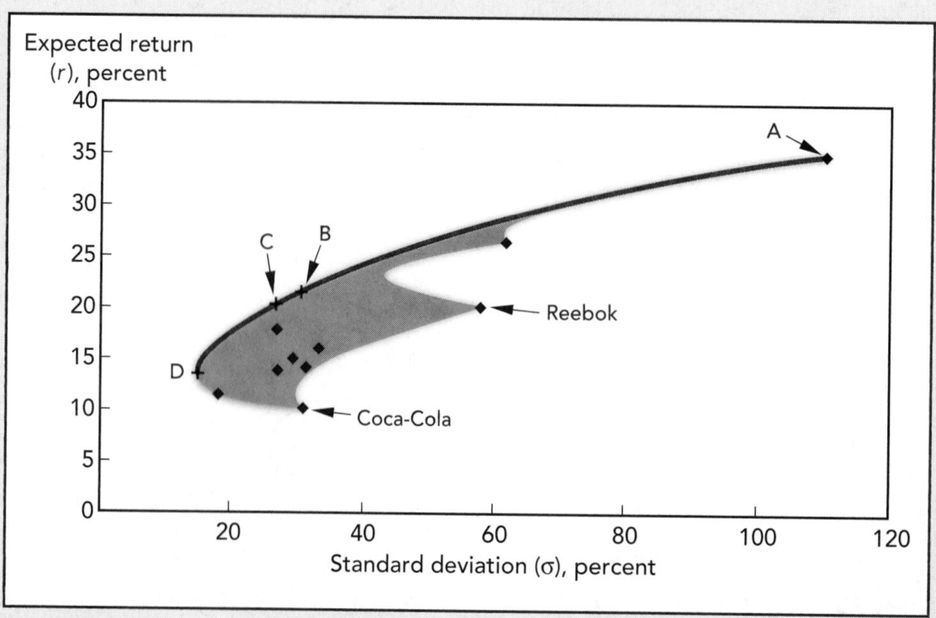

FIGURE 8.5

Each diamond shows the expected return and standard deviation of one of the 10 stocks in Table 8.1. The shaded area shows the possible combinations of expected return and standard deviation from investing in a *mixture* of these stocks. If you like high expected returns and dislike high standard deviations, you will prefer portfolios along the heavy line. These are *efficient* portfolios. We have marked the four efficient portfolios described in Table 8.1 (A, B, C, and D).

rationing problem, we can employ linear programming; to solve the portfolio problem, we would turn to a variant of linear programming known as *quadratic programming*. Given the expected return and standard deviation for each stock, as well as the correlation between each pair of stocks, we could give a computer a standard quadratic program and tell it to calculate the set of efficient portfolios.

Four of these efficient portfolios are marked in Figure 8.5. Their compositions are summarized in Table 8.1. Portfolio A offers the highest expected return; A is invested entirely in one stock, Amazon.com. Portfolio D offers the minimum risk; you can see from Table 8.1 that it has a large holding in Exxon Mobil, which has had the lowest standard deviation. Notice that D has only a small holding in Boeing and Coca-Cola but a much larger one in stocks such as General Motors, even though Boeing and Coca-Cola are individually of similar risk. The reason? On past evidence the fortunes of Boeing and Coca-Cola are more highly correlated with those of the other stocks in the portfolio and therefore provide less diversification.

Table 8.1 also shows the compositions of two other efficient portfolios B and C with intermediate levels of risk and expected return.

We Introduce Borrowing and Lending

Of course, large investment funds can choose from thousands of stocks and thereby achieve a wider choice of risk and return. This choice is represented in Figure 8.6 by the shaded, broken-egg-shaped area. The set of efficient portfolios is again marked by the heavy curved line.

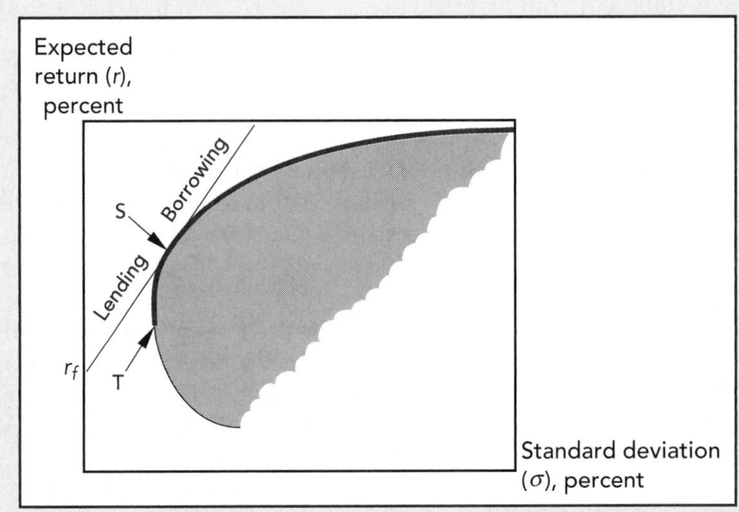

FIGURE 8.6

Lending and borrowing extend the range of investment possibilities. If you invest in portfolio S and lend or borrow at the risk-free interest rate, r_f, you can achieve any point along the straight line from r_f through S. This gives you a higher expected return for any level of risk than if you just invest in common stocks.

Now we introduce yet another possibility. Suppose that you can also lend and borrow money at some risk-free rate of interest r_f. If you invest some of your money in Treasury bills (i.e., lend money) and place the remainder in common stock portfolio S, you can obtain any combination of expected return and risk along the straight line joining r_f and S in Figure 8.6.[6] Since borrowing is merely negative lending, you can extend the range of possibilities to the right of S by borrowing funds at an interest rate of r_f and investing them as well as your own money in portfolio S.

Let us put some numbers on this. Suppose that portfolio S has an expected return of 15 percent and a standard deviation of 16 percent. Treasury bills offer an interest rate (r_f) of 5 percent and are risk-free (i.e., their standard deviation is zero). If you invest half your money in portfolio S and lend the remainder at 5 percent, the expected return on your investment is halfway between the expected return on S and the interest rate on Treasury bills:

$$\begin{aligned} r &= (\tfrac{1}{2} \times \text{expected return on S}) + (\tfrac{1}{2} \times \text{interest rate}) \\ &= 10\% \end{aligned}$$

And the standard deviation is halfway between the standard deviation of S and the standard deviation of Treasury bills:

$$\begin{aligned} \sigma &= (\tfrac{1}{2} \times \text{standard deviation of S}) + (\tfrac{1}{2} \times \text{standard deviation of bills}) \\ &= 8\% \end{aligned}$$

Or suppose that you decide to go for the big time: You borrow at the Treasury bill rate an amount equal to your initial wealth, and you invest everything in portfolio S. You have twice your own money invested in S, but you have to *pay* interest on the loan. Therefore your expected return is

$$\begin{aligned} r &= (2 \times \text{expected return on S}) - (1 \times \text{interest rate}) \\ &= 25\% \end{aligned}$$

[6]If you want to check this, write down the formula for the standard deviation of a two-stock portfolio:

$$\text{Standard deviation} = \sqrt{x_1^2\sigma_1^2 + x_2^2\sigma_2^2 + 2x_1x_2\rho_{12}\sigma_1\sigma_2}$$

Now see what happens when security 2 is riskless, i.e., when $\sigma_2 = 0$.

And the standard deviation of your investment is

$$\sigma = (2 \times \text{standard deviation of S}) - (1 \times \text{standard deviation of bills})$$
$$= 32\%$$

You can see from Figure 8.6 that when you lend a portion of your money, you end up partway between r_f and S; if you can borrow money at the risk-free rate, you can extend your possibilities beyond S. You can also see that regardless of the level of risk you choose, you can get the highest expected return by a mixture of portfolio S and borrowing or lending. S is the *best* efficient portfolio. There is no reason ever to hold, say, portfolio T.

If you have a graph of efficient portfolios, as in Figure 8.6, finding this best efficient portfolio is easy. Start on the vertical axis at r_f and draw the steepest line you can to the curved heavy line of efficient portfolios. That line will be tangent to the heavy line. The efficient portfolio at the tangency point is better than all the others. Notice that it offers the highest *ratio* of risk premium to standard deviation.

This means that we can separate the investor's job into two stages. First, the best portfolio of common stocks must be selected—S in our example.[7] Second, this portfolio must be blended with borrowing or lending to obtain an exposure to risk that suits the particular investor's taste. Each investor, therefore, should put money into just two benchmark investments—a risky portfolio S and a risk-free loan (borrowing or lending).[8]

What does portfolio S look like? If you have better information than your rivals, you will want the portfolio to include relatively large investments in the stocks you think are undervalued. But in a competitive market you are unlikely to have a monopoly of good ideas. In that case there is no reason to hold a different portfolio of common stocks from anybody else. In other words, you might just as well hold the market portfolio. That is why many professional investors invest in a market-index portfolio and why most others hold well-diversified portfolios.

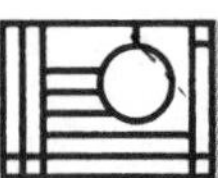

8.2 THE RELATIONSHIP BETWEEN RISK AND RETURN

In Chapter 7 we looked at the returns on selected investments. The least risky investment was U.S. Treasury bills. Since the return on Treasury bills is fixed, it is unaffected by what happens to the market. In other words, Treasury bills have a beta of 0. We also considered a much riskier investment, the market portfolio of common stocks. This has average market risk: Its beta is 1.0.

Wise investors don't take risks just for fun. They are playing with real money. Therefore, they require a higher return from the market portfolio than from Treasury bills. The difference between the return on the market and the interest rate is termed the *market risk premium.* Over a period of 75 years the market risk premium $(r_m - r_f)$ has averaged about 9 percent a year.

In Figure 8.7 we have plotted the risk and expected return from Treasury bills and the market portfolio. You can see that Treasury bills have a beta of 0 and a risk

[7]Portfolio S is the point of tangency to the set of efficient portfolios. It offers the highest expected risk premium $(r - r_f)$ per unit of standard deviation (σ).

[8]This *separation theorem* was first pointed out by J. Tobin in "Liquidity Preference as Behavior toward Risk," *Review of Economic Studies* 25 (February 1958), pp. 65–86.

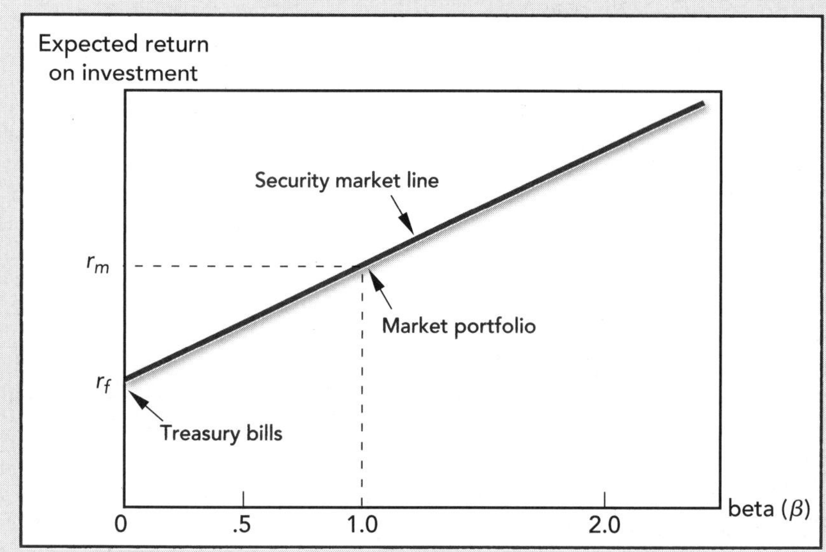

FIGURE 8.7

The capital asset pricing model states that the expected risk premium on each investment is proportional to its beta. This means that each investment should lie on the sloping security market line connecting Treasury bills and the market portfolio.

premium of 0.[9] The market portfolio has a beta of 1.0 and a risk premium of $r_m - r_f$. This gives us two benchmarks for the expected risk premium. But what is the expected risk premium when beta is not 0 or 1?

In the mid-1960s three economists—William Sharpe, John Lintner, and Jack Treynor—produced an answer to this question.[10] Their answer is known as the **capital asset pricing model,** or **CAPM.** The model's message is both startling and simple. In a competitive market, the expected risk premium varies in direct proportion to beta. This means that in Figure 8.7 all investments must plot along the sloping line, known as the **security market line.** The expected risk premium on an investment with a beta of .5 is, therefore, *half* the expected risk premium on the market; the expected risk premium on an investment with a beta of 2.0 is *twice* the expected risk premium on the market. We can write this relationship as

$$\text{Expected risk premium on stock} = \text{beta} \times \text{expected risk premium on market}$$
$$r - r_f = \beta(r_m - r_f)$$

Some Estimates of Expected Returns

Before we tell you where the formula comes from, let us use it to figure out what returns investors are looking for from particular stocks. To do this, we need three numbers: β, r_f, and $r_m - r_f$. We gave you estimates of the betas of 10 stocks in Table 7.5. In July 2001 the interest rate on Treasury bills was about 3.5 percent.

How about the market risk premium? As we pointed out in the last chapter, we can't measure $r_m - r_f$ with precision. From past evidence it appears to be about

[9]Remember that the risk premium is the difference between the investment's expected return and the risk-free rate. For Treasury bills, the difference is zero.

[10]W. F. Sharpe, "Capital Asset Prices: A Theory of Market Equilibrium under Conditions of Risk," *Journal of Finance* 19 (September 1964), pp. 425–442 and J. Lintner, "The Valuation of Risk Assets and the Selection of Risky Investments in Stock Portfolios and Capital Budgets," *Review of Economics and Statistics* 47 (February 1965), pp. 13–37. Treynor's article has not been published.

TABLE 8.2

These estimates of the returns *expected* by investors in July 2001 were based on the capital asset pricing model. We assumed 3.5 percent for the interest rate r_f and 8 percent for the expected risk premium $r_m - r_f$.

Stock	Beta (β)	Expected Return $[r_f + \beta(r_m - r_f)]$
Amazon.com	3.25	29.5%
Boeing	.56	8.0
Coca-Cola	.74	9.4
Dell Computer	2.21	21.2
Exxon Mobil	.40	6.7
General Electric	1.18	12.9
General Motors	.91	10.8
McDonald's	.68	8.9
Pfizer	.71	9.2
Reebok	.69	9.0

9 percent, although many economists and financial managers would forecast a lower figure. Let's use 8 percent in this example.

Table 8.2 puts these numbers together to give an estimate of the expected return on each stock. The stock with the lowest beta in our sample is Exxon Mobil. Our estimate of the expected return from Exxon Mobil is 6.7 percent. The stock with the highest beta is Amazon.com. Our estimate of its expected return is 29.5 percent, 26 percent more than the interest rate on Treasury bills.

You can also use the capital asset pricing model to find the discount rate for a new capital investment. For example, suppose that you are analyzing a proposal by Pfizer to expand its capacity. At what rate should you discount the forecast cash flows? According to Table 8.2, investors are looking for a return of 9.2 percent from businesses with the risk of Pfizer. So the cost of capital for a further investment in the same business is 9.2 percent.[11]

In practice, choosing a discount rate is seldom so easy. (After all, you can't expect to be paid a fat salary just for plugging numbers into a formula.) For example, you must learn how to adjust for the extra risk caused by company borrowing and how to estimate the discount rate for projects that do not have the same risk as the company's existing business. There are also tax issues. But these refinements can wait until later.[12]

Review of the Capital Asset Pricing Model

Let's review the basic principles of portfolio selection:

1. Investors like high expected return and low standard deviation. Common stock portfolios that offer the highest expected return for a given standard deviation are known as *efficient portfolios.*

[11]Remember that instead of investing in plant and machinery, the firm could return the money to the shareholders. The opportunity cost of investing is the return that shareholders could expect to earn by buying financial assets. This expected return depends on the market risk of the assets.

[12]Tax issues arise because a corporation must pay tax on income from an investment in Treasury bills or other interest-paying securities. It turns out that the correct discount rate for risk-free investments is the *after-tax* Treasury bill rate. We come back to this point in Chapters 19 and 26.

Various other points on the practical use of betas and the capital asset pricing model are covered in Chapter 9.

2. If the investor can lend or borrow at the risk-free rate of interest, one efficient portfolio is better than all the others: the portfolio that offers the highest ratio of risk premium to standard deviation (that is, portfolio S in Figure 8.6). A risk-averse investor will put part of his money in this efficient portfolio and part in the risk-free asset. A risk-tolerant investor may put all her money in this portfolio or she may borrow and put in even more.
3. The composition of this best efficient portfolio depends on the investor's assessments of expected returns, standard deviations, and correlations. But suppose everybody has the same information and the same assessments. If there is no superior information, each investor should hold the same portfolio as everybody else; in other words, everyone should hold the market portfolio.

Now let's go back to the risk of individual stocks:

4. Don't look at the risk of a stock in isolation but at its contribution to portfolio risk. This contribution depends on the stock's sensitivity to changes in the value of the portfolio.
5. A stock's sensitivity to changes in the value of the *market* portfolio is known as *beta.* Beta, therefore, measures the marginal contribution of a stock to the risk of the market portfolio.

Now if everyone holds the market portfolio, and if beta measures each security's contribution to the market portfolio risk, then it's no surprise that the risk premium demanded by investors is proportional to beta. That's what the CAPM says.

What If a Stock Did Not Lie on the Security Market Line?

Imagine that you encounter stock A in Figure 8.8. Would you buy it? We hope not[13]—if you want an investment with a beta of .5, you could get a higher expected return by investing half your money in Treasury bills and half in the market portfolio. If everybody shares your view of the stock's prospects, the price of A will have to fall until the expected return matches what you could get elsewhere.

What about stock B in Figure 8.8? Would you be tempted by its high return? You wouldn't if you were smart. You could get a higher expected return for the same beta by borrowing 50 cents for every dollar of your own money and investing in the market portfolio. Again, if everybody agrees with your assessment, the price of stock B cannot hold. It will have to fall until the expected return on B is equal to the expected return on the combination of borrowing and investment in the market portfolio.

We have made our point. An investor can always obtain an expected risk premium of $\beta(r_m - r_f)$ by holding a mixture of the market portfolio and a risk-free loan. So in well-functioning markets nobody will hold a stock that offers an expected risk premium of *less* than $\beta(r_m - r_f)$. But what about the other possibility? Are there stocks that offer a higher expected risk premium? In other words, are there any that lie above the security market line in Figure 8.8? If we take all stocks together, we have the market portfolio. Therefore, we know that stocks *on average* lie on the line. Since none lies *below* the line, then there also can't be any that lie *above* the line. Thus

[13]Unless, of course, we were trying to sell it.

FIGURE 8.8

In equilibrium no stock can lie below the security market line. For example, instead of buying stock A, investors would prefer to lend part of their money and put the balance in the market portfolio. And instead of buying stock B, they would prefer to borrow and invest in the market portfolio.

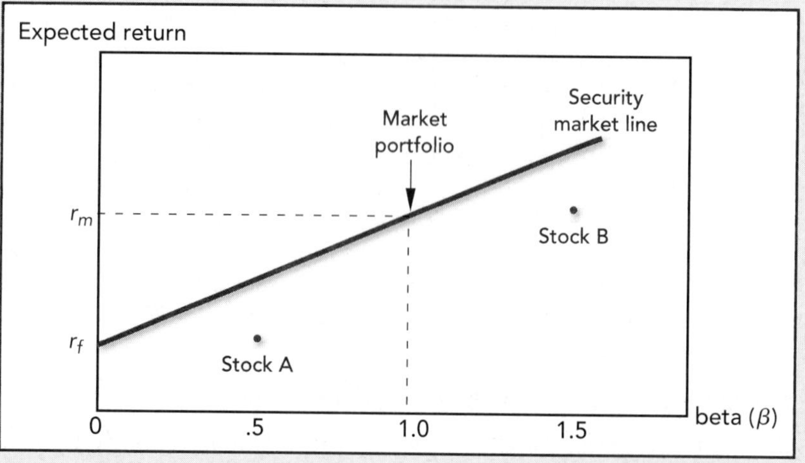

each and every stock must lie on the security market line and offer an expected risk premium of

$$r - r_f = \beta(r_m - r_f)$$

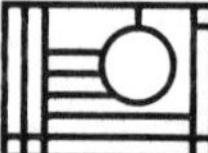

8.3 VALIDITY AND ROLE OF THE CAPITAL ASSET PRICING MODEL

Any economic model is a simplified statement of reality. We need to simplify in order to interpret what is going on around us. But we also need to know how much faith we can place in our model.

Let us begin with some matters about which there is broad agreement. First, few people quarrel with the idea that investors require some extra return for taking on risk. That is why common stocks have given on average a higher return than U.S. Treasury bills. Who would want to invest in risky common stocks if they offered only the *same* expected return as bills? We wouldn't, and we suspect you wouldn't either.

Second, investors do appear to be concerned principally with those risks that they cannot eliminate by diversification. If this were not so, we should find that stock prices increase whenever two companies merge to spread their risks. And we should find that investment companies which invest in the shares of other firms are more highly valued than the shares they hold. But we don't observe either phenomenon. Mergers undertaken just to spread risk don't increase stock prices, and investment companies are no more highly valued than the stocks they hold.

The capital asset pricing model captures these ideas in a simple way. That is why many financial managers find it the most convenient tool for coming to grips with the slippery notion of risk. And it is why economists often use the capital asset pricing model to demonstrate important ideas in finance even when there are other ways to prove these ideas. But that doesn't mean that the capital asset pricing model is ultimate truth. We will see later that it has several unsatisfactory features, and we will look at some alternative theories. Nobody knows whether one of these alternative theories is eventually going to come out on top or whether there are other, better models of risk and return that have not yet seen the light of day.

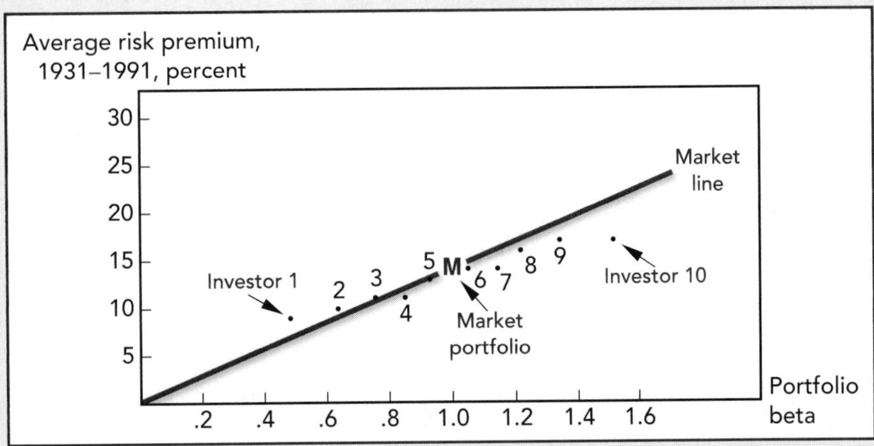

FIGURE 8.9

The capital asset pricing model states that the expected risk premium from any investment should lie on the market line. The dots show the actual average risk premiums from portfolios with different betas. The high-beta portfolios generated higher average returns, just as predicted by the CAPM. But the high-beta portfolios plotted below the market line, and four of the five low-beta portfolios plotted above. A line fitted to the 10 portfolio returns would be "flatter" than the market line.

Source: F. Black, "Beta and Return," *Journal of Portfolio Management* 20 (Fall 1993), pp. 8–18.

Tests of the Capital Asset Pricing Model

Imagine that in 1931 ten investors gathered together in a Wall Street bar to discuss their portfolios. Each agreed to follow a different investment strategy. Investor 1 opted to buy the 10 percent of New York Stock Exchange stocks with the lowest estimated betas; investor 2 chose the 10 percent with the next-lowest betas; and so on, up to investor 10, who agreed to buy the stocks with the highest betas. They also undertook that at the end of every year they would reestimate the betas of all NYSE stocks and reconstitute their portfolios.[14] Finally, they promised that they would return 60 years later to compare results, and so they parted with much cordiality and good wishes.

In 1991 the same 10 investors, now much older and wealthier, met again in the same bar. Figure 8.9 shows how they had fared. Investor 1's portfolio turned out to be much less risky than the market; its beta was only .49. However, investor 1 also realized the lowest return, 9 percent above the risk-free rate of interest. At the other extreme, the beta of investor 10's portfolio was 1.52, about three times that of investor 1's portfolio. But investor 10 was rewarded with the highest return, averaging 17 percent a year above the interest rate. So over this 60-year period returns did indeed increase with beta.

As you can see from Figure 8.9, the market portfolio over the same 60-year period provided an average return of 14 percent above the interest rate[15] and (of

[14]Betas were estimated using returns over the previous 60 months.

[15]In Figure 8.9 the stocks in the "market portfolio" are weighted equally. Since the stocks of small firms have provided higher average returns than those of large firms, the risk premium on an equally weighted index is higher than on a value-weighted index. This is one reason for the difference between the 14 percent market risk premium in Figure 8.9 and the 9.1 percent premium reported in Table 7.1.

FIGURE 8.10

The relationship between beta and actual average return has been much weaker since the mid-1960s. Compare Figure 8.9.

Source: F. Black, "Beta and Return," *Journal of Portfolio Management* 20 (Fall 1993), pp. 8–18.

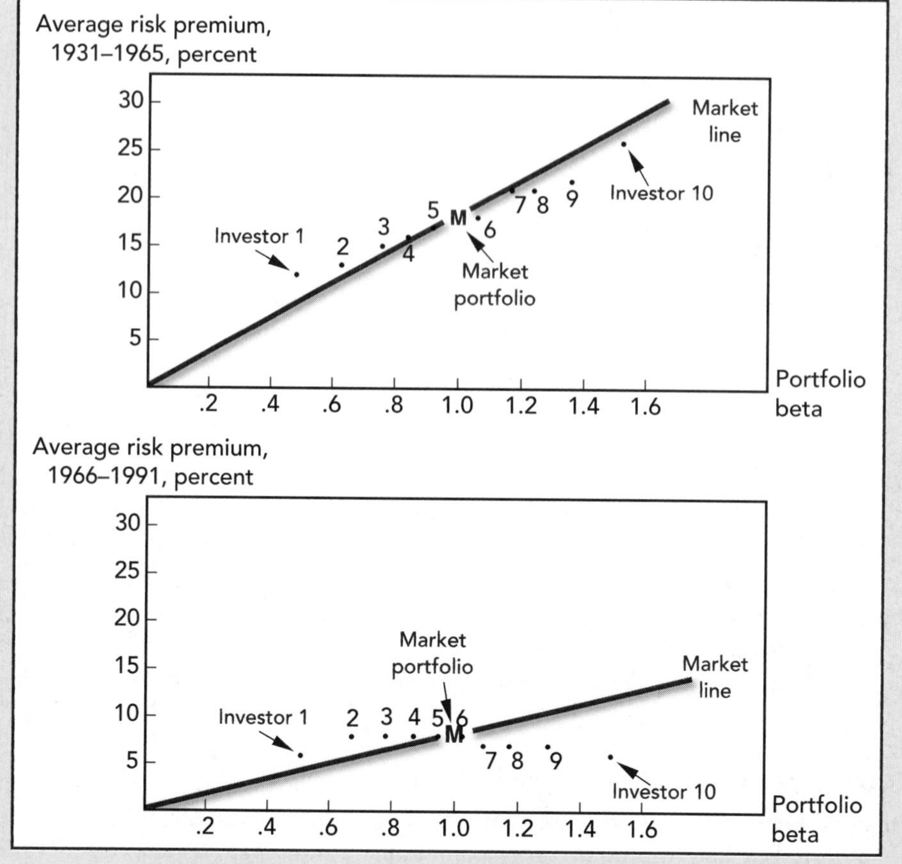

course) had a beta of 1.0. The CAPM predicts that the risk premium should increase in proportion to beta, so that the returns of each portfolio should lie on the upward-sloping security market line in Figure 8.9. Since the market provided a risk premium of 14 percent, investor 1's portfolio, with a beta of .49, should have provided a risk premium of a shade under 7 percent and investor 10's portfolio, with a beta of 1.52, should have given a premium of a shade over 21 percent. You can see that, while high-beta stocks performed better than low-beta stocks, the difference was not as great as the CAPM predicts.

Although Figure 8.9 provides broad support for the CAPM, critics have pointed out that the slope of the line has been particularly flat in recent years. For example, Figure 8.10 shows how our 10 investors fared between 1966 and 1991. Now it's less clear who is buying the drinks: The portfolios of investors 1 and 10 had very different betas but both earned the same average return over these 25 years. Of course, the line was correspondingly steeper before 1966. This is also shown in Figure 8.10

What's going on here? It is hard to say. Defenders of the capital asset pricing model emphasize that it is concerned with *expected* returns, whereas we can observe only *actual* returns. Actual stock returns reflect expectations, but they also embody lots of "noise"—the steady flow of surprises that conceal whether on av-

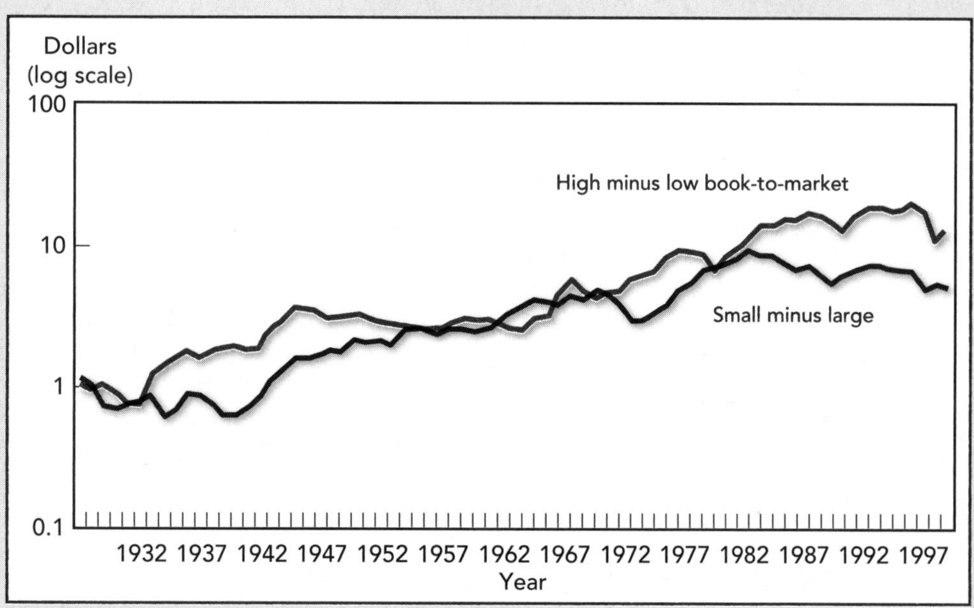

FIGURE 8.11

The burgundy line shows the cumulative difference between the returns on small-firm and large-firm stocks. The blue line shows the cumulative difference between the returns on high book-to-market-value stocks and low book-to-market-value stocks.

Source: **www.mba.tuck.dartmouth.edu/pages/faculty/ken.french/data_library.**

erage investors have received the returns they expected. This noise may make it impossible to judge whether the model holds better in one period than another.[16] Perhaps the best that we can do is to focus on the longest period for which there is reasonable data. This would take us back to Figure 8.9, which suggests that expected returns do indeed increase with beta, though less rapidly than the simple version of the CAPM predicts.[17]

The CAPM has also come under fire on a second front: Although return has not risen with beta in recent years, it has been related to other measures. For example, the burgundy line in Figure 8.11 shows the cumulative difference between the returns on small-firm stocks and large-firm stocks. If you had bought the shares with the smallest market capitalizations and sold those with the largest capitalizations, this is how your wealth would have changed. You can see that small-cap stocks did not always do well, but over the long haul their owners have made substantially

[16]A second problem with testing the model is that the market portfolio should contain all risky investments, including stocks, bonds, commodities, real estate—even human capital. Most market indexes contain only a sample of common stocks. See, for example, R. Roll, "A Critique of the Asset Pricing Theory's Tests; Part 1: On Past and Potential Testability of the Theory," *Journal of Financial Economics* 4 (March 1977), pp. 129–176.

[17]We say "simple version" because Fischer Black has shown that if there are borrowing restrictions, there should still exist a positive relationship between expected return and beta, but the security market line would be less steep as a result. See F. Black, "Capital Market Equilibrium with Restricted Borrowing," *Journal of Business* 45 (July 1972), pp. 444–455.

higher returns. Since 1928 the average annual difference between the returns on the two groups of stocks has been 3.1 percent.

Now look at the blue line in Figure 8.11 which shows the cumulative difference between the returns on value stocks and growth stocks. Value stocks here are defined as those with high ratios of book value to market value. Growth stocks are those with low ratios of book to market. Notice that value stocks have provided a higher long-run return than growth stocks.[18] Since 1928 the average annual difference between the returns on value and growth stocks has been 4.4 percent.

Figure 8.11 does not fit well with the CAPM, which predicts that beta is the *only* reason that expected returns differ. It seems that investors saw risks in "small-cap" stocks and value stocks that were not captured by beta.[19] Take value stocks, for example. Many of these stocks sold below book value because the firms were in serious trouble; if the economy slowed unexpectedly, the firms might have collapsed altogether. Therefore, investors, whose jobs could also be on the line in a recession, may have regarded these stocks as particularly risky and demanded compensation in the form of higher expected returns.[20] If that were the case, the simple version of the CAPM cannot be the whole truth.

Again, it is hard to judge how seriously the CAPM is damaged by this finding. The relationship among stock returns and firm size and book-to-market ratio has been well documented. However, if you look long and hard at past returns, you are bound to find some strategy that just by chance would have worked in the past. This practice is known as "data-mining" or "data snooping." Maybe the size and book-to-market effects are simply chance results that stem from data snooping. If so, they should have vanished once they were discovered. There is some evidence that this is the case. If you look again at Figure 8.11, you will see that in recent years small-firm stocks and value stocks have underperformed just about as often as they have overperformed.

There is no doubt that the evidence on the CAPM is less convincing than scholars once thought. But it will be hard to reject the CAPM beyond all reasonable doubt. Since data and statistics are unlikely to give final answers, the plausibility of the CAPM *theory* will have to be weighed along with the empirical "facts."

Assumptions behind the Capital Asset Pricing Model

The capital asset pricing model rests on several assumptions that we did not fully spell out. For example, we assumed that investment in U.S. Treasury bills is risk-free. It is true that there is little chance of default, but they don't guarantee a *real*

---

[18]The small-firm effect was first documented by Rolf Banz in 1981. See R. Banz, "The Relationship between Return and Market Values of Common Stock," *Journal of Financial Economics* 9 (March 1981), pp. 3–18. Fama and French calculated the returns on portfolios designed to take advantage of the size effect and the book-to-market effect. See E. F. Fama and K. R. French, "The Cross-Section of Expected Stock Returns," *Journal of Financial Economics* 47 (June 1992), pp. 427–465. When calculating the returns on these portfolios, Fama and French control for differences in firm size when comparing stocks with low and high book-to-market ratios. Similarly, they control for differences in the book-to-market ratio when comparing small- and large-firm stocks. For details of the methodology and updated returns on the size and book-to-market factors see Kenneth French's website (**www.mba.tuck.dartmouth.edu/pages/faculty/ken.french/data_library**).

[19]Small-firm stocks have higher betas, but the difference in betas is not sufficient to explain the difference in returns. There is no simple relationship between book-to-market ratios and beta.

[20]For a good review of the evidence on the CAPM, see J. H. Cochrane, "New Facts in Finance," *Journal of Economic Perspectives* 23 (1999), pp. 36–58.

return. There is still some uncertainty about inflation. Another assumption was that investors can *borrow* money at the same rate of interest at which they can lend. Generally borrowing rates are higher than lending rates.

It turns out that many of these assumptions are not crucial, and with a little pushing and pulling it is possible to modify the capital asset pricing model to handle them. The really important idea is that investors are content to invest their money in a limited number of benchmark portfolios. (In the basic CAPM these benchmarks are Treasury bills and the market portfolio.)

In these modified CAPMs expected return still depends on market risk, but the definition of market risk depends on the nature of the benchmark portfolios.[21] In practice, none of these alternative capital asset pricing models is as widely used as the standard version.

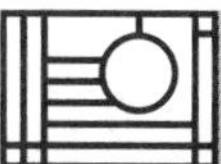

8.4 SOME ALTERNATIVE THEORIES

Consumption Betas versus Market Betas

The capital asset pricing model pictures investors as solely concerned with the level and uncertainty of their future wealth. But for most people wealth is not an end in itself. What good is wealth if you can't spend it? People invest now to provide future consumption for themselves or for their families and heirs. The most important risks are those that might force a cutback of future consumption.

Douglas Breeden has developed a model in which a security's risk is measured by its sensitivity to changes in investors' consumption. If he is right, a stock's expected return should move in line with its *consumption beta* rather than its market beta. Figure 8.12 summarizes the chief differences between the standard and consumption CAPMs. In the standard model investors are concerned exclusively with the amount and uncertainty of their future wealth. Each investor's wealth ends up perfectly correlated with the return on the market portfolio; the demand for stocks and other risky assets is thus determined by their market risk. The deeper motive for investing—to provide for consumption—is outside the model.

In the consumption CAPM, uncertainty about stock returns is connected directly to uncertainty about consumption. Of course, consumption depends on wealth (portfolio value), but wealth does not appear explicitly in the model.

The consumption CAPM has several appealing features. For example, you don't have to identify the market or any other benchmark portfolio. You don't have to worry that Standard and Poor's Composite Index doesn't track returns on bonds, commodities, and real estate.

However, you do have to be able to measure consumption. *Quick:* How much did you consume last month? It's easy to count the hamburgers and movie tickets, but what about the depreciation on your car or washing machine or the daily cost of your homeowner's insurance policy? We suspect that your estimate of total consumption will rest on rough or arbitrary allocations and assumptions. And if it's hard for you to put a dollar value on your total consumption, think of the

[21]For example, see M. C. Jensen (ed.), *Studies in the Theory of Capital Markets,* Frederick A. Praeger, Inc., New York, 1972. In the introduction Jensen provides a very useful summary of some of these variations on the capital asset pricing model.

FIGURE 8.12

(a) The standard CAPM concentrates on how stocks contribute to the level and uncertainty of investor's wealth. Consumption is outside the model. (b) The consumption CAPM defines risk as a stock's contribution to uncertainty about consumption. Wealth (the intermediate step between stock returns and consumption) drops out of the model.

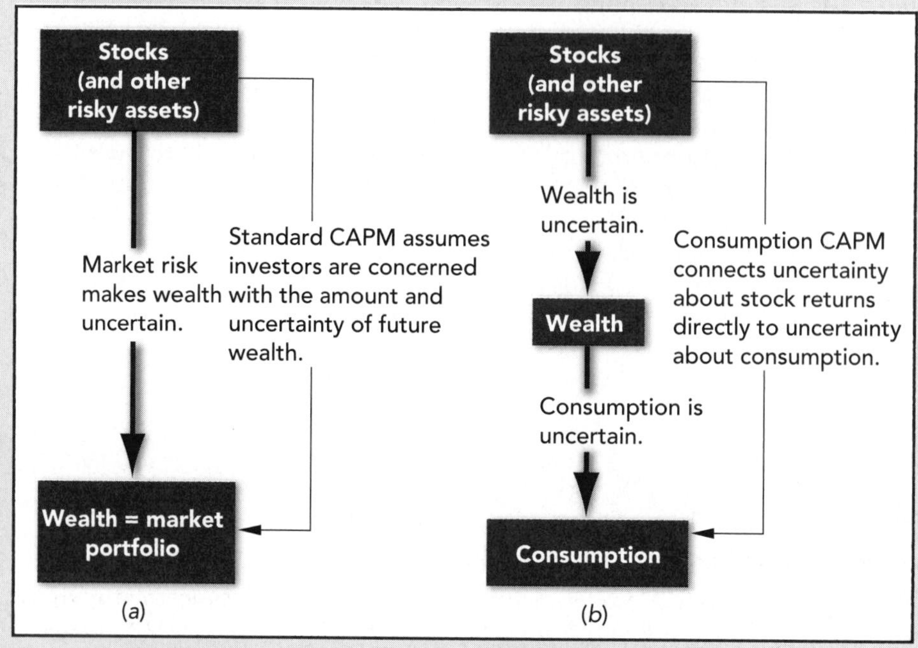

task facing a government statistician asked to estimate month-by-month consumption for all of us.

Compared to stock prices, estimated aggregate consumption changes smoothly and gradually over time. Changes in consumption often seem to be out of phase with the stock market. Individual stocks seem to have low or erratic consumption betas. Moreover, the volatility of consumption appears too low to explain the past average rates of return on common stocks unless one assumes unreasonably high investor risk aversion.[22] These problems may reflect our poor measures of consumption or perhaps poor models of how individuals distribute consumption over time. It seems too early for the consumption CAPM to see practical use.

Arbitrage Pricing Theory

The capital asset pricing theory begins with an analysis of how investors construct efficient portfolios. Stephen Ross's **arbitrage pricing theory,** or **APT,** comes from a different family entirely. It does not ask which portfolios are efficient. Instead, it starts by *assuming* that each stock's return depends partly on pervasive macroeconomic influences or "factors" and partly on "noise"—events that are unique to that company. Moreover, the return is assumed to obey the following simple relationship:

$$\text{Return} = a + b_1(r_{\text{factor 1}}) + b_2(r_{\text{factor 2}}) + b_3(r_{\text{factor 3}}) + \cdots + \text{noise}$$

The theory doesn't say what the factors are: There could be an oil price factor, an interest-rate factor, and so on. The return on the market portfolio *might* serve as one factor, but then again it might not.

[22]See R. Mehra and E. C. Prescott, "The Equity Risk Premium: A Puzzle," *Journal of Monetary Economics* 15 (1985), pp. 145–161.

Some stocks will be more sensitive to a particular factor than other stocks. Exxon Mobil would be more sensitive to an oil factor than, say, Coca-Cola. If factor 1 picks up unexpected changes in oil prices, b_1 will be higher for Exxon Mobil.

For any individual stock there are two sources of risk. First is the risk that stems from the pervasive macroeconomic factors which cannot be eliminated by diversification. Second is the risk arising from possible events that are unique to the company. Diversification *does* eliminate unique risk, and diversified investors can therefore ignore it when deciding whether to buy or sell a stock. The expected risk premium on a stock is affected by factor or macroeconomic risk; it is *not* affected by unique risk.

Arbitrage pricing theory states that the expected risk premium on a stock should depend on the expected risk premium associated with each factor and the stock's sensitivity to each of the factors (b_1, b_2, b_3, etc.). Thus the formula is[23]

$$\begin{aligned}\text{Expected risk premium} &= r - r_f \\ &= b_1(r_{\text{factor 1}} - r_f) + b_2(r_{\text{factor 2}} - r_f) + \cdots\end{aligned}$$

Notice that this formula makes two statements:

1. If you plug in a value of zero for each of the b's in the formula, the expected risk premium is zero. A diversified portfolio that is constructed to have zero sensitivity to each macroeconomic factor is essentially risk-free and therefore must be priced to offer the risk-free rate of interest. If the portfolio offered a higher return, investors could make a risk-free (or "arbitrage") profit by borrowing to buy the portfolio. If it offered a lower return, you could make an arbitrage profit by running the strategy in reverse; in other words, you would *sell* the diversified zero-sensitivity portfolio and *invest* the proceeds in U.S. Treasury bills.
2. A diversified portfolio that is constructed to have exposure to, say, factor 1, will offer a risk premium, which will vary in direct proportion to the portfolio's sensitivity to that factor. For example, imagine that you construct two portfolios, A and B, which are affected only by factor 1. If portfolio A is twice as sensitive to factor 1 as portfolio B, portfolio A must offer twice the risk premium. Therefore, if you divided your money equally between U.S. Treasury bills and portfolio A, your combined portfolio would have exactly the same sensitivity to factor 1 as portfolio B and would offer the same risk premium.

   Suppose that the arbitrage pricing formula did *not* hold. For example, suppose that the combination of Treasury bills and portfolio A offered a higher return. In that case investors could make an arbitrage profit by selling portfolio B and investing the proceeds in the mixture of bills and portfolio A.

The arbitrage that we have described applies to well-diversified portfolios, where the unique risk has been diversified away. But if the arbitrage pricing relationship holds for all diversified portfolios, it must generally hold for the individual stocks. Each stock must offer an expected return commensurate with its contribution to portfolio risk. In the APT, this contribution depends on the sensitivity of the stock's return to unexpected changes in the macroeconomic factors.

[23]There may be some macroeconomic factors that investors are simply not worried about. For example, some macroeconomists believe that money supply doesn't matter and therefore investors are not worried about inflation. Such factors would not command a risk premium. They would drop out of the APT formula for expected return.

A Comparison of the Capital Asset Pricing Model and Arbitrage Pricing Theory

Like the capital asset pricing model, arbitrage pricing theory stresses that expected return depends on the risk stemming from economywide influences and is not affected by unique risk. You can think of the factors in arbitrage pricing as representing special portfolios of stocks that tend to be subject to a common influence. If the expected risk premium on each of these portfolios is proportional to the portfolio's market beta, then the arbitrage pricing theory and the capital asset pricing model will give the same answer. In any other case they won't.

How do the two theories stack up? Arbitrage pricing has some attractive features. For example, the market portfolio that plays such a central role in the capital asset pricing model does not feature in arbitrage pricing theory.[24] So we don't have to worry about the problem of measuring the market portfolio, and in principle we can test the arbitrage pricing theory even if we have data on only a sample of risky assets.

Unfortunately you win some and lose some. Arbitrage pricing theory doesn't tell us what the underlying factors are—unlike the capital asset pricing model, which collapses *all* macroeconomic risks into a well-defined *single* factor, the return on the market portfolio.

APT Example

Arbitrage pricing theory will provide a good handle on expected returns only if we can (1) identify a reasonably short list of macroeconomic factors,[25] (2) measure the expected risk premium on each of these factors, and (3) measure the sensitivity of each stock to these factors. Let us look briefly at how Elton, Gruber, and Mei tackled each of these issues and estimated the cost of equity for a group of nine New York utilities.[26]

Step 1: Identify the Macroeconomic Factors Although APT doesn't tell us what the underlying economic factors are, Elton, Gruber, and Mei identified five principal factors that could affect either the cash flows themselves or the rate at which they are discounted. These factors are

Factor	Measured by
Yield spread	Return on long government bond *less* return on 30-day Treasury bills
Interest rate	Change in Treasury bill return
Exchange rate	Change in value of dollar relative to basket of currencies
Real GNP	Change in forecasts of real GNP
Inflation	Change in forecasts of inflation

[24]Of course, the market portfolio *may* turn out to be one of the factors, but that is not a necessary implication of arbitrage pricing theory.

[25]Some researchers have argued that there are four or five principal pervasive influences on stock prices, but others are not so sure. They point out that the more stocks you look at, the more factors you need to take into account. See, for example, P. J. Dhrymes, I. Friend, and N. B. Gultekin, "A Critical Reexamination of the Empirical Evidence on the Arbitrage Pricing Theory," *Journal of Finance* 39 (June 1984), pp. 323–346.

[26]See E. J. Elton, M. J. Gruber, and J. Mei, "Cost of Capital Using Arbitrage Pricing Theory: A Case Study of Nine New York Utilities," *Financial Markets, Institutions, and Instruments* 3 (August 1994), pp. 46–73. The study was prepared for the New York State Public Utility Commission. We described a parallel study in Chapter 4 which used the discounted-cash-flow model to estimate the cost of equity capital.

Factor	Estimated Risk Premium * ($r_{factor} - r_f$)
Yield spread	5.10%
Interest rate	−.61
Exchange rate	−.59
Real GNP	.49
Inflation	−.83
Market	6.36

TABLE 8.3

Estimated risk premiums for taking on factor risks, 1978–1990.

*The risk premiums have been scaled to represent the annual premiums for the average industrial stock in the Elton–Gruber–Mei sample.
Source: E. J. Elton, M. J. Gruber, and J. Mei, "Cost of Capital Using Arbitrage Pricing Theory: A Case Study of Nine New York Utilities," *Financial Markets, Institutions, and Instruments* 3 (August 1994), pp. 46–73.

To capture any remaining pervasive influences, Elton, Gruber, and Mei also included a sixth factor, the portion of the market return that could not be explained by the first five.

Step 2: Estimate the Risk Premium for Each Factor Some stocks are more exposed than others to a particular factor. So we can estimate the sensitivity of a sample of stocks to each factor and then measure how much extra return investors would have received in the past for taking on factor risk. The results are shown in Table 8.3.

For example, stocks with positive sensitivity to real GNP tended to have higher returns when real GNP increased. A stock with an average sensitivity gave investors an additional return of .49 percent a year compared with a stock that was completely unaffected by changes in real GNP. In other words, investors appeared to dislike "cyclical" stocks, whose returns were sensitive to economic activity, and demanded a higher return from these stocks.

By contrast, Table 8.3 shows that a stock with average exposure to *inflation* gave investors .83 percent a year *less* return than a stock with no exposure to inflation. Thus investors seemed to prefer stocks that protected them against inflation (stocks that did well when inflation accelerated), and they were willing to accept a lower expected return from such stocks.

Step 3: Estimate the Factor Sensitivities The estimates of the premiums for taking on factor risk can now be used to estimate the cost of equity for the group of New York State utilities. Remember, APT states that the risk premium for any asset depends on its sensitivities to factor risks (b) and the expected risk premium for each factor ($r_{factor} - r_f$). In this case there are six factors, so

$$r - r_f = b_1(r_{factor\ 1} - r_f) + b_2(r_{factor\ 2} - r_f) + \cdots + b_6(r_{factor\ 6} - r_f)$$

The first column of Table 8.4 shows the factor risks for the portfolio of utilities, and the second column shows the required risk premium for each factor (taken from Table 8.3). The third column is simply the product of these two numbers. It shows how much return investors demanded for taking on each factor risk. To find the expected risk premium, just add the figures in the final column:

$$\text{Expected risk premium} = r - r_f = 8.53\%$$

TABLE 8.4

Using APT to estimate the expected risk premium for a portfolio of nine New York State utility stocks.

Source: E. J. Elton, M. J. Gruber, and J. Mei, "Cost of Capital Using Arbitrage Pricing Theory: A Case Study of Nine New York Utilities," *Financial Markets, Institutions, and Instruments* 3 (August 1994), tables 3 and 4.

Factor	Factor Risk (b)	Expected Risk Premium ($r_{factor} - r_f$)	Factor Risk Premium $b(r_{factor} - r_f)$
Yield spread	1.04	5.10%	5.30%
Interest rate	−2.25	−.61	1.37
Exchange rate	.70	−.59	−.41
GNP	.17	.49	.08
Inflation	−.18	−.83	.15
Market	.32	6.36	2.04
Total			8.53%

The one-year Treasury bill rate in December 1990, the end of the Elton–Gruber–Mei sample period, was about 7 percent, so the APT estimate of the expected return on New York State utility stocks was[27]

$$\begin{aligned}\text{Expected return} &= \text{risk-free interest rate} + \text{expected risk premium}\\ &= 7 + 8.53\\ &= 15.53, \text{ or about } 15.5\%\end{aligned}$$

The Three-Factor Model

We noted earlier the research by Fama and French showing that stocks of small firms and those with a high book-to-market ratio have provided above-average returns. This could simply be a coincidence. But there is also evidence that these factors are related to company profitability and therefore may be picking up risk factors that are left out of the simple CAPM.[28]

If investors do demand an extra return for taking on exposure to these factors, then we have a measure of the expected return that looks very much like arbitrage pricing theory:

$$r - r_f = b_{\text{market}}(r_{\text{market factor}}) + b_{\text{size}}(r_{\text{size factor}}) + b_{\text{book-to-market}}(r_{\text{book-to-market factor}})$$

This is commonly known as the Fama–French three-factor model. Using it to estimate expected returns is exactly the same as applying the arbitrage pricing theory. Here's an example.[29]

Step 1: Identify the Factors Fama and French have already identified the three factors that appear to determine expected returns. The returns on each of these factors are

[27]This estimate rests on risk premiums actually earned from 1978 to 1990, an unusually rewarding period for common stock investors. Estimates based on long-run market risk premiums would be lower. See E. J. Elton, M. J. Gruber, and J. Mei, "Cost of Capital Using Arbitrage Pricing Theory: A Case Study of Nine New York Utilities," *Financial Markets, Institutions, and Instruments* 3 (August 1994), pp. 46–73.

[28]E. F. Fama and K. R. French, "Size and Book-to-Market Factors in Earnings and Returns," *Journal of Finance* 50 (1995), pp. 131–155.

[29]The example is taken from E. F. Fama and K. R. French, "Industry Costs of Equity," *Journal of Financial Economics* 43 (1997), pp. 153–193. Fama and French emphasize the imprecision involved in using either the CAPM or an APT-style model to estimate the returns that investors expect.

Factor	Measured by
Market factor	Return on market index *minus* risk-free interest rate
Size factor	Return on small-firm stocks *less* return on large-firm stocks
Book-to-market factor	Return on high book-to-market-ratio stocks *less* return on low book-to-market-ratio stocks

Step 2: Estimate the Risk Premium for Each Factor Here we need to rely on history. Fama and French find that between 1963 and 1994 the return on the market factor averaged about 5.2 percent per year, the difference between the return on small and large capitalization stocks was about 3.2 percent a year, while the difference between the annual return on stocks with high and low book-to-market ratios averaged 5.4 percent.[30]

Step 3: Estimate the Factor Sensitivities Some stocks are more sensitive than others to fluctuations in the returns on the three factors. Look, for example, at the first three columns of numbers in Table 8.5, which show some estimates by Fama and French of factor sensitivities for different industry groups. You can see, for example, that an increase of 1 percent in the return on the book-to-market factor *reduces* the return on computer stocks by .49 percent but *increases* the return on utility stocks by .38 percent.[31]

	Three-Factor Model				CAPM
	Factor Sensitivities				
	b_{market}	b_{size}	$b_{book\text{-}to\text{-}market}$	Expected Risk Premium*	Expected Risk Premium
Aircraft	1.15	.51	.00	7.54%	6.43%
Banks	1.13	.13	.35	8.08	5.55
Chemicals	1.13	−.03	.17	6.58	5.57
Computers	.90	.17	−.49	2.49	5.29
Construction	1.21	.21	−.09	6.42	6.52
Food	.88	−.07	−.03	4.09	4.44
Petroleum & gas	.96	−.35	.21	4.93	4.32
Pharmaceuticals	.84	−.25	−.63	.09	4.71
Tobacco	.86	−.04	.24	5.56	4.08
Utilities	.79	−.20	.38	5.41	3.39

TABLE 8.5

Estimates of industry risk premiums using the Fama–French three-factor model and the CAPM.

*The expected risk premium equals the factor sensitivities multiplied by the factor risk premiums, that is, $(b_{market} \times 5.2) + (b_{size} \times 3.2) + (b_{book\text{-}to\text{-}market} \times 5.4)$.

Source: E. F. Fama and K. R. French, "Industry Costs of Equity," *Journal of Financial Economics* 43 (1997), pp. 153–193.

[30]We saw earlier that over the longer period 1928–2000 the average annual difference between the returns on small and large capitalization stocks was 3.1 percent. The difference between the returns on stocks with high and low book-to-market ratios was 4.4 percent.

[31]A 1 percent return on the book-to-market factor means that stocks with a high book-to-market ratio provide a 1 percent higher return than those with a low ratio.

Once you have an estimate of the factor sensitivities, it is a simple matter to multiply each of them by the expected factor return and add up the results. For example, the fourth column of numbers shows that the expected risk premium on computer stocks is $r - r_f = (.90 \times 5.2) + (.17 \times 3.2) - (.49 \times 5.4) = 2.49$ percent. Compare this figure with the risk premium estimated using the capital asset pricing model (the final column of Table 8.5). The three-factor model provides a substantially lower estimate of the risk premium for computer stocks than the CAPM. Why? Largely because computer stocks have a low exposure (−.49) to the book-to-market factor.

SUMMARY

The basic principles of portfolio selection boil down to a commonsense statement that investors try to increase the expected return on their portfolios and to reduce the standard deviation of that return. A portfolio that gives the highest expected return for a given standard deviation, or the lowest standard deviation for a given expected return, is known as an *efficient portfolio.* To work out which portfolios are efficient, an investor must be able to state the expected return and standard deviation of each stock and the degree of correlation between each pair of stocks.

Investors who are restricted to holding common stocks should choose efficient portfolios that suit their attitudes to risk. But investors who can also borrow and lend at the risk-free rate of interest should choose the *best* common stock portfolio *regardless* of their attitudes to risk. Having done that, they can then set the risk of their overall portfolio by deciding what proportion of their money they are willing to invest in stocks. The best efficient portfolio offers the highest ratio of forecasted risk premium to portfolio standard deviation.

For an investor who has only the same opportunities and information as everybody else, the best stock portfolio is the same as the best stock portfolio for other investors. In other words, he or she should invest in a mixture of the market portfolio and a risk-free loan (i.e., borrowing or lending).

A stock's marginal contribution to portfolio risk is measured by its sensitivity to changes in the value of the portfolio. The marginal contribution of a stock to the risk of the *market portfolio* is measured by *beta.* That is the fundamental idea behind the capital asset pricing model (CAPM), which concludes that each security's expected risk premium should increase in proportion to its beta:

$$\text{Expected risk premium} = \text{beta} \times \text{market risk premium}$$
$$r - r_f = \beta(r_m - r_f)$$

The capital asset pricing theory is the best-known model of risk and return. It is plausible and widely used but far from perfect. Actual returns are related to beta over the long run, but the relationship is not as strong as the CAPM predicts, and other factors seem to explain returns better since the mid-1960s. Stocks of small companies, and stocks with high book values relative to market prices, appear to have risks not captured by the CAPM.

The CAPM has also been criticized for its strong simplifying assumptions. A new theory called the *consumption* capital asset pricing model suggests that security risk reflects the sensitivity of returns to changes in investors' *consumption.*

This theory calls for a consumption beta rather than a beta relative to the market portfolio.

The arbitrage pricing theory offers an alternative theory of risk and return. It states that the expected risk premium on a stock should depend on the stock's exposure to several pervasive macroeconomic factors that affect stock returns:

$$\text{Expected risk premium} = b_1(r_{\text{factor 1}} - r_f) + b_2(r_{\text{factor 2}} - r_f) + \cdots$$

Here b's represent the individual security's sensitivities to the factors, and $r_{\text{factor}} - r_f$ is the risk premium demanded by investors who are exposed to this factor.

Arbitrage pricing theory does not say what these factors are. It asks for economists to hunt for unknown game with their statistical tool kits. The hunters have returned with several candidates, including unanticipated changes in

- The level of industrial activity.
- The rate of inflation.
- The spread between short- and long-term interest rates.

Fama and French have suggested three different factors:

- The return on the market portfolio less the risk-free rate of interest.
- The difference between the return on small- and large-firm stocks.
- The difference between the return on stocks with high book-to-market ratios and stocks with low book-to-market ratios.

In the Fama–French three-factor model, the expected return on each stock depends on its exposure to these three factors.

Each of these different models of risk and return has its fan club. However, all financial economists agree on two basic ideas: (1) Investors require extra expected return for taking on risk, and (2) they appear to be concerned predominantly with the risk that they cannot eliminate by diversification.

Visit us at www.mhhe.com/bm7e

FURTHER READING

The pioneering article on portfolio selection is:

H. M. Markowitz: "Portfolio Selection," *Journal of Finance,* 7:77–91 (March 1952).

There are a number of textbooks on portfolio selection which explain both Markowitz's original theory and some ingenious simplified versions. See, for example:

E. J. Elton and M. J. Gruber: *Modern Portfolio Theory and Investment Analysis,* 5th ed., John Wiley & Sons, New York, 1995.

Of the three pioneering articles on the capital asset pricing model, Jack Treynor's has never been published. The other two articles are:

W. F. Sharpe: "Capital Asset Prices: A Theory of Market Equilibrium under Conditions of Risk," *Journal of Finance,* 19:425–442 (September 1964).

J. Lintner: "The Valuation of Risk Assets and the Selection of Risky Investments in Stock Portfolios and Capital Budgets," *Review of Economics and Statistics,* 47:13–37 (February 1965).

The subsequent literature on the capital asset pricing model is enormous. The following book provides a collection of some of the more important articles plus a very useful survey by Jensen:

M. C. Jensen (ed.): *Studies in the Theory of Capital Markets,* Frederick A. Praeger, Inc., New York, 1972.

The two most important early tests of the capital asset pricing model are:

E. F. Fama and J. D. MacBeth: "Risk, Return and Equilibrium: Empirical Tests," *Journal of Political Economy,* 81:607–636 (May 1973).

F. Black, M. C. Jensen, and M. Scholes: "The Capital Asset Pricing Model: Some Empirical Tests," in M. C. Jensen (ed.), *Studies in the Theory of Capital Markets,* Frederick A. Praeger, Inc., New York, 1972.

For a critique of empirical tests of the capital asset pricing model, see:

R. Roll: "A Critique of the Asset Pricing Theory's Tests; Part I: On Past and Potential Testability of the Theory," *Journal of Financial Economics,* 4:129–176 (March 1977).

Much of the recent controversy about the performance of the capital asset pricing model was prompted by Fama and French's paper. The paper by Black takes issue with Fama and French and updates the Black, Jensen, and Scholes test of the model:

E. F. Fama and K. R. French: "The Cross-Section of Expected Stock Returns," *Journal of Finance,* 47:427–465 (June 1992).

F. Black, "Beta and Return," *Journal of Portfolio Management,* 20:8–18 (Fall 1993).

Breeden's 1979 article describes the consumption asset pricing model, and the Breeden, Gibbons, and Litzenberger paper tests the model and compares it with the standard CAPM:

D. T. Breeden: "An Intertemporal Asset Pricing Model with Stochastic Consumption and Investment Opportunities," *Journal of Financial Economics,* 7:265–296 (September 1979).

D. T. Breeden, M. R. Gibbons, and R. H. Litzenberger: "Empirical Tests of the Consumption-Oriented CAPM," *Journal of Finance,* 44:231–262 (June 1989).

Arbitrage pricing theory is described in Ross's 1976 paper.

S. A. Ross: "The Arbitrage Theory of Capital Asset Pricing," *Journal of Economic Theory,* 13:341–360 (December 1976).

The most accessible recent implementation of APT is:

E. J. Elton, M. J. Gruber, and J. Mei, "Cost of Capital Using Arbitrage Pricing Theory: A Case Study of Nine New York Utilities," *Financial Markets, Institutions, and Instruments,* 3:46–73 (August 1994).

For an application of the Fama–French three-factor model, see:

E. F. Fama and K. R. French, "Industry Costs of Equity," *Journal of Financial Economics,* 43:153–193 (February 1997).

QUIZ

1. Here are returns and standard deviations for four investments.

	Return	Standard Deviation
Treasury bills	6%	0%
Stock P	10	14
Stock Q	14.5	28
Stock R	21.0	26

Calculate the standard deviations of the following portfolios.

a. 50 percent in Treasury bills, 50 percent in stock P.

b. 50 percent each in Q and R, assuming the shares have

- perfect positive correlation
- perfect negative correlation
- no correlation

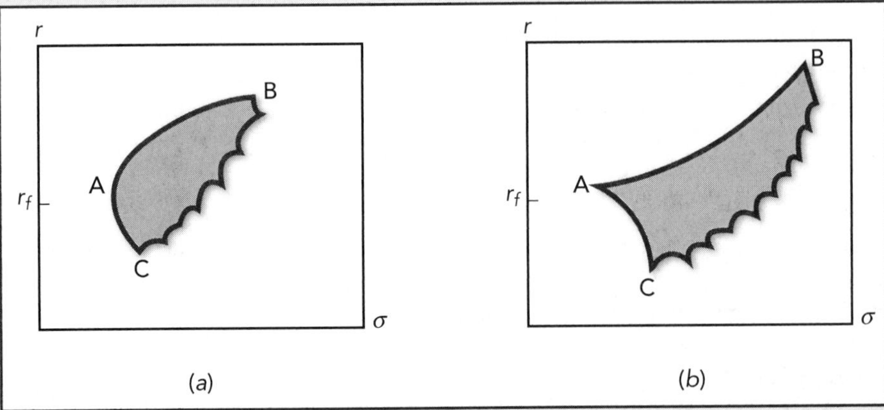

FIGURE 8.13

See Quiz Question 3.

c. Plot a figure like Figure 8.4 for Q and R, assuming a correlation coefficient of .5.
d. Stock Q has a lower return than R but a higher standard deviation. Does that mean that Q's price is too high or that R's price is too low?

2. For each of the following pairs of investments, state which would always be preferred by a rational investor (assuming that these are the *only* investments available to the investor):

a.	Portfolio A	r = 18 percent	σ = 20 percent
	Portfolio B	r = 14 percent	σ = 20 percent
b.	Portfolio C	r = 15 percent	σ = 18 percent
	Portfolio D	r = 13 percent	σ = 8 percent
c.	Portfolio E	r = 14 percent	σ = 16 percent
	Portfolio F	r = 14 percent	σ = 10 percent

3. Figures 8.13*a* and 8.13*b* purport to show the range of attainable combinations of expected return and standard deviation.
   a. Which diagram is incorrectly drawn and why?
   b. Which is the efficient set of portfolios?
   c. If r_f is the rate of interest, mark with an X the optimal stock portfolio.

4. **a.** Plot the following risky portfolios on a graph:

	Portfolio							
	A	**B**	**C**	**D**	**E**	**F**	**G**	**H**
Expected return (r), %	10	12.5	15	16	17	18	18	20
Standard deviation (σ), %	23	21	25	29	29	32	35	45

   b. Five of these portfolios are efficient, and three are not. Which are *in*efficient ones?
   c. Suppose you can also borrow and lend at an interest rate of 12 percent. Which of the above portfolios is best?
   d. Suppose you are prepared to tolerate a standard deviation of 25 percent. What is the maximum expected return that you can achieve if you cannot borrow or lend?
   e. What is your optimal strategy if you can borrow or lend at 12 percent and are prepared to tolerate a standard deviation of 25 percent? What is the maximum expected return that you can achieve?

5. How could an investor identify the *best* of a set of efficient portfolios of common stocks? What does "best" mean? Assume the investor can borrow or lend at the risk-free interest rate.
6. Suppose that the Treasury bill rate is 4 percent and the expected return on the market is 10 percent. Use the betas in Table 8.2.
   a. Calculate the expected return from McDonald's.
   b. Find the highest expected return that is offered by one of these stocks.
   c. Find the lowest expected return that is offered by one of these stocks.
   d. Would Dell offer a higher or lower expected return if the interest rate was 6 rather than 4 percent? Assume that the expected market return stays at 10 percent.
   e. Would Exxon Mobil offer a higher or lower expected return if the interest rate was 6 percent?
7. True or false?
   a. The CAPM implies that if you could find an investment with a negative beta, its expected return would be less than the interest rate.
   b. The expected return on an investment with a beta of 2.0 is twice as high as the expected return on the market.
   c. If a stock lies below the security market line, it is undervalued.
8. The CAPM has great theoretical, intuitive, and practical appeal. Nevertheless, many financial managers believe "beta is dead." Why?
9. Write out the APT equation for the expected rate of return on a risky stock.
10. Consider a three-factor APT model. The factors and associated risk premiums are

Factor	Risk Premium
Change in GNP	5%
Change in energy prices	−1
Change in long-term interest rates	+2

    Calculate expected rates of return on the following stocks. The risk-free interest rate is 7 percent.
    a. A stock whose return is uncorrelated with all three factors.
    b. A stock with average exposure to each factor (i.e., with $b = 1$ for each).
    c. A pure-play energy stock with high exposure to the energy factor ($b = 2$) but zero exposure to the other two factors.
    d. An aluminum company stock with average sensitivity to changes in interest rates and GNP, but negative exposure of $b = -1.5$ to the energy factor. (The aluminum company is energy-intensive and suffers when energy prices rise.)
11. Fama and French have proposed a three-factor model for expected returns. What are the three factors?

PRACTICE QUESTIONS

1. True or false? Explain or qualify as necessary.
   a. Investors demand higher expected rates of return on stocks with more variable rates of return.
   b. The CAPM predicts that a security with a beta of 0 will offer a zero expected return.
   c. An investor who puts \$10,000 in Treasury bills and \$20,000 in the market portfolio will have a beta of 2.0.

d. Investors demand higher expected rates of return from stocks with returns that are highly exposed to macroeconomic changes.
e. Investors demand higher expected rates of return from stocks with returns that are very sensitive to fluctuations in the stock market.

2. Look back at the calculation for Coca-Cola and Reebok in Section 8.1. Recalculate the expected portfolio return and standard deviation for different values of x_1 and x_2, assuming the correlation coefficient $\rho_{12} = 0$. Plot the range of possible combinations of expected return and standard deviation as in Figure 8.4. Repeat the problem for $\rho_{12} = +1$ and for $\rho_{12} = -1$.

3. Mark Harrywitz proposes to invest in two shares, X and Y. He expects a return of 12 percent from X and 8 percent from Y. The standard deviation of returns is 8 percent for X and 5 percent for Y. The correlation coefficient between the returns is .2.
a. Compute the expected return and standard deviation of the following portfolios:

Portfolio	Percentage in X	Percentage in Y
1	50	50
2	25	75
3	75	25

b. Sketch the set of portfolios composed of X and Y.
c. Suppose that Mr. Harrywitz can also borrow or lend at an interest rate of 5 percent. Show on your sketch how this alters his opportunities. Given that he can borrow or lend, what proportions of the common stock portfolio should be invested in X and Y?

4. M. Grandet has invested 60 percent of his money in share A and the remainder in share B. He assesses their prospects as follows:

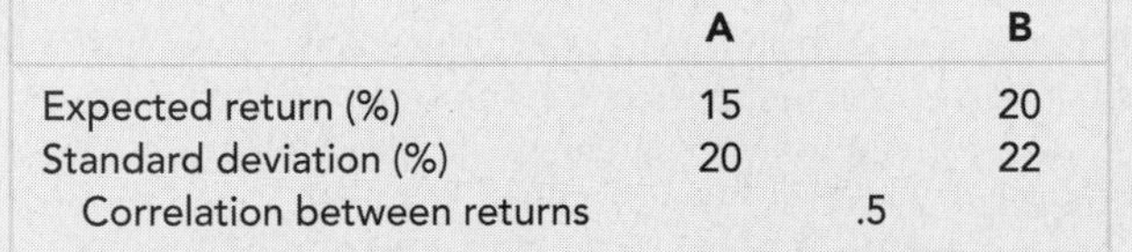

	A		B
Expected return (%)	15		20
Standard deviation (%)	20		22
Correlation between returns		.5	

a. What are the expected return and standard deviation of returns on his portfolio?
b. How would your answer change if the correlation coefficient was 0 or −.5?
c. Is M. Grandet's portfolio better or worse than one invested entirely in share A, or is it not possible to say?

5. Download "Monthly Adjusted Prices" for General Motors (GM) and Harley Davidson (HDI) from the Standard & Poor's Market Insight website (**www.mhhe.com/edumarketinsight**). Use the Excel function SLOPE to calculate beta for each company. (See Practice Question 7.13 for details.)

a. Suppose the S&P 500 index falls unexpectedly by 5 percent. By how much would you expect GM or HDI to fall?
b. Which is the riskier company for the well-diversified investor? How much riskier?
c. Suppose the Treasury bill rate is 4 percent and the expected return on the S&P 500 is 11 percent. Use the CAPM to forecast the expected rate of return on each stock.

STANDARD &POOR'S

6. Download the "Monthly Adjusted Prices" spreadsheets for Boeing and Pfizer from the Standard & Poor's Market Insight website (**www.mhhe.com/edumarketinsight**).
   a. Calculate the annual standard deviation for each company, using the most recent three years of monthly returns. Use the Excel function STDEV. Multiply by the square root of 12 to convert to annual units.
   b. Use the Excel function CORREL to calculate the correlation coefficient between the stocks' monthly returns.
   c. Use the CAPM to estimate expected rates of return. Calculate betas, or use the most recent beta reported under "Monthly Valuation Data" on the Market Insight website. Use the current Treasury bill rate and a reasonable estimate of the market risk premium.
   d. Construct a graph like Figure 8.5. What combination of Boeing and Pfizer has the lowest portfolio risk? What is the expected return for this minimum-risk portfolio?
7. The Treasury bill rate is 4 percent, and the expected return on the market portfolio is 12 percent. On the basis of the capital asset pricing model:
   a. Draw a graph similar to Figure 8.7 showing how the expected return varies with beta.
   b. What is the risk premium on the market?
   c. What is the required return on an investment with a beta of 1.5?
   d. If an investment with a beta of .8 offers an expected return of 9.8 percent, does it have a positive NPV?
   e. If the market expects a return of 11.2 percent from stock X, what is its beta?

STANDARD &POOR'S

8. Most of the companies in Table 8.2 are covered in the Standard & Poor's Market Insight website (**www.mhhe.com/edumarketinsight**). For those that are covered, use the Excel SLOPE function to recalculate betas from the monthly returns on the "Monthly Adjusted Prices" spreadsheets. Use as many monthly returns as available, up to a maximum of 60 months. Recalculate expected rates of return from the CAPM formula, using a current risk-free rate and a market risk premium of 8 percent. How have the expected returns changed from the figures reported in Table 8.2?

STANDARD &POOR'S

9. Go to the Standard & Poor's Market Insight website (**www.mhhe.com/edumarketinsight**), and find a low-risk income stock—Exxon Mobil or Kellogg might be good candidates. Estimate the company's beta to confirm that it is well below 1.0. Use monthly rates of return for the most recent three years. For the same period, estimate the annual standard deviation for the stock, the standard deviation for the S&P 500, and the correlation coefficient between returns on the stock and the S&P 500. (The Excel functions are given in Practice Questions above.) Forecast the expected rate of return for the stock, assuming the CAPM holds, with a market return of 12 percent and a risk-free rate of 5 percent.
   a. Plot a graph like Figure 8.5 showing the combinations of risk and return from a portfolio invested in your low-risk stock and in the market. Vary the fraction invested in the stock from zero to 100 percent.
   b. Suppose you can borrow or lend at 5 percent. Would you invest in some combination of your low-risk stock and the market? Or would you simply invest in the market? Explain.
   c. Suppose you forecast a return on the stock that is 5 percentage points higher than the CAPM return used in part (a). Redo parts (a) and (b) with this higher forecasted return.
   d. Find a high-beta stock and redo parts (a), (b), and (c).
10. Percival Hygiene has $10 million invested in long-term corporate bonds. This bond portfolio's expected annual rate of return is 9 percent, and the annual standard deviation is 10 percent.

    Amanda Reckonwith, Percival's financial adviser, recommends that Percival consider investing in an index fund which closely tracks the Standard and Poor's 500 index. The index has an expected return of 14 percent, and its standard deviation is 16 percent.

a. Suppose Percival puts all his money in a combination of the index fund and Treasury bills. Can he thereby improve his expected rate of return without changing the risk of his portfolio? The Treasury bill yield is 6 percent.

b. Could Percival do even better by investing equal amounts in the corporate bond portfolio and the index fund? The correlation between the bond portfolio and the index fund is +.1.

11. "There may be some truth in these CAPM and APT theories, but last year some stocks did much better than these theories predicted, and other stocks did much worse." Is this a valid criticism?

12. True or false?

a. Stocks of small companies have done better than predicted by the CAPM.

b. Stocks with high ratios of book value to market price have done better than predicted by the CAPM.

c. On average, stock returns have been positively related to beta.

13. Some true or false questions about the APT:

a. The APT factors cannot reflect diversifiable risks.

b. The market rate of return cannot be an APT factor.

c. Each APT factor must have a positive risk premium associated with it; otherwise the model is inconsistent.

d. There is no theory that specifically identifies the APT factors.

e. The APT model could be true but not very useful, for example, if the relevant factors change unpredictably.

14. Consider the following simplified APT model (compare Tables 8.3 and 8.4):

Factor	Expected Risk Premium
Market	6.4%
Interest rate	−.6
Yield spread	5.1

Calculate the expected return for the following stocks. Assume $r_f = 5$ percent.

	Factor Risk Exposures		
	Market	Interest Rate	Yield Spread
Stock	(b_1)	(b_2)	(b_3)
P	1.0	−2.0	−.2
P^2	1.2	0	.3
P^3	.3	.5	1.0

15. Look again at Practice Question 14. Consider a portfolio with equal investments in stocks P, P^2, and P^3.

a. What are the factor risk exposures for the portfolio?

b. What is the portfolio's expected return?

16. The following table shows the sensitivity of four stocks to the three Fama–French factors in the five years to 2001. Estimate the expected return on each stock assuming that the interest rate is 3.5 percent, the expected risk premium on the market is 8.8 percent, the expected risk premium on the size factor is 3.1 percent, and the expected risk premium on the book-to-market factor is 4.4 percent. (These were the realized premia from 1928–2000.)

	Factor Sensitivities			
Factor	**Coca-Cola**	**Exxon Mobil**	**Pfizer**	**Reebok**
Market	.82	.50	.66	1.17
Size*	−.29	.04	−.56	.73
Book-to-market†	.24	.27	−.07	1.14

*Return on small-firm stocks less return on large-firm stocks.
†Return on high book-to-market-ratio stocks less return on low book-to-market-ratio stocks.

CHALLENGE QUESTIONS

1. In footnote 4 we noted that the minimum-risk portfolio contained an investment of 21.4 percent in Reebok and 78.6 in Coca-Cola. Prove it. *Hint:* You need a little calculus to do so.
2. Look again at the set of efficient portfolios that we calculated in Section 8.1.
   a. If the interest rate is 10 percent, which of the four efficient portfolios should you hold?
   b. What is the beta of each holding relative to that portfolio? *Hint:* Remember that if a portfolio is efficient, the expected risk premium on each holding must be proportional to the beta of the stock *relative to that portfolio.*
   c. How would your answers to (a) and (b) change if the interest rate was 5 percent?
3. "Suppose you could forecast the behavior of APT factors, such as industrial production, interest rates, etc. You could then identify stocks' sensitivities to these factors, pick the right stocks, and make lots of money." Is this a good argument favoring the APT? Explain why or why not.
4. The following question illustrates the APT. Imagine that there are only two pervasive macroeconomic factors. Investments X, Y, and Z have the following sensitivities to these two factors:

Investment	b_1	b_2
X	1.75	.25
Y	−1.00	2.00
Z	2.00	1.00

   We assume that the expected risk premium is 4 percent on factor 1 and 8 percent on factor 2. Treasury bills obviously offer zero risk premium.
   a. According to the APT, what is the risk premium on each of the three stocks?
   b. Suppose you buy \$200 of X and \$50 of Y and sell \$150 of Z. What is the sensitivity of your portfolio to each of the two factors? What is the expected risk premium?
   c. Suppose you buy \$80 of X and \$60 of Y and sell \$40 of Z. What is the sensitivity of your portfolio to each of the two factors? What is the expected risk premium?

d. Finally, suppose you buy $160 of X and $20 of Y and sell $80 of Z. What is your portfolio's sensitivity now to each of the two factors? And what is the expected risk premium?

e. Suggest two possible ways that you could construct a fund that has a sensitivity of .5 to factor 1 only. Now compare the risk premiums on each of these two investments.

f. Suppose that the APT did *not* hold and that X offered a risk premium of 8 percent, Y offered a premium of 14 percent, and Z offered a premium of 16 percent. Devise an investment that has zero sensitivity to each factor and that has a positive risk premium.

CHAPTER NINE

CAPITAL BUDGETING AND RISK

LONG BEFORE THE development of modern theories linking risk and expected return, smart financial managers adjusted for risk in capital budgeting. They realized intuitively that, other things being equal, risky projects are less desirable than safe ones. Therefore, financial managers demanded a higher rate of return from risky projects, or they based their decisions on conservative estimates of the cash flows.

Various rules of thumb are often used to make these risk adjustments. For example, many companies estimate the rate of return required by investors in their securities and then use this **company cost of capital** to discount the cash flows on new projects. Our first task in this chapter is to explain when the company cost of capital can, and cannot, be used to discount a project's cash flows. We shall see that it is the right hurdle rate for those projects that have the same risk as the firm's existing business; however, if a project is more risky than the firm as a whole, the cost of capital needs to be adjusted upward and the project's cash flows discounted at this higher rate. Conversely, a lower discount rate is needed for projects that are safer than the firm as a whole.

The capital asset pricing model is widely used to estimate the return that investors require.[1] It states

$$\text{Expected return} = r = r_f + (\text{beta})\,(r_m - r_f)$$

We used this formula in the last chapter to figure out the return that investors expected from a sample of common stocks but we did not explain how to estimate beta. It turns out that we can gain some insight into beta by looking at how the stock price has responded in the past to market fluctuations. Beta is difficult to measure accurately for an individual firm: Greater accuracy can be achieved by looking at an average of similar companies. We will also look at what features make some investments riskier than others. If you know *why* Exxon Mobil has less risk than, say, Dell Computer, you will be in a better position to judge the relative risks of different capital investment opportunities.

Some companies are financed entirely by common stock. In these cases the company cost of capital and the expected return on the stock are the same thing. However, most firms finance themselves partly by debt and the return that they earn on their investments must be sufficient to satisfy both the stockholders and the debtholders. We will show you how to calculate the company cost of capital when the firm has more than one type of security outstanding.

There is still another complication: Project betas can shift over time. Some projects are safer in youth than in old age; others are riskier. In this case, what do we mean by the project beta? There may be a separate beta for each year of the project's life. To put it another way, can we jump from the capital asset pricing model, which looks one period into the future, to the discounted-cash-flow formula for valuing long-lived assets? Most of the time it is safe to do so, but you should be able to recognize and deal with the exceptions.

We will use the capital asset pricing model, or CAPM, throughout this chapter. But don't infer that it is therefore the last word on risk and return. The principles and procedures covered in this chapter work just as well with other models such as arbitrage pricing theory (APT).

[1]In a survey of financial practice, Graham and Harvey found that 74 percent of firms always, or almost always, used the capital asset pricing model to estimate the cost of capital. See J. Graham and C. Harvey, "The Theory and Practice of Corporate Finance: Evidence from the Field," *Journal of Financial Economics* 60 (May/June 2001), pp. 187–244.

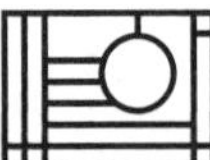

9.1 COMPANY AND PROJECT COSTS OF CAPITAL

The **company cost of capital** is defined as the expected return on a portfolio of all the company's existing securities. It is used to discount the cash flows on projects that have similar risk to that of the firm as a whole. For example, in Table 8.2 we estimated that investors require a return of 9.2 percent from Pfizer common stock. If Pfizer is contemplating an expansion of the firm's existing business, it would make sense to discount the forecasted cash flows at 9.2 percent.[2]

The company cost of capital is *not* the correct discount rate if the new projects are more or less risky than the firm's existing business. Each project should in principle be evaluated at its *own* opportunity cost of capital. This is a clear implication of the value-additivity principle introduced in Chapter 7. For a firm composed of assets A and B, the firm value is

$$\begin{aligned}\text{Firm value} &= \text{PV(AB)} = \text{PV(A)} + \text{PV(B)} \\ &= \text{sum of separate asset values}\end{aligned}$$

Here PV(A) and PV(B) are valued just as if they were mini-firms in which stockholders could invest directly. Investors would value A by discounting its forecasted cash flows at a rate reflecting the risk of A. They would value B by discounting at a rate reflecting the risk of B. The two discount rates will, in general, be different. If the present value of an asset depended on the identity of the company that bought it, present values would *not* add up. Remember, a good project is a good project is a good project.

If the firm considers investing in a third project C, it should also value C as if C were a mini-firm. That is, the firm should discount the cash flows of C at the expected rate of return that investors would demand to make a separate investment in C. *The true cost of capital depends on the use to which that capital is put.*

This means that Pfizer should accept any project that more than compensates for the *project's* beta. In other words, Pfizer should accept any project lying above the upward-sloping line that links expected return to risk in Figure 9.1. If the project has a high risk, Pfizer needs a higher prospective return than if the project has a low risk. Now contrast this with the company cost of capital rule, which is to accept any project *regardless of its risk* as long as it offers a higher return than the *company's* cost of capital. In terms of Figure 9.1, the rule tells Pfizer to accept any project above the horizontal cost of capital line, that is, any project offering a return of more than 9.2 percent.

It is clearly silly to suggest that Pfizer should demand the same rate of return from a very safe project as from a very risky one. If Pfizer used the company cost of capital rule, it would reject many good low-risk projects and accept many poor high-risk projects. It is also silly to suggest that just because another company has a low company cost of capital, it is justified in accepting projects that Pfizer would reject.

The notion that each company has some individual discount rate or cost of capital is widespread, but far from universal. Many firms require different returns

[2]Debt accounted for only about 0.3 percent of the total market value of Pfizer's securities. Thus, its cost of capital is effectively identical to the rate of return investors expect on its common stock. The complications caused by debt are discussed later in this chapter.

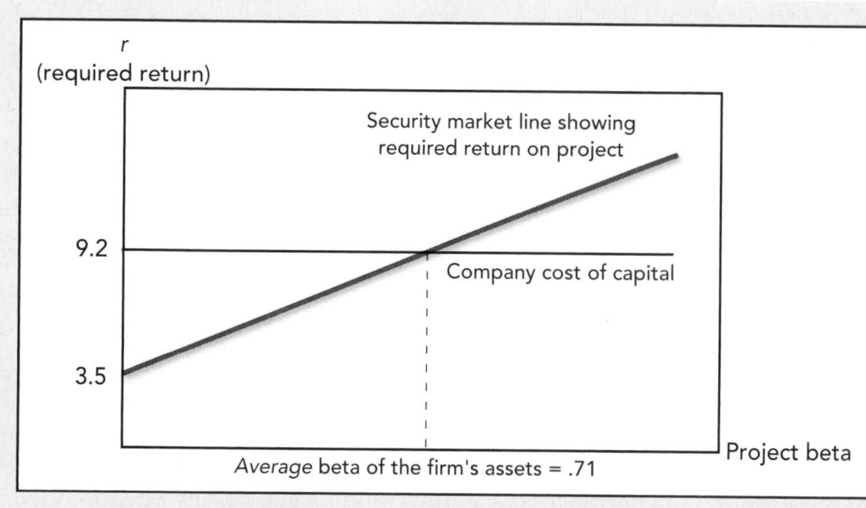

FIGURE 9.1

A comparison between the company cost of capital rule and the required return under the capital asset pricing model. Pfizer's company cost of capital is about 9.2 percent. This is the correct discount rate only if the project beta is .71. In general, the correct discount rate increases as project beta increases. Pfizer should accept projects with rates of return above the security market line relating required return to beta.

from different categories of investment. For example, discount rates might be set as follows:

Category	Discount Rate
Speculative ventures	30%
New products	20
Expansion of existing business	15 (company cost of capital)
Cost improvement, known technology	10

Perfect Pitch and the Cost of Capital

The true cost of capital depends on project risk, not on the company undertaking the project. So why is so much time spent estimating the company cost of capital?

There are two reasons. First, many (maybe, most) projects can be treated as average risk, that is, no more or less risky than the average of the company's other assets. For these projects the company cost of capital is the right discount rate. Second, the company cost of capital is a useful starting point for setting discount rates for unusually risky or safe projects. It is easier to add to, or subtract from, the company cost of capital than to estimate each project's cost of capital from scratch.

There is a good musical analogy here.[3] Most of us, lacking perfect pitch, need a well-defined reference point, like middle C, before we can sing on key. But anyone who can carry a tune gets *relative* pitches right. Businesspeople have good intuition about *relative* risks, at least in industries they are used to, but not about absolute risk or required rates of return. Therefore, they set a companywide cost of capital as a benchmark. This is not the right hurdle rate for everything the company does, but adjustments can be made for more or less risky ventures.

[3]The analogy is borrowed from S. C. Myers and L. S. Borucki, "Discounted Cash Flow Estimates of the Cost of Equity Capital—A Case Study," *Financial Markets, Institutions, and Investments* 3 (August 1994), p. 18.

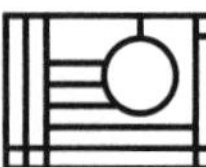

9.2 MEASURING THE COST OF EQUITY

Suppose that you are considering an across-the-board expansion by your firm. Such an investment would have about the same degree of risk as the existing business. Therefore you should discount the projected flows at the company cost of capital.

Companies generally start by estimating the return that investors require from the company's common stock. In Chapter 8 we used the capital asset pricing model to do this. This states

$$\text{Expected stock return} = r_f + \beta(r_m - r_f)$$

An obvious way to measure the beta (β) of a stock is to look at how its price has responded in the past to market movements. For example, look at the three left-hand scatter diagrams in Figure 9.2. In the top-left diagram we have calculated monthly returns from Dell Computer stock in the period after it went public in 1988, and we have plotted these returns against the market returns for the same month. The second diagram on the left shows a similar plot for the returns on General Motors stock, and the third shows a plot for Exxon Mobil. In each case we have fitted a line through the points. The slope of this line is an estimate of beta.[4] It tells us how much on average the stock price changed for each additional 1 percent change in the market index.

The right-hand diagrams show similar plots for the same three stocks during the subsequent period, February 1995 to July 2001. Although the slopes varied from the first period to the second, there is little doubt that Exxon Mobil's beta is much less than Dell's or that GM's beta falls somewhere between the two. If you had used the past beta of each stock to predict its future beta, you wouldn't have been too far off.

Only a small portion of each stock's total risk comes from movements in the market. The rest is unique risk, which shows up in the scatter of points around the fitted lines in Figure 9.2. *R-squared* (R^2) measures the proportion of the total variance in the stock's returns that can be explained by market movements. For example, from 1995 to 2001, the R^2 for GM was .25. In other words, a quarter of GM's risk was market risk and three-quarters was unique risk. The variance of the returns on GM stock was 964.[5] So we could say that the variance in stock returns that was due to the market was $.25 \times 964 = 241$, and the variance of unique returns was $.75 \times 964 = 723$.

The estimates of beta shown in Figure 9.2 are just that. They are based on the stocks' returns in 78 particular months. The noise in the returns can obscure the true beta. Therefore, statisticians calculate the *standard error* of the estimated beta to show the extent of possible mismeasurement. Then they set up a *confidence interval* of the estimated value plus or minus two standard errors. For example, the standard error of GM's estimated beta in the most recent period is .20. Thus the confidence interval for GM's beta is 1.00 plus or minus $2 \times .20$. If you state that the *true* beta for GM is between .60 and 1.40, you have a 95 percent chance of being right. Notice that we can be more confident of our estimate of Exxon Mobil's beta and less confident of Dell's.

Usually you will have more information (and thus more confidence) than this simple calculation suggests. For example, you know that Exxon Mobil's estimated

---

[4]Notice that you must regress the *returns* on the stock on the market *returns*. You would get a very similar estimate if you simply used the percentage *changes* in the stock price and the market index. But sometimes analysts make the mistake of regressing the stock price *level* on the *level* of the index and obtain nonsense results.

[5]This is an annual figure; we annualized the monthly variance by multiplying by 12 (see footnote 17 in Chapter 7). The standard deviation was $\sqrt{964} = 31.0$ percent.

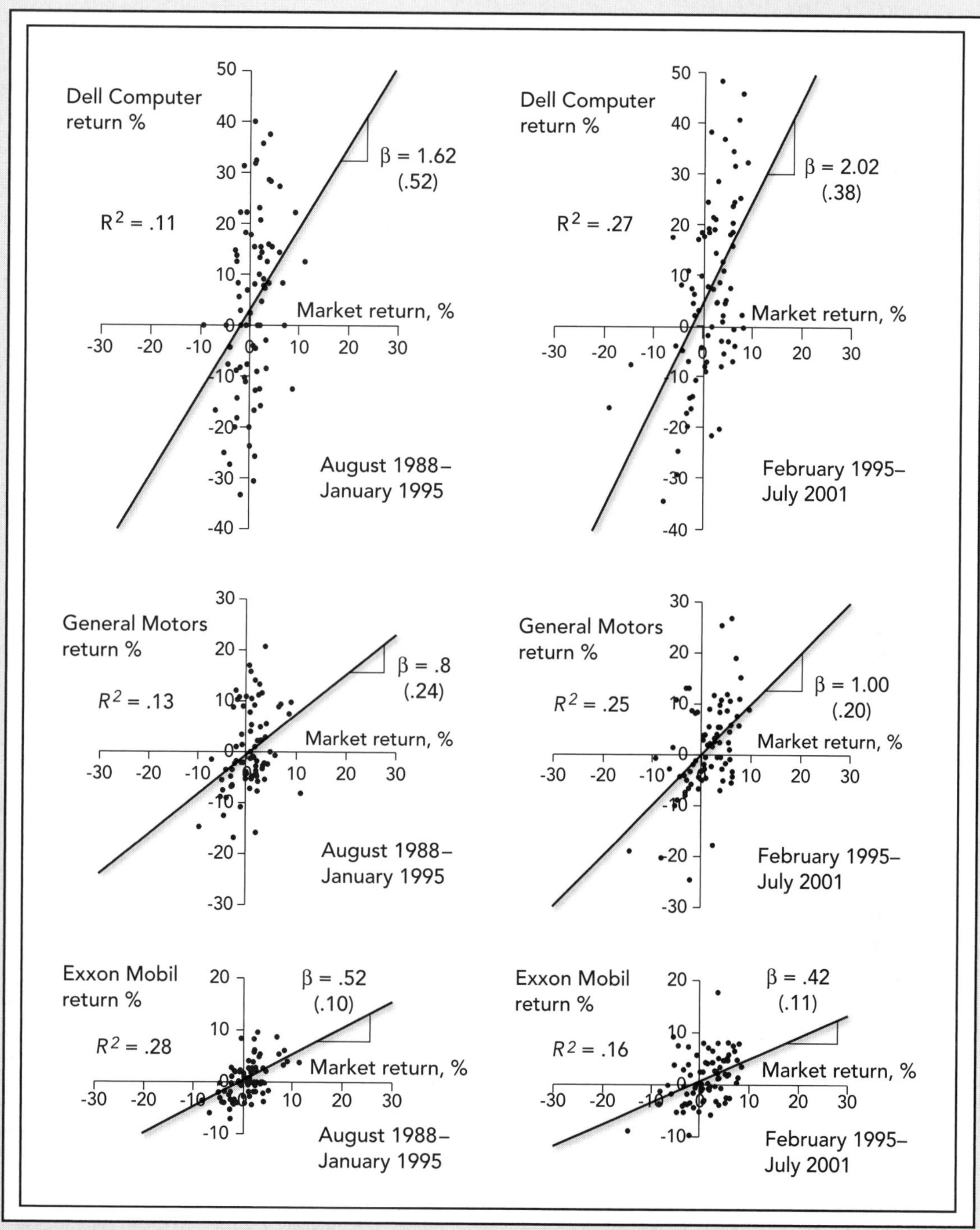

FIGURE 9.2

We have used past returns to estimate the betas of three stocks for the periods August 1988 to January 1995 (left-hand diagrams) and February 1995 to July 2001 (right-hand diagrams). Beta is the slope of the fitted line. Notice that in both periods Dell had the highest beta and Exxon Mobil the lowest. Standard errors are in parentheses below the betas. The standard error shows the range of possible error in the beta estimate. We also report the proportion of total risk that is due to market movements (R^2).

TABLE 9.1

Estimated betas and costs of (equity) capital for a sample of large railroad companies and for a portfolio of these companies. The precision of the portfolio beta is much better than that of the betas of the individual companies—note the lower standard error for the portfolio.

	β_{equity}	Standard Error
Burlington Northern & Santa Fe	.64	.20
CSX Transportation	.46	.24
Norfolk Southern	.52	.26
Union Pacific Corp.	.40	.21
Industry portfolio	.50	.17

beta was well below 1 in the previous period, while Dell's estimated beta was well above 1. Nevertheless, there is always a large margin for error when estimating the beta for individual stocks.

Fortunately, the estimation errors tend to cancel out when you estimate betas of *portfolios.*[6] That is why financial managers often turn to *industry betas.* For example, Table 9.1 shows estimates of beta and the standard errors of these estimates for the common stocks of four large railroad companies. Most of the standard errors are above .2, large enough to preclude a precise estimate of any particular utility's beta. However, the table also shows the estimated beta for a portfolio of all four railroad stocks. Notice that the estimated industry beta is more reliable. This shows up in the lower standard error.

The Expected Return on Union Pacific Corporation's Common Stock

Suppose that in mid-2001 you had been asked to estimate the company cost of capital of Union Pacific Corporation. Table 9.1 provides two clues about the true beta of Union Pacific's stock: the direct estimate of .40 and the average estimate for the industry of .50. We will use the industry average of .50.[7]

In mid-2001 the risk-free rate of interest r_f was about 3.5 percent. Therefore, if you had used 8 percent for the risk premium on the market, you would have concluded that the expected return on Union Pacific's stock was about 7.5 percent:[8]

[6]If the observations are independent, the standard error of the estimated mean beta declines in proportion to the square root of the number of stocks in the portfolio.

[7]Comparing the beta of Union Pacific with those of the other railroads would be misleading if Union Pacific had a materially higher or lower debt ratio. Fortunately, its debt ratio was about average for the sample in Table 9.1.

[8]This is really a discount rate for near-term cash flows, since it rests on a risk-free rate measured by the yield on Treasury bills with maturities less than one year. Is this, you may ask, the right discount rate for cash flows from an asset with, say, a 10- or 20-year expected life?

Well, now that you mention it, possibly not. In 2001 longer-term Treasury bonds yielded about 5.8 percent, that is, about 2.3 percent above the Treasury bill rate.

The risk-free rate could be defined as a long-term Treasury bond yield. If you do this, however, you should subtract the risk premium of Treasury bonds over bills, which we gave as 1.8 percent in Table 7.1. This gives a rough-and-ready estimate of the expected yield on short-term Treasury bills over the life of the bond:

$$\begin{aligned}\text{Expected average T-bill rate} &= \text{T-bond yield} - \text{premium of bonds over bills}\\ &= .058 - .019 = .039, \text{ or } 3.9\%\end{aligned}$$

The expected average future Treasury bill rate should be used in the CAPM if a discount rate is needed for an extended stream of cash flows. In 2001 this "long-term r_f" was a bit higher than the Treasury bill rate.

$$\text{Expected stock return} = r_f + \beta(r_m - r_f)$$
$$= 3.5 + .5(8.0) = 7.5\%$$

We have focused on using the capital asset pricing model to estimate the expected returns on Union Pacific's common stock. But it would be useful to get a check on this figure. For example, in Chapter 4 we used the constant-growth DCF formula to estimate the expected rate of return for a sample of utility stocks.[9] You could also use DCF models with varying future growth rates, or perhaps arbitrage pricing theory (APT). We showed in Section 8.4 how APT can be used to estimate expected returns.

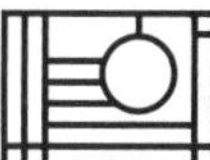

9.3 CAPITAL STRUCTURE AND THE COMPANY COST OF CAPITAL

In the last section, we used the capital asset pricing model to estimate the return that investors require from Union Pacific's common stock. Is this figure Union Pacific's company cost of capital? Not if Union Pacific has other securities outstanding. The company cost of capital also needs to reflect the returns demanded by the owners of these securities.

We will return shortly to the problem of Union Pacific's cost of capital, but first we need to look at the relationship between the cost of capital and the mix of debt and equity used to finance the company. Think again of what the *company* cost of capital is and what it is used for. We *define* it as the opportunity cost of capital for the firm's existing assets; we *use* it to value new assets that have the same risk as the old ones.

If you owned a portfolio of all the firm's securities—100 percent of the debt and 100 percent of the equity—you would own the firm's assets lock, stock, and barrel. You wouldn't share the cash flows with anyone; every dollar of cash the firm paid out would be paid to you. You can think of the company cost of capital as the expected return on this hypothetical portfolio. To calculate it, you just take a weighted average of the expected returns on the debt and the equity:

$$\text{Company cost of capital} = r_{\text{assets}} = r_{\text{portfolio}}$$
$$= \frac{\text{debt}}{\text{debt} + \text{equity}} r_{\text{debt}} + \frac{\text{equity}}{\text{debt} + \text{equity}} r_{\text{equity}}$$

For example, suppose that the firm's market-value balance sheet is as follows:

Asset value	100	Debt value (*D*)	30
		Equity value (*E*)	70
Asset value	100	Firm value (*V*)	100

Note that the values of debt and equity add up to the firm value ($D + E = V$) and that the firm value equals the asset value. (These figures are *market* values, not *book* values: The market value of the firm's equity is often substantially different from its book value.)

[9]The United States Surface Transportation Board uses the constant-growth model to estimate the cost of equity capital for railroad companies. We will review its findings in Chapter 19.

If investors expect a return of 7.5 percent on the debt and 15 percent on the equity, then the expected return on the assets is

$$r_{\text{assets}} = \frac{D}{V} r_{\text{debt}} + \frac{E}{V} r_{\text{equity}}$$

$$= \left(\frac{30}{100} \times 7.5\right) + \left(\frac{70}{100} \times 15\right) = 12.75\%$$

If the firm is contemplating investment in a project that has the same risk as the firm's existing business, the opportunity cost of capital for this project is the same as the firm's cost of capital; in other words, it is 12.75 percent.

What would happen if the firm issued an additional 10 of debt and used the cash to repurchase 10 of its equity? The revised market-value balance sheet is

Asset value	100	Debt value (*D*)	40
		Equity value (*E*)	60
Asset value	100	Firm value (*V*)	100

The change in financial structure does not affect the amount or risk of the cash flows on the total package of debt and equity. Therefore, if investors required a return of 12.75 percent on the total package before the refinancing, they must require a 12.75 percent return on the firm's assets afterward.

Although the required return on the *package* of debt and equity is unaffected, the change in financial structure does affect the required return on the individual securities. Since the company has more debt than before, the debtholders are likely to demand a higher interest rate. We will suppose that the expected return on the debt rises to 7.875 percent. Now you can write down the basic equation for the return on assets

$$r_{\text{assets}} = \frac{D}{V} r_{\text{debt}} + \frac{E}{V} r_{\text{equity}}$$

$$= \left(\frac{40}{100} \times 7.875\right) + \left(\frac{60}{100} \times r_{\text{equity}}\right) = 12.75\%$$

and solve for the return on equity

$$r_{\text{equity}} = 16.0\%$$

Increasing the amount of debt increased debtholder risk and led to a rise in the return that debtholders required (r_{debt} rose from 7.5 to 7.875 percent). The higher leverage also made the equity riskier and increased the return that shareholders required (r_{equity} rose from 15 to 16 percent). The weighted average return on debt and equity remained at 12.75 percent:

$$r_{\text{assets}} = (.4 \times r_{\text{debt}}) + (.6 \times r_{\text{equity}})$$

$$= (.4 \times 7.875) + (.6 \times 16) = 12.75\%$$

Suppose that the company decided instead to repay all its debt and to replace it with equity. In that case all the cash flows would go to the equity holders. The company cost of capital, r_{assets}, would stay at 12.75 percent, and r_{equity} would also be 12.75 percent.

How Changing Capital Structure Affects Beta

We have looked at how changes in financial structure affect expected return. Let us now look at the effect on beta.

The stockholders and debtholders both receive a share of the firm's cash flows, and both bear part of the risk. For example, if the firm's assets turn out to be worthless, there will be no cash to pay stockholders or debtholders. But debtholders usually bear much less risk than stockholders. Debt betas of large blue-chip firms are typically in the range of .1 to .3.[10]

If you owned a portfolio of all the firm's securities, you wouldn't share the cash flows with anyone. You wouldn't share the risks with anyone either; you would bear them all. Thus the firm's asset beta is equal to the beta of a portfolio of all the firm's debt and its equity.

The beta of this hypothetical portfolio is just a weighted average of the debt and equity betas:

$$\beta_{\text{assets}} = \beta_{\text{portfolio}} = \frac{D}{V}\beta_{\text{debt}} + \frac{E}{V}\beta_{\text{equity}}$$

Think back to our example. If the debt before the refinancing has a beta of .1 and the equity has a beta of 1.1, then

$$\beta_{\text{assets}} = (.3 \times .1) + (.7 \times 1.1) = .8$$

What happens after the refinancing? The risk of the total package is unaffected, but both the debt and the equity are now more risky. Suppose that the debt beta increases to .2. We can work out the new equity beta:

$$\beta_{\text{assets}} = \beta_{\text{portfolio}} = \frac{D}{V}\beta_{\text{dept}} + \frac{E}{V}\beta_{\text{equity}}$$

$$.8 = (.4 \times .2) + (.6 \times \beta_{\text{equity}})$$

$$\beta_{\text{equity}} = 1.2$$

You can see why borrowing is said to create *financial leverage* or *gearing.* Financial leverage does not affect the risk or the expected return on the firm's assets, but it does push up the risk of the common stock. Shareholders demand a correspondingly higher return because of this *financial risk.*

Figure 9.3 shows the expected return and beta of the firm's assets. It also shows how expected return and risk are shared between the debtholders and equity holders before the refinancing. Figure 9.4 shows what happens after the refinancing. Both debt and equity are now more risky, and therefore investors demand a higher return. But equity accounts for a smaller proportion of firm value than before. As a result, the weighted average of both the expected return and beta on the two components is unchanged.

Now you can see how to *unlever* betas, that is, how to go from an observed β_{equity} to β_{assets}. You have the equity beta, say, 1.2. You also need the debt beta, say, .2, and the relative market values of debt (D/V) and equity (E/V). If debt accounts for 40 percent of overall value V,

$$\beta_{\text{assets}} = (.4 \times .2) + (.6 \times 1.2) = .8$$

[10]For example, in Table 7.1 we reported average returns on a portfolio of high-grade corporate bonds. In the 10 years ending December 2000 the estimated beta of this bond portfolio was .17.

FIGURE 9.3

Expected returns and betas before refinancing. The expected return and beta of the firm's assets are weighted averages of the expected return and betas of the debt and equity.

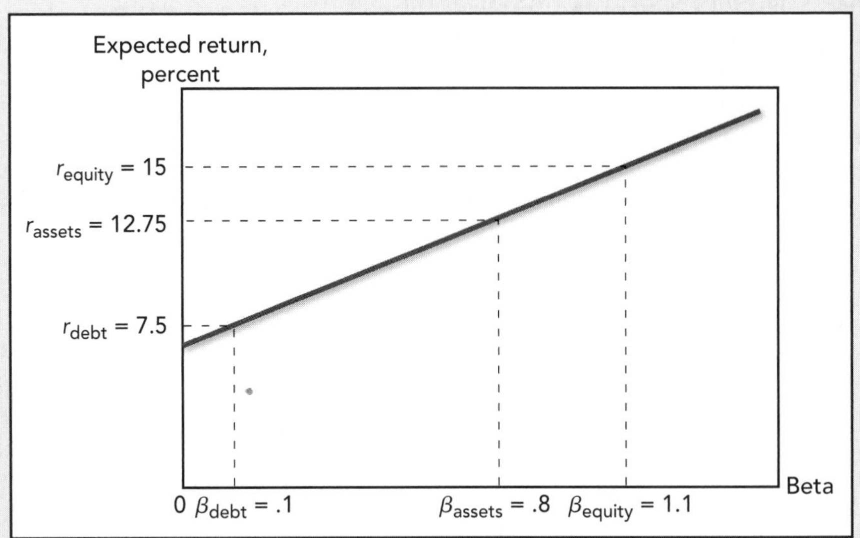

FIGURE 9.4

Expected returns and betas after refinancing.

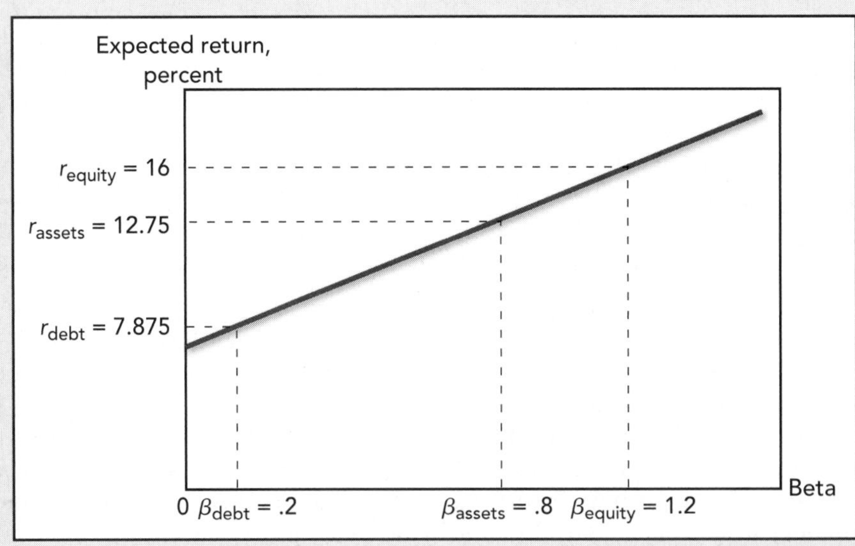

This runs the previous example in reverse. Just remember the basic relationship:

$$\beta_{assets} = \beta_{portfolio} = \frac{D}{V}\beta_{debt} + \frac{E}{V}\beta_{equity}$$

Capital Structure and Discount Rates

The company cost of capital is the opportunity cost of capital for the firm's assets. That's why we write it as r_{assets}. If a firm encounters a project that has the same beta as the firm's overall assets, then r_{assets} is the right discount rate for the project cash flows.

When the firm uses debt financing, the company cost of capital is not the same as r_{equity}, the expected rate of return on the firm's stock; r_{equity} is higher because of financial risk. However, the company cost of capital can be calculated as a weighted average of the returns expected by investors on the various debt and equity securities issued by the firm. You can also calculate the firm's asset beta as a weighted average of the betas of these securities.

When the firm changes its mix of debt and equity securities, the risk and expected returns of these securities change; however, the asset beta and the company cost of capital do not change.

Now, if you think all this is too neat and simple, you're right. The complications are spelled out in great detail in Chapters 17 through 19. But we must note one complication here: Interest paid on a firm's borrowing can be deducted from taxable income. Thus the after-tax cost of debt is $r_{\text{debt}}\,(1 - T_c)$, where T_c is the marginal corporate tax rate. When companies discount an average-risk project, they do not use the company cost of capital as we have computed it. They use the after-tax cost of debt to compute the after-tax weighted-average cost of capital or WACC:

$$\text{WACC} = r_{\text{debt}}(1 - T_c)\frac{D}{V} + r_{\text{equity}}\frac{E}{V}$$

More—lots more—on this in Chapter 19.

Back to Union Pacific's Cost of Capital

In the last section we estimated the return that investors required on Union Pacific's common stock. If Union Pacific were wholly equity-financed, the company cost of capital would be the same as the expected return on its stock. But in mid-2001 common stock accounted for only 60 percent of the market value of the company's securities. Debt accounted for the remaining 40 percent.[11] Union Pacific's company cost of capital is a weighted average of the expected returns on the different securities.

We estimated the expected return from Union Pacific's common stock at 7.5 percent. The yield on the company's debt in 2001 was about 5.5 percent.[12] Thus

$$\begin{aligned}\text{Company cost of capital} = r_{\text{assets}} &= \frac{D}{V}r_{\text{debt}} + \frac{E}{V}r_{\text{equity}} \\ &= \left(\frac{40}{100} \times 5.5\right) + \left(\frac{60}{100} \times 7.5\right) = 6.7\%\end{aligned}$$

Union Pacific's WACC is calculated in the same fashion, but using the after-tax cost of debt.

[11]Union Pacific had also issued preferred stock. Preferred stock is discussed in Chapter 14. To keep matters simple here, we have lumped the preferred stock in with Union Pacific's debt.

[12]This is a *promised* yield; that is, it is the yield if Union Pacific makes all the promised payments. Since there is some risk of default, the *expected* return is always less than the promised yield. Union Pacific debt has an investment-grade rating and the difference is small. But for a company that is hovering on the brink of bankruptcy, it can be important.

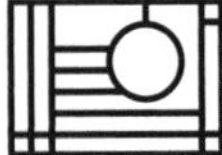

9.4 DISCOUNT RATES FOR INTERNATIONAL PROJECTS

We have shown how the CAPM can help to estimate the cost of capital for domestic investments by U.S. companies. But can we extend the procedure to allow for investments in different countries? The answer is yes in principle, but naturally there are complications.

Foreign Investments Are Not Always Riskier

Pop quiz: Which is riskier for an investor in the United States—the Standard and Poor's Composite Index or the stock market in Egypt? If you answer Egypt, you're right, but *only* if risk is defined as *total* volatility or variance. But does investment in Egypt have a high *beta?* How much does it add to the risk of a diversified portfolio held in the United States?

Table 9.2 shows estimated betas for the Egyptian market and for markets in Poland, Thailand, and Venezuela. The standard deviations of returns in these markets were two or three times more than the U.S. market, but only Thailand had a beta greater than 1. The reason is low correlation. For example, the standard deviation of the Egyptian market was 3.1 times that of the Standard and Poor's index, but the correlation coefficient was only .18. The beta was $3.1 \times .18 = .55$.

Table 9.2 does not prove that investment abroad is always safer than at home. But it should remind you always to distinguish between diversifiable and market risk. The opportunity cost of capital should depend on market risk.

Foreign Investment in the United States

Now let's turn the problem around. Suppose that the Swiss pharmaceutical company, Roche, is considering an investment in a new plant near Basel in Switzerland. The financial manager forecasts the Swiss franc cash flows from the project and discounts these cash flows at a discount rate measured in francs. Since the project is risky, the company requires a higher return than the Swiss franc interest rate. However, the project is average-risk compared to Roche's other Swiss assets. To estimate the cost of capital, the Swiss manager proceeds in the same way as her counterpart in a U.S. pharmaceutical company. In other words, she first measures the risk of the investment by estimating Roche's beta and the beta of other Swiss pharmaceutical companies. However, she calculates these betas *relative to the Swiss market index.* Suppose that both measures point to a beta of 1.1 and that the expected

TABLE 9.2

Betas of four country indexes versus the U.S. market, calculated from monthly returns, August 1996–July 2001. Despite high volatility, three of the four betas are less than 1. The reason is the relatively low correlation with the U.S. market.

	Ratio of Standard Deviations*	Correlation Coefficient	Beta†
Egypt	3.11	.18	.56
Poland	1.93	.42	.81
Thailand	2.91	.48	1.40
Venezuela	2.58	.30	.77

*Ratio of standard deviations of country index to Standard & Poor's Composite Index.

†Beta is the ratio of covariance to variance. Covariance can be written as $\sigma_{IM} = \rho_{IM}\,\sigma_I\,\sigma_M$; $\beta = \rho_{IM}\,\sigma_I\,\sigma_M/\sigma_M^2 = \rho\,(\sigma_I/\sigma_M)$, where I indicates the country index and M indicates the U.S. market.

risk premium on the Swiss market index is 6 percent.[13] Then Roche needs to discount the Swiss franc cash flows from its project at $1.1 \times 6 = 6.6$ percent above the Swiss franc interest rate.

That's straightforward. But now suppose that Roche considers construction of a plant in the United States. Once again the financial manager measures the risk of this investment by its beta relative to the Swiss market index. But notice that the value of Roche's business in the United States is likely to be much less closely tied to fluctuations in the Swiss market. So the beta of the U.S. project relative to the *Swiss* market is likely to be less than 1.1. How much less? One useful guide is the U.S. pharmaceutical industry beta calculated *relative to the Swiss market index.* It turns out that this beta has been .36.[14] If the expected risk premium on the Swiss market index is 6 percent, Roche should be discounting the Swiss franc cash flows from its U.S. project at $.36 \times 6 = 2.2$ percent above the Swiss franc interest rate.

Why does Roche's manager measure the beta of its investments relative to the Swiss index, whereas her U.S. counterpart measures the beta relative to the U.S. index? The answer lies in Section 7.4, where we explained that risk cannot be considered in isolation; it depends on the other securities in the investor's portfolio. Beta measures risk *relative to the investor's portfolio.* If U.S. investors already hold the U.S. market, an additional dollar invested at home is just more of the same. But, if Swiss investors hold the *Swiss* market, an investment in the United States can reduce their risk. That explains why an investment in the United States is likely to have lower risk for Roche's shareholders than it has for shareholders in Merck or Pfizer. It also explains why Roche's shareholders are willing to accept a lower return from such an investment than would the shareholders in the U.S. companies.[15]

When Merck measures risk relative to the U.S. market and Roche measures risk relative to the Swiss market, their managers are implicitly assuming that the shareholders simply hold domestic stocks. That's not a bad approximation, particularly in the case of the United States.[16] Although investors in the United States can reduce their risk by holding an internationally diversified portfolio of shares, they generally invest only a small proportion of their money overseas. Why they are so shy is a puzzle.[17] It looks as if they are worried about the costs of investing overseas, but we don't understand what those costs include. Maybe it is more difficult to figure out which foreign shares to buy. Or perhaps investors are worried that a

[13]Figure 7.3 showed that this is the historical risk premium on the Swiss market. The fact that the realized premium has been lower in Switzerland than the United States may be just a coincidence and may not mean that Swiss investors *expected* the lower premium. On the other hand, if Swiss firms are generally less risky, then investors may have been content with a lower premium.

[14]This is the beta of the Standard and Poor's pharmaceutical index calculated relative to the Swiss market for the period August 1996 to July 2001.

[15]When investors hold efficient portfolios, the expected reward for risk on each stock in the portfolio is proportional to its beta *relative to the portfolio.* So, if the Swiss market index is an efficient portfolio for Swiss investors, then Swiss investors will want Roche to invest in a new plant if the expected reward for risk is proportional to its beta relative to the Swiss market index.

[16]But it can be a bad assumption elsewhere. For small countries with open financial borders—Luxembourg, for example—a beta calculated relative to the local market has little value. Few investors in Luxembourg hold only local stocks.

[17]For an explanation of the cost of capital for international investments when there are costs to international diversification, see I. A. Cooper and E. Kaplanis, "Home Bias in Equity Portfolios and the Cost of Capital for Multinational Firms," *Journal of Applied Corporate Finance* 8 (Fall 1995), pp. 95–102.

foreign government will expropriate their shares, restrict dividend payments, or catch them by a change in the tax law.

However, the world is getting smaller, and investors everywhere are increasing their holdings of foreign securities. Large American financial institutions have substantially increased their overseas investments, and literally dozens of funds have been set up for individuals who want to invest abroad. For example, you can now buy funds that specialize in investment in emerging capital markets such as Vietnam, Peru, or Hungary. As investors increase their holdings of overseas stocks, it becomes less appropriate to measure risk relative to the domestic market and more important to measure the risk of any investment relative to the portfolios that they actually hold.

Who knows? Perhaps in a few years investors will hold internationally diversified portfolios, and in later editions of this book we will recommend that firms calculate betas relative to the world market. If investors throughout the world held the world portfolio, then Roche and Merck would both demand the same return from an investment in the United States, in Switzerland, or in Egypt.

Do Some Countries Have a Lower Cost of Capital?

Some countries enjoy much lower rates of interest than others. For example, as we write this the interest rate in Japan is effectively zero; in the United States it is above 3 percent. People often conclude from this that Japanese companies enjoy a lower cost of capital.

This view is one part confusion and one part probable truth. The confusion arises because the interest rate in Japan is measured in yen and the rate in the United States is measured in dollars. You wouldn't say that a 10-inch-high rabbit was taller than a 9-foot elephant. You would be comparing their height in different units. In the same way it makes no sense to compare an interest rate in yen with a rate in dollars. The units are different.

But suppose that in each case you measure the interest rate in *real* terms. Then you are comparing like with like, and it does make sense to ask whether the costs of overseas investment can cause the *real* cost of capital to be lower in Japan. Japanese citizens have for a long time been big savers, but as they moved into a new century they were very worried about the future and were saving more than ever. That money could not be absorbed by Japanese industry and therefore had to be invested overseas. Japanese investors were not *compelled* to invest overseas: They needed to be enticed to do so. So the expected real returns on Japanese investments fell to the point that Japanese investors were willing to incur the costs of buying foreign securities, and when a Japanese company wanted to finance a new project, it could tap into a pool of relatively low-cost funds.

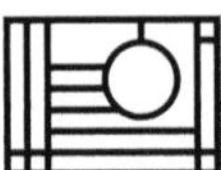

9.5 SETTING DISCOUNT RATES WHEN YOU CAN'T CALCULATE BETA

Stock or industry betas provide a rough guide to the risk encountered in various lines of business. But an asset beta for, say, the steel industry can take us only so far. Not all investments made in the steel industry are typical. What other kinds of evidence about business risk might a financial manager examine?

In some cases the asset is publicly traded. If so, we can simply estimate its beta from past price data. For example, suppose a firm wants to analyze the risks of holding a large inventory of copper. Because copper is a standardized, widely traded commodity, it is possible to calculate rates of return from holding copper and to calculate a beta for copper.

What should a manager do if the asset has no such convenient price record? What if the proposed investment is not close enough to business as usual to justify using a company cost of capital?

These cases clearly call for judgment. For managers making that kind of judgment, we offer two pieces of advice.

1. *Avoid fudge factors.* Don't give in to the temptation to add fudge factors to the discount rate to offset things that could go wrong with the proposed investment. Adjust cash-flow forecasts first.
2. *Think about the determinants of asset betas.* Often the characteristics of high- and low-beta assets can be observed when the beta itself cannot be.

Let us expand on these two points.

Avoid Fudge Factors in Discount Rates

We have defined risk, from the investor's viewpoint, as the standard deviation of portfolio return or the beta of a common stock or other security. But in everyday usage *risk* simply equals "bad outcome." People think of the risks of a project as a list of things that can go wrong. For example,

- A geologist looking for oil worries about the risk of a dry hole.
- A pharmaceutical manufacturer worries about the risk that a new drug which cures baldness may not be approved by the Food and Drug Administration.
- The owner of a hotel in a politically unstable part of the world worries about the political risk of expropriation.

Managers often add fudge factors to discount rates to offset worries such as these.

This sort of adjustment makes us nervous. First, the bad outcomes we cited appear to reflect unique (i.e., diversifiable) risks that would not affect the expected rate of return demanded by investors. Second, the need for a discount rate adjustment usually arises because managers fail to give bad outcomes their due weight in cash-flow forecasts. The managers then try to offset that mistake by adding a fudge factor to the discount rate.

Example Project Z will produce just one cash flow, forecasted at $1 million at year 1. It is regarded as average risk, suitable for discounting at a 10 percent company cost of capital:

$$PV = \frac{C_1}{1 + r} = \frac{1{,}000{,}000}{1.1} = \$909{,}100$$

But now you discover that the company's engineers are behind schedule in developing the technology required for the project. They're confident it will work, but they admit to a small chance that it won't. You still see the *most likely* outcome as $1 million, but you also see some chance that project Z will generate *zero* cash flow next year.

Now the project's prospects are clouded by your new worry about technology. It must be worth less than the $909,100 you calculated before that worry arose. But how much less? There is *some* discount rate (10 percent plus a fudge factor) that will give the right value, but we don't know what that adjusted discount rate is.

We suggest you reconsider your original $1 million forecast for project Z's cash flow. Project cash flows are supposed to be *unbiased* forecasts, which give due weight to all possible outcomes, favorable and unfavorable. Managers making unbiased forecasts are correct on average. Sometimes their forecasts will turn out high, other times low, but their errors will average out over many projects.

If you forecast cash flow of $1 million for projects like Z, you will overestimate the average cash flow, because every now and then you will hit a zero. Those zeros should be "averaged in" to your forecasts.

For many projects, the most likely cash flow is also the unbiased forecast. If there are three possible outcomes with the probabilities shown below, the unbiased forecast is $1 million. (The unbiased forecast is the sum of the probability-weighted cash flows.)

Possible Cash Flow	Probability	Probability-Weighted Cash Flow	Unbiased Forecast
1.2	.25	.3	
1.0	.50	.5	1.0, or $1 million
.8	.25	.2	

This might describe the initial prospects of project Z. But if technological uncertainty introduces a 10 percent chance of a zero cash flow, the unbiased forecast could drop to $900,000:

Possible Cash Flow	Probability	Probability-Weighted Cash Flow	Unbiased Forecast
1.2	.225	.27	
1.0	.45	.45	.90, or $900,000
.8	.225	.18	
0	.10	.0	

The present value is

$$\text{PV} = \frac{.90}{1.1} = .818, \text{ or } \$818{,}000$$

Now, of course, you can figure out the right fudge factor to add to the discount rate to apply to the original $1 million forecast to get the correct answer. But you have to think through possible cash flows to get that fudge factor; and once you have thought through the cash flows, you don't *need* the fudge factor.

Managers often work out a range of possible outcomes for major projects, sometimes with explicit probabilities attached. We give more elaborate examples and further discussion in Chapter 10. But even when a range of outcomes and probabilities is not explicitly written down, the manager can still consider the good and bad outcomes as well as the most likely one. When the bad outcomes outweigh the good, the cash-flow forecast should be reduced until balance is regained.

Step 1, then, is to do your best to make unbiased forecasts of a project's cash flows. Step 2 is to consider whether *investors* would regard the project as more or less risky than typical for a company or division. Here our advice is to search for characteristics of the asset that are associated with high or low betas. We wish we had a more fundamental scientific understanding of what these characteristics are. We see business risks surfacing in capital markets, but as yet there is no satisfactory theory describing how these risks are generated. Nevertheless, some things are known.

What Determines Asset Betas?

Cyclicality Many people intuitively associate risk with the variability of book, or accounting, earnings. But much of this variability reflects unique or diversifiable risk. Lone prospectors in search of gold look forward to extremely uncertain future earnings, but whether they strike it rich is not likely to depend on the performance of the market portfolio. Even if they do find gold, they do not bear much market risk. Therefore, an investment in gold has a high standard deviation but a relatively low beta.

What really counts is the strength of the relationship between the firm's earnings and the aggregate earnings on all real assets. We can measure this either by the *accounting beta* or by the *cash-flow beta.* These are just like a real beta except that changes in book earnings or cash flow are used in place of rates of return on securities. We would predict that firms with high accounting or cash-flow betas should also have high stock betas—and the prediction is correct.[18]

This means that cyclical firms—firms whose revenues and earnings are strongly dependent on the state of the business cycle—tend to be high-beta firms. Thus you should demand a higher rate of return from investments whose performance is strongly tied to the performance of the economy.

Operating Leverage We have already seen that financial leverage (i.e., the commitment to fixed-debt charges) increases the beta of an investor's portfolio. In just the same way, *operating leverage* (i.e., the commitment to fixed *production* charges) must add to the beta of a capital project. Let's see how this works.

The cash flows generated by any productive asset can be broken down into revenue, fixed costs, and variable costs:

$$\text{Cash flow} = \text{revenue} - \text{fixed cost} - \text{variable cost}$$

Costs are variable if they depend on the rate of output. Examples are raw materials, sales commissions, and some labor and maintenance costs. Fixed costs are cash outflows that occur regardless of whether the asset is active or idle (e.g., property taxes or the wages of workers under contract).

We can break down the asset's present value in the same way:

$$\text{PV(asset)} = \text{PV(revenue)} - \text{PV(fixed cost)} - \text{PV(variable cost)}$$

Or equivalently

$$\text{PV(revenue)} = \text{PV(fixed cost)} + \text{PV(variable cost)} + \text{PV(asset)}$$

[18]For example, see W. H. Beaver and J. Manegold, "The Association between Market-Determined and Accounting-Determined Measures of Systematic Risk: Some Further Evidence," *Journal of Financial and Quantitative Analysis* 10 (June 1979), pp. 231–284.

Those who *receive* the fixed costs are like debtholders in the project; they simply get a fixed payment. Those who receive the net cash flows from the asset are like holders of common stock; they get whatever is left after payment of the fixed costs.

We can now figure out how the asset's beta is related to the betas of the values of revenue and costs. We just use our previous formula with the betas relabeled:

$$\beta_{\text{revenue}} = \beta_{\text{fixed cost}} \frac{\text{PV(fixed cost)}}{\text{PV(revenue)}} + \beta_{\text{variable cost}} \frac{\text{PV(variable cost)}}{\text{PV(revenue)}} + \beta_{\text{asset}} \frac{\text{PV(asset)}}{\text{PV(revenue)}}$$

In other words, the beta of the value of the revenues is simply a weighted average of the beta of its component parts. Now the fixed-cost beta is zero by definition: Whoever receives the fixed costs holds a safe asset. The betas of the revenues and variable costs should be approximately the same, because they respond to the same underlying variable, the rate of output. Therefore, we can substitute $\beta_{\text{variable cost}}$ and solve for the asset beta. Remember that $\beta_{\text{fixed cost}} = 0$.

$$\begin{aligned}\beta_{\text{assets}} &= \beta_{\text{revenue}} \frac{\text{PV(revenue)} - \text{PV(variable cost)}}{\text{PV(asset)}} \\ &= \beta_{\text{revenue}} \left[1 + \frac{\text{PV(fixed cost)}}{\text{PV(asset)}}\right]\end{aligned}$$

Thus, given the cyclicality of revenues (reflected in β_{revenue}), the asset beta is proportional to the ratio of the present value of fixed costs to the present value of the project.

Now you have a rule of thumb for judging the relative risks of alternative designs or technologies for producing the same project. Other things being equal, the alternative with the higher ratio of fixed costs to project value will have the higher project beta. Empirical tests confirm that companies with high operating leverage actually do have high betas.[19]

Searching for Clues

Recent research suggests a variety of other factors that affect an asset's beta.[20] But going through a long list of these possible determinants would take us too far afield.

You cannot hope to estimate the relative risk of assets with any precision, but good managers examine any project from a variety of angles and look for clues as to its riskiness. They know that high market risk is a characteristic of cyclical ventures and of projects with high fixed costs. They think about the major uncertainties affecting the economy and consider how projects are affected by these uncertainties.[21]

---

[19] See B. Lev, "On the Association between Operating Leverage and Risk," *Journal of Financial and Quantitative Analysis* 9 (September 1974), pp. 627–642; and G. N. Mandelker and S. G. Rhee, "The Impact of the Degrees of Operating and Financial Leverage on Systematic Risk of Common Stock," *Journal of Financial and Quantitative Analysis* 19 (March 1984), pp. 45–57.

[20] This work is reviewed in G. Foster, *Financial Statement Analysis,* 2d ed., Prentice-Hall, Inc., Englewood Cliffs, N.J., 1986, chap. 10.

[21] Sharpe's article on a "multibeta" interpretation of market risk offers a useful way of thinking about these uncertainties and tracing their impact on a firm's or project's risk. See W. F. Sharpe, "The Capital Asset Pricing Model: A 'Multi-Beta' Interpretation," in H. Levy and M. Sarnat (eds.), *Financial Decision Making under Uncertainty,* Academic Press, New York, 1977.

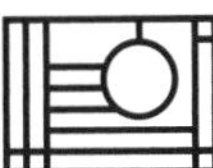

9.6 ANOTHER LOOK AT RISK AND DISCOUNTED CASH FLOW

In practical capital budgeting, a single discount rate is usually applied to all future cash flows. For example, the financial manager might use the capital asset pricing model to estimate the cost of capital and then use this figure to discount each year's expected cash flow.

Among other things, the use of a constant discount rate assumes that project risk does not change.[22] We know that this can't be strictly true, for the risks to which companies are exposed are constantly shifting. We are venturing here onto somewhat difficult ground, but there is a way to think about risk that can suggest a route through. It involves converting the expected cash flows to **certainty equivalents.** We will first explain what certainty equivalents are. Then we will use this knowledge to examine when it is reasonable to assume constant risk. Finally we will value a project whose risk *does* change.

Think back to the simple real estate investment that we used in Chapter 2 to introduce the concept of present value. You are considering construction of an office building that you plan to sell after one year for \$400,000. Since that cash flow is uncertain, you discount at a risk-adjusted discount rate of 12 percent rather than the 7 percent risk-free rate of interest. This gives a present value of 400,000/1.12 = \$357,143.

Suppose a real estate company now approaches and offers to fix the price at which it will buy the building from you at the end of the year. This guarantee would remove any uncertainty about the payoff on your investment. So you would accept a lower figure than the uncertain payoff of \$400,000. But how much less? If the building has a present value of \$357,143 and the interest rate is 7 percent, then

$$\text{PV} = \frac{\text{Certain cash flow}}{1.07} = \$357{,}143$$

$$\text{Certain cash flow} = \$382{,}143$$

In other words, a certain cash flow of \$382,143 has exactly the same present value as an expected but uncertain cash flow of \$400,000. The cash flow of \$382,143 is therefore known as the *certainty-equivalent cash flow.* To compensate for both the delayed payoff and the uncertainty in real estate prices, you need a return of 400,000 − 357,143 = \$42,857. To get rid of the risk, you would be prepared to take a cut in the return of 400,000 − 382,143 = \$17,857.

Our example illustrates two ways to value a risky cash flow C_1:

Method 1: Discount the risky cash flow at a *risk-adjusted discount rate* r that is greater than r_f.[23] The risk-adjusted discount rate adjusts for both time and risk. This is illustrated by the clockwise route in Figure 9.5.

Method 2: Find the certainty-equivalent cash flow and discount at the risk-free interest rate r_f. When you use this method, you need to ask, What is the smallest *certain* payoff for which I would exchange the risky cash flow C_1?

---

[22] See E. F. Fama, "Risk-Adjusted Discount Rates and Capital Budgeting under Uncertainty," *Journal of Financial Economics* 5 (August 1977), pp. 3–24; or S. C. Myers and S. M. Turnbull, "Capital Budgeting and the Capital Asset Pricing Model: Good News and Bad News," *Journal of Finance* 32 (May 1977), pp. 321–332.

[23] The quantity r can be less than r_f for assets with negative betas. But the betas of the assets that corporations hold are almost always positive.

FIGURE 9.5

Two ways to calculate present value. "Haircut for risk" refers to the reduction of the cash flow from its forecasted value to its certainty equivalent.

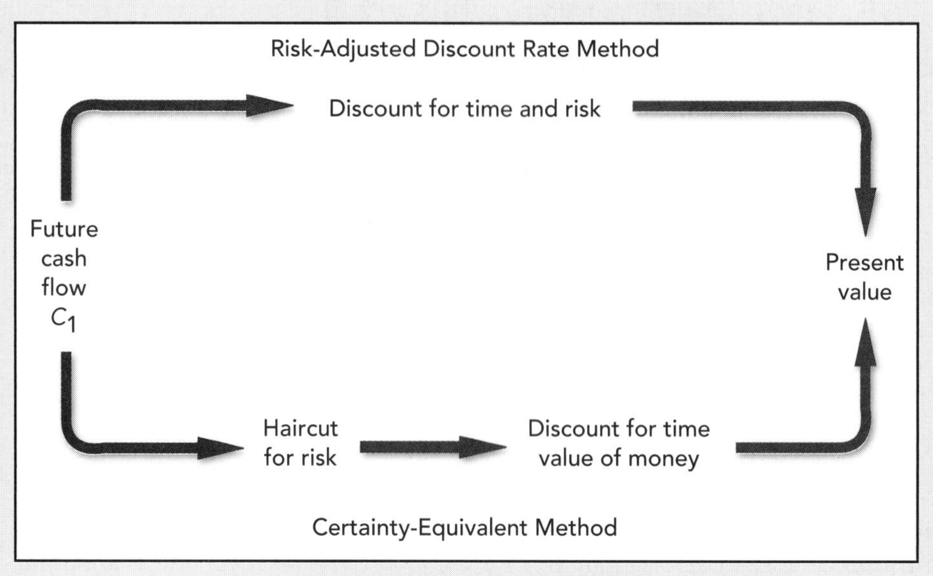

This is called the *certainty equivalent* of C_1 denoted by CEQ_1.[24] Since CEQ_1 is the value equivalent of a safe cash flow, it is discounted at the risk-free rate. The certainty-equivalent method makes *separate* adjustments for risk and time. This is illustrated by the counterclockwise route in Figure 9.5.

We now have two identical expressions for PV:

$$PV = \frac{C_1}{1+r} = \frac{CEQ_1}{1+r_f}$$

For cash flows two, three, or t years away,

$$PV = \frac{C_t}{(1+r)^t} = \frac{CEQ_t}{(1+r_f)^t}$$

When to Use a Single Risk-Adjusted Discount Rate for Long-Lived Assets

We are now in a position to examine what is implied when a constant risk-adjusted discount rate, r, is used to calculate a present value.

Consider two simple projects. Project A is expected to produce a cash flow of $100 million for each of three years. The risk-free interest rate is 6 percent, the market risk premium is 8 percent, and project A's beta is .75. You therefore calculate A's opportunity cost of capital as follows:

$$\begin{aligned} r &= r_f + \beta(r_m - r_f) \\ &= 6 + .75(8) = 12\% \end{aligned}$$

Discounting at 12 percent gives the following present value for each cash flow:

[24] CEQ_1 can be calculated directly from the capital asset pricing model. The certainty-equivalent form of the CAPM states that the certainty-equivalent value of the cash flow, C_1, is $PV = C_1 - \lambda \operatorname{cov}(\tilde{C}_1, \tilde{r}_m)$. Cov $(\tilde{C}_1, \tilde{r}_m)$ is the covariance between the uncertain cash flow, $\tilde{C}_1$, and the return on the market, r_m. Lambda, λ, is a measure of the market price of risk. It is defined as $(r_m - r_f)/\sigma_m^2$. For example, if $r_m - r_f = .08$ and the standard deviation of market returns is $\sigma_m = .20$, then lambda $= .08/.20^2 = 2$. We show on the Brealey-Myers website (**www.mhhe.com/bm7e**) how the CAPM formula can be twisted around into this certainty-equivalent form.

Project A		
Year	Cash Flow	PV at 12%
1	100	89.3
2	100	79.7
3	100	71.2
		Total PV 240.2

Now compare these figures with the cash flows of project B. Notice that B's cash flows are lower than A's; but B's flows are safe, and therefore they are discounted at the risk-free interest rate. The *present value* of each year's cash flow is identical for the two projects.

Project B		
Year	Cash Flow	PV at 6%
1	94.6	89.3
2	89.6	79.7
3	84.8	71.2
		Total PV 240.2

In year 1 project A has a risky cash flow of 100. This has the same PV as the safe cash flow of 94.6 from project B. Therefore 94.6 is the certainty equivalent of 100. Since the two cash flows have the same PV, investors must be willing to give up $100 - 94.6 = 5.4$ in expected year-1 income in order to get rid of the uncertainty.

In year 2 project A has a risky cash flow of 100, and B has a safe cash flow of 89.6. Again both flows have the same PV. Thus, to eliminate the uncertainty in year 2, investors are prepared to give up $100 - 89.6 = 10.4$ of future income. To eliminate uncertainty in year 3, they are willing to give up $100 - 84.8 = 15.2$ of future income.

To value project A, you discounted each cash flow at the same risk-adjusted discount rate of 12 percent. Now you can see what is implied when you did that. By using a constant rate, you effectively made a larger deduction for risk from the later cash flows:

Year	Forecasted Cash Flow for Project A	Certainty-Equivalent Cash Flow	Deduction for Risk
1	100	94.6	5.4
2	100	89.6	10.4
3	100	84.8	15.2

The second cash flow is riskier than the first because it is exposed to two years of market risk. The third cash flow is riskier still because it is exposed to three years of market risk. This increased risk is reflected in the steadily declining certainty equivalents:

Year	Forecasted Cash Flow for Project A (C_t)	Certainty-Equivalent Cash Flow (CEQ_t)	Ratio of CEQ_t to C_t
1	100	94.6	.946
2	100	89.6	$.896 = .946^2$
3	100	84.8	$.848 = .946^3$

Our example illustrates that if we are to use the same discount rate for every future cash flow, then the certainty equivalents must decline steadily as a fraction of the cash flow. There's no law of nature stating that certainty equivalents have to decrease in this smooth and regular way. It may be a fair assumption for most projects most of the time, but we'll sketch in a moment a real example in which that is not the case.

A Common Mistake

You sometimes hear people say that because distant cash flows are riskier, they should be discounted at a higher rate than earlier cash flows. That is quite wrong: We have just seen that using the same risk-adjusted discount rate for each year's cash flow implies a larger deduction for risk from the later cash flows. The reason is that the discount rate compensates for the risk borne *per period.* The more distant the cash flows, the greater the number of periods and the larger the *total* risk adjustment.

When You Cannot Use a Single Risk-Adjusted Discount Rate for Long-Lived Assets

Sometimes you will encounter problems where risk does change as time passes, and the use of a single risk-adjusted discount rate will then get you into trouble. For example, later in the book we will look at how options are valued. Because an option's risk is continually changing, the certainty-equivalent method needs to be used.

Here is a disguised, simplified, and somewhat exaggerated version of an actual project proposal that one of the authors was asked to analyze. The scientists at Vegetron have come up with an electric mop, and the firm is ready to go ahead with pilot production and test marketing. The preliminary phase will take one year and cost \$125,000. Management feels that there is only a 50 percent chance that pilot production and market tests will be successful. If they are, then Vegetron will build a \$1 million plant that would generate an expected annual cash flow in perpetuity of \$250,000 a year after taxes. If they are not successful, the project will have to be dropped.

The expected cash flows (in thousands of dollars) are

$$\begin{aligned} C_0 &= -125 \\ C_1 &= 50\% \text{ chance of } -1{,}000 \text{ and } 50\% \text{ chance of } 0 \\ &= .5(-1{,}000) + .5(0) = -500 \\ C_t \text{ for } t = 2, 3, \cdots &= 50\% \text{ chance of } 250 \text{ and } 50\% \text{ chance of } 0 \\ &= .5(250) + .5(0) = 125 \end{aligned}$$

Management has little experience with consumer products and considers this a project of extremely high risk.[25] Therefore management discounts the cash flows at 25 percent, rather than at Vegetron's normal 10 percent standard:

$$\text{NPV} = -125 - \frac{500}{1.25} + \sum_{t=2}^{\infty} \frac{125}{(1.25)^t} = -125, \text{ or } -\$125{,}000$$

This seems to show that the project is not worthwhile.

Management's analysis is open to criticism if the first year's experiment resolves a high proportion of the risk. If the test phase is a failure, then there's no risk at all—the project is *certain* to be worthless. If it is a success, there could well be only normal risk from then on. That means there is a 50 percent chance that in one year Vegetron will

[25] We will assume that they mean high *market* risk and that the difference between 25 and 10 percent is *not* a fudge factor introduced to offset optimistic cash-flow forecasts.

have the opportunity to invest in a project of *normal* risk, for which the *normal* discount rate of 10 percent would be appropriate. Thus the firm has a 50 percent chance to invest $1 million in a project with a net present value of $1.5 million:

$$\text{Success} \longrightarrow \text{NPV} = -1000 + \frac{250}{.10} = +1{,}500 \text{ (50\% chance)}$$

Pilot production and market tests

$$\text{Failure} \longrightarrow \text{NPV} = 0 \text{ (50\% chance)}$$

Thus we could view the project as offering an expected payoff of .5(1,500)+.5(0) = 750, or $750,000, at $t = 1$ on a $125,000 investment at $t = 0$. Of course, the certainty equivalent of the payoff is less than $750,000, but the difference would have to be very large to justify rejecting the project. For example, if the certainty equivalent is half the forecasted cash flow and the risk-free rate is 7 percent, the project is worth $225,500:

$$\text{NPV} = C_0 + \frac{\text{CEQ}_1}{1 + r}$$

$$= -125 + \frac{.5(750)}{1.07} = 225.5, \text{ or } \$225{,}500$$

This is not bad for a $125,000 investment—and quite a change from the negative-NPV that management got by discounting all future cash flows at 25 percent.

SUMMARY

In Chapter 8 we set out some basic principles for valuing risky assets. In this chapter we have shown you how to apply these principles to practical situations.

The problem is easiest when you believe that the project has the same market risk as the company's existing assets. In this case, the required return equals the required return on a portfolio of all the company's existing securities. This is called the *company cost of capital.*

Common sense tells us that the required return on any asset depends on its risk. In this chapter we have defined risk as beta and used the capital asset pricing model to calculate expected returns.

The most common way to estimate the beta of a stock is to figure out how the stock price has responded to market changes in the past. Of course, this will give you only an estimate of the stock's true beta. You may get a more reliable figure if you calculate an industry beta for a group of similar companies.

Suppose that you now have an estimate of the stock's beta. Can you plug that into the capital asset pricing model to find the company's cost of capital? No, the stock beta may reflect both business and financial risk. Whenever a company borrows money, it increases the beta (and the expected return) of its stock. Remember, the company cost of capital is the expected return on a portfolio of all the firm's securities, not just the common stock. You can calculate it by estimating the expected return on each of the securities and then taking a weighted average of these separate returns. Or you can calculate the beta of the portfolio of securities and then plug this *asset beta* into the capital asset pricing model.

The company cost of capital is the correct discount rate for projects that have the same risk as the company's existing business. Many firms, however, use the company cost of capital to discount the forecasted cash flows on all new projects. This

Visit us at www.mhhe.com/bm7e

is a dangerous procedure. In principle, each project should be evaluated at its own opportunity cost of capital; the true cost of capital depends on the use to which the capital is put. If we wish to estimate the cost of capital for a particular project, it is *project risk* that counts. Of course the company cost of capital is fine as a discount rate for average-risk projects. It is also a useful starting point for estimating discount rates for safer or riskier projects.

These basic principles apply internationally, but of course there are complications. The risk of a stock or real asset may depend on who's investing. For example, a Swiss investor would calculate a lower beta for Merck than an investor in the United States. Conversely, the U.S. investor would calculate a lower beta for a Swiss pharmaceutical company than a Swiss investor. Both investors see lower risk abroad because of the less-than-perfect correlation between the two countries' markets.

If all investors held the world market portfolio, none of this would matter. But there is a strong home-country bias. Perhaps some investors stay at home because they regard foreign investment as risky. We suspect they confuse total risk with market risk. For example, we showed examples of countries with extremely volatile stock markets. Most of these markets were nevertheless low-beta investments for an investor holding the U.S. market. Again, the reason was low correlation between markets.

Then we turned to the problem of assessing project risk. We provided several clues for managers seeking project betas. First, avoid adding fudge factors to discount rates to offset worries about bad project outcomes. Adjust cash-flow forecasts to give due weight to bad outcomes as well as good; *then* ask whether the chance of bad outcomes adds to the project's market risk. Second, you can often identify the characteristics of a high- or low-beta project even when the project beta cannot be calculated directly. For example, you can try to figure out how much the cash flows are affected by the overall performance of the economy: Cyclical investments are generally high-beta investments. You can also look at the project's operating leverage: Fixed production charges work like fixed debt charges; that is, they increase beta.

There is one more fence to jump. Most projects produce cash flows for several years. Firms generally use the same risk-adjusted rate to discount each of these cash flows. When they do this, they are implicitly assuming that cumulative risk increases at a constant rate as you look further into the future. That assumption is usually reasonable. It is precisely true when the project's future beta will be constant, that is, when risk *per period* is constant.

But exceptions sometimes prove the rule. Be on the alert for projects where risk clearly does not increase steadily. In these cases, you should break the project into segments within which the same discount rate can be reasonably used. Or you should use the certainty-equivalent version of the DCF model, which allows separate risk adjustments to each period's cash flow.

FURTHER READING

There is a good review article by Rubinstein on the application of the capital asset pricing model to capital investment decisions:

M. E. Rubinstein: "A Mean-Variance Synthesis of Corporate Financial Theory," *Journal of Finance,* 28:167–182 (March 1973).

There have been a number of studies of the relationship between accounting data and beta. Many of these are reviewed in:

G. Foster: *Financial Statement Analysis,* 2nd ed., Prentice-Hall, Inc., Englewood Cliffs, N.J., 1986.

For some ideas on how one might break down the problem of estimating beta, see:

W. F. Sharpe: "The Capital Asset Pricing Model: A 'Multi-Beta' Interpretation," in H. Levy and M. Sarnat (eds.), *Financial Decision Making under Uncertainty*, Academic Press, New York, 1977.

Fama and French present estimates of industry costs of equity capital from both the CAPM and APT models. The difficulties in obtaining precise estimates are discussed in:

E. F. Fama and K. R. French, "Industry Costs of Equity," *Journal of Financial Economics*, 43:153–193 (February 1997).

The assumptions required for use of risk-adjusted discount rates are discussed in:

E. F. Fama: "Risk-Adjusted Discount Rates and Capital Budgeting under Uncertainty," *Journal of Financial Economics*, 5:3–24 (August 1977).

S. C. Myers and S. M. Turnbull: "Capital Budgeting and the Capital Asset Pricing Model: Good News and Bad News," *Journal of Finance*, 32:321–332 (May 1977).

QUIZ

1. Suppose a firm uses its company cost of capital to evaluate all projects. Will it underestimate or overestimate the value of high-risk projects?
2. "A stock's beta can be estimated by plotting past prices against the level of the market index and drawing the line of best fit. Beta is the slope of this line." True or false? Explain.
3. Look back to the top-right panel of Figure 9.2. What proportion of Dell's return was explained by market movements? What proportion was unique or diversifiable risk? How does the unique risk show up in the plot? What is the range of possible error in the beta estimate?
4. A company is financed 40 percent by risk-free debt. The interest rate is 10 percent, the expected market return is 18 percent, and the stock's beta is .5. What is the company cost of capital?
5. The total market value of the common stock of the Okefenokee Real Estate Company is \$6 million, and the total value of its debt is \$4 million. The treasurer estimates that the beta of the stock is currently 1.5 and that the expected risk premium on the market is 9 percent. The Treasury bill rate is 8 percent. Assume for simplicity that Okefenokee debt is risk-free.
   a. What is the required return on Okefenokee stock?
   b. What is the beta of the company's existing portfolio of assets?
   c. Estimate the company cost of capital.
   d. Estimate the discount rate for an expansion of the company's present business.
   e. Suppose the company wants to diversify into the manufacture of rose-colored spectacles. The beta of unleveraged optical manufacturers is 1.2. Estimate the required return on Okefenokee's new venture.
6. Nero Violins has the following capital structure:

Security	Beta	Total Market Value, \$ millions
Debt	0	100
Preferred stock	.20	40
Common stock	1.20	200

   a. What is the firm's asset beta (i.e., the beta of a portfolio of all the firm's securities)?
   b. How would the asset beta change if Nero issued an additional \$140 million of common stock and used the cash to repurchase all the debt and preferred stock?
   c. Assume that the CAPM is correct. What discount rate should Nero set for investments that expand the scale of its operations without changing its asset beta? Assume a risk-free interest rate of 5 percent and a market risk premium of 6 percent.

7. True or false?
   a. Many foreign stock markets are much more volatile than the U.S. market.
   b. The betas of most foreign stock markets (calculated relative to the U.S. market) are usually greater than 1.0.
   c. Investors concentrate their holdings in their home countries. This means that companies domiciled in different countries may calculate different discount rates for the same project.
8. Which of these companies is likely to have the higher cost of capital?
   a. A's sales force is paid a fixed annual rate; B's is paid on a commission basis.
   b. C produces machine tools; D produces breakfast cereal.
9. Select the appropriate phrase from within each pair of brackets: "In calculating PV there are two ways to adjust for risk. One is to make a deduction from the expected cash flows. This is known as the [certainty-equivalent; risk-adjusted discount rate] method. It is usually written as PV = [$\text{CEQ}_t/(1 + r_f)^t$; $\text{CEQ}_t/(1 + r_m)^t$]. The certainty-equivalent cash flow, CEQ_t, is always [more than; less than] the forecasted risky cash flow. Another way to allow for risk is to discount the expected cash flows at a rate r. If we use the CAPM to calculate r, then r is [$r_f + \beta r_m$; $r_f + \beta(r_m - r_f)$; $r_m + \beta(r_m - r_f)$]. This method is exact only if the ratio of the certainty-equivalent cash flow to the forecasted risky cash flow [is constant; declines at a constant rate; increases at a constant rate]. For the majority of projects, the use of a single discount rate, r, is probably a perfectly acceptable approximation."
10. A project has a forecasted cash flow of $110 in year 1 and $121 in year 2. The interest rate is 5 percent, the estimated risk premium on the market is 10 percent, and the project has a beta of .5. If you use a constant risk-adjusted discount rate, what is
    a. The PV of the project?
    b. The certainty-equivalent cash flow in year 1 and year 2?
    c. The ratio of the certainty-equivalent cash flows to the expected cash flows in years 1 and 2?

PRACTICE QUESTIONS

1. "The cost of capital always depends on the risk of the project being evaluated. Therefore the company cost of capital is useless." Do you agree?

STANDARD &POOR'S

2. Look again at the companies listed in Table 8.2. Monthly rates of return for most of these companies can be found on the Standard & Poor's Market Insight website (**www.mhhe.com/edumarketinsight**)—see the "Monthly Adjusted Prices" spreadsheet. This spreadsheet also shows monthly returns for the Standard & Poor's 500 market index. What percentage of the variance of each company's return is explained by the index? Use the Excel function RSQ, which calculates R^2.

STANDARD &POOR'S

3. Pick at least five of the companies identified in Practice Question 2. The "Monthly Adjusted Prices" spreadsheets should contain about four years of monthly rates of return for the companies' stocks and for the Standard & Poor's 500 index.
   a. Split the rates of return into two consecutive two-year periods. Calculate betas for each period using the Excel SLOPE function. How stable was each company's beta?
   b. Suppose you had used these betas to estimate expected rates of return from the CAPM. Would your estimates have changed significantly from period to period?
   c. You may find it interesting to repeat your analysis using weekly returns from the "Weekly Adjusted Prices" spreadsheets. This will give more than 100 weekly rates of return for each two-year period.
4. The following table shows estimates of the risk of two well-known British stocks during the five years ending July 2001:

	Standard Deviation	R^2	Beta	Standard Error of Beta
British Petroleum (BP)	25	.25	.90	.17
British Airways	38	.25	1.37	.22

a. What proportion of each stock's risk was market risk, and what proportion was unique risk?
b. What is the variance of BP? What is the unique variance?
c. What is the confidence level on British Airways beta?
d. If the CAPM is correct, what is the expected return on British Airways? Assume a risk-free interest rate of 5 percent and an expected market return of 12 percent.
e. Suppose that next year the market provides a zero return. What return would you expect from British Airways?

5. Identify a sample of food companies on the Standard & Poor's Market Insight website (**www.mhhe.com/edumarketinsight**). For example, you could try Campbell Soup (CPB), General Mills (GIS), Kellogg (K), Kraft Foods (KFT), and Sara Lee (SLE).

STANDARD & POOR'S

a. Estimate beta and R^2 for each company from the returns given on the "Monthly Adjusted Prices" spreadsheet. The Excel functions are SLOPE and RSQ.
b. Calculate an industry beta. Here is the best procedure: First calculate the monthly returns on an equally weighted portfolio of the stocks in your sample. Then calculate the industry beta using these portfolio returns. How does the R^2 of this portfolio compare to the average R^2 for the individual stocks?
c. Use the CAPM to calculate an average cost of equity (r_{equity}) for the food industry. Use current interest rates—take a look at footnote 8 in this chapter—and a reasonable estimate of the market risk premium.

6. Look again at the companies you chose for Practice Question 5.
a. Calculate the market-value debt ratio (D/V) for each company. Note that $V = D + E$, where equity value E is the product of price per share and number of shares outstanding. E is also called "market capitalization"—see the "Monthly Valuation Data" spreadsheet. To keep things simple, look only at long-term debt as reported on the most recent quarterly or annual balance sheet for each company.
b. Calculate the beta for each company's assets (β_{assets}), using the betas estimated in Practice Question 5(a). Assume that $\beta_{debt} = .15$.
c. Calculate the company cost of capital for each company. Use the debt beta of .15 to estimate the cost of debt.
d. Calculate an *industry* cost of capital using your answer to question 5(c). *Hint:* What is the average debt ratio for your sample of food companies?
e. How would you use this food industry cost of capital in practice? Would you recommend that an individual food company, Campbell Soup, say, should use this industry rate to value its capital investment projects? Explain.

7. You are given the following information for Lorelei Motorwerke. Note: €300,000 means 300,000 euros.

Long-term debt outstanding:	€300,000
Current yield to maturity (r_{debt}):	8%
Number of shares of common stock:	10,000
Price per share:	€50
Book value per share:	€25
Expected rate of return on stock (r_{equity}):	15%

a. Calculate Lorelei's company cost of capital. Ignore taxes.
b. How would r_{equity} and the cost of capital change if Lorelei's stock price fell to €25 due to declining profits? Business risk is unchanged.

8. Look again at Table 9.1. This time we will concentrate on Burlington Northern.
a. Calculate Burlington's cost of equity from the CAPM using its own beta estimate and the industry beta estimate. How different are your answers? Assume a risk-free rate of 3.5 percent and a market risk premium of 8 percent.
b. Can you be confident that Burlington's true beta is *not* the industry average?
c. Under what circumstances might you advise Burlington to calculate its cost of equity based on its own beta estimate?

d. Burlington's cost of debt was 6 percent and its debt-to-value ratio, D/V, was .40. What was Burlington's company cost of capital? Use the industry average beta.

9. Amalgamated Products has three operating divisions:

Division	Percentage of Firm Value
Food	50
Electronics	30
Chemicals	20

To estimate the cost of capital for each division, Amalgamated has identified the following three principal competitors:

	Estimated Equity Beta	Debt/(Debt + Equity)
United Foods	.8	.3
General Electronics	1.6	.2
Associated Chemicals	1.2	.4

Assume these betas are accurate estimates and that the CAPM is correct.

a. Assuming that the debt of these firms is risk-free, estimate the asset beta for each of Amalgamated's divisions.

b. Amalgamated's ratio of debt to debt plus equity is .4. If your estimates of divisional betas are right, what is Amalgamated's equity beta?

c. Assume that the risk-free interest rate is 7 percent and that the expected return on the market index is 15 percent. Estimate the cost of capital for each of Amalgamated's divisions.

d. How much would your estimates of each division's cost of capital change if you assumed that debt has a beta of .2?

10. Look at Table 9.2. What would the four countries' betas be if the correlation coefficient for each was 0.5? Do the calculation and explain.

11. "Investors' home country bias is diminishing rapidly. Sooner or later most investors will hold the world market portfolio, or a close approximation to it." Suppose that statement is correct. What are the implications for evaluating foreign capital investment projects?

12. Consider the beta estimates for the country indexes shown in Table 9.2. Could this information be helpful to a U.S. company considering capital investment projects in these countries? Would a German company find this information useful? Explain.

13. Mom and Pop Groceries has just dispatched a year's supply of groceries to the government of the Central Antarctic Republic. Payment of $250,000 will be made one year hence after the shipment arrives by snow train. Unfortunately there is a good chance of a coup d'état, in which case the new government will not pay. Mom and Pop's controller therefore decides to discount the payment at 40 percent, rather than at the company's 12 percent cost of capital.

a. What's wrong with using a 40 percent rate to offset political risk?

b. How much is the $250,000 payment really worth if the odds of a coup d'état are 25 percent?

14. An oil company is drilling a series of new wells on the perimeter of a producing oil field. About 20 percent of the new wells will be dry holes. Even if a new well strikes oil, there is still uncertainty about the amount of oil produced: 40 percent of new wells which strike oil produce only 1,000 barrels a day; 60 percent produce 5,000 barrels per day.

a. Forecast the annual cash revenues from a new perimeter well. Use a future oil price of $15 per barrel.

b. A geologist proposes to discount the cash flows of the new wells at 30 percent to offset the risk of dry holes. The oil company's normal cost of capital is 10 percent. Does this proposal make sense? Briefly explain why or why not.

15. Look back at project A in Section 9.6. Now assume that
   a. Expected cash flow is $150 per year for five years.
   b. The risk-free rate of interest is 5 percent.
   c. The market risk premium is 6 percent.
   d. The estimated beta is 1.2.

   Recalculate the certainty-equivalent cash flows, and show that the ratio of these certainty-equivalent cash flows to the risky cash flows declines by a constant proportion each year.

16. A project has the following forecasted cash flows:

Cash Flows, $ Thousands			
C_0	C_1	C_2	C_3
−100	+40	+60	+50

   The estimated project beta is 1.5. The market return r_m is 16 percent, and the risk-free rate r_f is 7 percent.
   a. Estimate the opportunity cost of capital and the project's PV (using the same rate to discount each cash flow).
   b. What are the certainty-equivalent cash flows in each year?
   c. What is the ratio of the certainty-equivalent cash flow to the expected cash flow in each year?
   d. Explain why this ratio declines.

17. The McGregor Whisky Company is proposing to market diet scotch. The product will first be test-marketed for two years in southern California at an initial cost of $500,000. This test launch is not expected to produce any profits but should reveal consumer preferences. There is a 60 percent chance that demand will be satisfactory. In this case McGregor will spend $5 million to launch the scotch nationwide and will receive an expected annual profit of $700,000 in perpetuity. If demand is not satisfactory, diet scotch will be withdrawn.

   Once consumer preferences are known, the product will be subject to an average degree of risk, and, therefore, McGregor requires a return of 12 percent on its investment. However, the initial test-market phase is viewed as much riskier, and McGregor demands a return of 40 percent on this initial expenditure.

   What is the NPV of the diet scotch project?

CHALLENGE QUESTIONS

1. Suppose you are valuing a future stream of high-risk (high-beta) cash *out*flows. High risk means a high discount rate. But the higher the discount rate, the less the present value. This seems to say that the higher the risk of cash outflows, the less you should worry about them! Can that be right? Should the sign of the cash flow affect the appropriate discount rate? Explain.

2. U.S. pharmaceutical companies have an average beta of about .8. These companies have very little debt financing, so the asset beta is also about .8. Yet a European investor would calculate a beta of much less than .8 relative to returns on European stock markets. (How do you explain this?) Now consider some possible implications.
   a. Should German pharmaceutical companies move their R&D and production facilities to the United States?
   b. Suppose the German company uses the CAPM to calculate a cost of capital of 9 percent for investments in the United States and 12 percent at home. As a result it plans to invest large amounts of its shareholders' money in the United States. But its shareholders have already demonstrated their home country bias. Should the German company respect its shareholders' preferences and also invest mostly at home?

c. The German company can also buy shares of U.S. pharmaceutical companies. Suppose the expected rate of return in these shares is 13 percent, reflecting their beta of about 1.0 with respect to the U.S. market. Should the German company demand a 13 percent rate of return on investments in the United States?

3. An oil company executive is considering investing $10 million in one or both of two wells: Well 1 is expected to produce oil worth $3 million a year for 10 years; well 2 is expected to produce $2 million for 15 years. These are *real* (inflation-adjusted) cash flows.

The beta for *producing wells* is .9. The market risk premium is 8 percent, the nominal risk-free interest rate is 6 percent, and expected inflation is 4 percent.

The two wells are intended to develop a previously discovered oil field. Unfortunately there is still a 20 percent chance of a dry hole in each case. A dry hole means zero cash flows and a complete loss of the $10 million investment.

Ignore taxes and make further assumptions as necessary.

a. What is the correct real discount rate for cash flows from developed wells?
b. The oil company executive proposes to add 20 percentage points to the real discount rate to offset the risk of a dry hole. Calculate the NPV of each well with this adjusted discount rate.
c. What do *you* say the NPVs of the two wells are?
d. Is there any *single* fudge factor that could be added to the discount rate for developed wells that would yield the correct NPV for both wells? Explain.

4. If you have access to "Data Analysis Tools" in Excel, use the "regression" functions to investigate the reliability of the betas estimated in Practice Questions 3 and 5 and the industry cost of capital calculated in question 6.

a. What are the standard errors of the betas from questions 3(a) and 3(c)? Given the standard errors, do you regard the different beta estimates obtained for each company as signficantly different? (Perhaps the differences are just "noise.") What would you propose as the most reliable *forecast* of beta for each company?
b. How reliable are the beta estimates from question 5(a)?
c. Compare the standard error of the industry beta from question 5(b) to the standard errors for individual-company betas. Given these standard errors, would you change or amend your answer to question 6(e)?

MINI-CASE

Holiport Corporation

Holiport Corporation is a diversified company with three operating divisions:

- The construction division manages infrastructure projects such as roads and bridge construction.
- The food products division produces a range of confectionery and cookies.
- The pharmaceutical division develops and produces anti-infective drugs and animal healthcare products.

These divisions are largely autonomous. Holiport's small head-office financial staff is principally concerned with applying financial controls and allocating capital between the divisions. Table 9.3 summarizes each division's assets, revenues, and profits. Holiport has always been regarded as a conservative—some would say "stodgy"—company. Its bonds are highly rated and yield 7 percent, only 1.5 percent more than comparable government bonds.

Holiport's previous CFO, Sir Reginald Holiport-Bentley, retired last year after an autocratic 12-year reign. He insisted on a hurdle rate of 12 percent for all capital expenditures for all three divisions. This rate never changed, despite wide fluctuations in interest rates and inflation. However, the new CFO, Miss Florence Holiport-Bentley-Smythe (Sir Reginald's niece) had brought a breath of fresh air into the head office. She was determined to set dif-

	Construction	Food Products	Pharmaceuticals
Net working capital	47	373	168
Fixed assets	792	561	1083
Total net assets	839	934	1251
Revenues	1814	917	1271
Net profits	15	149	227

TABLE 9.3

Summary financial data for Holiport Corporation's three operating divisions (figures in £ millions).

	Holiport	Burchetts Green	Unifoods	Pharmichem
Cash and marketable securities	374	66	21	388
Other current assets	1596	408	377	1276
Fixed assets	2436	526	868	2077
Total assets	4406	1000	1266	3740
Short-term debt	340	66	81	21
Other current liabilities	1042	358	225	1273
Long-term debt	601	64	396	178
Equity	2423	512	564	2269
Total liabilities and equity	4406	1000	1266	3740
Number of shares, millions	1520	76	142	1299
Share price (£)	8.00	9.1	25.4	28.25
Dividend yield (%)	2.0	1.9	1.4	0.6
P/E ratio	31.1	14.5	27.6	46.6
Estimated β of stock	1.03	.80	1.15	.96

TABLE 9.4

Summary financial data for comparable companies (figures in £ millions, except as noted).

ferent costs of capital for each division. So when Henry Rodriguez returned from vacation, he was not surprised to find in his in-tray a memo from the new CFO. He was asked to determine how the company should establish divisional costs of capital and to provide estimates for the three divisions and for the company as a whole.

The new CFO's memo warned him not to confine himself to just one cookbook method, but to examine alternative estimates of the cost of capital. He also remembered a heated discussion between Florence and her uncle. Sir Reginald departed insisting that the only good forecast of the market risk premium was a long-run historical average; Florence argued strongly that alert, modern investors required much lower returns. Henry failed to see what "alert" and "modern" had to do with a market risk premium. Nevertheless, Henry decided that his report should address this question head on.

Henry started by identifying the three closest competitors to Holiport's divisions. Burchetts Green is a construction company, Unifoods produces candy, and Pharmichem is Holiport's main competitor in the animal healthcare business. Henry jotted down the summary data in Table 9.4 and poured himself a large cup of black coffee.

Questions

1. Help Henry Rogriguez by writing a memo to the CFO on Holiport's cost of capital. Your memo should (a) outline the merits of alternative methods for estimating the cost of capital, (b) explain your views on the market risk premium, and (c) provide an estimate of the cost of capital for each of Holiport's divisions.

PART TWO RELATED WEBSITES

Robert Shiller's home page includes long-term data on U.S. stock and bill returns:

www.aida.econ.yale.edu

Equity betas for individual stocks are found on Yahoo. (Or you can download the stock prices from Yahoo and calculate your own measures):

www.finance.yahoo.com

Aswath Damodoran's home page contains good long-term data on U.S. equities and average equity and asset betas for U.S. industries:

www.equity.stern.nyu.edu/~adamodar/New_Home_Page

Another useful site is Campbell Harvey's home page. It contains data on past stock returns and risk, and software to calculate mean-variance efficient frontiers:

www.duke.edu/~charvey

Data on the Fama-French factors are published on Ken French's website:

www.mba.tuck.dartmouth.edu/pages/faculty/ken.french

ValuePro provides software and data for estimating company cost of capital:

www.valuepro.net

For a collection of recent articles on the cost of capital see:

www.ibbotson.com

PART THREE

PRACTICAL PROBLEMS IN CAPITAL BUDGETING

EUROTUNNEL'S CONSTRUCTION OF a tunnel between England and France cost a record $15 billion. Before proceeding, the company developed cash flow forecasts that indicated a 14 percent return. Unfortunately, meticulous DCF calculations do not guarantee success. The tunnel proved more costly and took longer to build than anticipated. Also revenues were disappointing, and for some time the company did not even generate enough profits to pay the debt interest.

Of course, life is full of unpleasant surprises, but Part Three shows how companies can take steps to minimize the chance that a project will turn out a loser. Chapter 10 describes how companies identify factors that could put a project below water. It also shows how firms build in the flexibility to expand if things go well, and cut back if disaster threatens.

Chapter 11 looks at how managers satisfy themselves that a project truly does have a positive NPV. They do not simply check the NPV calculations. They ask fundamental economic questions about the project. Does the firm have some special advantage or headstart over other firms? How will competitors react? Will their responses erode the project's profitability? For example, Eurotunnel's management would have thought hard about the response of existing operators of channel ferries.

Finally, Chapter 12 shows how firms organize the investment process and provide managers and employees with the proper incentives to maximize firm value.

A PROJECT IS NOT A BLACK BOX

A BLACK BOX is something that we accept and use but do not understand. For most of us a computer is a black box. We may know what it is supposed to do, but we do not understand how it works and, if something breaks, we cannot fix it.

We have been treating capital projects as black boxes. In other words, we have talked as if managers are handed unbiased cash-flow forecasts and their only task is to assess risk, choose the right discount rate, and crank out net present value. Actual financial managers won't rest until they understand what makes the project tick and what could go wrong with it. Remember Murphy's law, "If anything can go wrong, it will," and O'Reilly's corollary, "at the worst possible time."

Even if the project's risk is wholly diversifiable, you still need to understand why the venture could fail. Once you know that, you can decide whether it is worth trying to resolve the uncertainty. Maybe further expenditure on market research would clear up those doubts about acceptance by consumers, maybe another drill hole would give you a better idea of the size of the ore body, and maybe some further work on the test bed would confirm the durability of those welds. If the project really has a negative NPV, the sooner you can identify it, the better. And even if you decide that it is worth going ahead on the basis of present information, you do not want to be caught by surprise if things subsequently go wrong. You want to know the danger signals and the actions you might take.

We will show you how to use *sensitivity analysis, break-even analysis,* and *Monte Carlo simulation* to identify crucial assumptions and to explore what can go wrong. There is no magic in these techniques, just computer-assisted common sense. You don't need a license to use them.

Discounted-cash-flow analysis commonly assumes that companies hold assets passively, and it ignores the opportunities to expand the project if it is successful or to bail out if it is not. However, wise managers value these opportunities. They look for ways to capitalize on success and to reduce the costs of failure, and they are prepared to pay up for projects that give them this flexibility. Opportunities to modify projects as the future unfolds are known as *real options.* We describe several important real options, and we show how to use *decision trees* to set out these options' attributes and implications.

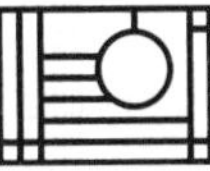

10.1 SENSITIVITY ANALYSIS

Uncertainty means that more things can happen than will happen. Whenever you are confronted with a cash-flow forecast, you should try to discover what else can happen.

Put yourself in the well-heeled shoes of the treasurer of the Otobai Company in Osaka, Japan. You are considering the introduction of an electrically powered motor scooter for city use. Your staff members have prepared the cash-flow forecasts shown in Table 10.1. Since NPV is positive at the 10 percent opportunity cost of capital, it appears to be worth going ahead.

$$\text{NPV} = -15 + \sum_{t=1}^{10} \frac{3}{(1.10)^t} = +¥3.43 \text{ billion}$$

Before you decide, you want to delve into these forecasts and identify the key variables that determine whether the project succeeds or fails. It turns out that the marketing department has estimated revenue as follows:

$$\begin{aligned}\text{Unit sales} &= \text{new product's share of market} \times \text{size of scooter market} \\ &= .1 \times 1 \text{ million} = 100{,}000 \text{ scooters}\end{aligned}$$

TABLE 10.1

Preliminary cash-flow forecasts for Otobai's electric scooter project (figures in ¥ billions).

Assumptions:
1. Investment is depreciated over 10 years straight-line.
2. Income is taxed at a rate of 50 percent.

	Year 0	Years 1–10
Investment	15	
1. Revenue		37.5
2. Variable cost		30
3. Fixed cost		3
4. Depreciation		1.5
5. Pretax profit (1 − 2 − 3 − 4)		3
6. Tax		1.5
7. Net profit (5 − 6)		1.5
8. Operating cash flow (4 + 7)		3
Net cash flow	−15	+3

$$\text{Revenue} = \text{unit sales} \times \text{price per unit}$$
$$= 100{,}000 \times 375{,}000 = ¥37.5 \text{ billion}$$

The production department has estimated variable costs per unit as ¥300,000. Since projected volume is 100,000 scooters per year, total variable cost is ¥30 billion. Fixed costs are ¥3 billion per year. The initial investment can be depreciated on a straight-line basis over the 10-year period, and profits are taxed at a rate of 50 percent.

These seem to be the important things you need to know, but look out for unidentified variables. Perhaps there are patent problems, or perhaps you will need to invest in service stations that will recharge the scooter batteries. The greatest dangers often lie in these *unknown* unknowns, or "unk-unks," as scientists call them.

Having found no unk-unks (no doubt you'll find them later), you conduct a **sensitivity analysis** with respect to market size, market share, and so on. To do this, the marketing and production staffs are asked to give optimistic and pessimistic estimates for the underlying variables. These are set out in the left-hand columns of Table 10.2. The right-hand side shows what happens to the project's net present value if the variables are set *one at a time* to their optimistic and pessimistic values. Your project appears to be by no means a sure thing. The most dangerous variables appear to be market share and unit variable cost. If market share is only .04 (and all other variables are as expected), then the project has an NPV of −¥10.4 billion. If unit variable cost is ¥360,000 (and all other variables are as expected), then the project has an NPV of −¥15 billion.

Value of Information

Now you can check whether an investment of time or money could resolve some of the uncertainty *before* your company parts with the ¥15 billion investment. Suppose that the pessimistic value for unit variable cost partly reflects the production department's worry that a particular machine will not work as designed and that the operation will have to be performed by other methods at an extra cost of ¥20,000 per unit. The chance that this will occur is only 1 in 10. But, if it does occur, the extra ¥20,000 unit cost will reduce after-tax cash flow by

$$\text{Unit sales} \times \text{additional unit cost} \times (1 - \text{tax rate})$$
$$= 100{,}000 \times 20{,}000 \times .50 = ¥1 \text{ billion}$$

Variable	Range			NPV, ¥ Billions		
	Pessimistic	Expected	Optimistic	Pessimistic	Expected	Optimistic
Market size	.9 million	1 million	1.1 million	+1.1	+3.4	+5.7
Market share	.04	.1	.16	−10.4	+3.4	+17.3
Unit price	¥350,000	¥375,000	¥380,000	−4.2	+3.4	+5.0
Unit variable cost	¥360,000	¥300,000	¥275,000	−15.0	+3.4	+11.1
Fixed cost	¥4 billion	¥3 billion	¥2 billion	+.4	+3.4	+6.5

TABLE 10.2

To undertake a sensitivity analysis of the electric scooter project, we set each variable *in turn* at its most pessimistic or optimistic value and recalculate the NPV of the project.

It would reduce the NPV of your project by

$$\sum_{t=1}^{10} \frac{1}{(1.10)^t} = ¥6.14 \text{ billion},$$

putting the NPV of the scooter project underwater at $+3.43 - 6.14 = -¥2.71$ billion.

Suppose further that a ¥10 million pretest of the machine will reveal whether it will work or not and allow you to clear up the problem. It clearly pays to invest ¥10 million to avoid a 10 percent probability of a ¥6.14 billion fall in NPV. You are ahead by $-10 + .10 \times 6{,}140 = +¥604$ million.

On the other hand, the value of additional information about market size is small. Because the project is acceptable even under pessimistic assumptions about market size, you are unlikely to be in trouble if you have misestimated that variable.

Limits to Sensitivity Analysis

Sensitivity analysis boils down to expressing cash flows in terms of key project variables and then calculating the consequences of misestimating the variables. It forces the manager to identify the underlying variables, indicates where additional information would be most useful, and helps to expose confused or inappropriate forecasts.

One drawback to sensitivity analysis is that it always gives somewhat ambiguous results. For example, what exactly does *optimistic* or *pessimistic* mean? The marketing department may be interpreting the terms in a different way from the production department. Ten years from now, after hundreds of projects, hindsight may show that the marketing department's pessimistic limit was exceeded twice as often as the production department's; but what you may discover 10 years hence is no help now. One solution is to ask the two departments for a *complete* description of the various odds. However, it is far from easy to extract a forecaster's subjective notion of the complete probability distribution of possible outcomes.[1]

Another problem with sensitivity analysis is that the underlying variables are likely to be interrelated. What sense does it make to look at the effect in isolation of an increase in market size? If market size exceeds expectations, it is likely that

[1]If you doubt this, try some simple experiments. Ask the person who repairs your television to state a numerical probability that your set will work for at least one more year. Or construct your own subjective probability distribution of the number of telephone calls you will receive next week. That ought to be easy. Try it.

	Cash Flows, Years 1–10, ¥ Billions	
	Base Case	High Oil Prices and Recession Case
1. Revenue	37.5	44.9
2. Variable cost	30.0	35.9
3. Fixed cost	3.0	3.5
4. Depreciation	1.5	1.5
5. Pretax profit (1 − 2 − 3 − 4)	3.0	4.0
6. Tax	1.5	2.0
7. Net profit (5 − 6)	1.5	2.0
8. Net cash flow (4 + 7)	3.0	3.5
PV of cash flows	+18.4	+21.5
NPV	+3.4	+6.5
	Assumptions	
	Base Case	High Oil Prices and Recession Case
Market size	1 million	.8 million
Market share	.1	.13
Unit price	¥375,000	¥431,300
Unit variable cost	¥300,000	¥345,000
Fixed cost	¥3 billion	¥3.5 billion

TABLE 10.3

How the NPV of the electric scooter project would be affected by higher oil prices and a world recession.

demand will be stronger than you anticipated and unit prices will be higher. And why look in isolation at the effect of an increase in price? If inflation pushes prices to the upper end of your range, it is quite probable that costs will also be inflated.

Sometimes the analyst can get around these problems by defining underlying variables so that they are roughly independent. But you cannot push *one-at-a-time* sensitivity analysis too far. It is impossible to obtain expected, optimistic, and pessimistic values for total *project* cash flows from the information in Table 10.2.

Scenario Analysis

If the variables are interrelated, it may help to consider some alternative plausible scenarios. For example, perhaps the company economist is worried about the possibility of another sharp rise in world oil prices. The direct effect of this would be to encourage the use of electrically powered transportation. The popularity of compact cars after the oil price increases in the 1970s leads you to estimate that an immediate 20 percent price rise in oil would enable you to capture an extra 3 percent of the scooter market. On the other hand, the economist also believes that higher oil prices would prompt a world recession and at the same time stimulate inflation. In that case, market size might be in the region of .8 million scooters and both prices and cost might be 15 percent higher than your initial estimates. Table 10.3 shows that this scenario of higher oil prices and recession would on balance help your new venture. Its NPV would increase to ¥6.5 billion.

Managers often find **scenario analysis** helpful. It allows them to look at different but *consistent* combinations of variables. Forecasters generally prefer to give an

	Inflows	Outflows						
		Year 0	Years 1–10					
Unit Sales, Thousands	Revenue, Years 1–10	Investment	Variable Costs	Fixed Costs	Taxes	PV Inflows	PV Outflows	NPV
0	0	15	0	3	−2.25	0	19.6	−19.6
100	37.5	15	30	3	1.5	230.4	227.0	3.4
200	75.0	15	60	3	5.25	460.8	434.4	26.4

TABLE 10.4

NPV of electric scooter project under different assumptions about unit sales (figures in ¥ billions except as noted).

estimate of revenues or costs under a particular scenario than to give some absolute optimistic or pessimistic value.

Break-Even Analysis

When we undertake a sensitivity analysis of a project or when we look at alternative scenarios, we are asking how serious it would be if sales or costs turned out to be worse than we forecasted. Managers sometimes prefer to rephrase this question and ask how bad sales can get before the project begins to lose money. This exercise is known as **break-even analysis.**

In the left-hand portion of Table 10.4 we set out the revenues and costs of the electric scooter project under different assumptions about annual sales.[2] In the right-hand portion of the table we discount these revenues and costs to give the *present value* of the inflows and the *present value* of the outflows. Net present value is of course the difference between these numbers.

You can see that NPV is strongly negative if the company does not produce a single scooter. It is just positive if (as expected) the company sells 100,000 scooters and is strongly positive if it sells 200,000. Clearly the *zero*-NPV point occurs at a little under 100,000 scooters.

In Figure 10.1 we have plotted the present value of the inflows and outflows under different assumptions about annual sales. The two lines cross when sales are 85,000 scooters. This is the point at which the project has zero NPV. As long as sales are greater than 85,000, the project has a positive NPV.[3]

Managers frequently calculate break-even points in terms of accounting profits rather than present values. Table 10.5 shows Otobai's after-tax profits at three levels of scooter sales. Figure 10.2 once again plots revenues and costs against sales. But the story this time is different. Figure 10.2, which is based on accounting profits, suggests a break-even of 60,000 scooters. Figure 10.1, which is based on present values, shows a break-even at 85,000 scooters. Why the difference?

When we work in terms of accounting profit, we deduct depreciation of ¥1.5 billion each year to cover the cost of the initial investment. If Otobai sells 60,000 scooters a year, revenues will be sufficient both to pay operating costs and to recover the

[2]Notice that if the project makes a loss, this loss can be used to reduce the tax bill on the rest of the company's business. In this case the project produces a tax saving—the tax outflow is negative.

[3]We could also calculate break-even sales by plotting equivalent annual costs and revenues. Of course, the break-even point would be identical at 85,000 scooters.

FIGURE 10.1

A break-even chart showing the present values of Otobai's cash inflows and outflows under different assumptions about unit sales. NPV is zero when sales are 85,000.

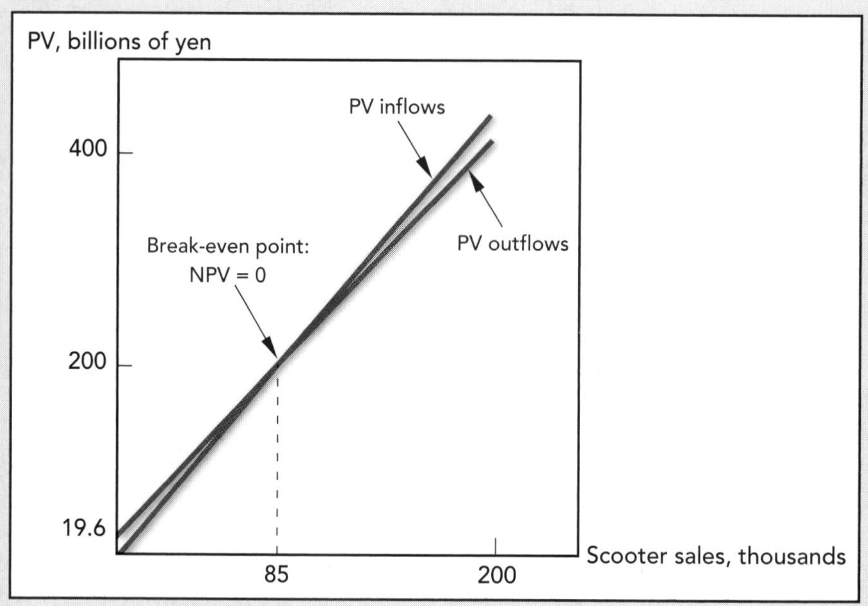

Unit Sales, Thousands	Revenue	Variable Costs	Fixed Costs	Depreciation	Taxes	Total Costs	Profit after Tax
0	0	0	3	1.5	−2.25	2.25	−2.25
100	37.5	30	3	1.5	1.5	36.0	1.5
200	75.0	60	3	1.5	5.25	69.75	5.25

TABLE 10.5

The electric scooter project's accounting profit under different assumptions about unit sales (figures in ¥ billions except as noted).

initial outlay of ¥15 billion. But they will *not* be sufficient to repay the *opportunity cost of capital* on that ¥15 billion. If we allow for the fact that the ¥15 billion could have been invested elsewhere to earn 10 percent, the equivalent annual cost of the investment is not ¥1.5 billion but ¥2.44 billion.[4]

[4]To calculate the equivalent annual cost of the initial ¥15 billion investment, we divide by the 10-year annuity factor for a 10 percent discount rate:

$$\text{Equivalent annual cost} = \frac{\text{investment}}{\text{10-year annuity factor}}$$
$$= \frac{15}{6.145} = \text{¥2.44 billion}$$

See Section 6.3.

The annual revenues at 85,000 scooters per year are about ¥31.9 billion. You can check that this is sufficient to cover variable costs, fixed costs, and taxes and still leave ¥2.44 billion per year to recover the ¥15 billion initial investment and a 10 percent return on that investment.

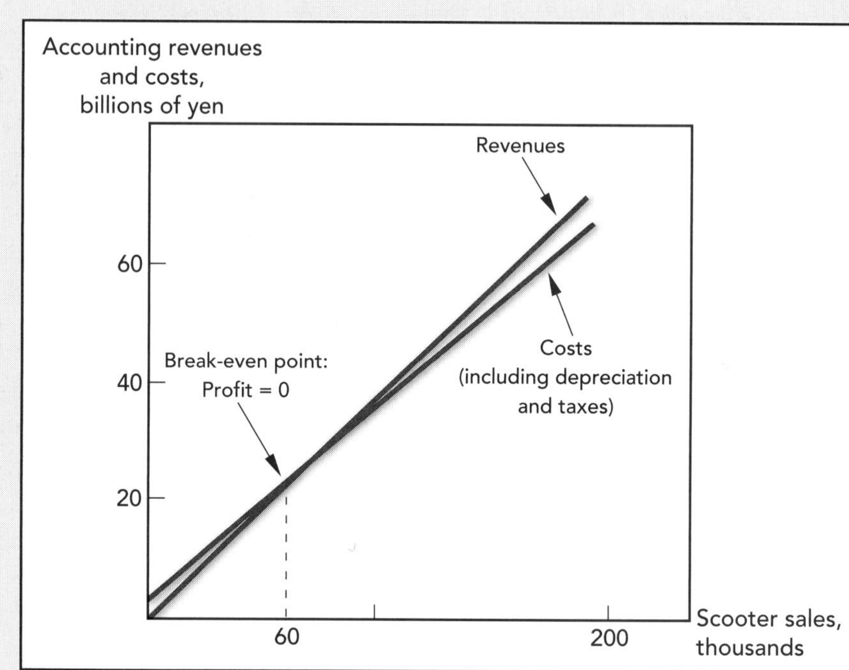

FIGURE 10.2

Sometimes break-even charts are constructed in terms of accounting numbers. After-tax profit is zero when sales are 60,000.

Companies that break even on an accounting basis are really making a loss—they are losing the opportunity cost of capital on their investment. Reinhardt has described a dramatic example of this mistake.[5] In 1971 Lockheed managers found themselves having to give evidence to Congress on the viability of the company's L-1011 TriStar program. They argued that the program appeared to be commercially attractive and that TriStar sales would eventually exceed the break-even point of about 200 aircraft. But in calculating this break-even point, Lockheed appears to have ignored the opportunity cost of the huge $1 billion capital investment on this project. Had it allowed for this cost, the break-even point would probably have been nearer to 500 aircraft.

Operating Leverage and Break-Even Points

Break-even charts like Figure 10.1 help managers appreciate *operating leverage,* that is, project exposure to fixed costs. Remember from Section 9.5 that high operating leverage means high risk, other things equal, of course.

The electric scooter project had low fixed costs, only ¥3 billion against projected revenues of ¥37.5 billion. But suppose Otobai now considers a different production technology with lower variable costs of only ¥120,000 per unit (versus ¥300,000 per unit) but higher fixed costs of ¥19 billion. Total forecasted production costs are lower (12 + 19 = ¥31 billion versus ¥33 billion), so profitability improves—compare Table 10.6 to Table 10.1. Project NPV increases to ¥9.6 billion.

Figure 10.3 is the new break-even chart. Break-even sales have *increased* to 88,000 (that's bad), even though total production costs have *fallen.* A new sensitivity analysis would show that project NPV is much more exposed to changes in market size,

[5]U. E. Reinhardt, "Break-Even Analysis for Lockheed's TriStar: An Application of Financial Theory," *Journal of Finance* 28 (September 1973), pp. 821–838.

TABLE 10.6

Cash-flow forecasts and PV for the electric scooter project, here assuming a production technology with high fixed costs but low total costs (figures in ¥ billions). Compare Table 10.1.

	Year 0	Years 1–10
Investment	15	
1. Revenue		37.5
2. Variable cost		12.0
3. Fixed cost		19.0
4. Depreciation		1.5
5. Pretax profit (1 − 2 − 3 − 4)		5.0
6. Tax		2.5
7. Net profit (5 − 6)		2.5
8. Operating cash flow (4 + 7)		4.0
Net cash flow	−15	+4.0

$$\text{NPV} = -15 + \sum_{t=1}^{10} \frac{4.0}{(1.1)^t} = +¥9.6 \text{ billion}$$

FIGURE 10.3

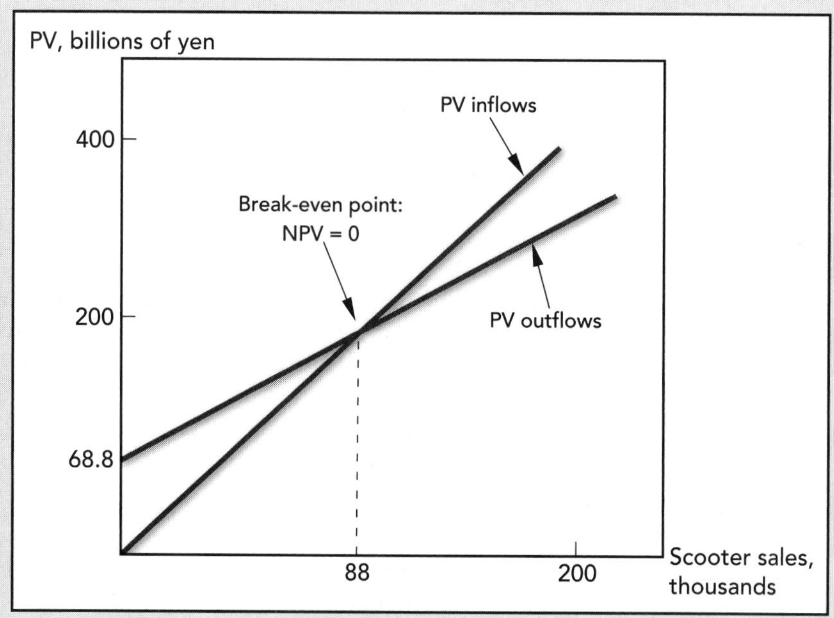

Break-even chart for an alternative production technology with higher fixed costs. Notice that break-even sales increase to 88,000. Compare Figure 10.1.

market share, or unit price. All of these differences can be traced to the higher fixed costs of the alternative production technology.

Is the alternative technology better than the original one? The financial manager would have to consider the alternative technology's higher business risk, and perhaps recompute NPV at a higher discount rate, before making a final decision.[6]

[6]He or she could use the procedures outlined in Section 9.5 to recalculate beta and come up with a new discount rate.

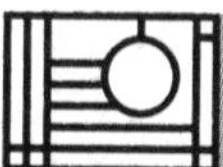

10.2 MONTE CARLO SIMULATION

Sensitivity analysis allows you to consider the effect of changing one variable at a time. By looking at the project under alternative scenarios, you can consider the effect of a *limited number* of plausible combinations of variables. **Monte Carlo simulation** is a tool for considering *all* possible combinations. It therefore enables you to inspect the entire distribution of project outcomes. The use of simulation in capital budgeting was first advocated by David Hertz[7] and McKinsey and Company, the management consultants.

Imagine that you are a gambler at Monte Carlo. You know nothing about the laws of probability (few casual gamblers do), but a friend has suggested to you a complicated strategy for playing roulette. Your friend has not actually tested the strategy but is confident that it will *on the average* give you a 2½ percent return for every 50 spins of the wheel. Your friend's optimistic estimate for any series of 50 spins is a profit of 55 percent; your friend's pessimistic estimate is a loss of 50 percent. How can you find out whether these really are the odds? An easy but possibly expensive way is to start playing and record the outcome at the end of each series of 50 spins. After, say, 100 series of 50 spins each, plot a frequency distribution of the outcomes and calculate the average and upper and lower limits. If things look good, you can then get down to some serious gambling.

An alternative is to tell a computer to simulate the roulette wheel and the strategy. In other words, you could instruct the computer to draw numbers out of its hat to determine the outcome of each spin of the wheel and then to calculate how much you would make or lose from the particular gambling strategy.

That would be an example of Monte Carlo simulation. In capital budgeting we replace the gambling strategy with a model of the project, and the roulette wheel with a model of the world in which the project operates. Let's see how this might work with our project for an electrically powered scooter.

Simulating the Electric Scooter Project

Step 1: Modeling the Project The first step in any simulation is to give the computer a precise model of the project. For example, the sensitivity analysis of the scooter project was based on the following implicit model of cash flow:

$$\text{Cash flow} = (\text{revenues} - \text{costs} - \text{depreciation}) \times (1 - \text{tax rate}) + \text{depreciation}$$
$$\text{Revenues} = \text{market size} \times \text{market share} \times \text{unit price}$$
$$\text{Costs} = (\text{market size} \times \text{market share} \times \text{variable unit cost}) + \text{fixed cost}$$

This model of the project was all that you needed for the simpleminded sensitivity analysis that we described above. But if you wish to simulate the whole project, you need to think about how the variables are interrelated.

For example, consider the first variable—market size. The marketing department has estimated a market size of 1 million scooters in the first year of the project's life, but of course you do not know how things will work out. Actual market

[7]See D. B. Hertz, "Investment Policies that Pay Off," *Harvard Business Review* 46 (January–February 1968), pp. 96–108.

size will exceed or fall short of expectations by the amount of the department's forecast error:

$$\text{Market size, year 1} = \text{expected market size, year 1} \times \left(1 + \begin{matrix}\text{forecast error,} \\ \text{year 1}\end{matrix}\right)$$

You *expect* the forecast error to be zero, but it could turn out to be positive or negative. Suppose, for example, that the actual market size turns out to be 1.1 million. That means a forecast error of 10 percent, or +.1:

$$\text{Market size, year 1} = 1 \times (1 + .1) = 1.1 \text{ million}$$

You can write the market size in the second year in exactly the same way:

$$\text{Market size, year 2} = \text{expected market size, year 2} \times \left(1 + \begin{matrix}\text{forecast error,} \\ \text{year 2}\end{matrix}\right)$$

But at this point you must consider how the expected market size in year 2 is affected by what happens in year 1. If scooter sales are below expectations in year 1, it is likely that they will continue to be below in subsequent years. Suppose that a shortfall in sales in year 1 would lead you to revise down your forecast of sales in year 2 by a like amount. Then

$$\text{Expected market size, year 2} = \text{actual market size, year 1}$$

Now you can rewrite the market size in year 2 in terms of the actual market size in the previous year plus a forecast error:

$$\text{Market size, year 2} = \text{market size, year 1} \times \left(1 + \begin{matrix}\text{forecast error,} \\ \text{year 2}\end{matrix}\right)$$

In the same way you can describe the expected market size in year 3 in terms of market size in year 2 and so on.

This set of equations illustrates how you can describe interdependence between different *periods*. But you also need to allow for interdependence between different *variables*. For example, the price of electrically powered scooters is likely to increase with market size. Suppose that this is the only uncertainty and that a 10 percent shortfall in market size would lead you to predict a 3 percent reduction in price. Then you could model the first year's price as follows:

$$\text{Price, year 1} = \text{expected price, year 1} \times \left(1 + \begin{matrix}.3 \times \text{error in} \\ \text{market size} \\ \text{forecast,} \\ \text{year 1}\end{matrix}\right)$$

Then, if variations in market size exert a permanent effect on price, you can define the second year's price as

$$\begin{aligned}\text{Price, year 2} &= \text{expected price, year 2} \times \left(1 + \begin{matrix}.3 \times \text{error in} \\ \text{market size} \\ \text{forecast,} \\ \text{year 2}\end{matrix}\right) \\ &= \text{actual price, year 1} \times \left(1 + \begin{matrix}.3 \times \text{error in} \\ \text{market size} \\ \text{forecast,} \\ \text{year 2}\end{matrix}\right)\end{aligned}$$

Notice how we have linked each period's selling price to the *actual* selling prices (including forecast error) in all previous periods. We used the same type of linkage for market size. These linkages mean that forecast errors accumulate; they do not cancel out over time. Thus, uncertainty *increases* with time: The farther out you look into the future, the more the actual price or market size may depart from your original forecast.

The complete model of your project would include a set of equations for each of the variables: market size, price, market share, unit variable cost, and fixed cost. Even if you allowed for only a few interdependencies between variables and across time, the result would be quite a complex list of equations.[8] Perhaps that is not a bad thing if it forces you to understand what the project is all about. Model building is like spinach: You may not like the taste, but it is good for you.

Step 2: Specifying Probabilities Remember the procedure for simulating the gambling strategy? The first step was to specify the strategy, the second was to specify the numbers on the roulette wheel, and the third was to tell the computer to select these numbers at random and calculate the results of the strategy:

The steps are just the same for your scooter project:

Think about how you might go about specifying your possible errors in forecasting market size. You *expect* market size to be 1 million scooters. You obviously don't think that you are underestimating or overestimating, so the expected forecast error is zero. On the other hand, the marketing department has given you a range of possible estimates. Market size could be as low as .85 million scooters or as high as 1.15 million scooters. Thus the forecast error has an expected value of 0 and a range of plus or minus 15 percent. If the marketing department has in fact given you the lowest and highest possible outcomes, actual market size should fall somewhere within this range with near certainty.[9]

That takes care of market size; now you need to draw up similar estimates of the possible forecast errors for each of the other variables that are in your model.

[8]Specifying the interdependencies is the hardest and most important part of a simulation. If all components of project cash flows were unrelated, simulation would rarely be necessary.

[9]Suppose "near certainty" means "99 percent of the time." If forecast errors are normally distributed, this degree of certainty requires a range of plus or minus three standard deviations.

Other distributions could, of course, be used. For example, the marketing department may view any market size between .85 and 1.15 million scooters as *equally likely*. In that case the simulation would require a uniform (rectangular) distribution of forecast errors.

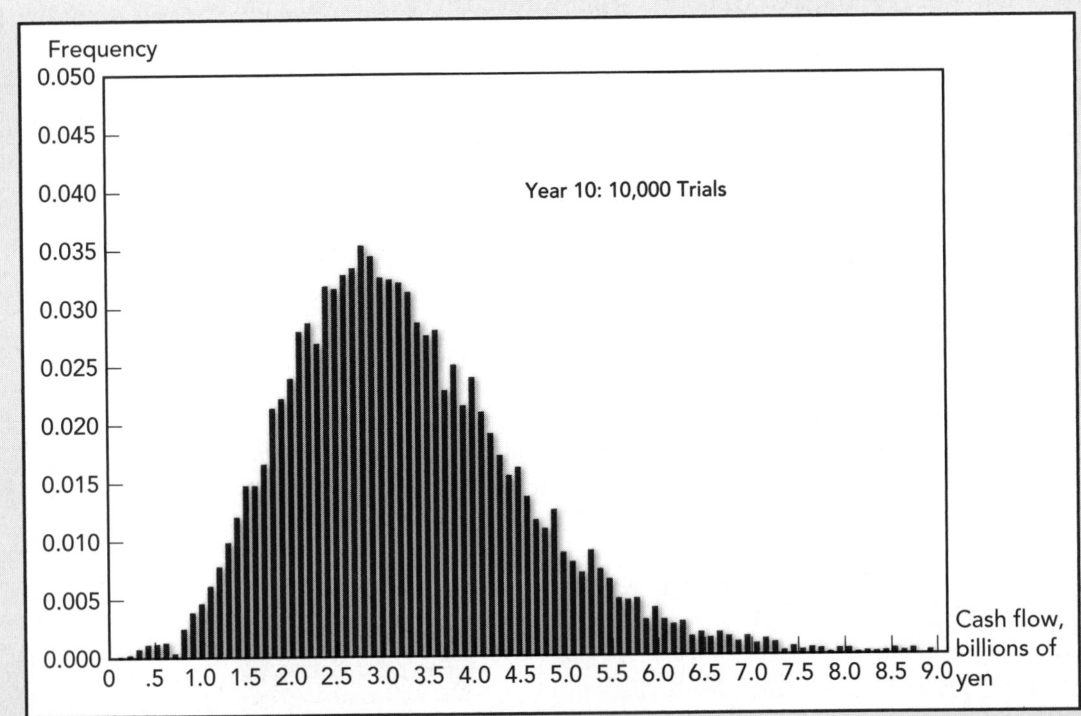

FIGURE 10.4

Simulation of cash flows for year 10 of the electric scooter project.

Step 3: Simulate the Cash Flows The computer now *samples* from the distribution of the forecast errors, calculates the resulting cash flows for each period, and records them. After many iterations you begin to get accurate estimates of the probability distributions of the project cash flows—accurate, that is, only to the extent that your model and the probability distributions of the forecast errors are accurate. Remember the GIGO principle: "Garbage in, garbage out."

Figure 10.4 shows part of the output from an actual simulation of the electric scooter project.[10] Note the positive skewness of the outcomes—very large outcomes are more likely than very small ones. This is common and realistic when forecast errors accumulate over time. Because of the skewness the average cash flow is somewhat higher than the most likely outcome; in other words, a bit to the right of the peak of the distribution.[11]

Step 4: Calculate Present Value The distributions of project cash flows should allow you to calculate the expected cash flows more accurately. In the final step you need to discount these expected cash flows to find present value.

[10]These are actual outputs from Crystal Ball™ software used with an EXCEL spreadsheet program. The simulation assumed annual forecast errors were normally distributed and ran through 10,000 trials. We thank Christopher Howe for running the simulation.

[11]When you are working with cash-flow forecasts, bear in mind the distinction between the expected value and the most likely (or modal) value. Present values are based on *expected* cash flows—that is, the probability-weighted average of the possible future cash flows. If the distribution of possible outcomes is skewed to the right as in Figure 10.4, the expected cash flow will be greater than the most likely cash flow.

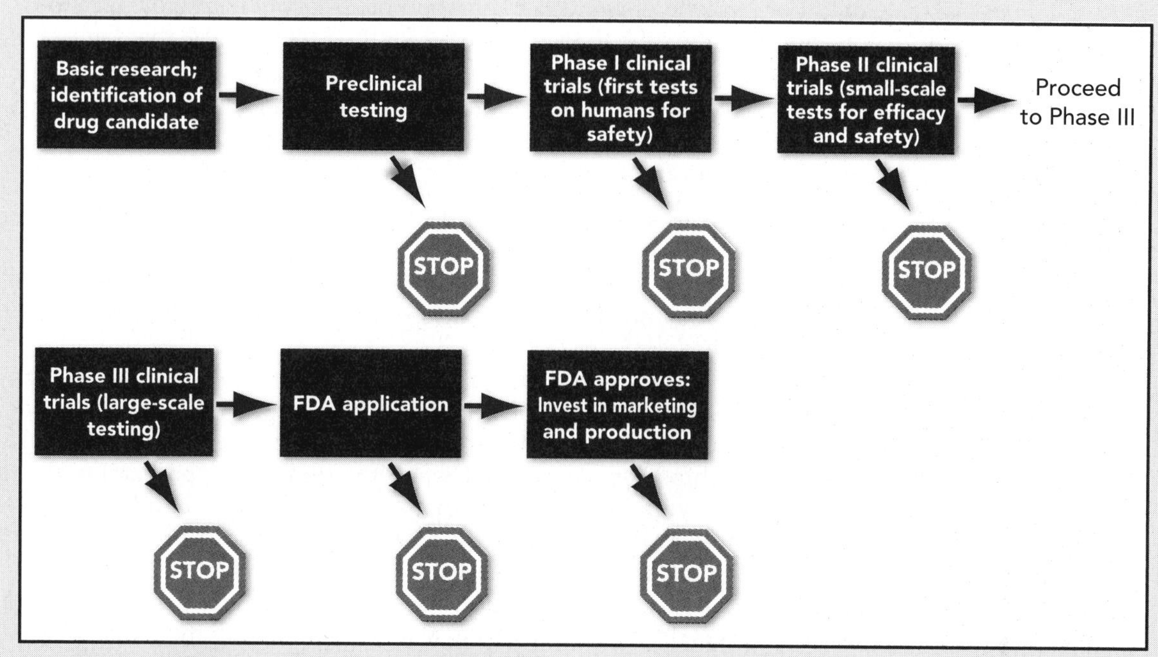

FIGURE 10.5

Research and testing of a potential new drug from discovery to initial sales. This figure concentrates on the odds that the drug will pass all required clinical tests and be approved by the Food and Drug Administration (FDA). Only a small fraction of drug candidates identified in basic research prove safe and effective and achieve profitable production. The "Stop" signs indicate failure and abandonment.

Simulation of Pharmaceutical Research and Development

Simulation, though sometimes costly and complicated, has the obvious merit of compelling the forecaster to face up to uncertainty and to interdependencies. By constructing a detailed Monte Carlo simulation, you will gain a better understanding of how the project works and what could go wrong with it. You will have confirmed, or improved, your forecasts of future cash flows, and your calculations of project NPV will be more confident.

Several large pharmaceutical companies have used Monte Carlo simulation to analyze investments in research and development (R&D) of new drugs. Figure 10.5 sketches the progression of a new drug from its infancy, when it is identified as a promising chemical compound, all the way through the R&D required for approval for sale by the Food and Drug Administration (FDA). At each phase of R&D, the company must decide whether to press on to the next phase or halt. The R&D effort lasts 10 to 12 years from preclinical testing to FDA approval and can cost $300 million or more.[12]

The pharmaceutical companies face two kinds of uncertainty:

1. *Will the compound work?* Will it have harmful side effects? Will it ultimately gain FDA approval? (Most drugs do not: Of 10,000 promising compounds,

[12]Myers and Howe estimated the average cost of bringing one new drug to market as about $300 million after tax. The estimate was based on R&D costs and success rates from the 1970s and 1980s, but adjusted for inflation through 1994. See S. C. Myers and C. Howe, "A Life-Cycle Model of Pharmaceutical R&D," MIT Program on the Pharmaceutical Industry, April 1997.

only 1 or 2 may ever get to market. The 1 or 2 that are marketed have to generate enough cash flow to make up for the 9,999 or 9,998 that fail.)

2. *Market success.* FDA approval does not guarantee that a drug will sell. A competitor may be there first with a similar (or better) drug. The company may or may not be able to sell the drug worldwide. Selling prices and marketing costs are unknown.

Imagine that you are standing at the top left of Figure 10.5. A proposed research program will investigate a promising class of compounds. Could you write down the expected cash inflows and outflows of the program up to 25 or 30 years in the future? We suggest that no mortal could do so without a model to help; simulation may provide the answer.[13]

Simulation may sound like a panacea for the world's ills, but, as usual, you pay for what you get. Sometimes you pay for more than you get. It is not just a matter of the time and money spent in building the model. It is extremely difficult to estimate interrelationships between variables and the underlying probability distributions, even when you are trying to be honest.[14] But in capital budgeting, forecasters are seldom completely impartial and the probability distributions on which simulations are based can be highly biased.

In practice, a simulation that attempts to be realistic will also be complex. Therefore the decision maker may delegate the task of constructing the model to management scientists or consultants. The danger here is that, even if the builders understand their creation, the decision maker cannot and therefore does not rely on it. This is a common but ironic experience: The model that was intended to open up black boxes ends up creating another one.

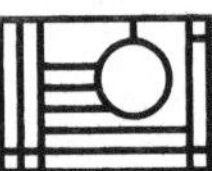

10.3 REAL OPTIONS AND DECISION TREES

If financial managers treat projects as black boxes, they may be tempted to think only of the first accept–reject decision and to ignore the subsequent investment decisions that may be tied to it. But if subsequent investment decisions depend on those made today, then today's decision may depend on what you plan to do tomorrow.

When you use discounted cash flow (DCF) to value a project, you implicitly assume that the firm will hold the assets passively. But managers are not paid to be dummies. After they have invested in a new project, they do not simply sit back and watch the future unfold. If things go well, the project may be expanded; if they go badly, the project may be cut back or abandoned altogether. Projects that can easily be modified in these ways are more valuable than those that don't provide such flexibility. The more uncertain the outlook, the more valuable this flexibility becomes.

That sounds obvious, but notice that sensitivity analysis and Monte Carlo simulation do not recognize the opportunity to modify projects.[15] For example,

[13] N. A. Nichols, "Scientific Management at Merck: An Interview with CFO Judy Lewent," *Harvard Business Review* 72 (January–February 1994), p. 91.

[14] These difficulties are less severe for the pharmaceutical industry than for most other industries. Pharmaceutical companies have accumulated a great deal of information on the probabilities of scientific and clinical success and on the time and money required for clinical testing and FDA approval.

[15] Some simulation models *do* recognize the possibility of changing policy. For example, when a pharmaceutical company uses simulation to analyze its R&D decisions, it allows for the possibility that the company can abandon the development at each phase.

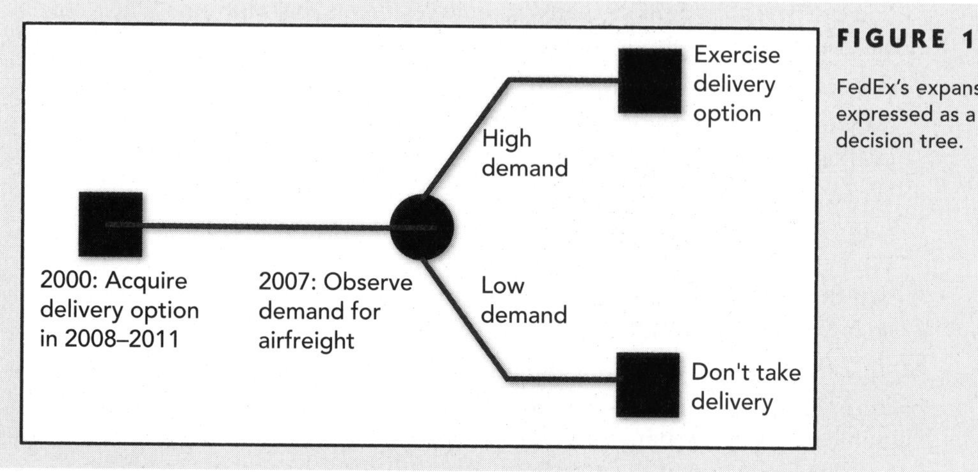

FIGURE 10.6

FedEx's expansion option expressed as a simple decision tree.

think back to the Otobai electric scooter project. In real life, if things go wrong with the project, Otobai would abandon to cut its losses. If so, the worst outcomes would not be as devastating as our sensitivity analysis and simulation suggested.

Options to modify projects are known as **real options.** Managers may not always use the term real option to describe these opportunities; for example, they may refer to "intangible advantages" of easy-to-modify projects. But when they review major investment proposals, these option intangibles are often the key to their decisions.

The Option to Expand

In 2000 FedEx placed an order for 10 Airbus A380 superjumbo transport planes for delivery in the years 2008–2011. Each flight of an A380 freighter will be capable of making a 200,000 pound dent in the massive volume of goods that FedEx carries each day, so the decision could have a huge impact on FedEx's worldwide business. If FedEx's long-haul airfreight business continues to expand and the superjumbo is efficient and reliable, the company will need more superjumbos. But it cannot be sure they will be needed.

Rather than placing further firm orders in 2000, FedEx has secured a place in the Airbus production line by acquiring *options* to buy a "substantial number" of additional aircraft at a predetermined price. These options do not commit the company to expand but give it the flexibility to do so.

Figure 10.6 displays FedEx's expansion option as a simple **decision tree.** You can think of it as a game between FedEx and fate. Each square represents an action or decision by the company. Each circle represents an outcome revealed by fate. In this case there is only one outcome in 2007,[16] when fate reveals the airfreight demand and FedEx's capacity needs. FedEx then decides whether to exercise its options and buy additional A380s. Here the future decision is easy: Buy the airplanes only if demand is high and the company can operate them profitably. If demand is low, FedEx walks away and leaves Airbus with the problem of selling the planes that were reserved for FedEx to some other customer.

[16]We assume that FedEx can wait until 2007 to decide whether to acquire the additional planes.

You can probably think of many other investments that take on added value because of the further options they provide. For example

- When launching a new product, companies often start with a pilot program to iron out possible design problems and to test the market. The company can evaluate the pilot and then decide whether to expand to full-scale production.
- When designing a factory, it can make sense to provide extra land or floor space to reduce the future cost of a second production line.
- When building a four-lane highway, it may pay to build six-lane bridges so that the road can be converted later to six lanes if traffic volumes turn out to be higher than expected.

Such options to expand do not show up in the assets that the company lists in its balance sheet, but investors are very aware of their existence. If a company has valuable real options that can allow it to invest in new profitable projects, its market value will be higher than the value of its physical assets now in place.

In Chapter 4 we showed how the present value of growth opportunities (PVGO) contributes to the value of a company's common stock. PVGO equals the forecasted total NPV of future investments. But it's better to think of PVGO as the value of the firm's *options* to invest and expand. The firm is not obliged to grow. It can invest more if the number of positive-NPV projects turns out high or slow down if that number turns out low. The flexibility to adapt investment to future opportunities is one of the factors that makes PVGO so valuable.

The Option to Abandon

If the option to expand has value, what about the decision to bail out? Projects don't just go on until assets expire of old age. The decision to terminate a project is usually taken by management, not by nature. Once the project is no longer profitable, the company will cut its losses and exercise its option to abandon the project.[17]

Some assets are easier to bail out of than others. Tangible assets are usually easier to sell than intangible ones. It helps to have active secondhand markets, which really exist only for standardized items. Real estate, airplanes, trucks, and certain machine tools are likely to be relatively easy to sell. On the other hand, the knowledge accumulated by a software company's research and development program is a specialized intangible asset and probably would not have significant abandonment value. (Some assets, such as old mattresses, even have *negative* abandonment value; you have to pay to get rid of them. It is costly to decommission nuclear power plants or to reclaim land that has been strip-mined.)

Example. Managers should recognize the option to abandon when they make the initial investment in a new project or venture. For example, suppose you must choose between two technologies for production of a Wankel-engine outboard motor.

1. Technology A uses computer-controlled machinery custom-designed to produce the complex shapes required for Wankel engines in high volumes and at low cost. But if the Wankel outboard doesn't sell, this equipment will be worthless.

[17]The abandonment option was first analyzed by A. A. Robichek and J. C. Van Horne, "Abandonment Value in Capital Budgeting," *Journal of Finance* 22 (December 1967), pp. 577–590.

2. Technology B uses standard machine tools. Labour costs are much higher, but the machinery can be sold for $10 million if the engine doesn't sell.

Technology A looks better in a DCF analysis of the new product because it was designed to have the lowest possible cost at the planned production volume. Yet you can sense the advantage of technology B's flexibility if you are unsure about whether the new outboard will sink or swim in the marketplace.

We can make the value of this flexibility concrete by expressing it as a real option. Just for simplicity, assume that the initial capital outlays for technologies A and B are the same. Technology A, with its low-cost customized machinery, will provide a payoff of $18.5 million if the outboard is popular with boat owners and $8.5 million if it is not. Think of these payoffs as the project's cash flow in its first year of production plus the present value of all subsequent cash flows. The corresponding payoffs to technology B are $18 million and $8 million.

	Payoffs from Producing Outboard ($ millions)	
	Technology A	Technology B
Buoyant demand	$18.5	$18
Sluggish demand	8.5	8

If you are obliged to continue in production regardless of how unprofitable the project turns out to be, then technology A is clearly the superior choice. But remember that at year-end you can bail out of technology B for $10 million. If the outboard is not a success in the market, you are better off selling the plant and equipment for $10 million than continuing with a project that has a present value of only $8 million.

Figure 10.7 summarizes this example as a decision tree. The abandonment option occurs at the right-hand boxes for Technology B. The decisions are obvious: continue if demand is buoyant, abandon otherwise. Thus the payoffs to Technology B are:

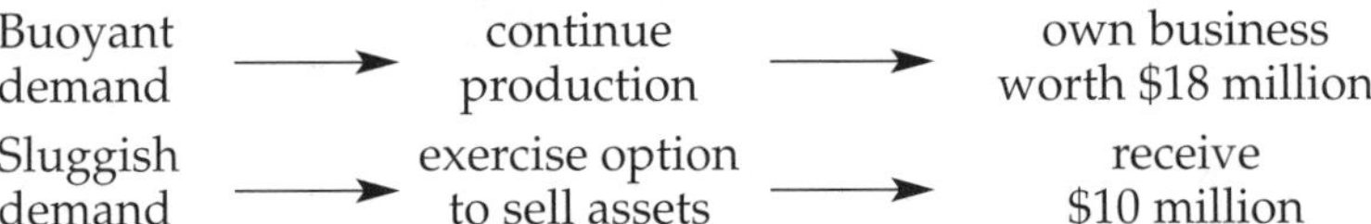

Technology B provides an insurance policy: If the outboard's sales are disappointing, you can abandon the project and recover $10 million. You can think of this abandonment option as an option to sell the assets for $10 million. The total value of the project using technology B is its DCF value, assuming that the company does not abandon, *plus* the value of the abandonment option. When you value this option, you are placing a value on flexibility.

Two Other Real Options

These are not the only real options. For example, companies with positive-NPV projects are not obliged to undertake them right away. If the outlook is uncertain, you may be able to avoid a costly mistake by waiting a bit. Such options to postpone investment are called *timing options.*

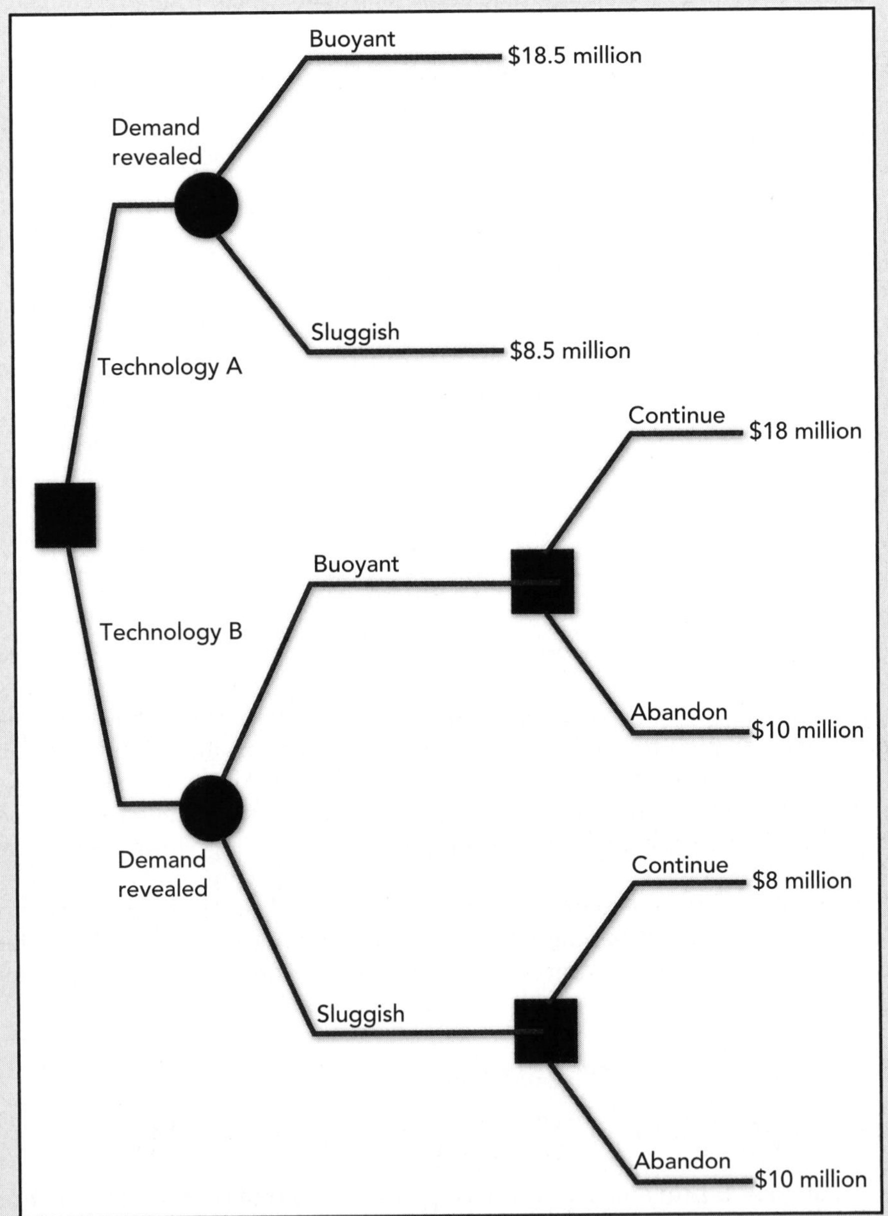

FIGURE 10.7

Decision tree for the Wankel outboard motor project. Technology B allows the firm to abandon the project and recover $10 million if demand is sluggish.

When companies undertake new investments, they generally think about the possibility that at a later stage they may wish to modify the project. After all, today everybody may be demanding round pegs, but, who knows, tomorrow square ones could be all the rage. In that case you need a plant that provides the flexibility to produce a variety of peg shapes. In just the same way, it may be worth paying up front for the flexibility to vary the inputs. For example, in Chapter 22 we will describe how electric utilities often build in the option to switch between burning oil to burning natural gas. We refer to these opportunities as *production options.*

More on Decision Trees

We will return to all these real options in Chapter 22, after we have covered the theory of option valuation in Chapters 20 and 21. But we will close this chapter with a closer look at decision trees.

Decision trees are commonly used to describe the real options imbedded in capital investment projects. But decision trees were used in the analysis of projects years before real options were first explicitly identified.[18] Decision trees can help to understand project risk and how future decisions will affect project cash flows. Even if you never learn or use option valuation theory, decision trees belong in your financial toolkit.

The best way to appreciate how decision trees can be used in project analysis is to work through a detailed example.

An Example: Magna Charter

Magna Charter is a new corporation formed by Agnes Magna to provide an executive flying service for the southeastern United States. The founder thinks there will be a ready demand from businesses that cannot justify a full-time company plane but nevertheless need one from time to time. However, the venture is not a sure thing. There is a 40 percent chance that demand in the first year will be low. If it is low, there is a 60 percent chance that it will remain low in subsequent years. On the other hand, if the initial demand is high, there is an 80 percent chance that it will stay high.

The immediate problem is to decide what kind of plane to buy. A turboprop costs $550,000. A piston-engine plane costs only $250,000 but has less capacity and customer appeal. Moreover, the piston-engine plane is an old design and likely to depreciate rapidly. Ms. Magna thinks that next year secondhand piston aircraft will be available for only $150,000.

That gives Ms. Magna an idea: Why not start out with one piston plane and buy another if demand is still high? It will cost only $150,000 to expand. If demand is low, Magna Charter can sit tight with one small, relatively inexpensive aircraft.

Figure 10.8 displays these choices. The square on the left marks the company's initial decision to purchase a turboprop for $550,000 or a piston aircraft for $250,000. After the company has made its decision, fate decides on the first year's demand. You can see in parentheses the probability that demand will be high or low, and you can see the expected cash flow for each combination of aircraft and demand level. At the end of the year the company has a second decision to make if it has a piston-engine aircraft: It can either expand or sit tight. This decision point is marked by the second square. Finally fate takes over again and selects the level of demand for year 2. Again you can see in parentheses the probability of high or low demand. Notice that the probabilities for the second year depend on the first-period outcomes. For example, if demand is high in the first period, then there is an 80 percent chance that it will also be high in the second. The chance of high

[18]The use of decision trees was first advocated by J. Magee in "How to Use Decision Trees in Capital Investment," *Harvard Business Review* 42(September–October 1964), pp. 79–96. Real options were first identified in S. C. Myers, "Determinants of Corporate Borrowing," *Journal of Financial Economics* 5 (November 1977), pp. 146–175.

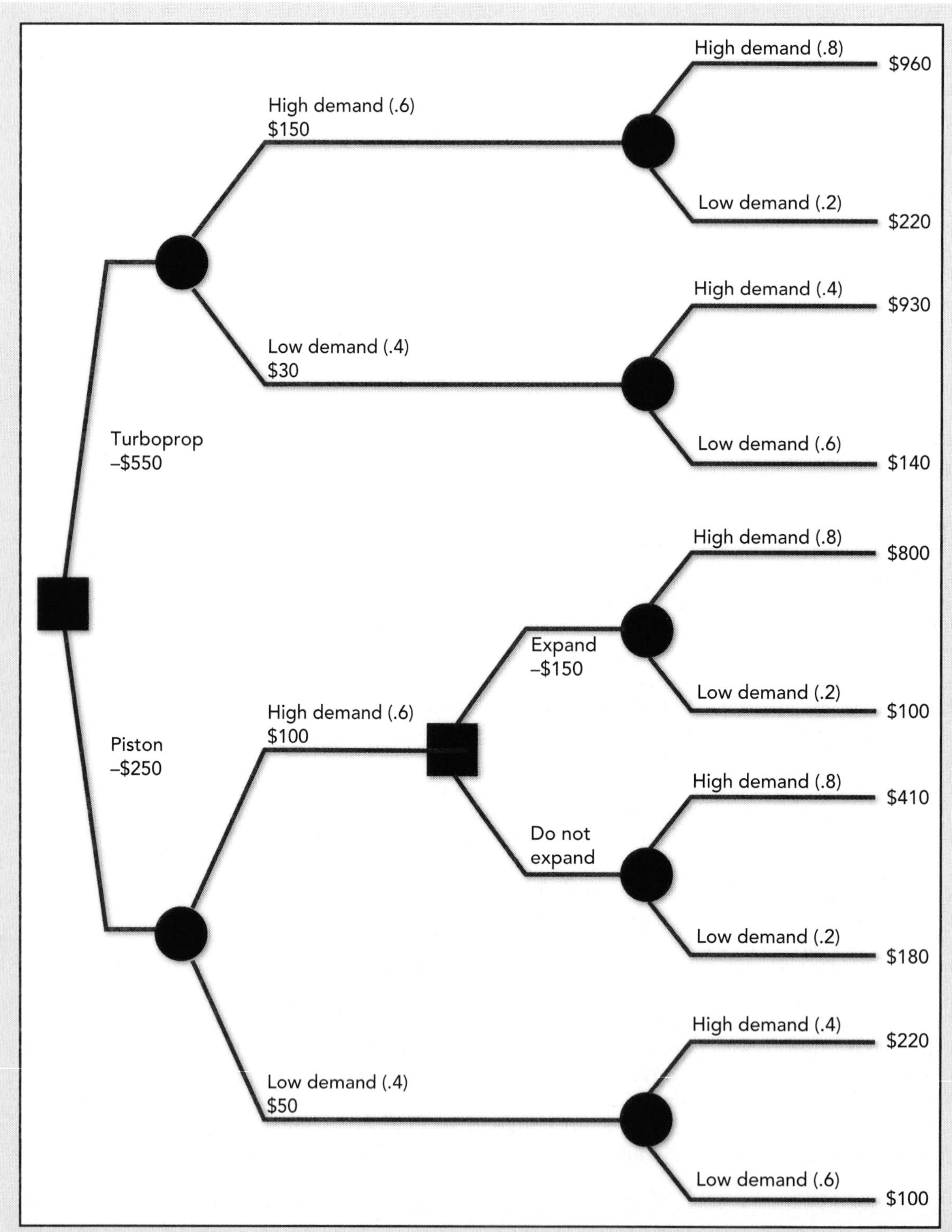

FIGURE 10.8

Decision tree for Magna Charter. Should it buy a turboprop or a smaller piston-engine plane? A second piston plane can be purchased in year 1 if demand turns out to be high. (All figures are in thousands. Probabilities are in parentheses.)

demand in *both* the first and second periods is .6 × .8 = .48. After the parentheses we again show the profitability of the project for each combination of aircraft and demand level. You can interpret each of these figures as the present value at the end of year 2 of the cash flows for that and all subsequent years.

The problem for Ms. Magna is to decide what to do today. We solve that problem by thinking first what she would do next year. This means that we start at the right side of the tree and work backward to the beginning on the left.

The only decision that Ms. Magna needs to make next year is whether to expand if purchase of a piston-engine plane is succeeded by high demand. If she expands, she invests \$150,000 and receives a payoff of \$800,000 if demand continues to be high and \$100,000 if demand falls. So her *expected* payoff is

$$\begin{aligned}&(\text{Probability high demand} \times \text{payoff with high demand})\\&\quad + (\text{probability low demand} \times \text{payoff with low demand})\\&\quad = (.8 \times 800) + (.2 \times 100) = +660, \text{ or } \$660{,}000\end{aligned}$$

If the opportunity cost of capital for this venture is 10 percent,[19] then the net present value of expanding, computed as of year 1, is

$$\text{NPV} = -150 + \frac{660}{1.10} = +450, \text{ or } \$450{,}000$$

If Ms. Magna does *not* expand, the expected payoff is

$$\begin{aligned}&(\text{Probability high demand} \times \text{payoff with high demand})\\&\quad + (\text{probability low demand} \times \text{payoff with low demand})\\&\quad = (.8 \times 410) + (.2 \times 180) = +364, \text{ or } \$364{,}000\end{aligned}$$

The net present value of *not* expanding, computed as of year 1, is

$$\text{NPV} = 0 + \frac{364}{1.10} = +331, \text{ or } \$331{,}000$$

Expansion obviously pays if market demand is high.

Now that we know what Magna Charter ought to do if faced with the expansion decision, we can roll back to today's decision. If the first piston-engine plane is bought, Magna can expect to receive cash worth \$550,000 in year 1 if demand is high and cash worth \$185,000 if it is low:

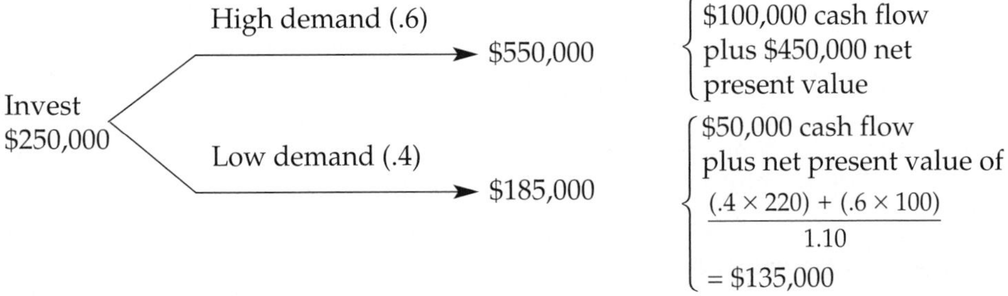

19We are guilty here of assuming away one of the most difficult questions. Just as in the Vegetron mop case in Chapter 9, the most risky part of Ms. Magna's venture is likely to be the initial prototype project. Perhaps we should use a lower discount rate for the second piston-engine plane than for the first.

The net present value of the investment in the piston-engine plane is therefore $117,000:

$$\text{NPV} = -250 + \frac{.6(550) + .4(185)}{1.10} = +117, \text{ or } \$117{,}000$$

If Magna buys the turboprop, there are no future decisions to analyze, and so there is no need to roll back. We just calculate expected cash flows and discount:

$$\begin{aligned}\text{NPV} &= -550 + \frac{.6(150) + .4(30)}{1.10} \\ &\quad + \frac{.6[.8(960) + .2(220)] + .4[.4(930) + .6(140)]}{(1.10)^2} \\ &= -550 + \frac{102}{1.10} + \frac{670}{(1.10)^2} = +96, \text{ or } \$96{,}000\end{aligned}$$

Thus the investment in the piston-engine plane has an NPV of $117,000; the investment in the turboprop has an NPV of $96,000. The piston-engine plane is the better bet. Note, however, that the choice would be different if we forgot to take account of the option to expand. In that case the NPV of the piston-engine plane would drop from $117,000 to $52,000:

$$\begin{aligned}\text{NPV} &= -250 + \frac{.6(100) + .4(50)}{1.10} \\ &\quad + \frac{.6[.8(410) + .2(180)] + .4[.4(220) + .6(100)]}{(1.10)^2} \\ &= +52, \text{ or } \$52{,}000\end{aligned}$$

The value of the option to expand is, therefore,

$$117 - 52 = +65, \text{ or } \$65{,}000$$

The decision tree in Figure 10.8 recognizes that, if Ms. Magna buys one piston-engine plane, she is not stuck with that decision. She has the option to expand by buying an additional plane if demand turns out to be unexpectedly high. But Figure 10.8 also assumes that, if Ms. Magna goes for the big time by buying a turboprop, there is nothing that she can do if demand turns out to be unexpectedly *low.* That is unrealistic. If business in the first year is poor, it may pay for Ms. Magna to sell the turboprop and abandon the venture entirely. In Figure 10.8 we could represent this option to bail out by adding an extra decision point (a further square) if the company buys the turboprop and first-year demand is low. If that happens, Ms. Magna could decide either to sell the plane or to hold on and hope demand recovers. If the abandonment option is sufficiently valuable, it may make sense to take the turboprop and shoot for the big payoff.

Pro and Con Decision Trees

Any cash-flow forecast rests on some assumption about the firm's future investment and operating strategy. Often that assumption is implicit. Decision trees force the underlying strategy into the open. By displaying the links between today's and tomorrow's decisions, they help the financial manager to find the strategy with the highest net present value.

The trouble with decision trees is that they get so _____ complex so _____ quickly (insert your own expletives). What will Magna Charter do if demand is neither high nor low but just middling? In that event Ms. Magna might sell the turboprop and buy a piston-engine plane, or she might defer expansion and abandonment decisions until year 2. Perhaps middling demand requires a decision about a price cut or an intensified sales campaign.

We could draw a new decision tree covering this expanded set of events and decisions. Try it if you like: You'll see how fast the circles, squares, and branches accumulate.

Life is complex, and there is very little we can do about it. It is therefore unfair to criticize decision trees because they can become complex. Our criticism is reserved for analysts who let the complexity become overwhelming. The point of decision trees is to allow explicit analysis of possible future events and decisions. They should be judged not on their comprehensiveness but on whether they show the most important links between today's and tomorrow's decisions. Decision trees used in real life will be more complex than Figure 10.8, but they will nevertheless display only a small fraction of possible future events and decisions. Decision trees are like grapevines: They are productive only if they are vigorously pruned.

Decision trees can help identify the future choices available to the manager and can give a clearer view of the cash flows and risks of a project. However, our analysis of the Magna Charter project begged an important question. The option to expand enlarged the spread of possible outcomes and therefore increased the risk of investing in a piston aircraft. Conversely, the option to bail out would narrow the spread of possible outcomes, reducing the risk of investment. We should have used different discount rates to recognize these changes in risk, but decision trees do not tell us how to do this. But the situation is not hopeless. Modern techniques of option pricing can value these investment options. We will describe these techniques in Chapters 20 and 21, and turn again to real options in Chapter 22.

Decision Trees and Monte Carlo Simulation

We have said that any cash-flow forecast rests on assumptions about future investment and operating strategy. Think back to the Monte Carlo simulation model that we constructed for Otobai's electric scooter project. What strategy was that based on? We don't know. Inevitably Otobai will face decisions about pricing, production, expansion, and abandonment, but the model builder's assumptions about these decisions are buried in the model's equations. The model builder may have implicitly identified a future strategy for Otobai, but it is clearly not the optimal one. There will be some runs of the model when nearly everything goes wrong and when in real life Otobai would abandon to cut its losses. Yet the model goes on period after period, heedless of the drain on Otobai's cash resources. The most unfavorable outcomes reported by the simulation model would never be encountered in real life.

On the other hand, the simulation model probably understates the project's potential value if nearly everything goes right: There is no provision for expanding to take advantage of good luck.

Most simulation models incorporate a business-as-usual strategy, which is fine as long as there are no major surprises. The greater the divergence from expected levels of market growth, market share, cost, etc., the less realistic is the simulation. Therefore the extreme high and low simulated values—the "tails" of the simulated distributions—should be treated with extreme caution. Don't take the area under the tails as realistic probabilities of disaster or bonanza.

SUMMARY

There is more to capital budgeting than grinding out calculations of net present value. If you can identify the major uncertainties, you may find that it is worth undertaking some additional preliminary research that will *confirm* whether the project is worthwhile. And even if you decide that you have done all you can to resolve the uncertainties, you still want to be aware of the potential problems. You do not want to be caught by surprise if things go wrong: You want to be ready to take corrective action.

There are three ways in which companies try to identify the principal threats to a project's success. The simplest is *sensitivity analysis.* In this case the manager considers in turn each of the determinants of the project's success and recalculates NPV at very optimistic and very pessimistic levels of that variable. This establishes a range of possible values. The project is "sensitive to" the variable if the range is wide, especially on the pessimistic side.

Sensitivity analysis of this kind is easy, but it is not always helpful. Variables do not usually change one at a time. If costs are higher than you expect, it is a good bet that prices will be higher also. And if prices are higher, it is a good bet that sales volume will be lower. If you don't allow for the dependencies between the swings and the merry-go-rounds, you may get a false idea of the hazards of the fairground business. Many companies try to cope with this problem by examining the effect on the project of alternative plausible combinations of variables. In other words, they will estimate the net present value of the project under different *scenarios* and compare these estimates with the base case.

In a sensitivity analysis you change variables one at a time: When you analyze scenarios, you look at a limited number of alternative combinations of variables. If you want to go whole hog and look at *all* possible combinations of variables, then you will probably use *Monte Carlo simulation* to cope with the complexity. In that case you must construct a complete model of the project and specify the probability distribution of each of the determinants of cash flow. You can then ask the computer to select a random number for each of these determinants and work out the cash flows that would result. After the computer has repeated this process a few thousand times, you should have a fair idea of the expected cash flow in each year and the spread of possible cash flows.

Simulation can be a very useful tool. The discipline of building a model of the project can in itself lead you to a deeper understanding of the project. And once you have constructed your model, it is a simple matter to see how the outcomes would be affected by altering the scope of the project or the distribution of any of the variables.

Elementary treatises on capital budgeting sometimes create the impression that, once the manager has made an investment decision, there is nothing to do but sit back and watch the cash flows unfold. In practice, companies are constantly modifying their operations. If cash flows are better than anticipated, the project may be expanded; if they are worse, it may be contracted or abandoned altogether. Options to modify projects are known as *real options.* In this chapter we introduced the main categories of real options: *expansion* options, *abandonment* options, *timing* options, and options providing *flexibility in production.*

Good managers take account of real options when they value a project. One convenient way to summarize real options and their cash flow consequences is to create a *decision tree.* You identify the things that could happen to the project and the main counteractions that you might take. Then, working back from the future to the present, you can consider which action you *should* take in each case.

Decision trees can help the financial manager to identify real options and their impacts on project risks and cash flows. The options may increase or decrease project risk. Because risk changes, standard discounted-cash-flow techniques can only approximate the present value of real options. We will cover option-valuation methods in Chapter 21 and revisit real options in Chapter 22.

FURTHER READING

For an excellent case study of break-even analysis, see:

U. E. Reinhardt: "Break-Even Analysis for Lockheed's TriStar: An Application of Financial Theory," *Journal of Finance,* 28:821–838 (September 1973).

Hax and Wiig discuss how Monte Carlo simulation and decision trees were used in an actual capital budgeting decision:

A. C. Hax and K. M. Wiig: "The Use of Decision Analysis in Capital Investment Problems," *Sloan Management Review,* 17:19–48 (Winter 1976).

Merck's use of Monte Carlo simulation is discussed in:

N. A. Nichols: "Scientific Management at Merck: An Interview with Judy Lewent," *Harvard Business Review,* 72:89–99 (January–February 1994).

Three not-too-technical references on real options are listed below. Additional references follow Chapter 22.

M. Amram and N. Kulatilaka: *Real Options: Managing Strategic Investments in an Uncertain World,* Harvard Business School Press, Boston, 1999.

A. Dixit and R. Pindyck: "The Options Approach to Capital Investment," *Harvard Business Review,* 73:105–115 (May–June 1995).

W. C. Kester: "Today's Options for Tomorrow's Growth," *Harvard Business Review,* 62:153–160 (March–April 1984).

QUIZ

1. Define and briefly explain each of the following terms or procedures:
   - **a.** Sensitivity analysis
   - **b.** Scenario analysis
   - **c.** Break-even analysis
   - **d.** Monte Carlo simulation
   - **e.** Decision tree
   - **f.** Real option
   - **g.** Abandonment value
   - **h.** Expansion value
2. True or false?
   - **a.** Sensitivity analysis is unnecessary for projects with asset betas that are equal to zero.

b. Sensitivity analysis can be used to identify the variables most crucial to a project's success.
c. If only one variable is uncertain, sensitivity analysis gives "optimistic" and "pessimistic" values for project cash flow and NPV.
d. The break-even sales level of a project is higher when *break even* is defined in terms of NPV rather than accounting income.
e. Monte Carlo simulation can be used to help forecast cash flows.
f. Monte Carlo simulation eliminates the need to estimate a project's opportunity cost of capital.

3. What are the advantages of scenario analysis compared to sensitivity analysis?
4. How should Monte Carlo simulation be used to help determine a project's NPV?
5. Suppose a manager has already estimated a project's cash flows, calculated its NPV, and done a sensitivity analysis like the one shown in Table 10.2. List the additional steps required to carry out a Monte Carlo simulation of project cash flows.
6. What are the four chief categories of real options?
7. True or false?
   a. Decision trees can help identify and describe real options.
   b. The option to expand increases NPV
   c. High abandonment value decreases NPV.
   d. If a project has positive NPV, the firm should always invest immediately.
8. Give an example of why flexible production facilities are valuable.

PRACTICE QUESTIONS

1. What is the NPV of the electric scooter project under the following scenario?

Market size	1.1 million
Market share	.1
Unit price	¥400,000
Unit variable cost	¥360,000
Fixed cost	¥2 billion

2. Otobai's staff has come up with the following revised estimates for the electric scooter project:

	Pessimistic	Expected	Optimistic
Market size	.8 million	1.0 million	1.2 million
Market share	.04	.1	.16
Unit price	¥300,000	¥375,000	¥400,000
Unit variable cost	¥350,000	¥300,000	¥275,000
Fixed cost	¥5 billion	¥3 billion	¥1 billion

Conduct a sensitivity analysis. What are the principal uncertainties in the project?

3. Otobai is considering still another production method for its electric scooter. It would require an additional investment of ¥15 billion but would reduce variable costs by ¥40,000 per unit. Other assumptions follow Table 10.1.
   a. What is the NPV of this alternative scheme?
   b. Draw break-even charts for this alternative scheme along the lines of Figure 10.1.
   c. Explain how you would interpret the break-even figure.

Now suppose Otobai's management would like to know the figure for variable cost per unit at which the electric scooter project in Section 10.1 would break even. Calculate the level of costs at which the project would earn zero profit and at which it would have zero NPV.

4. The Rustic Welt Company is proposing to replace its old welt-making machinery with more modern equipment. The new equipment costs $10 million and the company expects to sell its old equipment for $1 million. The attraction of the new machinery is that it is expected to cut manufacturing costs from their current level of $8 a welt to $4. However, as the following table shows, there is some uncertainty both about future sales and about the performance of the new machinery:

	Pessimistic	Expected	Optimistic
Sales, millions of welts	.4	.5	.7
Manufacturing cost with new machinery, dollars per welt	6	4	3
Economic life of new machinery, years	7	10	13

Conduct a sensitivity analysis of the replacement decision, assuming a discount rate of 12 percent. Rustic Welt does not pay taxes.

5. Rustic Welt could commission engineering tests to determine the actual improvement in manufacturing costs generated by the proposed new welt machines. (See problem 4 above.) The study would cost $450,000. Would you advise the company to go ahead with the study?

6. Summarize the problems that a manager would encounter in interpreting a standard sensitivity analysis, such as the one shown in Table 10.2. Which of these problems are alleviated by examining the project under alternative scenarios?

7. Operating leverage is often measured as the percentage increase in profits after depreciation for a 1 percent increase in sales.

   a. Calculate the operating leverage for the electric scooter project assuming unit sales are 100,000 (see Section 10.1).
   b. Now show that this figure is equal to 1 + (fixed costs/profits) including depreciation, divided by profits.
   c. Would operating leverage be higher or lower if sales were 200,000 scooters?

8. For what kinds of capital investment projects do you think Monte Carlo simulation would be most useful? For example, can you think of some industries in which this technique would be particularly attractive? Would it be more useful for large-scale investments than small ones? Discuss.

9. Look back at the Vegetron electric mop project in Section 9.6. Assume that if tests fail and Vegetron continues to go ahead with the project, the $1 million investment would generate only $75,000 a year. Display Vegetron's problem as a decision tree.

10. Describe the real option in each of the following cases:
   a. Deutsche Metall postpones a major plant expansion. The expansion has positive NPV on a discounted-cash-flow basis but top management wants to get a better fix on product demand before proceeding.
   b. Western Telecom commits to production of digital switching equipment specially designed for the European market. The project has a negative NPV, but it is justified on strategic grounds by the need for a strong market position in the rapidly growing, and potentially very profitable, market.
   c. Western Telecom vetoes a fully integrated, automated production line for the new digital switches. It relies on standard, less-expensive equipment. The automated

production line is more efficient overall, according to a discounted-cash-flow calculation.

d. Mount Fuji Airways buys a jumbo jet with special equipment that allows the plane to be switched quickly from freight to passenger use or vice versa.

e. The British–French treaty giving a concession to build a railroad link under the English Channel also required the concessionaire to propose by the year 2000 to build a "drive-through link" if "technical and economic conditions permit . . . and the decrease in traffic shall justify it without undermining the expected return on the first [rail] link." Other companies will not be permitted to build a link before the year 2020.

11. An auto plant that costs $100 million to build can produce a new line of cars that will generate cash flows with a present value of $140 million if the line is successful, but only $50 million if it is unsuccessful. You believe that the probability of success is only about 50 percent.
    a. Would you build the plant?
    b. Suppose that the plant can be sold for $90 million to another automaker if the line is not successful. Now would you build the plant?
    c. Illustrate this option to abandon using a decision tree.

12. Agnes Magna has found some errors in her data (see Section 10.3). The corrected figures are as follows:

Price of turbo, year 0	$350,000
Price of piston, year 0	$180,000
Discount rate	8 percent

Redraw the decision tree with the changed data. Calculate the value of the option to expand. Which plane should Ms. Magna buy?

13. Ms. Magna has thought of another possibility. She could abandon the venture entirely by selling the plane at the end of the first year. Suppose that the piston-engine plane can be sold for $150,000 and the turboprop can be sold for $500,000.
    a. In what circumstances would it pay for Ms. Magna to sell either plane?
    b. Redraw the decision tree in Figure 10.8 to recognize that there will be circumstances in which Ms. Magna will choose to take the money and bail out.
    c. Recalculate the value of the project recognizing the abandonment option.
    d. How much does the option to abandon add to the value of the piston-engine project? How much does it add to the value of the turboprop project?

14. How can decision trees help the financial manager to "open up the black box" and understand a capital investment project better? Why are decision trees *not* complete solutions to the valuation of real options?

CHALLENGE QUESTIONS

1. You own an unused gold mine that will cost $100,000 to reopen. If you open the mine, you expect to be able to extract 1,000 ounces of gold a year for each of three years. After that, the deposit will be exhausted. The gold price is currently $500 an ounce, and each year the price is equally likely to rise or fall by $50 from its level at the start of the year. The extraction cost is $460 an ounce and the discount rate is 10 percent.
    a. Should you open the mine now or delay one year in the hope of a rise in the gold price?
    b. What difference would it make to your decision if you could costlessly (but irreversibly) shut down the mine at any stage?

2. You are considering starting a company to provide a new Internet access service. There is a 60 percent chance the demand will be high in the first year. If it is high, there is an 80 percent chance that it will continue high indefinitely. If demand is low in the first year, there is a 60 percent chance that it will continue low indefinitely.

   If demand is high, forecasted revenue is $900,000 a year; if demand is low, forecasted revenue is $700,000 a year. You can cease to offer the service at any point, in which case, revenues are zero. Costs other than computing and telecommunications are forecasted at $500,000 a year regardless of demand. These costs also can be terminated at any point.

   You have a choice on computing and telecommunications. One possibility is to buy your own computers and software and to set up your own network and systems. This involves an initial outlay of $2,000,000 and no subsequent expenditure. The resulting system would have an economic life of 10 years and no salvage value. The alternative is to rent computer and telecommunications services as you need them from AT&T or one of the other major telecommunications companies. They propose to charge you 40 percent of your revenues.

   Assume that a decision to buy your own system cannot be reversed (i.e., if you buy a computer, you cannot resell it; if you do *not* buy it today, you cannot do so later). There are no taxes, and the opportunity cost of capital is 10 percent.

   Draw a decision tree showing your choices. Is it better to construct your own system or to rent it? State clearly any additional assumptions that you need to make.

3. Explain why real options are most valuable when forecasts of future cash flows are most uncertain.

MINI-CASE

Waldo County

Waldo County, the well-known real estate developer, worked long hours, and he expected his staff to do the same. So George Probit was not surprised to receive a call from the boss just as George was about to leave for a long summer's weekend.

Mr. County's success had been built on a remarkable instinct for a good site. He would exclaim "Location! Location! Location!" at some point in every planning meeting. Yet finance was not his strong suit. On this occasion he wanted George to go over the figures for a new $90 million outlet mall designed to intercept tourists heading downeast toward Maine. "First thing Monday will do just fine," he said as he handed George the file. "I'll be in my house in Bar Harbor if you need me."

George's first task was to draw up a summary of the projected revenues and costs. The results are shown in Table 10.7. Note that the mall's revenues would come from two sources: The company would charge retailers an annual rent for the space they occupied and in addition it would receive 5 percent of each store's gross sales.

Construction of the mall was likely to take three years. The construction costs could be depreciated straight-line over 15 years starting in year 3. As in the case of the company's other developments, the mall would be built to the highest specifications and would not need to be rebuilt until year 17. The land was expected to retain its value, but could not be depreciated for tax purposes.

Construction costs, revenues, operating and maintenance costs, and real estate taxes were all likely to rise in line with inflation, which was forecasted at 2 percent a year. The company's tax rate was 35 percent and the cost of capital was 9 percent in nominal terms.

	Year					
	0	1	2	3	4	5–17
Investment:						
Land	30					
Construction	20	30	10			
Operations:						
Rentals				12	12	12
Share of retail sales				24	24	24
Operating and maintenance costs	2	4	4	10	10	10
Real estate taxes	2	2	3	4	4	4

TABLE 10.7

Projected revenues and costs in real terms for the Downeast Tourist Mall (figures in $ millions).

George decided first to check that the project made financial sense. He then proposed to look at some of the things that might go wrong. His boss certainly had a nose for a good retail project, but he was not infallible. The Salome project had been a disaster because store sales had turned out to be 40 percent below forecast. What if that happened here? George wondered just how far sales could fall short of forecast before the project would be underwater.

Inflation was another source of uncertainty. Some people were talking about a zero long-term inflation rate, but George also wondered what would happen if inflation jumped to, say, 10 percent.

A third concern was possible construction cost overruns and delays due to required zoning changes and environmental approvals. George had seen cases of 25 percent construction cost overruns and delays up to 12 months between purchase of the land and the start of construction. He decided that he should examine the effect that this scenario would have on the project's profitability.

"Hey, this might be fun," George exclaimed to Mr. Waldo's secretary, Fifi, who was heading for Old Orchard Beach for the weekend. "I might even try Monte Carlo."

"Waldo went to Monte Carlo once," Fifi replied. "Lost a bundle at the roulette table. I wouldn't remind him. Just show him the bottom line. Will it make money or lose money? That's the bottom line."

"OK, no Monte Carlo," George agreed. But he realized that building a spreadsheet and running scenarios was not enough. He had to figure out how to summarize and present his results to Mr. County.

Questions

1. What is the project's NPV, given the projections in Table 10.7?
2. Conduct a sensitivity and a scenario analysis of the project. What do these analyses reveal about the project's risks and potential value?

CHAPTER ELEVEN

WHERE POSITIVE NET PRESENT VALUES COME FROM

WHY IS AN M.B.A. student who has learned about DCF like a baby with a hammer? Answer: Because to a baby with a hammer, everything looks like a nail.

Our point is that you should not focus on the arithmetic of DCF and thereby ignore the forecasts that are the basis of every investment decision. Senior managers are continuously bombarded with requests for funds for capital expenditures. All these requests are supported with detailed DCF analyses showing that the projects have positive NPVs.[1] How, then, can managers distinguish the NPVs that are truly positive from those that are merely the result of forecasting errors? We suggest that they should ask some probing questions about the possible sources of economic gain.

The first section in this chapter reviews certain common pitfalls in capital budgeting, notably the tendency to apply DCF when market values are already available and no DCF calculations are needed. The second section covers the *economic rents* that underlie all positive-NPV investments. The third section presents a case study describing how Marvin Enterprises, the gargle blaster company, analyzed the introduction of a radically new product.

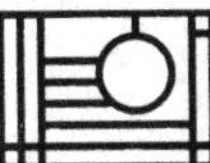

11.1 LOOK FIRST TO MARKET VALUES

Let us suppose that you have persuaded all your project sponsors to give honest forecasts. Although those forecasts are unbiased, they are still likely to contain errors, some positive and others negative. The average error will be zero, but that is little consolation because you want to accept only projects with *truly* superior profitability.

Think, for example, of what would happen if you were to jot down your estimates of the cash flows from operating various lines of business. You would probably find that about half *appeared* to have positive NPVs. This may not be because you personally possess any superior skill in operating jumbo jets or running a chain of laundromats but because you have inadvertently introduced large errors into your estimates of the cash flows. The more projects you contemplate, the more likely you are to uncover projects that *appear* to be extremely worthwhile. Indeed, if you were to extend your activities to making cash-flow estimates for various companies, you would also find a number of *apparently* attractive takeover candidates. In some of these cases you might have genuine information and the proposed investment really might have a positive NPV. But in many other cases the investment would look good only because you made a forecasting error.

What can you do to prevent forecast errors from swamping genuine information? We suggest that you begin by looking at market values.

The Cadillac and the Movie Star

The following parable should help to illustrate what we mean. Your local Cadillac dealer is announcing a special offer. For $45,001 you get not only a brand new Cadillac but also the chance to shake hands with your favorite movie star. You wonder how much you are paying for that handshake.

There are two possible approaches to the problem. You could evaluate the worth of the Cadillac's power steering, disappearing windshield wipers, and other features and conclude that the Cadillac is worth $46,000. This would seem to suggest that the dealership is willing to pay $999 to have a movie star shake hands with

[1]Here is another riddle. Are projects proposed because they have positive NPVs, or do they have positive NPVs because they are proposed? No prizes for the correct answer.

you. Alternatively, you might note that the market price for Cadillacs is $45,000, so that you are paying $1 for the handshake. As long as there is a competitive market for Cadillacs, the latter approach is more appropriate.

Security analysts face a similar problem whenever they value a company's stock. They must consider the information that is already known to the market about a company, *and* they must evaluate the information that is known only to them. The information that is known to the market is the Cadillac; the private information is the handshake with the movie star. Investors have already evaluated the information that is generally known. Security analysts do not need to evaluate this information again. They can *start* with the market price of the stock and concentrate on valuing their private information.

While lesser mortals would instinctively accept the Cadillac's market value of $45,000, the financial manager is trained to enumerate and value all the costs and benefits from an investment and is therefore tempted to substitute his or her own opinion for the market's. Unfortunately this approach increases the chance of error. Many capital assets are traded in a competitive market, so it makes sense to *start* with the market price and then ask why these assets should earn more in your hands than in your rivals'.

Example: Investing in a New Department Store

We encountered a department store chain that estimated the present value of the expected cash flows from each proposed store, including the price at which it could eventually sell the store. Although the firm took considerable care with these estimates, it was disturbed to find that its conclusions were heavily influenced by the forecasted selling price of each store. Management disclaimed any particular real estate expertise, but it discovered that its investment decisions were unintentionally dominated by its assumptions about future real estate prices.

Once the financial managers realized this, they always checked the decision to open a new store by asking the following question: "Let us assume that the property is fairly priced. What is the evidence that it is best suited to one of our department stores rather than to some other use? In other words, *if an asset is worth more to others than it is to you, then beware of bidding for the asset against them.*

Let us take the department store problem a little further. Suppose that the new store costs $100 million.[2] You forecast that it will generate after-tax cash flow of $8 million a year for 10 years. Real estate prices are estimated to grow by 3 percent a year, so the expected value of the real estate at the end of 10 years is $100 \times (1.03)^{10} = \$134$ million. At a discount rate of 10 percent, your proposed department store has an NPV of $1 million:

$$\text{NPV} = -100 + \frac{8}{1.10} + \frac{8}{(1.10)^2} + \cdots + \frac{8 + 134}{(1.10)^{10}} = \$1 \text{ million}$$

Notice how sensitive this NPV is to the ending value of the real estate. For example, an ending value of $120 million implies an NPV of −$5 million.

It is helpful to imagine such a business as divided into two parts—a real estate subsidiary which buys the building and a retailing subsidiary which rents and operates it. Then figure out how much rent the real estate subsidiary would have to charge, and ask whether the retailing subsidiary could afford to pay the rent.

[2]For simplicity we assume the $100 million goes entirely to real estate. In real life there would also be substantial investments in fixtures, information systems, training, and start-up costs.

In some cases a fair market rental can be estimated from real estate transactions. For example, we might observe that similar retail space recently rented for $10 million a year. In that case we would conclude that our department store was an unattractive use for the site. Once the site had been acquired, it would be better to rent it out at $10 million than to use it for a store generating only $8 million.

Suppose, on the other hand, that the property could be rented for only $7 million per year. The department store could pay this amount to the real estate subsidiary and still earn a net operating cash flow of $8 - 7 = \$1$ million. It is therefore the best *current* use for the real estate.[3]

Will it also be the best *future* use? Maybe not, depending on whether retail profits keep pace with any rent increases. Suppose that real estate prices and rents are expected to increase by 3 percent per year. The real estate subsidiary must charge $7 \times 1.03 = \$7.21$ million in year 2, $7.21 \times 1.03 = \$7.43$ million in year 3, and so on.[4] Figure 11.1 shows that the store's income fails to cover the rental after year 5.

If these forecasts are right, the store has only a five-year economic life; from that point on the real estate is more valuable in some other use. If you stubbornly believe that the department store is the best long-term use for the site, you must be ignoring potential growth in income from the store.[5]

There is a general point here. Whenever you make a capital investment decision, think what bets you are placing. Our department store example involved at least two bets—one on real estate prices and another on the firm's ability to run a successful department store. But that suggests some alternative strategies. For instance, it would be foolish to make a lousy department store investment just because you are optimistic about real estate prices. You would do better to buy real estate and rent it out to the highest bidders. The converse is also true. You shouldn't be deterred from going ahead with a profitable department store because you are pessimistic about real estate prices. You would do better to sell the real estate and *rent* it back for the department store. We suggest that you separate the two bets by first asking, "Should we open a department store on this site, assuming that the real estate is fairly priced?" and then deciding whether you also want to go into the real estate business.

Another Example: Opening a Gold Mine

Here is another example of how market prices can help you make better decisions. Kingsley Solomon is considering a proposal to open a new gold mine. He estimates that the mine will cost $200 million to develop and that in each of the next 10 years it will produce .1 million ounces of gold at a cost, after mining and refining, of $200 an ounce. Although the extraction costs can be predicted with reasonable accuracy, Mr. Solomon is much less confident about future gold prices. His best guess is that

[3]The fair market rent equals the profit generated by the real estate's *second*-best use.

[4]This rental stream yields a 10 percent rate of return to the real estate subsidiary. Each year it gets a 7 percent "dividend" and 3 percent capital gain. Growth at 3 percent would bring the value of the property to $134 million by year 10.

The present value (at $r = .10$) of the growing stream of rents is

$$PV = \frac{7}{r - g} = \frac{7}{.10 - .03} = \$100 \text{ million}$$

This PV is the initial market value of the property.

[5]Another possibility is that real estate rents and values are expected to grow at less than 3 percent a year. But in that case the real estate subsidiary would have to charge more than $7 million rent in year 1 to justify its $100 million real estate investment (see footnote 4 above). That would make the department store even less attractive.

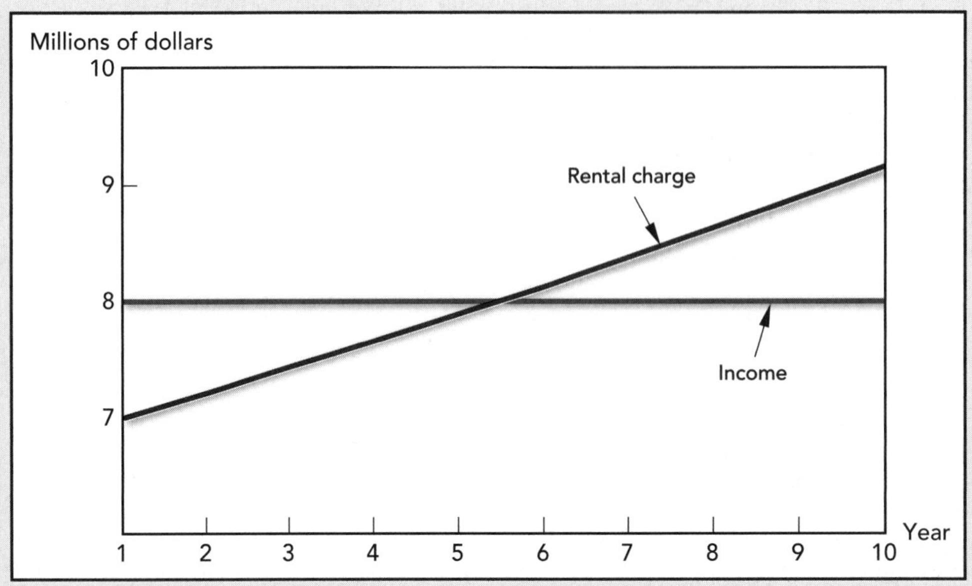

FIGURE 11.1

Beginning in year 6, the department store's income fails to cover the rental charge.

the price will rise by 5 percent per year from its current level of \$400 an ounce. At a discount rate of 10 percent, this gives the mine an NPV of −\$10 million:

$$\text{NPV} = -200 + \frac{.1(420 - 200)}{1.10} + \frac{.1(441 - 200)}{(1.10)^2} + \cdots + \frac{.1(652 - 200)}{(1.10)^{10}}$$
$$= -\$10 \text{ million}$$

Therefore the gold mine project is rejected.

Unfortunately, Mr. Solomon did not look at what the market was telling him. What is the PV of an ounce of gold? Clearly, if the gold market is functioning properly, it is the current price—\$400 an ounce. Gold does not produce any income, so \$400 is the discounted value of the expected future gold price.[6] Since the mine is

[6]Investing in an ounce of gold is like investing in a stock that pays no dividends: The investor's return comes entirely as capital gains. Look back at Section 4.2, where we showed that P_0, the price of the stock today, depends on DIV_1 and P_1, the expected dividend and price for next year, and the opportunity cost of capital r:

$$P_0 = \frac{\text{DIV}_1 + P_1}{1 + r}$$

But for gold $\text{DIV}_1 = 0$, so

$$P_0 = \frac{P_1}{1 + r}$$

In words, *today's price is the present value of next year's price.* Therefore, we don't have to know either P_1 or r to find the present value. Also since $\text{DIV}_2 = 0$,

$$P_1 = \frac{P_2}{1 + r}$$

expected to produce a total of 1 million ounces (.1 million ounces per year for 10 years), the present value of the revenue stream is $1 \times 400 = \$400$ million.[7] We assume that 10 percent is an appropriate discount rate for the relatively certain extraction costs. Thus

$$\begin{aligned} \text{NPV} &= -\text{initial investment} + \text{PV revenues} - \text{PV costs} \\ &= -200 + 400 - \sum_{t=1}^{10} \frac{.1 \times 200}{(1.10)^t} = \$77 \text{ million} \end{aligned}$$

It looks as if Kingsley Solomon's mine is not such a bad bet after all.[8]

Mr. Solomon's gold was just like anyone else's gold. So there was no point in trying to value it separately. By taking the PV of the gold sales as given, Mr. Solomon was able to focus on the crucial issue: Were the extraction costs sufficiently low to make the venture worthwhile? That brings us to another of those fundamental truths: If others are producing an article profitably and (like Mr. Solomon) you can make it more cheaply, then you don't need any NPV calculations to know that you are probably onto a good thing.

We confess that our example of Kingsley Solomon's mine is somewhat special. Unlike gold, most commodities are not kept solely for investment purposes, and therefore you cannot automatically assume that today's price is equal to the present value of the future price.[9]

---

and we can express P_0 as

$$P_0 = \frac{P_1}{1+r} = \frac{1}{1+r}\left(\frac{P_2}{1+r}\right) = \frac{P_2}{(1+r)^2}$$

In general,

$$P_0 = \frac{P_t}{(1+r)^t}$$

This holds for any asset which pays no dividends, is traded in a competitive market, and costs nothing to store. Storage costs for gold or common stocks are very small compared to asset value.

We also assume that guaranteed future delivery of gold is just as good as having gold in hand today. This is not quite right. As we will see in Chapter 27, gold in hand can generate a small "convenience yield."

[7]We assume that the extraction rate does not vary. If it can vary, Mr. Solomon has a valuable operating option to increase output when gold prices are high or to cut back when prices fall. Option pricing techniques are needed to value the mine when operating options are important. See Chapters 21 and 22.

[8]As in the case of our department store example, Mr. Solomon is placing two bets: one on his ability to mine gold at a low cost and the other on the price of gold. Suppose that he really does believe that gold is overvalued. That should not deter him from running a low-cost gold mine as long as he can place separate bets on gold prices. For example, he might be able to enter into a long-term contract to sell the mine's output or he could sell gold futures. (We explain *futures* in Chapter 27.)

[9]A more general guide to the relationship of current and future commodity prices was provided by Hotelling, who pointed out that if there are constant returns to scale in mining any mineral, the expected rise in the price of the mineral *less* extraction costs should equal the cost of capital. If the expected growth were faster, everyone would want to postpone extraction; if it were slower, everyone would want to exploit the resource today. In this case the value of a mine would be independent of when it was exploited, and you could value it by calculating the value of the mineral at today's price less the current cost of extraction. If (as is usually the case) there are declining returns to scale, then the expected price rise net of costs must be less than the cost of capital. For a review of Hotelling's Principle, see S. Devarajan and A. C. Fisher, "Hotelling's 'Economics of Exhaustible Resources': Fifty Years Later," *Journal of Economic Literature* 19 (March 1981), pp. 65–73. And for an application, see M. H. Miller and C. W. Upton, "A Test of the Hotelling Valuation Principle," *Journal of Political Economy* 93 (1985), pp. 1–25.

However, here's another way that you may be able to tackle the problem. Suppose that you are considering investment in a new copper mine and that someone offers to buy the mine's future output at a fixed price. If you accept the offer—and the buyer is completely creditworthy—the revenues from the mine are certain and can be discounted at the risk-free interest rate.[10] That takes us back to Chapter 9, where we explained that there are two ways to calculate PV:

- Estimate the expected cash flows and discount at a rate that reflects the risk of those flows.
- Estimate what sure-fire cash flows would have the same values as the risky cash flows. Then discount these *certainty-equivalent* cash flows at the risk-free interest rate.

When you discount the fixed-price revenues at the risk-free rate, you are using the certainty-equivalent method to value the mine's output. By doing so, you gain in two ways: You don't need to estimate future mineral prices, and you don't need to worry about the appropriate discount rate for risky cash flows.

But here's the question: What is the minimum fixed price at which you could agree today to sell your future output? In other words, what is the certainty-equivalent price? Fortunately, for many commodities there is an active market in which firms fix today the price at which they will buy or sell copper and other commodities in the future. This market is known as the *futures market*, which we will cover in Chapter 27. Futures prices are certainty equivalents, and you can look them up in the daily newspaper. So you don't need to make elaborate forecasts of copper prices to work out the PV of the mine's output. The market has already done the work for you; you simply calculate future revenues using the price in the newspaper of copper futures and discount these revenues at the risk-free interest rate.

Of course, things are never as easy as textbooks suggest. Trades in organized futures exchanges are largely confined to deliveries over the next year or so, and therefore your newspaper won't show the price at which you could sell output beyond this period. But financial economists have developed techniques for using the prices in the futures market to estimate the amount that buyers would agree to pay for more distant deliveries.[11]

Our two examples of gold and copper producers are illustrations of a universal principle of finance:

> When you have the market value of an asset, *use it*, at least as a starting point in your analysis.

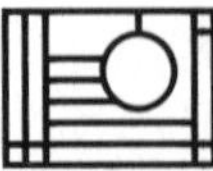

11.2 FORECASTING ECONOMIC RENTS

We recommend that financial managers ask themselves whether an asset is more valuable in their hands than in another's. A bit of classical microeconomics can help to answer that question. When an industry settles into long-run competitive

[10]We assume that the volume of output is certain (or does not have any market risk).

[11]After reading Chapter 27, check out E. S. Schwartz, "The Stochastic Behavior of Commodity Prices: Implications for Valuation and Hedging," *Journal of Finance* 52 (July 1997), pp. 923–973; and A. J. Neuberger, "Hedging Long-Term Exposures with Multiple Short-Term Contracts," *Review of Financial Studies* 12 (1999), pp. 429–459.

equilibrium, all its assets are expected to earn their opportunity costs of capital—no more and no less. If the assets earned more, firms in the industry would expand or firms outside the industry would try to enter it.

Profits that *more* than cover the opportunity cost of capital are known as *economic rents.* These rents may be either temporary (in the case of an industry that is not in long-run equilibrium) or persistent (in the case of a firm with some degree of monopoly or market power). The NPV of an investment is simply the discounted value of the economic rents that it will produce. Therefore when you are presented with a project that appears to have a positive NPV, don't just accept the calculations at face value. They may reflect simple estimation errors in forecasting cash flows. Probe behind the cash-flow estimates, and *try to identify the source of economic rents.* A positive NPV for a new project is believable only if *you* believe that your company has some special advantage.

Such advantages can arise in several ways. You may be smart or lucky enough to be first to the market with a new, improved product for which customers are prepared to pay premium prices (until your competitors enter and squeeze out excess profits). You may have a patent, proprietary technology, or production cost advantage that competitors cannot match, at least for several years. You may have some valuable contractual advantage, for example, the distributorship for gargle blasters in France.

Thinking about competitive advantage can also help ferret out negative-NPV calculations that are negative by mistake. If you are the lowest-cost producer of a profitable product in a growing market, then you should invest to expand along with the market. If your calculations show a negative NPV for such an expansion, then you have probably made a mistake.

How One Company Avoided a $100 Million Mistake

A U.S. chemical producer was about to modify an existing plant to produce a specialty product, polyzone, which was in short supply on world markets.[12] At prevailing raw material and finished-product prices the expansion would have been strongly profitable. Table 11.1 shows a simplified version of management's analysis. Note the NPV of about $64 million at the company's 8 percent real cost of capital—not bad for a $100 million outlay.

Then doubt began to creep in. Notice the outlay for transportation costs. Some of the project's raw materials were commodity chemicals, largely imported from Europe, and much of the polyzone production was exported back to Europe. Moreover, the U.S. company had no long-run technological edge over potential European competitors. It had a head start perhaps, but was that really enough to generate a positive NPV?

Notice the importance of the price spread between raw materials and finished product. The analysis in Table 11.1 forecasted the spread at a constant $1.20 per pound of polyzone for 10 years. That had to be wrong: European producers, who did not face the U.S. company's transportation costs, would see an even larger NPV and expand capacity. Increased competition would almost surely squeeze the spread. The U.S. company decided to calculate the *competitive* spread—the spread at which a European competitor would see polyzone capacity as zero NPV. Table 11.2 shows management's analysis. The resulting spread of $.95 per

[12]This is a true story, but names and details have been changed to protect the innocent.

TABLE 11.1

NPV calculation for proposed investment in polyzone production by a U.S. chemical company (figures in $ millions except as noted).

Note: For simplicity, we assume no inflation and no taxes. Plant and equipment have no salvage value after 10 years.
*Production capacity is 80 million pounds per year.
†Production costs are $.375 per pound after start-up ($.75 per pound in year 2, when production is only 40 million pounds).
‡Transportation costs are $.10 per pound to European ports.

	Year 0	Year 1	Year 2	Years 3–10
Investment	100			
Production, millions of pounds per year*	0	0	40	80
Spread, dollars per pound	1.20	1.20	1.20	1.20
Net revenues	0	0	48	96
Production costs†	0	0	30	30
Transport‡	0	0	4	8
Other costs	0	20	20	20
Cash flow	−100	−20	−6	+38
NPV (at r = 8%) = $63.6 million				

TABLE 11.2

What's the competitive spread to a European producer? About $.95 per pound of polyzone. Note that European producers face no transportation costs. Compare Table 11.1 (figures in $ millions except as noted).

	Year 0	Year 1	Year 2	Years 3–10
Investment	100			
Production, millions of pounds per year	0	0	40	80
Spread, dollars per pound	.95	.95	.95	.95
Net revenues	0	0	38	76
Production costs	0	0	30	30
Transport	0	0	0	0
Other costs	0	20	20	20
Cash flow	−100	−20	−12	+26
NPV (at r = 8%) = 0				

pound was the best *long-run* forecast for the polyzone market, other things constant of course.

How much of a head start did the U.S. producer have? How long before competitors forced the spread down to $.95? Management's best guess was five years. It prepared Table 11.3, which is identical to Table 11.1 except for the forecasted spread, which would shrink to $.95 by the start of year 5. Now the NPV was negative.

The project might have been saved if production could have been started in year 1 rather than 2 or if local markets could have been expanded, thus reducing transportation costs. But these changes were not feasible, so management canceled the project, albeit with a sigh of relief that its analysis hadn't stopped at Table 11.1.

This is a perfect example of the importance of thinking through sources of economic rents. Positive NPVs are suspect without some long-run competitive advantage. When a company contemplates investing in a new product or expanding production of an existing product, it should specifically identify its advantages or disadvantages over its most dangerous competitors. It should calculate NPV from

	Year					
	0	1	2	3	4	5–10
Investment	100					
Production, millions of pounds per year	0	0	40	80	80	80
Spread, dollars per pound	1.20	1.20	1.20	1.20	1.10	.95
Net revenues	0	0	48	96	88	76
Production costs	0	0	30	30	30	30
Transport	0	0	4	8	8	8
Other costs	0	20	20	20	20	20
Cash flow	−100	−20	−6	+38	+30	+18
NPV (at $r = 8\%$) = −$10.3						

TABLE 11.3

Recalculation of NPV for polyzone investment by U.S. company (figures in $ millions except as noted). If expansion by European producers forces competitive spreads by year 5, the U.S. producer's NPV falls to −$10.3 million. Compare Table 11.1.

those competitors' points of view. If competitors' NPVs come out strongly positive, the company had better expect decreasing prices (or spreads) and evaluate the proposed investment accordingly.

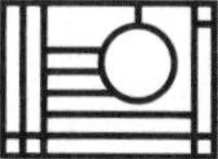

11.3 EXAMPLE—MARVIN ENTERPRISES DECIDES TO EXPLOIT A NEW TECHNOLOGY

To illustrate some of the problems involved in predicting economic rents, let us leap forward several years and look at the decision by Marvin Enterprises to exploit a new technology.[13]

One of the most unexpected developments of these years was the remarkable growth of a completely new industry. By 2023, annual sales of gargle blasters totaled $1.68 billion, or 240 million units. Although it controlled only 10 percent of the market, Marvin Enterprises was among the most exciting growth companies of the decade. Marvin had come late into the business, but it had pioneered the use of integrated microcircuits to control the genetic engineering processes used to manufacture gargle blasters. This development had enabled producers to cut the price of gargle blasters from $9 to $7 and had thereby contributed to the dramatic growth in the size of the market. The estimated demand curve in Figure 11.2 shows just how responsive demand is to such price reductions.

[13]We thank Stewart Hodges for permission to adapt this example from a case prepared by him, and we thank the BBC for permission to use the term *gargle blasters*.

FIGURE 11.2

The demand "curve" for gargle blasters shows that for each $1 cut in price there is an increase in demand of 80 million units.

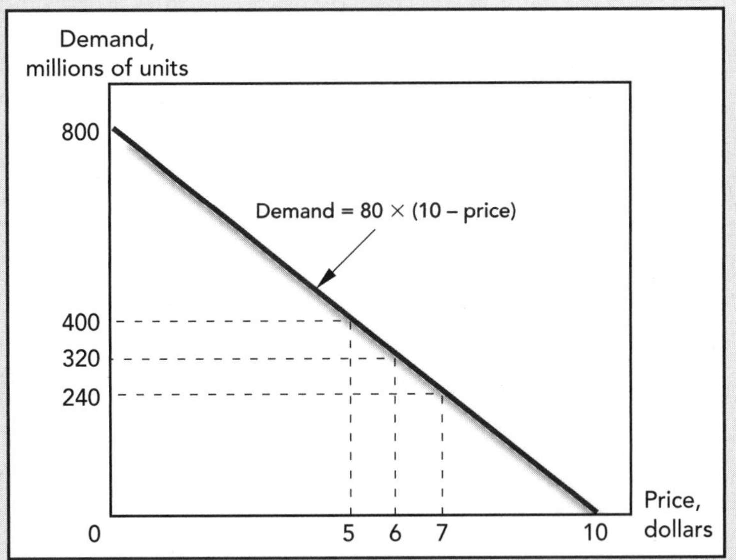

Table 11.4 summarizes the cost structure of the old and new technologies. While companies with the new technology were earning 20 percent on their initial investment, those with first-generation equipment had been hit by the successive price cuts. Since all Marvin's investment was in the 2019 technology, it had been particularly well placed during this period.

Rumors of new developments at Marvin had been circulating for some time, and the total market value of Marvin's stock had risen to $460 million by January 2024. At that point Marvin called a press conference to announce another technological breakthrough. Management claimed that its new third-generation process involving mutant neurons enabled the firm to reduce capital costs to $10 and manufacturing costs to $3 per unit. Marvin proposed to capitalize on this invention by embarking on a huge $1 billion expansion program that would add 100 million units to capacity. The company expected to be in full operation within 12 months.

Before deciding to go ahead with this development, Marvin had undertaken extensive calculations on the effect of the new investment. The basic assumptions were as follows:

1. The cost of capital was 20 percent.
2. The production facilities had an indefinite physical life.
3. The demand curve and the costs of each technology would not change.
4. There was no chance of a fourth-generation technology in the foreseeable future.
5. The corporate income tax, which had been abolished in 2014, was not likely to be reintroduced.

Marvin's competitors greeted the news with varying degrees of concern. There was general agreement that it would be five years before any of them would have access to the new technology. On the other hand, many consoled themselves with

Technology	Capacity, Millions of Units		Capital Cost per Unit ($)	Manufacturing Cost per Unit ($)	Salvage Value per Unit ($)
	Industry	Marvin			
First generation (2011)	120	—	17.50	5.50	2.50
Second generation (2019)	120	24	17.50	3.50	2.50

TABLE 11.4

Size and cost structure of the gargle blaster industry before Marvin announced its expansion plans.

Note: Selling price is $7 per unit. One unit means one gargle blaster.

the reflection that Marvin's new plant could not compete with an existing plant that had been fully depreciated.

Suppose that you were Marvin's financial manager. Would you have agreed with the decision to expand? Do you think it would have been better to go for a larger or smaller expansion? How do you think Marvin's announcement is likely to affect the price of its stock?

You have a choice. You can go on *immediately* to read *our* solution to these questions. But you will learn much more if you stop and work out your own answer first. Try it.

Forecasting Prices of Gargle Blasters

Up to this point in any capital budgeting problem we have always given you the set of cash-flow forecasts. In the present case you have to *derive* those forecasts.

The first problem is to decide what is going to happen to the price of gargle blasters. Marvin's new venture will increase industry capacity to 340 million units. From the demand curve in Figure 11.2, you can see that the industry can sell this number of gargle blasters only if the price declines to $5.75:

$$\begin{aligned}\text{Demand} &= 80 \times (10 - \text{price}) \\ &= 80 \times (10 - 5.75) = 340 \text{ million units}\end{aligned}$$

If the price falls to $5.75, what will happen to companies with the 2011 technology? They also have to make an investment decision: Should they stay in business, or should they sell their equipment for its salvage value of $2.50 per unit? With a 20 percent opportunity cost of capital, the NPV of staying in business is

$$\begin{aligned}\text{NPV} &= -\text{investment} + \text{PV}(\text{price} - \text{manufacturing cost}) \\ &= -2.50 + \frac{5.75 - 5.50}{.20} = -\$1.25 \text{ per unit}\end{aligned}$$

Smart companies with 2011 equipment will, therefore, see that it is better to sell off capacity. No matter what their equipment originally cost or how far it is depreciated, it is more profitable to sell the equipment for $2.50 per unit than to operate it and lose $1.25 per unit.

As capacity is sold off, the supply of gargle blasters will decline and the price will rise. An equilibrium is reached when the price gets to $6. At this point 2011 equipment has a zero NPV:

$$\text{NPV} = -2.50 + \frac{6.00 - 5.50}{.20} = \$0 \text{ per unit}$$

How much capacity will have to be sold off before the price reaches $6? You can check that by going back to the demand curve:

$$\begin{aligned} \text{Demand} &= 80 \times (10 - \text{price}) \\ &= 80 \times (10 - 6) = 320 \text{ million units} \end{aligned}$$

Therefore Marvin's expansion will cause the price to settle down at $6 a unit and will induce first-generation producers to withdraw 20 million units of capacity.

But after five years Marvin's competitors will also be in a position to build third-generation plants. As long as these plants have positive NPVs, companies will increase their capacity and force prices down once again. A new equilibrium will be reached when the price reaches $5. At this point, the NPV of new third-generation plants is zero, and there is no incentive for companies to expand further:

$$\text{NPV} = -10 + \frac{5.00 - 3.00}{.20} = \$0 \text{ per unit}$$

Looking back once more at our demand curve, you can see that with a price of $5 the industry can sell a total of 400 million gargle blasters:

$$\text{Demand} = 80 \times (10 - \text{price}) = 80 \times (10 - 5) = 400 \text{ million units}$$

The effect of the third-generation technology is, therefore, to cause industry sales to expand from 240 million units in 2023 to 400 million five years later. But that rapid growth is no protection against failure. By the end of five years any company that has only first-generation equipment will no longer be able to cover its manufacturing costs and will be *forced* out of business.

The Value of Marvin's New Expansion

We have shown that the introduction of third-generation technology is likely to cause gargle blaster prices to decline to $6 for the next five years and to $5 thereafter. We can now set down the expected cash flows from Marvin's new plant:

	Year 0 (Investment)	Years 1–5 (Revenue − Manufacturing Cost)	Year 6, 7, 8, . . . (Revenue − Manufacturing Cost)
Cash flow per unit ($)	−10	6 − 3 = 3	5 − 3 = 2
Cash flow, 100 million units ($ millions)	−1,000	600 − 300 = 300	500 − 300 = 200

Discounting these cash flows at 20 percent gives us

$$\text{NPV} = -1{,}000 + \sum_{t=1}^{5} \frac{300}{(1.20)^t} + \frac{1}{(1.20)^5}\left(\frac{200}{.20}\right) = \$299 \text{ million}$$

It looks as if Marvin's decision to go ahead was correct. But there is something we have forgotten. When we evaluate an investment, we must consider *all* incremental cash flows. One effect of Marvin's decision to expand is to reduce the value of its existing 2019 plant. If Marvin decided not to go ahead with the new technology, the \$7 price of gargle blasters would hold until Marvin's competitors started to cut prices in five years' time. Marvin's decision, therefore, leads to an immediate \$1 cut in price. This reduces the present value of its 2019 equipment by

$$24 \text{ million} \times \sum_{t=1}^{5} \frac{1.00}{(1.20)^t} = \$72 \text{ million}$$

Considered in isolation, Marvin's decision has an NPV of \$299 million. But it also reduces the value of existing plant by \$72 million. The net present value of Marvin's venture is, therefore, 299 − 72 = \$227 million.

Alternative Expansion Plans

Marvin's expansion has a positive NPV, but perhaps Marvin could do better to build a larger or smaller plant. You can check that by going through the same calculations as above. First you need to estimate how the additional capacity will affect gargle blaster prices. Then you can calculate the net present value of the new plant and the change in the present value of the existing plant. The total NPV of Marvin's expansion plan is

$$\text{Total NPV} = \text{NPV of new plant} + \text{change in PV of existing plant}$$

We have undertaken these calculations and plotted the results in Figure 11.3. You can see how total NPV would be affected by a smaller or larger expansion.

When the new technology becomes generally available in 2029, firms will construct a total of 280 million units of new capacity.[14] But Figure 11.3 shows that it would be foolish for Marvin to go that far. If Marvin added 280 million units of new capacity in 2024, the discounted value of the cash flows from the new plant would be zero *and* the company would have reduced the value of its old plant by \$144 million. To maximize NPV, Marvin should construct 200 million units of new capacity and set the price just below \$6 to drive out the 2011 manufacturers. Output is, therefore, less and price is higher than either would be under free competition.[15]

The Value of Marvin Stock

Let us think about the effect of Marvin's announcement on the value of its common stock. Marvin has 24 million units of second-generation capacity. In the absence of any

[14]Total industry capacity in 2029 will be 400 million units. Of this, 120 million units are second-generation capacity, and the remaining 280 million units are third-generation capacity.

[15]Notice that we are assuming that all customers have to pay the same price for their gargle blasters. If Marvin could charge each customer the maximum price which that customer would be willing to pay, output would be the same as under free competition. Such direct price discrimination is illegal and in any case difficult to enforce. But firms do search for indirect ways to differentiate between customers. For example, stores often offer free delivery which is equivalent to a price discount for customers who live at an inconvenient distance. Publishers differentiate their products by selling hardback copies to libraries and paperbacks to impecunious students. In the early years of electronic calculators, manufacturers put a high price on their product. Although buyers knew that the price would be reduced in a year or two, the convenience of having the machines for the extra time more than compensated for the additional outlay.

FIGURE 11.3

Effect on net present value of alternative expansion plans. Marvin's 100-million-unit expansion has a total NPV of $227 million (total NPV = NPV new plant + change in PV existing plant = 299 − 72 = 227). Total NPV is maximized if Marvin builds 200 million units of new capacity. If Marvin builds 280 million units of new capacity, total NPV is −$144 million.

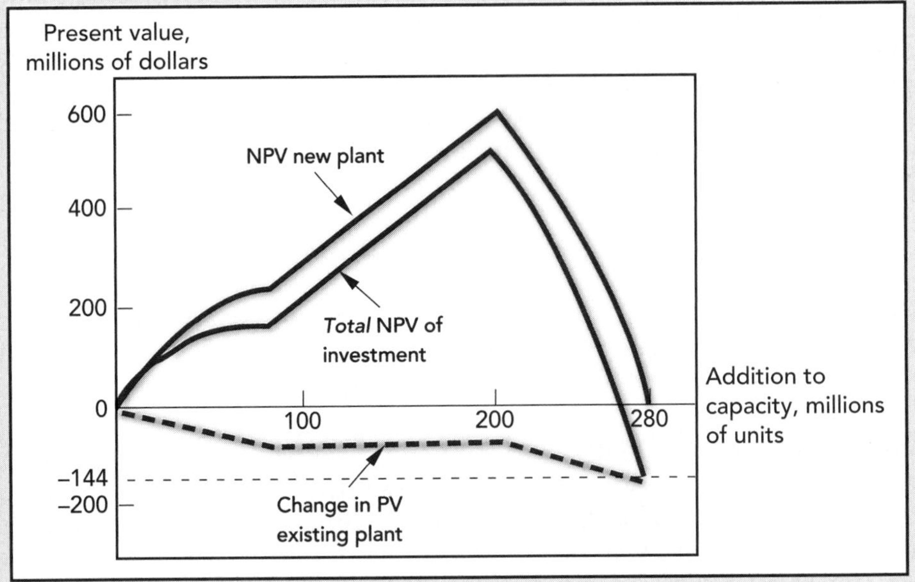

third-generation technology, gargle blaster prices would hold at $7 and Marvin's existing plant would be worth

$$\begin{aligned} PV &= 24 \text{ million} \times \frac{7.00 - 3.50}{.20} \\ &= \$420 \text{ million} \end{aligned}$$

Marvin's new technology reduces the price of gargle blasters initially to $6 and after five years to $5. Therefore the value of existing plant declines to

$$\begin{aligned} PV &= 24 \text{ million} \times \left[\sum_{t=1}^{5} \frac{6.00 - 3.50}{(1.20)^t} + \frac{5.00 - 3.50}{.20 \times (1.20)^5} \right] \\ &= \$252 \text{ million} \end{aligned}$$

But the *new* plant makes a net addition to shareholders' wealth of $299 million. So after Marvin's announcement its stock will be worth

$$252 + 299 = \$551 \text{ million}^{16}$$

Now here is an illustration of something we talked about in Chapter 4: Before the announcement, Marvin's stock was valued in the market at $460 million. The difference between this figure and the value of the existing plant represented the present value of Marvin's growth opportunities (PVGO). The market valued Mar-

[16]In order to finance the expansion, Marvin is going to have to sell $1,000 million of new stock. Therefore the *total* value of Marvin's stock will rise to $1,551 million. But investors who put up the new money will receive shares worth $1,000 million. The value of Marvin's old shares after the announcement is therefore $551 million.

vin's ability to stay ahead of the game at $40 million even before the announcement. After the announcement PVGO rose to $299 million.[17]

The Lessons of Marvin Enterprises

Marvin Enterprises may be just a piece of science fiction, but the problems that it confronts are very real. Whenever Intel considers developing a new microprocessor or Biogen considers developing a new drug, these firms must face up to exactly the same issues as Marvin. We have tried to illustrate the *kind* of questions that you should be asking when presented with a set of cash-flow forecasts. Of course, no economic model is going to predict the future with accuracy. Perhaps Marvin can hold the price above $6. Perhaps competitors will not appreciate the rich pickings to be had in the year 2029. In that case, Marvin's expansion would be even more profitable. But would you want to bet $1 billion on such possibilities? We don't think so.

Investments often turn out to earn far more than the cost of capital because of a favorable surprise. This surprise may in turn create a temporary opportunity for further investments earning more than the cost of capital. But anticipated and more prolonged rents will naturally lead to the entry of rival producers. That is why you should be suspicious of any investment proposal that predicts a stream of economic rents into the indefinite future. Try to estimate *when* competition will drive the NPV down to zero, and think what that implies for the price of your product.

Many companies try to identify the major growth areas in the economy and then concentrate their investment in these areas. But the sad fate of first-generation gargle blaster manufacturers illustrates how rapidly existing plants can be made obsolete by changes in technology. It is fun being in a growth industry when you are at the forefront of the new technology, but a growth industry has no mercy on technological laggards.

You can expect to earn economic rents only if you have some superior resource such as management, sales force, design team, or production facilities. Therefore, rather than trying to move into growth areas, you would do better to identify your firm's comparative advantages and try to capitalize on them. These issues came to the fore during the boom in New Economy stocks in the late 1990s. The optimists argued that the information revolution was opening up opportunities for companies to grow at unprecedented rates. The pessimists pointed out that competition in e-commerce was likely to be intense and that competition would ensure that the benefits of the information revolution would go largely to consumers. The Finance in the News box, which contains an extract from an article by Warren Buffett, emphasizes the point that rapid growth is no guarantee of superior profits.

We do not wish to imply that good investment opportunities don't exist. For example, such opportunities frequently arise because the firm has invested money in the past which gives it the option to expand cheaply in the future. Perhaps the firm can increase its output just by adding an extra production line, whereas its rivals would need to construct an entirely new factory. In such cases, you must take into account not only *whether* it is profitable to exercise your option, but also *when* it is best to do so.

Marvin also reminded us of project interactions, which we first discussed in Chapter 6. When you estimate the incremental cash flows from a project, you must remember to include the project's impact on the rest of the business. By introducing the new

[17]Notice that the market value of Marvin stock will be greater than $551 million if investors expect the company to expand again within the five-year period. In other words, PVGO after the expansion may still be positive. Investors may expect Marvin to stay one step ahead of its competitors or to successfully apply its special technology in other areas.

WARREN BUFFETT ON GROWTH AND PROFITABILITY

I thought it would be instructive to go back and look at a couple of industries that transformed this country much earlier in this century: automobiles and aviation. Take automobiles first: I have here one page, out of 70 in total, of car and truck manufacturers that have operated in this country. At one time, there was a Berkshire car and an Omaha car. Naturally I noticed those. But there was also a telephone book of others.

All told, there appear to have been at least 2,000 car makes, in an industry that had an incredible impact on people's lives. If you had foreseen in the early days of cars how this industry would develop, you would have said, "Here is the road to riches." So what did we progress to by the 1990s? After corporate carnage that never let up, we came down to three U.S. car companies—themselves no lollapaloozas for investors. So here is an industry that had an enormous impact on America—and also an enormous impact, though not the anticipated one, on investors. Sometimes, incidentally, it's much easier in these transforming events to figure out the losers. You could have grasped the importance of the auto when it came along but still found it hard to pick companies that would make you money. But there was one obvious decision you could have made back then—it's better sometimes to turn these things upside down—and that was to short horses. Frankly, I'm disappointed that the Buffett family was not short horses through this entire period. And we really had no excuse: Living in Nebraska, we would have found it super-easy to borrow horses and avoid a "short squeeze."

U.S. Horse Population

1900: 21 million

1998: 5 million

The other truly transforming business invention of the first quarter of the century, besides the car, was the airplane—another industry whose plainly brilliant future would have caused investors to salivate. So I went back to check out aircraft manufacturers and found that in the 1919–39 period, there were about 300 companies, only a handful still breathing today. Among the planes made then—we must have been the Silicon Valley of that age—were both the Nebraska and the Omaha, two aircraft that even the most loyal Nebraskan no longer relies upon.

Move on to failures of airlines. Here's a list of 129 airlines that in the past 20 years filed for bankruptcy. Continental was smart enough to make that list twice. As of 1992, in fact—though the picture would have improved since then—the money that had been made since the dawn of aviation by all of this country's airline companies was zero. Absolutely zero.

Sizing all this up, I like to think that if I'd been at Kitty Hawk in 1903 when Orville Wright took off, I would have been farsighted enough, and public-spirited enough—I owed this to future capitalists—to shoot him down. I mean, Karl Marx couldn't have done as much damage to capitalists as Orville did.

I won't dwell on other glamorous businesses that dramatically changed our lives but concurrently failed to deliver rewards to U.S. investors: the manufacture of radios and televisions, for example. But I will draw a lesson from these businesses: The key to investing is not assessing how much an industry is going to affect society, or how much it will grow, but rather determining the competitive advantage of any given company and, above all, the durability of that advantage. The products or services that have wide, sustainable moats around them are the ones that deliver rewards to investors.

Source: C. Loomis, "Mr. Buffett on the Stock Market," *Fortune* (November 22, 1999), pp. 110–115.

technology immediately, Marvin reduced the value of its existing plant by $72 million. Sometimes the losses on existing plants may completely offset the gains from a new technology. That is why we sometimes see established, technologically advanced companies deliberately slowing down the rate at which they introduce new products.

Notice that Marvin's economic rents were equal to the difference between its costs and those of the marginal producer. The costs of the marginal 2011-generation plant consisted of the manufacturing costs plus the opportunity cost of not selling the equipment. Therefore, if the salvage value of the 2011 equipment were higher, Marvin's competitors would incur higher costs and Marvin could earn higher rents. We took the salvage value as given, but it in turn depends on the cost savings from substituting outdated gargle blaster equipment for some other asset. In a well-functioning economy, assets will be used so as to minimize the *total* cost of producing the chosen set of outputs. The economic rents earned by any asset are equal to the total extra costs that would be incurred if that asset were withdrawn.

Here's another point about salvage value which takes us back to our discussion of Magna Charter in the last chapter: A high salvage value gives the firm an option to abandon a project if things start to go wrong. However, if competitors *know* that you can bail out easily, they are more likely to enter your market. If it is clear that you have no alternative but to stay and fight, they will be more cautious about competing.

When Marvin announced its expansion plans, many owners of first-generation equipment took comfort in the belief that Marvin could not compete with their fully depreciated plant. Their comfort was misplaced. Regardless of past depreciation policy, it paid to scrap first-generation equipment rather than keep it in production. Do not expect that numbers in your balance sheet can protect you from harsh economic reality.

SUMMARY

It helps to use present value when you are making investment decisions, but that is not the whole story. Good investment decisions depend both on a sensible criterion and on sensible forecasts. In this chapter we have looked at the problem of forecasting.

Projects may look attractive for two reasons: (1) There may be some errors in the sponsor's forecasts, and (2) the company can genuinely expect to earn excess profit from the project. Good managers, therefore, try to ensure that the odds are stacked in their favor by expanding in areas in which the company has a comparative advantage. We like to put this another way by saying that good managers try to identify projects that will generate economic rents. Good managers carefully avoid expansion when competitive advantages are absent and economic rents are unlikely. They do not project favorable current product prices into the future without checking whether entry or expansion by competitors will drive future prices down.

Our story of Marvin Enterprises illustrates the origin of rents and how they determine a project's cash flows and net present value.

Any present value calculation, including our calculation for Marvin Enterprises, is subject to error. That's life: There's no other sensible way to value most capital investment projects. But some assets, such as gold, real estate, crude oil, ships, and airplanes, and financial assets, such as stocks and bonds, are traded in reasonably competitive markets. When you have the market value of such an asset, *use it*, at least as a starting point for your analysis.

Visit us at www.mhhe.com/bm7e

FURTHER READING

For an interesting analysis of the likely effect of a new technology on the present value of existing assets, see:

S. P. Sobotka and C. Schnabel: "Linear Programming as a Device for Predicting Market Value: Prices of Used Commercial Aircraft, 1959–65," *Journal of Business,* 34:10–30 (January 1961).

QUIZ

1. You have inherited 250 acres of prime Iowa farmland. There is an active market in land of this type, and similar properties are selling for $1,000 per acre. Net cash returns per acre are $75 per year. These cash returns are expected to remain constant in real terms. How much is the land worth? A local banker has advised you to use a 12 percent discount rate.

2. True or false?

a. A firm that earns the opportunity cost of capital is earning economic rents.

b. A firm that invests in positive-NPV ventures expects to earn economic rents.

c. Financial managers should try to identify areas where their firms can earn economic rents, because it's there that positive-NPV projects are likely to be found.

d. Economic rent is the equivalent annual cost of operating capital equipment.

3. Demand for concave utility meters is expanding rapidly, but the industry is highly competitive. A utility meter plant costs $50 million to set up, and it has an annual capacity of 500,000 meters. The production cost is $5 per meter, and this cost is not expected to change. The machines have an indefinite physical life and the cost of capital is 10 percent. What is the competitive price of a utility meter?

a. $5 **b.** $10 **c.** $15

4. Look back to the polyzone example at the end of Section 11.2. Explain why it was necessary to calculate the NPV of investment in polyzone capacity from the point of view of a potential European competitor.

5. Your brother-in-law wants you to join him in purchasing a building on the outskirts of town. You and he would then develop and run a Taco Palace restaurant. Both of you are extremely optimistic about future real estate prices in this area, and your brother-in-law has prepared a cash-flow forecast that implies a large positive NPV. This calculation assumes sale of the property after 10 years.

What further calculations should you do before going ahead?

6. A new leaching process allows your company to recover some gold as a by-product of its aluminum mining operations. How would you calculate the PV of the future cash flows from gold sales?

7. On the London Metals Exchange the price for copper to be delivered in one year is $1,600 a ton. *Note:* Payment is made when the copper is delivered. The risk-free interest rate is 5 percent and the expected market return is 12 percent.

a. Suppose that you expect to produce and sell 100,000 tons of copper next year. What is the PV of this output? Assume that the sale occurs at the end of the year.

b. If copper has a beta of 1.2, what is the expected price of copper at the end of the year? What is the certainty-equivalent price?

8. New-model commercial airplanes are much more fuel-efficient than older models. How is it possible for airlines flying older models to make money when its competitors are flying newer planes? Explain briefly.

9. What are the lessons of Marvin Enterprises? Select from the following list. *Note:* Some of the following statements may be *partly* true, or true in some circumstances but not generally. Briefly explain your choices.

a. Companies should try to concentrate their investments in high-tech, high-growth sectors of the economy.

b. Think when your competition is likely to catch up, and what that will mean for product pricing and project cash flows.

c. Introduction of a new product may reduce the profits from an existing product but this project interaction should be ignored in calculating the new project's NPV.
d. In the long run, economic rents flow from some asset (usually intangible) or some advantage that your competitors do not have.
e. Do not attempt to enter a new market when your competitors can produce with fully depreciated plant.

PRACTICE QUESTIONS

1. Suppose that you are considering investing in an asset for which there is a reasonably good secondary market. Specifically, you're Delta Airlines, and the asset is a Boeing 757—a widely used airplane. How does the presence of a secondary market simplify your problem in principle? Do you think these simplifications could be realized in practice? Explain.
2. There is an active, competitive leasing (i.e., rental) market for most standard types of commercial jets. Many of the planes flown by the major domestic and international airlines are not owned by them but leased for periods ranging from a few months to several years.

   Gamma Airlines, however, owns two long-range DC-11s just withdrawn from Latin American service. Gamma is considering using these planes to develop the potentially lucrative new route from Akron to Yellowknife. A considerable investment in terminal facilities, training, and advertising will be required. Once committed, Gamma will have to operate the route for at least three years. One further complication: The manager of Gamma's international division is opposing commitment of the planes to the Akron–Yellowknife route because of anticipated future growth in traffic through Gamma's new hub in Ulan Bator.

   How would you evaluate the proposed Akron–Yellowknife project? Give a detailed list of the necessary steps in your analysis. Explain how the airplane leasing market would be taken into account. If the project is attractive, how would you respond to the manager of the international division?
3. Why is an M.B.A. student who has just learned about DCF like a baby with a hammer? What was the point of our answer?
4. Suppose the current price of gold is $280 per ounce. Hotshot Consultants advises you that gold prices will increase at an average rate of 12 percent for the next two years. After that the growth rate will fall to a long-run trend of 3 percent per year. What is the price of 1 million ounces of gold produced in eight years? Assume that gold prices have a beta of 0 and that the risk-free rate is 5.5 percent.
5. Thanks to acquisition of a key patent, your company now has exclusive production rights for barkelgassers (BGs) in North America. Production facilities for 200,000 BGs per year will require a $25 million immediate capital expenditure. Production costs are estimated at $65 per BG. The BG marketing manager is confident that all 200,000 units can be sold for $100 per unit (in real terms) until the patent runs out five years hence. After that the marketing manager hasn't a clue about what the selling price will be.

   What is the NPV of the BG project? Assume the real cost of capital is 9 percent. To keep things simple, also make the following assumptions:

   - The technology for making BGs will not change. Capital and production costs will stay the same in real terms.
   - Competitors know the technology and can enter as soon as the patent expires, that is, in year 6.
   - If your company invests immediately, full production begins after 12 months, that is, in year 1.
   - There are no taxes.
   - BG production facilities last 12 years. They have no salvage value at the end of their useful life.

6. How would your answer to question 5 change if:
   - Technological improvements reduce the cost of new BG production facilities by 3 percent per year?

   Thus a new plant built in year 1 would cost only 25 (1 − .03) = $24.25 million; a plant built in year 2 would cost $23.52 million; and so on. Assume that production costs per unit remain at $65.
7. Reevaluate the NPV of the proposed polyzone project under each of the following assumptions. Follow the format of Table 11.3. What's the right management decision in each case?
   a. Competitive entry does not begin until year 5, when the spread falls to $1.10 per pound, and is complete in year 6, when the spread is $.95 per pound.
   b. The U.S. chemical company can start up polyzone production at 40 million pounds in year 1 rather than year 2.
   c. The U.S. company makes a technological advance that reduces its annual production costs to $25 million. Competitors' production costs do not change.

8. Photographic laboratories recover and recycle the silver used in photographic film. Stikine River Photo is considering purchase of improved equipment for their laboratory at Telegraph Creek. Here is the information they have:
   - The equipment costs $100,000.
   - It will cost $80,000 per year to run.
   - It has an economic life of 10 years but can be depreciated over 5 years by the straight-line method (see Section 6.2).
   - It will recover an additional 5,000 ounces of silver per year.
   - Silver is selling for $20 per ounce. Over the past 10 years, the price of silver has appreciated by 4.5 percent per year in real terms. Silver is traded in an active, competitive market.
   - Stikine's marginal tax rate is 35 percent. Assume U.S. tax law.
   - Stikine's company cost of capital is 8 percent in real terms.

   What is the NPV of the new equipment? Make additional assumptions as necessary.
9. The Cambridge Opera Association has come up with a unique door prize for its December (2004) fund-raising ball: Twenty door prizes will be distributed, each one a ticket entitling the bearer to receive a cash award from the association on December 30, 2005. The cash award is to be determined by calculating the ratio of the level of the Standard and Poor's Composite Index of stock prices on December 30, 2005, to its level on June 30, 2005, and multiplying by $100. Thus, if the index turns out to be 1,000 on June 30, 2005, and 1,200 on December 30, 2005, the payoff will be 100 × (1,200/1,000) = $120.

   After the ball, a black market springs up in which the tickets are traded. What will the tickets sell for on January 1, 2005? On June 30, 2005? Assume the risk-free interest rate is 10 percent per year. Also assume the Cambridge Opera Association will be solvent at year-end 2005 and will, in fact, pay off on the tickets. Make other assumptions as necessary.

   Would ticket values be different if the tickets' payoffs depended on the Dow Jones Industrial index rather than the Standard and Poor's composite?

10. You are asked to value a large building in northern New Jersey. The valuation is needed for a bankruptcy settlement. Here are the facts:
    - The settlement *requires* that the building's value equal the PV value of the *net cash proceeds* the railroad would receive if it cleared the building and sold it for its highest and best nonrailroad use, which is as a warehouse.
    - The building has been appraised at $1 million. This figure is based on actual recent selling prices of a sample of similar New Jersey buildings used as, or available for use as, warehouses.

- If rented today as a warehouse, the building could generate $80,000 per year. This cash flow is calculated *after* out-of-pocket operating expenses and *after* real estate taxes of $50,000 per year:

Gross rents	$180,000
Operating expenses	50,000
Real estate taxes	50,000
Net	$80,000

Gross rents, operating expenses, and real estate taxes are uncertain but are expected to grow with inflation.

- However, it would take one year and $200,000 to clear out the railroad equipment and prepare the building for use as a warehouse. This expenditure would be spread evenly over the next year.
- The property will be put on the market when ready for use as a warehouse. Your real estate adviser says that properties of this type take, on average, 1 year to sell after they are put on the market. However, the railroad could rent the building as a warehouse while waiting for it to sell.
- The opportunity cost of capital for investment in real estate is 8 percent in *real* terms.
- Your real estate adviser notes that selling prices of comparable buildings in northern New Jersey have declined, in real terms, at an average rate of 2 percent per year over the last 10 years.
- A 5 percent sales commission would be paid by the railroad at the time of the sale.
- The railroad pays no income taxes. It would have to pay property taxes.

CHALLENGE QUESTIONS

1. The manufacture of polysyllabic acid is a competitive industry. Most plants have an annual output of 100,000 tons. Operating costs are $.90 a ton, and the sales price is $1 a ton. A 100,000-ton plant costs $100,000 and has an indefinite life. Its current scrap value of $60,000 is expected to decline to $57,900 over the next two years.

   Phlogiston, Inc., proposes to invest $100,000 in a plant that employs a new low-cost process to manufacture polysyllabic acid. The plant has the same capacity as existing units, but operating costs are $.85 a ton. Phlogiston estimates that it has two years' lead over each of its rivals in use of the process but is unable to build any more plants itself before year 2. Also it believes that demand over the next two years is likely to be sluggish and that its new plant will therefore cause temporary overcapacity.

   You can assume that there are no taxes and that the cost of capital is 10 percent.

   a. By the end of year 2, the prospective increase in acid demand will require the construction of several new plants using the Phlogiston process. What is the likely NPV of such plants?
   b. What does that imply for the price of polysyllabic acid in year 3 and beyond?
   c. Would you expect existing plant to be scrapped in year 2? How would your answer differ if scrap value were $40,000 or $80,000?
   d. The acid plants of United Alchemists, Inc., have been fully depreciated. Can it operate them profitably after year 2?
   e. Acidosis, Inc., purchased a new plant last year for $100,000 and is writing it down by $10,000 a year. Should it scrap this plant in year 2?
   f. What would be the NPV of Phlogiston's venture?

2. The world airline system is composed of the routes X and Y, each of which requires 10 aircraft. These routes can be serviced by three types of aircraft—A, B, and C. There are 5 type A aircraft available, 10 type B, and 10 type C. These aircraft are identical except for their operating costs, which are as follows:

Aircraft Type	Annual Operating Cost ($ millions)	
	Route X	Route Y
A	1.5	1.5
B	2.5	2.0
C	4.5	3.5

The aircraft have a useful life of five years and a salvage value of $1 million.

The aircraft owners do not operate the aircraft themselves but rent them to the operators. Owners act competitively to maximize their rental income, and operators attempt to minimize their operating costs. Airfares are also competitively determined.

Assume the cost of capital is 10 percent.

a. Which aircraft would be used on which route, and how much would each aircraft be worth?
b. What would happen to usage and prices of each aircraft if the number of type A aircraft increased to 10?
c. What would happen if the number of type A aircraft increased to 15?
d. What would happen if the number of type A aircraft increased to 20?

State any additional assumptions you need to make.

3. Taxes are a cost, and, therefore, changes in tax rates can affect consumer prices, project lives, and the value of existing firms. The following problem illustrates this. It also illustrates that tax changes that appear to be "good for business" do not always increase the value of existing firms. Indeed, unless new investment incentives increase consumer demand, they can work only by rendering existing equipment obsolete.

The manufacture of bucolic acid is a competitive business. Demand is steadily expanding, and new plants are constantly being opened. Expected cash flows from an investment in a new plant are as follows:

	0	1	2	3
1. Initial investment	100			
2. Revenues		100	100	100
3. Cash operating costs		50	50	50
4. Tax depreciation		33.33	33.33	33.33
5. Income pretax		16.67	16.67	16.67
6. Tax at 40%		6.67	6.67	6.67
7. Net income		10	10	10
8. After-tax salvage				15
9. Cash flow (7 + 8 + 4 − 1)	−100	+43.33	+43.33	+58.33
NPV at 20% = 0				

Assumptions:

1. Tax depreciation is straight-line over three years.
2. Pretax salvage value is 25 in year 3 and 50 if the asset is scrapped in year 2.
3. Tax on salvage value is 40 percent of the difference between salvage value and depreciated investment.
4. The cost of capital is 20 percent.

a. What is the value of a one-year-old plant? Of a two-year-old plant?
b. Suppose that the government now changes tax depreciation to allow a 100 percent writeoff in year 1. How does this affect the value of existing one- and two-year-old plants? Existing plants must continue using the original tax depreciation schedule.

c. Would it now make sense to scrap existing plants when they are two rather than three years old?
d. How would your answers change if the corporate income tax were abolished entirely?

MINI-CASE

Ecsy-Cola[18]

Libby Flannery, the regional manager of Ecsy-Cola, the international soft drinks empire, was reviewing her investment plans for Central Asia. She had contemplated launching Ecsy-Cola in the ex-Soviet republic of Inglistan in 2004. This would involve a capital outlay of $20 million in 2004 to build a bottling plant and set up a distribution system there. Fixed costs (for manufacturing, distribution, and marketing) would then be $3 million per year from 2003 onward. This would be sufficient to make and sell 200 million liters per year—enough for every man, woman, and child in Inglistan to drink four bottles per week! But there would be few savings from building a smaller plant, and import tariffs and transport costs in the region would keep all production within national borders.

The variable costs of production and distribution would be 12 cents per liter. Company policy requires a rate of return of 25 percent in nominal dollar terms, after local taxes but before deducting any costs of financing. The sales revenue is forecasted to be 35 cents per liter.

Bottling plants last almost forever, and all unit costs and revenues were expected to remain constant in nominal terms. Tax would be payable at a rate of 30 percent, and under the Inglistan corporate tax code, capital expenditures can be written off on a straight-line basis over four years.

All these inputs were reasonably clear. But Ms. Flannery racked her brain trying to forecast sales. Ecsy-Cola found that the "1-2-4" rule works in most new markets. Sales typically double in the second year, double again in the third year, and after that remain roughly constant. Libby's best guess was that, if she went ahead immediately, initial sales in Inglistan would be 12.5 million liters in 2005, ramping up to 50 million in 2007 and onward.

Ms. Flannery also worried whether it would be better to wait a year. The soft drink market was developing rapidly in neighboring countries, and in a year's time she should have a much better idea whether Ecsy-Cola would be likely to catch on in Inglistan. If it didn't catch on and sales stalled below 20 million liters, a large investment probably would not be justified.

Ms. Flannery had assumed that Ecsy-Cola's keen rival, Sparky-Cola, would not also enter the market. But last week she received a shock when in the lobby of the Kapitaliste Hotel she bumped into her opposite number at Sparky-Cola. Sparky-Cola would face costs similar to Ecsy-Cola. How would Sparky-Cola respond if Ecsy-Cola entered the market? Would it decide to enter also? If so, how would that affect the profitability of Ecsy-Cola's project?

Ms. Flannery thought again about postponing investment for a year. Suppose Sparky-Cola was interested in the Inglistan market. Would that favor delay or immediate action? Maybe Ecsy-Cola should announce its plans before Sparky-Cola had a chance to develop its own proposals. It seemed that the Inglistan project was becoming more complicated by the day.

Questions

1. Calculate the NPV of the proposed investment, using the inputs suggested in this case. How sensitive is this NPV to future sales volume?
2. What are the pros and cons of waiting for a year before deciding whether to invest? *Hint:* What happens if demand turns out high and Sparky-Cola also invests? What if Ecsy-Cola invests right away and gains a one-year head start on Sparky-Cola?

[18]We thank Anthony Neuberger for suggesting this topic.

CHAPTER TWELVE

MAKING SURE MANAGERS MAXIMIZE NPV

SO FAR WE'VE concentrated on criteria and procedures for identifying capital investments with positive NPVs. If a firm takes all (and only) positive-NPV projects, it maximizes the firm's value. But do the firm's managers *want* to maximize value?

Managers have no special gene or chromosome that automatically aligns their personal interests with outside investors' financial objectives. So how do shareholders ensure that top managers do not feather their own beds or grind their own axes? And how do top managers ensure that middle managers and employees try as hard as they can to find positive-NPV projects?

Here we circle back to the principal–agent problems first raised in Chapters 1 and 2. Shareholders are the ultimate principals; top managers are the stockholders' agents. But middle managers and employees are in turn agents of top management. Thus senior managers, including the chief financial officer, are simultaneously agents *vis-à-vis* shareholders and principals *vis-à-vis* the rest of the firm. The problem is to get everyone working together to maximize value.

This chapter summarizes how corporations grapple with that problem as they identify and commit to capital investment projects. We start with basic facts and tradeoffs and end with difficult problems in performance measurement. The main topics are as follows:

- **Process:** How companies develop plans and budgets for capital investments, how they authorize specific projects, and how they check whether projects perform as promised.
- **Information:** Getting accurate information and good forecasts to decision makers.
- **Incentives:** Making sure managers and employees are rewarded appropriately when they add value to the firm.
- **Performance Measurement:** You can't reward value added unless you can measure it. Since you get what you reward, and reward what you measure, you get what you measure. Make sure you are measuring the right thing.

In each case we will summarize standard practice and warn against common mistakes. The section on incentives probes more deeply into principal–agent relationships. The last two sections of the chapter describe performance measures, including residual income and economic value added. We also uncover the biases lurking in accounting rates of return. The pitfalls in measuring profitability are serious but are not as widely recognized as they should be.

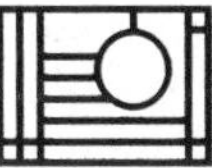

12.1 THE CAPITAL INVESTMENT PROCESS

For most large firms, the investment process starts with preparation of an annual **capital budget,** which is a list of investment projects planned for the coming year. Since the capital budget does not give the final go-ahead to spend money, the description of each project is not as detailed at this stage as it is later.

Most firms let project proposals bubble up from plants, product lines, or regional operations for review by divisional management and then from divisions for review by senior management and their planning staff. Of course middle managers cannot identify all worthwhile projects. For example, the managers of plants A and B cannot be expected to see the potential economies of closing their plants and consolidating production at a new plant C. Divisional managers would propose plant C. Similarly, divisions 1 and 2 may not be eager to give up their own computers to a corporationwide information system. That proposal would come from senior management.

Preparation of the capital budget is not a rigid, bureaucratic exercise. There is plenty of give-and-take and back-and-forth. Divisional managers negotiate with plant managers and fine-tune the division's list of projects. There may be special analyses of major outlays or ventures into new areas.

The final capital budget must also reflect the corporation's strategic planning. Strategic planning takes a top-down view of the company. It attempts to identify businesses in which the company has a competitive advantage. It also attempts to identify businesses to sell or liquidate and declining businesses that should be allowed to run down.

In other words, a firm's capital investment choices should reflect both bottom-up and top-down processes—capital budgeting and strategic planning, respectively. The two processes should complement each other. Plant and division managers, who do most of the work in bottom-up capital budgeting, may not see the forest for the trees. Strategic planners may have a mistaken view of the forest because they do not look at the trees one by one.

Project Authorizations

Once the capital budget has been approved by top management and the board of directors, it is the official plan for the ensuing year. However, it is not the final sign-off for specific projects. Most companies require **appropriation requests** for each proposal. These requests include detailed forecasts, discounted-cash-flow analyses, and backup information.

Because investment decisions are so important to the value of the firm, final approval of appropriation requests tends to be reserved for top management. Companies set ceilings on the size of projects that divisional managers can authorize. Often these ceilings are surprisingly low. For example, a large company, investing $400 million per year, might require top management approval of all projects over $500,000.

Some Investments May Not Show Up in the Capital Budget

The boundaries of capital expenditure are often imprecise. Consider the investments in information technology, or IT (computers, software and systems, training, and telecommunications), made by large banks and securities firms. These investments soak up *hundreds* of millions of dollars annually, and some multiyear IT projects have costs well over $1 billion. Yet much of this expenditure goes to intangibles such as system design, testing, or training. Such outlays often bypass capital expenditure controls, particularly if the outlays are made piecemeal rather than as large, discrete commitments.

Investments in IT may not appear in the capital budget, but for financial institutions they are much more important than outlays for plant and equipment. An efficient information system is a valuable asset for any company, especially if it allows the company to offer a special product or service to its customers. Therefore outlays for IT deserve careful financial analysis.

Here are some further examples of important investments that rarely appear on the capital budget.

Research and Development For many companies, the most important asset is technology. The technology is embodied in patents, licenses, unique products or services, or special production methods. The technology is generated by investment in research and development (R&D).

R&D budgets for major pharmaceutical companies routinely exceed $1 billion. Glaxo Smith Kline, one of the largest pharmaceutical companies, spent nearly $4 billion on R&D in 2000. The R&D cost of bringing *one* new prescription drug to market has been estimated at over $300 million.[1]

Marketing In 1998 Gillette launched the Mach3 safety razor. It had invested $750 million in new, custom machinery and renovated production facilities. It planned to spend $300 million on the initial marketing program. Its goal was to make the Mach3 a long-lived, brand-name, cash-cow consumer product. This marketing outlay was clearly a capital investment, because it was cash spent to generate future cash inflows.

Training and Personnel Development By launch of the Mach3, Gillette had hired 160 new workers and paid for 30,000 hours of training.

Small Decisions Add Up Operating managers make investment decisions every day. They may carry extra inventories of raw materials or spare parts, just to be sure they won't be caught short. Managers at the confabulator plant in Quayle City, Arkansas, may decide they need one more forklift or a cappuccino machine for the cafeteria. They may hold on to an idle machine tool or an empty warehouse that could have been sold. These are not big investments ($5,000 here, $40,000 there) but they add up.

How can the financial manager assure that small investments are made for the right reasons? Financial staff can't second-guess every operating decision. They can't demand a discounted-cash-flow analysis of a cappuccino machine. Instead they have to make operating managers conscious of the cost of investment and alert for investments that add value. We return to this problem later in the chapter.

Our general point is this: The financial manager has to consider all investments, regardless of whether they appear in the formal capital budget. The financial manager has to decide which investments are most important to the success of the company and where financial analysis is most likely to pay off. The financial manager in a pharmaceutical company should be deeply involved in decisions about R&D. In a consumer goods company, the financial manager should play a key role in marketing decisions to develop and launch new products.

Postaudits

Most firms keep a check on the progress of large projects by conducting postaudits shortly after the projects have begun to operate. Postaudits identify problems that need fixing, check the accuracy of forecasts, and suggest questions that should have been asked before the project was undertaken. Postaudits pay off mainly by helping managers to do a better job when it comes to the next round of investments. After a postaudit the controller may say, "We should have anticipated the extra working capital needed to support the project." When the next proposal arrives, working capital will get the attention it deserves.

Postaudits may not be able to measure all cash flows generated by a project. It may be impossible to split the project away from the rest of the business. Suppose

[1]This figure is for drugs developed in the late 1980s and early 1990s. It is after-tax, stated in 1994 dollars. The comparable pretax figure is over $400 million. See S. C. Myers and C. D. Howe, *A Life-Cycle Model of Pharmaceutical R&D,* MIT Program on the Pharmaceutical Industry, 1997.

that you have just taken over a trucking firm that operates a merchandise delivery service for local stores. You decide to revitalize the business by cutting costs and improving service. This requires three investments:

1. Buying five new diesel trucks.
2. Constructing a dispatching center.
3. Buying a computer and special software to keep track of packages and schedule trucks.

A year later you try a postaudit of the computer. You verify that it is working properly and check actual costs of purchase, installation, and training against projections. But how do you identify the incremental cash inflows generated by the computer? No one has kept records of the extra diesel fuel that *would have been* used or the extra shipments that *would have been* lost had the computer not been installed. You may be able to verify that service is better, but how much of the improvement comes from the new trucks, how much comes from the dispatching center, and how much comes from the new computer? It is impossible to say. The only meaningful way to judge the success or failure of your revitalization program is to examine the delivery business as a whole.[2]

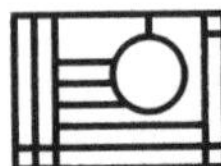

12.2 DECISION MAKERS NEED GOOD INFORMATION

Good investment decisions require good information. Decision makers get such information only if other managers are encouraged to supply it. Here are four information problems that financial managers need to think about.

Establishing Consistent Forecasts

Inconsistent assumptions often creep into investment proposals. Suppose the manager of your furniture division is bullish on housing starts but the manager of your appliance division is bearish. This inconsistency makes the furniture division's projects look better than the appliance division's. Senior management ought to negotiate a consensus estimate and make sure that all NPVs are recomputed using that joint estimate. Then projects can be evaluated consistently.

This is why many firms begin the capital budgeting process by establishing forecasts of economic indicators, such as inflation and growth in gross national product, as well as forecasts of particular items that are important to the firm's business, such as housing starts or the price of raw materials. These forecasts can then be used as the basis for all project analyses.

Reducing Forecast Bias

Anyone who is keen to get a project accepted is likely to look on the bright side when forecasting the project's cash flows. Such overoptimism seems to be a common feature in financial forecasts. Overoptimism afflicts governments too, probably more than private businesses. How often have you heard of a new dam, highway, or military aircraft that actually cost *less* than was originally forecasted?

[2]Even here you don't know the incremental cash flows unless you can establish what the business would have earned if you had not made the changes.

You will probably never be able to eliminate bias completely, but if you are aware of why bias occurs, you are at least part of the way there. Project sponsors are likely to overstate their case deliberately only if you, the manager, encourage them to do so. For example, if they believe that success depends on having the largest division rather than the most profitable one, they will propose large expansion projects that they do not truly believe have positive NPVs. Or if they believe that you won't listen to them unless they paint a rosy picture, you will be presented with rosy pictures. Or if you invite each division to compete for limited resources, you will find that each attempts to outbid the other for those resources. The fault in such cases is your own—if you hold up the hoop, others will try to jump through it.

Getting Senior Management the Information That It Needs

Valuing capital investment opportunities is hard enough when you can do the entire job yourself. In real life it is a cooperative effort. Although cooperation brings more knowledge to bear, it has its own problems. Some are unavoidable, just another cost of doing business. Others can be alleviated by adding checks and balances to the investment process.

Many of the problems stem from sponsors' eagerness to obtain approval for their favorite projects. As a proposal travels up the organization, alliances are formed. Preparation of the request inevitably involves compromises. But, once a division has agreed on its plants' proposals, the plants unite in competing against outsiders.

The competition among divisions can be put to good use if it forces division managers to develop a well-thought-out case for what they want to do. But the competition has its costs as well. Several thousand appropriation requests may reach the senior management level each year, all essentially sales documents presented by united fronts and designed to persuade. Alternative schemes have been filtered out at an earlier stage. The danger is that senior management cannot obtain (let alone absorb) the information to evaluate each project rationally.

The dangers are illustrated by the following practical question: Should we announce a definite opportunity cost of capital for computing the NPV of projects in our furniture division? The answer in theory is a clear yes, providing that the projects of the division are all in the same risk class. Remember that most project analysis is done at the plant or divisional level. Only a small proportion of project ideas analyzed survive for submission to top management. Plant and division managers cannot judge projects correctly unless they know the true opportunity cost of capital.

Suppose that senior management settles on 12 percent. That helps plant managers make rational decisions. But it also tells them exactly how optimistic they have to be to get their pet project accepted. Brealey and Myers's Second Law states: *The proportion of proposed projects having a positive NPV at the official corporate hurdle rate is independent of the hurdle rate.*[3]

This is not a facetious conjecture. The law was tested in a large oil company, whose capital budgeting staff kept careful statistics on forecasted profitability of proposed projects. One year top management announced a big push to conserve cash. It imposed discipline on capital expenditures by increasing the corporate hurdle rate by several percentage points. But staff statistics showed that the fraction of proposals

[3]There is no First Law; we thought that "Second Law" sounded better. There *is* a Third Law, but that is for another chapter.

with positive NPVs stayed rock-steady at about 85 percent of all proposals. Top management's tighter discipline was repaid with expanded optimism.

A firm that accepts poor information at the top faces two consequences. First, senior management cannot evaluate individual projects. In a study by Bower of a large multidivisional company, projects that had the approval of a division general manager were seldom turned down by his or her group of divisions, and those reaching top management were almost never rejected.[4] Second, since managers have limited control over project-by-project decisions, capital investment decisions are effectively decentralized regardless of what formal procedures specify.

Some senior managers try to impose discipline and offset optimism by setting rigid capital expenditure limits. This artificial capital rationing forces plant or division managers to set priorities. The firm ends up using capital rationing not because capital is truly unobtainable but as a way of decentralizing decisions.

Eliminating Conflicts of Interest

Plant and divisional managers are concerned about their own futures. Sometimes their interests conflict with stockholders' and that may lead to investment decisions that do not maximize shareholder wealth. For example, new plant managers naturally want to demonstrate good performance right away, in order to move up the corporate ladder, so they are tempted to propose quick-payback projects even if NPV is sacrificed. And if their performance is judged on book earnings, they will also be attracted by projects whose accounting results look good. That leads us to the next topic: how to motivate managers.

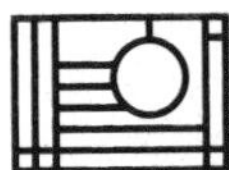

12.3 INCENTIVES

Managers will act in shareholders' interests only if they have the right incentives. Good capital investment decisions therefore depend on how managers' performance is measured and rewarded.

We start this section with an overview of agency problems encountered in capital investment, and then we look at how top management is actually compensated. Finally we consider how top management can set incentives for the middle managers and other employees who actually operate the business.

Overview: Agency Problems in Capital Budgeting

As you have surely guessed, there is no perfect system of incentives. But it's easy to see what *won't* work. Suppose shareholders decide to pay the financial managers a fixed salary—no bonuses, no stock options, just $X per month. The manager, as the stockholders' agent, is instructed to find and invest in all positive-NPV projects open to the firm. The manager may sincerely try to do so, but will face various tempting alternatives:

> **Reduced effort.** Finding and implementing investment in truly valuable projects is a high-effort, high-pressure activity. The financial manager will be tempted to slack off.

[4] J. L. Bower, *Managing the Resource Allocation Process: A Study of Corporate Planning and Investment*, Division of Research, Graduate School of Business Administration, Harvard University, Boston, 1970.

Perks. Our hypothetical financial manager gets no bonuses. Only $X per month. But he or she may take a bonus anyway, not in cash, but in tickets to sporting events, lavish office accommodations, planning meetings scheduled at luxury resorts, and so on. Economists refer to these nonpecuniary rewards as *private benefits.* Ordinary people call them *perks* (short for perquisites.)

Empire building. Other things equal, managers prefer to run large businesses rather than small ones. Getting from small to large may not be a positive-NPV undertaking.

Entrenching investment. Suppose manager Q considers two expansion plans. One plan will require a manager with special skills that manager Q just happens to have. The other plan requires only a general-purpose manager. Guess which plan Q will favor. Projects designed to require or reward the skills of existing managers are called *entrenching investments.*[5]

Entrenching investments and empire building are typical symptoms of overinvestment, that is, investing beyond the point where NPV falls to zero. The temptation to overinvest is highest when the firm has plenty of cash but limited investment opportunities. Michael Jensen calls this a *free-cash-flow* problem: "The problem is how to motivate managers to disgorge the cash rather than investing it below the cost of capital or wasting it in organizational inefficiencies."[6]

Avoiding risk. If a financial manager receives only a fixed salary, and cannot share in the upside of risky projects, then safe projects are, from the manager's viewpoint, better than risky ones. But risky projects can have large, positive NPVs.

A manager on a fixed salary could hardly avoid all these temptations all of the time. The resulting loss in value is an agency cost.

Monitoring

Agency costs can be reduced in two ways: by *monitoring* the managers' effort and actions and by giving them the right *incentives* to maximize value.

Monitoring can prevent the more obvious agency costs, such as blatant perks or empire building. It can confirm that the manager is putting sufficient time on the job. But monitoring costs time, effort, and money. Some monitoring is almost always worthwhile, but a limit is soon reached at which an extra dollar spent on monitoring would not return an extra dollar of value from reduced agency costs. Like all investments, monitoring encounters diminishing returns.

Some agency costs can't be prevented even with spendthrift monitoring. Suppose a shareholder undertakes to monitor capital investment decisions. How could he or she ever know for sure whether a capital budget approved by top management includes (1) *all* the positive-NPV opportunities open to the firm and (2) *no* projects with negative NPVs due to empire-building or entrenching investments? The managers obviously know more about the firm's prospects than outsiders ever can. If the shareholder could list all projects and their NPVs, then the managers would hardly be needed!

---

[5]A. Shleifer and R. W. Vishny, "Management Entrenchment: The Case of Manager-Specific Investments," *Journal of Financial Economics* 25 (November 1989), pp. 123–140.

[6]M. C. Jensen, "Agency Costs of Free Cash Flow, Corporate Finance and Takeovers," *American Economic Review* 76 (May 1986), p. 323.

Who actually does the monitoring? Ultimately it is the shareholders' responsibility, but in large, public companies, monitoring is *delegated* to the board of directors, who are elected by shareholders and are supposed to represent their interests. The board meets regularly, both formally and informally, with top management. Attentive directors come to know a great deal about the firm's prospects and performance and the strengths and weaknesses of its top management.

The board also hires independent accountants to audit the firm's financial statements. If the audit uncovers no problems, the auditors issue an opinion that the financial statements fairly represent the company's financial condition and are consistent with generally accepted accounting principles (GAAP, for short).

If problems are found, the auditors will negotiate changes in assumptions or procedures. Managers almost always agree, because if acceptable changes are not made, the auditors will issue a *qualified opinion,* which is bad news for the company and its shareholders. A qualified opinion suggests that managers are covering something up and undermines investors' confidence that they can monitor effectively.

A qualified opinion may be bad news, but when investors learn of accounting problems that have escaped detection by auditors, there's hell to pay. On April 15, 1998, Cendant Corporation announced discovery of serious accounting irregularities. The next day Cendant shares fell by about 46 percent, wiping $14 billion off the market value of the company.[7]

Lenders also monitor. If a company takes out a large bank loan, the bank will track the company's assets, earnings, and cash flow. By monitoring to protect its loan, the bank protects shareholders' interests also.[8]

Delegated monitoring is especially important when ownership is widely dispersed. If there is a dominant shareholder, he or she will generally keep a close eye on top management. But when the number of stockholders is large, and each stockholding is small, individual investors cannot justify much time and expense for monitoring. Each is tempted to leave the task to others, taking a free ride on others' efforts. But if everybody prefers to let somebody else do it, then it won't get done; that is, monitoring by shareholders will not be strong or effective. Economists call this the *free-rider problem.*[9]

Compensation

Because monitoring is necessarily imperfect, compensation plans must be designed to give managers the right incentives.

[7]Cendant was formed in 1997 by the merger of HFS, Inc., and CUC International, Inc. It appears that about $500 million of CUC revenue from 1995 to 1997 was just made up and that about 60 percent of CUC's income in 1997 was fake. By August 1998, several CUC managers were fired or had resigned, including Cendant's chairman, the founder of CUC. Over 70 lawsuits had been filed on behalf of investors in the company. Investigations were continuing. See E. Nelson and J. S. Lubin. "Buy the Numbers? How Whistle-Blowers Set Off a Fraud Probe That Crushed Cendant," *The Wall Street Journal* (August 13, 1998), pp. A1, A8.

[8]Lenders' and shareholders' interests are not always aligned—see Chapter 18. But a company's ability to satisfy lenders is normally good news for stockholders, particularly when lenders are well placed to monitor. See C. James "Some Evidence on the Uniqueness of Bank Loans," *Journal of Financial Economics* 19 (December 1987), pp. 217–235.

[9]The free-rider problem might seem to drive out all monitoring by dispersed shareholders. But investors have another reason to investigate: They want to make money on their common stock portfolios by buying undervalued companies and selling overvalued ones. To do this they must investigate companies' performance.

Compensation can be based on input (for example, the manager's effort or demonstrated willingness to bear risk) or on output (actual return or value added as a result of the manager's decisions). But input is so difficult to measure; for example, how does an outside investor observe effort? Therefore incentives are almost always based on output. The trouble is that output depends not just on the manager's decisions but also on many other events outside his or her control.

The fortunes of a business never depend only on the efforts of a few key individuals. The state of the economy or the industry is usually at least as important for the firm's success. Unless you can separate out these influences, you face a dilemma. You want to provide managers with a high-powered incentive, so that they capture all the benefits of their contributions to the firm, but such an arrangement would load onto the managers all the risk of fluctuations in the firm's value. Think of what this would mean in the case of GE, where in a recession income can fall by more than $1 billion. No group of managers would have the wealth to stump up a significant fraction of $1 billion, and they would certainly be reluctant to take on the risk of huge personal losses in a recession. A recession is not their fault.

The result is a compromise. Firms do link managers' pay to performance, but fluctuations in firm value are shared by managers and shareholders. Managers bear some of the risks that are outside their control and shareholders bear some of the agency costs if managers shirk, empire build, or otherwise fail to maximize value. Thus, some agency costs are inevitable. For example, since managers split the gains from hard work with the stockholders but reap all the personal benefits of an idle or indulgent life, they will be tempted to put in less effort than if shareholders could reward their effort perfectly.

If the firm's fortunes are largely outside managers' control, it makes sense to offer the managers low-powered incentives. In such cases the managers' compensation should be largely in the form of a fixed salary. If success depends almost exclusively on individual skill and effort, then managers are given high-powered incentives and end up bearing substantial risks. For example, a large part of the compensation of traders and salespeople in securities firms is in the form of bonuses or stock options.

How do managers of large corporations share in the fortunes of their firms? Michael Jensen and Kevin Murphy found that the median holding of chief executive officers (CEOs) in their firms was only .14 percent of the outstanding shares. On average, for every $1,000 addition to shareholder wealth, the CEO received $3.25 in extra compensation. Jensen and Murphy conclude that "corporate America pays its most important leaders like bureaucrats," and ask "Is it any wonder then that so many CEOs act like bureaucrats rather than the value-maximizing entrepreneurs companies need to enhance their standing in world markets?"[10]

Jensen and Murphy may overstate their case. It is true that managers bear only a small portion of the gains and losses in firm value. However, the payoff to the manager of a large, successful firm can still be very large. For example, when

[10]M. C. Jensen and K. Murphy, "CEO Incentives—It's Not How Much You Pay, But How," *Harvard Business Review* 68 (May–June 1990), p. 138. The data for Jensen and Murphy's study ended in 1983. Hall and Liebman have updated the study and argue that the sensitivity of compensation to changes in firm value has increased significantly. See B. J. Hall and J. B. Liebman, "Are CEOs Really Paid Like Bureaucrats?" Harvard University working paper, August 1997.

Michael Eisner was hired as CEO by the Walt Disney Company, his compensation package had three main components: a base annual salary of $750,000; an annual bonus of 2 percent of Disney's net income above a threshold of normal profitability; and a 10-year option that allowed him to purchase 2 million shares of stock for $14 a share, which was about the price of Disney stock at the time. As it turned out, by the end of Eisner's six-year contract the value of Disney shares had increased by $12 billion, more than sixfold. While Eisner received only 1.6 percent of that gain in value as compensation, this still amounted to $190 million.[11]

Because most CEOs own stock and stock options in their firms, managers of poorly performing firms often actually lose money; they also often lose their jobs. For example, a study of the remuneration of the chief executives of large U.S. firms found that the heads of firms that were in the top 10 percent in terms of stock market performance received over $9 million more in compensation than their brethren at the bottom 10 percent of the spectrum.[12]

Chief executives in the United States are generally paid more than those in other countries and their pay is more closely tied to stock returns. For example, Kaplan found that top managers in the United States earn salary plus bonus five times that of their Japanese counterparts, although Japanese managers receive more noncash compensation. The United States managers' stakes in their companies averaged more than double the Japanese managers' stakes.[13]

In the ideal incentive scheme, management should bear all the consequences of their own actions, but should not be exposed to the fluctuations in firm value over which they have no control. That raises a question: Managers are not responsible for fluctuations in the general level of the stock market. So why don't companies tie top management's compensation to stock returns relative to the market or to the firm's close competitors? This would tie managers' compensation somewhat more closely to their own contributions.

Tying top management compensation to stock prices raises another difficult issue. The market value of a company's shares reflects investors' expectations. The stockholders' return depends on how well the company performs relative to expectations. For example, suppose a company announces the appointment of an outstanding new manager. The stock price leaps up in anticipation of improved performance. Thenceforth, if the new manager delivers exactly the good performance that investors expected, the stock will earn only a normal, average rate of return. In this case a compensation scheme linked to the stock return would fail to recognize the manager's special contribution.

---

[11]We don't know whether Michael Eisner's contribution to the firm over the six-year period was more or less than $190 million. However, one of the benefits of paying such a large sum to the CEO is that it provides a wonderful incentive for junior managers to compete for the prize. In effect the firm runs a *tournament*, in which there is a large prize for the winner and considerably smaller prizes for runners-up. The incentive effects of tournaments show up dramatically in PGA golf tournaments. Players who enter the final round within striking distance of big prize money perform much better than their past records would predict. Those who receive only a small increase in prize money by moving up the ranking are more inclined to relax and deliver only average performance. See R. G. Ehrenberg and M. L. Bognanno, "Do Tournaments Have Incentive Effects?" *Journal of Political Economy* 6 (December 1990), pp. 1307–1324.

[12]See B. J. Hall and J. B. Liebman, op. cit.

[13]S. Kaplan, "Top Executive Rewards and Firm Performance: A Comparison of Japan and the USA," *Journal of Political Economy* 102 (June 1994), pp. 510–546.

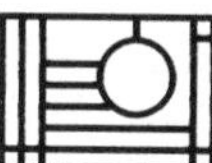

12.4 MEASURING AND REWARDING PERFORMANCE: RESIDUAL INCOME AND EVA

Almost all top executives of firms with publicly traded shares have compensation packages that depend in part on their firms' stock price performance. But their compensation also depends on increases in earnings or on other accounting measures of performance. For lower-level managers, compensation packages usually depend more on accounting measures and less on stock returns.

Accounting measures of performance have two advantages:

- They are based on absolute performance, rather than on performance relative to investors' expectations.
- They make it possible to measure the performance of junior managers whose responsibility extends to only a single division or plant.

Tying compensation to accounting profits also creates some obvious problems. First, accounting profits are partly within the control of management. For example, managers whose pay depends on near-term earnings may cut maintenance or staff training. This is not a recipe for adding value, but an ambitious manager hoping for a quick promotion will be tempted to pump up short-term profits, leaving longer-run problems to his or her successors.

Second, accounting earnings and rates of return can be severely biased measures of true profitability. We ignore this problem for now, but return to it in the next section.

Third, growth in earnings does not necessarily mean that shareholders are better off. Any investment with a positive rate of return (1 or 2 percent will do) will eventually increase earnings. Therefore, if managers are told to maximize growth in earnings, they will dutifully invest in projects offering 1 or 2 percent rates of return—projects that destroy value. But shareholders don't want growth in earnings for its own sake, and they are not content with 1 or 2 percent returns. They want positive-NPV investments, and *only* positive-NPV investments. They want the company to invest only if the expected rate of return exceeds the cost of capital.

In short, managers ought not to forget the cost of capital. In judging their performance, the focus should be on value added, that is, on returns over and above the cost of capital.

Look at Table 12.1, which contains a simplified income statement and balance sheet for your company's Quayle City confabulator plant. There are two methods for judging whether the plant has increased shareholder value.

Net Return on Investment Does the return on investment exceed the cost of capital? The net return to investment method calculates the difference between them.

As you can see from Table 12.1, your corporation has invested $1,000 million ($1 billion) in the Quayle City plant.[14] The plant's net earnings are $130 million. Therefore the firm is earning a return on investment (ROI) of 130/1,000 = .13 or

[14]In practice, investment would be measured as the average of beginning- and end-of-year assets. See Chapter 29.

TABLE 12.1

Simplified statements of income and assets for the Quayle City confabulator plant (figures in $ millions).

Income		Assets	
Sales	$550	Net working capital†	$80
Cost of goods sold*	275	Property, plant, and equipment investment	1,170
Selling, general, and administrative expenses	75	*Less* cumulative depreciation	360
	200	Net investment	810
Taxes at 35%	70	Other assets	110
Net income	$130	Total assets	$1,000

*Includes depreciation expense.
†Current assets less current liabilities.

13 percent.[15] If the cost of capital is (say) 10 percent, then the firm's activities are adding to shareholder value. The *net* return is 13 − 10 = 3 percent. If the cost of capital is (say) 20 percent, then shareholders would have been better off investing $1 billion somewhere else. In this case the net return is negative, at 13 − 20 = −7 percent.

Residual Income or Economic Value Added (EVA ©)[16] The second method calculates a net dollar return to shareholders. It asks, What are earnings after deducting a charge for the cost of capital?

When firms calculate income, they start with revenues and then deduct costs, such as wages, raw material costs, overhead, and taxes. But there is one cost that they do not commonly deduct: the cost of capital. True, they allow for depreciation of the assets financed by investors' capital, but investors also expect a positive return on their investment. As we pointed out in Chapter 10, a business that breaks even in terms of accounting profits is really making a loss; it is failing to cover the cost of capital.

To judge the net contribution to value, we need to deduct the cost of capital contributed to the plant by the parent company and its stockholders. For example, suppose that the cost of capital is 12 percent. Then the dollar cost of capital for the Quayle City plant is .12 × $1,000 = $120 million. The net gain is therefore 130 − 120 = $10 million. This is the addition to shareholder wealth due to management's hard work (or good luck).

Net income after deducting the dollar return required by investors is called *residual income, economic value added,* or *EVA.* The formula is

$$\begin{aligned}\text{EVA} &= \text{residual income} = \text{income earned} - \text{income required}\\ &= \text{income earned} - \text{cost of capital} \times \text{investment}\end{aligned}$$

For our example, the calculation is

$$\text{EVA} = \text{residual income} = 130 - (.12 \times 1{,}000) = +\$10 \text{ million}$$

[15]Notice that earnings are calculated after tax but with no deductions for interest paid. The plant is evaluated as if it were all-equity financed. This is standard practice (see Chapter 6). It helps to separate investment and financing decisions. The tax advantages of debt financing supported by the plant are picked up not in the plant's earnings or cash flows but in the discount rate. The cost of capital is the after-tax weighted average cost of capital, or WACC. WACC is explained in Chapter 19.

[16]EVA is the term used by the consulting firm Stern–Stewart, which has done much to popularize and implement this measure of residual income. With Stern–Stewart's permission, we omit the copyright symbol in what follows.

But if the cost of capital were 20 percent, EVA would be negative by $70 million.

Net return on investment and EVA are focusing on the same question. When return on investment equals the cost of capital, net return and EVA are both zero. But the net return is a percentage and ignores the scale of the company. EVA recognizes the amount of capital employed and the number of dollars of additional wealth created.

A growing number of firms now calculate EVA and tie management compensation to it.[17] They believe that a focus on EVA can help managers concentrate on increasing shareholder wealth. One example is Quaker Oats:

> Until Quaker adopted [EVA] in 1991, its businesses had one overriding goal—increasing quarterly earnings. To do it, they guzzled capital. They offered sharp price discounts at the end of each quarter, so plants ran overtime turning out huge shipments of Gatorade, Rice-A-Roni, 100% Natural Cereal, and other products. Managers led the late rush, since their bonuses depended on raising profits each quarter.
>
> This is the pernicious practice known as trade loading (because it loads up the trade, or retailers, with product) and many consumer product companies are finally admitting it damages long-run returns. An important reason is that it demands so much capital. Pumping up sales requires many warehouses (capital) to hold vast temporary inventories (more capital). But who cared? Quaker's operating businesses paid no charge for capital in internal accounting, so they barely noticed. It took EVA to spot the problem.[18]

When Quaker Oats implemented EVA, most of the capital-guzzling stopped.

The term *EVA* has been popularized by the consulting firm Stern–Stewart. But the concept of residual income has been around for some time,[19] and many companies that are not Stern–Stewart clients use this concept to measure and reward managers' performance.

Other consulting firms have their own versions of residual income. McKinsey & Company uses *economic profit (EP),* defined as capital invested multiplied by the spread between return on investment and the cost of capital. This is another expression of the concept of residual income. For the Quayle City plant, with a 12 percent cost of capital, economic profit is the same as EVA:

$$\begin{aligned}\text{Economic profit} &= \text{EP} = (\text{ROI} - r) \times \text{capital invested} \\ &= (.13 - .12) \times 1{,}000 = \$10 \text{ million}\end{aligned}$$

Pros and Cons of EVA

Let's start with the pros. EVA, economic profit, and other residual income measures are clearly better than earnings or earnings growth for measuring performance. A plant or division that's generating lots of EVA should generate accolades

[17]It can be shown that compensation plans that are linked to economic value added can induce a manager to choose the efficient investment level. See W. P. Rogerson, "International Cost Allocation and Managerial Incentives: A Theory Explaining the Use of Economic Value Added as a Performance Measure," *Journal of Political Economy* 4 (August 1977), pp. 770–795.

[18]Shawn Tully, "The Real Key to Creating Shareholder Wealth," *Fortune* (September 20, 1993), p. 48.

[19]EVA is conceptually the same as the residual income measure long advocated by some accounting scholars. See, for example, R. Anthony, "Accounting for the Cost of Equity," *Harvard Business Review* 51 (1973), pp. 88–102 and "Equity Interest—Its Time Has Come," *Journal of Accountancy* 154 (1982), pp. 76–93.

for its managers as well as value for shareholders. EVA may also highlight parts of the business that are not performing up to scratch. If a division is failing to earn a positive EVA, its management is likely to face some pointed questions about whether the division's assets could be better employed elsewhere.

EVA sends a message to managers: Invest if and only if the increase in earnings is enough to cover the cost of capital. For managers who are used to tracking earnings or growth in earnings, this is a relatively easy message to grasp. Therefore EVA can be used down deep in the organization as an incentive compensation system. It is a substitute for explicit monitoring by top management. Instead of *telling* plant and divisional managers not to waste capital and then trying to figure out whether they are complying, EVA rewards them for careful and thoughtful investment decisions. Of course, if you tie junior managers' compensation to their economic value added, you must also give them power over those decisions that affect EVA. Thus the use of EVA implies delegated decision-making.

EVA makes the cost of capital *visible* to operating managers. A plant manager can improve EVA by (a) increasing earnings or (b) *reducing* capital employed. Therefore underutilized assets tend to be flushed out and disposed of. Working capital may be reduced, or at least not added to casually, as Quaker Oats did by trade loading in its pre-EVA era. The plant managers in Quayle City may decide to do without that cappuccino machine or extra forklift.

Introduction of residual income measures often leads to surprising reductions in assets employed—not from one or two big capital disinvestment decisions, but from many small ones. Ehrbar quotes a sewing machine operator at Herman Miller Corporation:

> [EVA] lets you realize that even assets have a cost. . . . we used to have these stacks of fabric sitting here on the tables until we needed them. . . . We were going to use the fabric anyway, so who cares that we're buying it and stacking it up there? Now no one has excess fabric. They only have the stuff we're working on today. And it's changed the way we connect with suppliers, and we're having [them] deliver fabric more often.[20]

Now we come to the first limitation to EVA. It does not involve forecasts of future cash flows and does not measure present value. Instead, EVA depends on the *current* level of earnings. It may, therefore, reward managers who take on projects with quick paybacks and penalize those who invest in projects with long gestation periods. Think of the difficulties in applying EVA to a pharmaceutical research program, where it typically takes 10 to 12 years to bring a new drug from discovery to final regulatory approval and the drug's first revenues. That means 10 to 12 years of guaranteed losses, even if the managers in charge do everything right. Similar problems occur in startup ventures, where there may be heavy capital outlays but low or negative earnings in the first years of operation. This does not imply negative NPV, so long as operating earnings and cash flows are sufficiently high later on. But EVA would be negative in the startup years, even if the project were on track to a strong positive NPV.

The problem in these cases lies not so much in EVA as in the measurement of income. The pharmaceutical R&D program may be showing accounting losses, be-

[20] A. Ehrbar, *EVA: The Real Key to Creating Wealth*, John Wiley & Sons, Inc., New York, 1998, pp. 130–131.

TABLE 12.2

EVA performance of selected U.S. companies, 2000 (dollar figures in millions).

	Economic Value Added (EVA)	Capital Invested	Return on Capital	Cost of Capital
Philip Morris	$6,081	$57,220	17.4%	6.7%
General Electric	5,943	71,421	20.4	12.1
Microsoft	5,919	23,890	39.1	14.3
Exxon Mobil	5,357	181,344	10.5	7.6
Citigroup	4,646	73,890	19.0	12.7
Coca-Cola	1,266	19,523	15.7	9.2
Boeing	94	40,651	8.0	7.8
General Motors	−1,065	110,111	5.7	6.7
Viacom	−4,370	52,045	2.0	10.4
AT&T Corp	−9,972	206,700	4.5	9.3

Note: Economic value added is the rate of return on capital less the cost of capital times the amount of capital invested; e.g., for Coca-Cola EVA = (.157 − .092) × 19,523 = $1,266.
Source: Data provided by Stern–Stewart.

cause generally accepted accounting principles require that outlays for R&D be written off as a current expense. But from an economic point of view, the outlays are an investment, not an expense. If a proposal for a new business forecasts accounting losses during a startup period, but the proposal nevertheless shows positive NPV, then the startup losses are really an investment—cash outlays made to generate larger cash inflows when the new business hits its stride.

In short, EVA and other measures of residual income depend on accurate measures of economic income and investment. Applying EVA effectively requires major changes in income statements and balance sheets.[21] We will pick up this point in the next section.

Applying EVA to Companies

EVA's most important use is in measuring and rewarding performance inside the firm. But it can also be applied to firms as a whole. Business periodicals regularly report EVAs for companies and industries. Table 12.2 shows the economic value added in 2000 for a sample of U.S. companies.[22] Notice that the firms with the highest return on capital did not necessarily add the most economic value. For example, Philip Morris was top of the class in terms of economic value added, but its return on capital was less than half that of Microsoft. This is partly because Philip Morris has more capital invested and partly because it is less risky than Microsoft and its cost of capital is correspondingly lower.

[21]For example, R&D should not be treated as an immediate expense but as an investment to be added to the balance sheet and written off over a reasonable period. Eli Lilly, a large pharmaceutical company, did this so that it could use EVA. As a result, the net value of its assets at the end of 1996 increased from $6 to $13 billion.

[22]Stern–Stewart makes some adjustments to income and assets before calculating these EVAs, but it is almost impossible to include the value of all assets. For example, did Microsoft really earn a 39 percent true, economic rate of return? We suspect that the value of its assets is understated. The value of its intellectual property—the fruits of its investment over the years in software and operating systems—is not shown on the balance sheet. If the denominator in a return on capital calculation is too low, the resulting profitability measure is too high.

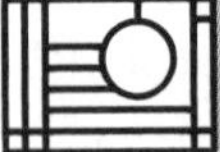

12.5 BIASES IN ACCOUNTING MEASURES OF PERFORMANCE

Any method of performance measurement that depends on accounting profitability measures had better hope those numbers are accurate. Unfortunately they are often not accurate, but biased. We referred to this problem in the last section and return to it now.

Biases in Accounting Rates of Return

Business periodicals regularly report book (accounting) rates of return on investment (ROIs) for companies and industries. ROI is just the ratio of after-tax operating income to the net (depreciated) book value of assets. We rejected book ROI as a capital investment criterion in Chapter 5, and in fact few companies now use it for that purpose. But they do use it to evaluate profitability of existing businesses.

Consider the pharmaceutical and chemical industries. According to Table 12.3, pharmaceutical companies have done much better than chemical companies. Are the pharmaceutical companies *really* that profitable? If so, lots of companies should be rushing into the pharmaceutical business. Or is there something wrong with the ROI measure?

Pharmaceutical companies have done well, but they look more profitable than they really are. Book ROIs are biased upward for companies with intangible investments such as R&D, simply because accountants don't put these outlays on the balance sheet.

Table 12.4 shows cash inflows and outflows for two mature companies. Neither is growing. Each must plow back $400 million to maintain its existing business. The *only* difference is that the chemical company's plowback goes mostly to plant and

TABLE 12.3

After-tax accounting rates of return for pharmaceutical and chemical companies, 2000.

Source: Datastream.

Pharmaceutical		Chemical	
Abbot Laboratories	19.2%	Du Pont	7.3%
Bristol-Myers Squibb	24.0	Dow Chemical	7.5
Merck	19.7	Ethyl Corporation	8.5
Pfizer	14.9	Hercules Inc.	5.4

TABLE 12.4

Comparison of a pharmaceutical company and a chemical company, each in a no-growth steady state (figures in $ millions). Revenues, costs, total investment, and annual cash flow are identical. But the pharmaceutical company invests more in R&D.

*Operating costs do *not* include any charge for depreciation.

†Cash flow = revenues − operating costs − total investment.

	Pharmaceutical	Chemical
Revenues	1,000	1,000
Operating costs, out-of-pocket*	500	500
Net operating cash flow	500	500
Investment in:		
Plant and equipment	100	300
R&D	300	100
Total investment	400	400
Annual cash flow†	+100	+100

	Pharmaceutical		Chemical	
Age, Years	Original Cost of Investment	Net Book Value	Original Cost of Investment	Net Book Value
0 (new)	100	100	300	300
1	100	90	300	270
2	100	80	300	240
3	100	70	300	210
4	100	60	300	180
5	100	50	300	150
6	100	40	300	120
7	100	30	300	90
8	100	20	300	60
9	100	10	300	30
Total net book value		550		1,650

	Pharmaceutical	Chemical
Annual depreciation*	100	300
R&D expense	300	100
Total depreciation and R&D	400	400

TABLE 12.5

Book asset values and annual depreciation for the pharmaceutical and chemical companies described in Table 12.4 (figures in $ millions).

*The pharmaceutical company has 10 vintages of assets, each depreciated by $10 per year. Total depreciation per year is $10 \times 10 = \$100$ million. The chemical company's depreciation is $10 \times 30 = \$300$ million.

	Pharmaceutical	Chemical
Revenues	1,000	1,000
Operating costs, out-of-pocket	500	500
R&D expense	300	100
Depreciation*	100	300
Net income	100	100
Net book value*	550	1,650
Book ROI	18%	6%

TABLE 12.6

Book ROIs for the companies described in Table 12.4 (figures in $ millions). The chemical and pharmaceutical companies' cash flows and values are identical. But the pharmaceutical's accounting rate of return is triple the chemical's. This bias occurs because accountants do not show the value of investment in R&D on the balance sheet.

*Calculated in Table 12.5.

equipment; the pharmaceutical company invests mostly in R&D. The chemical company invests only one-third as much in R&D ($100 versus $300 million) but triples the pharmaceutical company's investment in fixed assets.

Table 12.5 calculates the annual depreciation charges. Notice that the sum of R&D and total annual depreciation is identical for the two companies.

The companies' cash flows, true profitability, and true present values are also identical, but as Table 12.6 shows, the pharmaceutical company's book ROI is 18 percent, *triple* the chemical company's. The accountants would get annual income right (in this case it is identical to cash flow) but understate the value of the pharmaceutical company's assets relative to the chemical company's. Lower asset value creates the upward-biased pharmaceutical ROI.

The first moral is this: Do not assume that businesses with high book ROIs are necessarily performing better. They may just have more hidden assets, that is, assets which accountants do not put on balance sheets.

Measuring the Profitability of the Nodhead Supermarket—Another Example

Supermarket chains invest heavily in building and equipping new stores. The regional manager of a chain is about to propose investing $1 million in a new store in Nodhead. Projected cash flows are

	Year						
	1	2	3	4	5	6	after 6
Cash flow ($ thousands)	100	200	250	298	298	298	0

Of course, real supermarkets last more than six years. But these numbers are realistic in one important sense: It may take two or three years for a new store to catch on—that is, to build up a substantial, habitual clientele. Thus cash flow is low for the first few years even in the best locations.

We will assume the opportunity cost of capital is 10 percent. The Nodhead store's NPV at 10 percent is zero. It is an acceptable project, but not an unusually good one:

$$\text{NPV} = -1{,}000 + \frac{100}{1.10} + \frac{200}{(1.10)^2} + \frac{250}{(1.10)^3} + \frac{298}{(1.10)^4} + \frac{298}{(1.10)^5} + \frac{298}{(1.10)^6} = 0$$

With NPV = 0, the true (internal) rate of return of this cash-flow stream is also 10 percent.

Table 12.7 shows the store's forecasted *book* profitability, assuming straight-line depreciation over its six-year life. The book ROI is lower than the true return for the first two years and higher afterward.[23] This is the typical outcome: Accounting profitability measures are too low when a project or business is young and are too high as it matures.

At this point the regional manager steps up on stage for the following soliloquy:

> The Nodhead store's a decent investment. I really should propose it. But if we go ahead, I won't look very good at next year's performance review. And what if I also go ahead with the new stores in Russet, Gravenstein, and Sheepnose? Their cash-flow patterns are pretty much the same. I could actually appear to lose money next year. The stores I've got won't earn enough to cover the initial losses on four new ones.
>
> Of course, everyone knows new supermarkets lose money at first. The loss would be in the budget. My boss will understand—I think. But what about her boss? What if the board of directors starts asking pointed questions about profitability in my region? I'm under a lot of pressure to generate better earnings. Pamela Quince, the upstate manager, got a bonus for generating a 40 percent increase in book ROI. She didn't spend much on expansion.

The regional manager is getting conflicting signals. On one hand, he is told to find and propose good investment projects. *Good* is defined by discounted cash flow. On the other hand, he is also urged to increase book earnings. But the two goals conflict because book earnings do not measure true earnings. The greater the

[23] The errors in book ROI always catch up with you in the end. If the firm chooses a depreciation schedule that overstates a project's return in some years, it must also understate the return in other years. In fact, you can think of a project's IRR as a kind of average of the book returns. It is not a simple average, however. The weights are the project's book values discounted at the IRR. See J. A. Kay, "Accountants, Too, Could Be Happy in a Golden Age: The Accountant's Rate of Profit and the Internal Rate of Return," *Oxford Economic Papers* 28 (1976), pp. 447–460.

	Year					
	1	2	3	4	5	6
Cash flow	100	200	250	298	298	298
Book value at *start* of year, straight-line depreciation	1,000	833	667	500	333	167
Book value at *end* of year, straight-line depreciation	833	667	500	333	167	0
Change in book value during year	−167	−167	−167	−167	−167	−167
Book income	−67	+33	+83	+131	+131	+131
Book ROI	−.067	+.04	+.124	+.262	+.393	+.784
Book depreciation	167	167	167	167	167	167

TABLE 12.7

Forecasted book income and ROI for the proposed Nodhead store. Book ROI is lower than the true rate of return for the first two years and higher thereafter.

pressure for immediate book profits, the more the regional manager is tempted to forgo good investments or to favor quick-payback projects over longer-lived projects, even if the latter have higher NPVs.

Would EVA solve this problem? No, EVA would be negative in the first two years of the Nodhead store. In year 2, for example,

$$\text{EVA} = 33 - (.10 \times 833) = -50, \text{ or } -\$50{,}000$$

This calculation risks reinforcing the regional manager's qualms about the new Nodhead store.

Again, the fault here is not in the principle of EVA but in the measurement of income. If the project performs as projected in Table 12.7, the negative EVA in year 2 is really an investment.

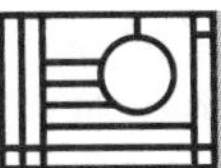

12.6 MEASURING ECONOMIC PROFITABILITY

Let us think for a moment about how profitability should be measured in principle. It is easy enough to compute the true, or economic, rate of return for a common stock that is continuously traded. We just record cash receipts (dividends) for the year, add the change in price over the year, and divide by the beginning price:

$$\text{Rate of return} = \frac{\text{cash receipts} + \text{change in price}}{\text{beginning price}} = \frac{C_1 + (P_1 - P_0)}{P_0}$$

The numerator of the expression for rate of return (cash flow plus change in value) is called **economic income:**

$$\text{Economic income} = \text{cash flow} + \text{change in present value}$$

Any reduction in present value represents **economic depreciation;** any increase in present value represents *negative* economic depreciation. Therefore

$$\text{Economic depreciation} = \text{reduction in present value}$$

and

$$\text{Economic income} = \text{cash flow} - \text{economic depreciation}$$

The concept works for any asset. Rate of return equals cash flow plus change in value divided by starting value:

$$\text{Rate of return} = \frac{C_1 + (PV_1 - PV_0)}{PV_0}$$

where PV_0 and PV_1 indicate the present values of the business at the ends of years 0 and 1.

The only hard part in measuring economic income and return is calculating present value. You can observe market value if shares in the asset are actively traded, but few plants, divisions, or capital projects have shares traded in the stock market. You can observe the present market value of *all* the firm's assets but not of any one of them taken separately.

Accountants rarely even attempt to measure present value. Instead they give us net book value (BV), which is original cost less depreciation computed according to some arbitrary schedule. Companies use the book value to calculate the book return on investment:

$$\begin{aligned}\text{Book income} &= \text{cash flow} - \text{book depreciation}\\ &= C_1 + (BV_1 - BV_0)\end{aligned}$$

Therefore

$$\text{Book ROI} = \frac{C_1 + (BV_1 - BV_0)}{BV_0}$$

If book depreciation and economic depreciation are different (they are rarely the same), then the book profitability measures will be wrong; that is, they will not measure true profitability. (In fact, it is not clear that accountants should even *try* to measure true profitability. They could not do so without heavy reliance on subjective estimates of value. Perhaps they should stick to supplying objective information and leave the estimation of value to managers and investors.)

It is not hard to forecast economic income and rate of return. Table 12.8 shows the calculations. From the cash-flow forecasts we can forecast present value at the start of periods 1 to 6. Cash flow plus *change* in present value equals economic income. Rate of return equals economic income divided by start-of-period value.

Of course, these are forecasts. Actual future cash flows and values will be higher or lower. Table 12.8 shows that investors *expect* to earn 10 percent in each year of the store's six-year life. In other words, investors expect to earn the opportunity cost of capital each year from holding this asset.[24]

Notice that EVA calculated using present value and economic income is zero in each year of the Nodhead project's life. For year 2, for example,

$$\text{EVA} = 100 - (.10 \times 100) = 0$$

[24]This is a general result. Forecasted profitability always equals the discount rate used to calculate the estimated future present values.

	Year					
	1	2	3	4	5	6
Cash flow	100	200	250	298	298	298
PV, at *start* of year, 10 percent discount rate	1,000	1,000	901	741	517	271
PV at *end* of year, 10 percent discount rate	1,000	900	741	517	271	0
Change in value during year	0	−100	−160	−224	−246	−271
Economic income	100	100	90	74	52	27
Rate of return	.10	.10	.10	.10	.10	.10
Economic depreciation	0	100	160	224	246	271

TABLE 12.8

Forecasted economic income and rate of return for the proposed Nodhead store. Economic income equals cash flow plus change in present value. Rate of return equals economic income divided by value at start of year.

Note: There are minor rounding errors in some annual figures.

EVA *should* be zero, because the project's true rate of return is only equal to the cost of capital. EVA will always give the right signal if income equals economic income and asset values are measured accurately.

Do the Biases Wash Out in the Long Run?

Some people downplay the problem we have just described. Is a temporary dip in book profits a major problem? Don't the errors wash out in the long run, when the region settles down to a steady state with an even mix of old and new stores?

It turns out that the errors diminish but do *not* exactly offset. The simplest steady-state condition occurs when the firm does not grow, but reinvests just enough each year to maintain earnings and asset values. Table 12.9 shows steady-state book ROIs for a regional division which opens one store a year. For simplicity we assume that the division starts from scratch and that each store's cash flows are carbon copies of the Nodhead store. The true rate of return on each store is, therefore, 10 percent. But as Table 12.9 demonstrates, steady-state book ROI, at 12.6 percent, overstates the true rate of return. Therefore, you cannot assume that the errors in book ROI will wash out in the long run.

Thus we still have a problem even in the long run. The extent of the error depends on how fast the business grows. We have just considered one steady state with a zero growth rate. Think of another firm with a 5 percent steady-state growth rate. Such a firm would invest $1,000 the first year, $1,050 the second, $1,102.50 the third, and so on. Clearly the faster growth means more new projects relative to old ones. The greater weight given to young projects, which have low book ROIs, the lower the business' apparent profitability. Figure 12.1 shows how this works out for a business composed of projects like the Nodhead store. Book ROI will either overestimate or underestimate the true rate of return unless the amount that the firm invests each year grows at the same rate as the true rate of return.[25]

[25]This also is a general result. Biases in steady-state book ROIs disappear when the growth rate equals the true rate of return. This was discovered by E. Solomon and J. Laya, "Measurement of Company Profitability: Some Systematic Errors in Accounting Rate of Return," in A. A. Robichek (ed.), *Financial Research and Management Decisions,* John Wiley & Sons, Inc., New York, 1967, pp. 152–183.

TABLE 12.9

Book ROI for a group of stores like the Nodhead store. The steady-state book ROI overstates the 10 percent *economic* rate of return.

	Year					
	1	2	3	4	5	6
Book income for store*						
1	−67	+33	+83	+131	+131	+131
2		−67	+33	+83	+131	+131
3			−67	+33	+83	+131
4				−67	+33	+83
5					−67	+33
6						−67
Total book income	−67	−34	+49	+180	+311	+442
Book value for store						
1	1,000	833	667	500	333	167
2		1,000	833	667	500	333
3			1,000	833	667	500
4				1,000	833	667
5					1,000	833
6						1,000
Total book value	1,000	1,833	2,500	3,000	3,333	3,500
Book ROI for all stores = $\frac{\text{total book income}}{\text{total book value}}$	−.067	−.019	+.02	+.06	+.093	+.126†

*Book income = cash flow + change in book value during year.
†Steady-state book ROI.

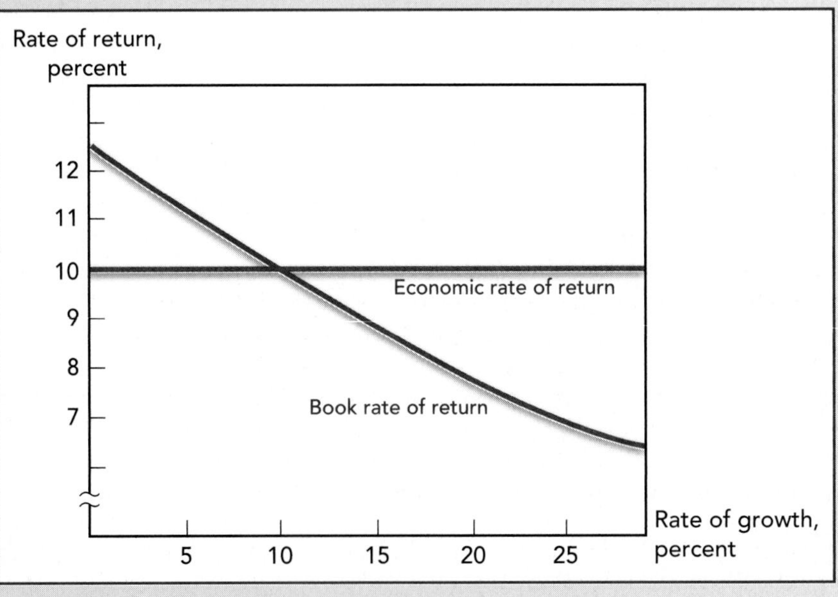

FIGURE 12.1

The faster a firm grows, the lower its book rate of return is, providing true profitability is constant and cash flows are constant or increasing over project life. This graph is drawn for a firm composed of identical projects, all like the Nodhead store (Table 12.7), but growing at a constant compound rate.

What Can We Do about Biases in Accounting Profitability Measures?

The dangers in judging profitability by accounting measures are clear from this chapter's discussion and examples. To be forewarned is to be forearmed. But we can say something beyond just "be careful."

It is natural for firms to set a standard of profitability for plants or divisions. Ideally that standard should be the opportunity cost of capital for investment in the plant or division. That's the whole point of EVA: to compare actual profits with the cost of capital. But if performance is measured by return on investment or EVA, then these measures need to recognize accounting biases. Ideally, the financial manager should identify and eliminate accounting biases before judging or rewarding performance.

This is easier said than done. Accounting biases are notoriously hard to get rid of. Thus, many firms end up asking not "Did the widget division earn more than its cost of capital last year?" but "Was the widget division's book ROI typical of a successful firm in the widget industry?" The underlying assumptions are that (1) similar accounting procedures are used by other widget manufacturers and (2) successful widget companies earn their cost of capital.

There are some simple accounting changes that could reduce biases in performance measures. Remember that the biases all stem from *not* using economic depreciation. Therefore why not switch to economic depreciation? The main reason is that each asset's present value would have to be reestimated every year. Imagine the confusion if this were attempted. You can understand why accountants set up a depreciation schedule when an investment is made and then stick to it apart from exceptional circumstances. But why restrict the choice of depreciation schedules to the old standbys, such as straight-line? Why not specify a depreciation pattern that at least matches *expected* economic depreciation? For example, the Nodhead store could be depreciated according to the expected economic depreciation schedule shown in Table 12.8. This would avoid any systematic biases.[26] It would break no law or accounting standard. This step seems so simple and effective that we are at a loss to explain why firms have not adopted it.[27]

One final comment: Suppose that you *do* conclude that a project has earned less than its cost of capital. This indicates that you made a mistake in taking on the project and, if you could have your time over again, you would not accept it. But does that mean you should bail out now? Not necessarily. That depends on how much the assets would be worth if you sold them or put them to an alternative use. A plant that produces low profits may still be worth operating if it has few alternative uses. Conversely, on some occasions it may pay to sell or redeploy a highly profitable plant.

Do Managers Worry Too Much about Book Profitability?

Book measures of profitability can be wrong or misleading because

1. Errors occur at different stages of project life. When true depreciation is decelerated, book measures are likely to understate true profitability for new projects and overstate it for old ones.

[26]Using expected economic depreciation will not generate book ROIs that are exactly right unless realized cash flows exactly match forecasted flows. But we expect forecasts to be right, on average.

[27]This procedure has been suggested by several authors, for example by Zvi Bodie in "Compound Interest Depreciation in Capital Investment," *Harvard Business Review* 60 (May–June 1982), pp. 58–60.

2. Errors also occur when firms or divisions have a balanced mix of old and new projects. Our steady-state analysis of Nodhead shows this.
3. Errors occur because of inflation, basically because inflation shows up in revenue faster than it shows up in costs. For example, a firm owning a plant built in 1980 will, under standard accounting procedures, calculate depreciation in terms of the plant's original cost in 1980 dollars. The plant's output is sold for current dollars. This is why the U.S. National Income and Product Accounts report corporate profits calculated under replacement cost accounting. This procedure bases depreciation not on the original cost of firms' assets, but on what it would cost to replace the assets at current prices.
4. Book measures are often confused by creative accounting. Some firms pick and choose among available accounting procedures, or even invent new ones, in order to make their income statements and balance sheets look good. This was done with particular imagination in the "go-go years" of the mid-1960s and the late 1990s.

Investors and financial managers have learned not to take accounting profitability at face value. Yet many people do not realize the depth of the problem. They think that if firms eschewed creative accounting, everything would be all right except perhaps for temporary problems with very old or very young projects. In other words, they worry about reason 4, and a little about reasons 1 and 3, but not at all about 2. We think reason 2 deserves more attention.

SUMMARY

We began this chapter by describing how capital budgeting is organized and ended by exposing serious biases in accounting measures of financial performance. Inevitably such discussions stress the mechanics of organization, control, accounting, and performance measurement. It is harder to talk about the informal procedures that reinforce the formal ones. But remember that it takes informal communication and personal initiative to make capital budgeting work. Also, the accounting biases are partly or wholly alleviated because managers and stockholders are smart enough to look behind book earnings.

Formal capital budgeting systems usually have four stages:

1. A *capital budget* for the firm is prepared. This is a plan for capital expenditure by plant, division, or other business unit.
2. *Project authorizations* are approved to give authority to go ahead with specific projects.
3. Procedures for *control of projects under construction* are established to warn if projects are behind schedule or are costing more than planned.
4. *Postaudits* are conducted to check on the progress of recent investments.

Capital budgeting is not entirely a bottom-up process. Strategic planners practice capital budgeting on a grand scale by attempting to identify those businesses in which the firm has a special advantage. Project proposals that support the firm's accepted overall strategy are much more likely to have clear sailing as they come up through the organization.

But don't assume that all important capital outlays appear as projects in the capital budgeting process. Many important investment decisions may never receive formal financial analysis. First, plant or division managers decide which projects to propose. Top management and financial staff may never see the alternatives. Second, investments in intangible assets, for example, marketing and R&D outlays, may bypass the capital budget. Third, there are countless routine investment decisions that must be made by middle management. These outlays are small if looked at one by one, but they add up.

Capital investment decisions must be decentralized to a large extent. Consequently agency problems are inevitable. Managers are tempted to slack off, to avoid risk, and to propose empire-building or entrenching investments. Empire building is a particular threat when plant and divisional managers' bonuses depend just on earnings or on growth in earnings.

Top management mitigates these agency problems by a combination of monitoring and incentives. Many large companies have implemented sophisticated incentive schemes based on residual income or economic value added (EVA). In these schemes, managers' bonuses depend on earnings minus a charge for capital employed. There is a strong incentive to dispose of unneeded assets and to acquire new ones only if additional earnings exceed the cost of capital. Of course EVA depends on accurate measures of earnings and capital employed.

Top management also create agency costs (e.g., empire building). In this case they are the agents and shareholders are the principals. Shareholders' interests are represented by the board of directors and are also protected by delegated monitors (e.g., the accountants who audit the company's books).

In most public corporations, top management's compensation is tied to the performance of the company's stock. This aligns their interests with shareholders'. But compensation tied to stock returns is not a complete solution. Stock returns respond to events outside management's control, and today's stock prices already reflect investors' expectations of managers' future performance.

Thus most firms also measure performance by accounting or book profitability. Unfortunately book income and return on investment (ROI) are often seriously biased measures of true profitability. For example, book ROIs are generally too low for new assets and too high for old ones. Businesses with important intangible assets generally have upward-biased ROIs because the intangibles don't appear on the balance sheet.

In principle, true or economic income is easy to calculate: You just subtract economic depreciation from the asset's cash flow. Economic depreciation is simply the decrease in the asset's present value during the period.

Unfortunately we can't ask accountants to recalculate each asset's present value every time income is calculated. But it does seem fair to ask why they don't try at least to match book depreciation schedules to typical patterns of economic depreciation.

Visit us at www.mhhe.com/bm7e

FURTHER READING

The most extensive study of the capital budgeting process is:

J. L. Bower: *Managing the Resource Allocation Process*, Division of Research, Graduate School of Business Administration, Harvard University, Boston, 1970.

The article by Pohlman, Santiago, and Markel is a more up-to-date survey of current practice:

R. A. Pohlman, E. S. Santiago, and F. L. Markel: "Cash Flow Estimation Practices of Large Firms," *Financial Management*, 17:71–79 (Summer 1988).

For an easy-to-read description of EVA, with lots of success stories, see
A. Ehrbar: *EVA: The Real Key to Creating Wealth,* John Wiley & Sons, Inc., New York, 1998.

Biases in book ROI and procedures for reducing the biases are discussed by:
E. Solomon and J. Laya: "Measurement of Company Profitability: Some Systematic Errors in the Accounting Rate of Return," in A. A. Robichek (ed.), *Financial Research and Management Decisions,* John Wiley & Sons, Inc., New York, 1967, pp. 152–183.

F. M. Fisher and J. I. McGowan: "On the Misuse of Accounting Rates of Return to Infer Monopoly Profits," *American Economic Review,* 73:82–97 (March 1983).

J. A. Kay: "Accountants, Too, Could Be Happy in a Golden Age: The Accountant's Rate of Profit and the Internal Rate of Return," *Oxford Economic Papers,* 28:447–460 (1976).

Z. Bodie: "Compound Interest Depreciation in Capital Investment," *Harvard Business Review,* 60:58–60 (May–June 1982).

QUIZ

1. True or false?
  a. The approval of a capital budget allows managers to go ahead with any project included in the budget.
  b. Capital budgets and project authorizations are mostly developed "bottom up." Strategic planning is a "top-down" process.
  c. Project sponsors are likely to be overoptimistic.
  d. Investments in marketing (for new products) and R&D are not capital outlays.
  e. Many capital investments are not included in the company's capital budget. (If true, give some examples.)
  f. Postaudits are typically undertaken about five years after project completion.

2. Explain how each of the following actions or problems can distort or disrupt the capital budgeting process.
  a. Overoptimism by project sponsors.
  b. Inconsistent forecasts of industry and macroeconomic variables.
  c. Capital budgeting organized solely as a bottom-up process.
  d. A demand for quick results from operating managers, e.g., requiring new capital expenditures to meet a payback constraint.

3. What is the practical implication of Brealey and Myers's Second Law? The law reads, "The proportion of proposed projects having a positive NPV at the corporate hurdle rate is independent of the hurdle rate."

4. Define the following: **(a)** Agency costs in capital investment, **(b)** private benefits, **(c)** empire building, **(d)** free-rider problem, **(e)** entrenching investment, **(f)** delegated monitoring.

5. Monitoring alone can never completely eliminate agency costs in capital investment. Briefly explain why.

6. Here are several questions about economic value added or EVA.
  a. Is EVA expressed as a percentage or a dollar amount?
  b. Write down the formula for calculating EVA.
  c. What is the difference, if any, between EVA and residual income?
  d. What is the point of EVA? Why do firms use it?
  e. Does the effectiveness of EVA depend on accurate measures of accounting income and assets?

7. The Modern Language Division earned $1.6 million on net assets of $20 million. The cost of capital is 11.5 percent. Calculate the net percentage return on investment and EVA.

8. True or false? Briefly explain your answers.
  a. Accountants require companies to write off outlays for R&D as current expenses. This makes R&D-intensive companies look less profitable than they really are.

b. Companies with valuable intangible assets will show upward-biased accounting rates of return.

9. Fill in the blanks:

"A project's economic income for a given year equals the project's _________ less its _________ depreciation. Book income is typically _________ than economic income early in the project's life and _________ than economic income later in its life."

10. Consider the following project:

	Period			
	0	1	2	3
Net cash flow	−100	0	78.55	78.55

The internal rate of return is 20 percent. The NPV, assuming a 20 percent opportunity cost of capital, is exactly zero. Calculate the expected *economic* income and economic depreciation in each year.

PRACTICE QUESTIONS

1. Discuss the value of postaudits. Who should conduct them? When? Should they consider solely financial performance? Should they be confined to the larger projects?

2. Draw up an outline or flowchart tracing the capital budgeting process from the initial idea for a new investment project to the completion of the project and the start of operations. Assume the idea for a new obfuscator machine comes from a plant manager in the Deconstruction Division of the Modern Language Corporation.

   Here are some questions your outline or flowchart should consider: Who will prepare the original proposal? What information will the proposal contain? Who will evaluate it? What approvals will be needed, and who will give them? What happens if the machine costs 40 percent more to purchase and install than originally forecasted? What will happen when the machine is finally up and running?

3. Compare typical compensation and incentive arrangements for **(a)** top management, for example, the CEO or CFO, and **(b)** plant or division managers. What are the chief differences? Can you explain them?

4. Suppose all plant and division managers were paid only a fixed salary—no other incentives or bonuses.
   a. Describe the agency problems that would appear in capital investment decisions.
   b. How would tying the managers' compensation to EVA alleviate these problems?

5. Table 12.10 shows a condensed income statement and balance sheet for Androscoggin Copper's Rumford smelting plant.
   a. Calculate the plant's EVA. Assume the cost of capital is 9 percent.
   b. As Table 12.10 shows, the plant is carried on Androscoggin's books at $48.32 million. However, it is a modern design, and could be sold to another copper company for $95 million. How should this fact change your calculation of EVA?

6. Here are a few questions about compensation schemes that tie top management's compensation to the rate of return earned on the company's common stock.
   a. Today's stock price depends on investors' expectations of future performance. What problems does this create?
   b. Stock returns depend on factors outside the managers' control, for example, changes in interest rates or prices of raw materials. Could this be a serious problem? If so, can you suggest a partial solution?
   c. Compensation schemes that depend on stock returns do *not* depend on accounting income or ROI. Is that an advantage? Why or why not?

TABLE 12.10

Condensed financial statements for the Rumford smelting plant. See practice question 5 (figures in $ millions).

Income Statement for 2001		Assets, December 31, 2001	
Revenue	$56.66	Net working capital	$7.08
Raw materials cost	18.72		
Operating cost	21.09	Investment in plant and equipment	69.33
Depreciation	4.50	*Less* accumulated depreciation	21.01
Pretax income	12.35	Net plant and equipment	48.32
Tax at 35%	4.32		
Net income	$8.03	Total assets	$55.40

7. Herbal Resources is a small but profitable producer of dietary supplements for pets. This is not a high-tech business, but Herbal's earnings have averaged around $1.2 million after tax, largely on the strength of its patented enzyme for making cats nonallergenic. The patent has eight years to run, and Herbal has been offered $4 million for the patent rights.

   Herbal's assets include $2 million of working capital and $8 million of property, plant, and equipment. The patent is not shown on Herbal's books. Suppose Herbal's cost of capital is 15 percent. What is its EVA?

8. List and define the agency problems likely to be encountered in a firm's capital investment decisions.

9. Large brokerage and investment companies, such as Merrill Lynch and Morgan Stanley Dean Witter, employ squadrons of security analysts. Each analyst devotes full time to an industry—aerospace, for example, or insurance—and issues reports and buy, hold, or sell recommendations for companies in the industry. How do security analysts help overcome free-rider problems in monitoring management? How do they help avoid agency problems in capital investment?

10. What is meant by *delegated monitoring?* Who are these monitors and what roles do they play?

11. True or false? Explain briefly.
    a. Book profitability measures are biased measures of true profitability for individual assets. However, these biases "wash out" when firms hold a balanced mix of old and new assets.
    b. Systematic biases in book profitability would be avoided if companies used depreciation schedules that matched expected economic depreciation. However, few, if any, firms have done this.

12. Calculate the year-by-year book and economic profitability for investment in polyzone production, as described in Chapter 11. Use the cash flows and competitive spreads shown in Table 11.2.

    What is the steady-state book rate of return (ROI) for a mature company producing polyzone? Assume no growth and competitive spreads.

13. Suppose that the cash flows from Nodhead's new supermarket are as follows:

	Year						
	0	1	2	3	4	5	6
Cash flows ($ thousands)	−1,000	+298	+298	+298	+138	+138	+138

    a. Recalculate economic depreciation. Is it accelerated or decelerated?
    b. Rework Tables 12.7 and 12.8 to show the relationship between the "true" rate of return and book ROI in each year of the project's life.

14. Use the Market Insight database (**www.mhhe.com/edumarketinsight**) to estimate the economic value added (EVA) for three firms. What problems did you encounter in doing this?

1. Is there an *optimal* level of agency costs? How would you define it?
2. Suppose it were possible to measure and track economic income and the true economic value of a firm's assets. Would there be any remaining need for EVA? Discuss.
3. Reconstruct Table 12.9 assuming a steady-state growth rate of 10 percent per year. Your answer will illustrate a fascinating theorem, namely, that book rate of return equals the economic rate of return when the economic rate of return and the steady-state growth rate are the same.
4. Consider an asset with the following cash flows:

	Year			
	0	**1**	**2**	**3**
Cash flows ($ millions)	−12	+5.20	+4.80	+4.40

The firm uses straight-line depreciation. Thus, for this project, it writes off $4 million per year in years 1, 2, and 3. The discount rate is 10 percent.

a. Show that economic depreciation equals book depreciation.
b. Show that the book rate of return is the same in each year.
c. Show that the project's book profitability is its true profitability.

You've just illustrated another interesting theorem. If the book rate of return is the same in each year of a project's life, the book rate of return equals the IRR.

5. The following are extracts from two newsletters sent to a stockbroker's clients:

Investment Letter—March 2001

Kipper Parlors was founded earlier this year by its president, Albert Herring. It plans to open a chain of kipper parlors where young people can get together over a kipper and a glass of wine in a pleasant, intimate atmosphere. In addition to the traditional grilled kipper, the parlors serve such delicacies as Kipper Schnitzel, Kipper Grandemere, and (for dessert) Kipper Sorbet.

The economics of the business are simple. Each new parlor requires an initial investment in fixtures and fittings of $200,000 (the property itself is rented). These fixtures and fittings have an estimated life of 5 years and are depreciated straight-line over that period. Each new parlor involves significant start-up costs and is not expected to reach full profitability until its fifth year. Profits per parlor are estimated as follows:

	Year after Opening				
	1	**2**	**3**	**4**	**5**
Profit	0	40	80	120	170
Depreciation	40	40	40	40	40
Profit after depreciation	–40	0	40	80	130
Book value at start of year	200	160	120	80	40
Return on investment (%)	–20	0	33	100	325

Kipper has just opened its first parlor and plans to open one new parlor each year. Despite the likely initial losses (which simply reflect start-up costs), our calculations show a dramatic profit growth and a long-term return on investment that is substantially higher than Kipper's 20 percent cost of capital.

The total market value of Kipper stock is currently only $250,000. In our opinion, this does not fully reflect the exciting growth prospects, and we strongly recommend clients to buy.

Investment Letter—April 2001

Albert Herring, president of Kipper Parlors, yesterday announced an ambitious new building plan. Kipper plans to open two new parlors next year, three the year after, and so on.

We have calculated the implications of this for Kipper's earnings per share and return on investment. The results are extremely disturbing, and under the new plan, there seems to be no prospect of Kipper's ever earning a satisfactory return on capital.

Since March, the value of Kipper's stock has fallen by 40 percent. Any investor who did not heed our earlier warnings should take the opportunity to sell the stock now.

Compare Kipper's accounting and economic income under the two expansion plans. How does the change in plan affect the company's return on investment? What is the PV of Kipper stock? Ignore taxes in your calculations.

6. In our Nodhead example, true depreciation was decelerated. That is not always the case. For instance, Figure 12.2 shows how on average the value of a Boeing 737 has varied with its age.[28] Table 12.11 shows the market value at different points in the plane's life and the cash flow needed in each year to provide a 10 percent return. (For example, if you bought a 737 for $19.69 million at the start of year 1 and sold it a year later, your total profit would be 17.99 + 3.67 − 19.69 = $1.97 million, 10 percent of the purchase cost.)

   Many airlines write off their aircraft straight-line over 15 years to a salvage value equal to 20 percent of the original cost.

   a. Calculate economic and book depreciation for each year of the plane's life.
   b. Compare the true and book rates of return in each year.
   c. Suppose an airline invested in a fixed number of Boeing 737s each year. Would steady-state book return overstate or understate true return?

FIGURE 12.2

Estimated value of Boeing 737 in January 1987 as a function of age.

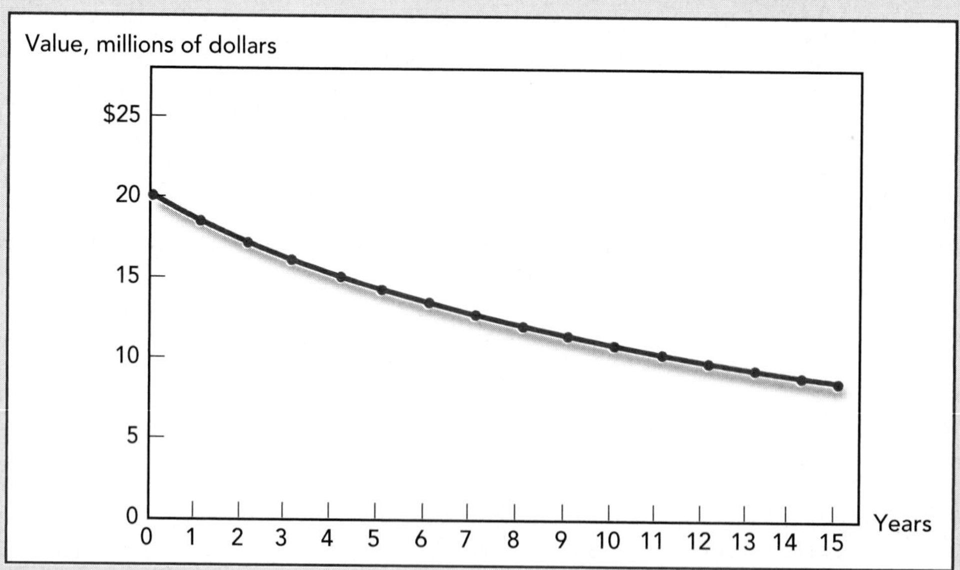

[28]We are grateful to Mike Staunton for providing us with these estimates.

TABLE 12.11

Estimated market values of a Boeing 737 in January 1987 as a function of age, plus the cash flows needed to provide a 10 percent true rate of return (figures in $ millions).

Start of Year	Market Value	Cash Flow
1	19.69	
2	17.99	$3.67
3	16.79	3.00
4	15.78	2.69
5	14.89	2.47
6	14.09	2.29
7	13.36	2.14
8	12.68	2.02
9	12.05	1.90
10	11.46	1.80
11	10.91	1.70
12	10.39	1.61
13	9.91	1.52
14	9.44	1.46
15	9.01	1.37
16	8.59	1.32

PART THREE RELATED WEBSITES

A discussion of capital budgeting procedures in the context of IT investments:

www.itpolicy.gsa.gov

Software for project analysis is available on:

www.decisioneering.com

www.kellogg.nwu.edu/faculty/myerson/ftp/addins.htm

The following sites provide articles and data on EVA:

www.sternstewart.com

www.financeadvisor.com

PART FOUR

FINANCING DECISIONS AND MARKET EFFICIENCY

SO FAR OUR focus has been on the investment decision. Now we turn to the problem of paying for these investments. This can be a challenging task. For example, in the introduction to Part Three we described how construction of the tunnel between England and France cost $15 billion. The financial manager was responsible for finding this huge sum. It involved borrowing from more than 200 banks as well as public issues of stock and bonds.

Later chapters will describe in detail the principal sources of finance, but Part Four sets the scene. We begin in Chapter 13 with a fundamental question, Can managers be confident that investors will pay a fair price for the firm's securities? Many scholars believe that securities are competitively priced, but we will also encounter some conflicting evidence.

Chapter 14 takes a first look at the firm's securities and their relative importance. It shows how they differ in their rights to payment and in the control that their holders can exercise.

Part Four concludes by showing how infant companies finance themselves and how, after reaching adulthood, they sell their securities to the public.

CHAPTER THIRTEEN

CORPORATE FINANCING AND THE SIX LESSONS OF MARKET EFFICIENCY

UP TO THIS point we have concentrated almost exclusively on the left-hand side of the balance sheet—the firm's capital expenditure decision. Now we move to the right-hand side and to the problems involved in financing the capital expenditures. To put it crudely, you've learned how to spend money, now learn how to raise it.

Of course, we haven't totally ignored financing in our discussion of capital budgeting. But we made the simplest possible assumption: all-equity financing. That means we assumed the firm raises its money by selling stock and then invests the proceeds in real assets. Later, when those assets generate cash flows, the cash is returned to the stockholders. Stockholders supply all the firm's capital, bear all the business risks, and receive all the rewards.

Now we are turning the problem around. We take the firm's present portfolio of real assets and its future investment strategy as given, and then we determine the best financing strategy. For example,

- Should the firm reinvest most of its earnings in the business, or should it pay them out as dividends?
- If the firm needs more money, should it issue more stock or should it borrow?
- Should it borrow short-term or long-term?
- Should it borrow by issuing a normal long-term bond or a convertible bond (i.e., a bond which can be exchanged for stock by the bondholders)?

There are countless other financing trade-offs, as you will see.

The purpose of holding the firm's capital budgeting decision constant is to separate that decision from the financing decision. Strictly speaking, this assumes that capital budgeting and financing decisions are *independent.* In many circumstances this is a reasonable assumption. The firm is generally free to change its capital structure by repurchasing one security and issuing another. In that case there is no need to associate a particular investment project with a particular source of cash. The firm can think, first, about which projects to accept and, second, about how they should be financed.

Sometimes decisions about capital structure depend on project choice or vice versa, and in those cases the investment and financing decisions have to be considered jointly. However, we defer discussion of such interactions of financing and investment decisions until later in the book.

We start this chapter by contrasting investment and financing decisions. The objective in each case is the same—to maximize NPV. However, it may be harder to find positive-NPV financing opportunities. The reason it is difficult to add value by clever financing decisions is that capital markets are efficient. By this we mean that fierce competition between investors eliminates profit opportunities and causes debt and equity issues to be fairly priced. If you think that sounds like a sweeping statement, you are right. That is why we have devoted this chapter to explaining and evaluating the efficient-market hypothesis.

You may ask why we start our discussion of financing issues with this conceptual point, before you have even the most basic knowledge about securities and issue procedures. We do it this way because financing decisions seem overwhelmingly complex if you don't learn to ask the right questions. We are afraid you might flee from confusion to the myths that often dominate popular discussion of corporate financing. You need to understand the efficient-market hypothesis not because it is *universally* true but because it leads you to ask the right questions.

We define the efficient-market hypothesis more carefully in Section 13.2. The hypothesis comes in different strengths, depending on the information available to investors. Sections 13.2 and 13.3 review the evidence for and against efficient markets. The evidence "for" is massive, but over the years a number of puzzling anomalies have accumulated.

The chapter closes with *the six lessons of market efficiency.*

13.1 WE ALWAYS COME BACK TO NPV

Although it is helpful to separate investment and financing decisions, there are basic similarities in the criteria for making them. The decisions to purchase a machine tool and to sell a bond each involve valuation of a risky asset. The fact that one asset is real and the other is financial doesn't matter. In both cases we end up computing net present value.

The phrase *net present value of borrowing* may seem odd to you. But the following example should help to explain what we mean: As part of its policy of encouraging small business, the government offers to lend your firm \$100,000 for 10 years at 3 percent. This means that the firm is liable for interest payments of \$3,000 in each of the years 1 through 10 and that it is responsible for repaying the \$100,000 in the final year. Should you accept this offer?

We can compute the NPV of the loan agreement in the usual way. The one difference is that the first cash flow is *positive* and the subsequent flows are *negative:*

$$\begin{aligned} \text{NPV} &= \text{amount borrowed} - \text{present value of interest payments} \\ &\quad - \text{present value of loan repayment} \\ &= +100{,}000 - \sum_{t=1}^{10} \frac{3{,}000}{(1+r)^t} - \frac{100{,}000}{(1+r)^{10}} \end{aligned}$$

The only missing variable is r, the opportunity cost of capital. You need that to value the liability created by the loan. We reason this way: The government's loan to you is a financial asset: a piece of paper representing your promise to pay \$3,000 per year plus the final repayment of \$100,000. How much would that paper sell for if freely traded in the capital market? It would sell for the present value of those cash flows, discounted at r, the rate of return offered by other securities issued by your firm. All you have to do to determine r is to answer the question, What interest rate would my firm have to pay to borrow money directly from the capital markets rather than from the government?

Suppose that this rate is 10 percent. Then

$$\begin{aligned} \text{NPV} &= +100{,}000 - \sum_{t=1}^{10} \frac{3{,}000}{(1.10)^t} - \frac{100{,}000}{(1.10)^{10}} \\ &= +100{,}000 - 56{,}988 = +\$43{,}012 \end{aligned}$$

Of course, you don't need any arithmetic to tell you that borrowing at 3 percent is a good deal when the fair rate is 10 percent. But the NPV calculations tell you just how much that opportunity is worth (\$43,012).[1] It also brings out the essential similarity of investment and financing decisions.

Differences between Investment and Financing Decisions

In some ways investment decisions are simpler than financing decisions. The number of different financing decisions (i.e., securities) is continually expanding. You will have to learn the major families, genera, and species. You will also need to become familiar with the vocabulary of financing. You will learn about such matters as caps, strips, swaps, and bookrunners; behind each of these terms lies an interesting story.

[1]We ignore here any tax consequences of borrowing. These are discussed in Chapter 18.

There are also ways in which financing decisions are much easier than investment decisions. First, financing decisions do not have the same degree of finality as investment decisions. They are easier to reverse. That is, their abandonment value is higher. Second, it's harder to make or lose money by smart or stupid financing strategies. That is, it is difficult to find financing schemes with NPVs significantly different from zero. This reflects the nature of the competition.

When the firm looks at capital investment decisions, it does *not* assume that it is facing perfect, competitive markets. It may have only a few competitors that specialize in the same line of business in the same geographical area. And it may own some unique assets that give it an edge over its competitors. Often these assets are intangible, such as patents, expertise, or reputation. All this opens up the opportunity to make superior profits and find projects with positive NPVs.

In financial markets your competition is all other corporations seeking funds, to say nothing of the state, local, and federal governments that go to New York, London, and other financial centers to raise money. The investors who supply financing are comparably numerous, and they are smart: Money attracts brains. The financial amateur often views capital markets as *segmented,* that is, broken down into distinct sectors. But money moves between those sectors, and it moves fast.

Remember that a good financing decision generates a positive NPV. It is one in which the amount of cash raised exceeds the value of the liability created. But turn that statement around. If selling a security generates a positive NPV for the seller, it must generate a negative NPV for the buyer. Thus, the loan we discussed was a good deal for your firm but a negative NPV from the government's point of view. By lending at 3 percent, it offered a $43,012 subsidy.

What are the chances that your firm could consistently trick or persuade investors into purchasing securities with negative NPVs to them? Pretty low. In general, firms should assume that the securities they issue are fairly priced. That takes us into the main topic of this chapter: efficient capital markets.

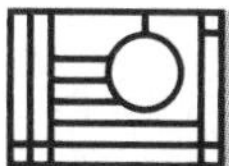

13.2 WHAT IS AN EFFICIENT MARKET?

A Startling Discovery: Price Changes Are Random

As is so often the case with important ideas, the concept of efficient capital markets stemmed from a chance discovery. In 1953 Maurice Kendall, a British statistician, presented a controversial paper to the Royal Statistical Society on the behavior of stock and commodity prices.[2] Kendall had expected to find regular price cycles, but to his surprise they did not seem to exist. Each series appeared to be "a 'wandering' one, almost as if once a week the Demon of Chance drew a random number . . . and added it to the current price to determine the next week's price." In other words, the prices of stocks and commodities seemed to follow a *random walk.*

---

[2]See M. G. Kendall, "The Analysis of Economic Time Series, Part I. Prices," *Journal of the Royal Statistical Society* 96 (1953), pp. 11–25. Kendall's idea was not wholly new. It had been proposed in an almost forgotten thesis written 53 years earlier by a French doctoral student, Louis Bachelier. Bachelier's accompanying development of the mathematical theory of random processes anticipated by five years Einstein's famous work on the random Brownian motion of colliding gas molecules. See L. Bachelier, *Theorie de la Speculation,* Gauthiers-Villars, Paris, 1900. Reprinted in English (A. J. Boness, trans.) in P. H. Cootner (ed.), *The Random Character of Stock Market Prices,* M.I.T. Press, Cambridge, MA, 1964, pp. 17–78.

If you are not sure what we mean by "random walk," you might like to think of the following example: You are given $100 to play a game. At the end of each week a coin is tossed. If it comes up heads, you win 3 percent of your investment; if it is tails, you lose 2.5 percent. Therefore, your capital at the end of the first week is either $103.00 or $97.50. At the end of the second week the coin is tossed again. Now the possible outcomes are:

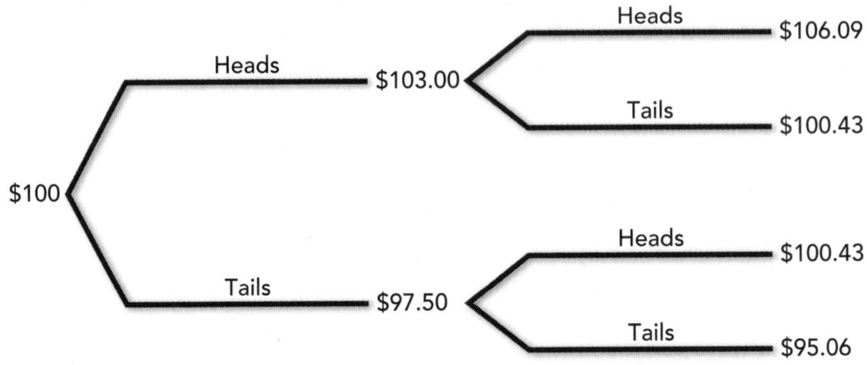

This process is a random walk with a positive drift of .25 percent per week.[3] It is a random walk because successive changes in value are independent. That is, the odds each week are the same, regardless of the value at the start of the week or of the pattern of heads and tails in the previous weeks.

If you find it difficult to believe that there are no patterns in share price changes, look at the two charts in Figure 13.1. One of these charts shows the outcome from playing our game for five years; the other shows the actual performance of the Standard and Poor's Index for a five-year period. Can you tell which one is which?[4]

When Maurice Kendall suggested that stock prices follow a random walk, he was implying that the price changes are independent of one another just as the gains and losses in our coin-tossing game were independent. Figure 13.2 illustrates this. Each dot shows the change in the price of Microsoft stock on successive days. The circled dot in the southeast quadrant refers to a pair of days in which a 1 percent increase was followed by a 1 percent decrease. If there was a systematic tendency for increases to be followed by decreases, there would be many dots in the southeast quadrant and few in the northeast quadrant. It is obvious from a glance that there is very little pattern in these price movements, but we can test this more precisely by calculating the coefficient of correlation between each day's price change and the next. If price movements persisted, the correlation would be positive; if there was no relationship, it would be 0. In our example, the correlation between successive price changes in Microsoft stock was +.022; there was a negligible tendency for price rises to be followed by further price rises.[5]

[3]The drift is equal to the expected outcome: $(1/2)(3) + (1/2)(-2.5) = .25\%$.

[4]The bottom chart in Figure 13.1 shows the real Standard and Poor's Index for the years 1980 through 1984; the top chart is a series of cumulated random numbers. Of course, 50 percent of you are likely to have guessed right, but we bet it was just a guess. A similar comparison between cumulated random numbers and actual price series was first suggested by H. V. Roberts, "Stock Market 'Patterns' and Financial Analysis: Methodological Suggestions," *Journal of Finance* 14 (March 1959), pp. 1–10.

[5]The correlation coefficient between successive observations is known as the *autocorrelation coefficient.* An autocorrelation of +.022 implies that, if Microsoft stock price rose by 1 percent more than average yesterday, your best forecast of today's price change would be a rise of .022 percent more than average.

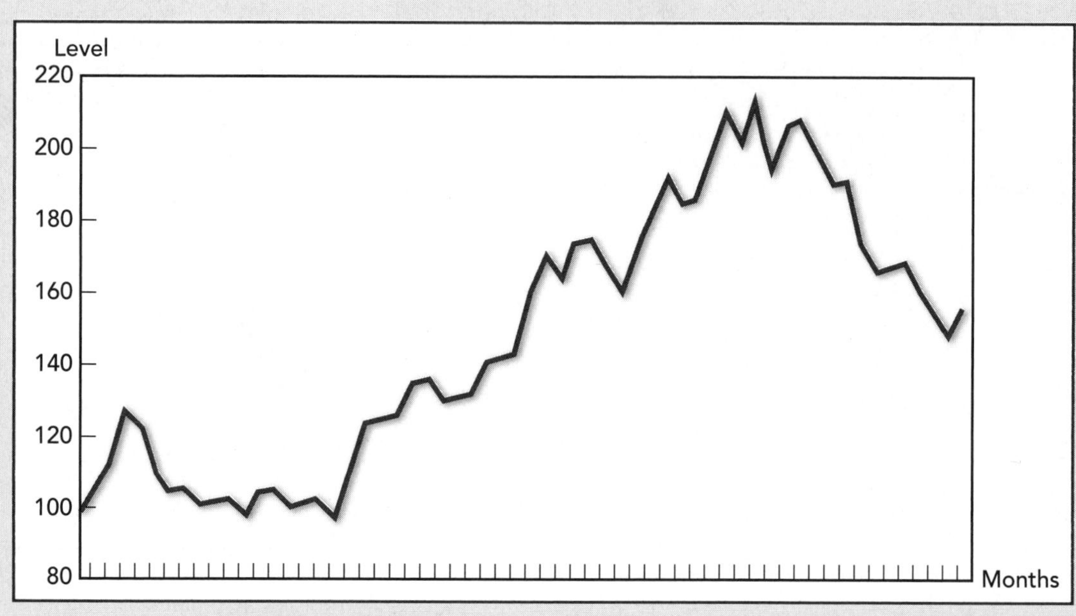

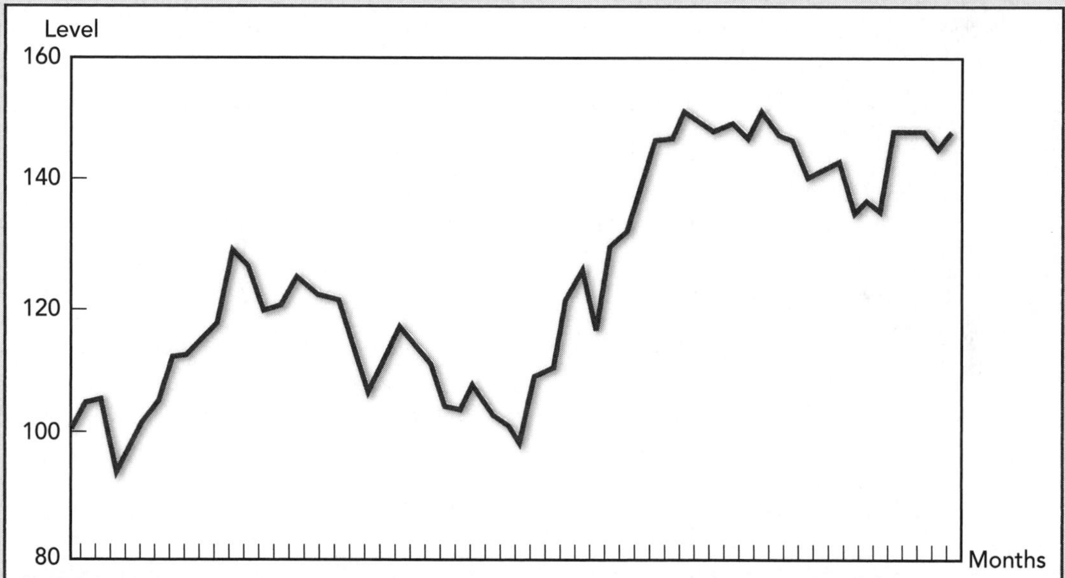

FIGURE 13.1

One of these charts shows the Standard and Poor's Index for a five-year period. The other shows the results of playing our coin-tossing game for five years. Can you tell which is which?

Figure 13.2 suggests that Microsoft's price changes were effectively uncorrelated. Today's price change gave investors almost no clue as to the likely change tomorrow. Does that surprise you? If so, imagine that it were not the case and that changes in Microsoft's stock price were expected to persist for several months. Figure 13.3 provides an example of such a predictable cycle. You can see that an

FIGURE 13.2

Each dot shows a pair of returns for Microsoft stock on two successive days between March 1990 and July 2001. The circled dot records a daily return of +1 percent and then −1 percent on the next day. The scatter diagram shows no significant relationship between returns on successive days.

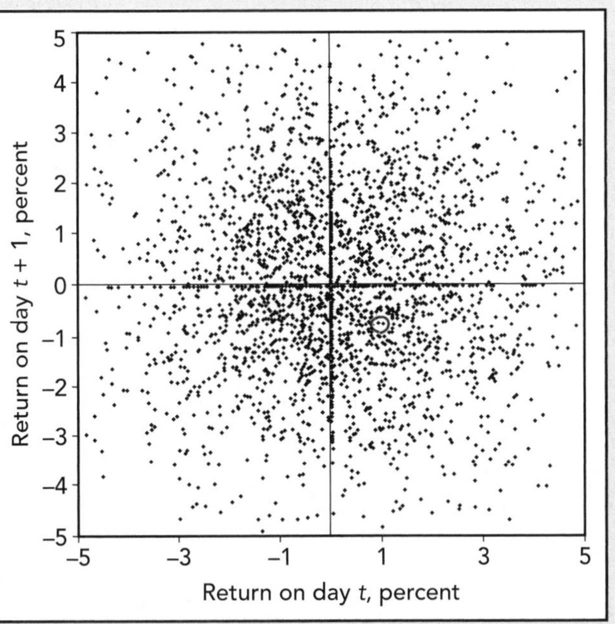

FIGURE 13.3

Cycles self-destruct as soon as they are recognized by investors. The stock price instantaneously jumps to the present value of the expected future price.

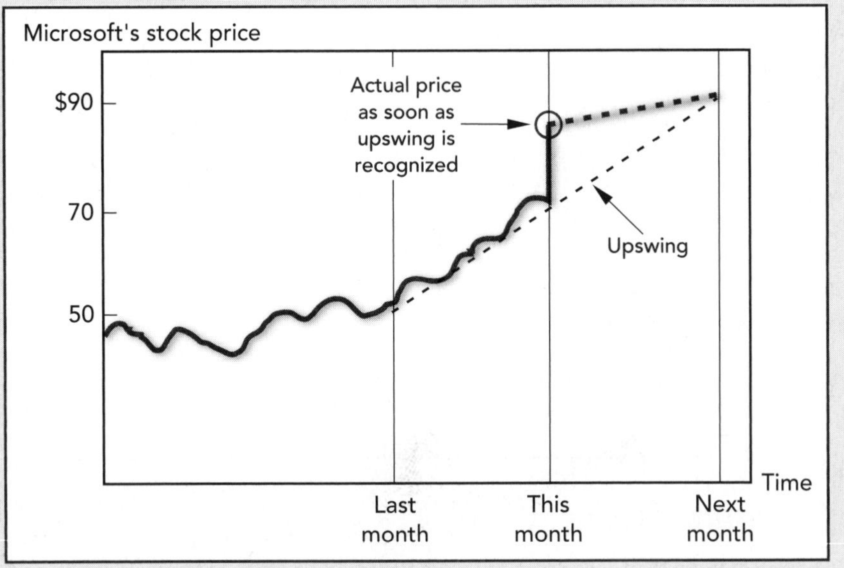

upswing in Microsoft's stock price started last month, when the price was $50, and it is expected to carry the price to $90 next month. What will happen when investors perceive this bonanza? It will self-destruct. Since Microsoft stock is a bargain at $70, investors will rush to buy. They will stop buying only when the stock offers a normal rate of return. Therefore, as soon as a cycle becomes apparent to investors, they immediately eliminate it by their trading.

Three Forms of Market Efficiency

You should see now why prices in competitive markets must follow a random walk. If past price changes could be used to predict future price changes, investors could make easy profits. But in competitive markets easy profits don't last. As investors try to take advantage of the information in past prices, prices adjust immediately until the superior profits from studying past price movements disappear. As a result, all the information in past prices will be reflected in *today's* stock price, not tomorrow's. Patterns in prices will no longer exist and price changes in one period will be independent of changes in the next. In other words, the share price will follow a random walk.

In competitive markets today's stock price must already reflect the information in past prices. But why stop there? If markets are competitive, shouldn't today's stock price reflect *all* the information that is available to investors? If so, securities will be fairly priced and security returns will be unpredictable, whatever information you consider.

Economists often define three levels of market efficiency, which are distinguished by the degree of information reflected in security prices. In the first level, prices reflect the information contained in the record of past prices. This is called the *weak* form of efficiency. If markets are efficient in the weak sense, then it is impossible to make consistently superior profits by studying past returns. Prices will follow a random walk.

The second level of efficiency requires that prices reflect not just past prices but all other published information, such as you might get from reading the financial press. This is known as the *semistrong* form of market efficiency. If markets are efficient in this sense, then prices will adjust immediately to public information such as the announcement of the last quarter's earnings, a new issue of stock, a proposal to merge two companies, and so on.

Finally, we might envisage a *strong* form of efficiency, in which prices reflect all the information that can be acquired by painstaking analysis of the company and the economy. In such a market we would observe lucky and unlucky investors, but we wouldn't find any superior investment managers who can consistently beat the market.

Efficient Markets: The Evidence

In the years that followed Maurice Kendall's discovery, financial journals were packed with tests of the efficient-market hypothesis. To test the weak form of the hypothesis, researchers measured the profitability of some of the trading rules used by those investors who claim to find patterns in security prices. They also employed statistical tests such as the one that we described when looking for patterns in the returns on Microsoft stock. For example, in Figure 13.4 we have used the same test to look for relationships between stock market returns in successive weeks. It appears that throughout the world there are few patterns in week-to-week returns.

To analyze the semistrong form of the efficient-market hypothesis, researchers have measured how rapidly security prices respond to different items of news, such as earnings or dividend announcements, news of a takeover, or macroeconomic information.

Before we describe what they found, we should explain how to isolate the effect of an announcement on the price of a stock. Suppose, for example, that you need

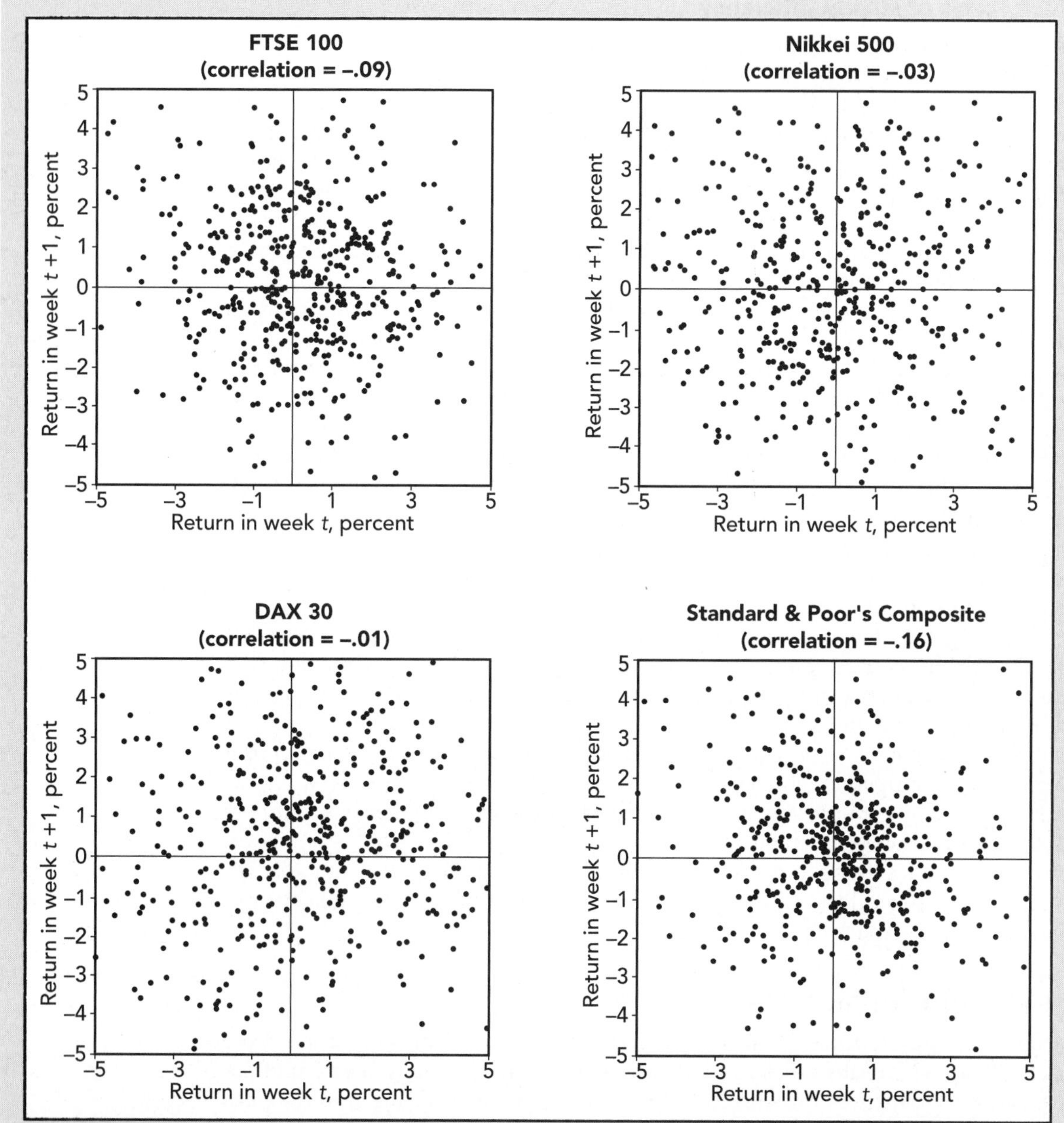

FIGURE 13.4

Each point in these scatter diagrams shows the return in successive weeks on four stock market indexes between September 1991 and July 2001. The wide scatter of points shows that there is almost no correlation between the return in one week and in the next. The four indexes are FTSE 100 (UK), the Nikkei 500 (Japan), DAX 30 (Germany), and Standard & Poor's Composite (USA).

to know how the stock price responds to news of a takeover. As a first stab, you could look at the returns on the stock in the months surrounding the announcement. But that would provide a very noisy measure, for the price would reflect among other things what was happening to the market as a whole. A second possibility would be to calculate a measure of relative performance.

Relative stock return = return on stock − return on market index

This is almost certainly better than simply looking at the returns on the stock. However, if you are concerned with performance over a period of several months or years, it would be preferable to recognize that fluctuations in the market have a larger effect on some stocks than others. For example, past experience might suggest that a change in the market index affected the value of a stock as follows:

Expected stock return = $\alpha + \beta \times$ return on market index[6]

Alpha (α) states how much on average the stock price changed when the market index was unchanged. Beta (β) tells us how much *extra* the stock price moved for each 1 percent change in the market index.[7] Suppose that subsequently the stock price provides a return of $\tilde{r}$ in a month when the market return is $\tilde{r}_m$. In that case we would conclude that the abnormal return for that month is

$$\text{Abnormal stock return} = \text{actual stock return} - \text{expected stock return}$$
$$= \tilde{r} - (\alpha + \beta\tilde{r}_m)$$

This abnormal return abstracts from the fluctuations in the stock price that result from marketwide influences.[8]

Figure 13.5 illustrates how the release of news affects abnormal returns. The graph shows the price run-up of a sample of 194 firms that were targets of takeover attempts. In most takeovers, the acquiring firm is willing to pay a large premium over the current market price of the acquired firm; therefore when a firm becomes the target of a takeover attempt, its stock price increases in anticipation of the takeover premium. Figure 13.5 shows that on the day the public become aware of a takeover attempt (Day 0 in the graph), the stock price of the typical target takes a big upward jump. The adjustment in stock price is immediate: After the big price move on the public announcement day, the run-up is over, and there is no further drift in the stock price, either upward or downward.[9] Thus within the day, the new stock prices apparently reflect (at least on average) the magnitude of the takeover premium.

A study by Patell and Wolfson shows just how fast prices move when new information becomes available.[10] They found that, when a firm publishes its latest earnings or announces a dividend change, the major part of the adjustment in price occurs within 5 to 10 minutes of the announcement.

---

[6]This relationship is often referred to as the *market model.*

[7]It is important when estimating α and β that you choose a period in which you believe that the stock behaved normally. If its performance was abnormal, then estimates of α and β cannot be used to measure the returns that investors expected. As a precaution, ask yourself whether your estimates of expected returns look sensible. Methods for estimating abnormal returns are analyzed in S. J. Brown and J. B. Warner, "Measuring Security Performance," *Journal of Financial Economics* 8 (1980), pp. 205–258.

[8]The market is not the only common influence on stock prices. For example, in Section 8.4 we described the Fama–French three-factor model, which states that a stock's return is influenced by three common factors—the market factor, a size factor, and a book-to-market factor. In this case we would calculate the expected stock return as $a + b_{\text{market}}(\tilde{r}_{\text{market factor}}) + b_{\text{size}}(\tilde{r}_{\text{size factor}}) + b_{\text{book-to-market}}(\tilde{r}_{\text{book-to-market factor}})$.

[9]See A. Keown and J. Pinkerton, "Merger Announcements and Insider Trading Activity," *Journal of Finance* 36 (September 1981), pp. 855–869. Note that prices on the days *before* the public announcement do show evidence of a sustained upward drift. This is evidence of a gradual leakage of information about a possible takeover attempt. Some investors begin to purchase the target firm in anticipation of a public announcement. Consistent with efficient markets, however, once the information becomes public, it is reflected fully and immediately in stock prices.

[10]See J. M. Patell and M. A. Wolfson, "The Intraday Speed of Adjustment of Stock Prices to Earnings and Dividend Announcements," *Journal of Financial Economics* 13 (June 1984), pp. 223–252.

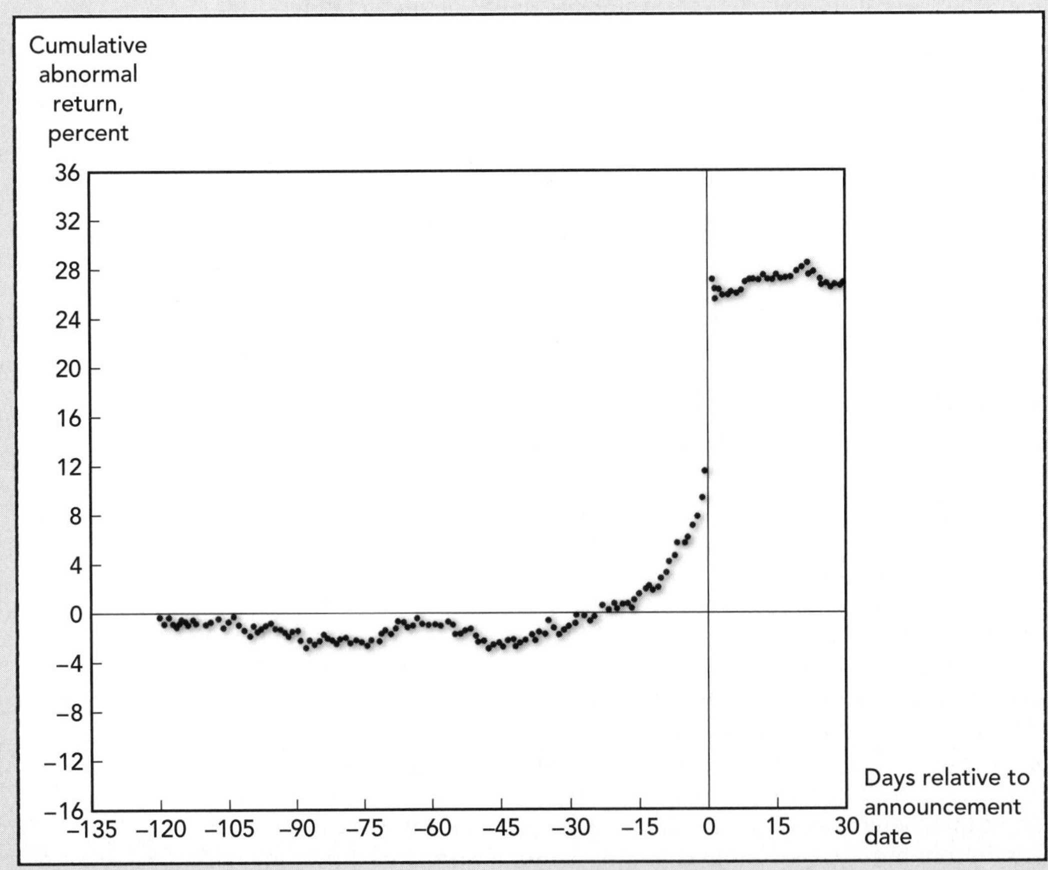

FIGURE 13.5

The performance of the stocks of target companies compared with that of the market. The prices of target stocks jump up on the announcement day, but from then on, there are no unusual price movements. The announcement of the takeover attempt seems to be fully reflected in the stock price on the announcement day.

Source: A. Keown and J. Pinkerton, "Merger Announcements and Insider Trading Activity," *Journal of Finance* 36 (September 1981), pp. 855–869.

Tests of the strong form of the hypothesis have examined the recommendations of professional security analysts and have looked for mutual funds or pension funds that could predictably outperform the market. Some researchers have found a slight persistent outperformance, but just as many have concluded that professionally managed funds fail to recoup the costs of management. Look, for example, at Figure 13.6, which is taken from a study by Mark Carhart of the average return on nearly 1,500 U.S. mutual funds. You can see that in some years the mutual funds beat the market, but as often as not it was the other way around. Figure 13.6 provides a fairly crude comparison, for mutual funds have tended to specialize in particular sectors of the market, such as low-beta stocks or large-firm stocks, that may have given below-average returns. To control for such differences, each fund needs to be compared with a benchmark portfolio of similar securities. The study by Mark Carhart did this, but the message was unchanged: The funds earned a lower return than the benchmark portfolios *after* expenses and roughly matched the benchmarks *before* expenses.

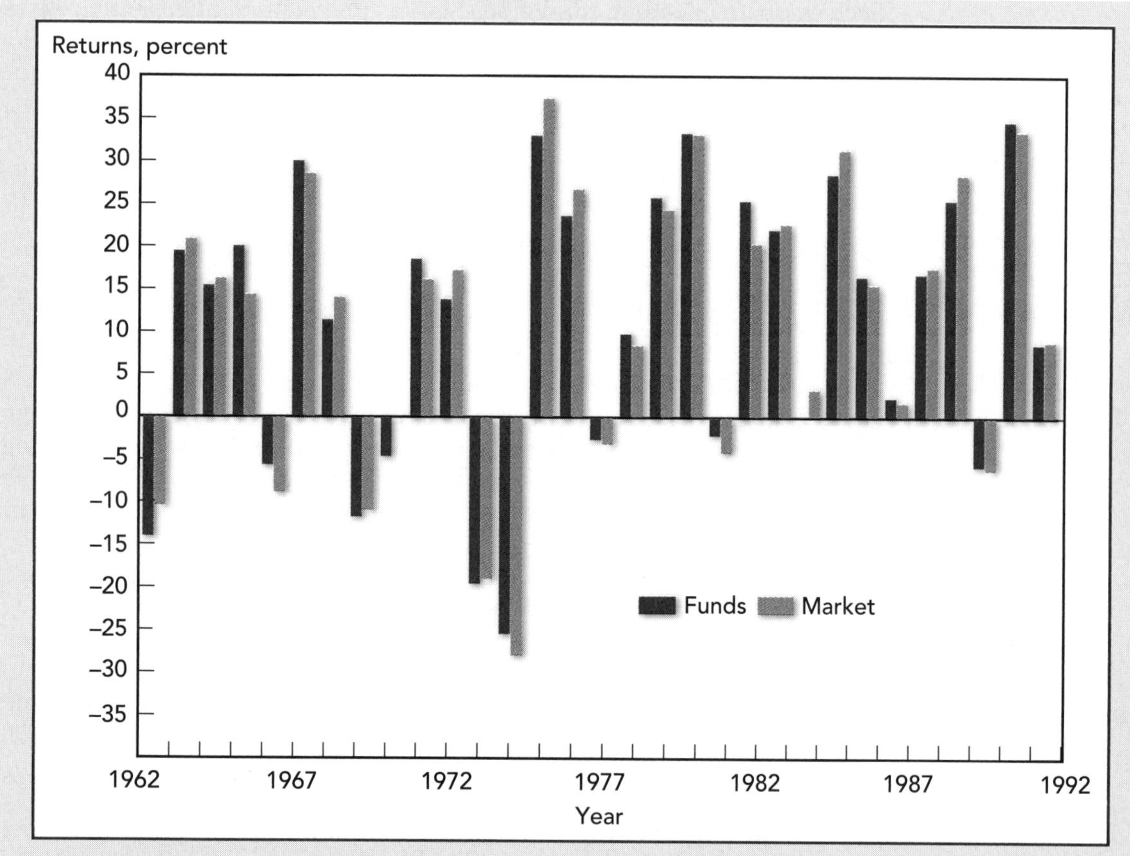

FIGURE 13.6

Average annual returns on 1,493 U.S. mutual funds and the market index, 1962–1992. Notice that mutual funds underperform the market in approximately half the years.

Source: M. M. Carhart, "On Persistence in Mutual Fund Performance," *Journal of Finance* 52 (March 1997), pp. 57–82.

It would be surprising if some managers were not smarter than others and could earn superior returns. But it seems difficult to spot the smart ones, and the top-performing managers one year have about an average chance of falling on their face the next year. For example, *Forbes Magazine,* a widely read investment periodical, has published annually since 1975 an "honor roll" of the most consistently successful mutual funds. Suppose that each year, when *Forbes* announced its honor roll, you had invested an equal sum in each of these exceptional funds. You would have outperformed the market in only 5 of the following 16 years, and your average annual return before paying any initial fees would have been more than 1 percent below the return on the market.[11]

[11]See B. G. Malkiel, "Returns from Investing in Equity Mutual Funds 1971 to 1991," *Journal of Finance* 50 (June 1995), pp. 549–572. It seems to be difficult to measure whether good performance does persist. Some contrary evidence is provided in E. J. Elton, M. J. Gruber, and C. R. Blake, "The Persistence of Risk-Adjusted Mutual Fund Performance," *Journal of Business* 69 (April 1996), pp. 133–157. There is, however, widespread agreement that the worst performing funds continue to underperform. That is not surprising, for they are shrinking and the costs of running them are proportionately higher.

Such evidence on strong-form efficiency has proved to be sufficiently convincing that many professionally managed funds have given up the pursuit of superior performance. They simply "buy the index," which maximizes diversification and minimizes the costs of managing the portfolio. Corporate pension plans now invest over a quarter of their United States equity holdings in index funds.

13.3 PUZZLES AND ANOMALIES—WHAT DO THEY MEAN FOR THE FINANCIAL MANAGER?

Almost without exception, early researchers concluded that the efficient-market hypothesis was a remarkably good description of reality. So powerful was the evidence that any dissenting research was regarded with suspicion. But eventually the readers of finance journals grew weary of hearing the same message. The interesting articles became those that turned up some puzzle. Soon the journals were packed with evidence of anomalies that investors have apparently failed to exploit.

We have already referred to one such puzzle—the abnormally high returns on the stocks of small firms. For example, look back at Figure 7.1, which shows the results of investing $1 in 1926 in the stocks of either small or large firms. (Notice that the portfolio values are plotted in Figure 7.1 on a logarithmic scale.) By 2000 the $1 invested in small company stocks had appreciated to $6,402, while the investment in large firms was worth only $2,587.[12] Although small firms had higher betas, the difference was not nearly large enough to explain the difference in returns.

Now this may mean one (or more) of three things. First, it could be that investors have demanded a higher expected return from small firms to compensate for some extra risk factor that is not captured in the simple capital asset pricing model. That is why we asked in Chapter 8 whether the small-firm effect is evidence against the CAPM.

Second, the superior performance of small firms could simply be a coincidence, a finding that stems from the efforts of many researchers to find interesting patterns in the data. There is evidence for and against the coincidence theory. Those who believe that the small-firm effect is a pervasive phenomenon can point to the fact that small-firm stocks have provided a higher return in many other countries. On the other hand, you can see from Figure 7.1 that the superior performance of small-firm stocks in the United States is limited to a relatively short period. Until the early 1960s small-firm and large-firm stocks were neck and neck. A wide gap then opened in the next two decades but it narrowed again in the 1980s when the small-firm effect first became known. If you looked simply at recent years, you might judge that there is a *large-firm* effect.

The third possibility is that we have here an important exception to the efficient-market theory, one that provided investors with an opportunity to make predictably superior profits over a period of two decades. If such anomalies offer easy pickings, you would expect to find a number of investors eager to take advantage of them. It turns out that, while many investors do try to exploit such anomalies, it is surprisingly difficult to get rich by doing so. For example, Professor Richard Roll, who probably knows as much as anyone about market anomalies, confesses

[12]In each case the portfolio values assume that dividends are reinvested.

> Over the past decade, I have attempted to exploit many of the seemingly most promising "inefficiencies" by actually trading significant amounts of money according to a trading rule suggested by the "inefficiencies"... I have never yet found one that worked in practice, in the sense that it returned more after cost than a buy-and-hold strategy.[13]

Do Investors Respond Slowly to New Information?

We have dwelt on the small-firm effect, but there is no shortage of other puzzles and anomalies. Some of them relate to the short-term behavior of stock prices. For example, returns appear to be higher in January than in other months, they seem to be lower on a Monday than on other days of the week, and most of the daily return comes at the beginning and end of the day.

To have any chance of making money from such short-term patterns, you need to be a professional trader, with one eye on the computer screen and the other on your annual bonus. If you are a corporate financial manager, these short-term patterns in stock prices may be intriguing conundrums, but they are unlikely to change the major financial decisions about which projects to invest in and how they should be financed. The more troubling concern for the corporate financial manager is the possibility that it may be several years before investors fully appreciate the significance of new information. The studies of daily and hourly price movements that we referred to above may not pick up this long-term mispricing, but here are two examples of an apparent long-term delay in the reaction to news.

The Earnings Announcement Puzzle The earnings announcement puzzle is summarized in Figure 13.7, which shows stock performance following the announcement of unexpectedly good or bad earnings during the years 1974 to 1986.[14] The 10 percent of the stocks of firms with the best earnings news outperform those with the worst news by more than 4 percent over the two months following the announcement. It seems that investors underreact to the earnings announcement and become aware of the full significance only as further information arrives.

The New-Issue Puzzle When firms issue stock to the public, investors typically rush to buy. On average those lucky enough to receive stock receive an immediate capital gain. However, researchers have found that these early gains often turn into losses. For example, suppose that you bought stock immediately following each initial public offering and then held that stock for five years. Over the period 1970–1998 your average annual return would have been 33 percent less than the return on a portfolio of similar-sized stocks.

The jury is still out on these studies of longer-term anomalies. Take, for example, the new-issue puzzle. Most new issues during the past 30 years have involved growth stocks with high market values and limited book assets. When the long-run performance of new issues is compared with a portfolio that is matched in terms of both size and book-to-market, the difference in performance disappears.[15] So

[13]R. Roll, "What Every CFO Should Know about Scientific Progress in Financial Economics: What Is Known and What Remains to be Resolved," *Financial Management* 23 (Summer 1994), pp. 69–75.

[14]V. L. Bernard and J. K. Thomas, "Post-Earnings Announcement Drift: Delayed Price Response or Risk Premium?" *Journal of Accounting Research* 27 (Supplement 1989), pp. 1–36.

[15]The long-run underperformance of new issues was described in R. Loughran and J. R. Ritter, "The New Issues Puzzle," *Journal of Finance* 50 (1995), pp. 23–51. The figures are updated on Jay Ritter's website and the returns compared with those of a portfolio which is matched in terms of size and book-to-market. (See **http://bear.cba.ufl.edu/ritter.**)

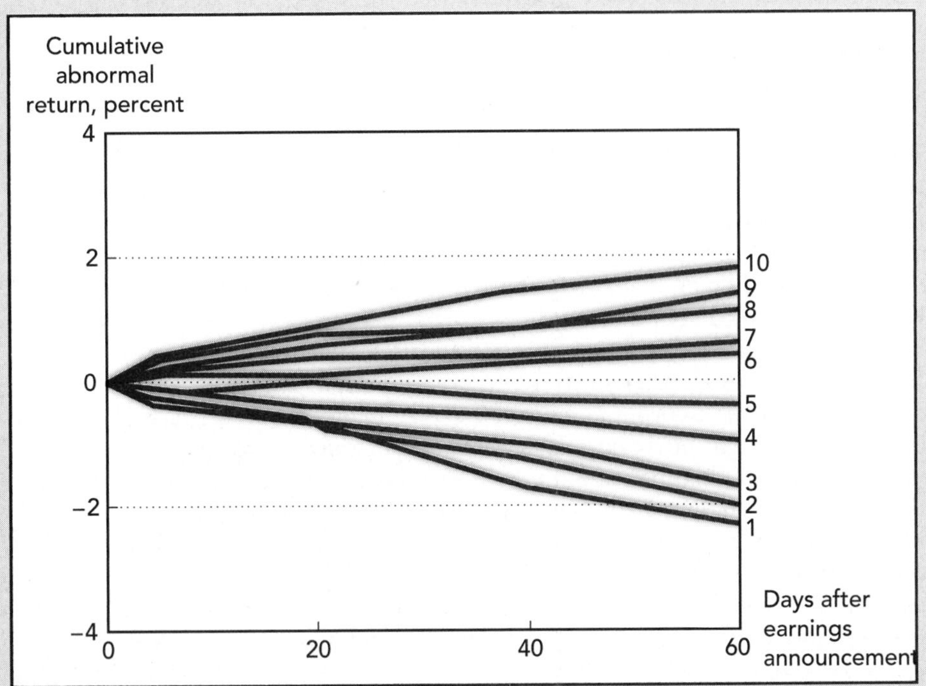

FIGURE 13.7

The cumulative abnormal returns of stocks of firms over the 60 days following an announcement of quarterly earnings. The 10 percent of the stocks with the best earnings news (Group 10) outperformed those with the worst news (Group 1) by more than 4 percent.

Source: V. L. Bernard and J. K. Thomas, "Post-Earnings-Announcement Drift: Delayed Price Response or Risk Premium?" *Journal of Accounting Research* 27 (Supplement 1989), pp. 1–36.

the new-issue puzzle could well turn out to be just the book-to-market puzzle in disguise.

Stock Market Anomalies and Behavioral Finance

In the meantime, some scholars are casting around for an alternative theory that might explain these apparent anomalies. Some argue that the answers lie in behavioral psychology. People are not 100 percent rational 100 percent of the time. This shows up in two broad areas—their attitudes to risk and the way that they assess probabilities.

1. *Attitudes toward risk* Psychologists have observed that, when making risky decisions, people are particularly loath to incur losses, even if those losses are small.[16] Losers tend to regret their actions and kick themselves for having been so foolish. To avoid this unpleasant possibility, individuals will tend to avoid those actions that may result in loss.

[16]This aversion to loss is modeled in D. Kahneman and A. Tversky, "Prospect Theory: An Analysis of Decision under Risk," *Econometrica* 47 (1979), pp. 263–291.

The pain of a loss seems to depend on whether it comes on the heels of earlier losses. Once investors have suffered a loss, they may be even more concerned not to risk a further loss and therefore they become particularly risk-averse. Conversely, just as gamblers are known to be more willing to make large bets when they are ahead, so investors may be more prepared to run the risk of a stock market dip after they have experienced a period of substantial gains.[17] If they do then suffer a small loss, they at least have the consolation of being up on the year.

When we discussed risk in Chapters 7 through 9, we pictured investors as concerned solely with the distribution of the possible returns, as summarized by the expected return and the variance. We did not allow for the possibility that investors may look back at the price at which they purchased stock and feel elated when their investment is in the black and depressed when it is in the red.

2. *Beliefs about probabilities* Most investors do not have a PhD in probability theory and may make systematic errors in assessing the probability of uncertain outcomes. Psychologists have found that, when judging the possible future outcomes, individuals commonly look back to what has happened in recent periods and then assume that this is representative of what may occur in the future. The temptation is to project recent experience into the future and to forget the lessons learned from the more distant past. Thus, an investor who places too much weight on recent events may judge that glamorous growth companies are very likely to continue to grow rapidly, even though very high rates of growth cannot persist indefinitely.

   A second systematic bias is that of overconfidence. Most of us believe that we are better-than-average drivers, and most investors think that they are better-than-average stock pickers. Two speculators who trade with one another cannot both make money from the deal; for every winner there must be a loser. But presumably investors are prepared to continue trading because each is confident that it is the other one who is the patsy.

Now these behavioral tendencies have been well documented by psychologists, and there is plenty of evidence that investors are not immune to irrational behavior. For example, most individuals are reluctant to sell stocks that show a loss. They also seem to be overconfident in their views and to trade excessively.[18] What is less clear is how far such behavioral traits help to explain stock market anomalies. Take, for example, the tendency to place too much emphasis on recent events and therefore to overreact to news. This phenomenon fits with one of our possible long-term puzzles (the long-term underperformance of new issues). It looks as if investors observe the hot new issues, get carried away by the apparent profits to be made, and then spend the next few years regretting their enthusiasm. However, the tendency to overreact doesn't help to explain our other long-term puzzle (the *underreaction* of investors to earnings announcements). Unless we have a theory of

[17] The effect is described in R. H. Thaler and E. J. Johnson, "Gambling with the House Money and Trying to Break Even: The Effects of Prior Outcomes on Risky Choice," *Management Science* 36 (1990), pp. 643–660. The implications for expected stock returns are explored in N. Barberis, M. Huang, and T. Santos, "Prospect Theory and Asset Prices," *Quarterly Journal of Economics* 116 (February 2001), pp. 1–53.

[18] See T. Odean, "Are Investors Reluctant to Realize their Losses?" *Journal of Finance* 53 (October 1998), pp. 1775–1798; and T. Odean, "Boys Will Be Boys: Gender, Overconfidence, and Common Stock Investment," *Quarterly Journal of Economics* 116 (February 2001), pp. 261–292.

human nature that can tell us when investors will overreact and when they will underreact, we are just as well off with the efficient-market theory which tells us that overreactions and underreactions are equally likely.[19]

There is another question that needs answering before we accept a behavioral bias as an explanation of an anomaly. It may well be true that many of us have a tendency to over- or underreact to recent events. However, hard-headed professional investors are constantly on the lookout for possible biases that may be a source of future profits.[20] So it is not enough to refer to irrationality on the part of individual investors; we also need to explain why professional investors have not competed away the apparent profit opportunities that such irrationality offers. The evidence on the performance of professionally managed portfolios suggests that many of these anomalies were not so easy to predict.

Professional Investors, Irrational Exuberance, and the Dot.com Bubble

Investors in technology stocks in the 1990s saw an extraordinary run-up in the value of their holdings. The Nasdaq Composite Index, which has a heavy weighting in high-tech stocks, rose 580 percent from the start of 1995 to its high in March 2000. Then even more rapidly than it began, the boom ended. By November 2001 the Nasdaq index had fallen 64 percent.

Some of the largest price gains and losses were experienced by the new "dot.com stocks." For example, Yahoo! shares, which began trading in April 1996, appreciated by 1,400 percent in just four years. At this point Yahoo! stock was valued at $124 billion, more than that of GM, Heinz, and Boeing combined. It was not, however, to last; just over a year later Yahoo!'s market capitalization was little more than $6 billion.

What caused the boom in high-tech stocks? Alan Greenspan, chairman of the Federal Reserve, attributed the run-up in prices to "irrational exuberance," a view that was shared by Professor Robert Shiller from Yale. In his book *Irrational Exuberance*[21] Shiller argued that, as the bull market developed, it generated optimism about the future and stimulated demand for shares.[22] Moreover, as investors racked up profits on their stocks, they became even more confident in their opinions.

But this brings us back to the $64,000 question. If Shiller was right and individual investors were carried away by irrational optimism, why didn't smart professional investors step in, sell high-tech stocks, and force their prices down to fair value? Were the pros also carried away on the same wave of euphoria? Or were they rationally reluctant to undertake more than a limited amount of selling if they could not be sure where and when the boom would end?

[19]This point is made in E. F. Fama, "Market Efficiency, Long-Term Returns, and Behavioral Finance," *Journal of Financial Economics* 49 (September 1998), pp. 283–306. One paper that does seek to model why investors may both underreact and overreact is N. Barberis, A. Shleifer, and R. Vishny, "A Model of Investor Sentiment," *Journal of Financial Economics* 49 (September 1998), pp. 307–343.

[20]Many financial institutions employ behavioral finance specialists to advise them on these biases.

[21]See R. J. Shiller, *Irrational Exuberance,* Broadway Books, 2001. Shiller also discusses behavioral explanations for the boom in R. J. Shiller, "Bubbles, Human Judgment, and Expert Opinion," Cowles Foundation Discussion Paper No. 1303, Cowles Foundation for Research in Economics, Yale University, New Haven, CT, May 2001.

[22]Some economists believe that the market price is prone to "bubbles"—situations in which price grows faster than fundamental value, but investors don't sell because they expect prices to keep rising. Of course, all such bubbles pop eventually, but they can in theory be self-sustaining for a while. The *Journal of Economic Perspectives* 4 (Spring 1990) contains several nontechnical articles on bubbles.

The Crash of 1987 and Relative Efficiency

On Monday, October 19, 1987, the Dow Jones Industrial Average (the Dow) fell 23 percent in *one day.* Immediately after the crash, everybody started to ask two questions: Who were the guilty parties? and Do prices reflect fundamental values?

As in most murder mysteries, the immediate suspects are not the ones "who done it." The first group of suspects included *index arbitrageurs,* who trade back and forth between index futures[23] and the stocks comprising the market index, taking advantage of any price discrepancies. On Black Monday futures fell first and fastest because investors found it easier to bail out of the stock market by way of futures than by selling individual stocks. This pushed the futures price below the stock market index.[24] The arbitrageurs tried to make money by selling stocks and buying futures, but they found it difficult to get up-to-date quotes on the stocks they wished to trade. Thus the futures and stock markets were for a time disconnected. Arbitrageurs contributed to the trading volume that swamped the New York Stock Exchange, but they did not cause the crash; they were the messengers who tried to transmit the selling pressure in the futures market back to the exchange.

The second suspects were large institutional investors who were trying to implement *portfolio insurance* schemes. Portfolio insurance aims to put a floor on the value of an equity portfolio by progressively selling stocks and buying safe, short-term debt securities as stock prices fall. Thus the selling pressure that drove prices down on Black Monday led portfolio insurers to sell still more. One institutional investor on October 19 sold stocks and futures totalling $1.7 billion. The immediate cause of the price fall on Black Monday may have been a herd of elephants all trying to leave by the same exit.

Perhaps some large portfolio insurers can be convicted of disorderly conduct, but why did stocks fall *worldwide,*[25] when portfolio insurance was significant only in the United States? Moreover, if sales were triggered mainly by portfolio insurance or trading tactics, they should have conveyed little fundamental information, and prices should have bounced back after Black Monday's confusion had dissipated.

So why did prices fall so sharply? There was no obvious, new fundamental information to justify such a sharp and widespread decline in share values. For this reason, the idea that the market price is the best estimate of intrinsic value seems less compelling than before the crash. It appears that either prices were irrationally high before Black Monday or irrationally low afterward. Could the theory of efficient markets be another casualty of the crash?

The events of October 1987 remind us how exceptionally difficult it is to value common stocks. For example, imagine that in November 2001 you wanted to check whether common stocks were fairly valued. At least as a first stab you might use the constant-growth formula that we introduced in Chapter 4. The annual expected dividend on the Standard and Poor's Composite Index was about 18.7.

[23]An index future provides a way of trading in the stock market as a whole. It is a contract that pays investors the value of the stocks in the index at a specified future date. We discuss futures in Chapter 27.

[24]That is, sellers pushed the futures prices below their *proper relation* to the index (again, see Chapter 27). The proper relation is not exact equality.

[25]Some countries experienced even larger falls than the United States. For example, prices fell by 46 percent in Hong Kong, 42 percent in Australia, and 35 percent in Mexico. For a discussion of the worldwide nature of the crash, see R. Roll, "The International Crash of October 1987," in R. Kamphuis (ed.), *Black Monday and the Future of Financial Markets,* Richard D. Irwin, Inc., Homewood, IL, 1989.

Suppose this dividend was expected to grow at a steady rate of 10 percent a year and investors required an annual return of 11.7 percent from common stocks. The constant growth formula gives a value for the index of

$$\text{PV(index)} = \frac{\text{DIV}}{r - g} = \frac{18.7}{.117 - .10} = 1{,}100$$

which was roughly the actual level of the index in mid-November 2001. But how confident could you be about any of these figures? Perhaps the likely dividend growth was only 9.5 percent per year. This would produce a 23 percent downward revision in your estimate of the right level of the index, from 1,100 to 850!

$$\text{PV(index)} = \frac{\text{DIV}}{r - g} = \frac{18.7}{.117 - .095} = 850$$

In other words, a price drop like Black Monday's could have occurred if investors had become just 0.5 percentage point less optimistic about future dividend growth.

The extreme difficulty of valuing common stocks from scratch has two important consequences. First, investors almost always price a common stock relative to yesterday's price or relative to today's price of comparable securities. In other words, they generally take yesterday's price as correct, adjusting upward or downward on the basis of today's information. If information arrives smoothly, then as time passes, investors become more and more confident that today's price level is correct. However, when investors lose confidence in the benchmark of yesterday's price, there may be a period of confused trading and volatile prices before a new benchmark is established.

Second, the hypothesis that stock price *always* equals intrinsic value is nearly impossible to test, because it is so difficult to calculate intrinsic value without referring to prices. Thus the crash did not conclusively disprove the hypothesis, but many people find it less plausible.

However, the crash does not undermine the evidence for market efficiency with respect to *relative* prices. Take, for example, Hershey stock, which sold for $66 in November 2001. Could we prove that true intrinsic value is $66? No, but we could be more confident that the price of Hershey should be roughly double that of Smucker ($33) since Hershey's earnings per share and dividend were about twice those of Smucker and the two shares had similar growth prospects. Moreover, if either company announced unexpectedly higher earnings, we could be quite confident that its share price would respond instantly and without bias. In other words, the subsequent price would be set correctly relative to the prior price. The most important lessons of market efficiency for the corporate financial manager are concerned with relative efficiency.

Market Anomalies and the Financial Manager

The financial manager needs to be confident that, when the firm issues new securities, it can do so at a fair price. There are two reasons that this may not be the case. First, the strong form of the efficient-market hypothesis may not be 100 percent true, so that the financial manager may have information that other investors do not have. Alternatively, investors may have the *same* information as management, but be slow to react to it. For example, we described above some evidence that new issues of stock tend to be followed by a prolonged period of low stock returns.

You sometimes hear managers say something along the following lines:

> Great! Our stock is clearly overpriced. This means we can raise capital cheaply and invest in Project X. Our high stock price gives us a big advantage over our competitors who could not possibly justify investing in Project X.

But that doesn't make sense. If your stock is truly overpriced, you can help your current shareholders by selling additional stock and using the cash to invest in other capital market securities. But you should *never* issue stock to invest in a project that offers a lower rate of return than you could earn elsewhere in the capital market. Such a project would have a negative NPV. You can always do better than investing in a negative-NPV project: Your company can go out and buy common stocks. In an efficient market, such purchases are always *zero* NPV.

What about the reverse? Suppose you know that your stock is *underpriced.* In that case, it certainly would not help your current shareholders to sell additional "cheap" stock to invest in other fairly priced stocks. If your stock is sufficiently underpriced, it may even pay to forego an opportunity to invest in a positive-NPV project rather than to allow new investors to buy into your firm at a low price. Financial managers who believe that their firm's stock is underpriced may be justifiably reluctant to issue more stock, but they may instead be able to finance their investment program by an issue of debt. In this case the market inefficiency would affect the firm's choice of financing but not its real investment decisions. In Chapter 15 we will have more to say about the financing choice when managers believe their stock is mispriced.

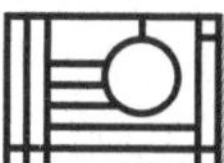

13.4 THE SIX LESSONS OF MARKET EFFICIENCY

Sorting out the puzzles will take time, but we believe that there is now widespread agreement that capital markets function sufficiently well that opportunities for easy profits are rare. So nowadays when economists come across instances where market prices apparently don't make sense, they don't throw the efficient-market hypothesis onto the economic garbage heap. Instead, they think carefully about whether there is some missing ingredient that their theories ignore.

We suggest therefore that financial managers should assume, at least as a starting point, that security prices are fair and that it is very difficult to outguess the market. This has some important implications for the financial manager.

Lesson 1: Markets Have No Memory

The weak form of the efficient-market hypothesis states that the sequence of past price changes contains no information about future changes. Economists express the same idea more concisely when they say that the market has no memory. Sometimes financial managers *seem* to act as if this were not the case. For example, studies by Taggart and others in the United States and by Marsh in the United Kingdom show that managers generally favor equity rather than debt financing after an abnormal price rise.[26] The idea is to catch the market while it is high. Similarly, they

[26]R. A. Taggart, "A Model of Corporate Financing Decisions," *Journal of Finance* 32 (December 1977), pp. 1467–1484; P. Asquith and D. W. Mullins, Jr., "Equity Issues and Offering Dilution," *Journal of Financial Economics* 15 (January–February 1986), pp. 16–89; P. R. Marsh, "The Choice between Debt and Equity: An Empirical Study," *Journal of Finance* 37 (March 1982), pp. 121–144.

are often reluctant to issue stock after a fall in price. They are inclined to wait for a rebound. But we know that the market has no memory and the cycles that financial managers seem to rely on do not exist.[27]

Sometimes a financial manager will have inside information indicating that the firm's stock is overpriced or underpriced. Suppose, for example, that there is some good news which the market does not know but you do. The stock price will rise sharply when the news is revealed. Therefore, if the company sold shares at the current price, it would be offering a bargain to new investors at the expense of present stockholders.

Naturally, managers are reluctant to sell new shares when they have favorable inside information. But such information has nothing to do with the history of the stock price. Your firm's stock could be selling at half its price of a year ago, and yet you could have special information suggesting that it is *still* grossly overvalued. Or it may be undervalued at twice last year's price.

Lesson 2: Trust Market Prices

In an efficient market you can trust prices, for they impound all available information about the value of each security. This means that in an efficient market, there is no way for most investors to achieve consistently superior rates of return. To do so, you not only need to know more than *anyone* else, but you also need to know more than *everyone* else. This message is important for the financial manager who is responsible for the firm's exchange-rate policy or for its purchases and sales of debt. If you operate on the basis that you are smarter than others at predicting currency changes or interest-rate moves, you will trade a consistent financial policy for an elusive will-o'-the-wisp.

The company's assets may also be directly affected by management's faith in its investment skills. For example, one company may purchase another simply because its management thinks that the stock is undervalued. On approximately half the occasions the stock of the acquired firm will with hindsight turn out to be undervalued. But on the other half it will be overvalued. On average the value will be correct, so the acquiring company is playing a fair game except for the costs of the acquisition.

Example—Orange County In December 1994, Orange County, one of the wealthiest counties in the United States, announced that it had lost $1.7 billion on its investment portfolio. The losses arose because the county treasurer, Robert Citron, had raised large short-term loans which he then used to bet on a rise in long-term bond prices.[28] The bonds that the county bought were backed by government-guaranteed mortgage loans. However, some of them were of an unusual type known as *reverse*

[27]If high stock prices signal expanded investment opportunities and the need to finance these new investments, we would expect to see firms raise more money *in total* when stock prices are historically high. But this does not explain why firms prefer to raise the extra cash at these times by an issue of equity rather than debt.

[28]Orange County borrowed money in the following way. Suppose it bought bond A and then sold it to a bank with a promise to buy it back at a slightly higher price. The cash from this sale was then invested in bond B. If bond prices fell, the county lost twice over: Its investment in bond B was worth less than the purchase price, and it was obliged to repurchase bond A for more than the bond was now worth. The sale and repurchase of bond A is known as a reverse repurchase agreement, or reverse "repo." We describe repos in Chapter 31.

floaters, which means that as interest rates rise, the interest payment on each bond is reduced, and vice versa.

Reverse floaters are riskier than normal bonds. When interest rates rise, prices of all bonds fall, but prices of reverse floaters suffer a double whammy because the interest rate payments decline as the discount rate rises. Thus Robert Citron's policy of borrowing to invest in reverse floaters ensured that when, contrary to his forecast, interest rates subsequently rose, the fund suffered huge losses.

Like Robert Citron, financial managers sometimes take large bets because they believe that they can spot the direction of interest rates, stock prices, or exchange rates, and sometimes their employers may encourage them to speculate.[29] We do not mean to imply that such speculation always results in losses, as in Orange County's case, for in an efficient market speculators win as often as they lose.[30] But corporate and municipal treasurers would do better to trust market prices rather than incur large risks in the quest for trading profits.

Lesson 3: Read the Entrails

If the market is efficient, prices impound all available information. Therefore, if we can only learn to read the entrails, security prices can tell us a lot about the future. For example, in Chapter 29 we will show how information in a company's financial statements can help the financial manager to estimate the probability of bankruptcy. But the market's assessment of the company's securities can also provide important information about the firm's prospects. Thus, if the company's bonds are offering a much higher yield than the average, you can deduce that the firm is probably in trouble.

Here is another example: Suppose that investors are confident that interest rates are set to rise over the next year. In that case, they will prefer to wait before they make long-term loans, and any firm that wants to borrow long-term money today will have to offer the inducement of a higher rate of interest. In other words, the long-term rate of interest will have to be higher than the one-year rate. Differences between the long-term interest rate and the short-term rate tell you something about what investors expect to happen to short-term rates in the future.[31]

Example—Hewlett Packard Proposes to Merge with Compaq On September 3, 2001, two computer companies, Hewlett Packard and Compaq, revealed plans to merge. Announcing the proposal, Carly Fiorina, the chief executive of Hewlett Packard, stated: "This combination vaults us into a leadership role" and creates "substantial shareowner value through significant cost structure improvements and access to new growth opportunities." But investors and analysts gave the proposal a big thumbs-down. Figure 13.8 shows that over the following two days the shares of Hewlett Packard underperformed the market by 21 percent, while Compaq shares underperformed by 16 percent. Investors, it seems, believed that the merger had a negative net present value of $13 billion. When on November 6 the Hewlett family announced that it would vote against the proposal, investors took

[29]We don't know why Robert Citron gambled with Orange County's money, but he was under pressure to make up for a shortfall in tax revenues.

[30]Watch out for the speculators who are making very large profits; they are almost certainly taking correspondingly large risks.

[31]We will discuss the relationship between short-term and long-term interest rates in Chapter 24. Notice, however, that in an efficient market the difference between the prices of *any* short-term and long-term contracts always says something about how participants expect prices to move.

FIGURE 13.8

Cumulative abnormal returns on Hewlett Packard and Compaq stocks during four-month period surrounding the announcement on September 3, 2001, of a proposed merger. Hewlett Packard stock recovered after the Hewlett family announced on November 6 that it would vote against the merger.

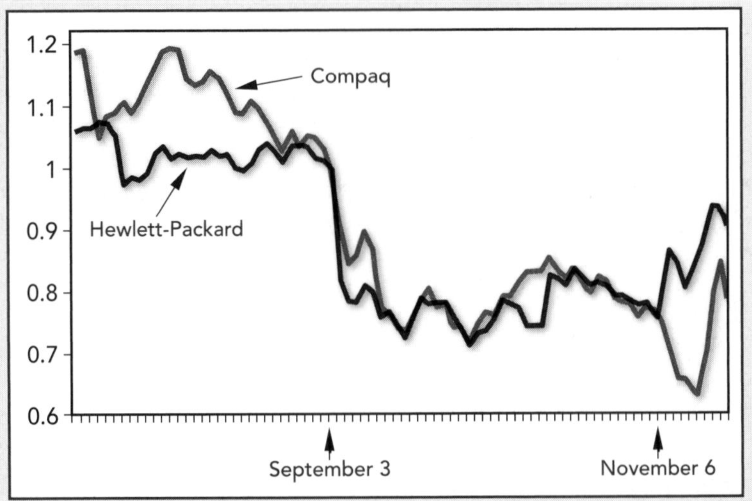

heart, and the next day Hewlett Packard shares gained 16 percent.[32] We do not wish to imply that investor concerns about the merger were justified, for management may have had important information that investors lacked. Our point is simply that the price reaction of the two stocks provided a potentially valuable summary of investor opinion about the effect of the merger on firm value.

Lesson 4: There Are No Financial Illusions

In an efficient market there are no financial illusions. Investors are unromantically concerned with the firm's cash flows and the portion of those cash flows to which they are entitled.

Example—Stock Dividends and Splits We can illustrate our fourth lesson by looking at the effect of stock dividends and splits. Every year hundreds of companies increase the number of shares outstanding either by subdividing the existing shares or by distributing more shares as dividends. This does not affect the company's future cash flows or the proportion of these cash flows attributable to each shareholder. For example, suppose the stock of Chaste Manhattan is selling for $210 per share. A 3-for-1 stock split would replace each outstanding share with three new shares. Chaste would probably arrange this by printing two new shares for each original share and distributing the new shares to its stockholders as a "free gift." After the split we would expect each share to sell for 210/3 = $70. Dividends per share, earnings per share, and all other per-share variables would be one-third their previous levels.

Figure 13.9 summarizes the results of a classic study of stock splits during the years 1926 to 1960.[33] It shows the cumulative abnormal performance of stocks

[32] The stock of Compaq, which was thought to be less badly affected by the merger, fell on the news, before also rising.

[33] See E. F. Fama, L. Fisher, M. Jensen, and R. Roll, "The Adjustment of Stock Prices to New Information," *International Economic Review* 10 (February 1969), pp. 1–21. Later researchers have discovered that shareholders make abnormal gains both when the split or stock dividend is announced and when it takes place. Nobody has offered a convincing explanation for the latter phenomenon. See, for example, M. S. Grinblatt, R. W. Masulis, and S. Titman, "The Valuation Effects of Stock Splits and Stock Dividends," *Journal of Financial Economics* 13 (December 1984), pp. 461–490.

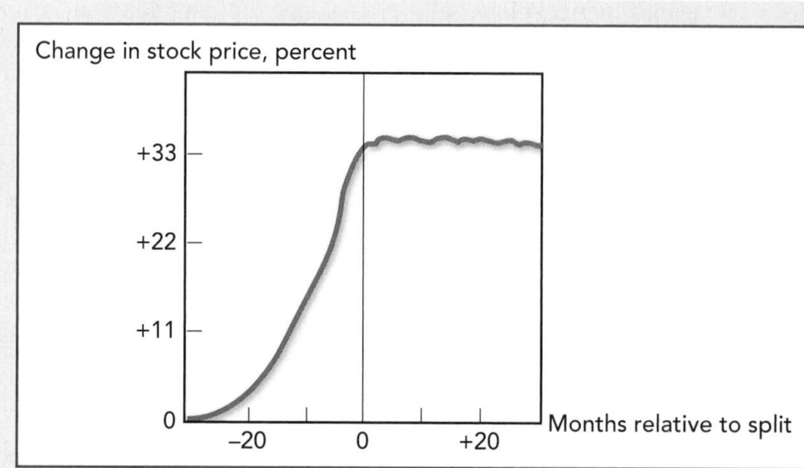

FIGURE 13.9

Cumulative abnormal returns at the time of a stock split. (Returns are adjusted for the increase in the number of shares.) Notice the rise before the split and the absence of abnormal changes after the split.

Source: E. Fama, L. Fisher, M. Jensen, and R. Roll, "The Adjustment of Stock Prices to New Information," *International Economic Review* 10 (February 1969), fig. 2b, p. 13.

around the time of the split after adjustment for the increase in the number of shares.[34] Notice the rise in price before the split. The announcement of the split would have occurred in the last month or two of this period. That means the decision to split is both the consequence of a rise in price and the cause of a further rise. It looks as if shareholders are not as hard-headed as we have been making out. They do seem to care about the form as well as the substance. However, during the subsequent year two-thirds of the splitting companies announced above-average increases in cash dividends. Normally such an announcement would cause an unusual rise in the stock price, but in the case of the splitting companies there was no such occurrence at any time after the split. The apparent explanation is that the split was accompanied by an explicit or implicit promise of a dividend increase and the rise in price at the time of the split had nothing to do with a predilection for splits as such but with the information that it was thought to convey.

This behavior does not imply that investors like the dividend increases for their own sake, for companies that split their stocks appear to be unusually successful in other ways. For example, Asquith, Healy, and Palepu found that stock splits are frequently preceded by sharp increases in earnings.[35] Such earnings increases are very often transitory, and investors rightly regard them with suspicion. However, the stock split appears to provide investors with an assurance that in this case the rise in earnings is indeed permanent.

Example—Accounting Changes There are other occasions on which managers seem to assume that investors suffer from financial illusion. For example, some firms devote considerable ingenuity to the task of manipulating earnings reported to stockholders. This is done by "creative accounting," that is, by choosing accounting methods that stabilize and increase reported earnings. Presumably firms

[34]By this we mean that the study looked at the change in the shareholders' wealth. A decline in the price of Chaste Manhattan stock from $210 to $70 at the time of the split would not affect shareholders' wealth.

[35]See P. Asquith, P. Healy, and K. Palepu, "Earnings and Stock Splits," *Accounting Review* 64 (July 1989), pp. 387–403.

go to this trouble because management believes that stockholders take the figures at face value.[36]

One way that companies can affect their reported earnings is through the way that they cost the goods taken out of inventory. Companies can choose between two methods. Under the FIFO (first-in, first-out) method, the firm deducts the cost of the first goods to have been placed in inventory. Under the LIFO (last-in, first-out) method companies deduct the cost of the latest goods to arrive in the warehouse. When inflation is high, the cost of the goods that were bought first is likely to be lower than the cost of those that were bought last. So earnings calculated under FIFO appear higher than those calculated under LIFO.

Now, if it were just a matter of presentation, there would be no harm in switching from LIFO to FIFO. But the IRS insists that the same method that is used to report to shareholders also be used to calculate the firm's taxes. So the lower immediate tax payments from using the LIFO method also bring lower apparent earnings.

If markets are efficient, investors should welcome a change to LIFO accounting, even though it reduces earnings. Biddle and Lindahl, who studied the matter, concluded that this is exactly what happens, so that the move to LIFO is associated with an abnormal rise in the stock price.[37] It seems that shareholders look behind the figures and focus on the amount of the tax savings.

Lesson 5: The Do-It-Yourself Alternative

In an efficient market investors will not pay others for what they can do equally well themselves. As we shall see, many of the controversies in corporate financing center on how well individuals can replicate corporate financial decisions. For example, companies often justify mergers on the grounds that they produce a more diversified and hence more stable firm. But if investors can hold the stocks of both companies why should they thank the companies for diversifying? It is much easier and cheaper for them to diversify than it is for the firm.

The financial manager needs to ask the same question when considering whether it is better to issue debt or common stock. If the firm issues debt, it will create financial leverage. As a result, the stock will be more risky and it will offer a higher expected return. But stockholders can obtain financial leverage without the firm's issuing debt; they can borrow on their own accounts. The problem for the financial manager is, therefore, to decide whether the company can issue debt more cheaply than the individual shareholder.

Lesson 6: Seen One Stock, Seen Them All

The elasticity of demand for any article measures the percentage change in the quantity demanded for each percentage addition to the price. If the article has close substitutes, the elasticity will be strongly negative; if not, it will be near zero. For example, coffee, which is a staple commodity, has a demand elasticity of about $-.2$. This means that a 5 percent increase in the price of coffee changes sales by $-.2 \times .05 = -.01$; in other words, it reduces demand by only 1 percent. Consumers are likely to regard

[36]For a discussion of the evidence that investors are not fooled by earnings manipulation, see R. Watts, "Does It Pay to Manipulate EPS?" in J. M. Stern and D. H. Chew, Jr. (eds.), *The Revolution in Corporate Finance*, Oxford, Basil Blackwell, 1986.

[37]G. C. Biddle and F. W. Lindahl, "Stock Price Reactions to LIFO Adoptions: The Association between Excess Returns and LIFO Tax Savings," *Journal of Accounting Research* 20 (Autumn 1982, Part 2), pp. 551–588.

different *brands* of coffee as much closer substitutes for each other. Therefore, the demand elasticity for a particular brand could be in the region of, say, −2.0. A 5 percent increase in the price of Maxwell House relative to that of Folgers would in this case reduce demand by 10 percent.

Investors don't buy a stock for its unique qualities; they buy it because it offers the prospect of a fair return for its risk. This means that stocks should be like *very* similar brands of coffee, almost perfect substitutes. Therefore, the demand for a company's stock should be highly elastic. If its prospective return is too low relative to its risk, *nobody* will want to hold that stock. If the reverse is true, *everybody* will scramble to buy.

Suppose that you want to sell a large block of stock. Since demand is elastic, you naturally conclude that you need only to cut the offering price very slightly to sell your stock. Unfortunately, that doesn't necessarily follow. When you come to sell your stock, other investors may suspect that you want to get rid of it because you know something they don't. Therefore, they will revise their assessment of the stock's value downward. Demand is still elastic, but the whole demand curve moves down. Elastic demand does not imply that stock prices never change when a large sale or purchase occurs; it *does* imply that you can sell large blocks of stock at close to the market price *as long as you can convince other investors that you have no private information.*

Here is one case that supports this view: In June 1977 the Bank of England offered its holding of BP shares for sale at 845 pence each. The bank owned nearly 67 million shares of BP, so the total value of the holding was £564 million, or about $970 million. It was a huge sum to ask the public to find.

Anyone who wished to apply for BP stock had nearly two weeks within which to do so. Just before the Bank's announcement the price of BP stock was 912 pence. Over the next two weeks the price drifted down to 898 pence, largely in line with the British equity market. Therefore, by the final application date, the discount being offered by the Bank was only 6 percent. In return for this discount, any applicant had to raise the necessary cash, taking the risk that the price of BP would decline before the result of the application was known, and had to pass over to the Bank of England the next dividend on BP.

If Maxwell House coffee is offered at a discount of 6 percent, the demand is unlikely to be overwhelming. But the discount on BP stock was enough to bring in applications for $4.6 billion worth of stock, 4.7 times the amount on offer.

We admit that this case was unusual in some respects, but an important study by Myron Scholes of a large sample of secondary offerings confirmed the ability of the market to absorb blocks of stock. The average effect of the offerings was a slight reduction in the stock price, but the decline was almost independent of the amount offered. Scholes's estimate of the demand elasticity for a company's stock was −3,000. Of course, this figure was not meant to be precise, and some researchers have argued that demand is not as elastic as Scholes's study suggests.[38] However, there seems to be widespread agreement with the general point that you can sell large quantities of stock at close to the market price as long as other investors do not deduce that you have some private information.

[38]For example, see W. H. Mikkelson and M. M. Partch, "Stock Price Effects and Costs of Secondary Distributions," *Journal of Financial Economics* 14 (June 1985), pp. 165–194. Scholes's study is M. S. Scholes, "The Market for Securities: Substitution versus Price Pressure and the Effects of Information on Share Prices," *Journal of Business* 45 (April 1972), pp. 179–211.

Here again we encounter an apparent contradiction with practice. Many corporations seem to believe not only that the demand elasticity is low but also that it varies with the stock price, so that when the price is relatively low, new stock can be sold only at a substantial discount. State and federal regulatory commissions, which set the prices charged by local telephone companies, electric companies, and other utilities, have sometimes allowed significantly higher earnings to compensate the firm for price "pressure." This pressure is the decline in the firm's stock price that is supposed to occur when new shares are offered to investors. Yet Paul Asquith and David Mullins, who searched for evidence of pressure, found that new stock issues by utilities drove down their stock prices on average by only .9 percent.[39] We will come back to the subject of pressure when we discuss stock issues in Chapter 15.

[39]See P. Asquith and D. W. Mullins, "Equity Issues and Offering Dilution," *Journal of Financial Economics* 15 (January–February 1986), pp. 61–89.

Visit us at www.mhhe.com/bm7e

SUMMARY

The patron saint of the Bolsa (stock exchange) in Barcelona, Spain, is Nuestra Senora de la Esperanza—Our Lady of Hope. She is the perfect patroness, for we all hope for superior returns when we invest. But competition between investors will tend to produce an efficient market. In such a market, prices will rapidly impound any new information, and it will be difficult to make consistently superior returns. We may indeed hope, but all we can rationally *expect* in an efficient market is a return just sufficient to compensate us for the time value of money and for the risks we bear.

The efficient-market hypothesis comes in three different flavors. The weak form of the hypothesis states that prices efficiently reflect all the information in the past series of stock prices. In this case it is impossible to earn superior returns simply by looking for patterns in stock prices; in other words, price changes are random. The semistrong form of the hypothesis states that prices reflect all published information. That means it is impossible to make consistently superior returns just by reading the newspaper, looking at the company's annual accounts, and so on. The strong form of the hypothesis states that stock prices effectively impound all available information. It tells us that superior information is hard to find because in pursuing it you are in competition with thousands, perhaps millions, of active, intelligent, and greedy investors. The best you can do in this case is to assume that securities are fairly priced and to hope that one day Nuestra Senora will reward your humility.

While there remain plenty of unsolved puzzles, there seems to be widespread agreement that consistently superior returns are hard to attain. Thirty years ago any suggestion that security investment is a fair game was generally regarded as bizarre. Today it is not only widely discussed in business schools but also permeates investment practice and government policy toward the securities markets.

For the corporate treasurer who is concerned with issuing or purchasing securities, the efficient-market theory has obvious implications. In one sense, however, it raises more questions than it answers. The existence of efficient markets does not mean that the financial manager can let financing take care of itself. It provides only a starting point for analysis. It is time to get down to details about securities and issue procedures. We start in Chapter 14.

FURTHER READING

The classic review articles on market efficiency are:

E. F. Fama: "Efficient Capital Markets: A Review of Theory and Empirical Work," *Journal of Finance,* 25:383–417 (May 1970).

E. F. Fama: "Efficient Capital Markets: II," *Journal of Finance,* 46:1575–1617 (December 1991).

For evidence on possible exceptions to the efficient-market theory, we suggest:

G. Hawawini and D. B. Keim: "On the Predictability of Common Stock Returns: World-Wide Evidence," in R. A. Jarrow, V. Maksimovic, and W. T. Ziemba (eds.), *Finance,* North-Holland, Amsterdam, Netherlands, 1994.

Martin Gruber's Presidential Address to the American Finance Association is an interesting overview of the performance of mutual fund managers.

M. Gruber: "Another Puzzle: The Growth in Actively Managed Mutual Funds," *Journal of Finance,* 51:783–810 (July 1996).

Andre Shleifer's book and Robert Shiller's paper provide a good introduction to behavioral finance. A useful collection of papers on behavioral explanations for market anomalies is provided in Richard Thaler's book of readings, while Eugene Fama's paper offers a more skeptical view of these behavioral theories.

A. Shleifer: *Inefficient Markets: An Introduction to Behavioral Finance,* Oxford University Press, Oxford, 2000.

R. J. Shiller: "Human Behavior and the Efficiency of the Financial System," in J. B. Taylor and M. Woodford (eds.), *Handbook of Macroeconomics,* North-Holland, Amsterdam, 1999.

R. H. Thaler (ed.): *Advances in Behavioral Finance,* Russell Sage Foundation, New York, 1993.

E. F. Fama: "Market Efficiency, Long-Term Returns, and Behavioral Finance," *Journal of Financial Economics,* 49:283–306 (September 1998).

The following book contains an interesting collection of articles on the crash of 1987:

R. W. Kamphuis, Jr., et al. (eds.): *Black Monday and the Future of Financial Markets,* Dow-Jones Irwin, Inc., Homewood, IL, 1989.

Visit us at www.mhhe.com/bm7e

QUIZ

1. Which (if any) of these statements are true? Stock prices appear to behave as though successive values **(a)** are random numbers, **(b)** follow regular cycles, **(c)** differ by a random number.

2. Supply the missing words:

   "There are three forms of the efficient-market hypothesis. Tests of randomness in stock returns provide evidence for the _________ form of the hypothesis. Tests of stock price reaction to well-publicized news provide evidence for the _________ form, and tests of the performance of professionally managed funds provide evidence for the _________ form. Market efficiency results from competition between investors. Many investors search for new information about the company's business that would help them to value the stock more accurately. Such research helps to ensure that prices reflect all available information; in other words, it helps to keep the market efficient in the _________ form. Other investors study past stock prices for recurrent patterns that would allow them to make superior profits. Such research helps to ensure that prices reflect all the information contained in past stock prices; in other words, it helps to keep the market efficient in the _________ form."

3. True or false? The efficient-market hypothesis assumes that
   a. There are no taxes.
   b. There is perfect foresight.
   c. Successive price changes are independent.
   d. Investors are irrational.

e. There are no transaction costs.
f. Forecasts are unbiased.

4. The stock of United Boot is priced at $400 and offers a dividend yield of 2 percent. The company has a 2-for-1 stock split.
   a. Other things equal, what would you expect to happen to the stock price?
   b. In practice would you expect the stock price to fall by more or less than this amount?
   c. Suppose that a few months later United Boot announces a rise in dividends that is exactly in line with that of other companies. Would you expect the announcement to lead to a slight abnormal rise in the stock price, a slight abnormal fall, or no change?
5. True or false?
   a. Financing decisions are less easily reversed than investment decisions.
   b. Financing decisions don't affect the total size of the cash flows; they just affect who receives the flows.
   c. Tests have shown that there is almost perfect negative correlation between successive price changes.
   d. The semistrong form of the efficient-market hypothesis states that prices reflect all publicly available information.
   e. In efficient markets the expected return on each stock is the same.
   f. Myron Scholes's study of the effect of secondary distributions provided evidence that the demand schedule for a single company's shares is highly elastic.
6. Analysis of 60 monthly rates of return on United Futon common stock indicates a beta of 1.45 and an alpha of −.2 percent per month. A month later, the market is up by 5 percent, and United Futon is up by 6 percent. What is Futon's abnormal rate of return?
7. True or false?
   a. Analysis by security analysts and investors helps keep markets efficient.
   b. Psychologists have found that, once people have suffered a loss, they are more relaxed about the possibility of incurring further losses.
   c. Psychologists have observed that people tend to regard recent events as representative of what might happen in the future.
   d. If the efficient-market hypothesis is correct, managers will not be able to increase stock prices by creative accounting that boosts reported earnings.
8. Geothermal Corporation has just received good news: its earnings increased by 20 percent from last year's value. Most investors are anticipating an increase of 25 percent. Will Geothermal's stock price increase or decrease when the announcement is made?
9. Here again are the six lessons of market efficiency. For each lesson give an example showing the lesson's relevance to financial managers.
   a. Markets have no memory.
   b. Trust market prices.
   c. Read the entrails.
   d. There are no financial illusions.
   e. The do-it-yourself alternative.
   f. Seen one stock, seen them all.

PRACTICE QUESTIONS

1. How would you respond to the following comments?
   a. "Efficient market, my eye! I know lots of investors who do crazy things."
   b. "Efficient market? Balderdash! I know at least a dozen people who have made a bundle in the stock market."
   c. "The trouble with the efficient-market theory is that it ignores investors' psychology."

d. "Despite all the limitations, the best guide to a company's value is its written-down book value. It is much more stable than market value, which depends on temporary fashions."

2. Respond to the following comments:
   a. "The random-walk theory, with its implication that investing in stocks is like playing roulette, is a powerful indictment of our capital markets."
   b. "If everyone believes you can make money by charting stock prices, then price changes won't be random."
   c. "The random-walk theory implies that events are random, but many events are not random. If it rains today, there's a fair bet that it will rain again tomorrow."

3. Which of the following observations *appear* to indicate market inefficiency? Explain whether the observation appears to contradict the weak, semistrong, or strong form of the efficient-market hypothesis.
   a. Tax-exempt municipal bonds offer lower pretax returns than taxable government bonds.
   b. Managers make superior returns on their purchases of their company's stock.
   c. There is a positive relationship between the return on the market in one quarter and the change in aggregate profits in the next quarter.
   d. There is disputed evidence that stocks which have appreciated unusually in the recent past continue to do so in the future.
   e. The stock of an acquired firm tends to appreciate in the period before the merger announcement.
   f. Stocks of companies with unexpectedly high earnings *appear* to offer high returns for several months after the earnings announcement.
   g. Very risky stocks on average give higher returns than safe stocks.

4. Look again at Figure 13.9.
   a. Is the steady rise in the stock price before the split evidence of market inefficiency?
   b. How do you think those stocks performed that did *not* increase their dividends by an above-average amount?

5. Stock splits are important because they convey information. Can you suggest some other financial decisions that do so?

6. Here are alphas and betas for Intel and Conagra for the 60 months ending October 2001. Alpha is expressed as a percent per month.

	Alpha	Beta
Intel	.77	1.61
Conagra	.17	.47

   Explain how these estimates would be used to calculate an abnormal return.

7. It is sometimes suggested that stocks with low price–earnings ratios tend to be underpriced. Describe a possible test of this view. Be as precise as possible.

8. "If the efficient-market hypothesis is true, then it makes no difference what securities a company issues. All are fairly priced." Does this follow?

9. "If the efficient-market hypothesis is true, the pension fund manager might as well select a portfolio with a pin." Explain why this is not so.

10. The bottom graph in Figure 13.1 shows the actual performance of the Standard and Poor's 500 Index for a five-year period. Two financial managers, Alpha and Beta, are contemplating this chart. Each manager's company needs to issue new shares of common stock sometime in the next year.

Alpha: My company's going to issue right away. The stock market cycle has obviously topped out, and the next move is almost surely down. Better to issue now and get a decent price for the shares.

Beta: You're too nervous; we're waiting. It's true that the market's been going nowhere for the past year or so, but the figure clearly shows a basic upward trend. The market's on the way up to a new plateau.

What would you say to Alpha and Beta?

11. What does the efficient-market hypothesis have to say about these two statements?
    a. "I notice that short-term interest rates are about 1 percent below long-term rates. We should borrow short-term."
    b. "I notice that interest rates in Japan are lower than rates in the United States. We would do better to borrow Japanese yen rather than U.S. dollars."
12. We suggested that there are three possible interpretations of the small-firm effect: a required return for some unidentified risk factor, a coincidence, or market inefficiency. Write three brief memos, arguing each point of view.
13. "It may be true that in an efficient market there *should* be no patterns in stock prices, but, if everyone believes that they *do* exist, then this belief will be self-fulfilling." Discuss.
14. Column (a) in Table 13.1 shows the monthly return on the British FTSE 100 index from August 1999 through July 2001. Columns (b) and (c) show the returns on the stocks of two firms. Both announced dividend increases during this period—Executive Cheese

Visit us at www.mhhe.com/bm7e

TABLE 13.1

See practice question 14. Rates of return in percent per month.

Month	(A) Market Return	(B) Executive Cheese Return	(C) Paddington Beer Return
1999:			
Aug.	.2	−1.9	−.5
Sept.	−3.5	−10.1	−6.1
Oct.	3.7	8.1	9.8
Nov.	5.5	7.5	16.5
Dec.	5.0	4.3	6.7
2000:			
Jan.	−9.5	−5.3	−11.1
Feb.	−.6	5.7	−7.3
Mar.	4.9	−9.7	4.5
Apr.	−3.3	−4.7	−14.8
May	.5	−10.0	−1.1
June	−.7	−2.7	−1.2
July	.8	.1	−2.6
Aug.	4.8	3.4	12.4
Sept.	−5.7	5.6	−7.9
Oct.	2.3	−2.2	11.5
Nov.	−4.6	−6.5	−14.4
Dec.	1.3	−.2	3.4
2001:			
Jan.	1.2	−3.7	4.1
Feb.	−6.0	−9.0	−14.1
Mar.	−4.8	7.3	−6.5
Apr.	5.9	4.7	12.6
May	−2.9	−7.1	−.7
June	−2.7	0.5	−14.5
July	−2.0	−0.5	−11.4

in September 2000 and Paddington Beer in January 2000. Calculate the average abnormal return of the two stocks during the month of the dividend announcement.

15. On May 15, 1997, the government of Kuwait offered to sell 170 million BP shares, worth about $2 billion. Goldman Sachs was contacted after the stock market closed in London and given one hour to decide whether to bid on the stock. They decided to offer 710.5 pence ($11.59) per share, and Kuwait accepted. Then Goldman Sachs went looking for buyers. They lined up 500 institutional and individual investors worldwide, and resold all the shares at 716 pence ($11.70). The resale was complete before the London Stock Exchange opened the next morning. Goldman Sachs made $15 million overnight.[40]

What does this deal say about market efficiency? Discuss.

CHALLENGE QUESTIONS

1. Bond dealers buy and sell bonds at very low spreads. In other words, they are willing to sell at a price only slightly higher than the price at which they buy. Used-car dealers buy and sell cars at very wide spreads. What has this got to do with the strong form of the efficient-market hypothesis?

2. "An analysis of the behavior of exchange rates and bond prices around the time of international assistance for countries in balance of payments difficulties suggests that on average prices decline sharply for a number of months before the announcement of the assistance and are largely stable after the announcement. This suggests that the assistance is effective but comes too late." Does this follow?

3. Use either the Market Insight database (**www.mhhe.com/edumarketinsight**) or (**www.finance.yahoo.com**) to download daily prices for 5 U.S. stocks for a recent 12-month period. For each stock construct a scatter diagram of successive returns as in Figure 13.2. Then calculate the correlation between the returns on successive days. Do you find any consistent patterns?

[40] "Goldman Sachs Earns a Quick $15 Million Sale of BP Shares," *The Wall Street Journal,* May 16, 1997, p. A4.

CHAPTER FOURTEEN

AN OVERVIEW OF CORPORATE FINANCING

WE NOW BEGIN our analysis of long-term financing decisions—an undertaking we will not complete until Chapter 26. This chapter provides an introduction to corporate financing. It reviews with a broad brush several topics that will be explored more carefully later on.

We start the chapter by looking at aggregate data on the sources of financing for U.S. corporations. Much of the money for new investments comes from profits that companies retain and reinvest. The remainder comes from selling new debt or equity securities. These financing patterns raise several interesting questions. Do companies rely too heavily on internal financing rather than on new issues of debt or equity? Are debt ratios of U.S. corporations dangerously high? How do patterns of financing differ across the major industrialized countries?

Our second task in the chapter is to review some of the essential features of debt and equity. Lenders and stockholders have different *cash flow rights* and also different *control rights*. The lenders have first claim on cash flow, because they are promised definite cash payments for interest and principal. The stockholder receives whatever cash is left over after the lenders are paid. Stockholders, on the other hand, have complete control of the firm, providing that they keep their promises to lenders. As owners of the business, stockholders have the ultimate control over what assets the company buys, how the assets are financed, and how they are used. Of course, in large public corporations the stockholders delegate these decisions to the board of directors, who in turn appoint senior management. In these cases *effective* control often ends up with the company's management.

The simple division of sources of cash into debt and equity glosses over the many different types of debt that companies issue. Therefore, we close our discussion of debt and equity with a brief canter through the main categories of debt. We also pause to describe certain less common forms of equity, particularly preferred stock.

Financial institutions play an important role in supplying finance to companies. For example, banks provide short- and medium-term debt, help to arrange new public issues of securities, buy and sell foreign currencies, and so on. We introduce you to the major financial institutions and look at the roles that they play in corporate financing and in the economy at large.

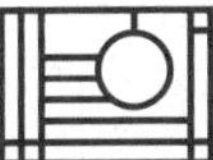

14.1 PATTERNS OF CORPORATE FINANCING

Companies invest in long-term assets (mainly property, plant, and equipment) and net working capital. Table 14.1 shows where they get the cash to pay for these investments. You can see that by far the greater part of the money is generated internally. In other words, it comes from cash that the company has set aside as depreciation and from retained earnings (earnings not paid out as dividends).[1] Shareholders are happy for companies to plow back this money into the firm, so long as it goes to positive-NPV investments. Every positive-NPV investment generates a higher price for their shares.

In most years there is a gap between the cash that companies need and the cash that they generate internally. This gap is the financial deficit. To make up the deficit, companies must either sell new equity or borrow. So companies face two basic financing decisions: How much profit should be plowed back into the

[1]In Table 14.1, internally generated cash was calculated by adding depreciation to retained earnings. Depreciation is a noncash expense. Thus, retained earnings understate the cash flow available for reinvestment.

	1990	1991	1992	1993	1994	1995	1996	1997	1998	1999	2000
1. Capital expenditure	87.1%	104.5%	87.5%	87.3%	83.2%	77.6%	87.6%	81.0%	89.1%	80.4%	86.6%
2. Investment in net working capital and other uses	12.9%	−4.5%	12.5%	12.7%	16.8%	22.4%	12.4%	19.0%	10.9%	19.6%	13.4%
3. Total investment	100.0%	100.0%	100.0%	100.0%	100.0%	100.0%	100.0%	100.0%	100.0%	100.0%	100.0%
Total investment, billions	**$ 498**	**$ 412**	**$ 517**	**$ 567**	**$ 754**	**$ 789**	**$ 755**	**$ 880**	**$ 872**	**$ 1,116**	**$ 1,162**
4. Internally generated cash	86.8%	108.6%	90.0%	90.2%	87.7%	78.6%	89.5%	82.7%	85.7%	72.1%	76.7%
5. Financial deficit	13.2%	−8.6%	10.0%	9.8%	12.3%	21.4%	10.5%	17.3%	14.3%	27.9%	23.3%
Financial deficit covered by											
6. Net stock issues	−12.7%	4.4%	5.2%	3.8%	−6.9%	−7.4%	−9.2%	−13.0%	−30.6%	−12.9%	−14.3%
7. Net increase in debt	25.9%	−13.0%	4.8%	6.1%	19.3%	28.8%	19.7%	30.3%	45.0%	40.8%	37.6%

TABLE 14.1

Sources and uses of funds in nonfinancial corporations expressed as percentages of each year's total investment.

Source: Board of Governors of the Federal Reserve System, Division of Research and Statistics, Flow of Funds Accounts Table F.102 for Nonfarm, Nonfinancial Corporate Business, at **www.federalreserve.gov/releases/z1/current/data.htm**.

business rather than paid out as dividends? and What proportion of the deficit should be financed by borrowing rather than by an issue of equity? To answer the first question the firm requires a dividend policy (we discuss this in Chapter 16); and to answer the second it needs a debt policy (this is the topic of Chapters 17 and 18).

Notice that net stock issues were negative in most years. That means that the amount of new money raised by companies issuing equity was more than offset by the amount of money returned to shareholders by repurchase of previously outstanding shares. (Companies can buy back their own shares, or they may repurchase and retire other companies' shares in the course of mergers and acquisitions.) We discuss share repurchases in Chapter 16 and mergers and acquisitions in Chapter 33.

Net stock issues were positive in the early 1990s. Companies had entered the decade with uncomfortably high debt levels, so they paid down debt in 1991 and replenished equity in 1991, 1992, and 1993. But net stock issues turned negative in 1994 and stayed negative for the rest of the decade. Aggregate debt issues increased to cover both the financial deficit and the net retirements of equity.

Companies in the United States are not alone in their heavy reliance on internal funds. Internal funds make up more than two-thirds of corporate financing in Germany, Japan, and the United Kingdom.[2]

Do Firms Rely Too Much on Internal Funds?

We have seen that on average internal funds (retained earnings plus depreciation) cover most of the cash firms need for investment. It seems that internal financing is more convenient than external financing by stock and debt issues. But some observers worry that managers have an irrational or self-serving aversion to external finance. A manager seeking comfortable employment could be tempted to forego a risky but positive-NPV project if it involved launching a new stock issue and facing awkward questions from potential investors. Perhaps managers take the line of least resistance and dodge the "discipline of capital markets."

But there are also some good reasons for relying on internally generated funds. The cost of issuing new securities is avoided, for example. Moreover, the announcement of a new equity issue is usually bad news for investors, who worry that the decision signals lower future profits or higher risk.[3] If issues of shares are costly and send a bad-news signal to investors, companies may be justified in looking more carefully at those projects that would require a new stock issue.

Has Capital Structure Changed?

We commented that in recent years firms have, in the aggregate, issued much more debt than equity. But is there a long-run trend to heavier reliance on debt finance? This is a hard question to answer in general, because financing policy varies so

[2]See, for example, J. Corbett and T. Jenkinson, "How Is Investment Financed? A Study of Germany, Japan, the United Kingdom and the United States," *The Manchester School* 65 (Supplement 1997), pp. 69–93.

[3]Managers do have insiders' insights and naturally are tempted to issue stock when the price looks good to them, that is, when they are less optimistic than outside investors. The outside investors realize this and will buy a new issue only at a discount from the pre-announcement price. More on stock issues in Chapter 15.

Current assets[†]		$1,547	Current liabilities[†]		$1,234
Fixed assets	$2,361		Long-term debt	$1,038	
Less depreciation	1,166		Other long-term liabilities[‡]	679	
Net fixed assets		1,195	Total long-term liabilities		1,717
Other long-term assets		2,160	Stockholders' equity		1,951
Total assets[§]		$4,903	Total liabilities and stockholders' equity[§]		$4,903

TABLE 14.2

Aggregate balance sheet for manufacturing corporations in the United States, 1st quarter, 2001 (figures in $ billions)*.

*Excludes companies with less than $250,000 in assets.
[†]See Table 30.1 for a breakdown of current assets and liabilities.
[‡]Includes deferred taxes and several miscellaneous categories.
[§]Columns may not add up because of rounding.
Source: U.S. Census Bureau, *Quarterly Financial Report for Manufacturing, Mining and Trade Corporations*, 1st Quarter, 2001 (**www.census.gov/csd/qfr**).

much from industry to industry and from firm to firm. But a few statistics will do no harm as long as you keep these difficulties in mind.

Table 14.2 shows the aggregate balance sheet of all manufacturing corporations in the United States in 2001. If all manufacturing corporations were merged into one gigantic firm, Table 14.2 would be its balance sheet.

Assets and liabilities in Table 14.2 are entered at book, that is, accounting values. These do not generally equal market values. The numbers are nevertheless instructive. The table shows that manufacturing corporations had total book assets of $4,903 billion. On the right-hand side of the balance sheet, we find total long-term liabilities of $1,717 billion and stockholders' equity of $1,951 billion.

So what was the book debt ratio of manufacturing corporations in 2001? It depends on what you mean by *debt*. If all liabilities are counted as debt, the debt ratio is .60:

$$\frac{\text{Debt}}{\text{Total assets}} = \frac{1{,}234 + 1{,}717}{4{,}903} = .60$$

This measure of debt includes both current liabilities and long-term obligations. Sometimes financial analysts focus on the proportions of debt and equity in *long-term* financing. The proportion of debt in long-term financing is

$$\frac{\text{Long-term liabilities}}{\text{Long-term liabilities} + \text{stockholders' equity}} = \frac{1{,}717}{1{,}717 + 1{,}951} = .47$$

The sum of long-term liabilities and stockholders' equity is called *total capitalization*. Figure 14.1 plots these two ratios from 1954 to 2001. There is a clear upward trend. But before we conclude that industry is becoming weighed down by a crippling debt burden, we need to put these changes in perspective.

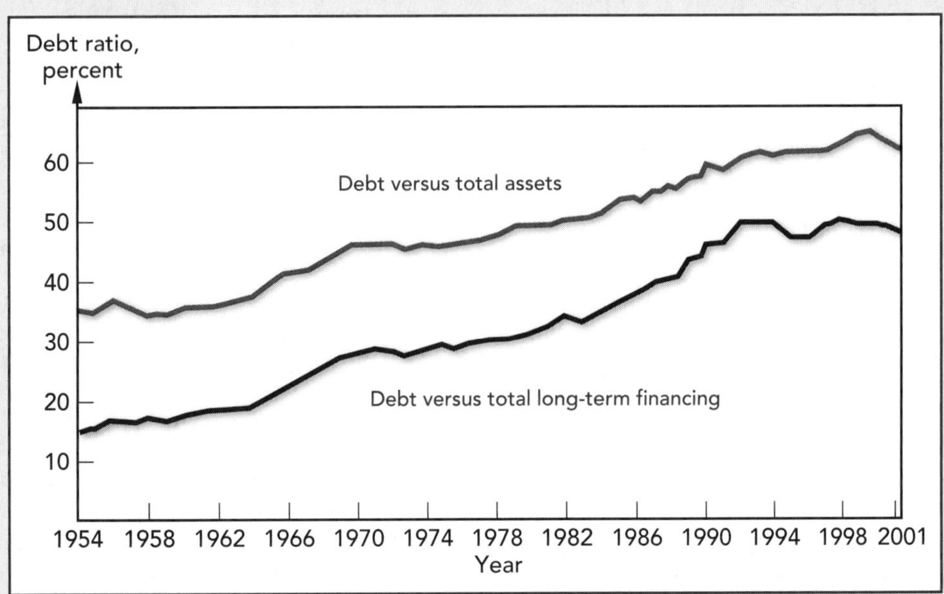

FIGURE 14.1

Average debt ratios for manufacturing corporations in the United States have increased in the postwar period. However, note that these ratios compare debt with the *book* value of total assets and total long-term financing. The actual value of corporate assets is higher as a result of inflation.

Source: U.S. Census Bureau, *Quarterly Financial Report for Manufacturing, Mining and Trade Corporations,* various issues.

1990 versus 1920 Debt ratios in the 1990s, though clearly higher than in the early postwar period, are no higher than in the 1920s and 1930s. You could argue that Figure 14.1 starts from an abnormally low point.[4]

Inflation Some of the upward movement in Figure 14.1 may have reflected inflation, which was especially rapid—by U.S. standards—throughout the 1970s and early 1980s. Rapid inflation means that the *book* value of corporate assets falls behind the actual value of those assets. If corporations were borrowing against *actual* value, it would not be surprising to observe rising ratios of debt-to-book asset values.

To illustrate, suppose that you bought a house 10 years ago for $60,000. You financed the purchase in part with a $30,000 mortgage, 50 percent of the purchase price. Today the house is worth $120,000. Suppose that you repay the remaining balance of your original mortgage and take out a new mortgage of $60,000, which is again 50 percent of current market value. Your *book* debt ratio would be 100 percent. The reason is that the book value of the house is its *original* cost of $60,000 (we assume no depreciation). An analyst having only book values to work with would observe that 10 years ago your book debt ratio was only 50 percent and might conclude

[4]See Figure 1.3 on p. 25 in R. A. Taggart, Jr., "Secular Patterns in the Financing of U.S. Corporations," in B. M. Friedman (ed.), *Corporate Capital Structures in the United States,* University of Chicago Press, 1985.

TABLE 14.3

Median debt-to-total-capital ratios in 1991 for samples of traded companies in the major countries. Debt includes short- and long-term debt. Total capital is defined as the sum of all debt and equity. The adjusted figures correct for some international differences in accounting.

Source: R. G. Rajan and L. Zingales, "What Do We Know about Capital Structure? Some Evidence from International Data," *Journal of Finance* 50 (December 1995), pp. 1421–1460.

	Debt to Total Capital			
	Book	Book, Adjusted	Market	Market, Adjusted
Canada	39%	37%	35%	32%
France	48	34	41	28
Germany	38	18	23	15
Italy	47	39	46	36
Japan	53	37	29	17
United Kingdom	28	16	19	11
United States	37	33	28	23

that you had decided to "use more debt." But you have no more debt relative to the actual value of your house.

Despite such qualifications, it's still the case that many U.S. corporations are carrying a lot more debt than they used to. Should we be worried? It's true that higher debt ratios mean that more companies will fall into financial distress if a serious recession hits the economy. But all companies live with this risk to some degree, and it does not follow that less risk is better. Finding the optimal debt ratio is like finding the optimal speed limit. We can agree that accidents at 30 miles per hour are generally less dangerous than accidents at 60 miles per hour, but we do not therefore set the speed limit on all roads at 30. Speed has benefits as well as risks. So does debt, as we will see in Chapter 18.

There is no God-given, correct debt ratio, and if there were, it would change. It may be that some of the new tools that allow firms to manage their risks have made higher debt ratios practicable.

International Comparisons Corporations in the United States are generally viewed as having less debt than many of their foreign counterparts. That was surely true in the 1950s and 1960s. Now it is not so clear.

Rajan and Zingales examined the balance sheets of a large sample of publicly traded firms in the seven largest industrialized countries. They calculated debt ratios using both book and market values of shareholders' equity. (The book value of debt was assumed to approximate market value.) A taste of their results is given in Table 14.3. Notice that the debt ratios for the United States sample fall in the middle of the pack.

International comparisons of this sort are always muddied by differences in accounting methods. For example, German companies show pension liabilities as a debtlike obligation on their balance sheets, with no offsetting entry for pension assets.[5] They also report "reserves" separately from equity. These reserves do not cover any specific obligations but serve as equity for a rainy day. Reserves might be drawn down to offset a future drop in operating earnings, for example. (This would be unacceptably creative accounting in the United States.) When Rajan and Zingales crossed out the pension liabilities and added back reserves to equity, the *adjusted* debt ratios for German companies dropped to the low levels reported in Table 14.3.

[5]United States companies show a net liability only if the pension plan is underfunded.

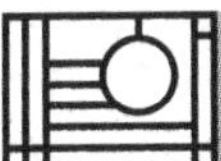

14.2 COMMON STOCK

Corporations raise cash in two principal ways—by issuing equity or by issuing debt. The equity consists largely of common stock, but companies may also issue preferred stock. As we shall see, there is a much greater diversity of debt securities.

We start our brief tour of corporate securities by taking a closer look at common stock. Table 14.4 shows the common equity of H.J. Heinz Company. The maximum number of shares that can be issued is known as the *authorized share capital;* for Heinz it was 600 million shares. If management wishes to increase the number of authorized shares, it needs the agreement of shareholders to do so. By May 2000 Heinz had already issued 431 million shares, and so it could issue 169 million more without further shareholder approval.

Most of the issued shares were held by investors. These shares are said to be *issued and outstanding.* But Heinz has also bought back 84 million shares from investors. Repurchased shares are held in the company's treasury until they are either canceled or resold. Treasury shares are said to be *issued but not outstanding.*

The issued shares are entered into the company's books at their par value. Each Heinz share had a par value of $.25. Thus the total book value of the issued shares was 431 × $.25 = $108 million. Par value has little economic significance.[6] Some companies issue shares with no par value. In this case, the stock is listed in the accounts at an arbitrarily determined figure.

The price of new shares sold to the public almost always exceeds par value. The difference is entered in the company's accounts as additional paid-in capital or capital surplus. Thus, if Heinz had sold an additional 100,000 shares at $40 a share, the common stock account would have increased by 100,000 × $.25 = $25,000, and the capital surplus account would have increased by 100,000 × $39.75 = $3,975,000.

Heinz distributed about 50 percent of its earnings as dividends. The remainder was retained in the business and used to finance new investments. The cumulative amount of retained earnings was $4,757 million.

TABLE 14.4

Book value of common stockholders' equity of H.J. Heinz Company, May 3, 2000 (figures in millions).

Sources: H.J. Heinz Company, *Annual Reports.*

Common shares ($.25 par value per share)	$ 108
Additional paid-in capital	304
Retained earnings	4,757
Treasury shares	(2,920)
Other adjustments	(652)
Net common equity	$1,596
Note:	
Authorized shares	600
Issued shares, of which:	431
Outstanding shares	347
Treasury shares	84

[6]Because some states do not allow companies to sell shares below par value, par value is generally set at a low figure.

FIGURE 14.2

Holdings of corporate equities, 2000.

Source: Board of Governors of the Federal Reserve System, Division of Research and Statistics, Flow of Funds Accounts Table L.213 at **www.federalreserve.gov/releases/z1/current/data.htm**.

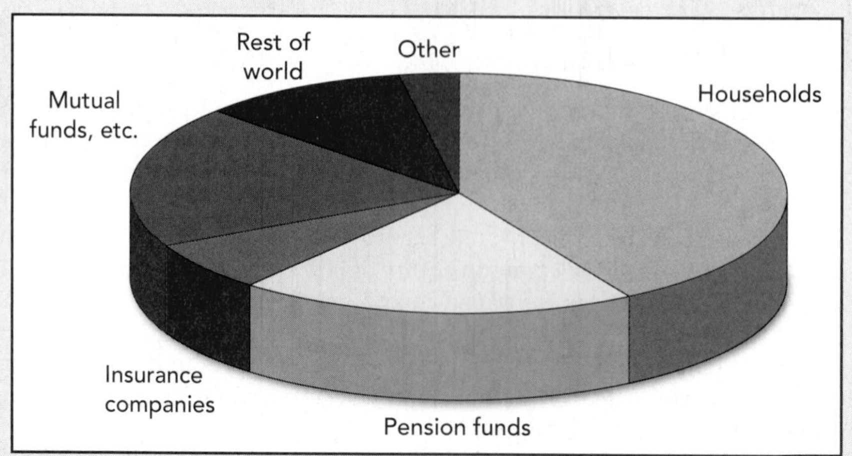

The next entry in the common stock account shows the amount that the company has spent on repurchasing its common stock. The repurchases have *reduced* the stockholders' equity by $2,920 million. Finally, there is an entry for other adjustments, principally currency losses stemming from Heinz's foreign operations. We would rather not get into these accounting adjustments here.

Heinz's net common equity had a book value in May 2000 of $1,596 million. That works out at 1,596/347 = $4.60 per share. But in May 2000, Heinz's shares were priced at about $35 each. So the *market value* of the common stock was 347 million × $35 = $12.1 billion, over $10 billion higher than book.

Ownership of the Corporation

A corporation is owned by its common stockholders. Some of this common stock is held directly by individual investors, but the greater proportion belongs to **financial institutions** such as banks, pension funds, and insurance companies. For example, look at Figure 14.2. You can see that in the United States just over 60 percent of common stock is held by financial institutions, with pension funds and mutual funds each holding about 20 percent.

What do we mean when we say that these stockholders *own* the corporation? The answer is obvious if the company has issued no other securities. Consider the simplest possible case of a corporation financed solely by common stock, all of which is owned by the firm's chief executive officer (CEO). This lucky owner–manager receives all the cash flows and makes all investment and operating decisions. She has complete *cash-flow rights* and also complete *control rights.*

These rights are split up and reallocated as soon as the company borrows money. If it takes out a bank loan, it enters into a contract with the bank promising to pay interest and eventually repay the principal. The bank gets a privileged, but limited, right to cash flows; the residual cash-flow rights are left to the stockholder.

The bank will typically protect its claim by imposing restrictions on what the firm can or cannot do. For example, it may require the firm to limit future borrowing, and it may forbid the firm to sell off assets or to pay excessive dividends. The stockholders' control rights are thereby limited. However, the contract with the bank can never restrict or determine all the operating and investment decisions necessary to run the firm efficiently. (No team of lawyers, no matter how long they scribbled, could ever write a contract covering all possible contingencies.[7]) The owner of the common stock retains the rights of control over these decisions. For example, she may choose to increase the selling price of the firm's products, to hire temporary rather than permanent employees, or to construct a new plant in Miami Beach rather than Hollywood.[8]

Ownership of the firm can of course change. If the firm fails to make the promised payments to the bank, it may be forced into bankruptcy. Once the firm is under the "protection" of a bankruptcy court, shareholders' cash-flow and control rights are tightly restricted and may be extinguished altogether. Unless some rescue or reorganization plan can be implemented, the bank will become the new owner of the firm and will acquire the cash-flow and control rights of ownership. (We discuss bankruptcy in Chapter 25.)

There is no law of nature that says residual cash-flow rights and residual control rights have to go together. For example, one could imagine a situation where the debtholder gets to make all the decisions. But this would be inefficient. Since the benefits of good decisions are felt mainly by the common stockholders, it makes sense to give them control over how the firm's assets are used.

We have focused so far on a firm that is owned by a single stockholder. In many countries, such as Italy, Hong Kong, or Mexico, there is generally a dominant stockholder who controls 20 percent or more of the votes of even the largest corporations.[9] There are also a few major businesses in the United States that are controlled by one or two large stockholders. For example, at the beginning of 2001 Bill Gates owned 21 percent of the common stock of Microsoft as well as being chairman and chief executive. However, such concentration of control is the exception. Ownership of most major corporations in the United States is widely dispersed.

The common stockholders in widely held corporations still have the residual rights over the cash flows and have the ultimate right of control over the company's affairs. In practice, however, their control is limited to an entitlement to vote, either in person or by proxy, on appointments to the *board of directors,* and on other crucial matters such as the decision to merge. Many shareholders do not bother to vote. They reason that, since they own so few shares, their vote will have little impact on the outcome. The problem is that, if all shareholders think in the same way, they cede effective control and management gets a free hand to look after its own interests.

Voting Procedures and the Value of Votes

If the company's articles of incorporation specify a *majority voting* system, each director is voted upon separately and stockholders can cast one vote for each share that they own. If a company's articles permit *cumulative voting,* the directors are voted upon jointly and stockholders can, if they wish, allot all their votes to just

[7]Theoretical economists therefore stress the importance of *incomplete contracts.* Their point is that contracts pertaining to the management of the firm *must* be incomplete and that someone must exercise residual rights of control. See O. Hart, *Firms, Contracts, and Financial Structure,* Clarendon Press, Oxford, 1995.

[8]Of course, the bank manager may suggest that a particular decision is unwise, or even threaten to cut off future lending, but the bank does not have any *right* to make these decisions.

[9]See R. La Porta, F. Lopez-de-Silanes, and A. Shleifer, "Corporate Ownership around the World," *Journal of Finance* 54 (1999), pp. 471–517.

one candidate.[10] Cumulative voting makes it easier for a minority group among the stockholders to elect directors who will represent the group's interests. That is why some shareholder groups campaign for cumulative voting.

On many issues a simple majority of votes cast is sufficient to carry the day, but the company charter may specify some decisions that require a *supermajority* of, say, 75 percent of those eligible to vote. For example, a supermajority vote is sometimes needed to approve a merger. Managers, who believe that their jobs may be threatened by a merger, are often anxious to persuade shareholders to agree that the charter should be amended to require a supermajority vote.[11]

The issues on which stockholders are asked to vote are rarely contested, particularly in the case of large, publicly traded firms. Occasionally, there are *proxy contests* in which the firm's existing management and directors compete with outsiders for effective control of the corporation. But the odds are stacked against the outsiders, for the insiders can get the firm to pay all the costs of presenting their case and obtaining votes.

Usually companies have one class of common stock and each share has one vote. Occasionally, however, a firm may have two classes of stock outstanding, which differ in their right to vote. Suppose that a firm needs fresh equity capital, but its present shareholders do not wish to relinquish their control of the firm. The existing shares could be labeled "class A," and then "class B" shares with limited voting privileges could be issued to outsiders.

Both classes of shareholders would have the same cash-flow rights but they would have different control rights. For example, each A share could have five votes, the B shares only one. However, the two classes would have identical claims to the corporation's assets, earnings, and dividends.

Holders of the A shares would have extra voting power to toss out bad management or to force management to adopt value-enhancing investment or operating policies. But both the A and B shares should benefit equally from such changes, since the two classes of shares have identical cash-flow rights. So here's the question: If everyone gains equally from better management, why would investors be prepared to pay more for one class of shares than for another? The only plausible reason is *private benefits* captured by the A shares. For example, a holder of a block of A shares might be able to obtain a seat on the board of directors or access to perquisites provided by the company. (How about a ride to Bermuda on the corporate jet?) The A shares might have extra bargaining power in an acquisition. The A shares might be held by another company, which could use its voting power and influence to secure a business advantage. These are some of the reasons why the A shares could sell for a higher price.

These private benefits of control seem to be much larger in some countries than others. For example, Luigi Zingales has looked at companies in the United States and Italy that have two classes of stock. In the United States investors were on average prepared to pay an extra 11 percent for the shares with the superior voting

[10] For example, suppose there are five directors to be elected and you own 100 shares. You therefore have a total of $5 \times 100 = 500$ votes. Under the majority voting system, you can cast a maximum of 100 votes for any one candidate. Under a cumulative voting system, you can cast all 500 votes for your favorite candidate.

[11] See, for example, R. M. Stulz, "Managerial Control of Voting Rights: Financing Policies and the Market for Corporate Control," *Journal of Financial Economics* 20 (January–March 1988), pp. 25–54.

A CONTEST OVER VOTING RIGHTS

"Not so long ago," wrote *The Economist* magazine, "shareholder friendly companies in Switzerland were as rare as Swiss admirals. Safe behind anti-takeover defences, most managers treated their shareholders with disdain." However, *The Economist* perceived one encouraging sign that these attitudes were changing. This was a proposal by the Union Bank of Switzerland (UBS) to change the rights of its equity holders.

UBS had two classes of shares—bearer shares, which are anonymous, and registered shares, which are not. In Switzerland, where anonymity is prized, bearer shares usually traded at a premium. UBS's bearer shares had sold at a premium for many years. However, there was another important distinction between the two share classes. The registered shares carried five times as many votes as an equivalent investment in the bearer shares. Presumably attracted by this feature, an investment company, BK Vision, began to accumulate a large position in the registered shares, and their price rose to a 38 percent premium over the bearer shares.

At this point UBS announced its plan to merge the two classes of share, so that the registered shares would become bearer shares and would lose their superior voting rights. Since all UBS's shares would then sell for the same price, UBS's announcement led to a rise in the price of the bearer shares and a fall in the price of the registered.

Martin Ebner, the president of BK Vision, objected to the change, complaining that it stripped the registered shareholders of some of their voting rights without providing compensation. The dispute highlighted the question of the value of superior voting stock. If the votes are used to secure benefits for *all* shareholders, then the stock should not sell at a premium. However, a premium would arise if holders of the superior voting stock expected to secure benefits for themselves alone.

To many observers UBS's proposal was a welcome attempt to prevent one group of shareholders from profiting at the expense of others and to unite all shareholders in the common aim of maximizing firm value. To others it represented an attempt to take away their rights. In any event, the debate over the proposal was never fully resolved, for UBS shortly afterward agreed to merge with SBC, another Swiss bank.

rights, but in Italy the average premium for a vote was 82 percent.[12] The Finance in the News box describes a major dispute in Switzerland over the value of superior voting rights.

Even when there is only one class of shares, minority stockholders may be at a disadvantage; the company's cash flow and potential value may be diverted to management or to one or a few dominant stockholders holding large blocks of shares. In the United States, the law protects minority stockholders from blatant or extreme exploitation. Minority stockholders in other countries do not always fare so well.[13]

[12]L. Zingales, "What Determines the Value of Corporate Votes?" *Quarterly Journal of Economics* 110 (1995), pp. 1047–1073; and L. Zingales, "The Value of the Voting Right: A Study of the Milan Stock Exchange," *Review of Financial Studies* 7 (1994), pp. 125–148. The data for the United States were for the period 1984–1990. This was the height of the leveraged buyout boom, when the value of control was likely to have been unusually large. An earlier study that looked at the period 1940–1978 found a premium of only 4 percent. See R. C. Lease, J. J. McConnell, and W. H. Mikkelson, "The Market Value of Control in Publicly-Traded Corporations," *Journal of Financial Economics* 11 (April 1983), pp. 439–471.

[13]International differences in the opportunities for dominant shareholders to exploit their position is discussed in S. Johnson et al., "Tunnelling," American Economic Review 90 (May 2000), pp. 22–27.

Example Financial economists sometimes refer to the exploitation of minority shareholders as *tunneling;* the majority shareholder tunnels into the firm and acquires control of the assets for himself. Let us look at an example of tunneling Russian-style.

To grasp how the scam works, you first need to understand *reverse stock splits.* These are often used by companies with a large number of low-priced shares. The company making the reverse split simply combines its existing shares into a smaller (and, hopefully, more convenient) number of new shares. For example, the shareholders might be given 2 new shares in place of the 3 shares that they currently own. As long as all shareholdings are reduced by the same proportion, nobody gains or loses by such a move.

However, the majority shareholder of one Russian company realized that the reverse stock split could be used to loot the company's assets. He therefore proposed that existing shareholders receive 1 new share in place of every 136,000 shares they currently held.[14]

Why did the majority shareholder pick the number "136,000"? Answer: because the two minority shareholders owned less than 136,000 shares and therefore did not have the right to *any* shares. Instead they were simply paid off with the par value of their shares and the majority shareholder was left owning the entire company. The majority shareholders of several other companies were so impressed with this device that they also proposed similar reverse stock splits to squeeze out their minority shareholders.

Needless to say such blatant exploitation would not be permitted in the United States.

Equity in Disguise

Common stocks are issued by corporations. But a few equity securities are issued not by corporations but by partnerships or trusts. We will give some brief examples.

Partnerships Newhall Land and Farming is a *master limited partnership* which owns large tracts of real estate, mostly in southern California. You can buy "units" in this partnership on the New York Stock Exchange, thus becoming a *limited* partner in Newhall. The most the limited partners can lose is their investment in the company.[15] In this and most other respects, the Newhall partnership units are just like the shares in an ordinary corporation. They share in the profits of the business and receive cash distributions (like dividends) from time to time.

Partnerships avoid corporate income tax; any profits or losses are passed straight through to the partners' tax returns. Offsetting this tax advantage are various limitations of partnerships. For example, the law regards a partnership merely as a voluntary association of individuals; like its partners, it is expected to have a limited life. A corporation, on the other hand, is an independent legal "person" that can, and often does, outlive all its original shareholders.

[14]Since a reverse stock split required only the approval of a simple majority of the shareholders, the proposal was voted through.

[15]A partnership can offer limited liability *only* to its limited partners. The partnership must also have one or more general partners, who have unlimited liability. However, general partners can be corporations. This puts the corporation's shield of limited liability between the partnership and the human beings who ultimately own the general partner.

Trusts and REITs Would you like to own a part of the oil in the Prudhoe Bay field on the north slope of Alaska? Just call your broker and buy a few units of the Prudhoe Bay Royalty Trust. British Petroleum (BP) set up this trust and gave it a royalty interest in production from BP's share of the Prudhoe Bay revenues. As the oil is produced, each trust unit gets its share of the revenues.

This trust is the passive owner of a single asset: the right to a share of the revenues from BP's Prudhoe Bay production. Operating businesses, which cannot be passive, are rarely organized as trusts, though there are exceptions, notably *real estate investment trusts,* or *REITs* (pronounced "reets").

REITs were created to facilitate public investment in commercial real estate; there are shopping center REITs, office building REITs, apartment REITs, and REITs that specialize in lending to real estate developers. REIT "shares" are traded just like common stocks.[16] The REITs themselves are not taxed, so long as they pay out at least 95 percent of earnings to the REITs' owners, who must pay whatever taxes are due on the dividends. However, REITs are tightly restricted to real estate investment. You cannot set up a widget factory and avoid corporate taxes by calling it a REIT.

Preferred Stock

Usually when investors talk about equity or stock, they are referring to common stock. But Heinz has also issued $139,000 of **preferred stock,** and this too is part of the company's equity. Despite its name, preferred stock provides only a small part of most companies' cash needs and it will occupy less time in later chapters. However, it can be a useful method of financing in mergers and certain other special situations.

Like debt, preferred stock offers a series of fixed payments to the investor. The company can choose *not* to pay a preferred dividend, but in that case it may not pay a dividend to its common stockholders. Most issues of preferred are known as *cumulative preferred stock.* This means that the firm must pay *all* past preferred dividends before common stockholders get a cent. If the company does miss a preferred dividend, the preferred stockholders generally gain some voting rights, so that the common stockholders are obliged to share control of the company with the preferred holders. Directors are also aware that failure to pay the preferred dividend earns the company a black mark with investors, so they do not take such a decision lightly.

14.3 DEBT

When companies borrow money, they promise to make regular interest payments and to repay the principal. However, this liability is limited. Stockholders have the right to default on the debt if they are willing to hand over the corporation's assets to the lenders. Clearly, they will choose to do this only if the value of the assets is less than the amount of the debt.[17]

[16]There are also some private REITs, whose shares are not publicly traded.

[17]In practice this handover of assets is far from straightforward. Sometimes there may be thousands of lenders with different claims on the firm. Administration of the handover is usually left to the bankruptcy court (see Chapter 25).

FIGURE 14.3

Holdings of corporate and foreign bonds, end 2000.

Source: Board of Governors of the Federal Reserve System, Division of Research and Statistics, Flow of Funds Accounts Table L.212 at **www.federalreserve.gov/releases/z1/current/data.htm**.

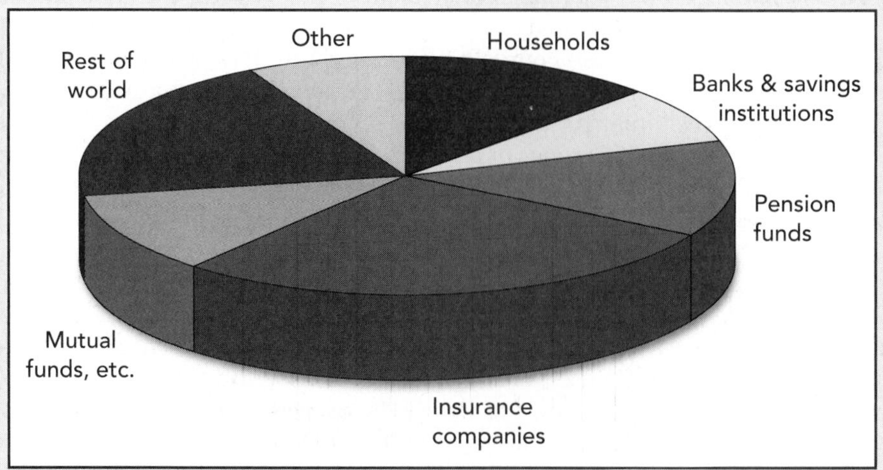

Because lenders are not regarded as owners of the firm, they do not normally have any voting power. The company's payments of interest are regarded as a cost and are deducted from taxable income. Thus interest is paid from *before-tax* income, whereas dividends on common and preferred stock are paid from *after-tax* income. Therefore the government provides a tax subsidy on the use of debt which it does not provide on equity. We will discuss debt and taxes in detail in Chapter 18.

We have seen that financial institutions own the majority of corporate equity. Figure 14.3 shows that this is also true of the company's bonds. In this case it is the insurance companies that own the largest stake.[18]

Debt Comes in Many Forms

The financial manager is faced with an almost bewildering choice of debt securities. For example, look at Table 14.5, which shows the many ways that H.J. Heinz has borrowed money. Heinz has also entered into a number of other arrangements that are not shown on the balance sheet. For example, it has arranged lines of credit that allow it to take out further short-term bank loans. Also it has entered into a swap that converts its fixed-rate sterling notes into floating-rate debt.

You are probably wondering what a swap or floating-rate debt is. Relax—later in the book we will spend several chapters explaining the various features of corporate debt. For the moment, simply notice that the mixture of loans that each company issues reflects the financial manager's response to a number of questions:

1. *Should the company borrow short-term or long-term?* If your company simply needs to finance a temporary increase in inventories ahead of the Christmas season, then it may make sense to take out a short-term bank loan. But suppose that the cash is needed to pay for expansion of an oil refinery. Refinery facilities can operate more or less continuously for

[18]Figure 14.3 does not include shorter-term debt such as bank loans. Almost all short-term debt issued by corporations is held by financial institutions.

US Dollar Debt	Foreign Currency Debt
Bank loans	Sterling notes
Commercial paper	Euro notes
Senior unsecured notes and debentures	Lire notes
Eurodollar notes	Australian dollar notes
Revenue bonds	

TABLE 14.5

Large firms issue many different securities. This table shows some of the debt securities on Heinz's balance sheet in May 2000.

15 or 20 years. In that case it would be more appropriate to issue a long-term bond.[19]

Some loans are repaid in a steady regular way; in other cases the entire loan is repaid at maturity. Occasionally either the borrower or the lender has the option to terminate the loan early and to demand that it be repaid immediately.

2. *Should the debt be fixed or floating rate?* The interest payment, or coupon, on long-term bonds is commonly fixed at the time of issue. If a $1,000 bond is issued when long-term interest rates are 10 percent, the firm continues to pay $100 per year regardless of how interest rates fluctuate.

   Most bank loans and some bonds offer a variable, or *floating,* rate. For example, the interest rate in each period may be set at 1 percent above LIBOR (London Interbank Offered Rate), which is the interest rate at which major international banks lend dollars to each other. When LIBOR changes, the interest rate on your loan also changes.

3. *Should you borrow dollars or some other currency?* Many firms in the United States borrow abroad. Often they may borrow dollars abroad (foreign investors have large holdings of dollars), but firms with large overseas operations may decide to issue debt in a foreign currency. After all, if you need to spend foreign currency, it probably makes sense to borrow foreign currency.

   Because these international bonds have usually been marketed by the London branches of international banks they have traditionally been known as **eurobonds** and the debt is called **eurocurrency** debt. A eurobond may be denominated in dollars, yen, or any other currency. Unfortunately, when the single European currency was established, it was called the *euro.* It is, therefore, easy to confuse a *eurobond* (a bond that is sold internationally) with a bond that is denominated in euros. (Notice that Heinz has issued both eurodollar debt and euro debt.)

4. *What promises should you make to the lender?* Lenders want to make sure that their debt is as safe as possible. Therefore, they may demand that their debt is senior to other debt. If default occurs, *senior* debt is first in line to be repaid. The *junior,* or *subordinated,* debtholders are paid only after all senior

[19]A company might choose to finance a long-term project with short-term debt if it wished to signal its confidence in the future. Investors would deduce that, if the company anticipated declining profits, it would not take the risk of being unable to take out a fresh loan when the first one matured. See D. Diamond, "Debt Maturity Structure and Liquidity Risk," *Quarterly Journal of Economics* 106 (1991), pp. 709–737.

debtholders are satisfied (though all debtholders rank ahead of the preferred and common stockholders).

The firm may also set aside some of its assets specifically for the protection of particular creditors. Such debt is said to be **secured** and the assets that are set aside are know as **collateral.** Thus a retailer might offer inventory or accounts receivable as collateral for a bank loan. If the retailer defaults on the loan, the bank can seize the collateral and use it to help pay off the debt.

Usually the firm also provides assurances to the lender that it will use the money well and not take unreasonable risks. For example, a firm that borrows in moderation is less likely to get into difficulties than one that is up to its gunwales in debt. So the borrower may agree to limit the amount of extra debt that it can issue. Lenders are also concerned that, if trouble occurs, others will push ahead of them in the queue. Therefore, the firm may agree not to create new debt that is senior to existing debtholders or to put aside assets for other lenders.

5. *Should you issue straight or convertible bonds?* Companies often issue securities that give the owner an option to convert them into other securities. These options may have a substantial effect on value. The most dramatic example is provided by a **warrant,** which is *nothing but* an option. The owner of a warrant can purchase a set number of the company's shares at a set price before a set date. Warrants and bonds are often sold together as a package.

   A **convertible bond** gives its owner the option to exchange the bond for a predetermined number of shares. The convertible bondholder hopes that the issuing company's share price will zoom up so that the bond can be converted at a big profit. But if the shares zoom down, there is no obligation to convert; the bondholder remains a bondholder.[20]

Variety's the Very Spice of Life

We have indicated several dimensions along which corporate securities can be classified. That gives the financial manager plenty of choice in designing securities. As long as you can convince investors of its attractions, you can issue a convertible, subordinated, floating-rate bond denominated in Swedish kronor. Rather than combining features of existing securities, you may create an entirely new one. We can imagine a coal mining company issuing convertible bonds on which the payment fluctuates with coal prices. We know of no such security, but it is perfectly legal to issue it—and who knows?—it might generate considerable interest among investors.

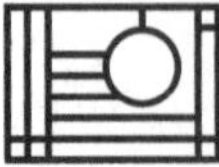

14.4 FINANCIAL MARKETS AND INSTITUTIONS

That completes our tour of corporate securities. You may feel like the tourist who has just seen 12 cathedrals in five days. But there will be plenty of time in later chapters for reflection and analysis. It is now time to move on and to look briefly

[20]Companies may also issue convertible preferred stock. The Heinz preferred stock that we mentioned earlier is convertible.

at the markets in which the firm's securities are traded and at the financial institutions that hold them.

We have explained that corporations raise money by selling financial assets such as stocks and bonds. This increases the amount of cash held by the company and the amount of stocks and bonds held by the public. Such an issue of securities is known as a *primary issue* and it is sold in the **primary market.** But in addition to helping companies to raise cash, financial markets also allow investors to trade stocks or bonds between themselves. For example, Ms. Watanabe might decide to raise some cash by selling her Sony stock at the same time that Mr. Hashimoto invests his savings in Sony. So they make a trade. The result is simply a transfer of ownership from one person to another, which has no effect on the company's cash, assets, or operations. Such purchases and sales are known as *secondary transactions* and they take place in the **secondary market.**

Some financial assets have less active secondary markets than others. For example, when a company borrows money from the bank, the bank acquires a financial asset (the company's promise to repay the loan with interest). Banks do sometimes sell packages of loans to other banks, but usually they retain the loan until it is repaid by the borrower. Other financial assets are regularly traded and their prices are shown each day in the newspaper. Some, such as shares of stock, are traded on organized exchanges like the New York, London, or Tokyo stock exchanges. In other cases there is no organized exchange and the financial assets are traded by a network of dealers. For example, if General Motors needs to buy foreign currency for an overseas investment, it will do so from one of the major banks that deals regularly in currency. Markets where there is no organized exchange are known as *over-the-counter (OTC)* markets.

Financial Institutions

We have referred to the fact that a large proportion of the company's equity and debt is owned by financial institutions. Since we will be meeting some of these financial institutions in the following chapters, we should introduce them to you here and explain what functions they serve.

Financial institutions act as *financial intermediaries* that gather the savings of many individuals and reinvest them in the financial markets. For example, banks raise money by taking deposits and by selling debt and common stock to investors. They then lend the money to companies and individuals. Of course banks must charge sufficient interest to cover their costs and to compensate depositors and other investors.

Banks and their immediate relatives, such as savings and loan companies, are the most familiar intermediaries. But there are many others, such as insurance companies and mutual funds. In the United States insurance companies are more important than banks for the *long-term* financing of business. They are massive investors in corporate stocks and bonds, and they often make long-term loans directly to corporations. Most of the money for these loans comes from the sale of insurance policies. Say you buy a fire insurance policy on your home. You pay cash to the insurance company, which it invests in the financial markets. In exchange you get a financial asset (the insurance policy). You receive no interest on this asset, but if a fire does strike, the company is obliged to cover the damages up to the policy limit. This is the return on your investment. Of course, the company will issue not just one policy but thousands. Normally the incidence of fires averages out, leaving the company with a predictable obligation to its policyholders as a group.

Why are financial intermediaries different from a manufacturing corporation? First, the financial intermediary may raise money in special ways, for example, by taking deposits or by selling insurance policies. Second, the financial intermediary invests in *financial assets,* such as stocks, bonds, or loans to businesses or individuals. By contrast, the manufacturing company's main investments are in *real* assets, such as plant and equipment. Thus the intermediary receives cash flows from its investment in one set of financial assets (stocks, bonds, etc.) and repackages those flows as a different set of financial assets (bank deposits, insurance policies, etc.). The intermediary hopes that investors will find the cash flows on this new package more attractive than those provided by the original security.

Financial intermediaries contribute in many ways to our individual well-being and the smooth functioning of the economy. Here are some examples.

The Payment Mechanism Think how inconvenient life would be if all payments had to be made in cash. Fortunately, checking accounts, credit cards, and electronic transfers allow individuals and firms to send and receive payments quickly and safely over long distances. Banks are the obvious providers of payments services, but they are not alone. For example, if you buy shares in a money-market mutual fund, your money is pooled with that of other investors and is used to buy safe, short-term securities. You can then write checks on this mutual fund investment, just as if you had a bank deposit.

Borrowing and Lending Almost all financial institutions are involved in channeling savings toward those who can best use them. Thus, if Ms. Jones has more money now than she needs and wishes to save for a rainy day, she can put the money in a bank savings deposit. If Mr. Smith wants to buy a car now and pay for it later, he can borrow money from the bank. Both the lender and borrower are happier than if they were forced to spend cash as it arrived. Of course, individuals are not alone in needing to raise cash. Companies with profitable investment opportunities may also wish to borrow from the bank, or they may raise the finance by selling new shares or bonds. Governments also often run at a deficit, which they fund by issuing large quantities of debt.

In principle, individuals or firms with cash surpluses could take out newspaper advertisements or surf the Net looking for those with cash shortages. But it can be cheaper and more convenient to use a financial intermediary, such as a bank, to link up the borrower and lender. For example, banks are equipped to check out the would-be borrower's creditworthiness and to monitor the use of cash lent out. Would you lend money to a stranger contacted over the Internet? You would be safer lending the money to the bank and letting the bank decide what to do with it.

Notice that banks promise their checking account customers instant access to their money and at the same time make long-term loans to companies and individuals. Since there is no marketplace in which bank loans are regularly bought and sold, most of the loans that banks make are illiquid. This mismatch between the liquidity of the bank's liabilities (the deposits) and most of its assets (the loans) is possible only because the number of depositors is sufficiently large so banks can be fairly sure that they won't all want to withdraw their money simultaneously.

Pooling Risk Financial markets and institutions allow firms and individuals to pool their risks. For instance, insurance companies make it possible to share the risk of an automobile accident or a household fire. Here is another example. Suppose that you have only a small sum to invest. You could buy the stock of a single company, but then you would be wiped out if that company went belly-up. It's generally better to buy shares in a mutual fund that invests in a diversified portfolio of common stocks or other securities. In this case you are exposed only to the risk that security prices as a whole will fall.

The basic functions of financial markets are the same the world over. So it is not surprising that similar institutions have emerged to perform these functions. In almost every country you will find banks accepting deposits, making loans, and looking after the payments system. You will also encounter insurance companies offering life insurance and protection against accident. If the country is relatively prosperous, other institutions, such as pension funds and mutual funds, will also have been established to help manage people's savings.

Of course there are differences in institutional structure. Take banks, for example. In many countries where securities markets are relatively undeveloped, banks play a much more dominant role in financing industry. Often the banks undertake a wider range of activities than they do in the United States. For example, they may take large equity stakes in industrial companies; this would not generally be allowed in the United States.[21]

[21]U.S. banks are permitted to acquire temporary equity holdings as a result of company bankruptcy.

SUMMARY

Financial managers are faced with two broad financing decisions:

1. What proportion of profits should the corporation reinvest in the business rather than distribute as dividends to its shareholders?
2. What proportion of the deficit should be financed by borrowing rather than by an issue of equity?

The answer to the first question reflects the firm's dividend policy and the answer to the second depends on its debt policy.

Table 14.1 summarized the ways that companies raise and spend money. Have another look at it and try to get a feel for the numbers. Notice that

1. Internally generated cash is the principal source of funds. Some people worry about this; they think that if management does not have to go to the trouble of raising the money, it won't think so hard when it comes to spending it.
2. The mix of financing changes from year to year. Sometimes companies prefer to issue equity and pay back part of their debt. At other times, they raise more debt than they need for investment and they use the balance to repurchase equity.

Common stock is the simplest form of finance. The common stockholders own the corporation. They are therefore entitled to whatever earnings are left over after all the firm's debts are paid. Stockholders also have the ultimate control over how the firm's assets are used. They exercise this control by voting on important matters, such as membership of the board of directors.

The second source of finance is preferred stock. Preferred is like debt in that it promises a fixed dividend, but preferred dividends are within the discretion of the board of directors. The firm must pay any dividends on the preferred before it is allowed to pay a dividend on the common stock. Lawyers and tax experts treat preferred stock as part of the company's equity. This means that preferred dividends are not tax-deductible. That is one reason that preferred is less popular than debt.

The third important source of finance is debt. Debtholders are entitled to a regular payment of interest and the final repayment of principal. If the company cannot make these payments, it can file for bankruptcy. The usual result is that the debtholders then take over and either sell the company's assets or continue to operate them under new management.

Note that the tax authorities treat interest payments as a cost and therefore the company can deduct interest when calculating its taxable income. Interest is paid from pretax income, whereas dividends and retained earnings come from after-tax income.

Debt ratios in the United States have generally increased over the post–World War II period. However, they are not appreciably higher than the ratios in the other major industrialized countries.

The variety of debt instruments is almost endless. The instruments differ by maturity, interest rate (fixed or floating), currency, seniority, security, and whether the debt can be converted into equity.

The majority of the firm's debt and equity is owned by financial institutions—notably banks, insurance companies, pension funds, and mutual funds. These institutions provide a variety of services. They run the payment system, channel savings to those who can best use them, and help firms to manage their risk. These basic functions do not change but the ways that financial markets and institutions perform these functions is constantly changing.

Visit us at www.mhhe.com/bm7e

FURTHER READING

A useful article for comparing financial structure in the United States and other major industrial countries is:

R. G. Rajan and L. Zingales: "What Do We Know about Capital Structure? Some Evidence from International Data," *Journal of Finance,* 50:1421–1460 (December 1995).

For a discussion of the allocation of control rights and cash-flow rights between stockholders and debtholders, see:

O. Hart: *Firms, Contracts, and Financial Structure,* Clarendon Press, Oxford, 1995.

Robert Merton gives an excellent overview of the functions of financial institutions in:

R. Merton: "A Functional Perspective of Financial Intermediation," *Financial Management,* 24: 23–41 (Summer 1995).

QUIZ

1. The figures in the following table are in the wrong order. Can you place them in their correct order?

	Percent of Total Sources, 2000
Internally generated cash	23
Financial deficit	−14
Net share issues	77
Debt issues	38

2. True or false?
   a. Net stock issues by U.S. nonfinancial corporations are in most years small but positive.
   b. Most capital investment by U.S. companies is funded by retained earnings and reinvested depreciation.
   c. Debt ratios in the U.S. have generally increased over the past 40 years.
   d. Debt ratios in the U.S. are lower than in other industrial countries.

3. The authorized share capital of the Alfred Cake Company is 100,000 shares. The equity is currently shown in the company's books as follows:

Common stock ($.50 par value)	$40,000
Additional paid-in capital	10,000
Retained earnings	30,000
Common equity	80,000
Treasury stock (2,000 shares)	5,000
Net common equity	$75,000

   a. How many shares are issued?
   b. How many are outstanding?
   c. Explain the difference between your answers to (a) and (b).
   d. How many more shares can be issued without the approval of shareholders?
   e. Suppose that Alfred Cake issues 10,000 shares at $2 a share. Which of the above figures would be changed?
   f. Suppose instead that the company bought back 5,000 shares at $5 a share. Which of the above figures would be changed?

4. There are 10 directors to be elected. A shareholder owns 80 shares. What is the maximum number of votes that he or she can cast for a favorite candidate under (a) majority voting? (b) cumulative voting?

5. In what ways is preferred stock like debt? In what ways is it like common stock?

6. Fill in the blanks, using the following terms: floating rate, common stock, convertible, subordinated, preferred stock, senior, warrant.
   a. If a lender ranks behind the firm's general creditors in the event of default, his or her loan is said to be ________.
   b. Interest on many bank loans is based on a ________ of interest.
   c. A(n) ________ bond can be exchanged for shares of the issuing corporation.
   d. A(n) ________ gives its owner the right to buy shares in the issuing company at a predetermined price.
   e. Dividends on ________ cannot be paid unless the firm has also paid any dividends on its ________.

7. True or false?
   a. In the United States, most common shares are owned by individual investors.
   b. An insurance company is a financial intermediary.
   c. Investments in partnerships cannot be publicly traded.
8. What is the traditional meaning of the term *eurobond?*
9. How do financial intermediaries contribute to the smooth functioning of the economy? Give three examples.

PRACTICE QUESTIONS

1. Use the Market Insight database (**www.mhhe.com/edumarketinsight**) to work out the financing proportions given in Table 14.1 for a particular industrial company for some recent year.

2. In Table 14.3 Rajan and Zingales use both book and market values of equity to measure debt ratios. Which measure results in the lower ratio? Why?
3. It is sometimes suggested that since retained earnings provide the bulk of industry's capital needs, the securities markets are largely redundant. Do you agree?

4. In 1999 Pfizer had 9,000 million shares of common stock authorized, 4,260 million in issue, and 3,847 million outstanding (figures rounded to the nearest million). Its equity account was as follows:

Common stock	$ 213
Additional paid-in capital	5,416
Retained earnings	10,109
Treasury shares	6,851

   Currency translation adjustment and contributions to an employee benefit trust have been deducted from retained earnings.
   a. What is the par value of each share?
   b. What was the average price at which shares were sold?
   c. How many shares have been repurchased?
   d. What was the average price at which the shares were repurchased?
   e. What is the value of the net common equity?

5. Inbox Software was founded in 1998. Its founder put up $2 million for 500,000 shares of common stock. Each share had a par value of $.10.
   a. Construct an equity account (like the one in Table 14.4) for Inbox on the day after its founding. Ignore any legal or administrative costs of setting up the company.
   b. After two years of operation, Inbox generated earnings of $120,000 and paid no dividends. What was the equity account at this point?
   c. After three years the company sold one million additional shares for $5 per share. It earned $250,000 during the year and paid no dividends. What was the equity account?

6. Look back at Table 14.4.
   a. Suppose that Heinz issued an additional 50 million shares at $30 a share. Rework Table 14.4 to show the company's equity after the issue.
   b. Suppose that Heinz *subsequently* repurchased 20 million shares at $35 a share. Rework Table 14.4 to show the effect of this further change.
7. Suppose that East Corporation has issued voting and nonvoting stock. Investors hope that holders of the voting stock will use their power to vote out the company's incompetent management. Would you expect the voting stock to sell for a higher price? Explain.

Visit us at www.mhhe.com/bm7e

8. In 2001 Beta Corporation earned gross profits of $760,000.
   a. Suppose that it is financed by a combination of common stock and $1 million of debt. The interest rate on the debt is 10 percent, and the corporate tax rate is 35 percent. How much profit is available for common stockholders after payment of interest and corporate taxes?
   b. Now suppose instead that Beta is financed by a combination of common stock and $1 million of preferred stock. The dividend yield on the preferred is 8 percent and the corporate tax rate is still 35 percent. How much profit is now available for common stockholders after payment of preferred dividends and corporate taxes?
9. Look up the financial statements for a U.S. corporation on the Internet and construct a table like Table 14.5 showing the types of debt that the company has issued. What arrangements has it made that would allow it to borrow more in the future? (You will need to look at the notes to the accounts to answer this.)
10. Which of the following features would increase the value of a corporate bond? Which would reduce its value?
    a. The borrower has the option to repay the loan before maturity.
    b. The bond is convertible into shares.
    c. The bond is secured by a mortgage on real estate.
    d. The bond is subordinated.

CHALLENGE QUESTIONS

1. The shareholders of the Pickwick Paper Company need to elect five directors. There are 200,000 shares outstanding. How many shares do you need to own to *ensure* that you can elect at least one director if **(a)** the company has majority voting? **(b)** it has cumulative voting?
2. Can you think of any new kinds of security that might appeal to investors? Why do you think they have not been issued?

Visit us at www.mhhe.com/bm7e

CHAPTER FIFTEEN

HOW CORPORATIONS ISSUE SECURITIES

IN CHAPTER 11 we encountered Marvin Enterprises, one of the most remarkable growth companies of the twenty-first century. It was founded by George and Mildred Marvin, two high-school dropouts, together with their chum Charles P. (Chip) Norton. To get the company off the ground the three entrepreneurs relied on their own savings together with personal loans from a bank. However, the company's rapid growth meant that they had soon borrowed to the hilt and needed more equity capital. Equity investment in young private companies is generally known as **venture capital.** Such venture capital may be provided by investment institutions or by wealthy individuals who are prepared to back an untried company in return for a piece of the action. In the first part of this chapter we will explain how companies like Marvin go about raising venture capital.

Venture capital organizations aim to help growing firms over that awkward adolescent period before they are large enough to go public. For a successful firm such as Marvin, there is likely to come a time when it needs to tap a wider source of capital and therefore decides to make its first public issue of common stock. The next section of the chapter describes what is involved in such an issue. We will explain the process for registering the offering with the Securities and Exchange Commission and we will introduce you to the underwriters who buy the issue and resell it to the public. We will also see that new issues are generally sold below the price at which they subsequently trade. To understand *why* that is so, we will need to make a brief sortie into the field of auction procedures.

A company's first issue of stock is seldom its last. In Chapter 14 we saw that corporations face a persistent financial deficit which they meet by selling securities. We will therefore look at how established corporations go about raising more capital. In the process we will encounter another puzzle: When companies announce a new issue of stock, the stock price generally falls. We suggest that the explanation lies in the information that investors read into the announcement.

If a stock or bond is sold publicly, it can then be traded on the securities markets. But sometimes investors intend to hold onto their securities and are not concerned about whether they can sell them. In these cases there is little advantage to a public issue, and the firm may prefer to place the securities directly with one or two financial institutions. At the end of this chapter we will explain how companies arrange a private placement.

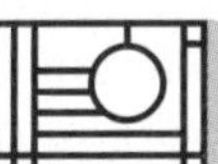

15.1 VENTURE CAPITAL

On April 1, 2013, George and Mildred Marvin met with Chip Norton in their research lab (which also doubled as a bicycle shed) to celebrate the incorporation of Marvin Enterprises. The three entrepreneurs had raised $100,000 from savings and personal bank loans and had purchased one million shares in the new company. At this *zero-stage* investment, the company's assets were $90,000 in the bank ($10,000 had been spent for legal and other expenses of setting up the company), plus the *idea* for a new product, the household gargle blaster. George Marvin was the first to see that the gargle blaster, up to that point an expensive curiosity, could be commercially produced using microgenetic refenestrators.

Marvin Enterprises' bank account steadily drained away as design and testing proceeded. Local banks did not see Marvin's idea as adequate collateral, so a transfusion of equity capital was clearly needed. Preparation of a *business plan* was a necessary first step. The plan was a confidential document describing the proposed product, its potential market, the underlying technology, and the resources (time, money, employees, plant, and equipment) needed for success.

Most entrepreneurs are able to spin a plausible yarn about their company. But it is as hard to convince a venture capitalist that your business plan is sound as to get a first novel published. Marvin's managers were able to point to the fact that they were prepared to put their money where their mouths were. Not only had they staked all their savings in the company but they were mortgaged to the hilt. This *signaled* their faith in the business.[1]

First Meriam Venture Partners was impressed with Marvin's presentation and agreed to buy one million new shares for $1 each. After this *first-stage* financing, the company's market-value balance sheet looked like this:

Marvin Enterprises First-Stage Balance Sheet (Market Values in $ Millions)

Cash from new equity	$1	$1	New equity from venture capital
Other assets, mostly intangible	1	1	Original equity held by entrepreneurs
Value	$2	$2	Value

By accepting a $2 million *after-the-money* valuation, First Meriam implicitly put a $1 million value on the entrepreneurs' idea and their commitment to the enterprise. It also handed the entrepreneurs a $900,000 paper gain over their original $100,000 investment. In exchange, the entrepreneurs gave up half their company and accepted First Meriam's representatives to the board of directors.[2]

The success of a new business depends critically on the effort put in by the managers. Therefore venture capital firms try to structure a deal so that management has a strong incentive to work hard. That takes us back to Chapters 1 and 12, where we showed how the shareholders of a firm (who are the principals) need to provide incentives for the managers (who are their agents) to work to maximize firm value.

If Marvin's management had demanded watertight employment contracts and fat salaries, they would not have found it easy to raise venture capital. Instead the Marvin team agreed to put up with modest salaries. They could cash in only from appreciation of their stock. If Marvin failed they would get nothing, because First Meriam actually bought *preferred* stock designed to convert automatically into common stock when and if Marvin Enterprises succeeded in an initial public offering or consistently generated more than a target level of earnings. But if Marvin Enterprises had failed, First Meriam would have been first in line to claim any salvageable assets. This raised even further the stakes for the company's management.[3]

[1]For a formal analysis of how management's investment in the business can provide a reliable signal of the company's value, see H. E. Leland and D. H. Pyle, "Informational Asymmetries, Financial Structure, and Financial Intermediation," *Journal of Finance* 32 (May 1977), pp. 371–387.

[2]Venture capital investors do not necessarily demand a majority on the board of directors. Whether they do depends, for example, on how mature the business is and on what fraction they own. A common compromise gives an equal number of seats to the founders and to outside investors; the two parties then agree to one or more additional directors to serve as tie-breakers in case a conflict arises. Regardless of whether they have a majority of directors, venture capital companies are seldom silent partners; their judgment and contacts can often prove useful to a relatively inexperienced management team.

[3]Notice the trade-off here. Marvin's management is being asked to put all its eggs into one basket. That creates pressure for managers to work hard, but it also means that they take on risk that could have been diversified away.

Venture capitalists rarely give a young company all the money it will need all at once. At each stage they give enough to reach the next major checkpoint. Thus in spring 2015, having designed and tested a prototype, Marvin Enterprises was back asking for more money for pilot production and test marketing. Its *second-stage* financing was $4 million, of which $1.5 million came from First Meriam, its original backers, and $2.5 million came from two other venture capital partnerships and wealthy individual investors. The balance sheet just after the second stage was as follows:

Marvin Enterprises Second-Stage Balance Sheet (Market Values in $ Millions)

Cash from new equity	$4	$4	New equity, second stage
Fixed assets	1	5	Equity from first stage
Other assets, mostly intangible	9	5	Original equity held by entrepreneurs
Value	$14	$14	Value

Now the after-the-money valuation was $14 million. First Meriam marked up its original investment to $5 million, and the founders noted an additional $4 million paper gain.

Does this begin to sound like a (paper) money machine? It was so only with hindsight. At stage 1 it wasn't clear whether Marvin would ever get to stage 2; if the prototype hadn't worked, First Meriam could have refused to put up more funds and effectively closed the business down.[4] Or it could have advanced stage 2 money in a smaller amount on less favorable terms. The board of directors could also have fired George, Mildred, and Chip and gotten someone else to try to develop the business.

In Chapter 14 we pointed out that stockholders and lenders differ in their cash-flow rights and control rights. The stockholders are entitled to whatever cash flows remain after paying off the other security holders. They also have control over how the company uses its money, and it is only if the company defaults that the lenders can step in and take control of the company. When a new business raises venture capital, these cash-flow rights and control rights are usually negotiated separately. The venture capital firm will want a say in how that business is run and will demand representation on the board and a significant number of votes. The venture capitalist may agree that it will relinquish some of these rights if the business subsequently performs well. However, if performance turns out to be poor, the venture capitalist may automatically get a greater say in how the business is run and whether the existing management should be replaced.

For Marvin, fortunately, everything went like clockwork. Third-stage *mezzanine financing* was arranged,[5] full-scale production began on schedule, and gargle blasters were acclaimed by music critics worldwide. Marvin Enterprises went public on February 3, 2019. Once its shares were traded, the paper gains earned by First Meriam

[4]If First Meriam had refused to invest at stage 2, it would have been an exceptionally hard sell convincing another investor to step in its place. The other outside investors knew they had less information about Marvin than First Meriam and would have read its refusal as a bad omen for Marvin's prospects.

[5]Mezzanine financing does not necessarily come in the third stage; there may be four or five stages. The point is that mezzanine investors come in late, in contrast to venture capitalists who get in on the ground floor.

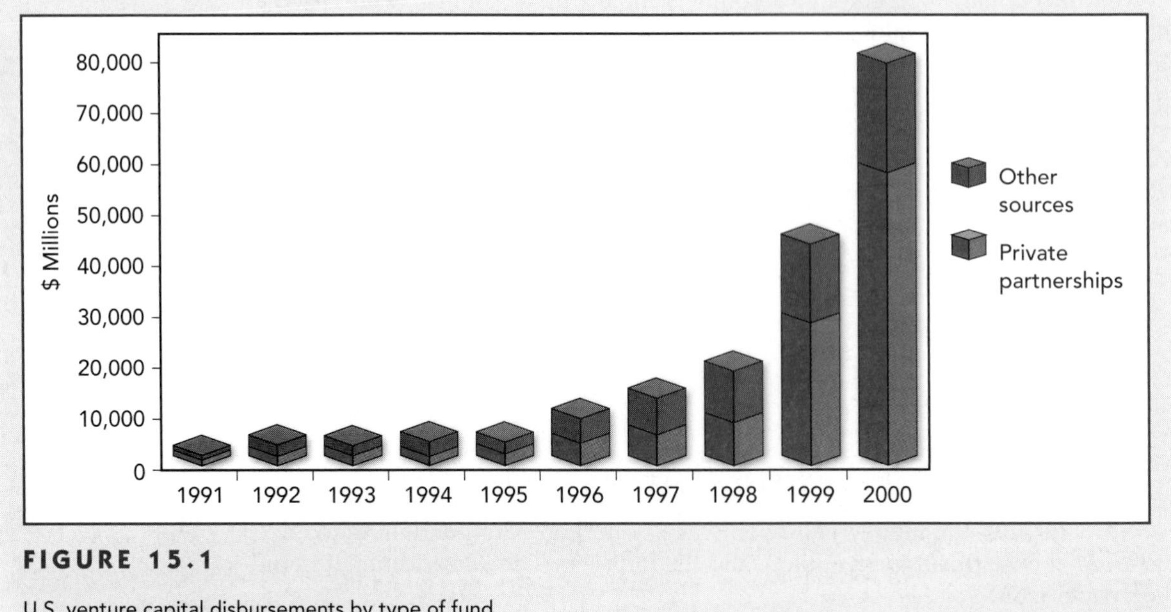

FIGURE 15.1

U.S. venture capital disbursements by type of fund.

Source: Venture Economics/National Venture Capital Association.

and the company's founders turned into fungible wealth. Before we go on to this initial public offering, let us look briefly at the venture capital markets today.

The Venture Capital Market

Most new companies rely initially on family funds and bank loans. Some of them continue to grow with the aid of equity investment provided by wealthy individuals, known as *angel investors*. However, the bulk of the capital for adolescent companies comes from specialist venture-capital firms, which pool funds from a variety of investors, seek out fledgling companies to invest in, and then work with these companies as they try to grow. Figure 15.1 shows how the amount of venture capital investment has increased. During the heady days of 2000 venture capital funds invested nearly $140 billion in some 16,000 different companies.

Most venture capital funds are organized as limited private partnerships with a fixed life of about 10 years. The management company is the general partner, and the pension funds and other investors are limited partners. Some large industrial firms, such as Intel, General Electric, and Sun Microsystems also act as *corporate venturers* by providing equity capital to new innovative companies.[6] Finally, in the United States the government provides cheap loans to small-business investment companies (SBICs) that then relend the money to deserving entrepreneurs. SBICs occupy a small, specialized niche in the venture capital markets.

Venture capital firms are not passive investors. They provide ongoing advice to the firms that they invest in and often play a major role in recruiting the senior

[6]See, for example, H. Chesbrough, "Designing Corporate Ventures in the Shadow of Private Venture Capital," *California Management Review* 42 (Spring 2000), pp. 31–49.

management team. This advice can be valuable to businesses in their early years and helps them to bring their products more quickly to market.[7]

Venture capitalists may cash in on their investment in two ways. Sometimes, once the new business has established a track record, it may be sold out to a larger firm. However, many entrepreneurs do not fit easily into a corporate bureaucracy and would prefer instead to remain the boss. In this case, the company may decide, like Marvin, to go public and so provide the original backers with an opportunity to "cash out," selling their stock and leaving the original entrepreneurs in control. A thriving venture capital market therefore needs an active stock exchange, such as Nasdaq, that specializes in trading the shares of young, rapidly growing firms.[8]

In many countries, such as those of continental Europe, venture capital markets have been slower to develop. But this is changing and investment in high-tech ventures in Europe has begun to blossom. This has been helped by the formation of new European exchanges that model themselves on Nasdaq. These mini-Nasdaqs inlcude Aim in London, Neuer Markt in Frankfurt, and Nouveau Marché in Paris.

For every 10 first-stage venture capital investments, only two or three may survive as successful, self-sufficient businesses, and rarely will they pay off as big as Marvin Enterprises. From these statistics come two rules for success in venture capital investment. First, don't shy away from uncertainty; accept a low probability of success. But don't buy into a business unless you can see the *chance* of a big, public company in a profitable market. There's no sense taking a long shot unless it pays off handsomely if you win. Second, cut your losses; identify losers early, and if you can't fix the problem—by replacing management, for example—throw no good money after bad.

How successful is venture capital investment? Since you can't look up the value of new start-up businesses in *The Wall Street Journal,* it is difficult to say with confidence. However, *Venture Economics,* which tracks the performance of over 1,200 venture capital funds, calculated that from 1980 to 2000 investors in these funds would have earned an average annual return of nearly 20 percent after expenses.[9] That is about 3 percent a year more than they would have earned from investing in the stocks of large public corporations.

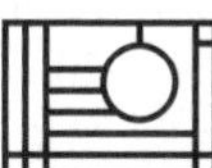

15.2 THE INITIAL PUBLIC OFFERING

Very few new businesses make it big, but venture capitalists keep sane by forgetting about the many failures and reminding themselves of the success stories—the investors who got in on the ground floor of firms like Federal Express, Genentech,

[7]For evidence on the role of venture capitalists in assisting new businesses, see T. Hellman and Manju Puri, "The Interaction between Product Market and Financial Strategy: The Role of Venture Capital," *Review of Financial Studies* 13 (2000), pp. 959–984; and S. N. Kaplan and P. Stromberg, "How Do Venture Capitalists Choose Investments," working paper, Graduate School of Business, University of Chicago, August 2000.

[8]This argument is developed in B. Black and R. Gilson, "Venture Capital and the Structure of Capital Markets: Banks versus Stock Markets," *Journal of Financial Economics* 47 (March 1998), pp. 243–277.

[9]See **www.ventureeconomics.com/news_ve.** Gompers and Lerner, who studied the period 1979–1997, found somewhat higher returns (see P. A. Gompers and J. Lerner, "Risk and Reward in Private Equity Investments: The Challenge of Performance Assessment," *Journal of Private Equity,* Winter 1997, pp. 5–12). In a study of a large sample of individual venture capital investments Cochrane tackles the problem of measuring returns on investments that remain unmarketable. The average *annually compounded* return on his sample is 57 percent, though the average *continuously compounded* return is much lower (see J. Cochrane, "The Risk and Return of Venture Capital," NBER Working Paper No. 8066, 2001).

Compaq, Intel, and Sun Microsystems. When First Meriam invested in Marvin Enterprises, it was not looking for cash dividends from its investment; instead it was hoping for rapid growth that would allow Marvin to go public and give First Meriam an opportunity to cash in on some of its gains.

By 2019 Marvin had grown to the point at which it needed still more capital to implement its second-generation production technology. At this point it decided to make an **initial public offering** of stock or **IPO.** This was to be partly a *primary* offering; that is, new shares were to be sold to raise additional cash for the company. It was also to be partly a *secondary* offering; that is, the venture capitalists and the company's founders were looking to sell some of their existing shares.

Often when companies go public, the issue is solely intended to raise new capital for the company. But there are also occasions when no new capital is raised and all the shares on offer are being sold as a secondary offering by existing shareholders. For example, in 1998 Du Pont sold off a large part of its holding in Conoco for $4.4 billion.[10]

Some of the biggest IPOs occur when governments sell off their shareholdings in companies. For example, the British government raised $9 billion from its sale of British Gas stock, while the secondary offering of Nippon Telegraph and Telephone by the Japanese government brought in nearly $13 billion.

For Marvin there were other benefits from going public. The market value of its stock would provide a readily available measure of the company's performance and would allow Marvin to reward its management team with stock options. Because information about the company would become more widely available, Marvin could diversify its sources of finance and reduce its costs of borrowing. These benefits outweighed the expense of the public issue and the continuing costs of administering a public company and communicating with its shareholders.

Instead of going public, many successful entrepreneurs may decide to sell out to a larger firm or they may continue to operate successfully as private, unlisted companies. Some very large companies in the United States are private. They include Bechtel, Cargill, and Levi Strauss. In other countries it is more common for large companies to remain privately owned. For example, since 1988 there have been only 70 listings of new, independent, nonfinancial companies on the Milan Stock Exchange.[11]

Arranging an Initial Public Offering[12]

Once Marvin had made the decision to go public, its first task was to select the *underwriters.* Underwriters act as financial midwives to a new issue. Usually they play a triple role: First they provide the company with procedural and financial advice, then they buy the issue, and finally they resell it to the public.

After some discussion Marvin settled on Klein Merrick as the managing underwriter and Goldman Stanley as the co-manager. Klein Merrick then formed a syndicate of underwriters who would buy the entire issue and reoffer it to the public.

---

[10]This is the largest U.S. IPO, but it is dwarfed by the Japanese telecom company NTT DoCoMo, which sold $18 billion of stock in 1998 and handed out $500 million in fees to the underwriters.

[11]The reasons for going public in Italy are analyzed in M. Pagano, F. Panetta, and L. Zingales, "Why Do Companies Go Public? An Empirical Analysis," *Journal of Finance* 53 (February 1998), pp. 27–64.

[12]For an excellent case study of how one company went public, see B. Uttal, "Inside the Deal That Made Bill Gates $350,000,000," *Fortune,* July 21, 1986.

Together with Klein Merrick and firms of lawyers and accountants, Marvin prepared a **registration statement** for the approval of the Securities and Exchange Commission (SEC).[13] This statement is a detailed and somewhat cumbersome document that presents information about the proposed financing and the firm's history, existing business, and plans for the future.

The most important sections of the registration statement are distributed to investors in the form of a **prospectus.** In Appendix B to this chapter we have reproduced the prospectus for Marvin's first public issue of stock.[14] Real prospectuses would go into much more detail on each topic, but this example should give you some feel for the mixture of valuable information and redundant qualification that characterizes these documents. The Marvin prospectus also illustrates how the SEC insists that investors' eyes are opened to the dangers of purchase (see "Certain Considerations" of the prospectus). Some investors have joked that if they read each prospectus carefully, they would not dare buy any new issue.

In addition to registering the issue with the SEC, Marvin needed to check that the issue complied with the so-called *blue-sky laws* of each state that regulate sales of securities within the state.[15] It also arranged for its newly issued shares to be traded on the Nasdaq exchange.

The Sale of Marvin Stock

While the registration statement was awaiting approval, Marvin and its underwriters began to firm up the issue price. First they looked at the price–earnings ratios of the shares of Marvin's principal competitors. Then they worked through a number of discounted-cash-flow calculations like the ones we described in Chapters 4 and 11. Most of the evidence pointed to a market value of $75 a share.

Marvin and Klein Merrick arranged a *road show* to talk to potential investors. Mostly these were institutional investors, such as managers of mutual funds and pension funds. The investors gave their reactions to the issue and indicated to the underwriters how much stock they wished to buy. Some stated the maximum price that they were prepared to pay, but others said that they just wanted to invest so many dollars in Marvin at whatever issue price was chosen. These discussions with fund managers allowed Klein Merrick to build up a book of potential orders.[16] Although the managers were not bound by their responses, they knew that, if they wanted to keep in the underwriters' good books, they should be careful not to go back on their expressions of interest. The underwriters also were not bound to treat all investors equally. Some investors who were keen to

[13]The rules governing the sale of securities derive principally from the Securities Act of 1933. The SEC is concerned solely with disclosure and it has no power to prevent an issue as long as there has been proper disclosure. Some public issues are exempt from registration. These include issues by small businesses and loans maturing within nine months.

[14]The company is allowed to circulate a preliminary version of the prospectus (known as a *red herring*) before the SEC has approved the registration statement.

[15]In 1980, when Apple Computer Inc. went public, the Massachusetts state government decided the offering was too risky and barred the sale of the shares to individual investors in the state. The state relented later after the issue was out and the price had risen. Needless to say, this action was not acclaimed by Massachusetts investors.

States do not usually reject security issues by honest firms through established underwriters. We cite the example to illustrate the potential power of state securities laws and to show why underwriters keep careful track of them.

[16]The managing underwriter is therefore often known as the *bookrunner.*

buy Marvin stock were disappointed in the allotment that they subsequently received.

Immediately after it received clearance from the SEC, Marvin and the underwriters met to fix the issue price. Investors had been enthusiastic about the story that the company had to tell and it was clear that they were prepared to pay more than $75 for the stock. Marvin's managers were tempted to go for the highest possible price, but the underwriters were more cautious. Not only would they be left with any unsold stock if they overestimated investor demand but they also argued that some degree of underpricing was needed to tempt investors to buy the stock. Marvin and the underwriters therefore compromised on an issue price of $80.

Although Marvin's underwriters were committed to buy only 900,000 shares from the company, they chose to sell 1,035,000 shares to investors. This left the underwriters short of 135,000 shares or 15 percent of the issue. If Marvin's stock had proved unpopular with investors and traded below the issue price, the underwriters could have bought back these shares in the marketplace. This would have helped to stabilize the price and would have given the underwriters a profit on these extra shares that they sold. As it turned out, investors fell over themselves to buy Marvin stock and by the end of the first day the stock was trading at $105. The underwriters would have incurred a heavy loss if they had been obliged to buy back the shares at $105. However, Marvin had provided underwriters with a *greenshoe* option which allowed them to buy an additional 135,000 shares from the company. This ensured that the underwriters were able to sell the extra shares to investors without fear of loss.

In choosing Klein Merrick to manage its IPO, Marvin was influenced by Merrick's proposals for making an active market in the stock in the weeks after the issue.[17] Merrick also planned to generate continuing investor interest in the stock by distributing a major research report on Marvin's prospects.[18]

The Underwriters

Companies get to make only one IPO, but underwriters are in the business all the time. Established underwriters are, therefore, careful of their reputation and will not handle a new issue unless they believe the facts have been presented fairly to investors. Thus, in addition to handling the sale of Marvin's issue, the underwriters in effect gave their seal of approval to it. This implied endorsement was worth quite a bit to a company like Marvin that was coming to the market for the first time.

Marvin's underwriters were prepared to enter into a firm commitment to buy the stock and then offer it to the public. Thus they took the risk that the issue might flop and they would be left with unwanted stock. Occasionally, where the sale of common stock is regarded as particularly risky, the underwriters may be

[17]On average the managing underwriter accounts for 40 to 60 percent of trading volume in the stock during the first 60 days after an IPO. See K. Ellis, R. Michaely, and M. O'Hara, "When the Underwriter is the Market Maker: An Examination of Trading in the IPO Aftermarket," *Journal of Finance* 55 (June 2000), pp. 1039–1074.

[18]The 25 days after the offer is designated as a *quiet period*. Merrick is obliged to wait until after this period before commenting on the valuation of the company. Survey evidence suggests that, in choosing an underwriter, firms place considerable importance on its ability to provide follow-up research reports. See L. Krigman, W. H. Shaw, and K. L. Womack, "Why Do Firms Switch Underwriters?" *Journal of Financial Economics* 60 (May–June 2001), pp. 245–284.

Underwriter	Value of Issues	Number of Issues
Merrill Lynch	$353	1,566
Citigroup/Salomon Smith Barney	334	1,039
Credit Suisse First Boston	252	996
JP Morgan	232	818
Morgan Stanley Dean Witter	211	656
Lehman Brothers	193	660
Goldman Sachs	189	598
UBS Warburg	172	690
Deutsche Bank	166	573
Banc of America Securities	125	571

TABLE 15.1

The top managing underwriters January 2001 to September 2001. Values include global debt and equity issues. Figures in billions.

Source: Thomson Financial Investment Banking/Capital Markets (www.tfibcm.com).

prepared to handle the sale only on a best-efforts basis. In this case the underwriters promise to sell as much of the issue as possible but do not guarantee to sell the entire amount.[19]

Successful underwriting requires financial muscle, considerable experience, and an established reputation. The names of Marvin's underwriters are of course fictitious, but Table 15.1 shows that underwriting in the United States is dominated by the major investment banks and large commercial banks. Foreign players are also heavily involved in underwriting securities that are sold internationally.

Underwriting is not always fun. On October 15, 1987, the British government finalized arrangements to sell its holding of BP shares at £3.30 a share.[20] This huge issue involved more than $12 billion and was underwritten by an international group of underwriters who marketed it in a number of countries. Four days after the underwriting was agreed, the October crash caused stock prices around the world to nose-dive. The underwriters unsuccessfully appealed to the British government to cancel the issue.[21] By the closing date of the offer, the price of BP stock had fallen to £2.96, and the underwriters had lost more than a billion dollars.

Underwriters face another danger. When a new issue goes wrong and the stock performs badly, they may be blamed for overhyping the issue. For example, in December 1999 the software company Va Linux went public at $30 a share. Next-day trading opened at $299 a share, but then the stock price began to sag. As we write this in November 2001, the stock is selling for less than $2. Disgruntled Va Linux investors sued the underwriters, complaining that the prospectus was "materially false." These underwriters had plenty of company; following the collapse of the "new economy" stocks in 2000, investors in almost one in three recent high-tech IPOs sued the underwriters.

[19]The alternative is to enter into an *all-or-none* arrangement. In this case, either the entire issue is sold at the offering price or the deal is called off and the issuing company receives nothing.

[20]The issue was partly a secondary issue (the sale of the British government's shares) and partly a primary issue (BP took the opportunity to raise additional capital by selling new shares).

[21]The government's only concession was to put a floor on the underwriters' losses by giving them the opportunity to resell their stock to the government at £2.80 a share.

Costs of a New Issue

We have described Marvin's underwriters as filling a triple role—providing advice, buying the new issue, and reselling it to the public. In return they received payment in the form of a *spread*; that is, they were allowed to buy the shares for less than the *offering price* at which the shares were sold to investors.[22] Klein Merrick as syndicate manager kept 20 percent of this spread. A further 25 percent of the spread was used to pay those underwriters who bought the issue. The remaining 55 percent went to the firms that provided the salesforce.

The underwriting spread on the Marvin issue amounted to 7 percent of the total sum raised from investors. Since many of the costs incurred by underwriters are fixed, you would expect that the percentage spread would decline with issue size. This in part is what we find. For example, a $5 million IPO might carry a spread of 10 percent, while the spread on a $300 million issue might be only 5 percent. However, Chen and Ritter found that with almost every IPO between $20 and $80 million the spread was exactly 7 percent.[23] Since it is difficult to believe that all these issues were equally costly to underwrite, this clustering at 7 percent is a puzzle.[24]

In addition to the underwriting fee, Marvin's new issue entailed substantial administrative costs. Preparation of the registration statement and prospectus involved management, legal counsel, and accountants, as well as the underwriters and their advisers. In addition, the firm had to pay fees for registering the new securities, printing and mailing costs, and so on. You can see from the first page of the Marvin prospectus (Appendix B) that these administrative costs totaled $820,000.

Underpricing of IPOs

Marvin's issue was costly in yet another way. Since the offering price was less than the true value of the issued securities, investors who bought the issue got a bargain at the expense of the firm's original shareholders.

These costs of *underpricing* are hidden but nevertheless real. For IPOs they generally exceed all other issue costs. Whenever any company goes public, it is very difficult for the underwriters to judge how much investors will be willing to pay for the stock. Sometimes they misjudge demand dramatically. For example, when the prospectus for the IPO of Netscape stock was first published, the underwriters indicated that the company would sell 3.5 million shares at a price between $12 and $14 each. However, the enthusiasm for Netscape's Internet browser system was such that the underwriters increased the shares available to 5 million and set an issue price of $28. The next morning the volume of orders was so large that trading was delayed by an hour and a half and, when trading did begin, the shares were quoted at $71, over five times the underwriters' initial estimates.

---

[22]In the more risky cases the underwriter usually receives some extra noncash compensation, such as warrants to buy additional common stock in the future.

[23]H. C. Chen and J. R. Ritter, "The Seven Percent Solution," *Journal of Finance* 55 (June 2000), pp. 1105–1132.

[24]Chen and Ritter argue that the fixed spread suggests the underwriting market is not competitive and the Justice Department was led to investigate whether the spread constituted evidence of price-fixing. Robert Hansen disagrees that the market is not competitive. See R. Hansen, "Do Investment Banks Compete in IPOs?: The Advent of the Seven Percent Plus Contract," *Journal of Financial Economics* 59 (2001) pp. 313–346.

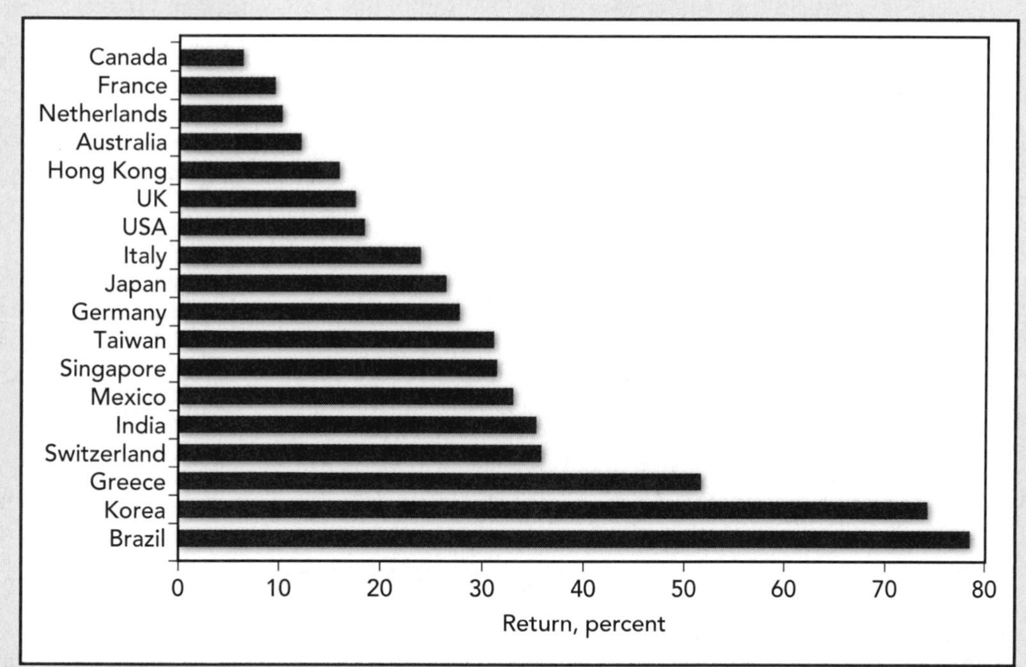

FIGURE 15.2

Average initial returns from investing in IPOs in different countries.

Source: T. Loughran, J. R. Ritter, and K. Rydqvist, "Initial Public Offerings: International Insights," *Pacific-Basin Finance Journal* 2 (1994), pp. 165–199, updated on **www.bear.cba.ufl.edu/ritter**.

We admit that the Netscape issue was unusual[25] but researchers have found that investors who buy at the issue price on average commonly realize very high returns over the following weeks. For example, a study by Ibbotson, Sindelar, and Ritter of nearly 15,000 U.S. new issues from 1960 to 2000 found average underpricing of 18.4 percent.[26] Figure 15.2 shows that the United States is not the only country in which IPOs are underpriced. In Brazil the gains from buying IPOs have averaged nearly 80 percent.[27]

You might think that shareholders would prefer not to sell their stock for less than its market price, but many investment bankers and institutional investors argue that underpricing is in the interests of the issuing firm. They say that a low offering price on the initial offer raises the price of the stock when it is subsequently traded in the market and enhances the firm's ability to raise further capital.[28] Skeptics respond that investment bankers push for a low offering price because it

[25]It does not, however, hold the record. That honor goes to Va Linux.

[26]R. G. Ibbotson, J. L. Sindelar, and J. R. Ritter, "The Market's Problems with the Pricing of Initial Public Offerings," *Journal of Applied Corporate Finance* 7 (Spring 1994), pp. 66–74, updated on **http://bear.cba.ufl.edu/ritter**. As we saw in Chapter 13, there is some evidence that these early gains are not maintained and in the five years following an IPO the shares underperform the market.

[27]There wasn't room on the chart to plot Chinese IPOs; their initial returns have averaged 257 percent.

[28]For an analysis of how a firm could rationally underprice to facilitate subsequent stock issues, see I. Welch, "Seasoned Offerings, Imitation Costs and the Underpricing of Initial Public Offerings," *Journal of Finance* 44 (June 1989), pp. 421–449.

reduces the risk that they will be left with unwanted stock and makes them popular with their clients who are allotted stock.

Winner's Curse

Here is another reason that new issues may be underpriced. Suppose that you bid successfully for a painting at an art auction. Should you be pleased? It is true that you now own the painting, which was presumably what you wanted, but everybody else at the auction apparently thought that the picture was worth less than you did. In other words, your success suggests that you may have overpaid.

This problem is known as the *winner's curse.* The highest bidder in an auction is most likely to have overestimated the object's value and, unless bidders recognize this in their bids, the buyer will on average overpay. If bidders are aware of the danger, they are likely to adjust their bids down correspondingly.

The same problem arises when you apply for a new issue of securities. For example, suppose that you decide to apply for every new issue of common stock. You will find that you have no difficulty in getting stock in the issues that no one else wants. But, when the issue is attractive, the underwriters will not have enough stock to go around, and you will receive less stock than you wanted. The result is that your money-making strategy may turn out to be a loser. If you are smart, you will play the game only if there is substantial underpricing on average.

Here then we have a possible rationale for the underpricing of new issues. Uninformed investors who cannot distinguish which issues are attractive are exposed to the winner's curse. Companies and their underwriters are aware of this and need to underprice on average to attract the uninformed investors.[29]

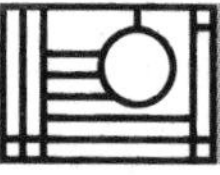

15.3 OTHER NEW-ISSUE PROCEDURES

Table 15.2 summarizes the main steps involved in making an initial public offering of stock in the United States. You can see that Marvin's new issue was a typical IPO in almost every respect. In particular most IPOs in the United States use the *bookbuilding* method in which the underwriter builds a book of likely orders and uses this information to set the issue price.

Although bookbuilding is rapidly gaining in popularity throughout the world,[30] firms and governments in different countries employ a variety of techniques for selling their securities. The main alternatives to bookbuilding are a fixed price offer or an auction. The fixed price offer is often used for IPOs in the UK. In this case the firm fixes the selling price and then advertises the number of shares on offer. If the price is set too high, investors will not apply for all the shares on offer and the underwriters will be obliged to buy the unsold shares. If the price is set too low, the applications will exceed the number of shares on offer and investors

[29]Notice that the winner's curse would disappear if only investors knew what the market price was going to be. One response is to allow trading in a security before it has been issued. This is known as a *gray market* and is most common for debt issues. Investors can observe the price in the gray market and can be more confident that they are not overbidding when the actual issue takes place.

[30]The growth in bookbuilding is discussed in A. E. Sherman, "Global Trends in IPO Methods: Book Building vs. Auctions," working paper, Department of Finance and Business Economics, University of Notre Dame, March 2001.

1. Company appoints managing underwriter (bookrunner) and co-manager(s). Underwriting syndicate formed.
2. Arrangement with underwriters includes agreement on spread (typically 7% for medium-sized IPOs) and on greenshoe option (typically allowing the underwriters to increase the number of shares bought by 15%).
3. Issue registered with SEC and preliminary prospectus (red herring) issued.
4. Roadshow arranged to market the issue to potential investors. Managing underwriter builds book of potential demand.
5. SEC approves registration. Company and underwriters agree on issue price.
6. Underwriters allot stock (typically with overallotment).
7. Trading starts. Underwriters cover short position by buying stock in the market or by exercising greenshoe option.
8. Managing underwriter makes liquid market in stock and provides research coverage.

TABLE 15.2

The main steps involved in making an initial public offering of stock in the United States.

will receive only a proportion of the shares that they applied for. Since the most underpriced offers are likely to be heavily oversubscribed, the fixed price offer leaves investors very exposed to the winner's curse.[31]

The alternative is to sell new securities by auction. In this case investors are invited to submit their bids, stating both how many securities they wish to buy and the price. The securities are then sold to the highest bidders. Most governments, including the U.S. Treasury, sell their bonds by auction. In recent years a few companies in the United States have made an IPO by auctioning stock on the Internet.

Notice that the bookbuilding method is in some ways like an auction, since potential buyers state how many shares they are prepared to buy at given prices. However, the bids are not binding and are used only as a guide to fix the price of the issue. Thus the issue price is commonly set below the price that is needed to sell the issue, and the underwriters are more likely to allot stock to their favorite clients and to those investors whose bids are most helpful in setting the issue price.[32]

Types of Auction

Suppose that a government wishes to auction four million bonds and three would-be buyers submit bids. Investor *A* bids $1,020 each for one million bonds, *B* bids $1,000 for three million bonds, and *C* bids $980 for two million bonds. The bids of the two highest bidders (*A* and *B*) absorb all the bonds on offer and *C* is left empty-handed. What price do the winning bidders, *A* and *B*, pay?

The answer depends on whether the sale is a *discriminatory auction* or a *uniform-price auction.* In a discriminatory auction every winner is required to pay the price that he or she bid. In this case *A* would pay $1,020 and *B* would pay $1,000. In a uniform-price auction both would pay $1,000, which is the price of the lowest winning bidder (investor *B*).

[31]Mario Levis found that, though IPOs in the UK offered an average first-day return of nearly 9 percent in the period 1985–1988, an investor who applied for an equal amount of each IPO would have done little better than break even. See M. Levis, "The Winner's Curse Problem, Interest Costs and the Underpricing of Initial Public Offerings," *Economics Journal* 100 (1990), pp. 76–89.

[32]F. Cornelli and D. Goldreich, "Bookbuilding and Strategic Allocation," *Journal of Finance* 56 (December 2001), pp. 2337–2369.

It might seem from our example that the proceeds from a uniform-price auction would be lower than from a discriminatory auction. But this ignores the fact that the uniform-price auction provides better protection against the winner's curse. Wise bidders know that there is little cost to overbidding in a uniform-price auction, but there is potentially a very high cost to doing so in a discriminatory auction.[33] Economists therefore often argue that the uniform-price auction should result in higher proceeds.[34]

Sales of bonds by the U.S. Treasury used to take the form of discriminatory auctions so that successful buyers paid their bid. However, governments do occasionally listen to economists, and the Treasury has now switched to a uniform-price auction. The Mexican government has also been sufficiently convinced to change from a discriminatory auction to a uniform-price auction.[35]

15.4 SECURITY SALES BY PUBLIC COMPANIES

For most companies their first public issue of stock is seldom their last. As they grow, they are likely to make further issues of debt and equity. Public companies can issue securities either by offering them to investors at large or by making a rights issue that is limited to existing stockholders. General cash offers are now used for virtually all debt and equity issues in the United States, but rights issues are widespread in other countries and you should understand how they work. Therefore in Appendix A to this chapter we describe rights issues.

General Cash Offers

When a corporation makes a general cash offer of debt or equity in the United States, it goes through much the same procedure as when it first went public. In other words, it registers the issue with the SEC and then sells the securities to an underwriter (or a syndicate of underwriters), who in turn offers the securities to the public. Before the price of the issue is fixed the underwriter will build up a book of likely demand for the securities just as in the case of Marvin's IPO.

The SEC allows large companies to file a single registration statement covering financing plans for up to two years into the future. The actual issues can then be done with scant additional paperwork, whenever the firm needs the cash or thinks it can issue securities at an attractive price. This is called *shelf registra-*

[33]In addition, the price in the uniform-price auction depends not only on the views of *B* but also on those of *A* (for example, if *A* had bid $990 rather than $1,020, then both *A* and *B* would have paid $990 for each bond). Since the uniform-price auction takes advantage of the views of both *A* and *B*, it reduces the winner's curse.

[34]Sometimes auctions reduce the winner's curse by allowing uninformed bidders to enter noncompetitive bids, whereby they submit a quantity but not a price. For example, in U.S. Treasury auctions investors may submit noncompetitive bids and receive their full allocation at the average price paid by competitive bidders.

[35]Experience in the United States and Mexico with uniform-price auctions suggests that they do indeed reduce the winner's curse problem and realize higher prices for the seller. See K. G. Nyborg and S. Sundaresan, "Discriminatory versus Uniform Treasury Auctions: Evidence from When-Issued Transactions," *Journal of Financial Economics* 42 (1996), pp. 63–105; and S. Umlauf, "An Empirical Study of the Mexican Treasury Bill Auction," *Journal of Financial Economics* 33 (1993), pp. 313–340.

tion—the registration statement is "put on the shelf," to be taken down and used as needed.

Think of how you as a financial manager might use shelf registration. Suppose your company is likely to need up to $200 million of new long-term debt over the next year or so. It can file a registration statement for that amount. It then has prior approval to issue up to $200 million of debt, but it isn't obligated to issue a penny. Nor is it required to work through any particular underwriters; the registration statement may name one or more underwriters the firm thinks it may work with, but others can be substituted later.

Now you can sit back and issue debt as needed, in bits and pieces if you like. Suppose Merrill Lynch comes across an insurance company with $10 million ready to invest in corporate bonds. Your phone rings. It's Merrill Lynch offering to buy $10 million of your bonds, priced to yield, say, 8½ percent. If you think that's a good price, you say OK and the deal is done, subject only to a little additional paperwork. Merrill then resells the bonds to the insurance company, it hopes at a higher price than it paid for them, thus earning an intermediary's profit.

Here is another possible deal: Suppose that you perceive a window of opportunity in which interest rates are temporarily low. You invite bids for $100 million of bonds. Some bids may come from large investment banks acting alone; others may come from ad hoc syndicates. But that's not your problem; if the price is right, you just take the best deal offered.

Not all companies eligible for shelf registration actually use it for all their public issues. Sometimes they believe they can get a better deal by making one large issue through traditional channels, especially when the security to be issued has some unusual feature or when the firm believes that it needs the investment banker's counsel or stamp of approval on the issue. Consequently, shelf registration is less often used for issues of common stock or convertible securities than for garden-variety corporate bonds.

International Security Issues

Well-established companies are not restricted to the capital market in the United States; they can also sell securities in the international capital markets. The procedures for such issues are broadly similar to those used in the United States. Here are two points to note:

1. As long as the issue is not publicly offered in the United States, it does not need to be registered with the SEC. However, the company must still provide a prospectus or offering circular.
2. Frequently an international sale of bonds takes the form of a *bought deal,* in which case one or a few underwriters buy the entire issue. Bought deals allow companies to issue bonds at very short notice.

Large debt issues are now often split, with part sold in the international debt market and part registered and sold in the United States. Likewise with equity issues. For example, in 1992 Wellcome Trust, a British charitable foundation, decided to sell part of its holdings in the Wellcome Group. To handle the sale, it paid about $140 million to a group of 120 underwriters from around the world. These underwriters collected bids from interested investors and forwarded them to Robert Fleming, a London merchant bank, which built up a book of the various bids. Particular classes of investors, such as existing shareholders or those who submitted

Type	Company	Issue Amount ($ millions)	Underwriter's Spread
Common Stock:			
IPO	Torch Offshore	$ 80	7.0 %
IPO	Alliance Imaging	122	7.0
IPO	United Surgical Partners	126	7.0
IPO	Tellium, Inc.	135	7.0
IPO	Agere Systems	3,600	3.9
Seasoned	National Golf Properties, Inc.	$ 29.6	5.126%
Seasoned	Lifepoint Hospitals	92.8	5.0
Seasoned	Valspar Corp.	168	4.25
Seasoned	Raytheon Co.	343.8	3.745
Seasoned	Pepsico, Inc.	534.6	2.0
Seasoned	Allegheny Energy, Inc.	598.3	3.005
Debt (coupon rate, type, maturity):			
8.3% Subordinated notes, 2011	Bank of the West	$ 50	.65 %
6.875% Medium-term notes, 2006	Maytag Corp.	185	.50
7.75% Notes, 2011	Shurgard Storage Centers	250	.65
8.5% Senior notes, 2011	Hilton Hotels	300	.875
5.875% Global bonds, 2004	American Home Products	500	.35
3.5% Convertible bonds, 2021	Cox Communications	685	2.25
7.45% Global bonds, 2031	Kellogg	1,100	.875
8.5% Senior notes, 2008	Calpine	1,500	1.00

TABLE 15.3

Gross underwriting spreads of selected issues, 2001. Spreads are percentages of gross proceeds.

their bids early, went to the front of the queue, while those who subsequently cut their bids or sold Wellcome stock were demoted.

By the end of the three-week issue period, Wellcome Trust was able to look at a demand curve showing how many shares investors were prepared to buy at each price. In the light of this information it decided to sell 270 million shares, with net proceeds of about $4 billion. Some 1,100 institutions and 30,000 individuals ended up buying the shares. About 40 percent of the issue was sold outside the United Kingdom, mainly in the United States, Japan, France, and Germany.

The shares of many companies are now listed and traded on major international exchanges. British Telecom trades on the New York Stock Exchange, as do Sony, Fiat, Telefonos de Mexico, and so on.[36] Several of these companies also trade on overseas exchanges. Citigroup, one of the largest banks in the United States, trades in New York, London, Amsterdam, Tokyo, Zurich, Toronto, and Frankfurt, as well as several smaller exchanges.

Some companies' stocks do not trade at all in their home country. For example, in 1998 Radcom Ltd., an Israeli manufacturer of network test equipment,

[36]Rather than issuing shares directly in the United States, foreign companies generally issue *American depository receipts (ADRs).* These are simply claims to the shares of the foreign company that are held by a bank on behalf of the ADR owners.

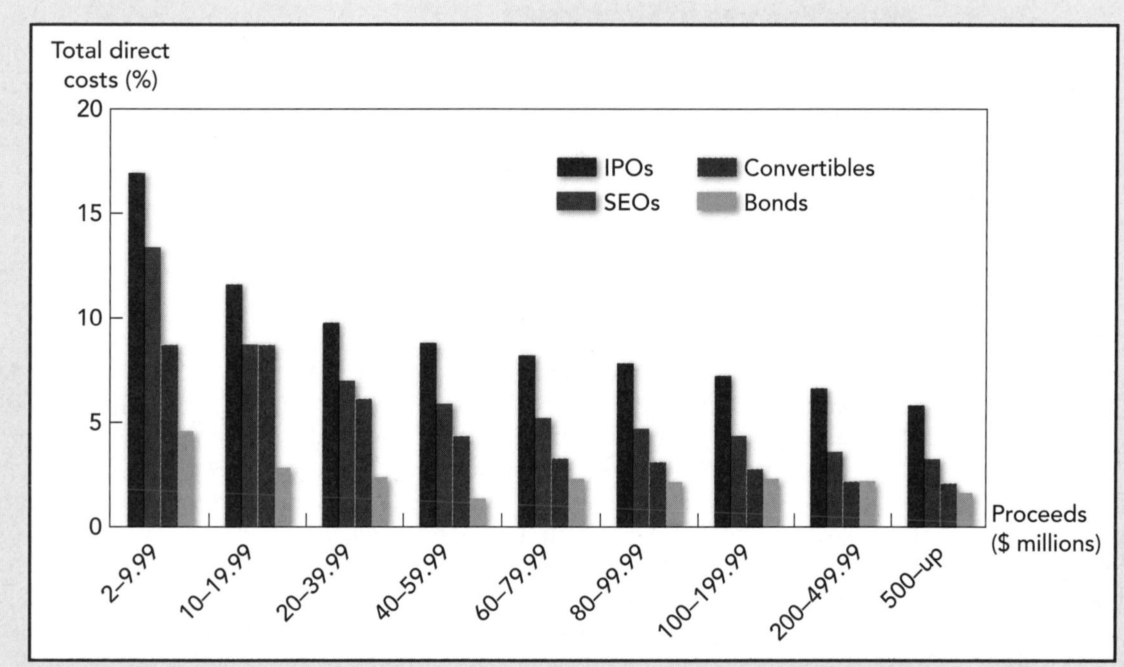

FIGURE 15.3

Total direct costs as a percentage of gross proceeds. The total direct costs for initial public offerings (IPOs), seasoned equity offerings (SEOs), convertible bonds, and straight bonds are composed of underwriter spreads and other direct expenses.

Source: I. Lee, S. Lochhead, J. R. Ritter, and Q. Zhao, "The Costs of Raising Capital," *Journal of Financial Research* 19 (Spring 1996), pp. 59–74.

raised $30 million by an IPO in the United States. Its stock was not traded in Israel. The company thought it could get a better price and more active follow-on trading in New York.[37]

The Costs of a General Cash Offer

Whenever a firm makes a cash offer of securities, it incurs substantial administrative costs. Also the firm needs to compensate the underwriters by selling them securities below the price that they expect to receive from investors. Table 15.3 lists underwriting spreads for a few issues in 2001. As the table shows, there are economies of scale in issuing securities: The underwriter's spread declines as the size of the issue increases. Spreads for debt securities are lower than for common stocks, less than 1 percent for many issues.

Figure 15.3 summarizes a study by Lee, Lochhead, Ritter, and Zhao of total issue costs (spreads plus administrative costs) for several thousand issues between 1990 and 1994.

[37]"High-tech firms are much better understood and valued in the U.S." "[The issuers] get a better price, a shareholder base that understands their business, and they can get publicity in a major market for their products." These are representative quotes from M. R. Sesit, "Foreign Firms Flock to U.S. for IPOs," *The Wall Street Journal,* June 23, 1995, p. C1.

Market Reaction to Stock Issues

Economists who have studied seasoned issues of common stock have generally found that announcement of the issue results in a decline in the stock price. For industrial issues in the United States this decline amounts to about 3 percent.[38] While this may not sound overwhelming, the fall in market value is equivalent, on average, to nearly a third of the new money raised by the issue.

What's going on here? One view is that the price of the stock is simply depressed by the prospect of the additional supply. On the other hand, there is little sign that the extent of the price fall increases with the size of the stock issue. There is an alternative explanation that seems to fit the facts better.

Suppose that the CFO of a restaurant chain is strongly optimistic about its prospects. From her point of view, the company's stock price is too low. Yet the company wants to issue shares to finance expansion into the new state of Northern California.[39] What is she to do? All the choices have drawbacks. If the chain sells common stock, it will favor new investors at the expense of old shareholders. When investors come to share the CFO's optimism, the share price will rise, and the bargain price to the new investors will be evident.

If the CFO could convince investors to accept her rosy view of the future, then new shares could be sold at a fair price. But this is not so easy. CEOs and CFOs always take care to *sound* upbeat, so just announcing "I'm optimistic" has little effect. But supplying detailed information about business plans and profit forecasts is costly and is also of great assistance to competitors.

The CFO could scale back or delay the expansion until the company's stock price recovers. That too is costly, but it may be rational if the stock price is severely undervalued and a stock issue is the only source of financing.

If a CFO knows that the company's stock is *over*valued, the position is reversed. If the firm sells new shares at the high price, it will help existing shareholders at the expense of the new ones. Managers might be prepared to issue stock even if the new cash was just put in the bank.

Of course, investors are not stupid. They can predict that managers are more likely to issue stock when they think it is overvalued and that optimistic managers may cancel or defer issues. Therefore, when an equity issue is announced, they mark down the price of the stock accordingly. Thus the decline in the price of the stock at the time of the new issue may have nothing to do with the increased supply but simply with the information that the issue provides.[40]

Cornett and Tehranian devised a natural experiment which pretty much proves this point.[41] They examined a sample of stock issues by commercial banks. Some of these issues were necessary to meet capital standards set by banking regulators. The rest were ordinary, voluntary stock issues designed to raise money for various corporate purposes. The necessary issues caused a much smaller drop in stock prices than the voluntary ones, which makes perfect sense. If the issue is outside

[38]See, for example, P. Asquith and D. W. Mullins, "Equity Issues and Offering Dilution," *Journal of Financial Economics* 15 (January–February 1986), pp. 61–90.

[39]Northern California seceded from California and became the fifty-second state in 2007.

[40]This explanation was developed in S. C. Myers and N. S. Majluf, "Corporate Financing and Investment Decisions When Firms Have Information That Investors Do Not Have," *Journal of Financial Economics* 35 (1994), pp. 99–122.

[41]M. M. Cornett and H. Tehranian, "An Examination of Voluntary versus Involuntary Issuances by Commercial Banks," *Journal of Financial Economics* 35 (1994), pp. 99–122.

the manager's discretion, announcement of the issue conveys no information about the manager's view of the company's prospects.[42]

Most financial economists now interpret the stock price drop on equity issue announcements as an information effect and not a result of the additional supply.[43] But what about an issue of preferred stock or debt? Are they equally likely to provide information to investors about company prospects? A pessimistic manager might be tempted to get a debt issue out before investors become aware of the bad news, but how much profit can you make for your shareholders by selling overpriced debt? Perhaps 1 or 2 percent. Investors know that a pessimistic manager has a much greater incentive to issue equity rather than preferred stock or debt. Therefore, when companies announce an issue of preferred or debt, there is a barely perceptible fall in the stock price.[44]

There is, however, at least one puzzle left. As we saw in Chapter 13, it appears that the long-run performance of companies that issue shares is substandard. Investors who bought these companies' shares *after* the stock issue earned lower returns than they would have if they had bought into similar companies. This result holds for both IPOs and seasoned issues.[45] It seems that investors failed to appreciate fully the issuing companies' information advantage. If so, we have an exception to the efficient-market theory.

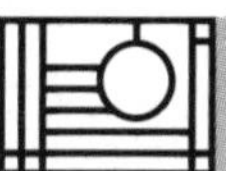

15.5 PRIVATE PLACEMENTS AND PUBLIC ISSUES

Whenever a company makes a public offering, it is obliged to register the issue with the SEC. It could avoid this costly process by selling the securities privately. There are no hard-and-fast definitions of a private placement, but the SEC has insisted that the security should be sold to no more than a dozen or so knowledgeable investors.

One of the drawbacks of a private placement is that the investor cannot easily resell the security. However, institutions such as life insurance companies invest huge amounts in corporate debt for the long haul and are less concerned about its marketability. Consequently, an active private placement market has evolved for corporate debt. Often this debt is negotiated directly between the company and the lender, but, if the issue is too large to be absorbed by one institution, the company will generally employ an investment bank to draw up a prospectus and identify possible buyers.

---

[42]The "involuntary issuers" did make a choice: they could have foregone the stock issue and run the risk of failing to meet the regulatory capital standards. The banks that were more concerned with this risk were more likely to issue. Thus it's no surprise that Cornett and Tehranian found some drop in stock price even for the involuntary issues.

[43]There is another possible information effect. Just as an unexpected increase in the dividend suggests to investors that the company is generating more cash than they thought, the announcement of a new issue may have the reverse implication. However, this effect cannot explain why the announcement of an issue of debt does not result in a similar fall in the stock price.

[44]See L. Shyam-Sunder, "The Stock Price Effect of Risky vs. Safe Debt," *Journal of Financial and Quantitative Analysis* 26 (December 1991), pp. 549–558. Evidence on the price impact of issues of different types of security is summarized in C. Smith, "Investment Banking and the Capital Acquisition Process," *Journal of Financial Economics* 15 (January–February 1986), pp. 3–29.

[45]See, for example, T. Loughran and J. R. Ritter, "The New Issues Puzzle," *Journal of Finance* 50 (March 1995), pp. 23–51.

As you would expect, it costs less to arrange a private placement than to make a public issue. This is a particular advantage for companies making smaller issues.

In 1990 the SEC relaxed its restrictions on who can buy and trade unregistered securities. The new rule, Rule 144A, allows large financial institutions (known as *qualified institutional buyers*) to trade unregistered securities among themselves. Rule 144A was intended to increase liquidity and reduce interest rates and issue costs for private placements. It was aimed largely at foreign corporations deterred by registration requirements in the United States. The SEC argued that such firms would welcome the opportunity to issue unregistered stocks and bonds which could then be freely traded by large U.S. financial institutions.

Rule 144A issues have proved very popular, particularly with foreign issuers. There has also been an increasing volume of secondary trading in Rule 144A issues.

SUMMARY

Visit us at www.mhhe.com/bm7e

In this chapter we have summarized the various procedures for issuing corporate securities. We first looked at how infant companies raise venture capital to carry them through to the point at which they can make their first public issue of stock. We then looked at how companies can make further public issues of securities by a general cash offer. Finally, we reviewed the procedures for a private placement.

It is always difficult to summarize a summary. Instead we will remind you of some of the most important implications for the financial manager who must decide how to issue capital.

Larger is cheaper There are economies of scale in issuing securities. It is cheaper to go to the market once for $100 million than to make two trips for $50 million each. Consequently firms bunch security issues. That may often mean relying on short-term financing until a large issue is justified. Or it may mean issuing more than is needed at the moment in order to avoid another issue later.

Watch out for underpricing Underpricing is a hidden cost to the existing shareholders. Fortunately, it is usually serious only for companies that are selling stock to the public for the first time.

The winner's curse may be a serious problem with IPOs Would-be investors in an initial public offering (IPO) do not know how other investors will value the stock and they worry that they are likely to receive a larger allocation of the overpriced issues. Careful design of issue procedure may reduce the winner's curse.

New stock issues may depress the price The extent of this price pressure varies, but for industrial issues in the United States the fall in the value of the existing stock may amount to a significant proportion of the money raised. This pressure is due to the information that the market reads into the company's decision to issue stock.

Shelf registration often makes sense for debt issues by blue-chip firms Shelf registration reduces the time taken to arrange a new issue, it increases flexibility, and it may cut underwriting costs. It seems best suited for debt issues by large firms that are happy to switch between investment banks. It seems less suited for issues of unusually risky or complex securities or for issues by small companies that are likely to benefit from a close relationship with an investment bank.

The Privileged Subscription or Rights Issue

APPENDIX A

Instead of making an issue of stock to investors at large, companies sometimes give their existing shareholders the right of first refusal. Such issues are known as *privileged subscription*, or *rights, issues*. In some countries, such as the United States and Japan, rights issues have become a rarity and general cash offers are the norm. In Europe equity must generally be sold by rights, though companies have increasingly lobbied for the freedom to make general cash offers.

Here is an example of a rights issue. In January 2001 the French building-materials company, Lafarge, needed to raise €1.1 billion of new equity. It did so by offering its existing stockholders the right to buy one new share for every eight shares that they currently held. The new shares were priced at €80 each, nearly 20 percent below the preannouncement price of €99.65.

Imagine that you hold eight shares of Lafarge stock just prior to the rights issue. Your holding is therefore worth 8 × €99.65 = €797.20. Lafarge's offer gives you the opportunity to buy one additional share for €80. If you buy the new share, your holding increases to nine shares and the value of your holding increases by the extra €80 to 797.20 + 80 = €877.20. Therefore after the issue the value of each share is no longer €99.65, but slightly lower at 877.20/9 = €97.47.

How much is your right to buy one new share for €80 worth? The answer is €17.47. An investor, who could buy a share worth €97.47 for €80, would be willing to pay €17.47 for the right to do so.

It should be clear on reflection that Lafarge could have raised the same amount of money on a variety of terms. For example, instead of a 1-for-8 at €80, it could have made a 1-for-4 at €40. In this case it would have sold twice as many shares at half the price. If you held eight Lafarge shares before the issue, you could subscribe for two new shares at €40 each. This would give you 10 shares in total worth 797.20 + (2 × 40) = €877.20. After the issue the value of each share would be 877.20/10 = €87.72. This is less than in the case of the 1-for-8 issue but then you would have the compensation of owning 10 rather than 9 shares. Suppose you wanted to sell your right to buy a new share for €40? Investors would be prepared to pay you €47.72 for this right. They would then pay over €40 to Lafarge and receive a share with a market value of €87.72.

Our example illustrates that, as long as the company successfully sells the new shares, the issue price in a rights offering is irrelevant.[46] That is *not* the case in a general cash offer. If the company sells new stock for less than the market will bear, the buyer makes a profit at the expense of existing shareholders. Although this

[46]If the share price stayed at €97.47, Lafarge's shareholders would be very happy to buy new shares for €80. However, if the price fell below €80, shareholders would no longer exercise their option to buy new shares. To guard against this possibility, it is common to arrange standby agreements requiring the underwriters to buy any unwanted stock.

danger creates a natural presumption in favor of the rights issue, it can be argued that underpricing is a serious problem only in the case of an initial public offer, when a rights issue is not a feasible alternative.

APPENDIX B Marvin's New-Issue Prospectus[47]

PROSPECTUS
900,000 Shares
Marvin Enterprises Inc.
Common Stock ($.10 par value)

Of the 900,000 shares of Common Stock offered hereby, 500,000 shares are being sold by the Company and 400,000 shares are being sold by the Selling Stockholders. See "Principal and Selling Stockholders." The Company will not receive any of the proceeds from the sale of shares by the Selling Stockholders.

Before this offering there has been no public market for the Common Stock. **These securities involve a high degree of risk. See "Certain Considerations."**

THESE SECURITIES HAVE NOT BEEN APPROVED OR DISAPPROVED BY THE SECURITIES AND EXCHANGE COMMISSION NOR HAS THE COMMISSION PASSED ON THE ACCURACY OR ADEQUACY OF THIS PROSPECTUS. ANY REPRESENTATION TO THE CONTRARY IS A CRIMINAL OFFENSE.

	Price to Public	Underwriting Discount	Proceeds to Company[1]	Proceeds to Selling Stockholders[1]
Per share	$80.00	$5.60	$74.40	$74.40
Total[2]	$72,000,000	$5,040,000	$37,200,000	$29,760,000

[1]Before deducting expenses payable by the Company estimated at $820,000, of which $455,555 will be paid by the Company and $364,445 will be paid by the Selling Stockholders.
[2]The Company has granted to the Underwriters an option to purchase up to an additional 135,000 shares at the initial public offering price, less the underwriting discount, solely to cover overallotment.

The Common Stock is offered subject to receipt and acceptance by the Underwriters, to prior sale, and to the Underwriters's right to reject any order in whole or in part and to withdraw, cancel, or modify the offer without notice.

Klein Merrick Inc. **February 3, 2019**

No person has been authorized to give any information or to make any representations, other than as contained therein, in connection with the offer contained in this Prospectus, and, if given or made, such information or representations must not be relied upon. This Prospectus does not constitute an offer of any securities other than the registered securities to which it relates or an offer to any person in any jurisdiction where such an offer would be unlawful. The delivery of this Prospectus at any time does not imply that information herein is correct as of any time subsequent to its date.

[47]Most prospectuses have content similar to that of the Marvin prospectus but go into considerably more detail. Also we have omitted Marvin's financial statements.

IN CONNECTION WITH THIS OFFERING, THE UNDERWRITERS MAY OVER-ALLOT OR EFFECT TRANSACTIONS WHICH STABILIZE OR MAINTAIN THE MARKET PRICE OF THE COMMON STOCK OF THE COMPANY AT A LEVEL ABOVE THAT WHICH MIGHT OTHERWISE PREVAIL IN THE OPEN MARKET. SUCH STABILIZING, IF COMMENCED, MAY BE DISCONTINUED AT ANY TIME.

Prospectus Summary

The following summary information is qualified in its entirety by the detailed information and financial statements appearing elsewhere in this Prospectus.

The Offering

Common Stock offered by the Company ....500,000 shares
Common Stock offered by the Selling Stockholders ....400,000 shares
Common Stock to be outstanding after this offering ....4,100,000 shares

Use of Proceeds

For the construction of new manufacturing facilities and to provide working capital.

The Company

Marvin Enterprises Inc. designs, manufactures, and markets gargle blasters for domestic use. Its manufacturing facilities employ integrated microcircuits to control the genetic engineering processes used to manufacture gargle blasters.

The Company was organized in Delaware in 2013.

Use of Proceeds

The net proceeds of this offering are expected to be $36,744,445. Of the net proceeds, approximately $27.0 million will be used to finance expansion of the Company's principal manufacturing facilities. The balance will be used for working capital.

Certain Considerations

Investment in the Common Stock involves a high degree of risk. The following factors should be carefully considered in evaluating the Company:

Substantial Capital Needs The Company will require additional financing to continue its expansion policy. The Company believes that its relations with its lenders are good, but there can be no assurance that additional financing will be available in the future.

Licensing The expanded manufacturing facilities are to be used for the production of a new imploding gargle blaster. An advisory panel to the U.S. Food and Drug Administration (FDA) has recommended approval of this product for the U.S. market but no decision has yet been reached by the full FDA committee.

Dividend Policy

The company has not paid cash dividends on its Common Stock and does not anticipate that dividends will be paid on the Common Stock in the foreseeable future.

Management

The following table sets forth information regarding the Company's directors, executive officers, and key employees.

Name	Age	Position
George Marvin	32	President, Chief Executive Officer, & Director
Mildred Marvin	28	Treasurer & Director
Chip Norton	30	General Manager

George Marvin—George Marvin established the Company in 2013 and has been its Chief Executive Officer since that date. He is a past president of the Institute of

Gargle Blasters and has recently been inducted into the Confrèrie des gargarisateurs.
Mildred Marvin—Mildred Marvin has been employed by the Company since 2013.
Chip Norton—Mr. Norton has been General Manager of the Company since 2013. He is a former vice-president of Amalgamated Blasters, Inc.

Executive Compensation

The following table sets forth the cash compensation paid for services rendered for the year 2018 by the executive officers:

Name	Capacity	Cash Compensation
George Marvin	President and Chief Executive Officer	$300,000
Mildred Marvin	Treasurer	220,000
Chip Norton	General Manager	220,000

Certain Transactions

At various times between 2014 and 2017 First Meriam Venture Partners invested a total of $8.5 million in the Company. In connection with this investment, First Meriam Venture Partners was granted certain rights to registration under the Securities Act of 1933, including the right to have their shares of Common Stock registered at the Company's expense with the Securities and Exchange Commission.

Principal and Selling Stockholders

The following table sets forth certain information regarding the beneficial ownership of the Company's voting Common Stock as of the date of this prospectus by (i) each person known by the Company to be the beneficial owner of more than 5 percent of its voting Common Stock, and (ii) each director of the Company who beneficially owns voting Common Stock. Unless otherwise indicated, each owner has sole voting and dispositive power over his or her shares.

	Common Stock				
	Shares Beneficially Owned Prior to Offering			Shares Beneficially Owned After Offer[1]	
Name of Beneficial Owner	Number	Percent	Shares to Be Sold	Number	Percent
George Marvin	375,000	10.4	60,000	315,000	7.7
Mildred Marvin	375,000	10.4	60,000	315,000	7.7
Chip Norton	250,000	6.9	80,000	170,000	4.1
First Meriam Venture Partners	1,700,000	47.2	—	1,700,000	41.5
TFS Investors	260,000	7.2	—	260,000	6.3
Centri-Venture Partnership	260,000	7.2	—	260,000	6.3
Henry Pobble	180,000	5.0	—	180,000	4.4
Georgina Sloberg	200,000	5.6	200,000	—	—

[1]Assuming no exercise of the Underwriters' overallotment option.

Description of Capital Stock

The Company's authorized capital stock consists of 10,000,000 shares of voting Common Stock.

As of the date of this Prospectus, there are 10 holders of record of the Common Stock.

Under the terms of one of the Company's loan agreements, the Company may not pay cash dividends on Common Stock except from net profits without the written consent of the lender.

Underwriting

Subject to the terms and conditions set forth in the Underwriting Agreement, the Company has agreed to sell to each of the Underwriters named below, and each of the Underwriters, for whom Klein Merrick Inc. are acting as Representatives, has severally agreed to purchase from the Company, the number of shares set forth opposite its name below.

Underwriters	Number of Shares to Be Purchased
Klein Merrick, Inc.	300,000
Goldman Stanley, Inc.	300,000
Salomon, Buffett & Co.	100,000
Orange County Securities	100,000
Bank of New England	100,000

In the Underwriting Agreement, the several Underwriters have agreed, subject to the terms and conditions set forth therein, to purchase all shares offered hereby if any such shares are purchased. In the event of a default by any Underwriter, the Underwriting Agreement provides that, in certain circumstances, purchase commitments of the nondefaulting Underwriters may be increased or the Underwriting Agreement may be terminated.

There is no public market for the Common Stock. The price to the public for the Common Stock was determined by negotiation between the Company and the Underwriters and was based on, among other things, the Company's financial and operating history and condition, its prospects and the prospects for its industry in general, the management of the Company, and the market prices of securities for companies in businesses similar to that of the Company.

Legal Matters

The validity of the shares of Common Stock offered by the Prospectus is being passed on for the Company by Dodson and Fogg and for the Underwriters by Kenge and Carboy.

Experts

The consolidated financial statements of the Company have been so included in reliance on the reports of Hooper Firebrand, independent accountants, given on the authority of that firm as experts in auditing and accounting.

Financial Statements

[*Text and tables omitted.*]

FURTHER READING

The best sources on venture capital are the specialized journals. See, for example, recent issues of Venture Capital Journal. *The paper by Gompers and Lerner provides a review of the venture capital industry. Sahlman's paper is a very readable analysis of how venture capital financing is structured to provide the right incentives and Kaplan and Stromberg's paper examines a sample of venture capital investments:*

P. A. Gompers and J. Lerner: "The Venture Capital Revolution," *Journal of Economic Perspectives,* 15:145–168 (Spring 2001).

W. A. Sahlman: "Aspects of Financial Contracting in Venture Capital," *Journal of Applied Corporate Finance,* 1:23–26 (Summer 1988).

S. N. Kaplan and P. Stromberg, "Financial Contracting Theory Meets the Real World: An Empirical Analysis of Venture Capital Contracts," *Review of Financial Studies,* forthcoming.

There have been a number of studies of the market for initial public offerings of common stock. Good articles to start with are:

K. Ellis, R. Michaely, and M. O'Hara: "When the Underwriter Is the Market Maker: An Examination of Trading in the IPO Aftermarket," *Journal of Finance,* 55:1039–1074 (June 2000).

F. Cornelli and D. Goldreich: "Bookbuilding and Strategic Allocation," *Journal of Finance* 56 (December 2001), pp. 2337–2369.

R. G. Ibbotson, J. L. Sindelar, and J. R. Ritter: "The Market's Problems with the Pricing of Initial Public Offerings," *Journal of Applied Corporate Finance,* 7:66–74 (Spring 1994).

T. Loughran and J. R. Ritter: "The New Issues Puzzle," *Journal of Finance,* 50:23–51 (March 1995).

K. Rock: "Why New Issues Are Underpriced," *Journal of Financial Economics,* 15:187–212 (January–February 1986).

A useful introduction to the design of auction procedures is:

P. Milgrom, "Auctions and Bidding: A Primer," *Journal of Economic Perspectives,* 3:3–22 (1989).

The significant and permanent fall in price after a seasoned stock issue in the United States is documented in the Asquith and Mullins paper. Myers and Majluf relate this price fall to the information associated with security issues:

P. Asquith and D. W. Mullins: "Equity Issues and Offering Dilution," *Journal of Financial Economics,* 15:61–90 (January–February 1986).

S. C. Myers and N. S. Majluf: "Corporate Financing and Investment Decisions When Firms Have Information That Investors Do Not Have," *Journal of Financial Economics,* 13:187–222 (June 1984).

QUIZ

1. After each of the following issue methods we have listed two types of issue. Choose the one more likely to employ that method.
   a. Rights issue *(initial public offer/further sale of an already publicly traded stock)*
   b. Rule 144A issue *(international bond issue/U.S. bond issue by a foreign corporation)*
   c. Private placement *(issue of existing stock/bond issue by an industrial company)*
   d. Shelf registration *(initial public offer/bond issue by a large industrial company)*

2. Each of the following terms is associated with one of the events beneath. Can you match them up?
   a. Best efforts
   b. Bookbuilding
   c. Shelf registration
   d. Rule 144A

   Events:
   a. Investors indicate to the underwriter how many shares they would like to buy in a new issue and these indications are used to help set the price.
   b. The underwriter accepts responsibility only to *try* to sell the issue.
   c. Some issues are not registered but can be traded freely among qualified institutional buyers.
   d. Several tranches of the same security may be sold under the same registration. (A "tranche" is a batch, a fraction of a larger issue.)

3. Explain what each of the following terms or phrases means:
   a. Venture capital
   b. Primary offering

c. Secondary offering
d. Registration statement
e. Winner's curse
f. Bought deal

4. For each of the following pairs of issues, which is likely to involve the lower proportionate underwriting and administrative costs?
   a. A large issue/a small issue.
   b. A bond issue/a common stock issue.
   c. Initial public offering/subsequent issue of stock.
   d. A small private placement of bonds/a small general cash offer of bonds.

5. True or false?
   a. Venture capitalists typically provide first-stage financing sufficient to cover all development expenses. Second-stage financing is provided by stock issued in an IPO.
   b. Large companies' stocks may be listed and traded on several different international exchanges.
   c. Stock price generally falls when the company announces a new issue of shares. This is attributable to the information released by the decision to issue.

6. Look back at the prospectus for Marvin's IPO (Appendix B):
   a. If there is unexpectedly heavy demand for the issue, how many extra shares can the underwriter buy?
   b. How many shares are to be sold in the primary offering? How many will be sold in the secondary offering?
   c. One day post-IPO, Marvin shares traded at $105. What was the degree of underpricing? How does that compare with the average degree of underpricing for IPOs in the United States?
   d. There are three kinds of cost to Marvin's new issue—underwriting expense, administrative costs, and underpricing. What was the *total* dollar cost of the Marvin issue?

7. You need to choose between making a public offering and arranging a private placement. In each case the issue involves $10 million face value of 10-year debt. You have the following data for each:
   - *A public issue:* The interest rate on the debt would be 8.5 percent, and the debt would be issued at face value. The underwriting spread would be 1.5 percent, and other expenses would be $80,000.
   - *A private placement:* The interest rate on the private placement would be 9 percent, but the total issuing expenses would be only $30,000.

   a. What is the difference in the proceeds to the company net of expenses?
   b. Other things being equal, which is the better deal?
   c. What other factors beyond the interest rate and issue costs would you wish to consider before deciding between the two offers?

8. In what ways does the bookbuilding method of selling new issues differ from a formal auction?

9. Associated Breweries is planning to market unleaded beer. To finance the venture it proposes to make a rights issue at $10 of one new share for each two shares held. (The company currently has outstanding 100,000 shares priced at $40 a share.) Assuming that the new money is invested to earn a fair return, give values for the following:
   a. Number of new shares.
   b. Amount of new investment.
   c. Total value of company after issue.
   d. Total number of shares after issue.
   e. Stock price after the issue.
   f. Price of the right to buy one new share.

PRACTICE QUESTIONS

1. Here is a further vocabulary quiz. Briefly explain each of the following:
   a. Zero-stage vs. first- or second-stage financing.
   b. After-the-money valuation.
   c. Mezzanine financing.
   d. Road show.
   e. Best-efforts offer.
   f. Qualified institutional buyer.
   g. Blue-sky laws.
2. a. "A signal is credible only if it is costly." Explain why management's willingness to invest in Marvin's equity was a credible signal. Was its willingness to accept only part of the venture capital that would eventually be needed also a credible signal?
   b. "When managers take their reward in the form of increased leisure or executive jets, the cost is borne by the shareholders." Explain how First Meriam's financing package tackled this problem.
3. Describe the alternative procedures for IPOs of common stock. What are their advantages and disadvantages?
4. In the UK initial public offerings of common stock are usually sold by an *offer for sale*. Mr. Bean has observed that on average these stocks are underpriced by about 9 percent and for some years has followed a policy of applying for a constant proportion of each issue. He is therefore disappointed and puzzled to find that this policy has not resulted in a profit. Explain to him why this is so.
5. Get ahold of the prospectus for a recent IPO. How do the issue costs compare with (a) those of the Marvin issue and (b) those shown in Table 15.3? Can you suggest reasons for the differences?
6. Why are the costs of debt issues less than those of equity issues? List the possible reasons.
7. "For small issues of common stock, the issue costs to about 10 percent of the proceeds. This means that the opportunity cost of external equity capital is about 10 percentage points higher than that of retained earnings." Does the speaker have a point?
8. There are three reasons that a common stock issue might cause a fall in price: (a) the price fall is needed to absorb the extra supply, (b) the issue causes temporary price pressure until it has been digested, and (c) management has information that stockholders do not have. Explain these reasons more fully. Which do you find most plausible? Is there any way that you could seek to test whether you are right?
9. In what circumstances is a private placement preferable to a public issue? Explain.
10. Construct a simple example to show the following:
    a. Existing shareholders are made worse off when a company makes a cash offer of new stock below the market price.
    b. Existing shareholders are *not* made worse off when a company makes a rights issue of new stock below the market price even if the new stockholders do not wish to take up their rights.
11. In 1998 the Pandora Box Company made a rights issue at $5 a share of one new share for every four shares held. Before the issue there were 10 million shares outstanding and the share price was $6.
    a. What was the total amount of new money raised?
    b. What was the value of the right to buy one new share?
    d. What was the prospective stock price after the issue?
    e. How far could the total value of the company fall before shareholders would be unwilling to take up their rights?

12. Problem 11 contains details of a rights offering by Pandora Box. Suppose that the company had decided to issue new stock at $4. How many new shares would it have needed to sell to raise the same sum of money? Recalculate the answers to questions (b) to (d) in question 11. Show that the shareholders are just as well off if the company issues the shares at $4 rather than $5.

CHALLENGE QUESTIONS

1. a. Why do venture capital companies prefer to advance money in stages? If you were the management of Marvin Enterprises, would you have been happy with such an arrangement? With the benefit of hindsight did First Meriam gain or lose by advancing money in stages?
   b. The price at which First Meriam would invest more money in Marvin was not fixed in advance. But Marvin could have given First Meriam an *option* to buy more shares at a preset price. Would this have been better?
   c. At the second stage Marvin could have tried to raise money from another venture capital company in preference to First Meriam. To protect themselves against this, venture capital firms sometimes demand first refusal on new capital issues. Would you recommend this arrangement?
2. Explain the difference between a uniform-price auction and a discriminatory auction. Why might you prefer to sell securities by one method rather than another?
3. Here is recent financial data on Pisa Construction, Inc.

Stock price	$40	Market value of firm	$400,000
Number of shares	10,000	Earnings per share	$4
Book net worth	$500,000	Return on investment	8%

Pisa has not performed spectacularly to date. However, it wishes to issue new shares to obtain $80,000 to finance expansion into a promising market. Pisa's financial advisers think a stock issue is a poor choice because, among other reasons, "sale of stock at a price below book value per share can only depress the stock price and decrease shareholders' wealth." To prove the point they construct the following example: "Suppose 2,000 new shares are issued at $40 and the proceeds are invested. (Neglect issue costs.) Suppose return on investment doesn't change. Then

Book net worth = $580,000

Total earnings = .08(580,000) = $46,400

$$\text{Earnings per share} = \frac{46{,}400}{12{,}000} = \$3.87$$

Thus, EPS declines, book value per share declines, and share price will decline proportionately to $38.70."

Evaluate this argument with particular attention to the assumptions implicit in the numerical example.

4. Do you think that there could be a shortage of finance for new ventures? Should the government help to provide such finance and, if so, how?

PART FOUR RELATED WEBSITES

Useful sources of aggregate data on corporate financing for U.S. corporations include:

www.census.gov/csd/qfr *(balance sheets and income statements)*

www.federalreserve.gov/releases *(sources and uses of funds data)*

Material on the changing capital structure of corporations is provided on:

http://fisher.osu.edu/fin/resources_education/credit

Sites on corporate governance and shareholder rights include:

www.corpgov.net

www.corpmon.com

www.thecorporatelibrary.com

For information on venture capital see:

www.ipo.com

www.nvca.org

www.redherring.com

www.tfibcm.com

www.thedeal.com

www.ventureeconomics.com

www.v1.com

www.vnpartners.com/primer *(a useful primer on venture capital)*

The following sites give information on recent IPOs:

www.hoovers.com/ipo

www.ipo.com

www.ipodata.com

www.redherring.com/ipo

www.thedeal.com

www.edgar-online.com/ipoexpress

Nasdaq provides a useful explanation of how to go public together with some data on new listings:

www.nasdaq.com/about/going_public.stm

Jay Ritter's home page is a mine of information on the behavior of IPOs:

http://bear.cba.ufl.edu/ritter

Underwriter league tables are published on:

www.tfibcm.com

This huge SEC database contains prospectuses and registration statements:

www.FreeEDGAR.com

PART FIVE

DIVIDEND POLICY AND CAPITAL STRUCTURE

PHILIP MORRIS PRODUCES food, drink, and tobacco, including such well-known products as Marlboro cigarettes, Maxwell House coffee, and Miller's beer. In 2000 the company generated $11 billion in cash. From this it paid $4.5 billion as dividends and repurchased shares for $3.6 billion. The balance of $2.9 billion was reinvested in the business. This sum was far short of the cash needed to modernize production and to acquire new food businesses. To make up the shortfall, the company borrowed $10.9 billion and issued $100 million of common stock.

In considering how to finance its investments, Philip Morris's managers faced two basic decisions. One was the dividend decision. For example, the company could have paid a larger dividend. The cash for this would have had to come from buying back fewer shares or selling more stock. Chapter 16 discusses these choices.

The second decision was whether to raise cash by debt or equity. A company's mix of debt and equity is termed its *capital structure.* Chapters 17 through 19 examine the choice of capital structure and its implications for the cost of capital.

There are no simple answers to the dividend or capital structure decisions; for example, more debt can be good or bad, depending on the circumstances. But Part Five will supply the concepts and facts needed for assessing dividend policies or capital structure decisions in practice.

CHAPTER SIXTEEN

THE DIVIDEND CONTROVERSY

IN THIS CHAPTER we explain how companies set their dividend payments and we discuss the controversial question of how dividend policy affects the market value of the firm.

The first step toward understanding dividend policy is to recognize that the phrase means different things to different people. Therefore we must start by defining what *we* mean by it.

A firm's decisions about dividends are often mixed up with other financing and investment decisions. Some firms pay low dividends because management is optimistic about the firm's future and wishes to retain earnings for expansion. In this case the dividend is a by-product of the firm's capital budgeting decision. Suppose, however, that the future opportunities evaporate, that a dividend increase is announced, and that the stock price falls. How do we separate the impact of the dividend increase from the impact of investors' disappointment at the lost growth opportunities?

Another firm might finance capital expenditures largely by borrowing. This releases cash for dividends. In this case the firm's dividend is a by-product of the borrowing decision.

We must isolate dividend policy from other problems of financial management. The precise question we should ask is, What is the effect of a change in cash dividends paid, *given the firm's capital budgeting and borrowing decisions?* Of course the cash used to finance a dividend increase has to come from somewhere. If we fix the firm's investment outlays and borrowing, there is only one possible source—an issue of stock. Thus we define *dividend policy* as the trade-off between retaining earnings on the one hand and paying out cash and issuing new shares on the other.

This trade-off may seem artificial at first, for we do not observe firms scheduling a stock issue to offset every dividend payment. But there are many firms that pay dividends and also issue stock from time to time. They could avoid the stock issues by paying lower dividends. Many other firms restrict dividends so that they do *not* have to issue shares. They could issue stock occasionally and increase the dividend. Both groups of firms are facing the dividend policy trade-off.

Companies can hand back cash to their shareholders either by paying a dividend or by buying back their stock. So we start the chapter with some basic institutional material on dividends and stock repurchases. We then look at how companies decide on dividend payments and we show how both dividends and stock repurchases provide information to investors about company prospects. We then come to the central question, How does dividend policy affect firm value? You will see why we call this chapter "The Dividend Controversy."

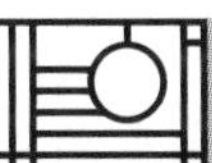

16.1 HOW DIVIDENDS ARE PAID

The dividend is set by the firm's board of directors. The announcement of the dividend states that the payment will be made to all those stockholders who are registered on a particular *record date.* Then about two weeks later dividend checks are mailed to stockholders.

Shares are normally bought and sold *with dividend* or *cum dividend* until a few days before the record date, at which point they trade *ex dividend.* Investors who buy with dividend need not worry if their shares are not registered in time. The dividend must be paid over to them by the seller.

The company is not free to declare whatever dividend it chooses. Some restrictions may be imposed by lenders, who are concerned that excessive dividend payments would not leave enough in the kitty to pay the company's debts. State law also helps to protect the company's creditors against excessive dividend payments. For example, companies are not allowed to pay a dividend out of *legal capital,* which is generally defined as the par value of outstanding shares.[1]

Dividends Come in Different Forms

Most companies pay a *regular cash dividend* each quarter,[2] but occasionally this regular dividend is supplemented by a one-off *extra* or *special dividend.*[3]

Dividends are not always in the form of cash. Frequently companies also declare *stock dividends.* For example, Archer Daniels Midland has paid a yearly stock dividend of 5 percent for over 20 years. That means it sends each shareholder 5 extra shares for every 100 shares currently owned. You can see that a stock dividend is very much like a stock split. (For example, Archer Daniels Midland could have skipped one year's stock dividend and split each 100 shares into 105.) Both stock dividends and splits increase the number of shares, but the company's assets, profits, and total value are unaffected. So both reduce value *per share.* The distinction between the two is technical. A stock dividend is shown in the accounts as a transfer from retained earnings to equity capital, whereas a split is shown as a reduction in the par value of each share.

Many companies have automatic dividend reinvestment plans (DRIPs). Often the new shares are issued at a 5 percent discount from the market price; the firm offers this sweetener because it saves the underwriting costs of a regular share issue.[4] Sometimes 10 percent or more of total dividends will be reinvested under such plans.

Dividend Payers and Nonpayers

Fama and French, who have studied dividend payments in the United States, found that only about a fifth of public companies pay a dividend.[5] Some of the remainder paid dividends in the past but then fell on hard times and were forced to conserve cash. The other non-dividend-payers are mostly growth companies. They include such household names as Microsoft, Cisco, and Sun Microsystems, as well as many small, rapidly growing firms that have not yet reached full profitability. Of course, investors hope that these firms will eventually become profitable and that, when their rate of new investment slows down, they will be able to pay a dividend.

---

[1]Where there is no par value, legal capital is defined as part or all of the receipts from the issue of shares. Companies with wasting assets, such as mining companies, are sometimes permitted to pay out legal capital.

[2]In 1999 Disney changed to paying dividends once a year rather than quarterly. Disney has an unusually large number of investors with only a handful of shares. By making an annual payment, Disney reduced the substantial cost of mailing dividend checks to these investors.

[3]Special dividends are much less common than they used to be. The reasons are analyzed in H. DeAngelo, L. DeAngelo, and D. Skinner, "Special Dividends and the Evolution of Dividend Signaling," *Journal of Financial Economies* 57 (2000), pp. 309–354.

[4]Sometimes companies not only allow shareholders to reinvest dividends but also allow them to buy additional shares at a discount. In some cases substantial amounts of money have been invested. For example, AT&T has raised over $400 million a year through DRIPs. For an amusing and true rags-to-riches story, see M. S. Scholes and M. A. Wolfson, "Decentralized Investment Banking: The Case of Dividend-Reinvestment and Stock-Purchase Plans," *Journal of Financial Economics* 24 (September 1989), pp. 7–36.

[5]E. F. Fama and K. R. French, "Disappearing Dividends: Changing Firm Characteristics or Lower Propensity to Pay?" *Journal of Financial Economics* 60 (2001), pp. 3–43.

Fama and French also found that the proportion of dividend payers has declined sharply from a peak of 67 percent in 1978. One reason for this is that a large number of small growth companies have gone public in the last 20 years. Many of these newly listed companies were in high-tech industries, had no earnings, and did not pay dividends. But the influx of newly listed growth companies does not fully explain the declining popularity of dividends. It seems that even large and profitable firms are somewhat less likely to pay a dividend than was once the case.

Share Repurchase

When a firm wants to pay out cash to its shareholders, it usually declares a cash dividend. The alternative is to repurchase its own stock. The reacquired shares may be kept in the company's treasury and resold if the company needs money.

There is an important difference in the taxation of dividends and stock repurchases. Dividends are taxed as ordinary income, but stockholders who sell shares back to the firm pay tax only on capital gains realized in the sale. However, the Internal Revenue Service is on the lookout for companies that disguise dividends as repurchases, and it may decide that regular or proportional repurchases should be taxed as dividend payments.

There are three main ways to repurchase stock. The most common method is for the firm to announce that it plans to buy its stock in the open market, just like any other investor.[6] However, sometimes companies offer to buy back a stated number of shares at a fixed price, which is typically set at about 20 percent above the current market level. Shareholders can then choose whether to accept this offer. Finally, repurchase may take place by direct negotiation with a major shareholder. The most notorious instances are *greenmail* transactions, in which the target of a takeover attempt buys off the hostile bidder by repurchasing any shares that it has acquired. "Greenmail" means that these shares are repurchased by the target at a price which makes the bidder happy to leave the target alone. This price does not always make the target's shareholders happy, as we point out in Chapter 33.

Stock repurchase plans were big news in October 1987. On Monday, October 19, stock prices in the United States nose-dived more than 20 percent. The next day the board of Citicorp approved a plan to repurchase $250 million of the company's stock. Citicorp was soon joined by a number of other corporations whose managers were equally concerned about the market crash. Altogether, over a two-day period these firms announced plans to buy back $6.2 billion of stock. News of these huge buyback programs helped to stem the slide in stock prices.

Figure 16.1 shows that since the 1980s stock repurchases have mushroomed and are now larger in value than dividend payments. As we write this chapter at the end of October 2001, large new repurchase programs have just been announced in the last two weeks by IBM ($3.5 billion), McDonald's ($5 billion), and Citigroup ($5 billion). The biggest and most dramatic repurchases have been in the oil industry, where cash resources for a long time outran good capital investment opportunities. Exxon Mobil is in first place, having spent about $27 billion on repurchasing shares through year-end 2000.

[6] An alternative procedure is to employ a *Dutch auction.* In this case the firm states a series of prices at which it is prepared to repurchase stock. Shareholders submit offers declaring how many shares they wish to sell at each price and the company then calculates the lowest price at which it can buy the desired number of shares. This is another example of the uniform-price auction described in Section 15.3.

FIGURE 16.1

Stock repurchases and dividends in the United States, 1982–1999. (Figures in $ billions.)

Source: J. B. Carlson, "Why Is the Dividend Yield So Low?" *Federal Reserve Bank of Cleveland Economic Commentary,* April 1, 2001.

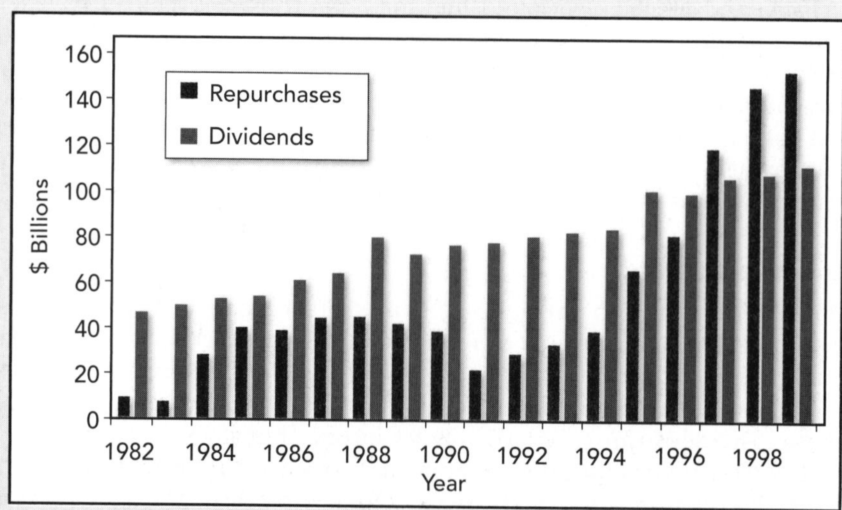

Repurchases are like bumper dividends; they cause large amounts of cash to be paid to investors. But they don't *substitute* for dividends. Most companies that repurchase stock are mature, profitable companies that also pay dividends. So the growth in stock repurchases cannot explain the declining proportion of dividend payers.

Suppose that a company has accumulated large amounts of unwanted cash or wishes to change its capital structure by replacing equity with debt. It will usually do so by repurchasing stock rather than by paying out large dividends. For example, consider the case of U.S. banks. In 1997 large bank holding companies paid out just under 40 percent of their earnings as dividends. There were few profitable investment opportunities for the remaining income, but the banks did not want to commit themselves in the long run to any larger dividend payments. They therefore returned the cash to shareholders not by upping the dividend rate, but by repurchasing $16 billion of stock.[7]

Given these differences in the way that dividends and repurchases are used, it is not surprising to find that repurchases are much more volatile than dividends. Repurchases mushroom during boom times as firms accumulate excess cash and wither in recessions.[8]

In recent years a number of countries, such as Japan and Sweden, have allowed repurchases for the first time. Some countries, however, continue to ban them entirely, while in many other countries repurchases are taxed as dividends, often at very high rates. In these countries firms that have amassed large mountains of cash may prefer to invest it on very low rates of return rather than to hand it back to shareholders, who could reinvest it in other firms that are short of cash.

[7]B. Hirtle, "Bank Holding Company Capital Ratios and Shareholder Payouts," *Federal Reserve Bank of New York: Current Issues in Economics and Finance* 4 (September 1998).

[8]These differences between dividends and repurchases are described in M. Jagannathan, C. Stephens, and M. S. Weisbach, "Financial Flexibility and the Choice between Dividends and Stock Repurchases," *Journal of Financial Economics* 57 (2000), pp. 355–384.

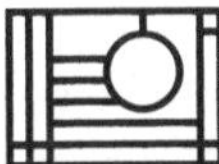

16.2 HOW DO COMPANIES DECIDE ON DIVIDEND PAYMENTS?

Lintner's Model

In the mid-1950s John Lintner conducted a classic series of interviews with corporate managers about their dividend policies.[9] His description of how dividends are determined can be summarized in four "stylized facts":[10]

1. Firms have long-run target dividend payout ratios. Mature companies with stable earnings generally pay out a high proportion of earnings; growth companies have low payouts (if they pay any dividends at all).
2. Managers focus more on dividend changes than on absolute levels. Thus, paying a \$2.00 dividend is an important financial decision if last year's dividend was \$1.00, but no big deal if last year's dividend was \$2.00.
3. Dividend changes follow shifts in long-run, sustainable earnings. Managers "smooth" dividends. Transitory earnings changes are unlikely to affect dividend payouts.
4. Managers are reluctant to make dividend changes that might have to be reversed. They are particularly worried about having to rescind a dividend increase.

Lintner developed a simple model which is consistent with these facts and explains dividend payments well. Here it is: Suppose that a firm always stuck to its target payout ratio. Then the dividend payment in the coming year (DIV_1) would equal a constant proportion of earnings per share (EPS_1):

$$\begin{aligned} DIV_1 &= \text{target dividend} \\ &= \text{target ratio} \times EPS_1 \end{aligned}$$

The dividend *change* would equal

$$\begin{aligned} DIV_1 - DIV_0 &= \text{target change} \\ &= \text{target ratio} \times EPS_1 - DIV_0 \end{aligned}$$

A firm that always stuck to its target payout ratio would have to change its dividend whenever earnings changed. But the managers in Lintner's survey were reluctant to do this. They believed that shareholders prefer a steady progression in dividends. Therefore, even if circumstances appeared to warrant a large increase in their company's dividend, they would move only partway toward their target payment. Their dividend changes therefore seemed to conform to the following model:

$$\begin{aligned} DIV_1 - DIV_0 &= \text{adjustment rate} \times \text{target change} \\ &= \text{adjustment rate} \times (\text{target ratio} \times EPS_1 - DIV_0) \end{aligned}$$

The more conservative the company, the more slowly it would move toward its target and, therefore, the *lower* would be its adjustment rate.

[9] J. Lintner, "Distribution of Incomes of Corporations among Dividends, Retained Earnings, and Taxes," *American Economic Review* 46 (May 1956), pp. 97–113.

[10] The stylized facts are given by Terry A. Marsh and Robert C. Merton, "Dividend Behavior for the Aggregate Stock Market," *Journal of Business* 60 (January 1987), pp. 1–40. See pp. 5–6. We have paraphrased and embellished.

Lintner's simple model suggests that the dividend depends in part on the firm's current earnings and in part on the dividend for the previous year, which in turn depends on that year's earnings and the dividend in the year before. Therefore, if Lintner is correct, we should be able to describe dividends in terms of a weighted average of current and past earnings.[11] The probability of an increase in the dividend rate should be greatest when *current* earnings have increased; it should be somewhat less when only the earnings from the previous year have increased; and so on. An extensive study by Fama and Babiak confirmed this hypothesis.[12] Their tests of Lintner's model suggest that it provides a fairly good explanation of how companies decide on the dividend rate, but it is not the whole story. We would expect managers to take future prospects as well as past achievements into account when setting the payment. As we shall see in the next section, that is indeed the case.

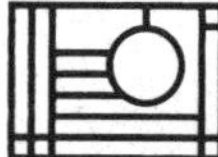

16.3 THE INFORMATION IN DIVIDENDS AND STOCK REPURCHASES

In some countries you cannot rely on the information that companies provide. Passion for secrecy and a tendency to construct multilayered corporate organizations produce asset and earnings figures that are next to meaningless. Some people say that, thanks to creative accounting, the situation is little better for some companies in the United States.

How does an investor in such a world separate marginally profitable firms from the real money makers? One clue is dividends. Investors can't read managers' minds, but they can learn from managers' actions. They know that a firm which reports good earnings and pays a generous dividend is putting its money where its mouth is. We can understand, therefore, why investors would value the information content of dividends and would refuse to believe a firm's reported earnings unless they were backed up by an appropriate dividend policy.

Of course, firms can cheat in the short run by overstating earnings and scraping up cash to pay a generous dividend. But it is hard to cheat in the long run, for a firm that is not making enough money will not have enough cash to pay out. If a firm chooses a high dividend payout without the cash flow to back it up, that firm will ultimately have to reduce its investment plans or turn to investors for additional debt or equity financing. All of these consequences are costly. Therefore, most managers don't increase dividends until they are confident that sufficient cash will flow in to pay them.

[11] This can be demonstrated as follows: Dividends per share in time t are

(1) $$\text{DIV}_t = aT(\text{EPS}_t) + (1 - a)\text{DIV}_{t-1}$$

where a is the adjustment rate and T is the target payout ratio. But the same relationship holds in $t - 1$:

(2) $$\text{DIV}_{t-1} = aT(\text{EPS}_{t-1}) + (1 - a)\text{DIV}_{t-2}$$

Substitute for DIV_{t-1} in (1):

$$\text{DIV}_t = aT(\text{EPS}_t) + aT(1 - a)(\text{EPS}_{t-1}) + (1 - a)^2\text{DIV}_{t-2}$$

We can make similar substitutions for DIV_{t-2}, DIV_{t-3}, etc., thereby obtaining

$$\text{DIV}_t = aT(\text{EPS}_t) + aT(1 - a)(\text{EPS}_{t-1}) + aT(1 - a)^2(\text{EPS}_{t-2}) + \cdots + aT(1 - a)^n(\text{EPS}_{t-n})$$

[12] E. F. Fama and H. Babiak, "Dividend Policy: An Empirical Analysis," *Journal of the American Statistical Association* 63 (December 1968), pp. 1132–1161.

There is some evidence that managers do look to the future when they set the dividend payment. For example, Benartzi, Michaely, and Thaler found that dividend increases generally followed a couple of years of unusual earnings growth.[13] Although this rapid growth did not persist beyond the year in which the dividend was changed, for the most part the higher level of earnings was maintained and declines in earnings were relatively uncommon. More striking evidence that dividends are set with an eye to the future is provided by Healy and Palepu, who focus on companies that pay a dividend for the first time.[14] On average earnings jumped 43 percent in the year that the dividend was paid. If managers thought that this was a temporary windfall, they might have been cautious about committing themselves to paying out cash. But it looks as if they had good reason to be confident about prospects, for over the next four years earnings grew on average by a further 164 percent.

If dividends provide some reassurance that the new level of earnings is likely to be sustained, it is no surprise to find that announcements of dividend cuts are usually taken by investors as bad news (stock price falls) and that dividend increases are good news (stock price rises). For example, in the case of the dividend initiations studied by Healy and Palepu, the announcement of the dividend resulted in an abnormal rise of 4 percent in the stock price.[15]

Notice that investors do not get excited about the *level* of a company's dividend; they worry about the *change,* which they view as an important indicator of the sustainability of earnings. In Finance in the News we illustrate how an unexpected change in dividends can cause the stock price to bounce back and forth as investors struggle to interpret the significance of the change.

It seems that in some other countries investors are less preoccupied with dividend changes. For example, in Japan there is a much closer relationship between corporations and major stockholders, and therefore information may be more easily shared with investors. Consequently, Japanese corporations are more prone to cut their dividends when there is a drop in earnings, but investors do not mark the stocks down as sharply as in the United States.[16]

The Information Content of Share Repurchase

Share repurchases, like dividends, are a way to hand cash back to shareholders. But unlike dividends, share repurchases are frequently a one-off event. So a company that announces a repurchase program is not making a long-term commitment to earn and distribute more cash. The information in the announcement of a share repurchase program is therefore likely to be different from the information in a dividend payment.

Companies repurchase shares when they have accumulated more cash than they can invest profitably or when they wish to increase their debt levels. Neither

[13]See L. Benartzi, R. Michaely, and R. H. Thaler, "Do Changes in Dividends Signal the Future or the Past," *Journal of Finance* 52 (July 1997), pp. 1007–1034. Similar results are reported in H. DeAngelo, L. DeAngelo, and D. Skinner, "Reversal of Fortune: Dividend Signaling and the Disappearance of Sustained Earnings Growth," *Journal of Financial Economics* 40 (1996), pp. 341–372.

[14]See P. Healy and K. Palepu, "Earnings Information Conveyed by Dividend Initiations and Omissions," *Journal of Financial Economics* 21 (1988), pp. 149–175.

[15]Healy and Palepu also looked at companies that *stopped* paying a dividend. In this case the stock price on average declined by an abnormal 9.5 percent on the announcement and earnings fell over the next four quarters.

[16]The dividend policies of Japanese *keiretsus* are analyzed in K. L. Dewenter and V. A. Warther, "Dividends, Asymmetric Information, and Agency Conflicts: Evidence from a Comparison of the Dividend Policies of Japanese and U.S. Firms," *Journal of Finance* 53 (June 1998), pp. 879–904.

FINANCE IN THE NEWS

THE DIVIDEND CUT HEARD 'ROUND THE WORLD

On May 9, 1994, FPL Group, the parent company of Florida Power & Light Company, announced a 32 percent reduction in its quarterly dividend payout, from 62 cents per share to 42 cents. In its announcement, FPL did its best to spell out to investors why it had taken such an unusual step. It stressed that it had studied the situation carefully and that, given the prospect of increased competition in the electric utility industry, the company's high dividend payout ratio (which had averaged 90 percent in the past 4 years) was no longer in the shareholders' best interests. The new policy resulted in a payout of about 60 percent of the previous year's earnings. Management also announced that, starting in 1995, the dividend payout would be reviewed in February instead of May to reinforce the linkage between dividends and annual earnings. In doing so, the company wanted to minimize unintended "signaling effects" from any future changes in dividends.

At the same time that it announced this change in dividend policy, FPL Group's board authorized the repurchase of up to 10 million shares of common stock over the next 3 years. In adopting this strategy, the company noted that changes in the U.S. tax code since 1990 had made capital gains more attractive than dividends to shareholders.

Besides providing a more tax-efficient means of distributing excess cash to its stockholders, FPL's substitution of stock repurchases for dividends was also designed to increase the company's financial flexibility in preparation for a new era of heightened competition among utilities. Although much of the cash savings from the dividend cut would be returned to shareholders in the form of stock repurchases, the rest would be used to retire debt and so reduce the company's leverage ratio. This deleveraging was intended to prepare the company for the likely increase in business risk and to provide some slack that would allow the company to take advantage of future business opportunities.

All this sounded logical, but investors' first reaction was dismay. On the day of the announcement, the stock price fell nearly 14 percent. But, as analysis digested the news and considered the reasons for the reduction, they concluded that the action was not a signal of financial distress but a well-considered strategic decision. This view spread throughout the financial community, and FPL's stock price began to recover. By the middle of the following month at least 15 major brokerage houses had placed FPL's common stock on their "buy" lists and the price had largely recovered from its earlier fall.

Source: Modified from D. Soter, E. Brigham, and P. Evanson, "The Dividend Cut 'Heard 'Round the World': The Case of FPL," *Journal of Applied Corporate Finance* 9 (Spring 1996), pp. 4–15.

circumstance is good news in itself, but shareholders are frequently relieved to see companies paying out the excess cash rather than frittering it away on unprofitable investments. Shareholders also know that firms with large quantities of debt to service are less likely to squander cash. A study by Comment and Jarrell, who looked at the announcements of open-market repurchase programs, found that on average they resulted in an abnormal price rise of 2 percent.[17]

[17]See R. Comment and G. Jarrell, "The Relative Signalling Power of Dutch-Auction and Fixed Price Self-Tender Offers and Open-Market Share Repurchases," *Journal of Finance* 46 (September 1991), pp. 1243–1271. There is also evidence of continuing superior performance during the years following a repurchase announcement. See D. Ikenberry, J. Lakonishok, and T. Vermaelen, "Market Underreaction to Open Market Share Repurchases," *Journal of Financial Economics* 39 (1995), pp. 181–208.

Stock repurchases may also be used to signal a manager's confidence in the future. Suppose that you, the manager, believe that your stock is substantially undervalued. You announce that the company is prepared to buy back a fifth of its stock at a price that is 20 percent above the current market price. But (you say) you are certainly not going to sell any of your own stock at that price. Investors jump to the obvious conclusion—you must believe that the stock is good value even at 20 percent above the current price.

When companies offer to repurchase their stock at a premium, senior management and directors usually commit to hold onto their stock.[18] So it is not surprising that researchers have found that announcements of offers to buy back shares above the market price have prompted a larger rise in the stock price, averaging about 11 percent.[19]

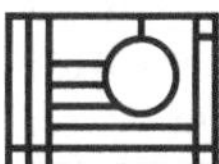

16.4 THE DIVIDEND CONTROVERSY

We have seen that a dividend increase indicates management's optimism about earnings and thus affects the stock price. But the jump in stock price that accompanies an unexpected dividend increase would happen eventually anyway as information about future earnings comes out through other channels. We now ask whether the dividend decision *changes* the value of the stock, rather than simply providing a *signal* of stock value.

One endearing feature of economics is that it can always accommodate not just two but three opposing points of view. And so it is with the controversy about dividend policy. On the right there is a conservative group which believes that an increase in dividend payout increases firm value. On the left, there is a radical group which believes that an increase in payout reduces value. And in the center there is a middle-of-the-road party which claims that dividend policy makes no difference.

The middle-of-the-road party was founded in 1961 by Miller and Modigliani (always referred to as "MM" or "M and M"), when they published a theoretical paper showing the irrelevance of dividend policy in a world without taxes, transaction costs, or other market imperfections.[20] By the standards of 1961 MM were leftist radicals, because at that time most people believed that even under idealized assumptions increased dividends made shareholders better off.[21] But now MM's proof is generally accepted as correct, and the argument has shifted to whether taxes or other market imperfections alter the situation. In the process MM have been pushed toward the center by a new leftist party which argues for *low* dividends. The leftists' position is based on MM's argument modified to take account

[18]Not only do managers' hold onto their stock; on average they also add to their holdings *before* the announcement of a repurchase. See D. S. Lee, W. Mikkelson, and M. M. Partch, "Managers Trading around Stock Repurchases," *Journal of Finance* 47 (1992), pp. 1947–1961.

[19]See R. Comment and G. Jarrell, *op. cit.*

[20]M. H. Miller and F. Modigliani: "Dividend Policy, Growth and the Valuation of Shares," *Journal of Business* 34 (October 1961), pp. 411–433.

[21]Not *everybody* believed dividends make shareholders better off. MM's arguments were anticipated in 1938 in J. B. Williams, *The Theory of Investment Value*, Harvard University Press, Cambridge, MA, 1938. Also, a proof very similar to MM's was developed by J. Lintner in "Dividends, Earnings, Leverage, Stock Prices and the Supply of Capital to Corporations," *Review of Economics and Statistics* 44 (August 1962), pp. 243–269.

of taxes and costs of issuing securities. The conservatives are still with us, relying on essentially the same arguments as in 1961.

Why should you care about this debate? Of course, if you help to decide your company's dividend payment, you will want to know how it affects value. But there is a more general reason than that. We have up to this point assumed that the company's investment decision is independent of its financing policy. In that case a good project is a good project is a good project, no matter who undertakes it or how it is ultimately financed. If dividend policy does not affect value, that is still true. But perhaps it *does* affect value. In that case the attractiveness of a new project may depend on where the money is coming from. For example, if investors prefer companies with high payouts, companies might be reluctant to take on investments financed by retained earnings.

We begin our discussion of dividend policy with a presentation of MM's original argument. Then we will undertake a critical appraisal of the positions of the three parties. Perhaps we should warn you before we start that our own position is mostly middle of the road but sometimes marginally leftist. (As investors we prefer low dividends because we don't like paying taxes!)

Dividend Policy Is Irrelevant in Perfect Capital Markets

In their classic 1961 article MM argued as follows: Suppose your firm has settled on its investment program. You have worked out how much of this program can be financed from borrowing, and you plan to meet the remaining funds requirement from retained earnings. Any surplus money is to be paid out as dividends.

Now think what happens if you want to increase the dividend payment without changing the investment and borrowing policy. The extra money must come from somewhere. If the firm fixes its borrowing, the only way it can finance the extra dividend is to print some more shares and sell them. The new stockholders are going to part with their money only if you can offer them shares that are worth as much as they cost. But how can the firm do this when its assets, earnings, investment opportunities, and, therefore, market value are all unchanged? The answer is that there must be a *transfer of value* from the old to the new stockholders. The new ones get the newly printed shares, each one worth less than before the dividend change was announced, and the old ones suffer a capital loss on their shares. The capital loss borne by the old shareholders just offsets the extra cash dividend they receive.

Figure 16.2 shows how this transfer of value occurs. Our hypothetical company pays out a third of its total value as a dividend and it raises the money to do so by selling new shares. The capital loss suffered by the old stockholders is represented by the reduction in the size of the burgundy boxes. But that capital loss is exactly offset by the fact that the new money raised (the blue boxes) is paid over to them as dividends.

Does it make any difference to the old stockholders that they receive an extra dividend payment plus an offsetting capital loss? It might if that were the only way they could get their hands on cash. But as long as there are efficient capital markets, they can raise the cash by selling shares. Thus the old shareholders can cash in either by persuading the management to pay a higher dividend or by selling some of their shares. In either case there will be a transfer of value from old to new shareholders. The only difference is that in the former case this transfer is caused

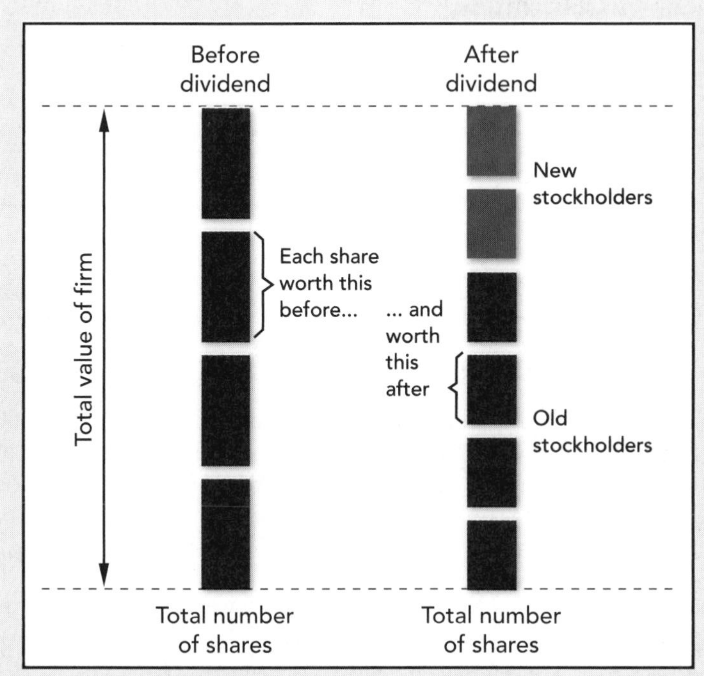

FIGURE 16.2

This firm pays out a third of its worth as a dividend and raises the money by selling new shares. The transfer of value to the new stockholders is equal to the dividend payment. The total value of the firm is unaffected.

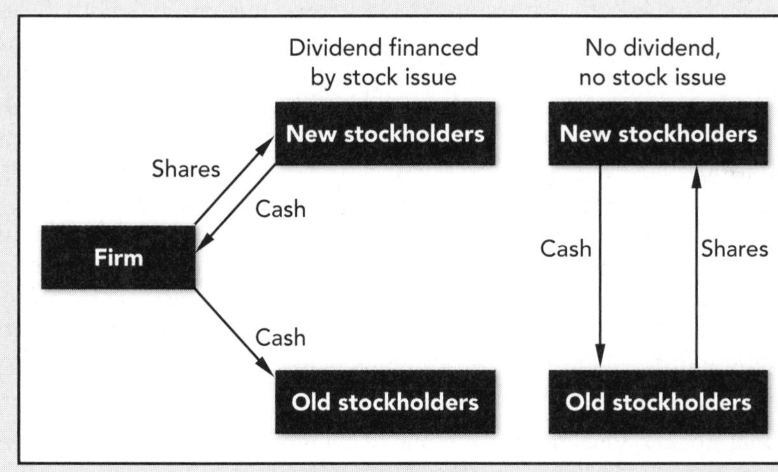

FIGURE 16.3

Two ways of raising cash for the firm's original shareholders. In each case the cash received is offset by a decline in the value of the old stockholders' claim on the firm. If the firm pays a dividend, each share is worth less because more shares have to be issued against the firm's assets. If the old stockholders sell some of their shares, each share is worth the same but the old stockholders have fewer shares.

by a dilution in the value of each of the firm's shares, and in the latter case it is caused by a reduction in the number of shares held by the old shareholders. The two alternatives are compared in Figure 16.3.

Because investors do not need dividends to get their hands on cash, they will not pay higher prices for the shares of firms with high payouts. Therefore firms ought not to worry about dividend policy. They should let dividends fluctuate as a by-product of their investment and financing decisions.

Dividend Irrelevance—An Illustration

Consider the case of Rational Demiconductor, which at this moment has the following balance sheet:

Rational Demiconductor's Balance Sheet (Market Values)

Cash ($1,000 held for investment)	1,000		0	Debt
Fixed assets	9,000		10,000 + NPV	Equity
Investment opportunity ($1,000 investment required)		NPV		
Total asset value	$10,000 + NPV		$10,000 + NPV	Value of firm

Rational Demiconductor has $1,000 cash earmarked for a project requiring $1,000 investment. We do not know how attractive the project is, and so we enter it at NPV; after the project is undertaken it will be worth $1,000 + NPV. Note that the balance sheet is constructed with market values; equity equals the market value of the firm's outstanding shares (price per share times number of shares outstanding). It is not necessarily equal to book net worth.

Now Rational Demiconductor uses the cash to pay a $1,000 dividend to its stockholders. The benefit to them is obvious: $1,000 of spendable cash. It is also obvious that there must be a cost. The cash is not free.

Where does the money for the dividend come from? Of course, the immediate source of funds is Rational Demiconductor's cash account. But this cash was earmarked for the investment project. Since we want to isolate the effects of dividend policy on shareholders' wealth, we assume that the company *continues* with the investment project. That means that $1,000 in cash must be raised by new financing. This could consist of an issue of either debt or stock. Again, we just want to look at dividend policy for now, and we defer discussion of the debt–equity choice until Chapters 17 and 18. Thus Rational Demiconductor ends up financing the dividend with a $1,000 stock issue.

Now we examine the balance sheet after the dividend is paid, the new stock is sold, and the investment is undertaken. Because Rational Demiconductor's investment and borrowing policies are unaffected by the dividend payment, its *overall* market value must be unchanged at $10,000 + NPV.[22] We know also that if the new stockholders pay a fair price, their stock is worth $1,000. That leaves us with only one missing number—the value of the stock held by the original stockholders. It is easy to see that this must be

$$
\begin{aligned}
\text{Value of original stockholders' shares} &= \text{value of company} - \text{value of new shares} \\
&= (10{,}000 + \text{NPV}) - 1{,}000 \\
&= \$9{,}000 + \text{NPV}
\end{aligned}
$$

The old shareholders have received a $1,000 cash dividend and incurred a $1,000 capital loss. Dividend policy doesn't matter.

By paying out $1,000 with one hand and taking it back with the other, Rational Demiconductor is recycling cash. To suggest that this makes shareholders better off is like advising a cook to cool the kitchen by leaving the refrigerator door open.

[22]All other factors that might affect Rational Demiconductor's value are assumed constant. This is not a necessary assumption, but it simplifies the proof of MM's theory.

Of course, our proof ignores taxes, issue costs, and a variety of other complications. We will turn to those items in a moment. The really crucial assumption in our proof is that the new shares are sold at a fair price. The shares sold to raise $1,000 must actually be *worth* $1,000.[23] In other words, we have assumed efficient capital markets.

Calculating Share Price

We have assumed that Rational Demiconductor's new shares can be sold at a fair price, but what is that price and how many new shares are issued?

Suppose that before this dividend payout the company had 1,000 shares outstanding and that the project had an NPV of $2,000. Then the old stock was worth in total $10,000 + NPV = $12,000, which works out at $12,000/1,000 = $12 per share. After the company has paid the dividend and completed the financing, this old stock is worth $9,000 + NPV = $11,000. That works out at $11,000/1,000 = $11 per share. In other words, the price of the old stock falls by the amount of the $1 per share dividend payment.

Now let us look at the new stock. Clearly, after the issue this must sell at the same price as the rest of the stock. In other words, it must be valued at $11. If the new stockholders get fair value, the company must issue $1,000/$11 or 91 new shares in order to raise the $1,000 that it needs.

Share Repurchase

We have seen that any increased cash dividend payment must be offset by a stock issue if the firm's investment and borrowing policies are held constant. In effect the stockholders finance the extra dividend by selling off part of their ownership of the firm. Consequently, the stock price falls by just enough to offset the extra dividend.

This process can also be run backward. With investment and borrowing policy given, any *reduction* in dividends must be balanced by a reduction in the number of shares issued or by repurchase of previously outstanding stock. But if the process has no effect on stockholders' wealth when run forward, it must likewise have no effect when run in reverse. We will confirm this by another numerical example.

Suppose that a technical discovery reveals that Rational Demiconductor's new project is not a positive-NPV venture but a sure loser. Management announces that the project is to be discarded and that the $1,000 earmarked for it will be paid out as an extra dividend of $1 per share. After the dividend payout, the balance sheet is

Rational Demiconductor's Balance Sheet (Market Values)

Cash	$ 0	$ 0	Debt
Existing fixed assets	9,000	9,000	Equity
New project	0		
Total asset value	$ 9,000	$ 9,000	Total firm value

Since there are 1,000 shares outstanding, the stock price is $10,000/1,000 = $10 before the dividend payment and $9,000/1,000 = $9 *after* the payment.

[23]The "old" shareholders get all the benefit of the positive NPV project. The new shareholders require only a fair rate of return. They are making a zero-NPV investment.

What if Rational Demiconductor uses the \$1,000 to repurchase stock instead? As long as the company pays a fair price for the stock, the \$1,000 buys \$1,000/\$10 = 100 shares. That leaves 900 shares worth 900 × \$10 = \$9,000.

As expected, we find that switching from cash dividends to share repurchase has no effect on shareholders' wealth. They forgo a \$1 cash dividend but end up holding shares worth \$10 instead of \$9.

Note that when shares are repurchased the transfer of value is in favor of those stockholders who do not sell. They forgo any cash dividend but end up owning a larger slice of the firm. In effect they are using their share of Rational Demiconductor's \$1,000 distribution to buy out some of their fellow shareholders.

Stock Repurchase and Valuation

Valuing the equity of a firm that repurchases its own stock can be confusing. Let's work through a simple example.

Company X has 100 shares outstanding. It earns \$1,000 a year, all of which is paid out as a dividend. The dividend per share is, therefore, \$1,000/100 = \$10. Suppose that investors expect the dividend to be maintained indefinitely and that they require a return of 10 percent. In this case the value of each share is PV_{share} = \$10/.10 = \$100. Since there are 100 shares outstanding, the *total* market value of the equity is PV_{equity} = 100 × \$100 = \$10,000. Note that we could reach the same conclusion by discounting the *total* dividend payments to shareholders (PV_{equity} = \$1,000/.10 = \$10,000).[24]

Now suppose the company announces that instead of paying a cash dividend in year 1, it will spend the same money repurchasing its shares in the open market. The total expected cash flows to shareholders (dividends and cash from stock repurchase) are unchanged at \$1,000. So the total value of the equity also remains at \$1,000/.10 = \$10,000. This is made up of the value of the \$1,000 received from the stock repurchase in year 1 ($PV_{repurchase}$ = \$1,000/1.1 = \$909.1) and the value of the \$1,000-a-year dividend starting in year 2 [$PV_{dividends}$ = \$1,000/(.10 × 1.1) = \$9,091]. Each share continues to be worth \$10,000/100 = \$100 just as before.

Think now about those shareholders who plan to sell their stock back to the company. They will demand a 10 percent return on their investment. So the price at which the firm buys back shares must be 10 percent higher than today's price, or \$110. The company spends \$1,000 buying back its stock, which is sufficient to buy \$1,000/\$110 = 9.09 shares.

The company starts with 100 shares, it buys back 9.09, and therefore 90.91 shares remain outstanding. Each of these shares can look forward to a dividend stream of \$1,000/90.91 = \$11 per share. So after the repurchase shareholders have 10 percent fewer shares, but earnings and dividends per share are 10 percent higher. An investor who owns one share today that is not repurchased will receive no dividends in year 1 but can look forward to \$11 a year thereafter. The value of each share is therefore 11/(.1 × 1.1) = \$100.

Our example illustrates several points. First, other things equal, company value is unaffected by the decision to repurchase stock rather than to pay a cash divi-

[24]When valuing the entire equity, remember that if the company is expected to issue additional shares in the future, we should include the dividend payments on these shares only if we also include the amount that investors pay for them. See Chapter 4.

dend. Second, when valuing the entire equity you need to include both the cash that is paid out as dividends and the cash that is used to repurchase stock. Third, when calculating the cash flow *per share*, it is double counting to include both the forecasted dividends per share *and* the cash received from repurchase (if you sell back your share, you don't get any subsequent dividends). Fourth, a firm that repurchases stock instead of paying dividends reduces the number of shares outstanding but produces an offsetting increase in earnings and dividends per share.

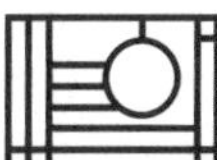

16.5 THE RIGHTISTS

Much of traditional finance literature has advocated high payout ratios. Here, for example, is a statement of the rightist position made by Graham and Dodd in 1951:

> The considered and continuous verdict of the stock market is overwhelmingly in favor of liberal dividends as against niggardly ones. The common stock investor must take this judgment into account in the valuation of stock for purchase. It is now becoming standard practice to evaluate common stock by applying one multiplier to that portion of the earnings paid out in dividends and a much smaller multiplier to the undistributed balance.[25]

This belief in the importance of dividend policy is common in the business and investment communities. Stockholders and investment advisers continually pressure corporate treasurers for increased dividends. When we had wage-price controls in the United States in 1974, it was deemed necessary to have dividend controls as well. As far as we know, no labor union objected that "dividend policy is irrelevant." After all, if wages are reduced, the employee is worse off. Dividends are the shareholders' wages, and so if the payout ratio is reduced the shareholder is worse off. Therefore fair play requires that wage controls be matched by dividend controls. Right?

Wrong! You should be able to see through that kind of argument by now. But there are more serious arguments for a high-payout policy that rely either on market imperfections or the effect of dividend policy on management incentives.

Market Imperfections

Those who favor large dividend payments point out that there is a natural clientele for high-payout stocks. For example, some financial institutions are legally restricted from holding stocks lacking established dividend records.[26] Trusts and endowment funds may prefer high-dividend stocks because dividends are regarded as spendable "income," whereas capital gains are "additions to principal." Some observers have argued that, although individuals are free to spend capital, they

[25]These authors later qualified this statement, recognizing the willingness of investors to pay high price–earnings multiples for growth stocks. But otherwise they stuck to their position. We quoted their 1951 statement because of its historical importance. Compare B. Graham and D. L. Dodd, *Security Analysis: Principles and Techniques*, 3rd ed., McGraw-Hill Book Company, New York, 1951, p. 432, with B. Graham, D. L. Dodd, and S. Cottle, *Security Analysis: Principles and Techniques*, 4th ed., McGraw-Hill Book Company, New York, 1962, p. 480.

[26]Most colleges and universities are legally free to spend capital gains from their endowments, but they usually restrict spending to a moderate percentage which can be covered by dividends and interest receipts.

may welcome the self-discipline that comes from spending only dividend income.[27] If so, they also may favor stocks that provide more spendable cash.

There is also a natural clientele of investors who look to their stock portfolios for a steady source of cash to live on. In principle this cash could be easily generated from stocks paying no dividends at all; the investor could just sell off a small fraction of his or her holdings from time to time. But it is simpler and cheaper for IBM to send a quarterly check than for its stockholders to sell, say, one share every three months. IBM's regular dividends relieve many of its shareholders of transaction costs and considerable inconvenience.[28]

Dividends, Investment Policy, and Management Incentives

If it is true that nobody gains or loses from shifts in dividend policy, why do shareholders often clamor for higher dividends? There is one good reason that applies particularly to mature companies with plenty of free cash flow but few profitable investment opportunities. Shareholders of such companies don't always trust managers to spend retained earnings wisely and they fear that the money will be plowed back into building a larger empire rather than a more profitable one. In such cases investors may clamor for generous dividends not because dividends are valuable in themselves, but because they signal a more careful, value-oriented investment policy.[29]

16.6 TAXES AND THE RADICAL LEFT

The left-wing dividend creed is simple: Whenever dividends are taxed more heavily than capital gains, firms should pay the lowest cash dividend they can get away with. Available cash should be retained or used to repurchase shares.

By shifting their distribution policies in this way, corporations can transmute dividends into capital gains. If this financial alchemy results in lower taxes, it should be welcomed by any taxpaying investor. That is the basic point made by the leftist party when it argues for low-dividend payout.

If dividends are taxed more heavily than capital gains, investors should pay more for stocks with low dividend yields. In other words, they should accept a lower *pretax* rate of return from securities offering returns in the form of capital gains rather than dividends. Table 16.1 illustrates this. The stocks of firms A and B are equally risky. Investors expect A to be worth $112.50 per share next year. The

[27]See H. Shefrin and M. Statman, "Explaining Investor Preference for Cash Dividends," *Journal of Financial Economics* 13 (June 1984), pp. 253–282.

[28]Those advocating generous dividends might go on to argue that a regular cash dividend relieves stockholders of the risk of having to sell shares at "temporarily depressed" prices. Of course, the firm will have to issue shares eventually to finance the dividend, but (the argument goes) the firm can pick the *right time* to sell. If firms really try to do this and if they are successful—two big *ifs*—then stockholders of high-payout firms might indeed get something for nothing.

[29]La Porta et al. argue that in countries such as the United States minority shareholders are able to pressure companies to disgorge cash and this prevents managers from using too high a proportion of earnings to benefit themselves. By contrast, companies pay out a smaller proportion of earnings in those countries where the law is more relaxed about overinvestment and empire building. See R. La Porta, F. Lopez-de-Silanes, A. Shleifer, and R. W. Vishny, "Agency Problems and Dividend Policies around the World," *Journal of Finance* 55 (February 2000), pp. 1–34.

	Firm A (No Dividend)	Firm B (High Dividend)
Next year's price	\$112.50	\$102.50
Dividend	\$0	\$10.00
Total pretax payoff	\$112.50	\$112.50
Today's stock price	\$100	\$97.78
Capital gain	\$12.50	\$4.72
Before-tax rate of return	$100 \times \left(\frac{12.5}{100}\right) = 12.5\%$	$100 \times \left(\frac{14.72}{97.78}\right) = 15.05\%$
Tax on dividend at 40%	\$0	$.40 \times 10 = \$4.00$
Tax on capital gains at 20%	$.20 \times 12.50 = \$2.50$	$.20 \times 4.72 = \$.94$
Total after-tax income (dividends plus capital gains less taxes)	$(0 + 12.50) - 2.50 = \$10.00$	$(10.00 + 4.72) - (4.00 + .94) = \$9.78$
After-tax rate of return	$100 \times \left(\frac{10}{100}\right) = 10.0\%$	$100 \times \left(\frac{9.78}{97.78}\right) = 10.0\%$

TABLE 16.1

Effects of a shift on dividend policy when dividends are taxed more heavily than capital gains. The high-payout stock (firm B) must sell at a lower price to provide the same after-tax return.

share price of B is expected to be only \$102.50, but a \$10 dividend is also forecasted, and so the total pretax payoff is the same, \$112.50.

Yet we find B's stock selling for less than A's and therefore offering a higher pretax rate of return. The reason is obvious: Investors prefer A because its return comes in the form of capital gains. Table 16.1 shows that A and B are equally attractive to investors who pay a 40 percent tax on dividends and a 20 percent tax on capital gains. Each offers a 10 percent return after all taxes. The difference between the stock prices of A and B is exactly the present value of the extra taxes the investors face if they buy B.[30]

The management of B could save these extra taxes by eliminating the \$10 dividend and using the released funds to repurchase stock instead. Its stock price should rise to \$100 as soon as the new policy is announced.

Why Pay Any Dividends at All?

It is true that when companies make very large one-off distributions of cash to shareholders, they generally choose to do so by share repurchase than by a large temporary hike in dividends. But if dividends attract more tax than capital gains, why should any firm ever pay a cash dividend? If cash is to be distributed to stockholders, isn't share repurchase always the best channel for doing so? The leftist position seems to call not just for low payouts but for *zero* payouts whenever capital gains have a tax advantage.

[30]Michael Brennan has modeled what happens when you introduce taxes into an otherwise perfect market. He found that the capital asset pricing model continues to hold, but on an *after-tax* basis. Thus, if A and B have the same beta, they should offer the same after-tax rate of return. The spread between pretax and post-tax returns is determined by a weighted average of investors' tax rates. See M. J. Brennan, "Taxes, Market Valuation and Corporate Financial Policy," *National Tax Journal* 23 (December 1970), pp. 417–427.

Few leftists would go quite that far. A firm that eliminates dividends and starts repurchasing stock on a regular basis may find that the Internal Revenue Service recognizes the repurchase program for what it really is and taxes the payments accordingly. That is why financial managers do not usually announce that they are repurchasing shares to save stockholders taxes; they give some other reason.[31]

The low-payout party has nevertheless maintained that the market rewards firms that have low-payout policies. They have claimed that firms which paid dividends and as a result had to issue shares from time to time were making a serious mistake. Any such firm was essentially financing its dividends by issuing stock; it should have cut its dividends at least to the point at which stock issues were unnecessary. This would not only have saved taxes for shareholders but it would also have avoided the transaction costs of the stock issues.[32]

Empirical Evidence on Dividends and Taxes

It is hard to deny that taxes are important to investors. You can see that in the bond market. Interest on municipal bonds is not taxed, and so municipals sell at low pretax yields. Interest on federal government bonds is taxed, and so these bonds sell at higher pretax yields. It does not seem likely that investors in bonds just forget about taxes when they enter the stock market. Thus, we would expect to find a historical tendency for high-dividend stocks to sell at lower prices and therefore to offer higher returns, just as in Table 16.1.

Unfortunately, there are difficulties in measuring this effect. For example, suppose that stock A is priced at $100 and is expected to pay a $5 dividend. The *expected* yield is, therefore, 5/100 = .05, or 5 percent. The company now announces bumper earnings and a $10 dividend. Thus with the benefit of hindsight, A's *actual* dividend yield is 10/100 = .10, or 10 percent. If the unexpected increase in earnings causes a rise in A's stock price, we will observe that a high actual yield is accompanied by a high actual return. But that would not tell us anything about whether a high *expected* yield was accompanied by a high *expected* return. In order to measure the effect of dividend policy, we need to estimate the dividends that investors expected.

A second problem is that nobody is quite sure what is meant by high dividend yield. For example, utility stocks have generally offered high yields. But did they have a high yield all year, or only in months or on days that dividends were paid? Perhaps for most of the year, they had zero yields and were perfect holdings for the highly taxed individuals.[33] Of course, high-tax investors did not want to hold a stock on the days dividends were paid, but they could sell their stock temporarily to a security dealer. Dealers are taxed equally on dividends and capital gains and therefore should not have demanded any extra return for holding stocks over the dividend period.[34] If shareholders could pass stocks freely between each other at the time of the dividend payment, we should not observe any tax effects at all.

---

[31]They might say, "Our stock is a good investment," or, "We want to have the shares available to finance acquisitions of other companies." What do you think of these rationales?

[32]These costs can be substantial. Refer back to Chapter 15, especially Figure 15.3.

[33]Suppose there are 250 trading days in a year. Think of a stock paying quarterly dividends. We could say that the stock offers a high dividend yield on 4 days but a zero dividend yield on the remaining 246 days.

[34]The stock could also be sold to a corporation, which could "capture" the dividend and then resell the shares. Corporations are natural buyers of dividends, because they pay tax only on 30 percent of dividends received from other corporations. (We say more on the taxation of intercorporate dividends later in this section.)

A number of researchers have attempted to tackle these problems and to measure whether investors demand a higher return from high-yielding stocks. Their findings offer some limited comfort to the dividends-are-bad school, for most of the researchers have suggested that high-yielding stocks have provided higher returns. However, the estimated tax rates differ substantially from one study to another. For example, while Litzenberger and Ramaswamy concluded that investors have priced stocks as if dividend income attracted an extra 14 to 23 percent rate of tax, Miller and Scholes using a different methodology came up with a negligible 4 percent difference in the rate of tax.[35]

The Taxation of Dividends and Capital Gains

Many of these attempts to measure the effect of dividends are of more historical than current interest, for they look back at the years before 1986 when there was a dramatic difference between the taxation of dividends and capital gains.[36] Today, the tax rate on capital gains for most shareholders is 20 percent, while for taxable incomes above $65,550 the tax rate on dividends ranges from 30.5 to 39.1 percent.[37]

Tax law favors capital gains in another way. Taxes on dividends have to be paid immediately, but taxes on capital gains can be deferred until shares are sold and capital gains are realized. Stockholders can choose when to sell their shares and thus when to pay the capital gains tax. The longer they wait, the less the present value of the capital gains tax liability.[38]

---

[35]See R. H. Litzenberger and K. Ramaswamy, "The Effects of Dividends on Common Stock Prices: Tax Effects or Information Effects," *Journal of Finance* 37 (May 1982), pp. 429–443; and M. H. Miller and M. Scholes, "Dividends and Taxes: Some Empirical Evidence," *Journal of Political Economy* 90 (1982), pp. 1118–1141. Merton Miller provides a broad review of the empirical literature in "Behavioral Rationality in Finance: The Case of Dividends," *Journal of Business* 59 (October 1986), pp. S451–S468.

[36]The Tax Reform Act of 1986 equalized the tax rates on dividends and capital gains. A gap began to open up again in 1992.

[37]Here are two examples of 2001 marginal tax rates by income bracket:

	Income Bracket	
Marginal Tax Rate	**Single**	**Married, Joint Return**
15%	$0–$27,050	$0–$45,200
27.5	$27,051–$65,550	$45,201–$109,250
30.5	$65,551–$136,750	$109,251–$166,500
35.5	$136,751–$297,350	$166,501–$297,350
39.1	Over $297,350	Over $297,350

Source: **http://taxes.yahoo.com/rates.html.**

There are different schedules for married taxpayers filing separately and for single taxpayers who are heads of households.

[38]When securities are sold capital gains tax is paid on the difference between the selling price and the initial purchase price or *basis.* Thus, shares purchased in 1996 for $20 (the basis) and sold for $30 in 2001 would generate $10 per share in capital gains and a tax of $2.00 at a 20 percent marginal rate.

Suppose the investor now decides to defer sale for one year. Then, if the interest rate is 8 percent, the present value of the tax, viewed from 2001, falls to $2.00/1.08 = \$1.85$. That is, the *effective* capital gains rate is 18.5 percent. The longer sale is deferred, the lower the effective rate will be.

The effective rate falls to zero if the investor dies before selling, because the investor's heirs get to "step up" the basis without recognizing any taxable gain. Suppose the price is still $30 when the investor dies. The heirs could sell for $30 and pay no tax, because they could claim a $30 basis. The $10 capital gain would escape tax entirely.

The distinction between capital gains and dividends is less important for financial institutions, many of which operate free of all taxes and therefore have no tax reason to prefer capital gains to dividends or vice versa. For example, pension funds are untaxed. These funds hold more than $3 trillion in common stocks, so they have enormous clout in the U.S. stock market. Only corporations have a tax reason to *prefer* dividends. They pay corporate income tax on only 30 percent of any dividends received. Thus the effective tax rate on dividends received by large corporations is 30 percent of 35 percent (the marginal corporate tax rate), or 10.5 percent. But they have to pay a 35 percent tax on the full amount of any realized capital gain.

The implications of these tax rules for dividend policy are pretty simple. Capital gains have advantages to many investors, but they are far less advantageous than they were 20 or 30 years ago. Thus, the leftist case for minimizing cash dividends is weaker than it used to be. At the same time, the middle-of-the-road party has increased its share of the vote.

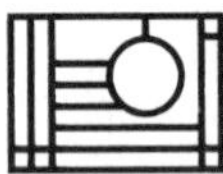

16.7 THE MIDDLE-OF-THE-ROADERS

The middle-of-the-road party, principally represented by Miller, Black, and Scholes, maintains that a company's value is not affected by its dividend policy.[39] We have already seen that this would be the case if there were no impediments such as transaction costs or taxes. The middle-of-the-roaders are aware of these phenomena but nevertheless raise the following disarming question: If companies could increase their share price by distributing more or less cash dividends, why have they not already done so? Perhaps dividends are where they are because no company believes that it could increase its stock price simply by changing its dividend policy.

This "supply effect" is not inconsistent with the existence of a clientele of investors who demand low-payout stocks. Firms recognized that clientele long ago. Enough firms may have switched to low-payout policies to satisfy fully the clientele's demand. If so, there is no incentive for *additional* firms to switch to low-payout policies.

Miller, Black, and Scholes similarly recognize possible high-payout clienteles but argue that they are satisfied also. If all clienteles are satisfied, their demands for high or low dividends have no effect on prices or returns. It doesn't matter which clientele a particular firm chooses to appeal to. If the middle-of-the-road party is right, we should not expect to observe any general association between dividend policy and market values, and the value of any individual company would be independent of its choice of dividend policy.

The middle-of-the-roaders stress that companies would not have generous payout policies unless they believed that this was what investors wanted. But this does not answer the question, Why *should* so many investors want high payouts?

[39]F. Black and M. S. Scholes, "The Effects of Dividend Yield and Dividend Policy on Common Stock Prices and Returns," *Journal of Financial Economics* 1 (May 1974), pp. 1–22; M. H. Miller and M. S. Scholes, "Dividends and Taxes," *Journal of Financial Economics* 6 (December 1978), pp. 333–364; and M. H. Miller, "Behavioral Rationality in Finance: The Case of Dividends," *Journal of Business* 59 (October 1986), pp. S451–S468.

Operating income	100	
Corporate tax at 35%	35	← Corporate tax
After-tax income (paid out as dividends)	65	
Income tax paid by investor at 39.1%	25.4	← Second tax paid by investor
Net income to shareholder	39.6	

TABLE 16.2

In the United States returns to shareholders are taxed twice. This example assumes that all income after corporate taxes is paid out as cash dividends to an investor in the top income tax bracket (figures in dollars per share).

This is the chink in the armor of the middle-of-the-roaders. If high dividends bring high taxes, it's difficult to believe that investors get what they want. The response of the middle-of-the-roaders has been to argue that there are plenty of wrinkles in the tax system which stockholders can use to avoid paying taxes on dividends. For example, instead of investing directly in common stocks, they can do so through a pension fund or insurance company, which receives more favorable tax treatment.

Here is another possible reason that U.S. companies may pay dividends even when these dividends result in higher tax bills. Companies that pay *low* dividends will be more attractive to highly taxed individuals; those that pay *high* dividends will have a greater proportion of pension funds or other tax-exempt institutions as their stockholders. These financial institutions are sophisticated investors; they monitor carefully the companies that they invest in and they bring pressure on poor managers to perform. Successful, well-managed companies are happy to have financial institutions as investors, but their poorly managed brethren would prefer unsophisticated and more docile stockholders.

You can probably see now where the argument is heading. Well-managed companies want to signal their worth. They can do so by having a high proportion of demanding institutions among their stockholders. How do they achieve this? By paying high dividends. Those shareholders who pay tax do not object to these high dividends as long as the effect is to encourage institutional investors who are prepared to put the time and effort into monitoring the management.[40]

Alternative Tax Systems

In the United States shareholders' returns are taxed twice. They are taxed at the corporate level (corporate tax) and in the hands of the shareholder (income tax or capital gains tax). These two tiers of tax are illustrated in Table 16.2, which shows the after-tax return to the shareholder if the company distributes all its income as dividends. We assume the company earns $100 a share before tax and therefore pays corporate tax of .35 × 100 = $35. This leaves $65 a share to be paid out as a dividend, which is then subject to a second layer of tax. For example, a shareholder who is taxed at the top marginal rate of 39.1 percent pays tax on this dividend of .391 × 65 = $25.4. Only a tax-exempt pension fund or charity would retain the full $65.

[40]This signaling argument is developed in F. Allen, A. E. Bernardo, and I. Welch, "A Theory of Dividends Based on Tax Clienteles," *Journal of Finance* 55 (December 2000), pp. 2499–2536.

TABLE 16.3

Under imputation tax systems, such as that in Australia, shareholders receive a tax credit for the corporate tax that the firm has paid (figures in Australian dollars per share).

	Rate of Income Tax		
	15%	30%	47%
Operating income	100	100	100
Corporate tax (T_c = .30)	30	30	30
After-tax income	70	70	70
Grossed-up dividend	100	100	100
Income tax	15	30	47
Tax credit for corporate payment	−30	−30	−30
Tax due from shareholder	−15	0	17
Available to shareholder	85	70	53

Of course, dividends are regularly paid by companies that operate under very different tax systems. In fact, the two-tier United States system is relatively rare. Some countries, such as Germany, tax investors at a higher rate on dividends than on capital gains, but they offset this by having a split-rate system of corporate taxes. Profits that are retained in the business attract a higher rate of corporate tax than profits that are distributed. Under this split-rate system, tax-exempt investors prefer that the company pay high dividends, whereas millionaires might vote to retain profits.

In some other countries, shareholders' returns are not taxed twice. For example, in Australia shareholders are taxed on dividends, but they may deduct from this tax bill their share of the corporate tax that the company has paid. This is known as an *imputation tax system.* Table 16.3 shows how the imputation system works. Suppose that an Australian company earns pretax profits of $A100 a share. After it pays corporate tax at 30 percent, the profit is $A70 a share. The company now declares a net dividend of $A70 and sends each shareholder a check for this amount. This dividend is accompanied by a tax credit saying that the company has already paid $A30 of tax on the shareholder's behalf. Thus shareholders are treated as if each received a total, or gross, dividend of 70 + 30 = $A100 and paid tax of $A30. If the shareholder's tax rate is 30 percent, there is no more tax to pay and the shareholder retains the net dividend of $A70. If the shareholder pays tax at the top personal rate of 47 percent, then he or she is required to pay an additional $17 of tax; if the tax rate is 15 percent (the rate at which Australian pension funds are taxed), then the shareholder receives a *refund* of 30 − 15 = $A15.[41]

Under an imputation tax system, millionaires have to cough up the extra personal tax on dividends. If this is more than the tax that they would pay on capital gains, then millionaires would prefer that the company does not distribute earnings. If it is the other way around, they would prefer dividends.[42] Investors with low tax rates have no doubts about the matter. If the company pays a dividend, these investors receive a check from the revenue service for the excess tax that the company has paid, and therefore they prefer high payout rates.

[41]In Australia, shareholders receive a credit for the full amount of corporate tax that has been paid on their behalf. In other countries the tax credit is less than the corporate tax rate. You can think of the tax system in these countries as lying between the Australian and United States systems.

[42]In the case of Australia the tax rate on capital gains is the same as the tax rate on dividends. However, for securities that are held for more than 12 months only half of the gain is taxed.

Look once again at Table 16.3 and think what would happen if the corporate tax rate was zero. The shareholder with a 15 percent tax rate would still end up with $A85, and the shareholder with the 47 percent rate would still receive $A53. Thus, under an imputation tax system, when a company pays out all its earnings, there is effectively only one layer of tax—the tax on the shareholder. The revenue service collects this tax through the company and then sends a demand to the shareholder for any excess tax or makes a refund for any overpayment.[43]

[43]This is only true for earnings that are paid out as dividends. Retained earnings are subject to corporate tax. Shareholders get the benefit of retained earnings in the form of capital gains.

SUMMARY

Dividends come in several forms. The most common is the regular cash dividend, but sometimes companies pay a dividend in the form of stock.

When managers decide on the dividend, their primary concern seems to be to give shareholders a "fair" level of dividends. Most managers have a conscious or subconscious long-term target payout rate. If firms simply applied the target payout rate to each year's earnings, dividends could fluctuate wildly. Managers therefore try to smooth dividend payments by moving only partway toward the target payout in each year. Also they don't just look at past earnings performance: They try to look into the future when they set the payment. Investors are aware of this and they know that a dividend increase is often a sign of optimism on the part of management.

As an alternative to dividend payments, the company can repurchase its own stock. Although this has the same effect of distributing cash to shareholders, the Internal Revenue Service taxes shareholders only on the capital gains that they may realize as a result of the repurchase.

In recent years many companies have bought back their stock in large quantities, but repurchases do not generally substitute for dividends. Instead, they are used to return unwanted cash to shareholders or to retire equity and replace it with debt. Investors usually interpret stock repurchases as an indication of managers' optimism.

If we hold the company's investment policy constant, then dividend policy is a trade-off between cash dividends and the issue or repurchase of common stock. Should firms retain whatever earnings are necessary to finance growth and pay out any residual as cash dividends? Or should they increase dividends and then (sooner or later) issue stock to make up the shortfall of equity capital? Or should they reduce dividends below the "residual" level and use the released cash to repurchase stock?

If we lived in an ideally simple and perfect world, there would be no problem, for the choice would have no effect on market value. The controversy centers on the effects of dividend policy in our flawed world. A common—though by no means universal—view in the investment community is that high payout enhances share price. Although there are natural clienteles for high-payout stocks, we find it difficult to explain a *general* preference for dividends. We suspect that investors often pressure companies to increase dividends when they do not trust management to spend free cash flow wisely. In this case a dividend increase may lead to a rise

Visit us at www.mhhe.com/bm7e

in the stock price not because investors like dividends as such but because they want management to run a tighter ship.

The most obvious and serious market imperfection has been the different tax treatment of dividends and capital gains. Currently in the United States the tax rate on dividend income can be almost 40 percent, whereas the rate of capital gains tax tops out at only 20 percent. Thus investors should have required a higher before-tax return on high-payout stocks to compensate for their tax disadvantage. High-income investors should have held mostly low-payout stocks.

This view has a respectable theoretical basis. It is supported by some evidence that gross returns have, on the average, reflected the tax differential. The weak link is the theory's silence on the question of why companies continue to distribute such large sums contrary to the preferences of investors.

The third view of dividend policy starts with the notion that the actions of companies *do* reflect investors' preferences; the fact that companies pay substantial dividends is the best evidence that investors want them. If the supply of dividends exactly meets the demand, no single company could improve its market value by changing its dividend policy. Although this explains corporate behavior, it is at a cost, for we cannot explain why dividends are what they are and not some other amount.

These theories are too incomplete and the evidence is too sensitive to minor changes in specification to warrant any dogmatism. Our sympathies, however, lie with the third, middle-of-the-road view. Our recommendations to companies would emphasize the following points: First, there is little doubt that sudden shifts in dividend policy can cause abrupt changes in stock price. The principal reason is the information that investors read into the company's actions. Given such problems, there is a clear case for smoothing dividends, for example, by defining the firm's target payout and making relatively slow adjustments toward it. If it is necessary to make a sharp dividend change, the company should provide as much forewarning as possible and take care to ensure that the action is not misinterpreted.

Subject to these strictures, we believe that, at the very least, a company should adopt a target payout that is sufficiently low as to minimize its reliance on external equity. Why pay out cash to stockholders if that requires issuing new shares to get the cash back? It's better to hold onto the cash in the first place.

If dividend policy doesn't affect firm value, then you don't need to worry about it when estimating the cost of capital. But if (say) you believe that tax effects are important, then in principle you should recognize that investors demand higher returns from high-payout stocks. Some financial managers do take dividend policy into account, but most become de facto middle-of-the-roaders when estimating the cost of capital. It seems that the effects of dividend policy are too uncertain to justify fine-tuning such estimates.

FURTHER READING

Lintner's classic analysis of how companies set their dividend payments is provided in:

J. Lintner: "Distribution of Incomes of Corporations among Dividends, Retained Earnings, and Taxes," *American Economic Review,* 46:97–113 (May 1956).

Marsh and Merton have reinterpreted Lintner's findings and used them to explain the aggregate dividends paid by U.S. corporations:

T. A. Marsh and R. C. Merton: "Dividend Behavior for the Aggregate Stock Market," *Journal of Business,* 60:1–40 (January 1987).

The pioneering article on dividend policy in the context of a perfect capital market is:
M. H. Miller and F. Modigliani: "Dividend Policy, Growth and the Valuation of Shares," *Journal of Business,* 34:411–433 (October 1961).

There are several interesting models explaining the information content of dividends. Two influential examples are:
S. Bhattacharya: "Imperfect Information, Dividend Policy and the Bird in the Hand Fallacy," *Bell Journal of Economics and Management Science,* 10:259–270 (Spring 1979).

M. H. Miller and K. Rock: "Dividend Policy under Asymmetric Information," *Journal of Finance,* 40:1031–1052 (September 1985).

Financial Management *published a special issue on dividend policy in Autumn 1998. It includes four articles on the information content of dividends.*

The effect of differential rates of tax on dividends and capital gains is analyzed rigorously in the context of the capital asset pricing model in:
M. J. Brennan: "Taxes, Market Valuation and Corporate Financial Policy," *National Tax Journal,* 23:417–427 (December 1970).

The argument that dividend policy is irrelevant even in the presence of taxes is presented in:
F. Black and M. S. Scholes: "The Effects of Dividend Yield and Dividend Policy on Common Stock Prices and Returns," *Journal of Financial Economics,* 1:1–22 (May 1974).

M. H. Miller and M. S. Scholes: "Dividends and Taxes," *Journal of Financial Economics,* 6:333–364 (December 1978).

A review of some of the empirical evidence is contained in:
R. Michaely and A. Kalay: "Dividends and Taxes: A Re-Examination," *Financial Management,* 29:55–75 (Summer 2000).

Merton Miller reviews research on the dividend controversy in:
M. H. Miller: "Behavioral Rationality in Finance: The Case of Dividends," *Journal of Business,* 59:S451–S468 (October 1986).

Visit us at www.mhhe.com/bm7e

QUIZ

1. In the 1st quarter of 2001 Merck paid a regular quarterly dividend of \$.34 a share.

a. Match each of the following sets of dates:

(A1) 27 February 2001	(B1) Record date
(A2) 6 March 2001	(B2) Payment date
(A3) 7 March 2001	(B3) Ex-dividend date
(A4) 9 March 2001	(B4) Last with-dividend date
(A5) 2 April 2001	(B5) Declaration date

b. On one of these dates the stock price is likely to fall by about the value of the dividend. Which date? Why?

c. Merck's stock price at the end of February was \$80.20. What was the dividend yield?

d. If earnings per share for 2001 are \$3.20, what is the percentage payout rate?

e. Suppose that in 2001 the company paid a 10 percent stock dividend. What would be the expected fall in price?

2. Between 1986 and 2000 Textron dividend changes were described by the following equation:

$$\text{DIV}_t - \text{DIV}_{t-1} = .36(.26\ \text{EPS}_t - \text{DIV}_{t-1})$$

What do you think were **(a)** Textron's target payout ratio? **(b)** the rate at which dividends adjusted toward the target?

3. True or false?
   a. Realized long-term gains are taxed at the marginal rate of income tax.
   b. The *effective* rate of tax on capital gains can be less than the tax rate on dividends.
4. Here are several "facts" about typical corporate dividend policies. Which are true and which false?
   a. Companies decide each year's dividend by looking at their capital expenditure requirements and then distributing whatever cash is left over.
   b. Most companies have some notion of a target payout ratio.
   c. They set each year's dividend equal to the target payout ratio times that year's earnings.
   d. Managers and investors seem more concerned with dividend changes than with dividend levels.
   e. Managers often increase dividends temporarily when earnings are unexpectedly high for a year or two.
   f. Companies undertaking substantial share repurchases usually finance them with an offsetting reduction in cash dividends.
5. a. Wotan owns 1,000 shares of a firm that has just announced an increase in its dividend from $2.00 to $2.50 a share. The share price is currently $150. If Wotan does not wish to spend the extra cash, what should he do to offset the dividend increase?
   b. Brunhilde owns 1,000 shares of a firm that has just announced a dividend cut from $8.00 a share to $5.00. The share price is currently $200. If Brunhilde wishes to maintain her consumption, what should she do to offset the dividend cut?
6. a. The London Match Company has 1 million shares outstanding, on which it currently pays an annual dividend of £5.00 a share. The chairman has proposed that the dividend should be increased to £7.00 a share. If investment policy and capital structure are not to be affected, what must the company do to offset the dividend increase?
   b. Patriot Games has 5 million shares outstanding. The president has proposed that, given the firm's large cash holdings, the annual dividend should be increased from $6.00 a share to $8.00. If you agree with the president's plans for investment and capital structure, what else must the company do as a consequence of the dividend increase?
7. House of Haddock has 5,000 shares outstanding and the stock price is $140. The company is expected to pay a dividend of $20 per share next year and thereafter the dividend is expected to grow indefinitely by 5 percent a year. The President, George Mullet, now makes a surprise announcement: He says that the company will henceforth distribute half the cash in the form of dividends and the remainder will be used to repurchase stock.
   a. What is the total value of the company before and after the announcement? What is the value of one share?
   b. What is the expected stream of dividends per share for an investor who plans to retain his shares rather than sell them back to the company? Check your estimate of share value by discounting this stream of dividends per share.
8. Here are key financial data for House of Herring, Inc.:

Earnings per share for 2009	$5.50
Number of shares outstanding	40 million
Target payout ratio	50%
Planned dividend per share	$2.75
Stock price, year-end 2009	$130

   House of Herring plans to pay the entire dividend early in January 2010. All corporate and personal taxes were repealed in 2008.

a. Other things equal, what will be House of Herring's stock price after the planned dividend payout?
b. Suppose the company cancels the dividend and announces that it will use the money saved to repurchase shares. What happens to the stock price on the announcement date? Assume that investors learn nothing about the company's prospects from the announcement. How many shares will the company need to repurchase?
c. Suppose the company increases dividends to $5.50 per share and then issues new shares to recoup the extra cash paid out as dividends. What happens to the with- and ex-dividend share prices? How many shares will need to be issued? Again, assume investors learn nothing from the announcement about House of Herring's prospects.

9. Answer the following question twice, once assuming current tax law and once assuming the same rate of tax on dividends and capital gains.

Suppose all investments offered the same expected return *before* tax. Consider two equally risky shares, Hi and Lo. Hi shares pay a generous dividend and offer low expected capital gains. Lo shares pay low dividends and offer high expected capital gains. Which of the following investors would prefer the Lo shares? Which would prefer the Hi shares? Which shouldn't care? (Assume that any stock purchased will be sold after one year.)
a. A pension fund.
b. An individual.
c. A corporation.
d. A charitable endowment.
e. A security dealer.

PRACTICE QUESTIONS

1. Look in a recent issue of *The Wall Street Journal* at "Dividend News" and choose a company reporting a regular dividend.
a. How frequently does the company pay a regular dividend?
b. What is the amount of the dividend?
c. By what date must your stock be registered for you to receive the dividend?
d. How many weeks later is the dividend paid?
e. Look up the stock price and calculate the annual yield on the stock.

2. "Risky companies tend to have lower target payout ratios and more gradual adjustment rates." Explain what is meant by this statement. Why do you think it is so?

3. Which types of companies would you expect to distribute a relatively high or low proportion of current earnings? Which would you expect to have a relatively high or low price–earnings ratio?
a. High-risk companies.
b. Companies that have experienced an unexpected decline in profits.
c. Companies that *expect* to experience a decline in profits.
d. Growth companies with valuable future investment opportunities.

4. Little Oil has outstanding 1 million shares with a total market value of $20 million. The firm is expected to pay $1 million of dividends next year, and thereafter the amount paid out is expected to grow by 5 percent a year in perpetuity. Thus the expected dividend is $1.05 million in year 2, $1.105 million in year 3, and so on. However, the company has heard that the value of a share depends on the flow of dividends, and therefore it announces that next year's dividend will be increased to $2 million and that the extra cash will be raised immediately by an issue of shares. After that, the total amount paid out each year will be as previously forecasted, that is, $1.05 million in year 2 and increasing by 5 percent in each subsequent year.

a. At what price will the new shares be issued in year 1?
b. How many shares will the firm need to issue?

c. What will be the expected dividend payments on these new shares, and what therefore will be paid out to the *old* shareholders after year 1?

d. Show that the present value of the cash flows to current shareholders remains $20 million.

5. We stated in Section 16.4 that MM's proof of dividend irrelevance assumes that new shares are sold at a fair price. Look back at question 4. Assume that new shares are issued in year 1 at $10 a share. Show who gains and who loses. Is dividend policy still irrelevant? Why or why not?

6. Respond to the following comment: "It's all very well saying that I can sell shares to cover cash needs, but that may mean selling at the bottom of the market. If the company pays a regular cash dividend, investors avoid that risk."

7. "Dividends are the shareholders' wages. Therefore, if a government adopts an incomes policy, restricting increases in wages, it should in all logic restrict increases in dividends." Does this make sense?

8. Refer to the first balance sheet prepared for Rational Demiconductor in Section 16.4. Again it uses cash to pay a $1,000 cash dividend, planning to issue stock to recover the cash required for investment. But this time catastrophe hits before the stock can be issued. A new pollution control regulation increases manufacturing costs to the extent that the value of Rational Demiconductor's existing business is cut in half, to $4,500. The NPV of the new investment opportunity is unaffected, however. Show that dividend policy is still irrelevant.

9. "Many companies use stock repurchases to increase earnings per share. For example, suppose that a company is in the following position:

Net profit	$10 million
Number of shares before repurchase	1 million
Earnings per share	$10
Price–earnings ratio	20
Share price	$200

The company now repurchases 200,000 shares at $200 a share. The number of shares declines to 800,000 shares and earnings per share increase to $12.50. Assuming the price–earnings ratio stays at 20, the share price must rise to $250." Discuss.

10. Hors d'Age Cheeseworks has been paying a regular cash dividend of $4 per share each year for over a decade. The company is paying out all its earnings as dividends and is not expected to grow. There are 100,000 shares outstanding selling for $80 per share. The company has sufficient cash on hand to pay the next annual dividend.

    Suppose that Hors d'Age decides to cut its cash dividend to zero and announces that it will repurchase shares instead.

    a. What is the immediate stock price reaction? Ignore taxes, and assume that the repurchase program conveys no information about operating profitability or business risk.

    b. How many shares will Hors d'Age purchase?

    c. Project and compare future stock prices for the old and new policies. Do this for at least years 1, 2, and 3.

11. An article on stock repurchase in the *Los Angeles Times* noted: "An increasing number of companies are finding that the best investment they can make these days is in themselves." Discuss this view. How is the desirability of repurchase affected by company prospects and the price of its stock?

12. It is well documented that stock prices tend to rise when firms announce increases in their dividend payouts. How, then, can it be said that dividend policy is irrelevant?

13. Comment briefly on each of the following statements:
    a. "Unlike American firms, which are always being pressured by their shareholders to increase dividends, Japanese companies pay out a much smaller proportion of earnings and so enjoy a lower cost of capital."
    b. "Unlike new capital, which needs a stream of new dividends to service it, retained earnings have zero cost."
    c. "If a company repurchases stock instead of paying a dividend, the number of shares falls and earnings per share rise. Thus stock repurchase must always be preferred to paying dividends."
14. Suppose the Miller–Modigliani (MM) theory of dividend policy is correct. How would a government-imposed dividend freeze affect **(a)** stock prices? **(b)** capital investment?
15. Formaggio Vecchio has just announced its regular quarterly cash dividend of $1 per share.
    a. When will the stock price fall to reflect this dividend payment—on the record date, the ex-dividend date, or the payment date?
    b. Assume that there are no taxes. By how much is the stock price likely to fall?
    c. Now assume that *all* investors pay tax of 30 percent on dividends and nothing on capital gains. What is the likely fall in the stock price?
    d. Suppose, finally, that everything is the same as in part (c), except that security dealers pay tax on *both* dividends and capital gains. How would you expect your answer to (c) to change? Explain.
16. Refer back to question 15. Assume no taxes and a stock price immediately after the dividend announcement of $100.
    a. If you own 100 shares, what is the value of your investment? How does the dividend payment affect your wealth?
    b. Now suppose that Formaggio Vecchio cancels the dividend payment and announces that it will repurchase 1 percent of its stock at $100. Do you rejoice or yawn? Explain.
17. The shares of A and B both sell for $100 and offer a pretax return of 10 percent. However, in the case of company A the return is entirely in the form of dividend yield (the company pays a regular annual dividend of $10 a share), while in the case of B the return comes entirely as capital gain (the shares appreciate by 10 percent a year). Suppose that dividends and capital gains are both taxed at 30 percent. What is the after-tax return on share A? What is the after-tax return on share B to an investor who sells after two years? What about an investor who sells after 10 years?
18. a. The Horner Pie Company pays a quarterly dividend of $1. Suppose that the stock price is expected to fall on the ex-dividend date by $.90. Would you prefer to buy on the with-dividend date or the ex-dividend date if you were (i) a tax-free investor, (ii) an investor with a marginal tax rate of 40 percent on income and 16 percent on capital gains?
    b. In a study of ex-dividend behavior, Elton and Gruber[44] estimate that the stock price fell on the average by 85 percent of the dividend. Assuming that the tax rate on capital gains was 40 percent of the rate on income tax, what did Elton and Gruber's result imply about investors' marginal rate of income tax?
    c. Elton and Gruber also observed that the ex-dividend price fall was different for high-payout stocks and for low-payout stocks. Which group would you expect to show the larger price fall as a proportion of the dividend?
    d. Would the fact that investors can trade stocks freely around the ex-dividend date alter your interpretation of Elton and Gruber's study?

[44] E. J. Elton and M. J. Gruber, "Marginal Stockholders' Tax Rates and the Clientele Effect," *Review of Economics and Statistics* 52 (1970), pp. 68–74.

e. Suppose Elton and Gruber repeat their tests for the period after the 1986 Tax Reform Act, when the tax rate was the same on dividends and capital gains. How would you expect their results to change?

19. In the United States, where there is a two-tier tax system, which investors are indifferent to the dividend payout ratio? How about investors in Australia, where there is an imputation tax system? Describe how the Australian system works and what it could imply for dividend policy.

20. The middle-of-the-road party holds that dividend policy doesn't matter because the *supply* of high-, medium-, and low-payout stocks has already adjusted to satisfy investors' demands. Investors who like generous dividends hold stocks which give them all the dividends that they want. Investors who want capital gains see a surfeit of low-payout stocks to choose from. Thus, high-payout firms cannot gain by transforming to low-payout firms, or vice versa.

Suppose the government equalizes the tax rates on dividends and capital gains. Suppose that before this change the supply of dividends matched investor needs. How would you expect the tax change to affect the total cash dividends paid by U.S. corporations and the proportion of high- versus low-payout companies? Would dividend policy still be irrelevant after any dividend supply adjustments are completed? Explain.

CHALLENGE QUESTIONS

1. Table 16.4 lists the dividends and earnings per share (EPS) for Merck and International Paper. Estimate the target payout for each company and the rate at which the dividend is adjusted toward the target. Suppose that in 2001 Merck's earnings increase to $5 a share and International Paper's earnings increase to $3 per share. How would you predict their dividends to change?

2. Consider the following two statements: "Dividend policy is irrelevant," and "Stock price is the present value of expected future dividends." (See Chapter 4.) They *sound* contradictory. This question is designed to show that they are fully consistent.

TABLE 16.4

See Challenge Question 1.

	Merck		International Paper	
Year	EPS	Dividend	EPS	Dividend
1983	.17	.08	1.16	.6
1984	.19	.09	.47	.6
1985	.21	.09	.54	.6
1986	.27	.11	1.45	.6
1987	.37	.14	1.84	.61
1988	.51	.22	3.28	.64
1989	.63	.28	3.86	.77
1990	.76	.32	2.60	.84
1991	.92	.39	1.80	.84
1992	1.56	.46	0.58	.84
1993	1.44	.52	1.17	.84
1994	1.19	.57	1.73	.84
1995	1.32	.62	4.50	.92
1996	1.56	.71	1.04	1.00
1997	1.87	.85	−.20	1.00
1998	2.15	.95	.60	1.00
1999	2.45	1.10	.48	1.00
2000	2.90	1.21	.32	1.00

The current price of the shares of Charles River Mining Corporation is \$50. Next year's earnings and dividends per share are \$4 and \$2, respectively. Investors expect perpetual growth at 8 percent per year. The expected rate of return demanded by investors is $r = 12$ percent.

We can use the perpetual-growth model to calculate stock price.

$$P_0 = \frac{\text{DIV}}{r - g} = \frac{2}{.12 - .08} = 50$$

Suppose that Charles River Mining announces that it will switch to a 100 percent payout policy, issuing shares as necessary to finance growth. Use the perpetual-growth model to show that current stock price is unchanged.

3. Suppose management is expected to make a fixed-price tender offer to repurchase half of the stock at a 20 percent premium. How, if at all, would that affect today's market price of the company's shares?
4. Adherents of the "dividends-are-good" school sometimes point to the fact that stocks with high yields tend to have above-average price–earnings multiples. Is this evidence convincing? Discuss.

CHAPTER SEVENTEEN

DOES DEBT POLICY MATTER?

A FIRM'S BASIC resource is the stream of cash flows produced by its assets. When the firm is financed entirely by common stock, all those cash flows belong to the stockholders. When it issues both debt and equity securities, it undertakes to split up the cash flows into two streams, a relatively safe stream that goes to the debtholders and a more risky one that goes to the stockholders.

The firm's mix of different securities is known as its **capital structure.** The choice of capital structure is fundamentally a marketing problem. The firm can issue dozens of distinct securities in countless combinations, but it attempts to find the particular combination that maximizes its overall market value.

Are these attempts worthwhile? We must consider the possibility that *no* combination has any greater appeal than any other. Perhaps the really important decisions concern the company's assets, and decisions about capital structure are mere details—matters to be attended to but not worried about.

Modigliani and Miller (MM), who showed that dividend policy doesn't matter in perfect capital markets, also showed that financing decisions don't matter in perfect markets.[1] Their famous "proposition I" states that a firm cannot change the *total* value of its securities just by splitting its cash flows into different streams: The firm's value is determined by its real assets, not by the securities it issues. Thus capital structure is irrelevant as long as the firm's investment decisions are taken as given.

MM's proposition I allows complete separation of investment and financing decisions. It implies that any firm could use the capital budgeting procedures presented in Chapters 2 through 12 without worrying about where the money for capital expenditures comes from. In those chapters, we assumed all-equity financing without really thinking about it. If proposition I holds, that is exactly the right approach.

We believe that in practice capital structure *does* matter, but we nevertheless devote all of this chapter to MM's argument. If you don't fully understand the conditions under which MM's theory holds, you won't fully understand why one capital structure is better than another. The financial manager needs to know what kinds of market imperfection to look for.

In Chapter 18 we will undertake a detailed analysis of the imperfections that are most likely to make a difference, including taxes, the costs of bankruptcy, and the costs of writing and enforcing complicated debt contracts. We will also argue that it is naive to suppose that investment and financing decisions can be completely separated.

But in this chapter we isolate the decision about capital structure by holding the decision about investment fixed. We also assume that dividend policy is irrelevant.

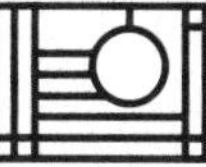

17.1 THE EFFECT OF LEVERAGE IN A COMPETITIVE TAX-FREE ECONOMY

We have referred to the firm's choice of capital structure as a *marketing problem.* The financial manager's problem is to find the combination of securities that has the greatest overall appeal to investors—the combination that maximizes the market value of the firm. Before tackling this problem, we ought to make sure that a policy which maximizes firm value also maximizes the wealth of the shareholders.

[1] F. Modigliani and M. H. Miller, "The Cost of Capital, Corporation Finance and the Theory of Investment," *American Economic Review* 48 (June 1958), pp. 261–297. MM's basic argument was anticipated in 1938 by J. B. Williams and to some extent by David Durand. See J. B. Williams, *The Theory of Investment Value,* Harvard University Press, Cambridge, MA, 1938; and D. Durand, "Cost of Debt and Equity Funds for Business: Trends and Problems of Measurement," in *Conference on Research in Business Finance,* National Bureau of Economic Research, New York, 1952.

Let D and E denote the market values of the outstanding debt and equity of the Wapshot Mining Company. Wapshot's 1,000 shares sell for \$50 apiece. Thus

$$E = 1{,}000 \times 50 = \$50{,}000$$

Wapshot has also borrowed \$25,000, and so V, the aggregate market value of all Wapshot's outstanding securities, is

$$V = D + E = \$75{,}000$$

Wapshot's stock is known as *levered equity*. Its stockholders face the benefits and costs of **financial leverage,** or *gearing*. Suppose that Wapshot "levers up" still further by borrowing an additional \$10,000 and paying the proceeds out to shareholders as a special dividend of \$10 per share. This substitutes debt for equity capital with no impact on Wapshot's assets.

What will Wapshot's equity be worth after the special dividend is paid? We have two unknowns, E and V:

Old debt	\$25,000	\$35,000 = D
New debt	\$10,000	
Equity		? = E
Firm value		? = V

If V is \$75,000 as before, then E must be $V - D = 75{,}000 - 35{,}000 = \$40{,}000$. Stockholders have suffered a capital loss which exactly offsets the \$10,000 special dividend. But if V *increases* to, say, \$80,000 as a result of the change in capital structure, then $E = \$45{,}000$ and the stockholders are \$5,000 ahead. In general, any increase or decrease in V caused by a shift in capital structure accrues to the firm's stockholders. We conclude that a policy which maximizes the market value of the firm is also best for the firm's stockholders.

This conclusion rests on two important assumptions: first, that Wapshot can ignore dividend policy and, second, that after the change in capital structure the old and new debt is *worth* \$35,000.

Dividend policy may or may not be relevant, but there is no need to repeat the discussion of Chapter 16. We need only note that shifts in capital structure sometimes force important decisions about dividend policy. Perhaps Wapshot's cash dividend has costs or benefits which should be considered in addition to any benefits achieved by its increased financial leverage.

Our second assumption that old and new debt ends up worth \$35,000 seems innocuous. But it could be wrong. Perhaps the new borrowing has increased the risk of the old bonds. If the holders of old bonds cannot demand a higher rate of interest to compensate for the increased risk, the value of their investment is reduced. In this case Wapshot's stockholders gain at the expense of the holders of old bonds even though the overall value of the debt and equity is unchanged.

But this anticipates issues better left to Chapter 18. In this chapter we will assume that any issue of debt has no effect on the market value of existing debt.[2]

[2]See E. F. Fama, "The Effects of a Firm's Investment and Financing Decisions," *American Economic Review* 68 (June 1978), pp. 272–284, for a rigorous analysis of the conditions under which a policy of maximizing the value of the firm is also best for the stockholders.

Enter Modigliani and Miller

Let us accept that the financial manager would like to find the combination of securities that maximizes the value of the firm. How is this done? MM's answer is that the financial manager should stop worrying: In a perfect market any combination of securities is as good as another. The value of the firm is unaffected by its choice of capital structure.

You can see this by imagining two firms that generate the same stream of operating income and differ only in their capital structure. Firm U is unlevered. Therefore the total value of its equity E_U is the same as the total value of the firm V_U. Firm, L, on the other hand, is levered. The value of its stock is, therefore, equal to the value of the firm less the value of the debt: $E_L = V_L - D_L$.

Now think which of these firms you would prefer to invest in. If you don't want to take much risk, you can buy common stock in the unlevered firm U. For example, if you buy 1 percent of firm U's shares, your investment is $.01\,V_U$ and you are entitled to 1 percent of the gross profits:

Dollar Investment	Dollar Return
$.01V_U$	.01 Profits

Now compare this with an alternative strategy. This is to purchase the same fraction of both the debt and the equity of firm L. Your investment and return would then be as follows:

	Dollar Investment	Dollar Return
Debt	$.01D_L$	.01 Interest
Equity	$.01E_L$	.01(Profits − interest)
Total	$.01(D_L + E_L)$ $= .01V_L$	.01 Profits

Both strategies offer the same payoff: 1 percent of the firm's profits. In well-functioning markets two investments that offer the same payoff must have the same cost. Therefore, $.01V_U$ must equal $.01V_L$: The value of the unlevered firm must equal the value of the levered firm.

Suppose that you are willing to run a little more risk. You decide to buy 1 percent of the outstanding shares in the *levered* firm. Your investment and return are now as follows:

Dollar Investment	Dollar Return
$.01E_L$ $= .01(V_L - D_L)$	.01(Profits − interest)

But there is an alternative strategy. This is to borrow $.01D_L$ on your own account and purchase 1 percent of the stock of the *unlevered* firm. In this case, your borrowing gives you an immediate cash *inflow* of $.01D_L$, but you have to pay interest on your loan equal to 1 percent of the interest that is paid by firm L. Your total investment and return are, therefore, as follows:

	Dollar Investment	Dollar Return
Borrowing	$-.01D_L$	$-.01$ Interest
Equity	$.01V_U$	.01 Profits
Total	$.01(V_U - D_L)$	.01(Profits − interest)

Again both strategies offer the same payoff: 1 percent of profits after interest. Therefore, both investments must have the same cost. The quantity $.01(V_U - D_L)$ must equal $.01(V_L - D_L)$ and V_U must equal V_L.

It does not matter whether the world is full of risk-averse chickens or venturesome lions. All would agree that the value of the unlevered firm U must be equal to the value of the levered firm L. As long as investors can borrow or lend on their own account on the same terms as the firm, they can "undo" the effect of any changes in the firm's capital structure. This is the basis for MM's famous proposition I: "The market value of any firm is independent of its capital structure."

The Law of the Conservation of Value

MM's argument that debt policy is irrelevant is an application of an astonishingly simple idea. If we have two streams of cash flow, A and B, then the present value of $A + B$ is equal to the present value of A plus the present value of B. We met this principle of *value additivity* in our discussion of capital budgeting, where we saw that in perfect capital markets the present value of two assets combined is equal to the sum of their present values considered separately.

In the present context we are not combining assets but splitting them up. But value additivity works just as well in reverse. We can slice a cash flow into as many parts as we like; the values of the parts will always sum back to the value of the unsliced stream. (Of course, we have to make sure that none of the stream is lost in the slicing. We cannot say, "The value of a pie is independent of how it is sliced," if the slicer is also a nibbler.)

This is really a *law of conservation of value.* The value of an asset is preserved regardless of the nature of the claims against it. Thus proposition I: Firm value is determined on the *left-hand* side of the balance sheet by real assets—not by the proportions of debt and equity securities issued by the firm.

The simplest ideas often have the widest application. For example, we could apply the law of conservation of value to the choice between issuing preferred stock, common stock, or some combination. The law implies that the choice is irrelevant, assuming perfect capital markets and providing that the choice does not affect the firm's investment, borrowing, and operating policies. If the total value of the equity "pie" (preferred and common combined) is fixed, the firm's owners (its common stockholders) do not care how this pie is sliced.

The law also applies to the *mix* of debt securities issued by the firm. The choices of long-term versus short-term, secured versus unsecured, senior versus subordinated, and convertible versus nonconvertible debt all should have no effect on the overall value of the firm.

Combining assets and splitting them up will not affect values as long as they do not affect an investor's choice. When we showed that capital structure does not af-

Data				
Number of shares	1,000			
Price per share	$10			
Market value of shares	$10,000			
			Outcomes	
Operating income ($)	500	1,000	**1,500**	2,000
Earnings per share ($)	.50	1.00	**1.50**	2.00
Return on shares (%)	5	10	**15**	20
			Expected outcome	

TABLE 17.1

Macbeth Spot Removers is entirely equity-financed. Although it *expects* to have an income of $1,500 a year in perpetuity, this income is not certain. This table shows the return to the stockholder under different assumptions about operating income. We assume no taxes.

fect choice, we implicitly assumed that both companies and individuals can borrow and lend at the same risk-free rate of interest. As long as this is so, individuals can undo the effect of any changes in the firm's capital structure.

In practice corporate debt is not risk-free and firms cannot escape with rates of interest appropriate to a government security. Some people's initial reaction is that this alone invalidates MM's proposition. It is a natural mistake, but capital structure can be irrelevant even when debt is risky.

If a company borrows money, it does not *guarantee* repayment: It repays the debt in full only if its assets are worth more than the debt obligation. The shareholders in the company, therefore, have limited liability.

Many individuals would like to borrow with limited liability. They might, therefore, be prepared to pay a small premium for levered shares *if the supply of levered shares were insufficient to meet their needs.*[3] But there are literally thousands of common stocks of companies that borrow. Therefore it is unlikely that an issue of debt would induce them to pay a premium for *your* shares.[4]

An Example of Proposition I

Macbeth Spot Removers is reviewing its capital structure. Table 17.1 shows its current position. The company has no leverage and all the operating income is paid as dividends to the common stockholders (we assume still that there are no taxes). The expected earnings and dividends per share are $1.50, but this figure is by no means certain—it could turn out to be more or less than $1.50. The price of each share is $10. Since the firm expects to produce a level stream of earnings in perpetuity, the expected return on the share is equal to the earnings–price ratio, $1.50/10.00 = .15$, or 15 percent.[5]

[3]Of course, individuals could *create* limited liability if they chose. In other words, the lender could agree that borrowers need repay their debt in full only if the assets of company X are worth more than a certain amount. Presumably individuals don't enter into such arrangements because they can obtain limited liability more simply by investing in the stocks of levered companies.

[4]Capital structure is also irrelevant if each investor holds a fully diversified portfolio. In that case he or she owns *all* the risky securities offered by a company (both debt and equity). But anybody who owns *all* the risky securities doesn't care about how the cash flows are divided between different securities.

[5]See Chapter 4, Section 4.

TABLE 17.2

Macbeth Spot Removers is wondering whether to issue $5,000 of debt at an interest rate of 10 percent and repurchase 500 shares. This table shows the return to the shareholder under different assumptions about operating income.

Data				
Number of shares	500			
Price per share	$10			
Market value of shares	$5,000			
Market value of debt	$5,000			
Interest at 10 percent	$500			
			Outcomes	
Operating income ($)	500	1,000	**1,500**	2,000
Interest ($)	500	500	**500**	500
Equity earnings ($)	0	500	**1,000**	1,500
Earnings per share ($)	0	1	**2**	3
Return on shares (%)	0	10	**20**	30
			Expected outcome	

Ms. Macbeth, the firm's president, has come to the conclusion that shareholders would be better off if the company had equal proportions of debt and equity. She therefore proposes to issue $5,000 of debt at an interest rate of 10 percent and use the proceeds to repurchase 500 shares. To support her proposal, Ms. Macbeth has analyzed the situation under different assumptions about operating income. The results of her calculations are shown in Table 17.2.

In order to see more clearly how leverage would affect earnings per share, Ms. Macbeth has also produced Figure 17.1. The burgundy line shows how earnings per share would vary with operating income under the firm's current all-equity financing. It is, therefore, simply a plot of the data in Table 17.1. The blue line shows how earnings per share would vary given equal proportions of debt and equity. It is, therefore, a plot of the data in Table 17.2.

Ms. Macbeth reasons as follows: "It is clear that the effect of leverage depends on the company's income. If income is greater than $1,000, the return to the equity holder is *increased* by leverage. If it is less than $1,000, the return is *reduced* by leverage. The return is unaffected when operating income is exactly $1,000. At this point the return on the market value of the assets is 10 percent, which is exactly equal to the interest rate on the debt. Our capital structure decision, therefore, boils down to what we think about income prospects. Since we expect operating income to be above the $1,000 break-even point, I believe we can best help our shareholders by going ahead with the $5,000 debt issue."

As financial manager of Macbeth Spot Removers, you reply as follows: "I agree that leverage will help the shareholder as long as our income is greater than $1,000. But your argument ignores the fact that Macbeth's shareholders have the alternative of borrowing on their own account. For example, suppose that an investor borrows $10 and then invests $20 in two unlevered Macbeth shares. This person has to put up only $10 of his or her own money. The payoff on the investment varies with Macbeth's operating income, as shown in Table 17.3. This is exactly the same set of payoffs as the investor would get by buying one share in the levered company. (Compare the last two lines of Tables 17.2 and 17.3.)

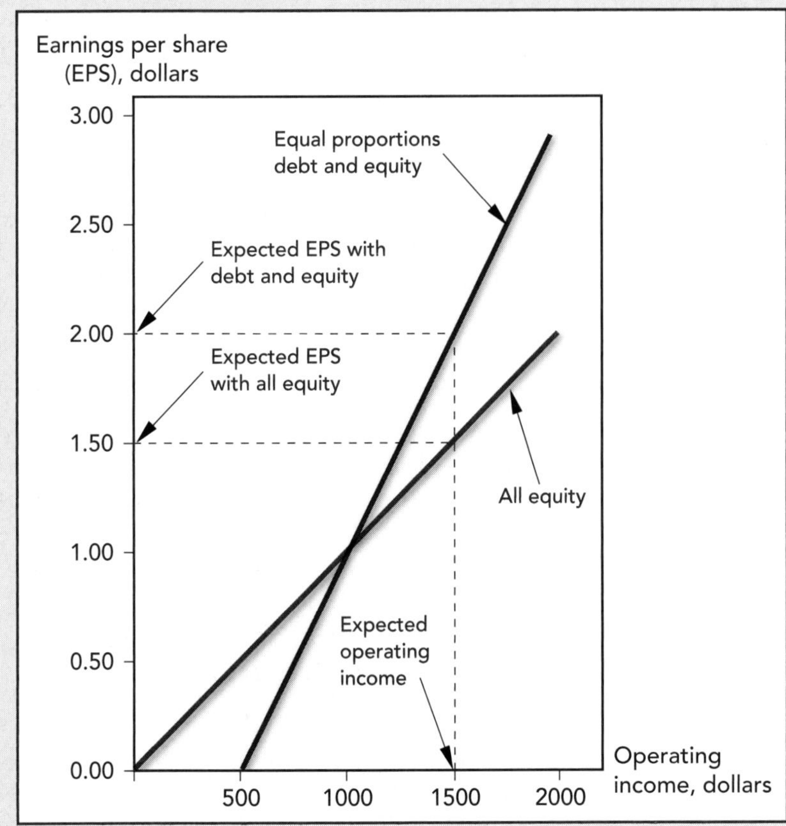

FIGURE 17.1

Borrowing increases Macbeth's EPS (earnings per share) when operating income is greater than $1,000 and reduces EPS when operating income is less than $1,000. Expected EPS rises from $1.50 to $2.

	Operating Income ($)			
	500	1,000	1,500	2,000
Earnings on two shares ($)	1	2	**3**	4
Less interest at 10% ($)	1	1	**1**	1
Net earnings on investment ($)	0	1	**2**	3
Return on $10 investment (%)	0	10	**20**	30
			Expected outcome	

TABLE 17.3

Individual investors can replicate Macbeth's leverage.

Therefore, a share in the levered company must also sell for $10. If Macbeth goes ahead and borrows, it will not allow investors to do anything that they could not do already, and so it will not increase value."

The argument that you are using is exactly the same as the one MM used to prove proposition I.

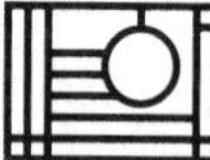

17.2 HOW LEVERAGE AFFECTS RETURNS

Implications of Proposition I

Consider now the implications of proposition I for the expected returns on Macbeth stock:

	Current Structure: All Equity	Proposed Structure: Equal Debt and Equity
Expected earnings per share ($)	1.50	2.00
Price per share ($)	10	10
Expected return on share (%)	15	20

Leverage increases the expected stream of earnings per share but *not* the share price. The reason is that the change in the expected earnings stream is exactly offset by a change in the rate at which the earnings are capitalized. The expected return on the share (which for a perpetuity is equal to the earnings–price ratio) increases from 15 to 20 percent. We now show how this comes about.

The expected return on Macbeth's assets r_A is equal to the expected operating income divided by the total market value of the firm's securities:

$$\text{Expected return on assets} = r_A = \frac{\text{expected operating income}}{\text{market value of all securities}}$$

We have seen that in perfect capital markets the company's borrowing decision does not affect *either* the firm's operating income *or* the total market value of its securities. Therefore the borrowing decision also does not affect the expected return on the firm's assets r_A.

Suppose that an investor holds all of a company's debt and all of its equity. This investor would be entitled to all the firm's operating income; therefore, the expected return on the portfolio would be equal to r_A.

The expected return on a portfolio is equal to a weighted average of the expected returns on the individual holdings. Therefore the expected return on a portfolio consisting of *all* the firm's securities is[6]

$$\begin{aligned}\text{Expected return on assets} &= \left(\text{proportion in debt} \times \text{expected return on debt}\right) \\ &+ \left(\text{proportion in equity} \times \text{expected return on equity}\right)\end{aligned}$$

$$r_A = \left(\frac{D}{D+E} \times r_D\right) + \left(\frac{E}{D+E} \times r_E\right)$$

We can rearrange this equation to obtain an expression for r_E, the expected return on the equity of a levered firm:

[6]This equation should look familiar. We introduced it in Chapter 9 when we showed that the company cost of capital is a weighted average of the expected returns on the debt and equity. (*Company cost of capital* is simply another term for the expected return on assets, r_A.) We also stated in Chapter 9 that changing the capital structure does not change the company cost of capital. In other words, we implicitly assumed MM's proposition I.

$$\text{Expected return on equity} = \text{expected return on assets} + \text{debt–equity ratio} \times \left(\text{expected return on assets} - \text{expected return on debt}\right)$$

$$r_E = r_A + \frac{D}{E}(r_A - r_D)$$

Proposition II

This is MM's proposition II: The expected rate of return on the common stock of a levered firm increases in proportion to the debt–equity ratio (D/E), expressed in market values; the rate of increase depends on the spread between r_A, the expected rate of return on a portfolio of all the firm's securities, and r_D, the expected return on the debt. Note that $r_E = r_A$ if the firm has no debt.

We can check out this formula for Macbeth Spot Removers. Before the decision to borrow

$$r_E = r_A = \frac{\text{expected operating income}}{\text{market value of all securities}}$$

$$= \frac{1{,}500}{10{,}000} = .15, \text{ or } 15\%$$

If the firm goes ahead with its plan to borrow, the expected return on assets r_A is still 15 percent. The expected return on equity is

$$r_E = r_A + \frac{D}{E}(r_A - r_D)$$

$$= .15 + \frac{5{,}000}{5{,}000}(.15 - .10)$$

$$= .20, \text{ or } 20\%$$

The general implications of MM's proposition II are shown in Figure 17.2. The figure assumes that the firm's bonds are essentially risk-free at low debt levels. Thus r_D is independent of D/E, and r_E increases linearly as D/E increases. As the firm borrows more, the risk of default increases and the firm is required to pay higher rates of interest. Proposition II predicts that when this occurs the rate of increase in r_E slows down. This is also shown in Figure 17.2. The more debt the firm has, the less sensitive r_E is to further borrowing.

Why does the slope of the r_E line in Figure 17.2 taper off as D/E increases? Essentially because holders of risky debt bear some of the firm's business risk. As the firm borrows more, more of that risk is transferred from stockholders to bondholders.

The Risk–Return Trade-off

Proposition I says that financial leverage has no effect on shareholders' wealth. Proposition II says that the rate of return they can expect to receive on their shares increases as the firm's debt–equity ratio increases. How can shareholders be indifferent to increased leverage when it increases expected return? The answer is that any increase in expected return is exactly offset by an increase in risk and therefore in shareholders' *required* rate of return.

FIGURE 17.2

MM's proposition II. The expected return on equity r_E increases linearly with the debt–equity ratio so long as debt is risk-free. But if leverage increases the risk of the debt, debtholders demand a higher return on the debt. This causes the rate of increase in r_E to slow down.

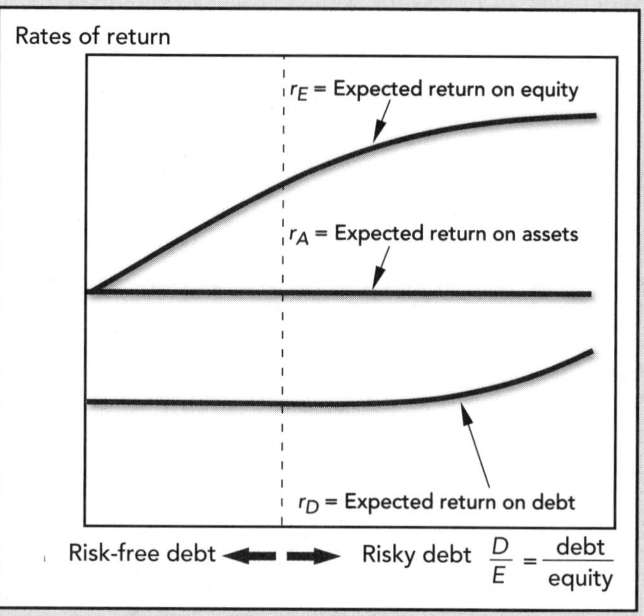

TABLE 17.4

Leverage increases the risk of Macbeth shares.

		Operating Income	
		$500	$1,500
All equity:	Earnings per share ($)	.50	1.50
	Return on shares (%)	5	15
50 percent debt:	Earnings per share ($)	0	2
	Return on shares (%)	0	20

Look at what happens to the risk of Macbeth shares if it moves to equal debt–equity proportions. Table 17.4 shows how a shortfall in operating income affects the payoff to the shareholders.

The debt–equity proportion does not affect the *dollar* risk borne by equityholders. Suppose operating income drops from $1,500 to $500. Under all-equity financing, equity earnings drop by $1 per share. There are 1,000 outstanding shares, and so *total* equity earnings fall by $1 × 1,000 = $1,000. With 50 percent debt, the same drop in operating income reduces earnings per share by $2. But there are only 500 shares outstanding, and so total equity income drops by $2 × 500 = $1,000, just as in the all-equity case.

However, the debt–equity choice does amplify the spread of *percentage* returns. If the firm is all-equity-financed, a decline of $1,000 in the operating income reduces the return on the shares by 10 percent. If the firm issues risk-free debt with a fixed interest payment of $500 a year, then a decline of $1,000 in the operating income reduces the return on the shares by 20 percent. In other words,

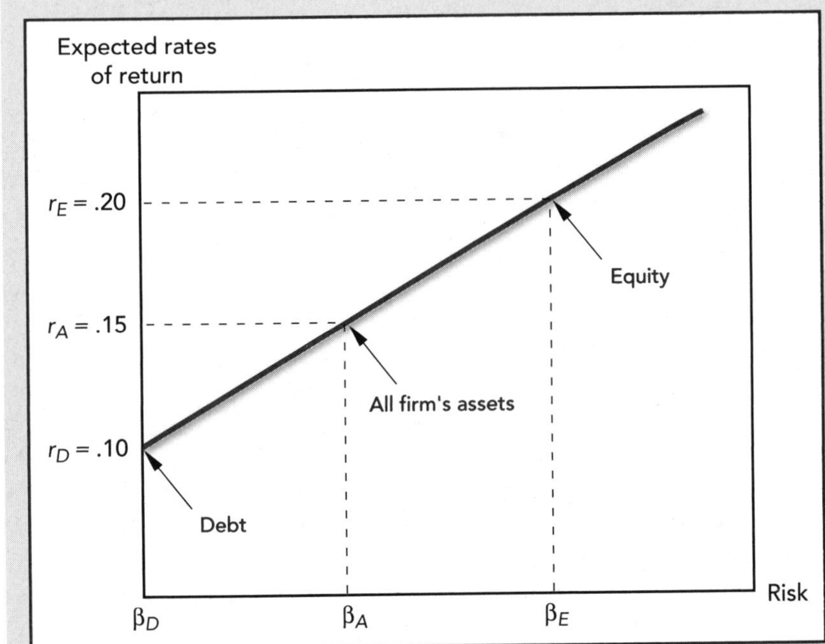

FIGURE 17.3

If Macbeth is unlevered, the expected return on its equity equals the expected return on its assets. Leverage increases both the expected return on equity (r_E) and the risk of equity (β_E).

the effect of leverage is to double the amplitude of the swings in Macbeth's shares. Whatever the beta of the firm's shares before the refinancing, it would be twice as high afterward.

Just as the expected return on the firm's assets is a weighted average of the expected return on the individual securities, so likewise is the beta of the firm's assets a weighted average of the betas of the individual securities:[7]

$$\text{Beta of assets} = \left(\text{proportion of debt} \times \text{beta of debt}\right) + \left(\text{proportion of equity} \times \text{beta of equity}\right)$$

$$\beta_A = \left(\frac{D}{D+E} \times \beta_D\right) + \left(\frac{E}{D+E} \times \beta_E\right)$$

We can rearrange this equation also to give an expression for β_E, the beta of the equity of a levered firm:

$$\text{Beta of equity} = \text{beta of assets} + \text{debt–equity ratio} \times \left(\text{beta of assets} - \text{beta of debt}\right)$$

$$\beta_E = \beta_A + \frac{D}{E}(\beta_A - \beta_D)$$

Now you can see why investors require higher returns on levered equity. The required return simply rises to match the increased risk.

In Figure 17.3, we have plotted the expected returns and the risk of Macbeth's securities, assuming that the interest on the debt is risk-free.[8]

[7]This equation should also look old-hat. We used it in Section 9.3 when we stated that changes in the capital structure change the beta of stock but not the asset beta.

[8]In this case $\beta_D = 0$ and $\beta_E = \beta_A + (D/E)\beta_A$.

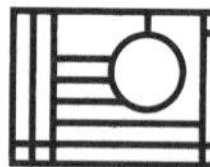

17.3 THE TRADITIONAL POSITION

What did financial experts think about debt policy before MM? It is not easy to say because with hindsight we see that they did not think too clearly.[9] However, a "traditional" position has emerged in response to MM. In order to understand it, we have to discuss the **weighted-average cost of capital.**

The expected return on a portfolio of all the company's securities is often referred to as the weighted-average cost of capital:[10]

$$\text{Weighted-average cost of capital} = r_A = \left(\frac{D}{V} \times r_D\right) + \left(\frac{E}{V} \times r_E\right)$$

The weighted-average cost of capital is used in capital budgeting decisions to find the net present value of projects that would not change the business risk of the firm.

For example, suppose that a firm has $2 million of outstanding debt and 100,000 shares selling at $30 per share. Its current borrowing rate is 8 percent, and the financial manager thinks that the stock is priced to offer a 15 percent return. Therefore $r_D = .08$ and $r_E = .15$. (The hard part is estimating r_E, of course.) This is all we need to calculate the weighted-average cost of capital:

$$D = \$2 \text{ million}$$
$$E = 100{,}000 \text{ shares} \times \$30 \text{ per share} = \$3 \text{ million}$$
$$V = D + E = 2 + 3 = \$5 \text{ million}$$

$$\begin{aligned}\text{Weighted-average cost of capital} &= \left(\frac{D}{V} \times r_D\right) + \left(\frac{E}{V} \times r_E\right) \\ &= \left(\frac{2}{5} \times .08\right) + \left(\frac{3}{5} \times .15\right) \\ &= .122, \text{ or } 12.2\%\end{aligned}$$

Note that we are still assuming that proposition I holds. If it doesn't, we can't use this simple weighted average as the discount rate even for projects that do not change the firm's business "risk class." As we will see in Chapter 19, the weighted-average cost of capital is only a starting point for setting discount rates.

Two Warnings

Sometimes the objective in financing decisions is stated not as "maximize overall market value" but as "minimize the weighted-average cost of capital." If MM's proposition I holds, then these are equivalent objectives. If MM's proposition I does *not* hold, then the capital structure that maximizes the value of the firm also minimizes the weighted-average cost of capital, *provided* that operating income is independent of capital structure. Remember that the weighted-average cost of capital is the expected rate of return on the market value of all of the firm's securities.

[9]Financial economists in 20 years may remark on Brealey and Myers's blind spots and clumsy reasoning. On the other hand, they may not remember us at all.

[10]Remember that in this chapter we ignore taxes. In Chapter 19, we shall see that the weighted-average cost of capital formula needs to be amended when debt interest can be deducted from taxable profits.

Anything that increases the value of the firm reduces the weighted-average cost of capital if operating income is constant. But if operating income is varying too, all bets are off.

In Chapter 18 we will show that financial leverage can affect operating income in several ways. Therefore maximizing the value of the firm is *not* always equivalent to minimizing the weighted-average cost of capital.

Warning 1 Shareholders want management to increase the firm's value. They are more interested in being rich than in owning a firm with a low weighted-average cost of capital.

Warning 2 Trying to minimize the weighted-average cost of capital seems to encourage logical short circuits like the following. Suppose that someone says, "Shareholders demand—and deserve—higher expected rates of return than bondholders do. Therefore debt is the cheaper capital source. We can reduce the weighted-average cost of capital by borrowing more." But this doesn't follow if the extra borrowing leads stockholders to demand a still higher expected rate of return. According to MM's proposition II the cost of equity capital r_E increases by just enough to keep the weighted-average cost of capital constant.

This is not the only logical short circuit you are likely to encounter. We have cited two more in practice question 5 at the end of this chapter.

Rates of Return on Levered Equity—The Traditional Position

You may ask why we have even mentioned the aim of minimizing the weighted-average cost of capital if it is often wrong or confusing. We had to because the traditionalists accept this objective and argue their case in terms of it.

The logical short circuit we just described rested on the assumption that r_E, the expected rate of return demanded by stockholders, does not rise as the firm borrows more. Suppose, just for the sake of argument, that this is true. Then r_A, the weighted-average cost of capital, must decline as the debt–equity ratio rises.

Take Figure 17.4, for example, which is drawn on the assumption that shareholders demand 12 percent no matter how much debt the firm has and that bondholders always want 8 percent. The weighted-average cost of capital starts at 12 percent and ends up at 8. Suppose that this firm's operating income is a level, perpetual stream of \$100,000 a year. Then firm value starts at

$$V = \frac{100{,}000}{.12} = \$833{,}333$$

and ends up at

$$V = \frac{100{,}000}{.08} = \$1{,}250{,}000$$

The gain of \$416,667 falls into the stockholders' pockets.[11]

Of course this is absurd: A firm that reaches 100 percent debt *has to be bankrupt*. If there is *any* chance that the firm could remain solvent, then the equity retains

[11]Note that Figure 17.4 relates r_E and r_D to D/V, the ratio of debt to firm value, rather than to the debt–equity ratio D/E. In this figure we wanted to show what happens when the firm is 100 percent debt-financed. At that point $E = 0$ and D/E is infinite.

FIGURE 17.4

If the expected rate of return demanded by stockholders r_E is unaffected by financial leverage, then the weighted-average cost of capital r_A declines as the firm borrows more. At 100 percent debt r_A equals the borrowing rate r_D. Of course this is an absurd and totally unrealistic case.

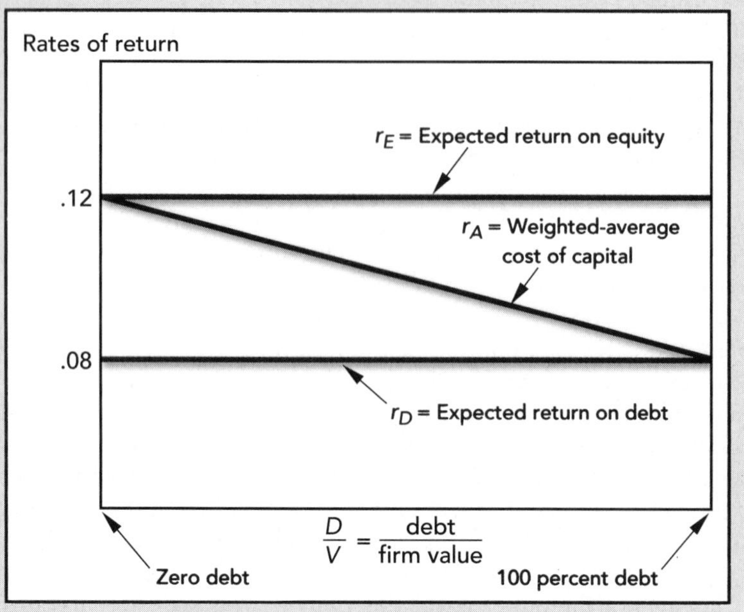

some value, and the firm cannot be 100 percent debt-financed. (Remember that we are working with the *market* values of debt and equity.)

But if the firm is bankrupt and its original shares are worthless pieces of paper, then its *lenders are its new shareholders.* The firm is back to all-equity financing! We assumed that the original stockholders demanded 12 percent—why should the new ones demand any less? They have to bear all of the firm's business risk.[12]

The situation described in Figure 17.4 is just impossible.[13] However, it is possible to stake out a position somewhere *between* Figures 17.3 and 17.4. That is exactly what the traditionalists have done. Their hypothesis is shown in Figure 17.5. They hold that a moderate degree of financial leverage may increase the expected equity return r_E, although not to the degree predicted by MM's proposition II. But irresponsible firms that borrow *excessively* find r_E shooting up faster than MM predict. Consequently, the weighted-average cost of capital r_A declines at first, then rises. Its minimum point is the point of optimal capital structure. Remember that minimizing r_A is equivalent to maximizing overall firm value if, as the traditionalists assume, operating income is unaffected by borrowing.

Two arguments might be advanced in support of the traditional position. First, it could be that investors don't notice or appreciate the financial risk created by "moderate" borrowing, although they wake up when debt is "excessive." If so, investors in moderately leveraged firms may accept a lower rate of return than they really should.

[12]We ignore the costs, delays, and other complications of bankruptcy. They are discussed in Chapter 18.

[13]This case is often termed the *net-income* (NI) approach because investors are assumed to capitalize income *after* interest at the same rate regardless of financial leverage. In contrast, MM's approach is a net-operating-income (NOI) approach because the value of the firm is fundamentally determined by operating income, the total dollar return to *both* bondholders and stockholders. This distinction was emphasized by D. Durand in his important, pre-MM paper, "Cost of Debt and Equity Funds for Business: Trends and Problems of Measurement," in *Conference on Research in Business Finance,* National Bureau of Economic Research, New York, 1952.

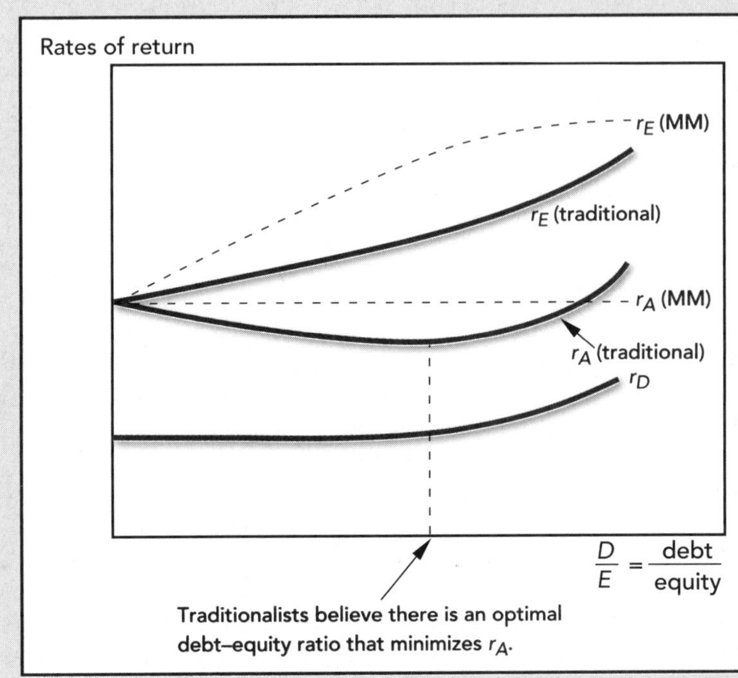

FIGURE 17.5

The dashed lines show MM's view of the effect of leverage on the expected return on equity r_E and the weighted-average cost of capital r_A. (See Figure 17.2.) The solid lines show the traditional view. Traditionalists say that borrowing at first increases r_E more slowly than MM predict but that r_E shoots up with excessive borrowing. If so, the weighted-average cost of capital can be minimized if you use just the right amount of debt.

That seems naive.[14] The second argument is better. It accepts MM's reasoning as applied to perfect capital markets but holds that actual markets are imperfect. Imperfections may allow firms that borrow to provide a valuable service for investors. If so, levered shares might trade at premium prices compared to their theoretical values in perfect markets.

Suppose that corporations can borrow more cheaply than individuals. Then it would pay investors who want to borrow to do so indirectly by holding the stock of levered firms. They would be willing to live with expected rates of return that do not fully compensate them for the business and financial risk they bear.

Is corporate borrowing really cheaper? It's hard to say. Interest rates on home mortgages are not too different from rates on high-grade corporate bonds.[15] Rates on margin debt (borrowing from a stockbroker with the investor's shares tendered as security) are not too different from the rates firms pay banks for short-term loans.

There are some individuals who face relatively high interest rates, largely because of the costs lenders incur in making and servicing small loans. There are economies of scale in borrowing. A group of small investors could do better by borrowing via a corporation, in effect pooling their loans and saving transaction costs.[16]

[14]This first argument may reflect a confusion between financial risk and the risk of default. Default is not a serious threat when borrowing is moderate; stockholders worry about it only when the firm goes "too far." But stockholders bear financial risk—in the form of increased volatility of rate of return and higher beta—even when the chance of default is nil. We demonstrated this in Figure 17.3.

[15]One of the authors once obtained a home mortgage at a rate ½ percentage point *less* than the contemporaneous yield on long-term AAA bonds.

[16]Even here there are alternatives to borrowing on personal account. Investors can draw down their savings accounts or sell a portion of their investment in bonds. The impact of reductions in lending on the investor's balance sheet and risk position is exactly the same as increases in borrowing.

But suppose that this class of investors is large, both in number and in the aggregate wealth it brings to capital markets. Shouldn't the investors' needs be fully satisfied by the thousands of levered firms already existing? Is there really an unsatisfied clientele of small investors standing ready to pay a premium for one more firm that borrows?

Maybe the market for corporate leverage is like the market for automobiles. Americans need millions of automobiles and are willing to pay thousands of dollars apiece for them. But that doesn't mean that you could strike it rich by going into the automobile business. You're at least 50 years too late.

Where to Look for Violations of MM's Propositions

MM's propositions depend on perfect capital markets. We believe capital markets are generally well-functioning, but they are not 100 percent perfect 100 percent of the time. Therefore, MM must be wrong some times in some places. The financial manager's problem is to figure out when and where.

That is not easy. Just finding market imperfections is insufficient.

Consider the traditionalists' claim that imperfections make borrowing costly and inconvenient for many individuals. That creates a clientele for whom corporate borrowing is better than personal borrowing. That clientele would, in principle, be willing to pay a premium for the shares of a levered firm.

But maybe it doesn't *have* to pay a premium. Perhaps smart financial managers long ago recognized this clientele and shifted the capital structures of their firms to meet its needs. The shifts would not have been difficult or costly to make. But if the clientele is now satisfied, it is no longer willing to pay a premium for levered shares. Only the financial managers who *first* recognized the clientele extracted any advantage from it.

Today's Unsatisfied Clienteles Are Probably Interested in Exotic Securities

So far we have made little progress in identifying cases where firm value might plausibly depend on financing. But our examples illustrate what smart financial managers look for. They look for an *unsatisfied* clientele, investors who want a particular kind of financial instrument but because of market imperfections can't get it or can't get it cheaply.

MM's proposition I is violated when the firm, by imaginative design of its capital structure, can offer some *financial service* that meets the needs of such a clientele. Either the service must be new and unique or the firm must find a way to provide some old service more cheaply than other firms or financial intermediaries can.

Now, is there an unsatisfied clientele for garden-variety debt or levered equity? We doubt it. But perhaps you can invent an exotic security and uncover a latent demand for it.

In the next several chapters we will encounter a number of new securities that have been invented by companies and advisers. These securities take the company's basic cash flows and repackage them in ways that are thought to be more attractive to investors. However, while inventing these new securities is easy, it is more difficult to find investors who will rush to buy them.[17]

Imperfections and Opportunities

The most serious capital market imperfections are often those created by government. An imperfection which supports a violation of MM's proposition I *also* cre-

[17]We return to the topic of security innovation in Section 25.8.

ates a money-making opportunity. Firms and intermediaries will find some way to reach the clientele of investors frustrated by the imperfection.

For many years the United States government imposed a limit on the rate of interest that could be paid on savings accounts. It did so to protect savings institutions by limiting competition for their depositors' money. The fear was that depositors would run off in search of higher yields, causing a cash drain that savings institutions would not be able to meet. This would cut off the supply of funds from those institutions for new real estate mortgages and knock the housing market for a loop. The savings institutions could not have afforded to offer higher interest rates on deposits—even if the government had allowed them to—because most of their past deposits had been locked up in fixed-rate mortgages issued when interest rates were much lower.

These regulations created an opportunity for firms and financial institutions to design new savings schemes that were not subject to the interest-rate ceilings. One invention was the *floating-rate note,* first issued on a large scale and with terms designed to appeal to individual investors by Citicorp in July 1974. Floating-rate notes are medium-term debt securities whose interest payments "float" with short-term interest rates. On the Citicorp issue, for example, the coupon rate used to calculate each semiannual interest payment was set at 1 percentage point above the contemporaneous yield on Treasury bills. The holder of the Citicorp note was therefore protected against fluctuating interest rates, because Citicorp sent a larger semiannual check when interest rates rose (and, of course, a smaller check when rates fell).

Citicorp evidently found an untapped clientele of investors, for it was able to raise $650 million in the first offering. The success of the issue suggests that Citicorp was able to add value by changing its capital structure. However, other companies were quick to jump on Citicorp's bandwagon, and within five months an additional $650 million of floating-rate notes were issued by other companies. By the mid-1980s about $43 billion of floating-rate securities were outstanding, though by that time the interest-rate ceiling was no longer a motive.

Interest-rate regulation also provided financial institutions with an opportunity to create value by offering money-market funds. These are mutual funds invested in Treasury bills, commercial paper, and other high-grade, short-term debt instruments. Any saver with a few thousand dollars to invest can gain access to these instruments through a money-market fund and can withdraw money at any time by writing a check against his or her fund balance. Thus the fund resembles a checking or savings account which pays close to market interest rates.[18] These money-market funds have become enormously popular. By 2001, their assets had increased to $2 trillion.

As floating-rate notes, money-market funds, and other instruments became more easily available, the protection given by government restrictions on savings account rates became less and less helpful. Finally the restrictions were lifted, and savings institutions met their competition head-on.

Long before interest-rate ceilings were finally removed, most of the gains had gone out of issuing the new securities to individual investors. Once the clientele was finally satisfied, MM's proposition I was restored (until the government creates a new imperfection). The moral of the story is this: If you ever find an unsatisfied clientele, do something right away, or capital markets will evolve and steal it from you.

[18]Money-market funds offer rates slightly lower than those on the securities they invest in. This spread covers the fund's operating costs and profits.

SUMMARY

At the start of this chapter we characterized the firm's financing decision as a marketing problem. Think of the financial manager as taking all of the firm's real assets and selling them to investors as a package of securities. Some financial managers choose the simplest package possible: all-equity financing. Some end up issuing dozens of debt and equity securities. The problem is to find the particular combination that maximizes the market value of the firm.

Modigliani and Miller's (MM's) famous proposition I states that no combination is better than any other—that the firm's overall market value (the value of all its securities) is independent of capital structure. Firms that borrow do offer investors a more complex menu of securities, but investors yawn in response. The menu is redundant. Any shift in capital structure can be duplicated or "undone" by investors. Why should they pay extra for borrowing indirectly (by holding shares in a levered firm) when they can borrow just as easily and cheaply on their own accounts?

MM agree that borrowing increases the expected rate of return on shareholders' investments. But it also increases the risk of the firm's shares. MM show that the risk increase exactly offsets the increase in expected return, leaving stockholders no better or worse off.

Proposition I is an extremely general result. It applies not just to the debt–equity trade-off but to *any* choice of financing instruments. For example, MM would say that the choice between long-term and short-term debt has no effect on firm value.

The formal proofs of proposition I all depend on the assumption of perfect capital markets.[19] MM's opponents, the "traditionalists," argue that market imperfections make personal borrowing excessively costly, risky, and inconvenient for some investors. This creates a natural clientele willing to pay a premium for shares of levered firms. The traditionalists say that firms should borrow to realize the premium.

But this argument is incomplete. There may be a clientele for levered equity, but that is not enough; the clientele has to be *unsatisfied.* There are already thousands of levered firms available for investment. Is there still an unsatiated clientele for garden-variety debt and equity? We doubt it.

Proposition I is violated when financial managers find an untapped demand and satisfy it by issuing something new and different. The argument between MM and the traditionalists finally boils down to whether this is difficult or easy. We lean toward MM's view: Finding unsatisfied clienteles and designing exotic securities to meet their needs is a game that's fun to play but hard to win.

[19] Proposition I can be proved umpteen different ways. The references at the end of this chapter include several more abstract and general proofs. Our formal proofs have been limited to MM's own arguments.

FURTHER READING

The pioneering work on the theory of capital structure is:

F. Modigliani and M. H. Miller: "The Cost of Capital, Corporation Finance and the Theory of Investment," *American Economic Review,* 48:261–297 (June 1958).

However, Durand deserves credit for setting out the issues that MM later solved:

D. Durand: "Cost of Debt and Equity Funds for Business: Trends and Problems in Measurement," in *Conference on Research in Business Finance,* National Bureau of Economic Research, New York, 1952, pp. 215–247.

MM provided a shorter and clearer proof of capital structure irrelevance in:

F. Modigliani and M. H. Miller: "Reply to Heins and Sprenkle," *American Economic Review,* 59:592–595 (September 1969).

A somewhat difficult article which analyzes capital structure in the context of capital asset pricing theory is:

R. S. Hamada: "Portfolio Analysis, Market Equilibrium and Corporation Finance," *Journal of Finance,* 24:13–31 (March 1969).

More abstract and general theoretical treatments can be found in:

J. E. Stiglitz: "On the Irrelevance of Corporate Financial Policy," *American Economic Review,* 64:851–866 (December 1974).

E. F. Fama: "The Effects of a Firm's Investment and Financing Decisions," *American Economic Review,* 68:272–284 (June 1978).

The fall 1988 issue of the Journal of Economic Perspectives *contains an anniversary collection of articles, including one by Modigliani and Miller, which review and assess the MM propositions. The summer 1989 issue of* Financial Management *contains three more articles under the heading "Reflections on the MM Propositions 30 Years Later."*

QUIZ

1. Assume a perfectly competitive market with no corporate or personal taxes. Companies A and B each earn gross profits of P and differ only in their capital structure—A is wholly equity-financed and B has debt outstanding on which it pays a certain $100 of interest each year. Investor X purchases 10 percent of the equity of A.
   a. What profits does X obtain?
   b. What alternative strategy would provide the same result?
   c. Suppose investor Y purchases 10 percent of the equity of B. What profits does Y obtain?
   d. What alternative strategy would provide the same result?
2. Ms. Kraft owns 50,000 shares of the common stock of Copperhead Corporation with a market value of $2 per share, or $100,000 overall. The company is currently financed as follows:

	Book Value
Common stock (8 million shares)	$2 million
Short-term loans	$2 million

   Copperhead now announces that it is replacing $1 million of short-term debt with an issue of common stock. What action can Ms. Kraft take to ensure that she is entitled to exactly the same proportion of profits as before? (Ignore taxes.)
3. The common stock and debt of Northern Sludge are valued at $50 million and $30 million, respectively. Investors currently require a 16 percent return on the common stock and an 8 percent return on the debt. If Northern Sludge issues an additional $10 million of common stock and uses this money to retire debt, what happens to the expected return on the stock? Assume that the change in capital structure does not affect the risk of the debt and that there are no taxes. If the risk of the debt did increase, would your answer underestimate or overestimate the expected return on the stock?
4. Company C is financed entirely by common stock and has a β of 1.0. The stock has a price–earnings multiple of 10 and is priced to offer a 10 percent expected return. The company decides to repurchase half the common stock and substitute an equal value of debt. Assume that the debt yields a risk-free 5 percent.
   a. Give
      i. The beta of the common stock after the refinancing.
      ii. The beta of the debt.
      iii. The beta of the company (i.e., stock and debt combined).

b. Give
   i. Investors' required return on the common stock before the refinancing.
   ii. The required return on the common stock after the refinancing.
   iii. The required return on the debt.
   iv. The required return on the company (i.e., stock and debt combined) after the refinancing.

c. Assume that the operating profit of firm C is expected to remain constant. Give
   i. The percentage increase in earnings per share.
   ii. The new price–earnings multiple.

5. Suppose that Macbeth Spot Removers issues $2,500 of debt and uses the proceeds to repurchase 250 shares.
   a. Rework Table 17.2 to show how earnings per share and share return now vary with operating income.
   b. If the beta of Macbeth's assets is .8 and its debt is risk-free, what would be the beta of the equity after the increased borrowing?

6. True or false? Explain briefly.
   a. Stockholders always benefit from an increase in company value.
   b. MM's proposition I assumes that actions which maximize firm value also maximize shareholder wealth.
   c. The reason that borrowing increases equity risk is because it increases the probability of bankruptcy.
   d. If firms did not have limited liability, the risk of their assets would be increased.
   e. If firms did not have limited liability, the risk of their equity would be increased.
   f. Borrowing does not affect the return on equity if the return on the firm's assets is equal to the interest rate.
   g. As long as the firm is certain that the return on assets will be higher than the interest rate, an issue of debt makes the shareholders better off.
   h. MM's proposition I implies that an issue of debt increases expected earnings per share and leads to an offsetting fall in the price–earnings ratio.
   i. MM's proposition II assumes increased borrowing does not affect the interest rate on the firm's debt.
   j. Borrowing increases firm value if there is a clientele of investors with a reason to prefer debt.

7. Note the two blank graphs in Figure 17.6. On graph *(a)*, assume MM are right, and plot the relationship between financial leverage and (i) the rates of return on debt and equity and (ii) the weighted-average cost of capital. Then fill in graph *(b)*, assuming the traditionalists are right.

8. Look back to Section 17.1. Suppose that Ms. Macbeth's investment bankers have informed her that since the new issue of debt is risky, debtholders will demand a return of 12.5 percent, which is 2.5 percent above the risk-free interest rate.
   a. What are r_A and r_E?
   b. Suppose that the beta of the unlevered stock was .6. What will be β_A, β_E, and β_D after the change to the capital structure?
   c. Assuming that the capital asset pricing model is correct, what is the expected return on the market?

9. Capitale Netto s.a. is financed solely by common stock, which offers an expected return of 13 percent. Suppose now that the company issues debt and repurchases stock so that its debt ratio is .4. Investors note the extra risk and raise their required return on the stock to 15 percent.
   a. What is the interest rate on the debt?
   b. If the debt is risk-free and the beta of the equity after the refinancing is 1.5, what is the expected return on the market?

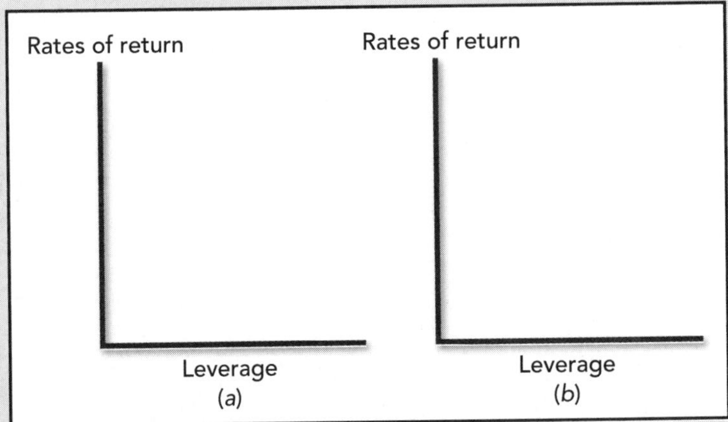

FIGURE 17.6

See quiz question 7.

10. Executive Chalk is financed solely by common stock and has outstanding 25 million shares with a market price of $10 a share. It now announces that it intends to issue $160 million of debt and to use the proceeds to buy back common stock.
    a. How is the market price of the stock affected by the announcement?
    b. How many shares can the company buy back with the $160 million of new debt that it issues?
    c. What is the market value of the firm (equity plus debt) after the change in capital structure?
    d. What is the debt ratio after the change in structure?
    e. Who (if anyone) gains or loses?

    Now try the next question.

11. Executive Cheese has issued debt with a market value of $100 million and has outstanding 15 million shares with a market price of $10 a share. It now announces that it intends to issue a further $60 million of debt and to use the proceeds to buy back common stock. Debtholders, seeing the extra risk, mark the value of the existing debt down to $70 million.
    a. How is the market price of the stock affected by the announcement?
    b. How many shares can the company buy back with the $60 million of new debt that it issues?
    c. What is the market value of the firm (equity plus debt) after the change in capital structure?
    d. What is the debt ratio after the change in structure?
    e. Who (if anyone) gains or loses?

PRACTICE QUESTIONS

1. Companies A and B differ only in their capital structure. A is financed 30 percent debt and 70 percent equity; B is financed 10 percent debt and 90 percent equity. The debt of both companies is risk-free.
    a. Rosencrantz owns 1 percent of the common stock of A. What other investment package would produce identical cash flows for Rosencrantz?
    b. Guildenstern owns 2 percent of the common stock of B. What other investment package would produce identical cash flows for Guildenstern?
    c. Show that neither Rosencrantz nor Guildenstern would invest in the common stock of B if the *total* value of company A were less than that of B.

2. Here is a limerick:

    There once was a man named Carruthers,
    Who kept cows with miraculous udders.

He said, "Isn't this neat?
They give cream from one teat,
And skim milk from each of the others!"

What is the analogy between Mr. Carruthers's cows and firms' financing decisions? What would MM's proposition I, suitably adapted, say about the value of Mr. Carruthers's cows? Explain.

3. Hubbard's Pet Foods is financed 80 percent by common stock and 20 percent by bonds. The expected return on the common stock is 12 percent and the rate of interest on the bonds is 6 percent. Assuming that the bonds are default-risk free, draw a graph that shows the expected return of Hubbard's common stock (r_E) and the expected return on the package of common stock and bonds (r_A) for different debt–equity ratios.

4. "MM totally ignore the fact that as you borrow more, you have to pay higher rates of interest." Explain carefully whether this is a valid objection.

5. Indicate what's wrong with the following arguments:
   a. "As the firm borrows more and debt becomes risky, both stockholders and bondholders demand higher rates of return. Thus by *reducing* the debt ratio we can reduce *both* the cost of debt and the cost of equity, making everybody better off."
   b. "Moderate borrowing doesn't significantly affect the probability of financial distress or bankruptcy. Consequently moderate borrowing won't increase the expected rate of return demanded by stockholders."

6. Each of the following statements is false or at least misleading. Explain why in each case.
   a. "A capital investment opportunity offering a 10 percent DCF rate of return is an attractive project if it can be 100 percent debt-financed at an 8 percent interest rate."
   b. "The more debt the firm issues, the higher the interest rate it must pay. That is one important reason why firms should operate at conservative debt levels."

7. Can you invent any new kinds of debt that might be attractive to investors? Why do you think they have not been issued?

8. It has been suggested that one disadvantage of common stock financing is that share prices tend to decline in recessions, thereby increasing the cost of capital and deterring investment. Discuss this view. Is it an argument for greater use of debt financing?

9. Figure 17.5 shows that r_D increases as the debt–equity ratio increases. In MM's world r_E also increases but at a declining rate. Explain why.

   Redraw Figure 17.5, showing how r_D and r_E change for increasingly high debt–equity ratios. Can r_D ever be higher than r_A? Can r_E decline beyond a certain debt–equity ratio?

10. Imagine a firm that is expected to produce a level stream of operating profits. As leverage is increased, what happens to
    a. The ratio of the market value of the equity to income after interest?
    b. The ratio of the market value of the *firm* to income before interest if (i) MM are right and (ii) the traditionalists are right?

11. Archimedes Levers is financed by a mixture of debt and equity. You have the following information about its cost of capital:

$r_E =$ ___	$r_D = 12\%$	$r_A =$ ___
$\beta_E = 1.5$	$\beta_D =$ ___	$\beta_A =$ ___
$r_f = 10\%$	$r_m = 18\%$	$D/V = .5$

    Can you fill in the blanks?

12. Look back at question 11. Suppose now that Archimedes repurchases debt and issues equity so that $D/V = .3$. The reduced borrowing causes r_D to fall to 11 percent. How do the other variables change?

13. Schuldenfrei a.g. pays no taxes and is financed entirely by common stock. The stock has a beta of .8, a price–earnings ratio of 12.5, and is priced to offer an 8 percent expected return. Schuldenfrei now decides to repurchase half the common stock and substitute an equal value of debt. If the debt yields a *risk-free* 5 percent, calculate
    a. The beta of the common stock after the refinancing.
    b. The required return and risk premium on the stock before the refinancing.
    c. The required return and risk premium on the stock after the refinancing.
    d. The required return on the debt.
    e. The required return on the company (i.e., stock and debt combined) after the refinancing.

    Assume that the operating profit of the firm is expected to remain constant in perpetuity. Give
    f. The percentage increase in expected earnings per share.
    g. The new price–earnings multiple.
14. Gamma Airlines is currently all-equity-financed, and its shares offer an expected return of 18 percent. The risk-free interest rate is 10 percent. Draw a graph with return on the vertical axis and debt–equity ratio (D/E) on the horizontal axis, and plot for different levels of leverage the expected return on assets (r_A), the expected return on equity (r_E), and the return on debt (r_D). Assume that the debt is risk-free. Now draw a similar graph with the debt ratio (D/V) on the horizontal axis.
15. Two firms, U and L, are identical except for their capital structure. Both will earn $150 in a boom and $50 in a slump. There is a 50 percent chance of each event. U is entirely equity-financed, and therefore shareholders receive the entire income. Its shares are valued at $500. L has issued $400 of risk-free debt at an interest rate of 10 percent, and therefore $40 of L's income is paid out as interest. There are no taxes or other market imperfections. Investors can borrow and lend at the risk-free rate of interest.
    a. What is the value of L's stock?
    b. Suppose that you invest $20 in U's stock. Is there an alternative investment in L that would give identical payoffs in boom and slump? What is the expected payoff from such a strategy?
    c. Now suppose that you invest $20 in L's stock. Design an alternative strategy with identical payoffs.
    d. Now show that MM's proposition II holds.

CHALLENGE QUESTIONS

1. Consider the following three tickets: ticket A pays $10 if ____ is elected as president, ticket B pays $10 if ____ is elected, and ticket C pays $10 if neither is elected. (Fill in the blanks yourself.) Could the three tickets sell for less than the present value of $10? Could they sell for more? Try auctioning off the tickets. What are the implications for MM's proposition I?
2. People often convey the idea behind MM's proposition I by various supermarket analogies, for example, "The value of a pie should not depend on how it is sliced," or, "The cost of a whole chicken should equal the cost of assembling one by buying two drumsticks, two wings, two breasts, and so on."

    Actually proposition I doesn't work in the supermarket. You'll pay less for an uncut whole pie than for a pie assembled from pieces purchased separately. Supermarkets charge more for chickens after they are cut up. Why? What costs or imperfections cause proposition I to fail in the supermarket? Are these costs or imperfections likely to be important for corporations issuing securities on the U.S. or world capital markets? Explain.

CHAPTER EIGHTEEN

HOW MUCH SHOULD A FIRM BORROW?

IN CHAPTER 17 we found that debt policy rarely matters in well-functioning capital markets. Few financial managers would accept that conclusion as a practical guideline. If debt policy doesn't matter, then they shouldn't worry about it—financing decisions should be delegated to underlings. Yet financial managers do worry about debt policy. This chapter explains why.

If debt policy were *completely* irrelevant, then actual debt ratios should vary randomly from firm to firm and industry to industry. Yet almost all airlines, utilities, banks, and real estate development companies rely heavily on debt. And so do many firms in capital-intensive industries like steel, aluminum, chemicals, petroleum, and mining. On the other hand, it is rare to find a drug company or advertising agency that is not predominantly equity-financed. Glamorous growth companies rarely use much debt despite rapid expansion and often heavy requirements for capital.

The explanation of these patterns lies partly in the things we left out of the last chapter. We ignored taxes. We assumed bankruptcy was cheap, quick, and painless. It isn't, and there are costs associated with financial distress even if legal bankruptcy is ultimately avoided. We ignored potential conflicts of interest between the firm's security holders. For example, we did not consider what happens to the firm's "old" creditors when new debt is issued or when a shift in investment strategy takes the firm into a riskier business. We ignored the information problems that favor debt over equity when cash must be raised from new security issues. We ignored the incentive effects of financial leverage on management's investment and payout decisions.

Now we will put all these things back in: taxes first, then the costs of bankruptcy and financial distress. This will lead us to conflicts of interest and to information and incentive problems. In the end we will have to admit that debt policy *does* matter.

However, we will *not* throw away the MM theory we developed so carefully in Chapter 17. We're shooting for a theory combining MM's insights *plus* the effects of taxes, costs of bankruptcy and financial distress, and various other complications. We're not dropping back to the traditional view based on inefficiencies in the capital market. Instead, we want to see how well-functioning capital markets *respond* to taxes and the other things covered in this chapter.

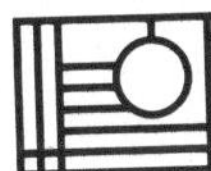

18.1 CORPORATE TAXES

Debt financing has one important advantage under the corporate income tax system in the United States. The interest that the company pays is a tax-deductible expense. Dividends and retained earnings are not. Thus the return to bondholders escapes taxation at the corporate level.

Table 18.1 shows simple income statements for firm U, which has no debt, and firm L, which has borrowed \$1,000 at 8 percent. The tax bill of L is \$28 less than that of U. This is the *tax shield* provided by the debt of L. In effect the government pays 35 percent of the interest expense of L. The total income that L can pay out to its bondholders and stockholders increases by that amount.

Tax shields can be valuable assets. Suppose that the debt of L is fixed and permanent. (That is, the company commits to refinance its present debt obligations when they mature and to keep rolling over its debt obligations indefinitely.) It looks forward to a permanent stream of cash flows of \$28 per year. The risk of these flows is likely to be less than the risk of the operating assets of L. The tax shields

TABLE 18.1

The tax deductibility of interest increases the total income that can be paid out to bondholders and stockholders.

	Income Statement of Firm U	Income Statement of Firm L
Earnings before interest and taxes	$1,000	$1,000
Interest paid to bondholders	0	80
Pretax income	1,000	920
Tax at 35%	350	322
Net income to stockholders	$ 650	$ 598
Total income to both bondholders and stockholders	$0 + 650 = $650	$80 + 598 = $678
Interest tax shield (.35 × interest)	$0	$28

depend only on the corporate tax rate[1] and on the ability of L to earn enough to cover interest payments. The corporate tax rate has been pretty stable. (It did fall from 46 to 34 percent after the Tax Reform Act of 1986, but that was the first material change since the 1950s.) And the ability of L to earn its interest payments must be reasonably sure; otherwise it could not have borrowed at 8 percent.[2] Therefore we should discount the interest tax shields at a relatively low rate.

But what rate? One common assumption is that the risk of the tax shields is the same as that of the interest payments generating them. Thus we discount at 8 percent, the expected rate of return demanded by investors who are holding the firm's debt:

$$\text{PV(tax shield)} = \frac{28}{.08} = \$350$$

In effect the government itself assumes 35 percent of the $1,000 debt obligation of L.

Under these assumptions, the present value of the tax shield is independent of the return on the debt r_D. It equals the corporate tax rate T_c times the amount borrowed D:

$$\begin{aligned}\text{Interest payment} &= \text{return on debt} \times \text{amount borrowed} \\ &= r_D \times D\end{aligned}$$

$$\begin{aligned}\text{PV(tax shield)} &= \frac{\text{corporate tax rate} \times \text{expected interest payment}}{\text{expected return on debt}} \\ &= \frac{T_c(r_D D)}{r_D} = T_c D\end{aligned}$$

Of course, PV(tax shield) is less if the firm does not plan to borrow permanently, or if it may not be able to use the tax shields in the future.

[1] Always use the marginal corporate tax rate, not the average rate. Average rates are often much lower than marginal rates because of accelerated depreciation and other tax adjustments. For large corporations, the marginal rate is usually taken as the statutory rate, which was 35 percent when this chapter was written (2001). However, effective marginal rates can be less than the statutory rate, especially for smaller, riskier companies which cannot be sure that they will earn taxable income in the future.

[2] If the income of L does not cover interest in some future year, the tax shield is not necessarily lost. L can carry back the loss and receive a tax refund up to the amount of taxes paid in the previous three years. If L has a string of losses, and thus no prior tax payments that can be refunded, then losses can be carried forward and used to shield income in subsequent years.

Normal Balance Sheet (Market Values)	
Asset value (present value of after-tax cash flows)	Debt Equity
Total assets	Total value
Expanded Balance Sheet (Market Values)	
Pretax asset value (present value of *pretax* cash flows)	Debt Government's claim (present value of future taxes) Equity
Total pretax assets	Total pretax value

TABLE 18.2

Normal and expanded market value balance sheets. In a normal balance sheet, assets are valued after tax. In the expanded balance sheet, assets are valued pretax, and the value of the government's tax claim is recognized on the right-hand side. Interest tax shields are valuable because they reduce the government's claim.

How Do Interest Tax Shields Contribute to the Value of Stockholders' Equity?

MM's proposition I amounts to saying that the value of a pie does not depend on how it is sliced. The pie is the firm's assets, and the slices are the debt and equity claims. If we hold the pie constant, then a dollar more of debt means a dollar less of equity value.

But there is really a third slice, the government's. Look at Table 18.2. It shows an *expanded* balance sheet with *pretax* asset value on the left and the value of the government's tax claim recognized as a liability on the right. MM would still say that the value of the pie—in this case *pretax* asset value—is not changed by slicing. But anything the firm can do to reduce the size of the government's slice obviously makes stockholders better off. One thing it can do is borrow money, which reduces its tax bill and, as we saw in Table 18.1, increases the cash flows to debt and equity investors. The *after-tax* value of the firm (the sum of its debt and equity values as shown in a normal market value balance sheet) goes up by PV(tax shield).

Recasting Pfizer's Capital Structure

Pfizer, Inc., is a large successful firm that uses essentially no long-term debt. Table 18.3(*a*) shows simplified book and market value balance sheets for Pfizer as of year-end 2000.

Suppose that you were Pfizer's financial manager in 2001 with complete responsibility for its capital structure. You decide to borrow $1 billion on a permanent basis and use the proceeds to repurchase shares.

Table 18.3(*b*) shows the new balance sheets. The book version simply has $1,000 million more long-term debt and $1,000 million less equity. But we know that Pfizer's assets must be worth more, for its tax bill has been reduced by 35 percent of the interest on the new debt. In other words, Pfizer has an increase in PV(tax shield), which is worth $T_cD = .35 \times \$1{,}000$ million = $350 million. If the MM theory holds *except* for taxes, firm value must increase by $350 million to $296,247 million. Pfizer's equity ends up worth $289,794 million.

TABLE 18.3(a)

Simplified balance sheets for Pfizer, Inc., December 31, 2000 (figures in millions).

Notes:

1. Market value is equal to book value for net working capital, long-term debt, and other long-term liabilities. Equity is entered at actual market value: number of shares times closing price on December 29, 2000. The difference between the market and book values of long-term assets is equal to the difference between the market and book values of equity.
2. The market value of the long-term assets includes the tax shield on the existing debt. This tax shield is worth .35 × 1,123 = $393 million.

Book Values			
Net working capital	$ 5,206	$ 1,123	Long-term debt
Long-term assets	16,323	4,330	Other long-term liabilities
		16,076	Equity
Total assets	$ 21,529	$ 21,529	Total value
Market Values			
Net working capital	$ 5,206	$ 1,123	Long-term debt
		4,330	Other long-term liabilities
Market value of long-term assets	290,691	290,444	Equity
Total assets	$295,897	$295,897	Total value

TABLE 18.3(b)

Balance sheets for Pfizer, Inc., with additional $1 billion of long-term debt substituted for stockholders' equity (figures in millions).

Notes:

1. The figures in Table 18.3(*b*) for net working capital, long-term assets, and other long-term liabilities are identical to those in Table 18.3(*a*).
2. Present value of tax shields assumed equal to corporate tax rate (35 percent) times additional long-term debt.

Book Values			
Net working capital	$ 5,206	$ 2,123	Long-term debt
Long-term assets	16,323	4,330	Other long-term liabilities
		15,076	Equity
Total assets	$ 21,529	$ 21,529	Total value
Market Values			
Net working capital	$ 5,206	$ 2,123	Long-term debt
		4,330	Other long-term liabilities
Market value of long-term assets	291,041	289,794	Equity
Total assets	$296,247	$296,247	Total value

Now you have repurchased $1,000 million worth of shares, but Pfizer's equity value has dropped by only $650 million. Therefore Pfizer's stockholders must be $350 million ahead. Not a bad day's work.[3]

MM and Taxes

We have just developed a version of MM's proposition I as corrected by them to reflect corporate income taxes.[4] The new proposition is

[3]Notice that as long as the bonds are sold at a fair price, all the benefits from the tax shield go to the shareholders.

[4]Interest tax shields are recognized in MM's original article, F. Modigliani and M. H. Miller, "The Cost of Capital, Corporation Finance and the Theory of Investment," *American Economic Review* 48 (June 1958), pp. 261–296. The valuation procedure used in Table 18.3(*b*) is presented in their 1963 article "Corporate Income Taxes and the Cost of Capital: A Correction," *American Economic Review* 53 (June 1963), pp. 433–443.

$$\text{Value of firm} = \text{value if all-equity-financed} + \text{PV(tax shield)}$$

In the special case of permanent debt,

$$\text{Value of firm} = \text{value if all-equity-financed} + T_cD$$

Our imaginary financial surgery on Pfizer provides the perfect illustration of the problems inherent in this "corrected" theory. That $350 million came too easily; it seems to violate the law that there is no such thing as a money machine. And if Pfizer's stockholders would be richer with $2,123 million of corporate debt, why not $3,123 or $17,199 million?[5] Our formula implies that firm value and stockholders' wealth continue to go up as D increases. The optimal debt policy appears to be embarrassingly extreme. All firms should be 100 percent debt-financed.

MM were not that fanatical about it. No one would expect the formula to apply at extreme debt ratios. There are several reasons why our calculations overstate the value of interest tax shields. First, it's wrong to think of debt as fixed and perpetual; a firm's ability to carry debt changes over time as profits and firm value fluctuate.[6] Second, many firms face marginal tax rates less than 35 percent. Third, you can't use interest tax shields unless there will be future profits to shield—and no firm can be absolutely sure of that.

But none of these qualifications explains why firms like Pfizer not only exist but also thrive with no debt at all. It is hard to believe that the management of Pfizer is simply missing the boat.

Therefore we have argued ourselves into a corner. There are just two ways out:

1. Perhaps a fuller examination of the U.S. system of corporate *and personal* taxation will uncover a tax disadvantage of corporate borrowing, offsetting the present value of the corporate tax shield.
2. Perhaps firms that borrow incur other costs—bankruptcy costs, for example—offsetting the present value of the tax shield.

We will now explore these two escape routes.

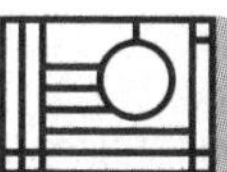

18.2 CORPORATE AND PERSONAL TAXES

When personal taxes are introduced, the firm's objective is no longer to minimize the *corporate* tax bill; the firm should try to minimize the present value of *all* taxes paid on corporate income. "All taxes" include *personal* taxes paid by bondholders and stockholders.

Figure 18.1 illustrates how corporate and personal taxes are affected by leverage. Depending on the firm's capital structure, a dollar of operating income will

---

[5]The last figure would correspond to a 100 percent book debt ratio. But Pfizer's *market* value would be $301,524 million according to our formula for firm value. Pfizer's common shares would have an aggregate value of $279,995 million.

[6]The valuation of interest tax shields is discussed again in Section 19.4. Our calculation here adheres to Chapter 19's "Financing Rule 1," which assumes that debt is fixed regardless of future performance of the project or the firm.

FIGURE 18.1

The firm's capital structure determines whether operating income is paid out as interest or equity income. Interest is taxed only at the personal level. Equity income is taxed at both the corporate and the personal levels. However, T_{pE}, the personal tax rate on equity income, can be less than T_p, the personal tax rate on interest income.

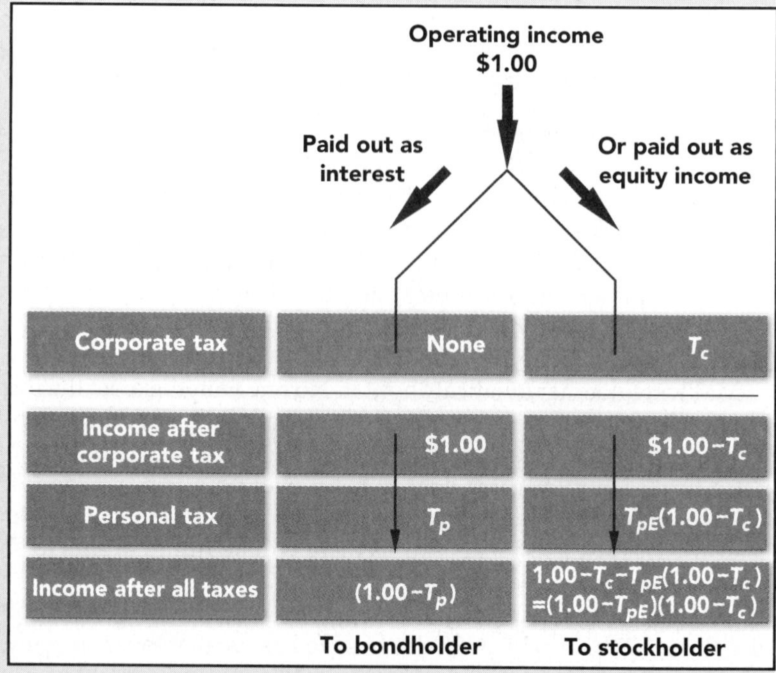

accrue to investors either as debt interest or equity income (dividends or capital gains). That is, the dollar can go down either branch of Figure 18.1.

Notice that Figure 18.1 distinguishes between T_p, the personal tax rate on interest, and T_{pE}, the effective personal rate on equity income. The two rates are equal if equity income comes entirely as dividends. But T_{pE} can be less than T_p if equity income comes as capital gains. In 2001 the top rate on ordinary income, including interest and dividends, was 39.1 percent. The rate on *realized* capital gains was 20 percent.[7] However, capital gains taxes can be deferred until shares are sold, so the top *effective* capital gains rate can be less than 20 percent.

The firm's objective should be to arrange its capital structure so as to maximize after-tax income. You can see from Figure 18.1 that corporate borrowing is better if $(1 - T_p)$ is more than $(1 - T_{pE}) \times (1 - T_c)$; otherwise it is worse. The *relative tax advantage* of debt over equity is

$$\text{Relative tax advantage of debt} = \frac{1 - T_p}{(1 - T_{pE})(1 - T_c)}$$

This suggests two special cases. First, suppose all equity income comes as dividends. Then debt and equity income are taxed at the same effective personal rate. But with $T_{pE} = T_p$, the relative advantage depends only on the *corporate rate*:

$$\text{Relative advantage} = \frac{1 - T_p}{(1 - T_{pE})(1 - T_c)} = \frac{1}{1 - T_c}$$

[7]See Section 16.6 for details. Note that we are simplifying by ignoring those corporate investors, such as banks, which pay top rates on capital gains of 35 percent.

In this case, we can forget about personal taxes. The tax advantage of corporate borrowing is exactly as MM calculated it.[8] They do not have to assume away personal taxes. Their theory of debt and taxes requires only that debt and equity be taxed at the same rate.

The second special case occurs when corporate and personal taxes cancel to make debt policy irrelevant. This requires

$$1 - T_p = (1 - T_{pE})(1 - T_c)$$

This case can happen only if T_c, the corporate rate, is less than the personal rate T_p *and* if T_{pE}, the effective rate on equity income, is small. Merton Miller explored this situation at a time when tax rates in the United States were very different from today, but we won't go into the details of his analysis here.[9]

In any event we seem to have a simple, practical decision rule. Arrange the firm's capital structure to shunt operating income down that branch of Figure 18.1 where the tax is least. Unfortunately that is not as simple as it sounds. What's T_{pE}, for example? The shareholder roster of any large corporation is likely to include tax-exempt investors (such as pension funds or university endowments) as well as millionaires. All possible tax brackets will be mixed together. And it's the same with T_p, the personal tax rate on interest. The large corporation's "typical" bondholder might be a tax-exempt pension fund, but many taxpaying investors also hold corporate debt.

Some investors may be much happier to buy your debt than others. For example, you should have no problems inducing pension funds to lend; they don't have to worry about personal tax. But taxpaying investors may be more reluctant to hold debt and will be prepared to do so only if they are compensated by a high rate of interest. Investors paying tax on interest at the top rate of 39.1 percent may be particularly unwilling to hold debt. They will prefer to hold common stock or municipal bonds whose interest is exempt from tax.

To determine the net tax advantage of debt, companies would need to know the tax rates faced by the marginal investor—that is, an investor who is equally happy to hold debt or equity. This makes it hard to put a precise figure on the tax benefit, but we can nevertheless provide a back-of-the-envelope calculation. One way to estimate the tax rate of the marginal debt investor is to see how much yield investors are prepared to give up when they invest in tax-exempt municipal bonds. As we write this in August 2001, short-term municipals yield 2.49 percent, while similar Treasury bonds yield 3.71 percent. An investor with a personal tax rate of 33 percent would receive exactly the same after-tax interest from the two securities and would be equally happy to hold them.[10]

---

[8]Of course, personal taxes reduce the dollar amount of corporate interest tax shields, but the appropriate discount rate for cash flows after personal tax is also lower. If investors are willing to lend at a prospective return *before* personal taxes of r_D, then they must also be willing to accept a return *after* personal taxes of $r_D(1 - T_p)$, where T_p is the marginal rate of personal tax. Thus we can compute the value after personal taxes of the tax shield on permanent debt:

$$\text{PV(tax shield)} = \frac{T_c \times (r_D D) \times (1 - T_p)}{r_D \times (1 - T_p)} = T_c D$$

This brings us back to our previous formula for firm value:

$$\text{Value of firm} = \text{value if all-equity-financed} + T_c D$$

[9]See M. H. Miller, "Debt and Taxes," *Journal of Finance* 32 (May 1977), pp. 261–276.

[10]That is, $(1 - .33) \times 3.71 = 2.49$ percent.

To work out how much tax such an investor would pay on equity income, we need to know the proportion of income that is in the form of capital gains and the tax that is paid on these gains. Companies currently (2001) pay out on average 28 percent of their earnings. So for each \$1.00 of equity income, \$.28 consists of dividends and the balance of \$.72 comprises capital gains. We assume that by not realizing these capital gains immediately, investors can cut the effective tax to one-half the statutory rate on realized gains, that is, $20/2 = 10$ percent[11] Therefore, if our marginal investor invests in common stock, the tax on each \$1.00 of equity income is $T_{pE} = (.28 \times .33) + (.72 \times .10) = .16$.

Now we can calculate the effect of shunting a dollar of income down each of the two branches in Figure 18.1:

	Interest	Equity Income
Income before tax	\$1.00	\$1.00
Less corporate tax at $T_c = .35$	0	.35
Income after corporate tax	1.00	.65
Personal tax at $T_p = .33$ and $T_{pE} = .16$	.33	.107
Income after all taxes	\$ .67	\$ .543
	Advantage to debt = \$.127	

The advantage to debt financing appears to be about \$.13 on the dollar.

We should emphasize that our back-of-the-envelope calculation is just that. Economists have come up with differing figures for the tax rate of the marginal debtholder and the effective rate of capital gains tax. These estimates may give higher or lower figures for the tax advantage of debt. Also our calculation of the benefits of debt financing assumed that the firm could be confident that it would have sufficient income to shield. In practice few firms can be *sure* they will show a taxable profit in the future. If a firm shows a loss and cannot carry the loss back against past taxes, its interest tax shield must be carried forward with the hope of using it later. The firm loses the time value of money while it waits. If its difficulties are deep enough, the wait may be permanent and the interest tax shield may be lost forever.

Notice also that borrowing is not the only way to shield income against tax. Firms have accelerated write-offs for plant and equipment. Investment in many intangible assets can be expensed immediately. So can contributions to the firm's pension fund. The more that firms shield income in these ways, the lower is the expected shield from corporate borrowing.[12] Even if the firm is confident that it will earn a taxable profit with the current level of debt, it is unlikely to be so positive if the amount of debt is increased.[13]

[11]For an analysis of the effective rate of capital gains tax, see R. C. Green and B. Hollifield, "The Personal Tax Advantages of Equity," working paper, Graduate School of Industrial Administration, Carnegie Mellon University, January 2001.

[12]For a discussion of these and other tax shields on company borrowing, see H. DeAngelo and R. Masulis, "Optimal Capital Structure under Corporate and Personal Taxation," *Journal of Financial Economics* 8 (March 1980), pp. 5–29.

[13]For some evidence on the average marginal tax rate of U.S. firms, see J. R. Graham, "Debt and the Marginal Tax Rate," *Journal of Financial Economics* 41 (May 1996), pp. 41–73, and "Proxies for the Corporate Marginal Tax Rate," *Journal of Financial Economics* 42 (October 1996), pp. 187–221.

Thus corporate tax shields are worth more to some firms than to others. Firms with plenty of noninterest tax shields and uncertain future profits should borrow less than consistently profitable firms with lots of taxable profits to shield. Firms with large accumulated tax-loss carry-forwards shouldn't borrow at all. Why should such a firm pay a high rate of interest to induce taxpaying investors to hold its debt when it can't use interest tax shields? All this suggests that there is a moderate tax advantage to corporate borrowing, at least for companies that are reasonably sure they can use the corporate tax shields. For companies that do not expect corporate tax shields there is probably a moderate tax disadvantage.

Do companies make full use of interest tax shields? John Graham argues that they don't. His estimates suggest that for the typical firm unused tax shields are worth nearly 5 percent of company value.[14] Presumably, well-established companies like Pfizer, with effectively no long-term debt, are leaving even more money on the table. It seems either that managers of these firms are missing out or that there are some offsetting disadvantages to increased borrowing. We will now explore this second escape route.

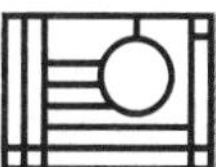

18.3 COSTS OF FINANCIAL DISTRESS

Financial distress occurs when promises to creditors are broken or honored with difficulty. Sometimes financial distress leads to bankruptcy. Sometimes it only means skating on thin ice.

As we will see, financial distress is costly. Investors know that levered firms may fall into financial distress, and they worry about it. That worry is reflected in the current market value of the levered firm's securities. Thus, the value of the firm can be broken down into three parts:

$$\begin{matrix}\text{Value} \\ \text{of firm}\end{matrix} = \begin{matrix}\text{value if} \\ \text{all-equity-financed}\end{matrix} + \text{PV(tax shield)} - \begin{matrix}\text{PV(costs of} \\ \text{financial distress)}\end{matrix}$$

The costs of financial distress depend on the probability of distress and the magnitude of costs encountered if distress occurs.

Figure 18.2 shows how the trade-off between the tax benefits and the costs of distress determines optimal capital structure. PV(tax shield) initially increases as the firm borrows more. At moderate debt levels the probability of financial distress is trivial, and so PV(cost of financial distress) is small and tax advantages dominate. But at some point the probability of financial distress increases rapidly with additional borrowing; the costs of distress begin to take a substantial bite out of firm value. Also, if the firm can't be sure of profiting from the corporate tax shield, the tax advantage of additional debt is likely to dwindle and eventually disappear. The theoretical optimum is reached when the present value of tax savings due to further borrowing is just offset by increases in the present value of costs of distress. This is called the *trade-off theory* of capital structure.

Costs of financial distress cover several specific items. Now we identify these costs and try to understand what causes them.

---

[14]Graham's estimates for individual firms recognize both the uncertainty in future profits and the existence of noninterest tax shields. See J. R. Graham, "How Big Are the Tax Benefits of Debt?" *Journal of Finance* 55 (October 2000), pp. 1901–1941.

FIGURE 18.2

The value of the firm is equal to its value if all-equity-financed plus PV(tax shield) minus PV(costs of financial distress). According to the trade-off theory of capital structure, the manager should choose the debt ratio that maximizes firm value.

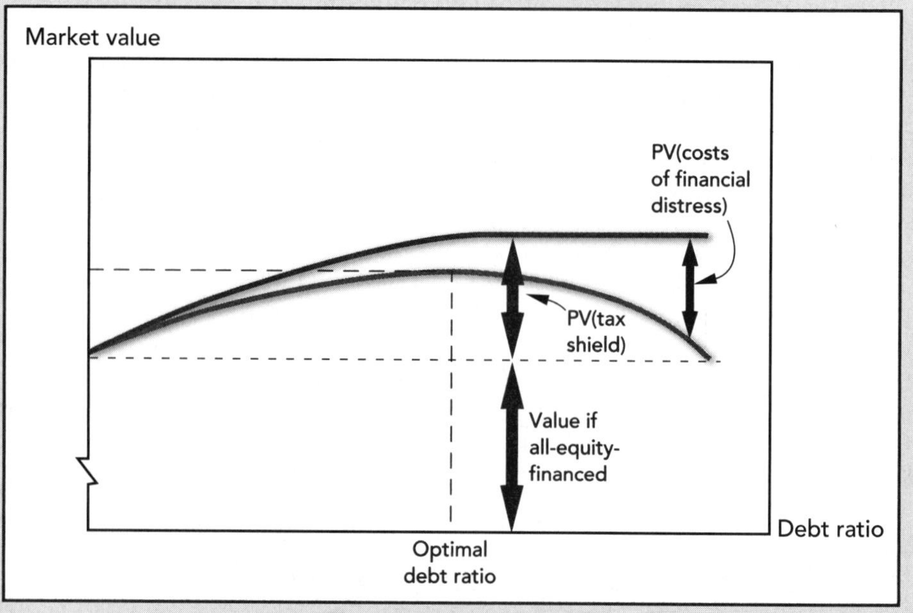

Bankruptcy Costs

You rarely hear anything nice said about corporate bankruptcy. But there is some good in almost everything. Corporate bankruptcies occur when stockholders exercise their *right to default*. That right is valuable; when a firm gets into trouble, limited liability allows stockholders simply to walk away from it, leaving all its troubles to its creditors. The former creditors become the new stockholders, and the old stockholders are left with nothing.

In our legal system all stockholders in corporations automatically enjoy limited liability. But suppose that this were not so. Suppose that there are two firms with identical assets and operations. Each firm has debt outstanding, and each has promised to repay $1,000 (principal and interest) next year. But only one of the firms, Ace Limited, enjoys limited liability. The other firm, Ace Unlimited, does not; its stockholders are personally liable for its debt.

Figure 18.3 compares next year's possible payoffs to the creditors and stockholders of these two firms. The only differences occur when next year's asset value turns out to be less than $1,000. Suppose that next year the assets of each company are worth only $500. In this case Ace Limited defaults. Its stockholders walk away; their payoff is zero. Bondholders get the assets worth $500. But Ace Unlimited's stockholders can't walk away. They have to cough up $500, the difference between asset value and the bondholders' claim. The debt is paid whatever happens.

Suppose that Ace Limited does go bankrupt. Of course, its stockholders are disappointed that their firm is worth so little, but that is an operating problem having nothing to do with financing. Given poor operating performance, the right to go bankrupt—the right to default—is a valuable privilege. As Figure 18.3 shows, Ace Limited's stockholders are in better shape than Unlimited's are.

The example illuminates a mistake people often make in thinking about the costs of bankruptcy. Bankruptcies are thought of as corporate funerals. The mourn-

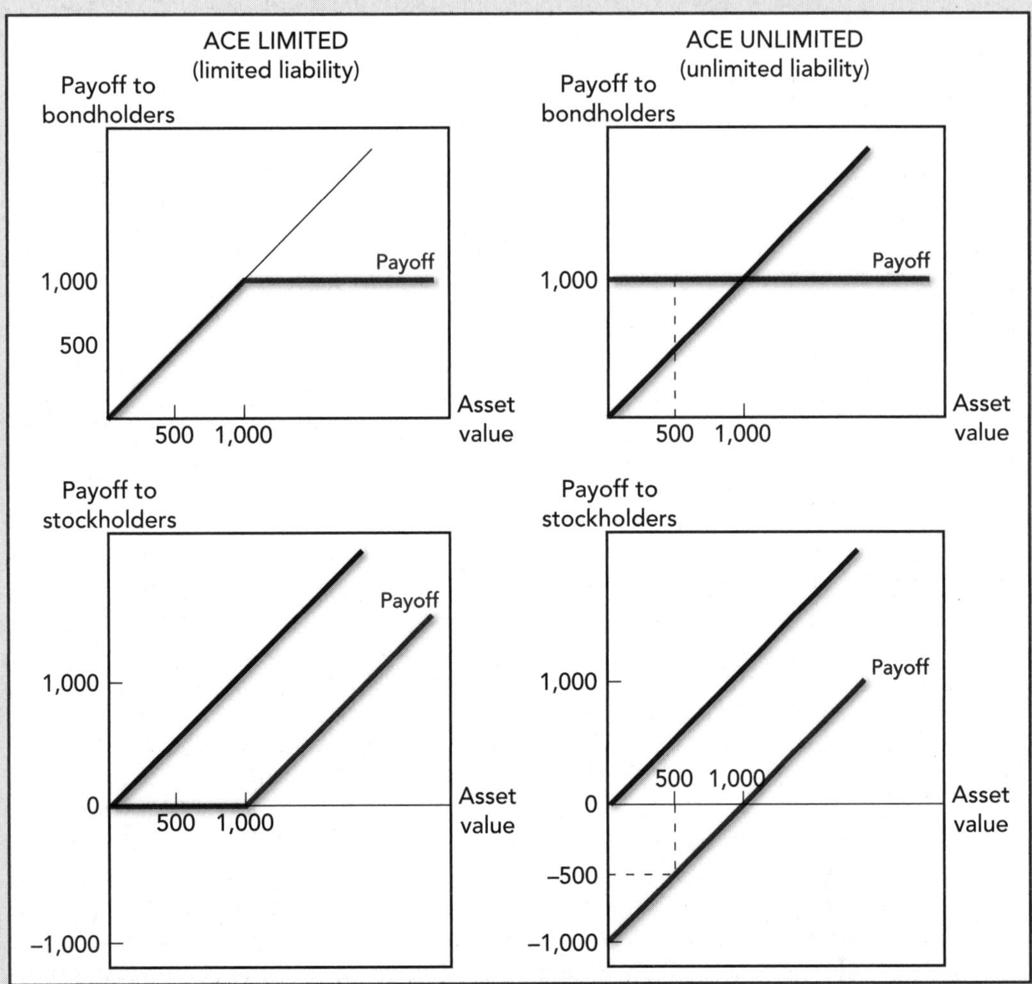

FIGURE 18.3

Comparison of limited and unlimited liability for two otherwise identical firms. If the two firms' asset values are less than $1,000, Ace Limited stockholders default and its bondholders take over the assets. Ace Unlimited stockholders keep the assets, but they must reach into their own pockets to pay off its bondholders. The total payoff to both stockholders and bondholders is the same for the two firms.

ers (creditors and especially shareholders) look at their firm's present sad state. They think of how valuable their securities used to be and how little is left. Moreover, they think of the lost value as a cost of bankruptcy. That is the mistake. The decline in the value of assets is what the mourning is really about. That has no necessary connection with financing. The bankruptcy is merely a legal mechanism for allowing creditors to take over when the decline in the value of assets triggers a default. Bankruptcy is not the *cause* of the decline in value. It is the result.

Be careful not to get cause and effect reversed. When a person dies, we do not cite the implementation of his or her will as the cause of death.

We said that bankruptcy is a legal mechanism allowing creditors to take over when a firm defaults. Bankruptcy costs are the costs of using this mechanism.

FIGURE 18.4

Total payoff to Ace Limited security holders. There is a $200 bankruptcy cost in the event of default (shaded area).

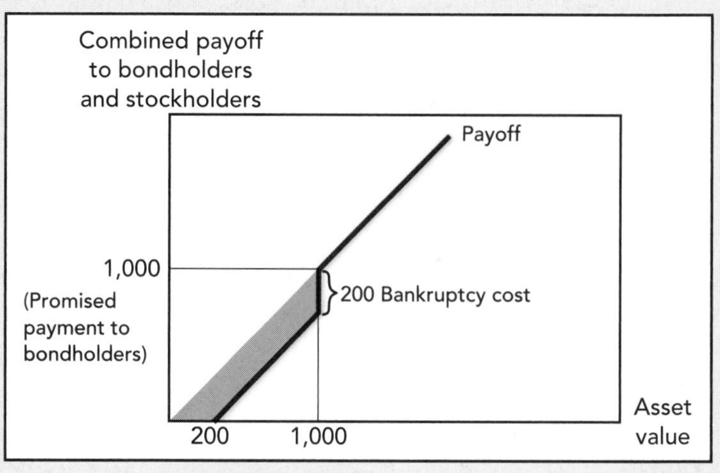

There are no bankruptcy costs at all shown in Figure 18.3. Note that only Ace Limited can default and go bankrupt. But, regardless of what happens to asset value, the *combined* payoff to the bondholders and stockholders of Ace Limited is always the same as the *combined* payoff to the bondholders and stockholders of Ace Unlimited. Thus the overall market values of the two firms now (this year) must be identical. Of course, Ace Limited's *stock* is worth more than Ace Unlimited's stock because of Ace Limited's right to default. Ace Limited's *debt* is worth correspondingly less.

Our example was not intended to be strictly realistic. Anything involving courts and lawyers cannot be free. Suppose that court and legal fees are $200 if Ace Limited defaults. The fees are paid out of the remaining value of Ace's assets. Thus if asset value turns out to be $500, creditors end up with only $300. Figure 18.4 shows next year's *total* payoff to bondholders and stockholders net of this bankruptcy cost. Ace Limited, by issuing risky debt, has given lawyers and the court system a claim on the firm if it defaults. The market value of the firm is reduced by the present value of this claim.

It is easy to see how increased leverage affects the present value of the costs of financial distress. If Ace Limited borrows more, it increases the probability of default and the value of the lawyers' claim. It increases PV (costs of financial distress) and reduces Ace's present market value.

The costs of bankruptcy come out of stockholders' pockets. Creditors foresee the costs and foresee that *they* will pay them if default occurs. For this they demand compensation in advance in the form of higher payoffs when the firm does *not* default; that is, they demand a higher promised interest rate. This reduces the possible payoffs to stockholders and reduces the present market value of their shares.

Evidence on Bankruptcy Costs

Bankruptcy costs can add up fast. Manville, which declared bankruptcy in 1982 because of expected liability for asbestos-related health claims, spent $200 million on fees before it emerged from bankruptcy in 1988.[15] While Eastern Airlines was in

[15] S. P. Sherman, "Bankruptcy's Spreading Blight," *Fortune*, June 3, 1991, pp. 123–132.

bankruptcy, it spent $114 million on professional fees.[16] Daunting as such numbers may seem, they are not a large fraction of the companies' asset values. For example, the fees incurred by Eastern amounted to only 3.5 percent of its assets when it entered bankruptcy, or about the equivalent of one jumbo jet.

Lawrence Weiss, who studied 31 firms that went bankrupt between 1980 and 1986, found average costs of about 3 percent of total book assets and 20 percent of the market value of equity in the year prior to bankruptcy. A study by Edward Altman found that costs were similar for retail companies but higher for industrial companies. Also, bankruptcy eats up a larger fraction of asset value for small companies than for large ones. There are significant economies of scale in going bankrupt.[17] Finally, a study by Andrade and Kaplan of a sample of troubled and highly leveraged firms estimated costs of financial distress amounting to 10 to 20 percent of predistress market value.[18] A breakdown of these costs of corporate bankruptcy is provided in the Finance in the News box.

Direct versus Indirect Costs of Bankruptcy

So far we have discussed the *direct* (that is, legal and administrative) costs of bankruptcy. There are indirect costs too, which are nearly impossible to measure. But we have circumstantial evidence indicating their importance.

Some of the indirect costs arise from the reluctance to do business with a firm that may not be around for long. Customers worry about the continuity of supplies and the difficulty of obtaining replacement parts if the firm ceases production. Suppliers are disinclined to put effort into servicing the firm's account and demand cash on the nail for their goods. Potential employees are unwilling to sign on and the existing staff keep slipping away from their desks for job interviews.

Managing a bankrupt firm is not easy. Consent of the bankruptcy court is required for many routine business decisions, such as the sale of assets or investment in new equipment. At best this involves time and effort; at worst the proposals are thwarted by the firm's creditors, who have little interest in the firm's long-term prosperity and would prefer the cash to be paid out to them.

Sometimes the problem is reversed: The bankruptcy court is so anxious to maintain the firm as a going concern that it allows the firm to engage in negative-NPV activities. When Eastern Airlines entered the "protection" of the bankruptcy court in 1989, it still had some valuable, profit-making routes and saleable assets such as planes and terminal facilities. The creditors would have been best served by a prompt liquidation, which probably would have generated enough cash to pay off all debt and preferred stockholders. But the bankruptcy judge was keen to keep Eastern's planes flying at all costs, so he allowed the company to sell many of its assets to fund

[16] L. Gibbs and A. Boardman, "A Billion Later, Eastern's Finally Gone," *American Lawyer Newspaper Groups*, February 6, 1995.

[17] The pioneering study of bankruptcy costs is J. B. Warner, "Bankruptcy Costs: Some Evidence," *Journal of Finance* 26 (May 1977), pp. 337–348. The Weiss and Altman papers are L. A. Weiss, "Bankruptcy Resolution: Direct Costs and Violation of Priority of Claims," *Journal of Financial Economics* 27 (October 1990), pp. 285–314, and E. I. Altman, "A Further Investigation of the Bankruptcy Cost Question," *Journal of Finance* 39 (September 1984), pp. 1067–1089.

[18] G. Andrade and S. N. Kaplan, "How Costly is Financial (not Economic) Distress? Evidence from Highly Leveraged Transactions that Became Distressed," *Journal of Finance* 53 (October 1998), pp. 1443–1493.

FINANCE IN THE NEWS

WHO CAN AFFORD TO GO BROKE?

The costs of going broke are spiralling. Consider what's happening to Pacific Gas & Electric Corp. Since seeking protection from creditors in April 2001, it has been billed more than $7 million in fees from lawyers, investment bankers, and accountants, according to court filings. The company's lead counsel has charged $2.6 million, its investment banker wants $350,000 a month and a $20 million success fee. PG&E will also have to pay the financial adviser to its creditors, which has proposed $900,000 in fees for two months' work. Industry sources figure PG&E's final tab could total $98 million.

On average a bankrupt company with $1 billion in assets pays advisers as much as $60 million to help strike a deal with creditors (see table).

Source: "Who Can Afford to Go Broke," *Business Week*, September 10, 2001, p. 116.

The High Cost of Chapter 11

Adviser	Debtor	Creditor
Lawyer	$500,000–$1 million per month	$300,000–$700,000 per month
Accountant	$200,000 per month	
Investment Banker	$200,000–$250,000 per month; $7 million–$10 million success fee	$175,000–$225,000 per month; $3 million–$8 million success fee
Total bill for $1 billion distressed company in 18 months	$23.2 million–$60.75 million	

hefty operating losses. When Eastern finally closed down after two years, it was not just bankrupt, but *administratively* insolvent: There was almost nothing for creditors, and the company was running out of cash to pay legal expenses.[19]

We do not know what the sum of direct and indirect costs of bankruptcy amounts to. We suspect it is a significant number, particularly for large firms for which proceedings would be lengthy and complex. Perhaps the best evidence is the reluctance of creditors to force bankruptcy. In principle, they would be better off to end the agony and seize the assets as soon as possible. Instead, creditors often overlook defaults in the hope of nursing the firm over a difficult period. They do this in part to avoid costs of bankruptcy.[20] There is an old financial saying, "Borrow $1,000 and you've got a banker. Borrow $10,000,000 and you've got a partner."

[19]The bankruptcy of Eastern Airlines is analyzed in L. A. Weiss and K. H. Wruck, "Information Problems, Conflicts of Interest, and Asset Stripping: Chapter 11's Failure in the Case of Eastern Airlines," *Journal of Financial Economics* 48 (1998), pp. 55–97.

[20]There is another reason. Creditors are not always given absolute priority in bankruptcy. *Absolute priority* means that creditors must be paid in full before stockholders receive a cent. Sometimes reorganizations are negotiated which provide something for everyone, even though creditors are *not* paid in full. Thus creditors can never be sure how they will fare in bankruptcy.

In all this discussion of bankruptcy costs we have said very little about bankruptcy *procedures*. These are described in the appendix at the end of Chapter 25.

Financial Distress without Bankruptcy

Not every firm that gets into trouble goes bankrupt. As long as the firm can scrape up enough cash to pay the interest on its debt, it may be able to postpone bankruptcy for many years. Eventually the firm may recover, pay off its debt, and escape bankruptcy altogether.

When a firm is in trouble, both bondholders and stockholders want it to recover, but in other respects their interests may be in conflict. In times of financial distress the security holders are like many political parties—united on generalities but threatened by squabbling on any specific issue.

Financial distress is costly when these conflicts of interest get in the way of proper operating, investment, and financing decisions. Stockholders are tempted to forsake the usual objective of maximizing the overall market value of the firm and to pursue narrower self-interest instead. They are tempted to play games at the expense of their creditors. We will now illustrate how such games can lead to costs of financial distress.

Here is the Circular File Company's book balance sheet:

Circular File Company (Book Values)

Net working capital	$ 20	$ 50	Bonds outstanding
Fixed assets	80	50	Common stock
Total assets	$100	$100	Total value

We will assume there is only one share and one bond outstanding. The stockholder is also the manager. The bondholder is somebody else.

Here is its balance sheet in market values—a clear case of financial distress, since the face value of Circular's debt ($50) exceeds the firm's total market value ($30):

Circular File Company (Market Values)

Net working capital	$20	$25	Bonds outstanding
Fixed assets	10	5	Common stock
Total assets	$30	$30	Total value

If the debt matured today, Circular's owner would default, leaving the firm bankrupt. But suppose that the bond actually matures one year hence, that there is enough cash for Circular to limp along for one year, and that the bondholder cannot "call the question" and force bankruptcy before then.

The one-year grace period explains why the Circular share still has value. Its owner is betting on a stroke of luck that will rescue the firm, allowing it to pay off the debt with something left over. The bet is a long shot—the owner wins only if firm value increases from $30 to more than $50.[21] But the owner has a secret weapon: He controls investment and operating strategy.

[21]We are not concerned here with how to work out whether $5 is a fair price for stockholders to pay for the bet. We will come to that in Chapter 20 when we discuss the valuation of options.

Risk Shifting: The First Game

Suppose that Circular has $10 cash. The following investment opportunity comes up:

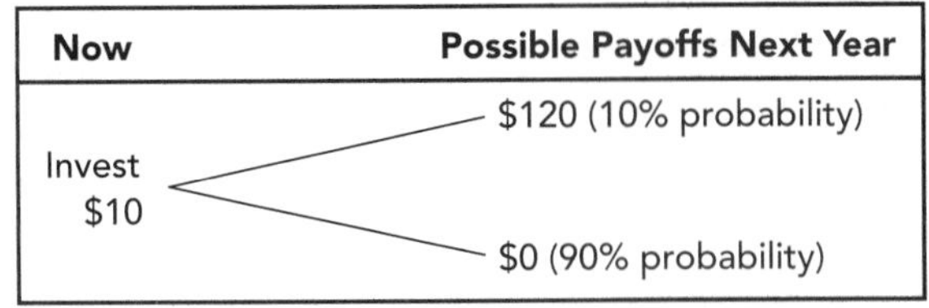

This is a wild gamble and probably a lousy project. But you can see why the owner would be tempted to take it anyway. Why not go for broke? Circular will probably go under anyway, so the owner is essentially betting with the bondholder's money. But the owner gets most of the loot if the project pays off.

Suppose that the project's NPV is −$2 but that it is undertaken anyway, thus depressing firm value by $2. Circular's new balance sheet might look like this:

Circular File Company (Market Values)

Net working capital	$10	$20	Bonds outstanding
Fixed assets	18	8	Common stock
Total assets	$28	$28	Total value

Firm value falls by $2, but the owner is $3 ahead because the bond's value has fallen by $5.[22] The $10 cash that used to stand behind the bond has been replaced by a very risky asset worth only $8.

Thus a game has been played at the expense of Circular's bondholder. The game illustrates the following general point: Stockholders of levered firms gain when business risk increases. Financial managers who act strictly in their shareholders' interests (and *against* the interests of creditors) will favor risky projects over safe ones. They may even take risky projects with negative NPVs.

This warped strategy for capital budgeting clearly is costly to the firm and to the economy as a whole. Why do we associate the costs with financial distress? Because the temptation to play is strongest when the odds of default are high. A blue-chip company like Exxon Mobil would never invest in our negative-NPV gamble. Its creditors are not vulnerable to this type of game.

Refusing to Contribute Equity Capital: The Second Game

We have seen how stockholders, acting in their immediate, narrow self-interest, may take projects that reduce the overall market value of their firm. These are errors of commission. Conflicts of interest may also lead to errors of omission.

Assume that Circular cannot scrape up any cash, and therefore cannot take that wild gamble. Instead a *good* opportunity comes up: a relatively safe asset costing $10 with a present value of $15 and NPV = +$5.

This project will not in itself rescue Circular, but it is a step in the right direction. We might therefore expect Circular to issue $10 of new stock and to go ahead with the investment. Suppose that two new shares are issued to the original owner for $10 cash. The project is taken. The new balance sheet might look like this:

[22]We are not calculating this $5 drop. We are simply using it as a plausible assumption. The tools necessary for a calculation come in Chapter 21.

Circular File Company (Market Values)

Net working capital	$20	$33	Bonds outstanding
Fixed assets	25	12	Common stock
Total assets	$45	$45	Total value

The total value of the firm goes up by $15 ($10 of new capital and $5 NPV). Notice that the Circular bond is no longer worth $25, but $33. The bondholder receives a capital gain of $8 because the firm's assets include a new, safe asset worth $15. The probability of default is less, and the payoff to the bondholder if default occurs is larger.

The stockholder loses what the bondholder gains. Equity value goes up not by $15 but by $15 − $8 = $7. The owner puts in $10 of fresh equity capital but gains only $7 in market value. Going ahead is in the firm's interest but not the owner's.

Again, our example illustrates a general point. If we hold business risk constant, any increase in firm value is shared among bondholders and stockholders. The value of any investment opportunity to the firm's *stockholders* is reduced because project benefits must be shared with bondholders. Thus it may not be in the stockholders' self-interest to contribute fresh equity capital even if that means forgoing positive-NPV investment opportunities.

This problem theoretically affects all levered firms, but it is most serious when firms land in financial distress. The greater the probability of default, the more bondholders have to gain from investments that increase firm value.

And Three More Games, Briefly

As with other games, the temptation to play the next three games is particularly strong in financial distress.

Cash In and Run Stockholders may be reluctant to put money into a firm in financial distress, but they are happy to take the money out—in the form of a cash dividend, for example. The market value of the firm's stock goes down by less than the amount of the dividend paid, because the decline in *firm* value is shared with creditors. This game is just "refusing to contribute equity capital" run in reverse.

Playing for Time When the firm is in financial distress, creditors would like to salvage what they can by forcing the firm to settle up. Naturally, stockholders want to delay this as long as they can. There are various devious ways of doing this, for example, through accounting changes designed to conceal the true extent of trouble, by encouraging false hopes of spontaneous recovery, or by cutting corners on maintenance, research and development, and so on, in order to make this year's operating performance look better.

Bait and Switch This game is not always played in financial distress, but it is a quick way to get *into* distress. You start with a conservative policy, issuing a limited amount of relatively safe debt. Then you suddenly switch and issue a lot more. That makes all your debt risky, imposing a capital loss on the "old" bondholders. Their capital loss is the stockholders' gain.

The most dramatic example of bait and switch occurred in October 1988, when the management of RJR Nabisco announced its intention to acquire the company in a *leveraged buy-out* (LBO). This put the company "in play" for a transaction in which existing shareholders would be bought out and the company would be "taken private." The cost of the buy-out would be almost entirely debt-financed. The new private company would start life with an extremely high debt ratio.

RJR Nabisco had debt outstanding with a market value of about $2.4 billion. The announcement of the coming LBO drove down this market value by $298 million.[23]

What the Games Cost

Why should anyone object to these games so long as they are played by consenting adults? Because playing them means poor decisions about investments and operations. These poor decisions are *agency costs* of borrowing.

The more the firm borrows, the greater is the temptation to play the games (assuming the financial manager acts in the stockholders' interest). The increased odds of poor decisions in the future prompt investors to mark down the present market value of the firm. The fall in value comes out of the shareholders' pockets. Therefore it is ultimately in their interest to avoid temptation. The easiest way to do this is to limit borrowing to levels at which the firm's debt is safe or close to it.

Banks and other corporate lenders are also not financial innocents. They realize that games may be played at their expense and so protect themselves by rationing the amount that they will lend or by imposing restrictions on the company's actions. For example, consider the case of Henrietta Ketchup, a budding entrepreneur with two possible investment projects that offer the following payoffs:

	Investment	Payoff	Probability of Payoff
Project 1	−12	+15	1.0
Project 2	−12	+24	.5
		0	.5

Project 1 is surefire and very profitable; project 2 is risky and a rotten project. Ms. Ketchup now approaches her bank and asks to borrow the present value of $10 (she will find the remaining money out of her own purse). The bank calculates that the payoff will be split as follows:

	Expected Payoff to Bank	Expected Payoff to Ms. Ketchup
Project 1	+10	+5
Project 2	$(.5 \times 10) + (.5 \times 0) = +5$	$.5 \times (24 - 10) = +7$

If Ms. Ketchup accepts project 1, the bank's debt is certain to be paid in full; if she accepts project 2, there is only a 50 percent chance of payment and the expected payoff to the bank is only $5. Unfortunately, Ms. Ketchup will prefer to take project 2, for if things go well, she gets most of the profit, and if they go badly, the bank bears most of the loss. Unless Ms. Ketchup can convince the bank that she will not gamble with its money, the bank will limit the amount that it is prepared to lend.[24]

[23]We thank Paul Asquith for these figures. RJR Nabisco was finally taken private not by its management but by another LBO partnership. We discuss this LBO in Chapter 34.

[24]You might think that, if the bank suspects Ms. Ketchup will undertake project 2, it should just raise the interest rate on its loan. In this case Ms. Ketchup will not want to take on project 2 (they can't both be happy with a lousy project). But Ms. Ketchup also would not want to pay a high rate of interest if she is going to take on project 1 (she would do better to borrow less money at the risk-free rate). So simply raising the interest rate is not the answer.

How can Ms. Ketchup reassure the bank of her intentions? The obvious answer is to give it veto power over potentially dangerous decisions. There we have the ultimate economic rationale for all that fine print backing up corporate debt. Debt contracts frequently limit dividends or equivalent transfers of wealth to stockholders; the firm may not be allowed to pay out more than it earns, for example. Additional borrowing is almost always limited. For example, many companies are prevented by existing bond indentures from issuing any additional long-term debt unless their ratio of earnings to interest charges exceeds 2.0.[25]

Sometimes firms are restricted from selling assets or making major investment outlays except with the lenders' consent. The risks of playing for time are reduced by specifying accounting procedures and by giving lenders access to the firm's books and its financial forecasts.

Of course, fine print cannot be a complete solution for firms that insist on issuing risky debt. The fine print has its own costs; you have to spend money to save money. Obviously a complex debt contract costs more to negotiate than a simple one. Afterward it costs the lender more to monitor the firm's performance. Lenders anticipate monitoring costs and demand compensation in the form of higher interest rates; thus the monitoring costs—another agency cost of debt—are ultimately paid by stockholders.

Perhaps the most severe costs of the fine print stem from the constraints it places on operating and investment decisions. For example, an attempt to prevent the risk-shifting game may also prevent the firm from pursuing *good* investment opportunities. At the minimum there are delays in clearing major investments with lenders. In some cases lenders may veto high-risk investments even if net present value is positive. Lenders can lose from risk shifting even when the firm's overall market value increases. In fact, the lenders may try to play a game of their own, forcing the firm to stay in cash or low-risk assets even if good projects are forgone.

Thus, debt contracts cannot cover every possible manifestation of the games we have just discussed. Any attempt to do so would be hopelessly expensive and doomed to failure in any event. Human imagination is insufficient to conceive of all the possible things that could go wrong. We will always find surprises coming at us on dimensions we never thought to think about.

We hope we have not left the impression that managers and stockholders always succumb to temptation unless restrained. Usually they refrain voluntarily, not only from a sense of fair play but also on pragmatic grounds: A firm or individual that makes a killing today at the expense of a creditor will be coldly received when the time comes to borrow again. Aggressive game playing is done only by out-and-out crooks and by firms in extreme financial distress. Firms limit borrowing precisely because they don't wish to land in distress and be exposed to the temptation to play.

Costs of Distress Vary with Type of Asset

Suppose your firm's only asset is a large downtown hotel, mortgaged to the hilt. The recession hits, occupancy rates fall, and the mortgage payments cannot be met. The lender takes over and sells the hotel to a new owner and operator. You use your firm's stock certificates for wallpaper.

What is the cost of bankruptcy? In this example, probably very little. The value of the hotel is, of course, much less than you hoped, but that is due to the lack of

[25]We discuss covenants and the rest of the fine print in debt contracts in Section 25.6.

guests, not to the bankruptcy. Bankruptcy doesn't damage the hotel itself. The direct bankruptcy costs are restricted to items such as legal and court fees, real estate commissions, and the time the lender spends sorting things out.[26]

Suppose we repeat the story of Heartbreak Hotel for Fledgling Electronics. Everything is the same, except for the underlying real assets—not real estate but a high-tech going concern, a growth company whose most valuable assets are technology, investment opportunities, and its employees' human capital.

If Fledgling gets into trouble, the stockholders may be reluctant to put up money to cash in on its growth opportunities. Failure to invest is likely to be much more serious for Fledgling than for a company like Heartbreak Hotel.

If Fledgling finally defaults on its debt, the lender will find it much more difficult to cash in by selling off the assets. Many of them are intangibles which have value only as a part of a going concern.

Could Fledgling be kept as a going concern through default and reorganization? It may not be as hopeless as putting a wedding cake through a car wash, but there are a number of serious difficulties. First, the odds of defections by key employees are higher than they would be if the firm had never gotten into financial trouble. Special guarantees may have to be given to customers who have doubts about whether the firm will be around to service its products. Aggressive investment in new products and technology will be difficult; each class of creditors will have to be convinced that it is in its interest for the firm to invest new money in risky ventures.

Some assets, like good commercial real estate, can pass through bankruptcy and reorganization largely unscathed; the values of other assets are likely to be considerably diminished. The losses are greatest for the intangible assets that are linked to the health of the firm as a going concern—for example, technology, human capital, and brand image. That may be why debt ratios are low in the pharmaceutical industry, where value depends on continued success in research and development, and in many service industries where value depends on human capital. We can also understand why highly profitable growth companies, such as Microsoft or Pfizer, use mostly equity finance.[27]

The moral of these examples is this: *Do not think only about the probability that borrowing will bring trouble. Think also of the value that may be lost if trouble comes.*

The Trade-off Theory of Capital Structure

Financial managers often think of the firm's debt–equity decision as a trade-off between interest tax shields and the costs of financial distress. Of course, there is controversy about how valuable interest tax shields are and what kinds of financial

---

[26]In 1989 the Rockefeller family sold 80 percent of Rockefeller Center—several acres of extremely valuable Manhattan real estate—to Mitsubishi Estate Company for $1.4 billion. A REIT, Rockefeller Center Properties, held a $1.3 billion mortgage loan (the REIT's only asset) secured by this real estate. But rents and occupancy rates did not meet forecasts, and by 1995 Mitsubishi had incurred losses of about $600 million. Then Mitsubishi quit, and Rockefeller Center was bankrupt. That triggered a complicated series of maneuvers and negotiations. But did this damage the value of the Rockefeller Center properties? Was Radio City Music Hall, one of the properties, any less valuable because of the bankruptcy? We doubt it.

[27]Empirical research confirms that firms holding largely intangible assets borrow less. See, for example, M. Long and I. Malitz, "The Investment-Financing Nexus: Some Empirical Evidence," *Midland Corporate Finance Journal* 3 (Fall 1985), pp. 53–59.

trouble are most threatening, but these disagreements are only variations on a theme. Thus, Figure 18.2 illustrates the debt–equity trade-off.

This *trade-off theory* of capital structure recognizes that target debt ratios may vary from firm to firm. Companies with safe, tangible assets and plenty of taxable income to shield ought to have high target ratios. Unprofitable companies with risky, intangible assets ought to rely primarily on equity financing.

If there were no costs of adjusting capital structure, then each firm should always be at its target debt ratio. However, there are costs, and therefore delays, in adjusting to the optimum. Firms cannot immediately offset the random events that bump them away from their capital structure targets, so we should see random differences in actual debt ratios among firms having the same target debt ratio.

All in all, this trade-off theory of capital structure choice tells a comforting story. Unlike MM's theory, which seemed to say that firms should take on as much debt as possible, it avoids extreme predictions and rationalizes moderate debt ratios.

But what are the facts? Can the trade-off theory of capital structure explain how companies actually behave?

The answer is "yes and no." On the "yes" side, the trade-off theory successfully explains many industry differences in capital structure. High-tech growth companies, for example, whose assets are risky and mostly intangible, normally use relatively little debt. Airlines can and do borrow heavily because their assets are tangible and relatively safe.[28]

The trade-off theory also helps explain what kinds of companies "go private" in LBOs. LBOs are acquisitions of public companies by private investors who finance a large fraction of the purchase price with debt. The target companies for LBO takeovers are usually mature, cash-cow businesses with established markets for their products but little in the way of high-NPV growth opportunities. That makes sense by the trade-off theory, because these are exactly the kind of companies that *ought* to have high debt ratios.

The trade-off theory also says that companies saddled with extra heavy debt—too much to pay down with a couple of years' internally generated cash—should issue stock, constrain dividends, or sell off assets to raise cash to rebalance capital structure. Here again, we can find plenty of confirming examples. When Texaco bought Getty Petroleum in January 1984, it borrowed $8 billion from a consortium of banks to help finance the acquisition. (The loan was arranged and paid over to Texaco within two weeks!) By the end of 1984, it had raised about $1.8 billion to pay down this debt, mostly by selling assets and forgoing dividend increases. Chrysler, when it emerged from near-bankruptcy in 1983, sold $432 million of new common stock to help regain a conservative capital structure.[29] In 1991, after a second brush with bankruptcy, it again sold shares to replenish equity, this time for $350 million.[30]

[28]We are not suggesting that all airline companies are safe; many are not. But air*craft* can support debt where air*lines* cannot. If Fly-by-Night Airlines fails, its planes retain their value in another airline's operations. There's a good secondary market in used aircraft, so a loan secured by aircraft can be well protected even if made to an airline flying on thin ice (and in the dark).

[29]Note that Chrysler issued stock *after* it emerged from financial distress. It did not *prevent* financial distress by raising equity money when trouble loomed on its horizon. Why not? Refer back to "Refusing to Contribute Equity Capital: The Second Game" or forward to the analysis of asymmetric information in Section 18.4.

[30]Chrysler simultaneously contributed $300 million of newly issued shares to its underfunded pension plans.

On the "no" side, there are a few things the trade-off theory cannot explain. It cannot explain why some of the most successful companies thrive with little debt. Think of Pfizer, which as Table 18.3(*a*) shows, is basically all-equity-financed. Granted, Pfizer's most valuable assets are intangible, the fruits of its pharmaceutical research and development. We know that intangible assets and conservative capital structures go together. But Pfizer also has a very large corporate income tax bill (over $2 billion in 2000) and the highest possible credit rating. It could borrow enough to save tens of millions of dollars without raising a whisker of concern about possible financial distress.

Pfizer illustrates an odd fact about real-life capital structures: The most profitable companies commonly borrow the least.[31] Here the trade-off theory fails, for it predicts exactly the reverse. Under the trade-off theory, high profits should mean more debt-servicing capacity and more taxable income to shield and so should give a *higher* target debt ratio.[32]

In general it appears that public companies rarely make major shifts in capital structure just because of taxes,[33] and it is hard to detect the present value of interest tax shields in firms' market values.[34]

A final point on the "no" side for the trade-off theory: Debt ratios today are no higher than they were in the early 1900s, when income tax rates were low (or zero). Debt ratios in other industrialized countries are equal to or higher than those in the United States. Many of these countries have imputation tax systems, which should eliminate the value of the interest tax shields.[35]

None of this disproves the trade-off theory. As George Stigler emphasized, theories are not rejected by circumstantial evidence; it takes a theory to beat a theory. So we now turn to a completely different theory of financing.

---

[31]For example, in an international comparison Wald found that profitability was the single largest determinant of firm capital structure. See J. K. Wald, "How Firm Characteristics Affect Capital Structure: An International Comparison," *Journal of Financial Research* 22 (Summer 1999), pp. 161–187.

[32]Here we mean debt as a fraction of the book or replacement value of the company's assets. Profitable companies might not borrow a greater fraction of their market value. Higher profits imply higher market value as well as stronger incentives to borrow.

[33]Mackie-Mason found that tax-paying companies are more likely to issue debt (vs. equity) than non-taxpaying companies. This shows that taxes do affect financing choices. However, it is not necessarily evidence for the static trade-off theory. Look back to Section 18.2, and note the special case where corporate and personal taxes cancel to make debt policy irrelevant. In that case, taxpaying firms would see no net tax advantage to debt: corporate interest tax shields would be offset by the taxes paid by investors in the firm's debt. But the balance would tip in favor of equity for a firm that was losing money and reaping no benefits from interest tax shields. See J. Mackie-Mason, "Do Taxes Affect Corporate Financing Decisions?" *Journal of Finance* 45 (December 1990), pp. 1471–1493.

[34]A study by E. F. Fama and K. R. French, covering over 2,000 firms from 1965 to 1992, failed to find any evidence that interest tax shields contributed to firm value. See "Taxes, Financing Decisions and Firm Value," *Journal of Finance* 53 (June 1998), pp. 819–843.

[35]We described the Australian imputation tax system in Section 16.7. Look again at Table 16.3, supposing that an Australian corporation pays $A10 of interest. This reduces the corporate tax by $A3.00; it also reduces the tax credit taken by the shareholders by $A3.00. The final tax does not depend on whether the corporation or the shareholder borrows.

You can check this by redrawing Figure 18.1 for the Australian system. The corporate tax rate T_c will cancel out. Since income after all taxes depends only on investors' tax rates, there is no special advantage to corporate borrowing.

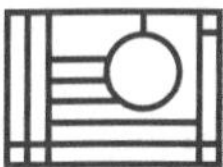

18.4 THE PECKING ORDER OF FINANCING CHOICES

The pecking-order theory starts with *asymmetric information*—a fancy term indicating that managers know more about their companies' prospects, risks, and values than do outside investors.

Managers obviously know more than investors. We can prove that by observing stock price changes caused by announcements by managers. When a company announces an increased regular dividend, stock price typically rises, because investors interpret the increase as a sign of management's confidence in future earnings. In other words, the dividend increase transfers information from managers to investors. This can happen only if managers know more in the first place.

Asymmetric information affects the choice between internal and external financing and between new issues of debt and equity securities. This leads to a *pecking order*, in which investment is financed first with internal funds, reinvested earnings primarily; then by new issues of debt; and finally with new issues of equity. New equity issues are a last resort when the company runs out of debt capacity, that is, when the threat of costs of financial distress brings regular insomnia to existing creditors and to the financial manager.

We will take a closer look at the pecking order in a moment. First, you must appreciate how asymmetric information can force the financial manager to issue debt rather than common stock.

Debt and Equity Issues with Asymmetric Information

To the outside world Smith & Company and Jones, Inc., our two example companies, are identical. Each runs a successful business with good growth opportunities. The two businesses are risky, however, and investors have learned from experience that current expectations are frequently bettered or disappointed. Current expectations price each company's stock at $100 per share, but the true values could be higher or lower:

	Smith & Co.	Jones, Inc.
True value could be higher, say	$120	$120
Best current estimate	100	100
True value could be lower, say	80	80

Now suppose that both companies need to raise new money from investors to fund capital investment. They can do this either by issuing bonds or by issuing new shares of common stock. How would the choice be made? One financial manager—we will not tell you which one—might reason as follows:

> Sell stock for $100 per share? Ridiculous! It's worth at least $120. A stock issue now would hand a free gift to new investors. I just wish those stupid, skeptical shareholders would appreciate the true value of this company. Our new factories will make us the world's lowest-cost producer. We've painted a rosy picture for the press and security analysts, but it just doesn't seem to be working. Oh well, the decision is obvious: we'll issue debt, not underpriced equity. A debt issue will save underwriting fees too.

The other financial manager is in a different mood:

> Beefalo burgers were a hit for a while, but it looks like the fad is fading. The fast-food division's gotta find some good new products or it's all downhill from here. Export markets are OK for now, but how are we going to compete with those new Siberian ranches? Fortunately the stock price has held up pretty well—we've had some good short-run news for the press and security analysts. Now's the time to issue stock. We have major investments underway, and why add increased debt service to my other worries?

Of course, outside investors can't read the financial managers' minds. If they could, one stock might trade at $120 and the other at $80.

Why doesn't the optimistic financial manager simply educate investors? Then the company could sell stock on fair terms, and there would be no reason to favor debt over equity or vice versa.

This is not so easy. (Note that both companies are issuing upbeat press releases.) Investors can't be told what to think; they have to be convinced. That takes a detailed layout of the company's plans and prospects, including the inside scoop on new technology, product design, marketing plans, and so on. Getting this across is expensive for the company and also valuable to its competitors. Why go to the trouble? Investors will learn soon enough, as revenues and earnings evolve. In the meantime the optimistic financial manager can finance growth by issuing debt.

Now suppose there are two press releases:

> Jones, Inc., will issue $120 million of five-year senior notes.
>
> Smith & Co. announced plans today to issue 1.2 million new shares of common stock. The company expects to raise $120 million.

As a rational investor, you immediately learn two things. First, Jones's financial manager is optimistic and Smith's is pessimistic. Second, Smith's financial manager is also stupid to think that investors would pay $100 per share. The *attempt* to sell stock shows that it must be worth less. Smith might sell stock at $80 per share, but certainly not at $100.[36]

Smart financial managers think this through ahead of time. The end result? Both Smith and Jones end up issuing debt. Jones, Inc., issues debt because its financial manager is optimistic and doesn't want to issue undervalued equity. A smart, but pessimistic, financial manager at Smith issues debt because an attempt to issue equity would force the stock price down and eliminate any advantage from doing so. (Issuing equity also reveals the manager's pessimism immediately. Most managers prefer to wait. A debt issue lets bad news come out later through other channels.)

The story of Smith and Jones illustrates how asymmetric information favors debt issues over equity issues. If managers are better informed than investors and both groups are rational, then any company that can borrow will do so rather than issuing fresh equity. In other words, debt issues will be higher in the pecking order.

Taken literally this reasoning seems to rule out any issue of equity. That's not right, because asymmetric information is not always important and there are other forces at work. For example, if Smith had already borrowed heavily, and would risk financial distress by borrowing more, then it would have a good reason to issue common stock. In this case announcement of a stock issue would not be en-

[36] A Smith stock issue might not succeed even at $80. Persistence in trying to sell at $80 could convince investors that the stock is worth even less!

tirely bad news. The announcement would still depress the stock price—it would highlight managers' concerns about financial distress—but the fall in price would not necessarily make the issue unwise or infeasible.

High-tech, high-growth companies can also be credible issuers of common stock. Such companies' assets are mostly intangible, and bankruptcy or financial distress would be especially costly. This calls for conservative financing. The only way to grow rapidly and keep a conservative debt ratio is to issue equity. If investors see equity issued for these reasons, problems of the sort encountered by Jones's financial manager become much less serious.

With such exceptions noted, asymmetric information can explain the dominance of debt financing over new equity issues in practice. Debt issues are frequent; equity issues, rare. The bulk of external financing comes from debt, even in the United States, where equity markets are highly information-efficient. Equity issues are even more difficult in countries with less well developed stock markets.

None of this says that firms ought to strive for high debt ratios—just that it's better to raise equity by plowing back earnings than issuing stock. In fact, a firm with ample internally generated funds doesn't have to sell any kind of security and thus avoids issue costs and information problems completely.[37]

Implications of the Pecking Order

The pecking-order theory of corporate financing goes like this.[38]

1. Firms prefer internal finance.
2. They adapt their target dividend payout ratios to their investment opportunities, while trying to avoid sudden changes in dividends.
3. Sticky dividend policies, plus unpredictable fluctuations in profitability and investment opportunities, mean that internally generated cash flow is sometimes more than capital expenditures and other times less. If it is more, the firm pays off debt or invests in marketable securities. If it is less, the firm first draws down its cash balance or sells its marketable securities.
4. If external finance is required, firms issue the safest security first. That is, they start with debt, then possibly hybrid securities such as convertible bonds, then perhaps equity as a last resort.

In this theory, there is no well-defined target debt–equity mix, because there are two kinds of equity, internal and external, one at the top of the pecking order and one at the bottom. Each firm's observed debt ratio reflects its cumulative requirements for external finance.

The pecking order explains why the most profitable firms generally borrow less—not because they have low target debt ratios but because they don't need outside money. Less profitable firms issue debt because they do not have internal funds sufficient for their capital investment programs and because debt financing is first on the pecking order of *external* financing.

[37]Even debt issues can create information problems if the odds of default are significant. A pessimistic manager may try to issue debt quickly, before bad news gets out. An optimistic manager will delay pending good news, perhaps arranging a short-term bank loan in the meantime. Rational investors will take this behavior into account in pricing the risky debt issue.

[38]The description is paraphrased from S. C. Myers, "The Capital Structure Puzzle," *Journal of Finance* 39 (July 1984), pp. 581–582. For the most part, this section follows Myers's arguments.

In the pecking-order theory, the attraction of interest tax shields is assumed to be a second-order effect. Debt ratios change when there is an imbalance of internal cash flow, net of dividends, and real investment opportunities. Highly profitable firms with limited investment opportunities work down to low debt ratios. Firms whose investment opportunities outrun internally generated funds are driven to borrow more and more.

This theory explains the inverse intraindustry relationship between profitability and financial leverage. Suppose firms generally invest to keep up with the growth of their industries. Then rates of investment will be similar within an industry. Given sticky dividend payouts, the least profitable firms will have less internal funds and will end up borrowing more.

The pecking order seems to predict changes in many mature firms' debt ratios to a T. These companies' debt ratios increase when the firms have financial deficits and decline when they have surpluses.[39] If asymmetric information makes major equity issues or retirements rare, this behavior is nearly inevitable.

The pecking order is less successful in explaining *inter*industry differences in debt ratios. For example, debt ratios tend to be low in high-tech, high-growth industries, even when the need for external capital is great. There are also mature, stable industries—electric utilities, for example—in which ample cash flow is *not* used to pay down debt. High dividend payout ratios give the cash flow back to investors instead.

Financial Slack

Other things equal, it's better to be at the top of the pecking order than at the bottom. Firms that have worked down the pecking order and need external equity may end up living with excessive debt or passing by good investments because shares can't be sold at what managers consider a fair price.

In other words, *financial slack* is valuable. Having financial slack means having cash, marketable securities, readily saleable real assets, and ready access to the debt markets or to bank financing. Ready access basically requires conservative financing so that potential lenders see the company's debt as a safe investment.

In the long run, a company's value rests more on its capital investment and operating decisions than on financing. Therefore, you want to make sure your firm has sufficient financial slack so that financing is quickly available for good investments. Financial slack is most valuable to firms with plenty of positive-NPV growth opportunities. That is another reason why growth companies usually aspire to conservative capital structures.

Free Cash Flow and the Dark Side of Financial Slack[40]

There is also a dark side to financial slack. Too much of it may encourage managers to take it easy, expand their perks, or empire-build with cash that should be paid back to stockholders. In other words, slack can make agency problems worse.

Michael Jensen has stressed the tendency of managers with ample free cash flow (or unnecessary financial slack) to plow too much cash into mature businesses or

---

[39]See L. Shyam Sunder and S. C. Myers, "Testing Static Tradeoff Against Pecking Order Models of Capital Structure," *Journal of Financial Economics* 51 (February 1999), pp. 219–244.

[40]Some of the following is drawn from S. C. Myers, "Still Searching for Optimal Capital Structure," *Journal of Applied Corporate Finance* 6 (Spring 1993), pp. 4–14.

ill-advised acquisitions. "The problem," Jensen says, "is how to motivate managers to disgorge the cash rather than investing it below the cost of capital or wasting it in organizational inefficiencies."[41]

If that's the problem, then maybe debt is an answer. Scheduled interest and principal payments are contractual obligations of the firm. Debt forces the firm to pay out cash. Perhaps the best debt level would leave just enough cash in the bank, after debt service, to finance all positive-NPV projects, with not a penny left over.

We do not recommend this degree of fine-tuning, but the idea is valid and important. Debt can discipline managers who are tempted to invest too much. It can also provide the pressure to force improvements in operating efficiency. We pick up this theme again in Chapters 33 and 34.

[41] M. C. Jensen, "Agency Costs of Free Cash Flow, Corporate Finance and Takeovers," *American Economic Review* 26 (May 1986), p. 323.

SUMMARY

Visit us at www.mhhe.com/bm7e

Our task in this chapter was to show why capital structure matters. We did not throw away MM's proposition I, that capital structure is irrelevant; we added to it. However, we did not arrive at any simple, satisfactory theory of optimal capital structure.

The traditional trade-off theory emphasizes taxes and financial distress. The value of the firm is broken down as

$$\text{Value if all-equity-financed} + \text{PV(tax shield)} - \text{PV(costs of financial distress)}$$

According to this theory, the firm should increase debt until the value from PV(tax shield) is just offset, at the margin, by increases in PV(costs of financial distress).

The costs of financial distress can be broken down as follows:

1. Bankruptcy costs
   a. Direct costs such as court fees.
   b. Indirect costs reflecting the difficulty of managing a company undergoing liquidation or reorganization.
2. Costs of financial distress short of bankruptcy
   a. Conflicts of interest between bondholders and stockholders of firms in financial distress may lead to poor operating and investment decisions. Stockholders acting in their narrow self-interest can gain at the expense of creditors by playing "games" that reduce the overall value of the firm.
   b. The fine print in debt contracts is designed to prevent these games. But fine print increases the costs of writing, monitoring, and enforcing the debt contract.

The value of the tax shield is more controversial. It would be easy to compute if we had only corporate taxes to worry about. In that case the net tax saving from borrowing would be just the marginal corporate tax rate T_c times $r_D D$, the interest payment. This tax shield is usually valued by discounting at the borrowing rate r_D. In the special case of fixed, permanent debt

$$\text{PV(tax shield)} = \frac{T_c(r_D D)}{r_D} = T_c D$$

However, corporate taxes are only part of the story. If investors are subject to higher taxes on interest income than on equity income (dividends and capital gains), they will be reluctant to hold corporate debt and will do so only if they are compensated by a sufficiently attractive rate of interest. Thus, ultimately firms end up paying for any additional personal taxes that are levied on debtholders. The personal tax disadvantage of debt is smaller today than it once was, but it probably still offsets to some degree the corporate tax advantage.

We suggest that borrowing may make sense for some firms but not for others. If a firm can be fairly sure of earning a profit, there is likely to be a net tax saving from borrowing. However, for firms that are unlikely to earn sufficient profits to benefit from the corporate tax shield, there is little, if any, net tax advantage to borrowing. For these firms the net tax saving could even be negative.

The trade-off theory balances the tax advantages of borrowing against the costs of financial distress. Corporations are supposed to pick a target capital structure that maximizes firm value. Firms with safe, tangible assets and plenty of taxable income to shield ought to have high targets. Unprofitable companies with risky, intangible assets ought to rely primarily on equity financing.

This theory of capital structure successfully explains many industry differences in capital structure, but it does not explain why the most profitable firms *within* an industry generally have the most conservative capital structures. Under the trade-off theory, high profitability should mean high debt capacity *and* a strong corporate tax incentive to use that capacity.

There is a competing, pecking-order theory, which states that firms use internal financing when available and choose debt over equity when external financing is required. This explains why the less profitable firms in an industry borrow more—not because they have higher target debt ratios but because they need more external financing and because debt is next on the pecking order when internal funds are exhausted.

The pecking order is a consequence of asymmetric information. Managers know more about their firms than outside investors do, and they are reluctant to issue stock when they believe the price is too low. They try to time issues when shares are fairly priced or overpriced. Investors understand this, and interpret a decision to issue shares as bad news. That explains why stock price usually falls when a stock issue is announced.

Debt is better than equity when these information problems are important. Optimistic managers will prefer debt to undervalued equity, and pessimistic managers will be pressed to follow suit. The pecking-order theory says that equity will be issued only when debt capacity is running out and financial distress threatens.

The pecking-order theory is clearly not 100 percent right. There are many examples of equity issued by companies that could easily have borrowed. But the theory does explain why most external financing comes from debt, and it explains why changes in debt ratios tend to follow requirements for external financing.

The pecking-order theory stresses the value of financial slack. Without sufficient slack, the firm may be caught at the bottom of the pecking order and be forced to choose between issuing undervalued shares, borrowing and risking financial distress, or passing up positive-NPV investment opportunities.

There is, however, a dark side to financial slack. Surplus cash or credit tempts managers to overinvest or to indulge an easy and glamorous corporate lifestyle. When temptation wins, or threatens to win, a high debt ratio can help: It forces the company to disgorge cash and prods managers and organizations to try harder to be more efficient.

FURTHER READING

Modigliani and Miller's analysis of the present value of interest tax shields at the corporate level is in:

F. Modigliani and M. H. Miller: "Corporate Income Taxes and the Cost of Capital: A Correction," *American Economic Review*, 53:433–443 (June 1963).

F. Modigliani and M. H. Miller: "Some Estimates of the Cost of Capital to the Electric Utility Industry, 1954–57," *American Economic Review*, 56:333–391 (June 1966).

Miller extends the MM model to personal as well as corporate taxes. DeAngelo and Masulis argue that firms with plenty of noninterest tax shields, for example, shields from depreciation, should borrow less. Graham's estimates of the tax benefits of debt recognize the possibility that firms will not earn taxable profits in the future:

M. H. Miller: "Debt and Taxes," *Journal of Finance*, 32:261–276 (May 1977).

H. DeAngelo and R. Masulis: "Optimal Capital Structure under Corporate Taxation," *Journal of Financial Economics*, 8:5–29 (March 1980).

J. R. Graham: "How Big Are the Tax Benefits of Debt?" *Journal of Finance*, 55:1901–1941 (October 2000).

The following articles analyze the conflicts of interest between bondholders and stockholders and their implications for financing policy (do not read the last article until you have read Chapter 20):

M. C. Jensen and W. H. Meckling: "Theory of the Firm: Managerial Behavior, Agency Costs and Ownership Structure," *Journal of Financial Economics*, 3:305–360 (October 1976).

S. C. Myers: "Determinants of Corporate Borrowing," *Journal of Financial Economics*, 5:146–175 (1977).

D. Galai and R. W. Masulis: "The Option Pricing Model and the Risk Factor of Stock," *Journal of Financial Economics*, 3:53–82 (January–March 1976).

Myers describes the pecking-order theory, which is in turn based on work by Myers and Majluf; Baskin and Shyam-Sunder and Myers survey some of the evidence for that theory:

S. C. Myers: "The Capital Structure Puzzle," *Journal of Finance*, 39:575–592 (July 1984).

S. C. Myers and N. S. Majluf: "Corporate Financing and Investment Decisions When Firms Have Information Investors Do Not Have," *Journal of Financial Economics*, 13:187–222 (June 1984).

J. Baskin: "An Empirical Investigation of the Pecking Order Hypothesis," *Financial Management*, 18:26–35 (Spring 1989).

L. Shyam-Sunder and S. C. Myers: "Testing Static Trade-Off Against Pecking-Order Models of Capital Structure," *Journal of Financial Economics*, 51:219–244 (February 1999).

Some useful reviews of theory and evidence on optimal capital structure are:

M. J. Barclay, C. W. Smith, and R. L. Watts: "The Determinants of Corporate Leverage and Dividend Policies," *Journal of Applied Corporate Finance*, 7:4–19 (Winter 1995).

M. Harris and A. Raviv: "The Theory of Optimal Capital Structure," *Journal of Finance*, 48:297–356 (March 1991).

S. C. Myers: "Capital Structure," *Journal of Economic Perspectives*, 15:81–102 (Spring 2000).

The Spring 1993 and Winter 1995 issues of the Journal of Applied Corporate Finance *contain several articles on the incentive effects of capital structure.*

The January–February 1986 issue of the Journal of Financial Economics *(vol. 15, no. 1/2) collects a series of empirical studies on the stock price impacts of debt and equity issues and capital structure changes.*

Visit us at www.mhhe.com/bm7e

QUIZ

1. Compute the present value of interest tax shields generated by these three debt issues. Consider corporate taxes only. The marginal tax rate is $T_c = .35$.
   a. A $1,000, one-year loan at 8 percent.

b. A five-year loan of $1,000 at 8 percent. Assume no principal is repaid until maturity.
c. A $1,000 perpetuity at 7 percent.

2. Here are book and market value balance sheets of the United Frypan Company (UF):

Book

Net working capital	$ 20	Debt	$ 40
Long-term assets	80	Equity	60
	$100		$100

Market

Net working capital	$ 20	Debt	$ 40
Long-term assets	140	Equity	120
	$160		$160

Assume that MM's theory holds with taxes. There is no growth, and the $40 of debt is expected to be permanent. Assume a 40 percent corporate tax rate.
a. How much of the firm's value is accounted for by the debt-generated tax shield?
b. How much better off will UF's shareholders be if the firm borrows $20 more and uses it to repurchase stock?
c. Now suppose that subsequently Congress passes a law which eliminates the deductibility of interest for tax purposes after a grace period of five years. What will be the new value of the firm, other things equal? (Assume an 8 percent borrowing rate.)

3. What is the relative tax advantage of corporate debt if the corporate tax rate is $T_c = .35$, the personal tax rate is $T_p = .31$, but all equity income is received as capital gains and escapes tax entirely ($T_{pE} = 0$)? How does the relative tax advantage change if the company decides to pay out all equity income as cash dividends?

4. This question tests your understanding of financial distress.
a. What are the costs of going bankrupt? Define these costs carefully.
b. "A company can incur costs of financial distress without ever going bankrupt." Explain how this can happen.
c. Explain how conflicts of interest between bondholders and stockholders can lead to costs of financial distress.

5. On February 29, 2003, when PDQ Computers announced bankruptcy, its share price fell from $3.00 to $.50 per share. There were 10 million shares outstanding. Does that imply bankruptcy costs of $10 \times (3.00 - .50) = \$25$ million? Explain.

6. "The firm can't use interest tax shields unless it has (taxable) income to shield." What does this statement imply for the debt policy? Explain briefly.

7. Let us go back to Circular File's market value balance sheet:

Net working capital	$20	$25	Bonds outstanding
Fixed assets	10	5	Common stock
Total assets	$30	$30	Total value

Who gains and who loses from the following maneuvers?
a. Circular scrapes up $5 in cash and pays a cash dividend.
b. Circular halts operations, sells its fixed assets, and converts net working capital into $20 cash. Unfortunately the fixed assets fetch only $6 on the secondhand market. The $26 cash is invested in Treasury bills.
c. Circular encounters an acceptable investment opportunity, NPV = 0, requiring an investment of $10. The firm borrows to finance the project. The new debt has the same security, seniority, etc., as the old.
d. Suppose that the new project has NPV = +$2 and is financed by an issue of preferred stock.
e. The lenders agree to extend the maturity of their loan from one year to two in order to give Circular a chance to recover.

8. What types of firms would be likely to incur heavy costs in the event of bankruptcy or financial distress? What types would incur relatively light costs? Give a few examples of each type.
9. The traditional theory of optimal capital structure states that firms trade off corporate interest tax shields against the possible costs of financial distress due to borrowing. What does this theory predict about the relationship between book profitability and target book debt ratios? Is the theory's prediction consistent with the facts?
10. What is meant by the pecking-order theory of capital structure? Could this theory explain the observed relationship between profitability and debt ratios? Explain briefly.
11. Why does asymmetric information push companies to raise external funds by borrowing rather than by issuing common stock?
12. For what kinds of companies is financial slack most valuable? Are there situations in which financial slack should be reduced by borrowing and paying out the proceeds to the stockholders? Explain.

PRACTICE QUESTIONS

1. Suppose that, in an effort to reduce the federal deficit, Congress increases the top personal tax rate on interest and dividends to 44 percent but retains a 20 percent tax rate on realized capital gains. The corporate tax rate stays at 35 percent. Compute the total corporate plus personal taxes paid on debt versus equity income if **(a)** all capital gains are realized immediately and **(b)** capital gains are deferred forever. Assume capital gains are half of equity income.
2. "The trouble with MM's argument is that it ignores the fact that individuals can deduct interest for personal income tax." Show why this is not an objection. What difference would it make if individuals were not allowed to deduct interest for personal tax?
3. Look back at the Pfizer example in Section 18.1. Suppose that Pfizer moves to a 40 percent book debt ratio by issuing debt and using the proceeds to repurchase shares. Consider only corporate taxes. Now reconstruct Table 18.3(*b*) to reflect the new capital structure.
4. Calculate the tax shield for an actual U.S. company assuming:
   a. Debt is permanent.
   b. Personal tax rates on debt and equity income are the same.

   How would the stock price change if the company announced tomorrow that it intended to replace all its debt with equity?
5. Tables 18.3(*a*) and 18.3(*b*), although pertaining to a real company, are really just a simplified numerical example. What factors would you expect to determine the value of interest tax shields in practice—not just for Pfizer, but for a range of companies with different profitability, risk, and types of business?
6. "The right of shareholders to default is a valuable privilege." Explain.
7. In Section 18.3, we briefly referred to three games: Playing for time, cash in and run, and bait and switch.

   For each game, construct a simple numerical example (like the example for the risk-shifting game) showing how shareholders can gain at the expense of creditors. Then explain how the temptation to play these games could lead to costs of financial distress.
8. Summarize the evidence pro and con the trade-off theory of capital structure.
9. Look at some real companies with different types of assets. What operating problems would each encounter in the event of financial distress? How well would the assets keep their value?

Visit us at www.mhhe.com/bm7e

10. The Salad Oil Storage (SOS) Company has financed a large part of its facilities with long-term debt. There is a significant risk of default, but the company is not on the ropes yet. Explain:
    a. Why SOS stockholders could lose by investing in a positive-NPV project financed by an equity issue.
    b. Why SOS stockholders could gain by investing in a negative-NPV project financed by cash.
    c. Why SOS stockholders could gain from paying out a large cash dividend.

    How might the firm's adherence to a target debt ratio mitigate some or all of the problems noted above?

11. a. Who benefits from the fine print in bond contracts when the firm gets into financial trouble? Give a one-sentence answer.
    b. Who benefits from the fine print when the bonds are issued? Suppose the firm is offered the choice of issuing (i) a bond with standard restrictions on dividend payout, additional borrowing, etc., and (ii) a bond with minimal restrictions but a much higher interest rate? Suppose the interest rates on both (i) and (ii) are fair from the viewpoint of lenders. Which bond would you expect the firm to issue? Why?

12. Caldor, the retailing chain, filed for bankruptcy in September 1995. Shortly after the bankruptcy its stock traded at $5.25 per share, down from about $20 earlier in the year. How much of this drop should be attributed to bankruptcy costs—all, part, or none? Explain.

13. "I was amazed to find that the announcement of a stock issue drives down the value of the issuing firm by *30 percent*, on average, of the proceeds of the issue. That issue cost dwarfs the underwriter's spread and the administrative costs of the issue. It makes common stock issues prohibitively expensive."
    a. You are contemplating a $100 million stock issue. On past evidence, you anticipate that announcement of this issue will drive down stock price by 3 percent and that the market value of your firm will fall by 30 percent of the amount to be raised. On the other hand, additional equity funds are necessary to fund an investment project which you believe has a positive NPV of $40 million. Should you proceed with the issue?
    b. Is the fall in market value on announcement of a stock issue an *issue cost* in the same sense as an underwriter's spread? Respond to the quote that begins this question.

    Use your answer to (a) as a numerical example to explain your response to (b).

14. Ronald Masulis[42] has analyzed the stock price impact of *exchange offers* of debt for equity or vice versa. In an exchange offer, the firm offers to trade freshly issued securities for seasoned securities in the hands of investors. Thus, a firm that wanted to move to a higher debt ratio could offer to trade new debt for outstanding shares. A firm that wanted to move to a more conservative capital structure could offer to trade new shares for outstanding debt securities.

    Masulis found that debt for equity exchanges were good news (stock price increased on announcement) and equity for debt exchanges were bad news.
    a. Are these results consistent with the trade-off theory of capital structure?
    b. Are the results consistent with the evidence that investors regard announcements of (i) stock issues as bad news, (ii) stock repurchases as good news, and (iii) debt issues as no news, or at most trifling disappointments?
    c. How could Masulis's results be explained?

---

[42]R. W. Masulis, "The Effects of Capital Structure Change on Security Prices: A Study of Exchange Offers," *Journal of Financial Economics* 8 (June 1980), pp. 139–177, and "The Impact of Capital Structure Change on Firm Value," *Journal of Finance* 38 (March 1983), pp. 107–126.

15. Suppose the trade-off theory of capital structure is true. Can you predict how companies' debt ratios should change over time? How do these predictions differ from the pecking-order theory's?

16. Summarize the evidence pro and con the pecking-order theory of capital structure.

17. "Why are personal taxes on bond interest important? They are the bondholder's problem." Explain why they are also indirectly the shareholder's problem.

18. The possible payoffs from Ms. Ketchup's projects (see Section 18.3) have not changed but there is now a 40 percent chance that project 2 will pay off $24 and a 60 percent chance that it will pay off $0.
    a. Recalculate the expected payoffs to the bank and Ms. Ketchup if the bank lends the present value of $10. Which project would Ms. Ketchup undertake?
    b. What is the maximum amount the bank could lend that would induce Ms. Ketchup to take project 1?

19. Select a dozen companies from the Market Insight database (**www.mhhe.com/edumarketinsight**). Estimate how much more these companies could borrow before they would exhaust taxable profits.

CHALLENGE QUESTION

STANDARD &POOR'S

1. Use the Market Insight database (**www.mhhe.com/edumarketinsight**) to see how well differences in company leverage seem to support the trade-off theory and the pecking-order theory.

CHAPTER NINETEEN

FINANCING AND VALUATION

WE FIRST ADDRESSED problems of capital budgeting in Chapter 2. At that point we said hardly a word about financing decisions; we proceeded under the simplest possible assumption about financing, namely, all-equity financing. We were really assuming an idealized Modigliani–Miller (MM) world in which all financing decisions are irrelevant. In a strict MM world, firms can analyze real investments as if they are to be all-equity-financed; the actual financing plan is a mere detail to be worked out later.

Under MM assumptions, decisions to spend money can be separated from decisions to raise money. In this chapter we reconsider the capital budgeting decision when investment and financing decisions *interact* and cannot be wholly separated.

In the early chapters you learned how to value a capital investment opportunity by a four-step procedure:

1. Forecast the project's incremental after-tax cash flow, assuming the project is entirely equity-financed.
2. Assess the project's risk.
3. Estimate the opportunity cost of capital, that is, the expected rate of return offered to investors by the equivalent-risk investments traded in capital markets.
4. Calculate NPV, using the discounted-cash-flow formula.

In effect, we were thinking of each project as a mini-firm, and asking, How much would that mini-firm be worth if we spun it off as a separate, all-equity-financed enterprise? How much would investors be willing to pay for shares in the project?

Of course, this procedure rests on the concept of *value additivity.* In well-functioning capital markets the market value of the firm is the sum of the present value of all the assets held by the firm[1]—the whole equals the sum of the parts.

In this chapter we stick with the value-additivity principle but extend it to include value contributed by financing decisions. There are two ways of doing this:

1. *Adjust the discount rate.* The adjustment is typically downward, to account for the value of interest tax shields. This is the most common approach. It is usually implemented via the after-tax weighted-average cost of capital or "WACC."
2. *Adjust the present value.* That is, start by estimating the project's "base-case" value as an all-equity-financed mini-firm, and then adjust this base-case NPV to account for the project's impact on the firm's capital structure. Thus

$$\text{Adjusted NPV (APV for short)} = \text{base-case NPV} + \text{NPV of financing decisions caused by project acceptance}$$

Once you identify and value the side effects of financing a project, calculating its APV (adjusted net present value) is no more than addition or subtraction.

This is a how-to-do-it chapter. In the next section, we explain and derive the after-tax weighted-average cost of capital, reviewing required assumptions and the too-common mistakes people make using this formula. Section 19.2 then covers the tricks of the trade: helpful tips on how to estimate

continued

[1]*All assets* means intangible as well as tangible assets. For example, a going concern is usually worth more than a haphazard pile of tangible assets. Thus, the aggregate value of a firm's tangible assets often falls short of its market value. The difference is accounted for by going-concern value or by other intangible assets such as accumulated technical expertise, an experienced sales force, or valuable growth opportunities.

inputs and how the formula is used in practice. Section 19.3 shows how to recalculate the weighted-average cost of capital when capital structure or asset mix changes.

Section 19.4 turns to the Adjusted Present Value or APV method. This is simple enough in concept: Just value the project by discounting at the opportunity cost of capital—not the WACC—and then add the present values gained or lost due to financing side effects. But identifying and valuing the side effects is sometimes tricky, so we'll have to work through some numerical examples.

Section 19.5 reexamines a basic and apparently simple issue: What should the discount rate be for a risk-free project? Once we recognize the tax deductibility of debt interest, we will find that all risk-free, or *debt-equivalent*, cash flows can be evaluated by discounting at the *after-tax* interest rate. We show that this rule is consistent with both the weighted-average cost of capital and with APV.

We conclude the chapter with a question and answer section designed to clarify points that managers and students often find confusing. An Appendix providing more details and more formulas can be obtained from the Brealey–Myers website.[2]

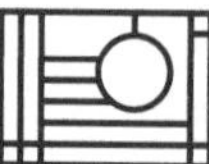

19.1 THE AFTER-TAX WEIGHTED-AVERAGE COST OF CAPITAL

Think back to Chapter 17 and Modigliani and Miller's (MM's) proposition I. MM showed that, without taxes or financial market imperfections, the cost of capital does not depend on financing. In other words, the weighted average of the expected returns to debt and equity investors equals the opportunity cost of capital, regardless of the debt ratio:

$$\text{Weighted-average return to debt and equity} = r_D \frac{D}{V} + r_E \frac{E}{V}$$
$$= r, \text{a constant, independent of } D/V$$

Here r is the opportunity cost of capital, the expected rate of return investors would demand if the firm had no debt at all; r_D and r_E are the expected rates of return on debt and equity, the "cost of debt" and "cost of equity." The weights D/V and E/V are the fractions of debt and equity, based on market values; V, the total market value of the firm, is the sum of D and E.

But you can't look up r, the opportunity cost of capital, in *The Wall Street Journal* or find it on the Internet. So financial managers turn the problem around: They start with the estimates of r_D and r_E and then infer r. Under MM's assumptions,

$$r = r_D \frac{D}{V} + r_E \frac{E}{V}$$

This formula calculates r, the opportunity cost of capital, as the expected rate of return on a portfolio of all the firm's outstanding securities.

[2]www.mhhe.com/bm7e.

We have discussed this weighted-average cost of capital formula in Chapters 9 and 17. However, the formula misses a crucial difference between debt and equity: Interest payments are tax-deductible. Therefore we move on to the *after-tax* weighted-average cost of capital, nicknamed WACC:

$$\text{WACC} = r_D(1 - T_c)\frac{D}{V} + r_E\frac{E}{V}$$

Here T_c is the marginal corporate tax rate.

Notice that the after-tax WACC is less than the opportunity cost of capital (r), because the "cost of debt" is calculated after tax as $r_D(1 - T_c)$. Thus the tax advantages of debt financing are reflected in a lower discount rate. Notice too that all the variables in the weighted-average formula refer to the firm as a whole. As a result, the formula gives the right discount rate only for projects that are just like the firm undertaking them. The formula works for the "average" project. It is incorrect for projects that are safer or riskier than the average of the firm's existing assets. It is incorrect for projects whose acceptance would lead to an increase or decrease in the firm's debt ratio.

Example: Sangria Corporation

Let's calculate WACC for the Sangria Corporation. Its book and market value balance sheets are

Sangria Corporation (Book Values, millions)

Asset value	\$100	\$ 50	Debt
		50	Equity
	\$100	\$100	

Sangria Corporation (Market Values, millions)

Asset value	\$125	\$ 50	Debt (D)
		75	Equity (E)
	\$125	\$125	Firm Value (V)

We calculated the market value of equity on Sangria's balance sheet by multiplying its current stock price (\$7.50) by 10 million, the number of its outstanding shares. The company has done well and future prospects are good, so the stock is trading above book value (\$5.00 per share). However, the book and market values of Sangria's debt are in this case equal.

Sangria's cost of debt (the interest rate on its existing debt and on any new borrowing) is 8 percent. Its cost of equity (the expected rate of return demanded by investors in Sangria's stock) is 14.6 percent.

The market value balance sheet shows assets worth \$125 million. Of course we can't observe this value directly, because the assets themselves are not traded. But we know what they are worth to debt and equity investors (50 + 75 = \$125 million). This value is entered on the left of the market value balance sheet.

Why did we show the book balance sheet? Only so you could draw a big **X** through it. Do so now.

When estimating the weighted-average cost of capital, you are not interested in past investments but in current values and expectations for the future. Sangria's true debt ratio is not 50 percent, the book ratio, but 40 percent, because its assets are worth \$125 million. The cost of equity, $r_E = .146$, is the expected rate of return from purchase of stock at \$7.50 per share, the current market price. It is not the return on book value per share. You can't buy shares in Sangria for \$5 anymore.

Sangria is consistently profitable and pays tax at the marginal rate of 35 percent. That is the final input for Sangria's WACC. The inputs are summarized here:

Cost of debt (r_D)	.08
Cost of equity (r_E)	.146
Marginal tax rate (T_c)	.35
Debt ratio (D/V)	50/125 = .4
Equity ratio (E/V)	75/125 = .6

The company's WACC is

$$\text{WACC} = .08(1 - .35)(.4) + .146(.6) = .1084, \text{or } 10.84\%$$

That's how you calculate the weighted-average cost of capital.[3]

Now let's see how Sangria would use this formula. Sangria's enologists have proposed investing \$12.5 million in construction of a perpetual crushing machine, which, conveniently for us, never depreciates and generates a perpetual stream of earnings and cash flow of \$2.085 million per year pretax. The after-tax cash flow is

Pretax cash flow	\$2.085
Tax at 35%	.730
After-tax cash flow	\$1.355 million

Notice: This after-tax cash flow takes no account of interest tax shields on debt supported by the perpetual crusher project. As we explained in Chapter 6, standard capital budgeting practice calculates after-tax cash flows as if the project were all-equity-financed. However, the interest tax shields will not be ignored: We are about to discount the project cash flows by Sangria's WACC, in which the cost of debt is entered after tax. The value of interest tax shields is picked up not as higher after-tax cash flows, but in a lower discount rate.

The crusher generates a perpetual cash flow of $C = \$1.355$ million, so NPV is

$$\text{NPV} = -12.5 + \frac{1.355}{.1084} = 0$$

NPV = 0 means a barely acceptable investment. The annual cash flow of \$1.355 million per year amounts to a 10.84% rate of return on investment (1.355/12.5 = .1084), exactly equal to Sangria's WACC.

If project NPV = 0, the return to equity investors must exactly equal the cost of equity, 14.6%. Let's confirm that Sangria shareholders could actually forecast a 14.6% return on their investment in the perpetual crusher project.

[3]In practice it's pointless to calculate discount rates to four decimal places. We do so here to avoid confusion from rounding errors. Earnings and cash flows are carried to three decimal places for the same reason.

Suppose Sangria sets up this project as a mini-firm. Its market-value balance sheet looks like this:

Perpetual Crusher (Market Values, millions)

Project value	\$12.5	\$ 5.0	Debt (D)
		7.5	Equity (E)
	\$12.5	\$12.5	Project Value (V)

Calculate the expected dollar return to shareholders:

$$\text{After-tax interest} = r_D(1 - T_c)D = .08(1 - .35)(5) = .26$$

$$\text{Expected equity income} = C - (1 - T_c)r_D D = 1.355 - .26 = 1.095$$

The project's earnings are level and perpetual, so the expected rate of return on equity is equal to the expected equity income divided by the equity value:

$$\text{Expected equity return} = r_E = \frac{\text{expected equity income}}{\text{equity value}}$$

$$= \frac{1.095}{7.5} = .146, \text{ or } 14.6\%$$

The expected return on equity equals the cost of equity, so it makes sense that the project's NPV is zero.

Review of Assumptions

By discounting the perpetual crusher's cash flows at Sangria's WACC, we assume that

- The project's business risks are the same as Sangria's other assets.
- The project supports the same fraction of debt to value as in Sangria's overall capital structure.

You can see the importance of these two assumptions: If the perpetual crusher had greater business risk than Sangria's other assets, or if acceptance of the project would lead to a permanent, material[4] change in Sangria's debt ratio, then Sangria's shareholders would not be content with a 14.6 percent expected return on their equity investment in the project.

We have illustrated the WACC formula only for a project offering perpetual cash flows. But Miles and Ezzell have shown that the formula works for any cash-flow pattern if the firm adjusts its borrowing to maintain a constant debt ratio over time. When the firm departs from this borrowing policy, WACC is only approximately correct.[5]

[4]Users of WACC need not worry about small or temporary fluctuations in debt-to-value ratios. Suppose that Sangria management decided for convenience to borrow \$12.5 million to allow immediate construction of the crusher. This does not necessarily change Sangria's long-term financing policy. If the crusher supports only \$5.0 million of debt, Sangria would have to pay down debt to restore its overall debt ratio to 40 percent. For example, it could fund later projects with less debt and more equity.

[5]J. Miles and R. Ezzell, "The Weighted Average Cost of Capital, Perfect Capital Markets, and Project Life: A Clarification," *Journal of Financial and Quantitative Analysis* 15 (September 1980), pp. 719–730.

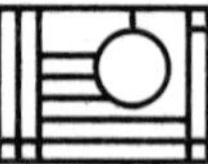

19.2 USING WACC—SOME TRICKS OF THE TRADE

Sangria had just one asset and two sources of financing. A real company's market value balance sheet has many more entries, for example:[6]

Current assets, including cash, inventory, and accounts receivable	Current liabilities, including accounts payable and short-term debt
Plant and equipment	Long-term debt (D)
	Preferred stock (P)
Growth opportunities	Equity (E)
	Firm value (V)

Several questions immediately arise:

1. *How does the formula change when there are more than two sources of financing?* Easy: There is one cost for each element. The weight for each element is proportional to its market value. For example, if the capital structure includes both preferred and common shares,

$$\text{WACC} = r_D(1 - T_c)\frac{D}{V} + r_P\frac{P}{V} + r_E\frac{E}{V}$$

where r_P is investors' expected rate of return on preferred stocks.

2. *What about short-term debt?* Many companies consider only long-term financing when calculating WACC. They leave out the cost of short-term debt. In principle this is incorrect. The lenders who hold short-term debt are investors who can claim their share of operating earnings. A company that ignores this claim will misstate the required return on capital investments.

   But "zeroing out" short-term debt is not a serious error if the debt is only temporary, seasonal, or incidental financing or if it is offset by holdings of cash and marketable securities.[7] Suppose, for example, that your company's Italian subsidiary takes out a six-month loan from an Italian bank to finance its inventory and accounts receivable. The dollar equivalent

---

[6]This balance sheet is for exposition and should not be confused with a real company's books. It includes the value of growth opportunities, which accountants do not recognize, though investors do. It excludes certain accounting entries, for example, deferred taxes.

Deferred taxes arise when a company uses faster depreciation for tax purposes than it uses in reports to investors. That means the company reports more taxes than it pays. The difference is accumulated as a liability for deferred taxes. In a sense there is a liability, because the Internal Revenue Service "catches up," collecting extra taxes, as assets age. But this is irrelevant in capital investment analysis, which focuses on actual after-tax cash flows and uses accelerated tax depreciation.

Deferred taxes should not be regarded as a source of financing or an element of the weighted-average cost of capital formula. The liability for deferred taxes is not a security held by investors. It is a balance sheet entry created to serve the needs of accounting.

Deferred taxes can be important in regulated industries, however. Regulators take deferred taxes into account in calculating allowed rates of return and the time patterns of revenues and consumer prices.

[7]Financial practitioners have rules of thumb for deciding whether short-term debt is worth including in the weighted-average cost of capital. Suppose, for example, that short-term debt is 10 percent of total liabilities and that net working capital is negative. Then short-term debt is almost surely being used to finance long-term assets and should be explicitly included in WACC.

of this loan will show up as a short-term debt on the parent's balance sheet. At the same time headquarters may be lending money by investing surplus dollars in short-term securities. If lending and borrowing offset, there is no point in including the cost of short-term debt in the weighted-average cost of capital, because the company is not a *net* short-term borrower.

3. *What about other current liabilities?* Current liabilities are usually "netted out" by subtracting them from current assets. The difference is entered as net working capital on the left-hand side of the balance sheet. The sum of long-term financing on the right is called *total capitalization.*

Net working capital = current assets − current liabilities	Long-term debt (D)
Plant and equipment	Preferred stock (P)
Growth opportunities	Equity (E)
	Total capitalization (V)

When net working capital is treated as an asset, forecasts of cash flows for capital investment projects must treat increases in net working capital as a cash outflow and decreases as an inflow. This is standard practice, which we followed in Section 6.2.

Since current liabilities include short-term debt, netting them out against current assets excludes the cost of short-term debt from the weighted-average cost of capital. We have just explained why this can be an acceptable approximation. But when short-term debt is an important, permanent source of financing—as is common for small firms and firms outside the United States—it should be shown explicitly on the right side of the balance sheet, not netted out against current assets. The interest cost of short-term debt is then one element of the weighted-average cost of capital.

4. *How are the costs of the financing elements calculated?* You can often use stock market data to get an estimate of r_E, the expected rate of return demanded by investors in the company's stock. With that estimate, WACC is not too hard to calculate, because the borrowing rate r_D and the debt and equity ratios D/V and E/V can be directly observed or estimated without too much trouble.[8] Estimating the value and required return for preferred shares is likewise usually not too complicated.

Estimating the required return on other security types can be troublesome. Convertible debt, where the investors' return comes partly from an option to exchange the debt for the company's stock, is one example. We will leave convertibles to Chapter 23.

Junk debt, where the risk of default is high, is likewise difficult. The higher the odds of default, the lower the market price of the debt and the higher the *promised* rate of interest. But the weighted-average cost of capital

[8]Most corporate debt is not actively traded, so its market value cannot be observed directly. But you can usually value a nontraded debt security by looking to securities that *are* traded and that have approximately the same default risk and maturity. See Chapter 24.

For healthy firms the market value of debt is usually not too far from book value, so many managers and analysts use book value for D in the weighted-average cost of capital formula. However, be sure to use *market,* not book, values for E.

is an *expected,* that is, average, rate of return, not a promised one. For example, in October 2001, Crown Cork bonds maturing in 2005 sold at only 76 percent of face value and offered an 18.6 percent promised yield, more than 14 percentage points above yields on the highest-quality debt issues maturing at the same time. The price and yield on the Crown Cork bond demonstrated investors' concern about the company's chronic financial ill-health. But the 18.6 percent yield was not an expected return, because it did not average in the losses to be incurred if Crown Cork defaults. Including 18.6 percent as a "cost of debt" in a calculation of WACC would therefore overstate Crown Cork's true cost of capital.

This is bad news: There is no easy or tractable way of estimating the expected rate of return on most junk debt issues.[9] The good news is that for most debt the odds of default are small. That means the promised and expected rates of return are close, and the promised rate can be used as an approximation in the weighted-average cost of capital.

Industry Costs of Capital

You can also calculate WACC for *industries.* Suppose that a pharmaceutical company has a subsidiary that produces specialty chemicals. What discount rate is better for the subsidiary's projects—the company WACC or a weighted-average cost of capital for a portfolio of "pure-play" specialty chemical companies? The latter rate is better in principle and also in practice if good data are available for firms with operations and markets similar to the subsidiary's.

An Application to the Railroad Industry Every year the United States Surface Transportation Board (STB) estimates a cost of capital for the railroad industry, defined as Class I (big) railroads. We will use the STB's data and estimates to calculate a railroad industry WACC for 1999.

The STB took care to estimate the market value of the railroads' common shares and all outstanding debt issues, including debt-equivalents such as equipment trust certificates and financial leases.[10] The aggregate industry capital structure was[11]

	Market Value (billions)	Financing Weights
Debt	$31,627.8	37.3%
Equity	53,210.0	62.7

The average cost of debt was 7.2 percent. To estimate the cost of equity, the STB used the constant-growth DCF model, which you will recall with pleasure from Section 4.3. If investors expect dividends to grow at a constant, perpetual rate, g, then the expected return is the sum of the dividend yield and the expected growth rate:

$$r_E = \frac{DIV_1}{P_0} + g$$

[9]When betas can be estimated for the junk issue or for a sample of similar issues, the expected return can be calculated from the capital asset pricing model. Otherwise, the yield should be adjusted for the probability of default. Evidence on historical default rates on junk bonds is described in Chapter 25.

[10]Equipment trust certificates are described in Section 25.3; financial leases are discussed in Chapter 26.

[11]There were three tiny preferred issues. For simplicity we have added them to debt.

An investor who bought a portfolio of the shares of Class I railroads in 1999 got a dividend yield of about 2.0 percent. A review of security analysts' forecasts gave an average expected growth rate for earnings and dividends of 10.9 percent. The cost of equity was thus estimated at $r_E = 2.0 + 10.9 = 12.9$ percent.

Using the statutory marginal tax rate of 35 percent,[12] the railroad industry WACC is

$$\text{WACC} = 0.072(1-.35)(.373) + .129(.627) = .098, \text{ or about } 10\%$$

Valuing Companies: WACC vs. the Flow-to-Equity Method

WACC is normally used as a hurdle rate or discount rate to value proposed capital investments. But sometimes it is used as a discount rate for valuing whole companies. For example, the financial manager may need to value a target company to decide whether to go ahead with a merger.

Valuing companies raises no new conceptual problems. You just treat the company as if it were one big project. Forecast the company's cash flows (the hardest part of the exercise) and discount back to present value. The company's WACC is the right discount rate if the company's debt ratio is expected to remain reasonably close to constant. But remember:

- If you discount at WACC, cash flows have to be projected just as you would for a capital investment project. Do not deduct interest. Calculate taxes as if the company were all-equity-financed. The value of interest tax shields is picked up in the WACC formula.
- The company's cash flows will probably not be forecasted to infinity. Financial managers usually forecast to a medium-term horizon—10 years, say—and add a terminal value to the cash flows in the horizon year. The terminal value is the present value at the horizon of post-horizon flows. Estimating the terminal value requires careful attention because it often accounts for the majority of the value of the company. See Section 4.5.
- Discounting at WACC values the assets and operations of the company. If the object is to value the company's equity, that is, its common stock, don't forget to subtract the value of the company's outstanding debt.

If the task is to value equity, there's an obvious alternative to discounting company cash flows at its WACC. Discount the cash flows to *equity,* after interest and after taxes, at the cost of equity. This is called the *flow-to-equity* method. If the company's debt ratio is constant over time, the flow-to-equity method should give the same answer as discounting company cash flows at the WACC and subtracting debt.

The flow-to-equity method seems simple, and it is simple if the proportions of debt and equity financing stay reasonably close to constant for the life of the company. But the cost of equity depends on financial leverage; it depends on financial risk as well as business risk. If financial leverage will change significantly, discounting flows to equity at today's cost of equity will not give the right answer.

A one-shot change in financing can usually be accommodated. Think again of a proposed takeover. Suppose the financial manager decides that the target's 20 percent debt-to-value ratio is stodgy and too conservative. She decides the company

[12]The STB actually uses a pretax cost of debt. If the STB's reported WACC is used as a discount rate, interest tax shields have to be valued separately, as in the adjusted-present-value method described in Section 19.4.

could easily support 40 percent debt and asks you to value the target's shares on that assumption. Unfortunately you have estimated the cost of equity at the existing 20 percent ratio. No problem! Adjust the cost of equity (we will revisit the formula in the next section) and proceed as usual. Of course you must forecast and discount cash flows to equity at the new 40 percent debt ratio. You also have to assume that this debt ratio will be maintained after the takeover.

Mistakes People Make in Using the Weighted-Average Formula

The weighted-average formula is very useful but also dangerous. It tempts people to make logical errors. For example, manager Q, who is campaigning for a pet project, might look at the formula

$$\text{WACC} = r_D(1 - T_c)\frac{D}{V} + r_E\frac{E}{V}$$

and think, Aha! My firm has a good credit rating. It could borrow, say, 90 percent of the project's cost if it likes. That means $D/V = .9$ and $E/V = .1$. My firm's borrowing rate r_D is 8 percent, and the required return on equity, r_E, is 15 percent. Therefore

$$\text{WACC} = .08(1 - .35)(.9) + .15(.1) = .062$$

or 6.2 percent. When I discount at that rate, my project looks great.

Manager Q is wrong on several counts. First, the weighted-average formula works only for projects that are carbon copies of the firm. The firm isn't 90 percent debt-financed.

Second, the immediate source of funds for a project has no necessary connection with the hurdle rate for the project. What matters is the project's overall contribution to the firm's borrowing power. A dollar invested in Q's pet project will not increase the firm's debt capacity by \$.90. If the firm borrows 90 percent of the project's cost, it is really borrowing in part against its *existing* assets. Any advantage from financing the new project with more debt than normal should be attributed to the old projects, not to the new one.

Third, even if the firm were willing and able to lever up to 90 percent debt, its cost of capital would not decline to 6.2 percent (as Q's naive calculation predicts). You cannot increase the debt ratio without creating financial risk for stockholders and thereby increasing r_E, the expected rate of return they demand from the firm's common stock. Going to 90 percent debt would certainly increase the borrowing rate, too.

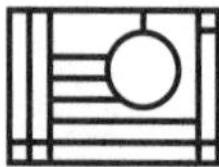

19.3 ADJUSTING WACC WHEN DEBT RATIOS OR BUSINESS RISKS CHANGE

The WACC formula assumes that the project to be valued will be financed in the same proportions of debt and equity as the firm as a whole. What if that is not true? What if the perpetual crusher project supports debt equal to, say, 20 percent of project value, versus 40 percent debt financing for the firm as a whole?

Moving from 40 to 20 percent debt changes all the elements of the WACC formula except the tax rate.[13] Obviously the financing weights change. But the cost

[13]It could change the tax rate too. For example, the firm might have enough pretax income to cover interest payments at 20 percent debt but not at 40 percent. In this case the effective marginal tax rate would be higher at 20 percent debt.

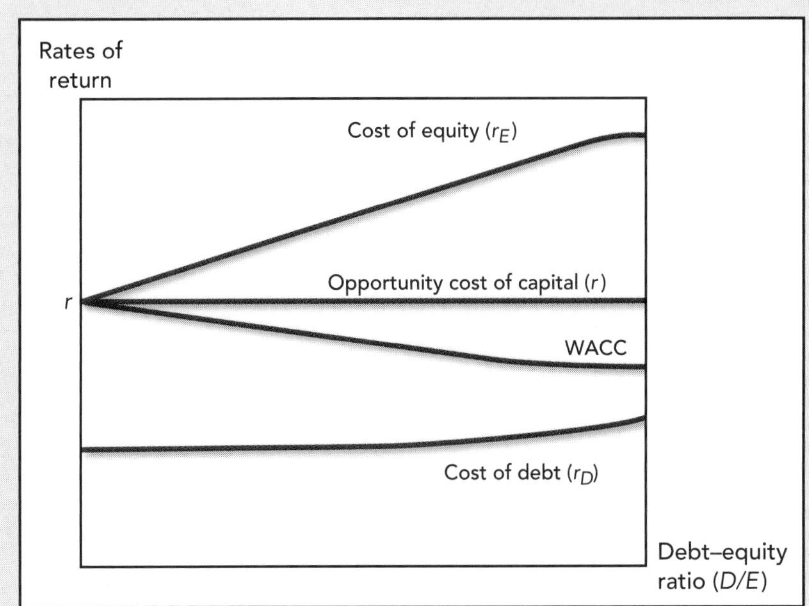

FIGURE 19.1

WACC plotted against the debt–equity ratio. WACC equals the opportunity cost of capital when there is no debt. WACC declines with financial leverage because of interest tax shields.

of equity r_E is less, because financial risk is reduced. The cost of debt may be lower too.

Figure 19.1 plots WACC and the costs of debt and equity as a function of the debt–equity ratio. The flat line is r, the opportunity cost of capital. Remember, this is the expected rate of return that investors would want from the project if it were all-equity-financed. The opportunity cost of capital depends only on business risk and is the natural reference point.

Suppose Sangria or the perpetual crusher project were all-equity-financed ($D/V = 0$). At that point WACC equals cost of equity, and both equal the opportunity cost of capital. Start from that point in Figure 19.1. As the debt ratio increases, the cost of equity increases, because of financial risk, but notice that WACC declines. The decline is *not* caused by use of "cheap" debt in place of "expensive" equity. It falls because of the tax shields on debt interest payments. If there were no corporate income taxes, the weighted-average cost of capital would be constant, and equal to the opportunity cost of capital, at all debt ratios. We showed this in Chapters 9 and 17.

Figure 19.1 shows the *shape* of the relationship between financing and WACC, but we have numbers only for Sangria's current 40 percent debt ratio. We want to recalculate WACC at a 20 percent ratio.

Here is the simplest way to do it. There are three steps.

Step 1 Calculate the opportunity cost of capital. In other words, calculate WACC and the cost of equity at zero debt. This step is called *unlevering* the WACC. The simplest unlevering formula is

$$\text{Opportunity cost of capital} = r = r_D D/V + r_E E/V$$

This formula comes directly from Modigliani and Miller's proposition I (see Section 17.1). If taxes are left out, the weighted-average cost of capital equals the opportunity cost of capital and is independent of leverage.

FIGURE 19.2

This plot shows WACC for the Sangria Corporation at debt-to-equity ratios of 25 and 67 percent. The corresponding debt-to-*value* ratios are 20 and 40 percent.

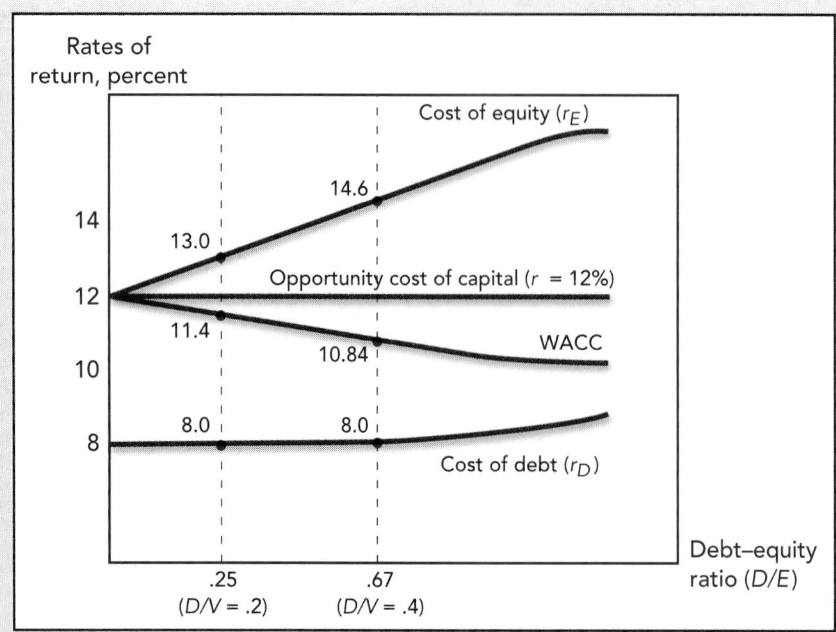

Step 2 Estimate the cost of debt, r_D, at the new debt ratio, and calculate the new cost of equity.

$$r_E = r + (r - r_D)D/E$$

This formula is Modigliani and Miller's proposition II (see Section 17.2). It calls for D/E, the ratio of debt to *equity*, not debt to value.

Step 3 Recalculate the weighted-average cost of capital at the new financing weights.

Let's do the numbers for the perpetual crusher project at $D/V = .20$ or 20 percent.

Step 1. Sangria's current debt ratio is $D/V = .4$

$$r = .08(.4) + .146(.6) = .12 \text{ or } 12\%$$

Step 2. We will assume that the debt cost stays at 8 percent when the debt ratio is 20 percent. Then

$$r_E = .12 + (.12 - .08)(.25) = .13 \text{ or } 13\%$$

Note that the debt–*equity* ratio is $.2/.8 = .25$.

Step 3. Recalculate WACC.

$$\text{WACC} = .08(1 - .35)(.2) + .13(.8) = .114 \text{ or } 11.4\%$$

Figure 19.2 enters these numbers on the plot of WACC versus debt ratio. The 11.4 percent project discount rate at 20 percent debt to value is .56 percentage points higher than at 40 percent.

Another Example: WACC for U.S. Railroads at 45 percent Debt Let's return to the WACC we calculated for large U.S. railroads. We assumed a debt-to-value ratio of 37.3 percent. How would the railroad industry WACC change at 45 percent debt?

Step 1. Calculate the unlevered opportunity cost of capital

$$r = .072(.373) + .129(.627) = .108$$

Step 2. Assume that the cost of debt increases to 8 percent at 45 percent debt. The cost of equity is

$$r_E = .108 + (.108 - .080)45/55 = .13$$

Step 3. Recalculate WACC. If the marginal tax rate stays at 35 percent,

$$\text{WACC} = .080(1 - .35).45 + .130(.55) = .095 \text{ or } 9.5\%$$

The cost of capital drops by more than one half percentage point. Is this a great deal? Not as good as it looks. In these simple calculations, the cost of capital drops as financial leverage increases, but only because of corporate interest tax shields. In Chapter 18 we reviewed all the reasons why just focusing on corporate interest tax shields overstates the advantages of debt. For example, costs of financial distress encountered at high debt levels appear nowhere in the WACC formula or in the standard formulas relating the cost of equity for leverage.[14]

Unlevering and Relevering Betas

Our three-step procedure (1) unlevers and then (2) relevers the cost of equity. Some financial managers find it convenient to (1) unlever and then (2) relever the equity beta. Given the beta of equity at the new debt ratio, the cost of equity is determined from the capital asset pricing model. Then WACC is recalculated.

The formula for unlevering beta was given in Section 9.2.

$$\beta_{\text{asset}} = \beta_{\text{debt}}(D/V) + \beta_{\text{equity}}(E/V)$$

This equation says that the beta of a firm's assets is revealed by the beta of a portfolio of all of the firm's outstanding debt and equity securities. An investor who bought such a portfolio would own the assets free and clear and absorb only business risks.

The formula for relevering beta closely resembles MM's proposition II, except that betas are substituted for rates of return:

$$\beta_{\text{equity}} = \beta_{\text{asset}} + (\beta_{\text{asset}} - \beta_{\text{debt}})D/E$$

The Importance of Rebalancing

The formulas for WACC and for unlevering and relevering expected returns are simple, but we must be careful to remember underlying assumptions. The most important point is *rebalancing.*

Calculating WACC for a company at its existing capital structure requires that the capital structure *not* change; in other words, the company must rebalance its capital structure to maintain the same market-value debt ratio for the relevant future. Take Sangria Corporation as an example. It starts with a debt-to-value ratio of 40 percent and a market value of $125 million. Suppose that Sangria's products do unexpectedly

[14]Some financial managers and analysts argue that the costs of debt and equity increase rapidly at high debt ratios because of costs of financial distress. This in turn would cause the WACC curve in Figure 19.1 to flatten out, and finally increase, as the debt ratio climbs. For practical purposes, this can be a sensible end result. However, formal modeling of the interactions between the cost of financial distress and the expected rates of return on the company's securities is not easy.

well in the marketplace and that market value increases to $150 million. Rebalancing means that it will then increase debt to .4 × 150 = $60 million,[15] thus regaining a 40 percent ratio. If market value instead falls, Sangria would have to pay down debt proportionally.

Of course real companies do not rebalance capital structure in such a mechanical and compulsive way. For practical purposes, it's sufficient to assume gradual but steady adjustment toward a long-run target. But if the firm plans significant changes in capital structure (for example, if it plans to pay off its debt), the WACC formula won't work. In such cases, you should turn to the APV method, which we describe in the next section.

Our three-step procedure for recalculating WACC makes a similar rebalancing assumption.[16] Whatever the starting debt ratio, the firm is assumed to rebalance to maintain that ratio in the future. The unlevering and relevering in steps 1 and 2 also ignore any impact of investors' personal income taxes on the costs of debt and equity.[17]

19.4 ADJUSTED PRESENT VALUE

We now take a different tack. Instead of messing around with the discount rate, we explicitly adjust cash flows and present values for costs or benefits of financing. This approach is called **adjusted present value,** or **APV.**

The adjusted-present-value rule is easiest to understand in the context of simple numerical examples. We start by analyzing a project under base-case assumptions and then consider possible financing side effects of accepting the project.

The Base Case

The APV method begins by valuing the project as if it were a mini-firm financed solely by equity. Consider a project to produce solar water heaters. It requires a $10 million investment and offers a level after-tax cash flow of $1.8 million per year for 10 years. The opportunity cost of capital is 12 percent, which reflects the project's business risk. Investors would demand a 12 percent expected return to invest in the mini-firm's shares.

Thus the mini-firm's base-case NPV is

$$\text{NPV} = -10 + \sum_{t=1}^{10} \frac{1.8}{(1.12)^t} = +\$.17 \text{ million, or } \$170{,}000$$

Considering the project's size, this figure is not much greater than zero. In a pure MM world where no financing decision matters, the financial manager would lean toward taking the project but would not be heartbroken if it were discarded.

[15]The proceeds of the additional borrowing would be paid out to shareholders or used, along with additional equity investment, to finance Sangria's growth.

[16]Similar, but not identical. The basic WACC formula assumes that rebalancing occurs at the end of each period. The unlevering and relevering formulas used in steps 1 and 2 of our three-step procedure are exact only if rebalancing is continuous so that the debt ratio stays constant day-to-day and week-to-week. However, the errors introduced from annual rebalancing are very small and can be ignored for practical purposes.

[17]The response of the cost of equity to changes in financial leverage can be affected by personal taxes. This is not covered here and is rarely adjusted for in practice.

Issue Costs

But suppose that the firm actually has to finance the $10 million investment by issuing stock (it will not have to issue stock if it rejects the project) and that issue costs soak up 5 percent of the gross proceeds of the issue. That means the firm has to issue $10,526,000 in order to obtain $10,000,000 cash. The $526,000 difference goes to underwriters, lawyers, and others involved in the issue process.

The project's APV is calculated by subtracting the issue cost from base-case NPV:

$$\begin{aligned}\text{APV} &= \text{base-case NPV} - \text{issue cost}\\ &= +170{,}000 - 526{,}000 = -\$356{,}000\end{aligned}$$

The firm would reject the project because APV is negative.

Additions to the Firm's Debt Capacity

Consider a different financing scenario. Suppose that the firm has a 50 percent target debt ratio. Its policy is to limit debt to 50 percent of its assets. Thus, if it invests more, it borrows more; in this sense investment adds to the firm's debt capacity.[18]

Is debt capacity worth anything? The most widely accepted answer is yes because of the tax shields generated by interest payments on corporate borrowing. (Look back to our discussion of debt and taxes in Chapter 18.) For example, MM's theory states that the value of the firm is independent of its capital structure *except* for the present value of interest tax shields:

$$\text{Firm value} = \text{value with all-equity financing} + \text{PV(tax shield)}$$

This theory tells us to compute the value of the firm in two steps: First compute its base-case value under all-equity financing, and then add the present value of taxes saved due to a departure from all-equity financing. This procedure is like an APV calculation for the firm as a whole.

We can repeat the calculation for a particular project. For example, suppose that the solar heater project increases the firm's assets by $10 million and therefore prompts it to borrow $5 million more. Suppose that this $5 million loan is repaid in equal installments, so that the amount borrowed declines with the depreciating book value of the solar heater project. We also assume that the loan carries an interest rate of 8 percent. Table 19.1 shows how the value of the interest tax shields is calculated. This is the value of the additional debt capacity contributed to the firm by the project. We obtain APV by adding this amount to the project's NPV:

$$\begin{aligned}\text{APV} &= \text{base-case NPV} + \text{PV(tax shield)}\\ &= +170{,}000 + 576{,}000 = \$746{,}000\end{aligned}$$

With these numbers, the solar heater project looks like a "go." But notice the differences between this APV calculation and an NPV calculated with a WACC used as the discount rate. The APV calculation assumes debt equal to 50 percent of book value, paid down on a fixed schedule. NPV using WACC assumes debt is a constant fraction of market value in each year of the project's life. Since the project's value will inevitably turn out higher or lower than expected, using WACC also assumes that

[18] *Debt capacity* is potentially misleading because it seems to imply an absolute limit to the amount the firm is *able* to borrow. That is not what we mean. The firm limits borrowing to 50 percent of assets as a rule of thumb for optimal capital structure. It could borrow more if it wanted to run increased risks of costs of financial distress.

Year	Debt Outstanding at Start of Year	Interest	Interest Tax Shield	Present Value of Tax Shield
1	$5,000	$400	$140	$129.6
2	4,500	360	126	108.0
3	4,000	320	112	88.9
4	3,500	280	98	72.0
5	3,000	240	84	57.2
6	2,500	200	70	44.1
7	2,000	160	56	32.6
8	1,500	120	42	22.7
9	1,000	80	28	14.0
10	500	40	14	6.5
			Total	$576

TABLE 19.1

Calculating the present value of interest tax shields on debt supported by the solar heater project (dollar figures in thousands).

Assumptions:

1. Marginal tax rate = T_c = .35; tax shield = $T_c \times$ interest.
2. Debt principal is repaid at end of year in ten $500,000 installments.
3. Interest rate on debt is 8 percent.
4. Present value is calculated at the 8 percent borrowing rate. The assumption here is that the tax shields are just as risky as the interest payments generating them.

future debt levels will be increased or reduced as necessary to keep the future debt ratio constant.

APV can be used when debt supported by a project is tied to the project's book value or has to be repaid on a fixed schedule. For example, Kaplan and Ruback used APV to analyze the prices paid for a sample of leveraged buyouts (LBOs). LBOs are takeovers, typically of mature companies, financed almost entirely with debt. However, the new debt is not intended to be permanent. LBO business plans call for generating extra cash by selling assets, shaving costs, and improving profit margins. The extra cash is used to pay down the LBO debt. Therefore you can't use WACC as a discount rate to evaluate an LBO because its debt ratio will not be constant.

APV works fine for LBOs. The company is first evaluated as if it were all-equity-financed. That means that cash flows are projected after tax, but without any interest tax shields generated by the LBO's debt. The tax shields are then valued separately. The debt repayment schedule is set down in the same format as Table 19.1 and the present value of interest tax shields is calculated and added to the all-equity value. Any other financing side effects are added also. The result is an APV valuation for the company.[19] Kaplan and Ruback found that APV did a pretty good job explaining prices paid in these hotly contested takeovers, considering that not all the information available to bidders had percolated into the public domain. Kaplan and Ruback were restricted to publicly available data.

[19]Kaplan and Ruback actually used "compressed" APV, in which all cash flows, including interest tax shields, are discounted at the opportunity cost of capital. S. N. Kaplan and R. S. Ruback, "The Valuation of Cash Flow Forecasts: An Empirical Analysis," *Journal of Finance* 50 (September 1995), pp. 1059–1093.

The Value of Interest Tax Shields

In Table 19.1, we boldly assume that the firm can fully capture interest tax shields of $.35 on every dollar of interest. We also treat the interest tax shields as safe cash inflows and discount them at a low 8 percent rate.

The true present value of the tax shields is almost surely less than $576,000:

- You can't use tax shields unless you pay taxes, and you don't pay taxes unless you make money. Few firms can be sure that future profitability will be sufficient to use up the interest tax shields.
- The government takes two bites out of corporate income: the corporate tax and the tax on bondholders' and stockholders' personal income. The corporate tax favors debt; the personal tax favors equity.
- A project's debt capacity depends on how well it does. When profits exceed expectations, the firm can borrow more; if the project fails, it won't support any debt. If the future amount of debt is tied to future project value, then the interest tax shields given in Table 19.1 are estimates, not fixed amounts.

In Chapter 18, we argued that the effective tax shield on interest was probably not 35 percent ($T_c = .35$) but some lower figure, call it T^*. We were unable to pin down an exact figure for T^*.

Suppose, for example, that we believe $T^* = .25$. We can easily recalculate the APV of the solar heater project. Just multiply the present value of the interest tax shields by 25/35. The bottom line of Table 19.1 drops from $576,000 to 576,000(25/35) = $411,000. APV drops to

$$\begin{aligned} \text{APV} &= \text{base-case NPV} + \text{PV(tax shield)} \\ &= +170{,}000 + 411{,}000 = \$581{,}000 \end{aligned}$$

PV(tax shield) drops still further if the tax shields are treated as forecasts and discounted at a higher rate. Suppose the firm ties the amount of debt to actual future project cash flows. Then the interest tax shields become just as risky as the project and should be discounted at the 12 percent opportunity cost of capital. PV(tax shield) drops to $362,000 at $T^* = .25$.

Review of the Adjusted-Present-Value Approach

If the decision to invest in a capital project has important side effects on other financial decisions made by the firm, those side effects should be taken into account when the project is evaluated. They include interest tax shields on debt supported by the project (a plus), any issue costs of raising financing for the project (a minus), or perhaps other side effects such as the value of a government-subsidized loan tied to the project.

The idea behind APV is to divide and conquer. The approach does not attempt to capture all the side effects in a single calculation. A series of present value calculations is made instead. The first establishes a base-case value for the project: its value as a separate, all-equity-financed mini-firm. Then each side effect is traced out, and the present value of its cost or benefit to the firm is calculated. Finally, all the present values are added together to estimate the project's total contribution to the value of the firm. Thus, in general,

$$\text{Project APV} = \text{base-case NPV} + \begin{array}{l}\text{sum of the present values of the side} \\ \text{effects of accepting the project}\end{array}$$

The wise financial manager will want to see not only the adjusted present value but also where that value is coming from. For example, suppose that base-case NPV is positive but the benefits are outweighed by the costs of issuing stock to finance the project. That should prompt the manager to look around to see if the project can be rescued by an alternative financing plan.

APV for International Projects

APV is most useful when financing side effects are numerous and important. This is frequently the case for large international projects, which may have custom-tailored *project financing* and special contracts with suppliers, customers, and governments.[20] Here are a few examples of financing side effects encountered in the international arena.

We explain project finance in Chapter 25. It typically means very high debt ratios to start, with most or all of a project's early cash flows committed to debt service. Equity investors have to wait. Since the debt ratio will not be constant, you have to turn to APV.

Project financing may include debt available at favorable interest rates. Most governments subsidize exports by making special financing packages available, and manufacturers of industrial equipment may stand ready to lend money to help close a sale. Suppose, for example, that your project requires construction of an on-site electricity generating plant. You solicit bids from suppliers in various countries. Don't be surprised if the competing suppliers sweeten their bids with offers of low interest rate project loans or if they offer to lease the plant on favorable terms. You should then calculate the NPVs of these loans or leases and include them in your project analysis.

Sometimes international projects are supported by contracts with suppliers or customers. Suppose a manufacturer wants to line up a reliable supply of a crucial raw material—powdered magnoosium, say. The manufacturer could subsidize a new magnoosium smelter by agreeing to buy 75 percent of production and guaranteeing a minimum purchase price. The guarantee is clearly a valuable addition to project APV: If the world price of powdered magnoosium falls below the minimum, the project doesn't suffer. You would calculate the value of this guarantee (by the methods explained in Chapters 20 and 21) and add it to APV.

Sometimes local governments impose costs or restrictions on investment or disinvestment. For example, Chile, in an attempt to slow down a flood of short-term capital inflows in the 1990s, required investors to "park" part of their incoming money in non-interest-bearing accounts for a period of two years. An investor in Chile during this period would calculate the cost of this requirement and subtract it from APV.

APV for the Perpetual Crusher Project

Discounting at WACC and calculating APV may seem like totally disconnected approaches to valuation. But we can show that, with consistent assumptions, they give nearly identical answers. We demonstrate this for the perpetual crusher project introduced in Section 19.1.

In the following calculations, we ignore any issue costs and concentrate on the value of interest tax shields. To keep things simple, we assume throughout this sec-

[20]Use of APV for international projects was first advocated by D. L. Lessard, "Valuing Foreign Cash Flows: An Adjusted Present Value Approach," in D. L. Lessard, ed., *International Financial Management: Theory and Application*, Warren, Gorham and Lamont, Boston, MA, 1979.

tion that the only financing side effects are the interest tax shields on debt supported by the perpetual crusher project, and we consider corporate taxes only. (In other words, $T^* = T_c$.) As in Section 19.1, we assume that the perpetual crusher is an exact match, in business risk and financing, to its parent, the Sangria Corporation.

Base-case NPV is found by discounting after-tax project cash flows of $1.355 million at the opportunity cost of capital r of 12 percent and then subtracting the $12.5 million outlay. The cash flows are perpetual, so

$$\text{Base-case NPV} = -12.5 + \frac{1.355}{.12} = -\$1.21 \text{ million}$$

Thus the project would not be worthwhile with all-equity financing. But it actually supports debt of $5 million. At an 8 percent borrowing rate ($r_D = .08$) and a 35 percent tax rate ($T_c = .35$), annual interest tax shields are $.35 \times .08 \times 5 = .14$, or $140,000.

What are those tax shields worth? It depends on the *financing rule* the company follows. There are two common rules:

- Financing Rule 1: *Debt fixed.* Borrow a fraction of *initial* project value and make any debt repayments on a predetermined schedule. We followed this rule in Table 19.1.
- Financing Rule 2: *Debt rebalanced.* Adjust the debt in each future period to keep it at a constant fraction of future project value.

What do these rules mean for the perpetual crusher project? Under Financing Rule 1, debt stays at $5 million come hell or high water, and interest tax shields stay at $140,000 per year. The tax shields are tied to fixed interest payments, so the 8 percent cost of debt is a reasonable discount rate:

$$\text{PV(tax shields, debt fixed)} = \frac{140{,}000}{.08} = \$1{,}750{,}000, \text{ or } \$1.75 \text{ million}$$

$$\begin{aligned} \text{APV} &= \text{base-case NPV} + \text{PV(tax shield)} \\ &= -1.21 + 1.75 = +\$.54 \text{ million} \end{aligned}$$

If the perpetual crusher were financed solely by equity, project value would be $11.29 million. With fixed debt of $5 million, value increases by PV(tax shield) to 11.29 + 1.75 = $13.04 million.

Under Financing Rule 2, debt is rebalanced to 40 percent of actual project value. That means future debt levels are not known at the start of the project. They shift up or down depending on the success or failure of the project. Interest tax shields therefore pick up the project's business risk.

If interest tax shields are just as risky as the project, they should be discounted at the project's opportunity cost of capital, in this case 12 percent.

$$\text{PV(tax shields, debt rebalanced)} = \frac{140{,}000}{.12} = 1{,}170{,}000, \text{ or } \$1.17 \text{ million}$$

$$\text{APV (debt rebalanced)} = -1.21 + 1.17 = -\$.04 \text{ million}$$

We have now valued the perpetual crusher project three different ways:

1. APV (debt fixed) = +$.54 million.
2. APV (debt rebalanced)= −$.04 million.
3. NPV (discounting at WACC)= $0 million.

The first APV is the highest, because it assumes that debt is fixed, not rebalanced, and that interest tax shields are as safe as the interest payments generating them.

A Technical Point on Financing Rule 2

But why don't APV calculations 2 and 3, which both follow Financing Rule 2, generate the same number? The answer is that our calculation of APV (debt rebalanced) gets the implications of Financing Rule 2 only approximately right.

Even when debt is rebalanced, *next year's* interest tax shields are fixed. Year 1's interest tax shield is fixed by the amount of debt at date 0, the start of the project. Therefore, year 1's interest tax shield should have been discounted at 8, not 12 percent.

Year 2's interest tax shield is not known at the start of the project, since debt is rebalanced at date 1, depending on the first year's performance. But once date 1's debt level is set, the interest tax shield is known. Therefore the forecasted interest tax shield at date 2 ($140,000) should be discounted for one year at 12 percent and one year at 8 percent.

The reasoning repeats. Every year, once debt is rebalanced, next year's interest tax shield is fixed. For example, year 15's interest tax shield is fixed once debt is rebalanced in year 14. Thus the present value of the year 15 tax shield is the date 0 forecast (again $140,000) discounted one year at 8 percent and 14 years at 12 percent.

So the procedure for calculating the exact value of tax shields under Financing Rule 2 is as follows:

1. Discount at the opportunity cost of capital, because future tax shields are tied to actual cash flows.
2. Multiply the resulting PV by $(1 + r)/(1 + r_D)$, because the tax shields are fixed one period before receipt.

For the perpetual crusher project, the forecasted interest tax shields are $140,000 or $.14 million. Their exact value is

$$\text{PV(approximate)} = \frac{.14}{.12} = \$1.17 \text{ million}$$

$$\text{PV(exact)} = 1.17 \times \left(\frac{1.12}{1.08}\right) = \$1.21 \text{ million}$$

The APV of the project, given these assumptions about future debt capacity, is

$$\begin{aligned} \text{APV} &= \text{base-case NPV} + \text{PV(tax shield)} \\ &= -1.21 + 1.21 = \$0 \text{ million} \end{aligned}$$

This calculation exactly matches our first valuation of the perpetual crusher project based on WACC. Discounting at WACC implicitly recognizes that next year's interest tax shield is fixed by this year's debt level.[21]

[21]Miles and Ezzell (see footnote 5) have come up with a useful formula for modifying WACC:

$$\text{WACC} = r - Lr_D T^*\left(\frac{1 + r}{1 + r_D}\right)$$

where L is the debt-to-value ratio and T^* is the net tax saving per dollar of interest paid. In practice T^* is hard to pin down, so the marginal tax rate T_c is used instead.

The Miles–Ezzell formula assumes Financing Rule 2, that is, that debt is rebalanced at the end of every period (although next year's interest tax shield is fixed). You can check that it values the Sangria project exactly (NPV = $0 million).

In Section 19.3, we used a three-step procedure to calculate WACC at different debt ratios. It turns out that this procedure is not exactly the same as the changes in WACC calculated by the Miles–Ezzell formula. However, the numerical differences are in practice very small. In the Sangria example they are lost in rounding.

Which Financing Rule?

In practice it rarely pays to worry whether interest tax shields are valued approximately (giving APV = −$.04 million) or exactly ($0 million). Your worrying time will be much better spent in refining forecasts of operating cash flows and thinking through what-if scenarios.

But which financing rule is better—debt fixed or debt rebalanced?

Sometimes debt has to be paid down on a fixed schedule, as for the solar heater project in Table 19.1. This is the case for most LBOs. But as a general rule we vote for the assumption of rebalancing, that is, for Financing Rule 2. Any capital budgeting procedure that assumes debt levels are *always* fixed after a project is undertaken is grossly oversimplified. Should we assume that the perpetual crusher project contributes $5 million to the firm's debt capacity not just when the project is undertaken but from here to eternity? That amounts to saying that the future value of the project will not change—a strong assumption indeed.

Financing Rule 2 is better: not "Always borrow $5 million," but "Always borrow 40 percent of the perpetual crusher project value." Then if project value increases, the firm borrows more. If it decreases, the firm borrows less. Under this policy you can no longer discount future interest tax shields at the borrowing rate because the shields are no longer certain. Their size depends on the amount actually borrowed and, therefore, on the actual future value of the project.

APV and Hurdle Rates

APV tells you whether a project makes a net contribution to the value of the firm. It can also tell you a project's *break-even* cash flow or internal rate of return. Let's check this for the perpetual crusher project. We first calculate the income at which APV = 0. We will then determine the project's minimum acceptable internal rate of return (IRR).

$$\text{APV} = \frac{\text{annual income}}{r} - \text{investment} + \text{PV(tax shield)}$$

$$= \frac{\text{annual income}}{.12} - 12.5 + 1.21 = 0$$

$$\text{Annual income} = \$1.355 \text{ million}$$

or 10.84 percent of the $12.5 million outlay. In other words, the minimum acceptable IRR for the project is 10.84 percent. At this IRR project APV is zero.

Suppose that we encounter another project with perpetual cash flows. Its opportunity cost of capital is also $r = .12$, and it also expands the firm's borrowing power by 40 percent of project value. We know that if such a project offers an IRR greater than 10.84 percent, it will have a positive APV. Therefore, we could shorten the analysis by just discounting the project's cash inflows at 10.84 percent.[22] This discount rate is the *adjusted cost of capital.* It reflects both the project's business risk and its contribution to the firm's debt capacity.

We will call the adjusted cost of capital r^*. To calculate r^* we find the minimum acceptable internal rate of return—the IRR at which APV = 0. The rule is this: *Accept projects which have a positive NPV at the adjusted cost of capital r^*.*

[22]Remember that forecasted project cash flows do *not* reflect the tax shields generated by any debt the project may support. Project taxes are calculated assuming all-equity financing.

The 10.84 percent adjusted cost of capital for the perpetual crusher project is (no surprise) identical to Sangria Corporation's WACC, calculated in Section 19.1.

A General Definition of the Adjusted Cost of Capital

We recapitulate the two concepts of cost of capital:

- Concept 1: *The opportunity cost of capital (r).* This is the expected rate of return offered in capital markets by equivalent-risk assets. This depends on the risk of the project's cash flows. The opportunity cost of capital is the correct discount rate for the project if it is all-equity-financed.
- Concept 2: *The adjusted cost of capital* (r^*). This is an adjusted opportunity cost or hurdle rate that reflects the financing side effects of an investment project.

Some people just say "cost of capital." Sometimes their meaning is clear in context. At other times, they don't know which concept they are referring to, and that can sow widespread confusion.

When financing side effects are important, you should accept projects with positive APVs. But if you know the adjusted discount rate, you don't have to calculate APV: You just calculate NPV at the adjusted rate. The weighted-average cost of capital formula is the most common way to calculate the adjusted cost of capital.

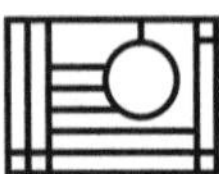

19.5 DISCOUNTING SAFE, NOMINAL CASH FLOWS

Suppose you're considering purchase of a $100,000 machine. The manufacturer sweetens the deal by offering to finance the purchase by lending you $100,000 for five years, with annual interest payments of 5 percent. You would have to pay 13 percent to borrow from a bank. Your marginal tax rate is 35 percent ($T_c = .35$).

How much is this loan worth? If you take it, the cash flows, in thousands of dollars, are

	Period					
	0	1	2	3	4	5
Cash flow	100	−5	−5	−5	−5	−105
Tax shield		+1.75	+1.75	+1.75	+1.75	+1.75
After-tax cash flow	100	−3.25	−3.25	−3.25	−3.25	−103.25

What is the right discount rate?

Here you are discounting *safe, nominal* cash flows—safe because your company must commit to pay if it takes the loan,[23] and nominal because the payments would be fixed regardless of future inflation. Now, the correct discount rate for safe, nominal cash flows is your company's *after-tax, un*subsidized borrowing rate.[24] In this case $r^* = r_D(1 - T_c) = .13(1 - .35) = .0845$. Therefore

[23]In theory, *safe* means literally "risk-free," like the cash returns on a Treasury bond. In practice, it means that the risk of not paying or receiving a cash flow is small.

[24]In Section 13.1 we calculated the NPV of subsidized financing using the *pretax* borrowing rate. Now you can see that was a mistake. Using the pretax rate implicitly defines the loan in terms of its pretax cash flows, violating a rule promulgated way back in Section 6.1: *Always* estimate cash flows on an after-tax basis.

$$\text{NPV} = +100 - \frac{3.25}{1.0845} - \frac{3.25}{(1.0845)^2} - \frac{3.25}{(1.0845)^3} - \frac{3.25}{(1.0845)^4} - \frac{103.25}{(1.0845)^5}$$
$$= +20.52, \text{ or } \$20{,}520$$

The manufacturer has effectively cut the machine's purchase price from $100,000 to $100,000 − $20,520 = $79,480. You can now go back and recalculate the machine's NPV using this fire-sale price, or you can use the NPV of the subsidized loan as one element of the machine's adjusted present value.

A General Rule

Clearly, we owe an explanation of why $r_D(1 - T_c)$ is the right discount rate for safe, nominal cash flows. It's no surprise that the rate depends on r_D, the unsubsidized borrowing rate, for that is investors' opportunity cost of capital, the rate they would demand from your company's debt. But why should r_D be converted to an *after-tax* figure?

Let's simplify by taking a *one-year* subsidized loan of $100,000 at 5 percent. The cash flows, in thousands of dollars, are

	Period 0	Period 1
Cash flow	100	−105
Tax shield		+1.75
After-tax cash flow	100	−103.25

Now ask, What is the maximum amount X that could be borrowed for one year through regular channels if $103,250 is set aside to service the loan?

"Regular channels" means borrowing at 13 percent pretax and 8.45 percent after tax. Therefore you will need 108.45 percent of the amount borrowed to pay back principal plus after-tax interest charges. If $1.0845X = 103{,}250$, then $X = 95{,}205$. Now if you can borrow $100,000 by a subsidized loan, but only $95,205 through normal channels, the difference ($4,795) is money in the bank. Therefore, it must also be the NPV of this one-period subsidized loan.

When you discount a safe, nominal cash flow at an after-tax borrowing rate, you are implicitly calculating the *equivalent loan*, the amount you could borrow through normal channels, using the cash flow as debt service. Note that

$$\text{Equivalent loan} = \text{PV}\begin{pmatrix}\text{cash flow available}\\ \text{for debt service}\end{pmatrix} = \frac{103{,}250}{1.0845} = 95{,}205$$

In some cases, it may be easier to think of taking the lender's side of the equivalent loan rather than the borrower's. For example, you could ask, How much would my company have to invest today in order to cover next year's debt service on the subsidized loan? The answer is $95,205: If you lend that amount at 13 percent, you will earn 8.45 percent after tax, and therefore have 95,205(1.0845) = $103,250. By this transaction, you can in effect cancel, or "zero out," the future obligation. If you can borrow $100,000 and then set aside only $95,205 to cover all the required debt service, you clearly have $4,795 to spend as you please. That amount is the NPV of the subsidized loan.

Therefore, regardless of whether it's easier to think of borrowing or lending, the correct discount rate for safe, nominal cash flows is an after-tax interest rate.[25]

In some ways, this is an obvious result once you think about it. Companies are free to borrow or lend money. If they *lend,* they receive the after-tax interest rate on their investment; if they *borrow* in the capital market, they pay the after-tax interest rate. Thus, the opportunity cost to companies of investing in debt-equivalent cash flows is the after-tax interest rate. This is the adjusted cost of capital for debt-equivalent cash flows.[26]

Some Further Examples

Here are some further examples of debt-equivalent cash flows.

Payout Fixed by Contract Suppose you sign a maintenance contract with a truck leasing firm, which agrees to keep your leased trucks in good working order for the next two years in exchange for 24 fixed monthly payments. These payments are debt-equivalent flows.[27]

Depreciation Tax Shields Capital projects are normally valued by discounting the total after-tax cash flows they are expected to generate. Depreciation tax shields contribute to project cash flow, but they are not valued separately; they are just folded into project cash flows along with dozens, or hundreds, of other specific inflows and outflows. The project's opportunity cost of capital reflects the average risk of the resulting aggregate.

However, suppose we ask what depreciation tax shields are worth *by themselves.* For a firm that's sure to pay taxes, depreciation tax shields are a safe, nominal flow. Therefore, they should be discounted at the firm's after-tax borrowing rate.[28]

Suppose we buy an asset with a depreciable basis of $200,000, which can be depreciated by the five-year tax depreciation schedule (see Table 6.4). The resulting tax shields are

[25]Borrowing and lending rates should not differ by much if the cash flows are truly safe, that is, if the chance of default is small. Usually your decision will not hinge on the rate used. If it does, ask which offsetting transaction—borrowing or lending—seems most natural and reasonable for the problem at hand. Then use the corresponding interest rate.

[26]All the examples in this section are forward-looking; they call for the value today of a stream of future debt-equivalent cash flows. But similar issues arise in legal and contractual disputes when a *past* cash flow has to be brought forward in time to a present value today. Suppose it's determined that company A should have paid B $1 million ten years ago. B clearly deserves more than $1 million today, because it has lost the time value of money. The time value of money should be expressed as an after-tax borrowing or lending rate, or if no risk enters, as the after-tax risk-free rate. The time value of money is *not* equal to B's overall cost of capital. Allowing B to "earn" its overall cost of capital on the payment allows it to earn a risk premium without bearing risk. For a broader discussion of these issues, see F. Fisher and C. Romaine, "Janis Joplin's Yearbook and Theory of Damages," *Journal of Accounting, Auditing & Finance* 5 (Winter/Spring 1990), pp. 145–157.

[27]We assume you are locked into the contract. If it can be canceled without penalty, you may have a valuable option.

[28]The depreciation tax shields are cash inflows, not outflows as for the contractual payout or the subsidized loan. For safe, nominal inflows, the relevant question is, How much could the firm borrow today if it uses the inflow for debt service? You could also ask, How much would the firm have to lend today to generate the same future inflow?

	Period					
	1	2	3	4	5	6
Percentage deductions	20	32	19.2	11.5	11.5	5.8
Dollar deductions (thousands)	\$40	\$64	\$38.4	\$23	\$23	\$11.6
Tax shields at $T_c = .35$ (thousands)	\$14	\$22.4	\$13.4	\$8.1	\$8.1	\$4.0

The after-tax discount rate is $r_D(1 - T_c) = .13(1 - .35) = .0845$. (We continue to assume a 13 percent pretax borrowing rate and a 35 percent marginal tax rate.) The present value of these shields is

$$\begin{aligned} \text{PV} &= \frac{14}{1.0845} + \frac{22.4}{(1.0845)^2} + \frac{13.4}{(1.0845)^3} + \frac{8.1}{(1.0845)^4} + \frac{8.1}{(1.0845)^5} + \frac{4.0}{(1.0845)^6} \\ &= +56.2, \text{ or } \$56{,}200 \end{aligned}$$

A Consistency Check

You may have wondered whether our procedure for valuing debt-equivalent cash flows is consistent with the WACC and APV approaches presented earlier in this chapter. Yes, it is consistent, as we will now illustrate.

Let's look at another very simple numerical example. You are asked to value a $1 million payment to be received from a blue-chip company one year hence. After taxes at 35 percent, the cash inflow is $650,000. The payment is fixed by contract.

Since the contract generates a debt-equivalent flow, the opportunity cost of capital is the rate investors would demand on a one-year note issued by the blue-chip company, which happens to be 8 percent. For simplicity, we'll assume this is your company's borrowing rate too. Our valuation rule for debt-equivalent flows is therefore to discount at $r^* = r_D(1 - T_c) = .08(1 - .35) = .052$:

$$\text{PV} = \frac{650{,}000}{1.052} = \$617{,}900$$

What is the *debt capacity* of this $650,000 payment? Exactly $617,900. Your company could borrow that amount and pay off the loan completely—principal and after-tax interest—with the $650,000 cash inflow. The debt capacity is 100 percent of the PV of the debt-equivalent cash flow.

If you think of it that way, our discount rate $r_D(1 - T_c)$ is just a special case of WACC with a 100 percent debt ratio ($D/V = 1$).

$$\begin{aligned} \text{WACC} &= r_D(1 - T_c)D/V + r_E E/V \\ &= r_D(1 - T_c) \text{ if } D/V = 1 \text{ and } E/V = 0 \end{aligned}$$

Now let's try an APV calculation. This is a two-part valuation. First, the $650,000 inflow is discounted at the opportunity cost of capital, 8 percent. Second, we add the present value of interest tax shields on debt supported by the project. Since the firm can borrow 100 percent of the cash flow's value, the tax shield is $r_D T_c \text{APV}$, and APV is

$$\text{APV} = \frac{650{,}000}{1.08} + \frac{.08(.35)\text{APV}}{1.08}$$

Solving for APV, we get \$617,900, the same answer we obtained by discounting at the after-tax borrowing rate. Thus our valuation rule for debt-equivalent flows is a special case of APV.

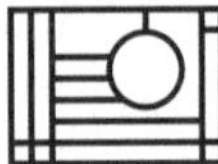

19.6 YOUR QUESTIONS ANSWERED

Question: All these cost of capital formulas—which ones do financial managers actually use?

Answer: The after-tax weighted-average cost of capital, most of the time. WACC is estimated for the company, or sometimes for an industry. We recommend industry WACCs when data are available for several closely comparable firms. The firms should have similar assets, operations, business risks, and growth opportunities.

Of course, conglomerate companies, with divisions operating in two or more unrelated industries, should not use a single company or industry WACC. Such firms should try to estimate a different industry WACC for each operating division.

Question: But WACC is the correct discount rate only for "average" projects. What if the project's financing differs from the company's or industry's?

Answer: Remember, investment projects are usually not separately financed. Even when they are, you should focus on the project's contribution to the firm's overall debt capacity, not on its immediate financing. (Suppose it's convenient to raise all the money for a particular project with a bank loan. That doesn't mean the project itself supports 100 percent debt financing. The company is borrowing against its existing assets as well as the project.)

But if the project's debt capacity is materially different from the company's existing assets, or if the company's overall debt policy changes, WACC should be adjusted. The adjustment can be done by the three-step procedure explained in Section 19.3.

Question: Could we do one more numerical example?

Answer: Sure. Suppose that WACC has been estimated as follows at a 30 percent debt ratio:

$$\begin{aligned} \text{WACC} &= r_D(1 - T_c)\frac{D}{V} + r_E\frac{E}{V} \\ &= .09(1 - .35)(.3) + .15(.7) = .1226, \text{ or } 12.26\% \end{aligned}$$

What is the correct discount rate at a 50 percent debt ratio?

First, let's repeat the three-step procedure.

Step 1. Calculate the opportunity cost of capital.

$$\begin{aligned} r &= r_D D/V + r_E E/V \\ &= .09(.3) + .15(.7) = .132 \text{ or } 13.2\% \end{aligned}$$

Step 2. Calculate the new costs of debt and equity. The cost of debt will be higher at 50 percent debt than 30 percent. Say it is $r_D = .095$. The new cost of equity is

$$\begin{aligned} r_E &= r + (r - r_D)D/E \\ &= .132 + (.132 - .095)50/50 \\ &= .169 \text{ or } 16.9\% \end{aligned}$$

Step 3. Recalculate WACC.

$$\text{WACC} = r_D(1 - T_c)D/V + r_E E/V$$
$$= .095(1 - .35)(.5) + .169(.5) = .1154, \text{ or about } 11.5\%$$

Question: How do I use the capital asset pricing model to calculate the after-tax weighted-average cost of capital?

Answer: First plug the equity beta into the capital asset pricing formula to calculate r_E, the expected return to equity. Then use this figure, along with the after-tax cost of debt and the debt-to-value and equity-to-value ratios, in the WACC formula. We covered this in Chapter 9. The only change here is use of the after-tax cost of debt, $r_D(1 - T_c)$.

Of course the CAPM is not the only way to estimate the cost of equity. For example, you might be able to use arbitrage pricing theory (APT—see Section 8.4) or the dividend-discount model (see Section 4.3).

Question: But suppose I do use the CAPM? What if I have to recalculate the equity beta for a different debt ratio?

Answer: The formula for the equity beta is

$$\beta_E = \beta_A + (\beta_A - \beta_D)\frac{D}{E}$$

where β_E is the equity beta, β_A is the asset beta, and β_D is the beta of the company's debt.

Question: Can I use the capital asset pricing model to calculate the asset beta and the opportunity cost of capital?

Answer: Sure. We covered this in Chapter 9. The asset beta is a weighted average of the debt and equity betas:[29]

$$\beta_A = \beta_D\frac{D}{V} + \beta_E\frac{E}{V}$$

Suppose you needed the opportunity cost of capital r. You could calculate β_A and then r from the capital asset pricing model.

Question: I think I understand how to adjust for differences in debt capacity or debt policy. How about differences in business risk?

Answer: If business risk is different, then r, the opportunity cost of capital, is different.

Figuring out the right r for an unusually safe or risky project is never easy. Sometimes the financial manager can use estimates of risk and expected return for companies similar to the project. Suppose, for example, that a traditional pharmaceutical company is considering a major commitment to biotech research. The financial manager could pick a sample of biotech companies, estimate their

[29]This formula assumes Financing Rule 2. If debt is fixed, taxes complicate the formulas. For example, if debt is fixed and permanent, and only corporate taxes are considered, the formula for β_E changes to

$$\beta_E = \beta_A + (\beta_A - \beta_D)(1 - T_c)D/E$$

average beta and cost of capital, and use these estimates as benchmarks for the biotech investment.

But in many cases it's difficult to find a good sample of matching companies for an unusually safe or risky project. Then the financial manager has to adjust the opportunity cost of capital by judgment.[30] Section 9.5 may be helpful in such cases.

Question: Let's go back to the cost of capital formulas. The tax rates are confusing. When should I use T_c and when T^*?

Answer: Always use T_c, the marginal corporate tax rate, (1) when calculating WACC as a weighted average of the costs of debt and equity and (2) when discounting safe, nominal cash flows. In each case the discount rate is adjusted *only* for corporate taxes.[31]

APV in principle calls for T^*, the net tax saving per dollar of interest paid by the firm. This depends on the effective personal tax rates on debt and equity income. T^* is almost surely less than T_c, but it is very difficult to pin down the numerical difference. Therefore in practice T_c is almost always used as an approximation.

Question: When do I need adjusted present value (APV)?

Answer: The WACC formula picks up only one financing side effect: the value of interest tax shields on debt supported by a project. If there are other side effects—subsidized financing tied to a project, for example—you should use APV.

You can also use APV to show the value of interest tax shields:

$$\text{APV} = \text{base-case NPV} + \text{PV(tax shield)}$$

where base-case NPV assumes all-equity financing. But it's usually easier to do this calculation in one step, by discounting project cash flows at an adjusted cost of capital (usually WACC). Remember, though, that discounting by WACC usually assumes Financing Rule 2, that is, debt rebalanced to a constant fraction of future project value. If this financing rule is not right, you may need APV to calculate PV(tax shield), as we did for the solar heater project in Table 19.1.[32]

Suppose, for example, that you are analyzing a company just after a leveraged recapitalization. The company has a very high initial debt level but plans to pay down the debt as rapidly as possible. APV could be used to obtain an accurate valuation.

[30]The judgment may be implicit. That is, the manager may not explicitly announce that the discount rate for a high-risk project is, say, 2.5 percentage points above the standard rate. But the project will not be approved unless it offers a higher-than-standard rate of return.

[31]Any effects of personal income taxes are reflected in r_D and r_E, the rates of return demanded by debt and equity investors.

[32]Having read Section 19.5, you may be wondering why we did not discount at the *after-tax* borrowing rate in Table 19.1. The answer is that we wanted to simplify and take one thing at a time. If debt is fixed and the odds of financial distress are low, interest tax shields are safe, nominal flows, and there is a case for using the after-tax rate. Doing so assumes that the firm will, or can, take out an additional loan with debt service exactly covered by the interest tax shields.

Investment decisions always have side effects on financing: Every dollar spent has to be raised somehow. Sometimes the side effects are irrelevant or at least unimportant. In an ideal world with no taxes, transaction costs, or other market imperfections, only investment decisions would affect firm value. In such a world firms could analyze all investment opportunities as if they were all-equity-financed. Firms would decide which assets to buy and then worry about getting the money to pay for them. No one making investment decisions would worry about where the money might come from because debt policy, dividend policy, and all other financing choices would have no impact on stockholders' wealth.

Side effects cannot be ignored in practice. There are two ways to take them into account. You can calculate NPV by discounting at an adjusted discount rate, or you can discount at the opportunity cost of capital and then add or subtract the present value of financing side effects. The second approach is called adjusted present value, or APV.

The most commonly used adjusted discount rate is the after-tax weighted-average cost of capital, or WACC:

$$\text{WACC} = r_D(1 - T_c)\frac{D}{V} + r_E\frac{E}{V}$$

Here r_D and r_E are the expected rates of return demanded by investors in the firm's debt and equity securities, respectively; D and E are the current *market values* of debt and equity; and V is the total market value of the firm ($V = D + E$).

Strictly speaking, this formula works only for projects that are carbon copies of the existing firm—projects with the same business risk that will be financed to maintain the firm's current, market debt ratio. But firms can use WACC as a benchmark rate to be adjusted for differences in business risk or financing. We suggested a three-step procedure for adjusting a company's WACC for differences between project and company debt ratios.

Discounting project cash flows at the WACC assumes that debt is rebalanced every period to keep a constant debt-to-market-value ratio. The amount of debt supported by a project is supposed to rise or fall with the project's after-the-fact success or failure. We called this Financing Rule 2. The WACC formula also assumes that financing matters *only* because of interest tax shields. When this or other assumptions are violated, only APV will give an absolutely correct answer.

APV is, in concept at least, simple. First calculate the present value of the project as if there are no important side effects. Then adjust present value to calculate the project's total impact on firm value. The rule is to accept the project if APV is positive:

$$\text{Accept project if APV} = \text{base-case NPV} + \begin{array}{c}\text{present value}\\ \text{of financing}\\ \text{side effects}\end{array} > 0$$

The base-case NPV is the project's NPV computed assuming all-equity financing and perfect capital markets. Think of it as the project's value if it were set up as a separate mini-firm. You would compute the mini-firm's value by forecasting its cash flows and discounting at the opportunity cost of capital for the project. The cash flows should be net of the taxes that an all-equity-financed mini-firm would pay.

Financing side effects are evaluated one by one and their present values are added to or subtracted from base-case NPV. We looked at several cases:

1. *Issue costs.* If accepting the project forces the firm to issue securities, then the present value of issue costs should be subtracted from base-case NPV.
2. *Interest tax shields.* Debt interest is a tax-deductible expense. Most people believe that interest tax shields contribute to firm value. Thus a project that prompts the firm to borrow more generates additional value. The project's APV is increased by the present value of interest tax shields on debt the project supports.
3. *Special financing.* Sometimes special financing opportunities are tied to project acceptance. For example, the government might offer subsidized financing for socially desirable projects. You simply compute the present value of the financing opportunity and add it to base-case NPV.

Remember not to confuse *contribution to corporate debt capacity* with the immediate source of funds for investment. For example, a firm might, as a matter of convenience, borrow \$1 million for a \$1 million research program. But the research would be unlikely to contribute \$1 million in debt capacity; a large part of the \$1 million new debt would be supported by the firm's other assets.

Also remember that *debt capacity* is not meant to imply an absolute limit on how much the firm *can* borrow. The phrase refers to how much it *chooses* to borrow. Normally the firm's optimal debt level increases as its assets expand; that is why we say that a new project contributes to corporate debt capacity.

Calculating APV may require several steps: one step for base-case NPV and one for each financing side effect. Many firms try to calculate APV in a single calculation. They do so by the following procedure: After-tax cash flows are forecasted in the usual way—that is, as if the project is all-equity-financed. But the discount rate is adjusted to reflect the financing side effects. If the discount rate is adjusted correctly, the result is APV:

$$\begin{array}{c}\text{NPV at adjusted}\\\text{discount rate}\end{array} = \text{APV} = \begin{array}{c}\text{NPV at opportunity}\\\text{cost of capital}\end{array} + \begin{array}{c}\text{present value of}\\\text{financing side effects}\end{array}$$

WACC is the leading example of an adjusted discount rate.

This chapter is almost 100 percent theory. The theory is difficult. If you think you understand all the formulas, assumptions, and relationships on the first reading, we suggest psychiatric assistance. We can, however, offer one simple, bullet-proof, easy-to-remember rule: Discount safe, nominal cash flows at the after-tax borrowing rate.

Visit us at www.mhhe.com/bm7e

FURTHER READING

The adjusted-present-value rule was developed in:

S. C. Myers: "Interactions of Corporate Financing and Investment Decisions—Implications for Capital Budgeting," *Journal of Finance,* 29:1–25 (March 1974).

The Harvard Business Review *has published a popular account of APV:*

T. A. Luehrman, "Using APV: A Better Tool for Valuing Operations," *Harvard Business Review* 75:145–154 (May–June 1997).

There have been dozens of articles on the weighted-average cost of capital and other issues discussed in this chapter. Here are two:

J. Miles and R. Ezzell: "The Weighted Average Cost of Capital, Perfect Capital Markets, and Project Life: A Clarification," *Journal of Financial and Quantitative Analysis,* 15:719–730 (September 1980).

R. A. Taggart, Jr.: "Consistent Valuation and Cost of Capital Expressions with Corporate and Personal Taxes," *Financial Management,* 20:8–20 (Autumn 1991).

The valuation rule for safe, nominal cash flows is developed in:

R. S. Ruback: "Calculating the Market Value of Risk-Free Cash Flows," *Journal of Financial Economics,* 15:323–339 (March 1986).

QUIZ

1. Calculate the weighted-average cost of capital (WACC) for Federated Junkyards of America, using the following information:
- Debt: $75,000,000 book value outstanding. The debt is trading at 90 percent of par. The yield to maturity is 9 percent.
- Equity: 2,500,000 shares selling at $42 per share. Assume the expected rate of return on Federated's stock is 18 percent.
- Taxes: Federated's marginal tax rate is $T_c = .35$.

What are the key assumptions underlying your calculation? For what type of project would Federated's weighted-average cost of capital be the right discount rate?

2. Suppose Federated Junkyards decides to move to a more conservative debt policy. A year later its debt ratio is down to 15 percent ($D/V = .15$). The interest rate has dropped to 8.6 percent. Recalculate Federated's WACC under these new assumptions. The company's business risk, opportunity cost of capital, and tax rate have not changed. Use the three-step procedure explained in Section 19.3.

3. True or false? Use of the WACC formula assumes
- **a.** A project supports a fixed amount of debt over the project's economic life.
- **b.** The *ratio* of the debt supported by a project to project value is constant over the project's economic life.
- **c.** The firm rebalances debt, each period, keeping the debt-to-value ratio constant.

4. What is meant by the flow-to-equity valuation method? What discount rate is used in this method? What assumptions are necessary for this method to give an accurate valuation?

5. True or false? The APV method
- **a.** Starts with a base-case value for the project.
- **b.** Calculates the base-case value by discounting project cash flows, forecasted assuming all-equity financing, at the WACC for the project.
- **c.** Is especially useful when debt is to be paid down on a fixed schedule.
- **d.** Can be used to calculate an adjusted discount rate for a company or a project.

6. Explain the difference between Financing Rules 1 (debt fixed) and 2 (debt rebalanced).

7. What is meant by financing "side effects" in an APV valuation? Give at least three examples of side effects encountered in practice.

8. A project costs $1 million and has a base-case NPV of exactly zero (NPV = 0). What is the project's APV in the following cases?
- **a.** If the firm invests, it has to raise $500,000 by stock issue. Issue costs are 15 percent of *net* proceeds.
- **b.** The firm has ample cash on hand. But if it invests, it will have access to $500,000 of debt financing at a subsidized interest rate. The present value of the subsidy is $175,000.

c. If the firm invests, its debt capacity increases by $500,000. The present value of interest tax shields on this debt is $76,000.

9. Whispering Pines, Inc., is all-equity-financed. The expected rate of return on the company's shares is 12 percent.
   a. What is the opportunity cost of capital for an average-risk Whispering Pines investment?
   b. Suppose the company issues debt, repurchases shares, and moves to a 30 percent debt-to-value ratio ($D/V = .30$). What will the company's weighted-average cost of capital be at the new capital structure? The borrowing rate is 7.5 percent and the tax rate is 35 percent.

10. Consider the APV of the solar heater project, as calculated in Table 19.1. How would the APV change if the net tax shield per dollar of interest were not $T_c = .35$, but $T^* = .10$?

11. Consider a project lasting one year only. The initial outlay is $1,000 and the expected inflow is $1,200. The opportunity cost of capital is $r = .20$. The borrowing rate is $r_D = .10$, and the net tax shield per dollar of interest is $T^* = T_c = .35$.
    a. What is the project's base-case NPV?
    b. What is its APV if the firm borrows 30 percent of the project's required investment?

12. The WACC formula seems to imply that debt is "cheaper" than equity—that is, that a firm with more debt could use a lower discount rate. Does this make sense? Explain briefly.

13. What discount rate should be used to value safe, nominal cash flows? Explain briefly.

14. The U.S. government has settled a dispute with your company for $16 million. It is committed to pay this amount in exactly 12 months. However, your company will have to pay tax on the award at a marginal tax rate of 35 percent. What is the award worth? The one-year Treasury rate is 5.5 percent.

Visit us at www.mhhe.com/bm7e

PRACTICE QUESTIONS

1. Table 19.2 shows a *book* balance sheet for the Wishing Well Motel chain. The company's long-term debt is secured by its real estate assets, but it also uses short-term bank financing. It pays 10 percent interest on the bank debt and 9 percent interest on the secured debt. Wishing Well has 10 million shares of stock outstanding, trading at $90 per share. The expected return on Wishing Well's common stock is 18 percent.

   Calculate Wishing Well's WACC. Assume that the book and market values of Wishing Well's debt are the same. The marginal tax rate is 35 percent.

2. Suppose Wishing Well is evaluating a new motel and resort on a romantic site in Madison County, Wisconsin. Explain how you would forecast the after-tax cash flows for this project. (*Hints:* How would you treat taxes? Interest expense? Changes in working capital?)

3. To finance the Madison County project, Wishing Well will have to arrange an additional $80 million of long-term debt and make a $20 million equity issue. Underwriting fees,

TABLE 19.2

Balance sheet for Wishing Well, Inc. (figures in $ millions).

Cash, marketable securities	100	Accounts payable	120
Inventory	50	Bank loan	280
Accounts receivable	200	Current liabilities	400
Current assets	350		
Real estate	2,100	Long-term debt	1,800
Other assets	150	Equity	400
Total	2,600	Total	2,600

TABLE 19.3

Simplified book balance sheet for Rensselaer Felt (figures in $ thousands).

Cash and marketable securities	1,500	Short-term debt	75,600
Accounts receivable	120,000	Accounts payable	62,000
Inventories	125,000	Current liabilities	137,600
Current assets	246,500		
Property, plant, and equipment	302,000	Long-term debt	208,600
		Deferred taxes	45,000
Other assets	89,000	Shareholders' equity	246,300
Total	637,500	Total	637,500

spreads, and other costs of this financing will total $4 million. How would you take this into account in valuing the proposed investment?

4. Table 19.3 shows a simplified balance sheet for Rensselaer Felt. Calculate this company's weighted-average cost of capital. The debt has just been refinanced at an interest rate of 6 percent (short term) and 8 percent (long term). The expected rate of return on the company's shares is 15 percent. There are 7.46 million shares outstanding, and the shares are trading at $46. The tax rate is 35 percent.

5. How will Rensselaer Felt's WACC and cost of equity change if it issues $50 million in new equity and uses the proceeds to retire long-term debt? Assume the company's borrowing rates are unchanged. Use the three-step procedure from Section 19.3.

6. Look one more time at practice question 4. Renssalaer Felt's pretax operating income is $100.5 million. Assume for simplicity that this figure is expected to remain constant forever. Value the company by the flow-to-equity method.

7. Rapidly growing companies may have to issue shares to finance capital expenditures. In doing so, they incur underwriting and other issue costs. Some analysts have tried to adjust WACC to account for these costs. For example, if issue costs are 8 percent of equity issue proceeds, and equity issues account for all of equity financing, the cost of equity might be divided by $1 - .08 = .92$. This would increase a 15 percent cost of equity to $15/.92 = 16.3$ percent.

   Explain why this sort of adjustment is *not* a smart idea. What is the correct way to take issue costs into account in project valuation?

8. Digital Organics (DO) has the opportunity to invest $1 million now ($t = 0$) and expects after-tax returns of $600,000 in $t = 1$ and $700,000 in $t = 2$. The project will last for two years only. The appropriate cost of capital is 12 percent with all-equity financing, the borrowing rate is 8 percent, and DO will borrow $300,000 against the project. This debt must be repaid in two equal installments. Assume debt tax shields have a net value of $.30 per dollar of interest paid. Calculate the project's APV using the procedure followed in Table 19.1.

9. You are considering a five-year lease of office space for R&D personnel. Once signed, the lease cannot be canceled. It would commit your firm to six annual $100,000 payments, with the first payment due immediately. What is the present value of the lease if your company's borrowing rate is 9 percent and its tax rate is 35 percent? *Note:* The lease payments would be tax-deductible.

10. Consider another perpetual project like the crusher described in Section 19.1. Its initial investment is $1,000,000, and the expected cash inflow is $85,000 a year in perpetuity. The opportunity cost of capital with all-equity financing is 10 percent, and the project allows the firm to borrow at 7 percent. Assume the net tax advantage to borrowing is $.35 per dollar of interest paid ($T^* = T_c = .35$).

    Use APV to calculate this project's value.

a. Assume first that the project will be partly financed with $400,000 of debt and that the debt amount is to be fixed and perpetual.

b. Then assume that the initial borrowing will be increased or reduced in proportion to changes in the future market value of this project.

Explain the difference between your answers to **(a)** and **(b).**

11. Suppose the project described in practice question 10 is to be undertaken by a university. Funds for the project will be withdrawn from the university's endowment, which is invested in a widely diversified portfolio of stocks and bonds. However, the university can also borrow at 7 percent. The university is tax exempt.

The university treasurer proposes to finance the project by issuing $400,000 of perpetual bonds at 7 percent and by selling $600,000 worth of common stocks from the endowment. The expected return on the common stocks is 10 percent. He therefore proposes to evaluate the project by discounting at a weighted-average cost of capital, calculated as

$$r = r_D \frac{D}{V} + r_E \frac{E}{V}$$

$$= .07\left(\frac{400{,}000}{1{,}000{,}000}\right) + .10\left(\frac{600{,}000}{1{,}000{,}000}\right)$$

$$= .088\text{, or } 8.8\%$$

What's right or wrong with the treasurer's approach? Should the university invest? Should it borrow? Would the project's value to the university change if the treasurer financed the project entirely by selling common stocks from the endowment?

12. What is meant by an adjusted discount rate (r^* in our notation)? In what circumstances would an adjusted discount rate *not* equal WACC?

13. The Bunsen Chemical Company is currently at its target debt ratio of 40 percent. It is contemplating a $1 million expansion of its existing business. This expansion is expected to produce a cash inflow of $130,000 a year in perpetuity.

The company is uncertain whether to undertake this expansion and how to finance it. The two options are a $1 million issue of common stock or a $1 million issue of 20-year debt. The flotation costs of a stock issue would be around 5 percent of the amount raised, and the flotation costs of a debt issue would be around 1½ percent.

Bunsen's financial manager, Miss Polly Ethylene, estimates that the required return on the company's equity is 14 percent, but she argues that the flotation costs increase the cost of new equity to 19 percent. On this basis, the project does not appear viable.

On the other hand, she points out that the company can raise new debt on a 7 percent yield which would make the cost of new debt 8½ percent. She therefore recommends that Bunsen should go ahead with the project and finance it with an issue of long-term debt.

Is Miss Ethylene right? How would you evaluate the project?

14. Curtis Bog, chief financial officer of Sphagnum Paper Corporation, is reviewing a consultant's analysis of Sphagnum's weighted-average cost of capital. The consultant proposes

$$\text{WACC} = (1 - T_c) r_D \frac{D}{V} + r_E \frac{E}{V}$$

$$= (1 - .35)(.103)(.55) + .183(.45)$$

$$= .1192\text{, or about } 12\%$$

Mr. Bog wants to check that this calculation is consistent with the capital asset pricing model. He has observed or estimated the following numbers:

Betas	$\beta_{debt} = .15$, $\beta_{equity} = 1.09$
Expected market risk premium ($r_m - r_f$)	.085
Risk-free rate of interest (r_f)	9 percent

Note: We suggest you simplify by ignoring personal income taxes and assuming that the promised and expected rates of returns on Sphagnum debt are equal.

15. Nevada Hydro is 40 percent debt-financed and has a weighted-average cost of capital of 9.7 percent:

$$\text{WACC} = (1 - T_c)r_D\frac{D}{V} + r_E\frac{E}{V}$$
$$= (1 - .35)(.085)(.40) + .125(.60) = .097$$

Banker's Tryst Company is advising Nevada Hydro to issue $75 million of preferred stock at a dividend yield of 9 percent. The proceeds would be used to repurchase and retire common stock. The preferred issue would account for 10 percent of the preissue market value of the firm.

Banker's Tryst argues that these transactions would reduce Nevada Hydro's WACC to 9.4 percent:

$$\text{WACC} = (1 - .35)(.085)(.40) + .09(.10) + .125(.50)$$
$$= .094, \text{ or } 9.4\%$$

Do you agree with this calculation? Explain.

16. Sometimes APV is particularly useful in international capital investment decisions. What kinds of tax or financing side effects are encountered in international projects?

17. Consider a different financing scenario for the solar water heater project discussed in Section 19.4. The project requires $10 million and has a base-case NPV of $170,000. Suppose the firm happens to have $5 million banked that could be used for the project.

The government, eager to encourage solar energy, offers to help finance the project by lending $5 million at a subsidized rate of 5 percent. The loan calls for the firm to pay the government $647,500 annually for 10 years (this amount includes both principal and interest).

a. What is the value of being able to borrow from the government at 5 percent? Assume the company's normal borrowing rate is 8 percent and the corporate tax rate is 35 percent.

b. Suppose the company's normal debt policy is to borrow 50 percent of the book value of its assets. It calculates the present value of interest tax shields by the procedure shown in Table 19.1 and includes this present value in APV. Should it do so here, given the government's offer of cheap financing?

18. Table 19.4 is a simplified book balance sheet for Phillips Petroleum in June 2001. Other information:

Number of outstanding shares (N)	256.2 million
Price per share (P)	$59
Beta based on 60 monthly returns, against the S&P Composite:	$\beta = .66$
Interest rates	
Treasury bills	3.5%
20-year Treasury bonds	5.8
New issue rate for Phillips assuming straight long-term debt	7.4
Marginal tax rate	35%

TABLE 19.4

Simplified book balance sheet for Phillips Petroleum, June 2001 (figures in $ millions).

Current assets	2,202	Current liabilities	2,780
Net property, plant, and equipment	15,124	Long-term debt	6,268
Investments and other assets	3,428	Deferred taxes	2,144
		Other liabilities	2,510
		Shareholders' equity	7,052
Total	20,754	Total	20,754

a. Calculate Phillips's WACC. Use the capital asset pricing model and the data given above. Make additional assumptions and approximations as necessary.

b. What would Phillips's WACC be if it moved to *and maintained* a debt—market value ratio (*D/V*) of 25 percent?

19. In question 18 you calculated a WACC for Phillips Petroleum. Phillips could also use an industry WACC. Under what conditions would the industry WACC be the better choice? Explain.

CHALLENGE QUESTIONS

1. In footnote 21 we referred to the Miles–Ezzell formula:

$$r^* = r - Lr_DT^*\left[\frac{1 + r}{1 + r_D}\right] = \text{WACC}$$

Derive this formula as the adjusted discount rate (r^*) for a one-period project. Then show that the formula correctly values projects of any life if the company follows Financing Rule 2.

2. In Section 19.3 we proposed a three-step procedure for calculating WACC at different debt ratios. The Miles–Ezzell formula can be used for the same purpose. Set up a numerical example and use these two approaches to calculate how WACC changes with financial leverage. Assume $T^* = T_c$. You will get slightly different numerical answers. Why?

3. Consider a project generating a level, perpetual stream of cash flows. The project is financed at an initial debt-to-value ratio *L*. The debt is likewise perpetual. But the company follows Financing Rule 1: The dollar amount of debt is kept constant. Derive a formula for the adjusted discount rate r^* to fit these assumptions.[33] What does this formula imply for **(a)** the difference between WACC and the opportunity cost of capital *r* and **(b)** the formulas for levering and relevering the cost of equity?

4. Financing Rule 2 ties the level of future interest tax shields to the future value of the project or company. That means the interest tax shields are risky and worth less than if the company followed Financing Rule 1. Does that mean that Financing Rule 1 is better for stockholders?

[33] Here you are following in MM's footsteps. See F. Modigliani and M. H. Miller, "Corporate Income Taxes and the Cost of Capital: A Correction," *American Economic Review* 53 (June 1963), pp. 433–443, and "Some Estimates of the Cost of Capital to the Electric Utility Industry," *American Economic Review* 56 (June 1966), pp. 333–391.

Some materials on cash and stock dividends is provided by:

www.e-analytics.com

www.dripcentral.com *(information on dividend reinvestment plans)*

John Graham's website contains material on capital structure:

www.duke.edu/~jgraham

ValuePro provides software and data for estimating WACCs:

www.valuepro.net

PART SIX

OPTIONS

POP QUIZ: WHAT do the following events have in common?

- Flatiron offers its president a bonus if the company's stock price exceeds $120.
- BJ Services issues 4.8 million warrants as partial payment for an acquisition.
- Tyco issues a $3.5 billion convertible bond.
- Blitzen Computer dips a toe in the water and enters a new market.
- Malted Herring postpones investment in a positive-NPV plant.
- Hewlett-Packard exports partially assembled printers even though it would be cheaper to ship the finished product.
- An investment uses standard machinery rather than efficient custom-designed machinery.

Answers: (1) each of these events involves an *option,* and (2) each is analyzed in the next four chapters. But you must walk before you can run. Therefore we start by focusing on a simple option to buy the stock of AOL Time-Warner. Chapter 20 examines the payoffs from this option, and Chapter 21 shows how it is valued.

Chapter 22 looks at the *real options* that arise in capital budgeting decisions. We encountered these in Chapter 10, when we used decision trees to set out future opportunities to modify a project. Now we place a value on this flexibility.

Chapter 23 looks at two sources of finance involving an option—warrants and convertible bonds. Later chapters will encounter many other securities with a built-in option.

CHAPTER TWENTY

UNDERSTANDING OPTIONS

FIGURE 20.1(A) SHOWS your payoff if you buy AOL Time Warner (AOL) stock at $55. You gain dollar-for-dollar if the stock price goes up and you lose dollar-for-dollar if it falls. That's trite; it doesn't take a genius to draw a 45-degree line.

Look now at panel (*b*), which shows the payoffs from an investment strategy that retains the upside potential of AOL stock but gives complete downside protection. In this case your payoff stays at $55 even if the AOL stock price falls to $50, $40, or zero. Panel (*b*)'s payoffs are clearly better than panel (*a*)'s. If a financial alchemist could turn panel (*a*) into (*b*), you'd be willing to pay for the service.

Of course alchemy has its dark side. Panel (*c*) shows an investment strategy for masochists. You lose if the stock price falls, but you give up any chance of profiting from a rise in the stock price. If you *like* to lose, or if somebody pays you enough to take the strategy on, this is the strategy for you.

Now, as you have probably suspected, all this financial alchemy is for real. You really can do all the transmutations shown in Figure 20.1. You do them with options, and we will show you how.

But why should the financial manager of an industrial company be interested in options? There are several reasons. First, companies regularly use commodity, currency, and interest-rate options to reduce risk. For example, a meatpacking company that wishes to put a ceiling on the cost of beef might take out an option to buy live cattle. A company that wishes to limit its future borrowing costs might take out an option to sell long-term bonds. And so on. In Chapter 27 we will explain how firms employ options to limit their risk.

Second, many capital investments include an embedded option to expand in the future. For instance, the company may invest in a patent that allows it to exploit a new technology or it may purchase adjoining land that gives it the option in the future to increase capacity. In each case the company is paying money today for the opportunity to make a further investment. To put it another way, the company is acquiring *growth opportunities.*

Here is another disguised option to invest: You are considering the purchase of a tract of desert land that is known to contain gold deposits. Unfortunately, the cost of extraction is higher than the current price of gold. Does this mean the land is almost worthless? Not at all. You are not obliged to mine the gold, but ownership of the land gives you the option to do so. Of course, if you know that the gold price will remain below the extraction cost, then the option is worthless. But if there is uncertainty about future gold prices, you could be lucky and make a killing.[1]

If the option to expand has value, what about the option to bail out? Projects don't usually go on until the equipment disintegrates. The decision to terminate a project is usually taken by management, not by nature. Once the project is no longer profitable, the company will cut its losses and exercise its option to abandon the project. Some projects have higher abandonment value than others. Those that use standardized equipment may offer a valuable abandonment option. Others may actually cost money to discontinue. For example, it is very costly to decommission an offshore oil rig.

We took a peek at these investment options in Chapter 10, and we showed there how to use decision trees to analyze Magna Charter's options to expand its airline operation or abandon it. In Chapter 22 we will take a more thorough look at these *real* options.

The other important reason why financial managers need to understand options is that they are often tacked on to an issue of corporate securities and so provide the investor or the company with the flexibility to change the terms of the issue. For example, in Chapter 23 we will show how warrants and

continued

[1]In Chapter 11 we valued Kingsley Solomon's gold mine by calculating the value of the gold in the ground and then subtracting the value of the extraction costs. That is correct only if we *know* that the gold will be mined. Otherwise, the value of the mine is increased by the value of the option to leave the gold in the ground if its price is less than the extraction cost.

convertibles give their holders an option to buy common stock in exchange for cash or bonds. Then in Chapter 25 we will see how corporate bonds may give the issuer or the investor the option of early repayment.

In fact, we shall see that whenever a company borrows, it creates an option. The reason is that the borrower is not *compelled* to repay the debt at maturity. If the value of the company's assets is less than the amount of the debt, the company will choose to default on the payment and the bondholders will get to keep the company's assets. Thus, when the firm borrows, the lender effectively acquires the company and the shareholders obtain the option to buy it back by paying off the debt. This is an extremely important insight. It means that anything that we can learn about traded options applies equally to corporate liabilities.[2]

In this chapter we use traded stock options to explain how options work, but we hope that our brief survey has convinced you that the interest of financial managers in options goes far beyond traded stock options. That is why we are asking you to invest here to acquire several important ideas for use later.

If you are unfamiliar with the wonderful world of options, it may seem baffling on first encounter. We will therefore divide this chapter into three bite-sized pieces. Our first task is to introduce you to call and put options and to show you how the payoff on these options depends on the price of the underlying asset. We will then show how financial alchemists can combine options to produce the interesting strategies depicted in Figure 20.1 (*b*) and (*c*).

We conclude the chapter by identifying the variables that determine option values. Here you will encounter some surprising and counterintuitive effects. For example, investors are used to thinking that increased risk reduces present value. But for options it is the other way around.

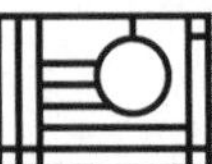

20.1 CALLS, PUTS, AND SHARES

The Chicago Board Options Exchange (CBOE) was founded in 1973 to allow investors to buy and sell options on shares of common stock. The CBOE was an almost instant success and other exchanges have since copied its example. In addition to options on individual common stocks, investors can now trade options on stock indexes, bonds, commodities, and foreign exchange.

Table 20.1 reproduces quotes from the CBOE for June 22, 2001. It shows the prices for two types of options on AOL stock—calls and puts. We will explain each in turn.

Call Options and Position Diagrams

A **call option** gives its owner the right to buy stock at a specified *exercise* or *strike price* on or before a specified exercise date. If the option can be exercised only on one particular day, it is conventionally known as a *European call;* in other cases

[2]This relationship was first recognized by Fischer Black and Myron Scholes, in "The Pricing of Options and Corporate Liabilities," *Journal of Political Economy* 81 (May–June 1973), pp. 637–654.

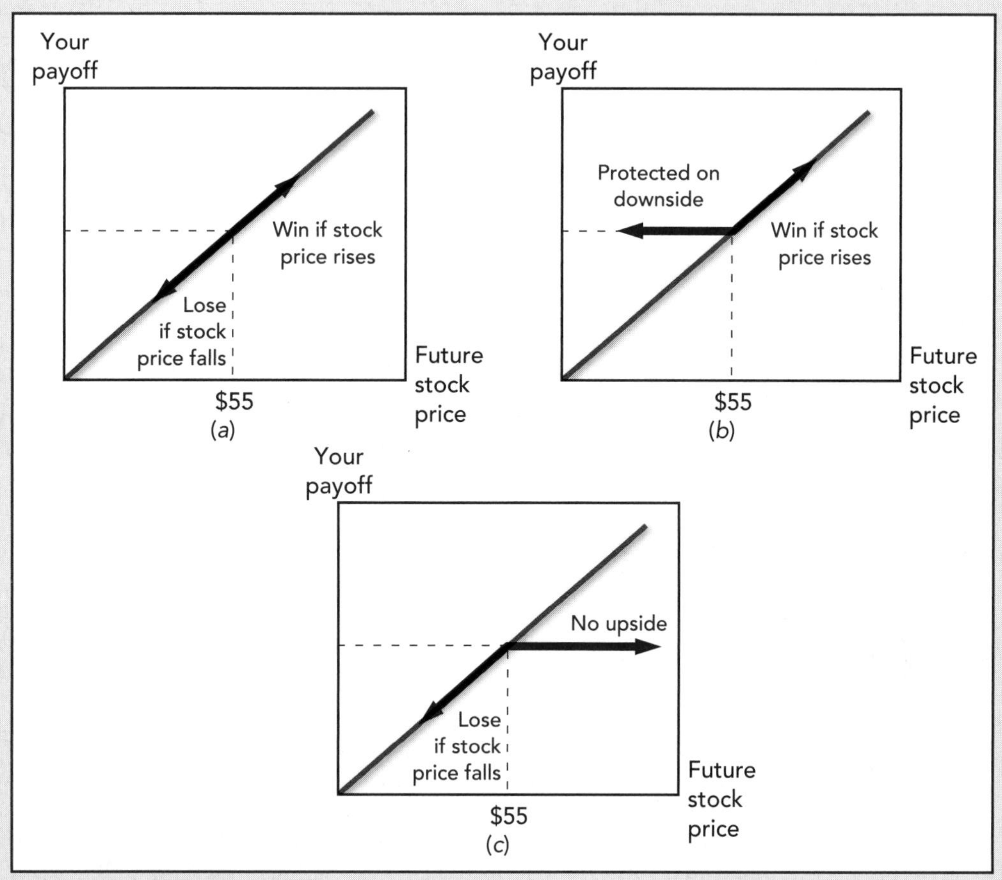

FIGURE 20.1

Payoffs to three investment strategies for AOL stock. (*a*) You buy one share for $55. (*b*) No downside. If stock price falls, your payoff stays at $55. (*c*) A strategy for masochists? You lose if stock price falls, but you don't gain if it rises.

(such as the AOL options shown in Table 20.1), the option can be exercised on or at any time before that day, and it is then known as an *American call.*

The third column of Table 20.1 sets out the prices of AOL Time Warner call options with different exercise prices and exercise dates. Look at the quotes for options maturing in October 2001. The first entry says that for $10.50 you could require an option to buy one share[3] of AOL stock for $45 on or before October 2001. Moving down to the next row, you can see that an option to buy for $5 more ($50 vs. $45) costs $3.75 less, that is $6.75. In general, the value of a call option goes down as the exercise price goes up.

Now look at the quotes for options maturing in January 2002 and 2003. Notice how the option price increases as option maturity is extended. For example, at an

[3]You can't actually buy an option on a single share. Trades are in multiples of 100. The minimum order would be for 100 options on 100 AOL shares.

TABLE 20.1

Prices of call and put options on AOL Time Warner stock on June 22, 2001. The closing stock price was $53.10.

*Long-term options are called "LEAPS."

Source: Chicago Board Options Exchange. Average of bid and asked quotes as reported at **www.cboe.com/MktQuote/DelayedQuotes.asp.**

Option Maturity	Exercise Price	Price of Call Option	Price of Put Option
October 2001	$ 45	$10.50	$ 1.97
	50	6.75	3.15
	55	3.85	5.25
	60	2.10	8.50
	65	1.07	12.50
	70	.52	17.10
January 2002	$ 45	$12.00	$ 2.90
	50	8.45	4.35
	55	**5.75**	**6.55**
	60	3.75	9.55
	65	2.25	13.20
	70	1.45	17.50
January 2003*	$ 50	$13.30	$ 7.30
	60	8.80	12.40
	70	5.90	19.40
	80	3.85	27.80
	100	1.70	47.00

exercise price of $60, the October 2001 call option costs $2.10, the January 2002 option costs $3.75, and the January 2003 option costs $8.80.

In Chapter 13 we met Louis Bachelier, who in 1900 first suggested that security prices follow a random walk. Bachelier also devised a very convenient shorthand to illustrate the effects of investing in different options.[4] We will use this shorthand to compare three possible investments in AOL—a call option, a put option, and the stock itself.

The *position diagram* in Figure 20.2(*a*) shows the possible consequences of investing in AOL January 2002 call options with an exercise price of $55 (boldfaced in Table 20.1). The outcome from investing in AOL calls depends on what happens to the stock price. If the stock price at the end of this six-month period turns out to be less than the $55 exercise price, nobody will pay $55 to obtain the share via the call option. Your call will in that case be valueless, and you will throw it away. On the other hand, if the stock price turns out to be greater than $55, it will pay to exercise your option to buy the share. In this case the call will be worth the market price of the share minus the $55 that you must pay to acquire it. For example, suppose that the price of AOL stock rises to $100. Your call will then be worth $100 − $55 = $45. That is your payoff, but of course it is not all profit. Table 20.1 shows that you had to pay $5.75 to buy the call.

Put Options

Now let us look at the AOL **put options** in the right-hand column of Table 20.1. Whereas the call option gives you the right to *buy* a share for a specified exercise price, the comparable put gives you the right to *sell* the share. For example, the

[4] L. Bachelier, *Théorie de la Speculation,* Gauthier-Villars, Paris, 1900. Reprinted in English in P. H. Cootner (ed.), *The Random Character of Stock Market Prices,* M.I.T. Press, Cambridge, MA, 1964.

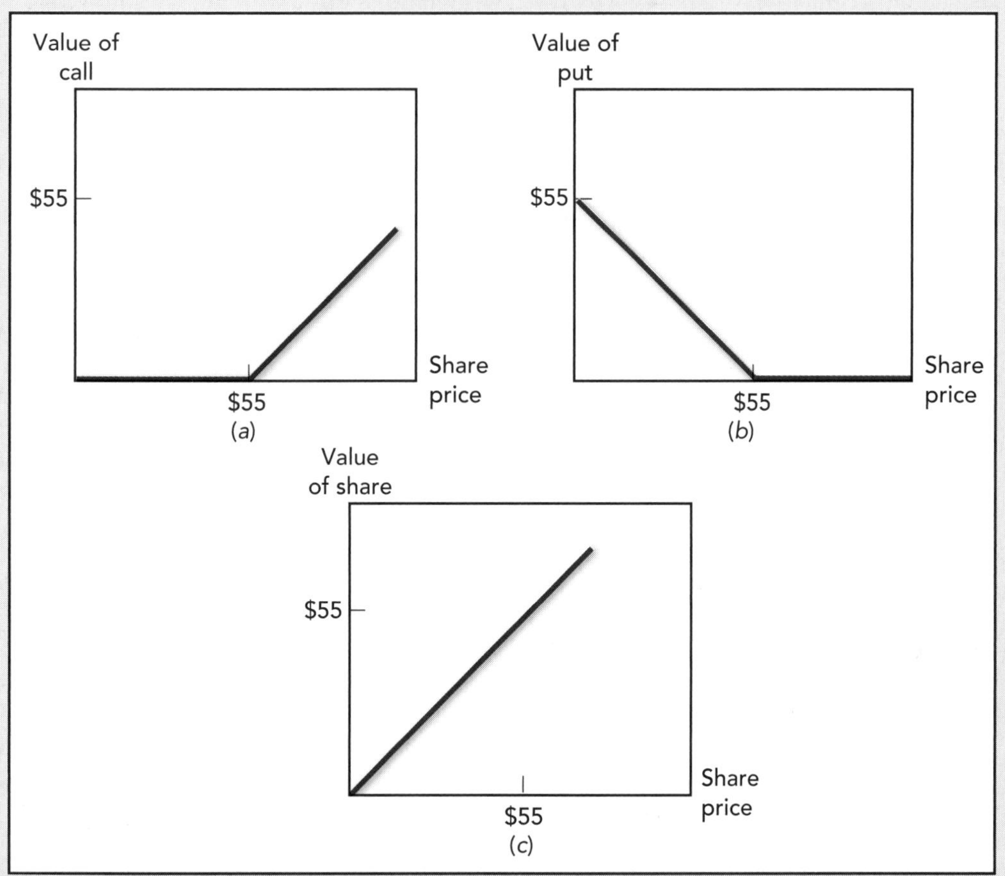

FIGURE 20.2

Position diagrams show how payoffs to owners of AOL calls, puts, and shares (shown by the colored lines) depend on the share price. (*a*) Result of buying AOL call exercisable at $55. (*b*) Result of buying AOL put exercisable at $55. (*c*) Result of buying AOL share.

boldfaced entry in the right-hand column of Table 20.1 shows that for $6.55 you could acquire an option to sell AOL stock for a price of $55 anytime before January 2002. The circumstances in which the put turns out to be profitable are just the opposite of those in which the call is profitable. You can see this from the position diagram in Figure 20.2(*b*). If AOL's share price immediately before expiration turns out to be *greater* than $55, you won't want to sell stock at that price. You would do better to sell the share in the market, and your put option will be worthless. Conversely, if the share price turns out to be *less* than $55, it will pay to buy stock at the low price and then take advantage of the option to sell it for $55. In this case, the value of the put option on the exercise date is the difference between the $55 proceeds of the sale and the market price of the share. For example, if the share is worth $35, the put is worth $20:

$$\begin{aligned}\text{Value of put option at expiration} &= \text{exercise price} - \text{market price of the share}\\ &= \$55 - \$35 = \$20\end{aligned}$$

Table 20.1 confirms that the value of a put *increases* when the exercise price is raised. However, extending the maturity date makes *both* puts and calls more valuable.

We have now reviewed position diagrams for investment in calls and puts. A third possible investment is directly in AOL stock. Figure 20.2(*c*) betrays few secrets when it shows that the value of this investment is always exactly equal to the market value of the share.

Selling Calls, Puts, and Shares

Let us now look at the position of an investor who *sells* these investments. If you sell, or "write," a call, you promise to deliver shares if asked to do so by the call buyer. In other words, the buyer's asset is the seller's liability. If by the exercise date the share price is below the exercise price, the buyer will not exercise the call and the seller's liability will be zero. If it rises above the exercise price, the buyer will exercise and the seller will give up the shares. The seller loses the difference between the share price and the exercise price received from the buyer. Notice that it is the buyer who always has the option to exercise; the seller simply does as he or she is told.

Suppose that the price of AOL stock turns out to be $80, which is above the option's exercise price of $55. In this case the buyer will exercise the call. The seller is forced to sell stock worth $80 for only $55 and so has a payoff of −$25.[5] Of course, that $25 loss is the buyer's gain. Figure 20.3(*a*) shows how the payoffs to the seller of the AOL call option vary with the stock price. Notice that for every dollar the buyer makes, the seller loses a dollar. Figure 20.3(*a*) is just Figure 20.2(*a*) drawn upside down.

In just the same way we can depict the position of an investor who sells, or writes, a put by standing Figure 20.2(*b*) on its head. The seller of the put has agreed to pay the exercise price of $55 for the share if the buyer of the put should request it. Clearly the seller will be safe as long as the share price remains above $55 but will lose money if the share price falls below this figure. The worst thing that can happen is that the stock becomes worthless. The seller would then be obliged to pay $55 for a stock worth $0. The "value" of the option position would be −$55.

Finally, Figure 20.3(*c*) shows the position of someone who sells AOL stock *short*. Short sellers sell stock which they do not yet own. As they say on Wall Street:

> He who sells what isn't his'n
> Buys it back or goes to prison.

Eventually, therefore, the short seller will have to buy the stock back. The short seller will make a profit if it has fallen in price and a loss if it has risen.[6] You can see that Figure 20.3(*c*) is simply an upside-down Figure 20.2(*c*).

Position Diagrams Are Not Profit Diagrams

Position diagrams show *only* the payoffs at option exercise; they do not account for the initial cost of buying the option or the initial proceeds from selling it.

This is a common point of confusion. For example, the position diagram in Figure 20.2(*a*) makes purchase of a call *look* like a sure thing—the payoff is at worst

[5]The seller has some consolation, for he or she was paid $5.75 in June for selling the call.

[6]Selling short is not as simple as we have described it. For example, a short seller usually has to put up margin, that is, deposit cash or securities with the broker. This assures the broker that the short seller will be able to repurchase the stock when the time comes to do so.

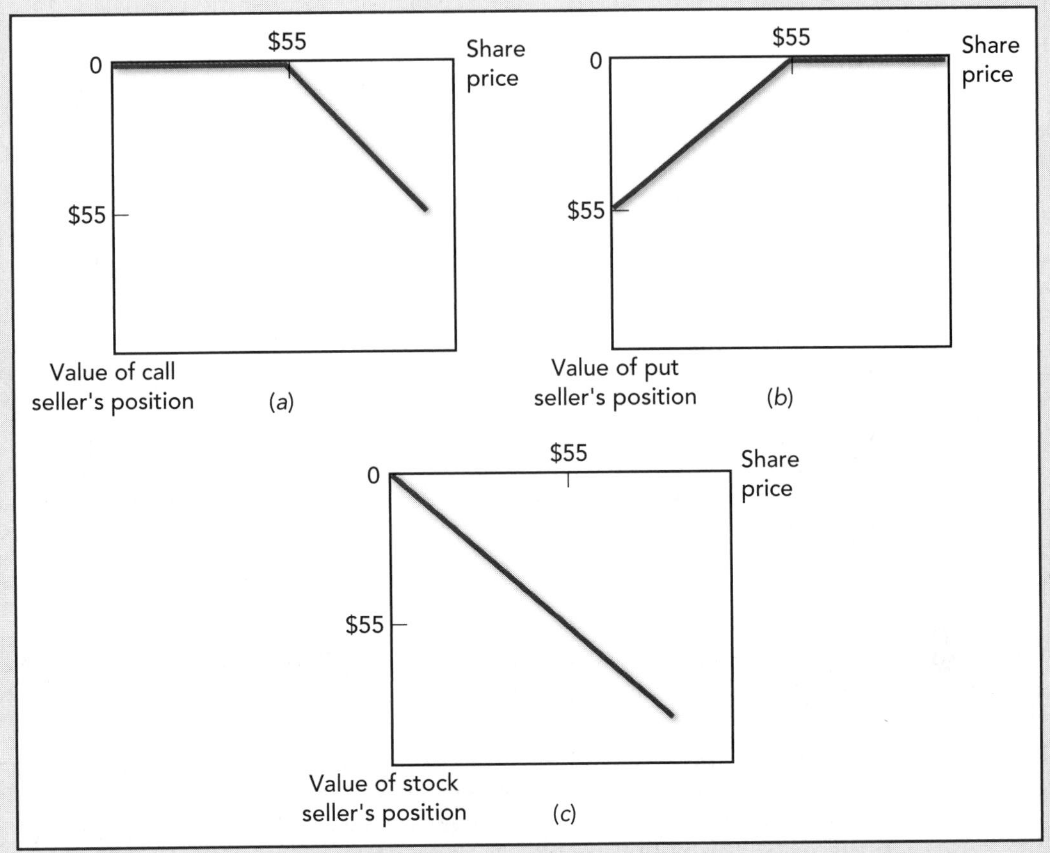

FIGURE 20.3

Payoffs to *sellers* of AOL calls, puts, and shares (shown by the colored lines) depend on the share price. (*a*) Result of selling AOL call exercisable at $55. (*b*) Result of selling AOL put exercisable at $55. (*c*) Result of selling AOL share short.

zero, with plenty of "upside" if AOL's stock price goes above $55 by January 2002. But compare the *profit diagram* in Figure 20.4(*a*), which subtracts the $5.75 *cost* of the call in June 2001 from the payoff at maturity. The call buyer loses money at all share prices less than $55 + 5.75 = $60.75. Take another example: The position diagram in Figure 20.3(*b*) makes selling a put *look* like a sure loss—the *best* payoff is zero. But the profit diagram in Figure 20.4(*b*), which recognizes the $6.55 received by the seller, shows that the seller gains at all prices above $55 − 6.55 = $48.45.[7]

Profit diagrams like those in Figure 20.4 may be helpful to the options beginner, but options experts rarely draw them. Now that you've graduated from the first options class we won't draw them either. We will stick to position diagrams, because you have to zero in on payoffs at exercise to understand options and to value them properly.

[7]Strictly speaking, the profit diagrams in Figure 20.4 should account for the time value of money, that is, the interest earned on the seller's initial proceeds and lost on the call buyer's outlay.

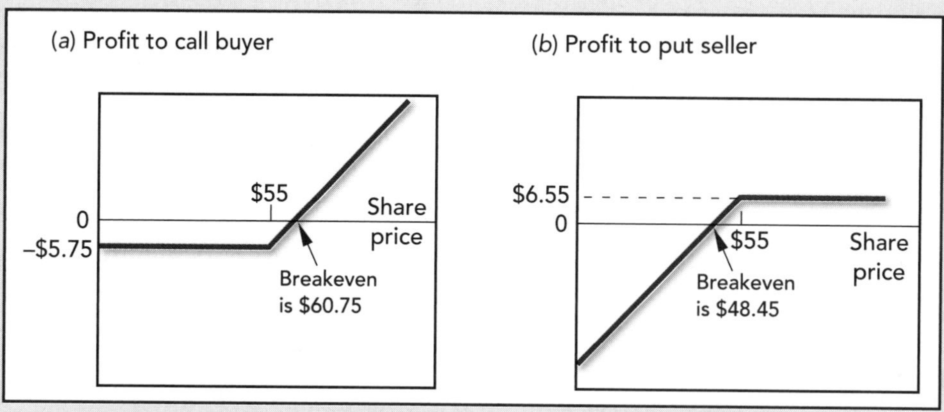

FIGURE 20.4

Profit diagrams incorporate the costs of buying an option or the proceeds from selling one. In panel (*a*), we substract the $5.75 cost of the AOL call from the payoffs plotted in Figure 20.2(*a*). In panel (*b*), we add the $6.55 proceeds from selling the AOL put to the payoffs in Figure 20.3(*b*).

20.2 FINANCIAL ALCHEMY WITH OPTIONS

Now that you understand the possible payoffs from calls and puts, we can start practicing some financial alchemy by conjuring up the strategies shown in Figure 20.1. Let's start with the strategy for masochists.

Look at row 1 of Figure 20.5. The first diagram shows the payoffs from buying a share of AOL stock, while the second shows the payoffs from *selling* a call option with a $55 exercise price. The third diagram shows what happens if you combine these two positions. The result is the no-win strategy that we depicted in panel (*c*) of Figure 20.1. You lose if the stock price declines below $55, but, if the stock price rises above $55, the owner of the call option will demand that you hand over your stock for the $55 exercise price. So you lose on the downside and give up any chance of a profit. That's the bad news. The good news is that you get paid for taking on this liability. In June 2001 you would have been paid $5.75, the price of a six-month call option.

Now, we'll create the downside protection shown in Figure 20.1(*b*). Look at row 2 of Figure 20.5. The first diagram again shows the payoff from buying a share of AOL stock, while the next diagram in row 2 shows the payoffs from buying an AOL put option with an exercise price of $55. The third diagram shows the effect of combining these two positions. You can see that, if AOL's stock price rises above $55, your put option is valueless, so you simply receive the gains from your investment in the share. However, if the stock price falls below $55, you can exercise your put option and sell your stock for $55. Thus, by adding a put option to your investment in the stock, you have protected yourself against loss.[8] This is the strategy that we depicted in panel (*b*) of Figure 20.1. Of course, there is no gain without pain. The *cost* of insuring yourself against loss is the amount that you pay for a put

[8]This combination of a stock and a put option is known as a *protective put*.

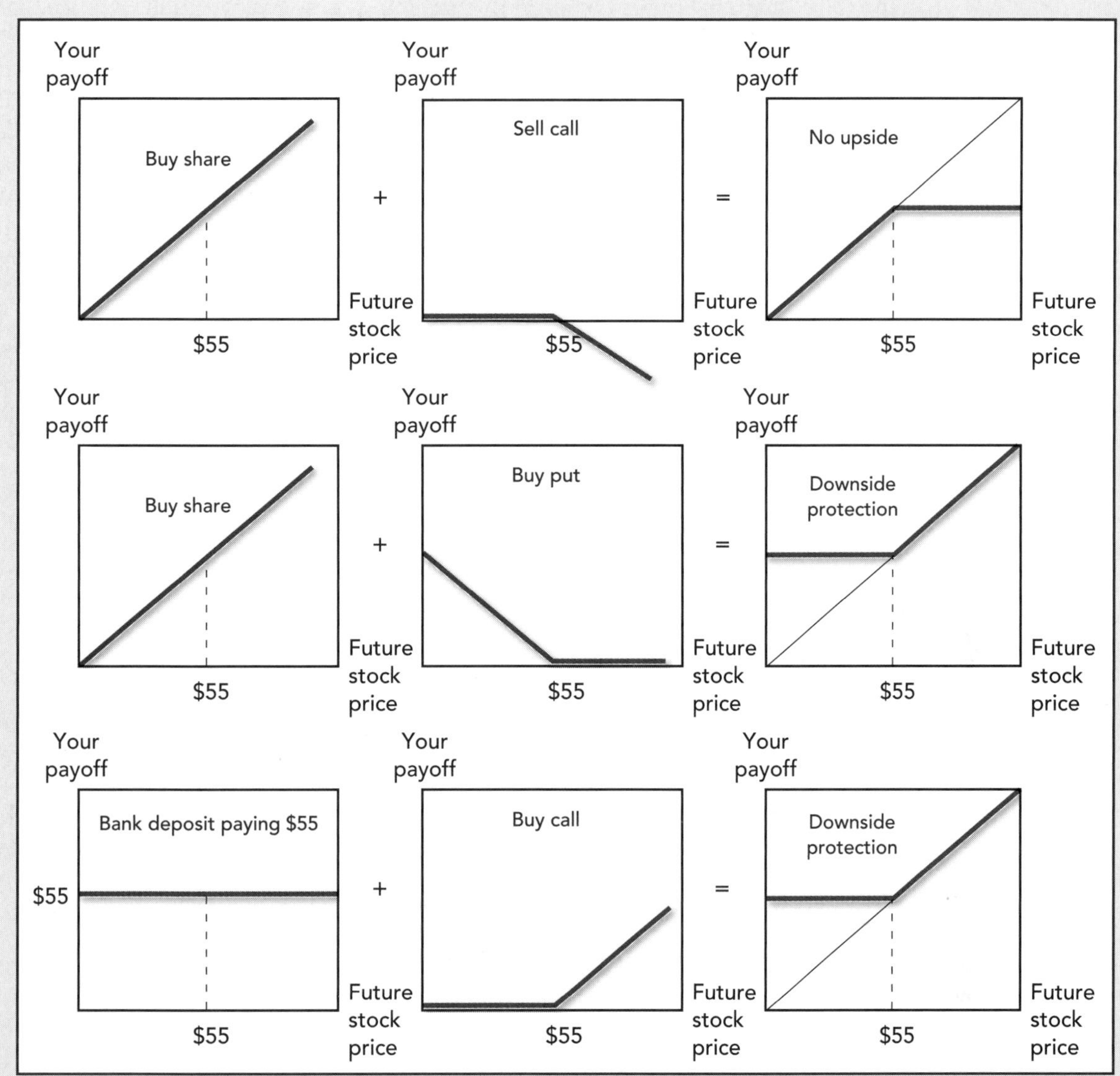

FIGURE 20.5

The first row shows how options can be used to create a strategy where you lose if the stock price falls but do not gain if it rises [strategy (*c*) in Figure 20.1]. The second and third rows show two ways to create the reverse strategy where you gain on the upside but are protected on the downside [strategy (*b*) in Figure 20.1].

option on AOL stock with an exercise price of $55. In June 2001 the price of this put was $6.55. This was the going rate for financial alchemists.

We have just seen how put options can be used to provide downside protection. We will now show you how call options can be used to get the same result. This is illustrated in row 3 of Figure 20.5. The first diagram shows the payoff from placing the present value of $55 in a bank deposit. Regardless of what happens to the price of AOL stock, your bank deposit will pay off $55. The second diagram in row 3 shows the payoff from a call option on AOL stock with an exercise price of $55, and the third diagram shows the effect of combining these two positions. Notice that, if the price of AOL stock falls, your call is worthless, but you still have your $55 in the bank. For every dollar that AOL stock price rises above $55, your investment in the call option pays off an extra dollar. For example, if the stock price rises to $100, you will have $55 in the bank and a call worth $45. Thus you participate fully in any rise in the price of the stock, while being fully protected against any fall. So we have just found another way to provide the downside protection depicted in panel (*b*) of Figure 20.1.

These last two rows of Figure 20.5 tell us something about the relationship between a call option and a put option. Regardless of the future stock price, both investment strategies provide identical payoffs. In other words, if you buy the share and a put option to sell it after six months for $55, you receive the same payoff as from buying a call option and setting enough money aside to pay the $55 exercise price. Therefore, if you are committed to holding the two packages until the options expire, the two packages should sell for the same price today. This gives us a fundamental relationship for European options:

$$\text{Value of call} + \text{present value of exercise price} = \text{value of put} + \text{share price}$$

To repeat, this relationship holds because the payoff of

[Buy call, invest present value of exercise price in safe asset[9]]

is identical to the payoff from

[Buy put, buy share]

This basic relationship among share price, call and put values, and the present value of the exercise price is called **put–call parity.**[10]

The relationship can be expressed in several ways. Each expression implies two investment strategies that give identical results. For example, suppose that you want to solve for the value of a put. You simply need to twist the put–call parity formula around to give

$$\text{Value of put} = \text{value of call} + \text{present value of exercise price} - \text{share price}$$

From this expression you can deduce that

[buy put]

is identical to

[Buy call, invest present value of exercise price in safe asset, sell share]

In other words, if puts are not available, you can create them by buying calls, putting cash in the bank, and selling shares.

[9]The present value is calculated at the *risk-free* rate of interest. It is the amount that you would have to invest today in a bank deposit or Treasury bills to realize the exercise price on the option's expiration date.

[10]Put–call parity holds only if you are committed to holding the options until the final exercise date. It therefore does not hold for American options, which you can exercise *before* the final date. We discuss possible reasons for early exercise in Chapter 21. Also if the stock makes a dividend payment before the final exercise date, you need to recognize that the investor who buys the call misses out on this dividend. In this case the relationship is

$$\text{Value of call} + \text{present value of exercise price} = \text{value of put} + \text{share price} - \text{present value of dividend.}$$

Default Puts and the Difference between Safe and Risky Bonds

In Chapter 18 we discussed the plight of Circular File Company, which borrowed \$50 per share. Unfortunately the firm fell on hard times and the market value of its assets fell to \$30. Circular's bond and stock prices fell to \$25 and \$5, respectively. Circular's *market* value balance sheet is now

Circular File Company (Market Values)

Asset value	\$30	\$25	Bonds
		5	Stock
	\$30	\$30	Firm value

If Circular's debt were due and payable now, the firm could not repay the \$50 it originally borrowed. It would default, bondholders receiving assets worth \$30 and shareholders receiving nothing. The reason Circular stock is worth \$5 is that the debt is *not* due now but rather is due a year from now. A stroke of good fortune could increase firm value enough to pay off the bondholders in full, with something left over for the stockholders.

Let us go back to a statement that we made at the start of the chapter. Whenever a firm borrows, the lender effectively acquires the company and the shareholders obtain the option to buy it back by paying off the debt. The stockholders have in effect purchased a call option on the assets of the firm. The bondholders have sold them this call option. Thus the balance sheet of Circular File can be expressed as follows:

Circular File Company (Market Values)

Asset value	\$30	\$25	Bond value = asset value − value of call
		5	Stock value = value of call
	\$30	\$30	Firm value = asset value

If this still sounds like a strange idea to you, try drawing one of Bachelier's position diagrams for Circular File. It should look like Figure 20.6. If the future value of the assets is less than \$50, Circular will default and the stock will be worthless. If the value of the assets exceeds \$50, the stockholders will receive asset value *less* the \$50 paid over to the bondholders. The payoffs in Figure 20.6 are identical to a call option on the firm's assets, with an exercise price of \$50.

Now look again at the basic relationship between calls and puts:

Value of call + present value of exercise price = value of put + value of share

To apply this to Circular File, we have to interpret "value of share" as "asset value," because the common stock is a call option on the firm's assets. Also, "present value of exercise price" is the present value of receiving the promised payment of \$50 to bondholders *for sure* next year. Thus

Value of call + present value of promised payment to bondholders
= value of put + asset value

Now we can solve for the value of Circular's bonds. This is equal to the firm's asset value less the value of the shareholders' call option on these assets:

Bond value = asset value − value of call
= present value of promised payment to bondholders − value of put

FIGURE 20.6

The value of Circular's common stock is the same as the value of a call option on the firm's assets with an exercise price of $50.

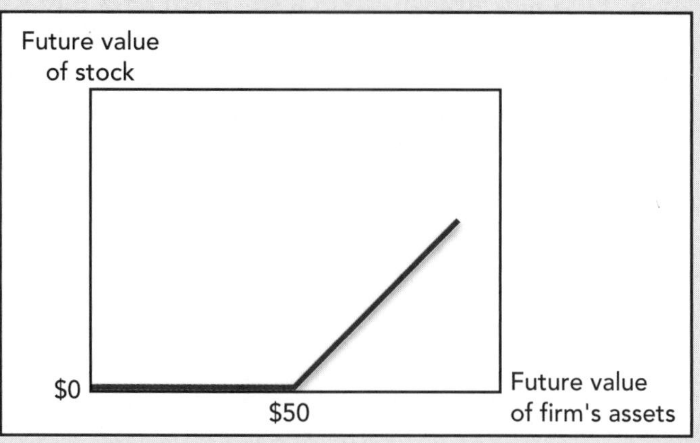

Circular's bondholders have in effect (1) bought a safe bond and (2) given the shareholders the option to sell them the firm's assets for the amount of the debt. You can think of the bondholders as receiving the $50 promised payment, but they have given the shareholders the option to take the $50 back in exchange for the assets of the company. If firm value turns out to be less than the $50 that is promised to bondholders, the shareholders will exercise their put option.

Circular's risky bond is equal to a safe bond less the value of the shareholders' option to default. To value this risky bond we need to value a safe bond and then subtract the value of the default option. The default option is equal to a put option on the firm's assets. Now you can see why bond traders, investors, and financial managers refer to *default puts.*

In the case of Circular File the option to default is extremely valuable because default is likely to occur. At the other extreme, the value of IBM's option to default is trivial compared to the value of IBM's assets. Default on IBM bonds is possible but extremely unlikely. Option traders would say that for Circular File the put option is "deep in the money" because today's asset value ($30) is well below the exercise price ($50). For IBM the put option is far "out of the money" because the value of IBM's assets substantially exceeds the value of IBM's debt.

We know that Circular's stock is equivalent to a call option on the firm's assets. It is also equal to (1) owning the firm's assets, (2) borrowing the present value of $50 with the obligation to repay regardless of what happens, but also (3) buying a put on the firm's assets with an exercise price of $50.

We can sum up by presenting Circular's balance sheet in terms of asset value, put value, and the present value of a sure $50 payment:

Circular File Company (Market Values)

Asset value	$30	$25	Bond value = present value of promised payment − value of default put
		5	Stock value = asset value − present value of promised payment + value of put
	$30	$30	Firm value = asset value

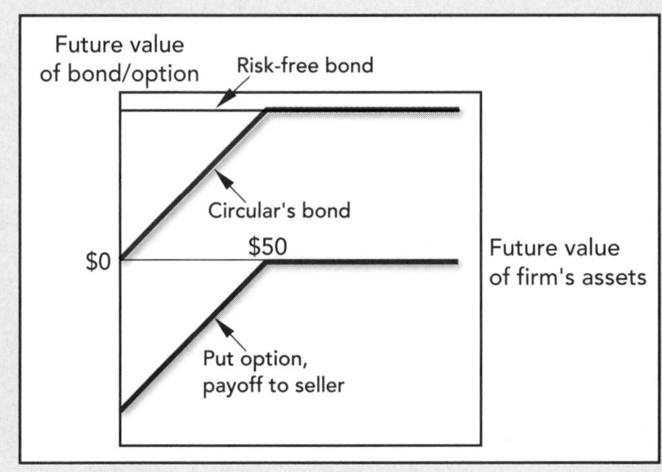

FIGURE 20.7

You can also think of Circular's bond (the colored line) as equivalent to a risk-free bond (the upper black line) *less* a put option on the firm's assets with an exercise price of $50 (the lower black line).

Again you can check this with a position diagram. The colored line in Figure 20.7 shows the payoffs to Circular's bondholders. If the firm's assets are worth more than $50, the bondholders are paid off in full; if the assets are worth less than $50, the firm defaults and the bondholders receive the value of the assets. You could get an identical payoff pattern by buying a safe bond (the upper black line) and selling a put option on the firm's assets (the lower black line).

Spotting the Option

Options rarely come with a large label attached. Often the trickiest part of the problem is to identify the option. For example, we suspect that until it was pointed out, you did not realize that every risky bond contains a hidden option. When you are not sure whether you are dealing with a put or a call or a complicated blend of the two, it is a good precaution to draw a position diagram. Here is an example.

The Flatiron and Mangle Corporation has offered its president, Ms. Higden, the following incentive scheme: At the end of the year Ms. Higden will be paid a bonus of $50,000 for every dollar that the price of Flatiron stock exceeds its current figure of $120. However, the maximum bonus that she can receive is set at $2 million.

You can think of Ms. Higden as owning 50,000 tickets, each of which pays nothing if the stock price fails to beat $120. The value of each ticket then rises by $1 for each dollar rise in the stock price up to the maximum of $2,000,000/50,000 = $40. Figure 20.8 shows the payoffs from just one of these tickets. The payoffs are not the same as those of the simple put and call options that we drew in Figure 20.2, but it is possible to find a combination of options that exactly replicates Figure 20.8. Before going on to read the answer, see if you can spot it yourself. (If you are someone who enjoys puzzles of the make-a-triangle-from-just-two-match-sticks type, this one should be a walkover.)

The answer is in Figure 20.9. The solid black line represents the purchase of a call option with an exercise price of $120, and the dotted line shows the sale of another call option with an exercise price of $160. The colored line shows the payoffs from a combination of the purchase and the sale—exactly the same as the payoffs from one of Ms. Higden's tickets.

FIGURE 20.8

The payoff from one of Ms. Higden's "tickets" depends on Flatiron's stock price.

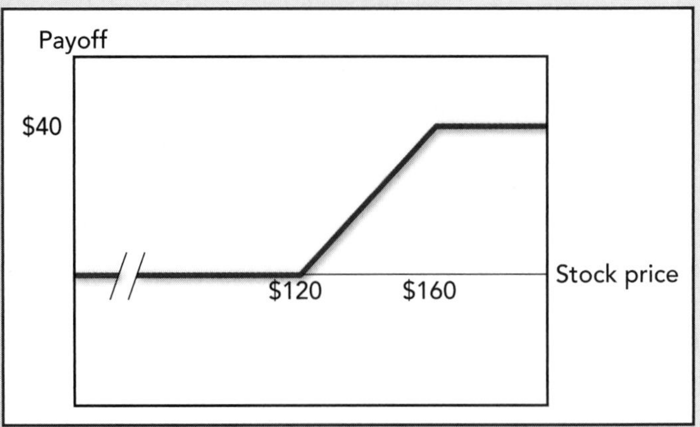

FIGURE 20.9

The solid black line shows the payoff from buying a call with an exercise price of \$120. The dotted line shows the *sale* of a call with an exercise price of \$160. The combined purchase and sale (shown by the colored line) is identical to one of Ms. Higden's "tickets."

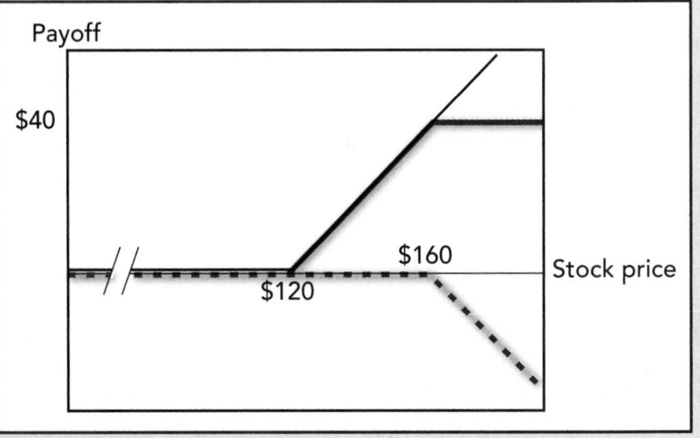

Thus, if we wish to know how much the incentive scheme is costing the company, we need to calculate the difference between the value of 50,000 call options with an exercise price of \$120 and the value of 50,000 calls with an exercise price of \$160.

We could have made the incentive scheme depend in a much more complicated way on the stock price. For example, the bonus could peak at \$2 million and then fall steadily back to zero as the stock price climbs above \$160. (Don't ask why anyone would want to offer such an arrangement—perhaps there's some tax angle.) You could still have represented this scheme as a combination of options. In fact, we can state a general theorem:

> Any set of contingent payoffs—that is, payoffs which depend on the value of some other asset—can be constructed with a mixture of simple options on that asset.

In other words, you can create any position diagram—with as many ups and downs or peaks and valleys as your imagination allows—by buying or selling the right combinations of puts and calls with different exercise prices.[11]

[11] In some cases you may also have to borrow or lend money to generate a position diagram with your desired pattern. Lending raises the payoff line in position diagrams, as in the bottom row of Figure 20.5. Borrowing lowers the payoff line.

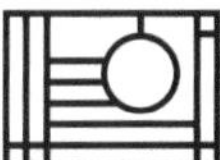

20.3 WHAT DETERMINES OPTION VALUES?

So far we have said nothing about how the market value of an option is determined. We do know what an option is worth when it matures, however. Consider, for instance, our earlier example of an option to buy AOL stock at $55. If AOL's stock price is below $55 on the exercise date, the call will be worthless; if the stock price is above $55, the call will be worth $55 less than the value of the stock. In terms of Bachelier's position diagram, the relationship is depicted by the heavy, lower line in Figure 20.10.

Even before maturity the price of the option can never remain *below* the heavy, lower-bound line in Figure 20.10. For example, if our option were priced at $5 and the stock were priced at $70, it would pay any investor to sell the stock and then buy it back by purchasing the option and exercising it for an additional $55. That would give a money machine with a profit of $10. The demand for options from investors using the money machine would quickly force the option price up, at least to the heavy line in the figure. For options that still have some time to run, the heavy line is therefore a *lower-bound* limit on the market price of the option.

The diagonal line in Figure 20.10 is the *upper-bound* limit to the option price. Why? Because the stock gives a higher ultimate payoff than the option. If at the option's expiration the stock price ends up above the exercise price, the option is worth the stock price *less* the exercise price. If the stock price ends up below the exercise price, the option is worthless, but the stock's owner still has a valuable security. Let P be the stock price at the option's expiration date, and assume the option's exercise price is $55. Then the extra dollar returns realized by stockholders are

	Stock Payoff	Option Payoff	Extra Payoff from Holding Stock Instead of Option
Option exercised (P greater than $55)	P	$P - 55$	$55
Option expires unexercised (P less than or equal to $55)	P	0	P

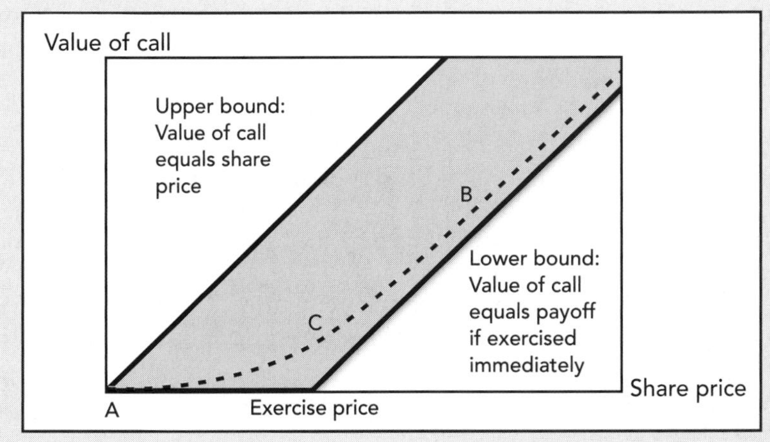

FIGURE 20.10

Value of a call before its expiration date (dashed line). The value depends on the stock price. It is always worth more than its value if exercised now (heavy line). It is never worth more than the stock price itself.

If the stock and the option have the same price, everyone will rush to sell the option and buy the stock. Therefore, the option price must be somewhere in the shaded region of Figure 20.10. In fact, it will lie on a curved, upward-sloping line like the dashed curve shown in the figure. This line begins its travels where the upper and lower bounds meet (at zero). Then it rises, gradually becoming parallel to the upward-sloping part of the lower bound. This line tells us an important fact about option values: *The value of an option increases as stock price increases,* if the exercise price is held constant.

That should be no surprise. Owners of call options clearly hope for the stock price to rise and are happy when it does. But let us look more carefully at the shape and location of the dashed line. Three points, *A*, *B*, and *C*, are marked on the dashed line. As we explain each point you will see why the option price has to behave as the dashed line predicts.

Point A *When the stock is worthless, the option is worthless:* A stock price of zero means that there is no possibility the stock will ever have any future value.[12] If so, the option is sure to expire unexercised and worthless, and it is worthless today.

Point B *When the stock price becomes large, the option price approaches the stock price less the present value of the exercise price:* Notice that the dashed line representing the option price in Figure 20.10 eventually becomes parallel to the ascending heavy line representing the lower bound on the option price. The reason is as follows: The higher the stock price is, the higher is the probability that the option will eventually be exercised. If the stock price is high enough, exercise becomes a virtual certainty; the probability that the stock price will fall below the exercise price before the option expires becomes trivially small.

If you own an option that you *know* will be exchanged for a share of stock, you effectively own the stock now. The only difference is that you don't have to pay for the stock (by handing over the exercise price) until later, when formal exercise occurs. In these circumstances, buying the call is equivalent to buying the stock but financing part of the purchase by borrowing. The amount implicitly borrowed is the present value of the exercise price. The value of the call is therefore equal to the stock price less the present value of the exercise price.

This brings us to another important point about options. Investors who acquire stock by way of a call option are buying on credit. They pay the purchase price of the option today, but they do not pay the exercise price until they actually take up the option. The delay in payment is particularly valuable if interest rates are high and the option has a long maturity. *Thus, the value of an option increases with both the rate of interest and the time to maturity.*

Point C *The option price always exceeds its minimum value* (except when stock price is zero): We have seen that the dashed and heavy lines in Figure 20.10 coincide when stock price is zero (point *A*), but elsewhere the lines diverge; that is, the option price must exceed the minimum value given by the heavy line. The reason for this can be understood by examining point *C*.

At point *C*, the stock price exactly equals the exercise price. The option is therefore worthless if exercised today. However, suppose that the option will not expire

[12]If a stock *can* be worth something in the future, then investors will pay *something* for it today, although possibly a very small amount.

until three months hence. Of course we do not know what the stock price will be at the expiration date. There is roughly a 50 percent chance that it will be higher than the exercise price and a 50 percent chance that it will be lower. The possible payoffs to the option are therefore

Outcome	Payoff
Stock price rises (50 percent probability)	Stock price less exercise price (option is exercised)
Stock price falls (50 percent probability)	Zero (option expires worthless)

If there is a positive probability of a positive payoff, and if the worst payoff is zero, then the option must be valuable. That means the option price at point C exceeds its lower bound, which at point C is zero. In general, the option prices will exceed their lower-bound values as long as there is time left before expiration.

One of the most important determinants of the *height* of the dashed curve (i.e., of the difference between actual and lower-bound value) is the likelihood of substantial movements in the stock price. An option on a stock whose price is unlikely to change by more than 1 or 2 percent is not worth much; an option on a stock whose price may halve or double is very valuable.

Panels (*a*) and (*b*) in Figure 20.11 illustrate this point. The panels compare the payoffs at expiration of two options with the same exercise price and the same stock price. The panels assume that stock price equals exercise price (like point C in Figure 20.10), although this is not a necessary assumption.[13] The only difference is that the price of stock Y at its option's expiration date is much harder to predict than the price of stock X at its option's expiration date. You can see this from the probability distributions superimposed on the figures.

In both cases there is roughly a 50 percent chance that the stock price will decline and make the options worthless, but if the prices of stocks X and Y rise, the odds are that Y will rise more than X. Thus there is a larger chance of a big payoff from the option on Y. Since the chance of a zero payoff is the same, the option on Y is worth more than the option on X. Figure 20.12 shows how the value of an option increases as stock price volatility increases. The upper curved line shows the values of the AOL call option assuming that the stock price is highly variable. The lower curved line assumes a lower (and more realistic) degree of volatility.[14]

The probability of large stock price changes during the remaining life of an option depends on two things: (1) the variance (i.e., volatility) of the stock price *per period* and (2) the number of periods until the option expires. If there are t remaining periods, and the variance per period is σ^2, the value of the option should depend on cumulative variability $\sigma^2 t$.[15] Other things equal, you would like to hold

[13]In drawing Figure 20.11 we have assumed that the distribution of possible stock prices is symmetric. This also is not a necessary assumption, and we will look more carefully at the distribution of price changes in the next chapter.

[14]The option values shown in Figure 20.12 were calculated by using the Black–Scholes option-valuation model. We explain this model in Chapter 21 and use it to value the AOL option.

[15]Here is an intuitive explanation: If the stock price follows a random walk (see Section 13.2), successive price changes are statistically independent. The cumulative price change before expiration is the sum of t random variables. The variance of a sum of independent random variables is the sum of the variances of those variables. Thus, if σ^2 is the variance of the daily price change, and there are t days until expiration, the variance of the cumulative price change is $\sigma^2 t$.

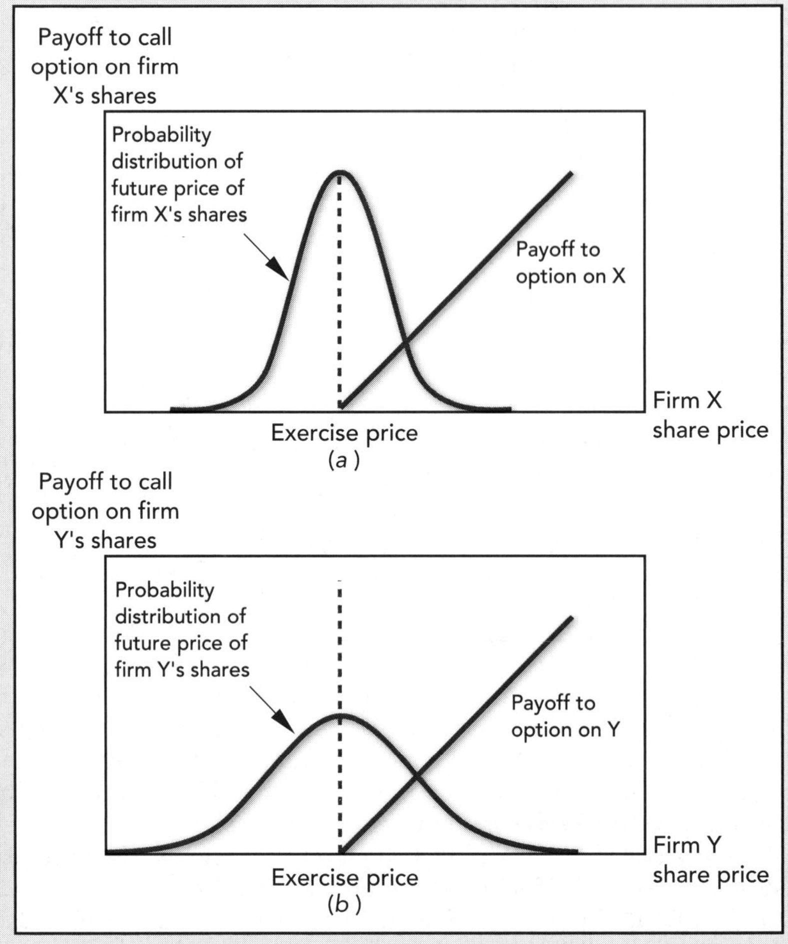

FIGURE 20.11

Call options are written against the shares of (*a*) firm X and (*b*) firm Y. In each case, the current share price equals the exercise price, so each option has a 50 percent chance of ending up worthless (if the share price falls) and a 50 percent chance of ending up "in the money" (if the share price rises). However, the chance of a *large* payoff is *greater* for the option on firm Y's share because Y's stock price is more volatile and therefore has more upside potential.

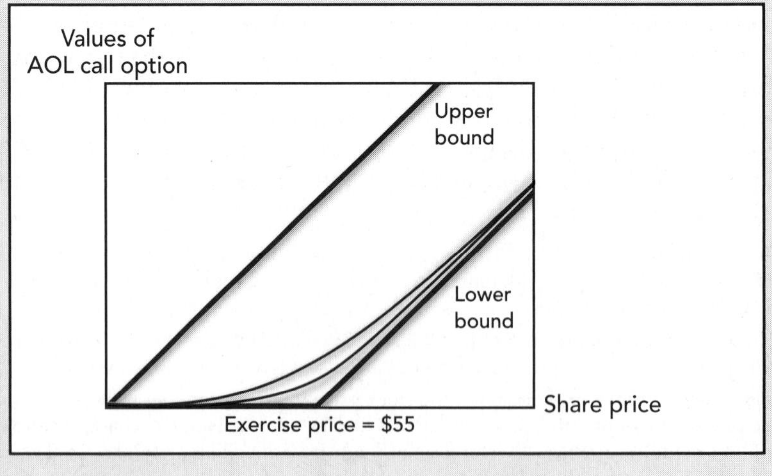

FIGURE 20.12

How the value of the AOL call option increases with the volatility of the stock price. Each of the curved lines shows the value of the option for different initial stock prices. The only difference is that the upper line assumes a much higher level of uncertainty about AOL's future stock price.

TABLE 20.2

What the price of a call option depends on.

1. If there is an *increase* in:	The change in the call option price is:
Stock price (P)	Positive
Exercise price (EX)	Negative
Interest rate (r_f)	Positive*
Time to expiration (t)	Positive
Volatility of stock price (σ)	Positive*

2. Other properties:
   a. *Upper bound.* The option price is always less than the stock price.
   b. *Lower bound.* The option price never falls below the payoff to immediate exercise (P − EX or zero, whichever is larger).
   c. If the stock is worthless, the option is worthless.
   d. As the stock price becomes very large, the option price approaches the stock price less the present value of the exercise price.

*The *direct* effects of increases in r_f or σ on option price are positive. There may also be *indirect* effects. For example, an increase in r_f could reduce stock price P. This in turn could reduce option price.

an option on a volatile stock (high σ^2). Given volatility, you would like to hold an option with a long life ahead of it (large t). Thus the value of an option increases *with both the volatility of the share price and the time to maturity.*

It's a rare person who can keep all these properties straight at first reading. Therefore, we have summed them up in Table 20.2.

Risk and Option Values

In most financial settings, risk is a bad thing; you have to be paid to bear it. Investors in risky (high-beta) stocks demand higher expected rates of return. High-risk capital investment projects have correspondingly high costs of capital and have to beat higher hurdle rates to achieve positive NPV.

For options it's the other way around. As we have just seen, options written on volatile assets are worth *more* than options written on safe assets. If you can understand and remember that one fact about options, you've come a long way.

Example. Suppose you have to choose between two job offers, as CFO of either Establishment Industries or Digital Organics. Establishment Industries' compensation package includes a grant of the stock options described on the left side of Table 20.3. You demand a similar package from Digital Organics, and they comply. In fact they match the Establishment Industries options in every respect, as you can see on the right side of Table 20.3. (The two companies' current stock prices just happen to be the same.) The only difference is that Digital Organics' stock is half again as volatile as Establishment Industries' stock (36 percent annual standard deviation vs. 24 percent for Establishment Industries).

If your job choice hinges on the value of the executive stock options, you should take the Digital Organics offer. The Digital Organics options are written on the more volatile asset and therefore are worth more. We will value the two stock-option packages in the next chapter.

Asset Risk and Equity Values In Section 18.3, we asserted that:

> Financial managers who act strictly in their shareholders' interests (and against the interests of creditors) will favor risky projects over safe ones.

TABLE 20.3

Which package of executive stock options would you choose? The package offered by Digital Organics is more valuable, because the volatility of that company's stock is higher.

	Establishment Industries	Digital Organics
Number of options	100,000	100,000
Exercise price	$25	$25
Maturity	5 years	5 years
Current stock price	$22	$22
Stock price volatility (standard deviation of return)	24%	36%

Now you can see why this statement is generally true. Common stock is a call option written on the firm's assets, and like all call options, its value depends on the risk of the underlying asset. If the financial manager can swap a risky asset for a safe one—holding everything else, including the value of the firm's assets, constant—then the value of the firm's common stock increases and shareholders are better off.[16]

There is, of course, an offsetting decrease in the value of the firm's debt. The debtholders have given up a default put. The riskier the firm's assets, the more that put is worth. Since the put value is subtracted from the default-free value of the debt, increased risk makes the debtholders worse off.

Although the assertion from Chapter 18 is generally true, it is not important for established, blue-chip companies where the odds of default are miniscule. For example, the value of the default put on Exxon Mobil's debt is trivial. But there are always companies, even large companies, in financial distress. Financial distress means that the odds of default are *not* trivial, that the default put is valuable, and that increased asset risk benefits shareholders.

[16] In this context, risk means all sources of uncertainty, not just market risk. Option prices depend on the standard deviation or variance of returns, not just on beta. You'll see this more explicitly in the next chapter.

SUMMARY

If you have managed to reach this point, you are probably in need of a rest and a stiff gin and tonic. So we will summarize what we have learned so far and take up the subject of options again in the next chapter when you are rested (or drunk).

There are two types of option. An American call is an option to buy an asset at a specified exercise price on or before a specified exercise date. Similarly, an American put is an option to sell the asset at a specified price on or before a specified date. European calls and puts are exactly the same except that they cannot be exercised before the specified exercise date. Calls and puts are the basic building blocks that can be combined to give any pattern of payoffs.

What determines the value of a call option? Common sense tells us that it ought to depend on three things:

1. To exercise an option you have to pay the exercise price. Other things being equal, the less you are obliged to pay, the better. Therefore, the value of an option increases with the ratio of the asset price to the exercise price.

2. You do not have to pay the exercise price until you decide to exercise the option. Therefore, an option gives you a free loan. The higher the rate of interest and the longer the time to maturity, the more this free loan is worth. Therefore the value of an option increases with the interest rate and time to maturity.
3. If the price of the asset falls short of the exercise price, you won't exercise the option. You will, therefore, lose 100 percent of your investment in the option no matter how far the asset depreciates below the exercise price. On the other hand, the more the price rises *above* the exercise price, the more profit you will make. Therefore the option holder does not lose from increased volatility if things go wrong, but gains if they go right. The value of an option increases with the variance per period of the stock return multiplied by the number of periods to maturity.

Always remember that an option written on a risky (high-variance) asset is worth more than an option on a safe asset. It's easy to forget, because in most other financial contexts increases in risk reduce present value.

Visit us at www.mhhe.com/bm7e

FURTHER READING

The classic articles on option valuation are:

F. Black and M. Scholes: "The Pricing of Options and Corporate Liabilities," *Journal of Political Economy,* 81:637–654 (May–June 1973).

R. C. Merton: "Theory of Rational Option Pricing," *Bell Journal of Economics and Management Science,* 4:141–183 (Spring 1973).

There are also a number of good texts on option valuation. They include:

J. Hull: *Options, Futures and Other Derivatives,* 5th ed., Prentice-Hall, Inc., Englewood Cliffs, NJ, 2003.

R. Jarrow and S. Turnbull: *Derivative Securities,* 2nd ed., South-Western College Publishing, Cincinnati, OH, 1999.

M. Rubinstein: *Derivatives: A PowerPlus Picture Book,* 1998.[17]

[17]This book is published by the author and is listed on **www.in-the-money.com**.

QUIZ

1. Complete the following passage:

   A ____ option gives its owner the opportunity to buy a stock at a specified price which is generally called the ____ price. A ____ option gives its owner the opportunity to sell stock at a specified price. Options that can be exercised only at maturity are called ____ options.

   The common stock of firms that borrow is a ____ option. Stockholders effectively sell the firm's ____ to ____, but retain the option to buy the ____ back. The exercise price is the ____.

2. Note Figure 20.13. Match each diagram, (*a*) and (*b*), with one of the following positions:
   - Call buyer
   - Call seller
   - Put buyer
   - Put seller

FIGURE 20.13

See Quiz question 2.

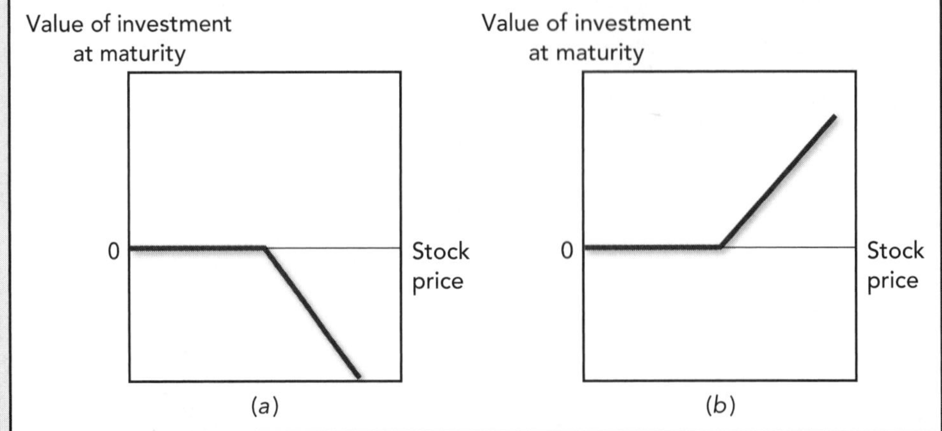

3. Suppose that you hold a share of stock and a put option on that share. What is the payoff when the option expires if **(a)** the stock price is below the exercise price? **(b)** the stock price is above the exercise price?
4. What is put–call parity and why does it hold? Could you apply the parity formula to a call and put with different exercise prices?
5. There is another strategy involving calls and borrowing and lending that gives the same payoffs as the strategy described in question 3. What is the alternative strategy?
6. Dr. Livingstone I. Presume holds £600,000 in East African gold stocks. Bullish as he is on gold mining, he requires absolute assurance that at least £500,000 will be available in six months to fund an expedition. Describe two ways for Dr. Presume to achieve this goal. There is an active market for puts and calls on East African gold stocks, and the rate of interest is 6 percent per year.
7. Suppose you buy a one-year European call option on Wombat stock with an exercise price of $100 and sell a one-year European put option with the same exercise price. The current stock price is $100, and the interest rate is 10 percent.
   a. Draw a position diagram showing the payoffs from your investments.
   b. How much will the combined position cost you? Explain.
8. Explain why the common stock of a firm that borrows is a call option. What is the underlying asset? What is the exercise price?
9. What does "default put" mean? When are default puts most important?
10. What is the lower bound to the price of a call option? If the price of a European call option were below the lower bound, how could you make a sure-fire profit? What is the upper bound to the price of a call option?
11. Look again at Figure 20.13. It appears that the call buyer in panel **(b)** can't lose and the call seller in panel **(a)** can't win. Is that correct? Explain. *Hint:* Draw a profit diagram for each panel.
12. What is a call option worth if **(a)** the stock price is zero? **(b)** the stock price is extremely high relative to the exercise price?
13. How does the price of a call option respond to the following changes, other things equal? Does the call price go up or down?
    a. Stock price increases.
    b. Exercise price is increased.
    c. Risk-free rate increases.
    d. Expiration date of the option is extended.

e. Volatility of the stock price falls.
f. Time passes, so the option's expiration date comes closer.

14. Respond to the following statements.
a. "I'm a conservative investor. I'd much rather hold a call option on a safe stock like Exxon Mobil than a volatile stock like AOL Time Warner."
b. "When a company lands in financial distress, stockholders are better off if the financial manager shifts to safer assets and operating strategies."

PRACTICE QUESTIONS

1. In everyday speech the term *option* often just means "choice," whereas in finance it refers specifically to the right to buy or sell an asset in the future on terms that are fixed today. Which of the following are the odd statements out? Are the options involved in the other statements puts or calls?
a. "The preferred stockholders in Chrysalis Motors have the option to redeem their shares at par value after 2009."
b. "What I like about Toit à Porcs is its large wine list. You have the option to choose from over 100 wines."
c. "I don't have to buy IBM stock now. I have the option to wait and see if the stock price goes lower over the next month or two."
d. "By constructing an assembly plant in Mexico, Chrysalis Motors gave itself the option to switch a substantial proportion of its production to that country if the dollar should appreciate in the future."

2. Discuss briefly the risks and payoffs of the following positions:
a. Buy stock and a put option on the stock.
b. Buy stock.
c. Buy call.
d. Buy stock and sell call option on the stock.
e. Buy bond.
f. Buy stock, buy put, and sell call.
g. Sell put.

3. "The buyer of the call and the seller of the put both hope that the stock price will rise. Therefore the two positions are identical." Is the speaker correct? Illustrate with a position diagram.

4. Pintail's stock price is currently $200. A one-year *American* call option has an exercise price of $50 and is priced at $75. How would you take advantage of this great opportunity? Now suppose the option is a *European* call. What would you do?

5. It is possible to buy three-month call options and three-month puts on stock Q. Both options have an exercise price for $60 and both are worth $10. Is a six-month call with an exercise price of $60 more or less valuable than a similar six-month put? *Hint:* Use put–call parity.

6. In June 2001 a six-month call on Intel stock, with an exercise price of $22.50, sold for $2.30. The stock price was $27.27. The risk-free interest rate was 3.9 percent. How much would you be willing to pay for a put on Intel stock with the same maturity and exercise price?

7. Go to the Chicago Board Options Exchange website at **www.cboe.com.** Check out the delayed quotes for AOL Time Warner for different exercise prices and maturities.
a. Confirm that higher exercise prices mean lower call prices and higher put prices.
b. Confirm that longer maturity means higher prices for both puts and calls.
c. Choose an AOL put and call with the same exercise price and maturity. Confirm that put–call parity holds (approximately). *Note:* You will have to use an up-to-date risk-free interest rate.

Visit us at www.mhhe.com/bm7e

8. The Rank and File Company is considering a rights issue to raise $50 million (see Chapter 15 Appendix A). An underwriter offers to "stand by" (i.e., to guarantee the success of the issue by buying any unwanted stock at the issue price). The underwriter's fee is $2 million.
   a. What kind of option does Rank and File acquire if it accepts the underwriter's offer?
   b. What determines the value of the option?
9. FX Bank has succeeded in hiring ace foreign exchange trader, Lucinda Cable. Her remuneration package reportedly includes an annual bonus of 20 percent of the profits that she generates in excess of $100 million. Does Ms. Cable have an option? Does it provide her with the appropriate incentives?
10. Suppose that Mr. Colleoni borrows the present value of $100, buys a six-month put option on stock Y with an exercise price of $150, and sells a six-month put option on Y with an exercise price of $50.
    a. Draw a position diagram showing the payoffs when the options expire.
    b. Suggest two other combinations of loans, options, and the underlying stock that would give Mr. Colleoni the same payoffs.
11. Which *one* of the following statements is correct?
    a. Value of put + present value of exercise price = value of call + share price.
    b. Value of put + share price = value of call+ present value of exercise price.
    c. Value of put − share price = present value of exercise price − value of call.
    d. Value of put + value of call = share price − present value of exercise price.

    The correct statement equates the value of two investment strategies. Plot the payoffs to each strategy as a function of the stock price. Show that the two strategies give identical payoffs.
12. Test the formula linking put and call prices by using it to explain the relative prices of traded puts and calls. (Note that the formula is exact only for European options. Most traded puts and calls are American.)
13. a. If you can't sell a share short, you can achieve exactly the same final payoff by a combination of options and borrowing or lending. What is this combination?
    b. Now work out the mixture of stock and options that gives the same final payoff as a risk-free loan.
14. The common stock of Triangular File Company is selling at $90. A 26-week call option written on Triangular File's stock is selling for $8. The call's exercise price is $100. The risk-free interest rate is 10 percent per year.
    a. Suppose that puts on Triangular stock are not traded, but you want to buy one. How would you do it?
    b. Suppose that puts *are* traded. What should a 26-week put with an exercise price of $100 sell for?
15. Digital Organics has 10 million outstanding shares trading at $25 per share. It also has a large amount of debt outstanding, all coming due in one year. The debt pays interest at 8 percent. It has a par (face) value of $350 million, but is trading at a market value of only $280 million. The one-year risk-free interest rate is 6 percent.
    a. Write out the put–call parity formula for Digital Organics' stock, debt, and assets.
    b. What is the value of the default put given up by Digital Organics' creditors?
16. Option traders often refer to "straddles" and "butterflies." Here is an example of each:
    - *Straddle:* Buy call with exercise price of $100 and simultaneously buy put with exercise price of $100.
    - *Butterfly:* Simultaneously buy one call with exercise price of $100, sell two calls with exercise price of $110, and buy one call with exercise price of $120.

Draw position diagrams for the straddle and butterfly, showing the payoffs from the investor's net position. Each strategy is a bet on variability. Explain briefly the nature of each bet.

17. Refer again to the Circular File balance sheet in Section 20.2. Suppose that the government suddenly offers to guarantee the $50 principal payment due bondholders next year and also to guarantee the interest payment. (In other words, if firm value falls short of the promised payments, the government will make up the difference.) This offer is a complete surprise to everyone. The government asks nothing in return, and so its offer is cheerfully accepted.
    a. Suppose that the promised interest rate on Circular's debt is 10 percent. The rate on one-year United States government notes is 8 percent. How will the guarantee affect bond value?
    b. The guarantee does *not* affect the value of Circular stock. Why? (*Note:* There could be some effect if the guarantee allows Circular to avoid costs of financial distress or bankruptcy. See Section 18.3.)
    c. How will the value of the firm (debt plus equity) change?

    Now suppose that the government offers the same guarantee for *new* debt issued by *Rectangular* File Company. Rectangular's assets are identical to Circular's, but Rectangular has no existing debt. Rectangular accepts the offer and uses the proceeds of a $50 debt issue to repurchase or retire stock.

    Will Rectangular stockholders gain from the opportunity to issue the guaranteed debt? By how much, approximately? (Ignore taxes.)

18. Look at actual trading prices of call options on stocks to check whether they behave as the theory presented in this chapter predicts. For example,
    a. Follow several options as they approach maturity. How would you expect their prices to behave? Do they actually behave that way?
    b. Compare two call options written on the same stock with the same maturity but different exercise prices.
    c. Compare two call options written on the same stock with the same exercise price but different maturities.

19. Is it more valuable to own an option to buy a portfolio of stocks or to own a portfolio of options to buy each of the individual stocks? Say briefly why.

20. Table 20.4 lists some prices of options on common stocks (prices are quoted to the nearest dollar). The interest rate is 10 percent a year. Can you spot any mispricing? What would you do to take advantage of it?

21. As manager of United Bedstead you own substantial executive stock options. These entitle you to buy the firm's shares during the next five years at a price of $100 a share. The plant manager has just outlined two alternative proposals to reequip the plant. Both proposals have the same net present value, but one is substantially riskier than the other. At first you are undecided about which to choose, but then you remember your stock options. How might these influence your choice?

Stock	Time to Exercise (months)	Exercise Price	Stock Price	Put Price	Call Price
Drongo Corp.	6	50	80	20	52
Ragwort, Inc.	6	100	80	10	15
Wombat Corp.	3	40	50	7	18
	6	40	50	5	17
	6	50	50	8	10

TABLE 20.4

Prices of options on common stocks (in dollars). See Practice Question 20.

22. You've just completed a month-long study of energy markets and conclude that energy prices will be *much* more volatile in the next year than historically. Assuming you're right, what types of option strategies should you undertake? *Note:* You can buy or sell options on oil-company stocks or on the price of future deliveries of crude oil, natural gas, fuel oil, etc.

CHALLENGE QUESTIONS

1. Figure 20.14 shows some complicated position diagrams. Work out the combination of stocks, bonds, and options that produces each of these positions.
2. In 1988 the Australian firm Bond Corporation sold a share in some land that it owned near Rome for $110 million and as a result boosted its 1988 earnings by $74 million. In 1989 a television program revealed that the buyer was given a put option to sell its share in the land back to Bond for $110 million and that Bond had paid $20 million for a call option to repurchase the share in the land for the same price.[18]
   a. What happens if the land is worth more than $110 million when the options expire? What if it is worth less than $110 million?
   b. Use position diagrams to show the net effect of the land sale and the option transactions.
   c. Assume a one-year maturity on the options. Can you deduce the interest rate?
   d. The television program argued that it was misleading to record a profit on the sale of land. What do you think?
3. Three six-month call options are traded on Hogswill stock:

Exercise Price	Call Option Price
$ 90	$ 5
100	11
110	15

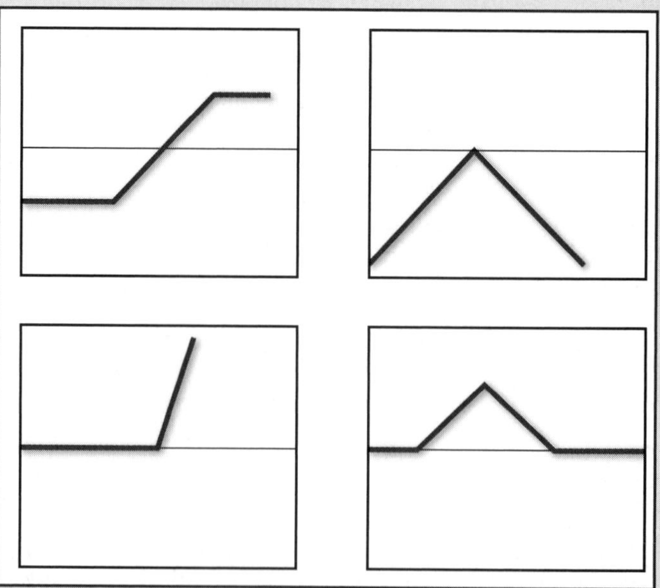

FIGURE 20.14

Some complicated position diagrams. See Challenge Question 1.

[18]See *Sydney Morning Herald,* March 14, 1989, p. 27. The options were subsequently renegotiated.

How would you make money by trading in Hogswill options? (*Hint:* Draw a graph with the option price on the vertical axis and the ratio of stock price to exercise price on the horizontal axis. Plot the three Hogswill options on your graph. Does this fit with what you know about how option prices should vary with the ratio of stock price to exercise price?) Now look in the newspaper at options with the same maturity but different exercise prices. Can you find any money-making opportunities?

4. Ms. Higden has been offered yet another incentive scheme (see Section 20.2). She will receive a bonus of $500,000 if the stock price at the end of the year is $120 or more; otherwise she will receive nothing.

a. Draw a position diagram illustrating the payoffs from such a scheme.

b. What combination of options would provide these payoffs? (*Hint:* You need to buy a large number of options with one exercise price and sell a similar number with a different exercise price.)

CHAPTER TWENTY-ONE

VALUING OPTIONS

IN THE LAST chapter we introduced you to call and put options. Call options give the owner the right to buy an asset at a specified exercise price; put options give the right to sell. We also took the first step toward understanding how options are valued. The value of a call option depends on five variables:

1. The higher the price of the asset, the more valuable an option to buy it.
2. The lower the price that you must pay to exercise the call, the more valuable the option.
3. You do not need to pay the exercise price until the option expires. This delay is most valuable when the interest rate is high.
4. If the stock price is *below* the exercise price at maturity, the call is valueless regardless of whether the price is $1 below or $100 below. However, for every dollar that the stock price rises *above* the exercise price, the option holder gains an additional dollar. Thus, the value of the call option increases with the volatility of the stock price.
5. Finally, a long-term option is more valuable than a short-term option. A distant maturity delays the point at which the holder needs to pay the exercise price and increases the chance of a large jump in the stock price before the option matures.

In this chapter we show how these variables can be combined into an exact option-valuation model—a formula we can plug numbers into to get a definite answer. We first describe a simple way to value options, known as the binomial model. We then introduce the Black–Scholes formula for valuing options. Finally, we provide a checklist showing how these two methods can be used to solve a number of practical option problems.

The only feasible way to value most options is to use a computer. But in this chapter we will work through some simple examples by hand. We do so because unless you understand the basic principles behind option valuation, you are likely to make mistakes in setting up an option problem and you won't know how to interpret the computer's answer and explain it to others.

In the last chapter we introduced you to the put and call options on AOL stock. In this chapter we will stick with that example and show you how to value the AOL options. But remember *why* you need to understand option valuation. It is not to make a quick buck trading on an options exchange. It is because many capital budgeting and financing decisions have options embedded in them. We will discuss a variety of these options in subsequent chapters.

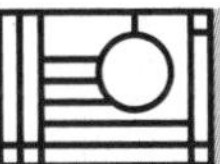

21.1 A SIMPLE OPTION-VALUATION MODEL

Why Discounted Cash Flow Won't Work for Options

For many years economists searched for a practical formula to value options until Fisher Black and Myron Scholes finally hit upon the solution. Later we will show you what they found, but first we should explain why the search was so difficult.

Our standard procedure for valuing an asset is to (1) figure out expected cash flows and (2) discount them at the opportunity cost of capital. Unfortunately, this is not practical for options. The first step is messy but feasible, but finding *the* opportunity cost of capital is impossible, because the risk of an option changes every time the stock price moves,[1] and we know it *will* move along a random walk through the option's lifetime.

[1]It also changes over time even with the stock price constant.

When you buy a call, you are taking a position in the stock but putting up less of your own money than if you had bought the stock directly. Thus, an option is always riskier than the underlying stock. It has a higher beta and a higher standard deviation of return.

How much riskier the option is depends on the stock price relative to the exercise price. A call option that is in the money (stock price greater than exercise price) is safer than one that is out of the money (stock price less than exercise price). Thus a stock price increase raises the option's price *and* reduces its risk. When the stock price falls, the option's price falls *and* its risk increases. That is why the expected rate of return investors demand from an option changes day by day, or hour by hour, every time the stock price moves.

We repeat the general rule: The higher the stock price is relative to the exercise price, the safer is the call option, although the option is always riskier than the stock. The option's risk changes every time the stock price changes.

Constructing Option Equivalents from Common Stocks and Borrowing

If you've digested what we've said so far, you can appreciate why options are hard to value by standard discounted-cash-flow formulas and why a rigorous option-valuation technique eluded economists for many years. The breakthrough came when Black and Scholes exclaimed, "Eureka! We have found it![2] The trick is to set up an *option equivalent* by combining common stock investment and borrowing. The net cost of buying the option equivalent must equal the value of the option."

We'll show you how this works with a simple numerical example. We'll travel back to the end of June 2001 and consider a six-month call option on AOL Time Warner (AOL) stock with an exercise price of $55. We'll pick a day when AOL stock was also trading at $55, so that this option is *at the money.* The short-term, risk-free interest rate was a bit less than 4 percent per year, or about 2 percent for six months.

To keep the example as simple as possible, we assume that AOL stock can do only two things over the option's six-month life: either the price will fall by a quarter to $41.25 or rise by one-third to $73.33.

If AOL's stock price falls to $41.25, the call option will be worthless, but if the price rises to $73.33, the option will be worth $73.33 − 55 = $18.33. The possible payoffs to the option are therefore

	Stock Price = $41.25	Stock Price = $73.33
1 call option	$0	$18.33

Now compare these payoffs with what you would get if you bought .5714 AOL shares and borrowed $23.11 from the bank:[3]

	Stock Price = $41.25	Stock Price = $73.33
.5714 shares	$23.57	$41.90
Repayment of loan + interest	−23.57	−23.57
Total payoff	$ 0	$18.33

[2]We do not know whether Black and Scholes, like Archimedes, were sitting in bathtubs at the time.

[3]The amount that you need to borrow from the bank is simply the present value of the difference between the payoffs from the option and the payoffs from the .5714 shares. In our example, amount borrowed = (55 − .5714 × 55)/1.02 = $23.11.

Notice that the payoffs from the levered investment in the stock are identical to the payoffs from the call option. Therefore, both investments must have the same value:

$$\begin{aligned}\text{Value of call} &= \text{value of .5714 shares} - \$23.11 \text{ bank loan}\\ &= (55 \times .5714) - 23.11 = \$8.32\end{aligned}$$

Presto! You've valued a call option.

To value the AOL option, we borrowed money and bought stock in such a way that we exactly replicated the payoff from a call option. This is called a **replicating portfolio.** The number of shares needed to replicate one call is called the **hedge ratio** or **option delta.** In our AOL example one call is replicated by a levered position in .5714 shares. The option delta is, therefore, .5714.

How did we know that AOL's call option was equivalent to a levered position in .5714 shares? We used a simple formula that says

$$\text{Option delta} = \frac{\text{spread of possible option prices}}{\text{spread of possible share prices}} = \frac{18.33 - 0}{73.33 - 41.25} = .5714$$

You have learned not only to value a simple option but also that you can replicate an investment in the option by a levered investment in the underlying asset. Thus, if you can't buy or sell an option on an asset, you can create a homemade option by a replicating strategy—that is, you buy or sell delta shares and borrow or lend the balance.

Risk-Neutral Valuation Notice why the AOL call option should sell for \$8.32. If the option price is higher than \$8.32, you could make a certain profit by buying .5714 shares of stock, selling a call option, and borrowing \$23.11. Similarly, if the option price is less than \$8.32, you could make an equally certain profit by selling .5714 shares, buying a call, and lending the balance. In either case there would be a money machine.[4]

If there's a money machine, everyone scurries to take advantage of it. So when we said that the option price had to be \$8.32 (or there would be a money machine), we did not have to know anything about investor attitudes to risk. The option price cannot depend on whether investors detest risk or do not care a jot.

This suggests an alternative way to value the option. We can *pretend* that all investors are *indifferent* about risk, work out the expected future value of the option in such a world, and discount it back at the risk-free interest rate to give the current value. Let us check that this method gives the same answer.

If investors are indifferent to risk, the expected return on the stock must be equal to the risk-free rate of interest:

$$\text{Expected return on AOL stock} = 2.0\% \text{ per six months}$$

We know that AOL stock can either rise by 33 percent to \$73.33 or fall by 25 percent to \$41.25. We can, therefore, calculate the probability of a price rise in our hypothetical risk-neutral world:

$$\begin{aligned}\text{Expected return} &= [\text{probability of rise} \times 33]\\ &\quad + [(1 - \text{probability of rise}) \times (-25)]\\ &= 2.0 \text{ percent}\end{aligned}$$

[4]Of course, you don't get seriously rich by dealing in .5714 shares. But if you multiply each of our transactions by a million, it begins to look like real money.

Therefore,[5]

$$\text{Probability of rise} = .463, \text{ or } 46.3\%$$

Notice that this is not the *true* probability that AOL stock will rise. Since investors dislike risk, they will almost surely require a higher expected return than the risk-free interest rate from AOL stock. Therefore the true probability is greater than .463.

We know that if the stock price rises, the call option will be worth $18.33; if it falls, the call will be worth nothing. Therefore, if investors are risk-neutral, the expected value of the call option is

$$\begin{aligned}&[\text{Probability of rise} \times 18.33] + [(1 - \text{probability of rise}) \times 0]\\&= (.463 \times 18.33) + (.537 \times 0)\\&= \$8.49\end{aligned}$$

And the current value of the call is

$$\frac{\text{Expected future value}}{1 + \text{interest rate}} = \frac{8.49}{1.02} = \$8.32$$

Exactly the same answer that we got earlier!

We now have two ways to calculate the value of an option:

1. Find the combination of stock and loan that replicates an investment in the option. Since the two strategies give identical payoffs in the future, they must sell for the same price today.
2. Pretend that investors do not care about risk, so that the expected return on the stock is equal to the interest rate. Calculate the expected future value of the option in this hypothetical *risk-neutral* world and discount it at the risk-free interest rate.[6]

Valuing the AOL Put Option

Valuing the AOL call option may well have seemed like pulling a rabbit out of a hat. To give you a second chance to watch how it is done, we will use the same method to value another option—this time, the six-month AOL put option with a $55 exercise price.[7] We continue to assume that the stock price will either rise to $73.33 or fall to $41.25.

[5]The general formula for calculating the risk-neutral probability of a rise in value is

$$p = \frac{\text{interest rate} - \text{downside change}}{\text{upside change} - \text{downside change}}$$

In the case of AOL stock

$$p = \frac{.02 - (-.25)}{.33 - (-.25)} = .463$$

[6]In Chapter 9 we showed how you can value an investment either by discounting the expected cash flows at a risk-adjusted discount rate or by adjusting the expected cash flows for risk and then discounting these *certainty-equivalent* flows at the risk-free interest rate. We have just used this second method to value the AOL option. The certainty-equivalent cash flows on the stock and option are the cash flows that would be expected in a risk-neutral world.

[7]When valuing *American* put options, you need to recognize the possibility that it will pay to exercise early. We discuss this complication later in the chapter, but it is not relevant for valuing the AOL put and we ignore it here.

If AOL's stock price rises to \$73.33, the option to sell for \$55 will be worthless. If the price falls to \$41.25, the put option will be worth \$55 − 41.25 = \$13.75. Thus the payoffs to the put are

	Stock Price = \$41.25	Stock Price = \$73.33
1 put option	\$13.75	\$0

We start by calculating the option delta using the formula that we presented above:[8]

$$\text{Option delta} = \frac{\text{spread of possible option prices}}{\text{spread of possible stock prices}} = \frac{0 - 13.75}{73.33 - 41.25} = -.4286$$

Notice that the delta of a put option is always negative; that is, you need to *sell* delta shares of stock to replicate the put. In the case of the AOL put you can replicate the option payoffs by *selling* .4286 AOL shares and *lending* \$30.81. Since you have sold the share short, you will need to lay out money at the end of six months to buy it back, but you will have money coming in from the loan. Your net payoffs are exactly the same as the payoffs you would get if you bought the put option:

	Stock Price = \$41.25	Stock Price = \$73.33
Sale of .4286 shares	−\$17.68	−\$31.43
Repayment of loan + interest	+31.43	+31.43
Total payoff	\$13.75	\$ 0

Since the two investments have the same payoffs, they must have the same value:

$$\begin{aligned}\text{Value of put} &= -.4286 \text{ shares} + \$30.81 \text{ bank loan} \\ &= -(.4286 \times 55) + 30.81 = \$7.24\end{aligned}$$

Valuing the Put Option by the Risk-Neutral Method Valuing the AOL put option with the risk-neutral method is a cinch. We already know that the probability of a rise in the stock price is .463. Therefore the expected value of the put option in a risk-neutral world is

$$\begin{aligned}&[\text{Probability of rise} \times 0] + [(1 - \text{probability of rise}) \times 13.75] \\ &= (.463 \times 0) + (.537 \times 13.75) \\ &= \$7.38\end{aligned}$$

And therefore the current value of the put is

$$\frac{\text{Expected future value}}{1 + \text{interest rate}} = \frac{7.38}{1.02} = \$7.24$$

The Relationship between Call and Put Prices We pointed out earlier that for European options there is a simple relationship between the value of the call and that of the put:[9]

$$\text{Value of put} = \text{value of call} - \text{share price} + \text{present value of exercise price}$$

[8] The delta of a put option is always equal to the delta of a call option with the same exercise price minus one. In our example, delta of put = .5714 − 1 = −.4286.

[9] *Reminder:* This formula applies only when the two options have the same exercise price and exercise date.

Since we had already calculated the value of the AOL call, we could also have used this relationship to find the value of the put:

$$\text{Value of put} = 8.32 - 55 + \frac{55}{1.02} = \$7.24$$

Everything checks.

21.2 THE BINOMIAL METHOD FOR VALUING OPTIONS

The essential trick in pricing any option is to set up a package of investments in the stock and the loan that will exactly replicate the payoffs from the option. If we can price the stock and the loan, then we can also price the option. Equivalently, we can pretend that investors are risk-neutral, calculate the expected payoff on the option in this fictitious risk-neutral world, and discount by the rate of interest to find the option's present value.

These *concepts* are completely general, but there are several ways to find the replicating package of investments. The example in the last section used a simplified version of what is known as the **binomial method.** The method starts by reducing the possible changes in next period's stock price to two, an "up" move and a "down" move. This simplification is OK if the time period is very short, so that a large number of small moves is accumulated over the life of the option. But it was fanciful to assume just two possible prices for AOL stock at the end of six months.

We could make the AOL problem a trifle more realistic by assuming that there are two possible price changes in each three-month period. This would give a wider variety of six-month prices. And there is no reason to stop at three-month periods. We could go on to take shorter and shorter intervals, with each interval showing two possible changes in AOL's stock price and giving an even wider selection of six-month prices.

This is illustrated in Figure 21.1. The two left-hand diagrams show our starting assumption: just two possible prices at the end of six months. Moving to the right, you can see what happens when there are two possible price changes every three months. This gives three possible stock prices when the option matures. In Figure 21.1(*c*) we have gone on to divide the six-month period into 26 weekly periods, in each of which the price can make one of two small moves. The distribution of prices at the end of six months is now looking much more realistic.

We could continue in this way to chop the period into shorter and shorter intervals, until eventually we would reach a situation in which the stock price is changing continuously and there is a continuum of possible future stock prices.

Example: The Two-Stage Binomial Method

Dividing the period into shorter intervals doesn't alter the basic method for valuing a call option. We can still replicate the call by a levered investment in the stock, but we need to adjust the degree of leverage at each stage. We will demonstrate first with our simple two-stage case in Figure 21.1 (*b*). Then we will work up to the situation where the stock price is changing continuously.

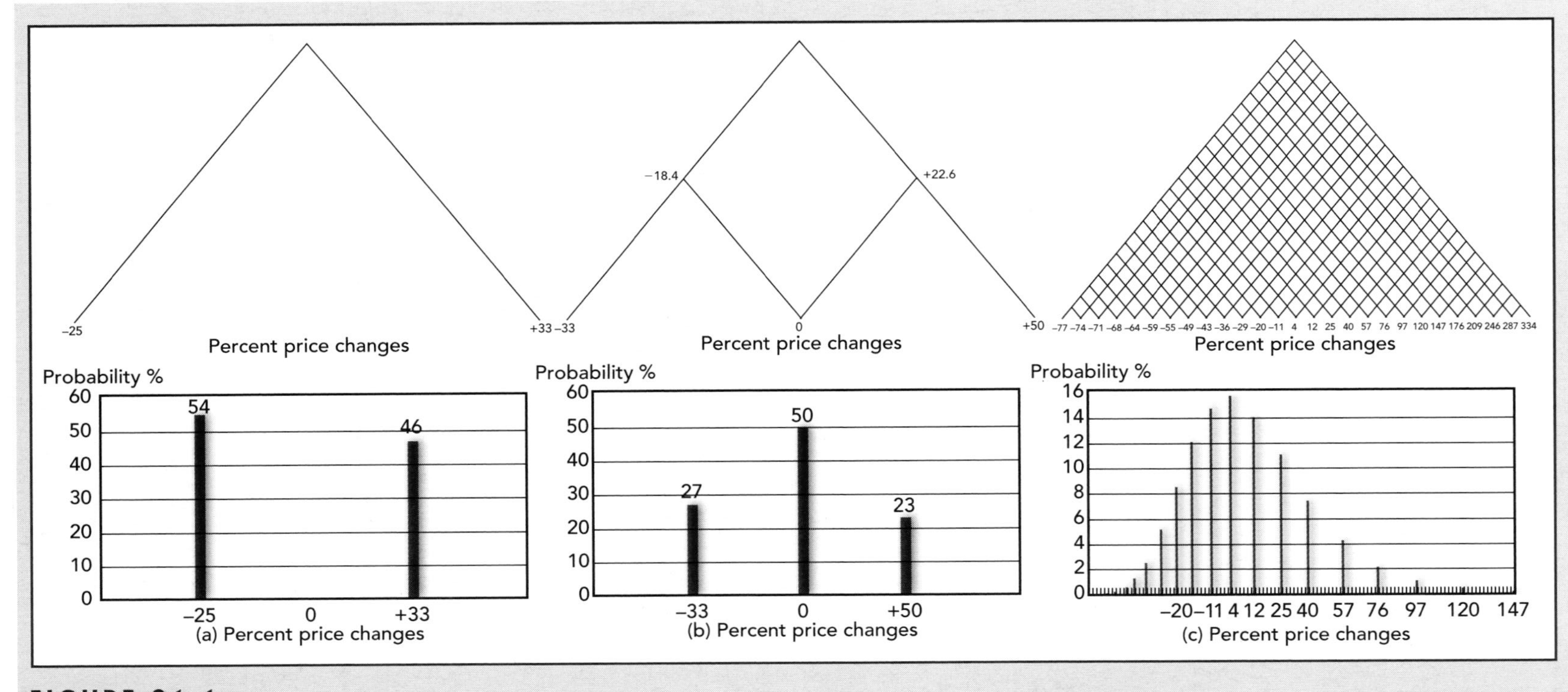

FIGURE 21.1

This figure shows the possible six-month price changes for AOL stock assuming that the stock makes a single up or down move each six months [Fig. 21.1(*a*)], each three months [Fig. 21.1(*b*)], or each week [Fig. 21.1(*c*)]. Beneath each tree we show a histogram of the possible six-month price changes, assuming investors are risk-neutral.

FIGURE 21.2

Present and possible future prices of AOL stock assuming that in each three-month period the price will either rise by 22.6% or fall by 18.4%. Figures in parentheses show the corresponding values of a six-month call option with an exercise price of $55.

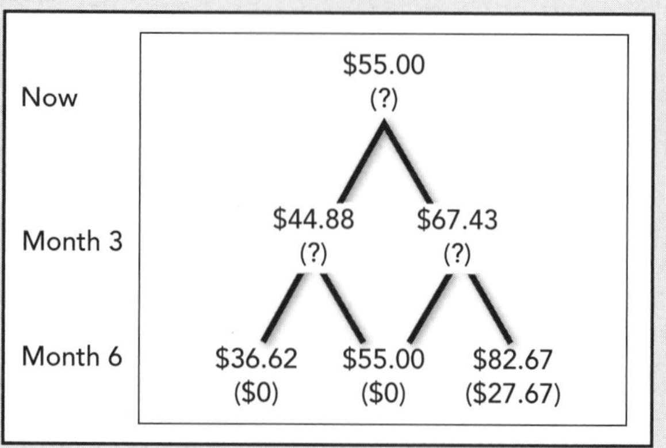

Figure 21.2 is taken from Figure 21.1 (*b*) and shows the possible prices of AOL stock, assuming that in each three-month period the price will either rise by 22.6 percent or fall by 18.4 percent. We show in parentheses the possible values at maturity of a six-month call option with an exercise price of $55. For example, if AOL's stock price turns out to be $36.62 in month 6, the call option will be worthless; at the other extreme, if the stock value is $82.67, the call will be worth $82.67 − $55 = $27.67. We haven't worked out yet what the option will be worth *before* maturity, so we just put question marks there for now.

Option Value in Month 3 To find the value of AOL's option today, we start by working out its possible values in month 3 and then work back to the present. Suppose that at the end of three months the stock price is $67.43. In this case investors know that, when the option finally matures in month 6, the stock price will be either $55 or $82.67, and the corresponding option price will be $0 or $27.67. We can therefore use our simple formula to find how many shares we need to buy in month 3 to replicate the option:

$$\text{Option delta} = \frac{\text{spread of possible option prices}}{\text{spread of possible stock prices}} = \frac{27.67 - 0}{82.67 - 55} = 1.0$$

Now we can construct a leveraged position in delta shares that would give identical payoffs to the option:

	Month 6 Stock Price = $55	Month 6 Stock Price = $82.67
Buy 1.0 shares	$55	$82.67
Borrow PV(55)	−55	−55
Total payoff	$ 0	$27.67

Since this portfolio provides identical payoffs to the option, we know that the value of the option in month 3 must be equal to the price of 1 share less the $55 loan discounted for 3 months at 4 percent per year, about 1 percent for 3 months:

$$\text{Value of call in month 3} = \$67.43 - \$55/1.01 = \$12.97$$

Therefore, if the share price rises in the first three months, the option will be worth $12.97. But what if the share price falls to $44.88? In that case the most that you can

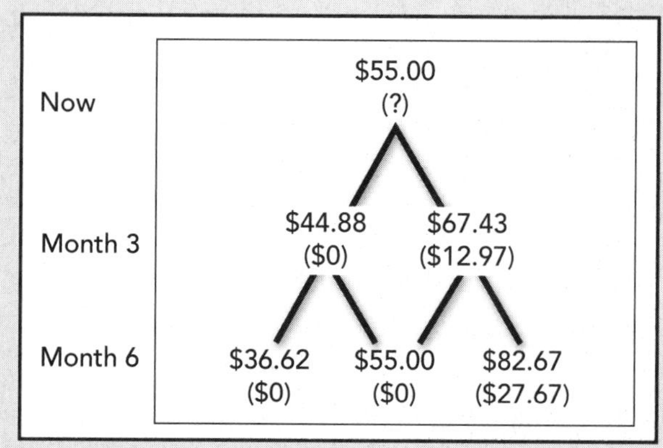

FIGURE 21.3

Present and possible future prices of AOL stock. Figures in parentheses show the corresponding values of a six-month call option with an exercise price of $55.

hope for is that the share price will recover to $55. Therefore the option is bound to be worthless when it matures and must be worthless at month 3.

Option Value Today We can now get rid of two of the question marks in Figure 21.2. Figure 21.3 shows that if the stock price in month 3 is $67.43, the option value is $12.97 and, if the stock price is $44.88, the option value is zero. It only remains to work back to the option value today.

We again begin by calculating the option delta:

$$\text{Option delta} = \frac{\text{spread of possible option prices}}{\text{spread of possible stock prices}} = \frac{12.97 - 0}{67.43 - 44.88} = .575$$

We can now find the leveraged position in delta shares that would give identical payoffs to the option:

	Month 3 Stock Price = $44.88	Month 3 Stock Price = $67.43
Buy .575 shares	$25.81	$38.78
Borrow PV(25.81)	−25.81	−25.81
Total payoff	$ 0	$12.97

The value of the AOL option today is equal to the value of this leveraged position:

$$\begin{aligned}\text{PV option} &= \text{PV}(.575 \text{ shares}) - \text{PV}(\$25.81)\\ &= .575 \times \$55 - \frac{\$25.81}{1.01} = \$6.07\end{aligned}$$

The General Binomial Method

Moving to two steps when valuing the AOL call probably added extra realism. But there is no reason to stop there. We could go on, as in Figure 21.1, to chop the period into smaller and smaller intervals. We could still use the binomial method to work back from the final date to the present. Of course, it would be tedious to do the calculations by hand, but simple to do so with a computer.

Since a stock can usually take on an almost limitless number of future values, the binomial method gives a more realistic and accurate measure of the option's value if

TABLE 21.1

As the number of intervals is increased, you must adjust the range of possible changes in the value of the asset to keep the same standard deviation. But you will get increasingly close to the Black–Scholes value of the AOL call option.

Note: The standard deviation is $\sigma = .4069$.

Intervals in a Year ($1/h$)	Change per Interval (%) Upside	Downside	Estimated Option Value
2	+33.3	−25.0	$8.32
4	+22.6	−18.4	6.07
12	+12.4	−11.1	6.65
52	+5.8	−5.5	6.75
		Black–Scholes value =	$6.78

we work with a large number of subperiods. But that raises an important question. How do we pick sensible figures for the up and down changes in value? For example, why did we pick figures of +22.6 percent and −18.4 percent when we revalued AOL's option with two subperiods? Fortunately, there is a neat little formula that relates the up and down changes to the standard deviation of stock returns:

$$1 + \text{upside change} = u = e^{\sigma\sqrt{h}}$$
$$1 + \text{downside change} = d = 1/u$$

where

e = base for natural logarithms = 2.718
σ = standard deviation of (continuously compounded) stock returns
h = interval as fraction of a year

When we said that AOL's stock could either rise by 33.3 percent or fall by 25 percent over six months ($h = .5$), our figures were consistent with a figure of 40.69 percent for the standard deviation of annual returns:

$$1 + \text{upside change (6-month interval)} = u = e^{.4069\sqrt{.5}} = 1.333$$
$$1 + \text{downside change} = d = 1/u = 1/1.333 = .75$$

To work out the equivalent upside and downside changes when we divide the period into two three-month intervals ($h = .25$), we use the same formula:

$$1 + \text{upside change (3-month interval)} = u = e^{.4069\sqrt{.25}} = 1.226$$
$$1 + \text{downside change} = d = 1/u = 1/1.226 = .816$$

The center columns in Table 21.1 show the equivalent up and down moves in the value of the firm if we chop the period into monthly or weekly periods, and the final column shows the effect on the estimated option value. (We will explain the Black–Scholes value shortly.)

The Binomial Method and Decision Trees

Calculating option values by the binomial method is basically a process of solving decision trees. You start at some future date and work back through the tree to the present. Eventually the possible cash flows generated by future events and actions are folded back to a present value.

Is the binomial method *merely* another application of decision trees, a tool of analysis that you learned about in Chapter 10? The answer is no, for at least two reasons. First, option pricing theory is absolutely essential for discounting within decision trees. Standard discounting doesn't work within decision trees for the same reason that it doesn't work for puts and calls. As we pointed out in Section 21.1, there is no single, constant discount rate for options because the risk of the option changes as time and the price of the underlying asset change. There is no single discount rate inside a decision tree, because if the tree contains meaningful future decisions, it also contains options. The market value of the future cash flows described by the decision tree has to be calculated by option pricing methods.

Second, option theory gives a simple, powerful framework for describing complex decision trees. For example, suppose that you have the option to postpone an investment for many years. The complete decision tree would overflow the largest classroom chalkboard. But now that you know about options, the opportunity to postpone investment might be summarized as "an American call on a perpetuity with a constant dividend yield." Of course, not all real problems have such easy option analogues, but we can often approximate complex decision trees by some simple package of assets and options. A custom decision tree may get closer to reality, but the time and expense may not be worth it. Most men buy their suits off the rack even though a custom-made suit from Saville Row would fit better and look nicer.

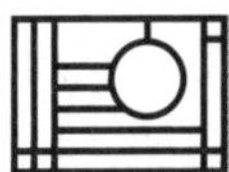

21.3 THE BLACK–SCHOLES FORMULA

Look back at Figure 21.1, which showed what happens to the distribution of possible AOL stock price changes as we divide the option's life into a larger and larger number of increasingly small subperiods. You can see that the distribution of price changes becomes increasingly smooth.

If we continued to chop up the option's life in this way, we would eventually reach the situation shown in Figure 21.4, where there is a continuum of possible stock price changes at maturity. Figure 21.4 is an example of a lognormal distribution. The lognormal distribution is often used to summarize the probability of different stock price changes.[10] It has a number of good commonsense features. For example, it recognizes the fact that the stock price can never fall by more than 100 percent, but that there is some, perhaps small, chance that it could rise by much more than 100 percent.

Subdividing the option life into indefinitely small slices does not affect the principle of option valuation. We could still replicate the call option by a levered investment in the stock, but we would need to adjust the degree of leverage continuously as time went by. Calculating option value when there is an infinite number of subperiods may sound a hopeless task. Fortunately, Black and Scholes derived a formula that does the trick. It is an unpleasant-looking formula, but on

[10]When we first looked at the distribution of stock price changes in Chapter 8, we assumed that these changes were normally distributed. We pointed out at the time that this is an acceptable approximation for very short intervals, but the distribution of changes over longer intervals is better approximated by the lognormal.

FIGURE 21.4

As the option's life is divided into more and more subperiods, the distribution of possible stock price changes approaches a lognormal distribution.

closer acquaintance you will find it exceptionally elegant and useful. The formula is

$$\text{Value of call option} = [\text{delta} \times \text{share price}] - [\text{bank loan}]$$

$$\uparrow \qquad \uparrow \qquad \uparrow$$

$$[N(d_1) \times P] - [N(d_2) \times \text{PV(EX)}]$$

where

$$d_1 = \frac{\log[P/\text{PV(EX)}]}{\sigma\sqrt{t}} + \frac{\sigma\sqrt{t}}{2}$$

$$d_2 = d_1 - \sigma\sqrt{t}$$

$N(d)$ = cumulative normal probability density function[11]

EX = exercise price of option; PV(EX) is calculated by discounting at the risk-free interest rate r_f

t = number of periods to exercise date

P = price of stock now

σ = standard deviation per period of (continuously compounded) rate of return on stock

Notice that the value of the call in the Black–Scholes formula has the same properties that we identified earlier. It increases with the level of the stock price P and decreases with the present value of the exercise price PV(EX), which in turn depends on the interest rate and time to maturity. It also increases with the time to maturity and the stock's variability ($\sigma\sqrt{t}$).

To derive their formula Black and Scholes assumed that there is a continuum of stock prices, and therefore to replicate an option investors must continuously adjust their holding in the stock. Of course this is not literally possible,

[11]That is, $N(d)$ is the probability that a normally distributed random variable $\tilde{x}$ will be less than or equal to d. $N(d_1)$ in the Black–Scholes formula is the option delta. Thus the formula tells us that the value of a call is equal to an investment of $N(d_1)$ in the common stock less borrowing of $N(d_2) \times \text{PV(EX)}$.

but even so the formula performs remarkably well in the real world, where stocks trade only intermittently and prices jump from one level to another. The Black–Scholes model has also proved very flexible; it can be adapted to value options on a variety of assets with special features, such as foreign currency, bonds, and commodities. It is not surprising therefore that it has been extremely influential and has become the standard model for valuing options. Every day dealers on the options exchanges use this formula to make huge trades. These dealers are not for the most part trained in the formula's mathematical derivation; they just use a computer or a specially programmed calculator to find the value of the option.

Using the Black–Scholes Formula

The Black–Scholes formula may look difficult, but it is very straightforward to apply. Let us practice using it to value the AOL call.

Here are the data that you need:

- Price of stock now $= P = 55$.
- Exercise price $= \text{EX} = 55$.
- Standard deviation of continuously compounded annual returns $= \sigma = .4069$.
- Years to maturity $= t = .5$.
- Interest rate per annum $= r_f = 4$ percent (equivalent to 1.98 percent for six months).[12]

Remember that the Black–Scholes formula for the value of a call is

$$[N(d_1) \times P] - [N(d_2) \times \text{PV(EX)}]$$

where

$$d_1 = \log\,[P/\text{PV(EX)}]/\sigma\sqrt{t} + \sigma\sqrt{t}/2$$
$$d_2 = d_1 - \sigma\sqrt{t}$$
$$N(d) = \text{cumulative normal probability function}$$

There are three steps to using the formula to value the AOL call:

Step 1 Calculate d_1 and d_2. This is just a matter of plugging numbers into the formula (noting that "log" means *natural* log):

$$\begin{aligned} d_1 &= \log\,[P/\text{PV(EX)}]/\sigma\sqrt{t} + \sigma\sqrt{t}/2 \\ &= \log\,[55/(55/1.0198)]/(.4069 \times \sqrt{.5}) + (.4069 \times \sqrt{.5})/2 \\ &= .2120 \end{aligned}$$
$$d_2 = d_1 - \sigma\sqrt{t} = .2120 - (.4069 \times \sqrt{.5}) = -.0757$$

---

[12]If the annually compounded rate of interest is 4 percent, the equivalent rate for six months is 1.98 percent. This will give $\text{PV(EX)} = 55/(1.04)^{.5} = \$53.93$. (In the earlier binomial examples, we used a 2 percent six-month rate.)

When valuing options, it is more common to use continuously compounded rates (see Section 3.3). If the annual rate is 4 percent, the equivalent continuously compounded rate is 3.92 percent. (The natural log of 1.04 is .0392, and $e^{.0392} = 1.04$.) Using continuous compounding, $55 \times e^{-.5 \times .0392} = \$53.93$.

There is only one trick here: If you are using a spreadsheet or computer program that calls for a continuously compounded interest rate, make sure that you *enter* a continuously compounded rate.

FIGURE 21.5

The curved line shows how the value of the AOL call option changs as the price of AOL stock changes.

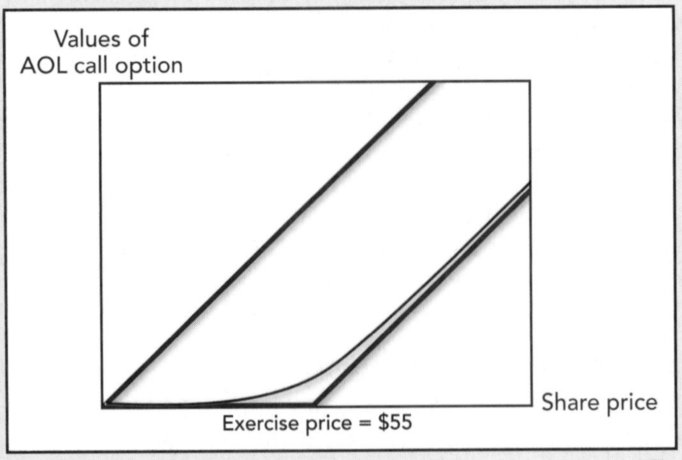

Step 2 Find $N(d_1)$ and $N(d_2)$. $N(d_1)$ is the probability that a normally distributed variable will be less than d_1 standard deviations above the mean. If d_1 is large, $N(d_1)$ is close to 1.0 (i.e., you can be almost certain that the variable will be less than d_1 standard deviations above the mean). If d_1 is zero, $N(d_1)$ is .5 (i.e., there is a 50 percent chance that a normally distributed variable will be below the average).

The simplest way to find $N(d_1)$ is to use the Excel function NORMSDIST. For example, if you enter NORMSDIST(.2120) into an Excel spreadsheet, you will see that there is a .5840 probability that a normally distributed variable will be less than .2120 standard deviations above the mean. Alternatively, you can use a set of normal probability tables such as those in Appendix Table 6, in which case you need to interpolate between the cumulative probabilities for $d_1 = .21$ and $d_1 = .22$.

Again you can use the Excel function to find $N(d_2)$. If you enter NORMSDIST(−.0757) into an Excel spreadsheet, you should get the answer .4698. In other words, there is a probability of .4698 that a normally distributed variable will be less than .0757 standard deviations *below* the mean. Alternatively, if you use Appendix Table 6, you need to look up the value for +.0757 and subtract it from 1.0:

$$\begin{aligned} N(d_2) &= N(-.0757) = 1 - N(+.0757) \\ &= 1 - .5302 = .4698 \end{aligned}$$

Step 3 Plug these numbers into the Black–Scholes formula. You can now calculate the value of the AOL call:

$$\begin{aligned} &[\text{Delta} \times \text{price}] - [\text{bank loan}] \\ &= [N(d_1) \times P] - [N(d_2) \times \text{PV(EX)}] \\ &= [.5840 \times 55] - [.4698 \times 55/(1.04)^{.5}] = \$6.78 \end{aligned}$$

Some More Practice Suppose you repeated the calculations for the AOL call for a wide range of stock prices. The result is shown in Figure 21.5. You can see that the option values lie along an upward-sloping curve that starts its travels in the bottom left-hand corner of the diagram. As the stock price increases, the option

	Establishment Industries	Digital Organics
Stock price (P)	\$22	\$22
Exercise price (EX)	\$25	\$25
Interest rate (r_f)	.04	.04
Maturity in years (t)	5	5
Standard deviation (σ)	.24	.36
$d_1 = \log[P/PV(EX)]/\sigma\sqrt{t} + \sigma\sqrt{t}/2$	.3955	.4873
$d_2 = d_1 - \sigma\sqrt{t}$	−.1411	−.3177
Value of call = $[N(d_1) \times P] - [N(d_2) \times PV(EX)]$	\$5.26	\$7.40
Value of 100,000 options	\$526,000	\$740,000

TABLE 21.2

Using the Black–Scholes formula to value the executive stock options for Establishment Industries and Digital Organics (see Table 20.3).

value rises and gradually becomes parallel to the lower bound for the option value. This is exactly the shape we deduced in Chapter 20 (see Figure 20.10).

The height of this curve of course depends on risk and time to maturity. For example, if the risk of AOL stock had suddenly decreased, the curve shown in Figure 21.5 would drop at every possible stock price.

Speaking of differences in risk, we can now use the Black–Scholes formula to value the executive stock option packages you were offered in Section 20.3 (see Table 20.3). Table 21.2 calculates the value of the package from safe-and-stodgy Establishment Industries at \$526,000. The package from risky-and-glamorous Digital Organics is worth \$740,000. Congratulations.

The Black–Scholes Formula and the Binomial Method

Look back at Table 21.1 where we used the binomial method to calculate the value of the AOL call. Notice that, as the number of intervals is increased, the values that you obtain from the binomial method begin to snuggle up to the Black–Scholes value of \$6.78.

The Black–Scholes formula recognizes a continuum of possible outcomes. This is usually more realistic than the limited number of outcomes assumed in the binomial method. The formula is also more accurate and quicker to use than the binomial method. So why use the binomial method at all? The answer is that there are circumstances in which you cannot use the Black–Scholes formula but the binomial method will still give you a good measure of the option's value. We will look at several such cases in the next section.

Using the Black–Scholes Formula to Estimate Variability

So far we have used our option pricing model to calculate the value of an option *given* the standard deviation of the asset's returns. Sometimes it is useful to turn the problem around and ask what the option price is telling us about the asset's variability. For example, the Chicago Board Options Exchange trades options on several market indexes. As we write this, the Standard and Poor's 100-share index is 575, while a six-month at-the-money call option on the index is priced at 42. If the Black–Scholes formula is correct, then an option value of 42 makes sense

FIGURE 21.6

Standard deviations of market returns implied by prices of options on stock indexes.

Source: **www.cboe.com.**

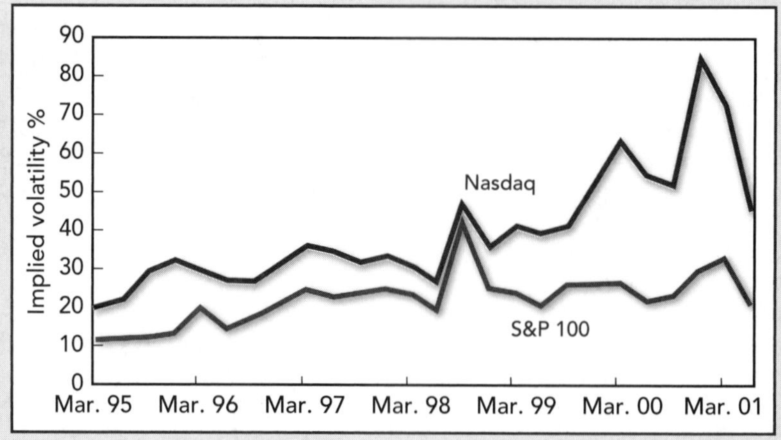

only if investors believe that the standard deviation of index returns is about 23 percent a year. You may be interested to compare this number with Figure 21.6, which shows the stock market volatility that was implied by the price of index options in earlier years. Notice the sharp increase in investor uncertainty about the value of Nasdaq stocks during the crash of the dot.com stocks in late 2000. This uncertainty showed up in the high price that investors were prepared to pay for options.

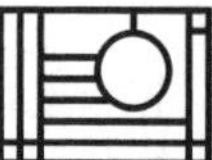

21.4 OPTION VALUES AT A GLANCE

So far our discussion of option values has assumed that investors hold the option until maturity. That is certainly the case with European options that *cannot* be exercised before maturity but may not be the case with American options that can be exercised at any time. Also, when we valued the AOL call, we could ignore dividends, because AOL did not pay any. Can the same valuation methods be extended to American options and to stocks that pay dividends? You may find it useful to have the following summary of how different combinations of features affect option value.

American Calls—No Dividends Unlike European options, American options can be exercised anytime. However, we know that in the absence of dividends the value of a call option increases with time to maturity. So, if you exercised an American call option early, you would needlessly reduce its value. Since an American call should not be exercised before maturity, its value is the same as that of a European call, and the Black–Scholes model applies to both options.

European Puts—No Dividends If we wish to value a European put, we can use the put–call parity formula from Chapter 20:

$$\text{Value of put} = \text{value of call} - \text{value of stock} + \text{PV(exercise price)}$$

American Puts—No Dividends It can sometimes pay to exercise an American put before maturity to reinvest the exercise price. For example, suppose that immediately after you buy an American put, the stock price falls to zero. In this case there is no advantage to holding onto the option since it *cannot* become more valuable. It is better to exercise the put and invest the exercise money. Thus an American put is always more valuable than a European put. In our extreme example, the difference is equal to the present value of the interest that you could earn on the exercise price. In all other cases the difference is less.

Because the Black–Scholes formula does not allow for early exercise, it cannot be used to value an American put exactly. But you can use the step-by-step binomial method as long as you check at each point whether the option is worth more dead than alive and then use the higher of the two values.

European Calls on Dividend-Paying Stocks Part of the share value comprises the present value of dividends. The option holder is not entitled to dividends. Therefore, when using the Black–Scholes model to value a European call on a dividend-paying stock, you should reduce the price of the stock by the present value of the dividends paid before the option's maturity.

Dividends don't always come with a big label attached, so look out for instances where the asset holder gets a benefit and the option holder does not. For example, when you buy foreign currency, you can invest it to earn interest; but if you own an option to buy foreign currency, you miss out on this income. Therefore, when valuing an option to buy foreign currency, you need to deduct the present value of this foreign interest from the current price of the currency.[13]

American Calls on Dividend-Paying Stocks We have seen that when the stock does not pay dividends, an American call option is *always* worth more alive than dead. By holding onto the option, you not only keep your option open but also earn interest on the exercise money. Even when there are dividends, you should never exercise early if the dividend you gain is less than the interest you lose by having to pay the exercise price early. However, if the dividend is sufficiently large, you might want to capture it by exercising the option just before the ex-dividend date.

The only general method for valuing an American call on a dividend-paying stock is to use the step-by-step binomial method. In this case you must check at each stage to see whether the option is more valuable if exercised just before the ex-dividend date than if held for at least one more period.

Example. Here is a last chance to practice your option valuation skills by valuing an American call on a dividend-paying stock. Figure 21.7 summarizes the possible price movements in Consolidated Pork Bellies stock. The stock price is currently \$100, but over the next year it could either fall by 20 percent to \$80 or rise by 25 percent to \$125. In either case the company will then pay its regular dividend of \$20. Immediately after payment of this dividend the stock price will fall to 80 − 20 = \$60, or 125 − 20 = \$105. Over the second year the

[13]For example, suppose that it currently costs \$2 to buy £1 and that this pound can be invested to earn interest of 5 percent. The option holder misses out on interest of .05 × \$2 = \$.10. So, before using the Black–Scholes formula to value an option to buy sterling, you must adjust the current price of sterling:

$$\text{Adjusted price of sterling} = \text{current price} - \text{PV(interest)}$$
$$= \$2 - .10/1.05 = \$1.905.$$

FIGURE 21.7

Possible values of Consolidated Pork Bellies stock.

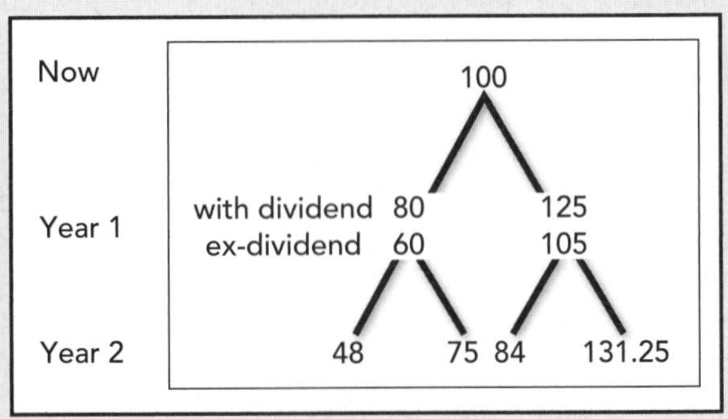

price will again either fall by 20 percent from the ex-dividend price or rise by 25 percent.[14]

Suppose that you wish to value a two-year American call option on Consolidated stock. Figure 21.8 shows the possible option values at each point, assuming an exercise price of \$70 and an interest rate of 12 percent. We won't go through all the calculations behind these figures, but we will focus on the option values at the end of year 1.

Suppose that the stock price has fallen in the first year. What is the option worth if you hold onto it for a further period? You should be used to this problem by now. First pretend that investors are risk-neutral and calculate the probability that the stock will rise in price. This probability turns out to be 71 percent.[15] Now calculate the expected payoff on the option and discount at 12 percent:

$$\text{Option value if not exercised in year 1} = \frac{(.71 \times 5) + (.29 \times 0)}{1.12} = \$3.18$$

Thus, if you hold onto the option, it is worth \$3.18. However, if you exercise the option just before the ex-dividend date, you pay an exercise price of \$70 for a stock worth \$80. This \$10 value from exercising is greater than the \$3.18 from holding onto the option. Therefore in Figure 21.8 we put in an option value of \$10 if the stock price falls in year 1.

You will also want to exercise if the stock price *rises* in year 1. The option is worth \$42.45 if you hold onto it but \$55 if you exercise. Therefore in Figure 21.8 we put in a value of \$55 if the stock price rises.

The rest of the calculation is routine. Calculate the expected option payoff in year 1 and discount by 12 percent to give the option value today:

$$\text{Option value today} = \frac{(.71 \times 55) + (.29 \times 10)}{1.12} = \$37.50$$

[14]Notice that the payment of a fixed dividend in year 1 results in four possible stock prices at the end of year 2. In other words, 60 × 1.25 does not equal 105 × .8. Don't let that put you off. You still start from the end and work back one step at a time to find the possible option values at each date.

[15]Using the formula given in footnote 5,

$$p = \frac{\text{interest rate} - \text{downside change}}{\text{upside change} - \text{downside change}} = \frac{12 - (-20)}{25 - (-20)} = .71$$

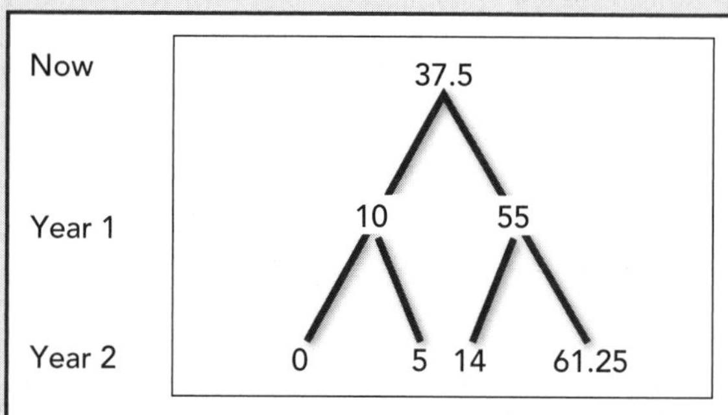

FIGURE 21.8

Values of a two-year call option on Consolidated Pork Bellies stock. Exercise price is $70. Although we show option values for year 2, the option will not be alive then. It will be exercised in year 1.

SUMMARY

In this chapter we introduced the basic principles of option valuation by considering a call option on a stock that could take on one of two possible values at the option's maturity. We showed that it is possible to construct a package of the stock and a loan that would provide exactly the same payoff as the option *regardless* of whether the stock price rises or falls. Therefore the value of the option must be the same as the value of this replicating portfolio.

We arrived at the same answer by pretending that investors are risk-neutral, so that the expected return on every asset is equal to the interest rate. We calculated the expected future value of the option in this imaginary risk-neutral world and then discounted this figure at the interest rate to find the option's present value.

The general binomial method adds realism by dividing the option's life into a number of subperiods in each of which the stock price can make one of two possible moves. Chopping the period into these shorter intervals doesn't alter the basic method for valuing a call option. We can still replicate the call by a package of the stock and a loan, but the package changes at each stage.

Finally, we introduced the Black–Scholes formula. This calculates the option's value when the stock price is constantly changing and takes on a continuum of possible future values.

When valuing options in practical situations there are a number of features to look out for. For example, you may need to recognize that the option value is reduced by the fact that the holder is not entitled to any dividends.

FURTHER READING

The classic articles on option valuation are:

F. Black and M. Scholes: "The Pricing of Options and Corporate Liabilities," *Journal of Political Economy,* 81:637–654 (May–June 1973).

R. C. Merton: "Theory of Rational Option Pricing," *Bell Journal of Economics and Management Science,* 4:141–183 (Spring 1973).

The texts listed under "Further Reading" in Chapter 20 can be referred to for discussion of option-valuation models and the practical complications of applying them.

QUIZ

1. The stock price of Deutsche Metall (DM) changes only once a month: either it goes up by 20 percent or it falls by 16.7 percent. Its price now is €40, that is, 40 euros. The interest rate is 12.7 percent per year, or about 1 percent per month.
   a. What is the value of a one-month call option with an exercise price of €40?
   b. What is the option delta?
   c. Show how the payoffs of this call option can be replicated by buying DM's stock and borrowing.
   d. What is the value of a two-month call option with an exercise price of €40?
   e. What is the option delta of the two-month call over the first one-month period?
2. Complete the following sentence and briefly explain: "The Black–Scholes formula gives the same answer as the binomial method when ____."
3. a. Can the delta of a call option be greater than 1.0? Explain.
   b. Can it be less than zero?
   c. How does the delta of a call change if the stock price rises?
   d. How does it change if the risk of the stock increases?
4. Why can't you value options using a standard discounted-cash-flow formula?
5. Use either the replicating-portfolio method or the risk-neutral method to value the six-month call and put options on AOL stock with an exercise price of $60 (see Table 20.1). Assume AOL stock price = $55.
6. Imagine that AOL's stock price will either rise by 25 percent or fall by 20 percent over the next six months (see Section 21.1). Recalculate the value of the call option (exercise price = $55) using (a) the replicating portfolio method and (b) the risk-neutral method. Explain intuitively why the option value falls from the value computed in Section 21.1.
7. Over the coming year Ragwort's stock price will halve to $50 from its current level of $100 or it will rise to $200. The one-year interest rate is 10 percent.
   a. What is the delta of a one-year call option on Ragwort stock with an exercise price of $100?
   b. Use the replicating-portfolio method to value this call.
   c. In a risk-neutral world what is the probability that Ragwort stock will rise in price?
   d. Use the risk-neutral method to check your valuation of the Ragwort option.
   e. If someone told you that in reality there is a 60 percent chance that Ragwort's stock price will rise to $200, would you change your view about the value of the option? Explain.
8. Use the Black–Scholes formula with Appendix Table 6 to value the following options:
   a. A call option written on a stock selling for $60 per share with a $60 exercise price. The stock's standard deviation is 6 percent per month. The option matures in three months. The risk-free interest rate is 1 percent per month.
   b. A put option written on the same stock at the same time, with the same exercise price and expiration date.

   Now for each of these options find the combination of stock and risk-free asset that would replicate the option.
9. "An option is always riskier than the stock it is written on." True or false? How does the risk of an option change when the stock price changes?
10. For which of the following options *might* it be rational to exercise before maturity? Explain briefly why or why not.
    a. American put on a non-dividend-paying stock.
    b. American call—the dividend payment is 50 pesos per annum, the exercise price is 1,000 pesos, and the interest rate is 10 percent.

c. American call—the interest rate is 10 percent, and the dividend payment is 5 percent of future stock price. *Hint:* The dividend depends on the stock price, which could either rise or fall.

PRACTICE QUESTIONS

1. Johnny Jones's high school derivatives homework asks for a binomial valuation of a 12-month call option on the common stock of the Overland Railroad. The stock is now selling for $45 per share and has a standard deviation of 24 percent. Johnny first constructs a binomial tree like Figure 21.2, in which stock price moves up or down every six months. Then he constructs a more realistic tree, assuming that the stock price moves up or down once every three months, or four times per year.
   a. Construct these two binomial trees.
   b. How would these trees change if Overland's standard deviation were 30 percent? *Hint:* Make sure to specify the right up and down percentage changes.
2. Suppose a stock price can go up by 15 percent or down by 13 percent over the next year. You own a one-year put on the stock. The interest rate is 10 percent, and the current stock price is $60.
   a. What exercise price leaves you indifferent between holding the put or exercising it now?
   b. How does this break-even exercise price change if the interest rate is increased?
3. Look back at Table 20.2. Now construct a similar table for put options. In each case construct a simple example to illustrate your point.
4. The price of Matterhorn Mining stock is 100 Swiss francs (SFr). During each of the next two six-month periods the price may either rise by 25 percent or fall by 20 percent (equivalent to a standard deviation of 31.5 percent a year). At month 6 the company will pay a dividend of SFr20. The interest rate is 10 percent per six-month period. What is the value of a one-year American call option with an exercise price of SFr80? Now recalculate the option value, assuming that the dividend is equal to 20 percent of the with-dividend stock price.
5. Buffelhead's stock price is $220 and could halve or double in each six-month period (equivalent to a standard deviation of 98 percent). A one-year call option on Buffelhead has an exercise price of $165. The interest rate is 21 percent a year.
   a. What is the value of the Buffelhead call?
   b. Now calculate the option delta for the second six months if (i) the stock price rises to $440 and (ii) the stock price falls to $110.
   c. How does the call option delta vary with the level of the stock price? Explain intuitively why.
   d. Suppose that in month 6 the Buffelhead stock price is $110. How at that point could you replicate an investment in the stock by a combination of call options and risk-free lending? Show that your strategy does indeed produce the same returns as those from an investment in the stock.
6. Suppose that you own an American put option on Buffelhead stock (see question 5) with an exercise price of $220.
   a. Would you ever want to exercise the put early?
   b. Calculate the value of the put.
   c. Now compare the value with that of an equivalent European put option.
7. Recalculate the value of the Buffelhead call option (see question 5), assuming that the option is American and that at the end of the first six months the company pays a dividend of $25. (Thus the price at the end of the year is either double or half the *ex*-dividend price in month 6.) How would your answer change if the option were European?

8. Suppose that you have an option which allows you to sell Buffelhead stock (see question 5) in month 6 for \$165 *or* to buy it in month 12 for \$165. What is the value of this unusual option?
9. The current price of the stock of Mont Tremblant Air is C\$100. During each six-month period it will either rise by 11.1 percent or fall by 10 percent (equivalent to an annual standard deviation of 14.9 percent). The interest rate is 5 percent per six-month period.
   a. Calculate the value of a one-year European put option on Mont Tremblant's stock with an exercise price of C\$102.
   b. Recalculate the value of the Mont Tremblant put option, assuming that it is an American option.
10. The current price of United Carbon (UC) stock is \$200. The standard deviation is 22.3 percent a year, and the interest rate is 21 percent a year. A one-year call option on UC has an exercise price of \$180.
    a. Use the Black–Scholes model to value the call option on UC.
    b. Use the formula given in Section 21.2 to calculate the up and down moves that you would use if you valued the UC option with the one-period binomial method. Now value the option by using that method.
    c. Recalculate the up and down moves and revalue the option by using the two-period binomial method.
    d. Use your answer to part (c) to calculate the option delta (i) today; (ii) next period if the stock price rises; and (iii) next period if the stock price falls. Show at each point how you would replicate a call option with a levered investment in the company's stock.
11. Suppose you construct an option hedge by buying a levered position in delta shares of stock and selling one call option. As the share price changes, the option delta changes, and you will need to adjust your hedge. You can minimize the cost of adjustments if changes in the stock price have only a small effect on the option delta. Construct an example to show whether the option delta is likely to vary more if you hedge with an in-the-money option, an at-the-money option, or an out-of-the-money option.
12. Other things equal, which of these American options are you most likely to want to exercise early?
    a. A put option on a stock with a large dividend or a call on the same stock.
    b. A put option on a stock that is selling below exercise price or a call on the same stock.
    c. A put option when the interest rate is high or the same put option when the interest rate is low.

    Illustrate your answer with examples.
13. Is it better to exercise a call option on the with-dividend date or on the ex-dividend date? How about a put option? Explain.
14. You can buy each of the following items of information about an American call option for \$10 apiece: PV (exercise price); exercise price; standard deviation × square root of time to maturity; interest rate (per annum); time to maturity; value of European put; expected return on stock.

    How much would you need to spend to value the option? Explain.

STANDARD &POOR'S

15. Look back to the companies listed in Table 7.3. Most of these companies are covered in the Standard & Poor's Market Insight website (**www.mhhe.com/edumarketinsight**), and most will have traded options. Pick at least three companies. For each company, download "Monthly Adjusted Prices" as an Excel spreadsheet. Calculate each company's standard deviation from the monthly returns given on the spreadsheet. The Excel function is STDEV. Convert the standard deviations from monthly to annual units by multiplying by the square root of 12.
    a. Use the Black–Scholes formula to value 3, 6, and 9 month call options on each stock. Assume the exercise price equals the current stock price, and use a current, risk-free, annual interest rate.

b. For each stock, pick a traded option with an exercise price approximately equal to the current stock price. Use the Black–Scholes formula and your estimate of standard deviation to value the option. How close is your calculated value to the traded price of the option?

c. Your answer to part (b) will not exactly match the traded price. Experiment with different values for standard deviation until your calculations match the traded options prices as closely as possible. What are these this implied volatilites? What do the implied volatilities say about investors' forecasts of future volatility?

CHALLENGE QUESTIONS

1. Use the formula that relates the value of the call and the put (see Section 21.1) and the one-period binomial model to show that the option delta for a put option is equal to the option delta for a call option minus 1.
2. Show how the option delta changes as the stock price rises relative to the exercise price. Explain intuitively why this is the case. (What happens to the option delta if the exercise price of an option is zero? What happens if the exercise price becomes indefinitely large?)
3. Write a spreadsheet program to value a call option using the Black–Scholes formula.
4. Your company has just awarded you a generous stock option scheme. You suspect that the board will either decide to increase the dividend or announce a stock repurchase program. Which do you secretly hope they will decide? Explain. (You may find it helpful to refer back to Chapter 16.)
5. In August 1986 Salomon Brothers issued four-year Standard and Poor's 500 Index Subordinated Notes (SPINS). The notes paid no interest, but at maturity investors received the face value plus a possible bonus. The bonus was equal to $1,000 times the proportionate appreciation in the market index.
   a. What would be the value of SPINS if issued today?
   b. If Salomon Brothers wished to hedge itself against a rise in the market index, how should it have done so?
6. Some corporations have issued *perpetual* warrants. Warrants are call options issued by a firm, allowing the warrant-holder to buy the firm's stock. We discuss warrants in Chapter 23. For now, just consider a perpetual call.
   a. What does the Black-Scholes formula predict for the value of an infinite-lived call option on a non-dividend paying stock? Explain the value you obtain. (*Hint:* what happens to the present value of the exercise price of a long-maturity option?)
   b. Do you think this prediction is realistic? If not, explain carefully why. (*Hint:* for one of several reasons: if a company's stock price followed the exact time-series process assumed by Black and Scholes, could the company ever be bankrupt, with a stock price of zero?)

MINI-CASE

Bruce Honiball's Invention

It was another disappointing year for Bruce Honiball, the manager of retail services at the Gibb River Bank. Sure, the retail side of Gibb River was making money, but it didn't grow at all in 2000. Gibb River had plenty of loyal depositors, but few new ones. Bruce had to

Year	Interest Rate	Market Return	End-Year Dividend Yield	Year	Interest Rate	Market Return	End-Year Dividend Yield
1981	13.3%	−20.2%	4.5%	1991	10.0%	37.8%	3.8%
1982	14.6	−10.7	5.6	1992	6.3	−.5	3.8
1983	11.1	70.1	4.0	1993	5.0	38.7	3.2
1984	11.0	−4.8	5.1	1994	5.7	−6.8	4.1
1985	15.3	46.5	4.6	1995	7.6	17.3	3.9
1986	15.4	47.7	3.9	1996	7.0	10.4	3.6
1987	12.8	1.6	4.8	1997	5.3	10.3	3.6
1988	12.1	16.8	5.4	1998	4.8	14.5	3.8
1989	16.8	19.9	5.5	1999	4.7	13.8	3.5
1990	14.2	−14.1	6.0	2000	5.9	−.9	3.2

TABLE 21.3

Australian interest rates and equity returns, 1981–2000.

figure out some new product or financial service—something that would generate some excitement and attention.

Bruce had been musing on one idea for some time. How about making it easy *and safe* for Gibb River's customers to put money in the stock market? How about giving them the upside of investing in equities—at least *some* of the upside—but none of the downside?

Bruce could see the advertisements now:

> How would you like to invest in Australian stocks completely risk-free? You can with the new Gibb River Bank *Equity-Linked Deposit*. You share in the good years; we take care of the bad ones.
>
> Here's how it works. Deposit $A100 with us for one year. At the end of that period you get back your $A100 *plus* $A5 for every 10 percent rise in the value of the Australian All Ordinaries stock index. But, if the market index falls during this period, the Bank will still refund your $A100 deposit in full.
>
> There's no risk of loss. Gibbs River Bank is your safety net.

Bruce had floated the idea before and encountered immediate skepticism, even derision: "Heads they win, tails we lose—is that what you're proposing, Mr. Honiball?" Bruce had no ready answer. Could the bank really afford to make such an attractive offer? How should it invest the money that would come in from customers? The bank had no appetite for major new risks.

Bruce has puzzled over these questions for the past two weeks but has been unable to come up with a satisfactory answer. He believes that the Australian equity market is currently fully valued, but he realizes that some of his colleagues are more bullish than he is about equity prices.

Fortunately, the bank had just recruited a smart new MBA graduate, Sheila Cox. Sheila was sure that she could find the answers to Bruce Honiball's questions. First she collected data on the Australian market to get a preliminary idea of whether equity-linked deposits could work. These data are shown in Table 21.3. She was just about to undertake some quick calculations when she received the following further memo from Bruce:

Sheila, I've got another idea. A lot of our customers probably share my view that the market is overvalued. Why don't we also offer them a chance to make some money by offering a "bear market deposit"? If the market goes up, they would just get back their $A100 deposit. If it goes down, they get their $A100 back plus $5 for each 10 percent that the market falls. Can you figure out whether we could do something like this? Bruce.

Questions

1. What kinds of options is Bruce proposing? How much would the options be worth? Would the equity-linked and bear-market deposits generate positive NPV for Gibb River Bank?

CHAPTER TWENTY-TWO

REAL OPTIONS

WHEN YOU USE discounted cash flow (DCF) to value a project, you implicitly assume that your firm will hold the project passively. In other words, you are ignoring the *real options* attached to the project—options that sophisticated managers can take advantage of. You could say that DCF does not reflect the value of management. Managers who hold real options do not have to be passive; they can make decisions to capitalize on good fortune or to mitigate loss. The opportunity to make such decisions clearly adds value whenever project outcomes are uncertain.

Chapter 10 introduced the four main types of real options:

- The option to expand if the immediate investment project succeeds.
- The option to wait (and learn) before investing.
- The option to shrink or abandon a project.
- The option to vary the mix of output or the firm's production methods.

Chapter 10 gave several simple examples of real options. We also showed you how to use decision trees to set out possible future outcomes and decisions. But we did not show you how to value real options. That is our task in this chapter. We will apply the concepts and valuation principles you learned in Chapter 21.

For the most part we will work with simple numerical examples. The art and science of valuing real options are illustrated just as well with simple calculations as complex ones. But we will also show you results for several more complex examples, including:

- A strategic investment in the computer business.
- The valuation of an aircraft purchase option.
- The option to develop commercial real estate.
- The decision to operate or mothball an oil tanker.

These examples show how financial managers value real options in real life.

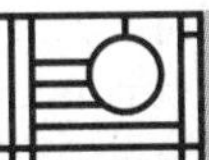

22.1 THE VALUE OF FOLLOW-ON INVESTMENT OPPORTUNITIES

It is 1982. You are assistant to the chief financial officer (CFO) of Blitzen Computers, an established computer manufacturer casting a profit-hungry eye on the rapidly developing personal computer market. You are helping the CFO evaluate the proposed introduction of the Blitzen Mark I Micro.

The Mark I's forecasted cash flows and NPV are shown in Table 22.1. Unfortunately the Mark I can't meet Blitzen's customary 20 percent hurdle rate and has a $46 million negative NPV, contrary to top management's strong gut feeling that Blitzen ought to be in the personal computer market.

The CFO has called you in to discuss the project:

"The Mark I just can't make it on financial grounds," the CFO says. "But we've got to do it for strategic reasons. I'm recommending we go ahead."

"But you're missing the all-important financial advantage, Chief," you reply.

"Don't call me 'Chief.' What financial advantage?"

"If we don't launch the Mark I, it will probably be too expensive to enter the micro market later, when Apple, IBM, and others are firmly established. If we go ahead, we have the opportunity to make follow-on investments which could be extremely profitable. The Mark I gives not only its own cash flows but also a call option to go on with a Mark II micro. That call option is the real source of strategic value."

TABLE 22.1

Summary of cash flows and financial analysis of the Mark I microcomputer ($ millions).

*After-tax operating cash flow is negative in 1982 because of R&D costs.

	Year					
	1982	1983	1984	1985	1986	1987
After-tax operating cash flow (1)*	−200	+110	+159	+295	+185	0
Capital investment (2)	250	0	0	0	0	0
Increase in working capital (3)	0	50	100	100	−125	−125
Net cash flow (1) − (2) − (3)	−450	+60	+59	+195	+310	+125
NPV at 20% = −$46.45, or about −$46 million						

"So it's strategic value by another name. That doesn't tell me what the Mark II investment's worth. The Mark II could be a great investment or a lousy one—we haven't got a clue."

"That's exactly when a call option is worth the most," you point out perceptively. "The call lets us invest in the Mark II if it's great and walk away from it if it's lousy."

"So what's it worth?"

"Hard to say precisely, but I've done a back-of-the-envelope calculation which suggests that the value of the option to invest in the Mark II could more than offset the Mark I's $46 million negative NPV. [The calculations are shown in Table 22.2.] If the option to invest is worth $55 million, the total value of the Mark I is its own NPV, −$46 million, plus the $55 million option attached to it, or +$9 million."

"You're just overestimating the Mark II," the CFO says gruffly. "It's easy to be optimistic when an investment is three years away."

"No, no," you reply patiently. "The Mark II is expected to be no more profitable than the Mark I—just twice as big and therefore twice as bad in terms of discounted cash flow. I'm forecasting it to have a negative NPV of about $100 million. But there's a chance the Mark II could be extremely valuable. The call option allows Blitzen to cash in on those upside outcomes. The chance to cash in could be worth $55 million."

"Of course, the $55 million is only a trial calculation, but it illustrates how valuable follow-on investment opportunities can be, especially when uncertainty is high and the product market is growing rapidly. Moreover, the Mark II will give us a call on the Mark III, the Mark III on the Mark IV, and so on. My calculations don't take subsequent calls into account."

"I think I'm beginning to understand a little bit of corporate strategy," mumbles the CFO.

Questions and Answers about Blitzen's Mark II

Question: I know how to use the Black–Scholes formula to value traded call options, but this case seems harder. What number do I use for the stock price? I don't see any traded shares.

Answer: With traded call options, you can see the value of the *underlying asset* that the call is written on. Here the option is to buy a nontraded real asset, the Mark II. We can't observe the Mark II's value; we have to compute it.

TABLE 22.2

Valuing the option to invest in the Mark II microcomputer.

Assumptions

1. The decision to invest in the Mark II must be made after 3 years, in 1985.
2. The Mark II investment is double the scale of the Mark I (note the expected rapid growth of the industry). Investment required is $900 million (the exercise price), which is taken as fixed.
3. Forecasted cash inflows of the Mark II are also double those of the Mark I, with present value of $807 million in 1985 and $807/(1.2)^3 = \$467$ million in 1982.
4. The future value of the Mark II cash flows is highly uncertain. This value evolves as a stock price does with a standard deviation of 35 percent per year. (Many high-technology stocks have standard deviations higher than 35 percent.)
5. The annual interest rate is 10 percent.

Interpretation

The opportunity to invest in the Mark II is a three-year call option on an asset worth $467 million with a $900 million exercise price.

Valuation

$$\text{PV(exercise price)} = \frac{900}{(1.1)^3} = 676$$

$$\text{Call value} = [N(d_1) \times P] - [N(d_2) \times \text{PV(EX)}]$$

$$d_1 = \log[P/\text{PV(EX)}]/\sigma\sqrt{t} + \sigma\sqrt{t}/2$$

$$= \log[.691]/.606 + .606/2 = -.3072$$

$$d_2 = d_1 - \sigma\sqrt{t} = -.3072 - .606 = -.9134$$

$$N(d_1) = .3793, N(d_2) = .1805$$

$$\text{Call value} = [.3793 \times 467] - [.1805 \times 676] = \$55.12 \text{ million}$$

The Mark II's forecasted cash flows are set out in Table 22.3. The project involves an initial outlay of $900 million in 1985. The cash inflows start in the following year and have a present value of $807 million in 1985, equivalent to $467 million in 1982 as shown in Table 22.3. So the real option to invest in the Mark II amounts to a three-year call on an underlying asset worth $467 million, with a $900 million exercise price.

Notice that real options analysis does *not* replace DCF. You typically need DCF to value the underlying asset.

Question: Table 22.2 uses a standard deviation of 35 percent per year. Where does that number come from?

Answer: We recommend you look for *comparables,* that is, traded stocks with business risks similar to the investment opportunity.[1] For the Mark II, the ideal comparables would be growth stocks in the personal computer business, or perhaps a broader sample of high-tech growth stocks. Use the average standard deviation of

[1]You could also use scenario analysis, which we described in Chapter 10. Work out "best" and "worst" scenarios to establish a range of possible future values. Then find the annual standard deviation that would generate this range over the life of the option. For the Mark II, a range from $300 million to $2 billion would cover about 90 percent of the possible outcomes. This range, shown in Figure 22.1, is consistent with an annual standard deviation of 35 percent.

	Year						
	1982	1985	1986	1987	1988	1989	1990
After-tax operating cash flow			+220	+318	+590	+370	0
Increase in working capital			100	200	200	−250	−250
Net cash flow			+120	+118	+390	+620	+250
Present value at 20%	+467 ←	+807					
Investment, PV at 10%	676 (PV in 1982) ←	900					
Forecasted NPV in 1985		−93					

TABLE 22.3

Cash flows of the Mark II microcomputer, as forecasted from 1982 ($ millions).

the comparable companies' returns as the benchmark for judging the risk of the investment opportunity.[2]

Question: Table 22.3 discounts the Mark II's cash flows at 20 percent. I understand the high discount rate, because the Mark II is risky. But why is the $900 million investment discounted at the risk-free interest rate of 10 percent? Table 22.3 shows the present value of the investment in 1982 of $676 million.

Answer: Black and Scholes assumed that the exercise price is a fixed, certain amount. We wanted to stick with their basic formula. If the exercise price is uncertain, you can switch to a slightly more complicated valuation formula.[3]

Question: Nevertheless, if I had to decide in 1982, once and for all, whether to invest in the Mark II, I wouldn't do it. Right?

Answer: Right. The NPV of a commitment to invest in the Mark II is negative:

$$\begin{aligned}\text{NPV}(1982) = \text{PV(cash inflows)} - \text{PV(investment)} &= \$467 - 676 \\ &= -\$209 \text{ million}\end{aligned}$$

The option to invest in the Mark II is "out of the money" because the Mark II's value is far less than the required investment. Nevertheless, the option is worth +$55 million. It is especially valuable because the Mark II is a risky project with lots of upside potential. Figure 22.1 shows the probability distribution of the

[2]Be sure to "unlever" the standard deviations, thereby eliminating volatility created by debt financing. Chapter 9 covered unlevering procedures for beta. The same principles apply for standard deviation: You want the standard deviation of a portfolio of all the debt and equity securities issued by the comparable firm.

[3]If the required investment is uncertain, you have, in effect, an option to exchange one risky asset (the future value of the exercise price) for another (the future value of the Mark II's cash inflows). See W. Margrabe, "The Value of an Option to Exchange One Asset for Another," *Journal of Finance* 33 (March 1978), pp. 177–186.

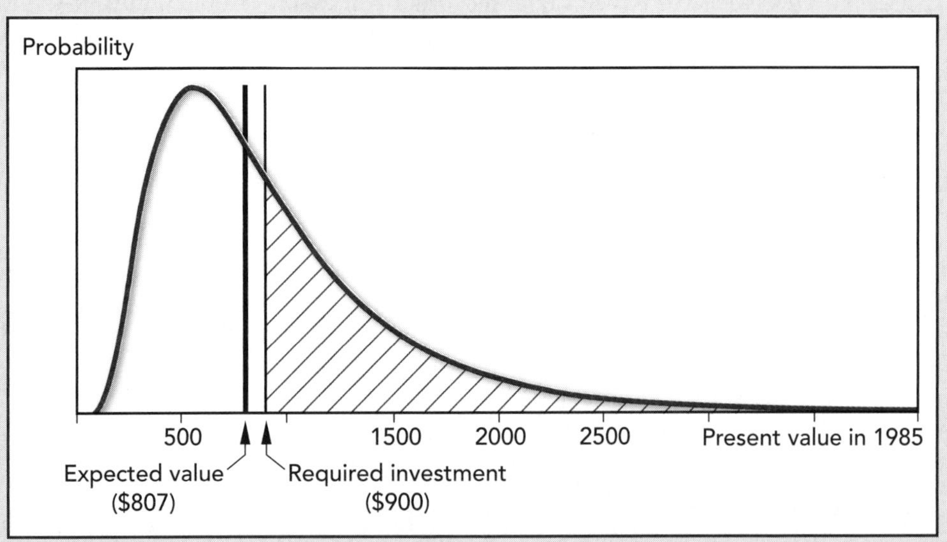

FIGURE 22.1

This distribution shows the range of possible present values for the Mark II project in 1985. The expected value is about $800 million, less than the required investment of $900 million. The *option* to invest pays off in the shaded area above $900 million.

possible present values of the Mark II in 1985. The expected (i.e., mean or average) outcome is our forecast of $807,[4] but the actual value could exceed $2 billion.

Question: Could it also be far below $807 million— $500 million or less?

Answer: The downside is irrelevant, because Blitzen won't invest unless the Mark II's actual value turns out higher than $900 million. The net option payoffs for all values less than $900 million are zero.

In a DCF analysis, you discount the expected outcome ($807 million), which averages the downside against the upside, the bad outcomes against the good. The value of a call option depends only on the upside. You can see the danger of trying to value a future investment option with DCF.

Question: What's the decision rule?

Answer: Adjusted present value. The Mark I project costs $46 million (NPV = −$46 million), but accepting it creates the expansion option for the Mark II. The expansion option is worth $55 million, so:

$$\text{APV} = -46 + 55 = +\$9 \text{ million}$$

[4]We have drawn the future values of the Mark II as a lognormal distribution, consistent with the assumptions of the Black–Scholes formula. Lognormal distributions are skewed to the right, so the average outcome is greater than the most likely outcome. (The most likely outcome is the highest point on the probability distribution.)

Of course we haven't counted other follow-on opportunities. If the Mark I and Mark II are successes, there will be an option to invest in the Mark III, possibly the Mark IV, and so on.

Other Expansion Options

You can probably think of many other cases where companies spend money today to create opportunities to expand in the future. A mining company may acquire rights to an ore body that is not worth developing today but could be very profitable if product prices increase. A real estate developer may invest in worn-out farmland that could be turned into a shopping mall if a new highway is built. A pharmaceutical company may acquire a patent that gives the right but not the obligation to market a new drug. In each case the company is acquiring a real option to expand.

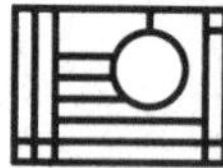

22.2 THE TIMING OPTION

The fact that a project has a positive NPV does not mean that you should take it today. It may be better to wait and see how the market develops.

Suppose that you are contemplating a now-or-never opportunity to build a malted herring factory. In this case you have an about-to-expire call option on the present value of the factory's future cash flows. If the present value exceeds the cost of the factory, the call option's payoff is the project's NPV. But if NPV is negative, the call option's payoff is zero, because in that case the firm will not make the investment.

Now suppose that you can delay construction of the plant. You still have the call option, but you face a trade-off. If the outlook is highly uncertain, it is tempting to wait and see whether the malted herring market takes off or nose-dives. On the other hand, if the project is truly profitable, the sooner you can capture the project's cash flows, the better. If the cash flows are high enough, you will want to exercise your option right away.

The cash flows from an investment project play the same role as dividend payments on a stock. When a stock pays no dividends, an American call is always worth more alive than dead and should never be exercised early. But payment of a dividend before the option matures reduces the ex-dividend price and the possible payoffs to the call option price at maturity. Think of the extreme case: If a company pays out all its assets in one bumper dividend, the stock price must be zero and the call worthless. Therefore, any in-the-money call would be exercised just before this liquidating dividend.

Dividends do not always prompt early exercise, but if they are sufficiently large, call option holders capture them by exercising just before the ex-dividend date. We see managers acting in the same way: When a project's forecasted cash flows are sufficiently large, managers capture the cash flows by investing right away.[5] But when forecasted cash flows are small, managers are inclined to hold onto their call

[5]In this case the call's value equals its lower-bound value because it is exercised immediately.

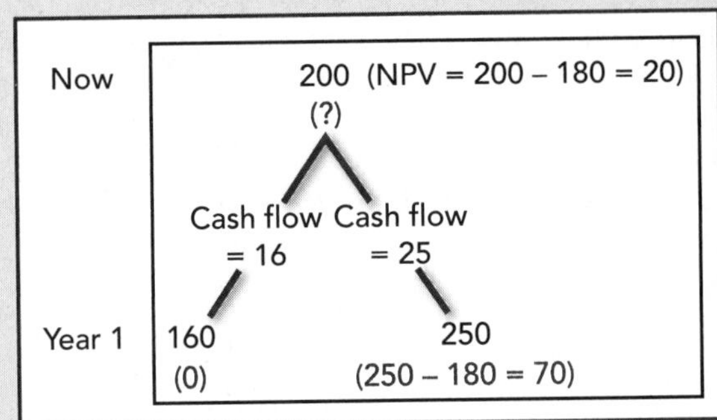

FIGURE 22.2

Possible cash flows and end-of-period values for the malted herring project are shown in blue. The project costs $180 million, either now or later. The burgundy figures in parentheses show payoffs from the option to wait and to invest later if the project is positive-NPV at year 1. Waiting means loss of the first year's cash flows. The problem is to figure out the current value of the option.

rather than to invest, even when project NPV is positive.[6] This explains why managers are sometimes reluctant to commit to positive-NPV projects. This caution is rational as long as the option to wait is open and sufficiently valuable.

Valuing the Malted Herring Option

Figure 22.2 shows the possible cash flows and end-of-year values for the malted herring project. If you commit and invest $180 million, you have a project worth $200 million. If demand turns out to be low in year 1, the cash flow is only $16 million and the value of the project falls to $160 million. But if demand is high in year 1, the cash flow is $25 million and value rises to $250 million. Although the project lasts indefinitely, we assume that investment cannot be postponed beyond the end of the first year, and therefore we show only the cash flows for the first year and the possible values at the end of the year. Notice that if you undertake the investment right away, you capture the first year's cash flow ($16 million or $25 million); if you delay, you miss out on this cash flow, but you will have more information on how the project is likely to work out.

We can use the binomial method to value this option. The first step is to pretend that investors are risk neutral and to calculate the probabilities of high and low demand in this risk-neutral world. If demand is high in the first year, the malted herring plant has a cash flow of $25 million and a year-end value of $250 million. The total return is $(25 + 250)/200 - 1 = .375$, or 37.5 percent. If demand is low, the plant has a cash flow of $16 million and a year-end value of $160 million. Total return is $(16 + 160)/200 - 1 = -.12$, or -12 percent. In a *risk-neutral* world, the expected return would be equal to the interest rate, which we assume is 5 percent:

$$\text{Expected return} = \begin{pmatrix}\text{Probability of}\\ \text{high demand}\end{pmatrix} \times 37.5 + \begin{pmatrix}1 - \text{probability of}\\ \text{high demand}\end{pmatrix} \times (-12) = 5\%$$

Therefore the (pretend) probability of high demand is 34.3 percent.

[6]We have been a bit vague about forecasted project cash flows. If competitors can enter and take away cash that you could have earned, the meaning is clear. But what about the decision to, say, develop an oil well? Here delay doesn't waste barrels of oil in the ground; it simply postpones production and the associated cash flow. The cost of waiting is the decline in today's *present value* of revenues from production. Present value declines if the future rate of increase in oil prices is not sufficiently high, that is, if the discounted price of oil is less than the current price.

We want to value a call option on the malted herring project with an exercise price of \$180 million. We begin as usual at the end and work backward. The bottom row of Figure 22.2 shows the possible values of this option at the end of the year. If project value is \$160 million, the option to invest is worthless. At the other extreme, if project value is \$250 million, option value is 250 − 180 = \$70 million.

To calculate the value of the option today, we work out the expected payoffs in a risk-neutral world and discount at the interest rate of 5 percent. Thus, the value of your option to invest in the malted herring plant is

$$\frac{(.343 \times 70) + (.657 \times 0)}{1.05} = \$22.9 \text{ million}$$

But here is where we need to recognize the opportunity to exercise the option immediately. The option is worth \$22.9 million if you keep it open, and it is worth the project's immediate NPV (200 − 180 = \$20 million) if exercised now. Thus the fact that the malted herring project has a positive NPV is not sufficient reason for investing. There is a still better strategy: Wait and see.

Optimal Timing for Real Estate Development

Sometimes it pays to wait for a long time, even for projects with large positive NPVs. Suppose you own a plot of vacant land in the suburbs.[7] The land can be used for a hotel or an office building, but not for both. A hotel could be later converted to an office building, or an office building to a hotel, but only at significant cost. You are therefore reluctant to invest, even if both investments have positive NPVs.

In this case you have two options to invest, but only one can be exercised. You therefore learn two things by waiting. First, you learn about the general *level* of cash flows from development, for example, by observing changes in the value of developed properties near your land. Second, you can update your estimates of the *relative* size of the hotel's future cash flows versus the office building's.

Figure 22.3 shows the conditions in which you would finally commit to build either the hotel or the office building. The horizontal axis shows the current cash flows that a hotel would generate. The vertical axis shows current cash flows for an office building. For simplicity, we will assume that each investment would have NPV of exactly zero at current cash flow of 100. Thus, if you were forced to invest today, you would choose the building with the higher cash flow, assuming the cash flow is greater than 100. (What if you were forced to decide today and each building could generate the same cash flow, say, 150? You would flip a coin.)

If the two buildings' cash flows plot in the colored area at the lower right of Figure 22.3, you build the hotel. To fall in this area, the hotel's cash flows have to beat two hurdles. First, they must exceed a minimum level of about 240. Second, they must exceed the office building's cash flows by a sufficient amount. If the situation is reversed, with office building cash flows above the minimum level of 240, and also sufficiently above the hotel's, then you build the office building. In this case, the cash flows plot in the colored area at the top left of the figure.

Notice how the "Delay development" region extends upward along the 45-degree line in Figure 22.3. When the cash flows from the hotel and office building are nearly the same, you become *very* cautious before choosing one over the other.

[7]The following example is based on P. D. Childs, T. J. Riddiough, and A. J. Triantis, "Mixed Uses and the Redevelopment Option," *Real Estate Economics* 24 (Fall 1996), pp. 317–339.

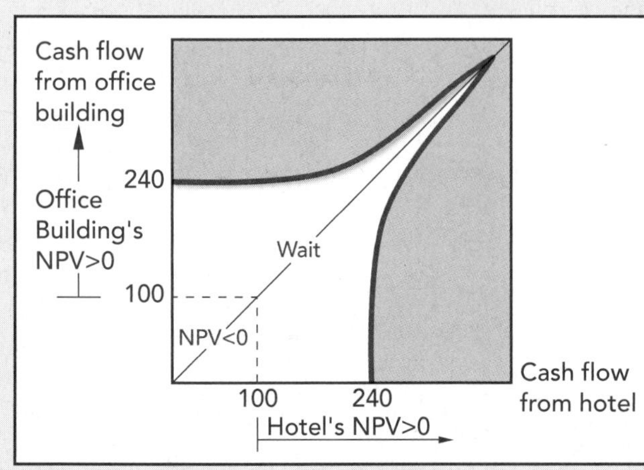

FIGURE 22.3

Development option for vacant land, assuming two mutually exclusive uses, either hotel or office building. The developer should "wait and see" unless the hotel's and office building's cash flows end up in one of the shaded areas.

Source: Adapted from Figure 1 in P. D. Childs, T. J. Riddiough, and A. J. Triantis, "Mixed Uses and the Redevelopment Option," *Real Estate Economics* 24 (Fall 1996), pp. 317–339.

You may be surprised at how high cash flows have to be in Figure 22.3 to justify investment. There are three reasons. First, building the office building means not building the hotel, and vice versa. Second, the calculations underlying Figure 22.3 assumed cash flows that were small, but growing; therefore, the costs of waiting to invest were small. Third, the calculations did not consider the threat that someone might build a competing hotel or office building right next door. In that case the "relax and wait" area of Figure 22.3 would shrink dramatically.

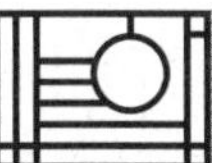

22.3 THE ABANDONMENT OPTION

Expansion value is important. When investments turn out well, the quicker and easier the business can be expanded, the better. But suppose bad news arrives, and cash flows are far below expectations. In that case it is useful to have the option to bail out and recover the value of the project's plant, equipment, or other assets. The option to abandon is equivalent to a put option. You exercise that abandonment option if the value recovered from the project's assets is greater than the present value of continuing the project for at least one more period.

The binomial method is tailor-made for most abandonment options. Here is an example.

The Zircon Subductor Project

Dawn East, the chief financial officer of Maine Subductor Corp., has to decide whether to start production of zircon subductors. The investment required is $12 million— $2 million for roads and site preparation and $10 million for equipment. The equipment costs $700,000 per year ($.7 million) to operate (a fixed cost). For simplicity, we will ignore other costs and taxes.

At today's prices, the project would generate revenues of $1.7 million per year. Annual output will be constant, so revenue is proportional to price. If the mine were operating today, cash flow would be $1.7 − .7 = $1.0 million.

FIGURE 22.4

Binomial tree for the Subductor project. Cash flow (top number) and end-of-period present value are shown for each node in millions of dollars. Abandonment occurs if cash flows drop to $.42 million (lighter shaded nodes) in years 3, 5, 7, or 9, and in year 10. Beginning present value is $ 13.84 million.

Year	0	1	2	3	4	5	6	7	8	9	10
Forecasted revenues		1.85	2.02	2.20	2.40	2.62	2.85	3.11	3.39	3.69	4.02
Present value	$17.00										
Fixed costs		0.70	0.70	0.70	0.70	0.70	0.70	0.70	0.70	0.70	0.70
Present value	$5.15										
NPV	-0.15										

Cash flow / Present value	0	1	2	3	4	5	6	7	8	9	10
											6.18 / 3.49
										5.28 / 8.61	
									4.50 / 12.22		4.50 / 3.49
								3.82 / 14.62		3.82 / 7.15	
							3.23 / 16.07		3.23 / 9.68		3.23 / 3.49
						2.72 / 16.75		2.72 / 11.31		2.72 / 6.05	
					2.27 / 16.86		2.27 / 12.23		2.27 / 7.77		2.27 / 3.49
				1.89 / 16.51		1.89 / 12.58		1.89 / 8.81		1.89 / 5.21	
			1.55 / 15.83		1.55 / 12.51		1.55 / 9.33		1.55 / 6.32		1.55 / 3.49
		1.26 / 14.91		1.26 / 12.10		1.26 / 9.43		1.26 / 6.92		1.26 / 4.58	
Cash flow / Present value	13.84		1.00 / 11.47		1.00 / 9.23		1.00 / 7.14		1.00 / 5.22		1.00 / 3.49
		0.78 / 10.73		0.78 / 8.83		0.78 / 7.09		0.78 / 5.50		0.78 / 4.11	
			0.59 / 8.49		0.59 / 6.95		0.59 / 5.60		0.59 / 4.43		0.59 / 3.49
				0.42 / 7.29		0.42 / 5.90		0.42 / 4.78		0.42 / 3.87	
					0.27 / 6.56		0.27 / 5.31		0.27 / 4.30		0.27 / 3.49
						0.15 / 5.90		0.15 / 4.78		0.15 / 3.87	
							0.03 / 5.31		0.03 / 4.30		0.03 / 3.49
								-0.06 / 4.78		-0.06 / 3.87	
									-0.14 / 4.30		-0.14 / 3.49
										-0.22 / 3.87	
											-0.28 / 3.49
Salvage value (years 1–10)		9.00	8.10	7.29	6.56	5.90	5.31	4.78	4.30	3.87	3.49

Calculate the Present Value of the Project The first step in a real options analysis is to value the underlying asset, that is, the project if it had no options attached. Usually this is done by discounted cash flow (DCF). In this case the chief source of uncertainty is the future selling price of zircon subductors. Therefore Ms. East starts by calculating the present value of future revenues. She notes a strong upward trend in subductor prices, and ends up forecasting annual growth at 9 percent for the next 10 years. Fixed costs are constant at $.7 million. The top panel of Figure 22.4 shows these cash-flow forecasts and calculates present values: $17 million for revenues, after discounting at a risk-adjusted rate of 9 percent, and $5.15 million for fixed costs, after discounting at a risk-free rate of 6 percent.[8] The NPV of the project, assuming no salvage value or abandonment over its 10-year life, is

$$\begin{aligned}\text{NPV} &= \text{PV(revenues)} - \text{PV(fixed costs)} - \text{investment required}\\ &= \$17.00 - 5.15 - 12.00 = -\$.15 \text{ million}\end{aligned}$$

This NPV is slightly negative, but Ms. East has so far made no provision for abandonment.

[8]Why calculate present values for revenues and fixed costs separately? Because it's easier to construct a binomial tree for revenues, which can be assumed to follow a random walk with constant standard deviation. We will subtract fixed costs after the binomial tree is constructed.

Build a Binomial Tree Now Ms. East constructs a binomial tree for revenues and PV(revenues). She notes that subductor prices have followed a random walk with an annual standard deviation of about 14 percent. She constructs a binomial tree with one step per year. The "up" values for revenues are 115 percent of the prior year's revenues. The "down" values are 87 percent of prior revenues.[9] Thus, the up and down revenues for year 1 are $1.70 × 1.15 = $1.96 and $1.70 × .87 = $1.48 million, respectively.[10] After deduction of fixed costs, the up and down cash flows are $1.26 and $.78 million, respectively. The first two years of the resulting tree are shown below (figures in millions of dollars).

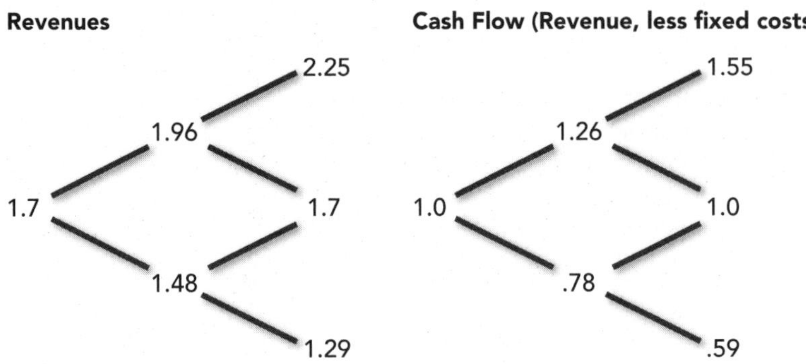

Figure 22.4 shows the whole tree, starting with cash flows in year 1. (Maine Subductor can't generate any revenues in year 0 because it hasn't started production yet.) The top number at each node is cash flow. The bottom number (in burgundy) is the *end*-of-year present value of *all* subsequent cash flows, including the value of the production equipment when the project ends or is abandoned. We will see in a moment how these present values are calculated.

Finally, Ms. East calculates the risk-neutral probabilities of up and down changes in revenues, p and $1 - p$, respectively. If the risk-free interest rate is 6 percent, $p = .6791$ and $1 - p = .3209$:

$$\text{Expected return} = .15p - .13(1 - p) = .06$$
$$\text{Probability of up change} = p = .6791$$
$$\text{Probability of down change} = 1 - p = .3209$$

Solve for Optimal Abandonment and Project Value Ms. East has assumed a project life of 10 years. At that time the production equipment, which normally depreciates by about 10 percent per year, should be worth $3.49 million. This salvage value represents what the equipment could be sold for, or its value to Maine Subductor if shifted to another use. Forecasted salvage values are shown year-by-year at the bottom of Figure 22.4.

Now let's calculate this project's value in the binomial tree. We start at the far right of Figure 22.4 (year 10) and work back to the present. The company will

[9]The formula (given in Section 21.2) for the up percentage is $u = e^{\sigma\sqrt{h}}$ where σ is the standard deviation per year and h is the interval as a fraction of a year. In this case, $h = 1$ and $e^{\sigma} = e^{.14} = 1.15$. The down value is $d = 1/u = .87$.

[10]We do not build the 9 percent forecasted growth rate into the up and down steps of the tree. However, the "up" probabilities will be greater than the "down" probabilities, enough greater that the present value of next period's revenue will equal this year's revenue, using a risk-free discount rate of 6 percent. In other words, the tree will assume a 6 percent *risk-neutral* expected growth rate.

abandon for sure in year 10, when the ore body is exhausted. Thus we enter the ending salvage value ($3.49 million) as the end-of-year value in year 10. Then we step back to year 9.

Suppose that Maine Subductor ends up in the best possible place in that year, where cash flow is $5.28 million. The upside payoff if the company does not abandon is the "up" node in year 10: 6.18 + 3.49 = $9.67 million. The downside payoff is 4.50 + 3.49 = $7.99 million. The present value, using the risk-neutral probabilities, is

$$PV = \frac{(.6791 \times 9.67) + (.3209 \times 7.99)}{1.06} = \$8.61 \text{ million}$$

The company could abandon at the end of year 9, realizing salvage value of $3.87 million, but continuing is better. We therefore enter $8.61 million as the end-of-year value at the top node for year 9 in Figure 22.4.

We can fill in the end-of-period values for the other nodes in year 9 by the same procedure. But at some point, as we step down to lower and lower cash flows, there will come a node where it's better to bail out than continue. This occurs when cash flow is $.42 million. The present value of continuing is only

$$PV = \frac{.6791 \times (.59 + 3.49) + .3209 \times (.27 + 3.49)}{1.06} = \$3.75 \text{ million}$$

The payoff to abandonment is $3.87 million, so that payoff is entered as the value in year 9 at all nodes with cash flows equal to or less than $.42 million.

The cash flows and end-of-year values for year 9 are the payoffs to continuing from year 8. We then calculate values in year 8, checking at each node whether to abandon, for year 7, and so on back to year zero.[11] In this example, Maine Subductor should abandon the project in any year when cash flows fall to $.42 million. This means that it never encounters cash flows less than $.42 million.

The present value at year 0 is $13.84 million, so the project is worthwhile: NPV = 13.84 − 12.00 = +$1.84 million.

How much of this NPV is due to abandonment value?[12] The DCF valuation at the top of Figure 22.4 (which ignores salvage and abandonment) gives NPV of −$.15 million, a drop of $1.99 million from the NPV with abandonment. Therefore, the value of the abandonment put is $1.99 million:

$$\begin{aligned} APV &= \text{NPV, no abandonment} + \text{value of abandonment option}^{13} \\ &= -.15 + 1.99 = \$1.84 \text{ million} \end{aligned}$$

The project looks good, although Ms. East may wish to check out the timing option. She could decide to wait.

---

[11]We will spare you the calculations. You can check them, however. The spreadsheet for Figure 22.4 is on this book's website (**www.mhhe.com/bm7e**).

[12]You could also revalue the binomial tree with all salvage values set to zero. The present value in year 0 then falls to $11.85 million, implying NPV = $11.85 − 12.00 = −$.15 million. You can do this calculation in the spreadsheet program on the website. Just set "Salvage t = 0" equal to zero.

[13]It turns out, however, that the value of *early* abandonment in this example is relatively small. Suppose that Maine Subductor could recover salvage value of $3.49 million in year 10, but not before. The present value of this recovery in year 0, using a 6 percent discount rate, is $1.95 million. APV in this case is −.15 + 1.95 = $1.8 million, only slightly less than the APV of $1.85 with early abandonment allowed.

Abandonment Value and Project Life

Ms. East assumed that the zircon subductor project had a definite 10 year life. But most projects' economic lives are not known at the start. Cash flows from a new product may last only a year or so if the product fails in the marketplace. But if it succeeds, that product, or variations or improvements of it, could be produced for decades.

A project's economic life can be just as hard to predict as the project's cash flows. Yet in standard DCF capital-budgeting analysis, that life is assumed to end at a fixed future date. Real options analysis allows us to relax that assumption. Here is the procedure.[14]

1. Forecast the range of possible cash flows well beyond your best guess of the project's economic life. Suppose, for example, that your guess is 10 years. You could prepare a binomial tree like Figure 22.4 stretching out 25 years into the future.
2. Then value the project, including its abandonment value. In the best upside scenarios, project life will be 25 years—it will never make sense to abandon before year 25. In the worst downside scenarios, project life will be much shorter, because the project will be more valuable dead than alive. If your original guess about project life is right, then in intermediate scenarios, where actual cash flows match expectations, abandonment will occur around year 10.

This procedure links project life to the performance of the project. It does not impose an arbitrary ending date, except in the far distant future.

Temporary Abandonment

Companies are often faced with complex options that allow them to abandon a project *temporarily,* that is, to mothball it until conditions improve. Suppose you own an oil tanker operating in the short-term spot market. (In other words, you charter the tanker voyage by voyage, at whatever short-term charter rates prevail at the start of the voyage.) The tanker costs $5 million a year to operate and at current tanker rates it produces charter revenues of $5.25 million per year. The tanker is therefore profitable but scarcely cause for celebration. Now tanker rates dip by about 10 percent, forcing revenues down to $4.7 million. Do you immediately lay off the crew and mothball the tanker until prices recover? The answer is clearly yes if the tanker business can be turned on and off like a faucet. But that is unrealistic. There is a fixed cost to mothballing the tanker. You don't want to incur this cost only to regret your decision next month if rates rebound to their earlier level. The higher the costs of mothballing and the more variable the level of charter rates, the greater the loss that you will be prepared to bear before you call it quits and lay up the boat.

Suppose that eventually you do decide to take the boat off the market. You lay up the tanker temporarily.[15] Two years later your faith is rewarded; charter rates rise, and the revenues from operating the tanker creep above the operating cost of

[14]See S. C. Myers and S. Majd, "Abandonment Value and Project Life," in F. J. Fabozzi (ed.), *Advances in Futures and Options Research,* JAI Press, 1990.

[15]We assume it makes sense to keep the tanker in mothballs. If rates fall sufficiently, it will pay to scrap the tanker.

FIGURE 22.5

An oil tanker should be mothballed when tanker rates fall to M, where the tanker's value if mothballed is enough above its value in operation to cover mothballing costs. The tanker is reactivated when rates recover to R.

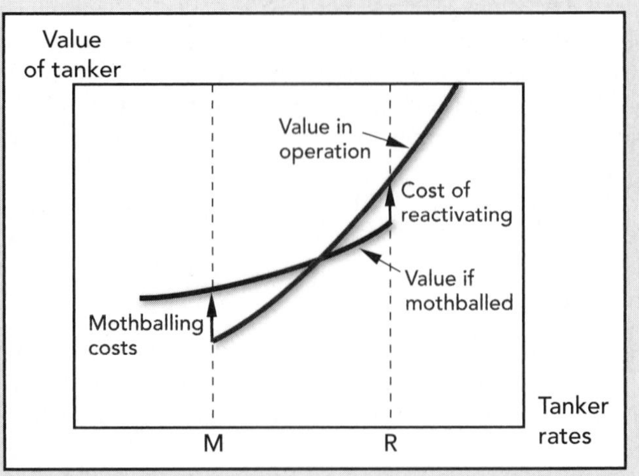

$5 million. Do you reactivate immediately? Not if there are costs to doing so. It makes more sense to wait until the project is well in the black and you can be fairly confident that you will not regret the cost of bringing the tanker back into operation.

These choices are illustrated in Figure 22.5. The colored line shows how the value of an operating tanker varies with the level of charter rates. The black line shows the value of the tanker when mothballed.[16] The level of rates at which it pays to mothball is given by M and the level at which it pays to reactivate is given by R. The higher the costs of mothballing and reactivating and the greater the variability in tanker rates, the further apart these points will be. You can see that it will pay for you to mothball as soon as the value of a mothballed tanker reaches the value of an operating tanker plus the costs of mothballing. It will pay to reactivate as soon as the value of a tanker that is operating in the spot market reaches the value of a mothballed tanker plus the costs of reactivating. If the level of rates falls below M, the value of the tanker is given by the black line; if the level is greater than R, value is given by the colored line. If rates lie between M and R, the tanker's value depends on whether it happens to be mothballed or operating.

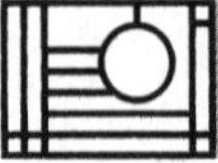

22.4 FLEXIBLE PRODUCTION—AND ANOTHER LOOK AT AIRCRAFT PURCHASE OPTIONS

Companies often have an option to vary either the inputs in the production process or the outputs. For example, an electric utility plant may be designed to operate on either oil or natural gas. Or a manufacturer may invest in computer-integrated manufacturing (CIM) systems that allow it to vary the production mix.

In such cases the firm has the option to acquire one asset in exchange for another. Consider the electric utility's decision to build an oil-fired generating plant that can be converted to run on natural gas. You can think of the utility as having

[16]Dixit and Pindyck estimate these thresholds for a medium-sized tanker and show how they depend on costs and the volatility of freight rates. See A. K. Dixit and R. S. Pindyck, *Investment under Uncertainty*, Princeton University Press, Princeton, NJ, 1994, Chapter 7.

an option to "buy" a gas-fired plant in exchange for the oil-fired plant. If oil prices were certain, this would be a simple call option on a gas-fired plant with a fixed exercise price (the value of an oil-fired plant plus the cost of conversion). If the price of gas is sufficiently low, it pays to exercise the option and switch to gas.

In practice both oil and gas prices are likely to vary. This means that the exercise price of the utility's call option changes as the price of oil changes. Uncertainty about this exercise price could reduce or enhance the value of the option, depending on the correlation between the prices of the two fuels. If oil prices and gas prices moved together dollar for dollar, your option to switch fuels would be valueless. The benefit of a rise in the value of the underlying asset (the gas-fired plant) would be exactly offset by a rise in the option's exercise price (the value of the oil-fired plant). The best of all worlds would occur if the prices of the two fuels were negatively correlated. In this case whenever oil became expensive, the gas would become cheap. In these (unlikely) circumstances the option to switch between the two fuels would be particularly valuable.

In this example, the output is the same (electricity); option value comes from flexibility in raw materials (gas or oil). In other cases, option value comes from the flexibility to switch from product to product using the same production facilities. For example, textile firms have invested heavily in computer-controlled knitting machines, which allow production to shift from product to product, or from design to design, as demand and fashion dictate.

Flexibility in *procurement* can also have option value. For example, a computer manufacturer planning next year's production must also plan to buy components, such as disc drives and microprocessors, in large quantities. Should it strike a deal today with the component manufacturer? This locks in the quantity, price, and delivery dates. But it also gives up flexibility, for example, the ability to switch suppliers next year or buy at a "spot" price if next year's prices are lower.

The Finance in the News box features another example of the value of flexibility in production or procurement.

Another Look at Aircraft Purchase Options

For our final example, we return to the problem confronting airlines that order new airplanes for future use. In this industry "lead times" between an order and delivery can extend to several years. Long lead times mean that airlines which order planes today may end up not needing them. You can see why an airline might negotiate for an aircraft purchase *option.*

In Section 10.3, we used aircraft purchase options to illustrate the option to expand. That's true, but not the whole truth. Let's take another look. Suppose an airline forecasts a need for a new Airbus A320 four years hence.[17] It has at least three choices.

- *Commit now.* It can commit now to buy the plane, in exchange for Airbus's offer of locked-in price and delivery date.
- *Acquire option.* It can seek a purchase option from Airbus, allowing the airline to decide later whether to buy. A purchase option fixes the price and delivery date if the option is exercised.

[17]The following example is based on J. E. Stonier, "What is an Aircraft Purchase Option Worth? Quantifying Asset Flexibility Created through Manufacturer Lead-Time Reductions and Product Commonality," in G. F. Butler and M. R. Keller (eds.), *Handbook of Airline Finance,* Aviation Week Books, 1999.

FINANCE IN THE NEWS

VALUING FLEXIBILITY

With the help of faculty from Stanford University, Hewlett-Packard has experimented with real options since the beginning of the 1990s. Example: In the '80s, HP customized inkjet printers for foreign markets at the factory, then shipped them in finished form to warehouses. Customizing at the factory is cheaper than customizing in the field. But HP kept guessing wrong on demand and ending up with, say, too many printers configured for French customers but not enough for Germans.

Executives realized that it would be smarter to ship partially assembled printers and then customize them at the warehouse, once it had firm orders. True, local customization costs more. But even though production costs rose, HP saved $3 million a month by more effectively matching supply to demand, says Corey A. Billington, a former Stanford professor who directs HP's Strategic Planning & Modeling group.

Common sense? Sure. But you can also view it as a neat solution of a real-options problem. Increasing the cost of production—anathema to your average engineer—was in effect the price HP paid for the option to delay configuration choices until the optimal time.

Source: P. Coy, "Exploiting Uncertainty," *Business Week*, June 7, 1999.

- *Wait and decide later.* Airbus will be happy to sell another A320 at any time in the future if the airline wants to buy one. However, the airline may have to pay a higher price and wait longer for delivery, especially if the airline industry is flying high and many planes are on order.

The top half of Figure 22.6 shows the terms of a typical purchase option for an Airbus A320. The option must be exercised at year 3, when final assembly of the plane will begin. The option fixes the purchase price and the delivery date in year 4. The bottom half of the figure shows the consequences of "wait and decide later." We assume that the decision will come at year 3. If the decision is "buy," the airline pays the year-3 price and joins the queue for delivery in year 5 or later.

The payoffs from "wait and decide later" can never be better than the payoffs from an aircraft purchase option, since the airline can discard the option and negotiate afresh with Airbus if it wishes. In most cases the airline will be better off in the future with the option than without it; the airline is at least guaranteed a place in the production line, and it may have locked in a favorable purchase price. But how much are these advantages worth today, compared to the wait-and-see strategy?

Figure 22.7 illustrates Airbus's answers to this problem. It assumes a three-year purchase option with an exercise price equal to the current A320 price of $45 million. The present value of the purchase option depends on both the NPV of purchasing an A320 at that price and on the forecasted wait for delivery if the airline does *not* have a purchase option but nevertheless decides to place an order in year 3. The longer the wait in year 3, the more valuable it is to have the purchase option today. (Remember that the purchase option holds a place in the A320 production line and guarantees delivery in year 4.)

	Year 0	Year 3	Year 4	Year 5 or later
Buy option	Airline and manufacturer set price and delivery date	Exercise? (Yes or no)	Aircraft delivered if option exercised	
Wait	Wait	Buy now? If yes, negotiate price and wait for delivery.		Aircraft delivered if purchased at year 3.

FIGURE 22.6

This aircraft purchase option, if exercised at year 3, guarantees delivery at year 4 at a fixed price. Without the option, the airline can still order the plane at year 3, but the price is uncertain and the wait for delivery longer.

Source: Adapted from Figure 17-17 in J. Stonier, "What is an Aircraft Purchase Option Worth? Quantifying Asset Flexibility Created through Manufacturer Lead-Time Reductions and Product Commonality," in G. F. Butler and M. R. Keller (eds.), *Handbook of Airline Finance*, Aviation Week Books, 1999.

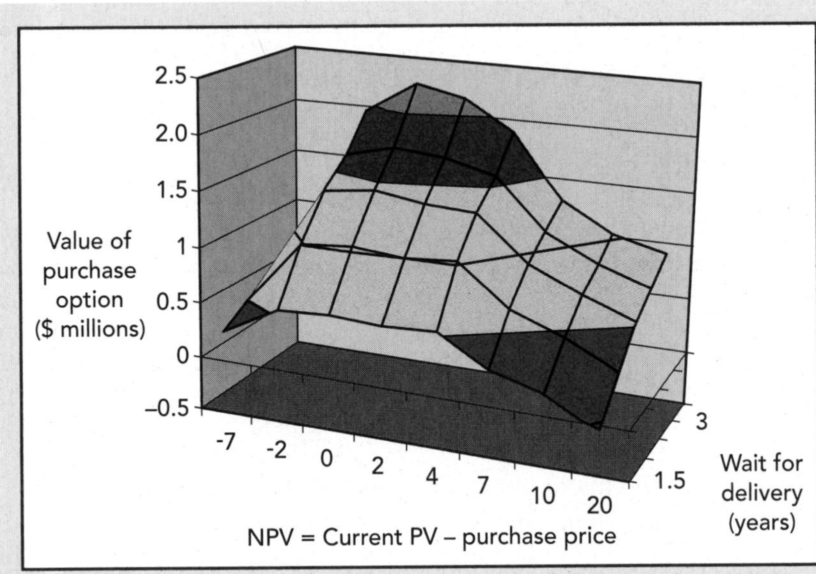

FIGURE 22.7

Value of aircraft purchase option—the *extra* value of the option versus waiting and possibly negotiating a purchase later. (See Figure 22.6.) The purchase option is worth most when NPV of purchase now is about zero and the forecasted wait for delivery is long.

Source: Adapted from Fig. 17-20 in J. Stonier, *op. cit.*

If the NPV of buying an A320 today is very high (the right-hand side of Figure 22.7), future NPV will probably be high as well, and the airline will want to buy regardless of whether it has a purchase option. In this case the value of the purchase option comes mostly from the value of guaranteed delivery in year 4.[18]

[18]The Airbus real-options model assumes that future A320 prices will be increased when demand is high, but only to an upper bound. Thus the airline that waits and decides later may still have a positive-NPV investment opportunity if future demand and NPV are high. Figure 22.7 plots the *difference* between the value of the purchase option and this wait-and-see opportunity. This difference can shrink when NPV is high, especially if forecasted waiting times are short.

If the NPV is very low, then the option has low value because the airline is unlikely to exercise it. (Low NPV today probably means low NPV in year 3.) The purchase option is worth the most, compared to the wait-and-decide-later strategy, when NPV is around zero. In this case the airline can exercise the option, getting a good price and early delivery, if future NPV is higher than expected, and walk away from the option if NPV disappoints. Of course, if it walks away, it may still wish to negotiate with Airbus for delivery at a price lower than the option's exercise price.

We have cruised by many of the technical details of Airbus's valuation model for purchase options. But the example does illustrate how real-options models are being built and used. By the way, Airbus offers more than just plain-vanilla purchase options. Airlines can negotiate "rolling options," which lock in price but do not guarantee a place on the production line. (Exercise of the rolling option means that the airline joins the end of the queue.) Airbus also offers a purchase option that includes the right to switch from delivery of an A320 to an A319, a somewhat smaller plane.

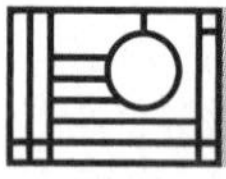

22.5 A CONCEPTUAL PROBLEM?

In this chapter we have suggested that option pricing models can help to value the real options embedded in capital investment decisions.

When we introduced option pricing models in Chapter 21, we suggested that the trick is to construct a package of the underlying asset and a loan that would give exactly the same payoffs as the option. If the two investments do not sell for the same price, then there are arbitrage possibilities. But many assets are not freely traded. This means that we can no longer rely on arbitrage arguments to justify the use of option models.

The risk-neutral method still makes practical sense, however. It's really just an application of the *certainty-equivalent* method introduced in Chapter 9.[19] The key assumption—implicit till now—is that the company's *shareholders* have access to assets with the same risk characteristics (e.g., the same beta) as the capital investments being evaluated by the firm.

Think of each real investment opportunity as having a "double," a security or portfolio with identical risk. Then the expected rate of return offered by the double is also the cost of capital for the real investment and the discount rate for a DCF valuation of the investment project. Now what would investors pay for a real *option* based on the project? The same as for an identical traded option written on the double. This traded option does not have to exist; it is enough to know how it would be valued by investors, who could employ either the arbitrage or the risk-neutral method. The two methods give the same answer, of course.

When we value a real option by the risk-neutral method, we are calculating the option's value if it could be traded. This exactly parallels standard capital budget-

[19]Use of risk-neutral probabilities converts future cash flows to certainty equivalents, which are then discounted to present value at a risk-free rate.

ing. If shareholders can buy traded securities or portfolios with the same risk characteristics as the real investments being evaluated by the firm, they would vote unanimous endorsement for any real investment whose market value if traded would exceed the investment required. This key assumption supports the use of both DCF and real-option-valuation methods.

SUMMARY

In Chapter 21 you learned the basics of option valuation. In this chapter we described four important real options:

1. *The option to make follow-on investments.* Companies often cite "strategic" value when taking on negative-NPV projects. A close look at the projects' payoffs reveals call options on follow-on projects in addition to the immediate projects' cash flows. Today's investments can generate tomorrow's opportunities.
2. *The option to wait (and learn) before investing.* This is equivalent to owning a call option on the investment project. The call is exercised when the firm commits to the project. But often it's better to defer a positive-NPV project in order to keep the call alive. Deferral is most attractive when uncertainty is great and immediate project cash flows—which are lost or postponed by waiting—are small.
3. *The option to abandon.* The option to abandon a project provides partial insurance against failure. This is a put option; the put's exercise price is the value of the project's assets if sold or shifted to a more valuable use.
4. *The option to vary the firm's output or its production methods.* Firms often build flexibility into their production facilities so that they can use the cheapest raw materials or produce the most valuable set of outputs. In this case they effectively acquire the option to exchange one asset for another.

We should offer here a healthy warning: The real options encountered in practice are often complex. Each real option brings its own issues and trade-offs. Nevertheless the tools that you have learned in this and previous chapters can be used in practice. The Black–Scholes formula often suffices to value expansion options. Problems of investment timing and optimal abandonment can be tackled with binomial trees.

Binomial trees are cousins of decision trees. You work back through binomial trees from future payoffs to present value. Whenever a future decision needs to be made, you figure out the value-maximizing choice, using the principles of option pricing theory, and record the resulting value at the appropriate node of the tree.

Don't jump to the conclusion that real-option-valuation methods can replace discounted cash flow (DCF). First, DCF works fine for safe cash flows. It also works fine for "cash cow" assets—that is, for assets or businesses whose value depends primarily on forecasted cash flows, not on real options. Second, the starting point in most real-option analyses is the present value of an underlying asset. To value the underlying asset, you typically have to use DCF.

Real options are rarely traded assets. When we value a real option, we are estimating its value if it could be traded. This is the standard approach in corporate finance, the same approach taken in DCF valuations. The key assumption is that shareholders can buy traded securities or portfolios with the same risk characteristics as the real investments being evaluated by the firm. If so, they would vote unanimously for any real investment whose market value if traded would exceed the investment required. This key assumption supports the use of both DCF and real-option-valuation methods.

FURTHER READING

Further reading for Chapter 10 lists several introductory articles on real options. The Summer 2001 issue of the Journal of Applied Corporate Finance *contains several additional articles, including the following survey of how real options are used in practice:*

A. Triantis and A. Borison: "Real Options: State of the Practice," *Journal of Applied Corporate Finance,* 14:8–24 (Summer 2001).

The standard texts on real options include:

T. Copeland and V. Antikarov: *Real Options: A Practitioner's Guide,* Texere, New York, 2001.

A. K. Dixit and R. S. Pindyck: *Investment under Uncertainty,* Princeton University Press, Princeton, NJ, 1994.

M. Amran and N. Kulatilaka: *Real Options: Managing Strategic Investments in an Uncertain World,* Harvard Business School Press, Boston, 1999.

L. Trigeorgis: *Real Options,* MIT Press, Cambridge, MA, 1996.

The Autumn 1993 issue of Financial Management *includes six articles on real options, including a description of how to value an industrial facility that can be fueled with gas or oil:*

N. Kulatilaka: "The Value of Flexibility: The Case of a Dual-Fuel Industrial Steam Boiler," *Financial Management,* 22:271–280 (Autumn 1993).

Mason and Merton review a range of option applications to corporate finance:

S. P. Mason and R. C. Merton: "The Role of Contingent Claims Analysis in Corporate Finance," in E. I. Altman and M. G. Subrahmanyan (eds.), *Recent Advances in Corporate Finance,* Richard D. Irwin, Inc., Homewood, IL, 1985.

Brennan and Schwartz have worked out an interesting application to natural resource investments:

M. J. Brennan and E. S. Schwartz: "Evaluating Natural Resource Investments," *Journal of Business,* 58:135–157 (April 1985).

QUIZ

1. What are the four types of real options?
2. Look again at the valuation in Table 22.2 of the option to invest in the Mark II project. Consider a change in each of the following inputs. Would the change increase or decrease the value of the expansion option?
   a. Increased uncertainty (higher standard deviation).
   b. More optimistic forecast (higher expected value) of the Mark II in 1985.
   c. Increase in the required investment in 1985.
3. Describe the real options in each of the following cases.
   a. United Airlines pays Boeing for the option to purchase ten 747 jets in 2005.
   b. United Airlines buys Boeing 767 passenger jets with reinforced floors, larger doors, and other features that would allow quick conversion to a cargo plane.

c. Exxon Mobil pays $75 million for oil drilling rights in Central Costaguana. The Costaguanan oil fields are too small and costly to develop now but development could be profitable if oil prices rise.
d. Forest Investors purchases a remote stand of Northern hardwoods. Harvest is positive-NPV now but the company nevertheless postpones logging.
e. Deutsche Motorwerke builds an automobile engine plant in China. The investment is negative-NPV. The company justifies the project as a strategic investment.
f. A biotech startup declines an opportunity to buy a building designed for biotech research. Instead it operates in a rented warehouse. It even rents its furniture and laboratory equipment.
g. A plot of land suitable for construction of an office building is left vacant, even though the present value of rents from a new office building would significantly exceed construction cost.

4. Respond to the following comments.
   a. "You don't need option pricing theories to value flexibility. Just use a decision tree. Discount the cash flows in the tree at the company cost of capital."
   b. "These option pricing methods are just plain nutty. They say that real options on risky assets are worth more than options on safe assets."
   c. "Real-options methods eliminate the need for DCF valuation of investment projects."

5. You own a parcel of vacant land. You can develop it now, or wait.
   a. What is the advantage of waiting?
   b. Why might you decide to develop the property immediately?

PRACTICE QUESTIONS

1. Describe each of the following situations in the language of options:
   a. Drilling rights to undeveloped heavy crude oil in Northern Alberta. Development and production of the oil is a negative-NPV endeavor. (The break-even oil price is C$32 per barrel, versus a spot price of C$20.) However, the decision to develop can be put off for up to five years. Development costs are expected to increase by 5 percent per year.
   b. A restaurant is producing net cash flows, after all out-of-pocket expenses, of $700,000 per year. There is no upward or downward trend in the cash flows, but they fluctuate, with an annual standard deviation of 15 percent. The real estate occupied by the restaurant is owned, not leased, and could be sold for $5 million. Ignore taxes.
   c. A variation on part (b): Assume the restaurant faces known fixed costs of $300,000 per year, incurred as long as the restaurant is operating. Thus

$$\text{Net cash flow} = \text{revenue less variable costs} - \text{fixed costs}$$
$$\$700{,}000 = 1{,}000{,}000 - 300{,}000$$

   The annual standard deviation of the forecast error of revenue less variable costs is 10.5 percent. The interest rate is 10 percent. Ignore taxes.
   d. A paper mill can be shut down in periods of low demand and restarted if demand improves sufficiently. The costs of closing and reopening the mill are fixed.
   e. A real-estate developer uses a parcel of urban land as a parking lot, although construction of either a hotel or an apartment building on the land would be a positive-NPV investment.
   f. Air France negotiates a purchase option for the first 10 Sonic Cruisers produced by Boeing. Air France must confirm its order in 2005. Otherwise, Boeing will be free to sell the aircraft to other airlines.

2. After a good night's sleep, your boss, the CFO in Section 22.1, still doesn't understand. Try again. Explain why the Mark I microcomputer has a positive NPV even though DCF analyses of both the Mark I and the Mark II seem to show *negative* NPVs.
3. Look again at Table 22.2. How does the value in 1982 of the option to invest in the Mark II change if:
   a. The investment required for the Mark II is $800 million (vs. $900 million)?
   b. The present value of the Mark II in 1982 is $500 million (vs. $467 million)?
   c. The standard deviation of the Mark II's present value is only 20 percent (vs. 35 percent)?
4. You own a one-year call option on 1 acre of Los Angeles real estate. The exercise price is $2 million, and the current, appraised market value of the land is $1.7 million. The land is currently used as a parking lot, generating just enough money to cover real estate taxes. The annual standard deviation is 15 percent and the interest rate 12 percent. How much is your call worth? Use the Black–Scholes formula.
5. A variation on question 4: Suppose the land is occupied by a warehouse generating rents of $150,000 after real estate taxes and all other out-of-pocket costs. The value of the land plus warehouse is again $1.7 million. Other facts are as in question 4. You have a *European* call option. What is it worth?
6. In Section 22.4 we described the problem faced by a utility that was contemplating an investment in equipment that would allow it to burn either oil or gas. How would the value of the option to cofire be affected if **(a)** the prices of both oil and gas were very variable, but **(b)** the prices of oil and gas were highly correlated?
7. Look again at the malted herring example in Section 22.3. Suppose that by postponing the project for a year, you do not miss out on any cash flows. Instead all cash flows are simply delayed by one year. What is the value of the option to invest in the malted herring plant?
8. Suppose investment in the malted herring project (see Section 22.3) can be postponed to the end of year 2.
   a. Build a two-year binomial tree with cash flows proportional to end-of-year values. Under what circumstances would you want to delay construction for two years?
   b. How does this additional choice affect project NPV?
   c. Would NPV change if you could undertake the project *only* in years 0 or 2?
9. You have an option to purchase all of the assets of the Overland Railroad for $2.5 billion. The option expires in 9 months. You estimate Overland's current (month 0) present value (PV) as $2.7 billion. Overland generates after-tax free cash flow (FCF) of $50 million at the end of each quarter (i.e., at the end of each three-month period). If you exercise your option at the start of the quarter, that quarter's cash flow is paid out to you. If you do not exercise, the cash flow goes to Overland's current owners.

   In each quarter, Overland's PV either increases by 10 percent or decreases by 9.09 percent. This PV includes the quarterly FCF of $50 million. After the $50 million is paid out, PV drops by $50 million. Thus the binomial tree for the first quarter is (figures in millions):

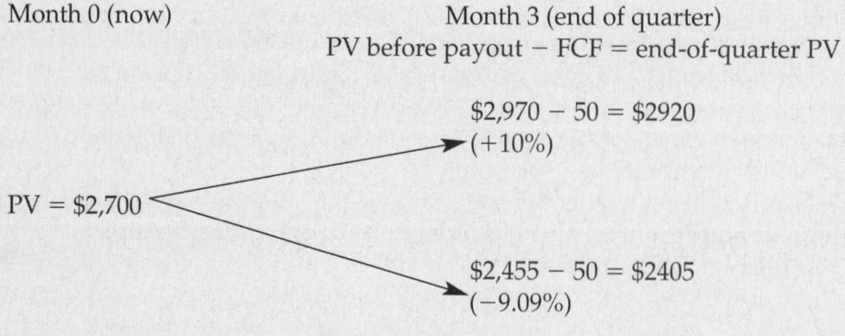

The risk-free interest rate is 2 percent per quarter.

a. Build a binomial tree for Overland, with one up or down change for each 3-month period (three steps to cover your 9-month option).

b. Suppose you can only exercise your option now, or after 9 months (not at month 3 or 6). Would you exercise now?

c. Suppose you can exercise now, or at month 3, 6, or 9. What is your option worth today? Should you exercise today, or wait?

10. In Section 10.3 we considered two production technologies for a new Wankel-engined outboard motor. Technology A was the most efficient but had no salvage value if the new outboards failed to sell. Technology B was less efficient but offered a salvage value of $10 million.

Figure 10.7 shows the present value of the project as either $18.5 or 8.5 million in year 1 if Technology A is used. Assume that the present value of these payoffs is $11.5 million at year 0.

a. With Technology B, the payoffs at year 1 are $18 or 8 million. What is the present value in year 0 if Technology B is used? (*Hint:* The payoffs with Technology B vs. A differ by a constant $.5 million.) The risk-free rate is 7 percent.

b. Technology B allows abandonment in year 1 for $10 million salvage value. Calculate abandonment value.

11. Look again at practice question 10. We will assume that Technology A has a salvage value of $7 million, rather than zero. The present value of the project with Technology A is $11.5 million at year 0, assuming no abandonment. The risk-free rate is 7 percent.

a. Construct a one-year binomial tree for this project, with one up or down step every three months (four steps total). The up steps are +25 percent, the down steps are −16.7 percent.

b. Suppose abandonment can only occur at year 1. In what circumstances would you abandon then? What is abandonment value at year 0?

12. How do the binomial trees used in this chapter differ from the decision trees discussed in Chapter 10?

13. Josh Kidding, who has only read part of Chapter 10, decides to value a real option by (1) setting out a decision tree, with cash flows and probabilities forecasted for each future outcome; (2) deciding what to do at each decision point in the tree; and (3) discounting the resulting expected cash flows at the company cost of capital. Will this procedure give the right answer? Why or why not?

14. Some argue that option pricing theory doesn't apply to real options, because the options are not traded in financial markets. Do you agree? Explain.

CHALLENGE QUESTIONS

1. Suppose you expect to need a new plant that will be ready to produce turbo-encabulators in 36 months. If design A is chosen, construction must begin immediately. Design B is more expensive, but you can wait 12 months before breaking ground. Figure 22.8 shows the cumulative present value of construction costs for the two designs up to the 36-month deadline. Assume that the designs, once built, will be equally efficient and have equal production capacity.

A standard discounted-cash-flow analysis ranks design A ahead of design B. But suppose the demand for turbo-encabulators falls and the new factory is not needed; then, as Figure 22.8 shows, the firm is better off with design B, provided the project is abandoned before month 24.

FIGURE 22.8

Cumulative construction cost of the two plant designs. Plant A takes 36 months to build; plant B, only 24. But plant B costs more.

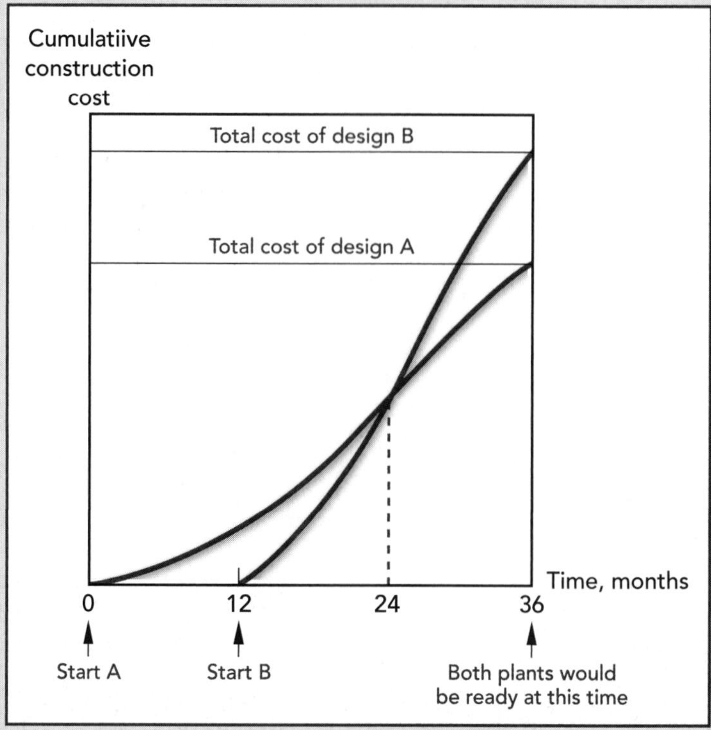

Describe this situation as the choice between two (complex) call options. Then describe the same situation in terms of (complex) abandonment options. The two descriptions should imply identical payoffs, given optimal exercise strategies.

2. Consumers appear to require returns of 25 percent or more before they are prepared to make energy-efficient investments, even though a more reasonable estimate of the cost of capital might be around 15 percent. Here is a highly simplified problem which illustrates that such behavior *could* be rational.[20]

   Suppose you have the opportunity to invest $1,000 in new space-heating equipment that would generate fuel savings of $250 a year forever given current fuel prices. What is the PV of this investment if the cost of capital is 15 percent? What is the NPV?

   Now recognize that fuel prices are uncertain and that the savings could well turn out to be $50 a year or $450 a year. If the risk-free interest rate is 10 percent, would you invest in the new equipment now or wait and see how fuel prices change? Explain.

3. In Chapter 4, we expressed the value of a share of stock as

$$P_0 = \frac{EPS_1}{r} + PVGO$$

[20]See, for example, A. H. Sanstad, C. Blumstein, and S. E. Stoft, "How High Are Option Values in Energy-Efficient Investments?" *Energy Policy* 9 (1995), pp. 739–743. However, the authors argue that the option to delay investment is not sufficiently valuable to explain consumer behavior.

where EPS_1 is earnings per share from existing assets, r is the expected rate of return required by investors, and PVGO is the present value of growth opportunities. PVGO really consists of a portfolio of expansion options.

a. What is the effect of an increase in PVGO on the standard deviation or beta of the stock's rate of return?

b. Suppose the CAPM is used to calculate the cost of capital for a growth (high-PVGO) firm. Assume all-equity financing. Will this cost of capital be the correct hurdle rate for investments to expand the firm's plant and equipment, or to introduce new products?

CHAPTER TWENTY-THREE

WARRANTS AND CONVERTIBLES

MANY DEBT ISSUES are either packages of bonds and warrants or convertibles. The warrant gives its owner the right to buy other company securities. A convertible bond gives its owner the right to exchange the bond for other securities.

There is also convertible preferred stock—it is often used to finance mergers, for example. Convertible preferred gives its owner the right to exchange the preferred share for other securities.

What are these strange hybrids, and how should you value them? Why are they issued? We will answer each of these questions in turn.

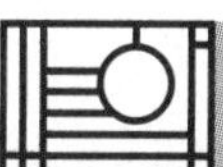

23.1 WHAT IS A WARRANT?

A significant proportion of private placement bonds and a smaller proportion of public issues are sold with warrants. In addition, warrants are sometimes sold with issues of common or preferred stock; they are also often given to investment bankers as compensation for underwriting services or used to compensate creditors in the case of bankruptcy.[1]

In April 1995 B.J. Services, a firm servicing the oil industry, issued 4.8 million warrants as partial payment for an acquisition. Each of these warrants allowed the holder to buy one share of B.J. Services for $30 at any time before April 2000. When the warrants were issued, the shares were priced at $19, so that the price needed to rise by more than 50 percent to make it worthwhile to exercise the warrants.

Warrant holders are not entitled to vote or to receive dividends. But the exercise price of a warrant is automatically adjusted for any stock dividends or stock splits. So, when in 1998 B.J. Services split its stock 2 for 1, each warrant holder was given the right to buy two shares and the exercise price was reduced to $30 \div 2 = \$15.00$ per share. By the time that the warrants finally expired in April 2000, the share price had reached $70 and so a warrant to buy two shares was worth $2 \times (\$70 - \$15) = \$110$.

Valuing Warrants

As a trained option spotter (having read Chapter 20), you have probably already classified the B.J. Services warrant as a five-year American call option exercisable at $15 (after adjustment for the 1998 stock split). You can depict the relationship between the value of the warrant and the value of the common stock with our standard option shorthand, as in Figure 23.1. The lower limit on the value of the warrant is the heavy line in the figure.[2] If the price of B.J. Services stock is less than $15, the lower limit on the warrant price is zero; if the price of the stock is greater than $15, the lower limit is equal to the stock price minus $15. Investors in warrants sometimes refer to this lower limit as the *theoretical* value of the warrant. It is a misleading term, because both theory and practice tell us that before the final exercise date the value of the warrant should lie *above* the lower limit, on a curve like the one shown in Figure 23.1.

[1]The term *warrant* usually refers to a long-term option issued by a company on its own stock or bonds, but investment banks and other financial institutions also issue "warrants" to buy the stock of another firm.

[2]Do you remember why this is a lower limit? What would happen if, by some accident, the warrant price was *less* than the stock price minus $15? (See Section 20.3.)

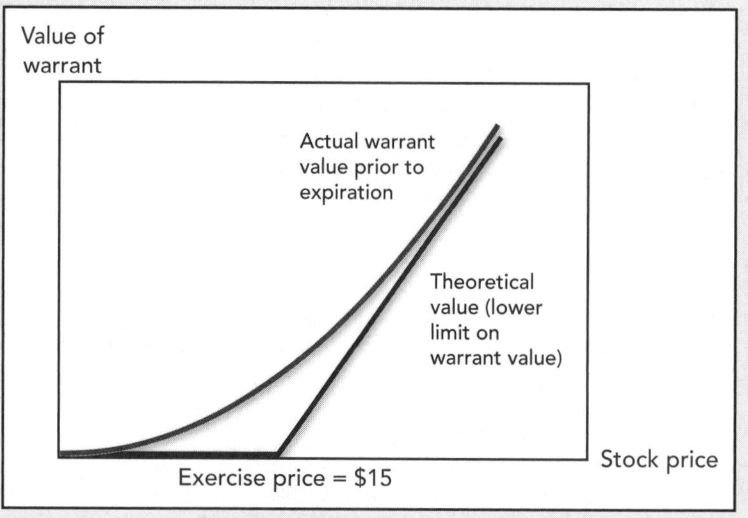

FIGURE 23.1

Relationship between the value of the B.J. Services warrant and stock price. The heavy line is the lower limit for warrant value. Warrant value falls to the lower limit just before the option expires. Before expiration, warrant value lies on a curve like the one shown here.

The height of this curve depends on two things. As we explained in Section 20.3, it depends on the variance of the stock returns per period (σ^2) times the number of periods before the option expires ($\sigma^2 t$). It also depends on the rate of interest (r_f) times the number of option periods (t). Of course as time runs out on a warrant, its price snuggles closer and closer to the lower bound. On the final day of its life, its price hits the lower bound.

Two Complications: Dividends and Dilution

If the warrant has no unusual features and the stock pays no dividends, then the value of the option can be estimated from the Black–Scholes formula described in Section 21.3.

But there is a problem when warrants are issued against dividend-paying stocks. The warrant holder is not entitled to dividends. In fact the warrant holder loses every time a cash dividend is paid because the dividend reduces stock price and thus reduces the value of the warrant. It may pay to exercise the warrant before maturity in order to capture the extra income.[3]

Remember that the Black–Scholes option-valuation formula assumes that the stock pays no dividends. Thus it will not give the theoretically correct value for a warrant issued by a dividend-paying firm. However, we showed in Chapter 21 how you can use the one-step-at-a-time binomial method to value options on dividend-paying stocks.

Another complication is that exercise of the warrants increases the number of shares. Therefore, exercise means that the firm's assets and profits are spread over a larger number of shares. Firms with significant amounts of warrants or convertibles outstanding are required to report earnings on a "fully diluted" basis, which recognizes the potential increase in the number of shares.

---

[3] This cannot make sense unless the dividend payment is larger than the interest that could be earned on the exercise price. By *not* exercising, the warrant holder keeps the exercise price and can put this money to work.

TABLE 23.1

United Glue's market value balance sheet (in $ millions).

Before the Issue			
Existing assets	$16	$ 4	Existing loans
		12	Common stock (1 million shares at $12 a share)
Total	$16	$16	Total
After the Issue			
Existing assets	$16	$ 4	Existing loans
New assets financed by debt and warrants	2	1.5	New loan without warrants
		5.5	Total debt
		.5	Warrants
		12	Common stock
		12.5	Total equity
Total	$18	$18.0	Total

This problem of *dilution* never arises with call options. If you buy or sell an option on the Chicago Board Options Exchange, you have no effect on the number of shares outstanding.

Example: Valuing United Glue's Warrants

United Glue has just issued a $2 million package of debt and warrants. Here are some basic data that we can use to value the warrants:

- Number of shares outstanding (N): 1 million
- Current stock price (P): $12
- Number of warrants issued per share outstanding (q): .10
- Total number of warrants issued (Nq): 100,000
- Exercise price of warrants (EX): $10
- Time to expiration of warrants (t): 4 years
- Annual standard deviation of stock price changes (σ): .40
- Rate of interest (r): 10%
- United stock pays no dividends.

Suppose that without the warrants the debt is worth $1.5 million. Then investors must be paying $.5 million for the warrants:

$$\begin{aligned}\text{Cost of warrants} &= \text{total amount of financing} - \text{value of loan without warrants}\\ 500{,}000 &= 2{,}000{,}000 - 1{,}500{,}000\end{aligned}$$

$$\text{Each warrant costs investors } \frac{500{,}000}{100{,}000} = \$5$$

Table 23.1 shows the market value of United's assets and liabilities both before and after the issue.

Now let us take a stab at checking whether the warrants are really worth the $500,000 that investors are paying for them. Since the warrant is a call option to buy the United stock, we can use the Black–Scholes formula to value the warrant. It turns out that a four-year call to buy United stock at \$10 is worth \$6.15.[4] Thus the warrant issue looks like a good deal for investors and a bad deal for United. Investors are paying \$5 a share for warrants that are worth \$6.15.

How the Value of United Warrants Is Affected by Dilution

Unfortunately, our calculations for United warrants do not tell the whole story. Remember that when investors exercise a traded call or put option, there is no change in either the company's assets or the number of shares outstanding. But, if United's warrants are exercised, the number of shares outstanding will increase by $Nq = 100{,}000$. Also the assets will increase by the amount of the exercise money ($Nq \times \text{EX} = 100{,}000 \times \$10 = \$1$ million). In other words, there will be dilution. We need to allow for this dilution when we value the warrants.

Let us call the value of United's equity V:

$$\text{Value of equity} = V = \text{value of United's total assets} - \text{value of debt}$$

If the warrants are exercised, equity value will increase by the amount of the exercise money to $V + Nq\text{EX}$. At the same time the number of shares will increase to $N + Nq$. So the share price after the warrants are exercised will be

$$\text{Share price after exercise} = \frac{V + Nq\text{EX}}{N + Nq}$$

At maturity the warrant holder can choose to let the warrants lapse or to exercise them and receive the share price less the exercise price. Thus the value of the warrants will be the share price minus the exercise price or zero, whichever is the higher. Another way to write this is

$$\begin{aligned}\text{Warrant value at maturity} &= \text{maximum (share price} - \text{exercise price, zero)}\\ &= \text{maximum}\left(\frac{V + Nq\text{EX}}{N + Nq} - \text{EX}, 0\right)\\ &= \text{maximum}\left(\frac{V/N - \text{EX}}{1 + q}, 0\right)\\ &= \frac{1}{1+q}\,\text{maximum}\left(\frac{V}{N} - \text{EX}, 0\right)\end{aligned}$$

This tells us the effect of dilution on the value of United's warrants. The warrant value is the value of $1/(1 + q)$ call options written on the stock of an alternative firm with the same total equity value V, *but with no outstanding warrants.* The alternative firm's stock price would be equal to V/N—that is, the total value of United's

[4]In Chapter 21 we saw that the Black–Scholes formula for the value of a call is

$$[N(d_1) \times P] - [N(d_2) \times \text{PV(EX)}]$$

where $d_1 = \log[P/\text{PV(EX)}]/\sigma\sqrt{t} + \sigma\sqrt{t}/2$

$d_2 = d_1 - \sigma\sqrt{t}$

$N(d_1)$ = cumulative normal probability function

Plugging the data for United into this formula gives

$$d_1 = \log[12/(10/1.1^4)]/(.40 \times \sqrt{4}) + .40 \times \sqrt{4}/2 = 1.104 \text{ and } d_2 = 1.104 - .40 \times \sqrt{4} = .304$$

Appendix Table 6 shows that $N(d_1) = .865$, and $N(d_2) = .620$. Therefore, estimated warrant value $= .865 \times 12 - .620 \times (10/1.1^4) = \$6.15$.

equity (V) divided by the number of shares outstanding (N).[5] The stock price of this alternative firm is more variable than United's stock price. So when we value the call option on the alternative firm, we must remember to use the standard deviation of the changes in V/N.

Now we can recalculate the value of United's warrants allowing for dilution. First we find the stock price of the alternative firm:

$$\begin{aligned}\text{Current equity value of alternative firm} &= V = \text{value of United's total assets} \\ &\quad - \text{value of loans} \\ &= 18 - 5.5 = \$12.5 \text{ million}\end{aligned}$$

$$\text{Current share price of alternative firm} = \frac{V}{N} = \frac{12.5 \text{ million}}{1 \text{ million}} = \$12.50$$

Also, suppose the standard deviation of the share price changes of this alternative firm is $\sigma^* = .41$.[6]

The Black–Scholes formula gives a value of \$6.64 for a call option on a stock with a price of \$12.50 and a standard deviation of .41. The value of United warrants is equal to the value of $1/(1 + q)$ call options on the stock of this alternative firm. Thus warrant value is

$$\frac{1}{1+q} \times \text{value of call on alternative firm} = \frac{1}{1.1} \times 6.64 = \$6.04$$

This is a somewhat lower value than the one we computed when we ignored dilution but still a bad deal for United.

[5]The modifications to allow for dilution when valuing warrants were originally proposed in F. Black and M. Scholes, "The Pricing of Options and Corporate Liabilities," *Journal of Political Economy* 81 (May–June 1973), pp. 637–654. Our exposition follows a discussion in D. Galai and M. I. Schneller, "Pricing of Warrants and the Valuation of the Firm," *Journal of Finance* 33 (December 1978), pp. 1333–1342.

[6]How in practice could we compute σ^*? It would be easy if we could wait until the warrants had been trading for some time. In that case σ^* could be computed from the returns on a package of *all* the company's shares and warrants. In the present case we need to value the warrants *before* they start trading. We argue as follows: The standard deviation of the *assets* before the issue is equal to the standard deviation of a package of the common stock and the existing loans. For example, suppose that the company's debt is risk-free and that the standard deviation of stock returns *before* the bond–warrant issue is 38 percent. Then we calculate the standard deviation of the initial assets as follows:

$$\begin{aligned}\begin{matrix}\text{Standard deviation} \\ \text{of initial assets}\end{matrix} &= \begin{matrix}\text{proportion in} \\ \text{common stock}\end{matrix} \times \begin{matrix}\text{standard deviation} \\ \text{of common stock}\end{matrix} \\ &= \frac{12}{16} \times 38 = 28.5\%\end{aligned}$$

Now suppose that the assets after the issue are equally risky. Then

$$\begin{matrix}\text{Standard deviation} \\ \text{of assets after issue}\end{matrix} = \begin{matrix}\text{proportion of equity} \\ \text{after issue}\end{matrix} \times \begin{matrix}\text{standard deviation} \\ \text{of equity } (\sigma^*)\end{matrix}$$

$$28.5 = \frac{12.5}{18} \times \text{standard deviation of equity } (\sigma^*)$$

$$\text{Standard deviation of equity } (\sigma^*) = 41\%$$

Notice that in our example the standard deviation of the stock returns *before* the warrant issue was slightly lower than the standard deviation of the package of stock and warrants. However, the warrant holders bear proportionately more of this risk than do the stockholders; so the bond–warrant package could either increase or reduce the risk of the stock.

It may sound from all this as if you need to know the value of United warrants to compute their value. This is not so. The formula does not call for warrant value but for *V*, the value of United's equity (that is, the shares *plus* warrants). Given equity value, the formula calculates how the overall value of equity should be split up between stock and warrants. Thus, suppose that United's underwriter advises that $500,000 extra can be raised by issuing a package of bonds and warrants rather than bonds alone. Is this a fair price? You can check using the Black–Scholes formula with the adjustment for dilution.

Finally, notice that these modifications are necessary to apply the Black–Scholes formula to value a warrant. They are not needed by the warrant holder, who must decide whether to exercise at maturity. If at maturity the price of the stock exceeds the exercise price of the warrant, the warrant holder will of course exercise.

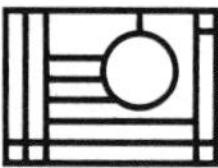

23.2 WHAT IS A CONVERTIBLE BOND?

The convertible bond is a close relative of the bond–warrant package. Many companies choose to issue convertible preferred as an alternative to issuing packages of preferred stock and warrants. We will concentrate on convertible bonds, but almost all our comments apply to convertible preferred issues.

In 1999 Amazon.com issued $1.25 billion of 4 3/4 percent convertible bonds due in 2009.[7] These could be converted at any time to 6.41 shares of common stock. In other words, the owner had a 10-year option to return the bond to the company and receive 6.41 shares of stock in exchange. The number of shares into which each bond can be converted is called the bond's *conversion ratio.* The conversion ratio of the Amazon bond was 6.41.

To receive 6.41 shares of Amazon stock, the owner had to surrender bonds with a face value of $1,000. This means that to receive one share, the owner had to surrender a face amount of $1,000/6.41 = $156.01. This figure is called the *conversion price.* Anybody who bought the bond at $1,000 to convert it into 6.41 shares paid the equivalent of $156.01 per share.

At the time of issue the price of Amazon stock was about $120 so the conversion price was 30 percent higher than the stock price.

Convertibles are usually protected against stock splits or stock dividends. When Amazon subsequently split its stock 2 for 1, the conversion ratio was increased to 12.82 and the conversion price dropped to $1,000/12.82 = $78.00.

The Convertible Menagerie

Amazon's convertible issue is typical, but you may come across more complicated cases. For example, in November 2000 Tyco raised the record sum of $3.5 billion from a convertible issue. The Tyco issue was an example of a LYON (liquid yield option note). A LYON is a callable and puttable, zero-coupon convertible bond (and you can't get much more complicated than that).

[7]The Amazon issue consisted of convertible subordinated notes. The term *subordinated* indicates that the issue is a junior debt; its holders will be at the bottom of the heap of creditors in the event of default. Notes are simply unsecured bonds. Therefore there are no specific assets that have been reserved to pay off the holders in the event of default. There is more about these terms in Section 25.3.

The Tyco issue was a 20-year zero-coupon bond that was convertible at any time into 10.3 shares. The bonds were issued at a price of $741.65, which gave bondholders a yield to maturity of 1.5 percent. When Tyco issued the convertible, corporate bonds were yielding roughly 8 percent. So an investor who converted immediately would be giving up a bond worth $\$1{,}000/1.08^{20} = \$215$. Investors who waited 20 years to convert would be relinquishing a bond worth $1,000 (as long as the firm is solvent). So the value of the bond that they give up increases each year.

The Tyco LYON contains two other options. Starting in 2007 the company has the right to call the bond for cash. The exercise price of this call option starts at 82.34 percent and increases by 1.5 percent each year until it reaches 100 percent in 2014. The bondholders also have an option, for there are five days between 2001 and 2014 on which they can demand repayment of their bonds. The repayment price starts at 75.28 percent and then is increased by 1.5 percent a year. These put options help to provide a more solid floor to the issue. Even if interest rates rise and prices of other bonds fall, LYON holders have a guaranteed price on these five days at which they can sell their bonds.[8] Obviously, investors who exercise the put give up the opportunity to convert their bonds into stock; it would be worth taking advantage of the guarantee only if the conversion price of the bonds was well below the exercise price of the put.[9]

Mandatory Convertibles

In recent years a number of companies have issued preferred stock or debt that is *automatically* converted into equity after several years. Investors in mandatory convertibles receive the benefit of a higher current income than common stockholders, but there is a limit on the value of the common stock that they ultimately receive. Thus they share in the appreciation of the common stock only up to this limit. As the stock price rises above this limit, the number of shares that the convertible holder receives is reduced proportionately.

Valuing Convertible Bonds

The owner of a convertible owns a bond and a call option on the firm's stock. So does the owner of a bond–warrant package. There are differences, of course, the most important being the requirement that a convertible owner give up the bond in order to exercise the call option. The owner of a bond–warrant package can (generally) exercise the warrant for cash and keep the bond. Nevertheless, understanding convertibles is easier if you analyze them first as bonds and then as call options.

Imagine that Eastman Kojak has issued convertible bonds with a total face value of $1 million and that these can be converted at any stage to one million shares of common stock. The price of Kojak's convertible bond depends on its *bond value* and its *conversion value*. The bond value is what each bond would sell for if it could not be converted. The conversion value is what the bond would sell for if it had to be converted immediately.

---

[8]Of course, this guarantee would not be worth much if the company was in financial distress and *couldn't* buy the bonds back.

[9]The reasons for issuing LYONs are discussed in J. J. McConnell and E. S. Schwartz, "The Origin of LYONs: A Case Study in Financial Innovation," *Journal of Applied Corporate Finance* 4 (Winter 1992), pp. 40–47. For a discussion of how to value an earlier LYON issue by Waste Management see J. McConnell and E. S. Schwartz, "Taming LYONs," *Journal of Finance* 41 (July 1986), pp. 561–576.

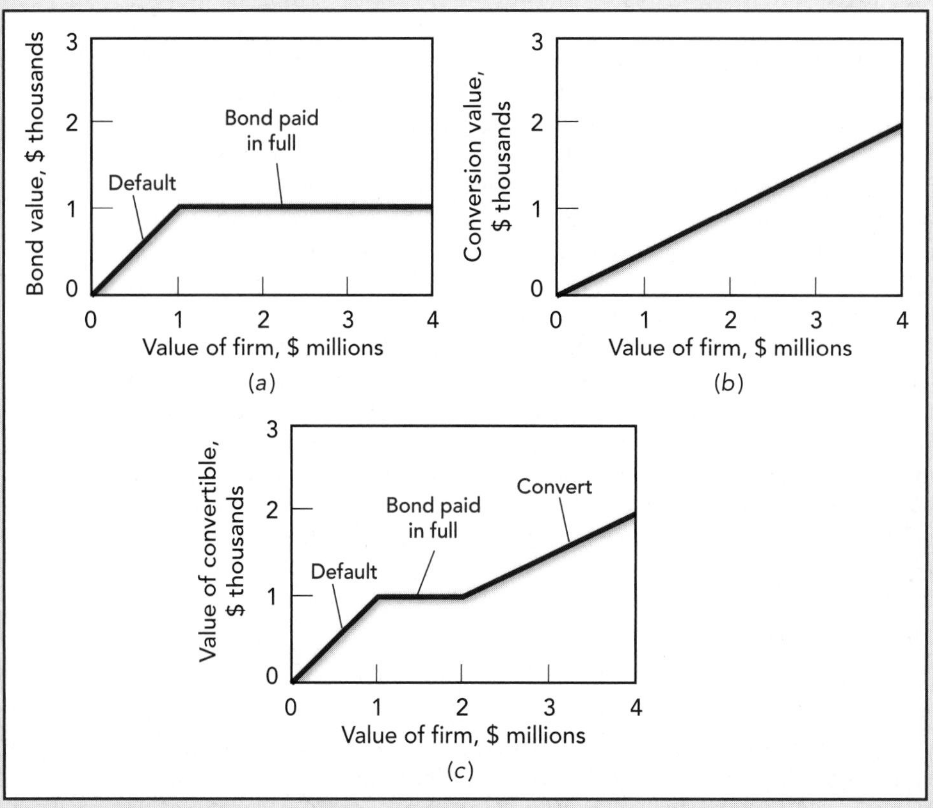

FIGURE 23.2

(*a*) The bond value when Eastman Kojak's convertible bond matures. If firm value is at least $1 million, the bond is paid off at its face value of $1000; if it is less than $1 million, the bondholders receive the value of the firm's assets. (*b*) The conversion value at maturity. If converted, the value of the convertible bond rises in proportion to firm value. (*c*) At maturity the convertible bondholder can choose to receive the principal repayment on the bond or convert to common stock. The value of the convertible bond is therefore the higher of its bond value and its conversion value.

Value at Maturity Figure 23.2(*a*) shows the possible *bond values* when the Kojak convertible matures. As long as the value of the firm's assets does not fall below $1 million, the bond will pay off in full. But if the firm value is *less* than $1 million, there will not be enough to pay off the bondholders. In the extreme case that the assets are worthless, the bondholders will receive nothing. Thus the horizontal line in Figure 23.2(*a*) shows the payoff if the bond is repaid in full, and the sloping line shows the payoffs if the firm defaults.[10]

You can think of the bond value as a lower bound, or "floor," to the price of the convertible. But that floor has a nasty slope and, when the company falls on hard times, the bonds may not be worth much. For example, we saw earlier how Amazon.com issued a convertible bond in 1999. Over the following two years

[10]You may recognize this as the position diagram for a default-free bond *minus* a put option on the assets with an exercise price equal to the face value of the bonds. See Section 20.1.

investors became disenchanted with dot.com companies and Amazon's stock price fell by 75 percent to $15. This was well below the conversion price of $78.03. Convertible bondholders might have hoped that the bond value would provide a secure floor to the value of their investment. Unfortunately, by early 2001 Amazon's bonds no longer looked as safe as they once had, and Moody's placed its convertible in the junk bond category Caa. By the spring of that year the price of the convertible had fallen to about $400 and offered a promised yield to maturity of 20 percent.

Figure 23.2(*b*) shows the possible *conversion values* at maturity of Kojak's convertible. We assume that Kojak already has one million shares of common stock outstanding, so the convertible holders will be entitled to half the value of the firm. For example, if the firm is worth $2 million,[11] the one million shares obtained by conversion would be worth $1 each. Each convertible bond can be exchanged for 1,000 shares of stock and therefore would have a conversion value of $1,000 \times 1 = \$1,000$.

Kojak's convertible also cannot sell for less than its conversion value. If it did, smart investors would buy the convertible, exchange it rapidly for stock, and sell the stock. Their profit would be equal to the difference between the conversion value and the price of the convertible.

Therefore, there are *two* lower bounds to the price of the convertible: its bond value and its conversion value. Investors will not convert if bond value exceeds conversion value; they will do so if conversion value exceeds bond value. In other words, the price of the convertible at maturity is represented by the higher of the two lines in Figure 23.2(*a*) and (*b*). This is shown in Figure 23.2(*c*).

Value before Maturity We can also draw a picture similar to Figure 23.2 when the convertible is *not* about to mature. Because even healthy companies may subsequently fall sick and default on their bonds, other things equal, the bond value will be lower when the bond has some time to run. Thus bond value before maturity is represented by the curved line in Figure 23.3(*a*).[12]

Figure 23.3(*b*) shows that the lower bound to the price of a convertible before maturity is again the higher of the bond value and conversion value. However, before maturity the convertible bondholders *do not have to make a now-or-never choice for or against conversion.* They can wait and then, with the benefit of hindsight, take whatever course turns out to give them the highest payoff. Thus before maturity a convertible is always worth more than its lower-bound value. Its actual selling price will behave as shown by the top line in Figure 23.3(*c*). The difference between the top line and the lower bound is the value of a call option on the firm. Remember, however, that this option can be exercised only by giving up the bond. In other words, the option to convert is a call option with an exercise price equal to the bond value.

Dilution and Dividends Revisited

If you want to value a convertible, it is easiest to break the problem down into two parts. First estimate bond value; then add the value of the conversion option.

When you value the conversion option, you need to look out for the same things that make warrants more tricky to value than traded options. For example,

[11]Firm value is equal to the value of Kojak's common stock *plus* the value of its convertible bonds.

[12]Remember, the value of a risky bond is the value of a safe bond *less* the value of a put option on the firm's assets. The value of this option increases with maturity.

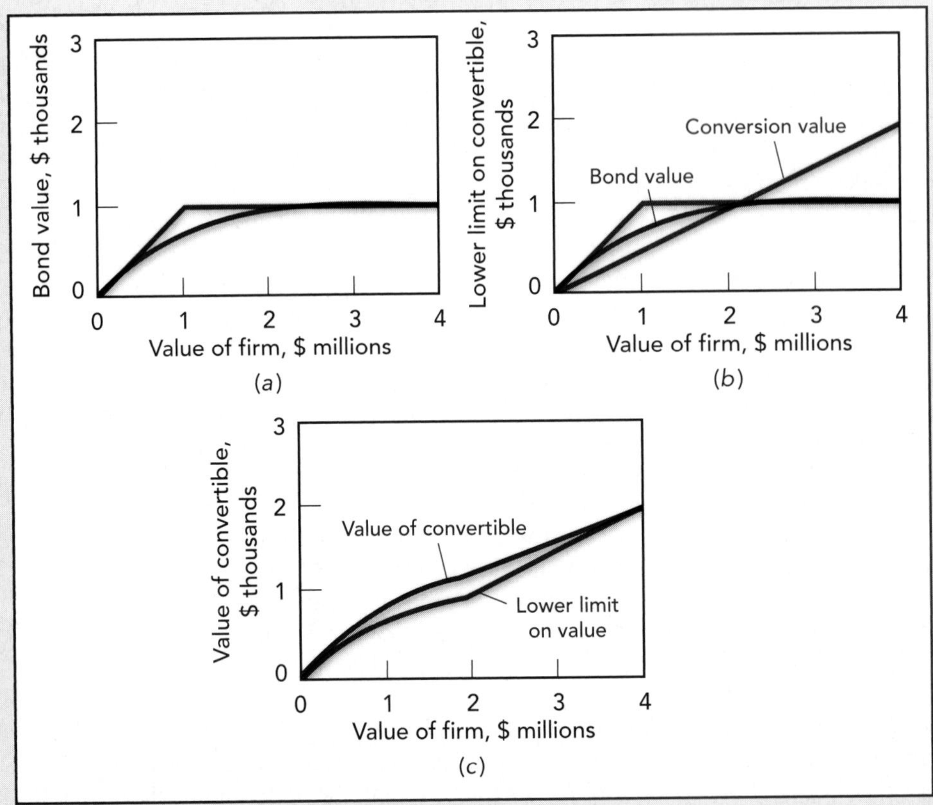

FIGURE 23.3

(*a*) Before maturity the bond value of Eastman Kojak's convertible bond is close to that of a similar default-free bond when firm value is high, but it falls sharply if firm value falls to a very low level. (*b*) If investors were obliged to make an immediate decision for or against conversion, the value of the convertible would be equal to the higher of bond value or conversion value. (*c*) Since convertible bondholders do not have to make a decision until maturity, (*b*) represents a lower limit. The value of the convertible bond is worth *more* than either bond value or conversion value.

dilution may be important. If the bonds are converted, the company saves on its interest payments and is relieved of having to eventually repay the loan; on the other hand, net profits have to be divided among a larger number of shares.[13] Companies are obliged to show in their financial statements how earnings would be affected by conversion.[14]

Also, you must remember that the convertible owner is missing out on the dividends on the common stock. If these dividends are higher than the interest on the

[13]In practice investors often ignore dilution and calculate conversion value as the share price times the number of shares into which the bonds can be converted. A convertible bond actually gives an option to acquire a fraction of the "new equity"—the equity *after* conversion. When we calculated the conversion value of Kojak's convertible, we recognized this by multiplying the proportion of common stock that the convertible bondholders would receive by the total value of the firm's assets (i.e., the value of the common stock plus the value of the convertible).

[14]These "diluted" earnings take into account the extra shares but not the savings in interest payments.

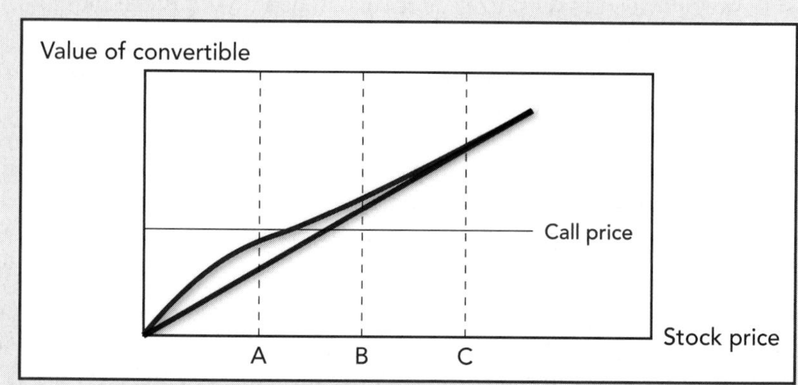

FIGURE 23.4

The decision to call a convertible. The financial manager should call at price C but wait at prices A and B. (*Note:* The conversion value is the straight upward-sloping line.)

bonds, it may pay to convert before the final exercise date in order to pick up the extra cash income.

Forcing Conversion

Companies usually retain an option to buy back or "call" the convertible bond at a preset price. If the company calls the bond, the owner has a brief period, usually about 30 days, within which to convert the bond or surrender it.[15] If a bond is surrendered, the investor receives the call price in cash. But if the share price is higher than the call price, the investor will convert the bond instead of surrendering it. Thus a call can *force conversion* if the stock price is high enough.

Most convertible bonds provide for two or more years of *call protection*. During this period the company is not permitted to call the bonds. However, many convertibles can be called early, before the end of the call protection, if the stock price has risen enough to provide a nice conversion profit. For example, a convertible with a call price of $40 might be callable early if the stock price trades above $65 for at least two weeks.

Calling the bond obviously does not affect the total size of the company pie, but it can affect the size of the individual slices. In other words, conversion has no effect on the total value of the firm's assets, but it does affect how asset value is *distributed* among the different classes of security holders. Therefore, if you want to maximize your shareholders' slice of the pie, you must minimize the convertible bondholders' slice. That means you must not call the bonds if they are worth *less* than the call price, for that would be giving the bondholders an unnecessary present. Similarly, you must not allow the bonds to remain uncalled if their value is *above* the call price, for that would not be minimizing the value of the bonds.

Let's apply this reasoning to specific cases. Refer to Figure 23.4, which matches Figure 23.3(*c*) but has the call price drawn in as a horizontal line. Consider the firm values corresponding to three stock prices, marked A, B, and C:

- At price A, the convertible is "out of the money." Calling the bond leads to redemption for cash and hands bondholders a free gift equal to the difference between the call price and the convertible value. Therefore the company should not call.

[15]Companies may also reserve the right to force conversion of warrants.

- Suppose call protection ends with price at level C. Then the financial manager should call immediately, forcing the convertible value down to the call price.[16]
- What if call protection ends with price at level B, barely above the call price? In this case the financial manager will probably wait. Remember, if a call is announced, bondholders have a 30-day period in which to decide whether to convert or redeem. The stock price could easily fall below the call price during this period, forcing the company to redeem for cash. Usually calls are not announced until the stock price is about 20 percent above the call price. This provides a safety margin to ensure conversion.[17]

Do companies follow these simple guidelines? On the surface they don't, for there are many instances of convertible bonds selling well above the call price. But the explanation seems to lie in the call-protection period, during which companies are not allowed to call their bonds. Paul Asquith found that most convertible bonds that are worth calling are called as soon as possible after this period ends.[18] The typical delay for bonds that can be called is slightly less than four months after the conversion value first exceeds the call price.

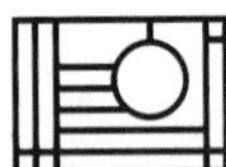

23.3 THE DIFFERENCE BETWEEN WARRANTS AND CONVERTIBLES

We have dwelt on the basic similarity between warrants and convertibles. Now let us look at some of the differences:

1. *Warrants are usually issued privately.* Packages of bonds with warrants or preferred stock with warrants tend to be more common in private placements. By contrast most convertible bonds are issued publicly.
2. *Warrants can be detached.* When you buy a convertible, the bond and the option are bundled up together. You cannot sell them separately. This may be inconvenient. If your tax position or attitude to risk inclines you to bonds, you may not want to hold options as well. Sometimes warrants are also "nondetachable," but usually you can keep the bond and sell the warrant.
3. *Warrants may be issued on their own.* Warrants do not have to be issued in conjunction with other securities. Often they are used to compensate investment bankers for underwriting services. Many companies also give their executives long-term options to buy stock. These executive stock options are not usually called warrants, but that is exactly what they are. Companies can also sell warrants on their own directly to investors, though they rarely do so.

[16]The financial manager might delay calling for a time at price C if interest payments on the convertible debt are less than the extra dividends that would be paid after conversion. This delay would reduce cash payments to bondholders. Nothing is lost if the financial manager always calls "on the way down" if stock price subsequently falls toward level B. Note that investors may convert voluntarily if dividends after conversion exceed interest on the convertible bond.

[17]See P. Asquith and D. Mullins, "Convertible Debt: Corporate Call Policy," *Journal of Finance* 46 (September 1991), pp. 1273–1290.

[18]See P. Asquith, "Convertible Bonds Are Not Called Late," *Journal of Finance* 50 (September 1995), pp. 1275–1289.

4. *Warrants are exercised for cash.* When you convert a bond, you simply exchange your bond for common stock. When you exercise warrants, you generally put up extra cash, though occasionally you have to surrender the bond or can choose to do so. This means that bond–warrant packages and convertible bonds usually have different effects on the company's cash flow and on its capital structure.
5. *A package of bonds and warrants may be taxed differently.* There are some tax differences between warrants and convertibles. Suppose that you are wondering whether to issue a convertible bond at 100. You can think of this convertible as a package of a straight bond worth, say, 90 and an option worth 10. If you issue the bond and option separately, the IRS will note that the bond is issued at a discount and that its price will rise by 10 points over its life. The IRS will allow you, the issuer, to spread this prospective price appreciation over the life of the bond and deduct it from your taxable profits. The IRS will also allocate the prospective price appreciation to the taxable income of the bondholder. Thus, by issuing a package of bonds and warrants rather than a convertible, you may reduce the tax paid by the issuing company and increase the tax paid by the investor.[19]

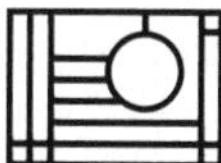

23.4 WHY DO COMPANIES ISSUE WARRANTS AND CONVERTIBLES?

You are approached by an investment banker who is anxious to persuade you that your company should issue warrants. She points out that the exercise price of the warrants could be set at 20 percent above the current stock price, so that you would effectively be selling stock at a hefty premium. And, if it turns out that the warrants are never exercised, the proceeds from their sale would become a clear profit to the company. Are you convinced?

You hear many similar arguments for issuing warrants and convertibles, but you should always be suspicious of any "Heads I win, tails you lose" argument. If the shareholder inevitably wins, the warrant holder must lose. But that doesn't make sense. Surely there must be some price at which it makes sense to buy warrants.[20]

Suppose that your company's stock is priced at $100 and that you are considering an issue of warrants exercisable at $120. You believe that you can sell these warrants at $10. If the stock price subsequently fails to reach $120, the warrants will not be exercised. You will have sold warrants for $10 each, which with the benefit of hindsight proved to be worthless to the buyer. If the stock price reaches $130, say, the warrants will be exercised. Your firm will have received the initial payment of $10 *plus* the exercise price of $120. On the other hand, it will have issued to the warrant holders stock worth $130 per share. The net result is a standoff. You have received a payment of $130 in exchange for a liability worth $130.

---

[19]See J. D. Finnerty, "The Case for Issuing Synthetic Convertible Bonds," *Midland Corporate Finance Journal* 4 (Fall 1986), pp. 73–82.

[20]Here is another "Heads I win, tails you lose" argument. You are an investor. Your broker calls you with an offer of ABC company warrants. ABC's share price is $10; the warrants expire in one year, have an exercise price of $10, and are selling at $1. Your broker points out that you are likely to make much larger percentage gains from buying the warrants rather than the shares. For example, if over the next year the share price rises by 20 percent to $12, the warrants will be worth $2, a gain of 100 percent. On the other hand, if the share price falls, the most that you can lose as a warrant holder is $1. How do you respond?

Think now what happens if the stock price rises above $130. Perhaps it goes to $200. In this case the warrant issue will end up producing a loss of $70. This is not a cash outflow but an opportunity loss. The firm receives $130, but in this case it could have sold stock for $200. On the other hand, the warrant holders gain $70: They invest $130 in cash to acquire stock that they can sell, if they like, for $200.

Our example is oversimplified—for instance, we have kept quiet about the time value of money and risk—but we hope it has made the basic point. When you sell warrants, you are selling options and getting cash in exchange. Options are valuable securities. If they are properly priced, this is a fair trade; in other words, it is a zero-NPV transaction.

Some managers look on convertibles as "cheap debt." Others regard them as a deferred sale of stock at an attractive price. These arguments also are misleading. We have seen that a convertible is like a package of a straight bond and an option. The difference between the market value of the convertible and that of the straight bond is therefore the price investors place on the call option. The convertible is "cheap" only if this price overvalues the option.

What then of the other managers—those who regard the issue as a deferred sale of common stock? A convertible bond gives you the right to buy stock by giving up a bond.[21] Bondholders may decide to do this, but then again they may not. Thus issue of a convertible bond *may* amount to a deferred stock issue. But if the firm *needs* equity capital, a convertible issue is an unreliable way of getting it.

Taken at their face value the motives of these managers are irrational. Convertibles are not just cheap debt, nor are they a deferred sale of stock. But we suspect that these simple phrases encapsulate some more complex and rational motives.

Notice that convertibles tend to be issued by the smaller and more speculative firms. They are almost invariably unsecured and generally subordinated. Now put yourself in the position of a potential investor. You are approached by a small firm with an untried product line that wants to issue some junior unsecured debt. You know that if things go well, you will get your money back, but if they do not, you could easily be left with nothing. Since the firm is in a new line of business, it is difficult to assess the chances of trouble. Therefore you don't know what the fair rate of interest is. Also, you may be worried that once you have made the loan, management will be tempted to run extra risks. It may take on additional senior debt, or it may decide to expand its operations and go for broke on your money. In fact, if you charge a very high rate of interest, you could be encouraging this to happen.

What can management do to protect you against a wrong estimate of the risk and to assure you that its intentions are honorable? In crude terms, it can give you a piece of the action. You don't mind the company running unanticipated risks as long as you share in the gains as well as the losses.[22]

---

[21]That is much the same as already having the stock together with the right to sell it for the convertible's bond value. In other words, instead of thinking of a convertible as a bond plus a call option, you could think of it as the stock plus a put option. Now you see why it is wrong to think of a convertible as equivalent to the sale of stock; it is equivalent to the sale of both stock *and* a put option. If there is any possibility that investors will want to hold onto their bond, the put option will have some value.

[22]See M. J. Brennan and E. S. Schwartz, "The Case for Convertibles," *Journal of Applied Corporate Finance* 1 (Summer 1988), pp. 55–64.

Convertible securities and warrants make sense whenever it is unusually costly to assess the risk of debt or whenever investors are worried that management may not act in the bondholders' interest.[23]

You can also think of a convertible issue as a *contingent* issue of equity. If a company's investment opportunities expand, its stock price is likely to increase, allowing the financial manager to call and force conversion of a convertible bond into equity. Thus the company gets fresh equity when it is most needed for expansion. Of course, it is also stuck with debt if the company does not prosper.[24]

The relatively low coupon rate on convertible bonds may also be a convenience for rapidly growing firms facing heavy capital expenditures. They may be willing to give up the conversion option to reduce immediate cash requirements for debt service. Without the conversion option, lenders might demand extremely high (promised) interest rates to compensate for the probability of default. This would not only force the firm to raise still more capital for debt service but also increase the risk of financial distress. Paradoxically, lenders' attempts to protect themselves against default may actually increase the probability of financial distress by increasing the burden of debt service on the firm.[25]

---

[23]Changes in risk ought to be more likely when the firm is small and its debt is low-grade. If so, we should find that the convertible bonds of such firms offer their owners a larger potential ownership share. This is indeed the case. See C. M. Lewis, R. J. Rogalski, and J. K. Seward, "Understanding the Design of Convertible Debt," *Journal of Applied Corporate Finance* 11 (Spring 1998), pp. 45–53.

[24]Jeremy Stein points out that an issue of a convertible sends a better signal to investors than a straight equity issue. As we explained in Chapter 15, announcement of a common stock issue prompts worries of overvaluation and usually depresses stock price. Convertibles are hybrids of debt and equity and send a less negative signal. If the company is likely to need equity, its willingness to issue a convertible, and to take the chance that stock price will rise enough to allow forced conversion, also signals management's confidence. See J. Stein, "Convertible Bonds as Backdoor Equity Financing," *Journal of Financial Economics* 32 (1992), pp. 3–21.

[25]This fact led to an extensive body of literature on "credit rationing." A lender rations credit if it is irrational to lend more to a firm regardless of the interest rate the firm is willing to *promise* to pay. Whether this can happen in efficient, competitive capital markets is controversial. We discussed credit rationing in Chapter 18. For a review of this literature, see E. Baltensperger, "Credit Rationing: Issues and Questions," *Journal of Money, Credit and Banking* 10 (May 1978), pp. 170–183.

SUMMARY

Instead of issuing straight bonds, companies may sell either packages of bonds and warrants or convertible bonds.

A warrant is just a long-term call option issued by the company. You already know a good deal about valuing call options. You know from Chapter 20 that call options must be worth at least as much as the stock price less the exercise price. You know that their value is greatest when they have a long time to expiration, when the underlying stock is risky, and when the interest rate is high.

Warrants are somewhat trickier to value than call options traded on the options exchanges. First, because they are long-term options, it is important to recognize that the warrant holder does not receive any dividends. Second, dilution must be allowed for.

A convertible bond gives its holder the right to swap the bond for common stock. The rate of exchange is usually measured by the *conversion ratio*—that is, the number of shares that the investor gets for each bond. Sometimes the rate of exchange is expressed in terms of the *conversion price*—that is, the face value of the bond that must be given up in order to receive one share.

Convertibles are like a package of a bond and a call option. When you evaluate the conversion option, you must again remember that the convertible holder does not receive dividends and that conversion results in dilution of the common stock. There are two other things to watch out for. One is the problem of default risk. If the company runs into trouble, you may have not only a worthless conversion option but also a worthless bond. Second, the company may be able to force conversion by calling the bond. It should do this when the market price of the convertible reaches the call price.

You hear a variety of arguments for issuing warrants or convertibles. Convertible bonds and bonds with warrants are almost always junior bonds and are frequently issued by risky companies. We think that this says something about the reasons for their issue. Suppose that you are lending to an untried company. You are worried that the company may turn out to be riskier than you thought or that it may issue additional senior bonds. You can try to protect yourself against such eventualities by imposing very restrictive conditions on the debt, but it is often simpler to allow some extra risk as long as you get a piece of the action. The convertible and bond–warrant package give you a chance to participate in the firm's successes as well as its failures. They diminish the possible conflicts of interest between bondholder and stockholder.

FURTHER READING

The items listed in Chapters 20 and 21 under "Further Reading" are also relevant to this chapter, in particular Black and Scholes's discussion of warrant valuation.

Ingersoll's work represents the "state of the art" in valuing convertibles:

J. E. Ingersoll: "A Contingent Claims Valuation of Convertible Securities," *Journal of Financial Economics,* 4:289–322 (May 1977).

Ingersoll also examines corporate call policies on convertible bonds in:

J. E. Ingersoll: "An Examination of Corporate Call Policies on Convertible Securities," *Journal of Finance,* 32:463–478 (May 1977).

Brennan and Schwartz's paper was written about the same time as Ingersoll's and reaches essentially the same conclusions; they also present a general procedure for valuing convertibles:

M. J. Brennan and E. S. Schwartz: "Convertible Bonds: Valuation and Optimal Strategies for Call and Conversion," *Journal of Finance,* 32:1699–1715 (December 1977).

Two useful articles on warrants are:

E. S. Schwartz: "The Valuation of Warrants: Implementing a New Approach," *Journal of Financial Economics,* 4:79–93 (January 1977).

D. Galai and M. A. Schneller: "Pricing of Warrants and the Value of the Firm," *Journal of Finance,* 33:1333–1342 (December 1978).

Asquith's analysis of the effect of call protection provides evidence that firms' decisions on calling convertibles are more rational than was previously believed:

P. Asquith: "Convertible Bonds Are Not Called Late," *Journal of Finance,* 50:1275–1289 (September 1995).

For nontechnical discussions of the pricing of convertibles and the reasons for their use, see:

M. J. Brennan and E. S. Schwartz: "The Case for Convertibles," *Journal of Applied Corporate Finance,* 1:55–64 (Summer 1988).

C. M. Lewis, R. J. Rogalski, and J. K. Seward, "Understanding the Design of Convertible Debt," *Journal of Applied Corporate Finance,* 11:45–53 (Spring 1998).

QUIZ

1. Associated Elk warrants entitle the owner to buy one share at $40.
   a. What is the "theoretical" value of the warrant if the stock price is: (i) $20? (ii) $30? (iii) $40? (iv) $50? (v) $60?
   b. Plot the theoretical value of the warrant against the stock price.
   c. Suppose the stock price is $60 and the warrant price is $5. What would you do?

2. In 1994 Viacom made a typical issue of warrants. Each warrant could be exercised before 1999 at a price of $70 per share. In September 1998 the stock price was $57 per share.
   a. Did the warrant holder have a vote?
   b. Did the warrant holder receive dividends?
   c. If the stock was split 3 for 1, how would the exercise price be adjusted?
   d. Suppose that instead of adjusting the exercise price after a 3-for-1 split, the company gives each warrant holder the right to buy *three* shares at $70 apiece. Would this have the same effect? Would it make the warrant holder better or worse off?
   e. What is the "theoretical" value of the warrant?
   f. Before maturity is the warrant worth more or less than the "theoretical" value?
   g. *Other things equal,* would the warrant be more or less valuable if:
      i. The company increased its rate of dividend payout?
      ii. The interest rate declined?
      iii. The stock became riskier?
      iv. The company extended the exercise period?
      v. The company reduced the exercise price?
   h. A few companies issue perpetual warrants that have no final exercise date. Suppose that Viacom warrants were perpetual. In what circumstances might it make sense for investors to exercise their warrants?
   i. If the stock price rises 5 percent, would you expect the price of a warrant to rise by more or less than 5 percent?

3. Company X has outstanding 1,000 shares and 200 warrants. Each warrant can be converted into one share at an exercise price of $20. What will be the *total* market value of X's shares after the warrants mature if the share price on that date is **(a)** $15, **(b)** $25?

4. Maple Aircraft has issued a 4 ¾ percent convertible subordinated debenture due 2008. The conversion price is $47.00 and the debenture is callable at $102.75 percent of face value. The market price of the convertible is 91 percent of face value, and the price of the common is $41.50. Assume that the value of the bond in the absence of a conversion feature is about 65 percent of face value.
   a. What is the conversion ratio of the debenture?
   b. If the conversion ratio were 50, what would be the conversion price?
   c. What is the conversion value?
   d. At what stock price is the conversion value equal to the bond value?
   e. Can the market price be less than the conversion value?
   f. How much is the convertible holder paying for the option to buy one share of common stock?
   g. By how much does the common have to rise by 2008 to justify conversion?
   h. When should Maple call the debenture?

5. **a.** Pi, Inc., has 30 million shares outstanding and has a net income of $210 million. Calculate Pi's earnings per share.
   b. Pi has also issued $50 million of 5 percent convertible bonds with a face value of $1,000 each and a conversion ratio of 3.142. How will earnings per share change if the bonds are converted?

6. True or false?
   a. Convertible bonds are usually senior claims on the firm.
   b. The higher the conversion ratio, the more valuable the convertible.

Visit us at www.mhhe.com/bm7e

c. The higher the conversion price, the more valuable the convertible.
d. If a company splits its stock, the conversion price is increased.
e. Other things equal, if dividend payments rise, bondholders are more likely to convert before maturity.
f. Convertible bonds do not share fully in a rise in the price of the common stock, but they provide some protection against a decline.

PRACTICE QUESTIONS

1. Associated Elk warrants have an exercise price of $40. The share price is $50. The dividend on the stock is $3, and the interest rate is 10 percent.
   a. Would you exercise your warrants now or later? State why.
   b. If the dividend increased to $5, it could pay to exercise now if the stock price has low variability and it could be better to exercise later if the stock price has high variability. Explain why.
2. Moose Stores has outstanding one million shares of common stock with a total market value of $40 million. It now announces an issue of one million warrants at $5 each. Each warrant entitles the owner to buy one Moose share for a price of $30 any time within the next five years. Moose Stores has stated that it will not pay a dividend within this period.
   The standard deviation of the returns on Moose's equity is 20 percent a year, and the interest rate is 8 percent.
   a. What is the market value of each warrant?
   b. What is the market value of each share after the warrant issue? (*Hint:* The value of the shares is equal to the total value of the equity less the value of the warrants.)
3. Look again at question 2. Suppose that Moose now forecasts the following dividend payments:

End of Year	Dividend
1	$2
2	3
3	4
4	5
5	6

   Reestimate the market values of the warrant and stock.
4. Occasionally firms extend the life of warrants that would otherwise expire unexercised. What is the cost of doing this?
5. The Surplus Value Company had $10 million (face value) of convertible bonds outstanding in 2001. Each bond has the following features:

Par or face value	$1000
Conversion price	$25
Current call price	105 (percent of face value)
Current trading price	130 (percent of face value)
Maturity	2011
Current stock price	$30 (per share)
Interest rate	10 (coupon as percent of face value)

   a. What is the bond's conversion value?
   b. Can you explain why the bond is selling above conversion value?
   c. Should Surplus call? What will happen if it does so?

6. Piglet Pies has issued a zero-coupon 10-year bond that can be converted into 10 Piglet shares. Comparable straight bonds are yielding 8 percent. Piglet stock is priced at $50 a share.
   a. Suppose that you had to make a now-or-never decision on whether to convert or to stay with the bond. Which would you do?
   b. If the convertible bond is priced at $550, how much are investors paying for the option to buy Piglet shares?
   c. If after one year the value of the conversion option is unchanged, what is the value of the convertible bond?
7. Iota Microsystems' 10 percent convertible is about to mature. The conversion ratio is 27.
   a. What is the conversion price?
   b. The stock price is $47. What is the conversion value?
   c. Should you convert?
8. In each case, state which of the two securities is likely to provide the higher return:
   a. When the stock price rises (stock *or* convertible bond?).
   b. When interest rates fall (straight bond *or* convertible bond?).
   c. When the specific risk of the stock decreases (straight bond *or* convertible bond?).
   d. When the dividend on the stock increases (stock *or* convertible bond?).
9. In 1996 Marriott International made an issue of LYONS. The bond matured in 2011, had a zero coupon, and was issued at $532.15. It could be converted into 8.76 shares. Beginning in 1999 the bonds could be called by Marriott. The call price was $603.71 in 1999 and increased by 4.3 percent a year thereafter. Holders had an option to put the bond back to Marriott in 1999 at $603.71 and in 2006 at $810.36. At the time of issue the price of the common stock was about $50.50.
   a. What was the yield to maturity on the bond?
   b. Assuming that comparable nonconvertible bonds yielded 10 percent, how much were investors paying for the conversion option?
   c. What was the conversion value of the bonds at the time of issue?
   d. What was the initial conversion price of the bonds?
   e. What is the conversion price in 2005? Why does it change?
   f. If the price of the bond in 2006 is less than $810.36, would you put the bond back to Marriott?
   g. At what price can Marriott call the bonds in 2006? If the price of the bond in 2006 is more than this, should Marriott call them?
10. "The company's decision to issue warrants should depend on the management's forecast of likely returns on the stock." Do you agree?
11. If the riskiness of the firm's assets increases, does the value of its convertible rise or fall, or can't you say?
12. Financing with convertible debt is especially appropriate for small, rapidly growing, or risky companies. Explain why.
13. The Pork Barrel Company has issued three-year warrants to buy 12 percent perpetual debentures at a price of 120 percent. The current interest rate is 12 percent and the standard deviation of returns on the bond is 20 percent. Use the Black–Scholes model to obtain a rough estimate of the value of Pork Barrel warrants.

Visit us at www.mhhe.com/bm7e

CHALLENGE QUESTIONS

1. The B.J. Services warrant is described in Section 23.1. How would you use the Black–Scholes formula to compute the value of the warrant immediately after its issue, assuming a stock price of $19 and a warrant price of $5? Begin by ignoring the problem of dilution. Then go on to describe how dilution would affect your calculations.

2. Here is a question about dilution. The Electric Bassoon Company has outstanding 2,000 shares with a total market value of $20,000 *plus* 1,000 warrants with a total market value of $5,000. Each warrant gives its holder the option to buy one share at $20.
   a. To value the warrants, you first need to value a call option on an alternative share. How might you calculate its standard deviation?
   b. Suppose that the value of a call option on this alternative share was $6. Calculate whether the Electric Bassoon warrants were undervalued or overvalued.
3. This question illustrates that when there is scope for the firm to vary its risk, lenders may be more prepared to lend if they are offered a piece of the action through the issue of a convertible bond.

   Ms. Blavatsky is proposing to form a new start-up firm with initial assets of $10 million. She can invest this money in one of two projects. Each has the same expected payoff, but one has more risk than the other. The relatively safe project offers a 40 percent chance of a $12.5 million payoff and a 60 percent chance of an $8 million payoff. The risky project offers a 40 percent chance of a $20 million payoff and a 60 percent chance of a $5 million payoff.

   Ms. Blavatsky initially proposes to finance the firm by an issue of straight debt with a promised payoff of $7 million. Ms. Blavatsky will receive any remaining payoff. Show the possible payoffs to the lender and to Ms. Blavatsky if (a) she chooses the safe project and (b) she chooses the risky project. Which project is Ms. Blavatsky likely to choose? Which will the lender want her to choose?

   Suppose now that Ms. Blavatsky offers to make the debt convertible into 50 percent of the value of the firm. Show that in this case the lender receives the same expected payoff from the two projects.
4. Occasionally it is said that issuing convertible bonds is better than issuing stock when the firm's shares are undervalued. Suppose that the financial manager of the Butternut Furniture Company does have inside information indicating that the Butternut stock price is too low. Butternut's future earnings will in fact be higher than investors expect. Suppose further that the inside information cannot be released without giving away a valuable competitive secret. Clearly, selling shares at the present low price would harm Butternut's existing shareholders. Will they also lose if convertible bonds are issued? If they do lose in this case, is the loss more or less than it would be if common stock were issued?

   Now suppose that investors forecast earnings accurately, but still undervalue the stock because they overestimate Butternut's actual business risk. Does this change your answers to the questions posed in the preceding paragraph? Explain.

MINI-CASE

The Shocking Demise of Mr. Thorndike

It was one of Morse's most puzzling cases. That morning Rupert Thorndike, the autocratic CEO of Thorndike Oil, was found dead in a pool of blood on his bedroom floor. He had been shot through the head, but the door and windows were bolted on the inside and there was no sign of the murder weapon.

Morse looked in vain for clues in Thorndike's office. He had to take another tack. He decided to investigate the financial circumstances surrounding Thorndike's demise.

The company's capital structure was as follows:

- *Debt:* $200 million face value. The bonds had a coupon of 5 percent, matured in 10 years, and offered a yield of 12 percent (the risk-free interest rate was 6 percent).

- *Stock:* 36 million shares, which closed at $10 per share on the day before the murder. The company had just announced a regular quarterly dividend of $.10 per share, and the shares were due to go ex-dividend in two weeks.
- *Warrants:* Warrants to buy an additional four million shares at $10 per share, expiring in three months time on December 31, 2003. The recent volatility of the shares had been around 50 percent per annum.

Yesterday Thorndike had flatly rejected an offer by T. Spoone Dickens to buy all Thorndike's assets for $1 billion cash, effective January 1, 2004. With Thorndike out of the way, it appeared that Dickens's offer would be accepted, much to the profit of Thorndike Oil's other shareholders.[26]

Thorndike's two nieces, Doris and Patsy, and his nephew John all had substantial investments in Thorndike Oil and had bitterly disagreed with Thorndike's dismissal of Dickens's offer. Their stakes are shown in the table below.

All debt issued by Thorndike Oil would be paid off at face value if Dickens's offer went through.

Morse kept coming back to the problem of motive. Which niece or nephew, he wondered, stood to gain most by eliminating Thorndike and allowing Dickens's offer to succeed?

	Debt (Face Value)	Stock (Number of Shares, in Millions)	Warrants (Number, in Millions)
Doris	$6 million	1.0	0
John	0	.5	2
Patsy	0	1.5	1

Questions

Help Morse by answering the following questions:

1. Value the company's debt, stock, and warrants both before and after Mr. Thorndike's death.
2. Which of Thorndike's relatives stood to gain most from his death?

[26]Rupert Thorndike's shares would go to a charitable foundation formed to "advance the study of financial engineering and its crucial role in world peace and progress." The managers of the foundation's endowment were not expected to oppose the takeover.

PART SIX RELATED WEBSITES

The Chicago Board site contains explanations of options markets and lots of data:

www.cboe.com

There are a number of good options sites, many of which provide data and calculators for Black–Scholes values and implied standard deviations:

www.cfo.com

www.fintools.net/options/optcalc.html *(very good calculators)*

www.numa.com

www.optionscentral.com

www.pcquote.com/options

www.pmpublishing.com *(includes historical implied volatilities)*

www.schaffersresearch.com/stock/calculator.asp

Two sites devoted to real options are:

www.real-options.com

www.puc-rio.br/marco.ind

Examples of journals specializing in options and other derivatives include:

www.appliederivatives.com

www.erivativesreview.com

www.futuresmag.com

www.risk.com

PART SEVEN

DEBT FINANCING

FALLING STOCK PRICES and low interest rates made 2001 a boom year for company borrowing. The largest issue was a record-breaking $11.9 billion issue by WorldCom. This involved bonds with different maturities.[1] The 3-year bonds paid interest of 6.5 percent, 2.2 percent above the yield on comparable government bonds. The 10-year bonds paid 7.5 percent, 2.4 percent above the government-bond yield, while the 30-year bonds paid 8.25 percent or nearly 2.7 percent above goverment-bond yields.

Why did WorldCom issue 30-year bonds, when the interest rate was lower on 3-year debt? Were the 3-year bonds cheap and the 30-year bonds expensive? And why did the company pay more in interest than the U.S. government? Part Seven first explains how bonds are priced, why short-term interest rates differ from long-term rates, and why companies pay more to borrow than governments.

Companies have an enormous choice in how they borrow. For example, the WorldCom issue pays a fixed interest rate; others pay a variable rate. The WorldCom issue consists of senior unsecured notes; others may be junior or secured. Chapter 25 explains these and other differences.

Finally, Chapter 26 explains leases and shows how they are valued. Leases have many of the characteristics of bonds.

[1]The package also included euro and sterling bonds.

CHAPTER TWENTY-FOUR

VALUING DEBT

HOW DO YOU estimate the present value of a company's bonds? The answer is simple: You take the cash flows and discount them at the opportunity cost of capital. Therefore, if a bond produces cash flows of C dollars per year for N years and is then repaid at its face value ($1,000), the present value is

$$PV = \frac{C}{1 + r_1} + \frac{C}{(1 + r_2)^2} + \cdots + \frac{C}{(1 + r_N)^N} + \frac{\$1{,}000}{(1 + r_N)^N}$$

where $r_1, r_2, \ldots, r_N$ are the appropriate discount rates for the cash flows to be received by the bond owners in periods 1, 2, . . . , N.

That is correct as far as it goes but it does not tell us anything about what *determines* the discount rates. For example,

- In 1945 U.S. Treasury bills offered a return of .4 percent: At their 1981 peak they offered a return of over 17 percent. Why does the same security offer radically different yields at different times?
- In mid-2001 the U.S. Treasury could borrow for one year at an interest rate of 3.4 percent, but it had to pay nearly 6 percent for a 30-year loan. Why do bonds maturing at different dates offer different rates of interest? In other words, why is there a *term structure* of interest rates?
- In mid-2001 the United States government could issue long-term bonds at a rate of nearly 6 percent. But even the most blue-chip corporate issuers had to pay at least 50 basis points (.5 percent) more on their long-term borrowing. What explains the premium that firms have to pay?

These questions lead to deep issues that will keep economists simmering for years. But we can give general answers and at the same time present some fundamental ideas.

Why should the financial manager care about these ideas? Who needs to know how bonds are priced as long as the bond market is active and efficient? Efficient markets protect the ignorant trader. If it is necessary to know whether the price is right for a proposed bond issue, you can check the prices of similar bonds. There is no need to worry about the historical behavior of interest rates, about the term structure, or about the other issues discussed in this chapter.

We do not believe that ignorance is desirable even when it is harmless. At least you ought to be able to read the bond tables in *The Wall Street Journal* and talk to investment bankers about the prices of recently issued bonds. More important, you will encounter many problems of bond pricing where there are no similar instruments already traded. How do you evaluate a private placement with a custom-tailored repayment schedule? How about financial leases? In Chapter 26 we will see that they are essentially debt contracts, but often extremely complicated ones, for which traded bonds are not close substitutes. Many companies, notably banks and insurance firms, are exposed to the risk of interest rate fluctuations. To control their exposure, these companies need to understand how interest rates change.[1] You will find that the terms, concepts, and facts presented in this chapter are essential to the analysis of these and other practical problems.

We start the chapter with our first question: Why does the general level of interest rates change over time? Next we turn to the relationship between short- and long-term interest rates. We consider three issues:

- Each period's cash flow on a bond potentially needs to be discounted at a different interest rate, but bond investors often calculate the yield to maturity as a summary measure of the interest rate on the bond. We first explain how these measures are related.

continued

[1] We discuss in Chapter 27 how firms protect themselves against interest rate risk.

- Second, we show why a change in interest rates has a greater impact on the price of long-term loans than on short-term loans.
- Finally, we look at some theories that explain why short- and long-term interest rates differ.

To close the chapter we shift the focus to corporate bonds and examine the risk of default and its effect on bond prices.

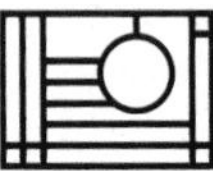

24.1 REAL AND NOMINAL RATES OF INTEREST

Indexed Bonds and the Real Rate of Interest

In Chapter 3 we drew the distinction between the real and nominal rate of interest. Most bonds promise a fixed *nominal* rate of interest. The *real* interest rate that you receive depends on the inflation rate. For example, if a one-year bond promises you a return of 10 percent and the expected inflation rate is 4 percent, the expected real return on your bond is $1.10/1.04 - 1 = .058$, or 5.8 percent. Since future inflation rates are uncertain, the real return on a bond is also uncertain. For example, if inflation turns out to be higher than the expected 4 percent, the real return will be *lower* than 5.8 percent.

You *can* nail down a real return; you do so by buying an indexed bond whose payments are linked to inflation. Indexed bonds have been around in many countries for decades, but they were almost unknown in the United States until 1997 when the U.S. Treasury began to issue inflation-indexed bonds known as TIPs (Treasury Inflation-Protected Securities).[2]

The real cash flows on TIPs are fixed, but the nominal cash flows (interest and principal) are increased as the Consumer Price Index increases. For example, suppose that the U.S. Treasury issues 3 percent 20-year TIPs at a price of 100. If during the first year the Consumer Price Index rises by (say) 10 percent, then the coupon payment on the bond would be increased by 10 percent to $(1.1 \times 3) = 3.3$ percent. And the final payment of principal would also be increased in the same proportion to $(1.1 \times 100) = 110$ percent. Thus, an investor who buys the bond at the issue price and holds it to maturity can be assured of a real yield of 3 percent.

As we write this in the summer of 2001, long-term TIPs offer a yield of 3.46 percent. This yield is a *real* yield: It measures how much extra goods your investment would allow you to buy. The 3.46 percent yield on TIPs was about 2.3 percent less than on nominal Treasury bonds. If the annual inflation rate proves to be higher than 2.3 percent, you will earn a higher return by holding long-term TIPs; if the inflation rate is lower than 2.3 percent, the reverse will be true.

What determines the real interest rate that investors demand? The classical economist's answer to this question is summed up in the title of Irving Fisher's great book: *The Theory of Interest: As Determined by Impatience to Spend Income and Opportunity to Invest It.*[3] The real interest rate, according to Fisher, is the price which equates

[2]In 1988 Franklin Savings Association had issued a 20-year bond whose interest (but not principal) was tied to the rate of inflation. Since then a trickle of companies has also issued indexed bonds.

[3]August M. Kelley, New York, 1965; originally published in 1930.

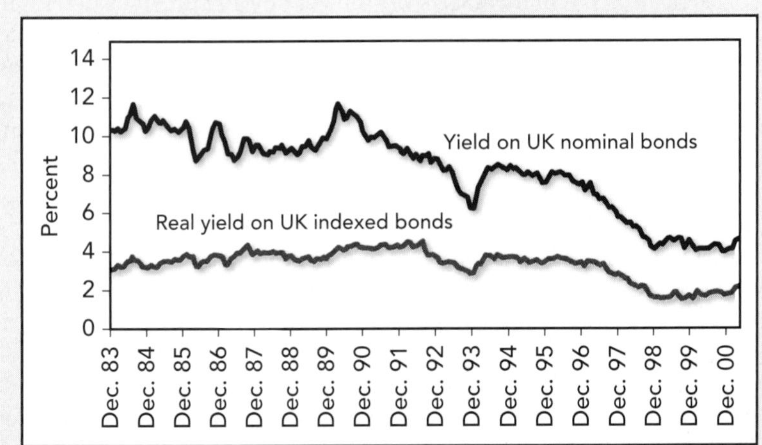

FIGURE 24.1

The burgundy line shows the real yield on long-term indexed bonds issued by the UK government. The blue line shows the yield on UK government long-term nominal bonds. Notice that the real yield has been much more stable than the nominal yield.

the supply and demand for capital. The supply depends on people's willingness to save.[4] The demand depends on the opportunities for productive investment.

For example, suppose that investment opportunities generally improve. Firms have more good projects, so they are willing to invest more than previously at any interest rate. Therefore, the rate has to rise to induce individuals to save the additional amount that firms want to invest.[5] Conversely, if investment opportunities deteriorate, there will be a fall in the real interest rate.

Fisher's theory emphasizes that the required real rate of interest depends on real phenomena. A high aggregate willingness to save may be associated with high aggregate wealth (because wealthy people usually save more), an uneven distribution of wealth (an even distribution would mean fewer rich people, who do most of the saving), and a high proportion of middle-aged people (the young don't need to save and the old don't want to—"You can't take it with you"). Correspondingly, a high propensity to invest may be associated with a high level of industrial activity or major technological advances.

Real interest rates do change but they do so gradually. We can see this by looking at the UK, where the government has issued indexed bonds since 1982. The colored line in Figure 24.1 shows that the (real) yield on these bonds has fluctuated within a relatively narrow range, while the yield on nominal government bonds has declined dramatically.

Inflation and Nominal Interest Rates

Now let us see what Irving Fisher had to say about inflation and interest rates. Suppose that consumers are equally happy with 100 apples today or 105 apples in a year's time. In this case the real or "apple" interest rate is 5 percent. Suppose also

[4]Some of this saving is done indirectly. For example, if you hold 100 shares of GM stock, and GM retains earnings of $1 per share, GM is saving $100 on your behalf.

[5]We assume that investors save more as interest rates rise. It doesn't have to be that way; here is an example of how a higher interest rate could mean *less* saving: Suppose that 20 years hence you will need $50,000 at current prices for your children's college expenses. How much will you have to set aside today to cover this obligation? The answer is the present value of a real expenditure of $50,000 after 20 years, or $50{,}000/(1 + \text{real interest rate})^{20}$. The higher the real interest rate, the lower the present value and the less you have to set aside.

that I know the price of apples will increase over the year by 10 percent. Then I will part with $100 today if I am repaid $115 at the end of the year. That $115 is needed to buy me 5 percent more apples than I can get for my $100 today. In other words, the nominal, or "money," rate of interest must equal the required real, or "apple," rate plus the prospective rate of inflation.[6] A change of 1 percent in the expected inflation rate produces a change of 1 percent in the nominal interest rate. That is Fisher's theory: A change in the expected inflation rate will cause the same change in the *nominal* interest rate; it has no effect on the required real interest rate.[7]

Nominal interest rates cannot be negative; if they were, everyone would prefer to hold cash, which pays zero interest.[8] But what about *real* rates? For example, is it possible for the money rate of interest to be 5 percent and the expected rate of inflation to be 10 percent, thus giving a negative real interest rate? If this happens, you may be able to make money in the following way: You borrow $100 at an interest rate of 5 percent and you use the money to buy apples. You store the apples and sell them at the end of the year for $110, which leaves you enough to pay off your loan plus $5 for yourself.

Since easy ways to make money are rare, we can conclude that if it doesn't cost anything to store goods, the money rate of interest can't be less than the expected rise in prices. But many goods are even more expensive to store than apples, and others can't be stored at all (you can't store haircuts, for example). For these goods, the money interest rate can be less than the expected price rise.

How Well Does Fisher's Theory Explain Interest Rates?

Not all economists would agree with Fisher that the real rate of interest is unaffected by the inflation rate. For example, if changes in prices are associated with changes in the level of industrial activity, then in inflationary conditions I might want more or less than 105 apples in a year's time to compensate me for the loss of 100 today.

We wish we could show you the past behavior of interest rates and *expected* inflation. Instead we have done the next best thing and plotted in Figure 24.2 the return on U.S. Treasury bills against actual inflation. Notice that between 1926 and 1981 the return on Treasury bills was below the inflation rate about as often as it

---

[6]We oversimplify. If apples cost $1.00 apiece today and $1.10 next year, you need 1.10 × 105 = $115.50 next year to buy 105 apples. The money rate of interest is 15.5 percent, not 15. Remember, the exact formula relating real and money rates is

$$1 + r_{\text{money}} = (1 + r_{\text{real}})(1 + i)$$

where i is the expected inflation rate. Thus

$$r_{\text{money}} = r_{\text{real}} + i + i(r_{\text{real}})$$

In our example, the money rate should be

$$r_{\text{money}} = .05 + .10 + .10(.05) = .155$$

When we said the money rate should be 15 percent, we ignored the cross-product term $i\,(r_{\text{real}})$. This is a common rule of thumb because the cross-product term is usually small. But there are countries where i is large (sometimes 100 percent or more). In such cases it pays to use the full formula.

[7]The apple example was taken from R. Roll, "Interest Rates on Monetary Assets and Commodity Price Index Changes," *Journal of Finance* 27 (May 1972), pp. 251–278.

[8]There seems to be an exception to almost every statement. In late 1998 concern about the solvency of some Japanese banks led to a large volume of yen deposits with Western banks. Some of these banks *charged* their customers interest on these deposits; the nominal interest rate was negative.

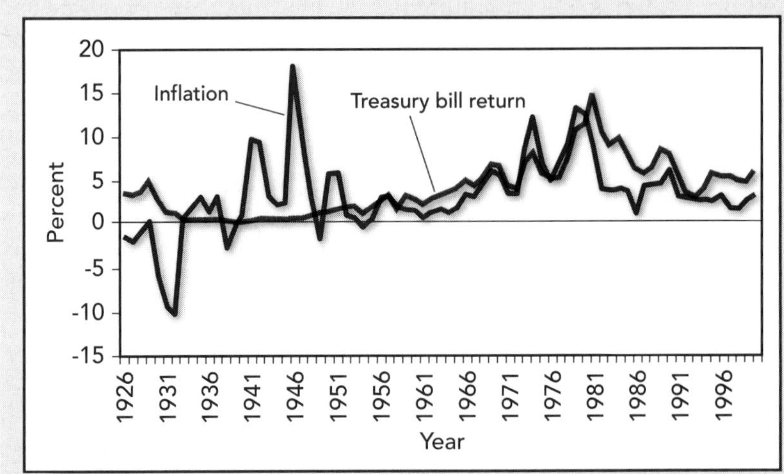

FIGURE 24.2

The return on U.S. Treasury bills and the rate of inflation, 1926–2000.

Source: Ibbotson Associates, Inc., Chicago, 2001.

was above. The average real interest rate during this period was a mere 0.1 percent. Since 1981 the return on bills has been significantly higher than the rate of inflation, so that investors have earned a positive real return on their savings.

Fisher's theory states that changes in anticipated inflation produce corresponding changes in the rate of interest. But Figure 24.2 offers little evidence of this in the 1930s and 1940s. During this period, the return on Treasury bills scarcely changed even though the inflation rate fluctuated sharply. Either these changes in inflation were unanticipated or Fisher's theory was wrong. Since the early 1950s, there appears to have been a closer relationship between interest rates and inflation in the United States.[9] Thus, for today's financial managers Fisher's theory provides a useful rule of thumb. If the expected inflation rate changes, it is a good bet that there will be a corresponding change in the interest rate.

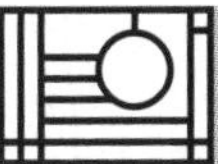

24.2 TERM STRUCTURE AND YIELDS TO MATURITY

We turn now to the relationship between short- and long-term rates of interest. Suppose that we have a simple loan that pays $1 at time 1. The present value of this loan is

$$PV = \frac{1}{1 + r_1}$$

Thus we discount the cash flow at r_1, the rate appropriate for a one-period loan. This rate, which is fixed today, is often called today's one-period **spot rate.**

If we have a loan that pays $1 at both time 1 and time 2, present value is

$$PV = \frac{1}{1 + r_1} + \frac{1}{(1 + r_2)^2}$$

[9]This probably reflects government policy, which before 1951 stabilized nominal interest rates. The 1951 "accord" between the Treasury and the Federal Reserve System permitted more flexible nominal interest rates after 1951.

Thus the first period's cash flow is discounted at today's one-period spot rate and the second period's flow is discounted at today's two-period spot rate. The series of spot rates r_1, r_2, etc., is one way of expressing the **term structure** of interest rates.

Yield to Maturity

Rather than discounting each of the payments at a different rate of interest, we could find a single rate of discount that would produce the same present value. Such a rate is known as the **yield to maturity,** though it is in fact no more than our old acquaintance, the internal rate of return (IRR), masquerading under another name. If we call the yield to maturity y, we can write the present value of the two-year loan as

$$\text{PV} = \frac{1}{1 + y} + \frac{1}{(1 + y)^2}$$

All you need to calculate y is the price of a bond, its annual payment, and its maturity. You can then rapidly work out the yield with the aid of a preprogrammed calculator.

The yield to maturity is unambiguous and easy to calculate. It is also the stock-in-trade of any bond dealer. By now, however, you should have learned to treat any internal rate of return with suspicion.[10] The more closely we examine the yield to maturity, the less informative it is seen to be. Here is an example.

Example. It is 2003. You are contemplating an investment in U.S. Treasury bonds and come across the following quotations for two bonds:[11]

Bond	Price	Yield to Maturity (IRR)
5s of '08	85.21%	8.78%
10s of '08	105.43	8.62

The phrase "5s of '08" refers to a bond maturing in 2008, paying annual interest of 5 percent of the bond's face value. The interest payment is called the *coupon* payment. In continental Europe coupons are usually paid annually; in the United States they are usually paid every six months, so the 5s of '08 would pay 2.5 percent of face value every six months. To simplify the arithmetic, we will pretend throughout this chapter that all coupon payments are annual. When the bonds mature in 2008, bondholders receive the bond's face value in addition to the final interest payment.

The price of each bond is quoted as a percent of face value. Therefore, if face value is $1,000, you would have to pay $852.11 to buy the bond and your yield would be 8.78 percent. Letting 2003 be $t = 0$, 2004 be $t = 1$, etc., we have the following discounted-cash-flow calculation:

	Cash Flows						
Bond	C_0	C_1	C_2	C_3	C_4	C_5	Yield
5s of '08	−852.11	+50	+50	+50	+50	+1,050	8.78%
10s of '08	−1,054.29	+100	+100	+100	+100	+1,100	8.62

[10]See Section 5.3.

[11]The quoted bond price is known as the *flat* (or *clean*) price. The price that the bond buyer pays (sometimes called the *dirty* price) is equal to the flat price *plus* the interest that the seller has already earned on the bond since the last interest payment date. You need to use the flat price to calculate yields to maturity.

		Present Value Calculations			
		5s of '08		10s of '08	
Period	Interest Rate	C_t	PV at r_t	C_t	PV at r_t
t = 1	$r_1 = .05$	$ 50	$ 47.62	$ 100	$ 95.24
t = 2	$r_2 = .06$	50	44.50	100	89.00
t = 3	$r_3 = .07$	50	40.81	100	81.63
t = 4	$r_4 = .08$	50	36.75	100	73.50
t = 5	$r_5 = .09$	1,050	682.43	1,100	714.92
	Totals		$852.11		$1,054.29

TABLE 24.1

Calculating present value of two bonds when long-term interest rates are higher than short-term rates.

Although the two bonds mature at the same date, they presumably were issued at different times—the 5s when interest rates were low and the 10s when interest rates were high.

Are the 5s of '08 a better buy? Is the market making a mistake by pricing these two issues at different yields? The only way you will know for sure is to calculate the bonds' present values by using spot rates of interest: r_1 for 2004, r_2 for 2005, etc. This is done in Table 24.1.

The important assumption in Table 24.1 is that long-term interest rates are higher than short-term interest rates. We have assumed that the one-year interest rate is $r_1 = .05$, the two-year rate is $r_2 = .06$, and so on. When each year's cash flow is discounted at the rate appropriate to that year, we see that each bond's present value is exactly equal to the quoted price. Thus each bond is fairly priced.

Why do the 5s have a higher yield? Because for each dollar that you invest in the 5s you receive relatively little cash inflow in the first four years and a relatively high cash inflow in the final year. Therefore, although the two bonds have identical maturity dates, the 5s provide a greater proportion of their cash flows in 2008. In this sense the 5s are a longer-term investment than the 10s. Their higher yield to maturity just reflects the fact that long-term interest rates are higher than short-term rates.

Notice why the yield to maturity can be misleading. When the yield is calculated, the *same* rate is used to discount *all* payments on the bond. But in our example bondholders actually demanded different rates of return (r_1, r_2, etc.) for cash flows that occurred at different times. Since the cash flows on the two bonds were not identical, the bonds had different yields to maturity. Therefore, the yield to maturity on the 5s of '08 offered only a rough guide to the appropriate yield on the 10s of '08.[12]

Measuring the Term Structure

Financial managers who just want a quick, summary measure of interest rates look in the financial press at the yields to maturity on government bonds. Thus managers will make broad generalizations such as "If we borrow money today, we will have to pay an interest rate of 8 percent." But if you wish to understand why different

[12]For a good analysis of the relationship between the yield to maturity and spot interest rates, see S. M. Schaefer, "The Problem with Redemption Yields," *Financial Analysts Journal* 33 (July–August 1977), pp. 59–67.

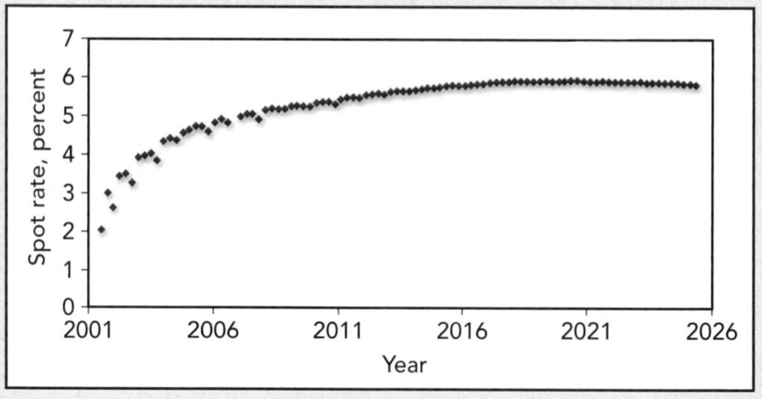

FIGURE 24.3

Spot rates on U.S. Treasury strips, June 2001.

bonds sell at different prices, you must dig deeper and look at the separate interest rates for one-year cash flows, for two-year cash flows, and so on. In other words, you must look at the spot rates of interest.

To find the spot interest rate, you need the price of a bond that simply makes one future payment. Fortunately, such bonds do exist. They are known as *stripped bonds* or *strips.* Strips originated in 1982 when several investment bankers came up with a novel idea. They bought U.S. Treasury bonds and reissued their own separate mini-bonds, each of which made only one payment. The idea proved to be popular with investors, who welcomed the opportunity to buy the mini-bonds rather than the complete package. If you've got a smart idea, you can be sure that others will soon clamber onto your bandwagon. It was therefore not long before the Treasury issued its own mini-bonds.[13] The prices of these bonds are shown each day in the daily press. For example, in the summer of 2001, a strip maturing in May 2021 cost $316.55 and 20 years later will give the investors a single payment of $1,000. Thus the 20-year spot rate was $(1000/316.55)^{1/20} - 1 = .0592$, or 5.92 percent.[14]

In Figure 24.3 we have used the prices of strips with different maturities to plot the term structure of spot rates from 1 to 24 years. You can see that investors required an interest rate of 3.4 percent from a bond that made a payment only at the end of one year and a rate of 5.8 percent from a bond that paid off only in year 2025.

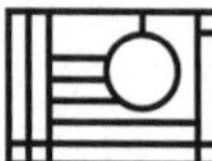

24.3 HOW INTEREST RATE CHANGES AFFECT BOND PRICES

Duration and Bond Volatility

In Chapter 7 we reviewed the historical performance of different security classes. We showed that since 1926 long-term government bonds have provided a higher average return than short-term bills, but have also been more variable. The stan-

[13]The Treasury continued to auction coupon bonds in the normal way, but investors could exchange them at the Federal Reserve Bank for stripped bonds.

[14]This is an annually compounded rate. The yields quoted by investment dealers are semiannually compounded rates.

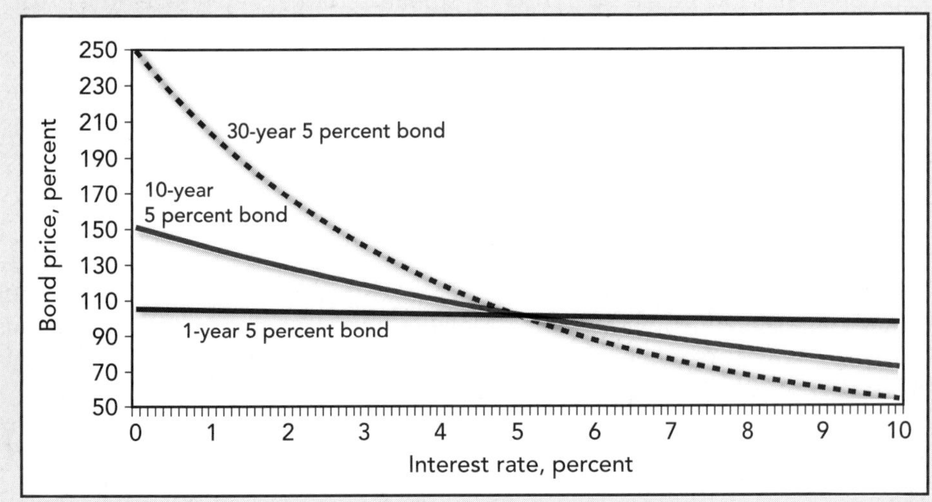

FIGURE 24.4

How bond prices change as interest rates change. Note that longer-term bonds are more sensitive to interest rate changes.

TABLE 24.2

The first four columns show that the cash flow in year 5 accounts for only 77.5 percent of the present value of the 6 7/8s of 2006. The final column shows how to calculate a weighted average of the time to each cash flow. This average is the bond's duration.

Year	C_t	PV(C_t) at 4.9%	Proportion of Total Value [PV(C_t)/V]	Proportion of Total Value × Time
1	68.75	65.54	0.060	0.060
2	68.75	62.48	0.058	0.115
3	68.75	59.56	0.055	0.165
4	68.75	56.78	0.052	0.209
5	1068.75	841.39	0.775	3.875
		V = 1085.74	1.000	Duration = 4.424 years

dard deviation of annual returns on a portfolio of long-term bonds was 9.4 percent compared with a standard deviation of 3.2 percent for bills.

Figure 24.4 illustrates why long-term bonds are more variable. Each line shows how the price of a 5-percent bond changes with the level of interest rates. You can see that the price of a longer-term bond is more sensitive to interest rate fluctuations than that of a shorter bond.

But what do we mean by long-term and short-term bonds? It is obvious in the case of strips that make payments in only one year. However, a coupon bond that matures in year 10 makes payments in *each* of years 1 through 10. Therefore, it is somewhat misleading to describe the bond as a 10-year bond; the average time to each cash flow is less than 10 years.

Consider the Treasury 6 7/8s of 2006. In mid-2001 these bonds had a present value of 108.57 percent of face value and yielded 4.9 percent. The third and fourth columns in Table 24.2 show where this present value comes from. Notice that the cash flow in year 5 accounts for only 77.5 percent of the bond's value. The remaining 22.5 percent of the value comes from the earlier cash flows.

Bond analysts often use the term **duration** to describe the average time to each payment. If we call the total value of the bond V, then duration is calculated as follows:[15]

$$\text{Duration} = \frac{[1 \times \text{PV}(C_1)]}{V} + \frac{[2 \times \text{PV}(C_2)]}{V} + \frac{[3 \times \text{PV}(C_3)]}{V} + \cdots$$

For the 6 7/8s of 2006,

$$\text{Duration} = (1 \times .060) + (2 \times .058) + (3 \times .055) + \cdots = 4.424 \text{ years}$$

The Treasury 4 5/8s of 2006 have the same maturity as the 6 7/8s, but the first four years' coupon payments account for a smaller fraction of the bond's value. In this sense the 4 5/8s are longer bonds than the 6 7/8s. The duration of the 4 5/8s is 4.574 years.

Consider now what happens to the prices of our two bonds as interest rates change:

	6 7/8s of 2006		4 5/8s of 2006	
	New Price	**Change**	**New Price**	**Change**
Yield falls .5%	1108.96	+2.14%	1009.91	+2.21%
Yield rises .5%	1063.16	−2.08%	966.81	−2.15%
Difference		4.22%		4.36%

Thus, a 1 percentage-point variation in yield causes the price of the 6 7/8s to change by 4.22 percent. We can say that the 6 7/8s have a **volatility** of 4.22 percent, while the 4 5/8s have a volatility of 4.36 percent.

Notice that the 4 5/8 percent bonds have the greater volatility and that they also have the longer duration. In fact, a bond's volatility is directly related to its duration:[16]

$$\text{Volatility (percent)} = \frac{\text{duration}}{1 + \text{yield}}$$

In the case of the 6 7/8s,

$$\text{Volatility (percent)} = \frac{4.424}{1.049} = 4.22$$

In Figure 24.4 we showed how bond prices vary with the level of interest rates. Each bond's volatility is simply the slope of the line relating the bond price to the interest rate. You can see this more clearly in Figure 24.5, where the convex curve shows the price of the 5 percent 30-year bond for different interest rates. The bond's volatility is measured by the slope of a tangent to this curve. For example, the dotted line in the figure shows that, if the interest rate is 5 percent, the curve has a slope of 15.4. At this point the change in bond price is 15.4 times a change in the interest rate. Notice that the bond's volatility changes as the interest rate changes. Volatility is higher at lower interest rates (the curve is steeper), and it is lower at higher rates (the curve is flatter).

[15]This measure is also known as *Macaulay duration* after its inventor. See F. Macaulay, *Some Theoretical Problems Suggested by the Movements of Interest Rates, Bond Yields, and Stock Prices in the United States since 1856,* National Bureau of Economic Research, New York, 1938.

[16]For this reason volatility is also called *modified duration.*

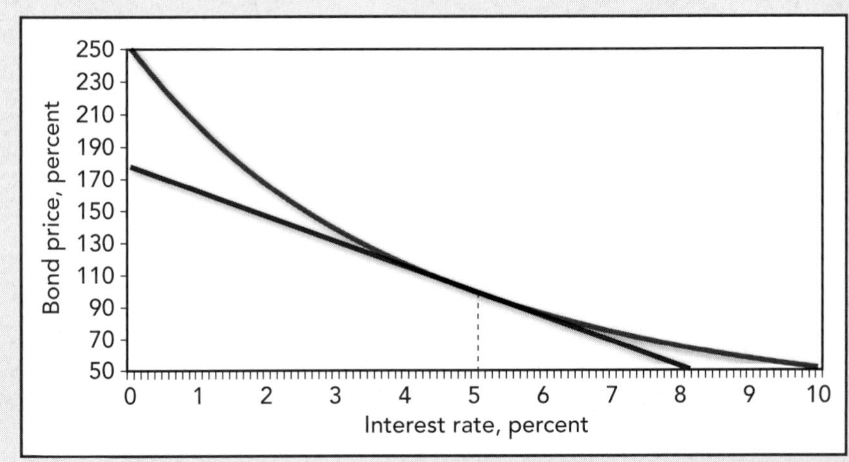

FIGURE 24.5

Volatility is the slope of the curve relating the bond price to the interest rate. For example, a 5 percent 30-year bond has a volatility of 15.4 when the interest rate is 5 percent. At this point the change in price is 15.4 times the change in the interest rate. Its volatility is higher at lower interest rates (the curve is steeper) and lower at higher rates (the curve is flatter).

Managing Interest Rate Risk

Volatility is a useful, summary measure of the likely effect of a change in interest rates on the value of a bond. The longer a bond's duration, the greater is its volatility. In Chapter 27 we will make use of this relationship between duration and volatility to describe how firms can protect themselves against interest rate changes. Here is an example that should give you a flavor of things to come.

Suppose your firm has promised to make pension payments to retired employees. The discounted value of these pension payments is $1 million; therefore, the firm puts aside $1 million in the pension fund and invests the money in government bonds. So the firm has a liability of $1 million and (through the pension fund) an offsetting asset of $1 million. But, as interest rates fluctuate, the value of the pension liability will change and so will the value of the bonds in the pension fund. How can the firm ensure that the value of the bonds in the fund is always sufficient to meet the liabilities? Answer: By making sure that the duration of the bonds is always the same as the duration of the pension liability.

A Cautionary Note

Bond volatility measures the effect on bond prices of a shift in interest rates. For example, we calculated that the 6 7/8s had a volatility of 4.22. This means a 1 percentage-point change in interest rates leads to a 4.22 percent change in bond price:

$$\text{Change in bond price} = 4.22 \times \text{change in interest rates}$$

This relationship is sometimes called a *one-factor model* of bond returns; it tells us how each bond's price changes in response to one factor—a change in the overall level of interest rates. One-factor models have proved very useful in helping firms to understand how they are affected by interest-rate changes and how they can protect themselves against these risks.

If the yields on all Treasury bonds moved in precise lockstep, then changes in the price of each bond would be exactly proportional to the bond's duration. For example, the price of a long-term bond with a duration of 20 years would always rise or fall twice as much as the price of a medium-term bond with a duration of 10 years. However, Figure 24.6 illustrates that short- and long-term interest rates do

FIGURE 24.6

Short-term and long-term interest rates do not always move in parallel. Between September 1992 and April 2000 short-term rates rose sharply while long-term rates declined.

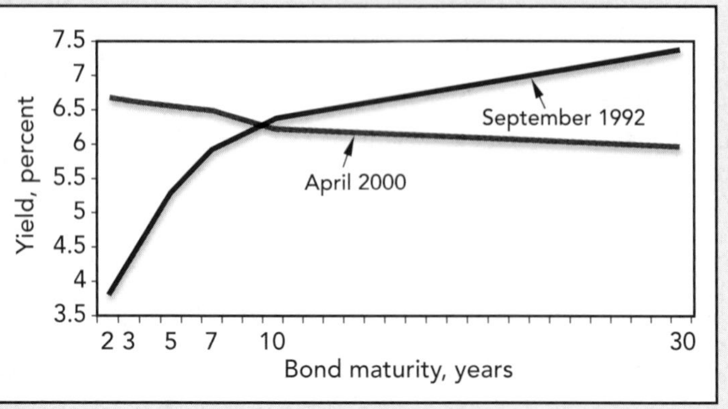

not always move in perfect unison. Between 1992 and 2000 short-term interest rates nearly doubled while long-term rates declined. As a result, the term structure, which initially sloped steeply upward, shifted to a downward slope. Because short- and long-term yields do not move in parallel, one-factor models cannot be the whole story, and managers need to worry not just about the risks of an overall change in interest rates but also about shifts in the term structure.

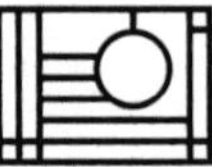

24.4 EXPLAINING THE TERM STRUCTURE

The term structure that we showed in Figure 24.3 was upward-sloping. In other words, long rates of interest are higher than short rates. This is the more common pattern but sometimes it is the other way around, with short rates higher than long rates. Why do we get these shifts in term structure?

Let us look at a simple example. Figure 24.3 showed that in the summer of 2001 the one-year spot rate (r_1) was about 3.5 percent. The two-year spot rate (r_2) was higher at 4 percent. Suppose that in 2001 you invest in a one-year U.S. Treasury strip. You would earn the one-year spot rate of interest and by the end of the year each dollar that you invested would have grown to $\$(1 + r_1) = \$1.035$. If instead you were prepared to invest for two years, you would earn the two-year spot rate of r_2 and by the end of the two years each dollar would have grown to $\$(1 + r_2)^2 = \$1.04^2 = \$1.0816$. By keeping your money invested for a further year, your savings grow from \$1.0350 to \$1.0816, an increase of 4.5 percent. This extra 4.5 percent that you earn by keeping your money invested for two years rather than one is termed the **forward interest rate** or f_2.

Notice how we calculated the forward rate. When you invest for one year, each dollar grows to $\$(1 + r_1)$. When you invest for two years, each dollar grows to $\$(1 + r_2)^2$. Therefore, the extra return that you earn for that second year is $f_2 = (1 + r_2)^2/(1 + r_1) - 1$. In our example,

$$f_2 = (1 + r_2)^2/(1 + r_1) - 1 = (1.04)^2/(1.035) - 1 = .045, \text{ or } 4.5\%$$

If you twist this equation around, you obtain an expression for the two-year spot rate, r_2, in terms of the one-year spot rate, r_1, and the forward rate, f_2:

$$(1 + r_2)^2 = (1 + r_1) \times (1 + f_2)$$

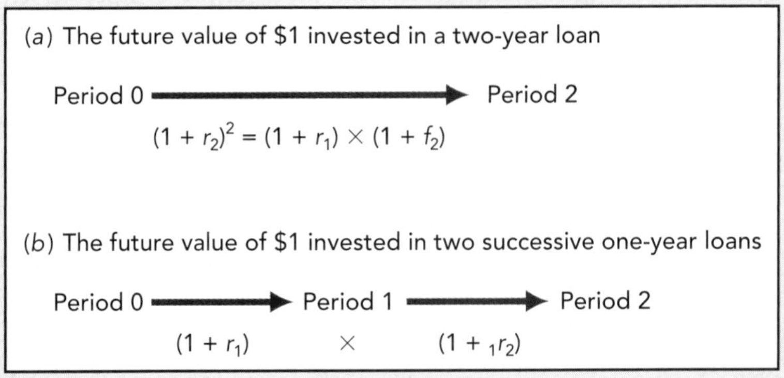

(*a*) The future value of $1 invested in a two-year loan

Period 0 → Period 2

$(1 + r_2)^2 = (1 + r_1) \times (1 + f_2)$

(*b*) The future value of $1 invested in two successive one-year loans

Period 0 → Period 1 → Period 2

$(1 + r_1) \quad \times \quad (1 + {}_1r_2)$

FIGURE 24.7

An investor can invest either in a two-year loan [*a*] or in two successive one-year loans [*b*]. The expectations theory says that in equilibrium the expected payoffs from these two strategies must be equal. In other words, the forward rate, f_2, must equal the expected spot rate, ${}_1r_2$.

In other words, you can think of the two-year investment as earning the one-year spot rate for the first year and the extra return, or forward rate, for the second year.

The Expectations Theory

Would you have been happy in the summer of 2001 to earn an extra 4.5 percent for investing for two years rather than one? The answer depends on how you expected interest rates to change over the coming year. Suppose, for example, that you were confident that interest rates would rise sharply, so that at the end of the year the one-year rate would be 5 percent. In that case rather than investing in a two-year bond and earning the extra 4.5 percent for the second year, you would do better to invest in a one-year bond and, when that matured, to reinvest the money for a further year at 5 percent. If other investors shared your view, no one would be prepared to hold the two-year bond and its price would fall. It would stop falling only when the extra return from holding the two-year bond equalled the expected future one-year rate. Let us call this expected rate ${}_1r_2$—that is, the spot rate of interest at year 1 on a loan maturing at the end of year 2.[17] Figure 24.7 shows that at that point investors would earn the same expected return from investing in a two-year loan as from investing in two successive one-year loans.

This is known as the **expectations theory** of term structure.[18] It states that in equilibrium the forward interest rate, f_2, must equal the expected one-year spot rate, ${}_1r_2$. The expectations theory implies that the *only* reason for an upward-sloping term structure, such as existed in the summer of 2001, is that investors expect short-term interest rates to rise; the *only* reason for a declining term structure is that investors expect short-term rates to fall.[19] The expectations theory also implies that investing in a succession of short-term bonds gives exactly the same expected return as investing in long-term bonds.

If short-term interest rates are significantly lower than long-term rates, it is often tempting to borrow short-term rather than long-term. The expectations theory

[17]Be careful to distinguish ${}_1r_2$ from r_2, the spot interest rate on a two-year bond held from time 0 to time 2. The quantity ${}_1r_2$ is a one-year spot rate established at time 1.

[18]The expectations theory is usually attributed to Lutz and Lutz. See F. A. Lutz and V. C. Lutz, *The Theory of Investment in the Firm*, Princeton University Press, Princeton, NJ, 1951.

[19]This follows from our example. If the two-year spot rate, r_2, exceeds the one-year rate, r_1, then the forward rate, f_2, also exceeds r_1. If the forward rate equals the expected spot rate, ${}_1r_2$ then ${}_1r_2$ must also exceed r_1. The converse is likewise true.

implies that such naïve strategies won't work. If short rates are lower than long rates, then investors must be expecting interest rates to rise. When the term structure is upward-sloping, you are likely to make money by borrowing short only if investors are *overestimating* future increases in interest rates.

Even on a casual glance the expectations theory does not seem to be the complete explanation of term structure. For example, if we look back over the period 1926–2000, we find that the return on long-term U.S. Treasury bonds was on average 1.9 percent higher than the return on short-term Treasury bills. Perhaps short-term interest rates did not go up as much as investors expected, but it seems more likely that investors wanted a higher expected return for holding long bonds and that on the average they got it. If so, the expectations theory is wrong.

The expectations theory has few strict adherents, but most economists believe that expectations about future interest rates have an important effect on term structure. For example, the expectations theory implies that if the forward rate of interest is 1 percent above the spot rate of interest, then your best estimate is that the spot rate of interest will rise by 1 percent. In a study of the U.S. Treasury bill market between 1959 and 1982, Eugene Fama found that a forward premium *does* on average precede a rise in the spot rate but the rise is less than the expectations theory would predict.[20]

The Liquidity-Preference Theory

What does the expectations theory leave out? The most obvious answer is "risk." If you are confident about the future level of interest rates, you will simply choose the strategy that offers the highest return. But, if you are not sure of your forecast, you may well opt for the less risky strategy even if it offers a lower expected return.

Remember that the prices of long-duration bonds are more volatile than those of short-term bonds. For some investors this extra volatility may not be a concern. For example, pension funds and life insurance companies with long-term liabilities may prefer to lock in future returns by investing in long-term bonds. However, the volatility of long-term bonds *does* create extra risk for investors who do not have such long-term fixed obligations.

Here we have the basis for the **liquidity-preference** theory of the term structure.[21] If investors incur extra risk from holding long-term bonds, they will demand the compensation of a higher expected return. In this case the forward rate must be higher than the expected spot rate. This difference between the forward rate and the expected spot rate is usually called the **liquidity premium.** If the liquidity-preference theory is right, the term structure should be upward-sloping more often than not. Of course, if future spot rates are expected to fall, the term structure could be downward-sloping and *still* reward investors for lending long. But the liquidity-preference theory would predict a less dramatic downward slope than the expectations theory.

[20]See E. F. Fama, "The Information in the Term Structure," *Journal of Financial Economics* 13 (December 1984), pp. 509–528. Evidence from the Treasury bond market that the forward premium has some power to predict changes in spot rates is provided in J. Y. Campbell, A. W. Lo, and A. C. MacKinlay, *The Econometrics of Financial Markets,* Princeton University Press, Princeton, NJ, 1997, pp. 421–422.

[21]The liquidity-preference hypothesis is usually attributed to Hicks. See J. R. Hicks, *Value and Capital: An Inquiry into Some Fundamental Principles of Economic Theory,* 2nd ed., Oxford University Press, Oxford, 1946. For a theoretical development, see R. Roll, *The Behavior of Interest Rates: An Application of the Efficient-Market Model to U.S. Treasury Bills,* Basic Books, Inc., New York, 1970.

Introducing Inflation

The money cash flows on a U.S. Treasury bond are certain, but the real cash flows are not. In other words, Treasury bonds are still subject to inflation risk. Let us look therefore at how uncertainty about inflation affects the risk of bonds with different maturities.[22]

Suppose that Irving Fisher is right and short rates of interest always incorporate fully the market's latest views about inflation. Suppose also that the market learns more as time passes about the likely inflation rate in a particular year. Perhaps today investors have only a very hazy idea about inflation in year 2, but in a year's time they expect to be able to make a much better prediction. Since investors expect to learn a good deal about the inflation rate in year 2 from experience in year 1, next year they will be in a much better position to judge the appropriate interest rate in year 2.

You are saving for your retirement. Which of the following strategies is the more risky? Invest in a succession of one-year Treasury bonds or invest in a 20-year bond?

If you buy the 20-year bond, you know what money you will have at the end of 20 years, but you will be making a long-term bet on inflation. Inflation may seem benign now, but who knows what it will be in 10 or 20 years? This uncertainty about inflation makes it more risky for you to fix today the rates at which you will lend in the distant future.

You can reduce this uncertainty by investing in successive short-term bonds. You do not know the interest rate at which you will be able to reinvest your money at the end of each year, but at least you know that it will incorporate the latest information about inflation in the coming year. So, if the prospects for inflation deteriorate, it is likely that you will be able to reinvest your money at a higher interest rate.

Inflation uncertainty may help to explain why long-term bonds provide a liquidity premium. If inflation creates additional risks for long-term lenders, borrowers must offer some incentive if they want investors to lend long. Therefore, the forward rate of interest f_2 must be greater than the expected spot rate $E({}_1r_2)$ by an amount that compensates investors for the extra risk of inflation.

Relationships between Bond Returns

These term structure theories tell us how bond prices may be determined at a point in time. More recently, financial economists have proposed some important theories of how price *movements* are related. These theories take advantage of the fact that the returns on bonds with different maturities tend to move together. For example, if short-term interest rates are high, it is a good bet that long-term rates will also be high. If short-term rates fall, long-term rates usually keep them company. Such linkages between interest rate movements can tell us something about relationships between bond prices.

The models that bond traders use to exploit these relationships can be quite complex and we can't get deeply into the subject here. However, the following example will give you a flavor of how the models work.

Suppose that you can invest in three possible government loans: a three-month Treasury bill, a medium-term bond, and a long-term bond. The return on

[22]See R. A. Brealey and S. M. Schaefer, "Term Structure and Uncertain Inflation," *Journal of Finance* 32 (May 1977), pp. 277–290.

TABLE 24.3

Illustrative payoffs from three government securities. Note the wider range of outcomes from the longer-duration loans. We don't know what the medium-term bond sells for; we need to figure it out from how its value *changes* when interest rates rise or fall.

	Beginning Price	Change in Value: If Interest Rates Rise	Change in Value: If Interest Rates Fall	Ending Value
Treasury bill	98	+2	+2	100
Medium-term bond	?	−6.5	+10	?
Long-term bond	105	−15	+18	90 or 123

the Treasury bill over the next three months is certain; we will assume it yields a 2 percent quarterly rate. The return on each of the other bonds depends on what happens to interest rates. Suppose that you foresee only two possible outcomes—a sharp rise in interest rates or a sharp fall. Table 24.3 summarizes how the prices of the three investments would be affected. Notice that the long-term bond has a longer duration and therefore a wider range of possible outcomes.

Here's the puzzle. You know the price of the Treasury bill and the long-term bond. But can you get rid of the two question marks in Table 24.3 and figure out what the medium-term bond should sell for?

Suppose that you start with \$100. You invest half of this money in the Treasury bill and half in the long-term bond. In this case the change in the value of your portfolio will be $(.5 \times 2) + [.5 \times (-15)] = -\$6.5$ if interest rates rise and $(.5 \times 2) + (.5 \times 18) = +\$10$ if interest rates fall. Thus, regardless of whether interest rates rise or fall, your portfolio will provide exactly the same payoffs as an investment in the medium-term bond. Since the two investments provide identical payoffs, they must sell for the same price or there will be a money machine. So, the value of the medium-term bond must be halfway between the value of a three-month bill and that of the long-term bond, that is, $(98 + 105)/2 = 101.5$. Knowing this, you can calculate what the yield to maturity on the medium-term bond has to be. You can also calculate its value next year, either $101.5 - 6.5 = 95$ or $101.5 + 10 = 111.5$.

Everything now checks; regardless of whether interest rates rise or fall, the medium-term bond will provide the same payoff as the package of Treasury bill and long-term bond and therefore it must cost the same:

	Initial Outlay	Ending Value: If Interest Rates Rise	Ending Value: If Interest Rates Fall
Equal holdings of Treasury bill & long-term bond	$(.5 \times 98) + (.5 \times 105) = 101.5$	$(.5 \times 100) + (.5 \times 90) = 95$	$(.5 \times 100) + (.5 \times 123) = 111.5$
Medium-term bond	101.5	$101.5 - 6.5 = 95$	$101.5 + 10 = 111.5$

Our example is grossly oversimplified, but you have probably already noticed that the basic idea is the same that we used when valuing an option. To value an option on a share, we constructed a portfolio of a risk-free loan and the common stock that would exactly replicate the payoffs from the option. That allowed us to price the option *given* the price of the risk-free loan and the share. Here we value a bond by constructing a portfolio of two or more other bonds that will provide exactly the same payoffs.[23] That allows us to value one bond *given* the prices of the other bonds.

Our example carries three messages. First, bond traders focus on *changes* in bond prices and on how the changes for different bonds are linked. Second, changes in bond prices can be related to a small number of factors (in our example, the change in the overall level of interest rates completely defined the change in the price of each bond). Third, once the linkages between bond prices can be pinned down, then each bond can be priced relative to a package of other bonds.

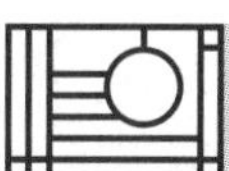

24.5 ALLOWING FOR THE RISK OF DEFAULT

You should by now be familiar with some of the basic ideas about why interest rates change and why short rates may differ from long rates. It only remains to consider our third question: Why do some borrowers have to pay a higher rate of interest than others?

The answer is obvious: Bond prices go down, and interest rates go up, when the probability of default increases. But when we say "interest rates go up," we mean *promised* interest rates. If the borrower defaults, the *actual* interest rate paid to the lender is less than the promised rate. The *expected* interest rate may go up with increasing probability of default, but this is not a logical necessity.

These points can be illustrated by a simple numerical example. Suppose that the interest rate on one-year, *risk-free* bonds is 9 percent. Backwoods Chemical Company has issued 9 percent notes with face values of $1,000, maturing in one year. What will the Backwoods notes sell for?

The answer is easy—if the notes are risk-free, just discount principal ($1,000) and interest ($90) at 9 percent:

$$\text{PV of notes} = \frac{\$1{,}000 + 90}{1.09} = \$1{,}000$$

Suppose instead that there is a 20 percent chance that Backwoods will default and that, if default does occur, holders of its notes receive nothing. In this case, the possible payoffs to the noteholders are

	Payoff	**Probability**
Full payment	$1,090	.8
No payment	0	.2

The expected payment is $.8(\$1,090) + .2(\$0) = \$872$.

We can value the Backwoods notes like any other risky asset, by discounting their expected payoff ($872) at the appropriate opportunity cost of capital. We might discount at the risk-free interest rate (9 percent) if Backwoods's possible default is

[23]Two early examples of models that use no-arbitrage conditions to model the term structure are O. Vasicek, "An Equilibrium Characterization of the Term Structure," *Journal of Financial Economics* 5 (November 1977), pp. 177–188; and J. C. Cox, J. E. Ingersoll, and S. A. Ross, "A Theory of the Term Structure of Interest Rates," *Econometrica* 53 (May 1985), pp. 385–407.

TABLE 24.4

Key to Moody's and Standard and Poor's bond ratings. The highest quality bonds are rated triple-A. Then come double-A bonds, and so on. Investment-grade bonds have to be Baa or higher. Bonds that don't make this cut are called junk bonds.

Moody's Ratings	Standard and Poor's Ratings
Investment-grade:	
Aaa	AAA
Aa	AA
A	A
Baa	BBB
Junk bonds:	
Ba	BB
B	B
Caa	CCC
Ca	CC
C	C

totally unrelated to other events in the economy. In this case the default risk is wholly diversifiable, and the beta of the notes is zero. The notes would sell for

$$\text{PV of notes} = \frac{\$872}{1.09} = \$800$$

An investor who purchased these notes for $800 would receive a *promised* yield of about 36 percent:

$$\text{Promised yield} = \frac{\$1{,}090}{\$800} - 1 = .363$$

That is, an investor who purchased the notes for $800 would earn a 36.3 percent rate of return if Backwoods does not default. Bond traders therefore might say that the Backwoods notes "yield 36 percent." But the smart investor would realize that the notes' *expected* yield is only 9 percent, the same as on risk-free bonds.

This of course assumes that risk of default with these notes is wholly diversifiable, so that they have no market risk. In general, risky bonds do have market risk (that is, positive betas) because default is more likely to occur in recessions when all businesses are doing poorly. Suppose that investors demand a 2 percent risk premium and an 11 percent expected rate of return. Then the Backwoods notes will sell for $872/1.11 = \$785.59$ and offer a promised yield of $(1{,}090/785.59) - 1 = .388$, or about 39 percent.

You rarely see traded bonds offering 39 percent yields, although we will soon encounter an example of one company's bonds that had a promised yield of 50 percent.

Bond Ratings

The relative quality of most traded bonds can be judged from bond ratings given by Moody's and Standard and Poor's. Table 24.4 summarizes these ratings. For example, the highest quality bonds are rated triple-A (Aaa) by Moody's, then come double-A (Aa) bonds, and so on. Bonds rated Baa or above are known as *investment-grade* bonds. Commercial banks, many pension funds, and other financial institutions are not allowed to invest in bonds unless they are investment-grade.[24]

[24]Investment-grade bonds can usually be entered at face value on the books of banks and life insurance companies.

Rating at Time of Issue	Percentage Defaulting within 1 Year after Issue	5 Years after Issue	10 Years after Issue
AAA	.0	.1	.1
AA	.0	.7	.7
A	.0	.2	.6
BBB	.0	1.6	2.8
BB	.4	8.3	16.4
B	1.5	22.0	33.0
CCC	2.3	35.4	47.5

TABLE 24.5

Default rates of corporate bonds 1971–1997 by Standard and Poor's rating at date of issue.

Source: R. A. Waldman, E. I. Altman, and A. R. Ginsberg, "Defaults and Returns on High Yield Bonds: Analysis through 1997," Salomon Smith Barney, New York, January 30, 1998.

Bond ratings are judgments about firms' financial and business prospects. There is no fixed formula by which ratings are calculated. Nevertheless, investment bankers, bond portfolio managers, and others who follow the bond market closely can get a fairly good idea of how a bond will be rated by looking at a few key numbers such as the firm's debt–equity ratio, the ratio of earnings to interest, and the return on assets.

Table 24.5 shows that bond ratings do reflect the probability of default. Since 1971 no bond that was initially rated triple-A by Standard and Poor's has defaulted in the year after issue and fewer than one in a thousand has defaulted within 10 years of issue. At the other extreme, over 2 percent of CCC bonds have defaulted in their first year and by year 10 almost half have done so. Of course, bonds rarely fall suddenly from grace. As time passes and the company becomes progressively more shaky, the agencies revise downward the bond's rating to reflect the increasing probability of default.

Since bond ratings reflect the probability of default, it is not surprising that there is also a close correspondence between a bond's rating and its promised yield. For example, in the postwar period the promised yield on Moody's Baa corporate bonds has been on average about .9 percent more than on Aaa's.

Firms and governments, having noticed the link between bond ratings and yields, worry that a reduction in rating will result in higher interest charges.[25] When the Asian currency crisis in 1998 led Moody's to downgrade the Malaysian government's risk rating, the government immediately canceled a much-needed $2 billion bond issue. Investors have a different concern; they worry that the rating agencies are slow to react when businesses are in trouble. When Enron went belly up in 2001, investors protested that only two months earlier the company's debt had an investment-grade rating.

Junk Bonds

Bonds rated below Baa are known as **junk bonds.** Most junk bonds used to be *fallen angels,* that is, bonds of companies that had fallen on hard times. But during the 1980s new issues of junk bonds multiplied tenfold as more and more companies issued large quantities of low-grade debt to finance takeovers or to defend themselves against being taken over.

[25] They almost certainly exaggerate the influence of the rating agencies, which are as much following investor opinion as leading it.

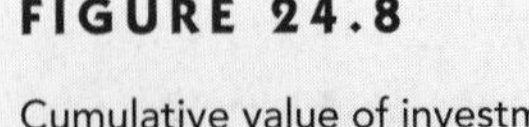

FIGURE 24.8

Cumulative value of investments in junk and Treasury bonds, 1978–2000. The plot assumes investment of $1 in 1977.

Source: E. I. Altman, "High Yield Bond and Default Study," Salomon Smith Barney, July 19, 2001.

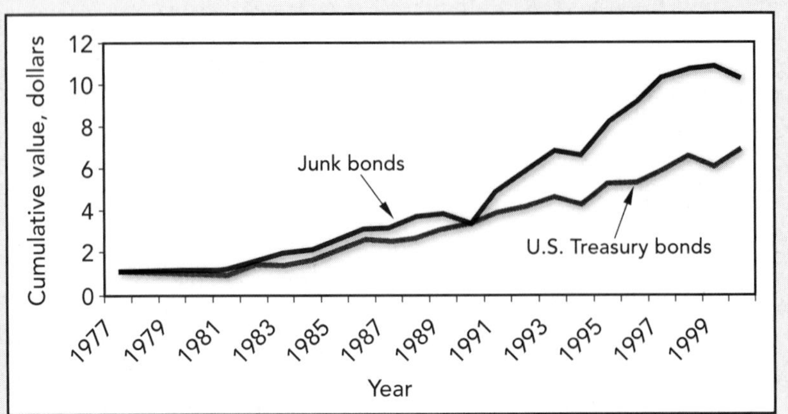

The development of this market for low-grade corporate bonds was largely the brainchild of the investment banking firm Drexel Burnham Lambert. The result was that for the first time corporate midgets were able to take control of corporate giants, because they could finance this activity by issues of debt. However, issuers of junk bonds often had debt ratios of 90 or 95 percent. Many worried that these high levels of leverage resulted in undue risk and pressed for legislation to ban junk bonds.

One of the largest issuers of junk bonds was Campeau Corporation. Between 1986 and 1988 Campeau amassed a huge retailing empire by acquiring major department store chains such as Federated Department Stores and Allied Stores. Unfortunately, it also amassed $10.9 billion in debt, which was supported by just $.9 billion of book equity. So when in September 1989 Campeau announced that it was having difficulties meeting the interest payments on its debt, the junk bond market took a nosedive and worries about the riskiness of junk bonds intensified. Campeau's own bonds fell to the point at which they offered a promised yield of nearly 50 percent. Campeau eventually filed for bankruptcy, and investors with holdings of junk bonds took large losses.

In 1990 and 1991 the default rate for junk bonds climbed to over 10 percent and the market for new issues of these bonds dried up. But later in the decade the market began to boom again and with increasing economic prosperity the annual default rate fell to below 2 percent before rising again in the new millenium.

Junk bonds promise a higher yield than U.S. Treasuries. When junk bonds were out of favor, their yields reached more than 9 percent above that of Treasuries, but the gap has since narrowed. Of course, companies can't always keep their promises. Many junk bonds have defaulted, while some of the more successful issuers have called their bonds, thus depriving their holders of the prospect of a continuing stream of high coupon payments. Figure 24.8 shows the performance since 1977 of a portfolio of junk bonds and 10-year Treasury bonds. On average, the *promised yield* on junk bonds was 4.8 percent higher than that on Treasuries, but the annual *realized return* was only 1.9 percent higher.

Option Pricing and Risky Debt

In Section 20.2 we showed that holding a corporate bond is equivalent to lending money with no chance of default *but* at the same time giving stockholders a put option on the firm's assets. When a firm defaults, its stockholders are in effect exercising their put. The put's value is the value of limited liability—the value of stockholders' right to walk away from their firm's debts in exchange for handing over the firm's assets to its creditors. Thus, valuing bonds should be a two-step process:

$$\text{Bond value} = \begin{array}{c}\text{bond value}\\ \text{assuming no chance}\\ \text{of default}\end{array} - \begin{array}{c}\text{value}\\ \text{of put}\\ \text{option}\end{array}$$

The first step is easy: Calculate the bond's value assuming no default risk. (Discount promised interest and principal payments at the rates offered by Treasury issues.) Second, calculate the value of a put written on the firm's assets, where the maturity of the put equals the maturity of the bond and the exercise price of the put equals the promised payments to bondholders.

Owning a corporate bond is also equivalent to owning the firm's assets *but* giving a call option on these assets to the firm's stockholders:

$$\text{Bond value} = \text{asset value} - \text{value of call option on assets}$$

Thus you can also calculate a bond's value, given the value of the firm's assets, by valuing a call option on these assets and subtracting the call value from the asset value. (The call value is just the value of the firm's common stock.) Therefore, if you can value puts and calls on a firm's assets, you can value its debt.[26]

Figure 24.9 shows a simple application of option theory to pricing corporate debt. It takes a company with average operating risk and shows how the promised interest rate on its debt should vary with its leverage and the maturity of the debt. For example, if the company has a 20 percent debt ratio and all its debt matures in 25 years, then it should pay about one-half percentage point above the government borrowing rate to compensate for default risk. Companies with more leverage ought to pay higher premiums. Notice that at relatively modest levels of leverage, promised yields increase with maturity. This makes sense, for the longer you have to wait for repayment, the greater is the chance that things will go wrong. However, if the company is already in distress and its assets are worth less than the face value of the debt, then promised yields are higher at low maturities. (In our example, they run off the top of the graph for maturities of less than four years.) This also makes sense, for in these cases the longer that you wait, the greater is the chance that the company will recover and avoid default.[27]

Notice that in constructing Figure 24.9 we made several artificial assumptions. One assumption is that the company does not pay dividends. If it does regularly pay out part of its assets to stockholders, there may be substantially fewer assets to protect the bondholder in the event of trouble. In this case, the market may be justified in requiring a higher yield on the company's bonds.

There are other complications that make the valuation of corporate debt and equity a good bit more difficult than it sounds. For example, in constructing Figure 24.9

[26]However, option-valuation procedures cannot value the *assets* of the firm. Puts and calls must be valued as a proportion of asset value. For example, note that the Black–Scholes formula (Section 21.3) requires stock price in order to compute the value of a call option.

[27]Sarig and Warga plot the difference between corporate bond yields and the yield on U.S. Treasuries. They confirm that the yield difference increases with maturity for high-grade bonds and declines for low-grade bonds. See O. Sarig and A. Warga, "Bond Price Data and Bond Market Liquidity," *Journal of Financial and Quantitative Analysis* 44 (1989), pp. 1351–1360. Incidentally, the shape of the curves in Figure 24.9 depends on how leverage is defined. If we had plotted curves for constant ratios of the *market* value of debt to debt plus equity, the curves would all have started at zero.

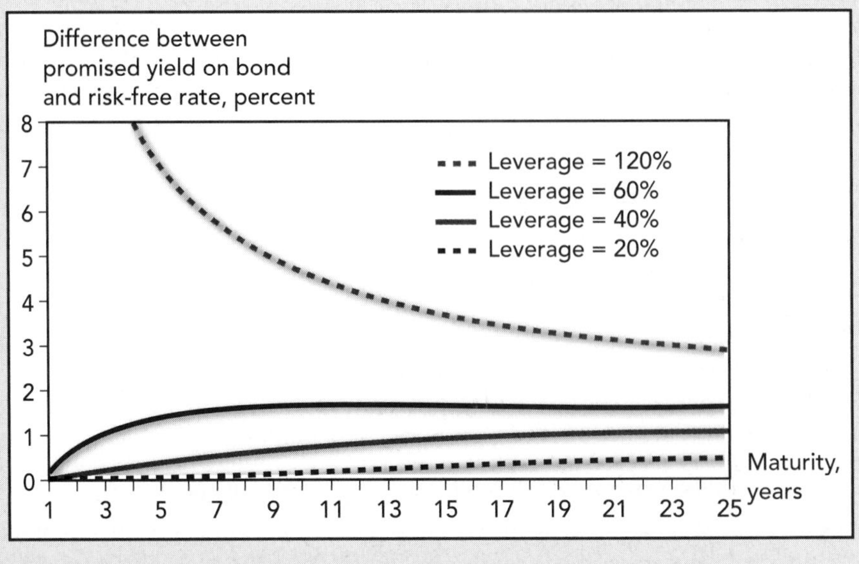

FIGURE 24.9

How the interest rate on risky corporate debt changes with leverage and maturity. These curves are calculated using option pricing theory under the following simplifying assumptions: (1) the risk-free interest rate is constant for all maturities; (2) the standard deviation of the returns on the company's assets is 25 percent per annum; (3) debt is in the form of zero-coupon bonds; and (4) leverage is the ratio $D/(D + E)$, where E is the market value of equity and D is the face value of the debt discounted at the risk-free interest rate.

we assumed that the company made only a single issue of zero-coupon debt. But suppose instead that it issues a 10-year bond which pays interest annually. We can still think of the company's stock as a call option that can be exercised by making the promised payments. But in this case there are 10 payments rather than just 1. To value the stock, we would have to value 10 sequential call options. The first option can be exercised by making the first interest payment when it comes due. By exercise the stockholders obtain a second call option, which can be exercised by making the second interest payment. The reward to exercising is that the stockholders get a third call option, and so on. Finally, in year 10 the stockholders can exercise the tenth option. By paying off both the principal and the last year's interest, the stockholders regain unencumbered ownership of the company's assets.

Of course, if the firm does not make any of these payments when due, bondholders take over and stockholders are left with nothing. In other words, by not exercising one call option, stockholders give up all subsequent call options.

Valuing the equity when the 10-year bond is issued is equivalent to valuing the first of the 10 call options. But you cannot value the first option without valuing the nine that follow.[28] Even this example understates the practical difficulties, because large firms may have dozens of outstanding debt issues with different interest rates and maturities, and before the current debt matures they may make further issues. But do not lose heart. Computers can solve these problems, more or less by brute force, even in the absence of simple, exact valuation formulas.

In practice, interest rate differentials tend to be greater than those shown in Figure 24.9. High-grade corporate bonds typically offer promised yields about 1 percentage point greater than U.S. Treasury bonds. It is very difficult to justify yield

[28]The other approach to valuing the company's debt (subtracting the value of a put option from risk-free bond value) is no easier. The analyst would be confronted by not one simple put but a package of 10 sequential puts.

differentials of this magnitude simply in terms of default risk.[29] So what is going on here? One possibility is that companies are paying too much for their debt, but it seems likely that the high yields on corporate bonds stem in part from some other drawback. One possibility is that investors demand additional yield to compensate for the illiquidity of corporate bonds. There is little doubt that investors prefer bonds that are easily bought and sold. We can even see small yield differences in the Treasury bond market, where the latest bonds to have been issued (known as "on-the-run" bonds) are traded much more heavily and typically yield a few basis points less than more seasoned issues.

Valuing Government Loan Guarantees

In the summer of 1971 Lockheed Corporation was in trouble. It was nearly out of cash after absorbing heavy cost overruns on military contracts and, at the same time, committing more than $800 million[30] to the development of the L1011 TriStar airliner. After months of suspense and controversy, the U.S. government rescued Lockheed by agreeing to guarantee up to $250 million of new bank loans. If Lockheed had defaulted on these loans, the banks could have gotten their money back directly from the government.

From the banks' point of view, these loans were as safe as Treasury notes. Thus, Lockheed was assured of being able to borrow up to $250 million at a favorable rate.[31] This assurance in turn gave Lockheed's banks the confidence to advance the rest of the money the firm needed.

The loan guarantee was a helping hand—a subsidy—to bring Lockheed through a difficult period. What was it worth? What did it cost the government?

This loan guarantee did not turn out to cost the government anything, because Lockheed survived, recovered, and paid off the loans that the government had guaranteed. Does that mean that the value of the guarantee to Lockheed was also zero? Does it mean the government absorbed no risks when it gave the guarantee in 1971, when Lockheed's survival was still uncertain? Of course not. The government absorbed the risk of default. Obviously the banks' loans to Lockheed were worth more with the guarantee than they would have been without it.

The present value of a loan guarantee is the amount lenders would be willing to pay to relieve themselves of all risk of default on an otherwise equivalent unguaranteed loan. It is the difference between the present value of the loan with the guarantee and its present value without the guarantee. A guarantee can clearly have substantial value on a large loan when the chance of default by the firm is high.

It turns out that a loan guarantee can be valued as a put on the firm's assets, where the put's maturity equals the loan's maturity and its exercise price equals the interest and principal payments promised to lenders. We can easily show the equivalence by starting with the definition of the value of the guarantee.

$$\text{Value of guarantee} = \text{value of guaranteed loan} - \text{loan value without the guarantee}$$

[29]See, for example, J. Huang and M. Huang, "How Much of the Corporate-Treasury Yield is Due to Credit Risk? Results from a New Calibration Approach," working paper, Pennsylvania State University, August 2000.

[30]See U. Reinhardt, "Break-Even Analysis for Lockheed's TriStar: An Application of Financial Theory," *Journal of Finance* 28 (September 1973), pp. 821–838.

[31]Lockheed paid the current Treasury bill rate plus a fee of roughly 2 percent to the government.

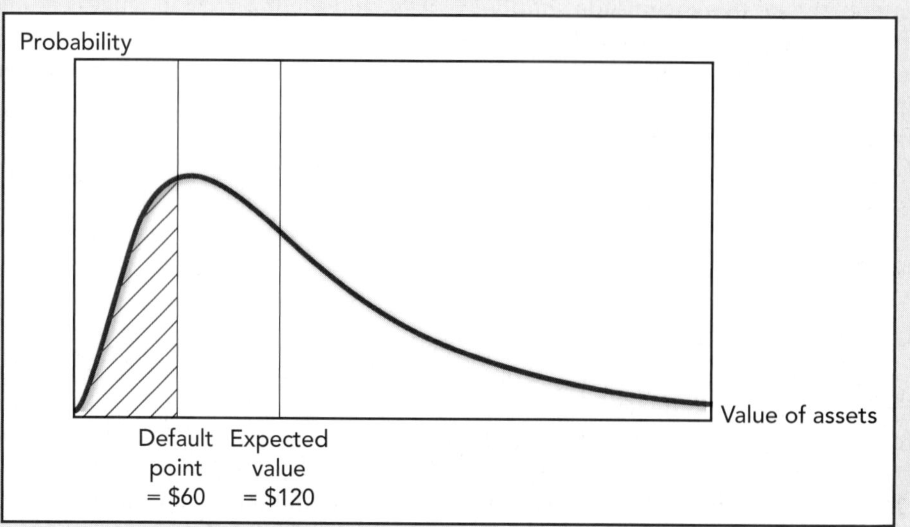

FIGURE 24.10

Backwoods Chemical has issued five-year debt with a face value of $60. The shaded area shows that there is a 20 percent probability that the value of the company's assets in year 5 will be less than $60, in which case the company will choose to default.

Without a guarantee, the loan becomes an ordinary debt obligation of the firm. We know from Section 20.2 that

$$\text{Value of ordinary loan} = \text{value assuming no chance of default} - \text{value of put option}$$

The loan's value, assuming no chance of default, is exactly its guaranteed value; thus, the put value equals the difference between the values of a guaranteed and an ordinary loan. This is the value of the loan guarantee.

Thus, option pricing theory should lead to a way of calculating the actual cost of the government's many loan guarantee programs. This will be a healthy thing. The government's possible liability under existing guarantee programs has been enormous. In 1987, for example, $4 billion in loans to shipowners had been guaranteed under the so-called Title IX program to support shipyards in the United States.[32] This program was one of dozens. Yet the true cost of these programs is not widely recognized. Because loan guarantees involve no immediate outlay, they do not appear in the federal budget. Members of Congress sponsoring loan guarantee programs do not, as far as we know, present careful estimates of the value of the programs to business and the present value of the programs' cost to the public.

Calculating the Probability of Default

Banks and other financial institutions not only want to know the value of the loans that they have made but they also need to know the risk that they are incurring. Suppose that the assets of Backwoods Chemical have a current market value of $100 and its debt has a face value of $60 (i.e., 60 percent leverage), all of which is due to be repaid at the end of five years. Figure 24.10 shows the range

[32] The actual figure on March 31, 1987, was $4,497,365,297.98. Since 1987 these government guarantees to shipowners have been substantially reduced.

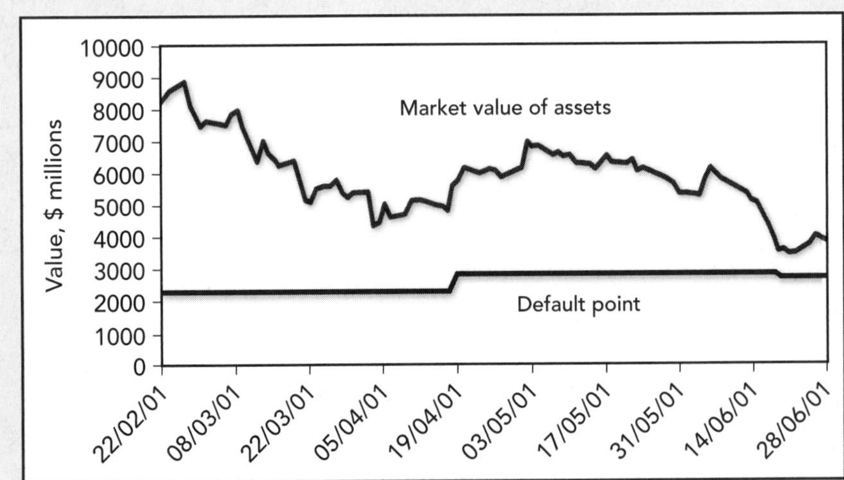

FIGURE 24.11

The market value of the assets of Metromedia Fiber Network crept closer to the point at which the firm would choose to default.

Source: KMV Credit Monitor.

of possible values of Backwoods's assets when the loan becomes due. The expected value of the assets is $120, but this value is by no means certain. There is a probability of 20 percent that the asset value could fall below $60, in which case the company will default on its debt. This probability is shown by the shaded area in Figure 24.10.

To calculate the probability that Backwoods will default, we need to know the expected growth in the market value of its assets, the face value and maturity of the debt, and the variability of future asset values. Real-world cases are likely to be more complex than our Backwoods example. For example, firms may have several classes of debt maturing on different dates. If so, shareholders have an option on an option. It may be worth their while to put up more money to pay off the short-term debt and thus keep alive the chance that the firm's fortunes will recover before the rest of the debt becomes due.

However, banks and consulting firms are now finding that they can use these ideas to measure the risk of actual loans.[33] For example, by mid-2001 the fiber-optics company, Metromedia Fiber Network, was a company in difficulties. Revenues had expanded rapidly, but so had losses. By 2000 the company was making operating losses of $329 million on revenues of $188 million. The stock price had fallen from a high of $50 to under $2, while the company's 8-year 10 percent notes were priced at 44 percent and offered a yield to maturity of 27 percent.

How close was Metromedia to default? Figure 24.11 provides an answer. The burgundy line shows the market value of Metromedia's assets, and the blue line shows the asset value at which the company would choose to default on its debts. You can see that during the first half of 2001 the value of the company's assets crept closer and closer to the default point.

[33]Banks are not just interested in the risk of individual loans; they would also like to know the risk of their entire portfolio. Therefore, specialists in credit risk also need to recognize the correlation between the outcomes. A portfolio of loans, all of which are to factory outlets in suburban Hicksville, is likely to be more risky than a portfolio with a wide variety of different borrowers.

FIGURE 24.12

Estimates by KMV Credit Monitor of the probability that Metromedia Fiber Network would default on its debt within a year.

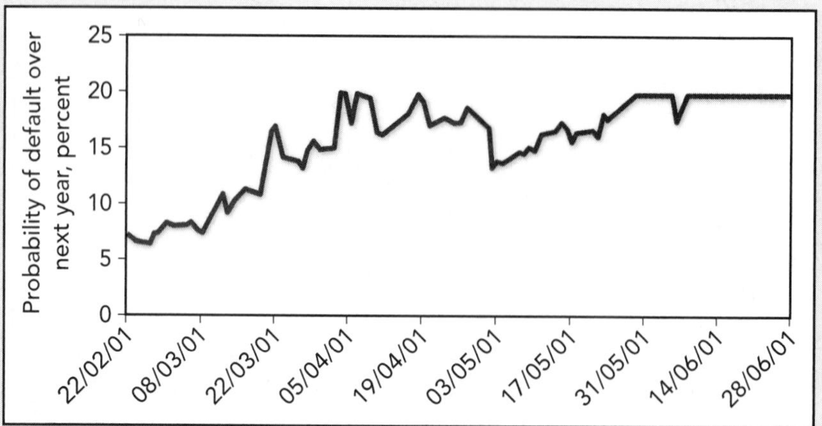

Of course, nobody had a crystal ball that could foresee what would happen to Metromedia, but KMV, a consulting firm specializing in the assessment of credit risk, estimated the *probability* at each point that the company would default in the next year. Figure 24.12 shows how KMV progressively increased its assessment of the probability of default.

SUMMARY

Efficient debt management presupposes that you understand how bonds are valued. That means you need to consider three problems:

1. What determines the general level of interest rates?
2. What determines the difference between long-term and short-term rates?
3. What determines the difference between the interest rates on company and government debt?

Here are some things to remember. The rate of interest depends on the demand for savings and the supply. The *demand* comes from firms who wish to invest in new plant and equipment. The supply of savings comes from individuals who are willing to consume tomorrow rather than today. The equilibrium interest rate is the rate that produces a *balance* between the demand and supply.

The best-known theory about the effect of inflation on interest rates was suggested by Irving Fisher. He argued that the nominal, or money, rate of interest is equal to the expected real rate plus the expected inflation rate. If the expected inflation rate increases by 1 percent, so too will the money rate of interest. During the past 50 years Fisher's simple theory has not done a bad job of explaining changes in short-term interest rates in the United States.

The value of any bond is equal to the cash payments discounted at the spot rates of interest. For example, the value of a 10-year bond with a 5 percent coupon equals

$$\text{PV(percent of face value)} = \frac{5}{1 + r_1} + \frac{5}{(1 + r_2)^2} + \cdots + \frac{105}{(1 + r_{10})^{10}}$$

Bond dealers generally look at the yield to maturity on a bond. This is simply the internal rate of return y, the discount rate at which

$$\text{Bond price} = \frac{5}{1+y} + \frac{5}{(1+y)^2} + \cdots + \frac{105}{(1+y)^{10}}$$

The yield to maturity y is a complex average of the spot interest rates r_1, r_2, etc. Like most averages it can be a useful summary measure, but it can also hide a lot of interesting information. We suggest you refer to yields on stripped bonds as measures of the spot rates of interest.

When you invest in a bond you usually receive a regular interest payment and then the final principal payment. Duration measures the *average* time to each payment. It is a useful summary measure of the length of a loan. It is also important because there is a direct relationship between the duration of a bond and its volatility. A change in interest rates has a greater effect on the price of a bond with a longer duration.

The one-period spot rate r_1 may be very different from the two-period spot rate r_2. In other words, investors often want a different annual rate of interest for lending for one year than for two years. Why is this? The *expectations theory* says that bonds are priced so that the expected rate of return from investing in bonds over any period is independent of the maturity of the bonds held by the investor. The expectations theory predicts that r_2 will exceed r_1 only if next year's one-period interest rate is expected to rise.

The expectations theory cannot be a complete explanation of the term structure if investors are worried about risk. Long bonds may be a safe haven for investors with long-term fixed liabilities. But other investors may not like the extra volatility of long-term bonds and may be concerned that a sudden burst in inflation could largely wipe out the real value of these bonds. Such investors will be prepared to hold long-term bonds only if they offer a liquidity premium—that is, a higher rate of interest.

Finally, we come to our third question: What determines the difference between interest rates on company and government debt? Company debt sells at a lower price than government debt. This discount represents the value of the company's option to default. We showed you how the value of this option varies with the degree of leverage and the time to maturity.

Ratings are widely used as a guide to the risk of loans. However, banks and consulting firms also recognize that the option to default is a put option and they have been developing models to estimate the probability that the borrower will exercise its option to default.

Visit us at www.mhhe.com/bm7e

FURTHER READING

A good general text on debt markets is:

A. Sundaresan and S. Sundaresan: *Fixed Income Markets and Their Derivatives,* South-Western College Publishing, Cincinnati, Ohio, 2nd ed., 2001.

Nelson provides a useful review of some of the standard theories of the term structure literature:

C. R. Nelson: "The Term Structure of Interest Rates: Theories and Evidence," in J. L. Bicksler (ed.), *Handbook of Financial Economics,* North-Holland Publishing Company, Amsterdam, 1980.

Empirical tests of term structure theories are provided by Fama and Shiller, Campbell, and Schoenholtz:

E. F. Fama: "The Information in the Term Structure," *Journal of Financial Economics,* 13:509–528 (December 1984).

E. F. Fama: "Term Premiums in Bond Returns," *Journal of Financial Economics,* 13:529–546 (December 1984).

R. J. Shiller, J. Y. Campbell, and K. L. Schoenholtz: "Forward Rates and Future Policy: Interpreting the Term Structure of Interest Rates," *Brookings Papers on Economic Activity,* 1:173–217 (1983).

The following paper by Schaefer is a good review of duration and of how it is used to hedge fixed liabilities:

S. M. Schaefer: "Immunisation and Duration: A Review of Theory, Performance and Application," *Midland Corporate Finance Journal,* 3:41–58 (Autumn 1984).

We referred briefly to modern models of the term structure, which exploit the relationship between the price changes of bonds with different maturities. For more on this topic we suggest:

T. S. Y. Ho: "Evolution of Interest Rate Models: A Comparison," *Journal of Derivatives,* 2:9–20 (Summer 1995).

The classic paper on the valuation of the option to default on corporate debt is:

R. Merton: "On the Pricing of Corporate Debt: The Risk Structure of Interest Rates," *Journal of Finance,* 29:449–470 (May 1974).

QUIZ

1. The real interest rate is determined by the demand for, and supply of, capital. Draw a diagram showing how the demand by companies for capital and the supply of capital by investors vary with the interest rate. Use this diagram to show the following:
   a. What will happen to the amount of investment and saving if firms' investment prospects improve? How will the equilibrium interest rate change?
   b. What will happen to the amount of investment and saving if individuals' willingness to save increases at each possible interest rate? How will the equilibrium interest rate change? Assume firms' investment opportunities do not change.
2. In 2001 Treasury 13 7/8s of 2011 offered a semiannually compounded yield of 8.04 percent. Recognizing that coupons are paid semiannually, calculate the bond's price.
3. Here are the prices in 1998 of four Scandinavian government bonds with similar maturities:

Bond	Price (%)
Denmark 7s of 2007	116.58
Finland 6s of 2008	111.58
Norway 6 3/4s of 2007	108.15
Sweden 6 1/2s of 2008	113.19

   a. If coupons are paid annually, which bond offered the highest yield to maturity? Which had the lowest?
   b. Which bonds had the longest and shortest durations?
4. a. What is the formula for the value of a two-year, 5 percent bond in terms of spot rates?
   b. What is the formula for its value in terms of yield to maturity?
   c. If the two-year spot rate is higher than the one-year rate, is the yield to maturity greater or less than the two-year spot rate?

d. In each of the following sentences choose the correct term from within the parentheses:

"The (yield-to-maturity/spot-rate) formula discounts all cash flows from one bond at the same rate even though they occur at different points in time."

"The (yield-to-maturity/spot-rate) formula discounts all cash flows received at the same point in time at the same rate even though the cash flows may come from different bonds."

5. Construct some simple examples to illustrate your answers to the following:

a. If interest rates rise, do bond prices rise or fall?

b. If the bond yield is greater than the coupon, is the price of the bond greater or less than 100?

c. If the price of a bond exceeds 100, is the yield greater or less than the coupon?

d. Do high-coupon bonds sell at higher or lower prices than low-coupon bonds?

e. If interest rates change, does the price of high-coupon bonds change proportionately more than that of low-coupon bonds?

6. The following table shows the prices of a sample of strips of UK gilts (government bonds) in December 1998. Each strip makes a single payment of £100 at maturity.

Maturity	Price (£)
December 2000	90.826
December 2005	73.565
December 2006	70.201
December 2007	67.787
December 2028	29.334

a. Calculate the annually compounded, spot interest rate for each year.

b. Is the term structure upward- or downward-sloping?

c. Would you expect the yield on a *coupon* bond maturing in December 2028 to be higher or lower than the yield on the 2028 strip?

d. Calculate the annually compounded, one-year forward rate of interest for December 2005. Now do the same for December 2006.

7. a. An 8 percent, five-year bond yields 6 percent. If the yield remains unchanged, what will be its price one year hence? Assume annual coupon payments.

b. What is the total return to an investor who held the bond over this year?

c. What can you deduce about the relationship between the bond return over a particular period and the yields to maturity at the start and end of that period?

8. True or false? Explain.

a. Longer-maturity bonds necessarily have longer durations.

b. The longer a bond's duration, the lower its volatility.

c. Other things equal, the lower the bond coupon, the higher its volatility.

d. If interest rates rise, bond durations rise also.

9. Calculate the durations and volatilities of securities A, B, and C. Their cash flows are shown below. The interest rate is 8 percent.

	Period 1	Period 2	Period 3
A	40	40	40
B	20	20	120
C	10	10	110

10. a. Suppose that the one-year spot rate of interest at time 0 is 1 percent and the two-year spot rate is 3 percent. What is the forward rate of interest for year 2?

b. What does the expectations theory of term structure say about the relationship between the forward rate and the one-year spot rate at time 1?
c. Over a very long period of time, the term structure in the United States has been on average upward-sloping. Is this evidence for or against the expectations theory?
d. What does the liquidity-preference theory say about the relationship between the forward rate and the one-year spot rate at time 1?
e. If the liquidity-preference theory is a good approximation and you have to meet long-term liabilities (college tuition for your children, for example), is it safer to invest in long- or short-term bonds? Assume inflation is predictable.
f. If inflation is very uncertain and you have to meet long-term real liabilities, is it safer to invest in long- or short-term bonds?

11. a. State the four Moody's ratings that are generally known as "investment-grade" ratings.
b. Other things equal, would you expect the yield to maturity on a corporate bond to increase or decrease with
i. The company's business risk?
ii. The expected rate of inflation?
iii. The risk-free rate of interest?
iv. The degree of leverage?

12. The difference between the price of a government bond and a simple corporate bond is equal to the value of an option. What is this option and what is its exercise price?

13. How in principle would you calculate the value of a government loan guarantee?

PRACTICE QUESTIONS

1. Why might Fisher's theory about inflation and interest rates *not* be true?
2. Under what conditions can the expected real interest rate be negative?
3. A 6 percent six-year bond yields 12 percent and a 10 percent six-year bond yields 8 percent. Calculate the six-year spot rate. (Assume annual coupon payments.)
4. Is the yield on high-coupon bonds more likely to be higher than that on low-coupon bonds when the term structure is upward-sloping or when it is downward-sloping?
5. The one-year spot rate is $r_1 = 6$ percent, and the forward rate for a one-year loan maturing in year 2 is $f_2 = 6.4$ percent. Similarly, $f_3 = 7.1$ percent, $f_4 = 7.3$ percent, and $f_5 = 8.2$ percent. What are the spot rates r_2, r_3, r_4, and r_5? If the expectations hypothesis holds, what can you say about expected future interest rates?
6. Suppose your company will receive $100 million at $t = 4$ but must make a $107 million payment at $t = 5$. Assume the spot and forward rates from question 5. Show how the company can lock in the interest rate at which it will invest at $t = 4$. Will the $100 million, invested at this locked-in rate, be sufficient to cover the $107 million liability?
7. Use the rates from question 5 one more time. Consider the following bonds, each with a five-year maturity. Calculate the yield to maturity for each. Which is the better investment (or are they equally attractive)? Each has $1,000 face value and pays coupons annually.

Coupon	Price
5	92.07%
7	100.31
12	120.92

8. You have estimated spot rates as follows:

Year	Spot Rate
1	$r_1 = 5.00\%$
2	$r_2 = 5.40$
3	$r_3 = 5.70$
4	$r_4 = 5.90$
5	$r_5 = 6.00$

   a. What are the discount factors for each date (that is, the present value of $1 paid in year t)?
   b. What are the forward rates for each period?
   c. Calculate the PV of the following Treasury notes:
      i. 5 percent, two-year note.
      ii. 5 percent, five-year note.
      iii. 10 percent, five-year note.
   d. Explain intuitively why the yield to maturity on the 10 percent bond is less than that on the 5 percent bond.
   e. What should be the yield to maturity on a five-year zero-coupon bond?
   f. Show that the correct yield to maturity on a five-year annuity is 5.75 percent.
   g. Explain intuitively why the yield on the five-year Treasury notes described in part (c) must lie between the yield on a five-year zero-coupon bond and a five-year annuity.

9. Look at the spot interest rates shown in question 8. Suppose that someone told you that the six-year spot interest rate was 4.80 percent. Why would you not believe him? How could you make money if he was right? What is the minimum sensible value for the six-year spot rate?

10. Look again at the spot interest rates shown in question 8. What can you deduce about the one-year spot interest rate in four years if
   a. The expectations theory of term structure is right?
   b. The liquidity-preference theory of term structure is right?
   c. The term structure contains an inflation uncertainty premium?

11. Look up prices of 10 U.S. Treasury bonds with different coupons and different maturities. Calculate how their prices would change if their yields to maturity increased by one percentage point. Are long- or short-term bonds most affected by the change in yields? Are high- or low-coupon bonds most affected?

12. Assume the term structure of interest rates is upward-sloping. How would you respond to the following comment? "The present term structure of interest rates makes short-term debt more attractive to corporate treasurers. Firms should avoid new long-term debt issues."

13. In Section 24.3 we stated that in 2001 the duration of the 4 5/8s of 2006 was 4.36 years. Construct a table like Table 24.2 to show that this is so.

14. The formula for the duration of a perpetual bond which makes an equal payment each year in perpetuity is (1 + yield)/yield. If bonds yield 5 percent, which has the longer duration—a perpetual bond or a 15-year zero-coupon bond? What if the yield is 10 percent?

15. You have just been fired as CEO. As consolation the board of directors gives you a five-year consulting contract at $150,000 per year. What is the duration of this contract if your personal borrowing rate is 9 percent? Use duration to calculate the change in the contract's present value for a .5 percent increase in your borrowing rate.

16. Look at the example in Section 24.4 of the Treasury bill and the medium- and long-term bonds. Now assume that the price of the medium-term bond can either fall by $10.75 or

rise by $14.0. What can you say now about the relationship between the value of the three bonds?

17. Explain carefully what factors determine the yield on corporate bonds.
18. Companies sometimes issue floating-rate bonds. In this case the interest rate might be set at (say) 1 percent above the Treasury bill rate. Would you expect the price of a company's floating-rate bonds to vary? If so, why?
19. Company A has issued a single zero-coupon bond maturing in 10 years. Company B has issued a coupon bond maturing in 10 years. Explain why it is more complicated to value B's debt than A's.
20. Company X has borrowed $150 maturing this year and $50 maturing in 10 years. Company Y has borrowed $200 maturing in five years. In both cases asset value is $140. Why might X not default while Y does?

CHALLENGE QUESTIONS

1. It has been suggested that the Fisher theory is a tautology. If the real rate of interest is defined as the difference between the nominal rate and the expected inflation rate, then the nominal rate *must* equal the real rate plus the expected inflation rate. In what sense is Fisher's theory *not* a tautology?
2. Find the arbitrage opportunity (opportunities?). Assume for simplicity that coupons are paid annually. In each case the face value of the bond is $1,000.

Bond	Maturity (years)	Coupon ($)	Price ($)
A	3	zero	751.30
B	4	50	842.30
C	4	120	1,065.28
D	4	100	980.57
E	3	140	1,120.12
F	3	70	1,001.62
G	2	zero	834.00

3. The duration of a bond which makes an equal payment each year in perpetuity is (1 + yield)/yield. Prove it.
4. What is the duration of a common stock whose dividends are expected to grow at a constant rate in perpetuity?
5. a. What spot and forward rates are embedded in the following Treasury bonds? The price of one-year (zero-coupon) Treasury bills is 93.46 percent. Assume for simplicity that bonds make only annual payments. *Hint:* Can you devise a mixture of long and short positions in these bonds that gives a cash payoff only in year 2? In year 3?

Coupon (%)	Maturity (years)	Price (%)
4	2	94.92
8	3	103.64

   b. A three-year bond with a 4 percent coupon is selling at 95.00 percent. Is there a profit opportunity here? If so, how would you take advantage of it?
6. Look back at our example in Section 24.4 of the short-, medium-, and long-term bonds. Remember that we said that the prices must stand in a particular relationship or there would be an arbitrage opportunity. This means that we can take advantage of the risk-

neutral trick that we used to value options. Pretend that investors are risk-neutral. Now answer the following questions:

a. Suppose that the price of the short bond is 98 and the price of the medium is 83. What is the price of the long bond?
b. What are the possible future prices of these three bonds at the end of three months if rates rise and if they fall?
c. What would be the expected return over the three months on each bond?
d. What is the probability of an interest rate rise?
e. Show that the expected return on each bond is equal.

7. Look up prices of 10 corporate bonds with different coupons and maturities. Be sure to include some low-rated bonds on your list. Now estimate what these bonds would sell for if the government had guaranteed them. Calculate the value of the guarantee for each bond. Can you explain the difference between the 10 guarantee values?

8. Bond rating services usually charge corporations for rating their bonds.
   a. Why do they do this, rather than charge those investors who use the information?
   b. Why will a company pay to have its bonds rated even when it knows the service is likely to assign a below-average rating?
   c. A few companies are not willing to pay for their bonds to be rated. What can investors deduce about the quality of these bonds?

9. Look back to the first Backwoods Chemical example at the start of Section 24.5. Suppose that the firm's book balance sheet is

Backwoods Chemical Company (Book Values)

Net working capital	$ 400	$1,000	Debt
Net fixed assets	1,600	1,000	Equity (net worth)
Total assets	$2,000	$2,000	Total value

The debt has a one-year maturity and a promised interest rate of 9 percent. Thus, the promised payment to Backwoods's creditors is $1,090. The market value of the assets is $1,200, and the standard deviation of asset value is 45 percent per year. The risk-free interest rate is 9 percent. Calculate the value of Backwoods debt and equity.

10. Refer again to question 9. Suppose that the continuously compounded return on Backwoods's assets over the next year is normally distributed with a mean of 10 percent. What is the probability that Backwoods will default?

CHAPTER TWENTY-FIVE

THE MANY DIFFERENT KINDS OF DEBT

IN CHAPTERS 17 and 18 we discussed how much a company should borrow. But companies also need to think about what *type* of debt to issue. They must decide whether to issue short- or long-term debt, whether to issue straight bonds or convertible bonds, whether to issue in the United States or in the international debt market, and whether to sell the debt publicly or place it privately with a few large investors.

As a financial manager, you need to choose the type of debt that makes sense for your company. For example, foreign currency debt may be best suited for firms with a substantial overseas business. Short-term debt is generally used when the firm has only a temporary need for funds.[1] Sometimes competition between lenders opens a window of opportunity in a particular sector of the debt market. The effect may be only a few basis-points reduction in yield, but on a large issue that can translate into savings of several million dollars. Remember the saying, "A million dollars here and a million there—pretty soon it begins to add up to real money."[2]

Our focus in this chapter is on straight long-term debt.[3] We begin our discussion by looking at the different types of bonds. We examine the differences between senior and junior bonds and between secured and unsecured bonds. Then we describe how bonds may be repaid by means of a sinking fund and how the borrower or the lender may have an option for early repayment. We also look at some of the restrictive provisions that deter the company from taking actions that would damage the bonds' value. We not only describe the different features of corporate debt but also try to explain *why* sinking funds, repayment options, and the like exist. They are not simply matters of custom; there are generally good economic reasons for their use.

Debt may be sold to the public or placed privately with large financial institutions. Because privately placed bonds are broadly similar to public issues, we will not discuss them at length. However, we will discuss another form of private debt known as project finance. This is the glamorous part of the debt market. The words *project finance* conjure up images of multi-million-dollar loans to finance huge ventures in exotic parts of the world. You'll find there's something to the popular image, but it's not the whole story.

Finally, we look at a few unusual bonds and consider the reasons for innovation in the debt markets.

If a company cannot service its debt, it will need to come to some arrangement with its creditors or file for bankruptcy. In the appendix to this chapter we explain the procedures involved in such cases. We will also consider the efficiency of the bankruptcy rules in the United States and look at how some European countries handle the problem.

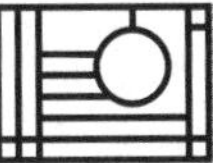

25.1 DOMESTIC BONDS AND INTERNATIONAL BONDS

A firm can issue a bond either in its home country or in another country. Of course, any firm that raises money abroad is subject to the rules of the country in which it does so. For example, any issue in the United States of publicly traded bonds needs to be registered with the SEC. Since the cost of registration can be particularly large for foreign firms, these firms often avoid registration by complying with the SEC's

[1]For example, Stohs and Mauer show that firms with a preponderance of short-term assets tend to issue short-term debt. See M. H. Stohs and D. C. Mauer, "The Determinants of Corporate Debt Maturity Structure," *Journal of Business* 69 (July 1996), pp. 279–312.

[2]The remark was made by the late Senator Everett Dirksen. However, he was talking billions.

[3]Short-term debt is discussed in Chapter 30.

Rule 144A for bond issues in the United States. Rule 144A bonds can be bought and sold only by large financial institutions.[4]

Bonds that are sold to local investors in another country's bond market are known as *foreign bonds.* The United States is by far the largest market for foreign bonds, but Japan and Switzerland are also important. These bonds have a variety of nicknames: A bond sold publicly by a foreign company in the United States is known as a *yankee bond;* a bond sold by a foreign firm in Japan is a *samurai.*

There is also a large international market for long-term bonds. These international bond issues are sold throughout the world by syndicates of underwriters, mainly located in London. They include the London branches of large U.S., European, and Japanese banks and security dealers. International issues are usually made in one of the major currencies. The U.S. dollar has been the most popular choice, but a high proportion of international bond issues are made in the euro, the currency of the European Monetary Union.

The international bond market arose during the 1960s because the U.S. government imposed an interest-equalization tax on the purchase of foreign securities and discouraged American corporations from exporting capital. Therefore both European and American multinationals were forced to tap an international market for capital.[5] This market came to be known as the *eurobond market,* but be careful not to confuse a eurobond (which may be in any currency) with a bond denominated in euros.

The interest-equalization tax was removed in 1974, and there are no longer any controls on capital exports from the United States. Since U.S. firms can now choose whether to borrow in New York or London, the interest rates in the two markets are usually similar. However, the international bond market is not directly subject to regulation by the U.S. authorities, and therefore the financial manager needs to be alert to small differences in the cost of borrowing in one market rather than another.

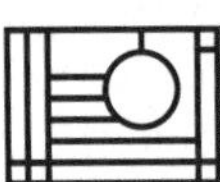

25.2 THE BOND CONTRACT

To give you some feel for the bond contract (and for some of the language in which it is couched), we have summarized in Table 25.1 the terms of an issue of 30-year bonds by Ralston Purina Company. We will look at each of the principal items in turn.

Indenture, or Trust Deed

The Ralston Purina offering was a public issue of bonds, which was registered with the SEC and listed on the New York Stock Exchange. In the case of a public issue, the bond agreement is in the form of an **indenture,** or **trust deed,** between the borrower and a trust company.[6] Continental Bank, which is the trust company for the Ralston

[4]We described Rule 144A in Section 15.5.

[5]Also, until 1984 the United States imposed a withholding tax on interest payments to foreign investors. Investors could avoid this tax by buying an international bond issued in London rather than a similar bond issued in New York.

[6]In the case of international bond issues, there is a *fiscal agent* who carries out somewhat similar functions to a bond trustee.

Listed	New York Stock Exchange
Trustee	Continental Bank, Chicago
Rights on default	The trustee or 25% of the debentures outstanding may declare interest due and payable.
Indenture modification	Indenture may not be modified except as provided with the consent of two-thirds of the debentures outstanding.
Registered	Fully registered
Denomination	$1,000
To be issued	$86.4 million
Issue date	June 4, 1986
Offered	Issued at a price of 97.60% plus accrued interest (proceeds to Company 96.725%) through First Boston Corporation, Goldman Sachs and Company, Shearson Lehman Brothers, Stifel Nicolaus and Company, and associates.
Interest	At a rate of 9½% per annum, payable June 1 and December 1 to holders registered on May 15 and November 15.
Security	Not secured. Company will not permit to have any lien on its property or assets without equally and ratably securing the debt securities.
Sale and lease-back	Company will not enter into any sale and lease-back transaction unless the Company within 120 days after the transfer of title to such principal property applies to the redemption of the debt securities at the then-applicable option redemption price an amount equal to the net proceeds received by the Company upon such sale.
Maturity	June 1, 2016
Sinking fund	Annually between June 2, 1996, and June 2, 2015, sufficient to redeem not less than $13.5 million principal amount, plus similar optional payments. Sinking fund is designed to redeem 90% of the debentures prior to maturity.
Callable	At whole or in part at any time at the option of the Company with at least 30, but not more than 60, days' notice on each May 31 as follows:

1989	106.390	1990	106.035	1991	105.680
1992	105.325	1993	104.970	1994	104.615
1995	104.260	1996	103.905	1997	103.550
1998	103.195	1999	102.840	2000	102.485
2001	102.130	2002	101.775	2003	101.420
2004	101.065	2005	100.710	2006	100.355

and thereafter at 100 plus accrued interest; provided, however, that prior to June 1, 1996, the Company may not redeem the bonds from, or in anticipation of, moneys borrowed having an effective interest cost of less than 9.748%.

TABLE 25.1

Summary of terms of 9½ percent sinking fund debenture 2016 issued by Ralston Purina Company.

Purina bond, represents the bondholders. It must see that the terms of the indenture are observed and look after the bondholders in the event of default. A copy of the bond indenture is included in the registration statement. It is a turgid legal document.[7] Its main provisions are summarized in the prospectus to the issue.

[7]For example, the indenture for one J.C. Penney bond stated: "In any case where several matters are required to be certified by, or covered by an opinion of, any specified Person, it is not necessary that all such matters be certified by, or covered by the opinion of, only one such Person, or that they be certified or covered by only one document, but one such Person may certify or give an opinion with respect to some matters and one or more such other Persons as to other matters, and any such Person may certify or give an opinion as to such matters in one or several documents." Try saying that three times fast.

Moving down Table 25.1, you will see that the Ralston Purina bonds are *registered.* This means that the company's registrar records the ownership of each bond and the company pays the interest and the final principal amount directly to each owner.[8]

Almost all bonds issued in the United States are issued in registered form, but in many countries bonds may be issued in *bearer* form. In this case, the certificate constitutes the primary evidence of ownership so the bondholder must send in coupons to claim interest and must send the certificate itself to claim the final repayment of principal. International bonds almost invariably allow the owner to hold them in bearer form. However, since the ownership of such bonds cannot be traced, the IRS has tried to deter U.S. residents from holding them.[9]

The Bond Terms

Like most dollar bonds, the Ralston Purina bonds have a face value of $1,000. Notice, however, that the bond price is shown as a percentage of face value. Also, the price is stated net of *accrued interest.* This means that the bond buyer must pay not only the quoted price but also the amount of any future interest that may have accrued. For example, an investor who bought bonds for delivery on (say) June 11, 1986, would be receiving them 10 days into the first interest period. Therefore, accrued interest would be $10/360 \times 9.5 = .26$ percent, and the investor would pay a price of 97.60 plus .26 percent of accrued interest.[10]

The Ralston Purina bonds were offered to the public at a price of 97.60 percent, but the company received only 96.725 percent. The difference represents the underwriters' spread. Of the $86.4 million raised, about $85.6 million went to the company and $.8 million went to the underwriters.

Since the bonds were issued at a price of 97.60 percent, investors who hold the bonds to maturity receive a capital gain over the 30 years of 2.40 percent.[11] However, the bulk of their return is provided by the regular interest payment. The annual interest or *coupon* payment on each bond is 9.50 percent of $1,000, or $95. This interest is payable semiannually, so every six months investors receive interest of 95/2 = $47.50. Most U.S. bonds pay interest semiannually, but a comparable international bond would generally pay interest annually.[12]

The regular interest payment on a bond is a hurdle that the company must keep jumping. If the company ever fails to pay the interest, lenders can demand their

[8]Often, investors do not physically hold the security; instead, their ownership is represented by a book entry. The "book" is in practice a computer.

[9]U.S. residents cannot generally deduct capital losses on bearer bonds. Also, payments on such bonds cannot be made to a bank account in the United States.

[10]In the U.S. corporate bond market accrued interest is calculated on the assumption that a year is composed of twelve 30-day months; in some other markets (such as the U.S. Treasury bond market) calculations recognize the actual number of days in each calendar month.

[11]This gain is not taxed as income as long as it amounts to less than .25 percent a year.

[12]If a bond pays interest semiannually, investors usually calculate a *semiannually* compounded yield to maturity on the bond. In other words, the yield is quoted as twice the six-month yield. Because international bonds pay interest annually, it is conventional to quote their yields to maturity on an *annually* compounded basis. Remember this when comparing yields.

money back instead of waiting until matters may have deteriorated further.[13] Thus, interest payments provide added protection for lenders.[14]

Sometimes bonds are sold with a lower interest payment but at a larger discount on their face value, so investors receive a significant part of their return in the form of capital appreciation.[15] The ultimate is the zero-coupon bond, which pays no interest at all; in this case the entire return consists of capital appreciation.[16]

The Ralston Purina interest payment is fixed for the life of the bond, but in some issues the payment varies with the general level of interest rates. For example, the payment may be tied to the U.S. Treasury bill rate or (more commonly) to the London interbank offered rate (LIBOR), which is the rate at which international banks lend to one another. Often these floating-rate notes specify a minimum (or floor) interest rate or they may specify a maximum (or cap) on the rate.[17] You may also come across "collars," which stipulate both a maximum and a minimum payment.

25.3 SECURITY AND SENIORITY

Almost all debt issues by industrial and financial companies are general unsecured obligations. Longer-term unsecured issues like the Ralston Purina bond are usually called **debentures;** shorter-term issues are usually called **notes.**

Utility company bonds are commonly secured. This means that if the company defaults on the debt, the trustee or lender may take possession of the relevant assets. If these are insufficient to satisfy the claim, the remaining debt will have a general claim, alongside any unsecured debt, against the other assets of the firm.

The majority of secured debt consists of **mortgage bonds.** These sometimes provide a claim against a specific building, but they are more often secured on all the firm's property.[18] Of course, the value of any mortgage depends on the extent of alternative uses of the property. A custom-built machine for producing buggy whips will not be worth much when the market for buggy whips dries up.

---

[13]There is one type of bond on which the borrower is obliged to pay interest only if it is covered by the year's earnings. These so-called *income bonds* are rare and have largely been issued as part of railroad reorganizations. For a discussion of the attraction of income bonds, see J. J. McConnell and G. G. Schlarbaum, "Returns, Risks, and Pricing of Income Bonds, 1956–1976 (Does Money Have an Odor?)," *Journal of Business* 54 (January 1981), pp. 33–64.

[14]See F. Black and J. C. Cox, "Valuing Corporate Securities: Some Effects of Bond Indenture Provisions," *Journal of Finance* 31 (May 1976), pp. 351–367. Black and Cox point out that the interest payment would be a trivial hurdle if the company could sell assets to make the payment. Such sales are, therefore, restricted.

[15]Any bond that is issued at a discount is known as an *original issue discount* (*OID*) bond. A zero coupon is often called a "pure discount bond."

[16]The ultimate of ultimates was an issue of a perpetual zero-coupon bond on behalf of a charity.

[17]Instead of issuing a capped floating-rate loan, a company will sometimes issue an uncapped loan and at the same time buy a cap from a bank. The bank pays the interest in excess of the specified level.

[18]If a mortgage is *closed*, no more bonds may be issued against the mortgage. However, usually there is no specific limit to the amount of bonds that may be secured (in which case the mortgage is said to be *open*). Many mortgage bonds are secured not only by existing property but also by "after-acquired" property. However, if the company buys only property that is already mortgaged, the bondholder would have only a junior claim on the new property. Therefore, mortgage bonds with after-acquired property clauses also limit the extent to which the company can purchase additional mortgaged property.

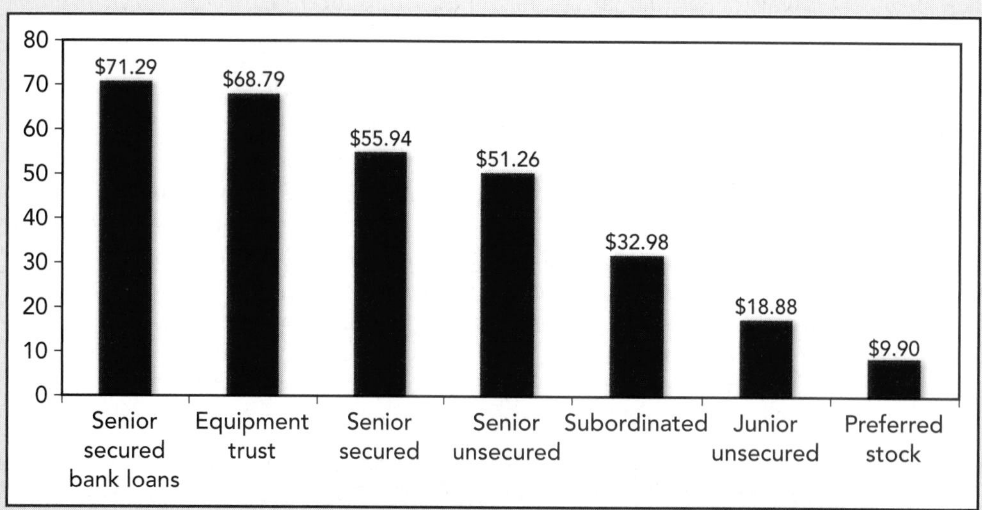

FIGURE 25.1

Average recovery rates per $100 face value on defaulting debt & preferred stock by seniority and security.

Source: "The Evolving Meaning of Moody's Bond Ratings," Moody's Investor Service, August 1999. See **www.moodys.com**.

Companies that own securities may use them as collateral for a loan. For example, holding companies are firms whose main assets consist of common stock in a number of subsidiaries. So, when holding companies wish to borrow, they generally use these investments as collateral. The problem for the lender is that this stock is junior to *all* other claims on the assets of the subsidiaries, and so these *collateral trust bonds* usually include detailed restrictions on the freedom of the subsidiaries to issue debt or preferred stock.

A third form of secured debt is the **equipment trust certificate.** This is most frequently used to finance new railroad rolling stock but may also be used to finance trucks, aircraft, and ships. Under this arrangement a trustee obtains formal ownership of the equipment. The company makes a down payment on the cost of the equipment, and the balance is provided by a package of equipment trust certificates with different maturities that might typically run from 1 to 15 years. Only when all these debts have finally been paid off does the company become the formal owner of the equipment. Bond rating agencies such as Moody's or Standard and Poor's usually rate equipment trust certificates one grade higher than the company's regular debt.

Bonds may be senior claims or they may be subordinated to the senior bonds or to *all* other creditors.[19] If the firm defaults, the senior bonds come first in the pecking order. The subordinated lender gets in line behind the firm's general creditors (but ahead of the preferred stockholder and the common stockholder).

As you can see from Figure 25.1, if default does occur, it pays to hold senior secured bonds. On average investors in these bonds can expect to recover over half of the amount of the loan. At the other extreme, recovery rates for junior unsecured bondholders are less than 20 percent of the face value of the debt.

[19]If a bond does not specifically state that it is junior, you can assume that it is senior.

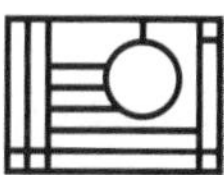

25.4 ASSET-BACKED SECURITIES

Instead of borrowing money directly, companies sometimes bundle up a group of assets and then sell the cash flows from these assets. These securities are known as **asset-backed** securities.

Suppose your company has made a large number of mortgage loans to buyers of homes or commercial real estate. However, you don't want to wait until the loans are paid off; you would like to get your hands on the money now. Here is what you do.

You establish a separate company that buys a package of the mortgage loans. To finance this purchase, the company sells *mortgage pass-through certificates.*[20] The holders of these certificates simply receive a share of the mortgage payments. For example, if interest rates fall and the mortgages are repaid early, holders of the pass-through certificates are also repaid early. That's not generally popular with these holders, for they get their money back just when they don't want it—when interest rates are low.[21]

Real estate companies are not unique in wanting to turn future cash receipts into up-front cash. Automobile loans, student loans, and credit card receivables are also often bundled together and re-marketed as a bond. Indeed, investment bankers seem able to repackage any set of cash flows into a loan. In 1997 David Bowie, the British rock star, established a company that then purchased the royalties from his current albums. The company financed the purchase by selling $55 million of 10-year notes at an interest rate of 7.9 percent. The royalty receipts were used to make the interest and principal payments on the notes. When asked about the singer's reaction to the idea, his manager replied, "He kind of looked at me cross-eyed and said 'What?' "[22]

25.5 REPAYMENT PROVISIONS

Sinking Funds

The maturity date of the Ralston Purina bond is June 1, 2016, but part of the issue is repaid on a regular basis before maturity. To do this, the company makes a regular repayment into a *sinking fund.* If the payment is in the form of cash, the trustee selects bonds by lottery and uses the cash to redeem them at their face value.[23]

---

[20]Mortgage-backed loans for commercial real estate are called (not surprisingly) *commercial mortgage backed securities* or *CMBS*.

[21]Sometimes, instead of issuing one class of pass-through certificates, the company will issue several different classes of security, known as *collateralized mortgage obligations* or *CMOs*. For example, any mortgage prepayments might be used first to pay off one class of security holders and only then will other classes start to be repaid.

[22]See J. Mathews, "David Bowie Reinvents Self, This Time as a Bond Issue," *Washington Post,* February 7, 1997.

[23]Every investor dreams of buying up the entire supply of a sinking-fund bond that is selling way below face value and then forcing the company to buy the bonds back at face value. Cornering the market in this way is fun to dream about but difficult to do. For a discussion, see K. B. Dunn and C. S. Spatt, "A Strategic Analysis of Sinking Fund Bonds," *Journal of Financial Economics* 13 (September 1984), pp. 399–424.

Instead of paying cash, the company can buy bonds in the marketplace and pay these into the fund.[24] This is a valuable option for the company. If the price of the bond is low, the firm will buy bonds in the market and hand them to the sinking fund; if the price is high, it will call the bonds by lottery.

Generally, there is a mandatory fund that *must* be satisfied and an optional fund which can be satisfied if the borrower chooses.[25] For example, Ralston Purina *must* contribute at least $13.5 million each year to the sinking fund but has the option to contribute a further $13.5 million.

As in the case of Ralston Purina, most "sinkers" begin to operate after about 10 years. For lower-quality issues the payments are usually sufficient to redeem the entire issue in equal installments over the life of the bond. In contrast, high-quality bonds often have light sinking fund requirements with large balloon payments at maturity.

We saw earlier that interest payments provide a regular test of the company's solvency. Sinking funds provide an additional hurdle that the firm must keep jumping. If it cannot pay the cash into the sinking fund, the lenders can demand their money back. That is why long-dated, low-quality issues usually involve larger sinking funds.

Unfortunately, a sinking fund is a weak test of solvency if the firm is allowed to repurchase bonds in the market. Since the *market* value of the debt must always be less than the value of the firm, financial distress reduces the cost of repurchasing debt in the market. The sinking fund, then, is a hurdle that gets progressively lower as the hurdler gets weaker.

Call Provisions

Corporate bonds sometimes include a call option that allows the company to pay back the debt early. Occasionally, you come across bonds that give the *investor* the repayment option. Retractable (or puttable) bonds give investors the option to demand early repayment, and extendible bonds give them the option to extend the bond's life.

For some companies callable bonds offer a natural form of insurance. For example, Fannie Mae and Freddie Mac are federal agencies that offer fixed- and floating-rate mortgages to home buyers. When interest rates fall, home owners are likely to repay their fixed-rate mortgage and take out a new mortgage at the lower interest rate. This can severely dent the income of the two agencies. Therefore, to protect themselves against the effect of falling interest rates, both agencies issue large quantities of long-term callable debt. When interest rates fall, the agencies can reduce their funding costs by calling their bonds and replacing them with new bonds at a lower rate. Ideally, the fall in bond interest payments should exactly offset the reduction in mortgage income.

These days, issues of straight bonds by industrial companies are much less likely to include a call provision.[26] However, Ralston Purina had the option to buy back the entire bond issue. The company was subject to two limitations on the use

[24] If the bonds are privately placed, the company cannot repurchase them in the marketplace; it *must* call them at their face value.

[25] A number of private placements (particularly those in extractive industries) require a payment only when net income exceeds some specified level.

[26] See, for example, L. Crabbe, "Callable Corporate Bonds: A Vanishing Breed," Board of Governors of the Federal Reserve System, Washington, D.C., 1991.

of this call option: Until 1989 the company was prohibited from calling the bond in any circumstances and from 1989 to 1996 it was not allowed to call the bond in order to replace it with new debt yielding less than the 9.748 percent yield on the original bond.

If interest rates fall and bond prices rise, the option to buy back the bond at a fixed price can be very attractive. The company can buy back the bond and issue another at a higher price and a lower interest rate. And so it proved with the Ralston Purina bond. By the time that the restrictions on calling the bonds were removed in 1996, interest rates had declined. The company was therefore able to repurchase the bond at the call price of 103.905, which was below the bond's potential value.

How does a company know when to call its bonds? The answer is simple: Other things equal, if it wishes to maximize the value of its stock, it must minimize the value of its bonds. Therefore, the company should never call the bond if its market value is less than the call price, for that would just be giving a present to the bondholders. Equally, a company *should* call the bond if it's worth *more* than the call price.

Of course, investors take the call option into account when they buy or sell the bond. They know that the company will call the bond as soon as it is worth more than the call price, so no investor will be willing to pay more than the call price for the bond. The market price of the bond may, therefore, reach the call price, but it will not rise above it. This gives the company the following rule for calling its bonds: *Call the bond when, and only when, the market price reaches the call price.*[27]

If we know how bond prices behave over time, we can modify the basic option-valuation model of Chapter 21 to find the value of the callable bond, *given* that investors know that the company will call the issue as soon as the market price reaches the call price. For example, look at Figure 25.2. It illustrates the relationship between the value of a straight 8 percent five-year bond and the value of a callable 8 percent five-year bond. Suppose that the value of the straight bond is very low. In this case there is little likelihood that the company will ever wish to call its bonds. (Remember that it will call the bonds only when their price equals the call price.) Therefore the value of the callable bond will be almost identical to the value of the straight bond. Now suppose that the straight bond is worth exactly 100. In this case there is a good chance that the company will wish at some time to call its bonds. Therefore the value of our callable bond will be slightly less than that of the straight bond. If interest rates decline further, the price of the straight bond will continue to rise, but nobody will ever pay more than the call price for the callable bond.

A call provision is not a free lunch. It provides the issuer with a valuable option, but that is recognized in a lower issue price. So why do companies bother with call provisions? One reason is that bond indentures often place a number of restrictions on what the company can do. Companies are happy to agree to these restrictions as long as they know they can escape from them if the restrictions prove too inhibiting. The call provision provides the escape route.

---

[27]See M. J. Brennan and E. S. Schwartz, "Savings Bonds, Retractable Bonds, and Callable Bonds," *Journal of Financial Economics* 5 (1997), pp. 67–88. Of course, this assumes that the bond is correctly priced, that investors are behaving rationally, and that investors expect the *firm* to behave rationally. Also, we ignore some complications. First, you may not wish to call a bond if you are prevented by a nonrefunding clause from issuing new debt. Second, the call premium is a tax-deductible expense for the company but is taxed as a capital gain to the bondholder. Third, there are other possible tax consequences to both the company and the investor from replacing a low-coupon bond with a higher-coupon bond. Fourth, there are costs to calling and reissuing debt.

FIGURE 25.2

Relationship between the value of a callable bond and that of a straight (noncallable) bond. Assumptions: (1) Both bonds have an 8 percent coupon and a five-year maturity; (2) the callable bond may be called at face value any time before maturity; (3) the short-term interest rate follows a random walk, and the expected returns on bonds of all maturities are equal.

Source: M. J. Brennan and E. S. Schwartz, "Savings Bonds, Retractable Bonds, and Callable Bonds," *Journal of Financial Economics* 5 (1977), pp. 67–88.

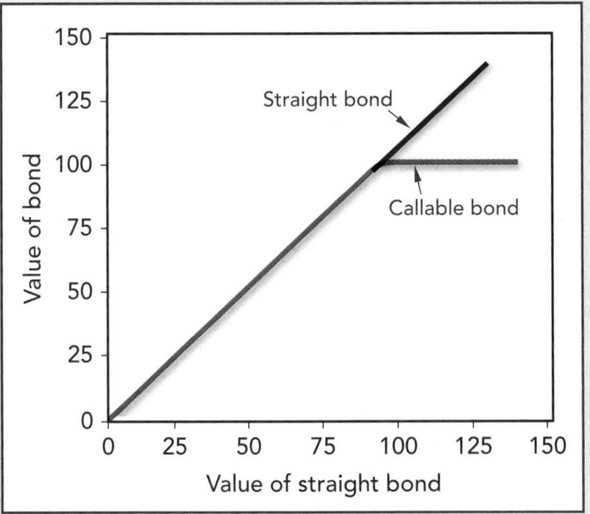

We mentioned earlier that some bonds also provide the investor with an option to demand early repayment. *Puttable* bonds exist largely because bond indentures cannot anticipate every action that the company may take which could harm the bondholder. If the value of the bonds is reduced, the put option allows bondholders to demand repayment.

Puttable loans can sometimes get their issuers into BIG trouble. During the 1990s many loans to Asian companies had given the lenders a repayment option. Consequently, when the Asian crisis struck in 1997, these companies were faced by a flood of lenders demanding their money back.

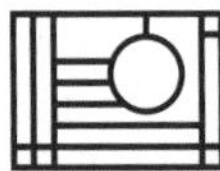

25.6 RESTRICTIVE COVENANTS

The difference between a corporate bond and a comparable Treasury bond is that the company has the option to default whereas the government supposedly doesn't. That is a valuable option. If you don't believe us, think about whether (other things equal) you would prefer to be a shareholder in a company with limited liability or in a company with unlimited liability. Of course you would prefer to have the option to walk away from your company's debts. Unfortunately, every silver lining has its cloud, and the drawback to having a default option is that corporate bondholders expect to be compensated for giving it to you. That is why corporate bonds sell at lower prices and therefore higher yields than government bonds.[28]

Investors know there is a risk of default when they buy a corporate bond. But they still want to make sure that the company plays fair. They don't want it to gam-

[28]In Chapters 20 and 24 we showed that this option to default is equivalent to a put option on the assets of the firm.

ble with their money or to take unreasonable risks. Therefore, the bond indenture may include a number of restrictive covenants to prevent the company from purposely increasing the value of its default option.[29]

After Ralston Purina had issued its bonds, the company had a total market value of $7.6 billion and total long-term debt of $2.1 billion. This meant that the company value would need to fall by over 70 percent before it would pay Ralston Purina to default. But suppose that after issuing the 9.5 percent bonds, Ralston Purina announced a bumper $3 billion bond issue. The company would have a market value of $10.6 billion and long-term debt of $5.1 billion. It would now pay the company to default if its value fell by little more than 50 percent ($1 - 5.1/10.6 = .52$, or 52 percent). The original bondholders would be worse off. If they had known about the new issue, they would not have been willing to pay such a high price for their bonds.

A new issue hurts the original bondholders because it increases the *ratio* of senior debt to company value. The bondholders would not object to an issue if the company kept the ratio the same by simultaneously issuing common stock. Therefore, the bond agreement often states that the company may issue more senior debt only if the ratio of senior debt to the value of net book assets is within a specified limit.

Why don't senior lenders demand limits on *subordinated* debt? The answer is that the subordinated lender does not get *any* money until the senior bondholders have been paid in full.[30] The senior bondholders, therefore, view subordinated bonds in much the same way that they view equity: They would be happy to see an issue of either. Of course, the converse is not true. Holders of subordinated debt *do* care both about the total amount of debt and the proportion that is senior to their claim. As a result, an issue of subordinated debt generally includes a restriction on both total debt and senior debt.

All bondholders worry that the company may issue more secured debt. An issue of mortgage bonds often imposes a limit on the amount of secured debt. This is not necessary when you are issuing unsecured debentures. As long as the debenture holders are given equal protection, they do not care how much you mortgage your assets. Therefore, the Ralston Purina debenture includes a so-called *negative pledge clause,* in which the debenture holders simply say, "Me, too."[31]

Instead of borrowing money to buy an asset, companies may enter into a long-term agreement to rent or lease it. For the debtholder this is very similar to secured borrowing. Therefore indentures also include limitations on leasing.

We have talked about how an unscrupulous borrower can try to increase the value of the default option by issuing more debt. But that is not the only way that such a company can exploit its existing bondholders. For example, we know that the value of an option is affected by dividend payments. If the company pays out large dividends to its shareholders and doesn't replace the cash by an issue of

[29]We described in Section 18.3 some of the games that managers can play at the expense of bondholders.

[30]In practice the courts do not always observe the strict rules of precedence (see the appendix to this chapter). Therefore the subordinated debtholder may receive *some* payment even when the senior debtholder is not fully paid off.

[31]"Me too" is not acceptable legal jargon. Instead the Ralston Purina bond agreement states that the company will not consent to any lien on its assets without securing the debentures "equally and ratably."

MARRIOTT PLAN ENRAGES HOLDERS OF ITS BONDS

Marriott Corp. has infuriated bond investors with a restructuring plan that may be a new way for companies to pull the rug out from under bondholders.

Prices of Marriott's existing bonds have plunged as much as 30% in the past two days in the wake of the hotel and food-services company's announcement that it plans to separate into two companies, one burdened with virtually all of Marriott's debt.

On Monday, Marriott said that it will divide its operations into two separate businesses. One, Marriott International Inc., is a healthy company that will manage Marriott's vast hotel chain; it will get most of the old company's revenue, a larger share of the cash flow and will be nearly debt-free.

The second business, called Host Marriott Corp., is a debt-laden company that will own Marriott hotels along with other real estate and retain essentially all of the old Marriott's $3 billion of debt.

The announcement stunned and infuriated bondholders, who watched nervously as the value of their Marriott bonds tumbled and as Moody's Investors Service Inc. downgraded the bonds to the junk-bond category from investment-grade.

PRICE PLUNGE

In trading, Marriott's 10% bonds that mature in 2012, which Marriott sold to investors just six months ago, were quoted yesterday at about 80 cents on the dollar, down from 110 Friday. The price decline translates into a stunning loss of $300 for a bond with a $1,000 face amount.

Marriott officials concede that the company's spinoff plan penalizes bondholders. However, the company notes that, like all public corporations, its fiduciary duty is to stockholders, not bondholders. Indeed, Marriott's stock jumped 12% Monday. (It fell a bit yesterday.)

Bond investors and analysts worry that if the Marriott spinoff goes through, other companies will soon follow suit by separating debt-laden units from the rest of the company. "Any company that fears it has underperforming divisions that are dragging down its stock price is a possible candidate [for such a restructuring]," says Dorothy K. Lee, an assistant vice president at Moody's.

If the trend heats up, investors said, the Marriott's structuring could be the worst news for corporate bondholders since RJR Nabisco Inc.'s managers shocked investors in 1987 by announcing they were taking the company private in a record $25 billion leveraged buyout. The move, which loaded RJR with debt and tanked the value of RJR bonds, triggered a deep slump of many investment-grade corporate bonds as investors backed away from the market.

STRONG COVENANTS MAY RE-EMERGE

Some analysts say the move by Marriott may trigger the re-emergence of strong covenants, or written protections in future corporate bond issues to protect bondholders against such restructurings as the one being engineered by Marriott. In the wake of the RJR buy-out, many investors demanded stronger covenants in new corporate bond issues.

Some investors blame themselves for not demanding stronger covenants. "It's our own fault," said Robert Hickey, a bond fund manager at Van Kampen Merritt. In their rush to buy bonds in an effort to lock in yields, many investors have allowed companies to sell bonds with covenants that have been "slim to none," Mr. Hickey said.

Source: Reprinted by permission of *The Wall Street Journal,*

stock, there are fewer assets available to cover the debt. Therefore many bond issues restrict the amount of dividends that the company may pay.[32]

Changes in Covenant Protection

Before 1980 most bonds had covenants limiting further issues of debt and payments of dividends. But then institutions relaxed their requirements for lending to large public companies and accepted bonds with no such restrictions. This was the case with RJR Nabisco, the food and tobacco giant, which in 1988 had $5 billion of A-rated debt outstanding. In that year the company was taken over, and $19 billion of additional debt was substituted for equity. As soon as the first plans for the takeover were announced, the value of the existing debt fell by about 12 percent, and it was downrated to BB. For one of the bondholders, Metropolitan Life Insurance, this meant a $40 million loss. Metropolitan sued the company, arguing that the bonds contained an *implied* covenant preventing major financing changes that would undercut existing bondholders.[33] However, Metropolitan lost: The courts held that only the written covenants count.

Restrictions on debt issues and dividend payments quietly returned to fashion.[34] Bond analysts and lawyers started to look more closely at *event risks* like the debt-financed takeover that socked Metropolitan. Some companies agreed to *poison-put* clauses that oblige the borrower to repay the bonds if a large quantity of stock is bought by a single investor and the firm's bonds are downrated.

Unfortunately, there are always nasty surprises around the next corner. The Finance in the News box describes how one such surprise came in 1992 when the hotel chain, Marriott, antagonized its bondholders.

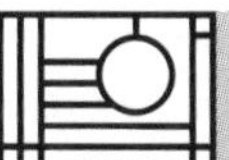

25.7 PRIVATE PLACEMENTS AND PROJECT FINANCE

The Ralston Purina debenture was registered with the SEC and sold to the public. However, debt is often placed privately with a small number of financial institutions. As we saw in Section 15.5, it costs less to arrange a private placement than to make a public debt issue. But there are three other ways in which the private placement bond may differ from its public counterpart.

First, if you place an issue privately with one or two financial institutions, it may be necessary to sign only a simple promissory note. This is just an IOU which lays down certain conditions that the borrower must observe. However, when you

[32]See A. Kalay, "Stockholder-Bondholder Conflict and Dividend Constraints," *Journal of Financial Economics* 10 (1982), pp. 211–233. A dividend restriction might typically prohibit the company from paying dividends if their cumulative amount would exceed the sum of (1) cumulative net income, (2) the proceeds from the sale of stock or conversion of debt, and (3) a dollar amount equal to one year's dividend.

[33]*Metropolitan Life Insurance Company* (plaintiff) *v. RJR Nabisco, Inc., and F. Ross Johnson* (defendants), Supreme Court of the State of New York, County of New York, Complaint, Nov. 16, 1988.

[34]A study by Paul Asquith and Thierry Wizman suggests that better covenants would have protected Metropolitan Life and other bondholders against loss. On average, the announcement of a leveraged buyout led to a fall of 5.2 percent in the value of the bond if there were no restrictions on further debt issues, dividend payments, or mergers. However, if the bond was protected by strong covenants, announcement of a leveraged buyout led to a *rise* in the bond price of 2.6 percent. See P. Asquith and T. A. Wizman, "Event Risk, Bond Covenants, and the Return to Existing Bondholders in Corporate Buyouts," *Journal of Financial Economics* 27 (September 1990), pp. 195–213.

make a public issue of debt, you must worry about who is to represent the bondholders in any subsequent negotiations and what procedures are needed for paying interest and principal. Therefore the contractual arrangement has to be that much more complicated.

The second characteristic of publicly issued bonds is that they are highly standardized products. They *have* to be—investors are constantly buying and selling without checking the fine print in the agreement. This is not so necessary in private placements and so the debt contract can be custom-tailored for firms with special problems or opportunities. The relationship between borrower and lender is much more intimate. Imagine a $20 million debt issue privately placed with an insurance company, and compare it with an equivalent public issue held by 200 anonymous investors. The insurance company can justify a more thorough investigation of the company's prospects and therefore may be more willing to accept unusual terms or conditions.[35]

All bond agreements seek to protect the lender by imposing a number of conditions on the borrower. These conditions tend to be more severe in the case of privately placed debt. The borrowers are willing to agree to these conditions because they know that, if the debt is privately placed, the conditions can be modified later if it makes sense. However, in the case of a public issue it can be extremely cumbersome to get the permission of all the existing bondholders.

These features give private placements a particular niche in the corporate debt market, namely, loans to small and medium-sized firms. These are the firms that face the highest issue costs in public issues, that require the most detailed investigation, and that may require specialized, flexible loan arrangements. However, many large companies also use private placements.

Of course, the advantages of private placements are not free, for the lenders demand a higher rate of interest to compensate them for holding an illiquid asset. It is difficult to generalize about the differences in interest rates between private placements and public issues, but a typical differential is on the order of 50 basis points or .50 percentage points.

Project Finance

We are not going to dwell further on the topic of private placement bonds, because the greater part of what we have had to say about public issues is also true of private placements. However, we do need to discuss a different form of private loan, one that is tied as closely as possible to the fortunes of a particular project and that minimizes the exposure of the parent. Such a loan is usually referred to as **project finance** and is a specialty of large international banks.

Project finance means debt supported by the project, not by the project's sponsoring companies. Debt ratios are nevertheless very high. They can be high because the debt is supported not just by the project's assets but also by a variety of contracts and guarantees provided by customers, suppliers, and local governments, as well as by the project's owners.

Example Here is how project finance was used to construct a large new oil-fired power plant in Pakistan. First, a separate firm, the Hub Power Company (Hubco), was established to own the power station. Hubco then engaged a consortium of

[35]Of course debt with the same terms could be offered publicly, but then 200 separate investigations would be required—a much more expensive proposition.

companies, headed by the Japanese company, Mitsui & Co., to build the power station, while the British company, National Power, became responsible for managing and running it. Hubco agreed to buy the fuel from the Pakistan State Oil Company and to sell the power station's output to another government body, the Water and Power Development Authority (WAPDA).

Hubco's lawyers drew up a complex series of contracts to make sure that each of these parties came up to scratch. For example, the contractors guaranteed to deliver the plant on time and to ensure that it would operate to specifications. National Power, the plant manager, agreed to maintain the plant and operate it efficiently. Pakistan State Oil Company entered into a long-term contract to supply oil to Hubco and WAPDA agreed to buy Hubco's output for the next 30 years.[36] Since WAPDA would pay for the electricity with rupees, Hubco was concerned about the possibility of a fall in the value of the rupee. The State Bank of Pakistan, therefore, arranged to provide Hubco with foreign exchange at guaranteed exchange rates.

The effect of these contracts was to ensure that each risk was borne by the party that was best able to measure and control it. For example, the contractors were best placed to ensure that the plant was completed on time, so it made sense to ask them to bear the risk of construction delays. Similarly, the plant operator was best placed to operate the plant efficiently and would be penalized if it failed to do so. The contractors and the plant manager were prepared to take on these risks because the project involved an established technology and there was relatively little chance of unpleasant surprises.

While these contracts sought to be as precise as possible about each party's responsibilities, they could not cover every eventuality; inevitably the contracts were incomplete. Therefore, to buttress the formal legal agreements, the contractors and the plant manager became major shareholders in Hubco. This meant that if they cut corners in building and running the plant, they would share in the losses.

The equity in Hubco was highly levered. Over 75 percent of the $1.8 billion investment in the project was financed by debt. Some of this was junior debt provided by a fund that was set up by the World Bank and western and Japanese government aid agencies. The bulk of the debt was senior debt provided by a group of major international banks.[37] The banks were encouraged to invest because they knew that the World Bank and several governments were in the frontline and would take a hit if the project were to fail. But they were still concerned that the government of Pakistan might prevent Hubco from paying out foreign currency or it might impose a special tax or prevent the company bringing in the specialist staff it needed. Therefore, to protect Hubco against these political risks, the government promised to pay compensation if it interfered in such ways with the operation of the project. Of course, the government could not be prevented from tearing up that agreement, but, if it did, Hubco was able to call on a $360 million guarantee by the

[36]WAPDA entered into a *take-or-pay* agreement with Hubco; if it did not take the electricity, it still had to pay for it. In the case of pipeline projects the contract with the customer is often in the form of a *throughput* agreement, whereby the customer agrees to make a minimum use of the pipeline. Another arrangement for transferring revenue risk to a customer is the tolling contract, whereby the customer agrees to deliver to the project company materials that it is to process and to return to the customer. One purpose of transferring revenue risk to customers is to encourage them to estimate their demand for the project's output thoroughly.

[37]Notice that the project was not financed by a public bond issue. The concentrated ownership of bank debt induces the lenders to evaluate the project carefully and to monitor its subsequent progress. It also facilitates the renegotiation of the debt if the project company runs into difficulties.

World Bank and the Export–Import Bank of Japan. This was supposed to keep the Pakistan government honest once the plant was built and operating. Governments can be surprisingly relaxed in the face of the wrath of a private corporation but are usually reluctant to break an agreement that lands the World Bank with a large bill.

The arrangements for the Hubco project were complex, costly, and time-consuming. Not everything was plain sailing. The project was suspended for over a year by the Gulf War and it looked at one time as if it would be spiked by a Pakistani court ruling that the interest on the loans contravened Islamic law. Ten years after the start of discussions the final agreement on financing the project was signed and within a short time Hubco was producing a fifth of all Pakistan's electricity.

However, that was not the end of the Hubco story. After the fall of Benazir Bhutto's government in Pakistan, the new government terminated the contract with Hubco and announced a 30 percent cut in electricity tariffs. This inevitably led to a dispute with the World Bank, which spelled out that, until the dispute could be resolved, nothing could move on new loans.[38]

Project Finance—Some Common Features

No two project financings are alike, but they have some common features:

- The project is established as a separate company.
- The contractors and the plant manager become major shareholders in the project and thus share in the risk of the project's failure.
- The project company enters into a complex series of contracts that distributes risk among the contractors, the plant manager, the suppliers, and the customers.
- The government may guarantee that it will provide the necessary permits, allow the purchase of foreign exchange, and so on.
- The detailed contractual arrangements and government guarantees allow a large part of the capital for the project to be provided in the form of bank debt or other privately placed borrowing.

The Role of Project Finance

Project finance is widely used in developing countries to fund power, telecommunication, and transportation projects, but it is also used in the major industrialized countries. In the United States project finance is most commonly used to fund power plants. For example, an electric utility company may get together with an industrial company to construct a cogeneration plant that provides electricity to the utility and waste heat to a nearby industrial plant. The utility stands behind the cogeneration project and guarantees its revenue stream. Banks are happy to lend as much as 90 percent of the cost of the project because they know that, once the project is up and running, the cash flow is insulated from most of the risks facing normal businesses.[39]

There are some interesting regulatory implications, however. When a utility builds a power plant, it is entitled to a fair return on its investment: Regulators are

[38]The confrontation between Hubco and the government of Pakistan is described in C. Hill, "Power Failure," *Institutional Investor* (November 1999), pp. 109–119.

[39]Such extremely high debt ratios must rest on the utility's creditworthiness. In a sense, the utility has borrowed money "off balance sheet."

TABLE 25.2

Some examples of innovation in bond design.

Liquid Yield Option Notes (LYONs)	Puttable, callable, convertible, zero-coupon debt
Asset-backed securities	Many small loans are packaged together and resold as a bond
Catastrophe (CAT) bonds	Payments are reduced in the event of a specified natural disaster
Reverse floaters (yield-curve notes)	Floating-rate bonds that pay a higher rate of interest when other interest rates fall and a lower rate when other rates rise
Equity-linked bonds	Payments are linked to the performance of a stock-market index
Pay-in-kind bonds (PIKs)	Issuer can choose to make interest payments either in cash or in more bonds with an equivalent face value
Rate-sensitive bonds	Coupon rate changes as company's credit rating changes
Ratchet bonds	Floating-rate bond whose coupon can only be reset downward

supposed to set customer charges that will allow the utility to earn its cost of capital. Unfortunately, the cost of capital is not easily measured and is a natural focus for argument in regulatory hearings. But when a utility buys electric power, the cost of capital is rolled into the contract price and treated as an operating cost. In this case the pass-through to customers may be less controversial.

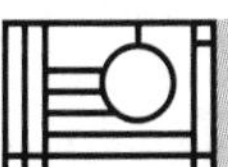

25.8 INNOVATION IN THE BOND MARKET

Domestic and international bonds, fixed- and floating-rate bonds, coupon bonds and zeros, callable and puttable bonds, secured and unsecured bonds, senior and junior bonds, privately placed bonds and project finance—you might think that all this would give you as much choice as you need. Yet almost every day some new type of bond seems to be issued.

Table 25.2 lists some of the more interesting bonds that have been invented in recent years.[40] We have already encountered some of these exotic bonds. For example, you may remember from Chapter 23 the convertible zero-coupon LYONs, and in this chapter we cited the "Bowie bonds" as an example of asset-backed bonds. In Chapter 27 we will also discuss catastrophe bonds whose payoffs are linked to the occurrence of natural disasters.

Here are a couple more examples of unusual bonds. The first is an issue of a three-year Japanese yen bond that combined the features of two types of exotic bond—the reverse floater and the equity-linked bond. The issue by the Norwegian Christiania Bank came in two parts or *tranches.* Tranche A paid interest equal to the prime rate but subject to a maximum (or *cap*) of 12.8 percent. Tranche B paid interest of 12.8 percent *less* the prime rate. Thus, if the general level of interest rates rose, the interest payment on tranche B fell but it was not allowed to fall below zero. If

[40]For a more comprehensive list of innovations, see K. A. Carrow and J. J. McConnell, "A Survey of U.S. Corporate Financing Innovations: 1970–1997," *Journal of Applied Corporate Finance* 12 (Spring 1999), pp. 55–69.

you had invested an equal amount in each tranche, the average interest rate on your two holdings would have been 6.4 percent.

That was not the end of tranche B's complications, since the principal payment was not fixed at 100 percent. Instead it declined if the Japanese stock market fell. If the index fell by about 50 percent, the bondholder did not receive any principal payment at all. Thus, investing in tranche B was like buying an unusual floating-rate note and also selling a put option on the Japanese stock market. To compensate for the possible capital loss, the bonds offered a relatively high rate of interest.

For several years the majority of international issues of yen bonds involved similar options. Why? One reason is that life insurance companies in Japan cannot distribute capital gains to policyholders and therefore had a powerful appetite for high-yielding bonds even if such investments involved the risk of a capital loss. Christiania Bank paid a high rate of interest on the package, but it obtained a put option in exchange. If it did not want to hold onto this put option, it could easily sell it to foreign investors who were worried that the Japanese equity market was overpriced and wanted protection against a fall in that market.

Our second example is a *pay-in-kind* bond (or *PIK*) issued by RJR Nabisco. The bond carried an attractive coupon of 15 percent, but for the first few years of the bond's life, RJR could choose to pay interest either in the form of cash or of bonds with an equivalent face value. This gave the company a valuable option. If RJR fell on hard times and bond prices dropped, it could hand over low-priced bonds instead of hard cash. RJR also had the right to call the bonds. That provided another valuable option: If interest rates fell and bond prices rose, the company could buy back the bond for the call price.

It is often difficult to foresee which new securities will become popular and which will never get off the ground. Sometimes new financial instruments succeed because they widen investor choice. Economists refer to such securities as helping to "complete the market." For example, the unusual weather in 1997–1998 resulting from El Niño encouraged a number of firms to market financial contracts that would pay off in unfavorable weather conditions. These firms hoped that *weather derivatives* would prove popular with the newly deregulated energy companies, the agricultural community, and many other businesses that might wish to protect themselves against the vagaries of the weather.

Governments may unwittingly play a major role in stimulating financial innovation, for new types of security are often designed to circumvent government regulations. For instance, we have already seen how one unusual bond, the equity-linked yen bond, was a consequence of Japanese insurance regulation. Unforeseen changes in the bond market can also result from changes in the tax rules. One of the most striking examples was the U.S. government's imposition of a tax on purchases of foreign securities, which brought about the development of the eurobond market in the 1960s.

SUMMARY

Now that you have read this chapter, you should have a fair idea of what you are letting yourself in for when you make a public issue of bonds. You can issue the bonds in the domestic U.S. market, in a foreign bond market, or in the international bond market. International bonds (also called eurobonds) are marketed simultaneously in a number of foreign countries, usually by the London branches of international banks and security dealers.

The detailed bond agreement is set out in the indenture between your company and a trustee, but the main provisions are summarized in the prospectus to the issue.

The indenture states whether the bonds are senior or subordinated and whether they are secured or unsecured. Most bonds are unsecured debentures or notes. This means that they are general claims on the corporation. The principal exceptions are utility mortgage bonds, collateral trust bonds, and equipment trust certificates. In the event of a default, the trustee to these issues can repossess the company's assets in order to pay off the debt.

Most long-term bond issues have a sinking fund. This means that the company must set aside enough money each year to retire a specified number of bonds. A sinking fund reduces the average life of the bond, and it provides a yearly test of the company's ability to service its debt. It therefore protects the bondholders against the risk of default.

Long-dated bonds may be callable before maturity. The company usually has to pay a call premium, which is initially equal to the coupon and which declines progressively to zero. The option to call the bond may be very valuable: If interest rates decline and bond values rise, you may be able to call a bond that would be worth substantially more than the call price. Of course, if investors know that you may call the bond, the call price will act as a ceiling on the market price. Your best strategy, therefore, is to call the bond as soon as the market price hits the call price. You are unlikely to do better than that.

The bond indenture also imposes certain conditions on the borrower. Here are some examples of covenants:

1. Issues of senior bonds prohibit the company from issuing further senior debt if the ratio of senior debt to net tangible assets is too high.
2. Issues of subordinated bonds may also prohibit the company from issuing further senior or junior debt if the ratio of *all* debt to net tangible assets is too high.
3. Unsecured bonds incorporate a negative pledge clause, which prohibits the company from securing additional debt without giving equal treatment to the existing unsecured bonds.
4. Many bonds place a limit on the company's dividend payments.

Private placements are less standardized than public issues, and they impose more stringent covenants. Otherwise, they are generally close counterparts of publicly issued bonds. Sometimes private debt takes the form of project finance. In this case the loan is tied to the fortunes of a particular project.

There is an enormous variety of bond issues, and new forms of bonds are spawned almost daily. By a principle of natural selection, some of these new instruments become popular and may even replace existing species. Others are ephemeral curiosities. Some innovations succeed because they widen investor choice and allow investors to manage their risks better. Others owe their origin to tax rules and government regulation.

APPENDIX

Bankruptcy Procedures

What do Pacific Gas and Electric, Global Crossing, Enron, Fruit of the Loom, and Kmart have in common? Answer: They have all filed for bankruptcy. In this appendix we will explain what this involves and we will look at some of the pros and cons of the U.S. bankruptcy laws.

Occasionally bankruptcy proceedings in the United States are initiated by the creditors, but usually it is the firm itself that decides to file. It can choose one of two procedures, which are set out in Chapters 7 and 11 of the 1978 Bankruptcy Reform Act. The purpose of Chapter 7 is to oversee the firm's death and dismemberment, while Chapter 11 seeks to nurse the firm back to health.

Most small firms make use of Chapter 7.[41] In this case the bankruptcy judge appoints a trustee, who then closes the firm down and auctions off the assets. The proceeds from the auction are used to pay off the creditors. There is a pecking order of unsecured creditors. The U.S. Treasury, court officers, and the trustee have first peck. Wages come next, followed by taxes and debts to some government agencies such as the Pension Benefit Guarantee Corporation. Frequently the trustee will need to prevent some creditors from trying to jump the gun and collect on their debts, and sometimes the trustee will retrieve property that a creditor has recently seized. Managers of small firms that are in trouble know that Chapter 7 bankruptcy means the end of the road and, therefore, will try to put off filing as long as possible. As a result, when the assets are eventually liquidated, the unsecured creditors usually receive only a few crumbs.[42]

Instead of agreeing to a liquidation, large public companies generally attempt to rehabilitate the business. This is in the shareholders' interests; they have nothing to lose if things deteriorate further and everything to gain if the firm recovers. The procedures for rehabilitation are set out in Chapter 11 of the 1978 act. Their purpose is to keep the firm alive and operating and to protect the value of its assets[43] while a plan of reorganization is worked out. During this period, other proceedings against the firm are halted, and the company usually continues to be run by its existing management.[44] The responsibility for developing the plan falls on the debtor firm but, if it cannot devise an acceptable plan, the court may invite anyone to do so—for example, a committee of creditors.

The plan goes into effect if it is accepted by the creditors and confirmed by the court. Acceptance requires approval by at least one-half of the creditors voting, and the creditors voting "aye" must represent two-thirds of the value of the creditors' aggregate claim against the firm. The plan also needs to be approved by two-thirds of the shareholders. Once the creditors and shareholders have accepted the plan, the court normally approves it, provided that *each class* of creditors is in favor and that the creditors will be no worse off under the plan than they would be if the firm's assets were liquidated and distributed. Under certain conditions the court may confirm a plan even if one or more classes of creditors votes against it,[45] but the rules for a "cram-down" are complicated and we will not attempt to cover them here.

The reorganization plan is basically a statement of who gets what; each class of creditors gives up its claim in exchange for new securities or a mixture of securities and cash. The problem is to design a new capital structure for the firm that will

---

[41]Sometimes small firms file under Chapter 11, but attempts to rehabilitate the firm are rarely successful and the assets eventually have to be liquidated.

[42]See M. J. White, "Survey Evidence on Business Bankruptcy," in J. S. Bhandari and L. A. Weiss (eds.), *Corporate Bankruptcy,* Cambridge University Press, Cambridge, 1996.

[43]To keep the firm alive, it may be necessary to continue to use assets that were offered as collateral, but this denies secured creditors access to their collateral. To resolve this problem, the Bankruptcy Reform Act makes it possible for firms operating under Chapter 11 to keep such assets as long as the creditors who have a claim on those assets are compensated for any decline in their value. Thus, the firm might make cash payments to the secured creditors to cover economic depreciation of the assets.

[44]Occasionally the court will appoint a trustee to manage the firm.

[45]But at least one class of creditors must vote for the plan; otherwise the court cannot approve it.

(1) satisfy the creditors and (2) allow the firm to solve the *business* problems that got the firm into trouble in the first place.[46] Sometimes satisfying these two conditions requires a plan of baroque complexity, involving the creation of a dozen or more new securities.

The Securities and Exchange Commission (SEC) plays a role in many reorganizations, particularly for large, public companies. Its interest is to ensure that all relevant and material information is disclosed to the creditors before they vote on a proposed plan of reorganization. The SEC may take part in a hearing before court approval of a plan, for example.

Chapter 11 proceedings are often successful, and the patient emerges fit and healthy. But in other cases rehabilitation proves impossible, and the assets are liquidated. Sometimes the firm may emerge from Chapter 11 for a brief period before it is once again submerged by disaster and back in the bankruptcy court. For example, TWA came out of Chapter 11 bankruptcy at the end of 1993, was back again less than two years later, and then for a third time in 1998, prompting jokes about "Chapter 22" and "Chapter 33."[47]

Is Chapter 11 Efficient?

Here is a simple view of the bankruptcy decision: Whenever a payment is due to creditors, management checks the value of the equity. If the value is positive, the firm pays the creditors (if necessary, raising the cash by an issue of shares). If the equity is valueless, the firm defaults on its debt and petitions for bankruptcy. If the assets of the bankrupt firm can be put to better use elsewhere, the firm is liquidated and the proceeds are used to pay off the creditors; otherwise the creditors simply become the new owners, and the firm continues to operate.[48]

In practice, matters are rarely so simple. For example, we observe that firms often petition for bankruptcy even when the equity has a positive value. And firms often continue to operate even when the assets could be used more efficiently elsewhere. The problems in Chapter 11 usually arise because the goal of paying off the creditors conflicts with the goal of maintaining the business as a going concern. We described in Chapter 18 how the assets of Eastern Airlines seeped away as the court attempted to keep the airline flying. When the company filed for bankruptcy, its assets were more than sufficient to repay in full its liabilities of $3.7 billion. But the bankruptcy judge was determined to keep Eastern flying. When it finally became clear that the airline was a terminal case, the assets were sold off and the creditors received less than $.9 billion. The creditors would clearly have been better off if Eastern had been liquidated immediately; the unsuccessful attempt at resuscitation cost the creditors $2.8 billion.[49]

[46]Although Chapter 11 is designed to keep the firm in business, the reorganization plan often involves the sale or closure of large parts of the business.

[47]One study found that after emerging from Chapter 11, about one in three firms reentered bankruptcy or privately restructured their debt. See E. S. Hotchkiss, "Postbankruptcy Reform and Management Turnover," *Journal of Finance* 50 (March 1995), pp. 3–21.

[48]If there are several classes of creditors, the junior creditors initially become the owners of the company and are responsible for paying off the senior debt. They now face exactly the same decision as the original owners. If their equity is valueless, they will also default and turn over ownership of the company to the next class of creditors.

[49]These estimates of creditor losses are taken from L. A. Weiss and K. H. Wruck, "Information Problems, Conflicts of Interest, and Asset Stripping: Chapter 11's Failure in the Case of Eastern Airlines," *Journal of Financial Economics* 48 (1998), pp. 55–97.

Here are some reasons that Chapter 11 proceedings do not always achieve an efficient solution:

1. Although the reorganized firm is legally a new entity, it is entitled to the tax-loss carryforwards belonging to the old firm. If the firm is liquidated rather than reorganized, the tax-loss carryforwards disappear. Thus there is a tax incentive to continue operating the firm even when its assets could be sold and put to better use elsewhere.
2. If the firm's assets are sold off, it is easy to determine what is available to pay the creditors. However, when the company is reorganized, it needs to conserve cash. Therefore, claimants are generally paid in a mixture of cash and securities. This makes it less easy to judge whether they receive a fair shake. For example, each bondholder may be offered $300 in cash and $700 in a new bond that pays no interest for the first two years and a low rate of interest thereafter. A bond of this kind in a company that is struggling to survive may not be worth much, but the bankruptcy court usually looks at the face value of the new bonds and may therefore regard the bondholders as paid off in full.
3. Senior creditors who know they are likely to get a raw deal in a reorganization are likely to press for a liquidation. Shareholders and junior creditors prefer a reorganization. They hope that the court will not interpret the pecking order too strictly and that they will receive some crumbs when the firm's remaining value is sliced up. In the majority of cases their hopes are realized; often they receive a substantial portion of the equity of the reorganized company even though the senior creditors receive less than they are owed.[50]
4. Although shareholders and junior creditors are at the bottom of the pecking order, they have a secret weapon—they can play for time. On average it takes two to three years before a plan is presented to the court and agreed to by each class of creditor. When they use delaying tactics, the junior claimants are betting on a stroke of luck that will rescue their investment. On the other hand, the senior claimants know that time is working against them, so they may be prepared to accept a smaller payoff as part of the price for getting a plan accepted. Also, prolonged bankruptcy cases are costly (the bankruptcy proceedings of Wickes Corporation involved about $250 million in legal and administrative costs).[51] Senior claimants may see their money seeping into lawyers' pockets and therefore decide to settle quickly.
5. While a reorganization plan is being drawn up, the company is likely to need additional working capital. It is therefore allowed to buy goods on credit and borrow money. The new creditors have priority over the old creditors, and their debt may even be secured by assets that are already mortgaged to existing debtholders. This also gives the old creditors an incentive to settle quickly, before their claims are diluted by the new debt.
6. While the firm is in Chapter 11, secured debt receives interest but unsecured debt does not. For unsecured debtholders that is another reason for a fast settlement.

[50]Franks and Torous found that stockholders received some payoff—usually securities—in two-thirds of Chapter 11 reorganizations. See J. R. Franks and W. N. Torous, "An Empirical Investigation of U.S. Firms in Reorganization," *Journal of Finance* 44 (July 1989), pp. 747–770. A similar study concluded that in a third of the cases shareholders received more than 25 percent of the equity in the new firm. See L. A. Weiss, "Bankruptcy Resolution: Direct Costs and Violation of Priority of Claims," *Journal of Financial Economics* 27 (October 1990), pp. 285–314.

[51]We reviewed these costs in Section 18.3.

7. Sometimes profitable companies have filed for Chapter 11 bankruptcy to protect themselves against burdensome suits.[52] For example, Continental Airlines, which was bedeviled by a costly labor contract, filed for Chapter 11 in 1982 and immediately cut pay by up to 50 percent.[53] In 1995 Dow Corning was threatened with costly litigation for damage allegedly caused by its silicone-gel breast implants. Dow filed for bankruptcy under Chapter 11, and the bankruptcy judge agreed to stay the damage suits. Needless to say, lawyers and legislators worry that these actions were contrary to the original intent of the bankruptcy acts.

Workouts

If Chapter 11 reorganizations are not efficient, why don't firms bypass the bankruptcy courts and get together with their creditors to work out a solution?

Many firms that are in distress *do* first seek a negotiated settlement. For example, they can seek to delay repayment of the debt or negotiate an interest rate holiday. However, shareholders and junior creditors know that senior creditors are anxious to avoid formal bankruptcy proceedings. So they are likely to be tough negotiators, and senior creditors generally need to make concessions to reach agreement.[54] The larger the firm, and the more complicated its capital structure, the less likely it is that everyone will agree to any proposal. For example, Wickes Corporation tried—and failed—to reach a negotiated settlement with its 250,000 creditors.

Sometimes the firm does agree to an informal workout with its creditors and then files under Chapter 11 to obtain the approval of the bankruptcy court.[55] Such *prepackaged bankruptcies* reduce the likelihood of subsequent litigation and allow the firm to gain the special tax advantages of Chapter 11.

Alternative Bankruptcy Procedures

The United States bankruptcy system is often described as a debtor-oriented system: Its principal focus is on rescuing firms in distress. But this comes at a cost, for there are many instances in which the firm's assets would be better redeployed in other uses. One critic of Chapter 11, Michael Jensen, has argued that "the U.S. bankruptcy system is fundamentally flawed. It is expensive, it exacerbates conflicts of interest among different classes of creditors, and it often takes years to resolve individual cases."[56] Jensen's proposed solution is to require that any bankrupt company be put immediately on the auction block and the proceeds distributed to claimants in accordance with the priority of their claims.[57]

[52]See, for example, A. Cifelli, "Management by Bankruptcy," *Fortune*, October 1983, pp. 69–73.

[53]The pay cut enabled Continental to reduce fares aggressively and improve its load factors, but it did not solve Continental's problems. Shortly after emerging from bankruptcy, it was back in the bankruptcy court.

[54]Franks and Torous show that creditors make even greater concessions to junior claimholders in informal workouts than in Chapter 11 reorganizations. See J. R. Franks and W. N. Torous, "How Shareholders and Creditors Fare in Workouts and Chapter 11 Reorganizations," *Journal of Financial Economics* 35 (May 1994), pp. 349–370.

[55]For example, when TWA reentered Chapter 11 in 1995, it had already agreed to a *prepack* with its creditors.

[56] M. C. Jensen, "Corporate Control and the Politics of Finance," *Journal of Applied Corporate Finance* 4 (Summer 1991), pp. 13–33.

[57]An ingenious alternative set of bankruptcy procedures is proposed in P. Aghion, O. Hart, and J. Moore, "The Economics of Bankruptcy Reform," *Journal of Law, Economics and Organization* 8 (1992), pp. 523–546.

In other countries the bankruptcy rules are often "creditor-oriented"; their object is to recover as much as possible for the lenders and to ensure that the senior claimants get first peck. For example, the bankruptcy procedures in Germany, Sweden, and the UK have much in common with Chapter 7 in the United States.[58] In other words, an outside official is appointed to take over the company and to sell the assets either piecemeal or as a going concern.[59] The proceeds are then distributed to creditors according to the priority of their claims.

Of course, the grass is always greener elsewhere. In the United States, critics of Chapter 11 complain about the costs of trying to save businesses that are no longer viable. By contrast, in Europe, bankruptcy laws are blamed for the demise of healthy businesses and governments there have looked for ways to encourage rehabilitation rather than liquidation.

---

[58] See, for example, M. J. White, "The Costs of Corporate Bankruptcy: A U.S.–European Comparison," in J. S. Bhandari and L. A. Weiss (eds.), *Corporate Bankruptcy*, Cambridge University Press, Cambridge, 1996; and P. Stromberg, "Conflicts of Interest and Market Illiquidity in Bankruptcy Auctions: Theory and Tests," *Journal of Finance* 55 (December 2000), pp. 2641–2692.

[59] Alhough the bankruptcy codes in these countries contain provisions to keep the firm operating, they are relatively rarely invoked.

FURTHER READING

A useful general work on debt securities is:

F. J. Fabozzi (ed.): *The Handbook of Fixed Income Securities*, Frank J. Fabozzi Associates, New Hope, PA, 2000.

The articles by Brennan and Schwartz and by Kraus are general discussions of call provisions:

M. J. Brennan and E. S. Schwartz: "Savings Bonds, Retractable Bonds and Callable Bonds," *Journal of Financial Economics*, 5:67–88 (1977).

A. Kraus: "An Analysis of Call Provisions and the Corporate Refunding Decision," *Midland Corporate Finance Journal*, 1:46–60 (Spring 1983).

Smith and Warner provide an extensive survey and analysis of covenants:

C. W. Smith and J. B. Warner: "On Financial Contracting: An Analysis of Bond Covenants," *Journal of Financial Economics*, 7:117–161 (June 1979).

Discussions of project finance include:

R. A. Brealey, I. A. Cooper, and M. Habib: "Using Project Finance to Fund Infrastructure Investments," *Journal of Applied Corporate Finance*, 9:25–38 (Fall 1996).

B. C. Esty: "Petrozuata: A Case Study on the Effective Use of Project Finance," *Journal of Applied Corporate Finance*, 12:26–42 (Fall 1999).

P. K. Nevitt and F. J. Fabozzi, *Project Financing*, American Educational Systems, London, 7th ed., 2000.

Altman's book is a general survey of the bankruptcy decision, while Bhandari and Weiss provide a useful collection of readings. Also listed below are several good studies of the conflicting interests of different security holders and the costs and consequences of reorganization:

E. A. Altman: *Corporate Financial Distress and Bankruptcy: A Complete Guide to Predicting and Avoiding Distress, and Profiting from Bankruptcy*, John Wiley & Sons, New York, 2nd ed., 1993.

J. S. Bhandari and L. A. Weiss (eds.), *Corporate Bankruptcy*, Cambridge University Press, Cambridge, 1996.

M. White: "The Corporate Bankruptcy Decision," *Journal of Economic Perspectives* 3:129–152 (Spring 1989).

J. R. Franks and W. N. Torous: "An Empirical Analysis of U.S. Firms in Reorganization," *Journal of Finance*, 44:747–770 (July 1989).

J. R. Franks and W. N. Torous: "How Shareholders and Creditors Fare in Workouts and Chapter 11 Reorganizations," *Journal of Financial Economics,* 35:349–370 (May 1994).

L. A. Weiss, "Bankruptcy Resolution: Direct Costs and Violation of Priority of Claims," *Journal of Financial Economics,* 27:285–314 (October 1990).

QUIZ

1. Select the most appropriate term from within the parentheses:
   a. (High-grade utility bonds/low-grade industrial bonds) generally have only light sinking-fund requirements.
   b. Collateral trust bonds are often issued by (utilities/industrial holding companies).
   c. (Utility bonds/industrial bonds) are usually unsecured.
   d. Equipment trust certificates are usually issued by (railroads/financial companies).
   e. Mortgage pass-through certificates are an example of (an asset-backed security/project finance).
2. *Vocabulary check.* Define the following terms: indenture or trust deed, debentures, mortgage bonds, call provision, sinking fund, foreign bond, negative pledge clause.
3. For each of the following sinking funds, state whether the fund increases or decreases the value of the bond at the time of issue (or whether it is impossible to say):
   a. An optional sinking fund operating by drawings at par.
   b. A mandatory sinking fund operating by drawings at par *or* by purchases in the market.
   c. A mandatory sinking fund operating by drawings at par.
4. **a.** As a senior bondholder, would you like the company to issue more junior debt, would you prefer it not to do so, or would you not care?
   b. You hold debt secured on the company's existing property. Would you like the company to issue more unsecured debt, would you prefer it not to do so, or would you not care?
5. Use Table 25.1 (but not the text) to answer the following questions:
   a. Who are the principal underwriters for the Ralston Purina bond issue?
   b. Who is the trustee for the issue?
   c. How many dollars does the company receive for each debenture after deduction of the underwriters' spread?
   d. Is the debenture "bearer" or "registered"?
   e. At what price was the issue callable in 1995?
   f. Could the company call the bond in 1990 and replace it with a debenture yielding 5 percent?
6. Look at Table 25.1:
   a. Suppose the debenture was issued on July 1, 1986, at 97.60 percent. How much would you have to pay to buy one bond delivered on July 1? Don't forget to include accrued interest.
   b. When is the first interest payment on the bond, and what is the amount of the payment?
   c. On what date do the bonds finally mature, and what is the principal amount of the bonds that is due to be repaid on that date?
   d. Suppose that the market price of the bonds rises to 102 and thereafter does not change. When should the company call the issue?
7. A security dealer in New York tells you that the yield to maturity on a 10 percent five-year corporate debenture is 7.80 percent. An international bond dealer in London tells you that the yield to maturity on an identical international bond (eurobond) is 7.90 percent. Which bond offers the higher return? Explain.
8. Explain the three principal ways in which the terms of private placement bonds commonly differ from those of public issues.

9. True or false? Briefly explain in each case.
   a. Lenders in project financings rarely have recourse against the project's owners if the project fails.
   b. Many new and exotic debt securities are triggered by government policies or regulations.
   c. Call provisions give a valuable option to debt investors.
   d. Restrictive covenants have been shown to protect debt investors when takeovers are financed with large amounts of debt.
   e. Privately placed debt issues often include stricter covenants than public debt. However, public debt covenants are more difficult and expensive to renegotiate.
10. What is the difference between Chapter 7 bankruptcy and Chapter 11 bankruptcy?
11. True or false?
   a. When a company becomes bankrupt, it is usually in the interests of the equityholders to seek a liquidation rather than a reorganization.
   b. A reorganization plan must be presented for approval by each class of creditor.
   c. The Internal Revenue Service has first claim on the company's assets in the event of bankruptcy.
   d. In a reorganization, creditors may be paid off with a mixture of cash and securities.
   e. When a company is liquidated, one of the most valuable assets to be sold is often the tax-loss carryforward.
12. Explain why equity can sometimes have a positive value even when companies petition for bankruptcy.

PRACTICE QUESTIONS

1. Suppose that the Ralston Purina bond was issued at face value and that investors continue to demand a yield of 9.5 percent. Sketch what you think would happen to the bond price as the first interest payment date approaches and then passes. What about the price of the bond plus accrued interest?
2. Find the terms and conditions of a recent bond issue and compare them with those of the Ralston Purina issue.
3. Bond prices can fall either because of a change in the general level of interest rates or because of an increased risk of default. To what extent do floating-rate bonds and puttable bonds protect the investor against each of these risks?
4. Proctor Power has fixed assets worth $200 million and net working capital worth $100 million. It is financed partly by equity and partly by three issues of debt. These consist of $250 million of First Mortgage Bonds secured only on the company's fixed assets, $100 million of senior debentures, and $120 million of subordinated debentures. If the debt were due today, how much would each debtholder be entitled to receive?
5. Elixir Corporation has just filed for bankruptcy. Elixir is a holding company whose assets consist of real estate worth $80 million and 100 percent of the equity of its two operating subsidiaries. It is financed partly by equity and partly by an issue of $400 million of senior collateral trust bonds that are just about to mature. Subsidiary A has issued directly $320 million of debentures and $15 million of preferred stock. Subsidiary B has issued $180 million of senior debentures and $60 million of subordinated debentures. A's assets have a market value of $500 million and B's have a value of $220 million. How much will each security holder receive if the assets are sold and distributed strictly according to precedence?
6. a. Residential mortgages may stipulate either a fixed rate or a variable rate. As a *borrower,* what considerations might cause you to prefer one rather than the other?
   b. Why might holders of mortgage pass-through certificates wish the mortgages to have a floating rate?

7. After a sharp change in interest rates, newly issued bonds generally sell at yields different from those of outstanding bonds of the same quality. One suggested explanation is that there is a difference in the value of the call provisions. Explain how this could arise.
8. Suppose that a company simultaneously issues a zero-coupon bond and a coupon bond with identical maturities. Both are callable at any time at their face values. Other things equal, which is likely to offer the higher yield? Why?
9. **a.** If interest rates rise, will callable or noncallable bonds fall more in price?
   b. Sometimes you encounter bonds that can be repaid after a fixed interval at the option of *either* the issuer or the bondholder. If the exercise price of each option is the same and both the issuer and bondholder act rationally, what will happen when the options can be exercised? (Ignore refinements such as transactions or issue costs.)
10. A puttable bond is a bond which may be repaid before maturity at the investor's option. Sketch a diagram similar to Figure 25.2 showing the relationship between the value of a straight bond and that of a puttable bond.
11. What restrictions are imposed on a company's freedom to issue further debt? Be as precise as possible. Explain carefully the reasons for such restrictions.
12. Does the issue of additional junior debt harm senior bondholders? Would your answer be the same if the junior debt matured *before* the senior debt? Explain.
13. Alpha Corp. is prohibited from issuing more senior debt unless net tangible assets exceed 200 percent of senior debt. Currently the company has outstanding $100 million of senior debt and has net tangible assets of $250 million. How much more senior debt can Alpha Corp. issue?
14. Explain carefully why bond indentures place limitations on the following actions:
   a. Sale of the company's assets.
   b. Payment of dividends to shareholders.
   c. Issue of additional senior debt.
15. Look up a recent issue of an unusual bond in, say, a recent issue of the periodical *Euromoney.* Why do you think this bond was issued? What investors do you think it would appeal to? How would you value the unusual features?
16. In Section 25.8 we referred to Christiania Bank's exotic bond. Explain how you would value tranche B. Assume that the principal repayment is fixed at 100 percent of par. *Hint:* Find a package of other securities that would produce identical cash flows.
17. Explain when it makes sense to use project finance rather than a direct debt issue by the parent company.
18. The appendix summarizes several problems with Chapter 11 bankruptcy. Which of these problems could be mitigated by negotiating a prepackaged bankruptcy?

CHALLENGE QUESTIONS

1. Dorlcote Milling has outstanding a $1 million 3 percent mortgage bond maturing in 10 years. The coupon on any new debt issued by the company is 10 percent. The finance director, Mr. Tulliver, cannot decide whether there is a tax benefit to repurchasing the existing bonds in the marketplace and replacing them with new 10 percent bonds. What do you think?
2. Refer back to the Hub Power project in Section 25.7. There were many other ways that the Hubco project could have been financed. For example, a government agency could have invested in the power plant and hired National Power to run it. Alternatively, National Power could have owned the power plant directly and funded its cost by a mixture of new borrowing and the sale of shares. What do you think were the advantages of setting up a separately financed company to undertake the project?

CHAPTER TWENTY-SIX

LEASING

MOST OF US occasionally rent a car, bicycle, or boat. Usually such personal rentals are short-lived; we may rent a car for a day or week. But in corporate finance longer-term rentals are common. A rental agreement that extends for a year or more and involves a series of fixed payments is called a **lease.**

Firms lease as an alternative to buying capital equipment. Computers are often leased; so are trucks, railroad cars, aircraft, and ships. Just about every kind of asset has been leased sometime by somebody, including electric power plants, nuclear fuel, handball courts, and zoo animals.

Every lease involves two parties. The *user* of the asset is called the *lessee.* The lessee makes periodic payments to the *owner* of the asset, who is called the *lessor.* For example, if you sign an agreement to rent an apartment for a year, you are the lessee and the owner is the lessor.

You often see references to the *leasing industry.* This refers to lessors. (Almost all firms are lessees to at least a minor extent.) Who are the lessors?

Some of the largest lessors are equipment manufacturers. For example, IBM is a large lessor of computers, and Deere is a large lessor of agricultural and construction equipment.

The other two major groups of lessors are banks and independent leasing companies. Leasing companies play an enormous role in the airline business. For example, in 2000 GE Capital Aviation Services, a subsidiary of GE Capital, owned and leased out 970 commercial aircraft. A large fraction of the world's airlines rely entirely on leasing to finance their fleets.

Leasing companies offer a variety of services. Some act as lease brokers (arranging lease deals) as well as lessors. Others specialize in leasing automobiles, trucks, and standardized industrial equipment; they succeed because they can buy equipment in quantity, service it efficiently, and if necessary resell it at a good price.

We begin this chapter by cataloging the different kinds of leases and some of the reasons for their use. Then we show how short-term, or cancelable, lease payments can be interpreted as equivalent annual costs. The remainder of the chapter analyzes long-term leases used as alternatives to debt financing.

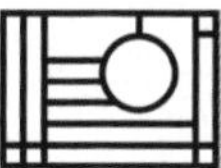

26.1 WHAT IS A LEASE?

Leases come in many forms, but in all cases the lessee (user) promises to make a series of payments to the lessor (owner). The lease contract specifies the monthly or semiannual payments, with the first payment usually due as soon as the contract is signed. The payments are usually level, but their time pattern can be tailored to the user's needs. For example, suppose that a manufacturer leases a machine to produce a complex new product. There will be a year's "shakedown" period before volume production starts. In this case, it might be possible to arrange for lower payments during the first year of the lease.

When a lease is terminated, the leased equipment reverts to the lessor. However, the lease agreement often gives the user the option to purchase the equipment or take out a new lease.

Some leases are short-term or cancelable during the contract period at the option of the lessee. These are generally known as *operating leases.* Others extend over most of the estimated economic life of the asset and cannot be canceled or can be canceled only if the lessor is reimbursed for any losses. These are called *capital, financial,* or *full-payout leases.*[1]

Financial leases are a *source of financing.* Signing a financial lease contract is like borrowing money. There is an immediate cash inflow because the lessee is relieved of having to pay for the asset. But the lessee also assumes a binding obligation to make the payments specified in the lease contract. The user could have borrowed the full purchase price of the asset by accepting a binding obligation to make interest and principal payments to the lender. Thus the cash-flow consequences of leasing and borrowing are similar. In either case, the firm raises cash now and pays it back later. A large part of this chapter will be devoted to comparing leasing and borrowing as financing alternatives.

Leases also differ in the services provided by the lessor. Under a *full-service,* or *rental,* lease, the lessor promises to maintain and insure the equipment and to pay any property taxes due on it. In a *net* lease, the lessee agrees to maintain the asset, insure it, and pay any property taxes. Financial leases are usually net leases.

Most financial leases are arranged for brand new assets. The lessee identifies the equipment, arranges for the leasing company to buy it from the manufacturer, and signs a contract with the leasing company. This is called a *direct* lease. In other cases, the firm sells an asset it already owns and leases it back from the buyer. These *sale and lease-back* arrangements are common in real estate. For example, firm X may wish to raise cash by selling a factory but still retain use of the factory. It could do this by selling the factory for cash to a leasing company and simultaneously signing a long-term lease contract for the factory. Legal ownership of the factory passes to the leasing company, but the right to use it stays with firm X.

You may also encounter *leveraged* leases. These are financial leases in which the lessor borrows part of the purchase price of the leased asset, using the lease contract as security for the loan. This does not change the lessee's obligations, but it can complicate the lessor's analysis considerably.

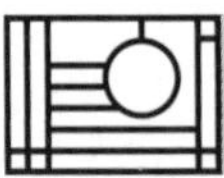

26.2 WHY LEASE?

You hear many suggestions about why companies should lease equipment rather than buy it. Let us look at some sensible reasons and then at four more dubious ones.

Sensible Reasons for Leasing

Short-Term Leases Are Convenient Suppose you want the use of a car for a week. You could buy one and sell it seven days later, but that would be silly. Quite apart from the fact that registering ownership is a nuisance, you would spend some time selecting a car, negotiating purchase, and arranging insurance. Then at the end of the week you would negotiate resale and cancel the registration and insurance. When you need a car only for a short time, it clearly makes sense to rent it. You save the trouble of registering ownership, and you know the effective cost. In the same way, it pays a company to lease equipment that it needs for only a year or two. Of course, this kind of lease is always an operating lease.

[1]In the shipping industry, a financial lease is called a *bareboat charter* or a *demise hire.*

Sometimes the cost of short-term rentals may seem prohibitively high, or you may find it difficult to rent at any price. This can happen for equipment that is easily damaged by careless use. The owner knows that short-term users are unlikely to take the same care they would with their own equipment. When the danger of abuse becomes too high, short-term rental markets do not survive. Thus, it is easy enough to buy a Lamborgini Diablo, provided your pockets are deep enough, but nearly impossible to rent one.

Cancellation Options Are Valuable Some leases that *appear* expensive really are fairly priced once the option to cancel is recognized. We return to this point in the next section.

Maintenance Is Provided Under a full-service lease, the user receives maintenance and other services. Many lessors are well equipped to provide efficient maintenance. However, bear in mind that these benefits will be reflected in higher lease payments.

Standardization Leads to Low Administrative and Transaction Costs Suppose that you operate a leasing company that specializes in financial leases for trucks. You are effectively lending money to a large number of firms (the lessees) which may differ considerably in size and risk. But, because the underlying asset is in each case the same saleable item (a truck), you can safely "lend" the money (lease the truck) without conducting a detailed analysis of each firm's business. You can also use a simple, standard lease contract. This standardization makes it possible to "lend" small sums of money without incurring large investigative, administrative, or legal costs.

For these reasons leasing is often a relatively cheap source of cash for the small company. It offers financing on a flexible, piecemeal basis, with lower transaction costs than in a bond or stock issue.

Tax Shields Can Be Used The lessor owns the leased asset and deducts its depreciation from taxable income. If the lessor can make better use of depreciation tax shields than an asset's user can, it may make sense for the leasing company to own the equipment and pass on some of the tax benefits to the lessee in the form of low lease payments.

Avoiding the Alternative Minimum Tax Red-blooded financial managers want to earn lots of money for their shareholders but *report* low profits to the tax authorities. Tax law in the United States allows this. A firm may use straight-line depreciation in its annual report but choose accelerated depreciation (and the shortest possible asset life) for its tax books. By this and other perfectly legal and ethical devices, profitable companies have occasionally managed to escape tax entirely. Almost all companies pay less tax than their public income statements suggest.[2]

But there is a trap for companies that shield too much income: the alternative minimum tax (*AMT*). Corporations must pay the AMT whenever it is higher than their tax computed in the regular way.

[2]Year-by-year differences between reported tax expense and taxes actually paid are explained in footnotes to the financial statements. The cumulative difference is shown on the balance sheet as a deferred tax liability. (Note that accelerated depreciation *postpones* taxes; it does not eliminate taxes.)

Here is how the AMT works: It requires a second calculation of taxable income, in which part of the benefit of accelerated depreciation and other tax-reducing items[3] is added back. The AMT is 20 percent of the result.

Suppose Yuppytech Services would have $10 million in taxable income but for the AMT, which forces it to add back $9 million of tax privileges:

	Regular Tax	Alternative Minimum Tax
Income	$10	10 + 9 = 19
Tax rate	.35	.20
Tax	$ 3.5	$3.8

Yuppytech must pay $3.8 million, not $3.5.[4]

How can this painful payment be avoided? How about leasing? Lease payments are *not* on the list of items added back in calculating the AMT. If you lease rather than buy, tax depreciation is less and the AMT is less. There is a net gain if the *lessor* is not subject to the AMT and can pass back depreciation tax shields in the form of lower lease payments.

Some Dubious Reasons for Leasing

Leasing Avoids Capital Expenditure Controls In many companies lease proposals are scrutinized as carefully as capital expenditure proposals, but in others leasing may enable an operating manager to avoid the elaborate approval procedures needed to buy an asset. Although this is a dubious reason for leasing, it may be influential, particularly in the public sector. For example, city hospitals have sometimes found it politically more convenient to lease their medical equipment than to ask the city government to provide funds for purchase. Another example is provided by the United States Navy, which once leased a fleet of new tankers and supply ships instead of asking Congress for the money to buy them.

Leasing Preserves Capital Leasing companies provide "100 percent financing"; they advance the full cost of the leased asset. Consequently, they often claim that leasing preserves capital, allowing the firm to save its cash for other things.

But the firm can also "preserve capital" by borrowing money. If Greymare Bus Lines leases a $100,000 bus rather than buying it, it does conserve $100,000 cash. It could also (1) buy the bus for cash and (2) borrow $100,000, using the bus as security. Its bank balance ends up the same whether it leases or buys and borrows. It has the bus in either case, and it incurs a $100,000 liability in either case. What's so special about leasing?

Leases May Be Off-Balance-Sheet Financing In some countries, such as Germany, financial leases are off-balance-sheet financing; that is, a firm can acquire an asset,

[3]Other items include some interest receipts from tax-exempt municipal securities and taxes deferred by use of completed contract accounting. (The completed contract method allows a manufacturer to postpone reporting taxable profits until a production contract is completed. Since contracts may span several years, this deferral can have a substantial positive NPV.)

[4]But Yuppytech can carry forward the $.3 million difference. If later years' AMTs are *lower* than regular taxes, the difference can be used as a tax credit. Suppose the AMT next year is $4 million and the regular tax is $5 million. Then Yuppytech pays only 5 − .3 = $4.7 million.

finance it through a financial lease, and show neither the asset nor the lease contract on its balance sheet.

In the United States, the Financial Accounting Standards Board (FASB) requires that all *capital* (i.e., financial) leases be capitalized. This means that the present value of the lease payments must be calculated and shown alongside debt on the right-hand side of the balance sheet. The same amount must be shown as an asset on the left-hand side.[5]

The FASB defines capital leases as leases which meet *any one* of the following requirements:

1. The lease agreement transfers ownership to the lessee before the lease expires.
2. The lessee can purchase the asset for a bargain price when the lease expires.
3. The lease lasts for at least 75 percent of the asset's estimated economic life.
4. The present value of the lease payments is at least 90 percent of the asset's value.

All other leases are operating leases as far as the accountants are concerned.

Many financial managers have tried to take advantage of this arbitrary boundary between operating and financial leases. Suppose that you want to finance a computer-controlled machine tool costing $1 million. The machine tool's life is expected to be 12 years. You could sign a lease contract for 8 years, 11 months (just missing requirement 3) with lease payments having a present value of $899,000 (just missing requirement 4). You could also make sure the lease contract avoids requirements 1 and 2. Result? You have off-balance-sheet financing. This lease would not have to be capitalized, although it is clearly a long-term, fixed obligation.

Now we come to the $64,000 question: Why should anyone *care* whether financing is off balance sheet or on balance sheet? Shouldn't the financial manager worry about substance rather than appearance?

When a firm obtains off-balance-sheet financing, the conventional measures of financial leverage, such as the debt–equity ratio, understate the true degree of financial leverage. Some believe that financial analysts do not always notice off-balance-sheet lease obligations (which are still referred to in footnotes) or the greater volatility of earnings that results from the fixed lease payments. They may be right, but we would not expect such an imperfection to be widespread.

When a company borrows money, it must usually consent to certain restrictions on future borrowing. Early bond indentures did not include any restrictions on financial leases. Therefore leasing was seen as a way to circumvent restrictive covenants. Loopholes such as these are easily stopped, and most bond indentures now include limits on leasing.

Long-term lease obligations ought to be regarded as debt whether or not they appear on the balance sheet. Financial analysts may overlook moderate leasing activity, just as they overlook minor debts. But major lease obligations are generally recognized and taken into account.

Leasing Affects Book Income Leasing can make the firm's balance sheet and income statement *look* better by increasing book income or decreasing book asset value, or both.

[5]This "asset" is then amortized over the life of the lease. The amortization is deducted from book income, just as depreciation is deducted for a purchased asset.

A lease which qualifies as off-balance-sheet financing affects book income in only one way: The lease payments are an expense. If the firm buys the asset instead and borrows to finance it, both depreciation and interest expense are deducted. Leases are usually set up so that payments in the early years are less than depreciation plus interest under the buy-and-borrow alternative. Consequently, leasing increases book income in the early years of an asset's life. The book rate of return can increase even more dramatically, because the book value of assets (the denominator in the book-rate-of-return calculation) is understated if the leased asset never appears on the firm's balance sheet.

Leasing's impact on book income should in itself have no effect on firm value. In efficient capital markets investors will look through the firm's accounting results to the true value of the asset and the liability incurred to finance it.

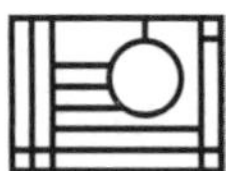

26.3 OPERATING LEASES

Remember our discussion of *equivalent annual costs* in Chapter 6? We defined the equivalent annual cost of, say, a machine as the annual rental payment sufficient to cover the present value of all the costs of owning and operating it.

In Chapter 6's examples, the rental payments were hypothetical—just a way of converting a present value to an annual cost. But in the leasing business the payments are real. Suppose you decide to lease a machine tool for one year. What will the rental payment be in a competitive leasing industry? The lessor's equivalent annual cost, of course.

Example of an Operating Lease

The boyfriend of the daughter of the CEO of Establishment Industries takes her to the senior prom in a pearly white stretch limo. The CEO is impressed. He decides Establishment Industries ought to have one for VIP transportation. Establishment's CFO prudently suggests a one-year operating lease instead and approaches Acme Limolease for a quote.

Table 26.1 shows Acme's analysis. Suppose it buys a new limo for $75,000 which it plans to lease out for seven years (years 0 through 6). The table gives Acme's forecasts of operating, maintenance, and administrative costs, the latter including the costs of negotiating the lease, keeping track of payments and paperwork, and finding a replacement lessee when Establishment's year is up. For simplicity we assume zero inflation and use a 7 percent real cost of capital. We also assume that the limo will have zero salvage value at the end of year 6. The present value of all costs, partially offset by the value of depreciation tax shields,[6] is $98,150. Now, how much does Acme have to charge to break even?

Acme can afford to buy and lease out the limo only if the rental payments forecasted over six years have a present value of at least $98,150. The problem, then, is

[6]The depreciation tax shields are safe cash flows if the tax rate does not change and Acme is sure to pay taxes. If 7 percent is the right discount rate for the other flows in Table 26.1, the depreciation tax shields deserve a lower rate. A more refined analysis would discount safe depreciation tax shields at an after-tax borrowing or lending rate. See Section 19.5 or the next section of this chapter.

	Year						
	0	1	2	3	4	5	6
Initial cost	−75						
Maintenance, insurance, selling, and administrative costs	−12	−12	−12	−12	−12	−12	−12
Tax shield on costs	+4.2	+4.2	+4.2	+4.2	+4.2	+4.2	+4.2
Depreciation tax shield*		+5.25	+8.40	+5.04	+3.02	+3.02	+1.51
Total	−82.80	−2.55	.60	−2.76	−4.78	−4.78	−6.29
PV at 7% = −$98.15†							
Break-even rent (level)	26.18	26.18	26.18	26.18	26.18	26.18	26.18
Tax	−9.16	−9.16	−9.16	−9.16	−9.16	−9.16	−9.16
Break-even rent after tax	17.02	17.02	17.02	17.02	17.02	17.02	17.02
PV at 7% = $98.15†							

TABLE 26.1

Calculating the zero-NPV rental rate (or equivalent annual cost) for Establishment Industries' pearly white stretch limo (figures in $ thousands).

Note: We assume no inflation and a 7 percent real cost of capital. The tax rate is 35 percent.
*Depreciation tax shields are calculated using the five-year schedule from Table 6.4.
†Note that the first payment of these annuities comes immediately. The standard annuity formula must be multiplied by $1 + r = 1.07$.

to calculate a six-year annuity with a present value of $98,150. We will follow common leasing practice and assume rental payments in advance.[7]

As Table 26.1 shows, the required annuity is $26,180, that is, about $26,000.[8] This annuity's present value (after taxes) exactly equals the present value of the after-tax costs of owning and operating the limo. The annuity provides Acme with a competitive expected rate of return (7 percent) on its investment. Acme could try to charge Establishment Industries more than $26,000, but if the CFO is smart enough to ask for bids from Acme's competitors, the winning lessor will end up receiving this amount.

Remember that Establishment Industries is not obligated to continue using the limo for more than one year. Acme may have to find several new lessees over the limo's economic life. Even if Establishment continues, it can renegotiate a new lease at whatever rates prevail in the future. Thus Acme does not know what it can charge in year 1 or afterward. If pearly white falls out of favor with teenagers and CEOs, Acme is probably out of luck.

In real life Acme would have several further things to worry about. For example, how long will the limo stand idle when it is returned at year 1? If idle time is likely before a new lessee is found, then lease rates have to be higher to compensate.[9]

[7]In Section 6.3 the hypothetical rentals were paid *in arrears*.

[8]This is a level annuity because we are assuming that (1) there is no inflation and (2) the services of a six-year-old limo are no different than a brand-new limo's. If users of aging limos see them as obsolete or unfashionable, or if new limos are cheaper, then lease rates for older limos would have to be cut. This would give a *declining* annuity: initial users would pay more than the amount shown in Table 26.1, later users, less.

[9]If, say, limos were off-lease and idle 20 percent of the time, lease rates would have to be 25 percent above those shown in Table 26.1.

In an operating lease, the *lessor* absorbs these risks, not the lessee. The discount rate used by the lessor must include a premium sufficient to compensate its shareholders for the risks of buying and holding the leased asset. In other words, Acme's 7 percent real discount rate must cover the risks of investing in stretch limos. (As we will see in the next section, risk bearing in *financial* leases is fundamentally different.)

Lease or Buy?

If you need a car or limo for only a day or a week you will surely rent it; if you need one for five years you will probably buy it. In between there is a gray region in which the choice of lease or buy is not obvious. The decision rule should be clear in concept, however: If you need an asset for your business, *buy it if the equivalent annual cost of ownership and operation is less than the best lease rate you can get from an outsider.* In other words, buy if you can "rent to yourself" cheaper than you can rent from others. (Again we stress that this rule applies to *operating* leases.)

If you plan to use the asset for an extended period, your equivalent annual cost of owning the asset will usually be less than the operating lease rate. The lessor has to mark up the lease rate to cover the costs of negotiating and administering the lease, the foregone revenues when the asset is off-lease and idle, and so on. These costs are avoided when the company buys and rents to itself.

There are two cases in which operating leases may make sense even when the company plans to use an asset for an extended period. First, the lessor may be able to buy and manage the asset at less expense than the lessee. For example, the major truck leasing companies buy thousands of new vehicles every year. That puts them in an excellent bargaining position with truck manufacturers. These companies also run very efficient service operations, and they know how to extract the most salvage value when trucks wear out and it is time to sell them. A small business, or a small division of a larger one, cannot achieve these economies and often finds it cheaper to lease trucks than to buy them.

Second, operating leases often contain useful options. Suppose Acme offers Establishment Industries the following two leases:

1. A one-year lease for $26,000.
2. A six-year lease for $28,000, *with the option to cancel the lease* at any time from year 1 on.[10]

The second lease has obvious attractions. Suppose Establishment's CEO becomes fond of the limo and wants to use it for a second year. If rates increase, lease 2 allows Establishment to continue at the old rate. If rates decrease, Establishment can cancel lease 2 and negotiate a lower rate with Acme or one of its competitors.

Of course, lease 2 is a more costly proposition for Acme: In effect it gives Establishment an insurance policy protecting it from increases in future lease rates. The difference between the costs of leases 1 and 2 is the annual insurance premium. But lessees may happily pay for insurance if they have no special knowledge of future asset values or lease rates. A leasing company acquires such knowledge in the course of its business and can generally sell such insurance at a profit.

[10]Acme might also offer a one-year lease for $28,000 but give the lessee an option to *extend* the lease on the same terms for up to five additional years. This is, of course, identical to lease 2. It doesn't matter whether the lessee has the (put) option to cancel or the (call) option to continue.

Airlines face fluctuating demand for their services and the mix of planes that they need is constantly changing. Most airlines, therefore, lease a proportion of their fleet on a short-term cancelable basis and are willing to pay a premium to lessors for bearing the cancelation risk. Specialist aircraft lessors are well-placed to bear this risk, for they will hope to find new customers for any aircraft that are returned to them.

Be sure to check out the options before you sign (or reject) an operating lease.[11]

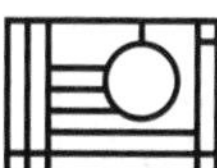

26.4 VALUING FINANCIAL LEASES

For operating leases the decision centers on "lease versus buy." For *financial* leases the decision amounts to "lease versus borrow." Financial leases extend over most of the economic life of the leased equipment. They are *not* cancelable. The lease payments are fixed obligations equivalent to debt service.

Financial leases make sense when the company is prepared to take on the business risks of owning and operating the leased asset. If Establishment Industries signs a *financial* lease for the stretch limo, it is stuck with that asset. The financial lease is just another way of borrowing money to pay for the limo.

Financial leases do offer special advantages to some firms in some circumstances. However, there is no point in further discussion of these advantages until you know how to value financial lease contracts.

Example of a Financial Lease

Imagine yourself in the position of Thomas Pierce III, president of Greymare Bus Lines. Your firm was established by your grandfather, who was quick to capitalize on the growing demand for transportation between Widdicombe and nearby townships. The company has owned all its vehicles from the time the company was formed; you are now reconsidering that policy. Your operating manager wants to buy a new bus costing $100,000. The bus will last only eight years before going to the scrap yard. You are convinced that investment in the additional equipment is worthwhile. However, the representative of the bus manufacturer has pointed out that her firm would also be willing to lease the bus to you for eight annual payments of $16,900 each. Greymare would remain responsible for all maintenance, insurance, and operating expenses.

Table 26.2 shows the direct cash-flow consequences of signing the lease contract. (An important indirect effect is considered later.) The consequences are

1. Greymare does not have to pay for the bus. This is equivalent to a cash inflow of $100,000.
2. Greymare no longer owns the bus, and so it cannot depreciate it. Therefore it gives up a valuable depreciation tax shield. In Table 26.2, we have assumed depreciation would be calculated using five-year tax depreciation schedules. (See Table 6.4.)
3. Greymare must pay $16,900 per year for eight years to the lessor. The first payment is due immediately.

[11]McConnell and Schallheim calculate the value of options in operating leases under various assumptions about asset risk, depreciation rates, etc. See J. J. McConnell and J. S. Schallheim, "Valuation of Asset Leasing Contracts," *Journal of Financial Economics* 12 (August 1983), pp. 237–261.

	Year							
	0	1	2	3	4	5	6	7
Cost of new bus	+100							
Lost depreciation tax shield		−7.00	−11.20	−6.72	−4.03	−4.03	−2.02	0
Lease payment	−16.9	−16.9	−16.9	−16.9	−16.9	−16.9	−16.9	−16.9
Tax shield of lease payment	+5.92	+5.92	+5.92	+5.92	+5.92	+5.92	+5.92	+5.92
Cash flow of lease	+89.02	−17.99	−22.19	−17.71	−15.02	−15.02	−13.00	−10.98

TABLE 26.2

Cash-flow consequences of the lease contract offered to Greymare Bus Lines (figures in $ thousands; some columns do not add due to rounding).

4. However, these lease payments are fully tax-deductible. At a 35 percent marginal tax rate, the lease payments generate tax shields of $5,920 per year. You could say that the after-tax cost of the lease payment is $16,900 − $5,920 = $10,980.

We must emphasize that Table 26.2 assumes that Greymare will pay taxes at the full 35 percent marginal rate. If the firm were sure to lose money, and therefore pay no taxes, lines 2 and 4 would be left blank. The depreciation tax shields are worth nothing to a firm that pays no taxes, for example.

Table 26.2 also assumes the bus will be worthless when it goes to the scrap yard at the end of year 7. Otherwise there would be an entry for salvage value lost.

Who Really Owns the Leased Asset?

To a lawyer or a tax accountant, that would be a silly question: The lessor is clearly the *legal* owner of the leased asset. That is why the lessor is allowed to deduct depreciation from taxable income.

From an *economic* point of view, you might say that the *user* is the real owner, because in a *financial* lease, the user faces the risks and receives the rewards of ownership. Greymare cannot cancel a financial lease. If the new bus turns out to be hopelessly costly and unsuited for Greymare's routes, that is Greymare's problem, not the lessor's. If it turns out to be a great success, the profit goes to Greymare, not the lessor. The success or failure of the firm's business operations does not depend on whether the buses are financed by leasing or some other financial instrument.

In many respects, a financial lease is equivalent to a secured loan. The lessee must make a series of fixed payments; if the lessee fails to do so, the lessor can repossess the asset. Thus we can think of a balance sheet like this

Greymare Bus Lines (Figures in $ Thousands)

Bus	100	100	Loan secured by bus
All other assets	1,000	450	Other loans
		550	Equity
Total assets	1,100	1,100	Total liabilities

as being economically equivalent to a balance sheet like this

Greymare Bus Lines (Figures in $ Thousands)

Bus	100	100	Financial lease
All other assets	1,000	450	Other loans
		550	Equity
Total assets	1,100	1,100	Total liabilities

Having said this, we must immediately add two qualifications. First, legal ownership can make a big difference when a financial lease expires because the lessor gets the salvage value of the asset. Once a secured loan is paid off, the user owns the asset free and clear.

Second, lessors and secured creditors may be treated differently in bankruptcy. If a company defaults on a lease payment, you might think that the lessor could pick up the leased asset and take it home. But if the bankruptcy court decides the asset is "essential" to the lessee's business, it "affirms" the lease. Then the bankrupt firm can continue to use the asset, *but* it must also continue to make the lease payments. This can be *good* news for the lessor: It is paid cash while other creditors cool their heels. Even secured creditors are not paid until the bankruptcy process works itself out.

If the lease is not affirmed but "rejected," the lessor can of course recover the leased asset. If it is worth less than the future payments the lessee had promised, the lessor can try to recoup this loss. But in this case the lender must get in line with the unsecured creditors.

Of course, neither the lessor nor the secured lender can be sure it will come out whole. Our point is that lessors and secured creditors have different rights when the asset user gets into trouble.

Leasing and the Internal Revenue Service

We have already noted that the lessee loses the tax depreciation of the leased asset but can deduct the lease payment in full. The *lessor,* as legal owner, uses the depreciation tax shield but must report the lease payments as taxable rental income.

However, the Internal Revenue Service is suspicious by nature and will not allow the lessee to deduct the entire lease payment unless it is satisfied that the arrangement is a genuine lease and not a disguised installment purchase or secured loan agreement. Here are examples of lease provisions that will arouse its suspicion:

1. Designating any part of the lease payment as "interest."
2. Giving the lessee the option to acquire the asset for, say, $1 when the lease expires. Such a provision would effectively give the asset's salvage value to the lessee.
3. Adopting a schedule of payments such that the lessee pays a large proportion of the cost over a short period and thereafter is able to use the asset for a nominal charge.
4. Including a so-called hell-or-high-water clause that obliges the lessee to make payments regardless of what subsequently happens to the lessor or the equipment.
5. Limiting the lessee's right to issue debt or pay dividends while the lease is in force.

6. Leasing "limited use" property—for example, leasing a machine or production facility which is custom-designed for the lessee's operations and which therefore will have scant secondhand value.

Some leases are designed *not* to qualify as a true lease for tax purposes. Suppose a manufacturer finds it convenient to lease a new computer but wants to keep the depreciation tax shields. This is easily accomplished by giving the manufacturer the option to purchase the computer for $1 at the end of the lease. Then the Internal Revenue Service treats the lease as an installment sale, and the manufacturer can deduct depreciation and the interest component of the lease payment for tax purposes. But the lease is still a lease for all other purposes.

A First Pass at Valuing a Lease Contract

When we left Thomas Pierce III, president of Greymare Bus Lines, he had just set down in Table 26.2 the cash flows of the financial lease proposed by the bus manufacturer.

These cash flows are typically assumed to be about as safe as the interest and principal payments on a secured loan issued by the lessee. This assumption is reasonable for the lease payments because the lessor is effectively lending money to the lessee. But the various tax shields might carry enough risk to deserve a higher discount rate. For example, Greymare might be confident that it could make the lease payments but not confident that it could earn enough taxable income to use these tax shields. In that case the cash flows generated by the tax shields would probably deserve a higher discount rate than the borrowing rate used for the lease payments.

A lessee might, in principle, end up using a separate discount rate for each line of Table 26.2, each rate chosen to fit the risk of that line's cash flow. But established, profitable firms usually find it reasonable to simplify by discounting the types of flows shown in Table 26.2 at a single rate based on the rate of interest the firm would pay if it borrowed rather than leased. We will assume Greymare's borrowing rate is 10 percent.

At this point we must go back to our discussion in Chapter 19 of debt-equivalent flows. When a company lends money, it pays tax on the interest it receives. Its net return is the after-tax interest rate. When a company borrows money, it can *deduct* interest payments from its taxable income. The net cost of borrowing is the after-tax interest rate. Thus the after-tax interest rate is the effective rate at which a company can transfer debt-equivalent flows from one time period to another. Therefore, to value the incremental cash flows stemming from the lease, we need to discount them at the after-tax interest rate.

Since Greymare can borrow at 10 percent, we should discount the lease cash flows at $r_D(1 - T_c) = .10(1 - .35) = .065$, or 6.5 percent. This gives

$$\begin{aligned}\text{NPV lease} &= +89.02 - \frac{17.99}{1.065} - \frac{22.19}{(1.065)^2} - \frac{17.71}{(1.065)^3} - \frac{15.02}{(1.065)^4} \\ &\quad - \frac{15.02}{(1.065)^5} - \frac{13.00}{(1.065)^6} - \frac{10.98}{(1.065)^7} \\ &= -.70, \text{ or } -\$700\end{aligned}$$

Since the lease has a negative NPV, Greymare is better off buying the bus.

A positive or negative NPV is not an abstract concept; in this case Greymare's shareholders really are $700 poorer if the company leases. Let us now check how this situation comes about.

Look once more at Table 26.2. The lease cash flows are

	Year							
	0	1	2	3	4	5	6	7
Lease cash flows, thousands	+89.02	−17.99	−22.19	−17.71	−15.02	−15.02	−13.00	−10.98

The lease payments are contractual obligations like the principal and interest payments on secured debt. Thus you can think of the incremental lease cash flows in years 1 through 7 as the "debt service" of the lease. Table 26.3 shows a loan with *exactly* the same debt service as the lease. The initial amount of the loan is 89.72 thousand dollars. If Greymare borrowed this sum, it would need to pay interest in the first year of $.10 \times 89.72 = 8.97$ and would *receive* a tax shield on this interest of $.35 \times 8.97 = 3.14$. Greymare could then repay 12.15 of the loan, leaving a net cash outflow of 17.99 (exactly the same as for the lease) in year 1 and an outstanding debt at the start of year 2 of 77.56.

As you walk through the calculations in Table 26.3, you see that it costs exactly the same to service a loan that brings an immediate inflow of 89.72 as it does to service the lease, which brings in only 89.02. That is why we say that the lease has a net present value of $89.02 - 89.72 = -.7$, or −$700. If Greymare leases the bus rather than raising an *equivalent loan*,[12] there will be $700 less in Greymare's bank account.

Our example illustrates two general points about leases and equivalent loans. First, if you can devise a borrowing plan that gives the same cash flow as the lease in every future period but a higher immediate cash flow, then you should not lease. If, however, the equivalent loan provides the same future cash outflows as the lease but a lower immediate inflow, then leasing is the better choice.

	Year							
	0	1	2	3	4	5	6	7
Amount borrowed at year-end	89.72	77.56	60.42	46.64	34.66	21.89	10.31	0
Interest paid at 10%		−8.97	−7.76	−6.04	−4.66	−3.47	−2.19	−1.03
Interest tax shield at 35%		+3.14	+2.71	+2.11	+1.63	+1.21	+.77	+.36
Interest paid after tax		−5.83	−5.04	−3.93	−3.03	−2.25	−1.42	−.67
Principal repaid		−12.15	−17.14	−13.78	−11.99	−12.76	−11.58	−10.31
Net cash flow of equivalent loan	89.72	−17.99	−22.19	−17.71	−15.02	−15.02	−13.00	−10.98

TABLE 26.3

Details of the equivalent loan to the lease offered to Greymare Bus Lines (figures in $ thousands; cash outflows shown with negative sign).

[12]When we compare the lease to its equivalent loan, we do not mean to imply that the bus alone could support all of that loan. Some part of the loan would be supported by Greymare's other assets. Some part of the lease would likewise be supported by the other assets.

Second, our example suggests two ways to value a lease:

1. *Hard way.* Construct a table like Table 26.3 showing the equivalent loan.
2. *Easy way.* Discount the lease cash flows at the *after-tax* interest rate that the firm would pay on an equivalent loan. Both methods give the same answer—in our case an NPV of −$700.

The Story So Far

We concluded that the lease contract offered to Greymare Bus Lines was *not* attractive because the lease provided $700 less financing than the equivalent loan. The underlying principle is as follows: A financial lease is superior to buying and borrowing if the financing provided by the lease exceeds the financing generated by the equivalent loan.

The principle implies this formula:

$$\text{Net value of lease} = \text{initial financing provided} - \sum_{t=1}^{N} \frac{\text{lease cash flow}}{[1 + r_D(1 - T_c)]^t}$$

where N is the length of the lease. Initial financing provided equals the cost of the leased asset minus any immediate lease payment or other cash outflow attributable to the lease.

Notice that the value of the lease is its incremental value relative to borrowing via an equivalent loan. A positive lease value means that *if* you acquire the asset, lease financing is advantageous. It does not prove you should acquire the asset.

However, sometimes favorable lease terms rescue a capital investment project. Suppose that Greymare had decided *against* buying a new bus because the NPV of the $100,000 investment was −$5,000 assuming normal financing. The bus manufacturer could rescue the deal by offering a lease with a value of, say, +$8,000. By offering such a lease, the manufacturer would in effect cut the price of the bus to $92,000, giving the bus-lease package a positive value to Greymare. We could express this more formally by treating the lease's NPV as a favorable financing side effect that adds to project adjusted present value (APV):[13]

$$\begin{aligned} \text{APV} &= \text{NPV of project} + \text{NPV of lease} \\ &= -5{,}000 + 8{,}000 = +\$3{,}000 \end{aligned}$$

Notice also that our formula applies to net financial leases. Any insurance, maintenance, and other operating costs picked up by the lessor have to be evaluated separately and added to the value of the lease. If the asset has salvage value at the end of the lease, that value should be taken into account also.

Suppose, for example, that the bus manufacturer offers to provide routine maintenance that would otherwise cost $2,000 per year after tax. However, Mr. Pierce reconsiders and decides that the bus will probably be worth $10,000 after eight years. (Previously he assumed the bus would be worthless at the end of the lease.) Then the value of the lease increases by the present value of the maintenance savings and decreases by the present value of the lost salvage value.

Maintenance and salvage value are harder to predict than the cash flows shown in Table 26.2, and normally deserve a higher discount rate. Suppose that Mr. Pierce uses 12 percent. Then the maintenance savings are worth

[13]See Chapter 19 for the general definition and discussion of APV.

$$\sum_{t=0}^{7} \frac{2000}{(1.12)^t} = \$11{,}100$$

The lost salvage value is worth $\$10{,}000/(1.12)^8 = \$4{,}000$.[14] Remember that we previously calculated the value of the lease as −$700. The revised value is therefore −700 + 11,100 − 4,000 = $6,400. Now the lease looks like a good deal.

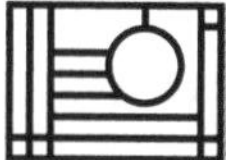

26.5 WHEN DO FINANCIAL LEASES PAY?

We have examined the value of a lease from the viewpoint of the lessee. However, the lessor's criterion is simply the reverse. As long as lessor and lessee are in the same tax bracket, every cash outflow to the lessee is an inflow to the lessor, and vice versa. In our numerical example, the bus manufacturer would project cash flows in a table like Table 26.2, but with the signs reversed. The value of the lease to the bus manufacturer would be

$$\begin{aligned}\text{Value of lease to lessor} &= -89.02 + \frac{17.99}{1.065} + \frac{22.19}{(1.065)^2} + \frac{17.71}{(1.065)^3} + \frac{15.02}{(1.065)^4} + \frac{15.02}{(1.065)^5} \\ &\quad + \frac{13.00}{(1.065)^6} + \frac{10.98}{(1.065)^7} \\ &= +.70\text{, or } \$700\end{aligned}$$

In this case, the values to lessee and lessor exactly offset (−$700 + $700 = 0). The lessor can win only at the lessee's expense.

But both lessee and lessor can win if their tax rates differ. Suppose that Greymare paid no tax ($T_c = 0$). Then the only cash flows of the bus lease would be

	Year							
	0	1	2	3	4	5	6	7
Cost of new bus	+100							
Lease payment	−16.9	−16.9	−16.9	−16.9	−16.9	−16.9	−16.9	−16.9

These flows would be discounted at 10 percent, because $r_D(1 - T_c) = r_D$ when $T_c = 0$. The value of the lease is

$$\begin{aligned}\text{Value of lease} &= +100 - \sum_{t=0}^{7} \frac{16.9}{(1.10)^t} \\ &= +100 - 99.18 = +.82\text{, or } \$820\end{aligned}$$

In this case there is a net gain of $700 to the lessor (who has the 35 percent tax rate) *and* a net gain of $820 to the lessee (who pays zero tax). This mutual gain is at the expense of the government. On one hand, the government gains from the lease contract because it can tax the lease payments. On the other hand, the contract allows the lessor to take advantage of depreciation and interest tax shields which are

[14] For simplicity, we have assumed that maintenance expenses are paid at the start of the year and that salvage value is measured at the *end* of year 8.

of no use to the lessee. However, because the depreciation is accelerated and the interest rate is positive, the government suffers a net loss in the present value of its tax receipts as a result of the lease.

Now you should begin to understand the circumstances in which the government incurs a loss on the lease and the other two parties gain. Other things being equal, the potential gains to lessor and lessee are highest when

- The lessor's tax rate is substantially higher than the lessee's.
- The depreciation tax shield is received early in the lease period.
- The lease period is long and the lease payments are concentrated toward the end of the period.
- The interest rate r_D is high—if it were zero, there would be no advantage in present value terms to postponing tax.

Lessors are constantly on the lookout for arrangements that increase the potential gains from leasing. Some of the most ingenious arrangements involve cross-border leases and take advantage of the fact that different tax authorities define "ownership" in different ways. For example, suppose that an asset is bought by a company in Switzerland, which then "leases" the asset to a firm in the United States. As the legal owner, the company can depreciate the asset for tax purposes in Switzerland. But the terms of the lease may be such that in the United States the user of the asset is regarded as the *effective* owner and therefore gets to depreciate it for tax purposes. Needless to say, the tax authorities are keen to prevent such "double-dipping," but, as soon as one opportunity is blocked off, another seems to arise.

Visit us at www.mhhe.com/bm7e

SUMMARY

A lease is just an extended rental agreement. The owner of the equipment (the *lessor*) allows the user (the *lessee*) to operate the equipment in exchange for regular lease payments.

There is a wide variety of possible arrangements. Short-term, cancelable leases are known as *operating leases*. In these leases the lessor bears the risks of ownership. Long-term, noncancelable leases are called *full-payout, financial*, or *capital* leases. In these leases the lessee bears the risks. Financial leases are *sources of financing* for assets the firm wishes to acquire and use for an extended period.

The key to understanding operating leases is equivalent annual cost. In a competitive leasing market, the annual operating lease payment will be forced down to the lessor's equivalent annual cost. Operating leases are attractive to equipment users if the lease payment is less than the *user's* equivalent annual cost of buying the equipment. Operating leases make sense when the user needs the equipment only for a short time, when the lessor is better able to bear the risks of obsolescence, or when the lessor can offer a good deal on maintenance. Remember too that operating leases often have valuable options attached.

A financial lease extends over most of the economic life of the leased asset and cannot be canceled by the lessee. Signing a financial lease is like signing a secured loan to finance purchase of the leased asset. With financial leases, the choice is not "lease versus buy" but "lease versus borrow."

Many companies have sound reasons for financing via leases. For example, companies that are not paying taxes can usually strike a favorable deal with a taxpaying lessor. Also, it may be less costly and time-consuming to sign a standardized lease contract than to negotiate a long-term secured loan.

When a firm borrows money, it pays the after-tax rate of interest on its debt. Therefore, the opportunity cost of lease financing is the after-tax rate of interest on the firm's bonds. To value a financial lease, we need to discount the incremental cash flows from leasing by the after-tax interest rate.

An equivalent loan is one that commits the firm to exactly the same future cash flows as a financial lease. When we calculate the net present value of the lease, we are measuring the difference between the amount of financing provided by the lease and the financing provided by the equivalent loan:

$$\text{Value of lease} = \text{financing provided by lease} - \text{value of equivalent loan}$$

We can also analyze leases from the lessor's side of the transaction, using the same approaches we developed for the lessee. If lessee and lessor are in the same tax bracket, they will receive exactly the same cash flows but with signs reversed. Thus, the lessee can gain only at the lessor's expense, and vice versa. However, if the lessee's tax rate is lower than the lessor's, then both can gain at the federal government's expense.

FURTHER READING

A useful general reference on leasing is:

J. S. Schallheim: *Lease or Buy? Principles for Sound Decisionmaking,* Harvard Business School Press, Boston, MA, 1994.

The approach to valuing financial leases presented in this chapter is based on:

S. C. Myers, D. A. Dill, and A. J. Bautista: "Valuation of Financial Lease Contracts," *Journal of Finance,* 31:799–819 (June 1976).

J. R. Franks and S. D. Hodges: "Valuation of Financial Lease Contracts: A Note," *Journal of Finance,* 33:647–669 (May 1978).

Other useful works include Nevitt and Fabozzi's book and the theoretical discussions of Miller and Upton and of Lewellen, Long, and McConnell:

P. K. Nevitt and F. J. Fabozzi: *Equipment Leasing,* 4th ed., Frank Fabozzi Associates, 2000.

M. H. Miller and C. W. Upton: "Leasing, Buying and the Cost of Capital Services," *Journal of Finance,* 31:761–786 (June 1976).

W. G. Lewellen, M. S. Long, and J. J. McConnell: "Asset Leasing in Competitive Capital Markets," *Journal of Finance,* 31:787–798 (June 1976).

Harold Bierman gives a detailed account of leasing and the AMT in:

H. Bierman: "Buy versus Lease with an Alternative Minimum Tax," *Financial Management,* 17:87–92 (Winter 1988).

The options embedded in many operating leases are discussed in:

T. E. Copeland and J. E. Weston: "A Note on the Evaluation of Cancelable Operating Leases," *Financial Management,* 11:68–72 (Summer 1982).

J. J. McConnell and J. S. Schallheim: "Valuation of Asset Leasing Contracts," *Journal of Financial Economics,* 12:237–261 (August 1983).

S. R. Grenadier, "Valuing Lease Contracts: A Real Options Approach," *Journal of Financial Economics,* 38:297–331 (July 1995).

QUIZ

1. The following terms are often used to describe leases:
   a. Direct
   b. Full-service
   c. Operating
   d. Financial
   e. Rental
   f. Net
   g. Leveraged
   h. Sale and lease-back
   i. Full-payout

   Match one or more of these terms with each of the following statements:
   A. The initial lease period is shorter than the economic life of the asset.
   B. The initial lease period is long enough for the lessor to recover the cost of the asset.
   C. The lessor provides maintenance and insurance.
   D. The lessee provides maintenance and insurance.
   E. The lessor buys the equipment from the manufacturer.
   F. The lessor buys the equipment from the prospective lessee.
   G. The lessor finances the lease contract by issuing debt and equity claims against it.
2. Some of the following reasons for leasing are rational. Others are irrational or assume imperfect or inefficient capital markets. Which of the following reasons are the rational ones?
   a. The lessee's need for the leased asset is only temporary.
   b. Specialized lessors are better able to bear the risk of obsolescence.
   c. Leasing provides 100 percent financing and thus preserves capital.
   d. Leasing allows firms with low marginal tax rates to "sell" depreciation tax shields.
   e. Leasing increases earnings per share.
   f. Leasing reduces the transaction cost of obtaining external financing.
   g. Leasing avoids restrictions on capital expenditures.
   h. Leasing can reduce the alternative minimum tax.
3. Explain why the following statements are true:
   a. In a competitive leasing market, the annual operating lease payment equals the lessor's equivalent annual cost.
   b. Operating leases are attractive to equipment users if the lease payment is less than the *user's* equivalent annual cost.
4. True or false?
   a. Lease payments are usually made at the start of each period. Thus the first payment is usually made as soon as the lease contract is signed.
   b. Financial leases can still provide off-balance-sheet financing.
   c. The cost of capital for a financial lease is the interest rate the company would pay on a bank loan.
   d. An equivalent loan's principal plus after-tax interest payments exactly match the after-tax cash flows of the lease.
   e. A financial lease should not be undertaken unless it provides more financing than the equivalent loan.
   f. It makes sense for firms that pay no taxes to lease from firms that do.
   g. Other things equal, the net tax advantage of leasing increases as nominal interest rates increase.
5. Acme has branched out to rentals of office furniture to start-up companies. Consider a $3,000 desk. Desks last for six years and can be depreciated on a five-year ACRS schedule (see Table 6.4). What is the break-even operating lease rate for a new desk? Assume that lease rates for old and new desks are the same and that Acme's pretax administrative costs are $400 per desk per year. The cost of capital is 9 percent and the tax rate is

35 percent. Lease payments are made in advance, that is, at the start of each year. The inflation rate is zero.

6. Refer again to quiz question 5. Suppose a blue-chip company requests a six-year *financial* lease for a $3,000 desk. The company has just issued five-year notes at an interest rate of 6 percent per year. What is the break-even rate in this case? Assume administrative costs drop to $200 per year. Explain why your answers to question 5 and this question differ.

7. Suppose that National Waferonics has before it a proposal for a four-year financial lease. The firm constructs a table like Table 26.2. The bottom line of its table shows the lease cash flows:

	Year 0	Year 1	Year 2	Year 3
Lease cash flow	+62,000	−26,800	−22,200	−17,600

These flows reflect the cost of the machine, depreciation tax shields, and the after-tax lease payments. Ignore salvage value. Assume the firm could borrow at 10 percent and faces a 35 percent marginal tax rate.

a. What is the value of the equivalent loan?
b. What is the value of the lease?
c. Suppose the machine's NPV under normal financing is −$5,000. Should National Waferonics invest? Should it sign the lease?

PRACTICE QUESTIONS

1. A lessee does not have to pay to buy the leased asset. Thus it's said that "leases provide 100 percent financing." Explain why this is *not* a true advantage to the lessee.

2. In quiz question 5 we assumed identical lease rates for old and new desks.
   a. How does the initial break-even lease rate change if the expected inflation rate is 5 percent per year? Assume that the *real* cost of capital does not change. *Hint:* Look at the discussion of equivalent annual costs in Chapter 6.
   b. How does your answer to part (a) change if wear and tear force Acme to cut lease rates by 10 percent in real terms for every year of a desk's age?

3. Look at Table 26.1. How would the initial break-even operating lease rate change if rapid technological change in limo manufacturing reduces the costs of new limos by 5 percent per year? *Hint:* We discussed technological change and equivalent annual costs in Chapter 6.

4. Why do you think that leasing of trucks, airplanes, and computers is such big business? What efficiencies offset the costs of running these leasing operations?

5. Financial leases make sense when the lessee faces a lower marginal tax rate than the lessor. Does this tax advantage carry over to *operating* leases?

The following questions all apply to financial leases.

6. Look again at the bus lease described in Table 26.2.
   a. What is the value of the lease if Greymare's marginal tax rate is $T_c = .20$?
   b. What would the lease value be if Greymare had to use straight-line depreciation for tax purposes?

7. In Section 26.4 we showed that the lease offered to Greymare Bus Lines had a positive NPV of $820 if Greymare paid no tax *and* a +$700 NPV to a lessor paying 35 percent tax. What is the minimum lease payment the lessor could accept under these assumptions? What is the maximum amount that Greymare could pay?

8. In Section 26.5 we listed four circumstances in which there are potential gains from leasing. Check them out by conducting a sensitivity analysis on the Greymare Bus Lines lease, assuming that Greymare does not pay tax. Try, in turn, (a) a lessor tax rate of 50 percent (rather than 35 percent), (b) immediate 100 percent depreciation in year 0 (rather than five-year ACRS), (c) a three-year lease with four annual rentals (rather than an eight-year lease), and (d) an interest rate of 20 percent (rather than 10 percent). In each case, find the minimum rental that would satisfy the lessor and calculate the NPV to the lessee.

9. In Section 26.5 we stated that if the interest rate were zero, there would be no advantage in postponing tax and therefore no advantage in leasing. Value the Greymare Bus Lines lease with an interest rate of zero. Assume that Greymare does not pay tax. Can you devise any lease terms that would make both a lessee and a lessor happy? (If you can, we would like to hear from you.)

10. A lease with a varying rental schedule is known as a *structured lease*. Try structuring the Greymare Bus Lines lease to increase value to the lessee while preserving the value to the lessor. Assume that Greymare does not pay tax. (*Note:* In practice the tax authorities will allow some structuring of rental payments but might be unhappy with some of the schemes you devise.)

11. Nodhead College needs a new computer. It can either buy it for $250,000 or lease it from Compulease. The lease terms require Nodhead to make six annual payments (prepaid) of $62,000. Nodhead pays no tax. Compulease pays tax at 35 percent. Compulease can depreciate the computer for tax purposes over five years. The computer will have no residual value at the end of year 5. The interest rate is 8 percent.
   a. What is the NPV of the lease for Nodhead College?
   b. What is the NPV for Compulease?
   c. What is the overall gain from leasing?

12. The Safety Razor Company has a large tax-loss carryforward and does not expect to pay taxes for another 10 years. The company is therefore proposing to lease $100,000 of new machinery. The lease terms consist of eight equal lease payments prepaid annually. The lessor can write the machinery off over seven years using the tax depreciation schedules given in Table 6.4. There is no salvage value at the end of the machinery's economic life. The tax rate is 35 percent, and the rate of interest is 10 percent. Wilbur Occam, the president of Safety Razor, wants to know the maximum lease payment that his company should be willing to make and the minimum payment that the lessor is likely to accept. Can you help him? How would your answer differ if the lessor was obliged to use straight-line depreciation?

13. The overall gain from leasing is the sum of the lease's value to the lessee and its value to the lessor. Construct simple numerical examples showing how this gain is affected by
   a. The rate of interest.
   b. The choice of depreciation schedule.
   c. The difference between the tax rates of the lessor and lessee.
   d. The length of the lease.

14. Many companies calculate the internal rate of return of the incremental after-tax cash flows from financial leases. What problems do you think this may give rise to? To what rate should the IRR be compared?

15. Discuss the following two opposite statements. Which do you think makes more sense?
   a. "Leasing is tax avoidance and should be legislated against."
   b. "Leasing ensures that the government's investment incentives work. It does so by allowing companies in nontaxpaying positions to take advantage of depreciation allowances."

Visit us at www.mhhe.com/bm7e

CHALLENGE QUESTIONS

1. Magna Charter has been asked to operate a Beaver bush plane for a mining company exploring north and west of Fort Liard. Magna will have a firm one-year contract with the mining company and expects that the contract will be renewed for the five-year duration of the exploration program. If the mining company renews at year 1, it will commit to use the plane for four more years.

   Magna Charter has the following choices.

   - Buy the plane for $500,000.
   - Take a one-year operating lease for the plane. The lease rate is $118,000, paid in advance.
   - Arrange a five-year, noncancelable financial lease at a rate of $75,000 per year, paid in advance.

   These are net leases: all operating costs are absorbed by Magna Charter.

   How would you advise Agnes Magna, the charter company's CEO? For simplicity assume five-year, straight-line depreciation for tax purposes. The company's tax rate is 35 percent. The weighted-average cost of capital for the bush-plane business is 14 percent, but Magna can borrow at 9 percent. The expected inflation rate is 4 percent.

   Ms. Magna thinks the plane will be worth $300,000 after five years. But if the contract with the mining company is not renewed (there is a 20 percent probability of this outcome at year 1), the plane will have to be sold on short notice for $400,000.

   If Magna Charter takes the five-year financial lease and the mining company cancels at year 1, Magna can sublet the plane, that is, rent it out to another user.

   Make additional assumptions as necessary.

2. Here is a variation on challenge question 1. Suppose Magna Charter is offered a five-year *cancelable* lease at an annual rate of $125,000, paid in advance. How would you go about analyzing this lease? You do not have enough information to do a full option pricing analysis, but you can calculate costs and present values for different scenarios.

3. Recalculate the value of the lease to Greymare Bus Lines if the company pays no taxes until year 3. Calculate the lease cash flows by modifying Table 26.2. Remember that the after-tax borrowing rate for periods 1 and 2 differs from the rate for periods 3 through 7.

Visit us at www.mhhe.com/bm7e

MINI-CASE

Halverton Corporation

Helen James, a newly recruited financial analyst at Halverton Corporation, had just been asked to analyze a proposal to acquire a new dredger.

She reviewed the capital appropriation request. The dredger would cost $3.5 million and was expected to generate cash flows of $470,000 a year for nine years. After that point, the dredger would almost surely be obsolete and have no significant salvage value. The company's weighted-average cost of capital was 16 percent.

Helen proposed a standard DCF analysis, but this suggestion was brushed off by Halverton's top management. They seemed to be convinced of the merits of the investment but were unsure of the best way to finance it. Halverton could raise the money by issuing a secured eight-year note at an interest rate of 12 percent. However, Halverton had large tax-loss carryforwards from a disastrous foray into foreign exchange options. As a result, the company was unlikely to be in a tax-paying position for many years. Halverton's CEO thought it might be better to lease the dredger than to buy it.

Helen's first step was to invite two leasing companies, Mount Zircon Finance and First Cookham Bank, to submit proposals. Both companies were in a tax-paying position and could write off their investment in the dredger using five-year MACRS tax depreciation.

Helen received the following letters, the first from Mount Zircon Finance:

February 29, 2006

Dear Helen,

We appreciated the opportunity to meet you the other day and to discuss the possibility of providing lease finance for your proposed new JLT4 dredger. As you know, Mount Zircon has extensive experience in this field and, because of our large volumes and low borrowing costs, we are able to offer very attractive terms.

We would envisage offering a 9-year lease with 10 annual payments of $544,300, with the initial lease payment due on entering into the lease contract. This is equivalent to a borrowing cost of 11.5 percent per annum (i.e., 10 payments of $544,300 paid at the beginning of each year discounted at 11.5 percent amounts to $3,500,000).

We hope that you agree with us that this is an attractive rate. It is well below your company's overall cost of capital. Our leasing proposal will cover the entire $3.5 million cost of the dredger, thereby preserving Halverton's capital for other uses. Leasing will also allow a very attractive return on equity from your company's acquisition of this new equipment.

This proposal is subject to a routine credit check and review of Halverton's financial statements. We expect no difficulties on that score, but you will understand the need for due diligence.

Thank you for contacting Mount Zircon Finance. We look forward to hearing your response.

Sincerely yours,
Henry Attinger
For and on behalf of Mount Zircon Finance

The next letter was from First Cookham.

February 29, 2006

Dear Helen,

It was an honor to meet you the other day and to discuss how First Cookham Bank can help your company to finance its new dredger. First Cookham has a small specialized leasing operation. This enables us to tailor our proposals to our clients' needs.

We recommend that Halverton consider leasing the dredger on a 7-year term. Subject to documentation and routine review of Halverton's financial statements, we could offer a 7-year lease on the basis of 8 payments of $619,400 due at the beginning of each year. This is equivalent to a loan at an interest rate of 11.41 percent.

We expect that this lease payment will be higher than quoted by the larger, mass-market leasing companies, but our financial analysts have determined that, by offering a shorter lease, we can quote a lower interest rate.

We are confident that this is a highly competitive offer, and we look forward to your response.

Yours sincerely,
George Bucknall,
First Cookham Bank

Both proposals appeared to be attractive. However, Helen realized the need to undertake careful calculations before deciding whether leasing made sense and which firm was offering the better deal. She also wondered whether the terms offered were really as attractive as the two lessors claimed. Perhaps she could persuade them to cut their prices.

Questions

1. Calculate the NPV to Halverton of the two lease proposals.
2. Does the dredger have a positive NPV with (a) ordinary financing, (b) lease financing?
3. Calculate the NPVs of the leases from the lessors' viewpoints. Is there a chance that they could offer more attractive terms?
4. Evaluate the arguments presented by each of the lessors.

Useful material and data on bond markets are available on:

www.bondmarkets.com *(website of the Bond Market Association. Includes useful statistics)*

www.bondsonline.com

www.bondresources.com/main.html

http://bonds.yahoo.com

www.duke.edu/~charvey/applets/Bond/test.html *(nice graphics illustrating effect of interest rate on bond prices)*

www.finpipe.com *(explanations of bond markets)*

www.hsh.com

www.investinginbonds.com *(also contains links to related sites)*

www.loanpricing.com *(useful statistics on corporate bond issuance)*

http://money.cnn.com/markets/bondcenter

http://ourworld.compuserve.com/homepages/martinhighmore *(bond calculator)*

The websites of the ratings services provide information and data on bond risk:

www.standardandpoors.com

www.moodys.com

For material on the estimation of default probabilities see:

www.kmv.com

www.riskmetrics.com

Here are some sites that focus on project finance:

www.hbs.edu/projfinportal

www.infrastructure.com

www.ipfa.org

For material on bankruptcies and bankruptcy procedures see:

www.abiworld.org

www.bankrupt.com

www.bankruptcydata.com

www.law.cornell.edu/uscode/11 *(a technical description of the bankruptcy code)*

The following sites contain material on leasing:

www.elaonline.com *(the site for the Equipment Leasing Association)*

www.gecapital.com

www.leasingcanada.com *(includes a lease calculator)*

PART EIGHT

RISK MANAGEMENT

TO ADD VALUE companies need to take risks. But they try to avoid those risks that carry no compensating gains. Consider, for example, Green Mountain Coffee, which buys and roasts each year about 11 million pounds of coffee. In the past four years the price of coffee has swung between about $.40 and $3.00 a pound. Green Mountain could be knocked badly off course by such fluctuations. It therefore fixes in advance the price for about 40 percent of its coffee needs and it uses coffee futures and options to reduce even further the risk of sudden price hikes.

No two companies are exposed to the same risks. Some financial managers lie awake worrying about the price of oil or copper; others may sweat about changes in interest rates or exchange rates. Part Eight explains how each can achieve peace of mind. We start in Chapter 27 with an overview of the objectives of risk management and with corporate purchases of insurance. The rest of the chapter focuses on the risk of changes in commodity prices and interest rates. You will discover there how commodity and financial futures markets work.

Chapter 28 turns to the special risks of doing business internationally. These largely follow from fluctuations in exchange rates, so we explain how exchange rates are related to international differences in interest rates and inflation.

CHAPTER TWENTY-SEVEN

MANAGING RISK

MOST OF THE time we take risk as God-given. An asset or business has its beta, and that's that. Its cash flow is exposed to unpredictable changes in raw material costs, tax rates, technology, and a long list of other variables. There's nothing the manager can do about it.

That's not wholly true. To some extent managers can choose the risks that the business takes. We have already come across one way that they can do so. In our discussion of real options in Chapter 22 we described how companies reduce risk by building flexibility into their operations. A company that uses standardized machine tools rather than specialized equipment lowers the cost of bailing out if things go wrong. A petrochemical plant that is designed to use either oil or natural gas as a feedstock reduces the impact of an unfavorable shift in relative fuel prices. And so on.

In this chapter we shall explain how companies also enter into financial contracts that insure against or hedge (i.e., offset) a variety of business hazards. But first we should give some reasons *why* they do so.

Insurance and hedging are seldom free: At best they are zero-NPV transactions.[1] Most businesses insure or hedge to reduce risk, not to make money. Why, then, bother to reduce risk in this way? For one thing, it makes financial planning easier and reduces the odds of an embarrassing cash shortfall. A shortfall might mean only an unexpected trip to the bank, but if financing is hard to obtain on short notice, the company might need to cut back its capital expenditure program. In extreme cases an unhedged setback could trigger financial distress or even bankruptcy. Banks and bondholders are aware of this possibility, and, before lending to your firm, they will often insist that it is properly insured.

In some cases hedging also makes it easier to decide whether an operating manager deserves a stern lecture or a pat on the back. Suppose your confectionery division shows a 60 percent profit increase in a period when cocoa prices decline by 12 percent. How much of the increase is due to the change in cocoa prices and how much to good management? If cocoa prices were hedged, it's probably good management. If they were not, things have to be sorted out with hindsight by asking, What would profits have been *if* cocoa prices had been hedged?[2]

Finally, hedging extraneous events can help focus the operating manager's attention. It's naive to expect the manager of the confectionery division *not* to worry about cocoa prices if her bottom line and bonus depend on them. That worrying time would be better spent if the prices were hedged.[3]

Of course, managers are not paid to avoid all risks, but if they can reduce their exposure to risks for which there are no compensating rewards, they can afford to place larger bets when the odds are in their favor.

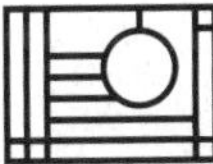

27.1 INSURANCE

Most businesses buy insurance against a variety of hazards—the risk that their plant will be damaged by fire; that their ships, planes, or vehicles will be involved in accidents; that the firm will be held liable for environmental damage; and so on.

---

[1]Hedging transactions are zero-NPV when trading is costless and markets are completely efficient. In practice the firm has to pay small trading costs at least.

[2]Many large firms insure or hedge away operating divisions' risk exposures by setting up internal, make-believe markets between each division and the treasurer's office. Trades in the internal markets are at real (external) market prices. The object is to relieve the operating managers of risks outside their control. The treasurer makes a separate decision on whether to offset the *firm's* exposure.

[3]A Texas oilman who lost hundreds of millions in ill-fated deals protested, "Why should I worry? Worry is for strong minds and weak characters." If there are any financial managers with weak minds and strong characters, we especially advise them to hedge whenever they can.

When a firm takes out insurance, it is simply transferring the risk to the insurance company. Insurance companies have some advantages in bearing risk. First, they may have considerable experience in insuring similar risks, so they are well placed to estimate the probability of loss and price the risk accurately. Second, they may be skilled at providing advice on measures that the firm can take to reduce the risk, and they may offer lower premiums to firms that take this advice. Third, an insurance company can *pool* risks by holding a large, diversified portfolio of policies. The claims on any individual policy can be highly uncertain, yet the claims on a portfolio of policies may be very stable. Of course, insurance companies cannot diversify away macroeconomic risks; firms use insurance policies to reduce their specific risk, and they find other ways to avoid macro risks.

Insurance companies also suffer some *disadvantages* in bearing risk, and these are reflected in the prices they charge. Suppose your firm owns a $1 billion offshore oil platform. A meteorologist has advised you that there is a 1-in-10,000 chance that in any year the platform will be destroyed as a result of a storm. Thus the *expected* loss from storm damage is $1 billion/10,000 = $100,000.

The risk of storm damage is almost certainly not a macroeconomic risk and can potentially be diversified away. So you might expect that an insurance company would be prepared to insure the platform against such destruction as long as the premium was sufficient to cover the expected loss. In other words, a fair premium for insuring the platform should be $100,000 a year.[4] Such a premium would make insurance a zero-NPV deal for your company. Unfortunately, no insurance company would offer a policy for only $100,000. Why not?

- *Reason 1: Administrative costs*. An insurance company, like any other business, incurs a variety of costs in arranging the insurance and handling any claims. For example, disputes about the liability for environmental damage can eat up millions of dollars in legal fees. Insurance companies need to recognize these costs when they set their premiums.
- *Reason 2: Adverse selection*. Suppose that an insurer offers life insurance policies with "no medical needed, no questions asked." There are no prizes for guessing who will be most tempted to buy this insurance. Our example is an extreme case of the problem of *adverse selection*. Unless the insurance company can distinguish between good and bad risks, the latter will always be most eager to take out insurance. Insurers increase premiums to compensate.
- *Reason 3: Moral hazard*. Two farmers met on the road to town. "George," said one, "I was sorry to hear about your barn burning down." "Shh," replied the other, "that's tomorrow night." The story is an example of another problem for insurers, known as *moral hazard*. Once a risk has been insured, the owner may be less careful to take proper precautions against damage. Insurance companies are aware of this and factor it into their pricing.

When these extra costs are small, insurance may be close to a zero-NPV transaction. When they are large, insurance may be a costly way to protect against risk.

Many insurance risks are *jump risks*; one day there is not a cloud on the horizon and the next day the hurricane hits. The risks can also be huge. For example, Hurricane Andrew, which devastated Florida, cost insurance companies $17 bil-

[4]This is imprecise. If the premium is paid at the beginning of the year and the claim is not settled until the end, then the zero-NPV premium equals the discounted value of the expected claim or $100,000/(1 + r)$.

lion; the attack on the World Trade Center is likely to involve payments of more than $35 billion.

Many in the industry worry that one day a major disaster will wipe out a large proportion of the capital of the U.S. insurance industry. Therefore, insurance companies have been looking for ways to share these risks with investors. One solution is for the insurance company to issue *catastrophe bonds* (or *Cat bonds*). The payment on a Cat bond depends on whether a catastrophe occurs and how much is lost.[5]

The first public issue of a Cat bond was made by the Swiss insurance giant, Winterthur. As a major provider of automobile insurance, Winterthur wanted to protect itself against the risk that storm damage could lead to an unusually large number of claims. Therefore, when it issued its bond, the company stated that it would not pay the annual interest if ever there was a hailstorm in Switzerland which damaged at least 6,000 cars that it had insured. In effect, owners of the Winterthur Cat bonds coinsured the company's risks.

How British Petroleum (BP) Changed Its Insurance Strategy[6]

Major public companies typically buy insurance against large potential losses and self-insure against routine ones. The idea is that large losses can trigger financial distress. On the other hand, routine losses for a corporation are predictable, so there is little point paying premiums to an insurance company and receiving back a fairly constant proportion as claims.

BP Amoco has challenged this conventional wisdom. Like all oil companies, BP is exposed to a variety of potential losses. Some arise from routine events such as vehicle accidents and industrial injuries. At the other extreme, they may result from catastrophes such as a major oil spill or the loss of an offshore oil rig. In the past BP purchased considerable external insurance.[7] During the 1980s it paid out an average of $115 million a year in insurance premiums and recovered $25 million a year in claims.

BP then took a hard look at its insurance strategy. It decided to allow local managers to insure against routine risks, for in those cases insurance companies have an advantage in assessing and pricing risk and compete vigorously against one another. However, it decided not to insure against most losses above $10 million. For these larger, more specialized risks BP felt that insurance companies had less ability to assess risk and were less well placed to advise on safety measures. As a result, BP concluded, insurance against large risks was not competitively priced.

How much extra risk did BP assume by its decision not to insure against major losses? BP estimated that large losses of above $500 million could be expected to occur once in 30 years. But BP is a huge company with equity worth about $180 billion. So even a $500 million loss, which could throw most companies into bankruptcy, would translate after tax into a fall of less than 1 percent in the value of

[5]For a discussion of Cat bonds and other techniques to spread insurance risk, see N. A. Doherty, "Financial Innovation in the Management of Catastrophe Risk," *Journal of Applied Corporate Finance* 10 (Fall 1997), pp. 84–95; and K. Froot, "The Market for Catastrophe Risk: A Clinical Examination," *Journal of Financial Economics* 60 (2001), pp. 529–571.

[6]Our description of BP's insurance strategy draws heavily on N. A. Doherty and C. W. Smith, Jr., "Corporate Insurance Strategy: The Case of British Petroleum," *Journal of Applied Corporate Finance* 6 (Fall 1993), pp. 4–15.

[7]However, with one or two exceptions insurance has not been available for the very largest losses of $500 million or more.

BP's equity. BP concluded that this was a risk worth taking. In other words, it concluded that for large, low-probability risks the stock market was a more efficient risk-absorber than the insurance industry.

BP Amoco is not the only company that has looked at the package of risks that it faces and the way that these risks should be managed. Here is how *The Economist* summarized risk management in Duke Energy:[8]

> Duke's risk managers are currently designing a model that examines different types of risk together: movements in exchange rates, changes in raw material prices, downtime caused by distribution failures, and so on. This is supposed to produce an "aggregate loss distribution," which estimates the likelihood that several events could happen at once and sink the company. With this better understanding of the company's aggregate risk, Duke's managers can make a more informed decision about how much of this potential loss should be absorbed by shareholders, how much hedged in the financial markets, and how much transferred to insurers.

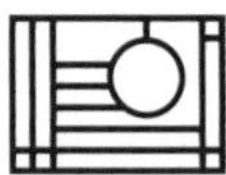

27.2 HEDGING WITH FUTURES

Hedging involves taking on one risk to offset another. We will explain shortly how to set up a hedge, but first we will give some examples and describe some tools that are specially designed for hedging. These are futures, forwards, and swaps. Together with options, they are known as *derivative instruments* or *derivatives* because their value depends on the value of another asset. You can think of them as side bets on the value of the underlying asset.[9]

We start with the oldest actively traded derivative instruments, **futures contracts.** Futures were originally developed for agricultural and other commodities. For example, suppose that a wheat farmer expects to have 100,000 bushels of wheat to sell next September. If he is worried that the price may decline in the interim, he can hedge by selling 100,000 bushels of September wheat futures. In this case he agrees to deliver 100,000 bushels of wheat in September at a price that is set today. Do not confuse this futures contract with an option, in which the holder has a choice whether to make delivery; the farmer's futures contract is a firm promise to deliver wheat.

A miller is in the opposite position. She needs to *buy* wheat after the harvest. If she would like to fix the price of this wheat ahead of time, she can do so by *buying* wheat futures. In other words, she agrees to take delivery of wheat in the future at a price that is fixed today. The miller also does not have an option; if she holds the contract to maturity, she is obliged to take delivery.

Both the farmer and the miller have less risk than before.[10] The farmer has hedged risk by *selling* wheat futures; this is termed a *short hedge*. The miller has hedged risk by *buying* wheat futures; this is known as a *long hedge*.

---

[8]"Meet the Riskmongers," *The Economist*, July 18, 1998, p. 93.

[9]"Side bet" conjures up an image of wicked speculators. Derivatives attract their share of speculators, some of whom may be wicked, but they are also used by sober and prudent businesspeople to reduce risk.

[10]We oversimplify. For example, the miller won't reduce risk if bread prices vary in proportion to the postharvest wheat price. In this case the miller is in the hazardous position of having fixed her cost but not her selling price. This point is discussed in A. C. Shapiro and S. Titman, "An Integrated Approach to Corporate Risk Management," *Midland Corporate Finance Journal* 3 (Summer 1985), pp. 41–56.

Future	Exchange	Future	Exchange
Barley	WPG	Orange juice	NYBOT
Corn	CBT, MCE	Sugar	LIFFE, NYBOT
Oats	CBT		
Wheat	CBT, KC, MCE, MPLS	Aluminum	LME
		Copper	COMEX, LME
		Gold	COMEX
Soybeans	CBT, MCE	Lead	LME
Soybean meal	CBT	Nickel	LME
Soybean oil	CBT	Silver	COMEX
		Tin	LME
Live cattle	CME	Zinc	LME
Lean hogs	CME		
		Crude oil	IPE, NYMEX
Cocoa	LIFFE, NYBOT	Gas oil	IPE
Coffee	LIFFE, NYBOT	Heating oil	NYMEX
Cotton	NYBOT	Natural gas	IPE, NYMEX
Lumber	CME	Unleaded gasoline	NYMEX

TABLE 27.1

Some commodity futures and the principal exchanges on which they are traded.

Key to abbreviations:

CBT	Chicago Board of Trade	LME	London Metal Exchange
CME	Chicago Mercantile Exchange	MCE	MidAmerica Commodity Exchange
COMEX	Commodity Exchange Division of NYMEX	MPLS	Minneapolis Grain Exchange
IPE	International Petroleum Exchange of London	NYBOT	New York Board of Trade
KC	Kansas City Board of Trade	NYMEX	New York Mercantile Exchange
LIFFE	London International Financial Futures and Options Exchange	WPG	Winnipeg Commodity Exchange

The price of wheat for immediate delivery is known as the *spot price*. When the farmer sells wheat futures, the price that he agrees to take for his wheat may be very different from the spot price. But as the date for delivery approaches, a futures contract becomes more and more like a spot contract and the price of the future snuggles up to the spot price.

The farmer may decide to wait until his futures contract matures and then deliver wheat to the buyer. In practice such delivery is very rare, for it is more convenient for the farmer to buy back the wheat futures just before maturity.[11] If he is properly hedged, any loss on his wheat crop will be exactly offset by the profit on his sale and subsequent repurchase of wheat futures.

Commodity and Financial Futures

Futures contracts are bought and sold on organized futures exchanges. Table 27.1 lists the principal commodity futures contracts and the exchanges on which they are traded. Notice that our farmer and miller are not the only businesses that can hedge

[11]In the case of some of the financial futures described below, you *cannot* deliver the asset. At maturity the buyer simply receives (or pays) the difference between the spot price and the price at which he or she agreed to purchase the asset.

Future	Exchange	Future	Exchange
U.S. Treasury bonds	CBT	Dow Jones Industrial Average	CBT
U.S. Treasury notes	CBT	S&P 500 Index	CME
U.S. agency notes	CBT	European equity index (Dow Jones Euro Stoxx)	Eurex
German government bonds (bunds)	Eurex		
Japanese government bonds (JGBs)	Simex, TSE	French equity index (CAC)	MATIF
British government bonds (gilts)	LIFFE	German equity index (DAX)	Eurex
		Japanese equity index (Nikkei)	CME, OSE, Simex
U.S. Treasury bills	CME		
		UK equity index (FTSE)	LIFFE
LIBOR	CME	Individual stocks	LIFFE
Eurodollar deposits	CME	Euro	CME
Euroyen deposits	CME, Simex, TIFFE		
		Japanese yen	CME

TABLE 27.2

Some financial futures and the principal exchanges on which they are traded.

Key to abbreviations:

CBT	Chicago Board of Trade
CME	Chicago Mercantile Exchange
LIFFE	London International Financial Futures and Options Exchange
MATIF	Marché à Terme d'Instruments Financiers
OSE	Osaka Securities Exchange
SIMEX	Singapore International Monetary Exchange
TIFFE	Tokyo International Financial Futures Exchange
TSE	Tokyo Stock Exchange

risk with commodity futures. The lumber company and the builder can hedge against changes in lumber prices, the copper producer and the cable manufacturer can hedge against changes in copper prices, the oil producer and the trucker can hedge against changes in gasoline prices, and so on.[12]

For many firms the wide fluctuations in interest rates and exchange rates have become at least as important a source of risk as changes in commodity prices. Financial futures are similar to commodity futures, but instead of placing an order to buy or sell a commodity at a future date, you place an order to buy or sell a financial asset at a future date. Table 27.2 lists some important financial futures. It is far from complete. You can trade futures on the Thailand stock market index, the South African rand, Finnish government bonds, and many other financial assets.

Financial futures have been a remarkably successful innovation. They were invented in 1972; within a few years, trading in financial futures significantly exceeded trading in commodity futures.

[12]By the time you read this, the list of futures contracts will almost certainly be out of date. Unsuccessful contracts are regularly dropped, and at any time the exchanges may be seeking approval for literally dozens of new contracts.

The Mechanics of Futures Trading

When you buy or sell a futures contract, the price is fixed today but payment is not made until later. You will, however, be asked to put up margin in the form of either cash or Treasury bills to demonstrate that you have the money to honor your side of the bargain. As long as you earn interest on the margined securities, there is no cost to you.

In addition, futures contracts are *marked to market*. This means that each day any profits or losses on the contract are calculated; you pay the exchange any losses and receive any profits. For example, suppose that our farmer agreed to deliver 100,000 bushels of wheat at \$2.80 a bushel. The next day the price of wheat futures declines to \$2.75 a bushel. The farmer now has a profit on his sale of $100{,}000 \times \$.05 = \$5{,}000$. The exchange's clearinghouse therefore pays this \$5,000 to the farmer. You can think of the farmer as closing out his position every day and then opening up a new position. Thus after the first day the farmer has realized a profit of \$5,000 on his trade and now has an obligation to deliver wheat for \$2.75 a bushel. The \$.05 that the farmer has already been paid *plus* the \$2.75 that remains to be paid equals the \$2.80 selling price at which the farmer originally agreed to deliver wheat.

Of course, our miller is in the opposite position. The fall in the futures price leaves her with a *loss* of \$.05 a bushel. She must, therefore, pay over this loss to the exchange's clearinghouse. In effect the miller closes out her initial purchase at a \$.05 loss and opens a new contract to take delivery at \$2.75 a bushel.[13]

Spot and Futures Prices—Financial Futures

If you want to buy a security, you have a choice. You can buy it for immediate delivery at the spot price. Alternatively, you can place an order for later delivery; in this case you buy at the futures price. When you buy a financial future, you end up with exactly the same security that you would have if you bought in the spot market. However, there are two differences. First, you don't pay for the security up front, and so you can earn interest on its purchase price. Second, you miss out on any dividend or interest that is paid in the interim. This tells us something about the relationship between the spot and futures prices:[14]

$$\frac{\text{Futures price}}{(1 + r_f)^t} = \begin{matrix}\text{spot}\\ \text{price}\end{matrix} - \text{PV}\begin{pmatrix}\text{dividends or}\\ \text{interest payments}\\ \text{forgone}\end{pmatrix}$$

Here r_f is the t-period risk-free interest rate. An example will show how and why this formula works.

Example: Stock Index Futures Suppose six-month stock index futures trade at 1,205 when the index is 1,190. The six-month interest rate is 4 percent, and the average dividend yield of stocks in the index is 1.6 percent per year. Are these numbers consistent?

---

[13]Notice that neither the farmer nor the miller need be concerned about whether the other party will honor his or her side of the bargain. The futures exchange guarantees the contract and protects itself by settling up profits and losses each day.

[14]This relationship is strictly true only if the contract is not marked to market. Otherwise the value of the future depends on the path of interest rates up to the delivery date. In practice this qualification is usually unimportant. See J. C. Cox, J. E. Ingersoll, and S. A. Ross, "The Relationship between Forward and Futures Prices," *Journal of Financial Economics* 9 (1981), pp. 321–346.

Suppose you buy the futures contract and set aside the money to exercise it. At a 4 percent annual rate, you'll earn about 2 percent interest over the next six months. Thus you invest

$$\frac{\text{Futures price}}{(1 + r_f)^t} = \frac{1{,}205}{1.02} = 1{,}181$$

What do you get in return? Everything you would have gotten by buying the index now at the spot price, except for the dividends paid over the next six months. If we assume, for simplicity, that a half-year's dividends are paid in month six (rather than evenly over six months), your payoff is

$$\text{Spot price} - \text{PV(dividends)} = 1{,}190 - \frac{1{,}190\,(.008)}{1.02} = 1{,}181$$

You get what you pay for.

Spot and Futures Prices—Commodities

The difference between buying *commodities* today and buying commodity futures is more complicated. First, because payment is again delayed, the buyer of the future earns interest on her money. Second, she does not need to store the commodities and, therefore, saves warehouse costs, wastage, and so on. On the other hand, the futures contract gives no *convenience yield*, which is the value of being able to get your hands on the real thing. The manager of a supermarket can't burn heating oil futures if there's a sudden cold snap, and he can't stock the shelves with orange juice futures if he runs out of inventory at 1 P.M. on a Saturday. All this means that for commodities,

$$\frac{\text{Futures price}}{(1 + r_f)^t} = \text{spot price} + \text{PV}\begin{pmatrix}\text{storage}\\ \text{costs}\end{pmatrix} - \text{PV}\begin{pmatrix}\text{convenience}\\ \text{yield}\end{pmatrix}$$

No one would be willing to hold the futures contract at a higher futures price or to hold the commodity at a lower futures price.[15]

It's interesting to compare the formulas for futures prices of commodities to the formulas for securities. PV(convenience yield) plays the same role as PV(dividends or interest payments forgone). But financial assets cost nothing to store, so PV(storage costs) does not appear in the formula for financial futures.

You can't observe PV(convenience yield) or PV(storage) separately, but you can infer the difference between them by comparing the spot price to the discounted futures price. This difference—that is, convenience yield less storage cost—is called *net convenience yield*.

Here is an example using quotes for August 2001. At that time the spot price of coffee was about 51 cents per pound. The futures price for March 2002 was 58.7 cents. Of course, if you bought and held the futures, you would not pay until March. The present value of this outlay is 57.4 cents, using a one-year interest rate of 4 percent. So PV(net convenience yield) is negative at 6.4 cents a pound:

$$\begin{aligned}\text{PV(net convenience yield)} &= \text{spot price} - \frac{\text{futures price}}{1 + r_f}\\ &= 51 - 57.4 = -6.4 \text{ cents}\end{aligned}$$

[15]Our formula could overstate the futures price if no one is willing to hold the commodity, that is, if inventories fall to zero or some absolute minimum.

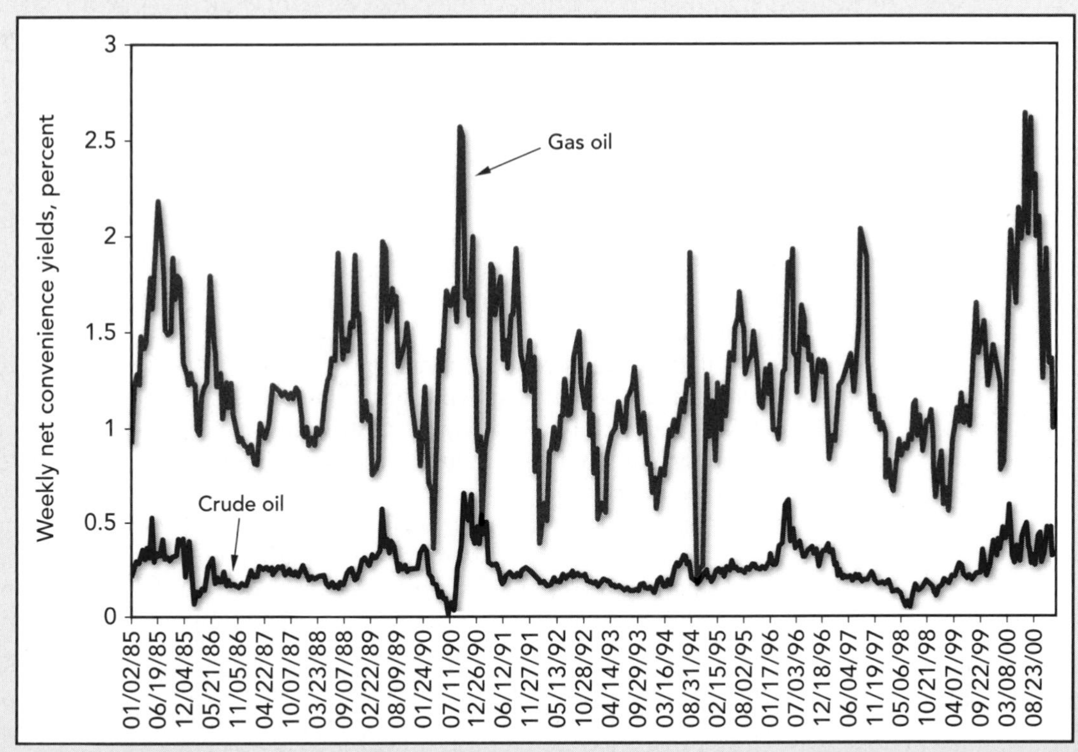

FIGURE 27.1

Weekly percentage net convenience yield (convenience yield *less* storage costs) for two commodities.

Source: R. S. Pindyck, "The Present Value Model of Rational Commodity Pricing," *Economic Journal* 103 (May 1993), pp. 511–530. We thank Professor Pindyck for updating the data.

Sometimes the net convenience yield is expressed as a percentage of the spot price, in this case as $-6.4/51 = -.125$, or -12.5 percent. Coffee in 2001 was in ample supply and evidently roasters had no worries that they would run short in the months ahead.

Figure 27.1 plots percentage net convenience yields for crude oil and gas oil (used for heating). Notice how much the spread between the spot and futures price for gas oil bounces around. When there are shortages or fears of an interruption of supply, traders may be prepared to pay 2 or more percent *per week* for the convenience of having oil in the tanks rather than the promise of future delivery.[16]

There is one further complication that we should note. There are some commodities that cannot be stored at all. You can't store electricity, for example. As a result, electricity supplied in, say, six-months' time is effectively a different commodity from electricity available now, and there is no simple link between today's price and that of a futures contract to buy or sell at the end of six months. Of course,

[16]For evidence that the net convenience yield is related to the level of inventories, see M. J. Brennan, "The Price of Convenience and the Valuation of Commodity Contingent Claims," in D. Lund and B. Øksendal (eds.), *Stochastic Models and Option Values*, North-Holland Publishing Company, Amsterdam, 1991.

generators and consumers will have their own views of what the spot price is likely to be when those six months have elapsed, and they may be more or less eager to fix today the price at which they buy or sell.

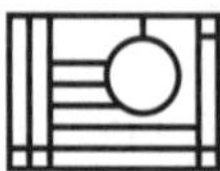

27.3 FORWARD CONTRACTS

Each day billions of dollars of futures contracts are bought and sold. This liquidity is possible only because futures contracts are standardized and mature on a limited number of dates each year.

Fortunately there is usually more than one way to skin a financial cat. If the terms of futures contracts do not suit your particular needs, you may be able to buy or sell a **forward contract.** Forward contracts are simply tailor-made futures contracts. The main forward market is in foreign currency. We will discuss forward exchange rates in the next chapter.

It is also possible to enter into a forward interest rate contract. For example, suppose that you know that at the end of six months you are going to need a three-month loan. You worry that interest rates will rise over the six-month period. You can lock in the interest rate on that loan by buying a *forward rate agreement (FRA)* from a bank.[17] For example, the bank might offer to sell you a six-month forward rate agreement on three-month LIBOR at 7 percent.[18] If at the end of six months the three-month LIBOR rate is greater than 7 percent, the bank will pay you the difference; if three-month LIBOR is less than 7 percent, you pay the bank the difference.[19]

Homemade Forward Contracts

Suppose that you borrow $90.91 for one year at 10 percent and lend $90.91 for two years at 12 percent. These interest rates are for loans made today; therefore, they are spot interest rates.

The cash flows on your transactions are as follows:

	Year 0	Year 1	Year 2
Borrow for 1 year at 10%	+90.91	−100	
Lend for 2 years at 12%	−90.91		+114.04
Net cash flow	0	−100	+114.04

Notice that you do not have any net cash outflow today but you have contracted to pay out money in year 1. The interest rate on this forward commitment is 14.04 percent. To calculate this forward interest rate, we simply worked out the extra return for lending for two years rather than one:

[17]Note that the party which profits from a rise in rates is described as the "buyer." In our example you would be said to "buy six against nine months" money, meaning that the forward rate agreement is for a three-month loan in six months' time.

[18]LIBOR (London interbank offered rate) is the interest rate at which major international banks in London lend each other dollars.

[19]Unlike futures contracts, forwards are not marked to market. Thus all profits or losses are settled when the contract matures.

$$\text{Forward interest rate} = \frac{(1 + \text{2-year spot rate})^2}{1 + \text{1-year spot rate}} - 1$$
$$= \frac{(1.12)^2}{1.10} - 1 = .1404, \text{ or } 14.04\%$$

In our example you manufactured a forward loan by borrowing short-term and lending long. But you can also run the process in reverse. If you wish to fix today the rate at which you borrow next year, you borrow long and lend the money until you need it next year.

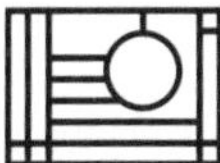

27.4 SWAPS

Some company cash flows are fixed. Others vary with the level of interest rates, rates of exchange, prices of commodities, and so on. These characteristics may not always result in the desired risk profile. For example, a company that pays a fixed rate of interest on its debt might prefer to pay a floating rate, while another company that receives cash flows in euros might prefer to receive them in yen. Swaps allow them to change their risk in these ways.

The market for swaps is huge. In 2000 the total notional amount of swaps outstanding was estimated at over $50 trillion. The major part of this figure consisted of interest rate swaps, but it is also possible to swap different currencies, equity indexes, and commodities.[20] We will show first how interest rate swaps work, and then describe a currency swap. We conclude with a brief look at *default swaps.* The default swap is an example of a *credit derivative,* a relatively new box of tools for managing risk.

Interest Rate Swaps

Friendly Bancorp has made a five-year, $50 million loan to fund part of the construction cost of a large cogeneration project. The loan carries a fixed interest rate of 8 percent. Annual interest payments are therefore $4 million. Interest payments are made annually, and all the principal will be repaid at year 5.

Suppose that instead of receiving fixed interest payments of $4 million a year, the bank would prefer to receive floating-rate payments. It can do so by swapping the $4 million, five-year annuity (the fixed interest payments) into a five-year floating-rate annuity. We will show first how Friendly Bancorp can make its own homemade swap. Then we will describe a simpler procedure.

The bank can borrow at a 6 percent fixed rate for five years.[21] Therefore, the $4 million interest it receives can support a fixed-rate loan of 4/.06 = $66.67 million. The bank can now construct the homemade swap as follows: It borrows $66.67 million at a fixed interest rate of 6 percent for five years and simultaneously lends

[20]Data on swaps are provided by the Bank for International Settlements (see **www.bis.org/statistics**). Equity swaps typically involve one party receiving the dividends and capital gains on an equity index, while the other party receives a fixed or floating rate of interest. Similarly, in a commodity swap one party receives a payment linked to the commodity price and the other receives the interest rate.

[21]The spread between the bank's 6 percent borrowing rate and the 8 percent lending rate is the bank's profit on the project financing.

	Year					
	0	1	2	3	4	5
Homemade swap:						
1. Borrow \$66.67 at 6% fixed rate	+66.67	−4	−4	−4	−4	−(4 + 66.67)
2. Lend \$66.67 at LIBOR floating rate	−66.67	+.05 × 66.67	$+\text{LIBOR}_1 \times 66.67$	$+\text{LIBOR}_2 \times 66.67$	$+\text{LIBOR}_3 \times 66.67$	$+\text{LIBOR}_4 \times 66.67 + 66.67$
Net cash flow	0	−4+.05 × 66.67	$-4 + \text{LIBOR}_1 \times 66.67$	$-4 + \text{LIBOR}_2 \times 66.67$	$-4 + \text{LIBOR}_3 \times 66.67$	$-4 + \text{LIBOR}_4 \times 66.67$
Standard fixed-to-floating swap:						
Net cash flow	0	−4 + .05 × 66.67	$-4 + \text{LIBOR}_1 \times 66.67$	$-4 + \text{LIBOR}_2 \times 66.67$	$-4 + \text{LIBOR}_3 \times 66.67$	$-4 + \text{LIBOR}_4 \times 66.67$

TABLE 27.3

The top panel shows the cash flows to a homemade fixed-to-floating interest rate swap. The bottom panel shows the cash flows to a standard swap transaction.

the same amount at LIBOR. We assume that LIBOR is initially 5 percent.[22] LIBOR is a short-term interest rate, so future interest receipts will fluctuate as the bank's investment is rolled over.

The net cash flows to this strategy are shown in the top portion of Table 27.3. Notice that there is no net cash flow in year 0 and that in year 5 the principal amount of the short-term investment is used to pay off the \$66.67 million loan. What's left? A cash flow equal to the *difference* between the interest earned (LIBOR × 66.67) and the \$4 million outlay on the fixed loan. The bank also has \$4 million per year coming in from the project financing, so it has transformed that fixed payment into a floating payment keyed to LIBOR.

Of course, there's an easier way to do this, shown in the bottom portion of Table 27.3. The bank can just enter into a five-year swap.[23] Naturally, Friendly Bancorp takes this easier route. Let's see what happens.

Friendly Bancorp calls a swap dealer, which is typically a large commercial or investment bank, and agrees to *swap* the payments on a \$66.67 million fixed-rate loan for the payments on an equivalent floating-rate loan. The swap is known as a fixed-to-floating interest rate swap and the \$66.67 million is termed the *notional principal* amount of the swap. Friendly Bancorp and the dealer are the *counterparties* to the swap.

The dealer is quoting a rate for five-year swaps of 6 percent against LIBOR.[24] This figure is sometimes quoted as a spread over the yield on U.S. Treasuries. For

[22]Maybe the short-term interest rate is below the five-year interest rate because investors expect interest rates to rise.

[23]Both strategies are equivalent to a series of forward contracts on LIBOR. The forward prices are \$4 million each for $\text{LIBOR}_1 \times 66.67$, $\text{LIBOR}_2 \times 66.67$, and so on. Separately negotiated forward prices would not be \$4 million for any one year, but the PVs of the "annuities" of forward prices would be identical.

[24]Notice that the swap rate always refers to the interest rate on the fixed leg of the swap. Rates are generally quoted against LIBOR, though dealers will also be prepared to quote rates against other short-term debt.

example, if the yield on five-year Treasury notes is 5.25 percent, the swap spread is .75 percent.[25]

The first payment on the swap occurs at the end of year 1 and is based on the starting LIBOR rate of 5 percent.[26] The dealer (who pays floating) owes the bank 5 percent of \$66.67 million, while the bank (which pays fixed) owes the dealer \$4 million (6 percent of \$66.67 million). The bank therefore makes a net payment to the dealer of $4 - (.05 \times 66.67) = \$.67$ million:

Bank	←	$.05 \times \$66.67 = \$3.33$	←	Counterparty
Bank	→	\$4	→	Counterparty
Bank	→	Net = \$.67	→	Counterparty

The second payment is based on LIBOR at year 1. Suppose it increases to 6 percent. Then the net payment is zero:

Bank	←	$.06 \times \$66.67 = \$4$	←	Counterparty
Bank	→	\$4	→	Counterparty
Bank	→	Net = 0	→	Counterparty

The third payment depends on LIBOR at year 2, and so on.

Notice that, when the two counterparties entered into the swap, the deal was fairly valued. In other words, the net cash flows had zero present value. What happens to the value of the swap as time passes? That depends on long-term interest rates. For example, suppose that after two years interest rates are unchanged, so a 6 percent note issued by the bank would continue to trade at its face value. In this case the swap still has zero value. (You can confirm this by checking that the NPV of a new three-year homemade swap is zero.) But if long rates increase over the two years to 7 percent (say), the value of a three-year note falls to

$$PV = \frac{4}{1.07} + \frac{4}{(1.07)^2} + \frac{4 + 66.67}{(1.07)^3} = \$64.92 \text{ million}$$

Now the fixed payments that the bank has agreed to make are less valuable and the swap is worth $66.67 - 64.92 = \$1.75$ million.

How do we know the swap is worth \$1.75 million? Consider the following strategy:

1. The bank can enter a new three-year swap deal in which it agrees to *pay* LIBOR on the same notional principal of \$66.67 million.
2. In return it receives fixed payments at the new 7 percent interest rate, that is, $.07 \times 66.67 = \$4.67$ per year.

The new swap cancels the cash flows of the old one, but it generates an extra. \$.67 million for three years. This extra cash flow is worth

$$PV = \sum_{t=1}^{3} \frac{.67}{(1.07)^t} = \$1.75 \text{ million}$$

[25]Swap spreads fluctuate. After Russia defaulted on its debt in 1998 and the U.S. hedge fund Long Term Capital Management (LTCM) came close to collapse, five-year swap spreads nearly doubled from 0.5 percent to 0.8 percent.

[26]More commonly, interest rate swaps are based on three-month LIBOR and involve quarterly cash payments.

Remember, ordinary interest rate swaps have no initial cost or value (NPV = 0), but their value drifts away from zero as time passes and long-term interest rates change. One counterparty wins as the other loses.

In our example, the swap dealer loses from the rise in interest rates. Dealers will try to hedge the risk of interest rate movements by engaging in a series of futures or forward contracts or by entering into an offsetting swap with a third party. As long as Friendly Bancorp and the other counterparty honor their promises, the dealer is fully protected against risk. The recurring nightmare for swap managers is that one party will default, leaving the dealer with a large unmatched position. This is called *counterparty risk.*

Currency Swaps

We now look briefly at an example of a currency swap.

Suppose that the Possum Company needs 11 million euros to help finance its European operations. We assume that the euro interest rate is about 5 percent, whereas the dollar rate is about 6 percent. Since Possum is better known in the United States, the financial manager decides not to borrow euros directly. Instead, the company issues $10 million of five-year 6 percent notes in the United States. Then it arranges with a counterparty to swap this dollar loan into euros. Under this arrangement the counterparty agrees to pay Possum sufficient dollars to service its dollar loan, and in exchange Possum agrees to make a series of annual payments in euros to the counterparty.

Here are Possum's cash flows (in millions):

	Year 0		Years 1–4		Year 5	
	Dollars	Euros	Dollars	Euros	Dollars	Euros
1. Issue dollar loan	+10		−.6		−10.6	
2. Swap dollars for euros	−10	+11	+.6	−.55	+10.6	−11.55
3. Net cash flow	0	+11	0	−.55	0	−11.55

Look first at the cash flows in year 0. Possum receives $10 million from its issue of dollar notes, which it then pays over to the swap counterparty. In return the counterparty sends Possum a check for €11 million. (We assume that at current rates of exchange $10 million is worth €11 million.)

Now move to years 1 through 4. Possum needs to pay interest of 6 percent on its debt issue, which works out at $.06 \times 10 = \$.6$ million. The swap counterparty agrees to provide Possum each year with sufficient cash to pay this interest and in return Possum makes an annual payment to the counterparty of 5 percent of €11 million, or €.55 million. Finally, in year 5 the swap counterparty pays Possum enough to make the final payment of interest and principal on its dollar notes ($10.6 million), while Possum pays the counterparty €11.55 million.

The combined effect of Possum's two steps (line 3) is to convert a 6 percent dollar loan into a 5 percent euro loan. You can think of the cash flows for the swap (line 2) as a series of contracts to buy euros in years 1 through 5. In each of years 1 through 4 Possum agrees to purchase $.6 million at a cost of .5 million euros; in year 5 it agrees to buy $10.6 million at a cost of 11.55 million euros.[27]

[27]Usually in a currency swap the two parties make an initial payment to each other (i.e., Possum pays the bank $10 million and receives €11 million). However, this is not necessary and Possum might prefer to buy the €11 million from another bank.

Credit Derivatives

In recent years there has been considerable growth in the use of *credit derivatives,* which protect lenders against the risk that a borrower will default. For example, bank A may be reluctant to refuse a loan to a major customer (customer X) but may be concerned about the total size of its exposure to that customer. Bank A can go ahead with the loan, but use credit derivatives to shuffle off the risk to bank B.

The most common credit derivative is known as a *default swap*. It works as follows. Bank A promises to pay a fixed sum each year to B as long as company X has not defaulted on its debts. If X defaults, B compensates A for the loss, but otherwise pays nothing. Thus you can think of B as providing A with long-term insurance against default in return for an annual insurance premium.[28]

Banks that have a portfolio of loans may be more concerned with the possibility of widespread defaults than with the risk of a single loan. In principle, they could negotiate a default swap on each individual loan. In practice, it is generally simpler to enter into a portfolio default swap that provides protection on the entire loan portfolio.

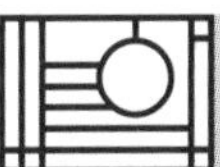

27.5 HOW TO SET UP A HEDGE

To hedge risk the firm buys one asset and sells an equal amount of another asset. For example, our farmer owned 100,000 bushels of wheat and sold 100,000 bushels of wheat futures. As long as the wheat that the farmer owns is identical to the wheat that he has promised to deliver, this strategy minimizes risk.

In practice the wheat that the farmer owns and the wheat that he sells in the futures markets are unlikely to be identical. For example, if he sells wheat futures on the Kansas City exchange, he agrees to deliver hard, red winter wheat in Kansas City in September. But perhaps he is growing northern spring wheat many miles from Kansas City; in this case the prices of the two wheats will not move exactly together.

Figure 27.2 shows how changes in the prices of the two types of wheat may have been related in the past. Notice two things about this figure. First, the scatter of points suggests that the price changes are imperfectly related. If so, it is not possible to construct a hedge that eliminates all risk. Some residual, or *basis,* risk will remain. Second, the slope of the fitted line shows that a 1 percent change in the price of Kansas wheat was on average associated with an .8 percent change in the price of the farmer's wheat. Because the price of the farmer's wheat is relatively insensitive to changes in Kansas prices, he needs to sell .8 × 100,000 bushels of wheat futures to minimize risk.

Let us generalize. Suppose that you already own an asset, A (e.g., wheat), and that you wish to hedge against changes in the value of A by making an offsetting sale of another asset, B (e.g., wheat futures). Suppose also that percentage changes in the value of A are related in the following way to percentage changes in the value of B:

$$\begin{matrix}\text{Expected change} \\ \text{in value of A}\end{matrix} = a + \delta\begin{pmatrix}\text{change in} \\ \text{value of B}\end{pmatrix}$$

[28]Another form of credit derivative is the credit option. In this case A would pay an up-front premium and B would assume the obligation to pay A in the event of X's default.

FIGURE 27.2

Hypothetical plot of past changes in the price of the farmer's wheat against changes in the price of Kansas City wheat futures. A 1 percent change in the futures price implies, on average, an .8 percent change in the price of the farmer's wheat.

Delta (δ) measures the sensitivity of A to changes in the value of B. It is also equal to the *hedge ratio*—that is, the number of units of B which should be sold to hedge the purchase of A. You minimize risk if you offset your position in A by the sale of delta units of B.[29]

The trick in setting up a hedge is to estimate the delta or hedge ratio. This often calls for a strong dose of judgment. For example, suppose that Antarctic Air would like to protect itself against a hike in oil prices. As the financial manager, you need to decide how much a rise in oil prices would affect firm value. Suppose the company spent \$200 million on fuel last year. Other things equal, a 10 percent increase in the price of oil will cost the company an extra $.1 \times 200 = \$20$ million. But perhaps you can partially offset the higher costs by higher ticket prices, in which case earnings will fall by *less* than \$20 million. Or perhaps an oil price rise will lead to a slowdown in business activity and therefore lower passenger numbers. In that case earnings will decline by *more* than \$20 million. Working out the likely effect on firm *value* is even more tricky, because that depends on whether the rise is likely to be permanent. Perhaps the price rise will induce an increase in production or encourage consumers to economize on energy usage.

Sometimes in such cases some history may help. For example, you could look at how firm value changed in the past as oil prices changed. In other cases it may be possible to call on a little theory to set up the hedge.

Using Theory to Set Up the Hedge: An Example

Potterton Leasing has just purchased some equipment and arranged to rent it out for \$2 million a year over eight years. At an interest rate of 12 percent, Potterton's rental income has a present value of \$9.94 million:[30]

$$\text{PV} = \frac{2}{1.12} + \frac{2}{(1.12)^2} + \cdots + \frac{2}{(1.12)^8} = \$9.94 \text{ million}$$

[29]Notice that A, the item that you wish to hedge, is the dependent variable. Delta measures the sensitivity of A to changes in B.

[30]We ignore taxes in this example.

Potterton proposes to finance the deal by issuing a package of \$1.91 million of one-year debt and \$8.03 million of six-year debt, each with a 12 percent coupon. Think of its new asset (the stream of rental income) and the new liability (the issue of debt) as a package. Does Potterton stand to gain or lose on this package if interest rates change?

To answer this question, it is helpful to go back to the concept of duration that we introduced in Chapter 24. Duration, you may remember, is the weighted-average time to each cash flow. Duration is important because it is directly related to volatility. If two assets have the same duration, their prices will be equally affected by any change in interest rates. If we call the total value of Potterton's rental income V, then the duration of Potterton's rental income is calculated as follows:

$$\begin{aligned}\text{Duration} &= \frac{1}{V}\{[\text{PV}(C_1) \times 1] + [\text{PV}(C_2) \times 2] + [\text{PV}(C_3) \times 3] + \cdots\} \\ &= \frac{1}{9.94}\left\{\left[\frac{2}{1.12} \times 1\right] + \left[\frac{2}{(1.12)^2} \times 2\right] + \cdots + \left[\frac{2}{(1.12)^8} \times 8\right]\right\} \\ &= 3.9 \text{ years}\end{aligned}$$

We can also calculate the duration of Potterton's new liabilities. The duration of the 1-year debt is 1 year, and the duration of the 6-year debt is 4.6 years. The duration of the package of 1- and 6-year debt is a weighted average of the durations of the individual issues:

$$\begin{aligned}\text{Duration of liability} &= (1.91/9.94) \times \text{duration of 1-year debt} \\ &\quad +(8.03/9.94) \times \text{duration of 6-year debt} \\ &= (.192 \times 1) + (.808 \times 4.6) = 3.9 \text{ years}\end{aligned}$$

Thus, both the asset (the lease) and the liability (the debt package) have a duration of 3.9 years. Therefore, both are affected equally by a change in interest rates. If rates rise, the present value of Potterton's rental income will decline, but the value of its debt obligation will also decline by the same amount. By equalizing the duration of the asset and that of the liability, Potterton has *immunized* itself against any change in interest rates. It looks as if Potterton's financial manager knows a thing or two about hedging.

When Potterton set up the hedge, it needed to find a package of loans that had a present value of \$9.94 million and a duration of 3.9 years. Call the proportion of the proceeds raised by the six-year loan x and the proportion raised by the one-year loan $(1 - x)$. Then

$$\begin{aligned}\text{Duration of package} &= (x \times \text{duration of 6-year loan}) + [(1 - x) \\ &\quad \times \text{duration of 1-year loan}] \\ 3.9 \text{ years} &= (x \times 4.6 \text{ years}) + [(1 - x) \times 1 \text{ year}] \\ x &= .808\end{aligned}$$

Since the package of loans must raise \$9.94 million, Potterton needs to issue $.808 \times 9.94 = \$8.03$ million of the six-year loan.

An important feature of this hedge is that it is dynamic. As interest rates change and time passes, the duration of Potterton's asset may no longer be the same as that of its liability. Thus, to remain hedged against interest rate changes, Potterton must be prepared to keep adjusting the duration of its debt.

Cash Flows ($ millions)								
	Year							
	1	2	3	4	5	6	7	8
Balance at start of year	9.94	9.13	8.23	7.22	6.08	4.81	3.39	1.79
Interest at 12%	1.19	1.10	.99	.87	.73	.58	.40	.21
Sinking fund payment	.81	.90	1.01	1.13	1.27	1.42	1.60	1.79
Interest plus sinking fund payment	2.00	2.00	2.00	2.00	2.00	2.00	2.00	2.00

TABLE 27.4

Potterton can hedge by issuing this sinking fund bond that pays out $2 million each year.

If Potterton is not disposed to follow this dynamic hedging strategy, it has an alternative. It can devise a debt issue whose cash flows exactly match the rental income from the lease. For example, suppose that it issues an eight-year sinking fund bond; the amount of the sinking fund is $810,000 in year 1, and the payment increases by 12 percent annually. Table 27.4 shows that the bond payments (interest plus sinking fund) are $2 million in each year.

Since the cash flows on the asset exactly match those on the liability, Potterton's financial manager can now relax. Each year the manager simply collects the $2 million rental income and hands it to the bondholders. Whatever happens to interest rates, the firm is always perfectly hedged.

Why wouldn't Potterton's financial manager *always* prefer to construct matching assets and liabilities? One reason is that it may be relatively costly to devise a bond with a specially tailored pattern of cash flows. Another may be that Potterton is continually entering into new lease agreements and issuing new debt. In this case the manager can never relax; it may be simpler to keep the durations of the assets and liabilities equal than to maintain an exact match between the cash flows.

Options, Deltas, and Betas

Here's another case where some theory can help you set up a hedge. In Chapter 20 we came across options. These give you the right, but not the obligation, to buy or sell an asset. Options are derivatives; their value depends only on what happens to the price of the underlying asset.

The *option delta* summarizes the link between the option and the asset. For example, if you own an option to buy a share of Walt Disney stock, the change in the value of your investment will be the same as it would be if you held delta shares of Disney.

Since the option price is tied to the asset price, options can be used for hedging. Thus, if you own an option to buy a share of Disney and at the same time you sell delta shares of Disney, any change in the value of your position in the stock will be exactly offset by the change in the value of your option position.[31] In other words, you will be perfectly hedged—hedged, that is, for the next short period of time.

[31] We are assuming that you hold one option and hedge by selling δ shares. If you owned one share and wanted to hedge by selling options, you would need to sell $1/\delta$ options.

Option deltas change as the stock price changes and time passes. Therefore, option-based hedges need to be adjusted frequently.

Options can be used to hedge commodities too. The miller could offset changes in the cost of future wheat purchases by buying call options on wheat (or on wheat futures). But this is not the simplest strategy if the miller is trying to lock in the future cost of wheat. She would have to check the option delta to determine how many options to buy, and she would have to keep track of changes in the option delta and reset the hedge as necessary.[32]

It's the same for financial assets. Suppose you hold a well-diversified portfolio of stocks with a beta of 1.0 and near-perfect correlation with the market return. You want to lock in the portfolio's value at year-end. You could accomplish this by selling call options on the index, but to maintain the hedge, the option position would have to be adjusted frequently. It's simpler just to sell index futures maturing at year-end.

Speaking of betas . . . what if your portfolio has a beta of .60, not 1.0? Then your hedge will require 40 percent fewer index futures contracts. And since your low-beta portfolio is probably not perfectly correlated with the market, there will be some basis risk as well. In this context our old friend beta (β) and the hedge ratio (δ) are one and the same. Remember, to hedge A with B, you need to know δ because

$$\text{Expected change in value of A} = a + \delta(\text{change in value of B})$$

When A is a stock or portfolio, and B is the market, we estimate beta from the same relationship:

$$\text{Expected change in stock or portfolio value} = a + \beta(\text{change in market index})$$

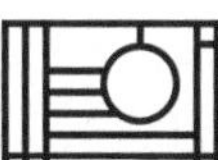

27.6 IS "DERIVATIVE" A FOUR-LETTER WORD?

Our earlier example of the farmer and miller showed how futures may be used to reduce business risk. However, if you were to copy the farmer and sell wheat futures without an offsetting holding of wheat, you would not be *reducing* risk: You would be *speculating*.

Speculators in search of large profits (and prepared to tolerate large losses) are attracted by the leverage that derivatives provide. By this we mean that it is not necessary to lay out much money up front and the profits or losses may be many times the initial outlay.[33] "Speculation" has an ugly ring, but a successful derivatives market needs speculators who are prepared to take on risk and provide more cautious people like our farmer and miller with the protection they need. For example, if an excess of farmers wish to sell wheat futures, the price of futures will be forced down until enough speculators are tempted to buy in the hope of a profit. If there is a surplus of millers wishing to buy wheat futures, the reverse will happen. The price of wheat futures will be forced *up* until speculators are drawn in to sell.

Speculation may be necessary to a thriving derivatives market, but it can get companies into serious trouble. Finance in the News describes how the German metals

[32]*Quiz:* What is the miller's position if she buys call options on wheat and simply holds them to maturity?

[33]For example, if you buy or sell forward, no money changes hands until the contract matures, though you may be required to put up margin to show that you can honor your commitment. This margin does not need to be cash; it can be in the form of safe securities.

THE DEBACLE AT METALLGESELLSCHAFT

In January 1994 the German industrial giant Metallgesellschaft shocked investors with news of huge losses in its U.S. oil subsidiary, MGRM. These losses, later estimated at over $1 billion, brought the firm to the brink of bankruptcy and it was saved only by a $1.9 billion rescue package from 120 banks.

The previous year MGRM had embarked on what looked like a sure-fire way to make money. It offered its customers forward contracts on deliveries of gasoline, heating oil, and diesel fuel for up to 10 years. These price guarantees proved extremely popular. By September 1993, MGRM had sold forward over 150 million barrels of oil at prices that were $3 to $5 a barrel over the prevailing spot prices.

As long as oil prices did not rise appreciably, MGRM stood to make a handsome profit from its forward sales, but if oil prices did return to their level of earlier years the result would be a calamitous loss. MGRM therefore sought to avoid such an outcome by buying energy futures. Unfortunately, the long-term futures contracts that were needed to offset MGRM's price guarantees did not exist. MGRM's solution was to enter into what is known as a "stack-and-roll" hedge. In other words, it bought a stack of short-dated futures contracts and, as these were about to expire, it rolled them over into a fresh stack of short-dated contracts.

MGRM was relaxed about the mismatch between the long-term maturity of its price guarantees and the much shorter maturity of its futures contracts. It could point to past history to justify its confidence, for in most years energy traders have placed a high value on owning the oil rather than having a promise of future delivery. In other words, the net convenience yield on oil has generally been positive (see Figure 27.1). As long as that continued to be the case, then each time that MGRM rolled over its futures contracts, it would be selling its maturing contracts at a higher price than it would need to pay for the stack of new contracts. However, if the net convenience yield were to become negative, the maturing futures contracts would sell for *less* than more distant ones. Unfortunately, this is what occurred in 1993. In that year there was a glut of oil, the storage tanks were full, and nobody was prepared to pay extra to get their hands on oil. The result was that MGRM was forced to pay a premium to roll over each stack of maturing contracts.

The fall in oil prices had another unfortunate consequence for MGRM. Futures contracts are marked to market. This means that the investor settles up the profits and losses on each contract as they arise. Therefore, as oil prices continued to fall in 1993, MGRM incurred losses on its purchases of oil futures. This resulted in huge margin calls.* The offsetting good news was that the fall in oil prices meant that its long-term forward contracts were looking increasingly profitable, but this profit was not money in the bank.

When Metallgesellschaft's board learned of these problems, it fired the chief executive and instructed the company to cease all hedging activities and to start negotiations with customers to cancel the long-term contracts. Almost immediately the fall in oil prices reversed. Within eight months the price had risen about 40 percent. If only MGRM had been able to hold on, it would have enjoyed a huge cash inflow.

Observers have continued to argue about the Metallgesellschaft debacle. Was the company's belief that the net convenience yield would remain positive a reasonable assumption or a gigantic speculation? How much did the company anticipate its cash needs and could it have financed them by borrowing on the strength of its long-term forward contracts? Did senior management mistake the margin calls for losses and just lose its nerve when it decided to liquidate the company's positions?

*In addition to buying futures contracts, MGRM also bought short-term over-the-counter forward contracts and commodity swaps. As these matured, MGRM had to make good the loss on them, even though it did not receive the gains on the price guarantees.

and oil trading company, Metallgesellschaft, took a $1 billion bath on its positions in oil futures. Metallgesellschaft had plenty of company. The Japanese company, Showa Shell, reported a loss of $1.5 billion on positions in foreign exchange futures. Another Japanese firm, Sumitomo Corporation, lost over $2 billion when a rogue trader tried to buy enough copper to control that market.[34] And in 1995 Baring Brothers, a blue-chip British merchant bank with a 200-year history, became insolvent. The reason: Nick Leeson, a trader in Baring's Singapore office, had placed very large bets on the Japanese stock market index resulting in losses of $1.4 billion.

These tales of woe have some cautionary messages for corporations. During the 1970s and 1980s many firms turned their treasury operations into profit centers and proudly announced their profits from trading in financial instruments. But it is not possible to make large profits in financial markets without also taking large risks, so these profits should have served as a warning rather than a matter for congratulation.

A Boeing 747 weighs 400 tons, flies at nearly 600 miles per hour, and is inherently very dangerous. But we don't ground 747s; we just take precautions to ensure that they are flown with care. Similarly, it is foolish to suggest that firms should ban the use of derivatives, but it makes obvious sense to take precautions against their misuse. Here are two bits of horse sense:

- *Precaution 1.* Don't be taken by surprise. By this we mean that senior management needs to monitor regularly the value of the firm's derivatives positions and to know what bets the firm has placed. At its simplest, this might involve asking what would happen if interest rates or exchange rates were to change by 1 percent. But large banks and consultants have also developed sophisticated models for measuring the risk of derivatives positions. J. P. Morgan, for example, offers corporate clients its *RiskMetrics* software to keep track of their risk.
- *Precaution 2.* Place bets only when you have some comparative advantage that ensures the odds are in your favor. If a bank were to announce that it was drilling for oil or launching a new soap powder, you would rightly be suspicious about whether it had what it takes to succeed. Conversely, when an industrial corporation places large bets on interest rates or exchange rates, it is competing against some highly paid pros in banks and other financial institutions. Unless it is better informed than they are about future interest rates or exchange rates, it should use derivatives for hedging, not for speculation.

Imprudent speculation in derivatives is undoubtedly an issue of concern for the company's shareholders, but is it a matter for more general concern? Some people believe so. They point to the huge volume of trading in derivatives and argue that speculative losses could lead to major defaults that might threaten the whole financial system. These worries have led to calls for increased regulation of derivatives markets.

Now, this is not the place for a discussion of regulation, but we should warn you about careless measures of the size of the derivatives markets and the possible losses. In December 2000 the notional value of outstanding derivative contracts was about $110 trillion.[35] This is a very large sum, but it tells you *nothing* about the

[34]The attempt failed, and the company later agreed to pay $150 million more in fines and restitution.

[35]Bank of International Settlements, *Derivatives Statistics* (**www.bis.org/statistics/derstats.htm**).

money that was being put at risk. For example, suppose that a bank enters into a $10 million interest rate swap and the other party goes bankrupt the next day. How much has the bank lost? Nothing. It hasn't paid anything up front; the two parties simply promised to pay sums to each other in the future. Now the deal is off.

Suppose that the other party does not go bankrupt until a year after the bank entered into the swap. In the meantime interest rates have moved in the bank's favor, so it should be receiving more money from the swap than it is paying out. When the other side defaults on the deal, the bank loses the difference between the interest that it is due to receive and the interest that it should pay. But it doesn't lose $10 million.[36]

The only meaningful measure of the potential loss from default is the amount that it would cost firms showing a profit to replace their swap positions. This figure is only a small fraction of the principal amount of swaps outstanding.[37]

[36]This does not mean that firms don't worry about the possibility of default, and there are a variety of ways that they try to protect themselves. In the case of swaps, firms are reluctant to deal with banks that do not have the highest credit rating.

[37]United States General Accounting Office, "Financial Derivatives: Actions Needed to Protect the Financial System," report to congressional requesters, May 1994. This does not mean that swaps have *increased* risk. If counterparties use swaps to hedge risk, they are *less likely* to default.

SUMMARY

As a manager, you are paid to take risks, but you are not paid to take *any* risks. Some are simply bad bets, and others could jeopardize the success of the firm. In these cases you should look for ways to insure or hedge.

Most businesses take out insurance against a variety of risks. Insurance companies have considerable expertise in assessing risk and may be able to pool risks by holding a diversified portfolio. Insurance works less well when the insurance policy attracts only the worst risks *(adverse selection)* or when the insured firm is tempted to skip on maintenance and safety procedures *(moral hazard).*

Insurance is generally purchased from specialist insurance companies, but sometimes firms issue specialized securities instead. Cat (catastrophe) bonds are an example.

The idea behind hedging is straightforward. You find two closely related assets. You then buy one and sell the other in proportions that minimize the risk of your net position. If the assets are *perfectly* correlated, you can make the net position risk-free.

The trick is to find the hedge ratio or delta—that is, the number of units of one asset that is needed to offset changes in the value of the other asset. Sometimes the best solution is to look at how the prices of the two assets have moved together in the past. For example, suppose you observe that a 1 percent change in the value of B has been accompanied on average by a 2 percent change in the value of A. Then delta equals 2.0; to hedge each dollar invested in A, you need to sell two dollars of B.

On other occasions a little theory can help to set up the hedge. For example, the effect of a change in interest rates on an asset's value depends on the asset's duration. If two assets have the same duration, they will be equally affected by fluctuations in interest rates.

Many of the hedges described in this chapter are static. Once you have set up the hedge, you can take a long vacation, confident that the firm is well protected. However, some hedges, such as those that match durations, are dynamic. As time passes and prices change, you need to rebalance your position to maintain the hedge.

Firms use a number of tools to hedge:

1. Futures contracts are advance orders to buy or sell an asset. The price is fixed today, but the final payment does not occur until the delivery date. The futures markets allow firms to place advance orders for dozens of different commodities, securities, and currencies.
2. Futures contracts are highly standardized and are traded in huge volumes on the futures exchanges. Instead of buying or selling a standardized futures contract, you may be able to arrange a tailor-made contract with a bank. These tailor-made futures contracts are called forward contracts. Firms regularly protect themselves against exchange rate changes by buying or selling forward currency contracts. Forward rate agreements (FRAs) provide protection against interest rate changes.
3. It is also possible to construct homemade forward contracts. For example, if you borrow for two years and at the same time lend for one year, you have effectively taken out a forward loan.
4. In recent years firms have entered into a variety of swap arrangements. For example, a firm may arrange for the bank to make all the future payments on its fixed-rate debt in exchange for paying the bank the cost of servicing a floating-rate loan.

Instead of using derivatives for hedging, some companies have decided that speculation is more fun, and this has sometimes gotten them into serious trouble. We do not believe that such speculation makes sense for an industrial company, but we caution against the view that derivatives are a threat to the financial system.

Visit us at www.mhhe.com/bm7e

FURTHER READING

Two general articles on corporate risk management are:

C. W. Smith and R. M. Stultz: "The Determinants of Firms' Hedging Policies," *Journal of Financial and Quantitative Analysis,* 20:391–405 (December 1985).

K. A. Froot, D. Scharfstein, and J. C. Stein: "A Framework for Risk Management," *Journal of Applied Corporate Finance,* 7:22–32 (Fall 1994).

Schaefer's paper is a useful review of how duration measures are used to immunize fixed liabilities:

S. M. Schaefer: "Immunisation and Duration: A Review of Theory, Performance and Applications," *Midland Corporate Finance Journal,* 3:41–58 (Autumn 1984).

The texts that we cited in the readings for Chapter 20 cover futures and swaps as well as options. There are also some useful texts that focus on futures and swaps. They include:

D. Duffie: *Futures Markets,* Prentice-Hall, Inc., Englewood Cliffs, NJ, 1989.

D. R. Siegel and D. F. Siegel: *Futures Markets,* Dryden Press, Chicago, 1990.

C. W. Smith, C. H. Smithson, and D. S. Wilford: *Managing Financial Risk,* 3rd ed., McGraw-Hill, Inc., New York, 1998.

The Metallgesellschaft debacle makes fascinating reading. The following three papers cover all sides of the debate:

C. Culp and M. H. Miller: "Metallgesellschaft and the Economics of Synthetic Storage," *Journal of Applied Corporate Finance,* 7:62–76 (Winter 1995).

F. Edwards: "The Collapse of Metallgesellschaft: Unhedgeable Risks, Poor Hedging Strategy, or Just Bad Luck?" *Journal of Futures Markets,* 15:211–264 (May 1995).

A. Mello and J. Parsons: "Maturity Structure of a Hedge Matters: Lessons from the Metallgesellschaft Debacle," *Journal of Applied Corporate Finance,* 7:106–120 (Spring 1995).

QUIZ

1. True or false?
   a. A perfect hedge of asset A requires an asset B that's perfectly correlated with A.
   b. Hedging transactions in an active futures market have zero or slightly negative NPVs.
   c. Longer maturity bonds necessarily have longer durations.
   d. The longer a bond's duration, the lower is its volatility.
   e. When you buy a futures contract, you pay now for delivery at a future date.
   f. The holder of a futures contract receives the convenience yield on the underlying commodity.
   g. The holder of a financial futures contract misses out on any dividend or interest payments made on the underlying security.
2. Yesterday you sold six-month futures on the German DAX stock market index at a price of 5,820. Today the DAX closed at 5,800 and DAX futures closed at 5,840. You get a call from your broker, who reminds you that your futures position is marked to market each day. Is she asking you to pay money, or is she about to offer to pay you?
3. Calculate the value of a six-month futures contract on a Treasury bond. You have the following information:
   - Six-month interest rate: 10 percent per year, or 4.9 percent for six months.
   - Spot price of bond: 95.
   - Coupon payments on the bond over the next six months: Present value of 4.
4. Calculate PV(convenience yield) for magnoosium scrap from the following information:
   - Spot price: $2,550 per ton.
   - Futures price: $2,408 for a one-year contract.
   - Interest rate: 12 percent.
   - PV(storage costs): $100 per year.
5. Residents of the northeastern United States suffered record-setting low temperatures throughout November and December 2015. Spot prices of heating oil rose 25 percent, to over $2 a gallon.
   a. What effect did this have on the net convenience yield and on the relationship between futures and spot prices?
   b. In late 2016 refiners and distributors were surprised by record-setting *high* temperatures. What was the effect on net convenience yield and spot and futures prices for heating oil?
6. After a record harvest, grain silos are full to the brim. Are storage costs likely to be high or low? What does this imply for the *net* convenience yield?
7. A year ago a British bank entered into a £50 million five-year interest rate swap. It agreed to pay company A each year a fixed rate of 6 percent and to receive in return LIBOR plus 1 percent. When the bank entered into this swap, LIBOR was 5 percent, but now interest rates have risen, so on a four-year interest rate swap the bank could expect to pay 6 1/2 percent and receive LIBOR plus 1 percent.
   a. Is the swap showing a profit or loss to the bank?
   b. Suppose that at this point company A approaches the bank and asks to terminate the swap. If there are four annual payments still remaining, how much should the bank charge A to terminate?
8. What is basis risk? In which of the following cases would you expect basis risk to be most serious?
   a. A broker owning a large block of Walt Disney common stock hedges by selling index futures.
   b. An Iowa corn farmer hedges the selling price of her crop by selling Chicago corn futures.
   c. An importer must pay 900 million euros in six months. He hedges by buying euros forward.

9. You own a $1 million portfolio of aerospace stocks with a beta of 1.2. You are very enthusiastic about aerospace but uncertain about the prospects for the overall stock market. Explain how you could hedge out your market exposure by selling the market short. How much would you sell? How in practice would you go about "selling the market"?

10. a. Marshall Arts has just invested one million euros in BTPs (long-term Italian government bonds). Marshall is concerned about increasing volatility in interest rates. He decides to hedge using bond futures contracts. Should he buy or sell such contracts?
    b. The treasurer of an Italian corporation plans to issue bonds in three months. She is also concerned about interest rate volatility and wants to lock in the price at which her company could sell 5 percent coupon bonds. How would she use bond futures contracts to hedge?

11. Securities A, B, and C have the following cash flows:

	Period 1	Period 2	Period 3
A	40	40	40
B	120	—	—
C	10	10	110

    a. Calculate their durations if the interest rate is 8 percent.
    b. Suppose that you have an investment of $10 million in A. What combination of B and C would immunize this investment against interest rate changes?
    c. Now suppose that you have a $10 million investment in B. How would you immunize?

PRACTICE QUESTIONS

1. Why might a large, multinational company choose to insure against common events, such as vehicle accidents, but not against rare events which could cause large losses? Explain briefly.
2. Large businesses spend millions of dollars annually on insurance. Why? Should they insure against all risks or does insurance make more sense for some risks than others?
3. What is meant by "moral hazard" and "adverse selection"? Explain why these effects tend to increase insurance premiums.
4. On some catastrophe bonds, payments are reduced if the claims against the issuer exceed a specified sum. In other cases payments are reduced only if claims against the entire industry exceed some sum. What are the advantages and disadvantages of the two structures? Which involves more basis risk? Which may create a problem of moral hazard?
5. "The farmer does not avoid risk by selling wheat futures. If wheat prices stay about $2.80 a bushel, then he will actually have lost by selling wheat futures at $2.50." Is this a fair comment?
6. Explain the chief differences between futures and forward contracts, e.g., for foreign exchange.
7. List some of the commodity futures contracts that are traded on exchanges. Who do you think could usefully reduce risk by buying each of these contracts? Who do you think might wish to sell each contract?
8. What is a currency swap? An interest rate swap? A default swap? Give an example of how each swap might be used.
9. In August 2001, six-month futures on the Brazilian Bovespa stock index traded at 15,330. Spot was 13,743. The interest rate was 19 percent and the dividend yield was about 4 percent. Were the futures fairly priced?

10. If you buy a nine-month T-bill future, you undertake to buy a three-month bill in nine months' time. Suppose that Treasury bills and notes currently offer the following yields:

Months to Maturity	Annual Yield
3	6%
6	6.5
9	7
12	8

What is the value of a nine-month bill future?

11. Table 27.5 contains spot and six-month futures prices for several commodities and financial instruments. There may be some money-making opportunities. See if you can find them, and explain how you would trade to take advantage of them. The interest rate is 14.5 percent, or 7 percent over the six-month life of the contracts.

12. The following table shows gold futures prices for varying contract lengths. Gold is predominantly an investment good, not an industrial commodity. Investors hold gold because it diversifies their portfolios and because they hope its price will rise. They do not hold it for its convenience yield.

Calculate the interest rate faced by traders in gold futures for each of the contract lengths shown below. The spot price is $295.2 per ounce.

	Contract Length (months)				
	1	**3**	**9**	**15**	**21**
Futures price	$296.49	$300.11	$312.32	$325.57	$339.65

13. In September 2001 swap dealers were quoting a rate for five-year euro interest-rate swaps of 4.5 percent against euribor (the short-term interest rate for euro loans). Euribor at the time was 4.1 percent. Suppose that A arranges with a dealer to swap a €10 million five-year fixed-rate loan for an equivalent floating-rate loan in euros.

Commodity	Spot Price	Futures Price	Comments
Magnoosium	$2,550 per ton	$2,728.50 per ton	PV(storage costs) = PV(convenience yield).
Frozen quiche	$.50 per pound	$.514 per pound	PV(storage costs) = $.10 per pound; PV(convenience yield) = $.05 per pound.
Nevada Hydro 8s of 2002	77	78.39	4% semiannual coupon payment is due just before futures contract expires.
Costaguanan pulgas (currency)	9,300 pulgas = $1	6,900 pulgas = $1	Costaguanan interest rate is 95% per year.
Establishment Industries common stock	$95	$97.54	Establishment pays dividends of $2 per quarter. Next dividend is paid 2 months from now.
Cheap white wine	$12,500 per 10,000-gal. tank	$14,200 per 10,000-gal. tank	PV(convenience yield) = $250 per tank. Your company unexpectedly has surplus storage and can store 50,000 gallons at no cost.

TABLE 27.5

Spot and six-month futures prices for selected commodities and securities. See problem 11.

a. What is the value of this swap at the time that it is entered into?
b. Suppose that immediately after A has entered into the swap, the long-term interest rate rises by 1 percent. Who gains and who loses?
c. What is now the value of the swap?

14. Firms A and B face the following borrowing rates for making a five-year fixed-rate debt issue in U.S. dollars or Swiss francs:

	U.S. Dollars	Swiss Francs
Firm A	10%	7%
Firm B	8	6

Suppose that A wishes to borrow U.S. dollars and B wishes to borrow Swiss francs. Show how a swap could be used to reduce the borrowing costs of each company. Assume a spot exchange rate of 2 Swiss francs per dollar.

15. What is meant by "delta" in the context of hedging? Give examples of how delta can be estimated or calculated.

16. A gold-mining firm is concerned about short-term volatility in its revenues. Gold currently sells for $300 an ounce, but the price is extremely volatile and could fall as low as $280 or rise as high as $320 in the next month. The company will bring 1,000 ounces to the market next month.
a. What will be total revenues if the firm remains unhedged for gold prices of $280, $300, and $320 an ounce?
b. The future price of gold for delivery one month ahead is $301. What will be the firm's total revenues at each gold price if the firm enters into a one-month futures contract to deliver 1,000 ounces of gold?
c. What will total revenues be if the firm buys a one-month put option to sell gold for $300 an ounce? The put option costs $2 per ounce.

17. Legs Diamond owns shares in Vanguard Index 500 mutual fund worth $1 million on July 15. (This is an index fund that tracks the Standard and Poor's 500 Index.) He wants to cash in now, but his accountant advises him to wait six months so as to defer a large capital gains tax. Explain to Legs how he can use stock index futures to hedge out his exposure to market movements over the next six months. Could Legs "cash in" without actually selling his shares?

18. Refer back to question 17. Suppose that the nearest index futures contract matures in seven months rather than in six. Show how Legs Diamond can still use index futures to hedge his position. How would the maturity date affect the hedge ratio?

19. Your investment bank has an investment of $100 million in the stock of the Swiss Roll Corporation and a short position in the stock of the Frankfurter Sausage Company. Here is the recent price history of the two stocks:

	Percentage Price Change	
Month	**Frankfurter Sausage**	**Swiss Roll**
January	−10	−10
February	−10	−5
March	−10	0
April	+10	0
May	+10	+5
June	+10	+10

On the evidence of these six months, how large would your short position in Frankfurter Sausage need to be to hedge you as far as possible against movements in the price of Swiss Roll?

20. Price changes on two gold-mining stocks have shown strong positive correlation. Their historical relationship is

$$\text{Average percentage change in A} = .001 + .75\,(\text{percentage change in B})$$

Changes in B explain 60 percent of the variation of the changes in A ($R^2 = .6$).

a. Suppose you own $100,000 of A. How much of B should you sell to minimize the risk of your net position?

b. What is the hedge ratio?

c. Here is the historical relationship between stock A and gold prices:

$$\text{Average percentage change in A} = -.002 + 1.2\,(\text{percentage change in gold price})$$

If $R^2 = .5$, can you lower the risk of your net position by hedging with gold (or gold futures) rather than with stock B? Explain.

21. In Section 27.5, we stated that the duration of Potterton's lease equals the duration of its debt.

a. Show that this is so.

b. Now suppose that the interest rate falls to 3 percent. Show how the value of the lease and the debt package are now affected by a .5 percent rise or fall in the interest rate. What would Potterton need to do to re-establish the interest rate hedge?

22. Line 1 of the following table shows cash payments that your company has just promised to make. Below that are the cash flows on a blue-chip corporate note. The interest rate is 10 percent. Your company can borrow at this rate if it wishes.

	Year 1	Year 2	Year 3	Year 4
Liability (millions)	0	0	−$20	−$20
Note's cash payments as percent of face value	12	12	12	112

a. What is the present value of your liability?

b. Calculate the durations of the liability and the note.

c. Suppose you wish to hedge the liability by investing in a combination of the note and a short-term bank deposit with a duration of zero. How much must you invest in each?

d. Would this hedge continue to protect your company if

i. Interest rates dropped by 3 percent?

ii. Short-term interest rates fluctuate while longer-term rates remain basically constant?

iii. Interest rates remain the same but two years pass?

e. Can you set up a hedge portfolio that relieves the financial manager of all the worries mentioned in (d)? Describe that portfolio.

23. Petrochemical Parfum (PP) is concerned about possible increases in the price of heavy fuel oil, which is one of its major inputs. Show how PP can use either options or futures contracts to protect itself against a rise in the price of crude oil. Show how the payoffs in each case would vary if the oil price were $14, $16, or $18 a barrel. What are the advantages and disadvantages for PP of using futures rather than options to reduce risk?

24. Explain the difference between insurance and hedging. Give an example of how options can be used for each.

25. "Speculators want futures contracts to be incorrectly priced; hedgers want them to be correctly priced." Why?

CHALLENGE QUESTIONS

1. Phillip's Screwdriver Company has borrowed $20 million from a bank at a floating interest rate of 2 percentage points above three-month Treasury bills, which now yield 5 percent. Assume that interest payments are made quarterly and that the entire principal of the loan is repaid after five years.

   Phillip's wants to convert the bank loan to fixed-rate debt. It could have issued a fixed-rate five-year note at a yield to maturity of 9 percent. Such a note would now trade at par. The five-year Treasury note's yield to maturity is 7 percent.

   a. Is Phillip's stupid to want long-term debt at an interest rate of 9 percent? It is borrowing from the bank at 7 percent.
   b. Explain how the conversion could be carried out by an interest rate swap. What will be the initial terms of the swap? (Ignore transaction costs and the swap dealer's profit.)

   One year from now medium- and long-term Treasury yields *decrease* to 6 percent, so the term structure then is flat. (The changes actually occur in month 5.) Phillip's credit standing is unchanged; it can still borrow at 2 percentage points over Treasury rates.

   c. What net swap payment will Phillip's make or receive?
   d. Suppose that Phillip's now wants to cancel the swap. How much would it need to pay the swap dealer? Or would the dealer pay Phillip's? Explain.

2. Hoopoe Corporation wants to borrow 100 million Canadian dollars at a fixed rate with a maturity of five years. It calculates that it can make an international bond issue with the following terms:

   - Interest: 10 5/8 percent payable annually.
   - Maturity: 5 years.
   - Issue expenses: .2 percent.

   A bank has presented Hoopoe with a proposal for a Swiss franc issue combined with a currency swap into Canadian dollars. The proposed terms for the Swiss franc issue are

   - Amount: 200 million Swiss francs.
   - Interest: 5 3/8 percent annually.
   - Maturity: 5 years.
   - Issue expenses: .2 percent.

   The counterparty of the swap would raise fixed dollars on the following terms:

   - Amount: 100 million Canadian dollars (equivalent to 200 million Swiss francs).
   - Interest: 10 5/8 percent annually.
   - Maturity: 5 years.
   - Issue expenses: .15 percent.

   The counterparty would be happy with an all-in cost in Swiss francs of 6.45 percent.

   a. Which alternative should Hoopoe take? (Ignore credit risk in your analysis.)
   b. Suppose that you are the corporate treasurer of Hoopoe. Discuss the credit risk issues involved in the alternatives.

3. Consider the commodities and financial assets listed in Table 27.6. The risk-free interest rate is 6 percent a year, and the term structure is flat.

   a. Calculate the six-month futures price for each case.
   b. Explain how a magnoosium producer would use a futures market to lock in the selling price of a planned shipment of 1,000 tons of magnoosium six months from now.
   c. Suppose the producer takes the actions recommended in your answer to (b), but after one month magnoosium prices have fallen to $2,200. What happens? Will the

TABLE 27.6

Spot prices for selected commodities and financial assets. See challenge question 3.

Asset	Spot Price	Comments
Magnoosium	$2,800 per ton	Net convenience yield = 4% per year
Oat bran	$.44 per bushel	Net convenience yield = .5% per month
Biotech stock index	140.2	Dividend = 0
Allen Wrench Co. common stock	$58.00	Cash dividend= $2.4 per year
5-year Treasury note	108.93	8% coupon
Westonian ruple	3.1 ruples= $1	12% interest rate in ruples

producer have to undertake additional futures market trades to restore its hedged position?

d. Does the biotech index futures price provide useful information about the expected future performance of biotech stocks?

e. Suppose Allen Wrench stock falls suddenly by $10 per share. Investors are confident that the cash dividend will not be reduced. What happens to the futures price?

f. Suppose interest rates suddenly fall. The spot rate for cash flows 6 months from now is 4 percent (per year); it is 4.5 percent for cash flows 12 months from now, 4.8 percent for cash flows 18 months from now, and 5 percent for all subsequent cash flows. What happens to the six-month futures price on the five-year Treasury note? What happens to a trader who shorted 100 notes at the futures price calculated in part (a)?

g. An importer must make a payment of one million ruples three months from now. Explain *two* strategies the importer could use to hedge against unfavorable shifts in the ruple–dollar exchange rate.

CHAPTER TWENTY-EIGHT

MANAGING INTERNATIONAL RISKS

IN THE LAST chapter we considered the risks that flow from changes in interest rates and commodity prices. But companies with substantial overseas interests encounter a variety of other hazards, including political risks and currency fluctuations. *Political risk* means the possibility that a hostile foreign government will expropriate your business without compensation or not allow profits to be taken out of the country.

To understand currency risk, you first need to understand how the foreign exchange market works and how prices for foreign currency are determined. We therefore start this chapter with some basic institutional detail about the foreign exchange market and we will look at some simple theories that link exchange rates, interest rates, and inflation. We will use these theories to show how firms assess and hedge their foreign currency exposure.

When we discussed investment decisions in Chapter 6, we showed that financial managers do not need to forecast exchange rates in order to evaluate overseas investment proposals. They can simply forecast the foreign currency cash flows and discount these flows at the foreign currency cost of capital. In this chapter we will explain *why* this rule makes sense. It turns out that it is the ability to hedge foreign exchange risk that allows companies to ignore future exchange rates when making investment decisions.

We conclude the chapter with a discussion of political risk. We show that, while companies cannot restrain a determined foreign government, they can structure their operations to reduce the risk of hostile actions.

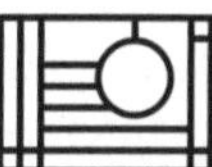

28.1 THE FOREIGN EXCHANGE MARKET

An American company that imports goods from France may need to buy euros to pay for the purchase. An American company exporting to France may receive euros, which it sells in exchange for dollars. Both firms make use of the foreign exchange market.

The foreign exchange market has no central marketplace. Business is conducted electronically. The principal dealers are the larger commercial banks and investment banks. A corporation that wants to buy or sell currency usually does so through a commercial bank. Turnover in the foreign exchange market is huge. In London in April 2001 $504 billion of currency changed hands each day. That is equivalent to an annual turnover of $126 trillion ($126,000,000,000,000). New York and Tokyo together accounted for a further $400 billion of turnover per day.[1]

Table 28.1 is adapted from the table of exchange rates in the *Financial Times*. Exchange rates are generally expressed in terms of the number of units of the foreign currency needed to buy one U.S. dollar. This is termed an *indirect quote*. In the first column of Table 28.1, the indirect quote for the yen shows that you can buy 120.700 yen for $1. This is often written as ¥120.700/$.

A *direct* exchange rate quote states how many dollars you can buy for one unit of foreign currency. The euro and the British pound sterling are usually shown as direct quotes.[2] For example, Table 28.1 shows that £1 is equivalent to $1.4483 or, more concisely, $1.4483/£. If £1 buys $1.4483, then $1 must buy 1/1.4483 = £.6905. Thus the indirect quote for the pound is £.6905/$.[3]

[1]The results of the triennial survey of foreign exchange business are published on **www.bis.org/publ.**

[2]The euro is the common currency of the European Monetary Union. The 12 members of the Union are Austria, Belgium, Finland, France, Germany, Greece, Ireland, Italy, Luxembourg, Netherlands, Portugal, and Spain.

[3]Foreign exchange dealers usually refer to the exchange rate between pounds and dollars as *cable*. In Table 28.1 cable is 1.4483.

TABLE 28.1

Spot and forward exchange rates, August 28, 2001.

*Rates show the number of units of foreign currency per U.S. dollar, except for the euro and the UK pound, which show the number of U.S. dollars per unit of foreign currency.

Source: *Financial Times*, August 29, 2001.

		Forward Rate*		
	Spot Rate*	1 Month	3 Months	1 Year
Europe:				
EMU (euro)	.9094	.9088	.9076	.9057
Norway (krone)	8.8756	8.9006	8.9594	9.1889
Sweden (krona)	10.3159	10.3221	10.3389	10.4034
Switzerland (franc)	1.6680	1.6677	1.6667	1.6563
United Kingdom (pound)	1.4483	1.4468	1.4432	1.4289
Americas:				
Canada (dollar)	1.5397	1.5403	1.5415	1.545
Mexico (peso)	9.1390	9.1865	9.307	9.924
Pacific/Africa:				
Hong Kong (dollar)	7.7999	7.7987	7.7962	7.7954
Japan (yen)	120.700	120.36	119.66	116.535
Singapore (dollar)	1.7542	1.7525	1.7491	1.7322
South Africa (rand)	8.3693	8.4102	8.4963	8.8278
Thailand (baht)	44.3450	44.39	44.555	45.295

The exchange rates in the first column of Table 28.1 are the prices of currency for immediate delivery. These are known as **spot rates of exchange.** The spot rate for the yen is ¥120.700/\$, and the spot rate for the pound is \$1.4483/£.

In addition to the spot exchange market, there is a *forward market.* In the forward market you buy and sell currency for future delivery. If you know that you are going to pay out or receive foreign currency at some future date, you can insure yourself against loss by buying or selling forward. Thus, if you need one million yen in three months, you can enter into a three-month *forward contract.* The **forward rate** on this contract is the price you agree to pay in three months when the one million yen are delivered. If you look again at Table 28.1, you will see that the three-month forward rate for the yen is quoted at ¥119.66/\$. If you buy yen for three months' delivery, you get fewer yen for your dollar than if you buy them spot. In this case the yen is said to trade at a forward *premium* relative to the dollar, because forward yen are more expensive than spot ones. Expressed as an annual rate, the forward premium is[4]

$$4 \times \left(\frac{120.700}{119.66} - 1\right) = .035, \text{ or } 3.5\%$$

You could also say that the dollar was selling at a *forward discount.*

A forward purchase or sale is a made-to-measure transaction between you and the bank. It can be for any currency, any amount, and any delivery day. You could buy, say, 99,999 Vietnamese dong or Haitian gourdes for a year and a day forward as long as you can find a bank ready to deal. Most forward transactions are for six months or less, but banks are prepared to buy and sell the major currencies for several years forward.[5]

[4]Here is an occasional point of confusion. Since the quote for the yen is indirect, we calculate the premium by taking the ratio of the spot rate to the forward rate. If we use *direct* quotes, then we need to calculate the ratio of the forward rate to the spot rate. In the case of the yen, the forward premium with direct quotes is $4 \times [(1/119.66)/(1/120.7) - 1] = .035$, or 3.5 percent.

[5]Forward and spot trades are often undertaken together. For example, a company might need the use of Japanese yen for one month. In this case it would buy the yen spot and simultaneously sell them forward. This is known as a *swap* trade, but do not confuse it with the longer-term interest rate and currency swaps described in Chapter 27.

There is also an organized market for currency for future delivery known as the currency *futures* market. Futures contracts are highly standardized; they exist only for the main currencies, and they are for specified amounts and for a limited choice of delivery dates.[6]

When you buy a forward or futures contract, you are committed to taking delivery of the currency. As an alternative, you can take out an *option* to buy or sell currency in the future at a price that is fixed today. Made-to-measure currency options can be bought from the major banks, and standardized options are traded on the options exchanges.

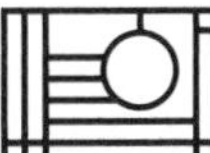

28.2 SOME BASIC RELATIONSHIPS

You can't develop a consistent international financial policy until you understand the reasons for the differences in exchange rates and interest rates. We will consider the following four problems:

- *Problem 1.* Why is the dollar rate of interest ($r_\$$) different from, say, the yen rate ($r_¥$)?
- *Problem 2.* Why is the forward rate of exchange ($f_{¥/\$}$) different from the spot rate ($s_{¥/\$}$)?
- *Problem 3.* What determines next year's expected spot rate of exchange between dollars and yen [$E(r_{¥/\$})$]?
- *Problem 4.* What is the relationship between the inflation rate in the United States ($i_\$$) and the inflation rate in Japan ($i_¥$)?

Suppose that individuals were not worried about risk and that there were no barriers or costs to international trade. In that case the spot exchange rates, forward exchange rates, interest rates, and inflation rates would stand in the following simple relationship to one another:

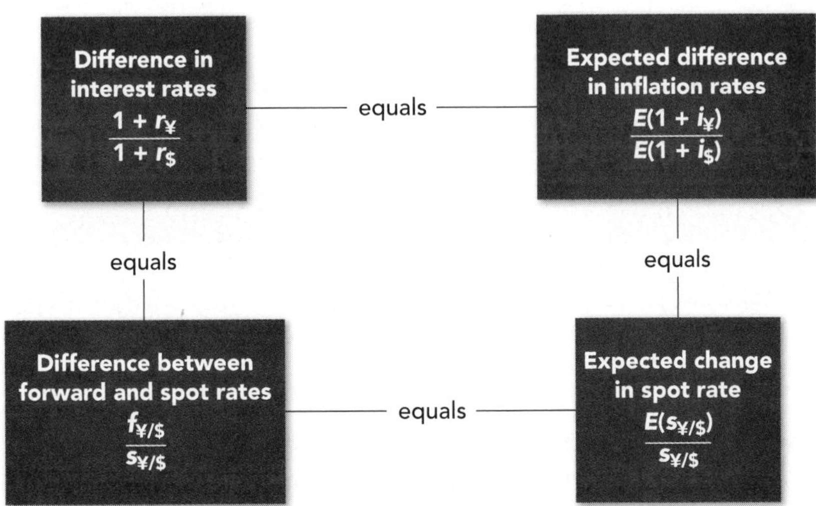

Why should this be so?

[6]See Chapter 27 for a further discussion of the difference between forward and futures contracts.

Interest Rates and Exchange Rates

It is August 2001 and you have $1 million to invest for one year. U.S. dollar deposits are offering an interest rate of about 3.65 percent; Japanese yen deposits are offering a meager .06 percent. Where should you put your money? Does the answer sound obvious? Let's check:

- *Dollar loan.* The rate of interest on one-year dollar deposits is 3.65 percent. Therefore at the end of the year you get 1,000,000 × 1.0365 = $1,036,500.
- *Yen loan.* The current exchange rate is ¥120.700/$. For $1 million, you can buy 1,000,000 × 120.700 = ¥120,700,000. The rate of interest on a one-year yen deposit is .06 percent. Therefore at the end of the year you get 120,700,000 × 1.0006 = ¥120,772,420. Of course, you don't know what the exchange rate is going to be in one year's time. But that doesn't matter. You can fix today the price at which you sell your yen. The one-year forward rate is ¥116.535/$. Therefore, by selling forward, you can make sure that you will receive 120,772,420/116.535 = $1,036,400 at the end of the year.

Thus, the two investments offer almost exactly the same rate of return.[7] They have to—they are both risk-free. If the domestic interest rate were different from the *covered* foreign rate, you would have a money machine.

When you make the yen loan, you receive a lower interest rate. But you get an offsetting gain because you sell yen forward at a higher price than you pay for them today. The interest rate differential is

$$\frac{1 + r_¥}{1 + r_\$}$$

And the differential between the forward and spot exchange rates is

$$\frac{f_{¥/\$}}{s_{¥/\$}}$$

Interest rate parity theory says that the difference in interest rates must equal the difference between the forward and spot exchange rates:

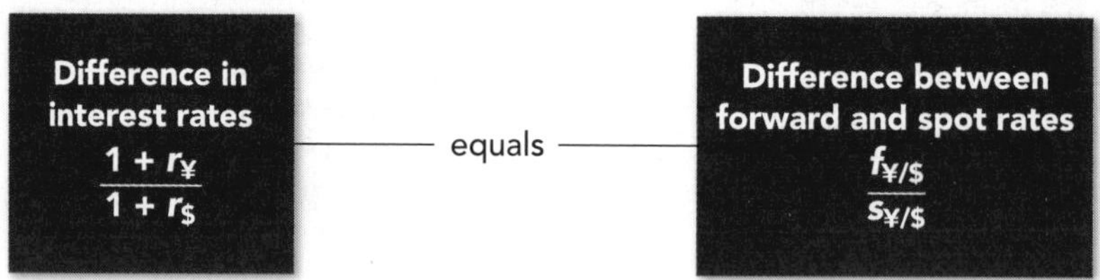

In our example,

$$\frac{1.0006}{1.0365} = \frac{116.535}{120.700}$$

The Forward Premium and Changes in Spot Rates

Now let's consider how the forward premium is related to changes in spot rates of exchange. If people didn't care about risk, the forward rate of exchange would depend solely on what people expected the spot rate to be. For example, if the one-

[7]The minor difference in our calculated end-of-year payoffs was mostly due to rounding in the interest rates.

year forward rate on yen is ¥116.535/$, that could only be because traders expect the spot rate in one year's time to be ¥116.535/$. If they expected it to be, say, ¥125/$, nobody would be willing to buy yen forward. They could get more yen for their dollar by waiting and buying spot.

Therefore the *expectations theory* of exchange rates tells us that the percentage difference between the forward rate and today's spot rate is equal to the expected change in the spot rate:

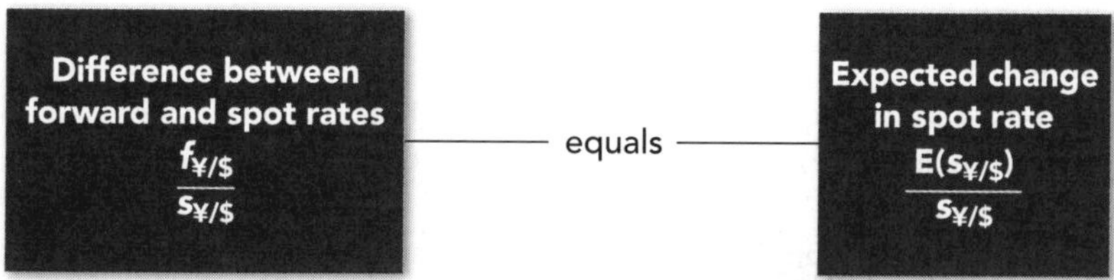

Of course, this assumes that traders don't care about risk. If they do care, the forward rate can be either higher or lower than the expected spot rate. For example, suppose that you have contracted to receive one million yen in three months, You can wait until you receive the money before you change it into dollars, but this leaves you open to the risk that the price of yen may fall over the next three months. Your alternative is to sell yen forward. In this case, you are fixing today the price at which you will sell your yen. Since you avoid risk by selling forward, you may be willing to do so even if the forward price of yen is a little *lower* than the expected spot price.

Other companies may be in the opposite position. They may have contracted to pay out yen in three months. They can wait until the end of the three months and then buy yen, but this leaves them open to the risk that the price of yen may rise. It is safer for these companies to fix the price today by *buying* yen forward. These companies may, therefore, be willing to buy forward even if the forward price of yen is a little *higher* than the expected spot price.

Thus some companies find it safer to sell yen forward, while others find it safer to buy yen forward. When the first group predominates, the forward price of yen is likely to be less than the expected spot price. When the second group predominates, the forward price is likely to be greater than the expected spot price. On average you would expect the forward price to underestimate the expected spot price just about as often as it overestimates it.

Changes in the Exchange Rate and Inflation Rates

Now we come to the third side of our quadrilateral—the relationship between changes in the spot exchange rate and inflation rates. Suppose that you notice that silver can be bought in the United States for $4.00 a troy ounce and sold in Japan for ¥675. You think you may be onto a good thing. You decide to buy silver for $4.00 and put it on the first plane to Tokyo, where you sell it for ¥675. Then you exchange your ¥675 for 675/120.700 = $5.59. You have made a gross profit of $1.59 an ounce. Of course, you have to pay transportation and insurance costs out of this, but there should still be something left over for you.

Money machines don't exist—not for long, anyway. As others notice the disparity between the price of silver in Japan and the price in the United States, the price will be forced down in Japan and up in the United States until the profit opportunity disappears. Arbitrage ensures that the dollar price of silver is about the same in the two countries. Of course, silver is a standard and easily transportable commodity, but the same forces should act to equalize the domestic and foreign prices of other goods. Those goods that can be bought more cheaply abroad will be imported, and that will force down the price of domestic products. Similarly, those goods that can be bought more cheaply in the United States will be exported, and that will force down the price of the foreign products.

This is often called *purchasing power parity.*[8] Just as the price of goods in Safeway must be roughly the same as the price of goods in A&P, so the price of goods in Japan when converted into dollars must be roughly the same as the price in the United States:

$$\text{Dollar price of goods in the USA} = \frac{\text{yen price of goods in Japan}}{\text{number of yen per dollar}}$$

Purchasing power parity implies that any differences in the rates of inflation will be offset by a change in the exchange rate. For example, if prices are rising by 2.6 percent in the United States while they are declining by −1.0 percent in Japan, the number of yen that you can buy for \$1 must fall by .99/1.026 − 1, or about 3.5 percent. Therefore purchasing power parity says that to estimate changes in the spot rate of exchange, you need to estimate differences in inflation rates:[9]

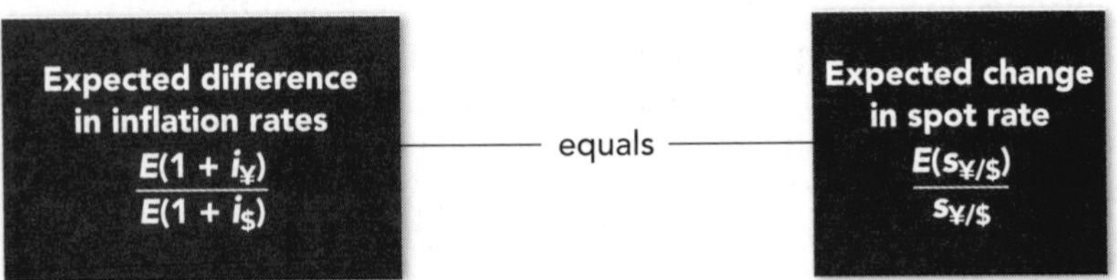

In our example,

Current spot rate	×	expected difference in inflation rates	=	expected spot rate
120.700	×	.99/1.026	=	116.5

Interest Rates and Inflation Rates

Now for the fourth leg! Just as water always flows downhill, so capital tends to flow where returns are greatest. But investors are not interested in *nominal* returns; they care about what their money will buy. So, if investors notice that real interest rates are higher in Japan than in the United States, they will shift their savings into Japan until the expected real returns are the same in the two countries. If the expected real interest rates are equal, then the difference in money rates must be equal to the difference in the expected inflation rates:[10]

[8]Economists use the term *purchasing power parity* to refer to the notion that the level of prices of goods in general must be the same in the two countries. They tend to use the phrase *law of one price* when they are talking about the price of a single good.

[9]In other words, the *expected* difference in inflation rates equals the *expected* change in the exchange rate. Strictly interpreted, purchasing power parity also implies that the *actual* difference in the inflation rates always equals the *actual* change in the exchange rate.

[10]In Section 24.1 we discussed Irving Fisher's theory that over time money interest rates change to reflect changes in anticipated inflation. Here we argue that international differences in money interest rates also reflect differences in anticipated inflation. This theory is sometimes known as the *international Fisher effect.*

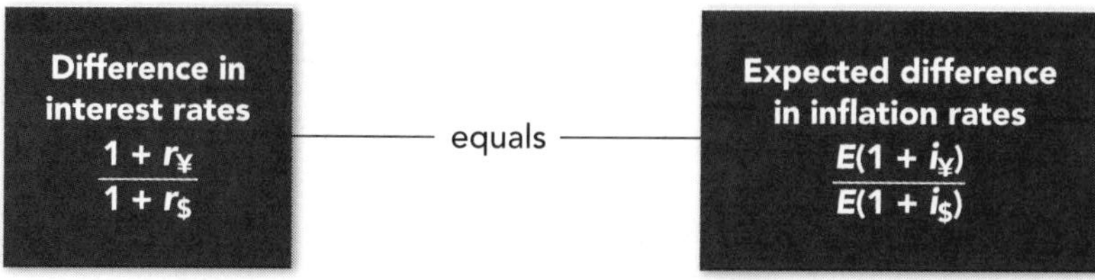

In Japan the real one-year interest rate is just over 1 percent:

$$r_{¥}(\text{real}) = \frac{1 + r_{¥}}{E(1 + i_{¥})} - 1 = \frac{1.0006}{.99} - 1 = .0107$$

Ditto for the United States:

$$r_{\$}(real) = \frac{1 + r_{\$}}{E(1 + i_{\$})} - 1 = \frac{1.0365}{1.026} - 1 = .0102$$

Is Life Really That Simple?

We have described above four theories that link interest rates, forward rates, spot exchange rates, and inflation rates. Of course, such simple economic theories are not going to provide an exact description of reality. We need to know how well they predict actual behavior. Let's check.

1. Interest Rate Parity Theory Interest rate parity theory says that the yen rate of interest covered for exchange risk should be the same as the dollar rate. In the example that we gave you earlier we used the rates of interest on dollar and yen deposits in London. Since money can be moved easily between these deposits, interest rate parity almost always holds. In fact, dealers *set* the forward price of yen by looking at the difference between the interest rates on deposits of dollars and yen.[11]

The relationship does not hold so exactly for deposits made in different domestic money markets. In these cases taxes and government regulations sometimes prevent the citizens of one country from switching out of one country's bank deposits and covering their exchange risk in the forward market.

2. The Expectations Theory of Forward Rates How well does the expectations theory explain the level of forward rates? Scholars who have studied exchange rates have found that forward rates typically exaggerate the likely change in the spot rate. When the forward rate appears to predict a sharp rise in the spot rate (a forward premium), the forward rate tends to overestimate the rise in the spot rate. Conversely, when the forward rate appears to predict a fall in the currency (a forward discount), it tends to overestimate this fall.[12]

This finding is *not* consistent with the expectations theory. Instead it looks as if sometimes companies are prepared to give up return to *buy* forward currency and other times they are prepared to give up return to *sell* forward currency. In

[11]The forward exchange rates shown in the *Financial Times* and reproduced in Table 28.1 are simply calculated from the differences in interest rates.

[12]Many researchers have even found that, when the forward rate predicts a rise, the spot rate is more likely to fall, and vice versa. For a readable discussion of this puzzling finding, see K. A. Froot and R. H. Thaler, "Anomalies: Foreign Exchange," *Journal of Political Economy* 4 (1990), pp. 179–192.

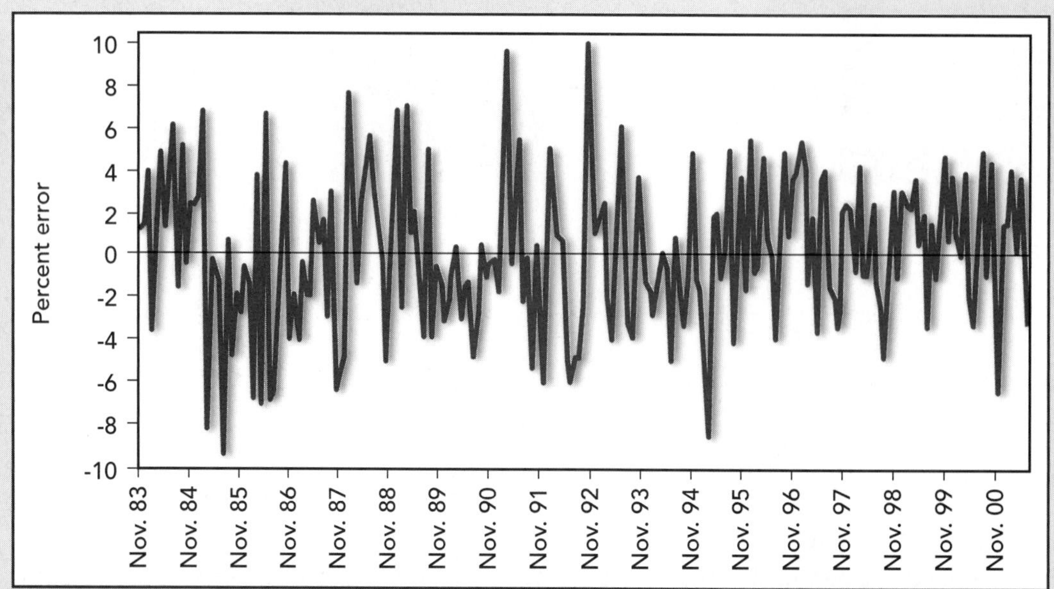

FIGURE 28.1

Percentage error from using the one-month forward rate for Swiss francs to forecast next month's spot rate. Note that the forward rate overestimates and underestimates the spot rate with about equal frequency.

other words, forward rates seem to contain a risk premium, but the sign of this premium swings backward and forward.[13] You can see this from Figure 28.1. Almost half the time the forward rate for the Swiss franc *overstates* the likely future spot rate and half the time it *understates* the likely spot rate. *On average* the forward rate and future spot rate are almost identical. This is important news for the financial manager; it means that a company which always uses the forward market to protect against exchange rate movements does not pay any extra for this insurance.

3. Purchasing Power Parity Theory What about the third side of our quadrilateral—purchasing power parity theory? No one who has compared prices in foreign stores with prices at home really believes that prices are the same throughout the world. Look, for example, at Table 28.2, which shows the price of a Big Mac in different countries. Notice that at current rates of exchange a Big Mac costs $3.65 in Switzerland but only $2.54 in the United States. To equalize prices in Switzerland and the United States, the number of Swiss francs that you could buy for your dollar would need to increase by $3.65/2.54 - 1 = .44$, or 44 percent.

This suggests a possible way to make a quick buck. Why don't you buy a hamburger-to-go in (say) the Philippines for the equivalent of $1.17 and take it for resale in Switzerland, where the price in dollars is $3.65? The answer, of course, is that the gain would not cover the costs. The same good can be sold for

[13]For evidence that forward exchange rates contain risk premia that are sometimes positive and sometimes negative, see, for example, E. F. Fama, "Forward and Spot Exchange Rates," *Journal of Monetary Economics* 14 (1984), pp. 319–338.

TABLE 28.2

Price of Big Mac hamburgers in different countries.

Source: "Big Mac Currencies," *The Economist*, April 21, 2001, p. 74.

Country	Local Price Converted to U.S. Dollars	Country	Local Price Converted to U.S. Dollars
Australia	1.52	Japan	2.38
Brazil	1.64	Mexico	2.36
Canada	2.14	Philippines	1.17
China	1.20	Russia	1.21
Denmark	2.93	Sweden	2.33
Germany	2.30	Switzerland	3.65
Hong Kong	1.37	United Kingdom	2.85
Hungary	1.32	United States	2.54

different prices in different countries because transportation is costly and inconvenient.[14]

On the other hand, there is clearly some relationship between inflation and changes in exchange rates. For example, between 1994 and 1999 prices in Turkey rose about 20 times. Or, to put it another way, you could say that the purchasing power of money in Turkey declined by about 95 percent. If exchange rates had not adjusted, Turkish exporters would have found it impossible to sell their goods. But, of course, exchange rates did adjust. In fact, the value of the Turkish currency declined by 92 percent relative to the U.S. dollar.

Turkey is an extreme case, but in Figure 28.2 we have plotted the relative change in purchasing power for a sample of countries against the change in the exchange rate. Turkey is tucked in the bottom left-hand corner; the United States is closer to the top right. You can see that although the relationship is far from exact, large differences in inflation rates are generally accompanied by an offsetting change in the exchange rate.

Strictly speaking, purchasing power parity theory implies that the differential inflation rate is always identical to the change in the spot rate. But we don't need to go as far as that. We should be content if the *expected* difference in the inflation rates equals the *expected* change in the spot rate. That's all we wrote on the third side of our quadrilateral. Look, for example, at Figure 28.3. The solid line shows that in 2000 £1 sterling bought almost 70 percent fewer dollars than it did at the beginning of the century. But this decline in the price of sterling was largely matched by the higher inflation rate in the United Kingdom. The thin line shows that the inflation-adjusted, or *real,* exchange rate ended the century at roughly the same level as it began.[15] Of course, the real exchange rate *does* change, sometimes dramatically. For example, the real value of sterling almost halved between 1980 and 1985 before recovering in the next five years. However, if you were a financial manager called on to make a long-term forecast of the exchange rate, you could not

[14]Of course, even within a currency area there may be considerable price variations. The price of a Big Mac, for example, differs substantially from one part of the United States to another. And even after the introduction of the euro, the price of Big Macs varied between \$1.96 in Italy and \$2.49 in France.

[15]The real exchange rate is equal to the nominal exchange rate multiplied by the inflation differential. For example, suppose that the value of sterling falls from \$1.54 = £1 to \$1.40 = £1 at the same time that the price of goods rises 10 percent faster in the United Kingdom than in the United States. The inflation-adjusted, or real, exchange rate is unchanged at

$$\text{Initial exchange rate} \times (1 + i_{£})/(1 + i_{\$}) = 1.40 \times 1.1 = \$1.54/£$$

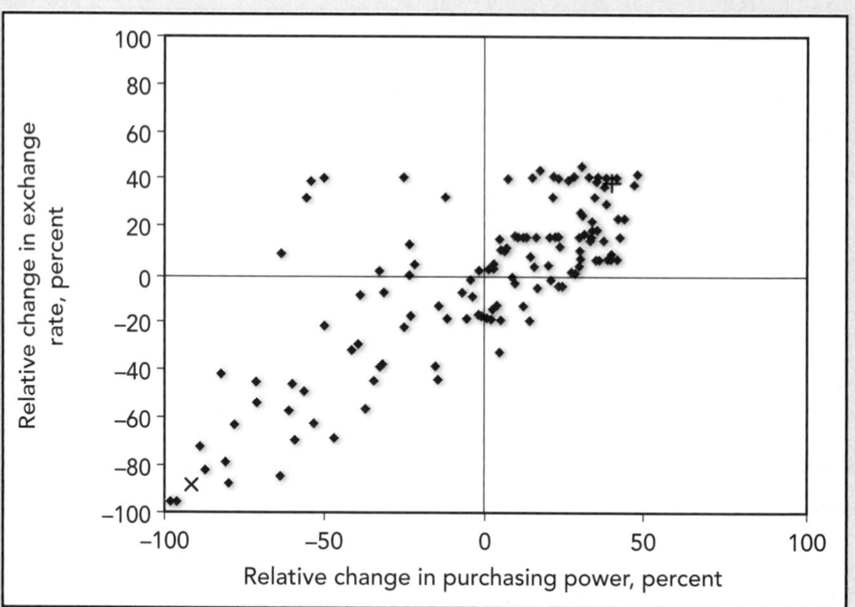

FIGURE 28.2

A decline in the exchange rate and a decline in a currency's purchasing power usually go hand in hand. In this diagram, each of the 138 points represents the experience of a different country between 1994 and 1999. The vertical axis shows the change in the value of the foreign currency relative to the average. The horizontal axis shows the change in purchasing power relative to the average. The × at the lower left is Turkey; the + at the upper right is the United States.

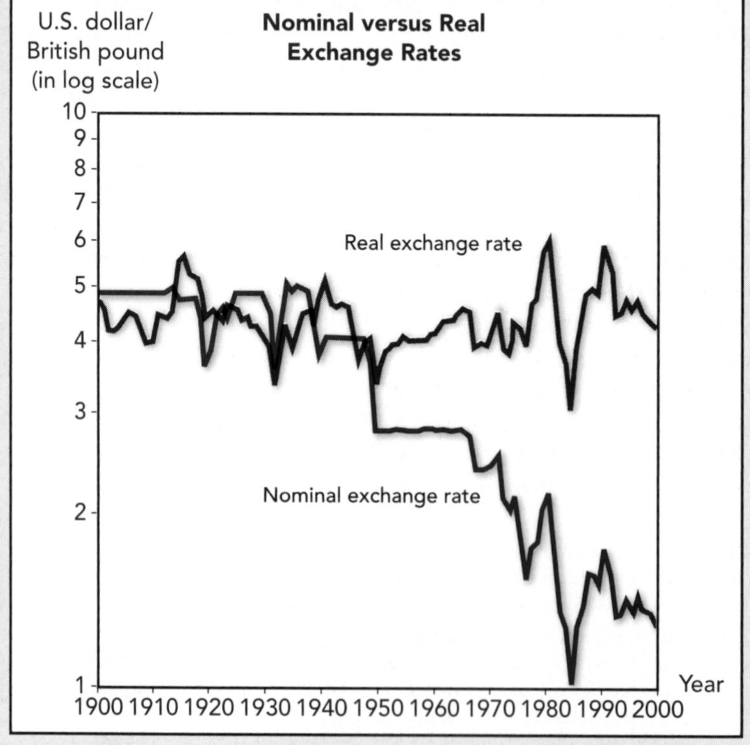

FIGURE 28.3

Since 1900 sterling has fallen sharply in value against the dollar. But this fall has largely offset the higher inflation rate in the UK. The *real* value of sterling has been roughly constant.

Source: N. Abuaf and P. Jorion, "Purchasing Power Parity in the Long Run," *Journal of Finance* 45 (March 1990), pp. 157–174. We are grateful to Li Jin for extending the data.

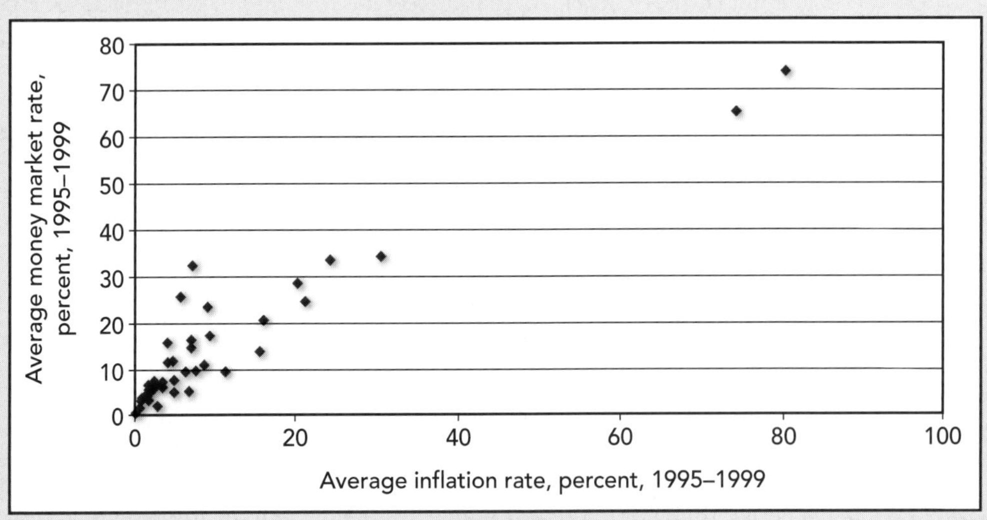

FIGURE 28.4

Countries with the highest interest rates generally have the highest inflation rates. In this diagram, each of the 51 points represents the experience of a different country.

have done much better than to assume that changes in the value of the currency would offset the difference in inflation rates.

4. Equal Real Interest Rates Finally we come to the relationship between interest rates in different countries. Do we have a single world capital market with the same *real* rate of interest in all countries? Does the difference in money interest rates equal the difference in the expected inflation rates?

This is not an easy question to answer since we cannot observe *expected* inflation. However, in Figure 28.4 we have plotted the average interest rate in each of 51 countries against the inflation that subsequently occurred. Japan is tucked into the bottom-left corner of the chart, while Turkey is represented by the dot in the top-right corner. You can see that, in general, the countries with the highest interest rates also had the highest inflation rates. In other words, there were much smaller differences between the real rates of interest than between the nominal (or money) rates.[16]

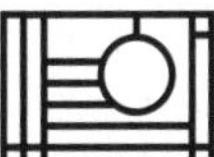

28.3 HEDGING CURRENCY RISK

Sharp exchange rate movements can make a large dent in corporate profits. To illustrate how companies cope with this problem, we will look at a typical company in the United States, Outland Steel, and walk through its foreign exchange operations.

[16]In Chapter 24 we saw that in some countries the government has issued indexed bonds promising a fixed real return. The annual interest payment and the amount repaid at maturity increase with the rate of inflation. In these cases, therefore, we can observe and compare the real rate of interest. As we write this, real interest rates in Australia, Canada, France, Sweden, and the United States cluster within the range of 3.3 to 3.7 percent. The exception is the UK, where the yield on indexed bonds is under 2.5 percent.

Example: Outland Steel Outland Steel has a small but profitable export business. Contracts involve substantial delays in payment, but since the company has a policy of always invoicing in dollars, it is fully protected against changes in exchange rates. Recently the export department has become unhappy with this practice and believes that it is causing the company to lose valuable export orders to firms that are willing to quote in the customer's own currency.

You sympathize with these arguments, but you are worried about how the firm should price long-term export contracts when payment is to be made in foreign currency. If the value of that currency declines before payment is made, the company may suffer a large loss. You want to take the currency risk into account, but you also want to give the sales force as much freedom of action as possible.

Notice that Outland can insure against its currency risk by selling the foreign currency forward. This means that it can separate the problem of negotiating sales contracts from that of managing the company's foreign exchange exposure. The sales force can allow for currency risk by pricing on the basis of the forward exchange rate. And you, as financial manager, can decide whether the company *ought* to hedge.

What is the cost of hedging? You sometimes hear managers say that it is equal to the difference between the forward rate and *today's* spot rate. That is wrong. If Outland does not hedge, it will receive the spot rate at the time that the customer pays for the steel. Therefore, the cost of insurance is the difference between the forward rate and the expected spot rate when payment is received.

Insure or speculate? We generally vote for insurance. First, it makes life simpler for the firm and allows it to concentrate on its main business.[17] Second, it does not cost much. (In fact, the cost is zero on average if the forward rate equals the expected spot rate, as the expectations theory of forward rates implies.) Third, the foreign currency market seems reasonably efficient, at least for the major currencies. Speculation should be a zero-NPV game, unless financial managers have information that is not available to the pros who make the market.

Is there any other way that Outland can protect itself against exchange loss? Of course. It can borrow foreign currency against its foreign receivables, sell the currency spot, and invest the proceeds in the United States. Interest rate parity theory tells us that in free markets the difference between selling forward and selling spot should be equal to the difference between the interest that you have to pay overseas and the interest that you can earn at home. However, in countries where capital markets are highly regulated, it may be cheaper to arrange foreign borrowing rather than forward cover.[18]

Our discussion of Outland's export business illustrates four practical implications of our simple theories about forward exchange rates. First, you can use forward rates to adjust for exchange risk in contract pricing. Second, the expectations theory suggests that protection against exchange risk is usually worth having. Third, interest rate parity theory reminds us that you can hedge either by selling forward or by borrowing foreign currency and selling spot. Fourth, the cost of for-

[17]It also relieves shareholders of worrying about the foreign exchange exposure they may have acquired by purchase of the firm's shares.

[18]Sometimes governments also attempt to prevent currency speculation by limiting the amount that companies can sell forward.

ward cover is not the difference between the forward rate and *today's* spot rate; it is the difference between the forward rate and the expected spot rate when the forward contract matures.

Perhaps we should add a fifth implication. You don't make money simply by buying currencies that go up in value and selling those that go down. For example, suppose that you buy Narnian leos and sell them after a year for 2 percent more than you paid for them. Should you give yourself a pat on the back? That depends on the interest that you have earned on your leos. If the interest rate on leos is 2 percentage points less than the interest rate on dollars, the profit on the currency is exactly canceled out by the reduction in interest income. Thus you make money from currency speculation only if you can predict whether the exchange rate will change by more or less than the interest rate differential. In other words, you must be able to predict whether the exchange rate will change by more or less than the forward premium or discount.

Transaction Exposure and Economic Exposure

The exchange risk from Outland Steel's export business is due to delays in foreign currency payments and is therefore referred to as *transaction exposure.* Transaction exposure can be easily identified and hedged. Since a 1 percent fall in the value of the foreign currency results in a 1 percent fall in Outland's dollar receipts, for every euro or yen that Outland is owed by its customers, it needs to sell forward one euro or one yen.[19]

However, Outland may still be affected by currency fluctuations even if its customers do not owe it a cent. For example, Outland may be in competition with Swedish steel producers. If the value of the Swedish krona falls, Outland will need to cut its prices in order to compete.[20] Outland can protect itself against such an eventuality by selling the krona forward. In this case the loss on Outland's steel business will be offset by the profit on its forward sale.

Notice that Outland's exposure to the krona is not limited to specific transactions that have already been entered into. Financial managers often refer to this broader type of exposure as *economic exposure.*[21] Economic exposure is less easy to measure than transaction exposure. For example, it is clear that the value of Outland Steel is positively related to the value of the krona, so to hedge its position it needs to sell krona forward. But in practice it may be hard to say exactly how many krona Outland needs to sell.

Economic exposure is a major source of risk for many firms. When the deutschemark appreciated in value in 1991 and 1992, German luxury carmakers such as Porsche and Mercedes took a bath on their overseas sales. So did American dealers that had a franchise to sell these cars. Competitors such as Jaguar, however, benefited from their rivals' discomfiture. Thus the German and British car producers and their dealers were affected by exchange rate changes even

[19]To put it another way, the hedge ratio is 1.0.

[20]Of course, if purchasing power parity always held, the fall in the value of the krona would be matched by higher inflation in Sweden. The risk for Outland is that the *real* value of the krona may decline, so that when measured in dollars Swedish costs are lower than previously. Unfortunately, it is much easier to hedge against a change in the *nominal* exchange rate than against a change in the *real* rate.

[21]Financial managers also refer to *translation exposure,* which measures the effect of an exchange rate change on the company's financial statements.

though they may have had no fixed obligation to pay or receive dollars. They had economic exposure as well as possible transaction exposure.[22]

Most firms do not attempt to quantify economic exposure, but that does not mean that they ignore it. For example, when a company makes a major overseas investment, it often finances it by foreign currency borrowing. A subsequent fall in the value of the foreign currency may reduce the dollar value of the investment, but this is compensated by the fall in the dollar cost of servicing the foreign debt.

Currency Speculation

Outland Steel's currency exposure arose naturally from its business activity, but the risk was avoidable; it could have been hedged using either the forward markets or the loan markets. Sometimes, however, companies deliberately take on currency risk in the hope of gain. Now there is nothing wrong with that if you truly do have a forecasting edge, but we should warn you against the dangers of naive strategies.

Suppose, for example, that a company in the United States notices that the interest rate on the Swiss franc is lower than on the dollar. Does this mean that it is "cheaper" to borrow Swiss francs? Before jumping to that conclusion, you need to ask *why* the Swiss interest rate is so low. Unless the Swiss government is deliberately holding the rate down by restrictions on the export of capital, you should suspect that the real cost of capital is roughly the same in Switzerland as anywhere else. The nominal interest rate is low only because investors expect a low domestic rate of inflation and a strong currency. Therefore, the advantage of the low rate of interest is likely to be offset by the additional dollars required to buy the Swiss francs required to pay off the loan.

You cannot reliably make a profit simply by borrowing in countries with low nominal rates of interest and you may be taking on considerable currency exposure by doing so. If the currency subsequently appreciates *more* rapidly than investors expect, it could turn out to be very costly to buy the currency that you need to service the loan. In 1989 several Australian banks learned this lesson the hard way. They had induced their clients to borrow at the low Swiss interest rates. When the value of the Swiss franc rose sharply, the banks found themselves sued by irate clients for not having warned them of the risk of a rise in the price of Swiss francs.

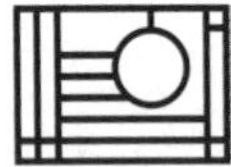

28.4 EXCHANGE RISK AND INTERNATIONAL INVESTMENT DECISIONS

Suppose that the Swiss pharmaceutical company, Roche, is evaluating a proposal to build a new plant in the United States. To calculate the project's net present value, Roche forecasts the following dollar cash flows from the project:

Cash Flows ($ millions)					
C_0	C_1	C_2	C_3	C_4	C_5
−1,300	400	450	510	575	650

[22]The German car producers could have hedged their exposure by borrowing dollars. As the deutschemark appreciated, their dollar income fell but the cost of servicing dollar loans would also have fallen. However, while borrowing dollars would have reduced the risk for German car producers, it should not have affected their decisions about where to produce and sell cars.

These cash flows are stated in dollars. So to calculate their net present value Roche discounts them at the dollar cost of capital. (Remember dollars need to be discounted at a *dollar* rate, not the Swiss franc rate.) Suppose this cost of capital is 12 percent. Then

$$\text{NPV} = -1{,}300 + \frac{400}{1.12} + \frac{450}{1.12^2} + \frac{510}{1.12^3} + \frac{575}{1.12^4} + \frac{650}{1.12^5} = \$513 \text{ million}$$

To convert this net present value to Swiss francs, the manager can simply multiply the dollar NPV by the spot rate of exchange. For example, if the spot rate is 2 SFr/$, then the NPV in Swiss francs is

$$\text{NPV in francs} = \text{NPV in dollars} \times \text{SFr/\$} = 513 \times 2 = 1{,}026 \text{ million francs}$$

Notice one very important feature of this calculation. Roche does not need to forecast whether the dollar is likely to strengthen or weaken against the Swiss franc. No currency forecast is needed, because the company can hedge its foreign exchange exposure. In that case, the decision to accept or reject the pharmaceutical project in the United States is totally separate from the decision to bet on the outlook for the dollar. For example, it would be foolish for Roche to accept a poor project in the United States just because management is optimistic about the outlook for the dollar; if Roche wishes to speculate in this way it can simply buy dollars forward. Equally, it would be foolish for Roche to reject a good project just because management is pessimistic about the dollar. The company would do much better to go ahead with the project and sell dollars forward. In that way, it would get the best of both worlds.[23]

When Roche ignores currency risk and discounts the dollar cash flows at a dollar cost of capital, it is implicitly assuming that the currency risk is hedged. Let us check this by calculating the number of Swiss francs that Roche would receive if it hedged the currency risk by selling forward each future dollar cash flow.

We need first to calculate the forward rate of exchange between dollars and francs. This depends on the interest rates in the United States and Switzerland. For example, suppose that the dollar interest rate is 6 percent and the Swiss franc interest rate is 4 percent. Then interest rate parity theory tells us that the one-year forward exchange rate is

$$s_{\text{SFr/\$}} \times (1 + r_{\text{SFr}})/(1 + r_{\$}) = \frac{2 \times 1.04}{1.06} = 1.962$$

Similarly, the two-year forward rate is

$$s_{\text{SFr/\$}} \times (1 + r_{\text{SFr}})^2/(1 + r_{\$})^2 = \frac{2 \times 1.04^2}{1.06^2} = 1.925$$

So, if Roche hedges its cash flows against exchange rate risk, the number of Swiss francs it will receive in each year is equal to the dollar cash flow times the forward rate of exchange:

[23] There is a general point here that is not confined to currency hedging. Whenever you face an investment that appears to have a positive NPV, decide what it is that you are betting on and then think whether there is a more direct way to place the bet. For example, if a copper mine looks profitable only because you are unusually optimistic about the price of copper, then maybe you would do better to buy copper futures or the shares of other copper producers rather than opening a copper mine.

Cash Flows (millions of Swiss francs)					
C_0	C_1	C_2	C_3	C_4	C_5
$-1{,}300 \times 2 = -2{,}600$	$400 \times 1.962 = 785$	$450 \times 1.925 = 866$	$510 \times 1.889 = 963$	$575 \times 1.853 = 1{,}066$	$650 \times 1.818 = 1{,}182$

These cash flows are in Swiss francs and therefore they need to be discounted at the risk-adjusted Swiss franc discount rate. Since the Swiss rate of interest is lower than the dollar rate, the risk-adjusted discount rate must also be correspondingly lower. The formula for converting from the required dollar return to the required Swiss franc return is[24]

$$(1 + \text{Swiss franc return}) = (1 + \text{dollar return}) \times \frac{(1 + \text{Swiss franc interest rate})}{(1 + \text{dollar interest rate})}$$

In our example

$$(1 + \text{Swiss franc return}) = 1.12 \times \frac{1.04}{1.06} = 1.099$$

Thus the risk-adjusted discount rate in dollars is 12 percent, but the discount rate in Swiss francs is only 9.9 percent.

All that remains is to discount the Swiss franc cash flows at the 9.9 percent risk-adjusted discount rate:

$$\begin{aligned} \text{NPV} &= -2{,}600 + \frac{785}{1.099} + \frac{866}{1.099^2} + \frac{963}{1.099^3} + \frac{1{,}066}{1.099^4} + \frac{1{,}182}{1.099^5} \\ &= 1{,}026 \text{ million francs} \end{aligned}$$

Everything checks. We obtain exactly the same net present value by (a) ignoring currency risk and discounting Roche's dollar cash flows at the dollar cost of capital and (b) calculating the cash flows in francs on the assumption that Roche hedges the currency risk and then discounting these Swiss franc cash flows at the franc cost of capital.

To repeat: When deciding whether to invest overseas, separate out the investment decision from the decision to take on currency risk. This means that your views about future exchange rates should NOT enter into the investment decision. The simplest way to calculate the NPV of an overseas investment is to forecast the cash flows in the foreign currency and discount them at the foreign currency cost of capital. The alternative is to calculate the cash flows that you would receive if you hedged the foreign currency risk. In this case you need to translate the foreign currency cash flows into your own currency *using the forward exchange rate* and then discount these domestic currency cash flows at the domestic cost of capital. If the two methods don't give the same answer, you have made a mistake.

When Roche analyzes the proposal to build a plant in the United States, it is able to ignore the outlook for the dollar *only because it is free to hedge the currency risk*. Be-

[24]The following example should give you a feel for the idea behind this formula. Suppose the spot rate for Swiss francs is 2 SFr = \$1. Interest rate parity tells us that the forward rate must be $2 \times 1.04/1.06 = 1.9623$ SFr/\$. Now suppose that a share costs \$100 and will pay an expected \$112 at the end of the year. The cost to Swiss investors of buying the share is $100 \times 2 = 200$ SFr. If the Swiss investors sell forward the expected payoff, they will receive an expected $112 \times 1.9623 = 219.8$ SFr. The expected return in Swiss francs is $219.8/200 - 1 = .099$ or 9.9 percent. More simply, the Swiss franc return is $1.12 \times 1.04/1.06 - 1 = .099$.

cause investment in a pharmaceutical plant does not come packaged with an investment in the dollar, the opportunity for firms to hedge allows for better investment decisions.

More about the Cost of Capital

In our discussion of Roche's investment decision we did not explain how Roche estimated the cost of capital for its investment in the United States. There is no simple agreed-upon procedure for doing this but we suggest that you first estimate the cost of capital in Swiss francs and then convert it to a dollar cost.

We discussed the problem of estimating the required return on Roche's overseas investment in Chapter 9. You need to decide how risky an investment in the U.S. pharmaceutical business would be to a Swiss investor. For example, a good starting point might be to look at the betas of a sample of U.S. pharmaceutical companies *relative to the Swiss market index.*[25]

Suppose that you decide that the investment's beta relative to the Swiss market is .7 and that the market risk premium in Switzerland is 8.4 percent. Then the required return on the project can be estimated as

$$\begin{aligned}\text{Required return} &= \text{Swiss interest rate} + (\text{beta} \times \text{Swiss market risk premium}) \\ &= 4 + (.7 \times 8.4) = 9.9\%\end{aligned}$$

This is the project's cost of capital measured in Swiss francs. We used it above to discount the expected *Swiss franc* cash flows if Roche hedged the project against currency risk. We cannot use it to discount the *dollar* cash flows from the project.

To discount the expected *dollar* cash flows, we need to convert the Swiss franc cost of capital to a dollar cost of capital. This means running our earlier calculation in reverse:

$$(1 + \text{dollar return}) = (1 + \text{Swiss franc return}) \times \frac{(1 + \text{dollar interest rate})}{(1 + \text{Swiss franc interest rate})}$$

In our example,

$$(1 + \text{dollar return}) = 1.099 \times \frac{1.06}{1.04} = 1.12$$

We used this 12 percent dollar cost of capital to discount the forecasted dollar cash flows from the project.

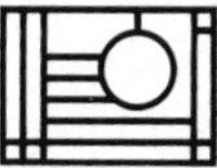

28.5 POLITICAL RISK

So far we have focused on the management of exchange rate risk, but managers also worry about political risk. By this they mean the threat that a government will change the rules of the game—that is, break a promise or understanding—*after* the

[25]We pointed out in Chapter 9 that when we use the beta relative to the U.S. index to estimate the returns required by U.S. investors, we are assuming that the U.S. market index is an efficient portfolio for these investors. Similarly, when we use the beta relative to the Swiss index to estimate the returns that Swiss investors require, we are assuming that the Swiss market index is an efficient portfolio for these investors. Investors do invest largely, but not exclusively, in their home markets.

	A	B	C	D	E	F	G	H	I	J	K	L	Total
Maximum score	12	12	12	12	12	6	6	6	6	6	6	4	100
Netherlands	9	10	10	12	12	6	6	6	6	6	6	4	93
USA	11	10	11	11	8	4	6	6	6	5	6	4	88
Germany	10	8	9	12	11	5	6	6	6	5	5	4	87
United Kingdom	11	10	11	9	9	5	6	6	6	4	6	4	87
France	10	7	9	10	11	3	5	6	5	5	5	4	80
Japan	10	6	6	12	10	2	6	5	6	6	5	4	78
Brazil	9	4	5	9	11	3	4	6	2	4	4	2	63
China	11	4	6	10	9	2	2	5	5	4	1	2	61
India	5	5	5	8	5	3	5	2	4	2	5	3	52
Russia	7	2	3	8	10	1	4	5	3	3	2	1	49
Indonesia	10	3	5	4	9	1	1	2	2	2	2	3	44
Iraq	8	3	4	3	4	1	0	5	2	2	0	0	32

TABLE 28.3

Political risk scores for a sample of countries, 1999.

Key:

A Government stability
B Socioeconomic conditions
C Investment profile
D Internal conflict
E External conflict
F Corruption
G Military in politics
H Religious tensions
I Law and order
J Ethnic tensions
K Democratic accountability
L Bureaucracy quality

Source: PRS Group (**www.prsgroup.com**).

investment is made. Of course political risks are not confined to overseas investments. Businesses in every country are exposed to the risk of unanticipated actions by governments or the courts. But in some parts of the world foreign companies are particularly vulnerable.

A number of consultancy services offer analyses of political and economic risks and draw up country rankings.[26] For example, Table 28.3 is an extract from the 1999 political risk rankings provided by the PRS Group. You can see that each country is scored on 12 separate dimensions. The Netherlands comes top of the class overall, while Iraq is near the bottom.

Some managers dismiss political risk as an act of God, like a hurricane or earthquake. But the most successful multinational companies structure their business to reduce political risk. Foreign governments are not likely to expropriate a local business if it cannot operate without the support of its parent. For example, the foreign subsidiaries of American computer manufacturers or pharmaceutical companies would have relatively little value if they were cut off from the know-how of their parents. Such operations are much less likely to be expropriated than, say, a mining operation that can be operated as a stand-alone venture.

We are not recommending that you turn your silver mine into a pharmaceutical company, but you may be able to plan your overseas manufacturing operations to

[26]For a discussion of these services see C. Erb, C. R. Harvey, and T. Viskanta, "Political Risk, Financial Risk, and Economic Risk," *Financial Analysts Journal* 52 (1996), pp. 28–46. Campbell Harvey's web page (**www.duke.edu/~charvey**) is also a useful source of information on political risk.

improve your bargaining position with foreign governments. For example, Ford has integrated its overseas operations so that the manufacture of components, subassemblies, and complete automobiles is spread across plants in a number of countries. None of these plants would have much value on its own, and Ford can switch production between plants if the political climate in one country deteriorates.

Multinational corporations have also devised financing arrangements to help keep foreign governments honest. For example, suppose your firm is contemplating an investment of $500 million to reopen the San Tomé silver mine in Costaguana with modern machinery, smelting equipment, and shipping facilities.[27] The Costaguanan government agrees to invest in roads and other infrastructure and to take 20 percent of the silver produced by the mine in lieu of taxes. The agreement is to run for 25 years.

The project's NPV on these assumptions is quite attractive. But what happens if a new government comes into power five years from now and imposes a 50 percent tax on "any precious metals exported from the Republic of Costaguana"? Or changes the government's share of output from 20 to 50 percent? Or simply takes over the mine "with fair compensation to be determined in due course by the Minister of Natural Resources of the Republic of Costaguana"?

No contract can absolutely restrain sovereign power. But you can arrange project financing to make these acts as painful as possible for the foreign government. For example, you might set up the mine as a subsidiary corporation, which then borrows a large fraction of the required investment from a consortium of major international banks. If your firm guarantees the loan, make sure the guarantee stands only if the Costaguanan government honors its contract. The government will be reluctant to break the contract if that causes a default on the loans and undercuts the country's credit standing with the international banking system.

If possible, you should arrange for the World Bank (or one of its affiliates) to finance part of the project or to guarantee your loans against political risk.[28] Few governments have the guts to take on the World Bank. Here is another variation on the same theme. Arrange to borrow, say, $450 million through the Costaguanan Development Agency. In other words, the development agency borrows in international capital markets and relends to the San Tomé mine. Your firm agrees to stand behind the loan as long as the government keeps its promises. If it does keep them, the loan is your liability. If not, the loan is *its* liability.

Political risk is not confined to the risk of expropriation. Multinational companies are always exposed to the criticism that they siphon funds out of countries in which they do business, and, therefore, governments are tempted to limit their freedom to repatriate profits. This is most likely to happen when there is considerable uncertainty about the rate of exchange, which is usually when you would most like to get your money out. Here again a little forethought can help. For example, there are often more onerous restrictions on the payment of dividends to the parent than on the payment of interest or principal on debt. Royalty payments and management fees are less sensitive than dividends, particularly if they are levied equally on all foreign operations. A company can also, within limits, alter the price of goods that are bought or sold within the group, and it can require more or less prompt payment for such goods.

[27]The early history of the San Tomé mine is described in Joseph Conrad's *Nostromo.*

[28]In Section 25.7 we described how the World Bank provided the Hubco power project with a guarantee against political risk.

The international financial manager has to cope with different currencies, interest rates, and inflation rates. To produce order out of chaos, the manager needs some model of how they are related. We described four very simple but useful theories.

Interest rate parity theory states that the interest differential between two countries must be equal to the difference between the forward and spot exchange rates. In the international markets, arbitrage ensures that parity almost always holds. There are two ways to hedge against exchange risk: One is to take out forward cover; the other is to borrow or lend abroad. Interest rate parity tells us that the costs of the two methods should be the same.

The expectations theory of exchange rates tells us that the forward rate equals the expected spot rate. In practice forward rates seem to incorporate a risk premium, but this premium is about equally likely to be negative as positive.

In its strict form, purchasing power parity states that \$1 must have the same purchasing power in every country. That doesn't square well with the facts, for differences in inflation rates are not perfectly related to changes in exchange rates. This means that there may be some genuine exchange risks in doing business overseas. On the other hand, the difference in inflation rates is just as likely to be above as below the change in the exchange rate.

Finally, we saw that in an integrated world capital market real rates of interest would have to be the same. In practice government regulation and taxes can cause differences in real interest rates. But do not simply borrow where interest rates are lowest. Those countries are also likely to have the lowest inflation rates and the strongest currencies.

With these precepts in mind we showed how you can use forward markets or the loan markets to hedge transactions exposure, which arises from delays in foreign currency payments and receipts. But the company's financing choices also need to reflect the impact of a change in the exchange rate on the value of the entire business. This is known as economic exposure.

Because companies can hedge their currency risk, the decision to invest overseas does not involve currency forecasts. There are two ways for a company to calculate the NPV of an overseas project. The first is to forecast the foreign currency cash flows and to discount them at the foreign currency cost of capital. The second is to translate the foreign currency cash flows into domestic currency assuming that they are hedged against exchange rate risk. These domestic currency flows can then be discounted at the domestic cost of capital. The answers should be identical.

In addition to currency risk, overseas operations may be exposed to extra political risk. However, firms may be able to structure the financing to reduce the chances that government will change the rules of the game.

FURTHER READING

There are a number of useful textbooks in international finance. Here is a small selection:

D. K. Eiteman and A. I. Stonehill: *Multinational Business Finance,* 8th ed., Addison-Wesley Publishing Company, Inc., Reading, MA, 1998.

J. O. Grabbe, *International Financial Markets,* 3rd ed., Prentice-Hall, Inc., Englewood Cliffs, NJ, 1995.

P. Sercu and R. Uppal: *International Financial Markets and the Firm,* South-Western College Publishing, Cincinnati, OH, 1995.

A. C. Shapiro: *Multinational Financial Management,* 6th ed., John Wiley & Sons, New York, 1999.

Here are some general discussions of international investment decisions and associated exchange risks:

G. W. Brown: "Managing Foreign Exchange Risk with Derivatives," *Journal of Financial Economics,* 60:401–448 (2001).

D. R. Lessard: "Global Competition and Corporate Finance in the 1990s," *Journal of Applied Corporate Finance,* 3:59–72 (Winter 1991).

M. D. Levi and P. Sercu: "Erroneous and Valid Reasons for Hedging Foreign Exchange Exposure," *Journal of Multinational Financial Management,* 1:25–37 (1991).

A. C. Shapiro: "International Capital Budgeting," *Midland Corporate Finance Journal,* 1:26–45 (Spring 1983).

Listed below are a few of the articles on the relationship between interest rates, exchange rates, and inflation:

Forward and spot exchange rates

M. D. D. Evans and K. K. Lewis: "Do Long-Term Swings in the Dollar Affect Estimates of the Risk Premia?" *Review of Financial Studies,* 8:709–742 (1995).

E. F. Fama: "Forward and Spot Exchange Rates," *Journal of Monetary Economics,* 14:319–338 (1984).

Interest-rate parity

K. Clinton: "Transaction Costs and Covered Interest Arbitrage: Theory and Evidence," *Journal of Political Economy,* 96:358–370 (April 1988).

J. A. Frenkel and R. M. Levich: "Covered Interest Arbitrage: Unexploited Profits?" *Journal of Political Economy,* 83:325–338 (April 1975).

Purchasing power parity

M. Adler and B. Lehmann: "Deviations from Purchasing Power Parity in the Long Run," *Journal of Finance,* 38:1471–1487 (December 1983).

K. Froot and K. Rogoff: "Perspectives on PPP and Long-run Real Exchange Rates," in G. Grossman and K. Rogoff (eds.), *Handbook of International Economics,* North-Holland Publishing Company, Amsterdam, 1995.

P. Jorion and R. Sweeney: "Mean Reversion in Real Exchange Rates: Evidence and Implications for Forecasting," *Journal of International Money and Finance,* 15:535–550 (1996).

K. Rogoff: "The Purchasing Power Parity Puzzle," *Review of Economic Literature,* 34:667–668 (June 1996).

QUIZ

1. Look at Table 28.1.
   a. How many Mexican pesos do you get for your dollar?
   b. What is the one-month forward rate for the peso?
   c. Is the dollar at a forward discount or premium on the peso?
   d. Use the one-year forward rate to calculate the annual percentage discount or premium on the peso.
   e. If the one-year interest rate on dollars is 3.7 percent annually compounded, what do you think is the one-year interest rate on pesos?
   f. According to the expectations theory, what is the expected spot rate for the peso in three months' time?
   g. According to the law of one price, what then is the expected difference in the rate of price inflation in the United States and Mexico?

2. Define each of the following theories in a sentence or simple equation:
   a. Interest rate parity theory.
   b. Expectations theory of forward rates.
   c. Purchasing power parity.
   d. International capital market equilibrium (relationship of real and nominal interest rates in different countries).
3. In March 1997 the exchange rate for the Indonesian rupiah was R2,419 = $1. Inflation in the year to March 1998 was about 30 percent in Indonesia and 2 percent in the United States.
   a. If purchasing power parity held, what should have been the nominal exchange rate in March 1998?
   b. The actual exchange rate in March 1998 (in the middle of the Asian currency crisis) was R8,325 = $1. What was the change in the *real* exchange rate?
4. The following table shows interest rates and exchange rates for the U.S. dollar and the Philippine peso. The spot exchange rate is 53.6 pesos = $1. Complete the missing entries:

	1 Month	3 Months	1 Year
Dollar interest rate (annually compounded)	3.60	3.50	?
Peso interest rate (annually compounded)	9.55	?	11.90
Forward pesos per dollar	?	?	57.844
Forward premium on peso (% per year)	?	−5.9	?

5. An importer in the United States is due to take delivery of clothing from Mexico in six months. The price is fixed in Mexican pesos. Which of the following transactions could eliminate the importer's exchange risk?
   a. Sell six-month call options on pesos.
   b. Buy pesos forward.
   c. Sell pesos forward.
   d. Sell pesos in the currency futures market.
   e. Borrow pesos; buy dollars at the spot exchange rate.
   f. Sell pesos at the spot exchange rate; lend dollars.
6. A U.S. company has committed to pay 10 million krona to a Swedish company in one year. What is the cost (in present value) of covering this liability by buying krona forward? The Swedish interest rate is 4.53 percent, and exchange rates are shown in Table 28.1. Briefly explain.
7. A firm in the United States is due to receive payment of €1 million in eight years' time. It would like to protect itself against a decline in the value of the euro, but finds it difficult to get forward cover for such a long period. Is there any other way in which it can protect itself?
8. In August 2001 short-term interest rates were about 3.65 percent in the United States and .06 percent in Japan. The spot exchange rate was ¥120.70/$. Suppose that one year later interest rates are 3 percent in both countries, while the value of the yen has appreciated to ¥115.00/$.
   a. Benjamin Pinkerton from New York invested in a U.S. two-year zero-coupon bond in August 2001 and sold it in August 2002. What was his return?
   b. Madame Butterfly from Osaka also invested in the two-year U.S. zero-coupon bond in August 2001 and sold it in August 2002. What was her return *in yen*?
   c. Suppose that Ms. Butterfly had correctly forecasted the price at which she sold her bond and that she hedged her investment against currency risk. How could she have done so? What would have been her return in yen?

9. It is the year 2006 and Pork Barrels Inc. is considering construction of a new barrel plant in Spain. The forecasted cash flows in millions of euros are as follows:

C_0	C_1	C_2	C_3	C_4	C_5
−80	+10	+20	+23	+27	+25

The spot exchange rate is \$1.2 = €1. The interest rate in the United States is 8 percent and the euro interest rate is 6 percent. You can assume that pork barrel production is effectively risk-free.

a. Calculate the NPV of the euro cash flows from the project. What is the NPV in dollars?
b. What are the dollar cash flows from the project if the company hedges against exchange rate changes?
c. Suppose that the company expects the euro to depreciate by 5 percent a year. How does this affect the value of the project?

PRACTICE QUESTIONS

1. Look at the foreign exchange table in a recent issue of *The Wall Street Journal* or the London *Financial Times.*
   a. How many U.S. dollars are worth one Canadian dollar today?
   b. How many Canadian dollars are worth one U.S. dollar today?
   c. Suppose that you arrange today to buy Canadian dollars in 90 days. How many Canadian dollars could you buy for each U.S. dollar?
   d. If forward rates simply reflect market expectations, what is the likely spot exchange rate for the New Zealand dollar in 90 days' time?
   e. Look at the table of money rates in the same issue. What is the three-month interest rate on dollars?
   f. Can you deduce the likely three-month interest rate for the Swiss franc?
   g. You can also buy currency for future delivery in the financial futures market. Look at the table of futures prices. What is the rate of exchange for Canadian dollars to be delivered in approximately six months' time?
2. Table 28.1 shows the 90-day forward rate on the Thai baht.
   a. Is the dollar at a forward discount or premium on the baht?
   b. What is the annual *percentage* discount or premium?
   c. If you have no other information about the two currencies, what is your best guess about the spot rate on the baht three months hence?
   d. Suppose that you expect to receive 100,000 baht in three months. How many dollars is this likely to be worth?
3. Look at Table 28.1. If the three-month interest rate on dollars is 3.5 percent, what do you think is the three-month interest rate on South African rands? Explain what would happen if the rate were substantially above your figure.
4. Look in *The Wall Street Journal* or the *Financial Times.* How many Swiss francs can you buy for \$1? How many Hong Kong dollars can you buy? What rate do you think a Swiss bank would quote for buying or selling Hong Kong dollars? Explain what would happen if it quoted a rate that was substantially above your figure.
5. What do our four basic relationships imply about the relationship between two countries' interest rates and the expected change in the exchange rate? Explain why you would or would not expect them to be related.
6. Ms. Rosetta Stone, the treasurer of International Reprints, Inc., has noticed that the interest rate in Japan is below the rates in most other countries. She is, therefore, sug-

Visit us at www.mhhe.com/bm7e

gesting that the company should make an issue of Japanese yen bonds. Does this make sense?

7. What considerations should an American company take into account when deciding how to finance its overseas subsidiaries?

8. Suppose you are the treasurer of Lufthansa, the German international airline. How is company value likely to be affected by exchange rate changes? What policies would you adopt to reduce exchange rate risk?

9. Companies may be affected by changes in the nominal exchange rate or in the real exchange rate. Explain how this can occur. Which risks are easiest to hedge against?

10. A Ford dealer in the United States may be exposed to a devaluation of the yen if this leads to a cut in the price of Japanese cars. Suppose that the dealer estimates that a 1 percent decline in the value of the yen would result in a permanent decline of 5 percent in the dealer's profits. How should she hedge against this risk, and how should she calculate the size of the hedge position? You may find it helpful to refer back to Section 27.5.

11. You have bid for a possible export order that would provide a cash inflow of €1 million in six months. The spot exchange rate is $.9094 = €1 and the six-month forward rate is $.9070 = €1. There are two sources of uncertainty: (1) the euro could appreciate or depreciate and (2) you may or may not receive the export order. Illustrate in each case the profits or losses that you would make if **(a)** you sell one million euros forward, and **(b)** you buy a six-month option to sell euros with an exercise price of $.9070/€.

12. In August 2001, an American investor buys 1,000 shares in a Mexican company at a price of 500 pesos each. The share does not pay any dividend. A year later she sells the shares for 550 pesos each. The exchange rates when she buys the stock are shown in Table 28.1. Suppose that the exchange rate at the time of sale is pesos 9.50/$.
    a. How many dollars does she invest?
    b. What is her total return in pesos? In dollars?
    c. Do you think that she has made an exchange rate profit or loss? Explain.

13. Table 28.4 shows the foreign exchange rate for the Australian dollar and the Australian and U.S. inflation rates. Using these data, plot the nominal and real exchange rates. Which was more volatile, the nominal or the real exchange rate?

14. Look again at Table 28.4. George and Bruce each have an equal share in a trust fund that provides them with an income of US$100,000 a year. George lives in Seattle, but Bruce emigrated to Sydney in 1983. What has happened to George's *real* income since 1983? What was Bruce's income in 1983 in Australian dollars? What was it in 2000? What has happened to Bruce's *real* income?

15. In 1992 a liter of scotch cost $22.84 in New York, S$69 in Singapore, and 3,240 roubles in Moscow.
    a. If the law of one price held, what was the exchange rate between U.S. dollars and Singapore dollars? Between U.S. dollars and roubles?
    b. The actual exchange rates in 1992 were S$1.63 = US$1 and 250 roubles = US$1. Where would you prefer to buy your scotch?

16. Table 28.5 shows the annual interest rate (annually compounded) and exchange rates against the dollar for different currencies. Are there any arbitrage opportunities? If so, how would you secure a positive cash flow today, while zeroing out all future cash flows?

17. "Last year we had a substantial income in sterling, which we hedged by selling sterling forward. In the event sterling rose, and our decision to sell forward cost us a lot of money. I think that in the future we should either stop hedging our currency exposure or just hedge when we think sterling is overvalued." As financial manager, how would you respond to your chief executive's comment?

18. In 1985 a German corporation bought $250 million forward to cover a future purchase of goods from the United States. However, the dollar subsequently depreciated and the company found that, if it had waited and then bought the dollars spot, it would have

TABLE 28.4

Comparative data for Australia and the United States, 1983–2000.

	Foreign Exchange Rate, A$/US$	Consumer Price Index: 1983 = 100	
		Australia	United States
1983	1.108	100	100
1984	1.137	104	104
1985	1.427	111	108
1986	1.491	121	110
1987	1.427	131	114
1988	1.275	141	117
1989	1.262	151	121
1990	1.280	163	125
1991	1.284	168	129
1992	1.360	169	132
1993	1.470	172	134
1994	1.287	175	138
1995	1.342	184	142
1996	1.255	189	146
1997	1.532	189	149
1998	1.633	191	158
1999	1.524	193	158
2000	1.799	202	163

TABLE 28.5

Interest rates and exchange rates.

	Interest Rate (%)	Spot Exchange Rate	1-Year Forward Exchange Rate*
United States (dollar)	3	—	—
Costaguana (pulga)	23	10,000	11,942
Westonia (ruple)	5	2.6	2.65
Gloccamorra (pint)	8	17.1	18.2
Anglosaxophonia (wasp)	4.1	2.3	2.28

*Number of units of foreign currency that can be exchanged for $1.

paid 225 million deutschmarks (DM) less. One financial manager pointed out that the company could have waited to buy the dollars and meanwhile covered its exposure by using options. In that case it would have saved itself 225 million DM and would have lost only the cost of the option—around 20 million DM.[29] Evaluate the company's decision and the financial manager's criticism.

19. Carpet Baggers, Inc., is proposing to construct a new bagging plant in Europe. The two prime candidates are Germany and Switzerland. The forecasted cash flows from the proposed plants are as follows:

	C_0	C_1	C_2	C_3	C_4	C_5	C_6	IRR (%)
Germany (millions of euros)	−60	+10	+15	+15	+20	+20	+20	18.8
Switzerland (millions of Swiss francs)	−120	+20	+30	+30	+35	+35	+35	12.8

[29]Example cited in *Managing Risks and Costs through Financial Innovation*, Business International Corporation, New York, 1987.

The spot exchange rate for euros is \$1.3/€, while the rate for Swiss francs is SFr1.5/\$. The interest rate is 5 percent in the United States, 4 percent in Switzerland, and 6 percent in the euro countries. The financial manager has suggested that, if the cash flows were stated in dollars, a return in excess of 10 percent would be acceptable.

Should the company go ahead with either project? If it must choose between them, which should it take?

CHALLENGE QUESTIONS

1. If investors recognize the impact of inflation and exchange rate changes on a firm's cash flows, changes in exchange rates should be reflected in stock prices. How would the stock price of each of the following Swiss companies be affected by an unanticipated appreciation of the Swiss franc of 10 percent? Assume that only 2 percent of the appreciation can be attributed to increased inflation in the rest of the world (relative to the Swiss inflation rate).
   a. *A Swiss airline*: More than two-thirds of its employees are Swiss. Most revenues come from international fares set in U.S. dollars.
   b. *Nestlé*: Fewer than 5 percent of its employees are Swiss. Most revenues are derived from sales of consumer goods in a wide range of countries with competition from local producers.
   c. *Union Bank of Switzerland:* Most employees are Swiss. All non-Swiss franc monetary positions are fully hedged.
2. Alpha and Omega are U.S. corporations. Alpha has a plant in Hamburg that imports components from the United States, assembles them, and then sells the finished product in Germany. Omega is at the opposite extreme. It also has a plant in Hamburg, but it buys its raw material in Germany and exports its output back to the United States. How is each firm likely to be affected by a fall in the value of the euro? How could each firm hedge itself against exchange risk?

MINI-CASE

Exacta, s.a.

Exacta, s.a., is a major French producer, based in Lyons, of precision machine tools. About two-thirds of its output is exported. The majority of these sales is within the European Union. However, the company also has a thriving business in the United States, despite strong competition from several U.S. firms. Exacta usually receives payment for exported goods within two months of the invoice date, so that at any point in time only about one-sixth of annual exports to the United States is exposed to currency risk.

The company believes that its North American business is now large enough to justify a local manufacturing operation, and it has recently decided to establish a plant in South Carolina. Most of the output from this plant will be sold in the United States, but the company believes that there should also be opportunities for future sales in Canada and Mexico.

The South Carolina plant will involve a total investment of \$380 million and is expected to be in operation by the year 2001. Annual revenues from the plant are expected to be about \$420 million and the company forecasts net profits of \$52 million a year. Once the plant is up and running, it should be able to operate for several years without substantial additional investment.

Although there is widespread enthusiasm for the project, several members of the management team have expressed anxiety about possible currency risk. M. Pangloss, the finance director, reassured them that the company was not a stranger to currency risk; after all, the company is already exporting about $320 million of machine tools each year to the United States and has managed to exchange its dollar revenue for French francs—and now for euros—without any major losses. But not everybody was convinced by this argument. For example, the CEO, M. B. Bardot, pointed out that the $380 million to be invested would substantially increase the amount of money at risk if the dollar fell relative to the euro. M. Bardot was notoriously risk-averse on financial matters and would push for complete hedging if practical.

M. Pangloss attempted to reassure the CEO. At the same time, he secretly shared some of the anxieties about exchange rate risk, particularly in the early years of the euro's existence. Nearly all the revenues from the South Carolina plant would be in U.S. dollars and the bulk of the $380 million investment would likewise be incurred in the United States. About two-thirds of the operating costs would be in dollars, but the remaining one-third would represent payment for components brought in from Lyons plus the charge by head office for management services and use of patents. The company has yet to decide whether to invoice its U.S. operation in dollars or euros for these purchases from the parent company.

M. Pangloss is optimistic that the company can hedge itself against currency risk. His favored solution is for Exacta to finance the plant by a $380 million issue of dollar bonds. That way the dollar investment would be offset by a matching dollar liability. An alternative is for the company to sell forward at the beginning of each year the expected revenues from the U.S. plant. But he realizes from experience that these simple solutions might carry hidden dangers. He decides to slow down and think more systematically about the additional exchange risk from the U.S. operation.

Questions

1. What would Exacta's true exposure be from its new U.S. operations, and how would it change from the company's current exposure?
2. Given that exposure, what would be the most effective and inexpensive approach to hedging?

PART EIGHT RELATED WEBSITES

The major futures exchanges have useful sites that provide data and explain how futures markets work:

www.cbot.com *(Chicago Board of Trade)*

www.cme.com *(Chicago Mercantile Exchange)*

www.eurexchange.com *(Eurex)*

www.liffe.com *(London International Financial Futures Exchange)*

The site for the Bank for International Settlements includes periodic surveys of derivative and currency markets:

www.bis.org

Commodity futures and options quotes and comment are available on:

www.cisco-futures.com

www.commoditytrader.net

www.io.com/~gibbonsb/wahoo *(links to derivative sites)*

Examples of journals specializing in derivatives include:

www.appliederivatives.com

www.erivativesreview.com

www.futuresmag.com

www.Risk.net

ISDA is the trade association for swap dealers:

www.isda.org

For data on companies in a number of countries and useful links to other finance-related sites for each country, see:

www.corporateinformation.com

A wonderful site for data and commentary on emerging markets is:

www.emgmkts.com

For sample rankings of countries by political risk see:

www.duke.edu/~charvey

www.prsgroup.com

PART NINE

FINANCIAL PLANNING AND SHORT-TERM MANAGEMENT

W. T. GRANT WAS a large successful department store chain with 1,200 stores and $1.8 billion of sales. Yet in 1975 the company filed for bankruptcy, in what *Business Week* termed "the most significant bankruptcy in U.S. history."

The company's problems stemmed from the mid-1960s when it embarked on a rapid expansion policy. New stores take time to reach full profitability, so while profits initially increased, return on capital fell. Since the company chose to increase dividends, the money for the new investment had to be raised largely from the capital market. Instead of selling more shares, W. T. Grant preferred to raise the money by borrowing.

As the country slipped into recession, profits evaporated. Yet Grant insisted on maintaining its dividend. Effectively it was borrowing to pay the dividend. Within a year the company was bankrupt.

W. T. Grant failed because its goals for growth were unsustainable, and it had no plans for surviving a recession. Part Nine shows how firms can check that their growth strategy is consistent with their financing plans. Chapter 29 explains how managers monitor the company's financial health and develop long-term financial plans. Chapter 30 turns to short-term planning and examines how firms forecast and manage their short-term cash requirements. The remaining two chapters focus on two short-term issues—the collection and disbursement of cash and the management of credit.

CHAPTER TWENTY-NINE

FINANCIAL ANALYSIS AND PLANNING

A CAMEL LOOKS like an animal designed by a committee. If a firm made all its financial decisions piecemeal, it would end up with a financial camel. Therefore, smart financial managers consider the overall effect of financing and investment decisions and ensure that they have the financial strategies in place to support the firm's plans for future growth.

Knowing where you stand today is a necessary prelude to contemplating where you might be in the future. Therefore we start the chapter with a brief review of a company's financial statements and we show how you can use these statements to assess the firm's overall performance and its current financial standing.

To produce order out of chaos, financial analysts calculate a few key financial ratios that summarize the company's financial strengths and weaknesses. These ratios are no substitute for a crystal ball, but they do help you to ask the right questions. For example, when the firm needs a loan from the bank, the financial manager can expect some searching questions about the firm's debt ratio and the proportion of profits that is absorbed by interest. Likewise, financial ratios may alert senior management to potential problem areas. If a division is earning a low rate of return on its capital or its profit margins are under pressure, you can be sure that management will demand an explanation.

Growing firms need to invest in working capital, plant and equipment, product development, and so on. All this requires cash. We will, therefore, explain how firms use financial planning models to help them understand the financial implications of their business plans and to explore the consequences of alternative financial strategies.

Our focus in this chapter is on the long-term future. For example, firms may have a planning horizon of 5 or 10 years. In the next chapter we will look at how firms also develop more detailed strategies to ensure that they can get safely through the next few months.

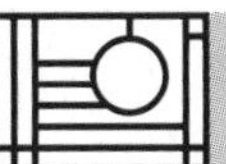

29.1 FINANCIAL STATEMENTS

Public companies have a variety of stakeholders, such as shareholders, bondholders, bankers, suppliers, employees, and management. All these stakeholders need to monitor the firm and to ensure that their interests are being served. They rely on the company's financial statements to provide the necessary information.

When reviewing a company's financial statements, it is important to remember that accountants still have a fair degree of leeway in reporting earnings and book values. For example, accountants have discretion in the way they treat intangible assets, such as patents or franchises. Some believe that including these items on the balance sheet provides the best measure of the company's value as a going concern. Others take a more conservative approach and exclude intangible assets. They reason that, if the firm were liquidated, these assets would be largely valueless.

Although accountants around the world are working toward common practices, there are considerable variations in the accounting rules of different countries. In Anglo-Saxon countries such as the United States or the UK which have large and active equity markets, the rules have been designed with the shareholder very much in mind. By contrast, in Germany the focus of accounting standards is to verify that the creditors are properly protected.

Ray Ball has pointed out that differences between German and U.S. practice also arise because "German laws and institutional arrangements closely link German corporations' reported earnings to their dividend payments and to bonuses paid to managers and employees alike. The economic role of reported earnings is analogous to an annually-baked pie that is divided among the important stakeholders (government, employees, shareholders and managers alike), the size of the pie having first been determined with prudential regard for the financial stability of the corporation. . . . Reporting a loss would eliminate bonus, dividend and tax distributions, to the chagrin of all the stakeholders."[1]

Another difference is the way that taxes are shown in the income statement. For example, in Germany taxes are paid on the published profits and the depreciation method must therefore be approved by the revenue service. That is not so in Anglo-Saxon countries, where the numbers shown in the published accounts are generally *not* the basis for calculating the company's tax payments. For instance, the depreciation method used to calculate the published profits may differ from the depreciation method used by the tax authorities.

Sometimes the effect of these differences in accounting rules can be substantial. When the German car manufacturer, Daimler-Benz, decided to list its shares on the New York Stock Exchange in 1993, it was required to revise its accounting practices to conform to U.S. standards. While it reported a modest profit in the first half of 1993 using German accounting rules, it reported a loss of $592 million under U.S. rules, primarily because of differences in the treatment of reserves.

Countries also differ in the amount and accuracy of the information disclosed in a company's financial statements. For example, the Russian company, Lukoil, owns some of the largest oil reserves in the world and has 120,000 employees. Yet until recently its income statement reported just four numbers, with no accompanying notes. A study by LaPorta et al. rated a sample of countries on the quality of their accounting standards.[2] Table 29.1 provides an extract from their results. In general, they concluded that company accounts were more informative in those countries with a Scandinavian or English legal tradition and less so in those with a French or German tradition. However, there was a huge variation within each of these groups.

TABLE 29.1

Country ratings on quality of accounting standards (a high figure indicates high quality).

Source: LaPorta et al., "Law and Finance," *Journal of Political Economy* 106 (December 1998), 1113–1155.

Country	Legal Tradition	Rating
Sweden	Scandinavian	83
United Kingdom	English	78
United States	English	71
France	French	69
Hong Kong	English	69
Switzerland	German	68
Japan	German	65
Germany	German	62
South Korea	German	62
Mexico	French	60
India	English	57
Peru	French	38
Egypt	French	24

[1]See R. J. Ball, "Daimler-Benz (DaimlerChrysler) AG: Evolution of Corporate Governance from a Code-law 'Stakeholder' to a Common-law 'Shareholder Value' System," Graduate School of Business, University of Chicago.

[2]LaPorta et al., "Law and Finance," *Journal of Political Economy* 106 (December 1998), pp. 1113–1155.

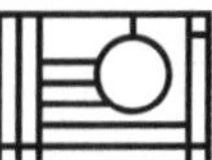

29.2 EXECUTIVE PAPER'S FINANCIAL STATEMENTS

Your task is to assess the financial standing of the Executive Paper Corporation. Perhaps you are a financial analyst with Executive Paper and are helping to develop a five-year financial plan. Perhaps you are employed by a rival company that is contemplating a takeover bid for Executive Paper. Or perhaps you are a banker who needs to assess whether the bank should lend to the company. In each case your first step is to assess the company's *current* condition. You have before you the latest balance sheet, income statement, and sources and uses of funds.

The Balance Sheet

Executive Paper's balance sheet in Table 29.2 provides a snapshot of the company's assets and the sources of the money used to buy those assets.

The items in the balance sheet are listed in declining order of liquidity. For example, you can see that the accountant lists first those assets which are most likely to be turned into cash in the near future. They include cash itself, marketable securities and receivables (that is, bills to be paid by the firm's customers), and

Assets	**Dec 1998**	**Dec 1999**	**Change**
Current assets:			
Cash & securities	75	110	+35
Receivables	433.1	440	+6.9
Inventory	339.9	350	+10.1
Total current assets	848	900	+52
Fixed assets:			
Property, plant, and equipment	929.5	1,000	+70.5
Less accumulated depreciation	396.7	450	+53.3
Net fixed assets	532.8	550	+17.2
Total assets	1,380.8	1,450	+69.2
Liabilities and Shareholders' Equity	**Dec 1998**	**Dec 1999**	**Change**
Current liabilities:			
Debt due within 1 year	96.6	100	+3.4
Payables	349.9	360	+10.1
Total current liabilities	446.5	460	+13.5
Long-term debt	425	450	+25
Shareholders' equity	509.3	540	+30.7
Total liabilities & shareholders' equity	1,380.8	1,450	+69.2
Other financial information:			
Market value of equity	598	708	
Average number of shares (millions)	14.16	14.16	
Share price ($)	42.25	50.00	

TABLE 29.2

The balance sheet of Executive Paper Corporation (figures in $ millions).

inventories of raw materials, work in process, and finished goods. These assets are all known as *current assets.*

The remaining assets on the balance sheet consist of long-term, usually illiquid, assets such as pulp and paper mills, office buildings, and timberlands. The balance sheet does not show up-to-date market values of these long-term assets. Instead, the accountant records the amount that each asset originally cost and then, in the case of plant and equipment, deducts a fixed annual amount for depreciation. The balance sheet does not include all the company's assets. Some of the most valuable ones are intangible, such as patents, reputation, a skilled management, and a well-trained labor force. Accountants are generally reluctant to record these assets in the balance sheet unless they can be readily identified and valued.

Now look at the right-hand portion of Executive Paper's balance sheet, which shows where the money to buy the assets came from.[3] The accountant starts by looking at the liabilities, that is, the money owed by the company. First come those liabilities that need to be paid off in the near future. These *current liabilities* include debts that are due to be repaid within the next year and payables (that is, amounts owed by the company to its suppliers).

The difference between the current assets and current liabilities is known as the *net current assets* or *net working capital.* It roughly measures the company's potential reservoir of cash. For Executive Paper in 1999

$$\begin{aligned}\text{Net working capital} &= \text{current assets} - \text{current liabilities}\\ &= 900 - 460 = \$440 \text{ million}\end{aligned}$$

The bottom portion of the balance sheet shows the sources of the cash that was used to acquire the net working capital and fixed assets. Some of the cash has come from the issue of bonds and leases that will not be repaid for many years. After all these long-term liabilities have been paid off, the remaining assets belong to the common stockholders. The company's equity is simply the total value of the net working capital and fixed assets less the long-term liabilities. Part of this equity has come from the sale of shares to investors and the remainder has come from earnings that the company has retained and invested on behalf of the shareholders.

Table 29.2 provides some other financial information about Executive Paper. For example, it shows the market value of the common stock. It is often helpful to compare the *book value* of the equity (shown in the company's accounts) with the *market value* established in the capital markets.

The Income Statement

If Executive Paper's balance sheet resembles a snapshot of the firm at a particular point in time, its income statement is like a video. It shows how profitable the firm has been over the past year.

Look at the summary income statement in Table 29.3. You can see that during 1999 Executive Paper sold goods worth \$2,200 million and that the total costs of producing and selling these goods were \$1,980 million. In addition to these out-of-pocket expenses, Executive Paper also made a deduction of \$53.3 million for the value of the fixed assets used up in producing the goods. Thus Executive Paper's earnings before interest and taxes (EBIT) were

[3]The British and Americans can never agree whether to keep to the left or the right. British accountants list liabilities on the left and assets on the right.

TABLE 29.3

The 1999 income statement of Executive Paper Corporation (figures in $ millions).

	$ Millions
Revenues	2,200
Costs	1,980
Depreciation	53.3
EBIT	166.7
Interest	42.5
Tax	49.7
Net income	74.5
Dividends	43.8
Retained earnings	30.7
Earnings per share, dollars	5.26
Dividend per share, dollars	3.09

TABLE 29.4

Sources and uses of funds for Executive Paper Corporation, 1999 (figures in $ millions).

	$ Millions	Notes:
Sources:		
Net income	74.5	See Table 29.3
Depreciation	53.3	See Table 29.3
Operating cash flow	127.8	
Issues of long-term debt	25.0	See Table 29.2: 450 − 425
Issues of equity	0	See Tables 29.2 and 29.3: 540 − 509.3 − (74.5 − 43.8)
Total sources	152.8	
Uses:		
Investment in net working capital	38.5	See Table 29.2: (900 − 460) − (848 − 446.5)
Investment in fixed assets	70.5	See Table 29.2: 1000 − 929.5
Dividends	43.8	See Table 29.3
Total uses	152.8	

$$
\begin{aligned}
\text{EBIT} &= \text{Total revenues} - \text{costs} - \text{depreciation} \\
&= 2{,}200 - 1{,}980 - 53.3 = \$166.7 \text{ million}
\end{aligned}
$$

Of this sum $42.5 million went to pay the interest on the short- and long-term debt (remember debt interest is paid out of pretax income) and a further $49.7 million went to the government in the form of taxes. The $74.5 million that was left over belonged to the shareholders. Executive Paper paid out $43.8 million as dividends and reinvested the remaining $30.7 million in the business.

Sources and Uses of Funds

Table 29.4 shows where Executive Paper raised funds and how it spent them.[4] Beside each row in the table we have added a brief note on how the figure is calculated. We will explain each item in turn.

[4]Notice that in a *Sources and Uses of Funds* table the different components of net working capital are not separated out. When we discuss short-term planning in Chapter 30, we will show how to draw up a *Sources and Uses of Cash* table, which separates out different items of net working capital.

Look first at the uses of funds. The money that Executive Paper generates is either invested in net working capital and fixed assets or it is paid out to shareholders as dividends. Thus

$$\text{Total uses of funds} = \text{investment in net working capital} + \text{investment in fixed assets} + \text{dividends paid to shareholders}$$

Table 29.2 shows that in 1999 Executive Paper started the year with net working capital of 848 − 446.5 = $401.5 million. By the end of the year it had grown to 900 − 460 = $440 million. So the company invested an additional $38.5 million in working capital. Over the same period fixed assets rose from $929.5 million to $1,000 million, an increase of $70.5 million. Finally, the income statement in Table 29.3 shows that Executive Paper distributed $43.8 million as dividends. Thus, in total, Executive Paper invested or paid out as dividends 38.5 + 70.5 + 43.8 = $152.8 million.

Where did the funds come from? There are two sources—the cash generated from operations and new money raised from investors:

$$\text{Total sources of funds} = \text{operating cash flow} + \text{new issues of long-term debt} + \text{new issues of equity}$$

The income statement shows that in 1999 the company generated $127.8 million from operations. This included $53.3 million of depreciation (remember depreciation is not a cash outflow) and $74.5 million of net income. This left a deficiency of 152.8 − 127.8 = $25 million that Executive Paper needed to raise from the capital market. You can see from the balance sheet that Executive Paper raised this $25 million by an issue of long-term debt (debt increased from $425 million to $450 million). Executive Paper did not issue new equity capital in 1999. So why does the balance sheet show an increase in equity of 540 − 509.3 = $30.7 million? The answer is that this increase in equity came from income that the company retained and plowed back on behalf of its shareholders (retained earnings = net income − dividends = 74.5 − 43.8 = $30.7 million).

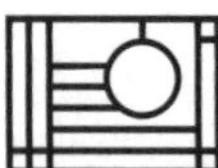

29.3 MEASURING EXECUTIVE PAPER'S FINANCIAL CONDITION

Executive Paper's financial statements provide you with the basic information to assess its current financial standing. However, financial statements typically contain large amounts of data—far more than is contained in the simplified statements for Executive Paper. To condense these data into a convenient form, financial managers generally focus on a few key financial ratios.

Table 29.5 summarizes the key financial ratios for Executive Paper.[5] We will explain how to calculate these ratios and use them to shed light on five questions:

- How much has the company borrowed? Is the amount of debt likely to result in financial distress?
- How liquid is the company? Can it easily lay its hands on cash if needed?

[5]In addition to the ratios that we describe below, Table 29.5 includes a few other ratios that you may well encounter. Some are simply alternative ways to express the same result; others are variations on a theme.

		Executive Paper	Paper Industry†
Leverage Ratios:			
Debt ratio	(Long-term debt + leases)/(long-term debt + leases + equity)	.45	.53
Debt ratio (including short-term debt)*	(Long-term debt + short-term debt + leases)/(long-term debt + short-term debt + leases + equity)	.50	.56
Debt–equity ratio	(Long-term debt + leases)/equity	.83	1.12
Times-interest-earned	(EBIT + depreciation)/interest	5.2	2.9
Liquidity Ratios:			
Net-working-capital-to-total assets*	(Current assets − current liabilities)/total assets	.30	.06
Current ratio	Current assets/current liabilities	2.0	1.3
Quick ratio	(Cash + short-term securities + receivables)/current liabilities	1.2	.7
Cash ratio	(Cash + short-term securities)/current liabilities	.2	.1
Interval measure*	(Cash + short-term securities + receivables)/(costs from operations/365)	101.4	61.7
Efficiency Ratios:			
Sales-to-assets ratio	Sales/average total assets	1.55	.90
Sales-to-net-working-capital*	Sales/average net working capital	5.2	14.1
Days in inventory	Average inventory/(cost of goods sold/365)	63.6	59.1
Inventory turnover*	Cost of goods sold/average inventory	5.7	6.2
Average collection period (days)	Average receivables/(sales/365)	72.4	45.9
Receivables turnover*	Sales/average receivables	5.0	8.0
Profitability Ratios:			
Net profit margin	(EBIT − tax)/sales	5.3%	−0.5%
Return on assets (ROA)	(EBIT − tax)/average total assets	8.3%	−0.4%
Return on equity (ROE)	Earnings available for common stockholders/average equity	14.2%	−10.3%
Payout ratio	Dividend per share/earnings per share	.6	n.a.
Market-Value Ratios:			
Price–earnings ratio (P/E)	Stock price/earnings per share	9.5	n.a
Dividend yield	Dividend per share/stock price	6.2%	1.8%
Market-to-book ratio	Stock price/book value per share	1.3	3.6

TABLE 29.5

Financial ratios for Executive Paper and the paper industry, 1999.

*This ratio is an extra bonus not discussed in Section 29.2.
†1999 ratios for U.S. paper and allied products.
Source: Compustat.

- How productively is the company using its assets? Are there any signs that the assets are not being used efficiently?
- How profitable is the company?
- How highly is the firm valued by investors? Are investors' expectations reasonable?

When you calculate a company's financial ratios, you need some criteria to decide whether they are a cause for concern or a matter for congratulation. Unfortunately, there is no "right" set of financial ratios to which all companies should aspire. Take, for example, the company's capital structure. Debt has both advantages and disadvantages, and, even if there were an optimal level of debt for company A, it would not be appropriate for company B.

When managers review a company's financial position, they often start by comparing the current year's ratios with equivalent figures for earlier years. It is also helpful to look at how the company's financial position measures up to that of other firms in the same industry. Therefore, in Table 29.5 we have compared the financial ratios of Executive Paper with those for the U.S. paper industry.[6]

How Much Has Executive Paper Borrowed?

When Executive Paper borrows, it promises to make a series of fixed payments. Because its shareholders get only what is left over after the debtholders have been paid, the debt is said to create *financial leverage.* In extreme cases, if hard times come, a company may be unable to pay its debts.

The company's bankers and bondholders also want to make certain that Executive Paper does not borrow excessively. So, if Executive wishes to take out a new loan, the lenders will scrutinize several measures of whether the company is borrowing too much and will demand that it *keep* its debt within reasonable bounds. Such borrowing limits are stated in terms of financial ratios.

Debt Ratio Financial leverage is usually measured by the ratio of long-term debt to total long-term capital. Since long-term lease agreements also commit the firm to a series of fixed payments, it makes sense to include the value of lease obligations with the long-term debt. For Executive Paper

$$\text{Debt ratio} = \frac{(\text{long-term debt} + \text{value of leases})}{(\text{long-term debt} + \text{value of leases} + \text{equity})}$$
$$= 450/(450 + 540) = .45$$

Another way to say the same thing is that Executive Paper has a debt-to-equity ratio of $450/540 = .83$:

$$\text{Debt–equity ratio} = \frac{(\text{long-term debt} + \text{value of leases})}{\text{equity}}$$
$$= 450/540 = .83$$

Notice that this measure makes use of book (i.e., accounting) values rather than market values.[7] The market value of the company finally determines whether the debtholders get their money back, so you might expect analysts to look at

[6]Financial ratios for different industries are published by the U.S. Department of Commerce, Dun and Bradstreet, The Risk Management Association, and others.

[7]In the case of leased assets accountants try to estimate the present value of the lease commitments. In the case of long-term debt they simply show the face value. This can sometimes be very different from present value. For example, the present value of low-coupon debt may be only a fraction of its face value. The difference between the book value of equity and its market value can be even more dramatic.

the face amount of the debt as a proportion of the total market value of debt and equity. On the other hand, the market value includes the value of intangible assets generated by research and development, advertising, staff training, and so on. These assets are not readily salable, and if the company falls on hard times, their value may disappear altogether. For some purposes, it may be just as good to follow the accountant and ignore these intangible assets. This is what lenders do when they insist that the borrower should not allow the book debt ratio to exceed a specified limit.

Debt ratios are sometimes defined in other ways. For example, analysts may include short-term debt or other obligations such as payables. There is a general point here. There are a variety of ways to define most financial ratios and there is no law stating how they *should* be defined. So be warned: Don't accept a ratio at face value without understanding how it has been calculated.

Times-Interest-Earned (or Interest Cover) Another measure of financial leverage is the extent to which interest is covered by earnings before interest and taxes (EBIT) plus depreciation. For Executive Paper,[8]

$$\text{Times-interest-earned} = \frac{(\text{EBIT} + \text{depreciation})}{\text{interest}}$$

$$= \frac{(166.7 + 53.3)}{42.5} = 5.2$$

The regular interest payment is a hurdle that companies must keep jumping if they are to avoid default. The times-interest-earned ratio measures how much clear air there is between hurdle and hurdler.

Is Executive Paper's borrowing in the ballpark of standard practice or is it a matter for concern? Table 29.5 provides some clues. You can see that the debt ratio is slightly lower than that of the rest of the paper industry and the times-interest-earned is significantly higher than that of most companies.

How Liquid Is Executive Paper?

If Executive Paper is borrowing for a short period or has some large bills coming up for payment, you want to make sure that it can lay its hands on the cash when it is needed. The company's bankers and suppliers also need to keep an eye on Executive's liquidity. They know that illiquid firms are more likely to fail and default on their debts.

Another reason that analysts focus on liquid assets is that the figures are often more reliable. The book value of Executive's newsprint mill may be a poor guide to its true value, but at least you know what its cash in the bank is worth. Liquidity ratios also have some *less* desirable characteristics. Because short-term assets and liabilities are easily changed, measures of liquidity can rapidly become out-of-date. You may not know what that newsprint mill is worth, but you can be fairly sure that it won't disappear overnight.

---

[8]The numerator of times-interest-earned can be defined in several ways. Sometimes depreciation is excluded. Sometimes it is just earnings plus interest, that is, earnings before interest but *after* tax. This last definition seems nutty to us, because the point of interest earned is to assess the risk that the firm won't have enough money to pay interest. If EBIT falls below interest obligations, the firm won't have to worry about taxes. Interest is paid before the firm pays taxes.

Current Ratio Executive Paper's current assets consist of cash and assets that can readily be turned into cash. Its current liabilities consist of payments that the company expects to make in the near future. Thus the ratio of the current assets to the current liabilities measures the margin of liquidity. It is known as the *current ratio:*

$$\text{Current ratio} = \frac{\text{current assets}}{\text{current liabilities}} = \frac{900}{460} = 1.96$$

Rapid decreases in the current ratio sometimes signify trouble. However, they can also be misleading. For example, suppose that a company borrows a large sum from the bank and invests it in short-term securities. If nothing else happens, net working capital is unaffected, but the current ratio changes. For this reason it might be preferable to net off the short-term investments and the short-term debt when calculating the current ratio.

Quick (or Acid-Test) Ratio Some assets are closer to cash than others. If trouble comes, inventories may not sell at anything above fire-sale prices. (Trouble typically comes *because* customers are not buying and the firm's warehouse is stuffed with unwanted goods.) Thus, managers often focus only on cash, short-term securities, and bills that customers have not yet paid:

$$\text{Quick ratio} = \frac{(\text{cash} + \text{short-term securities} + \text{receivables})}{\text{current liabilities}}$$

$$= \frac{110 + 440}{460} = 1.20$$

Cash Ratio A company's most liquid assets are its holdings of cash and marketable securities. That is why analysts also look at the cash ratio:

$$\text{Cash ratio} = \frac{(\text{cash} + \text{short-term securities})}{\text{current liabilities}} = \frac{110}{460} = .24$$

Of course, these summary measures of liquidity are just that. They are no substitute for detailed plans to ensure that the company can pay its bills. In the next chapter we will describe how companies forecast their cash needs and draw up a short-term financial plan to deal with any cash shortage.

How Productively Is Executive Paper Using Its Assets?

Financial analysts employ another set of ratios to judge how efficiently the firm is using its investment in current and fixed assets. Later in the chapter we will look at the financial implications of Executive's ambitious plans to expand output, but understanding the investment in fixed assets and working capital that is needed to support Executive Paper's *current* output may help to uncover any inconsistencies in these plans for the future.

Sales-to-Assets (or Asset Turnover) Ratio The sales-to-assets ratio shows how hard the firm's assets are being put to use:

$$\frac{\text{Sales}}{\text{average total assets}} = \frac{2{,}200}{(1{,}380.8 + 1{,}450)/2} = 1.55$$

Assets here are measured as the sum of current and fixed assets. Notice that since assets are likely to change over the course of a year, we use the *average* of the assets at the beginning and end of the year. Averages are commonly used whenever a *flow* figure (in this case, sales) is compared with a *stock* or snapshot figure (total assets).

Notice that for each dollar of investment Executive generates $1.55 of sales, a much higher figure than other paper companies. There are several possible explanations: (1) Executive uses its assets more efficiently; (2) Executive is working close to capacity, so that it may be difficult to increase sales without additional invested capital; or (3) compared with its rivals, Executive produces high volume, low margin products.[9] You need to dig deeper to know which explanation is correct. Remember our earlier comment—financial ratios help you to *ask* the right questions, not to *answer* them.

Instead of looking at the ratio of sales to *total assets,* managers sometimes look at how hard particular types of capital are being put to use. For example, it turns out that Executive's ratio of sales to *current assets* is less than that of other paper companies. It is the ratio of Executive's sales to its *fixed assets* that sets it apart from its rivals.

Days in Inventory The speed with which a company turns over its inventory is measured by the number of days that it takes for the goods to be produced and sold. First convert the cost of goods sold to a daily basis by dividing by 365. Then express inventories as a multiple of the daily cost of goods sold:

$$\text{Days in inventory} = \frac{\text{average inventory}}{\text{cost of goods sold} \div 365}$$
$$= \frac{(339.9 + 350)/2}{1{,}980/365} = 63.6 \text{ days}$$

Notice that Executive Paper appears to have a relatively low rate of inventory turnover. Perhaps there is scope for economizing on the company's investment in inventories.

Average Collection Period The average collection period measures how quickly customers pay their bills:

$$\text{Average collection period} = \frac{\text{average receivables}}{\text{sales} \div 365}$$
$$= \frac{(433.1 + 440)/2}{2{,}200/365} = 72.4 \text{ days}$$

The collection period for Executive Paper is somewhat longer than the industry average. The company may have a conscious policy of offering attractive credit terms to lure business, but it is worth looking at whether the credit manager is lax in chasing up the slow payers.

---

[9]We will see shortly that this last explanation does not hold up. The paper industry in 1999 earned a *negative* profit margin.

How Profitable Is Executive Paper?

Net Profit Margin If you want to know the proportion of sales that finds its way into profits, you look at the profit margin. Thus[10]

$$\text{Net profit margin} = \frac{(\text{EBIT} - \text{tax})}{\text{sales}} = .053, \text{ or } 5.3\%$$

Return on Assets (ROA) Managers often measure the performance of the firm by the ratio of income to total assets (income is usually defined as earnings before interest but after taxes). This is known as the firm's *return on assets* (ROA) or *return on investment* (ROI):[11]

$$\text{Return on assets} = \frac{(\text{EBIT} - \text{tax})}{(\text{average total assets})}$$

$$= \frac{(166.7 - 49.7)}{(1{,}380.8 + 1{,}450)/2} = .083, \text{ or } 8.3\%$$

Another measure focuses on the return on the firm's equity:

$$\text{Return on equity (ROE)} = \frac{(\text{earnings available for common stockholders})}{\text{average equity}}$$

$$= \frac{74.5}{(509.3 + 540)/2} = .142, \text{ or } 14.2\%$$

Executive Paper's return on assets and equity is in sharp contrast to the rest of the industry, which provided a negative return in 1999.

It is natural to compare the return earned by Executive Paper with the opportunity cost of capital. Of course, the assets in the financial statements are shown at *net book value,* that is, original cost less depreciation.[12] So a low ROA does not necessar-

---

[10]Net profit margin is sometimes measured as net income ÷ sales. This ignores the profits that are paid out to debtholders as interest and should therefore not be used to compare firms with different capital structures.

When making comparisons between firms, it makes sense to recognize that firms which pay more interest pay less tax. We suggest that you calculate the tax that the company would pay if it were all-equity-financed. To do this you need to adjust taxes by adding back interest tax shields (interest payments × marginal tax rate). Using an assumed tax rate of 40 percent,

$$\text{Net profit margin} = \frac{\text{EBIT} - (\text{tax} + \text{interest tax shields})}{\text{sales}}$$

$$= \frac{166.7 - [49.7 + (.4 \times 42.5)]}{2{,}200} = 0.45, \text{ or } 4.5\%$$

[11]When comparing the returns on total assets of firms with different capital structures, it makes sense to add back interest tax shields to tax payments (see footnote 10). This adjusted ratio then measures the returns that the company would have earned if it were all-equity-financed.

One other point about return on assets. Since profits are a flow figure and assets are a snapshot figure, analysts commonly divide profits by the average of assets at the start and end of the year. The reason that they do this is that the firm may raise large amounts of new capital during the year and then put it to work. Therefore part of the year's earnings is a return on this new capital.

However, this measure is potentially misleading and should not be compared closely with the cost of capital. After all, when we defined the return that shareholders require from investing in the capital market, we divided expected profit by the initial outlay, not by an average of starting and ending values.

[12]More careful comparisons between the return on assets and the cost of capital need to recognize the biases in accounting numbers. We discussed these biases in Chapter 12.

ily imply that those assets could be better employed elsewhere. Nor would a high ROA necessarily mean that you could buy similar assets today and get a high return.

In a competitive industry, firms can expect to earn only their cost of capital. Therefore, managers whose businesses are earning more than the cost of capital are likely to earn a pat on the back, while those that are earning a low return may face some tough questions or worse. Although shareholders like to see their companies earn a high return on assets, consumers' groups or regulators often regard a high return as evidence that the firm is charging excessive prices. Naturally, such conclusions are seldom cut and dried. There is plenty of room for argument as to whether the return on assets is properly measured or whether it exceeds the cost of capital.

Payout Ratio The payout ratio measures the proportion of earnings that is paid out as dividends. Thus

$$\text{Payout ratio} = \frac{\text{dividends}}{\text{earnings}} = \frac{43.8}{74.5} = .6$$

We saw in Section 16.2 that managers don't like to cut dividends if there is a shortfall in earnings. Therefore, if a company's earnings are particularly variable, management is likely to play it safe by setting a low average payout ratio. When earnings fall unexpectedly, the payout ratio will rise temporarily. Likewise, if earnings are expected to rise next year, management may feel that it can pay somewhat more generous dividends than it would otherwise have done.

How Highly Is Executive Paper Valued by Investors?

There is no law that prohibits you from introducing data that are not in the company accounts. For example, when you are assessing Executive Paper's efficiency, you might wish to look at the cost per ton of paper produced. Similarly, an airline might calculate revenues per passenger mile flown, and so on. If you want to gauge how highly Executive Paper is valued by investors, then you will need to calculate ratios that combine accounting and stock market data. Here are three examples.

Price–Earnings Ratio The price–earnings, or P/E, ratio measures the price that investors are prepared to pay for each dollar of earnings. In the case of Executive Paper

$$\text{P/E ratio} = \frac{\text{stock price}}{\text{earnings per share}} = \frac{50}{5.26} = 9.5$$

In Section 4.4 we explained that a high P/E ratio may indicate that investors think the firm has good growth opportunities or that its earnings are relatively safe and therefore more valuable. Of course, it may also mean that earnings are temporarily depressed. If a company just breaks even with zero earnings, its P/E ratio is infinite.

Dividend Yield Executive's dividend yield is simply its dividend as a proportion of the stock price. Thus

$$\text{Dividend yield} = \frac{\text{dividend per share}}{\text{stock price}} = \frac{3.09}{50} = .062, \text{ or } 6.2\%$$

Remember that the return to an investor comes in two forms—dividend yield and capital appreciation. Executive Paper's relatively high dividend yield may indicate that investors are demanding a relatively high rate of return or that they are not expecting rapid dividend growth with consequent capital gains.

Market-to-Book Ratio The market-to-book ratio is the ratio of the stock price to book value per share. For Executive Paper

$$\text{Market-to-book ratio} = \frac{\text{stock price}}{\text{book value per share}} = \frac{50}{540/14.16} = 1.3$$

Book value per share is just stockholders' book equity divided by the number of shares outstanding. Book equity equals common stock plus retained earnings—the net amount that the firm has received from stockholders or reinvested on their behalf.[13] Thus Executive Paper's market-to-book ratio of 1.3 means that the firm is worth 30 percent more than past and present stockholders have put into it.

The Dupont System

Some of the profitability and efficiency ratios that we described above can be linked in useful ways. These relationships are often referred to as the **Dupont system,** in recognition of the chemical company that popularized them.

The first relationship links the return on assets (ROA) with the firm's sales-to-assets ratio and its profit margin:

$$\text{ROA} = \frac{\text{EBIT} - \text{tax}}{\text{assets}} = \underset{\substack{\uparrow \\ \text{sales-to-} \\ \text{assets ratio}}}{\frac{\text{sales}}{\text{assets}}} \times \underset{\substack{\uparrow \\ \text{profit} \\ \text{margin}}}{\frac{\text{EBIT} - \text{tax}}{\text{sales}}}$$

All firms would like to earn a higher return on assets but their ability to do so is limited by competition. If the expected return on assets is fixed by competition, firms face a trade-off between the sales-to-assets ratio and the profit margin. For example, fast-food chains, which turn over their capital frequently, also tend to operate on low profit margins. Classy hotels have relatively high margins, but this is offset by lower sales-to-assets ratios.

Firms often seek to increase their profit margins by becoming more vertically integrated; for example, they may acquire a supplier or one of their sales outlets. Unfortunately, unless they have some special skill in running these new businesses, they are likely to find that any gain in profit margin is offset by a decline in the sales-to-assets ratio.

The return on equity (ROE) can be broken down as follows:

$$\begin{aligned}\text{ROE} &= \frac{\text{EBIT} - \text{tax} - \text{interest}}{\text{equity}} \\ &= \underset{\substack{\uparrow \\ \text{leverage} \\ \text{ratio}}}{\frac{\text{assets}}{\text{equity}}} \times \underset{\substack{\uparrow \\ \text{sales-to-} \\ \text{assets} \\ \text{ratio}}}{\frac{\text{sales}}{\text{assets}}} \times \underset{\substack{\uparrow \\ \text{profit} \\ \text{margin}}}{\frac{\text{EBIT} - \text{tax}}{\text{sales}}} \times \underset{\substack{\uparrow \\ \text{"debt} \\ \text{burden"}}}{\frac{\text{EBIT} - \text{tax} - \text{interest}}{(\text{EBIT} - \text{tax})}}\end{aligned}$$

[13]Retained earnings are measured net of depreciation. They represent stockholders' new investment in the business over and above the amount needed to maintain the firm's existing stock of assets.

Notice that the product of the two middle terms is the return on assets. This depends on the firm's production and marketing skills and is unaffected by the financing mix. However, the first and fourth terms do depend on the debt–equity mix.[14] The first term measures the ratio of gross assets to equity, while the last term measures the extent to which profits are reduced by interest. If the firm is leveraged, the first term is greater than 1.0 (assets are greater than equity) and the fourth term is less than 1.0 (part of the profits are absorbed by interest). Thus, leverage can either increase or reduce the return on equity. In the case of Executive Paper

$$\text{ROE} = \text{leverage ratio} \times \text{sales-to-assets ratio} \times \text{profit margin} \times \text{debt burden}$$
$$= 2.70 \times 1.55 \times .053 \times .637 = .14$$

So, for Executive Paper the leverage ratio (2.70) more than offsets the debt burden (.637). Executive's leverage increases its return on equity.

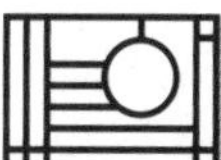

29.4 FINANCIAL PLANNING

Executive Paper's financial statements not only help you to understand the past, but they also provide the starting point for developing a financial plan for the future.

Financial plans begin with the firm's product development and sales objectives. For example, Executive Paper's corporate staff might ask each division to submit three alternative business plans covering the next five years:

1. A *best-case* or aggressive growth plan calling for heavy capital investment, new products, and an increased market share.
2. A *normal growth* plan in which the division grows with its markets but not at the expense of its competitors.
3. A plan of *retrenchment* designed to minimize capital outlays. This is planning for lean economic times.

Of course, the planners might also look at the opportunities for moving into a wholly new area where the company can exploit its existing strengths. Often they may recommend entering the market for strategic reasons, that is, not because the *immediate* investment is profitable but because it establishes the firm in the market and creates *options* for possibly valuable follow-on investments. In other words, there is a two-stage decision. At the second stage (the follow-on project) the financial manager faces a standard capital budgeting problem. But at the first stage projects may be valuable primarily for the options they bring with them.[15]

To see the financial consequences of the business plan, you need to develop forecasts of future cash flows. If the likely operating cash flow is insufficient to cover both the planned dividend payments and the investment in net working capital and fixed assets, then the firm needs to ensure that it can raise the balance by borrowing or by the sale of additional shares.

[14]There is a complication here because the amount of tax paid does depend on the financing mix. We suggested in footnote 10 that it would be better to add back any interest tax shields to the tax payment when calculating the firm's profit margin.

[15]The Blitzen Computers example in Section 22.1 illustrates how option theory can be used to quantify a project's strategic value.

Cash-flow forecasts should always be subjected to a reality check. For example, few companies can expect to continue to earn a high return on their investment without attracting competition. So firms are likely to find it difficult to maintain a high return on assets indefinitely. Conversely, those with a low return on assets may hope for some easing of competitive pressures and the arrival of more normal returns.[16]

When you prepare a financial plan, you shouldn't look just at the most likely financial consequences. You also need to plan for the unexpected. One way to do this is to work through the consequences of the plan under the most likely set of circumstances and then use *sensitivity analysis* to vary the assumptions one at a time. Another approach is to look at the implications of different plausible scenarios.[17] For example, one scenario might envisage high interest rates leading to a slowdown in world economic growth and lower commodity prices. The second scenario might involve a buoyant domestic economy, high inflation, and a weak currency.

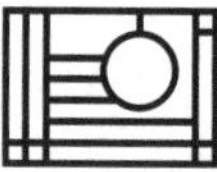

29.5 FINANCIAL PLANNING MODELS

Suppose that management has asked you to assume a 20 percent annual growth in Executive Paper's sales and profits over the next five years. Can the company realistically expect to finance this out of retained earnings and borrowing, or should it plan for an issue of equity? Spreadsheet programs are tailor-made for such questions. Let's investigate.

The basic sources and uses relationship tells us that

$$\begin{aligned}&\text{External capital required}\\&\quad = \text{operating cash flow}\\&\qquad - \text{investment in net working capital}\\&\qquad - \text{investment in fixed assets}\\&\qquad - \text{dividends}\end{aligned}$$

Thus there are four steps to finding how much extra cash Executive Paper will need and the implications for its debt ratio:

Step 1 Project next year's operating cash flow (depreciation provision plus net income) assuming the planned 20 percent increase in revenues. This gives the total sources of funds in the absence of any new issue of securities. Look, for example, at the second column of Table 29.6, which provides a forecast of operating cash flow in year 2000 for Executive Paper.

Step 2 Project what additional investment in net working capital and fixed assets will be needed to support this increased activity and how much of the net income will be paid out as dividends. The sum of these expenditures gives you the total

[16]For evidence that accounting returns tend to regress toward the mean, see Chapter 10 of K. G. Palepu, P. M. Healy, and V. L. Bernard, *Business Analysis and Valuation,* South-Western College Publishing, Cincinnati, OH, 2nd ed., 2000.

[17]For a description of the use of different planning scenarios in the Royal Dutch/Shell group, see P. Wack, "Scenarios: Uncharted Waters Ahead," *Harvard Business Review* 63 (September–October 1985) and "Scenarios: Shooting the Rapids," *Harvard Business Review* 64 (November–December 1985).

	1999	2000	2004
Revenues	2,200	2,640	5,474
Costs (90% of revenues)	1,980	2,376	4,927
Depreciation (10% of fixed assets at start of year)	53.3	55.0	114
EBIT	166.7	209.0	433.4
Interest (10% of long-term debt at start of year)	42.5	45	131.3
Tax (40% of pretax profit)	49.7	65.6	120.8
Net income	74.5	98.4	181.2
Operating cash flow	127.8	153.4	295.3

TABLE 29.6

Latest and pro forma income statements for Executive Paper (figures in $ millions).

	1999	2000	2004
Increase in net working capital (NWC) assuming NWC = 20% of revenues	38.5	88	182.5
Investment in fixed assets (FA) assuming FA = 25% of revenues	70.2	165	342.1
Dividend (60% of net income)	45.6	59.0	108.7
Total uses of funds	129.3	312.0	633.4
External capital required = total uses of funds − operating cash flow	25.0	158.6	338.1

TABLE 29.7

Latest and pro forma statements of sources and uses of funds for Executive Paper (figures in $ millions).

uses of funds. The second column of Table 29.7 provides a forecast of uses of funds for Executive Paper.

Step 3 Calculate the difference between the projected operating cash flow (from Step 1) and the projected uses (Step 2). This is the cash that will need to be raised from new sales of securities. For example, you can see from Table 29.7 that Executive Paper will need to issue $158.6 million of debt in 2000 if it is to expand at the planned rate and not sell more shares.

Step 4 Finally, construct a pro forma balance sheet that incorporates the additional assets and the increase in debt and equity. This is done in the second column of Table 29.8. Executive Paper's equity increases by the additional retained earnings (net income less dividends), while long-term debt is increased by the $158.6 million new issue.

Once you have set up the spreadsheet, it is easy to run out your projections for several years. The final columns in Tables 29.6–29.8 show the pro forma income statement, sources and uses of funds, and balance sheet for the year 2004, assuming Executive Paper continues to fund a 20 percent annual growth rate solely from retained earnings and new debt issues. Over the five-year period Executive Paper would need to borrow an additional $1.2 billion and by year 2004 its debt ratio would have increased to 67 percent. Most financial managers would regard this as sailing much too close to the wind, and the debt ratio would probably be above the limit set by the company's banks and bondholders.

TABLE 29.8

Latest and pro forma balance sheets for Executive Paper (figures in $ millions).

	1999	2000	2004
Net working capital (20% of revenues)	440	528	1,095
Net fixed assets (25% of revenues)	550	660	1,369
Total net assets	990	1,188	2,463
Long-term debt	450	608.6	1,651
Equity	540	579.4	812
Total long-term liabilities and equity	990	1,188	2,463

The obvious solution for Executive Paper is to issue a mix of debt and equity, but there are other possibilities that the financial manager may want to explore. One option may be to hold back dividends during this period of rapid growth, but it turns out that even a complete dividend freeze would still leave Executive Paper needing to raise just under $750 million of new funds. An alternative might be to investigate whether the company could cut back on net working capital. For example, we have seen that Executive Paper's customers take 72 days to pay their bills. Perhaps more careful control of credit collection could help to economize on capital.

We stated earlier that financial planning is not just about exploring how to cope with the most likely outcomes. It also needs to ensure that the firm is prepared for unlikely ones. For example, the paper industry is notoriously exposed to economic downturn. So you would certainly wish to check that Executive Paper could cope with a cyclical decline in sales and profit margins. Sensitivity analysis or scenario analysis can help you to do so.

Executive Paper's problem is not unique, for many companies find that rapid growth can bring burgeoning debt levels. Firms that fail to think through the financial consequences of their growth plans are liable to get into BIG trouble. Look, for example, at the Finance in the News box, which shows how British Telecom's attempt to become a global telecom company forced some hard thinking about how to finance this growth.

Pitfalls in Model Design

The Executive Paper model that we have developed is too simple for practical application. You probably have already thought of several ways to improve it—by keeping track of the outstanding shares, for example, and printing out earnings and dividends per share. Or you might want to distinguish between short-term lending and borrowing opportunities, now buried in working capital.

The model that we developed for Executive Paper is known as a *percentage of sales model.* Almost all the forecasts for the company are proportional to the forecasted level of sales. However, in reality many variables will *not* be proportional to sales. For example, important components of working capital such as inventory and cash balances will generally rise less rapidly than sales. In addition, fixed assets such as plant and equipment are typically not added in small increments as sales increase. Executive Paper's plant may well be operating at less than full capacity, so that the company can initially increase output without *any* additions to capacity. Eventually, however, if sales continue to increase, the firm may need to make a large new investment in plant and equipment.

INVESTORS QUESTION BRITISH TELECOM'S FINANCIAL PLANNING

As the country's principal telecom supplier, British Telecom (BT) was a safe, if somewhat uninspiring, investment. Including short-term loans, its debt ratio was a fairly conservative .38 and the volatility of its stock returns was well below the average for UK companies.

All that changed at the end of the 1990s when BT made a series of foreign acquisitions and paid several billion pounds for a license to offer third-generation mobile services in the UK. These expenditures were financed largely by new borrowing, including a record $10 billion bond issue in the United States. By December 2000 BT's debt had expanded to £30 billion and the debt ratio had climbed to .71. To reassure new bondholders BT had agreed that, if its debt rating were subsequently lowered, it would increase the interest payment on its bonds. Not long afterward the rating agencies announced that they were considering a downgrade, which would increase the cost of servicing BT's debt.

BT's aim was to reduce its debt by £10 billion, and it hoped to achieve this by selling off some recent acquisitions. Unfortunately, as the prices of high-tech stocks fell away in the spring of 2001, this plan began to look less and less attractive.

By March 2001 BT's share price had fallen 70 percent from its high, and anxious investors began to question whether the company had a coherent strategy to deal with its mountain of debt and to finance the heavy expenditures that would be needed to exploit its mobile licenses. Various questions were asked and debated. Should the company press ahead with its plans to sell off businesses? Could it live with its high debt ratio for the time being? Should it seek to build up equity by cutting its dividend or by issuing new equity? It was clear that for BT, financial planning had become central to the company's survival.

But beware of adding too much complexity: There is always the temptation to make a model bigger and more detailed. You may end up with an exhaustive model that is too cumbersome for routine use. The fascination of detail, if you give in to it, distracts attention from crucial decisions like stock issues and dividend policy.

There Is No Finance in Financial Planning Models

Why do we say there is no finance in these corporate financial models? The first reason is that they usually incorporate an accountant's view of the world. They are designed to forecast accounting statements. They do not emphasize the tools of financial analysis: incremental cash flow, present value, market risk, and so on.[18]

This may not matter as long as everyone recognizes the financial forecasts for what they are. However, you sometimes hear managers stating corporate goals in terms of accounting numbers. They may say, "Our objective is to achieve an

[18]Of course, there is no reason that the manager can't use the output to calculate the present value of the firm (given some assumption about growth beyond the planning period), and this is sometimes done.

annual sales growth of 20 percent," or "We want a 25 percent return on book equity and a profit margin of 10 percent." On the surface such objectives don't make sense. Shareholders want to be richer, not to have the satisfaction of a 10 percent profit margin. Also, a goal that is stated in terms of accounting ratios is not operational unless it is translated back into what the statement means for business decisions. For example, what does a 10 percent profit margin imply—higher prices, lower costs, increased vertical integration, or a move into new, high-margin products?

So why do managers define objectives in this way? In part such goals may be a mutual exhortation to try harder, like singing the company song before work. But we suspect that managers are often using a code to communicate real concerns. For example, the goal to increase sales rapidly may reflect managers' belief that increased market share is needed to achieve scale economies, or a target profit margin may be a way of saying that the firm has been pursuing sales growth at the expense of margins. The danger is that everyone may forget the code and the accounting targets may be seen as goals in themselves.

The second reason for saying that there is no finance in these planning models is that they produce no signposts pointing toward optimal decisions. They do not even tell us which alternatives are worth examining. For example, we saw that Executive Paper is planning for a rapid growth in sales and earnings per share. But is that good news for the shareholders? Well, not necessarily; it depends on the opportunity cost of the capital that Executive Paper needs to invest. If the new investment earns more than the cost of capital, it will have a positive NPV and add to shareholder wealth. However, the return that Executive Paper is forecasting to earn on its new investment is little more than the interest rate on its debt and almost certainly below Executive's cost of capital. In this case the company's planned investment will make shareholders worse off, even though the company expects steady growth in earnings per share.

The capital that Executive Paper needs to raise depends on its decision to pay out two-thirds of its earnings as a dividend. But the financial planning model does not tell us whether this dividend payment makes sense or what mixture of equity or debt the company should issue. In the end the management has to decide. We would like to tell you exactly how to make the choice, but we can't. There is no model that encompasses all the complexities encountered in financial planning.

As a matter of fact, there never will be one. This bold statement is based on Brealey and Myers's Third Law:[19]

- *Axiom:* The number of unsolved problems is infinite.
- *Axiom:* The number of unsolved problems that humans can hold in their minds is at any time limited to 10.
- *Law:* Therefore in any field there will always be 10 problems which can be addressed but which have no formal solution.

Brealey and Myers's Third Law implies that no model can find the best of all financial strategies.[20]

---

[19]The second law is presented in Section 12.2.

[20]It is possible to build linear programming models that help search for the best strategy subject to specified assumptions and constraints. These models can be more effective in screening alternative financial strategies.

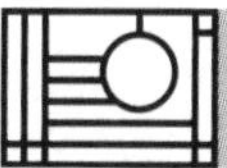

29.6 GROWTH AND EXTERNAL FINANCING

We started this chapter by noting that financial plans force managers to be consistent in their goals for growth, investment, and financing. Before leaving the topic of financial planning, we should look at some general relationships between a firm's growth objectives and its financing needs.

Recall that Executive Paper ended 1999 with fixed assets and net working capital of \$990 million. In 2000 it plans to plow back \$39.4 million, so net assets will increase by 39.4/990 or 3.98 percent. Thus Executive Paper can grow by 3.98 percent without needing to raise additional capital. The growth rate that a company can achieve without external funds is known as the *internal growth rate.* For Executive Paper

$$\text{Internal growth rate} = \frac{\text{retained earnings}}{\text{net assets}} = 3.98\%$$

We can gain more insight into what determines this growth rate by multiplying the top and bottom of the expression for internal growth rate by *net income* and *equity* as follows:

$$\begin{aligned}\text{Internal growth rate} &= \frac{\text{retained earnings}}{\text{net income}} \times \frac{\text{net income}}{\text{equity}} \times \frac{\text{equity}}{\text{net assets}} \\ &= \text{plowback ratio} \times \text{return on equity} \times \frac{\text{equity}}{\text{net assets}}\end{aligned}$$

In 2000 Executive Paper expects to plow back 40 percent of net income and to earn a return of 18.22 percent on the equity with which it began the year. At the start of the year equity finances 54.55 percent of Executive Paper's net assets. Therefore

$$\text{Internal growth rate} = .40 \times .1822 \times .5455 = .0398, \text{ or } 3.98\%$$

Notice that if Executive Paper wishes to grow faster than this without raising equity capital, it would need to (1) plow back a higher proportion of its earnings, (2) earn a higher return on equity (ROE), or (3) have a lower debt-to-equity ratio.[21]

Instead of focusing on how rapidly the company can grow without *any* external financing, Executive Paper's financial manager may be interested in the growth rate that can be sustained without additional *equity* issues. Of course, if the firm is able to raise enough debt, virtually any growth rate can be financed. It makes more sense to assume that the firm has settled on an optimal capital structure which it will maintain as equity is increased by the retained earnings. Thus the firm issues only enough debt to keep the debt–equity ratio constant. The *sustainable growth rate* is the highest growth rate the firm can maintain without increasing its financial leverage. It turns out that the sustainable growth rate depends only on the plowback rate and the return on equity:

$$\text{Sustainable growth rate} = \text{plowback ratio} \times \text{return on equity}$$

[21]Notice that the internal growth rate does not stay constant. As the firm plows back earnings, the debt-to-equity ratio declines and the internal growth rate increases.

For Executive Paper,

$$\text{Sustainable growth rate} = .40 \times .1822 = .0729, \text{ or } 7.29\%$$

We first encountered this formula in Chapter 4, where we used it to value the firm's equity.

These simple formulas remind us that financial plans need to be consistent. Firms may grow rapidly in the short term by relying on debt finance, but such growth cannot be maintained without incurring excessive debt levels.

SUMMARY

Managers use financial statements to monitor their own company's performance, to help understand the policies of a competitor, or to check on the health of a customer. But there is a danger of being overwhelmed by the sheer volume of data. That is why managers use a few salient ratios to summarize the firm's leverage, liquidity, efficiency, profitability, and market valuation. We have described some of the more popular financial ratios.

We offer the following general advice to users of these ratios:

1. Financial ratios seldom provide answers, but they do help you to ask the right questions.
2. There is no international standard for financial ratios. A little thought and common sense are worth far more than blind application of formulas.
3. You need a benchmark for assessing a company's financial position. Compare financial ratios with the company's ratios in earlier years and with the ratios of other firms in the same business.

Understanding the past is the first step to being prepared for the future. Most firms prepare a financial plan that describes the firm's strategy and projects its future consequences by means of pro forma balance sheets, income statements, and statements of sources and uses of funds. The plan establishes financial goals and is a benchmark for evaluating subsequent performance.

The plan is the end result, but the process that produces the plan is valuable in its own right. First, planning forces the financial manager to consider the combined effects of all the firm's investment and financing decisions. This is important because these decisions interact and should not be made independently. Second, planning requires the manager to consider events that could upset the firm's progress and to devise strategies to be held in reserve for counterattack when unhappy surprises occur.

There is no theory or model that leads straight to *the* optimal financial strategy. Consequently, financial planning proceeds by trial and error. Many different strategies may be projected under a range of assumptions about the future. The dozens of separate projections that may be made during this trial-and-error process generate a heavy load of arithmetic. Firms have responded by developing corporate financial planning models to forecast the financial consequences of different strategies. We showed how you can use a simple spreadsheet model to analyze Executive Paper's strategies. But remember there is no finance in these models. Their primary purpose is to produce accounting statements.

FURTHER READING

There are some good general texts on financial statement analysis. See, for example:

G. Foster: *Financial Statement Analysis,* 2nd ed., Prentice-Hall, Inc., Englewood Cliffs, NJ, 1986.

K. G. Palepu, V. L. Bernard, and P. M. Healy: *Business Analysis and Valuation,* South-Western College Publishing, Cincinnati, OH, 2nd ed., 2000.

Three classic articles on the application of financial ratios to specific problems are:

W. H. Beaver: "Financial Ratios as Predictors of Failure," *Empirical Research in Accounting: Selected Studies,* supplement to *Journal of Accounting Research,* 1966, pp. 77–111.

W. H. Beaver, P. Kettler, and M. Scholes: "The Association between Market-Determined and Accounting-Determined Risk Measures," *Accounting Review,* 45:654–682 (October 1970).

J. O. Horrigan: "The Determination of Long Term Credit Standing with Financial Ratios," *Empirical Research in Accounting: Selected Studies,* supplement to *Journal of Accounting Research,* 1966, pp. 44–62.

Corporate planning has an extensive literature of its own. Good books and articles include:

G. Donaldson: "Financial Goals and Strategic Consequences," *Harvard Business Review,* 63:57–66 (May–June 1985).

G. Donaldson: *Strategy for Financial Mobility,* Harvard Business School Press, Boston, 1986.

A. C. Hax and N. S. Majluf: *The Strategy Concept and Process—A Pragmatic Approach,* 2nd ed., Prentice-Hall, Inc., Englewood Cliffs, NJ, 1996.

The links between capital budgeting, strategy, and financial planning are discussed in:

S. C. Myers: "Finance Theory and Financial Strategy," *Interfaces,* 14:126–137 (January–February, 1984).

Here are three references on corporate planning models:

W. T. Carleton, C. L. Dick, Jr., and D. H. Downes: "Financial Policy Models: Theory and Practice," *Journal of Financial and Quantitative Analysis,* 8:691–709 (December 1973).

W. T. Carleton and J. M. McInnes: "Theory, Models and Implementation in Financial Management," *Management Science,* 28:957–978 (September 1982).

S. C. Myers and G. A. Pogue: "A Programming Approach to Corporate Financial Management," *Journal of Finance,* 29:579–599 (May 1974).

Visit us at www.mhhe.com/bm7e

QUIZ

1. Table 29.9 gives abbreviated balance sheets and income statements for Weyerhaeuser Company. Calculate the following ratios:
   a. Debt ratio.
   b. Times-interest-earned ratio.
   c. Current ratio.
   d. Quick ratio.
   e. Net profit margin.
   f. Days in inventory.
   g. Return on equity.
   h. Payout ratio.
2. There are no universally accepted definitions of financial ratios, but five of the following ratios make no sense at all. Substitute the correct definitions.
   a. Debt–equity ratio = (long-term debt + value of leases)/(long-term debt + value of leases + equity)
   b. Return on equity = (EBIT − tax)/average equity

TABLE 29.9

Income statement and balance sheet for Weyerhaeuser Company, 2000 (figures in millions).

Source: Weyerhaeuser Company, 2000 annual report.

Income Statement		
Net sales	$15,980	
Cost of goods sold	12,035	
Other expenses	1,412	
Depreciation	859	
Earnings before interest and tax (EBIT)	1,674	
Net interest	351	
Tax	483	
Earnings	$ 840	
Dividends	263	
Balance Sheet		
	End of Year	**Start of Year**
Cash and short-term securities	115	1,640
Receivables	1,247	1,296
Inventories	1,499	1,329
Other current assets	427	278
Total current assets	3,288	4,543
Tangible fixed assets	10,427	9,582
Other long-term assets	4,480	4,214
Total assets	$18,195	$18,339
Short-term debt	733	909
Payables	921	961
Other current liabilities	1,050	1,083
Total current liabilities	2,704	2,953
Long-term debt and capital leases	5,114	5,100
Other long-term liabilities	3,544	3,113
Common shareholders' equity	6,832	7,173
Total liabilities	$18,195	$18,339

c. Payout ratio = dividend/stock price
d. Profit margin = (EBIT − tax)/sales
e. Inventory turnover = sales/average inventory
f. Current ratio = current liabilities/current assets
g. Sales-to-net-working-capital = average sales/average net working capital
h. Average collection period = sales/(average receivables ÷ 365)
i. Quick ratio = (current assets − inventories)/current liabilities

3. True or false?
a. A company's debt–equity ratio is always less than 1.
b. The quick ratio is always less than the current ratio.
c. The return on equity is always less than the return on assets.
d. If a project is slow to reach full profitability, straight-line depreciation is likely to produce an overstatement of profits in the early years.
e. A substantial new advertising campaign by a cosmetics company will tend to depress earnings and cause the stock to sell at a low price–earnings multiple.

4. In each of the following cases, explain briefly which of the two companies is likely to be characterized by the higher ratio:
a. Debt–equity ratio: a shipping company or a computer software company.
b. Payout ratio: United Foods Inc. or Computer Graphics Inc.

c. Sales-to-assets ratio: an integrated pulp and paper manufacturer or a paper mill.
d. Average collection period: a supermarket chain or a mail-order company.
e. Price–earnings multiple: Basic Sludge Company or Fledgling Electronics.

5. A firm has $30,000 of inventory. If this represents 30 days' sales, what is the annual cost of goods sold? What is the inventory turnover ratio?

6. Keller Cosmetics maintains a profit margin of 4 percent and a sales-to-assets ratio of 3.
   a. What is its return on assets?
   b. If its debt–equity ratio is 1.0, its interest payments and taxes are each $10,000, and EBIT is $40,000, what is the return on equity?

7. A firm has a long-term debt–equity ratio of .4. Shareholders' equity is $1 million. Current assets are $200,000, and the current ratio is 2.0. Long-term assets total $1.5 million. What is the ratio of debt to total long-term capital?

8. Magic Flutes has total receivables of $3,000, which represent 20 days' sales. Average total assets are $75,000. The firm's profit margin is 5 percent. Find the firm's return on assets and sales-to-assets ratio.

9. Consider this simplified balance sheet for Geomorph Trading:

Current assets	100	60	Current liabilities
		280	Long-term debt
Long-term assets	500	70	Other liabilities
		190	Equity
	600	600	

   a. Calculate the ratio of debt to equity.
   b. What are Geomorph's net working capital and total long-term capital? Calculate the ratio of debt to total long-term capital.

10. Airlux Antarctica has current liabilities of $200 million and a crash—sorry—*cash* ratio of .05. How much cash and marketable securities does it hold?

11. On average, it takes Microlimp's customers 60 days to pay their bills. If Microlimp has annual sales of $500 million, what is the average value of unpaid bills?

12. Executive Paper's return on equity is higher than its return on assets. Is this always the case? Explain.

13. True or false?
   a. Financial planning should attempt to minimize risk.
   b. The primary aim of financial planning is to obtain better forecasts of future cash flows and earnings.
   c. Financial planning is necessary because financing and investment decisions interact and should not be made independently.
   d. Firms' planning horizons rarely exceed three years.
   e. Financial planning requires accurate forecasting.
   f. Financial planning models should include as much detail as possible.

14. Table 29.10 summarizes the 2002 income statement and end-year balance sheet of Drake's Bowling Alleys. Drake's financial manager forecasts a 10 percent increase in sales and costs in 2003. The ratio of sales to *average* assets is expected to remain at .40. Interest is forecasted at 5 percent of debt at start of year.
   a. What is the implied level of assets at the end of 2003?
   b. If the company pays out 50 percent of net income as dividends, how much cash will Drake need to raise in the capital markets in 2003?
   c. If Drake is unwilling to make an equity issue, what will be the debt ratio at the end of 2003?

TABLE 29.10

Financial statement for Drake's Bowling Alleys, 2002 (figures in thousands).

*Assets at end-2001 were $2,400,000.
†Debt at end-2001 was $500,000.

Income Statement			
Sales	$1,000 (40% of *average* assets)*		
Costs	750 (75% of sales)		
Interest	25 (5% of debt at start of year)†		
Pretax profit	225		
Tax	90 (40% of pretax profit)		
Net income	$ 135		
Balance Sheet			
Assets	$2,600	Debt	$ 500
		Equity	2,100
Total	$2,600	Total	$2,600

TABLE 29.11

Financial statements for Archimedes Levers, 2001.

Income Statement					
Sales	$4,000				
Costs, including interest	3,500				
Net income	$ 500				
Balance Sheet, Year-end					
	2001	**2000**		**2001**	**2000**
Assets	$3,200	$2,700	Debt	$1,200	$1,033
			Equity	2,000	1,667
Total	$3,200	$2,700	Total	$3,200	$2,700

15. Abbreviated financial statements for Archimedes Levers are shown in Table 29.11. If sales increase by 10 percent in 2002 and all other items, including debt, increase correspondingly, what must be the balancing item? What will be its value?
16. What is the maximum possible growth rate for Archimedes (see question 15) if the payout ratio is set at 50 percent and **(a)** no external debt or equity is to be issued? **(b)** the firm maintains a fixed debt ratio but issues no equity?

PRACTICE QUESTIONS

1. Look up the latest financial statements for any company on the Market Insight database (**www.mhhe.com/edumarketinsight**) and calculate a sources and uses of funds table for the latest year. Don't be put off by the fact that actual financial statements are more complicated than the simplified ones we showed for Executive Paper.
2. Look up the latest financial statements for any company on the Market Insight database (**www.mhhe.com/edumarketinsight**) and calculate the following ratios for the latest year:
   a. Debt ratio.
   b. Times-interest-earned.
   c. Current ratio.
   d. Quick ratio.
   e. Net profit margin.
   f. Days in inventory.

g. Return on equity.
h. Payout ratio.

STANDARD & POOR'S

3. Select a sample of companies with financial statements on the Market Insight database (**www.mhhe.com/edumarketinsight**) and compare the days in inventory and the average collection period for receivables. Can you explain these differences?

4. This question reviews some of the difficulties encountered in interpreting accounting numbers.
   a. Give four examples of important assets, liabilities, or transactions which may not be shown on the company's books.
   b. How does investment in intangible assets, such as research and development, distort accounting ratios? Give at least two examples.
   c. Explain the three ways in which accelerating inflation affects earnings and profitability ratios based on historical-cost accounting.

5. Use financial ratio analysis to compare two companies chosen from the same industry.

6. Discuss alternative measures of financial leverage. Should the market value of equity be used or the book value? Is it better to use the market value of debt, the book value, or the book value discounted at the risk-free interest rate? How should you treat off-balance-sheet obligations such as pension liabilities? How would you treat preferred stock, deferred tax reserves, and minority interest?

7. Suppose that at year-end 1999 Executive Paper had unused lines of credit that would have allowed it to borrow a further $300 million. Suppose also that it used this line of credit to raise short-term loans of $300 million and invested the proceeds in marketable securities. Would the company have appeared to be **(a)** more or less liquid? **(b)** more or less highly levered? Calculate the appropriate ratios.

8. How would the following actions affect a firm's current ratio?
   a. Inventory is sold.
   b. The firm takes out a bank loan to pay its suppliers.
   c. A customer pays its overdue bills.
   d. The firm uses cash to purchase additional inventories.

9. Sara Togas sells all its output to Federal Stores. The following table shows selected financial data, in millions, for the two firms:

	Sales	Profits	Assets
Federal Stores	$100	$10	$50
Sara Togas	20	4	20

   Calculate the sales-to-assets ratio, the profit margin, and the return on the two firms. Now assume that the two companies merge. If Federal continues to sell goods worth $100 million, how will the three financial ratios change?

10. United Ratio's common stock has a dividend yield of 4 percent. Its dividend per share is $2, and it has 10 million shares outstanding. If the market-to-book ratio is 1.5, what is the total book value of the equity?

11. As you can see, someone has spilled ink over some of the entries in the balance sheet and income statement of Transylvania Railroad (Table 29.12). Can you use the following information to work out the missing entries?
   - Financial leverage: .4.
   - Times-interest-earned: 8.
   - Current ratio: 1.4.
   - Quick ratio: 1.0.

Visit us at www.mhhe.com/bm7e

TABLE 29.12

Balance sheet and income statement of Transylvania Railroad (figures in $ millions).

	December 2001	December 2000
Balance Sheet		
Cash	■■■	20
Accounts receivable	■■■	34
Inventory	■■■	26
Total current assets	■■■	80
Fixed assets, net	■■■	25
Total	■■■	105
Notes payable	30	35
Accounts payable	25	20
Total current liabilities	■■■	55
Long-term debt	■■■	20
Equity	■■■	30
Total	115	105
Income Statement		
Sales	■■■	
Cost of goods sold	■■■	
Selling, general, and administrative expenses	10	
Depreciation	20	
EBIT	■■■	
Interest	■■■	
Earnings before tax	■■■	
Tax	■■■	
Earnings available for common stock	■■■	

- Cash ratio: .2.
- Return on total assets: .18.
- Return on equity: .41.
- Inventory turnover: 5.0.
- Receivables' collection period: 71.2 days.

12. Here are some data for five companies in the same industry:

	Company Code				
	A	B	C	D	E
Net income (millions)	$ 10	$ .5	$ 6.67	−$ 1	$ 6.67
Total book assets (millions)	$300	$30.0	$120.00	$50	$120.00
Shares outstanding (millions)	3	4	2	5	10
Share price	$100	$ 5	$ 50	$ 8	$ 10

You have been asked to calculate a measure of the industry price–earnings ratio. Discuss the possible ways that you might calculate such a measure. Does changing the method of calculation make a significant difference to the end result?

13. Describe some of the ways that the choice of accounting technique can temporarily depress or inflate earnings.

14. How would rapid inflation affect the accuracy and relevance of a manufacturing company's balance sheet and income statement? Does your answer depend on how much debt the company has issued?
15. In 1970 United Airlines bought four new jumbos for $21.8 million each. These planes were written down straight-line over 16 years to a residual value of $0.2 million each. However, they could have been sold in 1986 for about $20 million each.[22] How would the company's financial ratios have changed if it had used a depreciation schedule that more nearly reflected the actual decline in aircraft values?
16. The British food company Ranks Hovis McDougall (RHM) believed that some of its most valuable assets were its brand names. Yet these assets are not usually shown on the balance sheet. In 1988 RHM changed its accounting policy to include the value of brand names and thereby added £678 million (nearly $1.2 billion) to the balance sheet. Do you think that this change would facilitate comparisons between firms?
17. Suppose you wish to use financial ratios to estimate the risk of a company's stock. Which of those that we have described in this chapter are likely to be helpful? Can you think of other accounting measures of risk?
18. Look up some firms that have been in trouble. Plot the changes over the preceding years in the principal financial ratios. Are there any patterns?
19. List the major elements of a completed financial plan.
20. "There is no finance in financial planning models." Explain.
21. What are the dangers and disadvantages of using a financial model? Discuss.
22. Should a financial plan be considered an unbiased forecast of future cash flows, earnings, and other financial variables? Why or why not?
23. Our model of Executive Paper is an example of a top-down planning model. Some firms use a bottom-up financial planning model, which incorporates forecasts of revenues and costs for particular products, advertising plans, major investment projects, and so on. What sort of firms would you expect to use each type, and what would they use them for?
24. Corporate financial plans are often used as a basis for judging subsequent performance. What do you think can be learned from such comparisons? What problems are likely to arise, and how might you cope with these problems?
25. What problems are likely to be encountered in keeping the financial plan up-to-date?
26. The balancing item in the Executive Paper model is borrowing. What is meant by *balancing item*? How would the model change if dividends were made the balancing item instead? In that case how would you suggest that planned borrowing be determined?
27. Construct a new model for Executive Paper based on your answer to question 26. Does your model generate a feasible financial plan for 2000? (*Hint:* If it doesn't, you may have to allow the firm to issue stock.)
28. Executive Paper's financial manager believed that revenues in 2000 would rise by as much as 50 percent or by as little as 10 percent. Recalculate the pro forma financial statements under these two assumptions. How does the rate of growth in revenues affect the firm's borrowing requirement?

[22]See M. D. Staunton, *Pricing of Airline Assets and Their Valuation by Securities Markets*, unpublished PhD dissertation, London Business School, 1992.

TABLE 29.13

Financial statements for Executive Cheese Company, 2001 (figures in thousands).

Income Statement		
Revenue	$1,785	
Fixed costs	53	
Variable costs (80% of revenue)	1,428	
Depreciation	80	
Interest (at 11.8%)	24	
Taxes (at 40%)	80	
Net income	$ 120	
Sources and Uses of Funds		
Sources:		
Operating cash flow	$ 200	
Borrowing	36	
Stock issues	104	
Total sources	$ 340	
Uses:		
Increase in net working capital	$ 60	
Investment	200	
Dividends	80	
Total uses	$ 340	
Balance Sheet, Year-end		
	2001	**2000**
Assets:		
Net working capital	$ 400	$ 340
Fixed assets	800	680
Total assets	$1,200	$1,020
Liabilities:		
Debt	$ 240	$ 204
Book equity	960	816
Total liabilities	$1,200	$1,020

29. **a.** Use the Executive Paper model (Tables 29.6–29.8) to produce pro forma income statements, balance sheets, and sources and uses of funds statements for 2000 and 2001. Assume business as usual except that sales and costs were planned to expand by 30 percent per year, as were fixed assets and net working capital. The interest rate was forecasted to remain at 10 percent and stock issues were ruled out. Executive Paper also stuck to its 60 percent dividend payout ratio.

b. What are the firm's debt ratio and interest coverage under this plan?

c. Can the company continue to finance expansion by borrowing?

30. Table 29.13 shows the 2001 financial statements for the Executive Cheese Company. Annual depreciation is 10 percent of fixed assets at the beginning of the year, plus 10 percent of new investment. The company plans to invest a further $200 per year in fixed assets for the next five years and forecasts that the ratio of revenues to total assets at the start of each year will remain at 1.75. Fixed costs are expected to remain at $53, and variable costs, at 80 percent of revenue. The company's policy is to pay out two-thirds of net income as dividends and to maintain a book debt ratio of 20 percent.

TABLE 29.14

Financial statements for Dynastatics Corporation 2002 (figures in thousands).

Income Statement		
Revenue		$1,800
Fixed costs		56
Variable costs (80% of revenue)		1,440
Depreciation		80
Interest (8% of beginning-of-year debt)		24
Taxable income		200
Taxes (at 40%)		80
Net income		$ 120
Dividends	$80	
Retained earnings	$40	
Balance Sheet, Year-end		
	2002	**2001**
Assets:		
Net working capital	$ 400	$ 400
Fixed assets	800	800
Total assets	$1,200	$1,200
Liabilities and shareholders' equity:		
Debt	$ 300	$ 300
Equity	900	900
Total liabilities and shareholders' equity	$1,200	$1,200

TABLE 29.15

Financial statements for Eagle Sport Supply, 2002.

Income Statement	
Sales	$950
Costs	250
EBIT	700
Taxes	200
Net income	$500

Balance Sheet, Year-end	2001	2002		2001	2002
Assets	$2,700	$3,000	Debt	$ 900	$1,000
			Equity	1,800	2,000
Total	$2,700	$3,000	Total	$2,700	$3,000

a. Construct a model for Executive Cheese like the one in Tables 29.6–29.8.
b. Use your model to produce a set of financial statements for 2002.

31. Table 29.14 contains financial statements for Dynastatics Corporation. Although the company has not been growing, it now plans to expand and will increase net fixed assets (that is, assets net of depreciation) by $200 per year for the next five years. It forecasts that the ratio of revenues to total assets will remain fixed at 1.5. Annual

depreciation is 10 percent of fixed assets at the start of the year. Fixed costs are expected to remain at $56, and variable costs, at 80 percent of revenue. The company's policy is to pay out two-thirds of net income as dividends and to maintain a book debt ratio of 25 percent of total capital.

a. Produce a set of financial statements for 2007. Assume that net working capital will equal 50 percent of fixed assets.

b. Now assume that the balancing item is debt and that no equity is to be issued. Prepare a completed pro forma balance sheet for 2007. What is the projected debt ratio for 2003?

32. The financial statements of Eagle Sport Supply are shown in Table 29.15. For simplicity, "Costs" include interest. Assume that Eagle's assets are proportional to its sales.

a. Find Eagle's required external funds if it maintains a dividend payout ratio of 60 percent and plans a growth rate of 15 percent in 2003.

b. If Eagle chooses not to issue new shares of stock, what variable must be the balancing item? What will its value be?

c. Now suppose that the firm plans instead to increase long-term debt only to $1,100 and does not wish to issue any new shares of stock. Why must the dividend payment now be the balancing item? What will its value be?

33. a. What is the internal growth rate of Eagle Sports (see problem 32) if the dividend payout ratio is fixed at 60 percent and the equity-to-asset ratio is fixed at 2/3?

b. What is the sustainable growth rate?

34. Bio-Plasma Corp. is growing at 30 percent per year. It is all-equity-financed and has total assets of $1 million. Its return on equity is 20 percent. Its plowback ratio is 40 percent.

a. What is the internal growth rate?

b. What is the firm's need for external financing this year?

c. By how much would the firm increase its internal growth rate if it reduced its payout rate to zero?

d. By how much would such a move reduce the need for external financing? What do you conclude about the relationship between dividend policy and requirements for external financing?

CHALLENGE QUESTIONS

1. Take another look at Geomorph Trading's balance sheet in quiz question 9, and consider the following additional information:

Current Assets		Current Liabilities		Other Liabilities	
Cash	15	Payables	35	Deferred tax	32
Inventories	35	Taxes due	10	Unfunded pensions	22
Receivables	50	Bank loan	15	R&R reserve	16
	100		60		70

The "R&R reserve" covers the future costs of removal of an oil pipeline and environmental restoration of the pipeline route.

There are many ways to calculate a debt ratio for Geomorph. Suppose you are evaluating the safety of Geomorph's debt and want a debt ratio for comparison with the ratios of other companies in the same industry. Would you calculate the ratio in terms of total liabilities or total capitalization? What would you include in debt—the bank loan, the deferred tax account, the R&R reserve, the unfunded pension liability? Explain the pros and cons of these choices.

2. Take any firm whose financial statements are shown on the Market Insight database (**www.mhhe.com/edumarketinsight**) and make some plausible forecasts for future growth and the asset base needed to support that growth. Then use a spreadsheet program to develop a five-year financial plan. What financing is needed to support the planned growth? How vulnerable is the company to an error in your forecasts?

STANDARD
&POOR'S

CHAPTER THIRTY

SHORT-TERM FINANCIAL PLANNING

MOST OF THIS book is devoted to long-term financial decisions such as capital budgeting and the choice of capital structure. Such decisions are called *long-term* for two reasons. First, they usually involve long-lived assets or liabilities. Second, they are not easily reversed and therefore may commit the firm to a particular course of action for several years.

Short-term financial decisions generally involve short-lived assets and liabilities, and usually they are easily reversed. Compare, for example, a 60-day bank loan for $50 million with a $50 million issue of 20-year bonds. The bank loan is clearly a short-term decision. The firm can repay it two months later and be right back where it started. A firm might conceivably issue a 20-year bond in January and retire it in March, but it would be extremely inconvenient and expensive to do so. In practice, such a bond issue is a long-term decision, not only because of the bond's 20-year maturity but also because the decision to issue it cannot be reversed on short notice.

A financial manager responsible for short-term financial decisions does not have to look far into the future. The decision to take the 60-day bank loan could properly be based on cash-flow forecasts for the next few months only. The bond issue decision will normally reflect forecasted cash requirements 5, 10, or more years into the future.

Managers concerned with short-term financial decisions can avoid many of the difficult conceptual issues encountered elsewhere in this book. In a sense, short-term decisions are easier than long-term decisions, but they are not less important. A firm can identify extremely valuable capital investment opportunities, find the precise optimal debt ratio, follow the perfect dividend policy, and yet founder because no one bothers to raise the cash to pay this year's bills. Hence the need for short-term planning.

We start the chapter with an overview of the major classes of short-term assets and liabilities. We show how long-term financing decisions affect the firm's short-term financial planning problem. We describe how financial managers trace changes in cash and working capital, and we look at how they forecast month-by-month cash requirements or surpluses and develop short-term financing strategies. We conclude by examining more closely the principal sources of short-term finance.

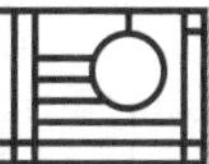

30.1 THE COMPONENTS OF WORKING CAPITAL

Short-term, or *current,* assets and liabilities are collectively known as **working capital.** Table 30.1 gives a breakdown of current assets and liabilities for all manufacturing corporations in the United States in 2000. Note that current assets are larger than current liabilities. **Net working capital** (current assets less current liabilities) was positive.

Current Assets

One important current asset is *accounts receivable.* When one company sells goods to another company or a government agency, it does not usually expect to be paid immediately. These unpaid bills, or *trade credit,* make up the bulk of accounts receivable. Companies also sell goods on credit to the final consumer. This *consumer credit* makes up the remainder of accounts receivable. We will discuss the management of receivables in Chapter 32. You will learn how companies decide which customers are good or bad credit risks and when it makes sense to offer credit.

Another important current asset is *inventory.* Inventories may consist of raw materials, work in process, or finished goods awaiting sale and shipment. Firms

TABLE 30.1

Current assets and liabilities for U.S. manufacturing corporations, first quarter, 2001 (figures in $ billions).

Source: U.S. Census Bureau, *Quarterly Financial Report for Manufacturing, Mining and Trade Corporations, First Quarter, 2001* (**www.census.gov/prod/www/abs/qfr-mm**).

Current Assets		Current Liabilities	
Cash	156.3	Short-term loans	228.4
Marketable securities	104.4	Accounts payable	357.3
Accounts receivable	527.2	Accrued income taxes	55.5
Inventories	510.7	Current payments due on long-term debt	85.3
Other current assets	248.9	Other current liabilities	507.4
Total	1547.5	Total	1233.9

Net working capital (current assets − current liabilities) = $1,547.5 − 1,233.9 = $313.6 billion

invest in inventory. The cost of holding inventory includes not only storage cost and the risk of spoilage or obsolescence but also the opportunity cost of capital, that is, the rate of return offered by other, equivalent-risk investment opportunities.[1] The benefits of holding inventory are often indirect. For example, a large inventory of finished goods (large relative to expected sales) reduces the chance of a "stockout" if demand is unexpectedly high. A producer holding a small finished-goods inventory is more likely to be caught short, unable to fill orders promptly. Similarly, large inventories of raw materials reduce the chance that an unexpected shortage would force the firm to shut down production or use a more costly substitute material.

Bulk orders for raw materials lead to large average inventories but may be worthwhile if the firm can obtain lower prices from suppliers. (That is, bulk orders may yield quantity discounts.) Firms are often willing to hold large inventories of finished goods for similar reasons. A large inventory of finished goods allows longer, more economical production runs. In effect, the production manager gives the firm a quantity discount.

The task of inventory management is to assess these benefits and costs and to strike a sensible balance. In manufacturing companies the production manager is best placed to make this judgment. Since the financial manager is not usually directly involved in inventory management, we will not discuss the inventory problem in detail.

The remaining current assets are cash and marketable securities. The cash consists of currency, demand deposits (funds in checking accounts), and time deposits (funds in savings accounts). The principal marketable security is commercial paper (short-term, unsecured notes sold by other firms). Other securities include U.S. Treasury bills and state and local government securities.

In choosing between cash and marketable securities, the financial manager faces a task like that of the production manager. There are always advantages to holding large "inventories" of cash—they reduce the risk of running out of cash and having to raise more on short notice. On the other hand, there is a cost to holding idle

[1]How risky are inventories? It is hard to generalize. Many firms just assume inventories have the same risk as typical capital investments and therefore calculate the cost of holding inventories using the firm's average opportunity cost of capital. You can think of many exceptions to this rule of thumb however. For example, some electronics components are made with gold connections. Should an electronics firm apply its average cost of capital to its inventory of gold? (See Section 11.1.)

cash balances rather than putting the money to work in marketable securities. In Chapter 31 we will tell you how the financial manager collects and pays out cash and decides on an optimal cash balance.

Current Liabilities

We have seen that a company's principal current asset consists of unpaid bills from other companies. One firm's credit must be another's debit. Therefore, it is not surprising that a company's principal current liability often consists of *accounts payable,* that is, outstanding payments to other companies. A firm that delays paying its bills is in effect borrowing money from its suppliers. So companies that are strapped for cash sometimes solve the problem by *stretching payables.*

To finance its investment in current assets, a company may rely on a variety of short-term loans. Banks and finance companies are the largest source of such loans, but companies may also issue short-term debt, called *commercial paper.* We will describe the different kinds of short-term debt toward the end of the chapter.

30.2 LINKS BETWEEN LONG-TERM AND SHORT-TERM FINANCING DECISIONS

All businesses require capital, that is, money invested in plant, machinery, inventories, accounts receivable, and all the other assets it takes to run a business efficiently. Typically, these assets are not purchased all at once but obtained gradually over time. Let us call the total cost of these assets the firm's *cumulative capital requirement.*

Most firms' cumulative capital requirement grows irregularly, like the wavy line in Figure 30.1. This line shows a clear upward trend as the firm's business grows. But there is also seasonal variation around the trend: In the figure the capital requirements peak late in each year. Finally, there would be unpredictable week-to-week and month-to-month fluctuations, but we have not attempted to show these in Figure 30.1.

The cumulative capital requirement can be met from either long-term or short-term financing. When long-term financing does not cover the cumulative capital requirement, the firm must raise short-term capital to make up the difference. When long-term financing *more* than covers the cumulative capital requirement, the firm has surplus cash available for short-term investment. Thus the amount of long-term financing raised, given the cumulative capital requirement, determines whether the firm is a short-term borrower or lender.

Lines *A*, *B*, and *C* in Figure 30.1 illustrate this. Each depicts a different long-term financing strategy. Strategy *A* always implies a short-term cash surplus. Strategy *C* implies a permanent need for short-term borrowing. Under *B*, which is probably the most common strategy, the firm is a short-term lender during part of the year and a borrower during the rest.

What is the *best* level of long-term financing relative to the cumulative capital requirement? It is hard to say. There is no convincing theoretical analysis of this question. We can make practical observations, however. First, most financial managers attempt to "match maturities" of assets and liabilities. That is, they finance long-lived assets like plant and machinery with long-term borrowing and equity. Second, most firms make a permanent investment in net working capital (current assets less current liabilities). This investment is financed from long-term sources.

FIGURE 30.1

The firm's cumulative capital requirement (colored line) is the cumulative investment in all the assets needed for the business. In this case the requirement grows year by year, but there is seasonal fluctuation within each year. The requirement for short-term financing is the difference between long-term financing (lines A^+, *A*, *B*, and *C*) and the cumulative capital requirement. If long-term financing follows line *C*, the firm always needs short-term financing. At line *B*, the need is seasonal. At lines *A* and A^+, the firm never needs short-term financing. There is always extra cash to invest.

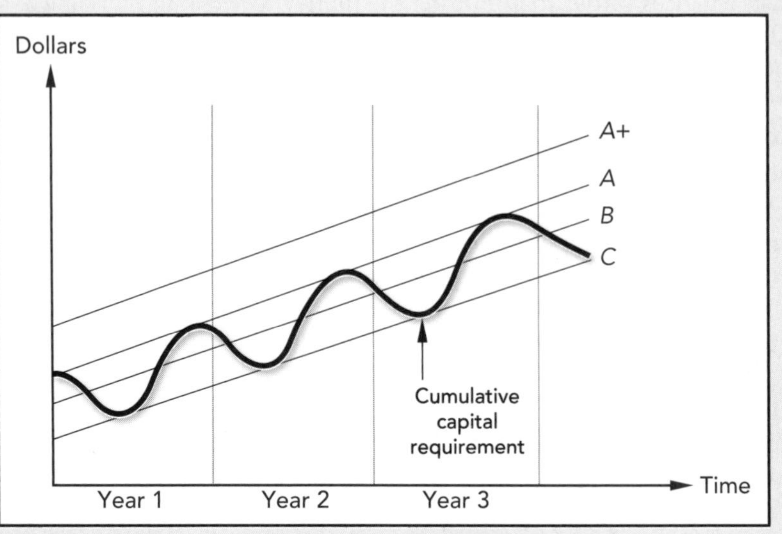

The Comforts of Surplus Cash

Many financial managers would feel more comfortable under strategy *A* than strategy *C*. Strategy A^+ (the highest line) would be still more relaxing. A firm with a surplus of long-term financing never has to worry about borrowing to pay next month's bills. But is the financial manager paid to be comfortable? Firms usually put surplus cash to work in Treasury bills or other marketable securities. This is at best a zero-NPV investment for a taxpaying firm.[2] Thus we think that firms with a *permanent* cash surplus ought to go on a diet, retiring long-term securities to reduce long-term financing to a level at or below the firm's cumulative capital requirement. That is, if the firm is on line A^+, it ought to move down to line *A*, or perhaps even lower.

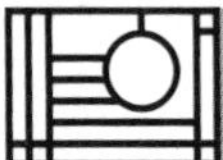

30.3 TRACING CHANGES IN CASH AND WORKING CAPITAL

Table 30.2 compares 2000 and 2001 year-end balance sheets for Dynamic Mattress Company. Table 30.3 shows the firm's income statement for 2001. Note that Dynamic's cash balance increased by $1 million during 2001. What caused this increase? Did the extra cash come from Dynamic Mattress Company's additional long-term borrowing, from reinvested earnings, from cash released by reducing inventory, or from extra credit extended by Dynamic's suppliers? (Note the increase in accounts payable.)

The correct answer is "all the above." Financial analysts often summarize sources and uses of cash in a statement like the one shown in Table 30.4. The statement shows that Dynamic *generated* cash from the following sources:

1. It issued $7 million of long-term debt.
2. It reduced inventory, releasing $1 million.

[2]If there is a tax advantage to borrowing, as most people believe, there must be a corresponding tax *disadvantage* to lending, and investment in Treasury bills has a negative NPV. See Section 18.1.

TABLE 30.2

Year-end balance sheets for 2000 and 2001 for Dynamic Mattress Company (figures in $ millions).

	2000	2001
Current assets:		
Cash	4	5
Marketable securities	0	5
Inventory	26	25
Accounts receivable	25	30
Total current assets	55	65
Fixed assets:		
Gross investment	56	70
Less depreciation	−16	−20
Net fixed assets	40	50
Total assets	95	115
Current liabilities:		
Bank loans	5	0
Accounts payable	20	27
Total current liabilities	25	27
Long-term debt	5	12
Net worth (equity and retained earnings)	65	76
Total liabilities and net worth	95	115

TABLE 30.3

Income statement for Dynamic Mattress Company, 2001 (figures in $ millions).

Note: Dividend = $1 million; retained earnings = $11 million.

Sales	350
Operating costs	−321
	29
Depreciation	−4
	25
Interest	−1
Pretax income	24
Tax at 50%	−12
Net income	12

3. It increased its accounts payable, in effect borrowing an additional $7 million from its suppliers.
4. By far the largest source of cash was Dynamic's operations, which generated $16 million. See Table 30.3, and note: Income ($12 million) understates cash flow because depreciation is deducted in calculating income. Depreciation is *not* a cash outlay. Thus, it must be added back in order to obtain operating cash flow.

Dynamic *used* cash for the following purposes:

1. It paid a $1 million dividend. (*Note:* The $11 million increase in Dynamic's equity is due to retained earnings: $12 million of equity income, less the $1 million dividend.)

TABLE 30.4

Sources and uses of cash for Dynamic Mattress Company, 2001 (figures in $ millions).

Sources:	
Issued long-term debt	7
Reduced inventories	1
Increased accounts payable	7
Cash from operations:	
Net income	12
Depreciation	4
Total sources	31
Uses:	
Repaid short-term bank loan	5
Invested in fixed assets	14
Purchased marketable securities	5
Increased accounts receivable	5
Dividend	1
Total uses	30
Increase in cash balance	1

2. It repaid a $5 million short-term bank loan.[3]
3. It invested $14 million. This shows up as the increase in gross fixed assets in Table 30.2.
4. It purchased $5 million of marketable securities.
5. It allowed accounts receivable to expand by $5 million. In effect, it lent this additional amount to its customers.

Tracing Changes in Net Working Capital

Financial analysts often find it useful to collapse all current assets and liabilities into a single figure for net working capital. Dynamic's net-working-capital balances were (in millions):

	Current Assets	Less	Current Liabilities	Equals	Net Working Capital
Year-end 2000	$55	–	$25	=	$30
Year-end 2001	$65	–	$27	=	$38

Table 30.5 gives balance sheets which report only net working capital, not individual current asset or liability items.

"Sources and uses" statements can likewise be simplified by defining *sources* as activities which contribute to net working capital and *uses* as activities which use up working capital. In this context working capital is usually referred to as *funds*, and a *sources and uses of funds statement* is presented.[4]

[3]This is principal repayment, not interest. Sometimes interest payments are explicitly recognized as a use of funds. If so, operating cash flow would be defined *before* interest, that is, as net income plus interest plus depreciation.

[4]We drew up a *sources and uses of funds* statement for Executive Paper in Section 29.1.

	2000	2001
Net working capital	30	38
Fixed assets:		
Gross investment	56	70
Less depreciation	−16	−20
Net fixed assets	40	50
Total net assets	70	88
Long-term debt	5	12
Net worth (equity and retained earnings)	65	76
Long-term liabilities and net worth*	70	88

TABLE 30.5

Condensed year-end balance sheets for 2000 and 2001 for Dynamic Mattress Company (figures in $ millions).

*When only *net* working capital appears on a firm's balance sheet, this figure (the sum of long-term liabilities and net worth) is often referred to as *total capitalization.*

Sources:	
Issued long-term debt	7
Cash from operations:	
Net income	12
Depreciation	4
	23
Uses:	
Invested in fixed assets	14
Dividend	1
	15
Increase in net working capital	8

TABLE 30.6

Sources and uses of funds (net working capital) for Dynamic Mattress Company, 2001 (figures in $ millions).

In 2000, Dynamic contributed to net working capital by

1. Issuing $7 million of long-term debt.
2. Generating $16 million from operations.

It used up net working capital by

1. Investing $14 million.
2. Paying a $1 million dividend.

The year's changes in net working capital are thus summarized by Dynamic Mattress Company's sources and uses of funds statement, given in Table 30.6.

Profits and Cash Flow

Now look back to Table 30.4, which shows sources and uses of *cash.* We want to register two warnings about the entry called *cash from operations.* It may not actually represent real dollars—dollars you can buy beer with.

First, depreciation may not be the only noncash expense deducted in calculating income. For example, most firms use different accounting procedures in their tax books than in their reports to shareholders. The point of special tax accounts is to minimize current taxable income. The effect is that the shareholder books overstate the firm's current cash tax liability,[5] and after-tax cash flow from operations is therefore understated.

Second, income statements record sales when made, not when the customer's payment is received. Think of what happens when Dynamic sells goods on credit. The company records a profit at the time of sale, but there is no cash inflow until the bills are paid. Since there is no cash inflow, there is no change in the company's cash balance, although there is an increase in working capital in the form of an increase in accounts receivable. No net addition to cash would be shown in a sources and uses statement like Table 30.4. The increase in cash from operations would be offset by an increase in accounts receivable.

Later, when the bills are paid, there is an increase in the cash balance. However, there is no further profit at this point and no increase in working capital. The increase in the cash balance is exactly matched by a decrease in accounts receivable.

That brings up an interesting characteristic of working capital. Imagine a company that conducts a very simple business. It buys raw materials for cash, processes them into finished goods, and then sells these goods on credit. The whole cycle of operations looks like this:

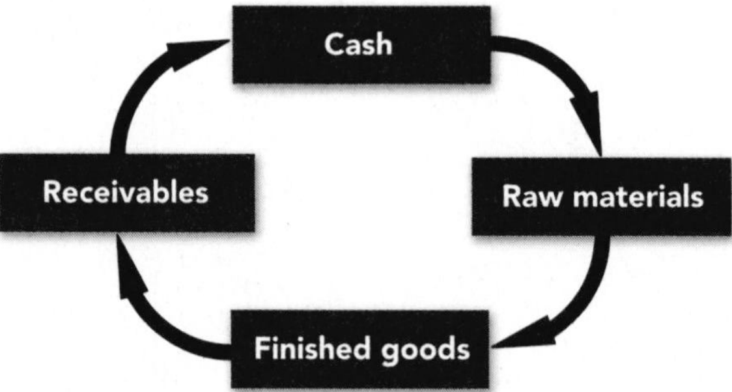

If you draw up a balance sheet at the beginning of the process, you see cash. If you delay a little, you find the cash replaced by inventories of raw materials and, still later, by inventories of finished goods. When the goods are sold, the inventories give way to accounts receivable, and finally, when the customers pay their bills, the firm draws out its profit and replenishes the cash balance.

There is only one constant in this process, namely, working capital. The components of working capital are constantly changing. That is one reason why (net) working capital is a useful summary measure of current assets and liabilities.

The strength of the working-capital measure is that it is unaffected by seasonal or other temporary movements between different current assets or liabilities. But the strength is also its weakness, for the working-capital figure hides a lot of interesting information. In our example cash was transformed into inventory, then into receivables, and back into cash again. But these assets have different degrees of risk and liquidity. You can't pay bills with inventory or with receivables, you must pay with cash.

[5]The difference between taxes reported and paid to the Internal Revenue Service shows up on the balance sheet as an increased deferred tax liability. The reason that a liability is recognized is that accelerated depreciation and other devices used to reduce current taxable income do not eliminate taxes; they only delay them. Of course, this reduces the present value of the firm's tax liability, but still the ultimate liability has to be recognized. In the sources and uses statements an increase in deferred taxes would be treated as a source of funds. In the Dynamic Mattress example we ignore deferred taxes.

FINANCE IN THE NEWS

FORD'S DISAPPEARING CASH MOUNTAIN

At the end of 1998 Ford had $23.8 billion in cash and marketable securities and only $9.8 billion in debt. But in the next three years Ford went on a shopping spree that resulted in the expenditure of more than $13 billion on acquisitions, such as Volvo Cars and Land Rover. In the same period Ford spent a total of $20 billion on new products and other capital projects. Within three years Ford's huge cash mountain had halved.

By most standards Ford remained relatively conservatively capitalized, but the outlook for the automobile industry was worsening rapidly. In the first nine months of 2001 Ford recorded a loss of nearly $5 billion, so that its operations became a cash drain rather than a source of cash. At the same time the company needed to set aside $3 billion to cover potential costs associated with alleged vehicle safety problems. As Ford faced a potential cash shortage, the company sought to conserve cash by halving its dividend payment and pruning its capital expenditure program.

Source: Ford Motor's cash drain is described in "Ford Motor's Cash Goes Subcompact," *The Wall Street Journal*, November 6, 2001.

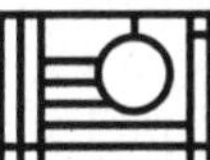

30.4 CASH BUDGETING

The past is interesting only for what one can learn from it. The financial manager's problem is to forecast *future* sources and uses of cash. These forecasts serve two purposes. First, they provide a standard, or budget, against which subsequent performance can be judged. Second, they alert the manager to future cash-flow needs. Cash, as we all know, has a habit of disappearing fast. Look, for example, at Finance in the News, which describes how Ford's large cash surplus rapidly turned into a shortage. Ford's financial manager needed to *plan* for this deficiency.

Preparing the Cash Budget: Inflow

There are at least as many ways to produce a quarterly cash budget as there are to skin a cat. Many large firms have developed elaborate corporate models; others use a spreadsheet program to plan their cash needs. The procedures of smaller firms may be less formal. But there are common issues that all firms must face when they forecast. We will illustrate these issues by continuing the example of Dynamic Mattress.

Most of Dynamic's cash inflow comes from the sale of mattresses. We therefore start with a sales forecast by quarter[6] for 2002:

	First Quarter	Second Quarter	Third Quarter	Fourth Quarter
Sales ($ millions)	87.5	78.5	116	131

[6]Most firms would forecast by month instead of by quarter. Sometimes weekly or even daily forecasts are made. But presenting a monthly forecast would triple the number of entries in Table 30.7 and subsequent tables. We wanted to keep the examples as simple as possible.

TABLE 30.7

To forecast Dynamic Mattress's collections on accounts receivable, you have to forecast sales and collection rates (figures in $ millions).

	First Quarter	Second Quarter	Third Quarter	Fourth Quarter
1. Receivables at start of period	30	32.5	30.7	38.2
2. Sales	87.5	78.5	116	131
3. Collections:				
Sales in current period (80%)	70	62.8	92.8	104.8
Sales in last period (20%)	15*	17.5	15.7	23.2
Total collections	85	80.3	108.5	128.0
4. Receivables at end of period 4 = 1 + 2 − 3	32.5	30.7	38.2	41.2

*Sales in the fourth quarter of the previous year were $75 million.

But sales become accounts receivable before they become cash. Cash flow comes from *collections* on accounts receivable.

Most firms keep track of the average time it takes customers to pay their bills. From this they can forecast what proportion of a quarter's sales is likely to be converted into cash in that quarter and what proportion is likely to be carried over to the next quarter as accounts receivable. Suppose that 80 percent of sales are "cashed in" in the immediate quarter and 20 percent are cashed in in the next. Table 30.7 shows forecasted collections under this assumption.

In the first quarter, for example, collections from current sales are 80 percent of $87.5, or $70 million. But the firm also collects 20 percent of the previous quarter's sales, or .2(75) = $15 million. Therefore total collections are $70 + $15 = $85 million.

Dynamic started the first quarter with $30 million of accounts receivable. The quarter's sales of $87.5 million were *added* to accounts receivable, but collections of $85 million were *subtracted*. Therefore, as Table 30.7 shows, Dynamic ended the quarter with accounts receivable of $30 + 87.5 − 85 = $32.5 million. The general formula is

$$\text{Ending accounts receivable} = \text{beginning accounts receivable} + \text{sales} - \text{collections}$$

The top section of Table 30.8 shows forecasted sources of cash for Dynamic Mattress. Collection of receivables is the main source, but it is not the only one. Perhaps the firm plans to dispose of some land or expects a tax refund or payment of an insurance claim. All such items are included as "other" sources. It is also possible that you may raise additional capital by borrowing or selling stock, but we don't want to prejudge that question. Therefore, for the moment we just assume that Dynamic will not raise further long-term finance.

Preparing the Cash Budget: Outflow

So much for the incoming cash. Now for the outgoing cash. There always seem to be many more uses for cash than there are sources. For simplicity, we have condensed the uses into four categories in Table 30.8.

1. *Payments on accounts payable.* You have to pay your bills for raw materials, parts, electricity, etc. The cash-flow forecast assumes all these bills are paid on time, although Dynamic could probably delay payment to some extent. Delayed payment is sometimes called *stretching your payables.* Stretching is one source of short-term financing, but for most firms it is an expensive

	First Quarter	Second Quarter	Third Quarter	Fourth Quarter
Sources of cash:				
Collections on accounts receivable	85	80.3	108.5	128
Other	0	0	12.5	0
Total sources	85	80.3	121	128
Uses of cash:				
Payments on accounts payable	65	60	55	50
Labor, administrative, and other expenses	30	30	30	30
Capital expenditures	32.5	1.3	5.5	8
Taxes, interest, and dividends	4	4	4.5	5
Total uses	131.5	95.3	95	93
Sources minus uses	−46.5	−15.0	+26	+35
Calculation of short-term financing requirement:				
1. Cash at start of period	5	−41.5	−56.5	−30.5
2. Change in cash balance (sources less uses)	−46.5	−15.0	+26	+35
3. Cash at end of period* 1 + 2 = 3	−41.5	−56.5	−30.5	+4.5
4. Minimum operating cash balance	5	5	5	5
5. Cumulative short-term financing required† 5 = 4 − 3	46.5	61.5	35.5	.5

TABLE 30.8

Dynamic Mattress's cash budget for 2002 (figures in $ millions).

*Of course, firms cannot literally hold a negative amount of cash. This is the amount the firm will have to raise to pay its bills.
†A negative sign would indicate a cash *surplus*. But in this example the firm must raise cash for all quarters.

source, because by stretching they lose discounts given to firms that pay promptly. This is discussed in more detail in Section 32.1.

2. *Labor, administrative, and other expenses.* This category includes all other regular business expenses.
3. *Capital expenditures.* Note that Dynamic Mattress plans a major capital outlay in the first quarter.
4. *Taxes, interest, and dividend payments.* This includes interest on presently outstanding long-term debt but does not include interest on any additional borrowing to meet cash requirements in 2002. At this stage in the analysis, Dynamic does not know how much it will have to borrow, or whether it will have to borrow at all.

The forecasted net inflow of cash (sources minus uses) is shown in the box in Table 30.8. Note the large negative figure for the first quarter: a $46.5 million forecasted *outflow.* There is a smaller forecasted outflow in the second quarter, and then substantial cash inflows in the second half of the year.

The bottom part of Table 30.8 (below the box) calculates how much financing Dynamic will have to raise if its cash-flow forecasts are right. It starts the year with $5 million in cash. There is a $46.5 million cash outflow in the first quarter, and so Dynamic will have to obtain at least $46.5 − 5 = $41.5 million of additional financing.

This would leave the firm with a forecasted cash balance of exactly zero at the start of the second quarter.

Most financial managers regard a planned cash balance of zero as driving too close to the edge of the cliff. They establish a *minimum operating cash balance* to absorb unexpected cash inflows and outflows. We will assume that Dynamic's minimum operating cash balance is $5 million. That means it will have to raise the full $46.5 million cash outflow in the first quarter and $15 million more in the second quarter. Thus its cumulative financing requirement is $61.5 million in the second quarter. This is the peak, fortunately: The cumulative requirement declines in the third quarter by $26 million to $35.5 million. In the final quarter Dynamic is almost out of the woods: Its cash balance is $4.5 million, just $.5 million shy of its minimum operating balance.

The next step is to develop a *short-term financing plan* that covers the forecasted requirements in the most economical way possible. We will move on to that topic after two general observations:

1. The large cash outflows in the first two quarters do not necessarily spell trouble for Dynamic Mattress. In part, they reflect the capital investment made in the first quarter: Dynamic is spending $32.5 million, but it should be acquiring an asset worth that much or more. In part, the cash outflows reflect low sales in the first half of the year; sales recover in the second half.[7] If this is a predictable seasonal pattern, the firm should have no trouble borrowing to tide it over the slow months.
2. Table 30.8 is only a best guess about future cash flows. It is a good idea to think about the *uncertainty* in your estimates. For example, you could undertake a sensitivity analysis, in which you inspect how Dynamic's cash requirements would be affected by a shortfall in sales or by a delay in collections. The trouble with such sensitivity analyses is that you are changing only one item at a time, whereas in practice a downturn in the economy might affect, say, sales levels *and* collection rates. An alternative but more complicated solution is to build a model of the cash budget and then to simulate to determine the probability of cash requirements significantly above or below the forecasts shown in Table 30.8.[8] If cash requirements are difficult to predict, you may wish to hold additional cash or marketable securities to cover a possible unexpected cash outflow.

30.5 THE SHORT-TERM FINANCING PLAN

Dynamic's cash budget defines its problem: Its financial manager must find short-term financing to cover the firm's forecasted cash requirements. There are dozens of sources of short-term financing, but for simplicity we assume that Dynamic has just two options.

Options for Short-Term Financing

1. *Bank loan:* Dynamic has an existing arrangement with its bank allowing it to borrow up to $38 million at an interest cost of 10 percent a year or 2.5

[7]Maybe people buy more mattresses late in the year when the nights are longer.

[8]In other words, you could use Monte Carlo simulation. See Section 10.2.

percent per quarter. The firm can borrow and repay whenever it wants to as long as it does not exceed its credit limit.

2. *Stretching payables:* Dynamic can also raise capital by putting off paying its bills. The financial manager believes that Dynamic can defer the following amounts in each quarter:

	First Quarter	Second Quarter	Third Quarter	Fourth Quarter
Amount deferrable ($ millions)	52	48	44	40

Thus, $52 million can be saved in the first quarter by *not* paying bills in that quarter. (Note that the cash-flow forecasts in Table 30.8 assumed that these bills *will* be paid in the first quarter.) If deferred, these payments *must* be made in the second quarter. Similarly, up to $48 million of the second quarter bills can be deferred to the third quarter, and so on.

Stretching payables is often costly, even if no ill will is incurred. The reason is that suppliers may offer discounts for prompt payment. Dynamic loses this discount if it pays late. In this example we assume the lost discount is 5 percent of the amount deferred. In other words, if a $100 payment is delayed, the firm must pay $105 in the next quarter.

Dynamic's Financing Plan

With these two options, the short-term financing strategy is obvious. Use the bank loan first, if necessary up to the $38 million limit. If there is still a shortage of cash, stretch payables.

Table 30.9 shows the resulting plan. In the first quarter the plan calls for borrowing the full amount available from the bank ($38 million) and stretching $3.5 million of payables (see lines 1 and 2 in the table). In addition the company sells the $5 million of marketable securities it held at the end of 1999 (line 8). Thus it raises 38 + 3.5 + 5 = $46.5 million of cash in the first quarter (line 10).

In the second quarter, the plan calls for Dynamic to continue to borrow $38 million from the bank and to stretch $19.7 million of payables. This raises a further $16.2 million after paying off the $3.5 million of bills deferred from the first quarter.

Why raise $16.2 million when Dynamic needs only an additional $15 million to finance its operations? The answer is that the company must pay interest on the borrowings that it undertook in the first quarter and it foregoes interest on the marketable securities that were sold.[9]

In the third and fourth quarters the plan calls for Dynamic to pay off its debt and to make a small purchase of marketable securities.

Evaluating the Plan

Does the plan shown in Table 30.9 solve Dynamic's short-term financing problem? No: The plan is feasible, but Dynamic can probably do better. The most glaring weakness is its reliance on stretching payables, an extremely expensive financing

[9]The bank loan calls for quarterly interest of .025 × 38 = $.95 million; the lost discount on the stretched payables amounts to .05 × 3.5 = $.175 million; and the interest lost on the marketable securities is .02 × 5 = $.1 million.

TABLE 30.9

Dynamic Mattress's financing plan (figures in $ millions).

Note: Column sums subject to rounding error.

*We assume that the first interest payment occurs one quarter after a loan is taken out.

†Dynamic sold $5 million of marketable securities in the first quarter. The yield is assumed to be 2 percent per quarter.

‡From Table 30.8.

	First Quarter	Second Quarter	Third Quarter	Fourth Quarter
New borrowing:				
1. Bank loan	38.0	0.0	0.0	0.0
2. Stretching payables	3.5	19.7	0.0	0.0
3. Total	41.5	19.7	0.0	0.0
Repayments:				
4. Bank loan	0.0	0.0	4.3	33.7
5. Stretching payables	0.0	3.5	19.7	0.0
6. Total	0.0	3.5	24.0	33.7
7. Net new borrowing	41.5	16.2	−24.0	−33.7
8. Plus securities sold	5.0	0.0	0.0	0.0
9. Less securities bought	0.0	0.0	0.0	0.4
10. Total cash raised	46.5	16.2	−24.0	−34.1
Interest payments*				
11. Bank loan	0.0	1.0	1.0	0.8
12. Stretching payables	0.0	0.2	1.0	0.0
13. Interest on securities sold†	0.0	0.1	0.1	0.1
14. Net interest paid	0.0	1.2	2.0	0.9
15. Cash required for operations‡	46.5	15.0	−26.0	−35.0
16. Total cash required	46.5	16.2	−24.0	−34.1

device. Remember that it costs Dynamic 5 percent *per quarter* to delay paying bills—20 percent per year at simple interest. The first plan would merely stimulate the financial manager to search for cheaper sources of short-term borrowing.

The financial manager would ask several other questions as well. For example:

1. Does the plan yield satisfactory current and quick ratios?[10] Its bankers may be worried if these ratios deteriorate.[11]
2. Are there intangible costs of stretching payables? Will suppliers begin to doubt Dynamic's creditworthiness?
3. Does the plan for 2002 leave Dynamic in good financial shape for 2003? (Here the answer is yes, since Dynamic will have paid off all short-term borrowing by the end of the year.)
4. Should Dynamic try to arrange long-term financing for the major capital expenditure in the first quarter? This seems sensible, following the rule of thumb that long-term assets deserve long-term financing. It would also reduce the need for short-term borrowing dramatically. A counterargument is that Dynamic is financing the capital investment *only temporarily* by short-term borrowing. By year-end, the investment is paid for by cash from operations. Thus Dynamic's initial decision not to seek immediate long-

[10]These ratios are discussed in Chapter 29.

[11]We have not worked out these ratios explicitly, but you can infer from Table 30.9 that they would be fine at the end of the year but relatively low in midyear, when Dynamic's borrowing is high.

term financing may reflect a preference for ultimately financing the investment with retained earnings.

5. Perhaps the firm's operating and investment plans can be adjusted to make the short-term financing problem easier. Is there any easy way of deferring the first quarter's large cash outflow? For example, suppose that the large capital investment in the first quarter is for new mattress-stuffing machines to be delivered and installed in the first half of the year. The new machines are not scheduled to be ready for full-scale use until August. Perhaps the machine manufacturer could be persuaded to accept 60 percent of the purchase price on delivery and 40 percent when the machines are installed and operating satisfactorily.
6. Dynamic may also be able to release cash by reducing the level of other current assets. For example, it could reduce receivables by getting tough with customers who are late paying their bills. (The cost is that in the future these customers may take their business elsewhere.) Or it may be able to get by with lower inventories of mattresses. (The cost is that it may lose business if there is a rush of orders that it cannot supply.)

Short-term financing plans are developed by trial and error. You lay out one plan, think about it, and then try again with different assumptions on financing and investment alternatives. You continue until you can think of no further improvements.

Trial and error is important because it helps you understand the real nature of the problem the firm faces. Here we can draw a useful analogy between the *process* of planning and Chapter 10, "A Project Is Not a Black Box." In Chapter 10 we described sensitivity analysis and other tools used by firms to find out what makes capital investment projects tick and what can go wrong with them. Dynamic's financial manager faces the same kind of task: not just to choose a plan but to understand what can go wrong with it and what will be done if conditions change unexpectedly.[12]

A Note on Short-Term Financial Planning Models

Working out a consistent short-term plan requires burdensome calculations.[13] Fortunately much of the arithmetic can be delegated to a computer. Many large firms have built *short-term financial planning models* to do this. Smaller companies like Dynamic Mattress do not face so much detail and complexity and find it easier to work with a spreadsheet program on a personal computer. In either case the financial manager specifies forecasted cash requirements or surpluses, interest rates, credit limits, etc., and the model grinds out a plan like the one shown in Table 30.9. The computer also produces balance sheets, income statements, and whatever special reports the financial manager may require.

Smaller firms that do not want custom-built models can rent general-purpose models offered by banks, accounting firms, management consultants, or specialized computer software firms.

[12]This point is even more important in *long-term* financial planning. See Chapter 29.

[13]If you doubt that, look again at Table 30.9. Notice that the cash requirements in each quarter depend on borrowing in the previous quarter, because borrowing creates an obligation to pay interest. Also, borrowing under a line of credit may require additional cash to meet compensating balance requirements; if so, that means still more borrowing and still higher interest charges in the next quarter. Moreover, the problem's complexity would have been tripled had we not simplified by forecasting per quarter rather than by month.

Most of these models are *simulation* programs.[14] They simply work out the consequences of the assumptions and policies specified by the financial manager. *Optimization* models for short-term financial planning are also available. These models are usually linear programming models. They search for the *best* plan from a range of alternative policies identified by the financial manager.

As a matter of fact, we used a linear programming model developed by Pogue and Bussard[15] to generate Dynamic Mattress's financial plans. Of course, in that simple example we hardly needed a linear programming model to identify the best strategy. It was obvious that Dynamic should always use the line of credit first, turning to the second-best alternative (stretching payables) only when the limit on the line of credit was reached. The Pogue–Bussard model nevertheless did the arithmetic quickly and easily.

Optimization helps when the firm faces complex problems with many interdependent alternatives and restrictions for which trial and error might never identify the *best* combination of alternatives.

Of course the best plan for one set of assumptions may prove disastrous if the assumptions are wrong. Thus the financial manager has to explore the implications of alternative assumptions about future cash flows, interest rates, and so on. Linear programming can help identify good strategies, but even with an optimization model the financial plan is still sought by trial and error.

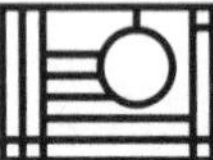

30.6 SOURCES OF SHORT-TERM BORROWING

Dynamic solved the greater part of its cash shortage by borrowing from a bank. But banks are not the only source of short-term loans. Finance companies are also a major source of cash, particularly for financing receivables and inventories.[16] In addition to borrowing from an intermediary like a bank or finance company, firms also sell short-term commercial paper or medium-term notes directly to investors. It is time to look more closely at these sources of short-term funds.

Bank Loans

To finance its investment in current assets, a company may rely on a variety of short-term loans. Obviously, if you approach a bank for a loan, the bank's lending officer is likely to ask searching questions about your firm's financial position and its plans for the future. Also, the bank will want to monitor the firm's subsequent progress. There is, however, a good side to this. Other investors know that banks

---

[14]Like the simulation models described in Section 10.2, except that the short-term planning models rarely include uncertainty explicitly. The models referred to here are built and used in the same way as the long-term financial planning models described in Section 29.4.

[15]G. A. Pogue and R. N. Bussard, "A Linear Programming Model for Short-Term Financial Planning under Uncertainty," *Sloan Management Review,* 13 (Spring 1972), pp. 69–99.

[16]*Finance companies* are firms that specialize in lending to businesses or individuals. They include independent firms, such as Household Finance, as well as subsidiaries of nonfinancial corporations, such as General Motors Acceptance Corporation (GMAC). In their lending finance companies compete with banks. However, they raise funds not by attracting deposits, as banks do, but by issuing commercial paper and other longer-term securities.

are hard to convince, and, therefore, when a company announces that it has arranged a large bank facility, the share price tends to rise.[17]

Bank loans come in a variety of flavors.[18] Here are a few of the ways that they differ.

Commitment Companies sometimes wait until they need the money before they apply for a bank loan, but nearly three-quarters of commercial bank loans are made under commitment. In this case the company establishes a line of credit that allows it to borrow from the bank up to an established limit. This line of credit may be an *evergreen credit* with no fixed maturity, but more commonly it is a *revolving credit* (*revolver*) with a fixed maturity of up to three years.

Credit lines are relatively expensive, for in addition to paying interest on any borrowings the company must pay a commitment fee on the unused amount. In exchange for this extra cost, the firm receives a valuable option: It has guaranteed access to the bank's money at a fixed spread over the general level of interest rates. This amounts to a put option, because the firm can sell its debt to the bank on fixed terms even if its own creditworthiness deteriorates or the cost of credit rises. The growth in the use of credit lines is changing the role of banks. They are no longer simply lenders; they are also in the business of providing companies with liquidity insurance.

Many companies discovered the value of this insurance in 1998, when Russia defaulted on its borrowings and created turmoil in the world's debt markets. Companies in the United States suddenly found it much more expensive to issue their own debt to investors. Those who had arranged lines of credit with their banks rushed to take advantage of them. As a result, new debt issues languished, while bank lending boomed.[19]

Maturity Most bank loans are for only a few months. For example, a company may need a short-term *bridge loan* to finance the purchase of new equipment or the acquisition of another firm. In this case the loan serves as interim financing until the purchase is completed and long-term financing is arranged. Often a short-term loan may be needed to finance a temporary increase in inventory. Such a loan is described as *self-liquidating;* in other words, the sale of goods provides the cash to repay the loan.

Banks also provide longer-term loans, known as *term loans.* A term loan typically has a maturity of four to five years. Usually the loan is repaid in level amounts over this period, though there is sometimes a large final balloon payment or just a single bullet payment at maturity. Banks can accommodate the repayment pattern to the anticipated cash flows of the borrower. For example, the first repayment might be delayed a year until the new factory is completed. Term loans are often renegotiated before maturity. Banks are willing to do this if the

[17]See C. James, "Some Evidence on the Uniqueness of Bank Loans," *Journal of Financial Economics* 19 (1987), pp. 217–235.

[18]The results of a survey of the terms of business lending by banks in the United States are published quarterly in the *Federal Reserve Bulletin* (see **www.federalreserve.gov/releases/E2/**).

[19]The rush to draw on bank lines of credit is described in M. R. Saidenberg and P. E. Strahan, "Are Banks Still Important for Financing Large Businesses?" *Federal Reserve Bank of New York, Current Issues in Economics and Finance* 5 (August 1999), pp. 1–6.

borrower is an established customer, remains creditworthy, and has a sound business reason for making the change.[20]

Rate of Interest Short-term bank loans are often made at a fixed rate of interest, which is often quoted as a discount. For example, if the interest rate on a one-year loan is stated as a discount of 5 percent, the borrower receives 100 − 5 = $95 and undertakes to pay $100 at the end of the year. The return on such a loan is not 5 percent, but 5/95 = .0526, or 5.26 percent.

For longer-term bank loans the interest rate is usually linked to the general level of interest rates. The most common benchmarks are the London Interbank Offered Rate (LIBOR), the federal funds rate,[21] or the bank's prime rate. Thus, if the rate is set at "1 percent over LIBOR," the borrower may pay 5 percent in the first three months when LIBOR is 4 percent, 6 percent in the next three months when LIBOR is 5 percent, and so on.[22]

Syndicated Loans Some bank loans are far too large for a single bank. In these cases the loan may be arranged by one or more lead banks and then parceled out among a syndicate of banks. For example, when Vodafone Airtouch needed to borrow $24 billion (€25 billion) to help finance its bid for the German telephone company, Mannesmann, it engaged 11 banks from around the world to arrange a large syndicate of banks that would lend the cash.

Loan Sales Large banks often have more demand for loans than they can satisfy; for smaller banks it is the other way around. Banks with an excess demand for loans may solve the problem by selling a portion of their existing loans to other institutions. Loan sales have mushroomed in recent years. In 1991 they totalled only $8 million; by 2000 they had reached $129 billion.[23]

These loan sales generally take one of two forms: *assignments* or *participations*. In the former case a portion of the loan is transferred with the agreement of the borrower. In the second case the lead bank maintains its relationship with its borrowers but agrees to pay over to the buyer a portion of the cash flows that it receives.

Participations often involve a single loan, but sometimes they can be huge deals involving hundreds of loans. Because these deals change a collection of nonmarketable bank loans into marketable securities, they are known as *securitizations*. For example, in 1996 the British bank, Natwest, securitized about one-sixth of its loan book. Natwest first put together a $5 billion package of about 200 loans to major firms in 17 different countries. It then sold notes, each of which promised to pay a proportion of the cash that it received from the package of loans. Because the notes provided the chance to share in a diversified portfolio of high-quality loans, they proved very popular with investors from around the world.

Security If a bank is concerned about a firm's credit risk, it will ask the firm to provide security for the loan. Since the bank is lending on a short-term basis, this

[20]Term loans typically allow the borrower to repay early, but in many cases the loan agreement specifies that the firm must pay a penalty for early repayment.

[21]The federal funds rate is the rate at which banks lend excess reserves to each other.

[22]In addition to paying interest, the borrower may be obliged to maintain a minimum interest-free deposit (*compensating balance*) with the bank. Compensating balances for bank loans are now relatively rare.

[23]Loan Pricing Corporation (**www.loanpricing.com**).

security usually consists of liquid assets such as receivables, inventories, or securities. Sometimes the bank will accept a *floating charge* against these assets.[24] This gives it a general claim if the firm defaults, but it does not specify the assets in detail, and it sets few restrictions on what the company can do with the assets.

More commonly, banks will require specific collateral. For example, suppose that there is a significant delay between the time that you ship your goods and when your customers pay you. If you need the money up front, you can borrow using these receivables as collateral. First, you must send the bank a copy of each invoice and provide it with a claim against the money that you receive from your customers. The bank will then lend up to 80 percent of the value of the receivables.

Each day, as you make more sales, your collateral increases and you can borrow more money. Each day also some customers pay their bills. This money is placed in a special collateral account under the bank's control and is periodically used to reduce the size of the loan. Therefore, as the firm's business fluctuates, so does the amount of the collateral and the size of the loan.[25]

You can also use inventories as security for a loan. For example, if your goods are stored in a warehouse, you need to arrange for an independent warehouse company to provide the bank with a receipt showing that the goods are held on the bank's behalf. When the loan is repaid, the bank returns the warehouse receipt and you are free to remove the goods.[26]

Banks are naturally choosy about the collateral that they will accept. They want to make sure that they can identify and sell the collateral if you default. For example, they may be happy to lend against a warehouse full of a standard nonperishable commodity, but they would turn up their nose at a warehouse of ripe Camemberts.

Banks also need to ensure that the collateral is kept safe and the borrower doesn't sell the assets and run off with the money. This is what happened in the great salad oil swindle. Fifty-one banks and companies made loans of nearly $200 million to the Allied Crude Vegetable Oil Refining Corporation. In return the company agreed to provide security in the form of storage tanks full of valuable salad oil. Unfortunately, the cursory inspections of the tanks failed to notice that they simply contained seawater and sludge. When the fraud was discovered, the president of Allied went to jail and the 51 lenders were left out in the cold, looking for their $200 million.[27] Lenders have been more careful since then, but Finance in the News shows that even old scams can still work.

Commercial Paper

Banks borrow money from one group of firms or individuals and relend the money to another group. They make their profit by charging the borrower a higher rate of interest than they offer the lender.

---

[24]Floating charges are common in other countries.

[25]In Chapter 32 we will describe how firms sometimes raise money by selling their receivables to a factor. The factor is responsible for collecting the debt and suffers any losses if the customers don't pay. When you pledge your receivables as collateral for a loan, *you* remain responsible for collecting the debt and *you* suffer if a customer is delinquent.

[26]It is not always practicable to keep inventory in a warehouse. For example, automobile dealers need to display their cars in a showroom. One solution is to enter into a floor-planning arrangement in which the finance company buys the cars and the dealer holds them in trust. When the cars are sold, the proceeds are used to redeem the cars from the finance company.

[27]See N.C. Miller, *The Great Salad Oil Swindle,* London, Gollancz, 1966.

FINANCE IN THE NEWS

THE HAZARDS OF SECURED BANK LENDING

The National Safety Council of Australia's Victoria Division had been a sleepy outfit until John Friedrich took over. Under its new management, NSC members trained like commandos and were prepared to go anywhere and do anything. They saved people from drowning, they fought fires, found lost bushwalkers and went down mines. Their lavish equipment included 22 helicopters, 8 aircraft and a mini-submarine. Soon the NSC began selling its services internationally.

Unfortunately the NSC's paramilitary outfit cost millions of dollars to run—far more than it earned in revenue. Friedrich bridged the gap by borrowing $A236 million of debt. The banks were happy to lend because the NSC's debt appeared well secured. At one point the company showed $A107 million of receivables (that is money owed by its customers), which it pledged as security for bank loans. Later checks revealed that many of these customers did not owe the NSC a cent. In other cases banks took comfort in the fact that their loans were secured by containers of valuable rescue gear. There were more than 100 containers stacked around the NSC's main base. Only a handful contained any equipment, but these were the ones that the bankers saw when they came to check that their loans were safe. Sometimes a suspicious banker would ask to inspect a particular container. Friedrich would then explain that it was away on exercise, fly the banker across the country in a light plane and point to a container well out in the bush. The container would of course be empty, but the banker had no way to know that.

Six years after Friedrich was appointed CEO, his massive fraud was uncovered. But a few days before a warrant could be issued, Friedrich disappeared. Although he was eventually caught and arrested, he shot himself before he could come to trial. Investigations revealed that Friedrich was operating under an assumed name, having fled from his native Germany, where he was wanted by the police. Many rumors continued to circulate about Friedrich. He was variously alleged to have been a plant of the CIA and the KGB and the NSC was said to have been behind an attempted counter-coup in Fiji. For the banks there was only one hard truth. Their loans to the NSC, which had appeared so well secured, would never be repaid.

Source: Adapted from Chapter 7 of T. Sykes, *The Bold Riders*, Allen & Unwin, St. Leonards, NSW, Australia, 1994.

Sometimes it is convenient to have a bank in the middle. It saves the lenders the trouble of looking for borrowers and assessing their creditworthiness, and it saves borrowers the trouble of looking for lenders. Depositors do not care whom the bank lends to: They need only satisfy themselves that the bank as a whole is safe.

There are also occasions on which it is *not* worth paying an intermediary to perform these functions. Large well-known companies can bypass the banking system by issuing their own short-term unsecured notes. These notes are known as **commercial paper (CP).** Financial institutions, such as bank holding companies and finance companies,[28] also issue commercial paper, sometimes in very large quantities. For example, GE Capital Corporation has nearly $70 billion of commercial paper in issue. The major issuers of commercial paper have set up their own marketing departments and sell their paper directly to investors, often

[28] *A bank holding company* is a firm that owns both a bank and nonbanking subsidiaries.

using the Web to do so. Smaller companies sell through dealers who receive a fee for marketing the issue.

Commercial paper in the United States has a maximum maturity of nine months, though most paper is for 60 days or less. Buyers of commercial paper generally hold it to maturity, but the company or dealer that sells the paper is usually prepared to repurchase it earlier.

The majority of commercial paper is issued by high-grade, nationally known companies.[29] Companies generally support their issue of commercial paper by arranging a backup line of credit with a bank, which guarantees that they can find the money to repay the paper.[30] The risk of default is, therefore, small.

Commercial paper is very popular with major companies. By cutting out the intermediary, they are able to borrow at rates that may be 1 to 1.5 percent below the prime rate charged by banks. Even after allowing for a dealer's commission and the cost of any backup line of credit, this is still a substantial savings. Banks have felt the competition from commercial paper and have been prepared to reduce their rates to blue-chip customers. As a result, "prime rate" doesn't mean what it used to. It once meant the rate banks charged their most creditworthy customers. Now the prime customers often pay less than the prime rate.

Medium-Term Notes

New issues of securities do not need to be registered with the SEC as long as they mature within 270 days. So by limiting the maturity of commercial paper issues, companies can avoid the delays and expense of registration. However, large blue-chip companies also make regular issues of unsecured **medium-term notes (MTNs).**

You can think of MTNs as a hybrid between corporate bonds and commercial paper. Like bonds, they are relatively long-term instruments; their maturity is never less than 270 days and may be as long as 30 years.[31] On the other hand, like commercial paper, MTNs are not underwritten but are sold on a regular basis either through dealers or, occasionally, direct to investors. Borrowers, such as finance companies, that are always needing cash, welcome the flexibility of MTNs. For example, a company may tell its dealer the amount of money that it needs to raise that week, the range of maturities that it can offer, and the maximum interest that it is prepared to pay. It is then up to the dealers to find the buyers.

[29]Moody's and Standard and Poor's publish quality ratings for commercial paper. For example, Moody's provides three ratings, from P-1 (denoting Prime 1, the highest-grade paper) to P-3. Most investors are reluctant to buy low-rated paper. For example, money-market funds are largely limited to holding P-1 paper.

[30]Banks often reserve the right to cancel this line of credit if there is a *material adverse change* in the company's condition. However, lower-rated companies may back their paper with an irrevocable line of credit.

[31]The Walt Disney Company has even used its MTN shelf registration to issue a 100-year bond.

SUMMARY

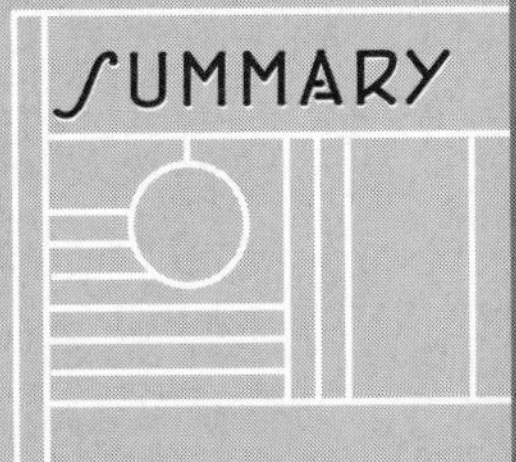

Short-term financial planning is concerned with the management of the firm's short-term, or current, assets and liabilities. The most important current assets are cash, marketable securities, inventory, and accounts receivable. The most important current liabilities are short-term loans and accounts payable. The difference between current assets and current liabilities is called (net) working capital.

Current assets and liabilities are turned over much more rapidly than the other items on the balance sheet. Short-term financing and investment decisions are more quickly and easily reversed than long-term decisions. Consequently, the financial manager does not need to look so far into the future when making them.

The nature of the firm's short-term financial planning problem is determined by the amount of long-term capital it raises. A firm that issues large amounts of long-term debt or common stock, or which retains a large part of its earnings, may find that it has permanent excess cash. In such cases there is never any problem paying bills, and short-term financial planning consists of managing the firm's portfolio of marketable securities. We think that firms with permanent cash surpluses ought to return the excess cash to their stockholders.

Other firms raise relatively little long-term capital and end up as permanent short-term debtors. Most firms attempt to find a golden mean by financing all fixed assets and part of current assets with equity and long-term debt. Such firms may invest cash surpluses during part of the year and borrow during the rest of the year.

The starting point for short-term financial planning is an understanding of sources and uses of cash.[32] Firms forecast their net cash requirements by forecasting collections on accounts receivable, adding other cash inflows, and subtracting all cash outlays. If the forecasted cash balance is insufficient to cover day-to-day operations and to provide a buffer against contingencies, the company will need to find additional finance. The search for the best short-term financial plan inevitably proceeds by trial and error. The financial manager must explore the consequences of different assumptions about cash requirements, interest rates, sources of finance, and so on. Firms are increasingly using computerized financial models to help in this process. The models range from simple spreadsheet programs that merely help with the arithmetic to linear programming models that help to find the best financial plan.

If you foresee a large and permanent cash deficiency, the financial plan may involve raising long-term finance. If the shortage is temporary, you may be able to finance it by not paying your bills for a while or you can choose from a variety of short- and medium-term loans.

Often firms arrange a *revolving line of credit* with a bank that allows them to borrow up to an agreed amount whenever they need financing. This is usually intended to tide the firm over a temporary shortage of cash and is therefore repaid in only a few months. However, banks also make *term loans* that sometimes extend for five years or more. In addition to borrowing from their domestic banks, companies may borrow dollars (or any other currency) from overseas banks or the foreign branches of U.S. banks. These international bank loans often involve huge sums of money and in this case they may be *syndicated* among a group of major banks.

Many bank loans are unsecured, but less-creditworthy borrowers may be asked to provide security. Sometimes this consists of a floating charge on receivables and inventories, but usually you will be asked to pledge specific assets. When you borrow against receivables, the bank is informed of all sales of goods

[32]We pointed out in Section 30.3 that sources and uses of *funds* are often analyzed rather than sources and uses of cash. Anything that contributes to working capital is called a *source of funds*; anything that diminishes working capital is called a *use of funds*. Sources and uses of funds statements are relatively simple because many sources and uses of cash are buried in changes in working capital. However, in forecasting, the emphasis is on cash flow. You pay bills with cash, not working capital.

and the resulting receivables are pledged to the bank. As the customers pay their bills, the money is paid into a special collateral account under the bank's control. Similarly, when you borrow against stocks of raw materials, the bank may insist that the goods are under the control of an independent warehouse company. As long as the bank holds the warehouse receipt for these goods, they cannot be released without the bank's permission.

The interest rate on very short-term bank loans is generally fixed for the life of the loan, but in other cases the rate floats with the general level of short-term interest rates. For example, it might be set at 1 percent over LIBOR (the London Interbank Offered Rate).

Of course, the interest rate that the bank charges must be sufficient to cover not only the opportunity cost of capital for the loan but also the costs of running the loan department. As a result, large regular borrowers have found it cheaper to bypass the banking system and issue their own short-term unsecured debt. This is called *commercial paper.* Longer-term loans that are marketed on a regular basis are known as *medium-term notes.*

FURTHER READING

Here are some general textbooks on working-capital management:

G. W. Gallinger and P. B. Healey: *Liquidity Analysis and Management,* 2nd. ed., Addison-Wesley Publishing Company, Inc., Reading, MA, 1991.

N. C. Hill and W. L. Sartoris: *Short-Term Financial Management: Text and Cases,* 3rd. ed., Prentice-Hall, Inc., Englewood Cliffs, NJ, 1995.

K. V. Smith and G. W. Gallinger: *Readings on Short-Term Financial Management,* 3rd ed., West Publishing Company, New York, 1988.

J. H. Vander Weide and S. F. Maier: *Managing Corporate Liquidity: An Introduction to Working Capital Management,* John Wiley & Sons, Inc., New York, 1985.

F. C. Scherr: *Modern Working Capital Management: Text and Cases,* Prentice-Hall, Inc., Englewood Cliffs, NJ, 1989.

Pogue and Bussard present a linear programming model for short-term financial planning:

G. A. Pogue and R. N. Bussard: "A Linear Programming Model for Short-Term Financial Planning under Uncertainty," *Sloan Management Review,* 13:69–99 (Spring 1972).

QUIZ

1. Fill in the blanks in the following statements:
   a. A firm has a cash surplus when its _____ exceeds its _____. The surplus is normally invested in _____.
   b. In developing the short-term financial plan, the financial manager starts with a budget for the next year. This budget shows the _____ generated or absorbed by the firm's operations and also the minimum _____ needed to support these operations. The financial manager may also wish to invest in _____ as a reserve for unexpected cash requirements.
   c. Short-term financing plans are developed by _____ and _____, often aided by computerized _____.
2. Listed below are six transactions that Dynamic Mattress might make. Indicate how each transaction would affect **(a)** cash and **(b)** working capital.

The transactions are

i. Pay out $2 million cash dividend.
ii. Receive $2,500 from a customer who pays a bill resulting from a previous sale.
iii. Pay $5,000 previously owed to one of its suppliers.
iv. Borrow $1 million long term and invest the proceeds in inventory.
v. Borrow $1 million short term and invest the proceeds in inventory.
vi. Sell $5 million of marketable securities for cash.

3. State how each of the following events would affect the firm's balance sheet. State whether each change is a source or use of cash.
   a. An automobile manufacturer increases production in response to a forecasted increase in demand. Unfortunately, the demand does not increase.
   b. Competition forces the firm to give customers more time to pay for their purchases.
   c. Inflation increases the value of raw material inventories by 20 percent.
   d. The firm sells a parcel of land for $100,000. The land was purchased five years earlier for $200,000.
   e. The firm repurchases its own common stock.
   f. The firm doubles its quarterly dividend.
   g. The firm issues $1 million of long-term debt and uses the proceeds to repay a short-term bank loan.

4. Here is a forecast of sales by National Bromide for the first four months of 2003 (figures in $ thousands):

	Month 1	Month 2	Month 3	Month 4
Cash sales	15	24	18	14
Sales on credit	100	120	90	70

On the average 50 percent of credit sales are paid for in the current month, 30 percent are paid in the next month, and the remainder are paid in the month after that. What is the expected cash inflow from operations in months 3 and 4?

5. Dynamic Futon forecasts the following purchases from suppliers:

	Jan.	Feb.	Mar.	Apr.	May	Jun.
Value of goods ($ millions)	32	28	25	22	20	20

   a. Forty percent of goods are supplied cash on delivery. The remainder are paid with an average delay of one month. If Dynamic Futon starts the year with payables of $22 million, what is the forecasted level of payables for each month?
   b. Suppose that from the start of the year the company stretches payables by paying 40 percent after one month and 20 percent after two months. (The remainder continue to be paid cash on delivery.) Recalculate payables for each month assuming that there are no cash penalties for late payment.

6. Each of the following events affects one or more tables in the chapter. Show the effects of each event by adjusting the tables listed in parentheses:
   a. Dynamic repays only $2 million of short-term debt in 2001. (Tables 30.2, 30.4–30.6)
   b. Dynamic issues an additional $10 million of long-term debt in 2001 and invests $12 million in a new warehouse. (Tables 30.2, 30.4–30.6)
   c. In 2001 Dynamic reduces the quantity of stuffing in each mattress. Customers don't notice, but operating costs fall by 10 percent. (Tables 30.2–30.6)

d. Starting in the third quarter of 2002, Dynamic employs new staff members who will prove very effective in persuading customers to pay more promptly. As a result, 90 percent of sales are paid for immediately, and 10 percent are paid in the following quarter. (Tables 30.7 and 30.8)
e. Starting in the first quarter of 2002, Dynamic cuts wages by $4 million a quarter. (Table 30.8)
f. In the second quarter of 2002 a disused warehouse mysteriously catches fire. Dynamic receives a $10 million check from the insurance company. (Table 30.8)
g. Dynamic's treasurer decides he can scrape by on a $2 million operating cash balance. (Table 30.8)

7. True or false?
   a. Most commercial bank loans are made under commitment.
   b. A line of credit provides the lender with a put option.
   c. Bank term loans typically have a maturity of several years.
   d. If the interest rate on a one-year bank loan is stated as a discount of 10 percent, the actual yield on the loan is less than 10 percent.
   e. The interest rate on term loans is usually linked to LIBOR, the federal funds rate, or the bank's prime rate.

8. Complete the passage below by selecting the most appropriate terms from the following list: *floating charge, commercial paper, warehouse receipt, collateral, commitment fee, line of credit, medium-term notes.*

   Companies with fluctuating capital needs often arrange a ______ with their bank. This is relatively expensive because companies need to pay a ______ on any unused amount.

   Secured short-term loans are sometimes covered by a ______ on all receivables and inventory. Generally, however, the borrower pledges specific assets as ______. For example, if goods are stored in a warehouse, an independent warehouse company may issue a ______ to the lender. The goods can then only be released with the lender's consent.

   Banks are not the only source of short-term debt. Many large companies issue their own unsecured debt directly to investors, often on a regular basis. If the maturity is less than nine months, this debt is generally known as ______. Companies also make regular issues of longer term debt to investors. These are called ______.

Visit us at www.mhhe.com/bm7e

PRACTICE QUESTIONS

1. Table 30.10 lists data from the budget of Ritewell Publishers. Half the company sales are for cash on the nail; the other half are paid for with a one-month delay. The company pays all its credit purchases with a one-month delay. Credit purchases in January were $30, and total sales in January were $180. Complete the cash budget in Table 30.11.

TABLE 30.10

Selected budget data for Ritewell Publishers.

	February	March	April
Total sales	200	220	180
Purchases of materials			
For cash	70	80	60
For credit	40	30	40
Other expenses	30	30	30
Taxes, interest, and dividends	10	10	10
Capital investment	100	0	0

TABLE 30.11

Cash budget for Ritewell Publishers.

	February	March	April
Sources of cash:			
Collections on cash sales			
Collections on accounts receivable	—	—	—
Total sources of cash			
Uses of cash:			
Payments of accounts payable			
Cash purchases of materials			
Other expenses			
Capital expenditures			
Taxes, interest, and dividends			
Total uses of cash	—	—	—
Net cash inflow			
Cash at start of period	100		
+ Net cash inflow			
= Cash at end of period			
+ Minimum operating cash balance	100	100	100
= Cumulative short-term financing required			

TABLE 30.12

Year-end balance sheet for 1999 (figures in $ millions).

Current assets:		Current liabilities:	
Cash	4	Bank loans	4
Marketable securities	2	Accounts payable	15
Inventory	20	Total current liabilities	19
Accounts receivable	22		
Total current assets	48	Long-term debt	5
		Net worth (equity and retained earnings)	60
Fixed assets:			
Gross investment	50		
Less depreciation	−14		
Net fixed assets	36	Total liabilities	
Total assets	84	and net worth	84

2. If a firm pays its bills with a 30-day delay, what fraction of its purchases will be paid in the current quarter? In the following quarter? What if the delay is 60 days?
3. Which items in Table 30.9 would be affected by the following events?
   a. There is a rise in interest rates.
   b. Suppliers demand interest for late payment.
   c. Dynamic receives an unexpected bill in the third quarter from the Internal Revenue Service for underpayment of taxes in previous years.
4. Table 30.12 shows Dynamic Mattress's year-end 1999 balance sheet, and Table 30.13 shows its income statement for 2000. Work out statements of sources and uses of cash and sources and uses of funds for 2000.

TABLE 30.13

Income statement for 2000 (figures in $ millions).

Sales	300
Operating costs	−285
	15
Depreciation	−2
	13
Interest	−1
Pretax income	12
Tax at 50%	−6
Net income	6

Note: Dividend = $1 million; retained earnings = $5 million.

5. Work out a short-term financing plan for Dynamic Mattress Company, assuming the limit on the line of credit is raised from $38 to $50 million. Otherwise keep to the assumptions used in developing Table 30.9.
6. Dynamic Mattress decides to lease its new mattress-stuffing machines rather than buy them. As a result, capital expenditure in the first quarter is reduced by $30 million, but the company must make lease payments of $1.5 million for each of the four quarters. Assume that the lease has no effect on tax payments until after the fourth quarter. Construct two tables like Tables 30.8 and 30.9 showing Dynamic's cumulative financing requirement and a new financing plan.
7. You need to borrow $10 million for 90 days. You have the following alternatives:
   a. Issue high-grade commercial paper, with a back-up line of credit costing .3 percent a year.
   b. Borrow from First Cookham Bank at an interest rate of .25 percent over LIBOR.
   c. Borrow from the Test Bank at prime.

   Given the rates currently prevailing in the market (see, for example, *The Wall Street Journal*), which alternative would you choose?
8. Suppose that you are a banker responsible for approving corporate loans. Nine firms are seeking secured loans. They offer the following assets as collateral:
   a. Firm A, a heating oil distributor, offers a tanker load of fuel in transit from the Middle East.
   b. Firm B, a wine wholesaler, offers 1,000 cases of Beaujolais Nouveau, located in a warehouse.
   c. Firm C, a stationer, offers an account receivable for office supplies sold to the City of New York.
   d. Firm D, a bookstore, offers its entire inventory of 15,000 used books.
   e. Firm E, a wholesale grocer, offers a boxcar full of bananas.
   f. Firm F, an appliance dealer, offers its inventory of electric typewriters.
   g. Firm G, a jeweler, offers 100 ounces of gold.
   h. Firm H, a government securities dealer, offers its portfolio of Treasury bills.
   i. Firm I, a boat builder, offers a half-completed luxury yacht. The yacht will take four months more to complete.

   Which of these assets are most likely to be good collateral? Which are likely to be bad collateral? Explain.
9. Any of the assets mentioned in the preceding question *could* be acceptable collateral under certain circumstances if appropriate safeguards were taken. What circumstances? What safeguards? Explain.
10. Interest rates on bank loans exceed rates on commercial paper. Why don't all firms issue commercial paper rather than borrow from banks?

11. Do you think you could make money by setting up a firm which would **(a)** issue commercial paper and **(b)** relend money to businesses at a rate slightly higher than the commercial paper rate but still less than the rate charged by banks?

STANDARD &POOR'S

12. Use the Market Insight database (**www.mhhe.com/edumarketinsight**) to find recent balance sheets and income statements for two companies. Draw up a sources and uses of cash statement and a sources and uses of funds statement as in Tables 30.4 and 30.6.

STANDARD &POOR'S

13. Use the Market Insight database (**www.mhhe.com/edumarketinsight**) to compare the investment in current assets of different companies. Which of these companies make a heavy investment in inventories or receivables? Can you explain why?

14. The Federal Reserve Bulletin publishes the results of a quarterly survey of bank lending (see **www.federalreserve.gov/releases/E2/**). Use the latest survey to describe the pattern of bank lending by domestic banks. Examine, for example, whether most loans are secured and whether they are made under commitment. What are the different characteristics of small and large loans? Now compare the results of this survey with an earlier one. Have there been any important changes?

CHALLENGE QUESTIONS

1. In some countries the market for long-term corporate debt is limited, and firms turn to short-term bank loans to finance long-term investments in plant and machinery. When a short-term loan comes due, it is replaced by another one, so that the firm is always a short-term debtor. What are the advantages and disadvantages?

2. Axle Chemical Corporation's treasurer has forecasted a $1 million cash deficit for the next quarter. However, there is only a 50 percent chance this deficit will actually occur. The treasurer estimates that there is a 20 percent probability the company will have no deficit at all and a 30 percent probability that it will actually need $2 million in short-term financing. The company can either take out a 90-day unsecured loan for $2 million at 1 percent per month or establish a line of credit, costing 1 percent per month on the amount borrowed plus a commitment fee of $20,000. If excess cash can be reinvested at 9 percent, which source of financing gives the lower expected cost?

3. Term loans usually require firms to pay a fluctuating interest rate. For example, the interest rate may be set at "1 percent above prime." The prime rate sometimes varies by several percentage points within a single year. Suppose that your firm has decided to borrow $40 million for five years. It has three alternatives. It can (a) borrow from a bank at the prime rate, currently 10 percent. The proposed loan agreement requires no principal repayments until the loan matures in five years. It can (b) issue 26-week commercial paper, currently yielding 9 percent. Since funds are required for five years, the commercial paper will have to be rolled over semiannually. That is, financing the $40 million requirement for five years will require 10 successive commercial paper sales. Or, finally, it can (c) borrow from an insurance company at a fixed rate of 11 percent. As in the bank loan, no principal has to be repaid until the end of the five-year period. What factors would you consider in analyzing these alternatives? Under what circumstances would you choose (a)? Under what circumstances would you choose (b) or (c)? (*Hint:* Don't forget Chapter 24.)

CHAPTER THIRTY-ONE

CASH MANAGEMENT

CHAPTER 30 PROVIDED an overall idea of what is involved in short-term financial management. Now it is time to get down to detail. We begin in this chapter by looking at how companies manage their holdings of cash and marketable securities. Then in the next chapter we look at the terms on which firms sell their goods and how they ensure that their customers pay promptly.

Out first task is to explain how cash is collected and paid out. In the United States small routine payments are commonly made by check. You want to ensure that when customers pay by check, you can convert these payments into usable cash in the bank quickly and cheaply. The use of checks is on the decline and large payments are almost always made electronically. You therefore need to understand how electronic payment systems work.

Our second task is to consider how much cash the firm should hold. Companies have a choice between holding cash in the bank and investing it in short-term securities. There is a trade-off here. Cash gives you a store of liquidity, which can be used to pay employees and suppliers. However, cash has the disadvantage that it does not pay interest. As we explain in the second section of this chapter, the trick is to strike a sensible balance.

In the last chapter we explained how companies raise short-term loans to tide them over a temporary cash shortage. If you are in the opposite position and have surplus cash, you need to know where you can park it to earn interest. So in the final section of this chapter we look at the menu of short-term investments that are available to the financial manager.

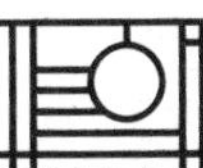

31.1 CASH COLLECTION AND DISBURSEMENT

The majority of small face-to-face purchases are made with coins or dollar bills. The most popular alternative in the United States for retail purchases is to pay by check. Each year individuals and firms write about 70 billion checks.

Notice that the United States is unusual in this heavy use of checks. For example, Figure 31.1 compares retail payment methods in the United States and Holland. You can see that checks are almost unknown in Holland: Most payments there are made by debit cards, direct debit, or credit transfer.[1]

How Checks Create Float

How does the firm's cash balance change when it writes or deposits a check? Suppose that the United Carbon Company has $1 million on demand deposit with its bank. It now pays one of its suppliers by writing and mailing a check for $200,000. The company's ledgers are immediately adjusted to show a cash balance of $800,000. But the company's bank won't learn anything about this check until it has been received by the supplier, deposited at the supplier's bank, and finally presented to United Carbon's bank for payment.[2] During this time United Carbon's bank continues to show

[1]Debit cards allow the cardholder to transfer money directly to the receiver's bank account. With a credit transfer the payer initiates the transaction, for example by giving her bank a standing order to make a regular payment. With a direct debit the transaction is initiated by the payee and is usually processed electronically.

[2]Checks deposited with a bank are cleared through the Federal Reserve clearing system, through a correspondent bank, or through a clearinghouse of local banks.

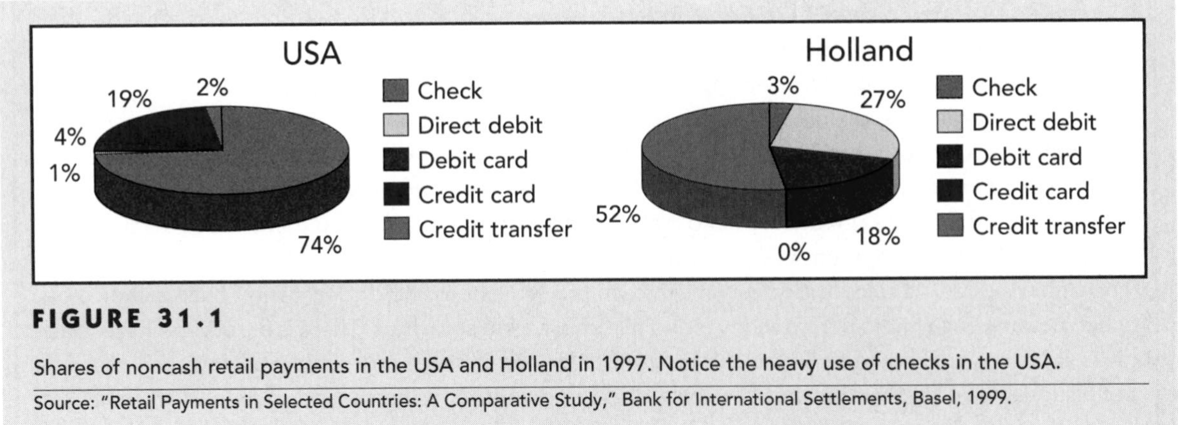

FIGURE 31.1

Shares of noncash retail payments in the USA and Holland in 1997. Notice the heavy use of checks in the USA.

Source: "Retail Payments in Selected Countries: A Comparative Study," Bank for International Settlements, Basel, 1999.

in its ledger that the company has a balance of $1 million. The company obtains the benefit of an extra $200,000 in the bank while the check is clearing. This sum is often called *payment*, or *disbursement float.*

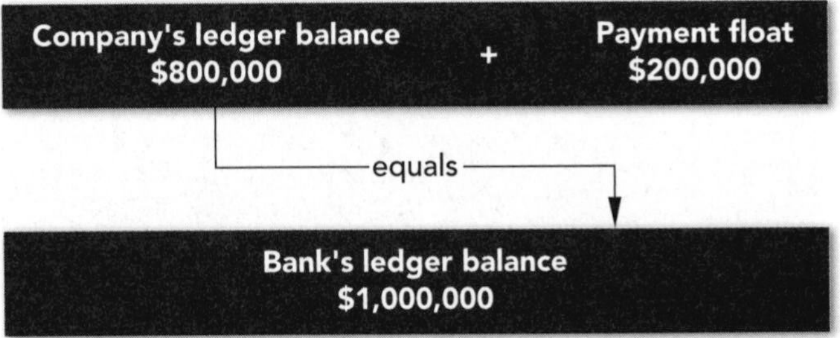

Float sounds like a marvelous invention, but unfortunately it can also work in reverse. Suppose that in addition to paying its supplier, United Carbon *receives* a check for $100,000 from a customer. It deposits the check, and both the company and the bank increase the ledger balance by $100,000:

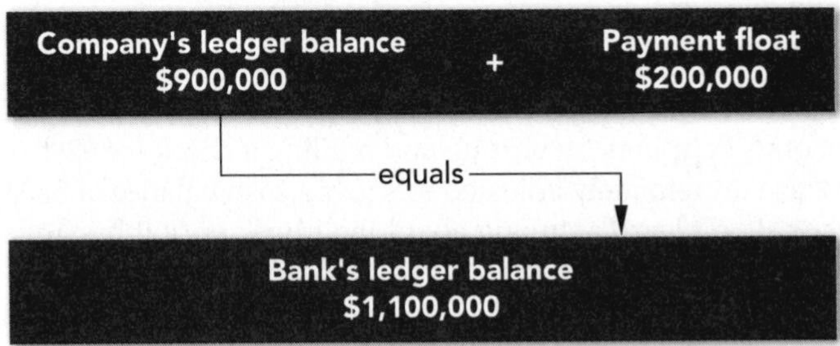

But this money isn't available to the company immediately. The bank doesn't actually have the money in hand until it has sent the check to, and received payment from, the customer's bank. Since the bank has to wait, it makes United Carbon wait too—usually one or two business days. In the meantime, the bank will show that United Carbon has an *available balance* of $1 million and an *availability float* of $100,000:

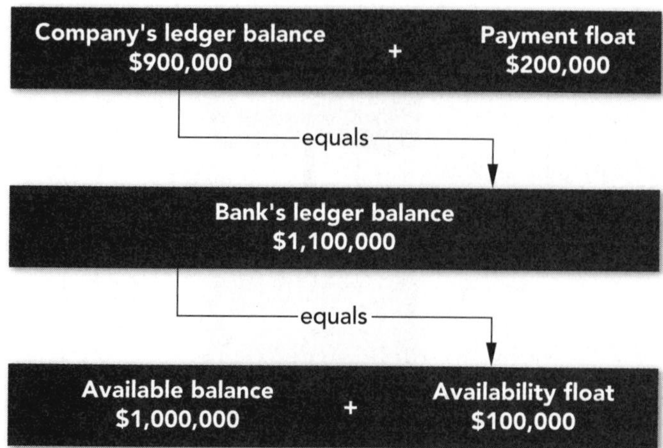

Notice that the company gains as a result of the payment float and loses as a result of the availability float. The difference is often termed the *net float.* In our example, the net float is $100,000. The company's available balance is therefore $100,000 greater than the balance shown in its ledger.

As financial manager you are concerned with the available balance, not with the company's ledger balance. If you know that it is going to be a week or two before some of your checks are presented for payment, you may be able to get by on a smaller cash balance. This game is often called *playing the float.*

You can increase your available cash balance by increasing your net float. This means that you want to ensure that checks paid in by customers are cleared rapidly and those paid to suppliers are cleared slowly. Perhaps this may sound like rather small beer, but think what it can mean to a company like Ford. Ford's daily sales average about $450 million. Therefore if it can speed up the collection process by one day, it frees $450 million, which is available for investment or payment to Ford's stockholders.

Some financial managers have become overenthusiastic in managing the float. In 1985, the brokerage firm E. F. Hutton pleaded guilty to 2,000 separate counts of mail and wire fraud. Hutton admitted that it had created nearly $1 billion of float by shuffling funds between its branches, and through various accounts at different banks. These activities cost the company a $2 million fine and its agreement to repay the banks any losses they may have incurred.

Managing Float

Float is the child of delay. Actually there are several kinds of delay, and so people in the cash management business refer to several kinds of float. Figure 31.2 summarizes.

Of course the delays that help the payer hurt the recipient. Recipients try to speed up collections. Payers try to slow down disbursements.

Speeding Up Collections

Many companies use **concentration banking** to speed up collections. In this case customers in a particular area make payment to a local branch office rather than to company headquarters. The local branch office then deposits the checks into a

FIGURE 31.2

Delays create float. Each heavy arrow represents a source of delay. Recipients try to reduce delay to get available cash sooner. Payers prefer delay because they can use their cash longer.

Note: The delays causing availability float and presentation float are equal on average but can differ from case to case.

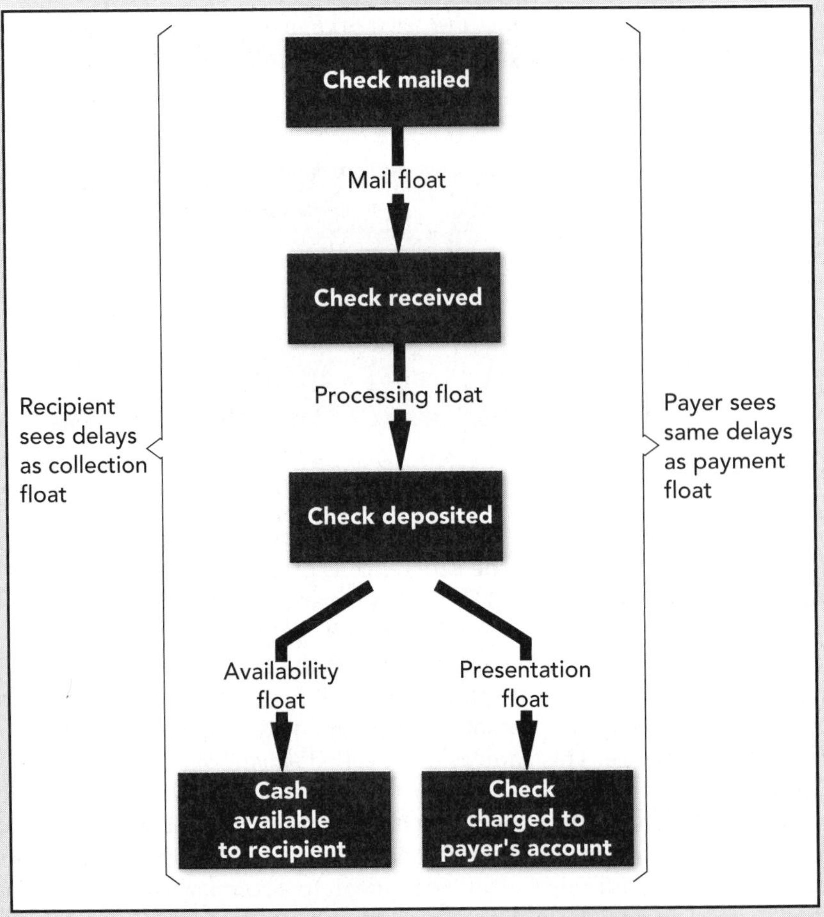

local bank account. Surplus funds are transferred to a *concentration account* at one of the company's principal banks.

Concentration banking reduces float in two ways. First, because the branch office is nearer to the customer, mailing time is reduced. Second, since the customer's check is likely to be drawn on a local bank, the time taken to clear the check is also reduced. Concentration banking brings many small balances together in one large, central balance, which can then be invested in interest-paying assets through a single transaction. For example, when Amoco streamlined its U.S. bank accounts in 1995, it was able to reduce its daily bank balances in non-interest-bearing accounts by almost 80 percent.[3]

Often concentration banking is combined with a **lock-box system.** In a lock-box system, you pay the local bank to take on the administrative chores. The system works as follows. The company rents a locked post office box in each principal region. All customers within a region are instructed to send their payments to the post office box. The local bank, as agent for the company, empties the box at regular intervals and deposits the checks in the company's local account. Surplus funds are transferred periodically to one of the company's principal banks.

[3]"Amoco Streamlines Treasury Operations," *The Citibank Globe,* November/December 1998.

How many collection points do you need if you use a lock-box system or concentration banking? The answer depends on where your customers are and on the speed of the U.S. mail. For example, suppose that you are thinking of opening a lock box. The local bank shows you a map of mail delivery times. From that and knowledge of your customers' locations, you come up with the following data:

- Average number of daily payments to lock box: 150
- Average size of payment: $1,200
- Rate of interest *per day:* .02 percent
- Saving in mailing time: 1.2 days
- Saving in processing time: .8 day

On this basis, the lock box would increase your collected balance by

$$150 \text{ items per day} \times \$1{,}200 \text{ per item} \times (1.2 + .8) \text{ days saved} = \$360{,}000$$

Invested at .02 percent per day, $360,000 gives a daily return of

$$.0002 \times \$360{,}000 = \$72$$

The bank's charge for operating the lock-box system depends on the number of checks processed. Suppose that the bank charges $.26 per check. That works out to $150 \times .26 = \$39$ per day. You are ahead by $\$72 - 39 = \$33$ per day, plus whatever your firm saves from not having to process the checks itself.

Our example assumes that the company has only two choices. It can do nothing, or it can operate the lock box. But maybe there is some other lock-box location, or some mixture of locations, that would be still more effective. Of course, you can always find this out by working through all possible combinations, but it may be simpler to solve the problem by linear programming. Many banks offer linear programming models to solve the problem of locating lock boxes.[4]

Controlling Disbursements

Speeding up collections is not the only way to increase the net float. You can also do so by slowing down disbursements. One tempting strategy is to increase mail time. For example, United Carbon could pay its New York suppliers with checks mailed from Nome, Alaska, and its Los Angeles suppliers with checks mailed from Vienna, Maine.

But on second thought you will realize that such post office tricks are unlikely to give more than a short-run payoff. Suppose you have promised to pay a New York supplier on February 29. Does it matter whether you mail the check from Alaska on the 26th or from New York on the 28th? Of course, you could use a remote mailing address as an excuse for paying late, but that's a trick easily seen through. If you have to pay late, you may as well mail late.[5]

There are effective ways of increasing presentation float, however. For example, suppose that United Carbon pays its suppliers with checks written on a New York City bank. From the time that the check has been deposited by the supplier, there

[4]See, for example, A. Kraus, C. Janssen, and A. McAdams, "The Lock-Box Location Problem," *Journal of Bank Research* 1 (Autumn 1970), pp. 50–58.

[5]Since the tax authorities look at the date of the postmark rather than the date of receipt, companies have been tempted to use a remote mailing address to pay their tax bills. But the tax authorities have reacted by demanding that large tax bills be paid by electronic transfer.

will be an average lapse of little more than a day before it is presented to United Carbon's bank for payment. The alternative is that United Carbon pays its suppliers with checks mailed to *arrive* on time but written on a bank in Helena, Montana; Midland, Texas; or Wilmington, Delaware. In these cases, it may take three or four days before each check is presented for payment. United Carbon, therefore, gains several days of additional float.[6]

Some firms even maintain disbursement accounts in different parts of the country. The computer looks up each supplier's zip code and automatically produces a check on the most distant bank.

The suppliers won't object to these machinations because the Federal Reserve guarantees a maximum clearing time of two days on all checks cleared through its system. The Federal Reserve, however, does object and has been trying to prevent remote disbursement.

A New York City bank receives several check deliveries each day from the Federal Reserve system as well as checks that come directly from other banks or through the local clearinghouse. Thus, if United Carbon uses a New York City bank for paying its suppliers, it will not know at the beginning of the day how many checks will be presented for payment. It must either keep a large cash balance to cover contingencies or be prepared to borrow. However, instead of having a disbursement account with a bank in New York, United Carbon could open a *zero-balance* account with a regional bank that receives almost all check deliveries in the form of a single, early-morning delivery from the Federal Reserve. Therefore, it can let the cash manager at United Carbon know early in the day exactly how much money will be paid out that day. The cash manager then arranges for this sum to be transferred from the company's concentration account to the disbursement account. Thus by the end of the day (and at the start of the next day), United Carbon has a zero balance in the disbursement account.

United Carbon's regional bank account has two advantages. First, by choosing a remote location, the company has gained several days of float. Second, because the bank can forecast early in the day how much money will be paid out, United Carbon does not need to keep extra cash in the account to cover contingencies.

The Finance in the News box describes how one Canadian company was able to reduce its cash needs by concentrating its cash holdings and using zero-balance accounts.

Electronic Funds Transfer

Throughout the world the use of checks is on the decline. For consumers they are being replaced by credit or debit cards. In the case of companies, payments are increasingly made electronically.[7] Electronic payments are relatively few in number but they account for the majority of transactions by value. Electronic payment systems may be of two kinds—a *gross* settlement system or a *net* settlement system. With gross settlement each payment is settled individually; with net settlement all payment instructions are accumulated and then at the end of the day any imbalances are settled.

---

[6]Remote disbursement accounts are described in I. Ross, "The Race Is to the Slow Payer," *Fortune*, April 18, 1983, pp. 75–80.

[7]Consumers also may receive and pay bills electronically via their personal computer. Currently Electronic Bill Presentment and Payment (EBPP) accounts for only a small proportion of payments but it is forecasted to grow rapidly.

HOW LAIDLAW RESTRUCTURED ITS CASH MANAGEMENT

The Canadian company, Laidlaw Inc., has more than 4,000 facilities throughout America, operating school bus services, ambulance services, and Greyhound coaches. During the 1990s the company expanded rapidly through acquisition, and its number of banking relationships multiplied until it had 1,000 separate bank accounts with more than 200 different banks. The head office had no way of knowing how much cash was stashed away in these accounts until the end of each quarter, when it was able to construct a consolidated balance sheet.

To economize on the use of cash, Laidlaw's financial manager sought to cut the company's average float from five days to two. At the same time management decided to consolidate cash management at five key banks. This enabled cash to be zero-balanced to a single account for each division and swept daily to Laidlaw's disbursement bank. Because the head office could obtain daily reports of the company's cash position, cash forecasting was improved and the company could reduce its cash needs still further.

Source: *Cash management at Laidlaw is described in G. Mann and S. Hutchison,* "Driving Down Working Capital: Laidlaw's Story," *Canadian Treasurer Magazine,* August/September 1999.

In the United States there are two systems for making large-value electronic payments—Fedwire (a gross system) and CHIPS (a net system). Fedwire is operated by the Federal Reserve system and connects over 10,000 financial institutions in the United States to the Fed and thereby to each other. Suppose Bank A instructs the Fed to transfer $1 million from its account with the Fed to the account of Bank B. Bank A's account is debited immediately and Bank B's account is credited at the same time. Fedwire is therefore an example of a *real-time gross settlement (RTGS)* system. Most developed countries now operate RTGS systems for large-value payments.

Real-time gross settlement suffers from a potential problem. If Bank A needs to pay Bank B, B needs to pay C, and C needs to pay A, there is a risk that the system could gridlock unless each bank kept a large reserve with the Fed. (A might not be able to pay B until it has been paid by C, C can't pay A until paid by B, and B in turn is awaiting payment by A.) To oil the wheels, therefore, the Fed takes on the credit risk by paying the receiving bank even if there are insufficient funds in the account of the payer. Since each payment is final and guaranteed by the Fed, each receiving bank can be sure that it has the money and can give its customer immediate access to the funds.

Cross-border high-value payments in dollars are handled by CHIPS, which is a privately owned system connecting 115 large domestic and foreign banks. CHIPS accumulates payment instructions throughout the day, and at the end of the day each bank settles up the net payment using Fedwire. This means that, if the bank receiving payments makes the funds available to its customers during the day, it would be at risk if the paying bank goes belly up during the day. Banks control this risk by imposing intraday credit limits on their exposure to each other.

Fedwire and CHIPS provide same-day settlement and are used to make high-value payments. Bulk payments such as wages, dividends, and payments to suppliers generally travel through the *Automated Clearinghouse (ACH)* system and take two to three days. In this case the company simply needs to provide a computer file of instructions to its bank, which then debits the corporation's account and forwards the payments to the ACH system. The ACH system is the largest payment system in the United States and in 1999 handled 6.2 billion payments with a value of $19 trillion.

For companies that are "wired" to their banks, customers, and suppliers, these electronic payment systems have at least three advantages:

- Record keeping and routine transactions are easy to automate when money moves electronically. Campbell Soup's Treasury Management Department discovered that it could handle cash management, short-term borrowing and lending, and bank relationships with a total staff of seven. The company's domestic cash flow was about $5 billion.[8]
- The marginal cost of transactions is very low. For example, it costs less than $10 to transfer huge sums of money using Fedwire and only a few cents to make an ACH transfer.
- Float is drastically reduced. Wire transfers generate no float at all. This can result in substantial savings. For example, cash managers at Occidental Petroleum found that one plant was paying out about $8 million per month three to five days early to avoid any risk of late fees if checks were delayed in the mail. The solution was obvious: The plant's managers switched to paying large bills electronically; that way they could ensure they arrived exactly on time.[9]

International Cash Management

Cash management in domestic firms is child's play compared with that in large multinational corporations operating in dozens of countries, each with its own currency, banking system, and legal structure.

A single, centralized cash management system is an unattainable ideal for these companies, although they are edging toward it. For example, suppose that you are the treasurer of a large multinational company with operations throughout Europe. You could allow the separate businesses to manage their own cash but that would be costly and would almost certainly result in each one accumulating little hoards of cash. The solution is to set up a regional system. In this case the company establishes a local concentration account with a bank in each country. Then any surplus cash is swept daily into central multicurrency accounts in London or another European banking center. This cash is then invested in marketable securities or used to finance any subsidiaries that have a cash shortage.

Payments also can be made out of the regional center. For example, to pay wages in each European country, the company just needs to send its principal bank a computer file with details of the payments to be made. The bank then finds the least costly way to transfer the cash from the company's central accounts and arranges for the funds to be credited on the correct day to the employees in each country.

[8]J. D. Moss, "Campbell Soup's Cutting-Edge Cash Management," *Financial Executive* 8 (September/October 1992), pp. 39–42.

[9]R. J. Pisapia, "The Cash Manager's Expanding Role: Working Capital," *Journal of Cash Management* 10 (November/December 1990), pp. 11–14.

Companies that maintain separate balances in each country are liable to find that they have a cash surplus in one country and a shortage in another. In this case the company could lend the surplus and borrow the deficit. However, that is likely to be costly, since banks need to charge a higher rate to borrowers than they pay to lenders. One alternative is to convert the surplus cash pool into the currency which is in short supply, but the simpler solution is to arrange for the bank to *pool* all your cash surpluses and shortages. In this case no money is transferred between accounts. Instead, the bank just adds together the credit and debit balances and pays you interest at its lending rate on the net surplus.

Most large multinationals have several banks in each country, but the more banks they use, the less control they have over their cash balances. So development of regional cash management systems favors banks that can offer a worldwide branch network. These banks also can afford to invest the several billion dollars that are needed to set up computer systems for handling cash payments and receipts in many different countries.

Paying for Bank Services

Much of the work of cash management—processing checks, transferring funds, running lock boxes, helping keep track of the company's accounts—is done by banks. And banks provide many other services not so directly linked to cash management, such as handling payments and receipts in foreign currency or acting as custodian for securities.[10]

All these services have to be paid for. Usually payment is in the form of a monthly fee, but banks may agree to waive the fee as long as the firm maintains a minimum average balance in an interest-free deposit. Banks are prepared to do this, because, after setting aside a portion of the money in a reserve account with the Fed, they can relend the money to earn interest. Demand deposits earmarked to pay for bank services are termed *compensating balances.* They used to be a very common way to pay for bank services, but there has been a steady trend away from using compensating balances and toward direct fees.

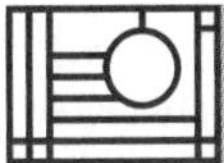

31.2 HOW MUCH CASH SHOULD THE FIRM HOLD?

Cash pays no interest. So why do individuals and corporations hold billions of dollars in cash and demand deposits? Why, for example, don't you take all your cash and invest it in interest-bearing securities? The answer of course is that cash gives you more *liquidity* than securities. You can use it to buy things. It is hard enough getting New York cab drivers to give you change for a $20 bill, but try asking them to split a Treasury bill.

In equilibrium all assets in the same risk class are priced to give the same expected marginal benefit. The benefit from holding Treasury bills is the interest that you receive; the benefit from holding cash is that it gives you a convenient store of liquidity. In equilibrium the marginal value of this liquidity is equal to the marginal value of the interest on Treasury bills. This is just another way of saying that Treasury bills are investments with zero net present value; they are fair value relative to cash.

[10]Of course, banks also lend money or give firms the *option* to borrow under a line of credit. See Section 30.6.

Does this mean that it does not matter how much cash you hold? Of course not. The marginal value of liquidity declines as you hold increasing amounts of cash. When you have only a small proportion of your assets in cash, a little extra can be extremely useful; when you have a substantial holding, any additional liquidity is not worth much. Therefore, as financial manager you want to hold cash balances up to the point where the marginal value of the liquidity is equal to the value of the interest forgone.

If that seems more easily said than done, you may be comforted to know that production managers must make a similar trade-off. Ask yourself why firms carry inventories of raw materials. They are not obliged to do so; they could simply buy materials day by day, as needed. But then they would pay higher prices for ordering in small lots, and they would risk production delays if the materials were not delivered on time. That is why they order more than the firm's immediate needs.[11]

But there is a cost to holding inventories. Interest is lost on the money that is tied up in inventories, storage must be paid for, and often there is spoilage and deterioration. Therefore production managers try to strike a sensible balance between the costs of holding too little inventory and those of holding too much.

It is exactly the same with cash. Cash is just another material that you require to carry on production. If you keep too small a proportion of your funds in the bank, you will need to make repeated sales of securities every time you want to pay your bills. On the other hand, if you keep excessive cash in the bank, you are losing interest.

The Inventory Decision

Let us look at what economists have had to say about managing inventories and then see whether some of these ideas may also help us to manage cash balances. Here is a simple inventory problem.

Everyman's Bookstore experiences a steady demand for *Principles of Corporate Finance* from customers who find that it makes a serviceable doorstop. There are two costs to holding an inventory of the book. First there is the *carrying cost.* This includes the cost of the capital that is tied up in the inventory, the cost of the shelf space, and so on. The second type of cost is the *order cost.* Each order involves a fixed handling expense and delivery charge.

These two costs are the kernel of the inventory problem. An increase in order size increases the average number of books in inventory, and therefore the carrying cost *rises.* However, as the store increases its order size, the number of orders falls, so that the order costs *decline.* The trick is to strike a sensible balance between these two costs. When carrying costs are high, you should hold a smaller inventory and replenish it more often. When order costs are high, you should hold a larger inventory and place orders less frequently.

Some numbers may help to illustrate. Suppose that the bookstore sells 100 copies of the book a year. Suppose also that the carrying cost of inventory works out at $4 per book and that each order placed with the publisher involves a fixed order cost of $2. The upward sloping line in Figure 31.3 shows that carrying costs increase in proportion to order size. The effect of order size on order costs is de-

[11]Not much more in many manufacturing operations. "Just-in-time" assembly systems provide for a continuous stream of parts deliveries, with no more than two or three hours' worth of parts inventory on hand. Financial managers likewise strive for just-in-time cash management systems, in which no cash lies idle anywhere in the company's business. This ideal is never quite reached because of the costs and delays discussed in this chapter. Large corporations get close, however.

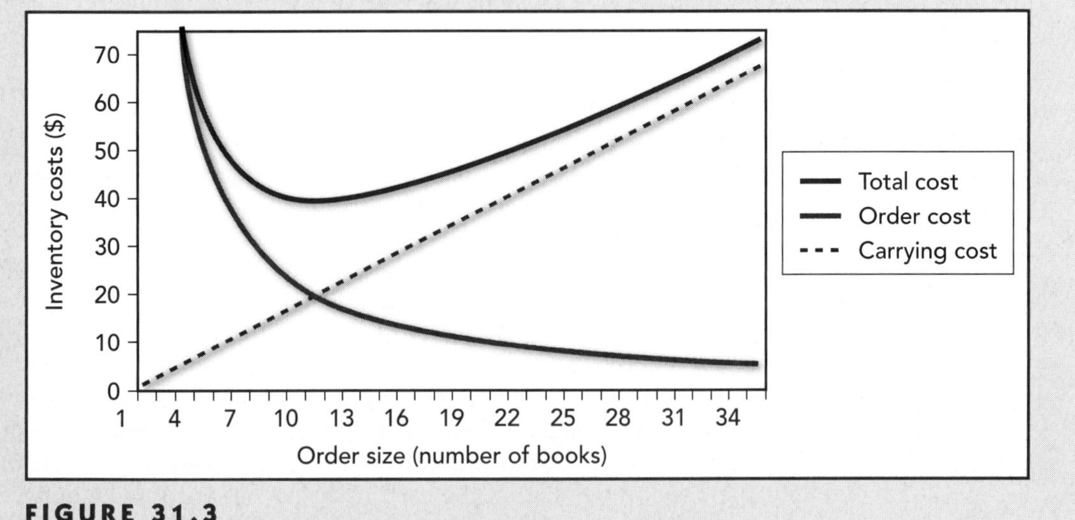

FIGURE 31.3

Optimal order size involves a trade-off between order costs and carrying costs.

picted by the downward sloping line. Order costs halve when the bookstore orders two books at a time rather than one, but thereafter the savings from increases in order size steadily diminish.

The upper curve in Figure 31.3 shows the sum of the carrying and order costs. You can see that total costs are minimized when the store orders 10 books at a time. Thus, 10 times a year the bookstore should place an order for 10 books and it should work off this inventory over the following five weeks.[12]

The Extension to Cash Balances

William Baumol was the first to point out that this simple inventory model can tell us something about the management of cash balances.[13] Suppose that you keep a reservoir of cash that is steadily drawn down to pay bills. When it runs out, you replenish the cash balance by selling Treasury bills. The order cost is the fixed administrative expense of each sale of Treasury bills. The main carrying cost of holding this cash is the interest that the firm is losing.

Deciding on the firm's cash holding is exactly analogous to the problem of optimum order size faced by Everyman's Bookstore. You just have to redefine the variables. For example, instead of referring to the number of books per order, order size becomes the amount of Treasury bills sold each time the cash balance is replenished. Order cost becomes cost per sale of Treasury bills, while carrying cost is just the interest lost from holding cash rather than bills.

If high interest rates increase the cost of carrying cash, you should hold a smaller inventory of cash and therefore make smaller and more frequent sales of Treasury

---

[12]See the *Principles of Corporate Finance* Web page (**www.mhhe.com/bm7e**) for an explanation of how to calculate the optimal order size.

[13]W. J. Baumol, "The Transactions Demand for Cash: An Inventory Theoretic Approach," *Quarterly Journal of Economics* 66 (November 1952), pp. 545–556.

bills. On the other hand, if the firm incurs high costs in selling securities, you should hold larger cash balances.

The Cash Management Trade-off

Baumol's model of cash balances is unrealistic in one important respect: It assumes that the firm is steadily using up its cash inventory. But that is not what usually happens. In some weeks the firm may collect some large unpaid bills and therefore receive a *net inflow* of cash. In other weeks it may pay its suppliers and so incur a net *outflow* of cash. Some of these cash flows can be forecasted with confidence; in other cases the amount of the flow or its timing is uncertain.

Economists and management scientists have developed a variety of more elaborate and realistic models that allow for the possibility of both cash inflows and outflows.[14] But no model will ever succeed in capturing all the intricacies of the firm's cash requirements or provide a substitute for the judgment of the cash manager. The importance of Baumol's model and its many offspring is that they all highlight the basic trade-off that the cash manager needs to make between the fixed costs of selling securities and the carrying costs of holding cash balances. Since there are economies of scale in buying or selling securities, the firm should wait and place a sufficiently large order rather than place a series of smaller orders.

Baumol's model helps us understand why small and medium-sized firms hold significant cash balances. But for very large firms, the transaction costs of buying and selling securities become trivial compared with the opportunity cost of holding idle cash balances.

Suppose that the interest rate is 8 percent per year, or roughly $8/365 = .022$ percent per day. Then the daily interest earned by \$1 million is $.00022 \times 1{,}000{,}000 =$ \$220. Even at a cost of \$50 per transaction, which is generously high, it pays to buy Treasury bills today and sell them tomorrow rather than to leave \$1 million idle overnight.

A corporation with \$1 billion of annual sales has an average daily cash flow of \$1,000,000,000/365, about \$2.7 million. Firms of this size end up buying or selling securities once a day, every day, unless by chance they have only a small positive cash balance at the end of the day.

Why do such firms hold any significant amounts of cash? There are basically two reasons. First, cash may be left in non-interest-bearing accounts to compensate banks for the services they provide. Second, large corporations may have literally hundreds of accounts with dozens of different banks. It is often better to leave idle cash in some of these accounts than to monitor each account daily and make daily transfers between them.

One major reason for the proliferation of bank accounts is decentralized management. You cannot give a subsidiary operating autonomy without giving its managers the right to spend and receive cash.

Good cash management nevertheless implies some degree of centralization. You cannot maintain your desired inventory of cash if all the subsidiaries in the group are responsible for their own private pools of cash. And you certainly want to avoid situations in which one subsidiary is investing its spare cash at 8 percent

[14]For example, the problem of cash management when inflows and outflows are unpredictable is analyzed in M. H. Miller and D. Orr, "A Model of the Demand for Money by Firms," *Quarterly Journal of Economics* 80 (August 1966), pp. 413–435. The Miller–Orr model is described in the *Principles of Corporate Finance* Web page.

while another is borrowing at 10 percent. It is not surprising, therefore, that even in highly decentralized companies there is generally central control over cash balances and bank relations.

31.3 INVESTING IDLE CASH

The Money Market

Temporary cash surpluses are generally invested in short-term securities. The market for these short-term investments is known as the **money market.** The money market has no physical marketplace. It consists of a loose agglomeration of banks and dealers linked together by telex, telephones, and computers. But a huge volume of securities is regularly traded on the money market, and competition is vigorous.

Most large corporations manage their own money-market investments, buying and selling through banks and dealers or over the Web. Small companies sometimes find it more convenient to hire a professional investment management firm or to put their cash into a money-market fund. This is a mutual fund that invests only in low-risk, short-term securities. We discussed money-market funds in Section 17.3.

Valuing Money-Market Investments

When we value long-term debt, it is important to take default risk into account. Almost anything may happen in 30 years, and even today's most respectable company may get into trouble eventually. This is the basic reason that corporate bonds offer higher yields than Treasury bonds.

Short-term debt is not risk-free either. When Penn Central failed, it had $82 million of short-term commercial paper outstanding.[15] After that shock, investors became much more discriminating in their purchases of commercial paper.

Such examples of failure are exceptions; in general, the danger of default is less for money-market securities issued by corporations than for corporate bonds. There are two reasons for this. First, the range of possible outcomes is smaller for short-term investments. Even though the distant future may be clouded, you can usually be confident that a particular company will survive for at least the next month. Second, for the most part only well-established companies can borrow in the money market. If you are going to lend money for only one day, you can't afford to spend too much time in evaluating the loan. Thus you will consider only blue-chip borrowers.

Despite the high quality of money-market investments, there are often significant differences in yield between corporate and U.S. government securities. Why is this? One answer is the risk of default. Another is that the investments have different degrees of liquidity or "moneyness." Investors like Treasury bills because they are easier to turn into cash on short notice. Securities that cannot be converted quickly and cheaply into cash need to offer relatively high yields.

During times of market turmoil investors often place a high value on having ready access to cash. On such occasions the yield on illiquid securities can increase dramatically. This happened in the fall of 1998 when a large hedge fund, Long

[15]Commercial paper is short-term debt issued by corporations. We described it in Section 30.6.

Term Capital Management (LTCM), came close to collapse.[16] Fearful that LTCM would be forced to liquidate its huge positions, investors shrank from securities that could not be converted easily into cash. The spread between the yield on commercial paper and Treasury bills rose to about 120 basis points (1.20 percent), almost four times its level at the beginning of the year.

Calculating the Yield on Money-Market Investments

Many money-market investments are pure discount securities. This means that they don't pay interest. The return consists of the difference between the amount you pay and the amount you receive at maturity. Unfortunately, it is no good trying to persuade the Internal Revenue Service that this difference represents capital gain. The IRS is wise to that one and will tax your return as ordinary income.

Interest rates on money-market investments are often quoted on a discount basis. For example, suppose that six-month bills are issued at a discount of 5 percent. This is rather a complicated way of saying that the price of a six-month bill is $100 - (6/12) \times 5 = \$97.50$. Therefore, for every $97.5 that you invest today, you receive $100 at the end of six months. The return over six months is $2.5/97.5 = .0256$, or 2.56 percent. This is equivalent to an annual yield of 5.12 percent simple interest or 5.19 percent if interest is compounded annually. Note that the return is always higher than the discount. When you read that an investment is selling at a discount of 5 percent, it is very easy to slip into the mistake of thinking that this is its return.[17]

The International Money Market

In Chapter 24 we pointed out that there are two main markets for dollar bonds. There is the domestic market in the United States and there is an international market. Similarly, in this chapter we shall see that in addition to the domestic money market, there is also an international market for short-term dollar investments. Since this market is based largely in Europe, it has traditionally been known as the *eurodollar* market. However, now that the European single currency has been called the euro, the term "eurodollar" is potentially confusing and we will just refer to "international dollars."

An international dollar is not some strange bank note; it is simply a dollar deposit in a bank outside the United States. For example, suppose that an American oil company buys crude oil from an Arab sheik and pays for it with a $1 million check drawn on Chase Manhattan Bank. The sheik then deposits the check into his account at Barclays Bank in London. As a result, Barclays has an asset in the form of a $1 million credit in its account with Chase Manhattan. It also has an offsetting liability in the form of a dollar deposit. That dollar deposit is placed in Europe; it is, therefore, an international dollar deposit.[18]

---

[16]Hedge funds specialize in making positive investments in securities that are believed to be undervalued, while selling short those that appear overvalued. The story of LTCM is told in R. Lowenstein, *When Genius Failed: The Rise and Fall of Long Term Capital Management*, Random House, New York, 2000; and N. Dunbar, *Inventing Money: The Story of Long Term Capital Management and the Legends behind It*, John Wiley, New York, 2000.

[17]To confuse things even more, dealers in the money market often quote rates as if there were only 360 days in a year. So a discount of 5 percent on a bill maturing in 182 days translates into a price of $100 - 5 \times (182/360) = 97.47$ percent.

[18]The sheik could equally well deposit the check with the London branch of a U.S. bank or a Japanese bank. He would still have made an international dollar deposit.

We will describe the principal domestic and international dollar investments shortly, but bear in mind that there is also an international market for investments in other currencies. For example, if a U.S. corporation wishes to make a short-term investment in yen, it can do so in the Tokyo money market or it can make an international yen deposit in London.

If we lived in a world without regulation and taxes, the interest rate on an international dollar loan would have to be the same as the rate on an equivalent domestic dollar loan, the rate on an international yen loan would have to be the same as that on a domestic yen loan, and so on. However, the international loan markets thrive because individual governments attempt to regulate domestic bank lending. For example, between 1963 and 1974 the U.S. government controlled the export of funds for corporate investment. Therefore, companies that wished to expand abroad were forced to borrow dollars outside the United States. This demand tended to push the interest rate on these loans above the domestic rate. At the same time the government limited the rate of interest that banks in the United States could pay on domestic deposits; this also tended to keep the rate of interest that you could earn on dollar deposits in Europe above the rate on domestic dollar deposits. By early 1974 the restrictions on the export of funds had been removed, and for large deposits the interest rate ceiling had also been abolished. In consequence, the difference between the interest rate on international dollar deposits and domestic deposits narrowed, but it did not disappear: Banks are not subject to Federal Reserve requirements on international dollar deposits and are not obliged to insure these deposits with the Federal Deposit Insurance Corporation. On the other hand, depositors are exposed to the (very low) risk that a foreign government could prohibit banks from repaying international dollar deposits. For these reasons international dollar investments continue to offer slightly higher rates of interest than domestic dollar deposits.

The U.S. government has become increasingly concerned that its regulations are driving banking business overseas to foreign banks and the overseas branches of American banks. To attract some of this business back to the States, the government in 1981 allowed U.S. and foreign banks to establish so-called *international banking facilities* (IBFs). An IBF is the financial equivalent of a free-trade zone; it is physically situated in the United States, but it is not required to maintain reserves with the Federal Reserve and depositors are not subject to any U.S. tax.[19] However, there are tight restrictions on what business an IBF can conduct. In particular, it cannot accept deposits from domestic United States corporations or make loans to them.

Banks in London lend dollars to one another at the *London interbank offered rate* (LIBOR). LIBOR is a benchmark for pricing many types of short-term loans in the United States and overseas. For example, a corporation in the United States may issue a floating-rate note with interest payments tied to LIBOR.

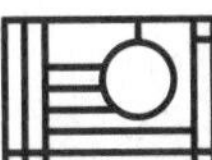

31.4 MONEY-MARKET INVESTMENTS

Table 31.1 summarizes the principal money-market investments. We will describe each in turn.

[19]For these reasons dollars held on deposit in an IBF are also classed as international dollars.

Investment	Borrower	Maturities When Issued	Marketability	Basis for Calculating Interest	Comments
Treasury bills	U.S. government	4 weeks, 3 months, or 6 months	Excellent secondary market	Discount	Auctioned weekly
Federal agency discount notes	FHLB, "Fannie Mae," "Sallie Mae," "Freddie Mac," etc.	Typically 3 to 6 months	Very good secondary market	Discount for securities of 6 months or less	Sold through dealers
Tax-exempt municipal notes	Municipalities, states, school districts, etc.	3 months to 1 year	Good secondary market	Usually interest-bearing; interest at maturity	Tax anticipation notes (TANs), revenue anticipation notes (RANs), bond anticipation notes (BANs), etc.
Tax-exempt variable-rate demand bonds (VRDBs)	Municipalities, states, state universities, etc.	20 to 40 years	Good secondary market	Variable interest rate	Long-term bonds but with put options to demand repayment
Non-negotiable time deposits and negotiable certificates of deposit (CDs)	Commercial banks, savings and loans	Usually 1 to 3 months; also longer-maturity variable-rate CDs	Poor secondary market for CDs	Interest-bearing with interest at maturity	Receipt for time deposit
Commercial paper (CP)	Industrial firms, finance companies, and bank holding companies; also municipalities	Maximum 270 days; usually 60 days or less	Dealers or issuer will repurchase paper	Usually discount	Unsecured promissory note; may be placed through dealer or directly with investor
Medium-term notes (MTNs)	Largely finance companies and banks; also industrial firms	Minimum 270 days; usually less than 10 years	Dealers will repurchase notes	Interest-bearing; usually fixed rate	Unsecured promissory note; placed through dealer
Bankers' acceptances (BAs)	Major commercial banks	1 to 6 months	Fair secondary market	Discount	Demands to pay that have been accepted by a bank
Repurchase agreements (repos)	Dealers in U.S. government securities	Overnight to about 3 months; also open repos (continuing contracts)	No secondary market	Repurchase price set higher than selling price; difference quoted as repo interest rate	Sales of government securities by dealer with simultaneous agreement to repurchase

TABLE 31.1

Money-market investments in the United States.

U.S. Treasury Bills

The first item in Table 31.1 is U.S. Treasury bills. These are usually issued weekly and mature in four weeks, three months, or six months.[20] Sales are by auction. You can enter a competitive bid and take your chance of receiving an allotment at your bid price. Alternatively, if you want to be sure of getting your bills, you can enter a noncompetitive bid. Noncompetitive bids are filled at the *average* price of the successful competitive bids. You don't have to participate in the auction to invest in Treasury bills. There is also an excellent secondary market in which billions of dollars of bills are bought and sold every day.

Federal Agency Securities

Agencies of the federal government such as the Federal Home Loan Bank (FHLB) and the Federal National Mortgage Association ("Fannie Mae") borrow both short and long term. The short-term debt consists of discount notes, which are similar to Treasury bills. They are very actively traded and are often held by corporations. Their yields are slightly above those on comparable Treasury securities. One reason for the slightly higher yields is that agency debt is not quite as marketable as Treasury issues.

Another is that most agency debt is backed not by the "full faith and credit" of the U.S. government but only by the agency itself.[21] Most investors do not believe that the U.S. government would allow one of its agencies to default, but in 2000 their faith and the price of agency debt both took a knock when a senior Treasury official reminded Congress that the government did *not* guarantee the debt. Soothing noises from the Treasury subsequently helped to reassure investors.

Short-Term Tax-Exempts

Short-term notes are also issued by municipalities, states, and agencies such as state universities and school districts.[22] These are slightly more risky than Treasury bills and not as easy to buy or sell.[23] Nevertheless they have one particular attraction—the interest is not subject to federal income tax.[24]

Pretax yields on tax-exempts are substantially lower than those on comparable taxed securities. But if your company pays tax at the standard 35 percent corporate rate, the lower gross yield of the municipals may be more than offset by the savings in tax.

Tax-exempt issues also include variable-rate demand bonds (VRDBs). These are long-term securities, whose interest payments are linked to the level of short-term interest rates. Whenever the interest rate is reset, investors have the right to sell the bonds back to the issuer for their face value. This ensures that on these reset dates the price of the bonds cannot be less than their face value. Therefore, although

---

[20]So-called three-month bills actually mature 91 days after issue, and six-month bills mature 182 days after issue.

[21]The exception is Ginnie Mae, whose debt is guaranteed by the U.S. government.

[22]Some of these notes are *general obligations* of the issuer; others are *revenue securities,* and in these cases payments are made from rent receipts or other user charges.

[23]Defaults on tax-exempts are rare but not unknown. For example, in 1983 the municipal utility Washington Public Power Supply System (unfortunately known as WPPSS) defaulted on $2.25 billion of bonds. The 1994 default of Orange County is described in Section 13.4.

[24]This advantage is partly offset by the fact that Treasury securities are free of state and local taxes.

VRDBs are long-term bonds, their prices are very stable and they compete with short-term tax-exempt notes as a home for spare cash.

Bank Time Deposits and Certificates of Deposit

If you make a time deposit with a bank, you are lending money to the bank for a fixed period. If you need the money before maturity, the bank will usually allow you to withdraw it but will exact a penalty in the form of a reduced rate of interest.

In the 1960s banks introduced the **negotiable certificate of deposit (CD)** for time deposits of $1 million or more. In this case, when the bank borrows, it issues a certificate of deposit, which is simply evidence of a time deposit with that bank. If a lender needs the money before maturity, it can sell the CD to another investor. When the loan matures, the new owner of the CD presents it to the bank and receives payment.

In recent years doubts about the creditworthiness of some banks have caused the secondary market in CDs to become less active, so that CDs are now much more like large non-negotiable time deposits.[25]

Instead of depositing dollars with a bank in the United States, a corporation can deposit them overseas with a foreign bank or the foreign branch of a U.S. bank. These deposits pay a fixed rate of interest, and either they are for a fixed term that may vary from one day to several years or they are for an undefined term but may be called at one or more days' notice. Since a time deposit is an illiquid investment, the London branches of the major banks also issue negotiable international dollar CDs.

Commercial Paper

We described commercial paper in the last chapter so we will not discuss it here beyond reminding you that it is short-term debt that is issued on a regular basis by both financial and nonfinancial companies. Commercial paper is popular with both industrial companies and money-market mutual funds as a parking place for short-term cash.

Bankers' Acceptances

In the next chapter we will explain how **bankers' acceptances (BAs)** may be used to finance exports or imports. An acceptance begins life as a written demand for the bank to pay a given sum at a future date. The bank then agrees to this demand by writing "accepted" on it. Once accepted, the draft becomes the bank's IOU and is a negotiable security that can be bought or sold through money-market dealers. Acceptances by the large U.S. banks generally mature in one to six months and involve very low credit risk.

Repurchase Agreements

Repurchase agreements, or *repos,* are effectively secured loans to a government security dealer. They work as follows: The investor buys part of the dealer's holding of Treasury securities and simultaneously arranges to sell them back again at a later date at a specified higher price. The borrower (the dealer) is said to have entered into a *repo;* the lender (who buys the securities) is said to have a *reverse repo.*

[25]Some CDs are not negotiable at all and are therefore *identical* to time deposits. For example, banks may sell low-value non-negotiable CDs to individuals.

Repos sometimes run for several months, but more frequently they are just overnight (24-hour) agreements. No other domestic money-market investment offers such liquidity. Corporations can treat overnight repos almost as if they were interest-bearing demand deposits.

Suppose that you decide to invest cash in repos for several days or weeks. You don't want to keep renegotiating agreements every day. One solution is to enter into an *open repo* with a security dealer. In this case there is no fixed maturity to the agreement; either side is free to withdraw at one day's notice. Alternatively, you may arrange with your bank to transfer any excess cash automatically into repos.

For many years repos appeared to be not only very liquid instruments but also very safe.[26] This reputation took a knock in 1982 when two money-market dealers went bankrupt. Each case involved heavy use of repos. One dealer, Drysdale Securities, had been in existence for only three months and had total capital of $20 million. However, it went bankrupt, owing Chase Bank $250 million. It's not easy to run up debts that fast, but Drysdale did it.

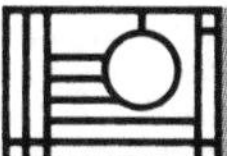

31.5 FLOATING-RATE PREFERRED STOCK—AN ALTERNATIVE TO MONEY-MARKET INVESTMENTS

There is no law preventing firms from making short-term investments in long-term securities. If a firm has $1 million set aside for an income tax payment, it could buy a long-term bond on January 1 and sell it on April 15, when the taxes must be paid. However, the danger in this strategy is obvious. What happens if bond prices fall by 10 percent between January and April? There you are, with a $1 million liability to the Internal Revenue Service, bonds worth only $900,000, and a very red face. Of course, bond prices could also go up, but why take the chance? Corporate treasurers entrusted with excess funds for short-term investment are naturally averse to the price volatility of long-term bonds.

We saw earlier how municipalities devised variable-rate demand bonds, which investors could periodically sell back to the issuer. The prices of these bonds are nearly immune to fluctuations in interest rates. In addition, the interest on municipal loans has the attraction of being tax-exempt. So a municipal variable-rate demand bond offers a safe, tax-free, short-term haven for your $1 million of cash.

Common stock and preferred stock also have an interesting tax advantage for corporations, since firms pay tax on only 30 percent of dividends received from other corporations. For each $1 of dividends received, the firm gets to keep $1 - .30 \times .35 = \$.895$. Thus the effective tax rate is only 10.5 percent. This is higher than the zero tax rate on the interest from municipal debt but much lower than the rate that the company pays on other debt interest.

Suppose you consider putting that $1 million in some other corporation's preferred shares.[27] The 10.5 percent tax rate is very tempting. On the other hand,

[26]To reduce the risk of repos, it is common to value the security at less than its market value. This difference is known as a *haircut*.

[27]Preferred shares are usually better short-term investments for a corporation than common shares. The preferred shares' expected return is virtually all dividends; most common shares are expected to generate capital gains, too. The corporate tax on capital gains is usually 35 percent. Corporations therefore have a strong incentive to like dividends and dislike capital gains.

since preferred dividends are fixed, the prices of preferred shares change when long-term interest rates change. A $1 million investment in preferred shares could be worth only $900,000 on April 15, when taxes are due. Wouldn't it be nice if someone invented a preferred share that was insulated from fluctuating interest rates?

Well, there are such securities, and you can probably guess how they work: Specify a dividend payment which goes up and down with the general level of interest rates.[28] The prices of these securities are less volatile than those of fixed-dividend preferreds.

Varying the dividend payment on preferred stock doesn't quite do the trick. For example, if investors become more concerned about the risk of preferred stock, they might demand a higher relative return and the price of the stock could fall. So companies sometimes add another wrinkle to floating-rate preferred. Instead of being tied rigidly to interest rates, the dividend can be reset periodically by means of an auction which is open to all investors. Existing shareholders can enter the auction by stating the minimum dividend they are prepared to accept; if this turns out to be higher than the rate that is needed to sell the issue, the shareholders sell the stock to the new investors at its face value. Alternatively, shareholders can simply enter a noncompetitive bid, keeping their shares and receiving whatever dividend is set by the other bidders. The result is similar to the variable-rate demand note: Because auction-rate preferred stock can be resold at regular intervals for its face value, its price cannot wander far in the interim.[29]

Why would any firm want to *issue* floating-rate preferreds? Dividends must be paid out of *after-tax* income, whereas interest comes out of before-tax income. Thus, if a taxpaying firm wants to issue a floating-rate security, it would normally choose to issue floating-rate debt to generate interest tax shields.

However, there are plenty of firms that are not paying taxes. These firms cannot make use of the interest tax shield. Moreover, they have been able to issue floating-rate preferreds at yields *lower* than what they would have to pay on a floating-rate debt issue. (The corporations buying the preferreds are happy with these lower yields because 70 percent of the dividends they receive escape tax.)

Floating-rate preferreds were invented in Canada in the mid-1970s, when several billion dollars' worth were issued before the Canadian tax authorities cooled off the market by limiting the dividend tax exclusion on some types of floating-rate issues. They were reinvented in the United States in May 1982, when Chemical New York Corporation, the holding company for Chemical Bank, raised $200 million. The securities proved so popular that over $4 billion of floating-rate preferreds were issued by the following spring. Then the novelty wore off, and the frequency of new issues slowed down. It was back to business as usual, with one important exception: There was one more item on the menu of investment opportunities open to corporate money managers.

[28]Usually there are limits on the maximum and minimum dividends that can be paid. Thus if interest rates leap to 100 percent, the preferred dividend would hit a ceiling of, say, 15 percent. If interest rates fall to 1 percent, the preferred dividend would hit a floor at say, 5 percent.

[29]See M. J. Alderson, K. C. Brown, and S. L. Lummer, "Dutch Auction Rate Preferred Stock," *Financial Management* 16 (Summer 1987), pp. 68–73.

In the United States a high proportion of small purchases are paid for by check. To make the best use of their cash, companies need to understand how a company's cash changes when it writes or deposits a check. The cash shown in the company's ledger is not the same as the available balance in your bank account. The difference is the net float. When you have written a large number of checks awaiting clearance, the available balance will be larger than the ledger balance. When you have just deposited a large number of checks that have not yet been cleared by the bank, the available balance will be smaller. If you can predict how long it will take checks to clear, you may be able to play the float and get by on a smaller cash balance.

You can also *manage* the float by speeding up collections and slowing down payments. One way to speed collections is to use concentration banking. Customers make payments to a regional office which then pays the checks into a local bank account. Surplus funds are transferred from the local account to a concentration bank. An alternative technique is lock-box banking. In this case customers send their payments to a local post office box. A local bank empties the box at regular intervals and clears the checks. Concentration banking and lock-box banking reduce mailing time and the time required to clear checks.

Large-value payments are almost always made electronically. In the United States there are two large-value systems—Fedwire (for dollar payments within the country) and CHIPS (for cross-border payments). Bulk payments, such as wages and dividends, are usually made by means of the Automated Clearinghouse (ACH) system.

Banks provide many services. They handle checks, manage lock boxes, provide advice, obtain references, and so on. Firms either pay cash for these services or pay by maintaining sufficient cash balances with the bank.

In many cases you will want to keep somewhat larger balances than are needed to pay for the tangible services. One reason is that the bank may be a valuable source of ideas and business connections. Another reason is that you may use the bank as a source of short-term funds. Leaving idle cash at your bank may be implicit compensation for the willingness of the bank to stand ready to advance credit when needed. A large cash balance may, therefore, be good insurance against a rainy day.

Cash provides liquidity, but it doesn't pay interest. Securities pay interest, but you can't use them to buy things. As financial manager you want to hold cash up to the point where the marginal value of liquidity is equal to the interest that you could earn on securities.

Cash is just one of the raw materials that you need to do business. It is expensive keeping your capital tied up in large inventories of raw materials when it could be earning interest. So why do you hold inventories at all? Why not order materials as and when you need them? The answer is that it is also expensive to keep placing many small orders. You need to strike a balance between holding too large an inventory of cash (and losing interest on the money) and making too many small adjustments to your stock of cash (and incurring additional administrative and transaction costs). If interest rates are high, you want to hold relatively small inventories of cash. If your cash needs are variable and your costs are high, you want to hold relatively large inventories.

If you have more cash than is currently needed, you can invest it in the money market. There is a wide choice of money-market investments, with different

FIGURE 31.4

Short-term assets held by U.S. nonfinancial corporations, 4th quarter, 2000.

Source: Federal Reserve System, Division of Research and Statistics, *Flow of Funds Accounts* (**www.federalreserve.gov/releases/Z1/current/data.htm**).

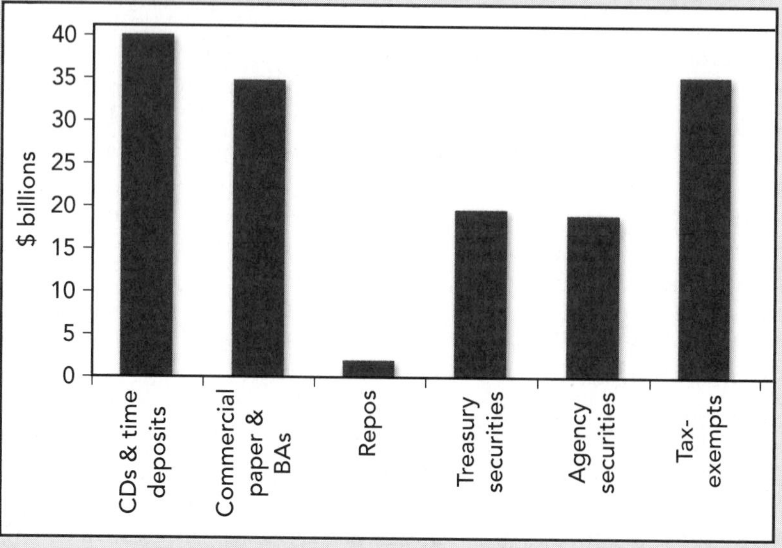

degrees of liquidity and risk. Remember that the interest rate on these investments is often quoted as a discount. The compound return is always higher than the rate of discount.

The principal money-market investments in the United States are

- U.S. Treasury bills
- Federal agency notes
- Short-term tax-exempts
- Time deposits and certificates of deposit
- Repurchase agreements
- Commercial paper
- Bankers' acceptances

Figure 31.4 should give you some feel for which of these investments are the most popular homes for surplus cash.

FURTHER READING

The next three articles analyze the design of lock-box and concentration banking systems:

A. Kraus, C. Janssen, and A. McAdams: "The Lock-Box Location Problem," *Journal of Bank Research,* 1:50–58 (Autumn 1970).

G. Cornuejols, M. L. Fisher, and G. L. Nemhauser: "Location of Bank Accounts to Optimize Float: An Analytic Study of Exact and Approximate Algorithms," *Management Science,* 23:789–810 (April 1977).

S. F. Maier and J. H. Vander Weide: "What Lock-Box and Disbursement Models Really Do," *Journal of Finance,* 37:361–371 (May 1983).

Baumol was the pioneer in applying inventory models to cash management. Miller and Orr extend the Baumol model to handling uncertain cash flows, and Mullins and Homonoff review tests of inventory models for cash management.

W. J. Baumol: "The Transactions Demand for Cash: An Inventory Theoretic Approach," *Quarterly Journal of Economics,* 66:545–556 (November 1952).

M. H. Miller and D. Orr: "A Model of the Demand for Money by Firms," *Quarterly Journal of Economics,* 80:413–435 (August 1966).

D. Mullins and R. Homonoff: "Applications of Inventory Cash Management Models," in S. C. Myers (ed.), *Modern Developments in Financial Management,* Frederick A. Praeger, Inc., New York, 1976.

The following article provides a useful description of electronic payments systems in the United States:

G. R. Junker, B. J. Summers, and F. M. Young: "A Primer on the Settlement of Payments in the United States," *Federal Reserve Bulletin,* 77:847–858 (November 1991).

Specialized "how-to" texts on cash management include:

J. E. Finnerty: *How to Manage Corporate Cash Effectively,* American Management Association, New York, 1991.

J. G. Kallberg and K. L. Parkinson: *Corporate Liquidity: Management and Measurement,* Richard D. Irwin, Homewood, IL, 1993.

C. R. Malburg: *The Cash Management Handbook,* Prentice-Hall, Englewood Cliffs, NJ, 1992.

For a detailed description of the money market and short-term lending opportunities, see:

L. Epstein: *Corporate Investing: A Treasurer's Reference,* John Wiley, New York, 2001.

F. J. Fabozzi, *The Handbook of Fixed Income Securities,* 6th ed., McGraw-Hill Companies, Inc., New York, 2000.

M. Stigum: *The Money Market,* 3rd ed., McGraw-Hill Professional Publishing, New York, 1990.

Chapter 4 of *U.S. Monetary Policy and Financial Markets,* which is available on the New York Federal Reserve website, **www.newyorkfed.org.**

QUIZ

1. A company has the following cash balances:

Company's ledger balance	$600,000
Bank's ledger balance	$625,000
Available balance	$550,000

   a. Calculate the payment float and availability float.
   b. Why does the company gain from the payment float?
   c. Suppose the company adopts a policy of writing checks on a remote bank. How is this likely to affect the three measures of cash balance?

2. Anne Teak, the financial manager of a furniture manufacturer, is considering operating a lock-box system. She forecasts that 300 payments a day will be made to lock boxes, with an average payment size of $1,500. The bank's charge for operating the lock boxes is *either* $.40 a check *or* compensating balances of $800,000.
   a. If the interest rate is 9 percent, which method of payment is cheaper?
   b. What reduction in the time to collect and process each check is needed to justify use of the lock-box system?

3. Complete the passage that follows by choosing the appropriate terms from the following list: *lock-box banking, Fedwire, CHIPS, payment float, concentration banking, availability float, net float.*

   The firm's available balance is equal to its ledger balance plus the _______ and minus the _______. The difference between the available balance and the ledger balance is often called the _______. Firms can increase their cash resources by speeding up collections. One way to do this is to arrange for payments to be made to regional offices which pay the checks into local banks. This is known as _______. Surplus funds are then transferred from the local bank to one of the company's main banks. Transfers can be made electronically by the _______ or _______ systems. Another technique is to arrange for a local bank to collect the checks directly from a post office box. This is known as _______.

4. Everyman's Bookstore has experienced an increased demand for *Principles of Corporate Finance.* It now expects to sell 216 books a year. Unfortunately, inventory carrying costs have increased to $6 per book per year, whereas order costs have remained steady at $2 per order. How many orders should the store place per year and what is its average inventory? You can answer the question either by plotting store costs as in Figure 31.1 or using the formula shown on the *Principles of Corporate Finance* Web page (**www.mhhe.com/bm7e**)

5. Now assume that Everyman's Bookstore uses up cash at a steady rate of $20,000 a year. The interest rate is 2 percent, and each sale of securities costs $2. How many times a year should the store sell securities and what is its average cash balance? Either plot the costs as in Figure 31.1 or use the formula shown on the *Principles of Corporate Finance* Web page (**www.mhhe.com/bm7e**)

6. Suppose that you can hold cash that pays no interest or invest in securities that pay interest at 8 percent. The securities are not easily sold on short notice; therefore, you must make up any cash deficiency by drawing on a bank line of credit which charges interest at 10 percent. Should you invest more or less in securities under each of the following circumstances?
   a. You are unusually uncertain about future cash flows.
   b. The interest rate on bank loans rises to 11 percent.
   c. The interest rates on securities and on bank loans both rise by the same proportion.
   d. You revise downward your forecast of future cash needs.

7. In January 2002 six-month (182-day) Treasury bills were issued at a discount of 1.75 percent. What is the annual yield?

8. For each item below, choose the investment that best fits the accompanying description:
   a. Maturity often overnight (repurchase agreements/bankers' acceptances).
   b. Maturity never more than 270 days (tax-exempts/commercial paper).
   c. Often directly placed with investors (finance company commercial paper/industrial commercial paper).
   d. Registered with the SEC (commercial paper/medium-term notes).
   e. Issued by the U.S. Treasury (tax-exempts/3-month bills).
   f. Quoted on a discount basis (certificates of deposit/Treasury bills).
   g. Sold by auction (tax-exempts/Treasury bills).

9. Consider three securities:
   a. A floating-rate bond.
   b. A preferred share paying a fixed dividend.
   c. A floating-rate preferred.

   A financial manager responsible for short-term investment of excess cash would probably choose the floating-rate preferred over *either* of the other two securities. Why? Explain briefly.

PRACTICE QUESTIONS

1. Every day, Consolidated Blancmange writes checks worth $100,000. These checks take an average of five days to clear. The company also receives payments of $150,000 every day. These take three days to clear.
   a. Calculate payment float, availability float, and net float.
   b. What would be the company's annual savings if it could reduce availability float to one day? The interest rate is 6 percent a year. What would be the present value of these savings?
2. On January 25, Coot Company has $250,000 deposited with a local bank. On January 27, the company writes and mails checks of $20,000 and $60,000 to suppliers. At the end of the month, Coot's financial manager deposits a $45,000 check received from a customer in the morning mail and picks up the end-of-month account summary from the bank. The manager notes that only the $20,000 payment of the 27th has cleared the bank. What are the company's ledger balance and payment float? What is the company's net float?
3. Knob, Inc., is a nationwide distributor of furniture hardware. The company now uses a central billing system for credit sales of $180 million annually. First National, Knob's principal bank, offers to establish a new concentration banking system for a flat fee of $100,000 per year. The bank estimates that mailing and collection time can be reduced by three days. By how much will Knob's availability float be reduced under the new system? How much extra interest income will the new system generate if the extra funds are used to reduce borrowing under Knob's line of credit with First National? Assume that the borrowing rate is 12 percent. Finally, should Knob accept First National's offer if collection costs under the old system are $40,000 per year?
4. Explain why companies use zero-balance accounts to make disbursements.
5. A parent company settles the collection account balances of its subsidiaries once a week. (That is, each week it transfers any balances in the accounts to a central account.) The cost of a wire transfer is $10. A check costs $.80. Cash transferred by wire is available the same day, but the parent must wait three days for checks to clear. Cash can be invested at 12 percent per year. How much money must be in a collection account before it pays to use a wire transfer?
6. The financial manager of JAC Cosmetics is considering opening a lock box in Pittsburgh. Checks cleared through the lock box will amount to $300,000 per month. The lock box will make cash available to the company three days earlier than is currently the case.
   a. Suppose that the bank offers to run the lock box for a $20,000 compensating balance. Is the lock box worthwhile?
   b. Suppose that the bank offers to run the lock box for a fee of $.10 per check cleared instead of a compensating balance. What must the average check size be for the fee alternative to be less costly? Assume an interest rate of 6 percent per year.
   c. Why did you need to know the interest rate to answer (b) but not to answer (a)?
7. Some years ago, Merrill Lynch increased its float by mailing checks drawn on west coast banks to customers in the east and checks drawn on east coast banks to customers in the west. A subsequent class action suit against Merrill Lynch revealed that in 28 months, from September 1976, Merrill Lynch disbursed $1.25 billion in 365,000 checks to New York State customers alone. The plaintiffs' lawyer calculated that by using a remote bank Merrill Lynch had increased its average float by 1.5 days.
   a. How much did Merrill Lynch disburse per day to New York State customers?
   b. What was the total gain to Merrill Lynch over the 28 months, assuming an interest rate of 8 percent?
   c. What was the present value of the increase in float if the benefits were expected to be permanent?

d. Suppose that the use of remote banks had involved Merrill Lynch in extra expenses. What was the maximum extra cost per check that Merrill Lynch would have been prepared to pay?

8. The processing cost of making a payment through the ACH system is roughly half the cost of making the same payment by check. Why, therefore, do firms often rationally choose to make payments by check?

9. How would you expect a firm's cash balance to respond to the following changes?
   a. Interest rates increase.
   b. The volatility of daily cash flow decreases.
   c. The transaction cost of buying or selling marketable securities goes up.

10. A firm maintains a separate account for cash disbursements. Total disbursements are $100,000 per month, spread evenly over the month. Administrative and transaction costs of transferring cash to the disbursement account are $10 per transfer. Marketable securities yield 1 percent per month. Determine the size and number of transfers that will minimize the cost of maintaining the special account.

11. Suppose that the rate of inflation accelerates from 5 to 10 percent per year. Would firms' cash balances go up or down relative to sales? Explain.

12. Suppose that interest rates double.
   a. What, according to the Baumol model, would happen to the firm's average cash balances?
   b. Recalculate the gain from operating the lock-box system described in Section 31.1 given the new level of interest rates.

13. A three-month Treasury bill and a six-month bill both sell at a discount of 10 percent. Which offers the higher annual yield?

14. In Section 31.3 we described a six-month bill that was issued on an annually compounded yield of 5.19 percent. Suppose that one month has passed and the investment still offers the same annually compounded return. What is the percentage discount? What was your return over the month?

15. Look again at question 14. Suppose another month has passed, so the bill has only one month left to run. It is now selling at a discount of 5 percent. What is the yield calculated on a simple interest basis? What was your realized return over the two months?

16. Look up current interest rates offered by short-term investment alternatives. Suppose that your firm has $1 million excess cash to invest for the next two months. How would you invest this cash? How would your answer change if the excess cash were $5,000, $20,000, $100,000, or $100 million?

17. In February 2002 high-grade corporate bonds sold at a yield of 5.89 percent, while tax-exempts of comparable maturity offered 3.99 percent annually. If an investor receives the same *after-tax* return from corporates and tax-exempts, what is that investor's marginal rate of tax? What other factors might affect an investor's choice between the two types of securities?

18. The IRS prohibits companies from borrowing money to buy tax-exempts and also deducting the interest payments on the borrowing from taxable income. Should the IRS prohibit such activity? If it didn't, would you advise the company to borrow to buy tax-exempts?

19. Suppose you are a wealthy individual paying 39.1 percent tax on income. What is the expected after-tax yield on each of the following investments?
   a. A municipal note yielding 6.5 percent pretax.
   b. A Treasury bill yielding 10 percent pretax.
   c. A floating-rate preferred stock yielding 7.5 percent pretax.

How would your answer change if the investor is a corporation paying tax at 35 percent? What other factors would you need to take into account when deciding where to invest the corporation's spare cash?

20. Most floating-rate preferreds have both a floor and a ceiling on their dividend rate. (See Section 31.5, footnote 28.) How do these limits affect the behavior of the *prices* of these securities as interest rates change? Why do you think the companies included the limits in the first place?

CHALLENGE QUESTION

1. The first floating-rate preferreds were successfully issued at initial yields *below* yields on Treasury bills. How was this possible? The preferreds were clearly riskier than the bills. What would you predict for the *long-run* relationship between yields on bills and on floating-rate preferreds? (We say "long-run" to give time for all firms that will want to issue floating-rate preferreds to get around to doing so.)

CHAPTER THIRTY-TWO

CREDIT MANAGEMENT

WHEN COMPANIES SELL their products, they sometimes demand cash on or before delivery, but in most cases they allow some delay in payment. If you turn back to the balance sheet in Table 30.1, you can see that for the average manufacturing company, *accounts receivable* constitute about one-third of its current assets. Receivables include both trade credit and consumer credit. The former is by far the larger and will, therefore, be the main focus of this chapter.

Companies that do not pay for their purchases immediately are effectively borrowing money from their suppliers. Such "debts" show up as *accounts payable* in the purchasing companies' balance sheets. Table 30.1 shows that payables are the most important source of short-term finance, much larger than short-term loans from banks and other institutions.

Management of trade credit requires answers to five sets of questions:

1. On what terms do you propose to sell your goods or services? How long are you going to give customers to pay their bills? Are you prepared to offer a cash discount for prompt payment?
2. What evidence do you need of indebtedness? Do you just ask the buyer to sign a receipt, or do you insist on some more formal commitment?
3. Which customers are likely to pay their bills? To find out, do you consult a credit agency or ask for a bank reference? Or do you analyze the customer's financial statements?
4. How much credit are you prepared to extend to each customer? Do you play it safe by turning down any doubtful prospects? Or do you accept the risk of a few bad debts as part of the cost of building up a large regular clientele?
5. How do you collect the money when it becomes due? How do you keep track of payments? What do you do about reluctant payers or deadbeats?

We will discuss each set of questions in turn.

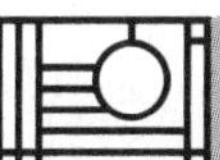

32.1 TERMS OF SALE

Not all sales involve credit. For example, if you are producing goods to the customer's specification or incurring substantial delivery costs, then it may be sensible to ask for cash before delivery (CBD). If you are supplying goods to a wide variety of irregular customers, you may prefer cash on delivery (COD).[1] If your product is expensive and custom-designed, you may require **progress payments** as work is carried out. For example, a large, extended consulting contract might call for 30 percent payment after completion of field research, 30 percent more on submission of a draft report, and the remaining 40 percent when the project is finally completed.

When we look at transactions that do involve credit, we find that each industry seems to have its own particular usage with regard to payment terms.[2] These norms have a rough logic. For example, firms selling consumer durables may allow the buyer a month to pay, while those selling perishable goods, such as cheese or fresh fruit, typically demand payment in a week. Similarly, a seller will generally allow more extended payment if its customers are in low-risk businesses, if

[1]Some goods *can't* be sold on credit—a glass of beer, for example.

[2]Standard credit terms in different industries are reported in O. K. Ng, J. K. Smith, and R. L. Smith, "Evidence on the Determinants of Credit Terms Used in Interfirm Trade," *Journal of Finance* 54 (June 1999), pp. 1109–1129.

their accounts are large, if the customers need time to ascertain the quality of the goods, and if the goods are not quickly resold.

To induce customers to pay before the final date, it is common to offer a cash discount for prompt settlement. For example, pharmaceutical manufacturers commonly require payment within 30 days but may offer a 2 percent discount to customers who pay within 10 days. These terms are referred to as "2/10, net 30."

Cash discounts are often very large. For example, a customer who buys on terms of 2/10, net 30 may decide to forgo the cash discount and pay on the thirtieth day. This means that the customer obtains an extra 20 days' credit but pays about 2 percent more for the goods. This is equivalent to borrowing money at a rate of 44.6 percent per annum.[3] Of course, any firm that delays payment beyond the due date gains a cheaper loan but damages its reputation for creditworthiness.

You can think of the terms of sale as fixing both the price for the cash buyer and the rate of interest charged for credit. For example, suppose that a firm reduces the cash discount from 2 to 1 percent. That would represent an *increase* in the price for the cash buyer of 1 percent but a *reduction* in the implicit rate of interest charged the credit buyer from just over 2 percent per 20 days to just over 1 percent per 20 days.

For many items that are bought on a recurrent basis, it is inconvenient to require separate payment for each delivery. A common solution is to pretend that all sales during the month in fact occur at the end of the month (EOM). Thus goods may be sold on terms of 8/10, EOM, net 60. This arrangement allows the customer a cash discount of 8 percent if the bill is paid within 10 days of the end of the month; otherwise, the full payment is due within 60 days of the invoice date.[4] When purchases are subject to seasonal fluctuations, manufacturers often encourage customers to take early delivery by allowing them to delay payment until the usual order season. This practice is known as "season dating."

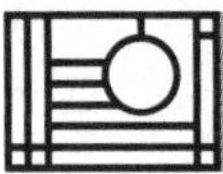

32.2 COMMERCIAL CREDIT INSTRUMENTS

The terms of sale define when payment is due but not the nature of the contract. Repetitive sales to domestic customers are almost always made on *open account* and involve only an implicit contract. There is simply a record in the seller's books and a receipt signed by the buyer.

If you want a clear commitment from the buyer, before you deliver the goods, you can arrange a **commercial draft.**[5] This works as follows: You draw a draft ordering payment by the customer and send this draft to the customer's bank together with the shipping documents. If immediate payment is required, the draft is termed a *sight draft;* otherwise, it is known as a *time draft.* Depending on whether it is a sight or a time

[3]The cash discount allows you to pay \$98 rather than \$100. If you do not take the discount, you get a 20-day loan, but you pay $2/98 = 2.04$ percent more for your goods. The number of 20-day periods in a year is $365/20 = 18.25$. A dollar invested for 18.25 periods at 2.04 percent per period grows to $(1.0204)^{18.25} = \$1.446$, a 44.6 percent return on the original investment. If a customer is happy to borrow at this rate, it's a good bet that he or she is desperate for cash (or can't work out compound interest). For a discussion of this issue, see J. K. Smith, "Trade Credit and Information Asymmetry," *Journal of Finance* 42 (September 1987), pp. 863–872.

[4]Terms of 8/10, prox., net 60 would entitle the customer to a discount if the bill is paid within 10 days of the end of the following (or "proximo") month.

[5]Commercial drafts are sometimes known by the more general term *bills of exchange.*

draft, the customer either pays up or acknowledges the debt by adding the word *accepted* and his or her signature. The bank then hands the shipping documents to the customer and forwards the money or the **trade acceptance** to you, the seller.[6] You may hold the trade acceptance to maturity or use it as security for a loan.

If your customer's credit is for any reason suspect, you may ask the customer to arrange for his or her bank to *accept* the time draft. In this case, the bank guarantees the customer's debt. These **bankers' acceptances** are often used in overseas trade; they have a higher standing and greater negotiability than trade acceptances.

If you are selling goods overseas, you may ask the customer to arrange for an *irrevocable letter of credit.* In this case the customer's bank sends you a letter stating that it has established a credit in your favor at a bank in the United States. You then draw a draft on the customer's bank and present it to your bank in the United States together with the letter of credit and the shipping documents. The bank in the United States arranges for this draft to be accepted or paid and forwards the documents to the customer's bank.

If you sell goods to a customer who proves unable to pay, you cannot get your goods back. You simply become a general creditor of the company, in common with other unfortunates. You can avoid this situation by making a *conditional sale,* whereby title to the goods remains with the seller until full payment is made. The conditional sale is common practice in Europe. In the United States it is used only for goods that are bought on an installment basis. In this case, if the customer fails to make the agreed number of payments, then the goods can be immediately repossessed by the seller.

32.3 CREDIT ANALYSIS

Firms are not allowed to discriminate between customers by charging them different prices. Neither may they discriminate by offering the same prices but different credit terms.[7] You *can* offer different terms of sale to different *classes* of buyers. You can offer volume discounts, for example, or discounts to customers willing to accept long-term purchase contracts. But as a rule, if you have a customer of doubtful standing, you should keep to your regular terms of sale and protect yourself by restricting the volume of goods that the customer may buy on credit.

There are a number of ways to find out whether customers are likely to pay their debts. For example, you are likely to have more confidence in those existing customers that have paid promptly in the past. For new customers there are three broad sources of information about their creditworthiness. You can seek the views of a specialist credit analyst, you can look at the information embedded in the firm's security prices, or you can use the firm's financial statements to make your own assessment.

Specialist Credit Analysts The simplest way to assess a customer's credit standing is to seek the views of a specialist in credit assessment. For example, in Chapter 24 we described how bond rating agencies, such as Moody's and Standard and Poor's, provide a useful guide to the riskiness of the firm's bonds.

---

[6]You often see the terms of sale defined as "SD-BL." This means that the bank will hand over the bill of lading in return for payment on a sight draft.

[7]Price discrimination, and by implication credit discrimination, is prohibited by the Robinson-Patman Act.

Bond ratings are usually available only for relatively large firms. However, you can obtain information on many smaller companies from a credit agency. Dun and Bradstreet is by far the largest of these agencies and its database contains reports on more than 10 million companies.

Credit agencies usually report the experience that other firms have had with your customer. Alternatively, you may be able to get this information by checking with a credit bureau or by contacting the firms directly. You can also ask your bank to undertake a credit check. It will contact the customer's bank and ask for information on the customer's average balance, access to bank credit, and general reputation.

Security Prices In addition to checking with a credit agency or your bank, it may make sense to check what everybody else in the financial community thinks about your customer's credit standing. Does that sound expensive? It isn't if your customer is a public company. For example, you can learn what other investors think by comparing the yield on the firm's bonds with the yields on those of other firms. (Of course, the comparison should be between bonds of similar maturity, coupon, etc.) You can also look at how the customer's stock price has been behaving. A sharp fall in stock price doesn't mean that the company is in trouble, but it does suggest that prospects are less bright than they were formerly.

In Chapter 24 we saw how information on security prices can be used to put a figure on the chances of default. Companies have an incentive to exercise their option to default when the value of their assets is less than the amount of their debt. So, if you know how much the value of the firm's assets may fluctuate, you can estimate the probability that the asset value will fall below the default point. In Chapter 24 we looked at an example of how one consulting firm, KMV, uses this market-based approach to estimate default probabilities.

Financial Statements Security price data may not be available for many customers, and in these cases you will need to rely on the customers' financial statements to make your own assessment of their credit standing. In Chapter 29 we saw how managers calculate a few key financial ratios to measure the firm's financial strength. Firms that are highly leveraged, illiquid, and unprofitable generally don't make dependable customers.

If you have a large number of customers, it may be useful to combine different financial indicators into a single measure of which companies or individuals are most likely to default. For example, if you apply for a credit card or a bank loan, you will be asked various questions about your financial position. The information that you provide is then used to calculate an overall credit score. One widely used system, designed by the consultancy firm Fair Isaacs, takes account of five factors: (1) How promptly the applicant has paid in the past (35 percent of score); (2) how much debt of each type is outstanding (30 percent of score); (3) the length of the applicant's credit history (15 percent of score); (4) the number of credit cards and recently opened credit accounts that the applicant has (10 percent of score); and (5) the mix of regular credit cards, store cards, and margin accounts (10 percent of score). Applicants who fail to make the grade on the score are likely to be refused credit or subjected to more detailed analysis.

Suppose you want to devise a scoring system that will help you to decide whether to extend credit to small businesses. You suspect that there is an above-average probability that firms with a low return on assets and a low current ratio

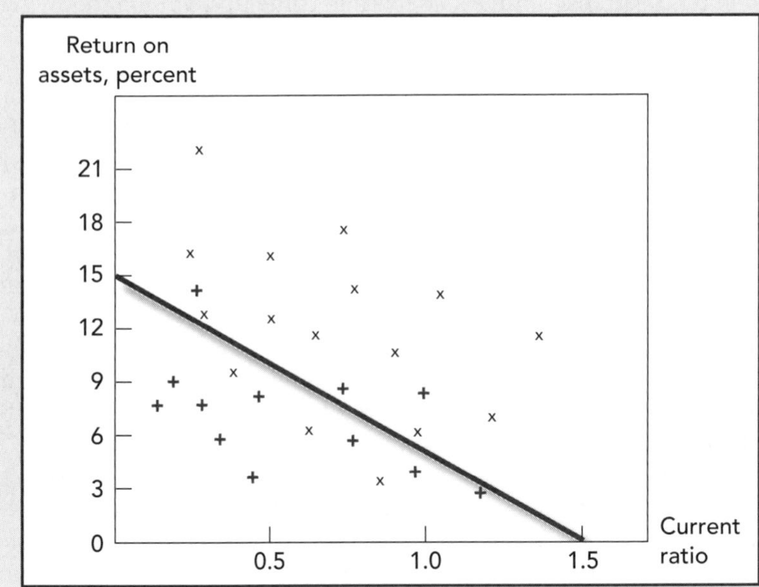

FIGURE 32.1

The black x's represent a hypothetical group of firms that subsequently repaid their loans; the burgundy +'s represent those that defaulted. The sloping line discriminates between the two groups on the basis of return on assets and current ratio. The line represents the equation

$$Z = \text{return on assets} + 10(\text{current ratio}) = 15$$

Firms that plot above the line have Z scores greater than 15.

will default on their debts.[8] To test this, you take a sample of past loans and construct a scatter diagram showing for each borrower the return on assets and the current ratio (see Figure 32.1). Those businesses that repaid their loans are shown by a blue x; the ones that defaulted are shown in burgundy. Now try to draw a straight dividing line between the two groups. You can't completely separate them, but the line in our diagram keeps the two groups as far apart as possible. (Note that there are only three blue x's below the line and three burgundy +'s above it.) This line tells us that if you wish to *discriminate* between the good and the bad risks, you should give 10 times as much weight to the current ratio as you give to return on assets. The index of creditworthiness is

$$\text{Index of creditworthiness} = Z = \text{return on assets, percent} + 10\,(\text{current ratio})$$

You minimize the degree of misclassification if you predict that applicants with Z scores over 15 will pay their debts and that those with Z scores below 15 will not pay.[9]

In practice you do not need to consider only two variables, nor do you need to estimate the equation by eye. *Multiple-discriminant analysis* (MDA) is a straightforward statistical technique for calculating how much weight to put on each variable to separate the creditworthy sheep from the impecunious goats.[10]

---

[8] The current ratio is the ratio of current assets to current liabilities. It is commonly used as a measure of the company's ability to lay its hands on cash. See Chapter 29.

[9] The quantity 15 is an arbitrary constant. We could just as well have used 150, in which case the Z score is

$$Z = 10(\text{return on assets, percent}) + 100(\text{current ratio})$$

[10] MDA is not the only statistical technique that you can use for this purpose. Probit and logit are two other potentially useful techniques. These estimate the probability of some event (e.g., default) as a function of observable attributes.

Edward Altman has used discriminant analysis to come up with the following index of creditworthiness:[11]

$$Z = .72\,\frac{\text{(net working capital)}}{\text{total assets}} + .85\,\frac{\text{(retained earnings)}}{\text{total assets}} + 3.1\,\frac{\text{(EBIT)}}{\text{total assets}}$$
$$+ .42\,\frac{\text{(shareholders' equity)}}{\text{total liabilities}} + 1.0\,\frac{\text{sales}}{\text{total assets}}$$

Those companies with a Z-score of less than 1.20 were predicted to go bankrupt. Companies with Z-scores between 1.20 and 2.90 were hovering in the grey area between decline and recovery.

Updated and refined versions of Altman's Z-score model are regularly used by banks and industrial companies. We wish we could show you one of these recent versions, but they are all top secret. A company with a superior method for identifying good and bad borrowers has a significant leg up on the competition.[12]

Credit scoring systems should carry a health warning. When you construct a risk index, it is tempting to experiment with many different combinations of variables until you find the equation that would have worked best in the past. Unfortunately, if you "mine" the data in this way, you are likely to find that the system works less well in the future than it did previously. If you are misled by the past successes into placing too much faith in your model, you may refuse credit to a number of potentially good customers. The profits that you lose by turning away these customers could more than offset the gains that you make from avoiding a few bad eggs. As a result, you could be worse off than if you had pretended that you could not tell one customer from another and extended credit to all of them.

Does this mean that you should not use credit scoring systems? Not a bit. It simply implies that it is not sufficient to have a good credit scoring system; you also need to know how much to rely on it. That is the topic of the next section.

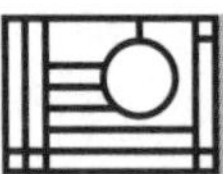

32.4 THE CREDIT DECISION

Let us suppose that you have taken the first three steps toward an effective credit operation. In other words, you have fixed your terms of sale; you have decided on the contract that customers must sign, and you have established a procedure for estimating the probability that they will pay up. Your next step is to work out which of your customers should be offered credit.

If there is no possibility of repeat orders, the decision is relatively simple. Figure 32.2 summarizes your choice. On one hand, you can refuse credit. In this case you make neither a profit nor a loss. The alternative is to offer credit. Suppose that the probability that the customer will pay up is p. If the customer does pay, you receive additional revenues (REV) and you incur additional costs; your

[11] EBIT is earnings before interest and taxes. Z-score models for predicting bankruptcy were originally developed in E. I. Altman, "Financial Ratios, Discriminant Analysis and the Prediction of Corporate Bankruptcy," *Journal of Finance* 23 (September 1968), pp. 589–609. The equation cited here comes from E. I. Altman, *Corporate Financial Distress,* John Wiley, New York, 1983.

[12] When a British bank laid off a number of employees, one unhappy staff member decided that the best way to retaliate was to leak details of the bank's credit scoring system to the press. See V. Orvice, "Would You Get a Loan?" *Daily Mail,* March 16, 1994, p. 29.

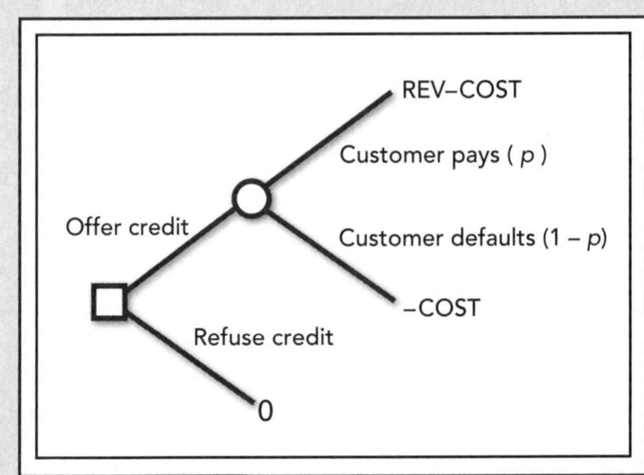

FIGURE 32.2

If you refuse credit, you make neither profit nor loss. If you offer credit, there is a probability p that the customer will pay and you will make REV − COST; there is a probability $(1 - p)$ that the customer will default and you will lose COST.

net gain is the present value of REV − COST. Unfortunately, you can't be certain that the customer will pay; there is a probability $(1 - p)$ of default. Default means you receive nothing and incur the additional costs. The *expected* profit from each course of action is therefore as follows:

	Expected Profit
Refuse credit	0
Grant credit	$p\text{PV(REV} - \text{COST)} - (1 - p)\text{PV(COST)}$

You should grant credit if the expected profit from doing so is greater than the expected profit from refusing.

Consider, for example, the case of the Cast Iron Company. On each nondelinquent sale Cast Iron receives revenues with a present value of \$1,200 and incurs costs with a value of \$1,000. Therefore the company's expected profit if it offers credit is

$$p\text{PV(REV} - \text{COST)} - (1 - p)\text{PV(COST)} = p \times 200 - (1 - p) \times 1{,}000$$

If the probability of collection is 5/6, Cast Iron can expect to break even:

$$\text{Expected profit} = \frac{5}{6} \times 200 - \left(1 - \frac{5}{6}\right) \times 1{,}000 = 0$$

Therefore Cast Iron's policy should be to grant credit whenever the chances of collection are better than 5 out of 6.

When to Stop Looking for Clues

We told you earlier where to *start* looking for clues about a customer's creditworthiness, but we never said anything about when to *stop*. Now we can work out how your profits would be affected by more detailed credit analysis.

Suppose that Cast Iron Company's credit department undertakes a study to determine which customers are most likely to default. It appears that 95 percent of its customers have been prompt payers and 5 percent have been slow payers. However, customers with a record of slow payment are much more likely to default on the next order than those with a record of prompt payment. On the average 20 percent of the slow payers subsequently default, but only 2 percent of the prompt payers do so.

Suppose Cast Iron reviews a sample of 1,000 customers, none of whom has defaulted yet. Of these, 950 have a record of prompt payment, and 50 have a record of slow payment. On the basis of past experience Cast Iron should expect 19 of the prompt payers to default in the future and 10 of the slow payers to do so:

Category	Number of Customers	Probability of Default	Expected Number of Defaults
Prompt payers	950	.02	19
Slow payers	50	.20	10
All customers	1,000	.029	29

Now the credit manager must make a decision: Should the company refuse to give any more credit to customers that have been slow payers in the past?

If you are aware that a customer has been a slow payer, the answer is clearly yes. Every sale to a slow payer has only an 80 percent chance of payment ($p = .8$). Selling to a *slow* payer, therefore, gives an expected *loss* of $40:

$$\text{Expected profit} = p\text{PV}(\text{REV} - \text{COST}) - (1 - p)\text{PV}(\text{COST})$$
$$= .8(200) - .2(1{,}000) = -\$40$$

But suppose that it costs $10 to search through Cast Iron's records to determine whether a customer has been a prompt or slow payer. Is it worth doing so? The expected payoff to such a check is

$$\begin{array}{c}\text{Expected payoff}\\ \text{to credit check}\end{array} = \begin{array}{l}\text{(probability of identifying a slow payer}\\ \times \text{ gain from not extending credit)} - \text{ cost of credit check}\end{array}$$
$$= (.05 \times 40) - 10 = -\$8$$

In this case checking isn't worth it. You are paying $10 to avoid a $40 loss 5 percent of the time. But suppose that a customer orders 10 units at once. Then checking is worthwhile because you are paying $10 to avoid a *$400* loss 5 percent of the time:

$$\text{Expected payoff to credit check} = (.05 \times 400) - 10 = \$10$$

The credit manager therefore decides to check customers' past payment records only on orders of more than five units. You can verify that a credit check on a five-unit order just pays for itself.

Our illustration is simplistic, but you have probably grasped the message: You don't want to subject each order to the same credit analysis. You want to concentrate your efforts on the large and doubtful orders.

Credit Decisions with Repeat Orders

So far we have ignored the possibility of repeat orders. But one of the reasons for offering credit today is that you may get yourself a good, regular customer by doing so.

Figure 32.3 illustrates the problem.[13] Cast Iron has been asked to extend credit to a new customer. You can find little information on the firm, and you believe that

[13]Our example is adapted from H. Bierman, Jr., and W. H. Hausman, "The Credit Granting Decision," *Management Science* 16 (April 1970), pp. B519–B532.

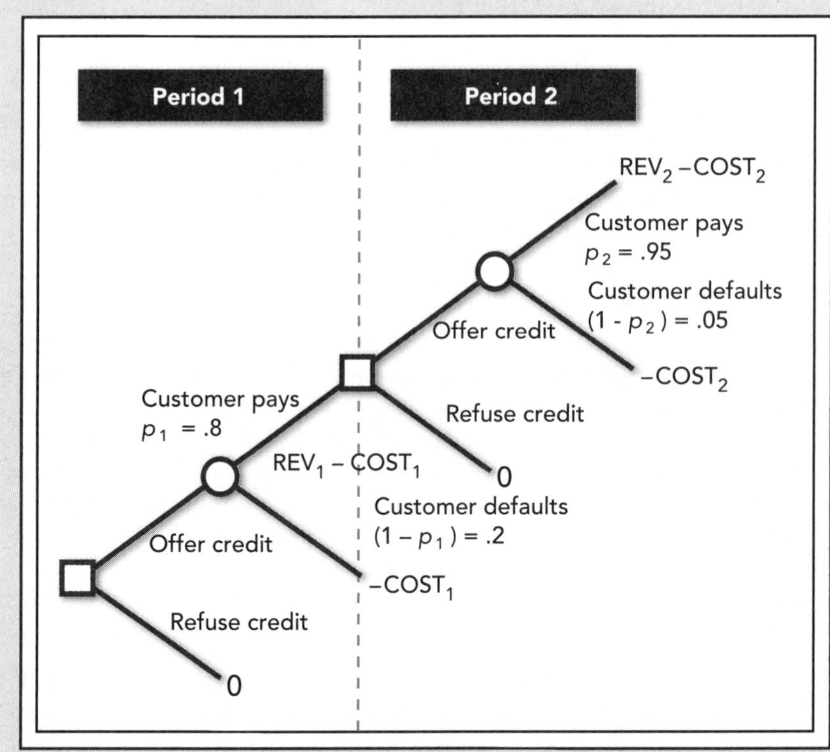

FIGURE 32.3

In this example there is only a .8 probability that your customer will pay in period 1; but if payment is made, there will be another order in period 2. The probability that the customer will pay for the second order is .95. The possibility of this good repeat order more than compensates for the expected loss in period 1.

the probability of payment is no better than .8. If you grant credit, the expected profit on this customer's order is

$$\begin{aligned}\text{Expected profit on initial order} &= p_1 \times \text{PV(REV} - \text{COST)} \\ &\quad - (1 - p_1) \times \text{PV(COST)} \\ &= (.8 \times 200) - (.2 \times 1{,}000) = -\$40\end{aligned}$$

You decide to refuse credit.

This is the correct decision if there is no chance of a repeat order. But look again at the decision tree in Figure 32.3. If the customer does pay up, there will be a reorder next year. Because the customer has paid once, you can be 95 percent sure that he or she will pay again. For this reason any repeat order is very profitable.

$$\begin{aligned}\text{Next year's expected profit on repeat order} &= p_2\text{PV}(\text{REV}_2 - \text{COST}_2) - (1 - p_2) \\ &\quad \text{PV}(\text{COST}_2) \\ &= (.95 \times 200) - (.05 \times 1{,}000) = \$140\end{aligned}$$

Now you can reexamine today's credit decision. If you grant credit today, you receive the expected profit on the initial order *plus* the possible opportunity to extend credit next year:

$$\begin{aligned}\text{Total expected profit} &= \text{expected profit on initial order} \\ &\quad + \text{probability of payment and repeat order} \\ &\quad \times \text{PV(next year's expected profit on repeat order)} \\ &= -40 + .80 \times \text{PV}(140)\end{aligned}$$

At any reasonable discount rate, you ought to extend credit. For example, if the discount rate is 20 percent,

$$\text{Total expected profit (present value)} = -40 + \frac{.8(140)}{1.2} = \$53.33$$

In this example you should grant credit even though you expect to take a loss on the order. The expected loss is more than outweighed by the possibility that you will secure a reliable and regular customer.

Some General Principles

Sometimes the credit manager faces clear-cut choices. In such circumstances it may be possible to estimate fairly precisely the consequences of a more liberal or a more stringent credit policy. But real-life situations are generally far more complex than our simple examples. Customers are not all good or all bad. Many of them pay consistently late; you get your money, but it costs more to collect and you lose a few months' interest. Then there is the question of risk: You may be able to measure the revenues and costs, but at what rate do you discount them?

Like almost all financial decisions, credit allocation involves a strong dose of judgment. Our examples are intended as reminders of the issues involved rather than as cookbook formulas. Here are the basic things to remember.

1. *Maximize profit.* As credit manager, you should not focus on minimizing the number of bad accounts; your job is to maximize expected profit. You must face up to the following facts: The best that can happen is that the customer pays promptly; the worst is default. In the best case, the firm receives the full additional revenues from the sale less the additional costs; in the worst, it receives nothing and loses the costs. You must weigh the chances of these alternative outcomes. If the margin of profit is high, you are justified in a liberal credit policy; if it is low, you cannot afford many bad debts.
2. *Concentrate on the dangerous accounts.* You should not expend the same effort on analyzing all credit applications. If an application is small or clear-cut, your decision should be largely routine; if it is large or doubtful, you may do better to move straight to a detailed credit appraisal. Most credit managers don't make credit decisions on an order-by-order basis. Instead, they set a credit limit for each customer. The sales representative is required to refer the order for approval only if the customer exceeds this limit.
3. *Look beyond the immediate order.* The credit decision is a dynamic problem. You cannot look only at the present. Sometimes it may be worth accepting a relatively poor risk as long as there is a likelihood that the customer will become a regular and reliable buyer. New businesses must, therefore, be prepared to incur more bad debts than established businesses. This is part of the cost of building up a good customer list.

32.5 COLLECTION POLICY

It would be nice if all customers paid their bills by the due date. But they don't—and since you may also occasionally "stretch" your payables, you can't altogether blame them.

The credit manager keeps a record of payment experiences with each customer. Thus the manager knows that company Alpha always takes the discount and that. Omega generally takes 90 days to pay. When a customer is in arrears, the usual procedure is to send a statement of account and to follow this at intervals with increasingly insistent letters or telephone calls. If none of these has any effect, most companies turn the debt over to a collection agency or an attorney. The fee for such services is usually between 15 and 40 percent of the amount collected.

There is always a potential conflict of interest between the collection department and the sales department. Sales representatives commonly complain that they no sooner win new customers than the collection department frightens them off with threatening letters. The collection manager, on the other hand, bemoans the fact that the sales force is concerned only with winning orders and does not care whether the goods are subsequently paid for.

There are also many instances of cooperation between sales managers and the financial managers who worry about collections. For example, the specialty chemicals division of a major pharmaceutical company actually made a business loan to an important customer that had been suddenly cut off by its bank. The pharmaceutical company bet that it knew its customer better than the customer's bank did. The bet paid off. The customer arranged alternative bank financing, paid back the pharmaceutical company, and became an even more loyal customer. It was a nice example of financial management supporting sales.

It is not common for suppliers to make business loans to customers in this way, but they lend money indirectly whenever they allow a delay in payment. Trade credit can be an important source of short-term funds for indigent customers that cannot obtain a bank loan. But that raises an important question: If the bank is unwilling to lend, does it make sense for you, the supplier, to continue to extend trade credit? Here are two possible reasons why it may make sense: First, as in the case of our pharmaceutical company, you may have more information than the bank does about the customer's business. Second, you need to look beyond the immediate transaction and recognize that your firm may stand to lose some profitable future sales if the customer goes out of business.[14]

Factoring and Credit Insurance

A large firm has some advantages in managing its accounts receivable. There are potential economies of scale in record keeping, billing, and so on. Also debt collection is a specialized business that calls for experience and judgment. The small firm may not be able to hire or train a specialized credit manager. However, it may be able to obtain some of these economies by farming out part of the job to a **factor.**

Factoring works as follows: The factor and the client agree on credit limits for each customer and on the average collection period. The client then notifies each customer that the factor has purchased the debt. Thereafter, for any sale, the client sends a copy of the invoice to the factor, the customer makes payment directly to the factor, and the factor pays the client on the basis of the agreed average collection period regardless of whether the customer has paid. There are, of course, costs

[14]Of course, banks also need to recognize future opportunities to make profitable loans to the firm. The question therefore is whether suppliers have a *greater* stake in the continued prosperity of the firm. For some evidence on the determinants of the supply and demand for trade credit, see M. A. Petersen and R. G. Rajan, "Trade Credit: Theories and Evidence," *Review of Financial Studies* 10 (1997), pp. 661–692.

to such an operation, and the factor typically charges a fee of 1 to 2 percent of the value of the invoice.[15]

This factoring arrangement, known as *maturity factoring*, provides assistance with collection and insurance against bad debts. Generally, the factor is also willing to advance 70 to 80 percent of the value of the accounts at an interest cost of 2 or 3 percent above the prime rate. Factoring that provides collection, insurance, and finance is generally termed *old-line factoring*.[16]

Factoring is most common in industries such as clothing and toys. These industries are characterized by many small producers and retailers that do not have long-established relationships with each other. Because a factor may be employed by a number of manufacturers, it sees a larger proportion of the transactions than any single firm and therefore is better placed to judge the creditworthiness of each customer.[17]

If you don't want help with collection but do want protection against bad debts, you can obtain credit insurance. The credit insurance company obviously wants to be certain that you do not throw caution to the winds by extending boundless credit to the most speculative accounts. It therefore generally imposes a maximum amount that it will cover for accounts with a particular credit rating. Thus it may agree to insure up to a total of $100,000 of sales to customers with the highest Dun and Bradstreet rating, up to $50,000 to those with the next-highest rating, and so on. You may claim not only if the customer actually becomes insolvent but also if an account is overdue. Such a delinquent account is then turned over to the insurance company, which makes vigorous efforts to collect.

Most governments have established agencies to insure export credits. In the United States this insurance is provided by the *Export–Import Bank* (*Ex–Im Bank*) in association with a group of insurance companies known as the *Foreign Credit Insurance Association* (*FCIA*). Banks are much more willing to lend against export credits that have been insured.

[15] Many factors are subsidiaries of commercial banks. Their typical client is a relatively small manufacturing company selling on a repetitive basis to a large number of industrial or retail customers.

[16] Under an arrangement known as *with-recourse factoring*, the company is liable for any delinquent accounts. In this case the factor provides collection, but not insurance.

[17] This point is made in S. L. Mian and C. W. Smith, Jr., "Accounts Receivable Management Policy: Theory and Evidence," *Journal of Finance* 47 (March 1992), pp. 169–200.

SUMMARY

Credit management involves five steps. The first is to establish normal terms of sale. This means that you must decide the length of the payment period and the size of any cash discounts. In most industries these conditions are standardized.

The second step is to decide the form of the contract with your customer. Most domestic sales are made on open account. In this case the only evidence that the customer owes you money is the entry in your ledger and a receipt signed by the customer. Particularly if the customer is located in a foreign country, you may require a more formal contract. We looked at two such devices—the trade acceptance and the letter of credit.

The third step is to assess each customer's creditworthiness. There are a variety of sources of information—your own experience with the customer, the experience of other creditors, the assessment of a credit agency, a check with the customer's bank, the market value of the customer's securities, and an analysis of the customer's financial statements. Firms that handle a large volume of credit information often use a formal system for combining the data from various sources into an overall credit score. Such numerical scoring systems help separate the borderline cases from the obvious sheep or goats. We showed how you can use statistical techniques such as multiple-discriminant analysis to give an efficient measure of default risk.

When you have made an assessment of the customer's credit standing, you can move to the fourth step in credit management, which is to establish sensible credit limits. The job of the credit manager is not to minimize the number of bad debts; it is to maximize profits. This means that you should increase the customer's credit limit as long as the probability of payment times the expected profit is greater than the probability of default times the cost of the goods. Remember not to be too shortsighted in reckoning the expected profit. It is often worth accepting the marginal applicant if there is a chance that the applicant may become a regular and reliable customer.

The fifth, and final, step is to *collect.* Doing so requires tact and judgment. You want to be firm with the truly delinquent customer, but you don't want to offend the good one by writing demanding letters just because a check has been delayed in the mail. You will find it easier to spot troublesome accounts if you keep a careful record of the aging of receivables.

These five steps are interrelated. For example, you can afford more liberal terms of sale if you are very careful about whom you grant credit to. You can accept higher-risk customers if you are very active in pursuing any late payers. A good credit policy is one that adds up to a sensible whole.

FURTHER READING

A standard text on the practice and institutional background of credit management is:

R. H. Cole and L. Mishler: *Consumer and Business Credit Management*, 11th ed., McGraw-Hill, New York, 1998.

For a more analytical discussion of credit policy, see:

S. Mian and C. W. Smith: "Extending Trade Credit and Financing," *Journal of Applied Corporate Finance*, 7:75–84 (Spring 1994).

M. A. Peterson and R. G. Rajan: "Trade Credit: Theories and Evidence," *Review of Financial Studies*, 10:661–692 (1997).

Altman's paper is the classic on numerical credit scoring:

E. I. Altman: "Financial Ratios, Discriminant Analysis and the Prediction of Corporate Bankruptcy," *Journal of Finance*, 23:589–609 (September 1968).

Altman also provides a review of credit scoring models in:

E. I. Altman: *Corporate Financial Distress and Bankruptcy*, 2nd ed., John Wiley, New York, 1993.

QUIZ

1. Company X sells on a 1/30, net 60 basis. Customer Y buys goods invoiced at $1,000.
   - **a.** How much can Y deduct from the bill if Y pays on day 30?
   - **b.** What is the effective annual rate of interest if Y pays on the due date rather than on day 30?
   - **c.** How would you expect payment terms to change if
     - **i.** The goods are perishable.
     - **ii.** The goods are not rapidly resold.
     - **iii.** The goods are sold to high-risk firms.
2. The lag between the purchase date and the date on which payment is due is known as the *terms lag.* The lag between the due date and the date on which the buyer actually

pays is the *due lag*, and the lag between the purchase and actual payment dates is the *pay lag*. Thus,

$$\text{Pay lag} = \text{terms lag} + \text{due lag}$$

State how you would expect the following events to affect each type of lag:

a. The company imposes a service charge on late payers.

b. A recession causes customers to be short of cash.

c. The company changes its terms from net 10 to net 20.

3. Complete the passage below by selecting the appropriate terms for each blank from the following list (some terms may be used more than once): *acceptance, open, commercial, trade, the United States, his or her own, draft, account, bank, the customer's, letter of credit, shipping documents.*

Most goods are sold on ______ ______. In this case the only evidence of the debt is a record in the seller's books and a signed receipt. If you wish to ensure that its buyer will pay, you can arrange a(n) ______ ______, ordering payment by the customer. In order to obtain the ______ ______, the customer must acknowledge this order and sign the document. The signed acknowledgment is known as a(n) ______ ______. Sometimes the seller may ask ______ ______ bank to sign the document. In this case it is known as a(n) ______ ______. The fourth form of contract is used principally in overseas trade. The customer's bank sends the exporter a(n) ______ ______ ______ stating that it has established a credit in his or her favor at a bank in the United States. The exporter then draws a draft on ______ bank and presents it to ______ ______ bank together with the ______ ______ and ______ ______. The bank then arranges for this draft to be accepted and forwards the ______ ______ to the customer's bank.

4. The Branding Iron Company sells its irons for $50 apiece wholesale. Production cost is $40 per iron. There is a 25 percent chance that wholesaler Q will go bankrupt within the next year. Q orders 1,000 irons and asks for six months' credit. Should you accept the order? Assume that the discount rate is 10 percent per year, there is no chance of a repeat order, and Q will pay either in full or not at all.

5. Look back at Section 32.4. Cast Iron's costs have increased from $1,000 to $1,050. Assuming there is no possibility of repeat orders, answer the following:

a. When should Cast Iron grant or refuse credit?

b. If it costs $12 to determine whether a customer has been a prompt or slow payer in the past, when should Cast Iron undertake such a check?

6. Look back at the discussion in Section 32.4 of credit decisions with repeat orders. If $p_1 = .8$, what is the minimum level of p_2 at which Cast Iron is justified in extending credit?

7. True or False?

a. Exporters who require greater certainty of payment arrange for the customers to sign a bill of lading in exchange for a sight draft.

b. Multiple-discriminant analysis is often used to construct an index of creditworthiness. This index is generally called a Z score.

c. It makes sense to monitor the credit manager's performance by looking at the proportion of bad debts.

d. If a customer refuses to pay despite repeated reminders, the company will usually turn the debt over to a factor or an attorney.

e. The Foreign Credit Insurance Association insures export credits.

PRACTICE QUESTIONS

1. Listed below are some common terms of sale. Can you explain what each means?

a. 2/30, net 60.

b. net 10.

c. 2/5, EOM, net 30.

2. Some of the items in question 1 involve a cash discount. For each of these, calculate the rate of interest paid by customers who pay on the due date instead of taking the cash discount.
3. Phoenix Lambert currently sells its goods cash on delivery. However, the financial manager believes that by offering credit terms of 2/10 net 30 the company can increase sales by 4 percent, without significant additional costs. If the interest rate is 6 percent and the profit margin is 5 percent, would you recommend offering credit? Assume first that all customers take the cash discount. Then assume that they all pay on day 30.
4. As treasurer of the Universal Bed Corporation, Aristotle Procrustes is worried about his bad debt ratio, which is currently running at 6 percent. He believes that imposing a more stringent credit policy might reduce sales by 5 percent and reduce the bad debt ratio to 4 percent. If the cost of goods sold is 80 percent of the selling price, should Mr. Procrustes adopt the more stringent policy?
5. Jim Khana, the credit manager of Velcro Saddles, is reappraising the company's credit policy. Velcro sells on terms of net 30. Cost of goods sold is 85 percent of sales, and fixed costs are a further 5 percent of sales. Velcro classifies customers on a scale of 1 to 4. During the past five years, the collection experience was as follows:

Classification	Defaults as Percent of Sales	Average Collection Period in Days for Nondefaulting Accounts
1	.0	45
2	2.0	42
3	10.0	40
4	20.0	80

The average interest rate was 15 percent.

What conclusions (if any) can you draw about Velcro's credit policy? What other factors should be taken into account before changing this policy?

6. Look again at question 5. Suppose (a) that it costs $95 to classify each new credit applicant and (b) that an almost equal proportion of new applicants falls into each of the four categories. In what circumstances should Mr. Khana not bother to undertake a credit check?
7. Until recently, Augean Cleaning Products sold its products on terms of net 60, with an average collection period of 75 days. In an attempt to induce customers to pay more promptly, it has changed its terms to 2/10, EOM, net 60. The initial effect of the changed terms is as follows:

	Average Collection Periods, Days	
Percent of Sales with Cash Discount	Cash Discount	Net
60	30*	80

*Some customers deduct the cash discount even though they pay after the specified date.

Calculate the effect of the changed terms. Assume
- Sales volume is unchanged.
- The interest rate is 12 percent.
- There are no defaults.
- Cost of goods sold is 80 percent of sales.

8. Look back at question 7. Assume that the change in credit terms results in a 2 percent increase in sales. Recalculate the effect of the changed credit terms.
9. Financial ratios were described in Chapter 29. If you were a credit manager, to which financial ratios would you pay most attention? Which do you think would be the least informative?

10. Discuss the problems with developing a numerical credit scoring system for evaluating personal loans. You can only test your system using data for applicants who have in the past been granted credit. Is this a potential problem?

11. Discuss ways in which real-life decisions are more complex than the decision illustrated in Figure 32.3. How do you think these differences ought to affect the credit decision?

12. How should your willingness to grant credit be affected by differences in **(a)** the profit margin, **(b)** the interest rate, **(c)** the probability of repeat orders? In each case illustrate your answer with a simple example.

STANDARD &POOR'S

13. Select two companies from the Market Insight database (**www.mhhe.com/edumarketinsight**). Use their latest financial statements to calculate some financial ratios that throw light on their relative creditworthiness. Calculate a Z-score for each, using the formula shown in Section 32.3. Now look at other indicators of creditworthiness, such as the company's bond rating or the return on its stock. Are the different indicators providing consistent messages?

STANDARD &POOR'S

14. Use the Market Insight database (**www.mhhe.com/edumarketinsight**) to compare the average collection periods (see Section 29.3) for different companies. Can you explain why some companies grant more credit than others?

CHALLENGE QUESTIONS

1. Why do firms grant "free" credit? Would it be more efficient if all sales were for cash and late payers were charged interest?

2. Sometimes a firm sells its receivables at a discount to a wholly owned captive finance company. This captive finance company is partly financed by the parent, but it also issues substantial amounts of debt. What are the possible advantages of such an arrangement?

3. Reliant Umbrellas has been approached by Plumpton Variety Stores of Nevada. Plumpton has expressed interest in an initial purchase of 5,000 umbrellas at $10 each on Reliant's standard terms of 2/30, net 60. Plumpton estimates that if the umbrellas prove popular with customers, its purchases could be in the region of 30,000 umbrellas a year. After deductions for variable costs, this account would add $47,000 per year to Reliant's profits.

   Reliant has been anxious for some time to break into the lucrative Nevada market, but its credit manager has some doubts about Plumpton. In the past five years, Plumpton had embarked on an aggressive program of store openings. In 2001, however, it went into reverse. The recession, combined with aggressive price competition, caused a cash shortage. Plumpton laid off employees, closed one store, and deferred store openings. The company's Dun and Bradstreet rating is only fair, and a check with Plumpton's other suppliers reveals that, although Plumpton traditionally took cash discounts, it has recently been paying 30 days slow. A check through Reliant's bank indicates that Plumpton has unused credit lines of $350,000 but has entered into discussions with the banks for a renewal of a $1,500,000 term loan due at the end of the year. Table 32.1 summarizes Plumpton's latest financial statements.

   As credit manager of Reliant, how do you feel about extending credit to Plumpton?

4. Galenic, Inc., is a wholesaler for a range of pharmaceutical products. Before deducting any losses from bad debts, Galenic operates on a profit margin of 5 percent. For a long time the firm has employed a numerical credit scoring system based on a small number of key ratios. This has resulted in a bad debt ratio of 1 percent.

   Galenic has recently commissioned a detailed statistical study of the payment record of its customers over the past eight years and, after considerable experimentation, has identified five variables that could form the basis of a new credit scoring system. On the evidence of the past eight years, Galenic calculates that for every 10,000 accounts it would have experienced the following default rates:

Credit Score under Proposed System	Number of Accounts		
	Defaulting	Paying	Total
Greater than 80	60	9,100	9,160
Less than 80	40	800	840
Total	100	9,900	10,000

By refusing credit to firms with a low credit score (less than 80), Galenic calculates that it would reduce its bad debt ratio to 60/9,160, or just under .7 percent. While this may not seem like a big deal, Galenic's credit manager reasons that this is equivalent to a decrease of one-third in the bad debt ratio and would result in a significant improvement in the profit margin.

a. What is Galenic's current profit margin, allowing for bad debts?

b. Assuming that the firm's estimates of default rates are right, how would the new credit scoring system affect profits?

c. Why might you suspect that Galenic's estimates of default rates will not be realized in practice? What are the likely consequences of overestimating the accuracy of such a credit scoring scheme?

d. Suppose that one of the variables in the proposed scoring system is whether the customer has an existing account with Galenic (new customers are more likely to default). How would this affect your assessment of the proposal?

TABLE 32.1

Plumpton Variety Stores: summary financial statements (figures in millions).

	2001	2000		2001	2000
Cash	$ 1.0	$ 1.2	Payables	$ 2.3	$ 2.5
Receivables	1.5	1.6	Short-term loans	3.9	1.9
Inventory	10.9	11.6	Long-term debt	1.8	2.6
Fixed assets	5.1	4.3	Equity	10.5	11.7
Total assets	$18.5	$18.7	Total liabilities	$18.5	$18.7

	2001	2000
Sales	$55.0	$59.0
Cost of goods sold	32.6	35.9
Selling, general, and administrative expenses	20.8	20.2
Interest	.5	.3
Tax	.5	1.3
Net income	$ .6	$ 1.3

PART NINE RELATED WEBSITES

For an introductory guide to understanding financial statements see:

www.ibm.com/investor/financialguide

For easy access to annual reports see:

www.reportgallery.com

www.prars.com

Downloadable software for short- and long-term financial planning is available on:

www.decisioneering.com

Journals with articles on short-term financial management include:

www.americanbanker.com

www.intltreasurer.com

www.treasuryandrisk.com

The Federal Reserve Bank sites are good general sources of reference for short-term interest rates and material on payment systems. See, for example:

www.federalreserve.gov

www.ny.frb.org

www.stls.frb.org

Sites on short-term debt markets include:

www.afponline.org *(money market and interest rate data)*

www.gecfosolutions.com *(GE Capital's website contains information on sources and costs of short-term finance)*

www.ny.frb.org/pihome/addpub/credit.pdf *(a guide to sources of credit)*

The websites of most major banks provide material on cash management services. See, for example:

www.bankone.com

www.bankofamerica.com

Other sites dealing with cash management include:

www.nacha.org *(material on electronic payment)*

www.phoenixhecht.com *(a comprehensive website on cash management with useful links)*

Some sites that are concerned with credit management:

www.creditworthy.com *(credit management)*

www.dnb.com *(examples of Dun and Bradstreet credit reports, articles on credit management, and an introductory guide to understanding financial statements)*

www.ftc.gov/bcp/conline/pubs/credit/scoring.htm *(a guide to credit scoring)*

www.nacm.org *(contains links to sites on credit-related issues)*

PART TEN

MERGERS, CORPORATE CONTROL, AND GOVERNANCE

THE JOURNAL *Mergers and Acquisitions* listed over 5,000 mergers involving U.S. corporations in 2000, and the total value of the companies acquired was $1.7 trillion. The year included the announcement of the U.S.'s largest merger, as AOL and Time Warner agreed to form a company valued at $350 billion.

What are the likely gains from mergers? How can managers calculate their benefits and costs? How can target companies defend themselves against unwelcome bidders? Who gains and who loses in mergers? Chapter 33 considers these questions.

Mergers are partly about economies from combining two businesses, but they are also about who gets to run the company. Chapter 34 circles back and considers other ways that companies may change their ownership and control. For example, we look at cases where a company spins off part of its business or where the firm is bought out by a group of investors who then take the business private. Chapter 34 also considers differences in the financial organization of corporations. For example, we contrast diversified conglomerates with more focused corporations and ask why conglomerates are more common outside the United States. Finally, we note some international differences in the financing and control of corporations.

CHAPTER THIRTY-THREE

MERGERS

THE SCALE AND pace of merger activity in the United States have been remarkable. In 2000, the peak of the merger boom, U.S. companies were involved in deals totaling more than $1.7 trillion. Table 33.1 lists just a few of the more important recent mergers, including several that involved overseas companies.

During these periods of intense merger activity, management spends significant amounts of time either searching for firms to acquire or worrying about whether some other firm will acquire their company.

A merger adds value only if the two companies are worth more together than apart. This chapter covers why two companies could be worth more together and how to get the merger deal done if they are. We proceed as follows.

- *Motives.* Sources of value added.
- *Dubious motives.* Don't be tempted.
- *Benefits and costs.* It's important to estimate them consistently.
- *Mechanics.* Legal, tax, and accounting issues.
- *Takeover battles and tactics.* We look back to several famous takeover battles. This history illustrates merger tactics and shows some of the economic forces driving merger activity.
- *Mergers and the economy.* How can we explain merger waves? Who gains and who loses as a result of mergers?

This chapter concentrates on ordinary mergers, that is, combinations of two established firms. We keep asking, What makes two firms worth more together than apart? We assume mergers are undertaken to cut costs, add revenues, or create growth opportunities.

But mergers also change *control* and *ownership.* Pick a merger, and you'll almost always find that one firm is the protagonist and the other is the target. The top management of the target firm usually departs after the merger.

Financial economists now view mergers as part of a broader *market for corporate control.* The activity in this market goes far beyond ordinary mergers. It includes spin-offs and divestitures, where a company splits off part of its assets and operations into an independent corporation. It includes restructurings, where a company reshapes its capital structure to change incentives for managers. It includes buyouts of public companies by groups of private investors.

When corporate control changes, the first questions to ask are: Who owns the business now? Who is running it? How closely do the owners control the managers? What incentives do the managers now have?

Such questions take us well beyond the analysis of ordinary mergers. In this chapter we concentrate on mergers. In the next, we move on to the market for corporate control.

TABLE 33.1

Some important mergers in 2000 and 2001.

Acquiring Company	Selling Company	Payment ($ billions)
Vodafone Air Touch (UK)	Mannesmann (Ger)	202.8
America Online	Time Warner	106.0
Pfizer	Warner-Lambert	89.2
Glaxo Wellcome (UK)	SmithKline Beecham (UK/US)	76.0
Bell Atlantic	GTE	53.4
Total Fina (Fr)	Elf Aquitaine (Fr)	50.1
AT&T	MediaOne	49.3
France Telecom (Fr)	Orange (UK)	46.0
Viacom	CBS	39.4
Chase Manhattan	J.P. Morgan	33.6
Citigroup	Associates First Capital	31.0
BP Amoco (UK)	Atlantic Richfield	27.2

Source: *Mergers and Acquisitions*, various issues.

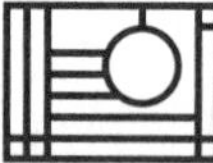

33.1 SENSIBLE MOTIVES FOR MERGERS

Mergers that take place between two firms in the same line of business are known as *horizontal mergers.* Recent examples include bank mergers, such as Chemical Bank's merger with Chase and Nationsbank's purchase of BankAmerica. Other headline-grabbing horizontal mergers include those between oil giants Exxon and Mobil, and between British Petroleum (BP) and Amoco.

A *vertical merger* involves companies at different stages of production. The buyer expands back toward the source of raw materials or forward in the direction of the ultimate consumer. An example is Walt Disney's acquisition of the ABC television network. Disney planned to use the ABC network to show *The Lion King* and other recent movies to huge audiences.

A *conglomerate merger* involves companies in unrelated lines of businesses. The majority of mergers in the 1960s and 1970s were conglomerate. They became less popular in the 1980s. In fact, much of the action since the 1980s has come from breaking up the conglomerates that had been formed 10 to 20 years earlier.

With these distinctions in mind, we are about to consider motives for mergers, that is, reasons why two firms may be worth more together than apart. We proceed with some trepidation. The motives, though they often lead the way to real benefits, are sometimes just mirages that tempt unwary or overconfident managers into takeover disasters. This was the case for AT&T, which spent $7.5 billion to buy NCR. The aim was to shore up AT&T's computer business and to "link people, organizations and their information into a seamless, global computer network."[1] It didn't work. Even more embarrassing (on a smaller scale) was the acquisition of Apex One, a sporting apparel company, by Converse Inc. The purchase was made on May 18, 1995. Apex One was closed down on August 11, after Converse failed to produce new designs quickly enough to satisfy retailers. Converse lost an investment of over $40 million in 85 days.[2]

Many mergers that seem to make economic sense fail because managers cannot handle the complex task of integrating two firms with different production processes, accounting methods, and corporate cultures. This was one of the problems in the AT&T–NCR merger. It also bedeviled Novell's acquisition of Wordperfect. That merger at first seemed a perfect fit between Novell's strengths in networks for personal computers and Wordperfect's applications software. But Wordperfect's postacquisition sales were horrible, partly because of competition from other word processing systems but also because of a series of battles over turf and strategy:

> Wordperfect executives came to view Novell executives as rude invaders of the corporate equivalent of Camelot. They repeatedly fought with . . . Novell's staff over everything from expenses and management assignments to Christmas bonuses. [This led to] a strategic mistake: dismantling a Wordperfect sales team . . . needed to push a long-awaited set of office software products.[3]

The value of most businesses depends on *human assets*—managers, skilled workers, scientists, and engineers. If these people are not happy in their new roles

[1]Robert E. Allen, AT&T chairman, quoted in J. J. Keller, "Disconnected Line: Why AT&T Takeover of NCR Hasn't Been a Real Bell Ringer," *The Wall Street Journal,* September 9, 1995, p. A1.

[2]Mark Maremount, "How Converse Got Its Laces All Tangled," *Business Week,* September 4, 1995, p. 37.

[3]D. Clark, "Software Firm Fights to Remake Business after Ill-Fated Merger," *The Wall Street Journal,* January 12, 1996, p. A1.

in the acquiring firm, the best of them will leave. One Portuguese bank (BCP) learned this lesson the hard way when it bought an investment management firm against the wishes of the firm's employees. The entire workforce immediately quit and set up a rival investment management firm with a similar name. Beware of paying too much for assets that go down in the elevator and out to the parking lot at the close of each business day. They may drive into the sunset and never return.

There are also occasions when the merger does achieve gains but the buyer nevertheless loses because it pays too much. For example, the buyer may overestimate the value of stale inventory or underestimate the costs of renovating old plant and equipment, or it may overlook the warranties on a defective product. Buyers need to be particularly careful about environmental liabilities. If there is pollution from the seller's operations or toxic waste on its property, the costs of cleaning up will probably fall on the buyer.

Economies of Scale

Just as most of us believe that we would be happier if only we were a little richer, so every manager seems to believe that his or her firm would be more competitive if only it were just a little bigger. Achieving *economies of scale* is the natural goal of horizontal mergers. But such economies have been claimed in conglomerate mergers, too. The architects of these mergers have pointed to the economies that come from sharing central services such as office management and accounting, financial control, executive development, and top-level management.[4]

The most prominent recent examples of mergers in pursuit of economies of scale come from the banking industry. The United States entered the 1990s with far too many banks, largely as a result of outdated regulations on interstate banking. As these regulations eroded and communications and technology improved, hundreds of small banks were bought out and merged into regional or "supra-regional" firms. When Chase and Chemical, two of the largest money-center banks, merged, they forecasted that the merger would reduce costs by 16 percent a year, or $1.5 billion. The savings would come from consolidating operations and eliminating redundant costs.[5]

Optimistic financial managers can see potential economies of scale in almost any industry. But it is easier to buy another business than to integrate it with yours afterward. Some companies that have gotten together in pursuit of scale economies still function as a collection of separate and sometimes competing operations with different production facilities, research efforts, and marketing forces.

Economies of Vertical Integration

Vertical mergers seek economies in vertical integration. Some companies try to gain control over the production process by expanding back toward the output of the raw material and forward to the ultimate consumer. One way to achieve this is to merge with a supplier or a customer.

---

[4]Economies of scale are enjoyed when the average unit cost of production goes down as production increases. One way to achieve economies of scale is to spread fixed costs over a larger volume of production.

[5]Houston et al. examine 41 large bank mergers in which the companies provided forecasts of cost savings. On average the estimated present value of these savings was about 12 percent of the market value of the combined companies. See J. F. Houston, C. M. James, and M. D. Ryngaert, "Where Do Merger Gains Come from? Bank Mergers from the Perspective of Insiders and Outsiders," *Journal of Financial Economics* 60 (2001), pp. 285–331.

Vertical integration facilitates coordination and administration. We illustrate via an extreme example. Think of an airline that does not own any planes. If it schedules a flight from Boston to San Francisco, it sells tickets and then rents a plane for that flight from a separate company. This strategy might work on a small scale, but it would be an administrative nightmare for a major carrier, which would have to coordinate hundreds of rental agreements daily. In view of these difficulties, it is not surprising that all major airlines have integrated backward, away from the consumer, by buying and flying airplanes rather than patronizing rent-a-plane companies.

Do not assume that more vertical integration is better than less. Carried to extremes, it is absurdly inefficient, as in the case of LOT, the Polish state airline, which in the late 1980s found itself raising pigs to make sure that its employees had fresh meat on their tables. (Of course, in a centrally managed economy it may be necessary to raise your own cattle or pigs, since you can't be sure you'll be able to buy meat.)

Nowadays the tide of vertical integration seems to be flowing out. Companies are finding it more efficient to *outsource* the provision of many services and various types of production. For example, back in the 1950s and 1960s, General Motors was deemed to have a cost advantage over its main competitors, Ford and Chrysler, because a greater fraction of the parts used in GM's automobiles were produced in-house. By the 1990s, Ford and Chrysler had the advantage: They could buy the parts cheaper from outside suppliers. This was partly because the outside suppliers tended to use nonunion labor at lower wages. But it also appears that manufacturers have more bargaining power versus independent suppliers than versus a production facility that's part of the corporate family. In 1998 GM decided to spin off Delphi, its automotive parts division, as a separate company.[6] After the spin-off, GM can continue to buy parts from Delphi in large volumes, but it negotiates the purchases at arm's length.[7]

Complementary Resources

Many small firms are acquired by large ones that can provide the missing ingredients necessary for the small firms' success. The small firm may have a unique product but lack the engineering and sales organization required to produce and market it on a large scale. The firm could develop engineering and sales talent from scratch, but it may be quicker and cheaper to merge with a firm that already has ample talent. The two firms have *complementary resources*—each has what the other needs—and so it may make sense for them to merge. The two firms are worth more together than apart because each acquires something it does not have and gets it cheaper than it would by acting on its own. Also, the merger may open up opportunities that neither firm would pursue otherwise.

Of course, two large firms may also merge because they have complementary resources. Consider the 1989 merger between two electric utilities, Utah Power & Light and PacifiCorp, which served customers in California. Utah Power's peak demand came in the summer, for air conditioning. PacifiCorp's peak came in the winter, for heating. The savings from combining the two firms' generating systems were estimated at $45 million annually.

[6]We cover spin-offs in the next chapter.

[7]In 2000 Ford followed GM by announcing plans to spin off its auto-parts business, Visteon Corporation.

Surplus Funds

Here's another argument for mergers: Suppose that your firm is in a mature industry. It is generating a substantial amount of cash, but it has few profitable investment opportunities. Ideally such a firm should distribute the surplus cash to shareholders by increasing its dividend payment or repurchasing stock. Unfortunately, energetic managers are often reluctant to adopt a policy of shrinking their firm in this way. If the firm is not willing to purchase its own shares, it can instead purchase another company's shares. Firms with a surplus of cash and a shortage of good investment opportunities often turn to mergers *financed by cash* as a way of redeploying their capital.

Some firms have excess cash and do not pay it out to stockholders or redeploy it by wise acquisitions. Such firms often find themselves targeted for takeover by other firms that propose to redeploy the cash for them.[8] During the oil price slump of the early 1980s, many cash-rich oil companies found themselves threatened by takeover. This was not because their cash was a unique asset. The acquirers wanted to capture the companies' cash flow to make sure it was not frittered away on negative-NPV oil exploration projects. We return to this *free-cash-flow* motive for takeovers later in this chapter.

Eliminating Inefficiencies

Cash is not the only asset that can be wasted by poor management. There are always firms with unexploited opportunities to cut costs and increase sales and earnings. Such firms are natural candidates for acquisition by other firms with better management. In some instances "better management" may simply mean the determination to force painful cuts or realign the company's operations. Notice that the motive for such acquisitions has nothing to do with benefits from combining two firms. Acquisition is simply the mechanism by which a new management team replaces the old one.

A merger is not the only way to improve management, but sometimes it is the only simple and practical way. Managers are naturally reluctant to fire or demote themselves, and stockholders of large public firms do not usually have much *direct* influence on how the firm is run or who runs it.[9]

If this motive for merger is important, one would expect to observe that acquisitions often precede a change in the management of the target firm. This seems to be the case. For example, Martin and McConnell found that the chief executive is four times more likely to be replaced in the year after a takeover than during earlier years.[10] The firms they studied had generally been poor performers; in the four years before acquisition their stock prices had lagged behind those of other firms in the same industry by 15 percent. Apparently many of these firms fell on bad times and were rescued, or reformed, by merger.

Of course, it is easy to criticize another firm's management but not so easy to improve it. Some of the self-appointed scourges of poor management turn out to be

---

[8]Takeovers in this case often take the form of leveraged buy-outs. See Chapter 34.

[9]It is difficult to assemble a large-enough block of stockholders to effectively challenge management and the incumbent board of directors. Stockholders can have enormous indirect influence, however. Their displeasure shows up in the firm's stock price. A low stock price may encourage a takeover bid by another firm.

[10]K. J. Martin and J. J. McConnell, "Corporate Performance, Corporate Takeovers, and Management Turnover," *Journal of Finance* 46 (June 1991), pp. 671–687.

less competent than those they replace. Here is how Warren Buffet, the chairman of Berkshire Hathaway, summarizes the matter:[11]

> Many managers were apparently over-exposed in impressionable childhood years to the story in which the imprisoned, handsome prince is released from the toad's body by a kiss from the beautiful princess. Consequently, they are certain that the managerial kiss will do wonders for the profitability of the target company. Such optimism is essential. Absent that rosy view, why else should the shareholders of company A want to own an interest in B at a takeover cost that is two times the market price they'd pay if they made direct purchases on their own? In other words investors can always buy toads at the going price for toads. If investors instead bankroll princesses who wish to pay double for the right to kiss the toad, those kisses better pack some real dynamite. We've observed many kisses, but very few miracles. Nevertheless, many managerial princesses remain serenely confident about the future potency of their kisses, even after their corporate backyards are knee-deep in unresponsive toads.

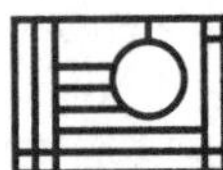

33.2 SOME DUBIOUS REASONS FOR MERGERS

The benefits that we have described so far all make economic sense. Other arguments sometimes given for mergers are dubious. Here are a few of the dubious ones.

To Diversify

We have suggested that the managers of a cash-rich company may prefer to see it use that cash for acquisitions rather than distribute it as extra dividends. That is why we often see cash-rich firms in stagnant industries merging their way into fresh woods and pastures new.

What about diversification as an end in itself? It is obvious that diversification reduces risk. Isn't that a gain from merging?

The trouble with this argument is that diversification is easier and cheaper for the stockholder than for the corporation. No one has shown that investors pay a premium for diversified firms; in fact, discounts are common. For example, Kaiser Industries was dissolved as a holding company because its diversification apparently *subtracted* from its value. Kaiser Industries' main assets were shares of Kaiser Steel, Kaiser Aluminum, and Kaiser Cement. These were independent companies, and the stock of each was publicly traded. Thus you could value Kaiser Industries by looking at the stock prices of Kaiser Steel, Kaiser Aluminum, and Kaiser Cement. But Kaiser Industries' stock was selling at a price reflecting a significant *discount* from the value of its investment in these companies. The discount vanished when Kaiser Industries revealed its plan to sell its holdings and distribute the proceeds to its stockholders.

Why the discount existed in the first place is a puzzle. But the example at least shows that diversification does not *increase* value. The appendix to this chapter provides a simple proof that corporate diversification does not affect value in perfect markets as long as investors' diversification opportunities are unrestricted. This is the *value-additivity* principle introduced in Chapter 7.

[11]Berkshire Hathaway 1981 Annual Report, cited in G. Foster, "Comments on M&A Analysis and the Role of Investment Bankers," *Midland Corporate Finance Journal* 1 (Winter 1983), pp. 36–38.

	World Enterprises before Merger	Muck and Slurry	World Enterprises after Merger
1. Earnings per share	$2.00	$2.00	$2.67
2. Price per share	$40	$20	$40
3. Price–earnings ratio	20	10	15
4. Number of shares	100,000	100,000	150,000
5. Total earnings	$200,000	$200,000	$400,000
6. Total market value	$4,000,000	$2,000,000	$6,000,000
7. Current earnings per dollar invested in stock (line 1 ÷ line 2)	$.05	$.10	$.067

TABLE 33.2

Impact of merger on market value and earnings per share of World Enterprises.

Note: When World Enterprises purchases Muck and Slurry, there are no gains. Therefore, total earnings and total market value should be unaffected by the merger. But earnings *per share* increase. World Enterprises issues only 50,000 of its shares (priced at $40) to acquire the 100,000 Muck and Slurry shares (priced at $20).

Increasing Earnings per Share: The Bootstrap Game

During the 1960s some conglomerate companies made acquisitions that offered no evident economic gains. Nevertheless the conglomerates' aggressive strategy produced several years of rising earnings per share. To see how this can happen, let us look at the acquisition of Muck and Slurry by the well-known conglomerate World Enterprises.[12]

The position before the merger is set out in the first two columns of Table 33.2. Notice that because Muck and Slurry has relatively poor growth prospects, its stock sells at a lower price–earnings ratio than does World Enterprises' stock (line 3). The merger, we assume, produces no economic benefits, and so the firms should be worth exactly the same together as they are apart. The market value of World Enterprises after the merger should be equal to the sum of the separate values of the two firms (line 6).

Since World Enterprises' stock is selling for double the price of Muck and Slurry stock (line 2), World Enterprises can acquire the 100,000 Muck and Slurry shares for 50,000 of its own shares. Thus World will have 150,000 shares outstanding after the merger.

Total earnings double as a result of the merger (line 5), but the number of shares increases by only 50 percent. Earnings *per share* rise from $2.00 to $2.67. We call this the *bootstrap effect* because there is no real gain created by the merger and no increase in the two firms' combined value. Since the stock price is unchanged, the price–earnings ratio falls (line 3).

Figure 33.1 illustrates what is going on here. Before the merger $1 invested in World Enterprises bought 5 cents of current earnings and rapid growth prospects. On the other hand, $1 invested in Muck and Slurry bought 10 cents of current earnings but slower growth prospects. If the *total* market value is not altered by the merger, then $1 invested in the merged firm gives 6.7 cents of immediate earnings but slower growth than World Enterprises offered alone. Muck and Slurry shareholders get lower immediate earnings but faster growth. Neither side gains or loses provided everybody understands the deal.

Financial manipulators sometimes try to ensure that the market does *not* understand the deal. Suppose that investors are fooled by the exuberance of the president

[12]The discussion of the bootstrap game follows S. C. Myers, "A Framework for Evaluating Mergers," in S. C. Myers (ed.), *Modern Developments in Financial Management*, Frederick A. Praeger, Inc., New York, 1976.

FIGURE 33.1

Effects of merger on earnings growth. By merging with Muck and Slurry, World Enterprises increases current earnings but accepts a slower rate of future growth. Its stockholders should be no better or worse off unless investors are fooled by the bootstrap effect.

Source: S. C. Myers, "A Framework for Evaluating Mergers," in S. C. Myers, ed., *Modern Developments in Financial Management*, Frederick A. Praeger, Inc., New York, 1976, Figure 1, p. 639.

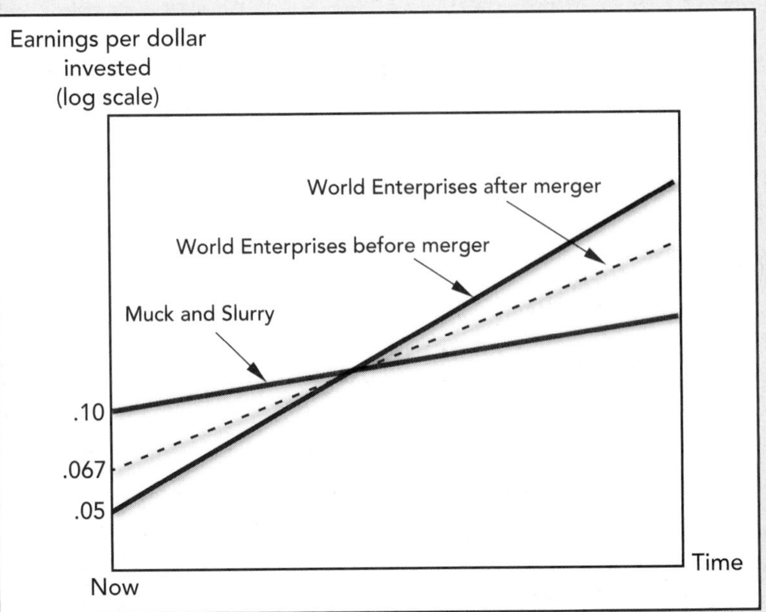

of World Enterprises and by plans to introduce modern management techniques into its new Earth Sciences Division (formerly known as Muck and Slurry). They could easily mistake the 33 percent postmerger increase in earnings per share for real growth. If they do, the price of World Enterprises stock rises and the shareholders of both companies receive something for nothing.

You should now see how to play the bootstrap, or "chain letter," game. Suppose that you manage a company enjoying a high price–earnings ratio. The reason why it is high is that investors anticipate rapid growth in future earnings. You achieve this growth not by capital investment, product improvement, or increased operating efficiency but by the purchase of slow-growing firms with low price–earnings ratios. The long-run result will be slower growth and a depressed price–earnings ratio, but in the short run earnings per share can increase dramatically. If this fools investors, you may be able to achieve higher earnings per share without suffering a decline in your price–earnings ratio. But to *keep* fooling investors, you must continue to expand by merger *at the same compound rate.* Obviously you cannot do this forever; one day expansion must slow down or stop. Then earnings growth will cease, and your house of cards will fall.

This kind of game is not played so often now. But there is still a widespread belief that a firm should not acquire companies with higher price–earnings ratios than its own. Of course you know better than to believe that low-P/E stocks are cheap and high-P/E stocks are dear. If life were as simple as that, we should all be wealthy by now. Beware of false prophets who suggest that you can appraise mergers just on the basis of their immediate impact on earnings per share.

Lower Financing Costs

You often hear it said that a merged firm is able to borrow more cheaply than its separate units could. In part this is true. We have already seen (in Section 15.4) that there are significant economies of scale in making new issues. Therefore, if firms can make fewer, larger security issues by merging, there are genuine savings.

But when people say that borrowing costs are lower for the merged firm, they usually mean something more than lower issue costs. They mean that when two firms merge, the combined company can borrow at lower interest rates than either firm could separately. This, of course, is exactly what we should expect in a well-functioning bond market. While the two firms are separate, they do not guarantee each other's debt; if one fails, the bondholder cannot ask the other for money. But after the merger each enterprise effectively does guarantee the other's debt; if one part of the business fails, the bondholders can still take their money out of the other part. Because these mutual guarantees make the debt less risky, lenders demand a lower interest rate.

Does the lower interest rate mean a net gain to the merger? Not necessarily. Compare the following two situations:

- *Separate issues.* Firm A and firm B each make a $50 million bond issue.
- *Single issue.* Firms A and B merge, and the new firm AB makes a single $100 million issue.

Of course AB would pay a lower interest rate, other things being equal. But it does not make sense for A and B to merge just to get that lower rate. Although AB's shareholders do gain from the lower rate, they lose by having to guarantee each other's debt. In other words, they get the lower interest rate only by giving bondholders better protection. There is no *net* gain.

In Sections 20.2 and 24.5 we showed that

$$\text{Bond value} = \begin{array}{c}\text{bond value}\\\text{assuming no}\\\text{chance of default}\end{array} - \begin{array}{c}\text{value of}\\\text{shareholders' (put)}\\\text{option to default}\end{array}$$

Merger increases bond value (or reduces the interest payments necessary to support a *given* bond value) only by reducing the value of stockholders' options to default. In other words, the value of the default option for AB's $100 million issue is less than the combined value of the two default options on A's and B's separate $50 million issues.

Now suppose that A and B each borrow $50 million and *then* merge. If the merger is a surprise, it is likely to be a happy one for the bondholders. The bonds they thought were guaranteed by one of the two firms end up guaranteed by both. The stockholders lose in this case because they have given bondholders better protection but have received nothing for it.

There is one situation in which mergers can create value by making debt safer. In Section 18.3 we described the choice of an optimal debt ratio as a trade-off of the value of tax shields on interest payments made by the firm against the present value of possible costs of financial distress due to borrowing too much. Merging decreases the probability of financial distress, other things being equal. If it allows increased borrowing, and increased value from the interest tax shields, there will be a net gain to the merger.[13]

[13]This merger rationale was first suggested by W. G. Lewellen, "A Pure Financial Rationale for the Conglomerate Merger," *Journal of Finance* 26 (May 1971), pp. 521–537. If you want to see some of the controversy and discussion that this idea led to, look at R. C. Higgins and L. D. Schall, "Corporate Bankruptcy and Conglomerate Merger," *Journal of Finance* 30 (March 1975), pp. 93–114; and D. Galai and R. W. Masulis, "The Option Pricing Model and the Risk Factor of Stock," *Journal of Financial Economics* 3 (January–March 1976), especially pp. 66–69.

33.3 ESTIMATING MERGER GAINS AND COSTS

Suppose that you are the financial manager of firm A and you want to analyze the possible purchase of firm B.[14] The first thing to think about is whether there is an *economic gain* from the merger. There is an economic gain *only if the two firms are worth more together than apart.* For example, if you think that the combined firm would be worth PV_{AB} and that the separate firms are worth PV_A and PV_B, then

$$\text{Gain} = PV_{AB} - (PV_A + PV_B) = \Delta PV_{AB}$$

If this gain is positive, there is an economic justification for merger. But you also have to think about the *cost* of acquiring firm B. Take the easy case in which payment is made in cash. Then the cost of acquiring B is equal to the cash payment minus B's value as a separate entity. Thus

$$\text{Cost} = \text{cash paid} - PV_B$$

The net present value to A of a merger with B is measured by the difference between the gain and the cost. Therefore, you should go ahead with the merger if its net present value, defined as

$$\begin{aligned} \text{NPV} &= \text{gain} - \text{cost} \\ &= \Delta PV_{AB} - (\text{cash} - PV_B) \end{aligned}$$

is positive.

We like to write the merger criterion in this way because it focuses attention on two distinct questions. When you estimate the benefit, you concentrate on whether there are any gains to be made from the merger. When you estimate cost, you are concerned with the division of these gains between the two companies.

An example may help make this clear. Firm A has a value of \$200 million, and B has a value of \$50 million. Merging the two would allow cost savings with a present value of \$25 million. This is the gain from the merger. Thus,

$$\begin{aligned} PV_A &= \$200 \\ PV_B &= \$50 \\ \text{Gain} &= \Delta PV_{AB} = +\$25 \\ PV_{AB} &= \$275 \text{ million} \end{aligned}$$

Suppose that B is bought for cash, say, for \$65 million. The cost of the merger is

$$\begin{aligned} \text{Cost} &= \text{cash paid} - PV_B \\ &= 65 - 50 = \$15 \text{ million} \end{aligned}$$

Note that the stockholders of firm B—the people on the other side of the transaction—are ahead by \$15 million. *Their* gain is *your* cost. They have captured \$15 million of the \$25 million merger gain. Thus when we write down the NPV of the merger from A's viewpoint, we are really calculating that part of the gain which A's stockholders get

[14]This chapter's definitions and interpretations of the gains and costs of merger follow those set out in S. C. Myers, "A Framework for Evaluating Mergers," op. cit.

to keep. The NPV to A's stockholders equals the overall gain from the merger less that part of the gain captured by B's stockholders:

$$\text{NPV} = 25 - 15 = +\$10 \text{ million}$$

Just as a check, let's confirm that A's stockholders really come out $10 million ahead. They start with a firm worth PV_A = $200 million. They end up with a firm worth $275 million and then have to pay out $65 million to B's stockholders.[15] Thus their net gain is

$$\begin{aligned}\text{NPV} &= \text{wealth with merger} - \text{wealth without merger}\\ &= (PV_{AB} - \text{cash}) - PV_A\\ &= (\$275 - \$65) - \$200 = +\$10 \text{ million}\end{aligned}$$

Suppose investors do not anticipate the merger between A and B. The announcement will cause the value of B's stock to rise from $50 million to $65 million, a 30 percent increase. If investors share management's assessment of the merger gains, the market value of A's stock will increase by $10 million, only a 5 percent increase.

It makes sense to keep an eye on what investors think the gains from merging are. If A's stock price falls when the deal is announced, then investors are sending the message that the merger benefits are doubtful or that A is paying too much for them.[16]

Right and Wrong Ways to Estimate the Benefits of Mergers

Some companies begin their merger analyses with a forecast of the target firm's future cash flows. Any revenue increases or cost reductions attributable to the merger are included in the forecasts, which are then discounted back to the present and compared with the purchase price:

$$\begin{matrix}\text{Estimated}\\ \text{net gain}\end{matrix} = \begin{matrix}\text{DCF valuation}\\ \text{of target, including}\\ \text{merger benefits}\end{matrix} - \begin{matrix}\text{cash required}\\ \text{for acquisition}\end{matrix}$$

This is a dangerous procedure. Even the brightest and best-trained analyst can make large errors in valuing a business. The estimated net gain may come up positive not because the merger makes sense but simply because the analyst's cash-flow forecasts are too optimistic. On the other hand, a good merger may not be pursued if the analyst fails to recognize the target's potential as a stand-alone business.

Our procedure *starts* with the target's stand-alone market value (PV_B) and concentrates on the *changes* in cash flow that would result from the merger. *Ask yourself why the two firms should be worth more together than apart.*

The same advice holds when you are contemplating the *sale* of part of your business. There is no point in saying to yourself, This is an unprofitable business and should be sold. Unless the buyer can run the business better than you can, the price you receive will reflect the poor prospects.

[15]We are assuming that PV_A includes enough cash to finance the deal, or that the cash can be borrowed at a market interest rate. Notice that the value to A's stockholders after the deal is done and paid for is $275 − 65 = $210 million—a gain of $10 million.

[16]Think back to Section 13.4, where we saw how Hewlett Packard's stock price fell when it announced its plans to merge with Compaq.

Sometimes you may come across managers who believe that there are simple rules for identifying good acquisitions. They may say, for example, that they always try to buy into growth industries or that they have a policy of acquiring companies that are selling below book value. But our comments in Chapter 11 about the characteristics of a good investment decision also hold true when you are buying a whole company. *You add value only if you can generate additional economic rents*—some competitive edge that other firms can't match and the target firm's managers can't achieve on their own.

One final piece of horse sense: Often two companies bid against each other to acquire the same target firm. In effect, the target firm puts itself up for auction. In such cases, ask yourself whether the target is worth more to you than to the other bidder. If the answer is no, you should be cautious about getting into a bidding contest. Winning such a contest may be more expensive than losing it. If you lose, you have simply wasted your time; if you win, you have probably paid too much.

More on Estimating Costs—What If the Target's Stock Price Anticipates the Merger?

The cost of a merger is the premium that the buyer pays over the seller's stand-alone value. How can that value be determined? If the target is a public company, you can start with its market value; just observe price per share and multiply by the number of shares outstanding. But bear in mind that if investors *expect* A to acquire B, or if they expect *somebody* to acquire B, the market value of B may overstate its stand-alone value.

This is one of the few places in this book where we draw an important distinction between market value (MV) and the true, or "intrinsic," value (PV) of the firm as a separate entity. The problem here is not that the market value of B is wrong but that it may not be the value of firm B as a separate entity. Potential investors in B's stock will see two possible outcomes and two possible values:

Outcome	Market Value of B's Stock
1. No merger	PV_B: Value of B as a separate firm
2. Merger occurs	PV_B *plus* some part of the benefits of the merger

If the second outcome is possible, MV_B, the stock market value we observe for B, will overstate PV_B. This is exactly what *should* happen in a competitive capital market. Unfortunately, it complicates the task of a financial manager who is evaluating a merger.

Here is an example: Suppose that just before A and B's merger announcement we observe the following:

	Firm A	Firm B
Market price per share	\$200	\$100
Number of shares	1,000,000	500,000
Market value of firm	\$200 million	\$50 million

Firm A intends to pay \$65 million cash for B. If B's market price reflects only its value as a separate entity, then

$$\text{Cost} = (\text{cash paid} - PV_B)$$
$$= (65 - 50) = \$15 \text{ million}$$

However, suppose that B's share price has already risen $12 because of rumors that B might get a favorable merger offer. That means that its intrinsic value is overstated by $12 \times 500{,}000 = \$6$ million. Its true value, PV_B, is only $44 million. Then

$$\text{Cost} = (65 - 44) = \$21 \text{ million}$$

Since the merger gain is $25 million, this deal still makes A's stockholders better off, but B's stockholders are now capturing the lion's share of the gain.

Notice that if the market made a mistake, and the market value of B was *less* than B's true value as a separate entity, the cost could be negative. In other words, B would be a *bargain* and the merger would be worthwhile from A's point of view, even if the two firms were worth no more together than apart. Of course, A's stockholders' gain would be B's stockholders' loss, because B would be sold for less than its true value.

Firms have made acquisitions just because their managers believed they had spotted a company whose intrinsic value was not fully appreciated by the stock market. However, we know from the evidence on market efficiency that "cheap" stocks often turn out to be expensive. It is not easy for outsiders, whether investors or managers, to find firms that are truly undervalued by the market. Moreover, if the shares are bargain-priced, A doesn't need a merger to profit by its special knowledge. It can just buy up B's shares on the open market and hold them passively, waiting for other investors to wake up to B's true value.

If firm A is wise, it will not go ahead with a merger if the cost exceeds the gain. Conversely, firm B will not consent to a merger if it thinks the cost to A is negative, for a negative cost to A means a negative gain to B. This gives us a range of possible cash payments that would allow the merger to take place. Whether the payment is at the top or the bottom of this range depends on the relative bargaining power of the two participants.

Estimating Cost When the Merger Is Financed by Stock

In recent years about 70 percent of mergers have involved payment wholly or partly in the form of the acquirer's stock. When a merger is financed by stock, cost depends on the value of the shares in the new company received by the shareholders of the selling company. If the sellers receive N shares, each worth P_{AB}, the cost is

$$\text{Cost} = N \times P_{AB} - PV_B$$

Just be sure to use the price per share *after the merger is announced* and its benefits are appreciated by investors.

Suppose that A offers 325,000 (.325 million) shares instead of $65 million in cash. A's share price before the deal is announced is $200. If B is worth $50 million stand-alone,[17] the cost of the merger *appears* to be

$$\text{Apparent cost} = .325 \times 200 - 50 = \$15 \text{ million}$$

However, the apparent cost may not be the true cost. A's stock price is $200 before the merger announcement. At the announcement it ought to go up.

Given the gain and the terms of the deal, we can calculate share prices and market values after the deal. The new firm will have 1.325 million shares outstanding

[17]In this case we assume that B's stock price has *not* risen on merger rumors and accurately reflects B's stand-alone value.

and will be worth \$275 million.[18] The new share price is 275/1.325 = \$207.55. The true cost is

$$\text{Cost} = .325 \times 207.55 - 50 = \$17.45 \text{ million}$$

This cost can also be calculated by figuring out the gain to B's shareholders. They end up with .325 million shares, or 24.5 percent of the new firm AB. Their gain is

$$.245(275) - 50 = \$17.45 \text{ million}$$

In general, if B's shareholders are given the fraction x of the combined firms,

$$\text{Cost} = x\text{PV}_{\text{AB}} - \text{PV}_{\text{B}}$$

We can now understand the first key distinction between cash and stock as financing instruments. If cash is offered, the cost of the merger is unaffected by the merger gains. If stock is offered, the cost depends on the gains because the gains show up in the postmerger share price.

Stock financing also mitigates the effect of overvaluation or undervaluation of either firm. Suppose, for example, that A overestimates B's value as a separate entity, perhaps because it has overlooked some hidden liability. Thus A makes too generous an offer. Other things being equal, A's stockholders are better off if it is a stock offer rather than a cash offer. With a stock offer, the inevitable bad news about B's value will fall partly on the shoulders of B's stockholders.

Asymmetric Information

There is a second key difference between cash and stock financing for mergers. A's managers will usually have access to information about A's prospects that is not available to outsiders. Economists call this *asymmetric information.*

Suppose A's managers are more optimistic than outside investors. They may think that A's shares will really be worth \$215 after the merger, \$7.45 higher than the \$207.55 market price we just calculated. If they are right, the true cost of a stock-financed merger with B is

$$\text{Cost} = .325 \times 215 - 50 = \$19.88$$

B's shareholders would get a "free gift" of \$7.45 for every A share they receive—an extra gain of \$7.45 × .325 = 2.42, that is, \$2.42 million.

Of course, if A's managers were really this optimistic, they would strongly prefer to finance the merger with cash. Financing with stock would be favored by *pessimistic* managers who think their company's shares are *over*valued.

Does this sound like "win-win" for A—just issue shares when overvalued, cash otherwise? No, it's not that easy, because B's shareholders, and outside investors generally, understand what's going on. Suppose you are negotiating on behalf of B. You find that A's managers keep suggesting stock rather than cash financing. You quickly infer A's managers' pessimism, mark down your own opinion of what the shares are worth, and drive a harder bargain.

[18]In this case no cash is leaving the firm to finance the merger. In our example of a cash offer, \$65 million would be paid out to B's stockholders, leaving the final value of the firm at 275 − 65 = \$210 million. There would only be one million shares outstanding, so share price would be \$210. The cash deal is better for A's shareholders.

This asymmetric-information story explains why buying-firms' share prices generally fall when stock-financed mergers are announced.[19] Andrade, Mitchell, and Stafford found an average market-adjusted fall of 1.5 percent on the announcement of stock-financed mergers between 1973 and 1998. There was a small *gain* (.4 percent) for a sample of cash-financed deals.[20]

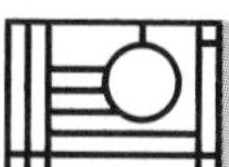

33.4 THE MECHANICS OF A MERGER

Buying a company is a much more complicated affair than buying a piece of machinery. Thus we should look at some of the problems encountered in arranging mergers. In practice, these problems are often *extremely* complex, and specialists must be consulted. We are not trying to replace those specialists; we simply want to alert you to the kinds of legal, tax, and accounting issues they deal with.

Mergers and Antitrust Law

Mergers can get bogged down in the federal antitrust laws. The most important statute here is the Clayton Act of 1914, which forbids an acquisition whenever "in any line of commerce or in any section of the country" the effect "*may be* substantially to lessen competition, or to *tend* to create a monopoly."

Antitrust law can be enforced by the federal government in either of two ways: by a civil suit brought by the Justice Department or by a proceeding initiated by the Federal Trade Commission (FTC).[21] The Hart–Scott–Rodino Antitrust Act of 1976 requires that these agencies be informed of all acquisitions of stock amounting to $15 million or 15 percent of the target's stock, whichever is less. Thus, almost all large mergers are reviewed at an early stage.[22] Both the Justice Department and the FTC then have the right to seek injunctions delaying a merger. Often this injunction is enough to scupper the companies' plans.

Both the FTC and the Justice Department have been flexing their muscles in recent years. Here is an example. After the end of the Cold War, sharp declines in defense budgets triggered consolidation in the U.S. aerospace industry. By 1998 there remained just three giant companies—Boeing, Lockheed Martin, and Raytheon—plus several smaller ones, including Northrup Grumman. Thus, when Lockheed Martin and Northrup Grumman announced plans to get together, the Departments of Justice and Defense decided that this was a merger too far. In the face of this opposition, the two companies broke off their engagement.

---

[19]The same reasoning applies to stock issues. See Sections 15.4 and 18.4.

[20]See G. Andrade, M. Mitchell, and E. Stafford, "New Evidence and Perspectives on Mergers," *Journal of Economic Perspectives* 15 (Spring 2001), pp. 103–120. This result confirms earlier work by Travlos and by Franks, Harris, and Titman. See N. Travlos, "Corporate Takeover Bids, Methods of Payment, and Bidding Firms' Stock Returns," *Journal of Finance* 42 (September 1987), pp. 943–963; and J. R. Franks, R. S. Harris, and S. Titman, "The Postmerger Share-Price Performance of Acquiring Firms," *Journal of Financial Economics* 29 (March 1991), pp. 81–96.

[21]Competitors or third parties who think they will be injured by the merger can also bring antitrust suits.

[22]The target has to be notified also, and it in turn informs investors. Thus the Hart–Scott–Rodino Act effectively forces an acquiring company to "go public" with its bid.

The merger boom of the late 1990s has kept antitrust regulators busy. Other industries in which large mergers have been blocked on antitrust grounds include aluminum (Reynolds and Alcoa), telecoms (WorldCom and Sprint), supermarkets (Kroger and WinnDixie), video rentals (Hollywood Entertainment and Blockbuster), and office equipment (Office Depot and Staples).

Companies that do business outside the USA also have to worry about foreign antitrust laws. For example, GE's $46 billion takeover bid for Honeywell was blocked by the European Commission, which argued that the combined company would have too much power in the aircraft industry.

Sometimes trustbusters will object to a merger, but then relent if the companies agree to divest certain assets and operations. For example, the Justice Department has insisted that any joint venture between American Airlines and British Airways would be permitted to go ahead only if the airlines relinquished some of their take-off and landing slots at London's Heathrow airport.

The Form of Acquisition

Suppose you are confident that the purchase of company B will not be challenged on antitrust grounds. Next you will want to consider the form of the acquisition.

One possibility is literally to *merge* the two companies, in which case one company automatically assumes *all* the assets and *all* the liabilities of the other. Such a merger must have the approval of at least 50 percent of the stockholders of each firm.[23]

An alternative is simply to buy the seller's stock in exchange for cash, shares, or other securities. In this case the buyer can deal individually with the shareholders of the selling company. The seller's managers may not be involved at all. Their approval and cooperation are generally sought, but if they resist, the buyer will attempt to acquire an effective majority of the outstanding shares. If successful, the buyer has control and can complete the merger and, if necessary, toss out the incumbent management.

The third approach is to buy some or all of the seller's assets. In this case ownership of the assets needs to be transferred, and payment is made to the selling firm rather than directly to its stockholders.

Merger Accounting

When one company buys another, its management worries about how the purchase will show up in its financial statements. Before 2001 the company had a choice of accounting method, but in that year the Financial Accounting Standards Board (FASB) introduced new rules that required the buyer to use the *purchase method* of merger accounting. This is illustrated in Table 33.3, which shows what happens when A Corporation buys B Corporation, leading to the new AB Corporation. The two firms' initial balance sheets are shown at the top of the table. Below this we show what happens to the balance sheet when the two firms merge. We assume that B Corporation has been purchased for $1.8 million, 180 percent of book value.

Why did A Corporation pay an $800,000 premium over B's book value? There are two possible reasons. First, the true values of B's *tangible* assets—its working capital, plant, and equipment—may be greater than $1 million. We will assume that this is *not* the reason; that is, we assume that the assets listed on its balance

[23]Corporate charters and state laws sometimes specify a higher percentage.

TABLE 33.3

Accounting for the merger of A Corporation and B Corporation assuming that A Corporation pays $1.8 million for B Corporation (figures in $ millions).

Key: NWC = net working capital; FA = net book value of fixed assets; D = debt; E = book value of equity.

Initial Balance Sheets

A Corporation				B Corporation			
NWC	2.0	3.0	D	NWC	.1	0	D
FA	8.0	7.0	E	FA	.9	1.0	E
	10.0	10.0			1.0	1.0	

Balance Sheet of AB Corporation

NWC	2.1	3.0	D
FA	8.9	8.8	E
Goodwill	.8		
	11.8	11.8	

sheet are valued there correctly.[24] Second, A Corporation may be paying for an *intangible* asset that is not listed on B Corporation's balance sheet. For example, the intangible asset may be a promising product or technology. Or it may be no more than B Corporation's share of the expected economic gains from the merger.

A Corporation is buying an asset worth $1.8 million. The problem is to show that asset on the left-hand side of AB Corporation's balance sheet. B Corporation's tangible assets are worth only $1 million. This leaves $.8 million. Under the purchase method, the accountant takes care of this by creating a new asset category called *goodwill* and assigning $.8 million to it.[25] As long as the goodwill continues to be worth at least $.8 million, it stays on the balance sheet and the company's earnings are unaffected. However, the company is obliged each year to estimate the fair value of the goodwill. If the estimated value ever falls below $.8 million, the amount shown on the balance sheet must be adjusted downward and the write-off deducted from that year's earnings. Some companies have found that this can make a nasty dent in profits. For example, when the new accounting rules were introduced, AOL announced that it would need to write down its assets by as much as $60 billion.

Some Tax Considerations

An acquisition may be either taxable or tax-free. If payment is in the form of cash, the acquisition is regarded as taxable. In this case the selling stockholders are treated as having *sold* their shares, and they must pay tax on any capital gains. If payment is largely in the form of shares, the acquisition is tax-free and the shareholders are viewed as *exchanging* their old shares for similar new ones; no capital gains or losses are recognized.

The tax status of the acquisition also affects the taxes paid by the merged firm afterward. After a tax-free acquisition, the merged firm is taxed as if the two firms had always been together. In a taxable acquisition, the assets of the selling firm are

[24] If B's tangible assets are worth more than their previous book values, they would be reappraised and their current values entered on AB Corporation's balance sheet.

[25] If part of the $.8 million consisted of payment for identifiable intangible assets such as patents, the accountant would place these under a separate category of assets. Identifiable intangible assets that have a finite life need to be written off over their life.

	Taxable Merger	Tax-free Merger
Impact on Captain B	Captain B must recognize a $30,000 capital gain.	Capital gain can be deferred until Captain B sells the Baycorp shares.
Impact on Baycorp	Boat is revalued at $280,000. Baycorp must pay tax on the $130,000 write-up, but tax depreciation increases to $280,000/10 = $28,000 per year (assuming 10 years of remaining life).	Boat's value remains at $150,000, and tax depreciation continues at $15,000 per year.

TABLE 33.4

Possible tax consequences when Baycorp buys Seacorp for $330,000. Captain B's original investment in Seacorp was $300,000. Just before the merger Seacorp's assets were $50,000 of marketable securities and one boat with a book value of $150,000 but a market value of $280,000.

revalued, the resulting write-up or write-down is treated as a taxable gain or loss, and tax depreciation is recalculated on the basis of the restated asset values.

A very simple example will illustrate these distinctions. In 1990 Captain B forms Seacorp, which purchases a fishing boat for $300,000. Assume, for simplicity, that the boat is depreciated for tax purposes over 20 years on a straight-line basis (no salvage value). Thus annual depreciation is $300,000/20 = $15,000, and in 2000 the boat has a net book value of $150,000. But in 2000, Captain B finds that, owing to careful maintenance, inflation, and good times in the local fishing industry, the boat is really worth $280,000. In addition, Seacorp holds $50,000 of marketable securities.

Now suppose that Captain B sells the firm to Baycorp for $330,000. The possible tax consequences of the acquisition are shown in Table 33.4. In this case, Captain B is better off with a tax-free deal because capital gains taxes can be deferred. Baycorp will probably go along; it covets the $13,000-per-year extra depreciation tax shield that a taxable merger would generate, but the increased annual tax shields do not justify forcing Captain B to pay taxes on a $130,000 write-up.

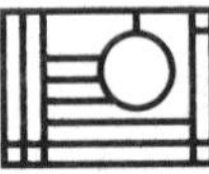

33.5 TAKEOVER BATTLES AND TACTICS

Many mergers are negotiated by the two firms' top managements and boards of directors. When the companies are similar in size, these friendly mergers are often presented as "a merger between equals." However, in practice one of the management teams usually comes out on top. Consider, for example, the merger between Daimler-Benz and Chrysler. As Chrysler's profits slumped, the plans to integrate the two management teams with co-chairmen in Stuttgart and Dearborn rapidly fell apart; many of Chrysler's senior executives left and Daimler's management took control.[26]

If a negotiated merger appears impossible the acquirer can instead go over the heads of the target firm's management and appeal directly to its stockholders. There

[26] The story of the Daimler/Chrysler merger is told in B. Vlasic and B. A. Stertz, *Taken for a Ride: How Daimler-Benz Drove Off with Chrysler,* William Morrow & Co., 2000.

are two ways of doing this. First, the acquirer can seek the support of the target firm's stockholders at the next annual meeting. This is called a *proxy fight* because the right to vote someone else's share is called a *proxy*.[27]

Proxy fights are expensive and difficult to win. The alternative for the would-be acquirer is to make a *tender offer* directly to the shareholders. The management of the target firm may advise its shareholders to accept the tender, or it may attempt to fight the bid.

Tender battles resemble a complex game of poker. The rules are set mostly by the Williams Act of 1968, by state law, and by the courts. The problem in setting the rules is that it is unclear who requires protection. Should the management of the target firm be given more weapons to defend itself against unwelcome predators? Or should it simply be encouraged to sit the game out? Or should it be obliged to conduct an auction to obtain the highest price for its shareholders? And what about would-be acquirers? Should they be forced to reveal their intentions at an early stage, or would that allow other firms to piggy-back on their good ideas and enter competing bids?[28]

Keep these questions in mind as we review one of the more interesting chapters in merger history.

Boone Pickens Tries to Take Over Cities Service, Gulf Oil, and Phillips Petroleum

The 1980s saw a series of pitched takeover battles in the oil industry. The most interesting and visible player in these battles was Boone Pickens, chairman of Mesa Petroleum and a self-styled advocate for shareholders everywhere. Pickens and Mesa didn't win many battles, but they made a lot of money losing them, and they helped force major changes in oil companies' investment and financing policies.

Mesa's attack on Cities Service[29] illustrates Pickens's *modus operandi*. The battle began in May 1982, when Mesa bought Cities shares in preparation for a takeover bid. Cities counterattacked. It issued more shares to dilute Mesa's holdings, and it made a retaliatory offer for Mesa. (This is called a *pacman defense*—try to take over the attacker before it takes over you!) Over the following month Mesa upped its bid for Cities, and Cities twice increased its bid for Mesa. But in the end Cities won: Mesa agreed to call off its bid and not to make another one for Cities for at least five years. In exchange, Cities agreed to repurchase Mesa's holdings at an $80 million profit to Mesa. This is called a *greenmail* payment.

Though Cities escaped Mesa, it was still in play. It looked for a *white knight*, that is, a friendly acquirer, and found one in Gulf Oil. But the Federal Trade Commission raised various objections to that deal, and Gulf backed out.

In the end, Cities was bought by Occidental Petroleum. Occidental made a tender offer of $55 per share in cash for 45 percent of Cities, followed by a package of fixed income securities for the remaining stock. This is called a *two-tier offer*. In effect, Occidental was saying, "Last one through the door does the washing up."

---

[27]Peter Dodd and Jerrold Warner have written a detailed description and analysis of proxy fights. See "On Corporate Governance: A Study of Proxy Contests," *Journal of Financial Economics* 2 (April 1985), pp. 401–438.

[28]The Williams Act obliges firms who own 5 percent or more of another company's shares to tip their hand by reporting their holding in a Schedule 13(d) filing with the SEC.

[29]See R. S. Ruback, "The Cities Service Takeover: A Case Study," *Journal of Finance* 38 (May 1983), pp. 319–330.

TABLE 33.5

Phillips's balance sheet was dramatically changed by its leveraged repurchase (figures in billions).

	1985	1984		1985	1984
Current assets	$ 3.1	$ 4.6	Current liabilities	$ 3.1	$ 5.3
Fixed assets	10.3	11.2	Long-term debt	6.5	2.8
Other	.6	1.2	Other long-term liabilities	2.8	2.3
			Equity	1.6	6.6
Total assets	$14.0	$17.0	Total liabilities	$14.0	$17.0

Almost all Cities stockholders rushed to take advantage of the cash offer, and Occidental gained control.

One year after its brief engagement with Cities, Gulf itself became a takeover target. Pickens and Mesa were again on the warpath. At this point Chevron came to the rescue and acquired Gulf for $13.2 billion, more than double its value six months earlier. Chevron's bid gave Mesa a profit of $760 million on the Gulf shares it had bought. Asked for his views, Pickens commented, "Shucks, I guess we lost another one."

But why was Gulf worth that much more to Chevron than to investors just a few months earlier? Where was the added value? The answer will emerge as we look at Pickens's next foray, against Phillips Petroleum.

By 1984 Mesa had accumulated 6 percent of Phillips at an average price of $38 per share and made a bid for a further 15 percent at $60 per share. Phillips's first response was predictable: It bought out Mesa's shareholding. This greenmail payment gave Mesa a profit of $89 million.[30]

The other two responses reveal why Phillips was such an attractive target. It raised its dividend by 25 percent, reduced capital spending, and announced a program to sell $2 billion of assets. It also agreed to repurchase about 50 percent of its stock and to issue instead $4.5 billion of debt. Table 33.5 shows how this *leveraged repurchase* changed Phillips's balance sheet. The new debt ratio was about 80 percent, and book equity shrank by $5 billion to $1.6 billion.

This massive debt burden put Phillips on a strict cash diet. It was forced to sell assets and pinch pennies wherever possible. Capital expenditures were cut back from $1,065 million in 1985 to $646 million in 1986. In the same years, the number of employees fell from 25,300 to 21,800. Austerity continued through the late 1980s.

How did this *restructuring* shield Phillips from takeover? Certainly not by making purchase of the company more expensive. On the contrary, restructuring drastically reduced the total market value of Phillips's outstanding stock and therefore reduced the likely cost of buying out its remaining shareholders.

But restructuring removed the chief *motive* for takeover, which was to force Phillips to generate and pay out more cash to investors. Before the restructuring, investors sensed that Phillips was not running a tight ship and worried that it would plow back its ample operating cash flow into mediocre capital investments or ill-advised expansion. They wanted Phillips to pay out its free cash flow rather than let it be soaked up by a too-comfortable organization or plowed into negative-

[30]Giving in to greenmail can be dangerous, as Phillips soon discovered. Just six weeks later another corporate raider, Carl Icahn, acquired nearly 5 percent of Phillips stock and made an offer for the remainder. Phillips responded with a second greenmail payment, buying out Icahn and his pals for a profit (to them) of about $35 million.

NPV investments. Consequently, Phillips's share price did not reflect the potential value of its assets and operations. *That* created the opportunity for a takeover. One can almost hear the potential raider thinking:

> So what if I have to pay a 30 or 40 percent premium to take over Phillips? I can borrow most of the purchase price and then pay off the loan by selling surplus assets, cutting out all but the best capital investments, and wringing out slack in the organization. It'll be a rough few years, but if surgery's necessary, I might as well be the doctor and get paid for doing it.

Phillips's managers did not agree that the company was slack or prone to overinvestment. Nevertheless, they bowed to pressure from the stock market and undertook the surgery themselves. They paid out billions to repurchase stock and to service the $6.5 billion in long-term debt. They sold assets, cut back capital investment, and put their organization on the diet investors were calling for.

There are two lessons here. First, when the merger motive is to eliminate inefficiency or to distribute excess cash, the target's best defense is to do what the bidder would do, and thus avoid the cost, confusion, and random casualties of a takeover battle. Second, you can see why a company with ample free cash flow can be a tempting target for takeover.

The oil industry entered the 1980s with more-than-ample free cash flow. Rising oil prices had greatly increased revenues and operating profits. Investment opportunities had not expanded proportionately. Many companies overinvested. Investors foresaw massive, negative-NPV outlays and marked down the companies' stock prices accordingly. This created the opportunity for takeovers. Pickens and other acquirers could afford to offer a premium over the prebid stock price, knowing that if they did gain control they could increase value by putting the target company on a diet.

Pickens never succeeded in taking over a major oil company, but he and other "raiders" helped force the industry to cut back investment, reduce operating costs, and return cash to investors. Much of the cash was returned by stock repurchases.

Takeover Defenses

The Cities Service case illustrates several tactics managers use to fight takeover bids. Frequently they don't wait for a bid before taking defensive action. Instead, they deter potential bidders by devising *poison pills* that make their companies unappetizing or they persuade shareholders to agree to *shark-repellent* changes to the company charter.[31] Table 33.6 summarizes the principal first and second levels of defense.

Why do managers contest takeover bids? One reason is to extract a higher price from the bidder. Another possible reason is that managers believe their jobs may be at risk in the merged company. These managers are not trying to obtain a better price; they want to stop the bid altogether.

Some companies reduce these conflicts of interest by offering their managers *golden parachutes,* that is, generous payoffs if the managers lose their jobs as the result of a takeover. It may seem odd to reward managers for being taken over. However, if a soft landing overcomes their opposition to takeover bids, a few million dollars may be a small price to pay.

[31]Since shareholders expect to gain if their company is taken over, it is no surprise that they do not welcome these impediments. See, for example, G. Jarrell and A. Poulsen, "Shark Repellents and Stock Prices: The Effects of Antitakeover Amendments since 1980," *Journal of Financial Economics* 19 (1987), pp. 127–168.

Type of Defense	Description
	Preoffer Defenses
Shark-repellent charter amendments:	
Staggered board	The board is classified into three equal groups. Only one group is elected each year. Therefore the bidder cannot gain control of the target immediately.
Supermajority	A high percentage of shares is needed to approve a merger, typically 80%.
Fair price	Mergers are restricted unless a fair price (determined by formula or appraisal) is paid.
Restricted voting rights	Shareholders who own more than a specified proportion of the target have no voting rights unless approved by the target's board.
Waiting period	Unwelcome acquirers must wait for a specified number of years before they can complete the merger.
Other:	
Poison pill	Existing shareholders are issued rights which, if there is a significant purchase of shares by a bidder, can be used to purchase additional stock in the company at a bargain price.
Poison put	Existing bondholders can demand repayment if there is a change of control as a result of a hostile takeover.
	Postoffer Defenses
Litigation	File suit against bidder for violating antitrust or securities laws.
Asset restructuring	Buy assets that bidder does not want or that will create an antitrust problem.
Liability restructuring	Issue shares to a friendly third party or increase the number of shareholders. Repurchase shares from existing shareholders at a premium.

TABLE 33.6

A summary of takeover defenses.

Source: This table is loosely adapted from R. S. Ruback, "An Overview of Takeover Defenses," working paper no. 1836–86, Sloan School of Management, MIT, Cambridge, MA, September 1986, tables 1 and 2. See also L. Herzel and R. W. Shepro, *Bidders and Targets: Mergers and Acquisitions in the U.S.*, Basil Blackwell, Inc., Cambridge, MA, 1990, chap. 8.

Any management team that tries to develop improved weapons of defense must expect challenge in the courts. In the early 1980s the courts tended to give managers the benefit of the doubt and respect their business judgment about whether a takeover should be resisted. But the courts' attitudes to takeover battles have changed. For example, in 1993 a court blocked Viacom's agreed takeover of Paramount on the grounds that Paramount's directors did not do their homework before turning down a higher offer from QVC. Paramount was forced to give up its poison-pill defense and the stock options that it had offered to Viacom. Because of such decisions, managers have become much more careful in opposing bids, and they do not throw themselves blindly into the arms of any white knight.[32]

At the same time, state governments have provided some new defensive weapons. In 1987 the Supreme Court upheld state laws that allow companies to deprive an investor of voting rights as soon as the investor's share in the company ex-

[32]In 1985 a shiver ran through many boardrooms when the directors of Trans Union Corporation were held personally liable for being too hasty in accepting a takeover bid. Changes in judicial attitudes to takeover defenses are reviewed in L. Herzel and R. W. Shepro, *Bidders and Targets: Mergers and Acquisitions in the U.S.*, Basil Blackwell, Inc., Cambridge, MA, 1990.

ceeds a certain level. Since then state antitakeover laws have proliferated. Many allow boards of directors to block mergers with hostile bidders for several years and to consider the interests of employees, customers, suppliers, and their communities in deciding whether to try to block a hostile bid.

AlliedSignal vs. AMP

The hostile attacks of the 1980s were rarely repeated in the 1990s, when most mergers were friendly.[33] But now and then a battle flared up. The following example illustrates takeover tactics and defenses near the end of the millennium.

In the first week of August 1998, AlliedSignal, Inc., announced that it would bid $44.50 per share, or $9.8 billion, for AMP, Inc. AMP's stock price immediately jumped by nearly 50 percent to about $43 per share.

AMP was the world's largest producer of cables and connectors for computers and other electronic equipment. It had just announced a fall of nearly 50 percent in quarterly profits from the previous year. The immediate cause for this bad news was economic troubles in Southeast Asia, one of AMP's most important export markets. But longer-run performance had also disappointed investors, and the company was widely viewed as ripe for change in operations and management. AlliedSignal was betting that it could make these changes faster and better than the incumbent management.

AMP at first seemed impregnable. It was chartered in Pennsylvania, which had passed tough antitakeover laws. Pennsylvania corporations could "just say no" to takeovers that might adversely affect employees and local communities. The company also had a strong poison pill.[34]

AlliedSignal held out an olive branch, hinting that price was flexible if AMP was ready to talk turkey. But the offer was rebuffed. A tender offer went out to AMP shareholders, and 72 percent accepted. However, the terms of the offer did not require AlliedSignal to buy any shares until the poison pill was removed. In order to do that, AlliedSignal would have to appeal again to AMP's shareholders, asking them to approve a *solicitation of consent* blocking AMP's directors from enforcing the pill.

AMP fought back vigorously and imaginatively. It announced a plan to borrow $3 billion to repurchase its shares at $55 per share—its management's view of the true value of AMP stock. It convinced a federal court to delay AlliedSignal's solicitation of consent. At the same time it asked the Pennsylvania legislature to pass a law which would effectively bar the merger. The governor announced his support. Both companies sent teams of lobbyists to the state capitol. In October the bill was approved in the Pennsylvania House of Representatives and sent to the Senate for consideration.

Yet AlliedSignal discovered it had powerful allies. About 80 percent of AMP's shares were owned by mutual funds, pension funds, and other institutional investors. Many of these institutions bluntly and publicly disagreed with AMP's intransigence. The College Retirement Equities Fund (CREF), one of the largest U.S. pension funds, called AMP's defensive tactics "entirely inimical to the principles of shareholder democracy and good corporate governance." CREF then took an extraordinary step: It filed a legal brief supporting AlliedSignal's case in the federal court.[35] Then the Hixon family, descendants of AMP's co-founder, made public a

[33]By contrast, a number of hostle takeovers took place in continental European countries where such activity had been almost unknown.

[34]It was a *dead-hand* poison pill: Even if AlliedSignal gained a majority of AMP's board of directors, only the *previous* directors were empowered to vote to remove the pill.

[35]G. Faircloth, "AMP's Tactics Against AlliedSignal Bid Are Criticized by Big Pension Fund," *The Wall Street Journal*, September 28, 1998, p. A17.

letter to AMP's management and directors expressing "dismay," and asking, "Who do management and the board work for? The central issue is that AMP's management will not permit shareholders to voice their will."[36]

AMP had complained all along that AlliedSignal's bid was too low. Robert Ripp, AMP's chairman, reiterated this point in his reply to the Hixons and also said, "As a board, we have an overarching responsibility to AMP, all of its shareholders, and its other constituencies—which we believe we are serving on a basis consistent with your interests."[37]

But as the weeks passed, AMP's defenses, while still intact, did not look quite so strong. By mid-October it became clear that AMP would not receive timely help from the Pennsylvania legislature. In November, the federal court finally gave AlliedSignal the go-ahead for its solicitation of consent to remove the poison pill. Remember, 72 percent of its stockholders had already accepted AlliedSignal's tender offer.

Then, suddenly, AMP gave up: It agreed to be acquired by a white knight, Tyco International, for $55 per AMP share, paid for in Tyco stock. AlliedSignal dropped out of the bidding; it didn't think AMP was worth that much.

What are the lessons? First is the strength of poison pills and other takeover defenses, especially in a state like Pennsylvania where the law leans in favor of local targets. AlliedSignal's offensive gained ground, but with great expense and effort and at a very slow pace.

The second lesson is the potential power of institutional investors. We believe AMP gave in not because its legal and procedural defenses failed but largely because of economic pressure from its major shareholders.

Did AMP's management and board act in shareholders' interests? In the end, yes. They said that AMP was worth more than AlliedSignal's offer, and they found another buyer to prove them right. However, they would not have searched for a white knight absent AlliedSignal's bid.

Who Gains Most in Mergers?

As our brief history illustrates, in mergers sellers generally do better than buyers. Andrade, Mitchell, and Stafford found that following the announcement of the bid, selling shareholders received a healthy gain averaging 16 percent.[38] On the other hand, it appears that investors expected acquiring companies to just about break even. The prices of their shares fell by .7 percent.[39] The value of the *total* package—buyer plus seller—increased by 1.8 percent. Of course, these are averages; selling shareholders sometimes obtain much higher returns. When IBM took over Lotus Corporation, it paid a premium of 100 percent, or about $1.7 billion, for Lotus stock.

Why do sellers earn higher returns? There are two reasons. First, buying firms are typically larger than selling firms. In many mergers the buyer is so much larger that even substantial net benefits would not show up clearly in the buyer's share price. Suppose, for example, that company A buys company B, which is only one-tenth A's size. Suppose the dollar value of the net gain from the merger is split

---

[36]S. Lipin and G. Faircloth, "AMP's Antitakeover Tactics Rile Holder," *The Wall Street Journal*, October 5, 1998, p. A18.

[37]Ibid.

[38]See G. Andrade, M. Mitchell, and E. Stafford, "New Evidence and Perspectives on Mergers," *Journal of Economic Perspectives* 15 (Spring 2001), pp. 103–120.

[39]The small loss to the shareholders of acquiring firms is not statistically significant. Other studies using different samples have observed a small positive return.

equally between A and B.[40] Each company's shareholders receive the same *dollar* profit, but B's receive 10 times A's *percentage* return.

The second, and more important, reason is the competition among potential bidders. Once the first bidder puts the target company "in play," one or more additional suitors often jump in, sometimes as white knights at the invitation of the target firm's management. Every time one suitor tops another's bid, more of the merger gain slides toward the target. At the same time, the target firm's management may mount various legal and financial counterattacks, ensuring that capitulation, if and when it comes, is at the highest attainable price.

Of course, bidders and targets are not the only possible winners. Unsuccessful bidders often win, too, by selling off their holdings in target companies at substantial profits.

Other winners include investment bankers, lawyers, accountants, and in some cases arbitrageurs, or "arbs," who speculate on the likely success of takeover bids.[41] "Speculate" has a negative ring, but it can be a useful social service. A tender offer may present shareholders with a difficult decision. Should they accept, should they wait to see if someone else produces a better offer, or should they sell their stock in the market? This dilemma presents an opportunity for the arbitrageurs, who specialize in answering such questions. In other words, they buy from the target's shareholders and take on the risk that the deal will not go through.

As Ivan Boesky demonstrated, arbitrageurs can make even more money if they learn about the offer *before* it is publicly announced. Because arbitrageurs may accumulate large amounts of stock, they can have an important effect on whether a deal goes through, and the bidding company or its investment bankers may be tempted to take the arbitrageurs into their confidence. This is the point at which a legitimate and useful activity becomes an illegal and harmful one.

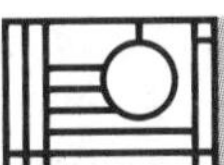

33.6 MERGERS AND THE ECONOMY

Merger Waves

Mergers come in waves. The first episode of intense merger activity occurred at the turn of the 20th century and the second occurred in the 1920s. There was a further boom from 1967 to 1969 and then again in the 1980s and 1990s (1999 and 2000 were record years). Each episode coincided with a period of buoyant stock prices, though there were substantial differences in the types of companies that merged and the ways they went about it.

We don't really understand why merger activity is so volatile. If mergers are prompted by economic motives, at least one of these motives must be "here today and gone tomorrow," and it must somehow be associated with high stock prices. But none of the economic motives that we review in this chapter has anything to do with the general level of the stock market. None burst on the scene in 1967, departed in 1970, and reappeared for most of the 1980s and again in the mid-1990s.

---

[40]In other words, the *cost* of the merger to A is one-half the gain ΔPV_{AB}.

[41]Strictly speaking, an arbitrageur is an investor who takes a fully hedged, that is, riskless, position. But arbitrageurs in merger battles often take very large risks indeed. Their activities are oxymoronicly known as "risk arbitrage."

Some mergers may result from mistakes in valuation on the part of the stock market. In other words, the buyer may believe that investors have underestimated the value of the seller or may hope that they *will* overestimate the value of the combined firm. But we see (with hindsight) that mistakes are made in bear markets as well as bull markets. Why don't we see just as many firms hunting for bargain acquisitions when the stock market is low? It is possible that "suckers are born every minute," but it is difficult to believe that they can be harvested only in bull markets.

Merger activity tends to be concentrated in a relatively small number of industries and is often prompted by deregulation and by changes in technology or the pattern of demand. Take the merger wave of the 1990s, for example. Deregulation of telecoms and banking earlier in the decade led to a spate of mergers in both industries. Elsewhere, the decline in military spending brought about a number of mergers between defense companies until the Department of Justice decided to call a halt. And in the entertainment industry the prospective advantages from controlling both content and distribution led to mergers between such giants as AOL and Time Warner.

Do Mergers Generate Net Benefits?

There are undoubtedly good acquisitions and bad acquisitions, but economists find it hard to agree on whether acquisitions are beneficial *on balance*. Indeed, since there seem to be transient fashions in mergers, it would be surprising if economists could come up with simple generalizations.

We do know that mergers generate substantial gains to acquired firms' stockholders. Since buyers roughly break even and sellers make substantial gains, it seems that there are positive overall benefits from mergers.[42] But not everybody is convinced. Some believe that investors analyzing mergers pay too much attention to short-term earnings gains and don't notice that these gains are at the expense of long-term prospects.[43]

Since we can't observe how companies would have fared in the absence of a merger, it is difficult to measure the effects on profitability. Ravenscroft and Scherer, who looked at mergers during the 1960s and early 1970s, argued that productivity declined in the years following a merger.[44] But studies of subsequent merger activity suggest that mergers *do* seem to improve real productivity. For example, Paul Healy, Krishna Palepu, and Richard Ruback examined 50 large mergers between 1979 and 1983 and found an average increase of 2.4 percentage points in the companies' pretax

[42]M. C. Jensen and R. S. Ruback, "The Market for Corporate Control: The Scientific Evidence," *Journal of Financial Economics* 11 (April 1983), pp. 5–50, after an extensive review of empirical work, conclude that "corporate takeovers generate positive gains" (p. 47). Richard Roll reviewed the same evidence and argues that "takeover gains may have been overestimated if they exist at all." See "The Hubris Hypothesis of Corporate Takeovers," *Journal of Business* 59 (April 1986), pp. 198–216.

[43]There have been a number of attempts to test whether investors are myopic. For example, McConnell and Muscarella examined the reaction of stock prices to announcements of capital expenditure plans. If investors were interested in short-term earnings, which are generally depressed by major capital expenditure programs, then these announcements should depress stock price. But they found that increases in capital spending were associated with *increases* in stock prices and reductions were associated with *falls*. Similarly, Jarrell, Lehn, and Marr found that announcements of expanded R&D spending prompted a *rise* in stock price. See J. McConnell and C. Muscarella, "Corporate Capital Expenditure Decisions and the Market Value of the Firm," *Journal of Financial Economics* 14 (July 1985), pp. 399–422; and G. Jarrell, K. Lehn, and W. Marr, "Institutional Ownership, Tender Offers, and Long-Term Investments," Office of the Chief Economist, Securities and Exchange Commission (April 1985).

[44]See D. J. Ravenscroft and F. M. Scherer, "Mergers and Managerial Performance," in J. C. Coffee, Jr., L. Lowenstein, and S. Rose-Ackerman (eds.), *Knights, Raiders, and Targets: The Impact of the Hostile Takeover,* Oxford University Press, New York, 1988.

returns.[45] They argue that this gain came from generating a higher level of sales from the same assets. There was no evidence indicating that the companies were mortgaging their long-term future by cutting back on long-term investments; expenditures on capital equipment and research and development tracked industry averages.[46]

Perhaps the most important effect of acquisitions is felt by the managers of companies that are *not* taken over. Perhaps the threat of takeover spurs the whole of corporate America to try harder. Unfortunately, we don't know whether, on balance, the threat of merger makes for active days or sleepless nights.

The threat of takeover may be a spur to inefficient management, but it is also costly. It can soak up large amounts of management time and effort. When a company is planning a takeover, it can be difficult to pay as much attention as one should to the firm's existing business.[47] In addition, the company needs to pay for the services provided by the investment bankers, lawyers, and accountants. In the year 2000 merging companies paid in total more than $2 billion for professional assistance.

---

[45] See P. Healy, K. Palepu, and R. Ruback, "Does Corporate Performance Improve after Mergers?" *Journal of Financial Economics* 31 (April 1992), pp. 135–175. The study examined the pretax returns of the merged companies relative to industry averages. A study by Lichtenberg and Siegel came to similar conclusions. Before merger, acquired companies had lower levels of productivity than did other firms in their industries, but by seven years after the control change, two-thirds of the productivity gap had been eliminated. See F. Lichtenberg and D. Siegel, "The Effect of Control Changes on the Productivity of U.S. Manufacturing Plants," *Journal of Applied Corporate Finance* 2 (Summer 1989), pp. 60–67.

[46] Maintained levels of capital spending and R&D are also observed by Lichtenberg and Siegel, op. cit.; and B. H. Hall, "The Effect of Takeover Activity on Corporate Research and Development," in A. J. Auerbach (ed.), *Corporate Takeover: Causes and Consequences,* University of Chicago Press, Chicago, 1988.

[47] There is some evidence that, while acquisitions lead to improvements in the productivity of the new plant, productivity in the firm's existing plant languishes. See R. McGuckin and S. Nguyen, "On Productivity and Plant Ownership Change: New Evidence from the Longitudinal Research Database," *Rand Journal of Economics* 26 (1995), pp. 257–276.

SUMMARY

A merger generates an economic gain if the two firms are worth more together than apart. Suppose that firms A and B merge to form a new entity, AB. Then the gain from the merger is

$$\text{Gain} = PV_{AB} - (PV_A + PV_B) = \Delta PV_{AB}$$

Gains from mergers may reflect economies of scale, economies of vertical integration, improved efficiency, the combination of complementary resources, or redeployment of surplus funds. In other cases there may be no advantage in combining two businesses, but the object of the acquisition is to install a more efficient management team. There are also dubious reasons for mergers. There is no value added by merging just to diversify risks, to reduce borrowing costs, or to pump up earnings per share.

In many cases the object of merging is to replace management or to force changes in investment or financing policies. Many of the takeovers in the 1980s were diet deals, in which companies were forced to sell assets, cut costs, or reduce capital expenditures. The changes added value when the target company had ample free cash flow but was overinvesting or not trying hard enough to reduce costs or dispose of underutilized assets.

You should go ahead with the acquisition if the gain exceeds the cost. Cost is the premium that the buyer pays for the selling firm over its value as a separate entity. It is easy to estimate when the merger is financed by cash. In that case,

$$\text{Cost} = \text{cash paid} - PV_B$$

When payment is in the form of shares, the cost naturally depends on what those shares are worth after the merger is complete. If the merger is a success, B's stockholders will share the merger gains.

The mechanics of buying a firm are much more complex than those of buying a machine. First, you have to make sure that the purchase does not fall afoul of the antitrust laws. Second, you have a choice of procedures: You can merge all the assets and liabilities of the seller into those of your own company; you can buy the stock of the seller rather than the company itself; or you can buy the individual assets of the seller. Third, you have to worry about the tax status of the merger. In a tax-free merger the tax position of the corporation and the stockholders is not changed. In a taxable merger the buyer can depreciate the full cost of the tangible assets acquired, but tax must be paid on any write-up of the assets' taxable value, and the stockholders in the selling corporation are taxed on any capital gains.

Mergers are often amicably negotiated between the management and directors of the two companies; but if the seller is reluctant, the would-be buyer can decide to make a tender offer or engage in a proxy fight. We sketched some of the offensive and defensive tactics used in takeover battles. We also observed that when the target firm loses, its shareholders typically win: Selling shareholders earn large abnormal returns, while the bidding firm's shareholders roughly break even. The typical merger appears to generate positive net benefits for investors, but competition among bidders, plus active defense by target management, pushes most of the gains toward the selling shareholders.

APPENDIX Conglomerate Mergers and Value Additivity

A pure conglomerate merger is one that has no effect on the operations or profitability of either firm. If corporate diversification is in stockholders' interests, a conglomerate merger would give a clear demonstration of its benefits. But if present values add up, the conglomerate merger would not make stockholders better or worse off.

In this appendix we examine more carefully our assertion that present values add. It turns out that values *do* add as long as capital markets are perfect and investors' diversification opportunities are unrestricted.

Call the merging firms A and B. Value additivity implies

$$PV_{AB} = PV_A + PV_B$$

where

$$PV_{AB} = \text{market value of combined firms just after merger;}$$
$$PV_A, PV_B = \text{separate market values of A and B just before merger.}$$

For example, we might have

$$PV_A = \$100 \text{ million } (\$200 \text{ per share} \times 500{,}000 \text{ shares outstanding})$$

and

$$PV_B = \$200 \text{ million } (\$200 \text{ per share} \times 1{,}000{,}000 \text{ shares outstanding})$$

Suppose A and B are merged into a new firm, AB, with one share in AB exchanged for each share of A or B. Thus there are 1,500,000 AB shares issued. *If* value additivity holds, then PV_{AB} must equal the sum of the separate values of A and B just before the merger, that is, \$300 million. That would imply a price of \$200 per share of AB stock.

But note that the AB shares represent a portfolio of the assets of A and B. Before the merger investors could have bought one share of A and two of B for \$600. Afterward they can obtain a claim on *exactly* the same real assets by buying three shares of AB.

Suppose that the opening price of AB shares just after the merger is \$200, so that $PV_{AB} = PV_A + PV_B$. Our problem is to determine if this is an equilibrium price, that is, whether we can rule out excess demand or supply at this price.

For there to be excess demand, there must be some investors who are willing to increase their holdings of A and B as a consequence of the merger. Who could they be? The only thing new created by the merger is diversification, but those investors who want to hold assets of A *and* B will have purchased A's and B's stock before the merger. The diversification is redundant and consequently won't attract new investment demand.

Is there a possibility of excess supply? The answer is yes. For example, there will be some shareholders in A who did not invest in B. After the merger they cannot invest solely in A, but only in a fixed combination of A and B. Their AB shares will be less attractive to them than the pure A shares, so they will sell part of or all their AB stock. In fact, the only AB shareholders who will *not* wish to sell are those who happened to hold A and B in exactly a 1:2 ratio in their premerger portfolios!

Since there is no possibility of excess demand but a definite possibility of excess supply, we seem to have

$$PV_{AB} \leq PV_A + PV_B$$

That is, corporate diversification can't help, but it may hurt investors by restricting the types of portfolios they can hold. This is not the whole story, however, since investment demand for AB shares might be attracted from other sources if PV_{AB} drops below $PV_A + PV_B$. To illustrate, suppose there are two other firms, A* and B*, which are judged by investors to have the same risk characteristics as A and B, respectively. Then before the merger,

$$r_A = r_{A^*} \quad \text{and} \quad r_B = r_{B^*}$$

where r is the rate of return expected by investors. We'll assume $r_A = r_{A^*} = .08$ and $r_B = r_{B^*} = .20$.

Consider a portfolio invested one-third in A* and two-thirds in B*. This portfolio offers an expected return of 16 percent:

$$\begin{aligned} r &= x_{A^*}r_{A^*} + x_{B^*}r_{B^*} \\ &= \tfrac{1}{3}(.08) + \tfrac{2}{3}(.20) = .16 \end{aligned}$$

A similar portfolio of A and B before their merger also offered a 16 percent return.

As we have noted, a new firm AB is really a portfolio of firms A and B, with portfolio weights of $\frac{1}{3}$ and $\frac{2}{3}$. Thus it is equivalent in risk to the portfolio of A* and B*. Thus the price of AB shares must adjust so that it likewise offers a 16 percent return.

What if AB shares drop below \$200, so that PV_{AB} is less than $PV_A + PV_B$? Since the assets and earnings of firms A and B are the same, the price drop means that the expected rate of return on AB shares has risen above the return offered by the A*B* portfolio. That is, if r_{AB} exceeds $\frac{1}{3}r_A + \frac{2}{3}r_B$, then r_{AB} must also exceed $\frac{1}{3}r_{A^*} + \frac{2}{3}r_{B^*}$. But this is untenable: Investors A* and B* could sell part of their holdings (in a 1:2 ratio), buy AB, and obtain a higher expected rate of return with no increase in risk.

On the other hand, if PV_{AB} rises above $PV_A + PV_B$, the AB shares will offer an expected return less than that offered by the A*B* portfolio. Investors will unload the AB shares, forcing their price down.

A stable result occurs only if AB shares stick at $200. Thus, value additivity will hold exactly in a perfect-market equilibrium if there are ample substitutes for the A and B assets. If A and B have unique risk characteristics, however, then PV_{AB} can fall below $PV_A + PV_B$. The reason is that the merger curtails investors' opportunity to custom-tailor their portfolios to their own needs and preferences. This makes investors worse off, reducing the attractiveness of holding the shares of firm AB.

In general, the condition for value additivity is that investors' opportunity set—that is, the range of risk characteristics attainable by investors through their portfolio choices—is independent of the particular portfolio of real assets held by the firm. Diversification per se can never expand the opportunity set given perfect security markets. Corporate diversification may reduce the investors' opportunity set, but only if the real assets the corporations hold lack substitutes among traded securities or portfolios.

In a few cases the firm may be able to expand the opportunity set. It can do so if it finds an investment opportunity that is unique—a real asset with risk characteristics shared by few or no other financial assets. In this lucky event the firm should not diversify, however. It should set up the unique asset as a separate firm so as to expand investors' opportunity set to the maximum extent. If Gallo by chance discovered that a small portion of its vineyards produced wine comparable to Chateau Margaux, it would not throw that wine into the Hearty Burgundy vat.

FURTHER READING

Here are two useful books on takeovers:

L. Herzel and R. Shepro: *Bidders and Targets: Mergers and Acquisitions in the U.S.*, Basil Blackwell, Inc., Cambridge, MA, 1990.

J. F. Weston, K. S. Chung, and J. A. Siu: *Takeovers, Restructuring and Corporate Finance*, 3rd ed., Prentice-Hall, Upper Saddle River, NJ, 2000.

A good review of the mechanics of acquisitions is provided in:

S. M. Litwin: "The Merger and Acquisition Process: A Primer on Getting the Deal Done," *The Financier: ACMT*, 2:6–17 (November 1995).

Recent merger waves are reviewed in:

G. Andrade, M. Mitchell, and E. Stafford: "New Evidence and Perspectives on Mergers," *Journal of Economic Perspectives*, 15:103–120 (Spring 2001).

Jensen and Ruback review the early empirical work on mergers. The April 1983 issue of the Journal of Financial Economics *also contains a collection of some of the more important empirical studies.*

M. C. Jensen and R. S. Ruback: "The Market for Corporate Control: The Scientific Evidence," *Journal of Financial Economics*, 11:5–50 (April 1983).

Finally, here are some informative case studies:

G. P. Baker: "Beatrice: A Study in the Creation and Destruction of Value," *Journal of Finance*, 47:1081–1119 (July 1992).

R. Bruner: "An Analysis of Value Destruction and Recovery in the Alliance and Proposed Merger of Volvo and Renault," *Journal of Financial Economics*, 51:125–166 (1999).

R. S. Ruback: "The Cities Service Takeover: A Case Study," *Journal of Finance*, 38:319–330 (May 1983).

B. Burrough and J. Helyar: *Barbarians at the Gate: The Fall of RJR Nabisco*, Harper & Row, New York, 1990.

QUIZ

1. Are the following hypothetical mergers horizontal, vertical, or conglomerate?
   a. IBM acquires Dell Computer.
   b. Dell Computer acquires Kroger.
   c. Kroger acquires H. J. Heinz.
   d. H. J. Heinz acquires IBM.
2. Which of the following motives for mergers make economic sense?
   a. Merging to achieve economies of scale.
   b. Merging to reduce risk by diversification.
   c. Merging to redeploy cash generated by a firm with ample profits but limited growth opportunities.
   d. Merging to combine complementary resources.
   e. Merging just to increase earnings per share.
3. Velcro Saddles is contemplating the acquisition of Pogo Ski Sticks, Inc. The values of the two companies as separate entities are $20 million and $10 million, respectively. Velcro Saddles estimates that by combining the two companies, it will reduce marketing and administrative costs by $500,000 per year in perpetuity. Velcro Saddles can either pay $14 million cash for Pogo or offer Pogo a 50 percent holding in Velcro Saddles. The opportunity cost of capital is 10 percent.
   a. What is the gain from merger?
   b. What is the cost of the cash offer?
   c. What is the cost of the stock alternative?
   d. What is the NPV of the acquisition under the cash offer?
   e. What is its NPV under the stock offer?
4. Which of the following transactions are *not* likely to be classed as tax-free?
   a. An acquisition of assets.
   b. A merger in which payment is entirely in the form of voting stock.
5. True or false?
   a. Sellers almost always gain in mergers.
   b. Buyers usually gain more than sellers.
   c. Firms that do unusually well tend to be acquisition targets.
   d. Merger activity in the United States varies dramatically from year to year.
   e. On the average, mergers produce large economic gains.
   f. Tender offers require the approval of the selling firm's management.
   g. The cost of a merger to the buyer equals the gain realized by the seller.
6. Mature companies with ample free cash flow are often targets for takeovers. Briefly explain why.
7. Briefly define the following terms:
   a. Purchase accounting
   b. Tender offer
   c. Poison pill
   d. Greenmail
   e. White knight

PRACTICE QUESTIONS

1. Examine several recent mergers and suggest the principal motives for merging in each case.
2. Examine a recent merger in which at least part of the payment made to the seller was in the form of stock. Use stock market prices to obtain an estimate of the gain from the merger and the cost of the merger.
3. Respond to the following comments.
   a. "Our cost of debt is too darn high, but our banks won't reduce interest rates as long as we're stuck in this volatile widget-trading business. We've got to acquire other companies with safer income streams."

b. "Merge with Fledgling Electronics? No way! Their P/E's too high. That deal would knock 20 percent off our earnings per share."

c. "Our stock's at an all-time high. It's time to make our offer for Digital Organics. Sure, we'll have to offer a hefty premium to Digital stockholders, but we don't have to pay in cash. We'll give them new shares of our stock."

4. Explain how you would estimate the gain and cost of a merger financed by stock. What stock price should be used to calculate the cost?

5. Sometimes the stock price of a possible target company rises in anticipation of a merger bid. Explain how this complicates the bidder's evaluation of the target company.

6. Suppose you obtain special information—information unavailable to investors—indicating that Backwoods Chemical's stock price is 40 percent undervalued. Is that a reason to launch a takeover bid for Backwoods? Explain carefully.

7. As treasurer of Leisure Products, Inc., you are investigating the possible acquisition of Plastitoys. You have the following basic data:

	Leisure Products	Plastitoys
Earnings per share	$ 5.00	$ 1.50
Dividend per share	$ 3.00	$ .80
Number of shares	1,000,000	600,000
Stock price	$90	$20

You estimate that investors currently expect a steady growth of about 6 percent in Plastitoys' earnings and dividends. Under new management this growth rate would be increased to 8 percent per year, without any additional capital investment required.

a. What is the gain from the acquisition?

b. What is the cost of the acquisition if Leisure Products pays $25 in cash for each share of Plastitoys?

c. What is the cost of the acquisition if Leisure Products offers one share of Leisure Products for every three shares of Plastitoys?

d. How would the cost of the cash offer and the share offer alter if the expected growth rate of Plastitoys were not changed by the merger?

8. The Muck and Slurry merger has fallen through (see Section 33.2). But World Enterprises is determined to report earnings per share of $2.67. It therefore acquires the Wheelrim and Axle Company. You are given the following facts:

	World Enterprises	Wheelrim and Axle	Merged Firm
Earnings per share	$2.00	$2.50	$2.67
Price per share	$40	$25	?
Price–earnings ratio	20	10	?
Number of shares	100,000	200,000	?
Total earnings	$200,000	$500,000	?
Total market value	$4,000,000	$5,000,000	?

Once again there are no gains from merging. In exchange for Wheelrim and Axle shares, World Enterprises issues just enough of its own shares to ensure its $2.67 earnings per share objective.

a. Complete the above table for the merged firm.

b. How many shares of World Enterprises are exchanged for each share of Wheelrim and Axle?

c. What is the cost of the merger to World Enterprises?

d. What is the change in the total market value of the World Enterprises shares that were outstanding before the merger?

9. Explain the distinction between a tax-free and a taxable merger. Are there circumstances in which you would expect buyer and seller to agree to a taxable merger?

10. Look again at Table 33.3. Suppose that B Corporation's fixed assets are reexamined and found to be worth $1.2 million instead of $.9 million. How would this affect the AB Corporation's balance sheet under purchase accounting? How would the value of AB Corporation change? Would your answer depend on whether the merger is taxable?

11. What was the common theme in Boone Pickens's attempts to take over Cities Service, Gulf Oil, and Phillips Petroleum? Did his efforts create value for these companies' shareholders? How? Was economic efficiency enhanced?

12. In July 1994 the top managers of Sovereign Bancorp were at loggerheads:[48]
- Jay Sidhu, president and chief executive officer of the $5 billion bank, wants to be an acquirer. Only by buying up other banks, he argues, will Sovereign gain the financial clout it needs to survive in the increasingly competitive industry.
- But Fred Jaindl, the bank's chairman and largest stockholder, wants it to *be* acquired. A buy-out, he figures, would deliver big profits to stockholders, including $50 million on his own stock.

a. Are shareholders generally better off as sellers, rather than buyers, in mergers and acquisitions? Why?

b. Under what conditions would the active acquisition strategy advocated by Sidhu make sense for Sovereign *and* its shareholders?

13. In December 1995 NatWest, one of the largest British banks, sold its U.S. retail banking operations to Fleet Financial for about $3.5 billion. This price was much less than industry observers had expected, but NatWest's stock price nevertheless sharply increased. "The central explanation [for the stock price rise] was found in the strong hints in NatWest's announcement that it would not rush out immediately and spend the sale money on some ill-judged and overpriced acquisition."[49] NatWest also announced that it was considering repurchasing shares.

How would you interpret this episode?

CHALLENGE QUESTIONS

1. Examine a hostile acquisition and discuss the tactics employed by both the predator and the target companies. Do you think that the management of the target firm was trying to defeat the bid or to secure the highest price for its stockholders? How did each announcement by the protagonists affect their stock prices?

2. How do you think mergers should be regulated? For example, what defenses should target companies be allowed to employ? Should managers of target firms be compelled to seek out the highest bids? Should they simply be passive and watch from the sidelines?

3. In Italy the first firm to bid for a target is allowed to revise its offer, but subsequent bidders may enter only one bid and they are not allowed to revise it. What do you think is the reason for this rule? Do you think that it should be introduced in the United States?

4. Do you have any rational explanation for the great fluctuations in aggregate merger activity and the apparent relationship between merger activity and stock prices?

[48] G. Bruce Knecht, "Nationwide Banking Is around the Corner, but Obstacles Remain," *The Wall Street Journal*, July 26, 1994, p. A1.

[49] George Graham, "NatWest Bids Farewell to an Albatross," *Financial Times*, December 23–24, 1995, p. 2.

CHAPTER THIRTY-FOUR

CONTROL, GOVERNANCE, AND FINANCIAL ARCHITECTURE

FIRST, SOME DEFINITIONS. *Corporate control* means the power to make investment and financing decisions. A hostile takeover bid is an attempt to force a change in corporate control. In popular usage, *corporate governance* refers to the role of the board of directors, shareholder voting, proxy fights, and to other actions taken by shareholders to influence corporate decisions. In the last chapter we saw a striking example: Pressure from institutional shareholders helped force AMP Corporation to abandon its legal defenses and accept a takeover.

Economists use the term governance more generally to cover all the mechanisms by which managers are led to act in the interests of the corporation's owners. A perfect system of corporate governance would give managers all the right incentives to make value-maximizing investment and financing decisions. It would assure that cash is paid out to investors when the company runs out of positive-NPV investment opportunities. It would give managers and employees fair compensation but prevent excessive perks and other private benefits.

This chapter considers control and governance in the United States and other industrialized countries. It picks up where the last chapter left off—mergers and acquisitions are, after all, changes in corporate control. We will cover other mechanisms for changing or exercising control, including leveraged buyouts (LBOs), spin-offs and carve-outs, and conglomerates versus private equity partnerships.

The first section starts with yet another famous takeover battle, the leveraged buyout of RJR Nabisco. Then we move to a general evaluation of LBOs, leveraged restructurings, privatizations, and spin-offs. The main point of these transactions is not just to change control, although existing management is often booted out, but also to change incentives for managers and improve financial performance.

Section 34.3 looks at conglomerates. "Conglomerate" usually means a large, public company with operations in several unrelated businesses or markets. We ask why conglomerates in the United States are a declining species, while in some other countries, for example Korea and India, they seem to be the dominant corporate form. Even in the United States, there are many successful *temporary* conglomerates, although they are not public companies.[1]

Section 34.4 shows how ownership and control vary internationally. We use Germany and Japan as the main examples.

There is a common theme to these three sections. You can't think about control and governance without thinking still more broadly about *financial architecture,* that is, about the financial organization of the business. Financial architecture is partly corporate control (who runs the business?) and partly governance (making sure managers act in shareholders' interests). But it also includes the legal form of organization (e.g., corporation vs. partnership), sources of financing (e.g., public vs. private equity), and relationships with financial institutions. The financial architectures of LBOs and most public corporations are fundamentally different. The financial architecture of a Korean conglomerate (a *chaebol*) is fundamentally different from a conglomerate in the United States. Where financial architecture differs, governance and control are different too.

Much of corporate finance (and much of this book) assumes a particular financial architecture—that of a public corporation with actively traded shares, dispersed ownership, and relatively easy access to financial markets. But there are other ways to organize and finance a business. Arrangements for ownership and control vary greatly country by country. Even in the United States many successful businesses are not corporations, many corporations are not public, and many public corporations have concentrated, not dispersed, ownership.

[1]What's a temporary conglomerate? Sorry, you'll have to wait for the punch line.

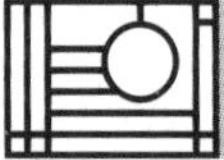

34.1 LEVERAGED BUYOUTS, SPIN-OFFS, AND RESTRUCTURINGS

Leveraged buyouts differ from ordinary acquisitions in two immediately obvious ways. First, a large fraction of the purchase price is debt-financed. Some, often all, of this debt is junk, that is, below investment-grade. Second, the LBO goes private, and its shares no longer trade on the open market.[2] The LBO's stock is held by a partnership of (usually institutional) investors. When this group is led by the company's management, the acquisition is called a **management buyout (MBO).**

In the 1970s and 1980s many management buyouts were arranged for unwanted divisions of large, diversified companies. Smaller divisions outside the companies' main lines of business sometimes lacked top management's interest and commitment, and divisional management chafed under corporate bureaucracy. Many such divisions flowered when spun off as MBOs. Their managers, pushed by the need to generate cash for debt service and encouraged by a substantial personal stake in the business, found ways to cut costs and compete more effectively.

In the 1980s MBO/LBO activity shifted to buyouts of entire businesses, including large, mature public corporations. Table 34.1 lists the largest LBOs of the 1980s plus examples of transactions from 1997 to 2001. More recent LBOs are generally smaller and not leveraged as aggressively as the deals of the 1980s. But LBO activity is still impressive in aggregate: Buyout firms raised over $60 billion in new capital in 2000.[3]

Acquirer	Target	Industry	Year	Price
KKR	RJR Nabisco	Food, tobacco	1989	$24,720
KKR	Beatrice	Food	1986	6,250
KKR	Safeway	Supermarkets	1986	4,240
Thompson Co.	Southland (7-11)	Convenience stores	1987	4,000
Wings Holdings	NWA, Inc.	Airlines	1989	3,690
KKR	Owens-Illinois	Glass	1987	3,690
TF Investments	Hospital Corp of America	Hospitals	1989	3,690
Macy Acquisitions Corp.	R. H. Macy & Co.	Department stores	1986	3,500
Bain Capital	Sealy Corp.	Mattresses	1997	811
Cyprus Group, with management*	WESCO Distribution, Inc.	Data communications	1998	1,100
Clayton, Dubilier, & Rice	North American Van Lines	Trucking	1998	200
Berkshire Partners	William Carter Co.	Children's clothing	2001	450
Heartland Industrial Partners	Springs Industries	Household textiles	2001	846

TABLE 34.1

The 10 largest LBOs of the 1980s, plus examples of more recent deals. Price in $ millions.

*Management participated in the buyout—a partial MBO.
Source: A. Kaufman and E. J. Englander, "Kohlberg Kravis Roberts & Co. and the Restructuring of American Capitalism," *Business History Review* 67 (Spring 1993), p. 78; *Mergers and Acquisitions* 33 (November/December 1998), p. 43, and various later issues.

[2] Sometimes a small *stub* of stock is not acquired and continues to trade.

[3] LBO Signposts, *Mergers & Acquisitions,* March 2001, p. 24.

Table 34.1 starts with the largest, most dramatic, and best-documented LBO of all time: the $25 billion takeover of RJR Nabisco by Kohlberg, Kravis, Roberts (KKR). The players, tactics, and controversies of LBOs are writ large in this case.

RJR Nabisco

On October 28, 1988, the board of directors of RJR Nabisco revealed that Ross Johnson, the company's chief executive officer, had formed a group of investors that was prepared to buy all RJR's stock for $75 per share in cash and take the company private. Johnson's group was backed up and advised by Shearson Lehman Hutton, the investment banking subsidiary of American Express. RJR's share price immediately moved to about $75, handing shareholders a 36 percent gain over the previous day's price of $56. At the same time RJR's bonds fell, since it was clear that existing bondholders would soon have a lot more company.[4]

Johnson's offer lifted RJR onto the auction block. Once the company was in play, its board of directors was obliged to consider other offers, which were not long in coming. Four days later KKR bid $90 per share, $79 in cash plus PIK preferred valued at $11. (PIK means "pay in kind." The preferred dividends would be paid not in cash but in more preferred shares.)[5]

The resulting bidding contest had as many turns and surprises as a Dickens novel. In the end it was Johnson's group against KKR. KKR offered $109 per share, after adding $1 per share (roughly $230 million) in the last hour.[6] The KKR bid was $81 in cash, convertible subordinated debentures valued at about $10, and PIK preferred shares valued at about $18. Johnson's group bid $112 in cash and securities.

But the RJR board chose KKR. Although Johnson's group had offered $3 per share more, its security valuations were viewed as "softer" and perhaps overstated. The Johnson group's proposal also contained a management compensation package that seemed extremely generous and had generated an avalanche of bad press.

But where did the merger benefits come from? What could justify offering $109 per share, about $25 billion in all, for a company that only 33 days previously was selling for $56 per share? KKR and the other bidders were betting on two things. First, they expected to generate billions in additional cash from interest tax shields, reduced capital expenditures, and sales of assets not strictly necessary to RJR's core businesses. Asset sales alone were projected to generate $5 billion. Second, they expected to make the core businesses significantly more profitable, mainly by cutting back on expenses and bureaucracy. Apparently there was plenty to cut, including the RJR "Air Force," which at one point included 10 corporate jets.

In the year after KKR took over, new management was installed that sold assets and cut back operating expenses and capital spending. There were also layoffs. As expected, high interest charges meant a net loss of $976 million for 1989, but pretax operating income actually increased, despite extensive asset sales, including the sale of RJR's European food operations.

Inside the firm, things were going well. But outside there was confusion, and prices in the junk bond market were rapidly declining, implying much higher future

---

[4]N. Mohan and C. R. Chen track the abnormal returns of RJR securities in "A Review of the RJR Nabisco Buyout," *Journal of Applied Corporate Finance* 3 (Summer 1990), pp. 102–108.

[5]See Section 25.8.

[6]The whole story is reconstructed by B. Burrough and J. Helyar in *Barbarians at the Gate: The Fall of RJR Nabisco*, Harper & Row, New York, 1990—see especially Ch. 18—and in a movie with the same title.

interest charges for RJR and stricter terms on any refinancing. In mid-1990 KKR made an additional equity investment, and in December 1990 it announced an offer of cash and new shares in exchange for $753 million of junk bonds. RJR's chief financial officer described the exchange offer as "one further step in the deleveraging of the company."[7] For RJR, the world's largest LBO, it seemed that high debt was a temporary, not permanent, virtue.

RJR, like many other firms that were taken private through LBOs, enjoyed only a short period as a private company. In 1991 RJR went public again with the sale of $1.1 billion of stock.[8] KKR progressively sold off its investment, and its remaining stake in the company was sold in 1995 at roughly the original purchase price.

Barbarians at the Gate?

The RJR Nabisco LBO crystallized views on LBOs, the junk bond market, and the takeover business. For many it exemplified all that was wrong with finance in the 1980s, especially the willingness of "raiders" to carve up established companies, leaving them with enormous debt burdens, basically in order to get rich quick.

There was plenty of confusion, stupidity, and greed in the LBO business. Not all the people involved were nice. On the other hand, LBOs generated enormous increases in market value, and most of the gains went to the selling stockholders, not to the raiders. For example, the biggest winners in the RJR Nabisco LBO were the company's stockholders.

The most important sources of added value came from making RJR Nabisco leaner and meaner. The company's new management was obliged to pay out massive amounts of cash to service the LBO debt. It also had an equity stake in the business and therefore had strong incentives to sell off nonessential assets, cut costs, and improve operating profits.

LBOs are almost by definition *diet deals.* But there were other motives. Here are some of them.

The Junk Bond Markets LBOs and debt-financed takeovers may have been driven by artificially cheap funding from the junk bond markets. With hindsight, it seems that investors in junk bonds underestimated the risks of default in junk bonds. Default rates climbed painfully from 1988 through 1991, when 10 percent of outstanding junk bonds with a face value of $18.9 billion defaulted.[9] The junk bond market also became much less liquid after the demise in 1990 of Drexel Burnham, the chief market maker, although the market recovered in the mid-1990s.

Leverage and Taxes Borrowing money saves taxes, as we explained in Chapter 18. But taxes were not the main driving force behind LBOs. The value of interest tax shields was just not big enough to explain the observed gains in market value.[10]

[7]G. Andress, "RJR Swallows Hard, Offers $5-a-Share Stock," *The Wall Street Journal,* December 18, 1990, pp. C1–C2.

[8]Northwest Airlines, Safeway Stores, Kaiser Aluminum, and Burlington Industries are other examples of LBOs that reverted to being public companies.

[9]See R. A. Waldman, E. I. Altman, and A. R. Ginsberg, "Defaults and Returns on High Yield Bonds: Analysis through 1997," Salomon Smith Barney, New York, January 30, 1998. See also Section 24.5.

[10]Moreover, there are some tax costs to LBOs. For example, selling shareholders realize capital gains and pay taxes that otherwise could be deferred. See L. Stiglin, S. N. Kaplan, and M. C. Jensen, "Effects of LBOs on Tax Revenues of the U.S. Treasury," *Tax Notes* 42 (February 6, 1989), pp. 727–733.

For example, Richard Ruback estimated the present value of additional interest tax shields generated by the RJR LBO at $1.8 billion.[11] But the gain in market value to RJR stockholders was about $8 billion.

Of course, if interest tax shields were the main motive for LBOs' high debt, then LBO managers would not be so concerned to pay off debt. We saw that this was one of the first tasks facing RJR Nabisco's new management.

Other Stakeholders We should look at the total gain to *all* investors in an LBO, not just to the selling stockholders. It's possible that the latter's gain is just someone else's loss and that no value is generated overall.

Bondholders are the obvious losers. The debt they thought was well secured may turn into junk when the borrower goes through an LBO. We noted how market prices of RJR Nabisco debt fell sharply when Ross Johnson's first LBO offer was announced. But again, the value losses suffered by bondholders in LBOs are not nearly large enough to explain stockholder gains. For example, Mohan and Chen's estimate[12] of losses to RJR bondholders was at most $575 million—painful to the bondholders, but far below the stockholders' gain.

Leverage and Incentives Managers and employees of LBOs work harder and often smarter. They have to generate cash for debt service. Moreover, managers' personal fortunes are riding on the LBO's success. They become owners rather than organization men and women.

It's hard to measure the payoff from better incentives, but there is some preliminary evidence of improved operating efficiency in LBOs. Kaplan, who studied 48 MBOs between 1980 and 1986, found average increases in operating income of 24 percent three years after the LBO. Ratios of operating income and net cash flow to assets and sales increased dramatically. He observed cutbacks in capital expenditures but not in employment. Kaplan suggests that these "operating changes are due to improved incentives rather than layoffs or managerial exploitation of shareholders through inside information."[13]

We have reviewed several motives for LBOs. We do not say that all LBOs are good. On the contrary, there have been many mistakes, and even soundly motivated LBOs are dangerous, at least for the buyers, as the bankruptcies of Campeau, Revco, National Gypsum, and other highly leveraged transactions (*HLTs*) proved. Yet, we do quarrel with those who portray LBOs solely as undertaken by Wall Street barbarians breaking up the traditional strengths of corporate America.

Leveraged Restructurings

The essence of a leveraged buyout is of course leverage. Why not take on the leverage and dispense with the buyout?

We reviewed one prominent example in the last chapter. Phillips Petroleum was attacked by Boone Pickens and Mesa Petroleum. Phillips dodged the takeover with a *leveraged restructuring*. It borrowed $4.5 billion and repurchased one-half of its outstanding shares. To service this debt, it sold assets for $2 billion and cut back

[11]R. S. Ruback, "RJR Nabisco," case study, Harvard Business School, Cambridge, MA, 1989.

[12]Mohan and Chen, op. cit.

[13]S. Kaplan, "The Effects of Management Buyouts on Operating Performance and Value," *Journal of Financial Economics* 24 (October 1989), pp. 217–254.

capital expenditure and operating costs. It put itself on a cash diet. The demands of servicing $4.5 billion of extra debt made sure it stayed on the diet.

Let's look at another *diet deal.*

Sealed Air's Leveraged Restructuring[14] In 1989 Sealed Air Corporation undertook a *leveraged restructuring.* It borrowed the money to pay a $328 million special cash dividend. In one stroke the company's debt increased 10 times. Its book equity (accounting net worth) went from $162 million to *minus* $161 million. Debt went from 13 percent of total book assets to 136 percent.

Sealed Air was a profitable company. The problem was that its profits were coming too easily because its main products were protected by patents. When the patents expired, strong competition was inevitable, and the company was not ready for it. In the meantime, there was too much financial slack:

> We didn't need to manufacture efficiently; we didn't need to worry about cash. At Sealed Air, capital tended to have limited value attached to it—cash was perceived as being free and abundant.

So the leveraged recap was used to "disrupt the status quo, promote internal change," and simulate "the pressures of Sealed Air's more competitive future." This shakeup was reinforced by new performance measures and incentives, including increases in stock ownership by employees.

It worked. Sales and operating profits increased steadily without major new capital investments, and net working capital *fell* by half, releasing cash to help service the company's debt. The company's stock price quadrupled in the five years after the restructuring.

Sealed Air's restructuring was not typical. It is an exemplar chosen with hindsight. It was also undertaken by a successful firm under no outside pressure. But it clearly shows the motive for most leveraged restructurings. They are designed to force mature, successful, but overweight companies to disgorge cash, reduce operating costs, and use assets more efficiently.

Financial Architecture of LBOs and Leveraged Restructurings

The financial structures of LBOs and leveraged restructurings are similar. The three main characteristics of LBOs are

1. *High debt.* The debt is not intended to be permanent. It is designed to be paid down. The requirement to generate cash for debt service is designed to curb wasteful investment and force improvements in operating efficiency.
2. *Incentives.* Managers are given a greater stake in the business via stock options or direct ownership of shares.
3. *Private ownership.* The LBO *goes private.* It is owned by a partnership of private investors who monitor performance and can act right away if something goes awry. But private ownership is not intended to be permanent. The most successful LBOs go public again as soon as debt has been paid down sufficiently and improvements in operating performance have been demonstrated.

Leveraged restructurings share the first two characteristics but continue as public companies.

[14]See K. H. Wruck, "Financial Policy as a Catalyst for Organizational Change: Sealed Air's Leveraged Special Dividend," *Journal of Applied Corporate Finance* 7 (Winter 1995), pp. 20–37.

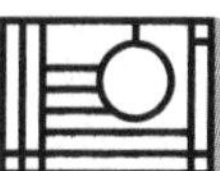

34.2 FUSION AND FISSION IN CORPORATE FINANCE

Figure 34.1 shows some of AT&T's acquisitions and divestitures. Prior to 1984, AT&T controlled most of the local, and virtually all of the long-distance telephone service in the United States. (Customers used to speak of the ubiquitous "Ma [Mother] Bell.") In 1984 the company accepted an antitrust settlement requiring local telephone service to be spun off to seven new, independent companies.[15] AT&T was left with its long-distance business plus Bell Laboratories, Western Electric (telecommunications manufacturing), and various other assets. As the communications industry became increasingly competitive, AT&T acquired several other businesses, notably in computers, cellular telephone service, and cable television. Some of these acquisitions are shown as the burgundy incoming arrows in Figure 34.1.

AT&T was an unusually active acquirer. It was a giant company trying to respond to rapidly changing technologies and markets. But AT&T was simultaneously *divesting* dozens of other businesses. For example, its credit card operations (the AT&T Universal Card) were sold to Citicorp. In 1996, AT&T created two new companies by spinning off Lucent (incorporating Bell Laboratories and Western Electric) and its computer business (NCR). AT&T had paid $7.5 billion to acquire NCR in 1990. These and several other important divestitures are shown as the burgundy outgoing arrows in Figure 34.1.

In the market for corporate control, fusion—mergers and acquisitions—gets the most publicity. But fission—the separation of assets and operations from the whole—can be just as important. We will now see how these separations are carried out by spin-offs, carve-outs, asset sales, and privatizations.

Spin-offs

A **spin-off** is a new, independent company created by detaching part of a parent company's assets and operations. Shares in the new company are distributed to the parent company's stockholders. Here are some recent examples.

- Sears Roebuck spun off Allstate, its insurance subsidiary, in 1995.
- In 1998 the Brazilian government completed privatization of Telebras, the Brazilian national telecommunications company. Before the final auction, the company was split into 12 separate pieces—one long-distance, three local, and eight wireless communications companies. In other words, 12 companies were spun out of the one original.
- In 2001 Thermo Electron spun off its healthcare and paper machinery and systems divisions as two new companies, Viasys and Kadant, respectively.
- In 2001 Canadian Pacific Ltd. spun off its oil and gas, shipping, coal mining, and hotel businesses as four new companies traded on the Toronto stock exchange.

Spin-offs are not taxed so long as shareholders in the parent are given at least 80 percent of the shares in the new company.[16]

[15]Subsequent mergers reduced these seven companies to four: Bell South, SBC Communications, Qwest, and Verizon.

[16]If less than 80 percent of the shares are distributed, the value of the distribution is taxed as a dividend to the investor.

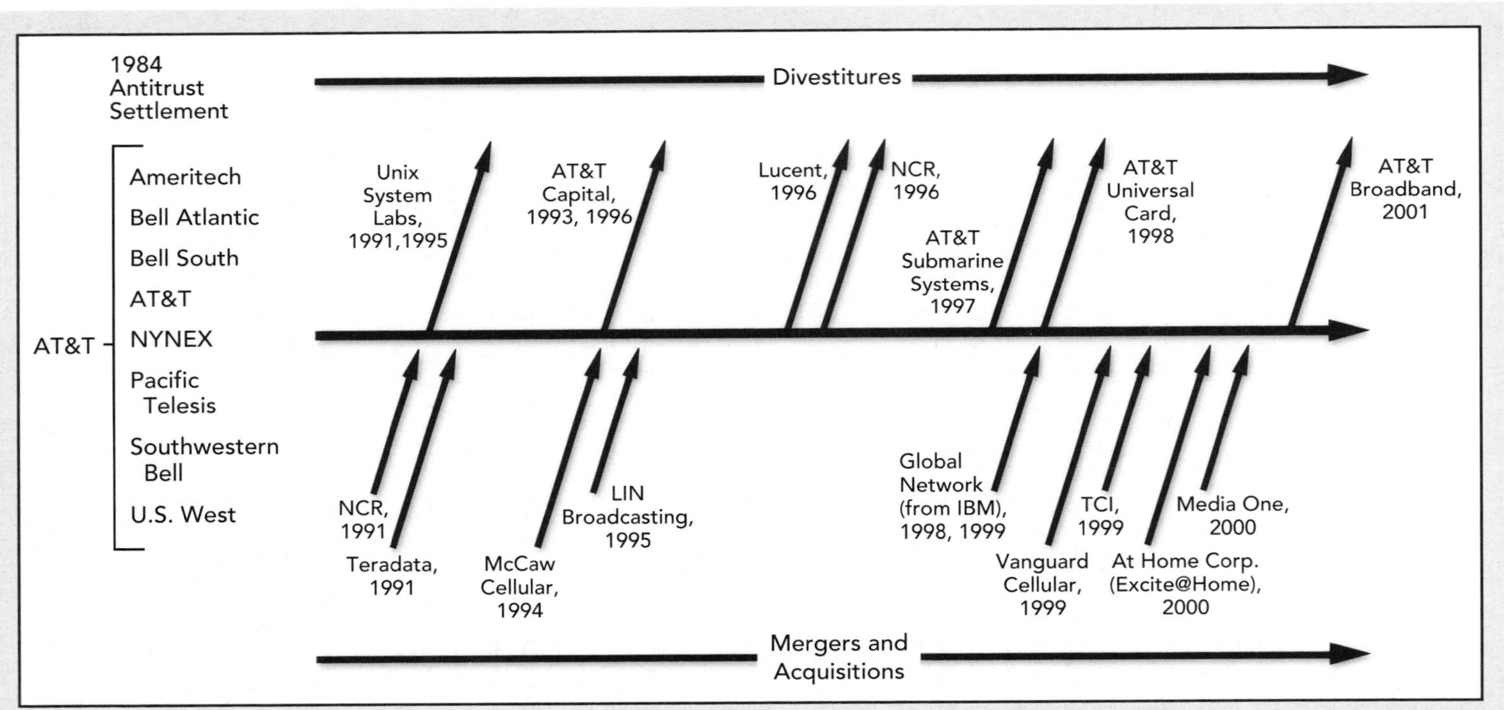

FIGURE 34.1

The effects of AT&T's antitrust settlement in 1984, and a few of AT&T's acquisitions and divestitures from 1991 to 2001. Divestitures are shown by the outgoing burgundy arrows. When two years are given, the transaction was completed in two steps.

Spin-offs widen investors' choice by allowing them to invest in just one part of the business. More important, spin-offs can improve incentives for managers. Companies sometimes refer to divisions or lines of business as "poor fits." By spinning these businesses off, management of the parent company can concentrate on its main activity.[17] If the businesses are independent, it is easier to see the value and performance of each and reward managers accordingly. Managers can be given stock or stock options in the spun-off company. Also, spin-offs relieve investors of the worry that funds will be siphoned from one business to support unprofitable capital investments in another.

Announcement of a spin-off is generally greeted as good news by investors.[18] Investors in U.S. companies seem to reward focus and penalize diversification. Consider the dissolution of John D. Rockefeller's Standard Oil trust in 1911. The company he founded, Standard Oil of New Jersey, was split up into seven separate corporations. Within a year of the breakup, the combined value of the successor companies' shares had more than doubled, increasing Rockefeller's personal fortune to about $900 million (about $15 billion in 2002 dollars). Theodore Roosevelt, who as president had led the trustbusters, ran again for president in 1912:[19]

> "The price of stock has gone up over 100 percent, so that Mr. Rockefeller and his associates have actually seen their fortunes doubled," he thundered during the campaign. "No wonder that Wall Street's prayer now is: 'Oh Merciful Providence, give us another dissolution.' "

Why is the value of the parts so often greater than the value of the whole? The best place to look for an answer to that question is in the financial architecture of conglomerates. But first, we take a brief look at carve-outs, asset sales, and privatizations.

Carve-outs

Carve-outs are similar to spin-offs, except that shares in the new company are not given to existing shareholders but are sold in a public offering. Recent carve-outs include Pharmacia's sale of part of its Monsanto subsidiary, and Philip Morris's sale of part of its Kraft Foods subsidiary. The latter sale raised $8.7 billion.

Most carve-outs leave the parent with majority control of the subsidiary, usually about 80 percent ownership.[20] This may not reassure investors who worry about

---

[17]The other way of getting rid of "poor fits" is to sell them to another company. One study found that over 30 percent of assets acquired in a sample of hostile takeovers from 1984 to 1986 were subsequently sold. See S. Bhagat, A. Shleifer, and R. Vishny, "Hostile Takeovers in the 1980s: The Return to Corporate Specialization," *Brookings Papers on Economic Activity: Microeconomics* (1990), pp. 1–12.

[18]Research on spin-offs includes K. Schipper and A. Smith, "Effects of Recontracting on Shareholder Wealth: The Case of Voluntary Spin-offs," *Journal of Financial Economics* 12 (December 1983), pp. 409–436; G. Hite and J. Owers, "Security Price Reactions around Corporate Spin-off Announcements," *Journal of Financial Economics* 12 (December 1983), pp. 437–467; and J. Miles and J. Rosenfeld, "An Empirical Analysis of the Effects of Spin-off Announcements on Shareholder Wealth," *Journal of Finance* 38 (December 1983), pp. 1597–1615. P. Cusatis, J. Miles, and J. R. Woolridge report improvements of operating performance in spun-off companies. See "Some New Evidence that Spin-offs Create Value," *Journal of Applied Corporate Finance* 7 (Summer 1994), pp. 100–107.

[19]D. Yergin: *The Prize,* Simon & Schuster, New York, 1991, p. 113.

[20]The parent must retain an 80 percent interest to consolidate the subsidiary with the parent's tax accounts. Otherwise the subsidiary is taxed as a freestanding corporation.

lack of focus or a poor fit, but it does allow the parent to set managers' compensation based on the performance of the subsidiary's stock price.

Some companies carve out a minority interest in a subsidiary and later sell or spin off the remaining shares. For example, Sara Lee, the food company, carved out a 19.5 percent stake in the luxury leather goods retailer Coach in 2000. The remaining 80.5 percent of the Coach shares were sold to Sara Lee stockholders in 2001.[21]

Perhaps the most enthusiastic carver-outer of the 1980s and 1990s was Thermo Electron, with operations in healthcare, power generation equipment, instrumentation, environmental monitoring and cleanup, and various other areas. At year-end 1997, it had seven publicly traded subsidiaries, which in turn had carved out 15 further public companies. The 15 were grandchildren of the ultimate parent, Thermo Electron.[22]

Some companies have distributed *tracking stock* tied to the performance of particular divisions. This does not require a spin-off or carve-out, only the creation of a new class of common stock. For example, in 1997 Georgia Pacific distributed a special class of shares tied to the performance of its Timber Group. The company noted that having two classes of shares "provides the opportunity to structure incentives for employees of each Group that are tied directly to the share price performance of that Group."[23]

Asset Sales

The simplest way to divest an asset is to sell it. **Asset sale** refers to the acquisition of *part* of one firm by another. The record asset sale is Comcast's acquisition of AT&T Broadband, AT&T's cable television division, for $42 billion in 2001.

We have mentioned the sale of AT&T's credit card division to Citibank. Asset sales are common in the credit card business. The largest credit card issuers, including Citibank, MBNA, and First USA, grew during the 1980s and 1990s by acquiring the credit card operations of hundreds of smaller banks.

Asset sales are also common in manufacturing. Maksimovic and Phillips examined a sample of about 50,000 U.S. manufacturing plants each year from 1974 to 1992. About 35,000 plants in the sample changed hands during that period. About one-half of the ownership changes were the result of mergers or acquisitions of entire firms. The other half of the ownership changes came about by asset sales, that is, sale of part or all of a division. On average, about 4 percent of the plants in the sample changed hands each year, about 2 percent by merger or acquisition, and about 2 percent by asset sales.[24]

---

[21]Sara Lee stockholders were allowed to exchange Sara Lee shares for Coach shares. The terms of the exchange gave Sara Lee's stockholders the opportunity to get Coach shares at a discount, so all of the Coach shares were issued in short order.

[22]In 1998 Thermo Electron announced a plan to consolidate several of its children and grandchildren in order to move to a less complicated structure. In 2001, it began to spin off some of its peripheral operations as separate companies.

[23]Georgia Pacific Corporation, Proxy Statement and Prospectus, November 11, 1997, p. 35. The Timber Group was sold to Plum Creek Timber Company in 2001. Timber Group tracking stock was exchanged for Plum Creek shares.

[24]V. Maksimovic and G. Phillips, "The Market for Corporate Assets: Who Engages in Mergers and Asset Sales and Are There Efficiency Gains?" *Journal of Finance* 56 (December 2001), Table I, p. 2030.

Announcements of asset sales are good news for investors in the selling firm, and productivity of the assets sold increases, on average, after the sale.[25] It appears that asset sales transfer business units to the companies that can manage them most effectively.

Privatization

A **privatization** is a sale of a government-owned company to private investors. For example, the government of Germany originally owned Volkswagen but sold it in 1961. Britain sold British Telecom in 1984. The United States sold Conrail in 1987.

Most privatizations are more like carve-outs than spin-offs, because shares are sold for cash, not distributed to the ultimate "shareholders," that is, to the people of the selling country. But several former Communist countries, including Russia, Poland, and the Czech Republic, privatized by means of vouchers distributed to citizens. The vouchers could be used to bid for shares in newly privatized companies. Thus the companies were not sold for cash, but for vouchers.[26]

Privatizations raised enormous sums for selling governments. France raised $17.6 billion in two share issues for France Telecom in 1997 and 1998. Japan raised over $80 billion in the privatization of NTT (Nippon Telephone and Telegraph) in 1987 and 1988. Privatizations have also been common in airlines (e.g., Japan Airlines and Air New Zealand) and banking (e.g., the French bank Paribas).

The motives for privatization seem to boil down to the following three points:

1. *Increased efficiency.* Through privatization, the enterprise is exposed to the discipline of competition and insulated from political influence on investment and operating decisions. Managers and employees can be given stronger incentives to cut costs and add economic value.
2. *Share ownership.* Privatizations encourage share ownership. Many privatizations give special terms or allotments to employees or small investors.
3. *Revenue for the government.* Last but not least!

There were fears that privatizations would lead to massive layoffs and unemployment, but that does not appear to be the case. While it is true that privatized companies operate more efficiently and thus reduce employment, they also grow faster as privatized companies, which increases employment. In many cases the net effect on employment is positive.

On other dimensions, the impact of privatization is almost always positive. A review of research on privatization concludes that privatized firms "almost always become more efficient, more profitable, . . . financially healthier and increase their capital investment spending."[27] It seems clear that changing from state to private ownership is in general a valuable change in financial architecture.

---

[25]See Maksimovic and Phillips, op. cit.

[26]There is extensive research on voucher privatizations. See, for example, M. Boyco, A. Shleifer, and R. Vishny, "Voucher Privatizations," *Journal of Financial Economics* 35 (April 1994), pp. 249–266; and R. Aggarwal and J. T. Harper, "Equity Valuation in the Czech Voucher Privatization Auctions," *Financial Management* 29 (Winter 2000), pp. 77–100.

[27]W. L. Megginson and J. M. Netter, "From State to Market: A Survey of Empirical Studies on Privatization," *Journal of Economic Literature* 39 (June 2001), p. 381.

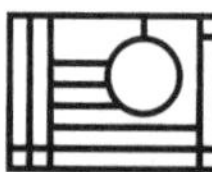

34.3 CONGLOMERATES

We now examine a different form of financial architecture, the conglomerate. Conglomerates are firms investing in several unrelated industries. Large public conglomerates are now rare in the United States, though common elsewhere. We will try to figure out why. We will also examine the financial architecture of the private conglomerates that invest in venture capital and LBOs.

Pros and (Mostly) Cons of U.S. Conglomerates

Conglomerates were the corporate celebrities of the 1960s. They grew by leaps and bounds through aggressive programs of acquisitions in unrelated industries. By the 1970s, the largest conglomerates had achieved amazing scopes and spans. Table 34.2 shows that by 1979 ITT was operating in 38 different industries and ranked eighth in total sales among U.S. corporations.

In 1995 ITT, which had already sold or spun off several lines of business, split its remaining operations into three separate firms. One acquired ITT's interests in hotels and gambling; a second took over ITT's automotive parts, defense, and electronics businesses; and a third specialized in insurance and financial services (ITT Hartford). Most of the conglomerates created in the 1960s were broken up in the 1980s and early 1990s; however, a few successful new conglomerates have sprung up. Tyco International, AMP's white knight, is one of these.[28]

What advantages were claimed for conglomerates? First, diversification across industries was supposed to stabilize earnings and reduce risk. That's hardly compelling, because shareholders can diversify much more efficiently and flexibly on their own.[29] Second, and more important, was the idea that good managers were fungible; in other words, that modern management would work as well in the manufacture of auto parts as in running a hotel chain. Neil Jacoby, writing in 1969, argued that computers and new methods of quantitative, scientific management had "created opportunities for profits through mergers that remove assets from the

TABLE 34.2

The largest U.S. conglomerates in 1979, ranked by sales compared to all U.S. industrial corporations. Most of these companies have been broken up.

Source: A. Chandler and R. S. Tetlow, eds., *The Coming of Managerial Capitalism*, Richard D. Irwin, Inc., Homewood, IL, 1985, p. 772; see also J. Baskin and P. J. Miranti, Jr., *A History of Corporate Finance*, Cambridge University Press, Cambridge, UK: 1997, chap. 7.

Sales Rank	Company	Number of Industries
8	International Telephone & Telegraph (ITT)	38
15	Tenneco	28
42	Gulf & Western Industries	41
51	Litton Industries	19
66	LTV	18
73	Illinois Central Industries	26
103	Textron	16
104	Greyhound	19
128	Martin Marietta	14

[28]See Section 33.5.

[29]See the Appendix to Chapter 33.

inefficient control of old-fashioned managers and place them under men schooled in the new management science."[30]

There was some truth in this. The most successful early conglomerates did force dramatic improvements in some mature and slackly managed businesses. The problem is, of course, that a company doesn't need to be diversified to take over and improve a lagging business.

Third, conglomerates' wide diversification meant that their top managements could operate an *internal capital market.* Free cash flow generated by divisions in mature industries could be funneled within the company to other divisions with profitable growth opportunities. There was no need for fast-growing divisions to raise financing from outside investors.

There are some good arguments for internal capital markets. The company's own managers probably know more about its investment opportunities than do outside investors, and transaction costs of issuing securities are avoided. Nevertheless, it appears that attempts by conglomerates to allocate capital investment across many unrelated industries are more likely to subtract value than add it. Trouble is, internal capital markets are not really markets but combinations of central planning (by the conglomerates' top management and financial staff) and intracompany bargaining. Divisional capital budgets depend on politics as well as pure economics. Large, profitable divisions with plenty of free cash flow may have more bargaining power than growth opportunities; they may get generous capital budgets while smaller divisions with good prospects but less bargaining power are reined in.

Berger and Ofek estimate the average conglomerate discount at 12 to 15 percent.[31] *Conglomerate discount* means that the market value of the whole conglomerate is less than the sum of the values of its parts. The chief cause of this discount, at least in Berger and Ofek's sample, seemed to be overinvestment and misallocation of investment. In other words, investors were marking down the value of the conglomerates' shares from worry that their managements would make negative-NPV investments in mature divisions and forego positive-NPV opportunities elsewhere.

Conglomerates face further problems. Their divisions' market values can't be observed independently, and it is difficult to set incentives for division managers. This is particularly serious when managers are asked to commit to risky ventures. For example, how would a biotech startup fare as a division of a traditional conglomerate? Would the conglomerate be as patient and risk-tolerant as investors in the stock market? How are the scientists and clinicians doing the biotech R&D rewarded if they succeed? We don't mean to say that high-tech innovation and risk-taking is impossible in public conglomerates, but the difficulties are evident.

Internal Capital Markets in the Oil Business Misallocations in internal capital markets are not restricted to pure conglomerates. For example, Lamont found that, when oil prices fell by half in 1986, diversified oil companies cut back capital investment in their *non-oil* divisions.[32] The non-oil divisions were forced to "share

---

[30]Quoted in A. Chandler and R. S. Tetlow, eds., *The Coming of Managerial Capitalism,* Richard D. Irwin, Inc., Homewood, IL: 1985, p. 746.

[31]P. Berger and E. Ofek, "Diversification's Effect on Firm Value," *Journal of Financial Economics* 37 (January 1995), pp. 39–65.

[32]O. Lamont, "Cash Flow and Investment: Evidence from Internal Capital Markets," *Journal of Finance* 52 (March 1997), pp. 83–109.

the pain," even though the drop in oil prices did not diminish their investment opportunities. *The Wall Street Journal* reported one example:[33]

> Chevron Corp. cut its planned 1986 capital and exploratory budget by about 30 percent because of the plunge in oil prices . . . A Chevron spokesman said that spending cuts would be across the board and that no particular operations will bear the brunt.
>
> About 65 percent of the $3.5 billion budget will be spent on oil and gas exploration and production—about the same proportion as before the budget revision.
>
> Chevron also will cut spending for refining and marketing, oil and natural gas pipelines, minerals, chemicals, and shipping operations.

Why cut back on capital outlays for minerals, say, or chemicals? Low oil prices are generally good news, not bad, for chemical manufacturing, because oil distillates are an important raw material.

By the way, most of the oil companies in Lamont's sample were large, blue-chip companies. They could have raised additional capital from investors to maintain spending in their non-oil divisions. They chose not to. We do not understand why.

All large companies must allocate capital among divisions or lines of business. Therefore they all have internal capital markets and must worry about mistakes and misallocations. But this danger probably increases as a company moves from a focus on one, or a few related industries, to unrelated conglomerate diversification. Look again at Table 34.2: How could the top management of ITT keep accurate track of investment opportunities in 38 different industries?

Fifteen Years after Reading this Chapter

You have just seized control of Establishment Industries, the blue-chip conglomerate, after a high-stakes, high-profile takeover battle. You are a financial celebrity, hounded by business reporters every time you step out of your stretch limo. You're contemplating a Ferrari and a trophy spouse. Fundraisers from your college or university are suddenly very attentive. But first you've got to deliver on promises to add shareholder value to your renamed New Establishment Corporation.

Fortunately you remember *Principles of Corporate Finance.* First you identify New Establishment's neglected divisions—the poor fits that have not received their share of capital or top management attention. These you spin off; no more internal capital market. As independent companies, these divisions can set their own capital budgets, but to obtain financing, they have to convince outside investors that their growth opportunities are truly positive-NPV. The managers of these spun-off companies can buy stock or be given stock options as part of their compensation packages. Therefore incentives to maximize value are stronger. Investors understand this, so New Establishment's stock price jumps as soon as the spin-offs are announced.

Establishment Industries also has some large, mature, cash-cow businesses. You add still more value by selling some of these divisions to LBO partnerships. You bargain hard and get a good price, so the stock price jumps again.

The remaining divisions will be the core of New Establishment. You consider pushing through a leveraged restructuring of these core activities to make sure that free cash flow is paid out to investors rather than invested in negative-NPV ventures. But you decide instead to implement a performance measurement and com-

[33]Cited in Lamont, op. cit., pp. 89–90.

pensation system based on residual income.[34] You also make sure managers and key employees have significant equity stakes. You take over as CEO, and New Establishment survives and prospers. Your celebrity status fades away, except that once a year you are listed in *Forbes* magazine's annual compilation of the 400 wealthiest executives and investors. It could happen.

Financial Architecture of Traditional U.S. Conglomerates

This fanciful tale sums up the argument for *focus* and against conglomerate diversification. We must be careful not to push the argument too far, however. GE, an exceptionally successful company, operates in a wide range of unrelated industries, including jet engines, equipment leasing, broadcasting, home appliances, and medical equipment.

But we can confidently identify the challenges set by the financial architecture of conglomerates.

To add value in the long run, the conglomerate structure sets two tasks for top management: (1) Make sure divisional management and operating performance are better than could be achieved if the divisions were independent and (2) operate an internal capital market that beats the external capital market. In other words, conglomerate management has to make better capital investment decisions than could be achieved by independent companies responsible for their own financing.

Task (1) is difficult because divisions' market values can't be observed separately, and it is difficult to set incentives for divisional managers. Task (2) is difficult because the conglomerate's central planners have to fully understand investment opportunities in many different industries and because internal capital markets are prone to allocations by bargaining and politics.

Now we turn to a class of conglomerates that does seem to add value. We will find, however, that they have a different financial architecture.

Temporary Conglomerates

Table 34.3 lists the businesses in which a Kohlberg, Kravis, Roberts (KKR) LBO fund operated in 1998. Looks like a conglomerate, right? But this fund is not a public company. It is a private partnership.

TABLE 34.3

KKR formed an LBO partnership in 1993. By 1998 this fund held companies in the following industries. The partnership was a (temporary) conglomerate.

Books, cards, other publishing (2 companies)
Communications
Consumer services (Kindercare Learning Centers)
Fiber optics (coupling and connections)
General food products
Golf and healthcare products (1 company)
Hospital and institutional management
Insurance (in Canada)
Other consumer products (1 company)
Printing and binding
Transportation equipment and parts

[34]That is, on EVA. See Section 12.4.

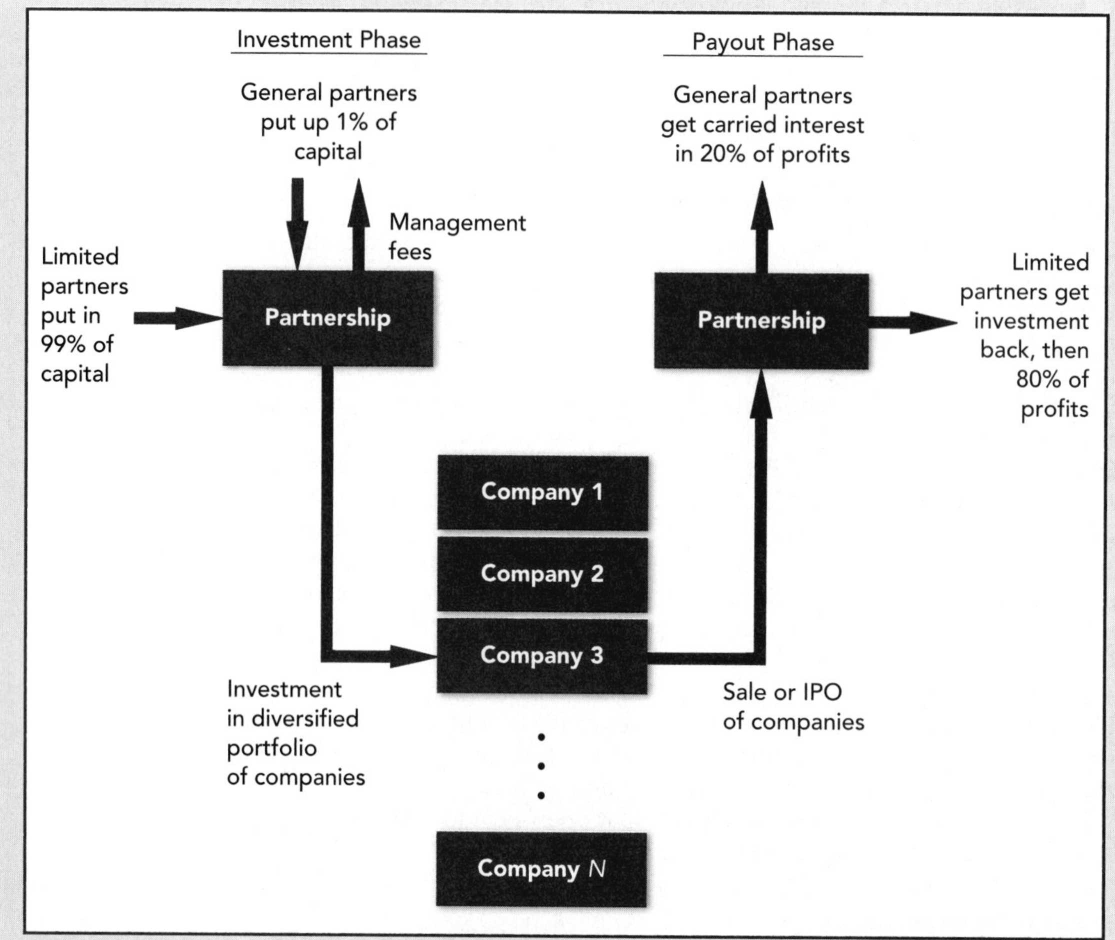

FIGURE 34.2

Organization of a typical private equity partnership. The limited partners, having put up almost all of the money, get first crack at the proceeds from sale or IPO of the portfolio companies. Once their investment is returned, they get 80 percent of any profits. The general partners, who organize and manage the partnership, get a 20 percent carried interest in profits.

This KKR fund is a private investment partnership and a *temporary conglomerate.* It buys up companies, generally in unrelated industries, but it does not buy and hold. It tries to buy, fix, and sell. It buys to restructure, to dispose of incidental assets, and to improve operations and management. If the program of improvement is a success, it sells out, either by taking the company public again or by selling it to another firm.

KKR is famous for LBOs. But its financial structure is shared by venture capital partnerships formed to invest in startup companies and by partnerships formed to buy up private companies without LBO financing. These are all *private equity partnerships.* Figure 34.2 shows how such a partnership is organized. The *general partners* organize and manage the venture. The *limited partners*[35] put up most of the

[35]Limited partners enjoy limited liability. See Section 14.2.

money. Limited partners are generally institutional investors, such as pension funds, endowments, and insurance companies. Wealthy individuals or families may also participate.

Once the partnership is formed, the general partners seek out companies to invest in. Venture capital partnerships look for high-tech startups, LBO partnerships for mature businesses with ample free cash flow and a need for new or reinvigorated management. Some partnerships specialize in particular industries, for example biotechnology or real estate. But most end up with a portfolio of companies in different industries.

The partnership agreement has a limited term, 10 years or less. The portfolio companies must be sold and the proceeds must be distributed. The general partners *cannot reinvest* the limited partners' money. Of course, once a fund is proved successful, the general partners can usually go back to the limited partners, or to other institutional investors, and form another one.

The general partners get a management fee, typically 1 or 2 percent of capital committed, plus a *carried interest,* usually 20 percent of the fund's profits. In other words the limited partners get paid off first, but then get only 80 percent of any further returns. (The general partners have a call option on 20 percent of the partnership's value, with an exercise price equal to the limited partners' investment.)

Table 34.4 summarizes a comparison by Baker and Montgomery of the financial structures of an LBO fund and a typical public conglomerate. Both are diversified, but the fund's limited partners do not have to worry that free cash flow will be plowed back into unprofitable investments. The fund has no internal capital market. Monitoring and compensation of management also differ. In the LBO fund, each company is run as a separate business. The managers report directly to the owners, the fund's partners. Each company's managers own shares or stock options in that company, not in the fund. Their compensation depends on their company's market value in a sale or IPO.

In a public conglomerate, these businesses would be divisions, not freestanding companies. Ownership of the conglomerate would be dispersed, not concentrated. The divisions would not be valued by investors in the stock market, but by the conglomerate's corporate staff, the very people who run the internal capital market.

LBO Partnerships	Public Conglomerates
Widely diversified, investment in unrelated industries	Widely diversified, investment in unrelated industries
Limited-life partnership forces sale of portfolio companies.	Public corporations designed to operate divisions for the long run
No financial links or transfers between portfolio companies	Internal capital market
General partners "do the deal," then monitor; lenders also monitor.	Hierarchy of corporate staff evaluates divisions' plans and performance.
Managers' compensation depends on exit value of company.	Divisional managers' compensation depends mostly on earnings—"smaller upside, softer downside."

TABLE 34.4

LBO funds vs. public conglomerates. Both diversify, investing in a portfolio of unrelated businesses, but their financial structures are otherwise fundamentally different.

Source: Adapted from G. Baker and C. Montgomery, "Conglomerates and LBO Associations: A Comparison of Organizational Forms," working paper, Harvard Business School, Cambridge, MA, July 1996.

Managers' compensation wouldn't depend on divisions' market values because no shares in the divisions would be traded and plans for sale or spin-off would not be part of the conglomerate's financial architecture.

The advantages of LBO partnerships are obvious: strong incentives to managers, concentrated ownership (no separation of ownership and control), and limited life, which reassures limited partners that cash flow will not be reinvested wastefully.

These advantages carry over to other types of private equity partnerships, including venture capital funds. We do not say that this financial structure is appropriate for most businesses. It is designed for change, not for the long run. But traditional conglomerates don't seem to work well for the long run, either.

Conglomerates around the World

Nevertheless, conglomerates are common outside the United States. In some emerging economies, they are the dominant financial structure. In Korea, for example, the 10 largest conglomerates control roughly two-thirds of the corporate economy. These *chaebols* are also strong exporters so that names like Samsung and Hyundai are recognized worldwide.

Conglomerates are common in Latin America. One of the more successful, the holding company[36] Quinenco, is in a dizzying variety of businesses, including hotels and brewing in Chile, pasta making in Peru, and the manufacture of copper and fiber optic cable in Brazil.

Why are conglomerates so common in such countries? There are several possible reasons.

Size You can't be big *and* focused in a small, closed economy: The scale of one-industry companies is limited by the local market. Scale may require diversification. There are various reasons why size can be an advantage. For example, larger companies have easier access to international financial markets. This is important if local financial markets are inefficient.

Size means political power; this is especially important in managed economies or in countries where the government economic policy is unpredictable. In Korea, for example, the government has controlled access to bank loans. Bank lending has been directed to government-approved uses. The Korean conglomerate chaebols have usually been first in line.

Undeveloped Financial Markets If a country's financial markets are substandard, an internal capital market may not be so bad after all.

"Substandard" does not just mean lack of scale or trading activity. It may mean government regulations limiting access to bank financing or requiring government approval before bonds or shares are issued.[37] It may mean information inefficiency: If accounting standards are loose and companies are secretive, monitoring by outside investors becomes especially costly and difficult, and agency costs proliferate.

[36]A holding company owns controlling blocks of shares in two or more subsidiary companies. The holding company and its subsidiaries operate as a group under common top management.

[37]In the United States, the SEC does *not* have the power to deny share issues. Its mandate is only to assure that investors are given adequate information.

In many countries, including some advanced economies, minority investors are not well protected by law and securities regulation. Sometimes there are blatant transfers of wealth from outside shareholders to insiders' pockets. It's no surprise that financial markets in such countries are relatively small.

Recent research by Rafael LaPorta and his colleagues finds a strong association between legal systems and the development of financial markets and the volume of external finance.[38] Minority shareholders seem to be best protected in common-law systems such as those in the United States, Great Britain, and other English-speaking countries. Civil-law systems, such as those in France and Spanish-speaking countries, offer less effective protection; consequently, financial markets are less important in such countries. The volume of external financing is low. Financing tends to flow instead through banks, within large, diversified companies, or among members of groups of associated companies. Many of these companies or groups are controlled by families.

The Bottom Line on Conglomerates

Are conglomerates good or bad? Does corporate diversification make sense? It depends on the task at hand and on the business, financial, and legal environments.

If the task is fundamental change, then the required management skills and knowledge may not be industry-specific. For example, the general partners in LBO funds are not industry experts. They specialize in identifying potential diet deals, negotiating financing, buying and selling assets, setting incentives, and choosing and monitoring management. It's no surprise that LBO funds end up with diversified portfolios; they invest wherever opportunities crop up. But these same skills are not best for long-run operation and growth. Thus LBO funds and other private equity partnerships are designed to force the managers of change to hand over the reins once change is accomplished.

If the task is managing for the long run, and the company has access to well-functioning financial markets, then focus usually beats diversification. Conglomerates have a hard time setting the right incentives for divisional managers and avoiding cross-subsidies and overinvestment in the internal capital market.

In less developed countries, conglomerates can be effective. Local history and practice have led to diversified companies or groups of companies. Also, diversification means scale, and size counts when local financial markets are small or undeveloped, when the company needs to attract the best professional managers, and when assistance or protection from the government is required.

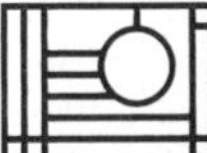

34.4 GOVERNANCE AND CONTROL IN THE UNITED STATES, GERMANY, AND JAPAN

For public corporations in the United States, the agency problems created by the separation of ownership and control are offset by

- Incentives for management, particularly compensation tied to changes in earnings and stock price.

[38] R. LaPorta, F. Lopez-de-Silanes, A. Shleifer, and R. Vishny, "Law and Finance," *Journal of Political Economy* 106 (December 1998), pp. 1113–1155 and "Legal Determinants of External Finance," *Journal of Finance* 52 (July 1997), pp. 1131–1150.

- The legal duty of managers and directors to act in shareholders' interest, backed up by monitoring by auditors, lenders, security analysts, and large institutional investors.
- The threat of a takeover, either by another public company or a private investment partnership.

But don't assume that ownership and control are always separated. A large block of shares may give effective control even when there is no majority owner.[39] For example, Bill Gates owns over 20 percent of Microsoft. Barring some extreme catastrophe, that block means that he can run the company as he wants to and as long as he wants to. Henry Ford's descendants still hold a class of Ford Motor Company shares with extra voting rights and thereby retain great power should they decide to exercise it.[40]

Nevertheless, the concentration of ownership of public U.S. corporations is much less than in some other industrialized countries. The differences are not so apparent in Canada, Britain, Australia, and other English-speaking countries, but there are dramatic differences in Japan and continental Europe. We start with Germany.

Ownership and Control in Germany

Figure 34.3 summarizes the ownership in 1990 of Daimler-Benz, one of the largest German companies. The immediate owners were Deutsche Bank, the largest German bank, with 28 percent; Mercedes Automobil Holding, with 25 percent; and the Kuwait government, with 14 percent. The remaining 32 percent of the shares were widely held by about 300,000 individual and institutional investors.

But this was only the top layer. Mercedes Automobil Holding was half owned by two holding companies, "Stella" and "Stern" for short. The rest of its shares were widely held. Stella's shares were in turn split four ways: between two banks; Robert Bosch, an industrial company; and another holding company, "Komet." Stern's ownership was split four ways too, but we ran out of space.[41]

The differences between German and U.S. ownership patterns leap out from Figure 34.3. Note the concentration of ownership of Daimler-Benz shares in large blocks and the several layers of owners. A similar figure for General Motors would just say, "General Motors, 100 percent widely held."

In Germany these blocks are often held by other companies—a *cross-holding* of shares—or by holding companies for families. Franks and Mayer, who examined the ownership of 171 large German companies in 1990, found 47 with blocks of

[39]A surprising number of public U.S. corporations do have majority owners. A study by Clifford Holderness and Dennis Sheehan identified over 650. See "The Role of Majority Shareholders in Publicly Held Corporations: An Exploratory Analysis," *Journal of Financial Economics* 20 (January/March 1988), pp. 317–346.

[40]You would predict that companies with concentrated ownership would show better financial performance simply because the blockholders face less of a free-rider problem when they represent shareholders' interests. This prediction appears to be true. However, investors who accumulate very large stakes and gain effective control of the firm may act in their own interests and against the interests of the remaining minority shareholders. See R. Morck, A. Shleifer, and R. Vishny, "Management Ownership and Market Valuation: An Empirical Analysis," *Journal of Financial Economics* 20 (January/March 1988), pp. 293–315.

[41]A five-layer ownership tree for Daimler-Benz is given in S. Prowse, "Corporate Governance in an International Perspective: A Survey of Corporate Control Mechanisms among Large Firms in the U.S., U.K., Japan and Germany," *Financial Markets, Institutions, and Instruments* 4 (February 1995), Table 16.

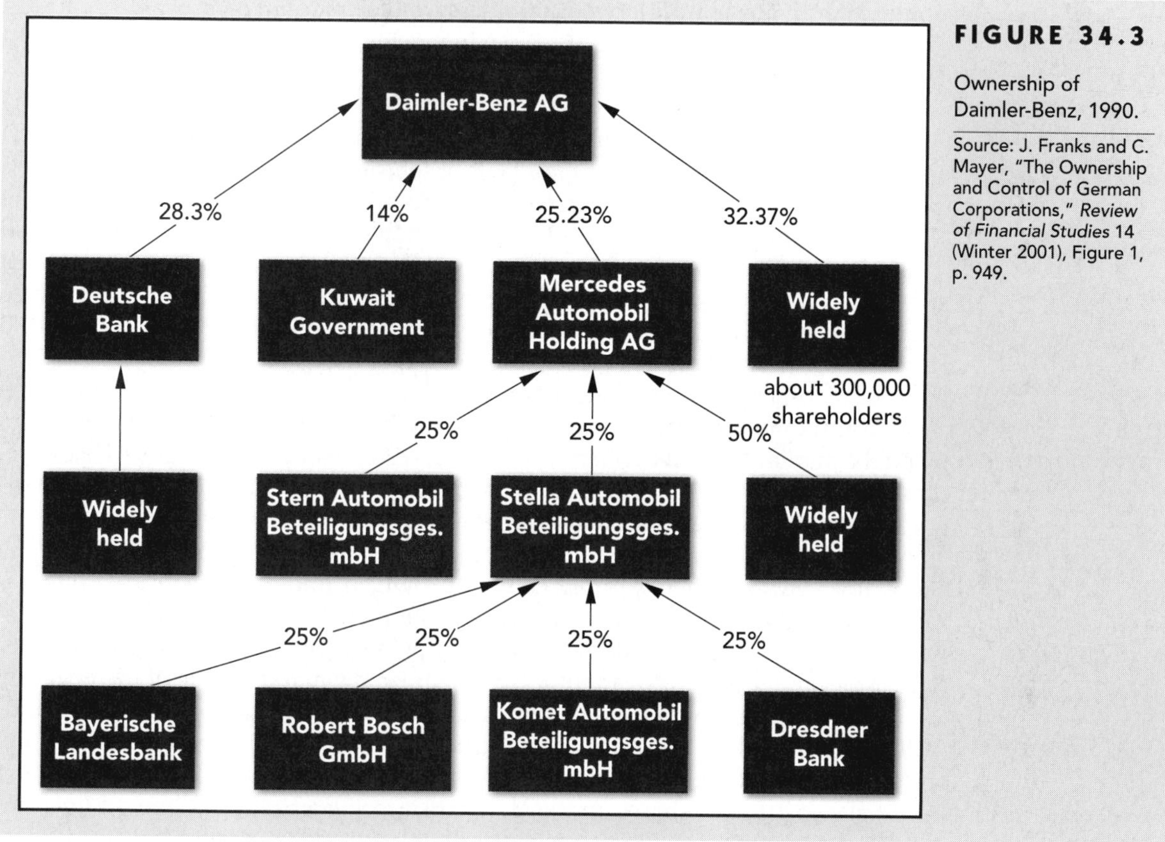

FIGURE 34.3

Ownership of Daimler-Benz, 1990.

Source: J. Franks and C. Mayer, "The Ownership and Control of German Corporations," *Review of Financial Studies* 14 (Winter 2001), Figure 1, p. 949.

shares held by other companies and 35 with blocks owned by families. Only 26 of the companies did *not* have a substantial block of stock held by some company or institution.[42]

Note also the bank ownership of Daimler-Benz. This would be impossible in the United States, where federal law prohibits equity investments by banks in nonfinancial corporations. Germany's *universal banking* system allows such investments. Moreover, German banks customarily hold shares for safekeeping on behalf of individual and institutional investors and often acquire proxies to vote these shares on the investors' behalf. For example, Deutsche Bank held 28 percent of Daimler-Benz for its own account and had proxies for 14 percent more. Therefore it *voted* 42 percent, which approaches a majority.

The ownership structures illustrated in Figure 34.3 are common for large German corporations. Control rests mainly with banks and blockholders, not with ordinary stockholders. Corporate control is achieved by buying or assembling blocks of shares. When control changes, selling blockholders receive premiums of 9 to 16 percent over the trading price of the shares. That price increases by 2 or 3 percent

[42]See J. Franks and C. Mayer, "The Ownership and Control of German Corporations," *Review of Financial Studies* 14 (Winter 2001), Table 1, p. 947. A block was defined as at least 25 percent ownership. In Germany, a block of this size can veto certain corporate actions, including share issues and changes in corporate charters.

only, so the gains to ordinary stockholders from changes in control are small.[43] In the United States, by contrast, the big winners in acquisitions are usually the selling firm's ordinary stockholders.

Blockholders in Germany do not have unchecked power, however. Large German companies have *two* boards of directors: the supervisory board (*Aufsichtsrat*) and management board (*Vorstand*). Half of the supervisory board's members are elected by employees, including management and staff as well as labor unions. The other half represents stockholders, often including bank executives. (There is also a chairman who can cast tie-breaking votes if necessary.) The supervisory board oversees strategy and elects and monitors the management board which operates the company. Thus control of shares does not mean control of the company—100 percent ownership controls only half of the supervisory board.

This two-tier governance structure reflects a belief, widespread in Europe, that the firm should act in the interests of all its stakeholders, including its employees and the public at large, and not just seek to maximize shareholder value. This structure does not mean poor financial performance or an easy life for management—poor performance leads to management turnover, just as in the United States,[44] and the German economy has, in general, thrived over the last 50 years. One may ask, however, whether German companies which undertake extensive international operations, and seek financing in international capital markets, are best served by a financial architecture that skimps on protection for outside minority investors and discourages attempts to maximize the market value of the firm.

Daimler-Benz, now DaimlerChrysler, is an interesting case study. In the mid-1990s it reversed an unsuccessful diversification strategy that had led it into several other industries, including aerospace and defense. In 1998 it took over Chrysler. It listed its shares on the New York Stock Exchange and issued financial statements conforming to U.S. accounting standards. It turned to international capital markets for financing, including a share issue in the U.S. At the same time Deutsche Bank was reducing its stake in the company. DaimlerChrysler has formally announced a commitment to increasing shareholder value.

. . . And in Japan

Japan's system of corporate governance is in some ways in between the systems of Germany and the United States and in other ways different from both.

The most notable feature of Japanese corporate finance is the **keiretsu.** A keiretsu is a network of companies, usually organized around a major bank. There are long-standing business relationships between the group companies; a manufacturing company might buy a substantial part of its raw materials from group suppliers and in turn sell much of its output to other group companies.

The bank and other financial institutions at the keiretsu's center own shares in most of the group companies (though a commercial bank in Japan is limited to 5 percent ownership of each company). Those companies may in turn hold the bank's shares or each others' shares. Here are the cross-holdings at the end of 1991 between Sumitomo Bank; the Sumitomo Corporation, a trading company; and Sumitomo Trust, which concentrates on investment management:

[43]Franks and Mayer, op. cit., Table 9, p. 969.

[44]See Franks and Mayer, op. cit.; and S. Kaplan, "Top Executives, Turnover and Firm Performance in Germany," *Journal of Law and Economics* 10 (1994), pp. 142–159.

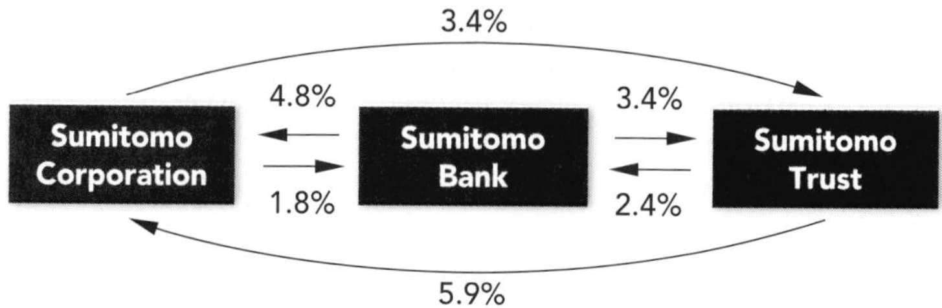

Thus the bank owns 4.8 percent of Sumitomo Corporation, which owns 1.8 percent of the bank. Both own shares in Sumitomo Trust . . . and so on. Table 34.5 illustrates the myriad of cross-holdings in a keiretsu. Because of the cross-holdings, the supply of shares available for purchase by outside investors is much less than the total number outstanding.

The keiretsu is tied together in other ways. Most debt financing comes from the keiretsu's banks or from elsewhere in the group. (Until the mid-1980s, all but a handful of Japanese companies were forbidden access to public debt markets. The fraction of debt provided by banks is still much greater than that in the United States.) Managers may sit on the boards of directors of other group companies, and a "presidents' council" of the CEOs of the most important group companies meets regularly.

Think of the keiretsu as a system of corporate governance, where power is split between the main bank, the largest companies, and the group as a whole. This confers certain financial advantages. First, firms have access to additional "internal" financing—internal to the group, that is. Thus a company with capital budgets exceeding

	Percentage of Shares Held in:					
Shareholder	**Sumitomo Bank**	**Sumitomo Metal Industries**	**Sumitomo Chemical**	**Sumitomo Trust**	**Sumitomo Corporation**	**NEC**
S. Bank	—	4.1	4.6	3.4	4.8	5.0
S. Metal Industries	*	—	*	2.5	2.8	*
S. Chemical	*	*	—	*	*	*
S. Trust	2.4	5.9	4.4	—	5.9	5.8
S. Corporation	1.8	1.6	*	3.4	—	2.2
NEC	*	*	*	2.9	3.7	—
Other†	9.7	4.8	9.8	10.4	9.5	11.6
Total†	13.9	16.4	18.8	22.6	26.7	24.6

TABLE 34.5

Cross-holdings of common stock between six companies in the Sumitomo group in 1991. Read *down* the columns to see holdings of each of the companies by the five others. Thus 4.6 percent of Sumitomo Chemical was owned by Sumitomo Bank, 4.4 percent by Sumitomo Trust, and 9.8 percent by other Sumitomo companies. These figures were compiled by examining the 10 largest shareholders of each company. Smaller cross-holdings are not reflected.

*Cross-holding does not appear in the 10 largest shareholdings.

†Based on the 10 largest shareholdings in 1991.

Source: Compiled from Dodwell Marketing Consultants, *Industrial Groupings in Japan,* 10th ed., Tokyo, 1992.

operating cash flows can turn to the main bank or other keiretsu companies for financing. This avoids the cost or possible bad-news signal of a public sale of securities. Second, when a keiretsu firm falls into financial distress, with insufficient cash to pay bills or fund necessary capital investments, a "workout" can usually be arranged. New management can be brought in from elsewhere in the group, and financing can be obtained, again "internally."

Hoshi, Kashyap, and Scharfstein tracked capital expenditure programs of a large sample of Japanese firms—many, but not all, members of keiretsus. The keiretsu companies' investments were more stable and less exposed to the ups and downs of operating cash flows or to episodes of financial distress.[45] It seems that the financial support of the keiretsus enabled their members to invest for the long run.

The Japanese system of corporate control has its disadvantages too, notably for outside investors, who have very little influence. Japanese managers' compensation is rarely tied to shareholder returns. Takeovers are unthinkable. Japanese companies have been particularly stingy with cash dividends; this was hardly a concern when growth was rapid and stock prices were stratospheric but is a serious issue for the future.

Corporate Ownership around the World

The theory of modern finance is most readily applied to public corporations with shares traded in active and efficient capital markets. The theory assumes that stockholders' interests are protected, so that ownership can be dispersed across thousands of minority stockholders. The protection comes from managers' incentives, particularly compensation tied to stock price; from supervision by the board of directors; and by the threat of hostile takeover of poorly performing companies.

This is a reasonable description of the corporate sector in the U.S., UK, and other "Anglo-Saxon" countries such as Canada and Australia. But as Germany and Japan illustrate, it is not an accurate description elsewhere. Corporate ownership in Germany is typical of continental Europe. The ownership diagram for a large French company would resemble Figure 34.3.[46]

The financial architecture of public companies in "Anglo-Saxon" economies may be the exception, not the rule. La Porta, Lopez-de-Silanes, and Shleifer surveyed the ownership of the largest companies in 27 developed countries. They found that "except in economies with very good shareholder protection, relatively few of these firms are widely held. Rather these firms are typically controlled by families or the State," or in some cases by financial institutions.[47]

This finding has various possible interpretations. The first is obvious: Protection for outside minority stockholders is a prerequisite for dispersed ownership and a broad and active stock market. Second, in countries that lack effective legal protection for minority stockholders, concentrated ownership may be the only feasible financial architecture.

[45]T. Hoshi, A. Kashyap, and D. Scharfstein, "Corporate Structure, Liquidity and Investment: Evidence from Japanese Industrial Groups," *Quarterly Journal of Economics* 106 (February 1991), pp. 33–60, and "The Role of Banks in Reducing the Costs of Financial Distress in Japan," *Journal of Financial Economics* 27 (September 1990), pp. 67–88.

[46]See J. Franks and C. Mayer, "Corporate Ownership and Control in the U. K., Germany and France," *Journal of Applied Corporate Finance* 9 (Winter 1997), pp. 30–45.

[47]R. La Porta, F. Lopez-de-Silanes, and A. Shleifer, "Corporate Ownership around the World," *Journal of Finance* 59 (April 1999), pp. 471–517.

SUMMARY

We started with LBOs. An LBO is a takeover or buyout financed mostly with debt. The LBO is owned privately, usually by an investment partnership. Debt financing is not the objective of most LBOs; it is a means to an end. Most LBOs are diet deals. The cash requirements for debt service force managers to shed unneeded assets, improve operating efficiency, and forego wasteful capital expenditure. The managers and key employees are given a significant equity stake in the business, so they have strong incentives to make these improvements.

Leveraged restructurings are in many ways similar to LBOs. Large amounts of debt are added and the proceeds are paid out. The company is forced to generate cash to cover debt service, but there is no change in control and the company stays public.

Most investments in LBOs are made by private equity partnerships. We called these temporary conglomerates. They are conglomerates because they assemble a portfolio of companies in several unrelated industries. They are temporary because the partnership has limited life, usually about 10 years. At the end of this period, the partnership's investments must be sold or taken public again in IPOs. Private equity funds do not buy and hold; they buy, fix, and sell. Investors in the partnership therefore do not have to worry about wasteful reinvestment of free cash flow. LBO managers know that they will be able to cash out their equity stakes if their company succeeds in improving efficiency and paying down debt.

The private equity partnership (or fund) is also common in venture capital and other areas of private investment. The limited partners, who put up almost all of the money, are mostly institutional investors such as pension funds, endowments, and insurance companies. The limited partners are first in line when the partnership's investments are sold. The general partners, who organize and manage the fund, get a carried interest in the fund's profits.

The private equity market has been growing steadily. In contrast to these temporary conglomerates, public conglomerates have been declining in the United States. In public companies, unrelated diversification seems to destroy value—the whole is worth less than the sum of its parts. There are two possible reasons for this conglomerate discount. First, the value of the parts can't be observed separately and it is difficult to set incentives for divisional managers. Second, conglomerates' internal capital markets are inefficient. It is difficult for management to appreciate investment opportunities in many different industries, and internal capital markets are prone to overinvestment and cross-subsidies. The difficulties of running internal capital markets are not restricted to pure conglomerates, but they are most acute there.

Of course corporations shed assets as well as acquire them. Divisions are divested by asset sales, carve-outs, or spin-offs. These divestitures are generally good news to investors; it appears that the divisions are moving to better homes, where they can be better managed and more profitable. The same improvements in efficiency and profitability are observed in privatizations, which are spin-offs or carve-outs of businesses owned by governments.

Although conglomerates are a declining species in the United States, they are common elsewhere, particularly in emerging economies. An internal capital market can make sense when a country's financial markets are not well developed. Diversification also brings scale, which may make it easier to attract professional management, to gain access to international financial markets, or to gain political power in countries where the government tries to manage the economy or where laws and regulations are erratically enforced.

We wonder, though, whether some of these emerging-market conglomerates will be temporary rather than permanent. In a rapidly growing and modernizing

Visit us at www.mhhe.com/bm7e

economy, opportunities to buy and fix are spread across many industries. If these investments are successful, the next logical step may be to sell and focus on one or a few core businesses.

Our discussion of LBOs, private equity partnerships, and conglomerates illustrates how much financial architecture varies and how it depends on the financial and business environment and on the task at hand. The conglomerate financial architecture thrives in much of the world but not in the United States. LBOs are designed to force change in mature businesses. Private equity partnerships eliminate the separation of ownership and control and make sure that the general partners have strong incentives to achieve high exit values for the partnership's investments.

We also sketched typical arrangements for ownership and control in Germany and Japan. We did so especially for readers in the United States, who may regard their system as natural. In some circumstances the German or Japanese system can work better. Here are two key differences.

First, corporate finance in the United States, Britain, and the other English-speaking countries relies more on financial markets and less on banks or other financial intermediaries than is the case in most other countries. United States corporations routinely issue publicly traded debt in situations where Japanese or European companies borrow from banks.

Second, U.S.-style corporate finance puts fewer buffers between managers and the stock market. The block holdings and layered ownership structure of German companies are rare in the United States, and of course there is nothing remotely like a Japanese keiretsu. So CEOs and CFOs in the United States usually find their paychecks tied to stockholder returns. Negative returns may bring insomnia or bad dreams about takeovers.

These international comparisons illustrate different approaches to the problem of corporate governance—the problem of ensuring that managers act in shareholders' interest.

FURTHER READING

Some of the ideas in this chapter were drawn from:

S. C. Myers: "Financial Architecture," *European Financial Management,* 5:133–142 (July 1999).

The papers by Kaplan and by Kaplan and Stein provide evidence on the evolution and performance of LBOs; Jensen, the chief proponent of the free-cash-flow theory of takeovers, gives a spirited and controversial defense of LBOs:

S. N. Kaplan: "The Effects of Management Buyouts on Operating Performance and Value," *Journal of Financial Economics,* 24:217–254 (October 1989).

S. N. Kaplan and J. C. Stein: "The Evolution of Buyout Pricing and Financial Structure (Or, What Went Wrong) in the 1980s," *Journal of Applied Corporate Finance,* 6:72–88 (Spring 1993).

M. C. Jensen: "The Eclipse of the Public Corporation," *Harvard Business Review,* 67:61–74 (September/October 1989).

Privatization is reviewed in:

W. L. Megginson and J. M. Nutter: "From State to Market: A Survey of Empirical Studies on Privatization," *Journal of Economic Literature,* 39:321–389 (June 2001).

The Winter 1997 issue of the Journal of Applied Corporate Finance *contains several articles on governance and control in different countries. See also the following survey article:*

A. Shleifer and R. Vishny: "A Survey of Corporate Governance," *Journal of Finance*, 52:737–783 (June 1997).

Here are five useful articles on corporate finance in Germany and Japan:

S. Prowse: "Corporate Governance in an International Perspective: A Survey of Corporate Control Mechanisms among Large Firms in the U.S., U.K., Japan and Germany," *Financial Markets, Institutions, and Investments*, 4:1–63 (1995).

J. Franks and C. Mayer: "Ownership and Control of German Corporations," *Review of Financial Studies*, 14:943–977 (Winter 2001).

T. Jenkinson and A. Ljungqvist: "The Role of Hostile Stakes in German Corporate Performance," *Journal of Corporate Finance*, 7:397–446 (December 2001).

D. E. Logue and J. K. Seward: "Anatomy of a Governance Transformation: The Case of Daimler-Benz," *Law and Contemporary Problems*, 62:87–111 (Summer 1999).

E. Berglof and E. Perotti: "The Governance Structure of the Japanese Keiretsu," *Journal of Financial Economics*, 36:259–284 (October 1994).

Here are some interesting case studies pertinent to this chapter.

J. Allen: "Reinventing the Corporation: The Satellite Structure of Thermo Electron," *Journal of Applied Corporate Finance*, 11:38–47 (Summer 1998).

R. Parrino: "Spinoffs and Wealth Transfers: the Marriott Case," *Journal of Financial Economics*, 43:241–274 (February 1997).

C. Eckel, D. Eckel, and V. Singal: "Privatization and Efficiency: Industry Effects of the Sale of British Airways," *Journal of Financial Economics*, 43:275–298 (February 1997).

B. Burrough and J. Helyar: *Barbarians at the Gate: The Fall of RJR Nabisco*, Harper & Row, New York, 1990.

G. P. Baker: "Beatrice: A Study in the Creation and Destruction of Value," *Journal of Finance*, 47:1081–1120 (July 1992).

D. J. Denis: "Organizational Form and the Consequences of Highly Leveraged Transactions," *Journal of Financial Economics*, 36:193–224 (October 1994).

Visit us at www.mhhe.com/bm7e

QUIZ

1. Define the following terms: (a) LBO, (b) MBO, (c) spin-off, (d) carve-out, (e) asset sale, (f) privatization, and (g) leveraged restructuring.
2. True or false?
   - **a.** One of the first tasks of an LBO's financial manager is to pay down debt.
   - **b.** Once an LBO or MBO goes private it almost always stays private.
   - **c.** Privatizations are generally followed by massive layoffs.
   - **d.** On average, privatization seems to improve efficiency and add value.
   - **e.** Targets for LBOs in the 1980s tended to be profitable companies in mature industries.
   - **f.** "Carried interest" refers to the deferral of interest payments on LBO debt.
   - **g.** By the late 1990s, new LBO transactions were extremely rare.
3. What are the government's motives in a privatization?
4. **a.** List the *disadvantages* of a traditional conglomerate in the United States.
   b. What advantages might a conglomerate have in other countries, particularly less-developed economies? List some examples.
5. What are the chief differences in the role of banks in corporate governance in the United States, Germany, and Japan?
6. What is meant by a "temporary conglomerate"? Give an example.

PRACTICE QUESTIONS

1. True, false, or "It depends on . . ."?
   a. Most large corporations are controlled by families, governments, or financial institutions.
   b. Top managers in Germany are much more secure in their jobs than managers in the U.S. because German shareholders have less power than U.S. shareholders.
   c. Carve-out or spin-off of a division improves incentives for the division's managers.
   d. Private-equity partnerships have limited lives. The main purpose is to force the general partners to seek out quick-payout investments.
   e. Managers of private-equity partnerships have an incentive to make risky investments.
2. For what kinds of companies would an LBO or MBO transaction *not* be productive?
3. What was the common theme in both the Phillips Petroleum restructuring and the RJR Nabisco LBO? Why was financial leverage a necessary part of both deals?
4. Outline the similarities and differences between the RJR Nabisco LBO and the Sealed Air leveraged restructuring. Were the economic motives the same? Were the results the same? Do you think it was an advantage for Sealed Air to remain a public company?
5. Examine some recent examples of divestitures and spin-offs. What do you think were the underlying reasons for them? How did investors react to the news?
6. Read *Barbarians at the Gate* (Further Reading). What agency costs can you identify? *Hint:* See Chapter 12. Do you think the LBO was well designed to reduce these costs?
7. Explain the financial architecture of a private-equity partnership. Pay particular attention to incentives and compensation. What types of investments were such partnerships designed to make?
8. Traditional conglomerates are now rare in the United States, but in many other countries, conglomerates are the dominant firms. Explain why.
9. What is meant by an internal capital market? When would you expect such a market to add value? When and why would it be expected to misallocate capital?

CHALLENGE QUESTION

1. We devoted considerable space in this chapter to the problems encountered in the financial management of conglomerates. Could these problems be cured by basing performance measurement and compensation on residual income or EVA? See Chapter 12.

PART TEN RELATED WEBSITES

The sites that provide market commentary (see list at end of Part One) contain material on recent mergers. Other sites concerned with mergers include:

www.thedeal.com

www.mergernetwork.com *(information on businesses for sale)*

www.mergerstat.com *(articles and some data on merger activity)*

PART ELEVEN

CONCLUSION

The end is nigh!

CHAPTER THIRTY-FIVE

CONCLUSION: WHAT WE DO AND DO NOT KNOW ABOUT FINANCE

IT IS TIME to sign off. Let us finish by thinking about some of the things that we do and do not know about finance.

35.1 WHAT WE DO KNOW: THE SEVEN MOST IMPORTANT IDEAS IN FINANCE

What would you say if you were asked to name the seven most important ideas in finance? Here is our list.

1. Net Present Value

When you wish to know the value of a used car, you look at prices in the secondhand car market. Similarly, when you wish to know the value of a future cash flow, you look at prices quoted in the capital markets, where claims to future cash flows are traded (remember, those highly paid investment bankers are just secondhand cash-flow dealers). If you can buy cash flows for your shareholders at a cheaper price than they would have to pay in the capital market, you have increased the value of their investment.

This is the simple idea behind *net present value* (NPV). When we calculate a project's NPV, we are asking whether the project is worth more than it costs. We are estimating its value by calculating what its cash flows would be worth if a claim on them were offered separately to investors and traded in the capital markets.

That is why we calculate NPV by discounting future cash flows at the opportunity cost of capital—that is, at the expected rate of return offered by securities having the same degree of risk as the project. In well-functioning capital markets, all equivalent-risk assets are priced to offer the same expected return. By discounting at the opportunity cost of capital, we calculate the price at which investors in the project could expect to earn that rate of return.

Like most good ideas, the net present value rule is "obvious when you think about it." But notice what an important idea it is. The NPV rule allows thousands of shareholders, who may have vastly different levels of wealth and attitudes toward risk, to participate in the same enterprise and to delegate its operation to a professional manager. They give the manager one simple instruction: "Maximize present value."

2. The Capital Asset Pricing Model

Some people say that modern finance is all about the capital asset pricing model. That's nonsense. If the capital asset pricing model had never been invented, our advice to financial managers would be essentially the same. The attraction of the model is that it gives us a manageable way of thinking about the required return on a risky investment.

Again, it is an attractively simple idea. There are two kinds of risk: risks that you can diversify away and those that you can't. You can measure the *nondiversifiable,* or *market,* risk of an investment by the extent to which the value of the investment is affected by a change in the *aggregate* value of all the assets in the economy. This is called the *beta* of the investment. The only risks that people care about are the ones that they can't get rid of—the nondiversifiable ones. This is why the required return on an asset increases in line with its beta.

Many people are worried by some of the rather strong assumptions behind the capital asset pricing model, or they are concerned about the difficulties of estimating a project's beta. They are right to be worried about these things. In 10 or 20 years' time we will probably have much better theories than we do now. But we will be extremely surprised if those future theories do not still insist on the crucial distinction between diversifiable and nondiversifiable risks—and that, after all, is the main idea underlying the capital asset pricing model.

3. Efficient Capital Markets

The third fundamental idea is that security prices accurately reflect available information and respond rapidly to new information as soon as it becomes available. This *efficient-market theory* comes in three flavors, corresponding to different definitions of "available information." The weak form (or random-walk theory) says that prices reflect all the information in past prices. The semistrong form says that prices reflect all publicly available information, and the strong form holds that prices reflect all acquirable information.

Don't misunderstand the efficient-market idea. It doesn't say that there are no taxes or costs; it doesn't say that there aren't some clever people and some stupid ones. It merely implies that competition in capital markets is very tough—there are no money machines, and security prices reflect the true underlying values of assets.

Extensive empirical testing of the efficient-market hypothesis began around 1970. By 2001, after 30 years of work, the tests have uncovered dozens of statistically significant anomalies. Sorry, but this work does *not* translate into dozens of ways to make easy money. Superior returns are elusive. For example, only a few mutual fund managers can generate superior returns for a few years in a row, and then only in small amounts.[1] Statisticians can beat the market, but real investors have a much harder time of it.

4. Value Additivity and the Law of Conservation of Value

The principle of *value additivity* states that the value of the whole is equal to the sum of the values of the parts. It is sometimes called the *law of the conservation of value.*

When we appraise a project that produces a succession of cash flows, we always assume that values add up. In other words, we assume

$$\begin{aligned} \text{PV(project)} &= \text{PV}(C_1) + \text{PV}(C_2) + \cdots + \text{PV}(C_t) + \cdots \\ &= \frac{C_1}{1+r} + \frac{C_2}{(1+r)^2} + \cdots + \frac{C_t}{(1+r)^t} + \cdots \end{aligned}$$

We similarly assume that the sum of the present values of projects A and B equals the present value of a composite project AB.[2] But value additivity also means that you can't increase value by putting two whole companies together unless you thereby increase the total cash flow. In other words, there are no benefits to mergers solely for diversification.

[1]See, for example, M. J. Gruber, "Another Puzzle: The Growth in Actively Managed Mutual Funds," *Journal of Finance* 51 (July 1996), pp. 783–810.

[2]That is, if

$$\text{PV(A)} = \text{PV}[C_1(\text{A})] + \text{PV}[C_2(\text{A})] + \cdots + \text{PV}[C_t(\text{A})] + \cdots$$
$$\text{PV(B)} = \text{PV}[C_1(\text{B})] + \text{PV}[C_2(\text{B})] + \cdots + \text{PV}[C_t(\text{B})] + \cdots$$

and if for each period t, $C_t(\text{AB}) = C_t(\text{A}) + C_t(\text{B})$, then

$$\text{PV(AB)} = \text{PV(A)} + \text{PV(B)}$$

5. Capital Structure Theory

If the law of the conservation of value works when you add up cash flows, it must also work when you subtract them.[3] Therefore, financing decisions that simply divide up operating cash flows don't increase overall firm value. This is the basic idea behind Modigliani and Miller's famous proposition I: In perfect markets changes in capital structure do not affect value. As long as the *total* cash flow generated by the firm's assets is unchanged by capital structure, value is independent of capital structure. The value of the whole pie does not depend on how it is sliced.

Of course, MM's proposition is not The Answer, but it does tell us where to look for reasons why capital structure decisions may matter. Taxes are one possibility. Debt provides a corporate interest tax shield, and this tax shield may more than compensate for any extra personal tax that the investor has to pay on debt interest. Also, high debt levels may spur managers to work harder and to run a tighter ship. But debt has its drawbacks if it leads to costly financial distress.

6. Option Theory

In everyday conversation we often use the word *option* as synonymous with *choice* or *alternative;* thus we speak of someone as "having a number of options." In finance *option* refers specifically to the opportunity to trade in the future on terms that are fixed today. Smart managers know that it is often worth paying today for the option to buy or sell an asset tomorrow.

Since options are so important, the financial manager needs to know how to value them. Finance experts always knew the relevant variables—the exercise price and the exercise date of the option, the risk of the underlying asset, and the rate of interest. But it was Black and Scholes who first showed how these can be put together in a usable formula.

The Black–Scholes formula was developed for simple call options and does not directly apply to the more complicated options often encountered in corporate finance. But Black and Scholes's most basic ideas—for example, the risk-neutral valuation method implied by their formula—work even where the formula doesn't. Valuing the real options described in Chapter 22 may require extra number crunching but no extra concepts.

7. Agency Theory

A modern corporation is a team effort involving a number of players, such as managers, employees, shareholders, and bondholders. For a long time economists used to assume without question that all these players acted for the common good, but in the last 30 years they have had a lot more to say about the possible conflicts of interest and how companies attempt to overcome such conflicts. These ideas are known collectively as *agency theory.*

Consider, for example, the relationship between the shareholders and the managers. The shareholders (the *principals*) want managers (their *agents*) to maximize firm value. In the United States the ownership of major corporations is widely dispersed and no single shareholder can check on the managers or reprimand those who are slacking. So, to encourage managers to pull their weight, firms seek to tie the managers' compensation to the value that they have added. For those managers

[3] If you *start* with the cash flow $C_t(AB)$ and split it into two pieces, $C_t(A)$ and $C_t(B)$, then total value is unchanged. That is, $PV[C_t(A)] + PV[C_t(B)] = PV[C_t(AB)]$. See footnote 2.

who persistently neglect shareholders' interests, there is the threat that their firm will be taken over and they will be turfed out.

In some other countries corporations are more likely to be owned by a few major shareholders and therefore there is less distance between ownership and control. For example, the families, companies, and banks which hold large stakes in many German companies can review top management's plans and decisions as insiders. In most cases they have the power to force changes as necessary. However, hostile takeovers in Germany are very rare.

We discussed the problems of management incentives and corporate control in Chapters 12, 14, and 34, but they were not the only places in the book where agency issues arose. For example, in Chapters 18 and 25 we looked at some of the conflicts that arise between shareholders and bondholders, and we described how loan agreements try to anticipate and minimize these conflicts.

Are these seven ideas exciting theories or plain common sense? Call them what you will, they are basic to the financial manager's job. If by reading this book you really understand these ideas and know how to apply them, you have learned a great deal.

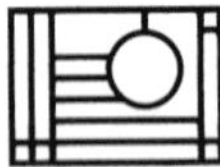

35.2 WHAT WE DO NOT KNOW: 10 UNSOLVED PROBLEMS IN FINANCE

Since the unknown is never exhausted, the list of what we do not know about finance could go on forever. But, following Brealey and Myers's Third Law (see Section 29.4), we will list and briefly discuss 10 unsolved problems that seem ripe for productive research.

1. What Determines Project Risk and Present Value?

A good capital investment is one that has a positive NPV. We have talked at some length about how to calculate NPV, but we have given you very little guidance about how to find positive-NPV projects, except to say in Section 11.2 that projects have positive NPVs when the firm can earn economic rents. But why do some companies earn economic rents while others in the same industry do not? Are the rents merely windfall gains, or can they be anticipated and planned for? What is their source, and how long do they persist before competition destroys them? Very little is known about any of these important questions.

Here is a related question: Why are some real assets risky and others relatively safe? In Section 9.5 we suggested a few reasons for differences in project betas—differences in operating leverage, for example, or in the extent to which a project's cash flows respond to the performance of the national economy. These are useful clues, but we have as yet no general procedure for estimating project betas. Assessing project risk is therefore still largely a seat-of-the-pants matter.

2. Risk and Return—What Have We Missed?

In 1848 John Stuart Mill wrote, "Happily there is nothing in the laws of value which remains for the present or any future writer to clear up; the theory is complete." Economists today are not so sure about that. For example, the capital asset pricing model is an enormous step toward understanding the effect of risk on the value of an asset, but there are many puzzles left, some statistical and some theoretical.

The statistical problems arise because the capital asset pricing model is hard to prove or disprove conclusively. It appears that average returns from low-beta stocks are too high (that is, higher than the capital asset pricing model predicts) and that those from high-beta stocks are too low; but this could be a problem with the way that the tests are conducted and not with the model itself.[4] We also described the puzzling discovery by Fama and French that expected returns appear to be related to the firm's size and to the ratio of the book value of the stock to its market value. Nobody understands why this should be so; perhaps these variables are related to variable x, that mysterious second risk variable that investors may rationally take into account in pricing shares.[5]

Meanwhile scholars toil on the theoretical front. We discussed some of their work in Section 8.4. But just for fun, here is another example: Suppose that you love fine wine. It may make sense for you to buy shares in a grand cru chateau, even if doing so soaks up a large fraction of your personal wealth and leaves you with a relatively undiversified portfolio. However, you are *hedged* against a rise in the price of fine wine: Your hobby will cost you more in a bull market for wine, but your stake in the chateau will make you correspondingly richer. Thus you are holding a relatively undiversified portfolio for a good reason. We would not expect you to demand a premium for bearing that portfolio's undiversifiable risk.

In general, if two people have different tastes, it may make sense for them to hold different portfolios. You may hedge your consumption needs with an investment in wine making, whereas somebody else may do better to invest in Baskin-Robbins. The capital asset pricing model isn't rich enough to deal with such a world. It assumes that all investors have similar tastes: The "hedging motive" does not enter, and therefore they hold the same portfolio of risky assets.

Merton has extended the capital asset pricing model to accommodate the hedging motive.[6] If enough investors are attempting to hedge against the same thing, the model implies a more complicated risk–return relationship. However, it is not yet clear who is hedging against what, and so the model remains difficult to test.

So the capital asset pricing model survives not from a lack of competition but from a surfeit. There are too many plausible alternative risk measures, and so far no consensus exists on the right course to plot if we abandon beta.

In the meantime we must recognize the capital asset pricing model for what it is: an incomplete but extremely useful way of linking risk and return. Recognize too that the model's most basic message, that diversifiable risk doesn't matter, is accepted by nearly everyone.

---

[4]See R. Roll, "A Critique of the Asset Pricing Theory's Tests: Part 1: On Past and Potential Testability of the Theory," *Journal of Financial Economics* 4 (March 1977), pp. 129–176; and, for a critique of the critique, see D. Mayers and E. M. Rice, "Measuring Portfolio Performance and the Empirical Content of Asset Pricing Models," *Journal of Financial Economics* 7 (March 1979), pp. 3–28.

[5]Fama and French point out that small firms, and firms with high book-to-market ratios, are also low-profitability firms. Such firms may suffer more in downturns in the economy. Thus size and book-to-market measures may be proxies for exposure to business-cycle risk. See E. F. Fama and K. R. French, "Size and Book-to-Market Factors in Earnings and Returns," *Journal of Finance* 50 (March 1995), pp. 131–155.

[6]See R. Merton, "An Intertemporal Capital Asset Pricing Model," *Econometrica* 41 (1973), pp. 867–887.

3. How Important Are the Exceptions to the Efficient-Market Theory?

The efficient-market theory is strong, but no theory is perfect; there must be exceptions.

Now some of the apparent exceptions could simply be coincidences, for the more that researchers study stock performance, the more strange coincidences they are likely to find. For example, there is evidence that daily returns around new moons have been roughly double those around full moons.[7] It seems difficult to believe that this is anything other than a chance relationship—fun to read about but not a concern for serious investors or financial managers. But not all exceptions can be dismissed so easily. We saw that the stocks of firms which announce unexpectedly good earnings continue to perform well for a couple of months after the announcement date. Some scholars believe that this may mean that the stock market is inefficient and investors have consistently been slow to react to earnings announcements. Of course, we can't expect investors never to make mistakes. If they have been slow to react in the past, it will be interesting to see whether they learn from their mistake and price the stocks more efficiently in the future.

If stocks are fairly priced, there are no easy ways to make superior profits. Unfortunately, the converse does *not* hold: Stock prices could deviate substantially from fair value, and yet it could be difficult to make superior profits. For example, suppose that the price of IBM stock is always one-half of its fair value. As long as IBM is *consistently* underpriced, the percentage capital gain is the same as it would be if the stock always sold at a fair price. Of course, if IBM stock is underpriced, you get correspondingly more future dividends for your money, but for low-yield stocks that does not make much difference to your total returns. So, while the bulk of the evidence shows that it is difficult to earn high returns, we should be cautious about assuming that stocks are necessarily fairly priced.

Some researchers believe that the efficient-market hypothesis ignores important aspects of human behavior. For example, psychologists find that people tend to place too much emphasis on recent events when they are predicting the future. If so, we may find that investors are liable to overreact to new information. It will be interesting to see how far such behavioral observations can help us to understand apparent anomalies.

4. Is Management an Off-Balance-Sheet Liability?

Closed-end funds are firms whose only asset is a portfolio of common stocks. One might think that if you knew the value of these common stocks, you would also know the value of the firm. However, this is not the case. The stock of the closed-end fund often sells for substantially less than the value of the fund's portfolio.[8]

All this might not matter much except that it could be just the tip of the iceberg. For example, real estate stocks appear to sell for less than the market values of the firms' net assets. In the late 1970s and early 1980s the market values of many large oil companies were less than the market values of their oil reserves. Analysts joked that you could buy oil cheaper on Wall Street than in west Texas.

All these are special cases in which it was possible to compare the market value of the whole firm with the values of its separate assets. But perhaps if we could ob-

[7]K. Yuan, L. Zheng, and Q. Zhu, "Are Investors Moonstruck? Lunar Phases and Stock Returns," working paper, University of Michigan, September 2001.

[8]There are relatively few closed-end funds. Most mutual funds are *open-end*. This means that they stand ready to buy or sell additional shares at a price equal to the fund's net asset value per share. Therefore the share price of an open-end fund always equals net asset value.

serve the values of other firms' separate parts, we might find that the value of the whole was often less than the sum of the values of the parts.

Whenever firms calculate the net present value of a project, they implicitly assume that the value of the whole project is simply the sum of the values of all the years' cash flows. We referred to this earlier as the law of the conservation of value. If we cannot rely on that law, the tip of the iceberg could turn out to be a hot potato.

We don't understand why closed-end investment companies or any of the other firms sell at a discount on the market values of their assets. One explanation is that the value added by the firm's management is less than the cost of the management. That is why we suggest that management may be an off-balance-sheet liability. For example, the discount of oil company shares from oil-in-the-ground value can be explained if investors expected the profits from oil production to be frittered away in negative-NPV investments and bureaucratic excess. The present value of growth opportunities (PVGO) was negative!

We do not mean to portray managers as leeches soaking up cash flows meant for investors. Managers commit their human capital to the firm and rightfully expect a reasonable cash return on these personal investments. If investors extract too great a share of the firm's cash flow, the personal investments are discouraged, and the long-run health and growth of the firm can be damaged.

In most firms, managers and employees coinvest with stockholders and creditors—human capital from the insiders and financial capital from outside investors. So far we know very little about how this coinvestment works.

5. How Can We Explain the Success of New Securities and New Markets?

In the last 20 years companies and the securities exchanges have created an enormous number of new securities: options, futures, options on futures; zero-coupon bonds, floating-rate bonds; bonds with collars and caps, asset-backed bonds; catastrophe bonds, . . . the list is endless. In some cases, it is easy to explain the success of new markets or securities; perhaps they allow investors to insure themselves against new risks or they result from a change in tax or in regulation. Sometimes a market develops because of a change in the costs of issuing or trading different securities. But there are many successful innovations that cannot be explained so easily. Why do investment bankers continue to invent, and successfully sell, complex new securities that outstrip our ability to value them? The truth is we don't understand why some innovations in markets succeed and others never get off the ground.

6. How Can We Resolve the Dividend Controversy?

We spent all of Chapter 16 on dividend policy without being able to resolve the dividend controversy. Many people believe dividends are good; others believe they are bad; and still others believe they are irrelevant. If pressed, we stand somewhere in the middle, but we can't be dogmatic about it.

We don't mean to disparage existing research; rather, we say that more is in order. Whether future research will change anybody's mind is another matter. The problem is to disentangle several possible reasons that dividend policy *may* matter. For example, a firm that pays dividends rather than repurchases stock is likely to land its shareholders with heavier tax bills. On the other hand, a commitment to pay regular dividends may also provide a signal of the company's prosperity; in effect, a company that pays dividends is putting its money where its mouth is.

The way that companies distribute cash has been changing. An increasing number of companies do not pay any dividends, while the volume of stock repurchases has mushroomed. However, these repurchases are not substitutes for dividends; companies that repurchase stock do not at the same time reduce their dividend payments. Thus we need to understand better both how companies determine their payout policy and how that policy affects firm value.

7. What Risks Should a Firm Take?

Financial managers end up managing risk. For example,

- When a firm expands production, managers often reduce the cost of failure by building in the option to alter the product mix or to bail out of the project altogether.
- By reducing the firm's borrowing, managers can spread operating risks over a larger equity base.
- Most businesses take out insurance against a variety of specific hazards.
- Managers often use futures or other derivatives to protect against adverse movements in commodity prices, interest rates, and exchange rates.

All these actions reduce risk. But less risk can't always be better. The point of risk management is not to reduce risk but to add value. We wish we could give general guidance on what bets the firm should place and what the *appropriate* level of risk is.

In practice, risk management decisions interact in complicated ways. For example, firms that are hedged against commodity price fluctuations may be able to afford more debt than those that are not hedged. Hedging can make sense if it allows the firm to take greater advantage of interest tax shields, provided the costs of hedging are sufficiently low.

How can a company set a risk management strategy that adds up to a sensible whole?

8. What Is the Value of Liquidity?

Unlike Treasury bills, cash pays no interest. On the other hand, cash provides more liquidity than Treasury bills. People who hold cash must believe that this additional liquidity offsets the loss of interest. In equilibrium, the marginal value of the additional liquidity must equal the interest rate on bills.

Now what can we say about corporate holdings of cash? It is wrong to ignore the liquidity gain and to say that the cost of holding cash is the lost interest. This would imply that cash always has a *negative* NPV. It is equally foolish to say that, because the marginal value of liquidity is equal to the loss of interest, it doesn't matter how much cash the firm holds. This would imply that cash always has a *zero* NPV. We know that the marginal value of cash to a holder declines with the size of the cash holding, but we don't really understand how to value the liquidity service of cash and therefore we can't say how much cash is enough or how readily the firm should be able to raise it. To complicate matters further, we note that cash can be raised on short notice by borrowing, or by issuing other new securities, as well as by selling assets. The financial manager with a $1 million unused line of credit may sleep just as soundly as one whose firm holds $1 million in marketable securities. In our chapters on working-capital management we largely finessed these questions by presenting models that are really too simple or by speaking vaguely of the need to ensure an "adequate" liquidity reserve.

A better knowledge of liquidity would also help us to understand better how corporate bonds are priced. We already know part of the reason that corporate bonds sell for lower prices than Treasury bonds—companies have the option to walk away from their debts. However, the differences between the prices of corporate bonds and Treasury bonds are too large to be explained just by the company's default option. It seems likely that the price difference is partly due to the fact that corporate bonds are less liquid than Treasury bonds. But, until we know how to price differences in liquidity, we can't really say much more than this.

Investors seem to value liquidity much more highly at some times than at others. When liquidity suddenly dries up, asset prices can become very volatile. This happened in 1998 when Long-Term Capital Management, a large hedge fund, collapsed.[9] Since its formation four years earlier LTCM had generated high returns by holding large positions in "cheap" illiquid assets, which it hedged by selling liquid assets. LTCM, therefore, served as a supplier of liquidity to other investors. When Russia defaulted on its debt in 1998, there was a rush by investors to get out of illiquid assets. As the value of LTCM's holdings declined, its banks demanded additional collateral for their loans and LTCM was forced to liquidate its positions in a market that was already short of liquidity. Eventually, the New York Fed encouraged a group of institutions to take over LTCM, but not before there had been very sharp swings in asset prices.

9. How Can We Explain Merger Waves?

In 1968 at the first peak of the postwar merger movement, Joel Segall noted: "There is no single hypothesis which is both plausible and general and which shows promise of explaining the current merger movement. If so, it is correct to say that there is nothing known about mergers; there are no useful generalizations."[10] Of course there are many plausible motives for merging. If you single out a *particular* merger, it is usually possible to think up a reason why that merger could make sense. But that leaves us with a special hypothesis for each merger. What we need is a general hypothesis to explain merger waves. For example, in the late 1990s everybody seemed to be merging, while at the beginning of the twenty-first century mergers were out of fashion.

There are other instances of apparent financial fashions. For example, from time to time there are hot new-issue periods when there seems to be an insatiable supply of speculative new issues and an equally insatiable demand for them. We don't understand why hard-headed businessmen sometimes seem to behave like a flock of sheep, but the following story may contain the seeds of an explanation.

It is early evening and George is trying to decide between two restaurants, the Hungry Horse and the Golden Trough. Both are empty and, since there seems to be little reason to prefer one to the other, George tosses a coin and opts for the Hungry Horse. Shortly afterward Georgina pauses outside the two restaurants. She somewhat prefers the Golden Trough, but observing George inside the Hungry Horse while the other restaurant is empty, she decides that George may know something that she doesn't and therefore the rational decision is to copy George. Fred is the third person to arrive. He sees that George and Georgina have both chosen the Hungry Horse, and, putting aside his own judgment, decides to go with the flow. And so it is with subsequent diners, who simply look at the packed tables in the one restaurant and the empty tables elsewhere and draw the obvious conclusions. Each diner

[9]Hedge funds attempt to buy underpriced securities and to sell short overpriced ones. They are typically organized as partnerships and owned by a small number of institutions or wealthy individuals.

[10]J. Segall, "Merging for Fun and Profit," *Industrial Management Review* 9 (Winter 1968), pp. 17–30.

behaves fully rationally in balancing his or her own views with the revealed preferences of the other diners. Yet the popularity of the Hungry Horse owed much to the toss of George's coin. If Georgina had been the first to arrive or if all diners could have pooled their information before coming to a decision, the Hungry Horse might not have scooped the jackpot.

Economists refer to this imitative behavior as a cascade.[11] It remains to be seen how far cascades or some alternative theory can help to explain financial fashions.

10. How Can We Explain International Differences in Financial Architecture?

In Chapter 34 we showed how financial architecture varies internationally. By this we mean that there are important international differences in the legal form of the business, its ownership, governance, and sources of financing. In the United States and most other English-speaking countries large firms are commonly organized as public corporations with actively traded shares, dispersed ownership, and relatively easy access to financial markets. In other countries businesses are often more closely held, and the owners have more say in how the business is run. Banks often play a much larger role in financing businesses and keeping an eye on their progress. Also, in many countries businesses are combined together into diversified conglomerates which can allocate capital from the parts that have a capital surplus to those that are short of capital.

We don't fully understand why these differences in organizational structure exist, though we suggested that part of the answer may lie in differences in legal and accounting systems. We also made some qualitative statements about the advantages and disadvantages of different structures, but commentators continue to debate which arrangements are most efficient. Some worry that the preoccupation of managers in the United States with enhancing shareholder value leads to a focus on short-term profits; others assert that too cozy a relationship between a company and its sources of capital can lead to a lack of discipline in managers.

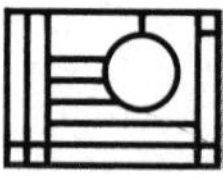

35.3 A FINAL WORD

That concludes our list of unsolved problems. We have given you the 10 uppermost in our minds. If there are others that you find more interesting and challenging, by all means construct your own list and start thinking about it.

It will take years for our 10 problems to be finally solved and replaced with a fresh list. In the meantime, we invite you to go on to further study what we *already* know about finance. We also invite you to apply what you have learned from reading this book.

Now that the book is done, we sympathize with Huckleberry Finn. At the end of his book he says:

> So there ain't nothing more to write, and I am rotten glad of it, because if I'd a'knowed what a trouble it was to make a book I wouldn't a' tackled it, and I ain't a'going to no more.

[11]For an introduction to cascades, see S. Bikhchandani, D. Hirschleifer, and I. Welch, "Learning from the Behavior of Others: Conformity, Fads, and Informational Cascades," *Journal of Economic Perspectives* 12 (Summer 1998), pp. 151–170.

APPENDIX A

PRESENT VALUE TABLES

APPENDIX TABLE 1

Discount factors: Present value of $1 to be received after t years = $1/(1 + r)^t$.

Number of Years	Interest Rate per Year														
	1%	2%	3%	4%	5%	6%	7%	8%	9%	10%	11%	12%	13%	14%	15%
1	.990	.980	.971	.962	.952	.943	.935	.926	.917	.909	.901	.893	.885	.877	.870
2	.980	.961	.943	.925	.907	.890	.873	.857	.842	.826	.812	.797	.783	.769	.756
3	.971	.942	.915	.889	.864	.840	.816	.794	.772	.751	.731	.712	.693	.675	.658
4	.961	.924	.888	.855	.823	.792	.763	.735	.708	.683	.659	.636	.613	.592	.572
5	.951	.906	.863	.822	.784	.747	.713	.681	.650	.621	.593	.567	.543	.519	.497
6	.942	.888	.837	.790	.746	.705	.666	.630	.596	.564	.535	.507	.480	.456	.432
7	.933	.871	.813	.760	.711	.665	.623	.583	.547	.513	.482	.452	.425	.400	.376
8	.923	.853	.789	.731	.677	.627	.582	.540	.502	.467	.434	.404	.376	.351	.327
9	.914	.837	.766	.703	.645	.592	.544	.500	.460	.424	.391	.361	.333	.308	.284
10	.905	.820	.744	.676	.614	.558	.508	.463	.422	.386	.352	.322	.295	.270	.247
11	.896	.804	.722	.650	.585	.527	.475	.429	.388	.350	.317	.287	.261	.237	.215
12	.887	.788	.701	.625	.557	.497	.444	.397	.356	.319	.286	.257	.231	.208	.187
13	.879	.773	.681	.601	.530	.469	.415	.368	.326	.290	.258	.229	.204	.182	.163
14	.870	.758	.661	.577	.505	.442	.388	.340	.299	.263	.232	.205	.181	.160	.141
15	.861	.743	.642	.555	.481	.417	.362	.315	.275	.239	.209	.183	.160	.140	.123
16	.853	.728	.623	.534	.458	.394	.339	.292	.252	.218	.188	.163	.141	.123	.107
17	.844	.714	.605	.513	.436	.371	.317	.270	.231	.198	.170	.146	.125	.108	.093
18	.836	.700	.587	.494	.416	.350	.296	.250	.212	.180	.153	.130	.111	.095	.081
19	.828	.686	.570	.475	.396	.331	.277	.232	.194	.164	.138	.116	.098	.083	.070
20	.820	.673	.554	.456	.377	.312	.258	.215	.178	.149	.124	.104	.087	.073	.061
25	.780	.610	.478	.375	.295	.233	.184	.146	.116	.092	.074	.059	.047	.038	.030
30	.742	.552	.412	.308	.231	.174	.131	.099	.075	.057	.044	.033	.026	.020	.015

Note: For example, if the interest rate is 10 percent per year, the present value of $1 received at year 5 is $.621.

Number of Years	Interest Rate per Year														
	16%	17%	18%	19%	20%	21%	22%	23%	24%	25%	26%	27%	28%	29%	30%
1	.862	.855	.847	.840	.833	.826	.820	.813	.806	.800	.794	.787	.781	.775	.769
2	.743	.731	.718	.706	.694	.683	.672	.661	.650	.640	.630	.620	.610	.601	.592
3	.641	.624	.609	.593	.579	.564	.551	.537	.524	.512	.500	.488	.477	.466	.455
4	.552	.534	.516	.499	.482	.467	.451	.437	.423	.410	.397	.384	.373	.361	.350
5	.476	.456	.437	.419	.402	.386	.370	.355	.341	.328	.315	.303	.291	.280	.269
6	.410	.390	.370	.352	.335	.319	.303	.289	.275	.262	.250	.238	.227	.217	.207
7	.354	.333	.314	.296	.279	.263	.249	.235	.222	.210	.198	.188	.178	.168	.159
8	.305	.285	.266	.249	.233	.218	.204	.191	.179	.168	.157	.148	.139	.130	.123
9	.263	.243	.225	.209	.194	.180	.167	.155	.144	.134	.125	.116	.108	.101	.094
10	.227	.208	.191	.176	.162	.149	.137	.126	.116	.107	.099	.092	.085	.078	.073
11	.195	.178	.162	.148	.135	.123	.112	.103	.094	.086	.079	.072	.066	.061	.056
12	.168	.152	.137	.124	.112	.102	.092	.083	.076	.069	.062	.057	.052	.047	.043
13	.145	.130	.116	.104	.093	.084	.075	.068	.061	.055	.050	.045	.040	.037	.033
14	.125	.111	.099	.088	.078	.069	.062	.055	.049	.044	.039	.035	.032	.028	.025
15	.108	.095	.084	.074	.065	.057	.051	.045	.040	.035	.031	.028	.025	.022	.020
16	.093	.081	.071	.062	.054	.047	.042	.036	.032	.028	.025	.022	.019	.017	.015
17	.080	.069	.060	.052	.045	.039	.034	.030	.026	.023	.020	.017	.015	.013	.012
18	.069	.059	.051	.044	.038	.032	.028	.024	.021	.018	.016	.014	.012	.010	.009
19	.060	.051	.043	.037	.031	.027	.023	.020	.017	.014	.012	.011	.009	.008	.007
20	.051	.043	.037	.031	.026	.022	.019	.016	.014	.012	.010	.008	.007	.006	.005
25	.024	.020	.016	.013	.010	.009	.007	.006	.005	.004	.003	.003	.002	.002	.001
30	.012	.009	.007	.005	.004	.003	.003	.002	.002	.001	.001	.001	.001	.000	.000

APPENDIX TABLE 2

Future value of $1 after t years $= (1 + r)^t$.

Number of Years	Interest Rate per Year														
	1%	2%	3%	4%	5%	6%	7%	8%	9%	10%	11%	12%	13%	14%	15%
1	1.010	1.020	1.030	1.040	1.050	1.060	1.070	1.080	1.090	1.100	1.110	1.120	1.130	1.140	1.150
2	1.020	1.040	1.061	1.082	1.102	1.124	1.145	1.166	1.188	1.210	1.232	1.254	1.277	1.300	1.323
3	1.030	1.061	1.093	1.125	1.158	1.191	1.225	1.260	1.295	1.331	1.368	1.405	1.443	1.482	1.521
4	1.041	1.082	1.126	1.170	1.216	1.262	1.311	1.360	1.412	1.464	1.518	1.574	1.630	1.689	1.749
5	1.051	1.104	1.159	1.217	1.276	1.338	1.403	1.469	1.539	1.611	1.685	1.762	1.842	1.925	2.011
6	1.062	1.126	1.194	1.265	1.340	1.419	1.501	1.587	1.677	1.772	1.870	1.974	2.082	2.195	2.313
7	1.072	1.149	1.230	1.316	1.407	1.504	1.606	1.714	1.828	1.949	2.076	2.211	2.353	2.502	2.660
8	1.083	1.172	1.267	1.369	1.477	1.594	1.718	1.851	1.993	2.144	2.305	2.476	2.658	2.853	3.059
9	1.094	1.195	1.305	1.423	1.551	1.689	1.838	1.999	2.172	2.358	2.558	2.773	3.004	3.252	3.518
10	1.105	1.219	1.344	1.480	1.629	1.791	1.967	2.159	2.367	2.594	2.839	3.106	3.395	3.707	4.046
11	1.116	1.243	1.384	1.539	1.710	1.898	2.105	2.332	2.580	2.853	3.152	3.479	3.836	4.226	4.652
12	1.127	1.268	1.426	1.601	1.796	2.012	2.252	2.518	2.813	3.138	3.498	3.896	4.335	4.818	5.350
13	1.138	1.294	1.469	1.665	1.886	2.133	2.410	2.720	3.066	3.452	3.883	4.363	4.898	5.492	6.153
14	1.149	1.319	1.513	1.732	1.980	2.261	2.579	2.937	3.342	3.797	4.310	4.887	5.535	6.261	7.076
15	1.161	1.346	1.558	1.801	2.079	2.397	2.759	3.172	3.642	4.177	4.785	5.474	6.254	7.138	8.137
16	1.173	1.373	1.605	1.873	2.183	2.540	2.952	3.426	3.970	4.595	5.311	6.130	7.067	8.137	9.358
17	1.184	1.400	1.653	1.948	2.292	2.693	3.159	3.700	4.328	5.054	5.895	6.866	7.986	9.276	10.76
18	1.196	1.428	1.702	2.026	2.407	2.854	3.380	3.996	4.717	5.560	6.544	7.690	9.024	10.58	12.38
19	1.208	1.457	1.754	2.107	2.527	3.026	3.617	4.316	5.142	6.116	7.263	8.613	10.20	12.06	14.23
20	1.220	1.486	1.806	2.191	2.653	3.207	3.870	4.661	5.604	6.727	8.062	9.646	11.52	13.74	16.37
25	1.282	1.641	2.094	2.666	3.386	4.292	5.427	6.848	8.623	10.83	13.59	17.00	21.23	26.46	32.92
30	1.348	1.811	2.427	3.243	4.322	5.743	7.612	10.06	13.27	17.45	22.89	29.96	39.12	50.95	66.21

Note: For example, if the interest rate is 10 percent per year, the investment of $1 today will be worth $1.611 at year 5.

Number of Years	Interest Rate per Year 16%	17%	18%	19%	20%	21%	22%	23%	24%	25%	26%	27%	28%	29%	30%
1	1.160	1.170	1.180	1.190	1.200	1.210	1.220	1.230	1.240	1.250	1.260	1.270	1.280	1.290	1.300
2	1.346	1.369	1.392	1.416	1.440	1.464	1.488	1.513	1.538	1.563	1.588	1.613	1.638	1.664	1.690
3	1.561	1.602	1.643	1.685	1.728	1.772	1.816	1.861	1.907	1.953	2.000	2.048	2.097	2.147	2.197
4	1.811	1.874	1.939	2.005	2.074	2.144	2.215	2.289	2.364	2.441	2.520	2.601	2.684	2.769	2.856
5	2.100	2.192	2.288	2.386	2.488	2.594	2.703	2.815	2.932	3.052	3.176	3.304	3.436	3.572	3.713
6	2.436	2.565	2.700	2.840	2.986	3.138	3.297	3.463	3.635	3.815	4.002	4.196	4.398	4.608	4.827
7	2.826	3.001	3.185	3.379	3.583	3.797	4.023	4.259	4.508	4.768	5.042	5.329	5.629	5.945	6.275
8	3.278	3.511	3.759	4.021	4.300	4.595	4.908	5.239	5.590	5.960	6.353	6.768	7.206	7.669	8.157
9	3.803	4.108	4.435	4.785	5.160	5.560	5.987	6.444	6.931	7.451	8.005	8.595	9.223	9.893	10.60
10	4.411	4.807	5.234	5.695	6.192	6.728	7.305	7.926	8.594	9.313	10.09	10.92	11.81	12.76	13.79
11	5.117	5.624	6.176	6.777	7.430	8.140	8.912	9.749	10.66	11.64	12.71	13.86	15.11	16.46	17.92
12	5.936	6.580	7.288	8.064	8.916	9.850	10.87	11.99	13.21	14.55	16.01	17.61	19.34	21.24	23.30
13	6.886	7.699	8.599	9.596	10.70	11.92	13.26	14.75	16.39	18.19	20.18	22.36	24.76	27.39	30.29
14	7.988	9.007	10.15	11.42	12.84	14.42	16.18	18.14	20.32	22.74	25.42	28.40	31.69	35.34	39.37
15	9.266	10.54	11.97	13.59	15.41	17.45	19.74	22.31	25.20	28.42	32.03	36.06	40.56	45.59	51.19
16	10.75	12.33	14.13	16.17	18.49	21.11	24.09	27.45	31.24	35.53	40.36	45.80	51.92	58.81	66.54
17	12.47	14.43	16.67	19.24	22.19	25.55	29.38	33.76	38.74	44.41	50.85	58.17	66.46	75.86	86.50
18	14.46	16.88	19.67	22.90	26.62	30.91	35.85	41.52	48.04	55.51	64.07	73.87	85.07	97.86	112.5
19	16.78	19.75	23.21	27.25	31.95	37.40	43.74	51.07	59.57	69.39	80.73	93.81	108.9	126.2	146.2
20	19.46	23.11	27.39	32.43	38.34	45.26	53.36	62.82	73.86	86.74	101.7	119.1	139.4	162.9	190.0
25	40.87	50.66	62.67	77.39	95.40	117.4	144.2	176.9	216.5	264.7	323.0	393.6	478.9	581.8	705.6
30	85.85	111.1	143.4	184.7	237.4	304.5	389.8	497.9	634.8	807.8	1026	1301	1646	2078	2620

APPENDIX TABLE 3

Annuity table: Present value of \$1 *per year* for each of *t* years = $1/r - 1/[r(1 + r)^t]$.

Number of Years	Interest Rate per Year														
	1%	2%	3%	4%	5%	6%	7%	8%	9%	10%	11%	12%	13%	14%	15%
1	.990	.980	.971	.962	.952	.943	.935	.926	.917	.909	.901	.893	.885	.877	.870
2	1.970	1.942	1.913	1.886	1.859	1.833	1.808	1.783	1.759	1.736	1.713	1.690	1.668	1.647	1.626
3	2.941	2.884	2.829	2.775	2.723	2.673	2.624	2.577	2.531	2.487	2.444	2.402	2.361	2.322	2.283
4	3.902	3.808	3.717	3.630	3.546	3.465	3.387	3.312	3.240	3.170	3.102	3.037	2.974	2.914	2.855
5	4.853	4.713	4.580	4.452	4.329	4.212	4.100	3.993	3.890	3.791	3.696	3.605	3.517	3.433	3.352
6	5.795	5.601	5.417	5.242	5.076	4.917	4.767	4.623	4.486	4.355	4.231	4.111	3.998	3.889	3.784
7	6.728	6.472	6.230	6.002	5.786	5.582	5.389	5.206	5.033	4.868	4.712	4.564	4.423	4.288	4.160
8	7.652	7.325	7.020	6.733	6.463	6.210	5.971	5.747	5.535	5.335	5.146	4.968	4.799	4.639	4.487
9	8.566	8.162	7.786	7.435	7.108	6.802	6.515	6.247	5.995	5.759	5.537	5.328	5.132	4.946	4.772
10	9.471	8.983	8.530	8.111	7.722	7.360	7.024	6.710	6.418	6.145	5.889	5.650	5.426	5.216	5.019
11	10.37	9.787	9.253	8.760	8.306	7.887	7.499	7.139	6.805	6.495	6.207	5.938	5.687	5.453	5.234
12	11.26	10.58	9.954	9.385	8.863	8.384	7.943	7.536	7.161	6.814	6.492	6.194	5.918	5.660	5.421
13	12.13	11.35	10.63	9.986	9.394	8.853	8.358	7.904	7.487	7.103	6.750	6.424	6.122	5.842	5.583
14	13.00	12.11	11.30	10.56	9.899	9.295	8.745	8.244	7.786	7.367	6.982	6.628	6.302	6.002	5.724
15	13.87	12.85	11.94	11.12	10.38	9.712	9.108	8.559	8.061	7.606	7.191	6.811	6.462	6.142	5.847
16	14.72	13.58	12.56	11.65	10.84	10.11	9.447	8.851	8.313	7.824	7.379	6.974	6.604	6.265	5.954
17	15.56	14.29	13.17	12.17	11.27	10.48	9.763	9.122	8.544	8.022	7.549	7.120	6.729	6.373	6.047
18	16.40	14.99	13.75	12.66	11.69	10.83	10.06	9.372	8.756	8.201	7.702	7.250	6.840	6.467	6.128
19	17.23	15.68	14.32	13.13	12.09	11.16	10.34	9.604	8.950	8.365	7.839	7.366	6.938	6.550	6.198
20	18.05	16.35	14.88	13.59	12.46	11.47	10.59	9.818	9.129	8.514	7.963	7.469	7.025	6.623	6.259
25	22.02	19.52	17.41	15.62	14.09	12.78	11.65	10.67	9.823	9.077	8.422	7.843	7.330	6.873	6.464
30	25.81	22.40	19.60	17.29	15.37	13.76	12.41	11.26	10.27	9.427	8.694	8.055	7.496	7.003	6.566

Note: For example, if the interest rate is 10 percent per year, the present value of \$1 received in each of the next 5 years is \$3.791.

Number of Years	Interest Rate per Year														
	16%	17%	18%	19%	20%	21%	22%	23%	24%	25%	26%	27%	28%	29%	30%
1	.862	.855	.847	.840	.833	.826	.820	.813	.806	.800	.794	.787	.781	.775	.769
2	1.605	1.585	1.566	1.547	1.528	1.509	1.492	1.474	1.457	1.440	1.424	1.407	1.392	1.376	1.361
3	2.246	2.210	2.174	2.140	2.106	2.074	2.042	2.011	1.981	1.952	1.923	1.896	1.868	1.842	1.816
4	2.798	2.743	2.690	2.639	2.589	2.540	2.494	2.448	2.404	2.362	2.320	2.280	2.241	2.203	2.166
5	3.274	3.199	3.127	3.058	2.991	2.926	2.864	2.803	2.745	2.689	2.635	2.583	2.532	2.483	2.436
6	3.685	3.589	3.498	3.410	3.326	3.245	3.167	3.092	3.020	2.951	2.885	2.821	2.759	2.700	2.643
7	4.039	3.922	3.812	3.706	3.605	3.508	3.416	3.327	3.242	3.161	3.083	3.009	2.937	2.868	2.802
8	4.344	4.207	4.078	3.954	3.837	3.726	3.619	3.518	3.421	3.329	3.241	3.156	3.076	2.999	2.925
9	4.607	4.451	4.303	4.163	4.031	3.905	3.786	3.673	3.566	3.463	3.366	3.273	3.184	3.100	3.019
10	4.833	4.659	4.494	4.339	4.192	4.054	3.923	3.799	3.682	3.571	3.465	3.364	3.269	3.178	3.092
11	5.029	4.836	4.656	4.486	4.327	4.177	4.035	3.902	3.776	3.656	3.543	3.437	3.335	3.239	3.147
12	5.197	4.988	4.793	4.611	4.439	4.278	4.127	3.985	3.851	3.725	3.606	3.493	3.387	3.286	3.190
13	5.342	5.118	4.910	4.715	4.533	4.362	4.203	4.053	3.912	3.780	3.656	3.538	3.427	3.322	3.223
14	5.468	5.229	5.008	4.802	4.611	4.432	4.265	4.108	3.962	3.824	3.695	3.573	3.459	3.351	3.249
15	5.575	5.324	5.092	4.876	4.675	4.489	4.315	4.153	4.001	3.859	3.726	3.601	3.483	3.373	3.268
16	5.668	5.405	5.162	4.938	4.730	4.536	4.357	4.189	4.033	3.887	3.751	3.623	3.503	3.390	3.283
17	5.749	5.475	5.222	4.990	4.775	4.576	4.391	4.219	4.059	3.910	3.771	3.640	3.518	3.403	3.295
18	5.818	5.534	5.273	5.033	4.812	4.608	4.419	4.243	4.080	3.928	3.786	3.654	3.529	3.413	3.304
19	5.877	5.584	5.316	5.070	4.843	4.635	4.442	4.263	4.097	3.942	3.799	3.664	3.539	3.421	3.311
20	5.929	5.628	5.353	5.101	4.870	4.657	4.460	4.279	4.110	3.954	3.808	3.673	3.546	3.427	3.316
25	6.097	5.766	5.467	5.195	4.948	4.721	4.514	4.323	4.147	3.985	3.834	3.694	3.564	3.442	3.329
30	6.177	5.829	5.517	5.235	4.979	4.746	4.534	4.339	4.160	3.995	3.842	3.701	3.569	3.447	3.332

APPENDIX TABLE 4

Values of e^{rt}. Future value of $1 invested at a *continuously compounded* rate *r* for *t* years.

rt	.00	.01	.02	.03	.04	.05	.06	.07	.08	.09
.00	1.000	1.010	1.020	1.030	1.041	1.051	1.062	1.073	1.083	1.094
.10	1.105	1.116	1.127	1.139	1.150	1.162	1.174	1.185	1.197	1.209
.20	1.221	1.234	1.246	1.259	1.271	1.284	1.297	1.310	1.323	1.336
.30	1.350	1.363	1.377	1.391	1.405	1.419	1.433	1.448	1.462	1.477
.40	1.492	1.507	1.522	1.537	1.553	1.568	1.584	1.600	1.616	1.632
.50	1.649	1.665	1.682	1.699	1.716	1.733	1.751	1.768	1.786	1.804
.60	1.822	1.840	1.859	1.878	1.896	1.916	1.935	1.954	1.974	1.994
.70	2.014	2.034	2.054	2.075	2.096	2.117	2.138	2.160	2.181	2.203
.80	2.226	2.248	2.271	2.293	2.316	2.340	2.363	2.387	2.411	2.435
.90	2.460	2.484	2.509	2.535	2.560	2.586	2.612	2.638	2.664	2.691
1.00	2.718	2.746	2.773	2.801	2.829	2.858	2.886	2.915	2.945	2.974
1.10	3.004	3.034	3.065	3.096	3.127	3.158	3.190	3.222	3.254	3.287
1.20	3.320	3.353	3.387	3.421	3.456	3.490	3.525	3.561	3.597	3.633
1.30	3.669	3.706	3.743	3.781	3.819	3.857	3.896	3.935	3.975	4.015
1.40	4.055	4.096	4.137	4.179	4.221	4.263	4.306	4.349	4.393	4.437
1.50	4.482	4.527	4.572	4.618	4.665	4.711	4.759	4.807	4.855	4.904
1.60	4.953	5.003	5.053	5.104	5.155	5.207	5.259	5.312	5.366	5.419
1.70	5.474	5.529	5.585	5.641	5.697	5.755	5.812	5.871	5.930	5.989
1.80	6.050	6.110	6.172	6.234	6.297	6.360	6.424	6.488	6.553	6.619
1.90	6.686	6.753	6.821	6.890	6.959	7.029	7.099	7.171	7.243	7.316

Note: For example, if the continuously compounded interest rate is 10 percent per year, the investment of $1 today will be worth $1.105 at year 1 and $1.221 at year 2.

rt	.00	.01	.02	.03	.04	.05	.06	.07	.08	.09
2.00	7.389	7.463	7.538	7.614	7.691	7.768	7.846	7.925	8.004	8.085
2.10	8.166	8.248	8.331	8.415	8.499	8.585	8.671	8.758	8.846	8.935
2.20	9.025	9.116	9.207	9.300	9.393	9.488	9.583	9.679	9.777	9.875
2.30	9.974	10.07	10.18	10.28	10.38	10.49	10.59	10.70	10.80	10.91
2.40	11.02	11.13	11.25	11.36	11.47	11.59	11.70	11.82	11.94	12.06
2.50	12.18	12.30	12.43	12.55	12.68	12.81	12.94	13.07	13.20	13.33
2.60	13.46	13.60	13.74	13.87	14.01	14.15	14.30	14.44	14.59	14.73
2.70	14.88	15.03	15.18	15.33	15.49	15.64	15.80	15.96	16.12	16.28
2.80	16.44	16.61	16.78	16.95	17.12	17.29	17.46	17.64	17.81	17.99
2.90	18.17	18.36	18.54	18.73	18.92	19.11	19.30	19.49	19.69	19.89
3.00	20.09	20.29	20.49	20.70	20.91	21.12	21.33	21.54	21.76	21.98
3.10	22.20	22.42	22.65	22.87	23.10	23.34	23.57	23.81	24.05	24.29
3.20	24.53	24.78	25.03	25.28	25.53	25.79	26.05	26.31	26.58	26.84
3.30	27.11	27.39	27.66	27.94	28.22	28.50	28.79	29.08	29.37	29.67
3.40	29.96	30.27	30.57	30.88	31.19	31.50	31.82	32.14	32.46	32.79
3.50	33.12	33.45	33.78	34.12	34.47	34.81	35.16	35.52	35.87	36.23
3.60	36.60	36.97	37.34	37.71	38.09	38.47	38.86	39.25	39.65	40.04
3.70	40.45	40.85	41.26	41.68	42.10	42.52	42.95	43.38	43.82	44.26
3.80	44.70	45.15	45.60	46.06	46.53	46.99	47.47	47.94	48.42	48.91
3.90	49.40	49.90	50.40	50.91	51.42	51.94	52.46	52.98	53.52	54.05

APPENDIX TABLE 5

Present value of $1 per year received in a continuous stream for each of t years (discounted at an *annually compounded* rate r) $= \{1 - 1/(1 + r)^t\}/\{\ln(1 + r)\}$.

Number of Years	Interest Rate per Year														
	1%	2%	3%	4%	5%	6%	7%	8%	9%	10%	11%	12%	13%	14%	15%
1	.995	.990	.985	.981	.976	.971	.967	.962	.958	.954	.950	.945	.941	.937	.933
2	1.980	1.961	1.942	1.924	1.906	1.888	1.871	1.854	1.837	1.821	1.805	1.790	1.774	1.759	1.745
3	2.956	2.913	2.871	2.830	2.791	2.752	2.715	2.679	2.644	2.609	2.576	2.543	2.512	2.481	2.450
4	3.922	3.846	3.773	3.702	3.634	3.568	3.504	3.443	3.383	3.326	3.270	3.216	3.164	3.113	3.064
5	4.878	4.760	4.648	4.540	4.437	4.337	4.242	4.150	4.062	3.977	3.896	3.817	3.741	3.668	3.598
6	5.825	5.657	5.498	5.346	5.202	5.063	4.931	4.805	4.685	4.570	4.459	4.353	4.252	4.155	4.062
7	6.762	6.536	6.323	6.121	5.930	5.748	5.576	5.412	5.256	5.108	4.967	4.832	4.704	4.582	4.465
8	7.690	7.398	7.124	6.867	6.623	6.394	6.178	5.974	5.780	5.597	5.424	5.260	5.104	4.956	4.816
9	8.609	8.243	7.902	7.583	7.284	7.004	6.741	6.494	6.261	6.042	5.836	5.642	5.458	5.285	5.121
10	9.519	9.072	8.657	8.272	7.913	7.579	7.267	6.975	6.702	6.447	6.208	5.983	5.772	5.573	5.386
11	10.42	9.884	9.391	8.935	8.512	8.121	7.758	7.421	7.107	6.815	6.542	6.287	6.049	5.826	5.617
12	11.31	10.68	10.10	9.572	9.083	8.633	8.218	7.834	7.478	7.149	6.843	6.559	6.294	6.048	5.818
13	12.19	11.46	10.79	10.18	9.627	9.116	8.647	8.216	7.819	7.453	7.115	6.802	6.512	6.242	5.992
14	13.07	12.23	11.46	10.77	10.14	9.571	9.048	8.570	8.131	7.729	7.359	7.018	6.704	6.413	6.144
15	13.93	12.98	12.12	11.34	10.64	10.00	9.423	8.897	8.418	7.980	7.579	7.212	6.874	6.563	6.276
16	14.79	13.71	12.75	11.88	11.11	10.41	9.774	9.201	8.681	8.209	7.778	7.385	7.024	6.694	6.390
17	15.64	14.43	13.36	12.41	11.55	10.79	10.10	9.482	8.923	8.416	7.957	7.539	7.158	6.809	6.490
18	16.48	15.14	13.96	12.91	11.98	11.15	10.41	9.742	9.144	8.605	8.118	7.676	7.275	6.910	6.577
19	17.31	15.83	14.54	13.39	12.39	11.49	10.69	9.983	9.347	8.777	8.263	7.799	7.380	6.999	6.652
20	18.14	16.51	15.10	13.86	12.77	11.81	10.96	10.21	9.533	8.932	8.394	7.909	7.472	7.077	6.718
25	22.13	19.72	17.67	15.93	14.44	13.16	12.06	11.10	10.26	9.524	8.877	8.305	7.797	7.344	6.938
30	25.94	22.62	19.89	17.64	15.75	14.17	12.84	11.70	10.73	9.891	9.164	8.529	7.973	7.482	7.047

Note: For example, if the interest rate is 10 percent per year, a continuous cash flow of $1 a year for each of 5 years is worth $3.977. A continuous flow of $1 in year 5 only is worth $3.977 − $3.326 = $.651.

Number of Years	Interest Rate per Year														
	16%	17%	18%	19%	20%	21%	22%	23%	24%	25%	26%	27%	28%	29%	30%
1	.929	.925	.922	.918	.914	.910	.907	.903	.900	.896	.893	.889	.886	.883	.880
2	1.730	1.716	1.703	1.689	1.676	1.663	1.650	1.638	1.625	1.613	1.601	1.590	1.578	1.567	1.556
3	2.421	2.392	2.365	2.337	2.311	2.285	2.259	2.235	2.211	2.187	2.164	2.141	2.119	2.098	2.077
4	3.016	2.970	2.925	2.882	2.840	2.799	2.759	2.720	2.682	2.646	2.610	2.576	2.542	2.509	2.477
5	3.530	3.464	3.401	3.340	3.281	3.223	3.168	3.115	3.063	3.013	2.964	2.917	2.872	2.828	2.785
6	3.972	3.886	3.804	3.724	3.648	3.574	3.504	3.436	3.370	3.307	3.246	3.187	3.130	3.075	3.022
7	4.354	4.247	4.145	4.048	3.954	3.865	3.779	3.696	3.617	3.542	3.469	3.399	3.331	3.266	3.204
8	4.682	4.555	4.434	4.319	4.209	4.104	4.004	3.909	3.817	3.730	3.646	3.566	3.489	3.415	3.344
9	4.966	4.819	4.680	4.547	4.422	4.302	4.189	4.081	3.978	3.880	3.786	3.697	3.612	3.530	3.452
10	5.210	5.044	4.887	4.739	4.599	4.466	4.340	4.221	4.108	4.000	3.898	3.801	3.708	3.619	3.535
11	5.421	5.237	5.063	4.900	4.747	4.602	4.465	4.335	4.213	4.096	3.986	3.882	3.783	3.689	3.599
12	5.603	5.401	5.213	5.036	4.870	4.713	4.566	4.428	4.297	4.173	4.057	3.946	3.841	3.742	3.648
13	5.759	5.542	5.339	5.150	4.972	4.806	4.650	4.503	4.365	4.235	4.112	3.997	3.887	3.784	3.686
14	5.894	5.662	5.446	5.245	5.058	4.882	4.718	4.564	4.420	4.284	4.157	4.036	3.923	3.816	3.715
15	6.010	5.765	5.537	5.326	5.129	4.945	4.774	4.614	4.464	4.324	4.192	4.068	3.951	3.841	3.737
16	6.111	5.853	5.614	5.393	5.188	4.998	4.820	4.655	4.500	4.355	4.220	4.092	3.973	3.860	3.754
17	6.197	5.928	5.679	5.450	5.238	5.041	4.858	4.687	4.529	4.381	4.242	4.112	3.990	3.875	3.767
18	6.272	5.992	5.735	5.498	5.279	5.076	4.889	4.714	4.552	4.401	4.259	4.127	4.003	3.887	3.778
19	6.336	6.047	5.781	5.538	5.313	5.106	4.914	4.736	4.571	4.417	4.273	4.139	4.014	3.896	3.785
20	6.391	6.094	5.821	5.571	5.342	5.130	4.935	4.754	4.586	4.430	4.284	4.149	4.022	3.903	3.791
25	6.573	6.244	5.945	5.674	5.427	5.201	4.994	4.803	4.627	4.464	4.314	4.173	4.042	3.920	3.806
30	6.659	6.312	6.000	5.718	5.462	5.229	5.016	4.821	4.641	4.476	4.323	4.181	4.048	3.925	3.810

APPENDIX TABLE 6

Cumulative probability [$N(d)$] that a normally distributed variable will be less than d standard deviations above the mean.

d	0	0.01	0.02	0.03	0.04	0.05	0.06	0.07	0.08	0.09
0	.5000	.5040	.5080	.5120	.5160	.5199	.5239	.5279	.5319	.5359
0.1	.5398	.5438	.5478	.5517	.5557	.5596	.5636	.5675	.5714	.5753
0.2	.5793	.5832	.5871	.5910	.5948	.5987	.6026	.6064	.6103	.6141
0.3	.6179	.6217	.6255	.6293	.6331	.6368	.6406	.6443	.6480	.6517
0.4	.6554	.6591	.6628	.6664	.6700	.6736	.6772	.6808	.6844	.6879
0.5	.6915	.6950	.6985	.7019	.7054	.7088	.7123	.7157	.7190	.7224
0.6	.7257	.7291	.7324	.7357	.7389	.7422	.7454	.7486	.7517	.7549
0.7	.7580	.7611	.7642	.7673	.7704	.7734	.7764	.7794	.7823	.7852
0.8	.7881	.7910	.7939	.7967	.7995	.8023	.8051	.8078	.8106	.8133
0.9	.8159	.8186	.8212	.8238	.8264	.8289	.8315	.8340	.8365	.8389
1	.8413	.8438	.8461	.8485	.8508	.8531	.8554	.8577	.8599	.8621
1.1	.8643	.8665	.8686	.8708	.8729	.8749	.8770	.8790	.8810	.8830
1.2	.8849	.8869	.8888	.8907	.8925	.8944	.8962	.8980	.8997	.9015
1.3	.9032	.9049	.9066	.9082	.9099	.9115	.9131	.9147	.9162	.9177
1.4	.9192	.9207	.9222	.9236	.9251	.9265	.9279	.9292	.9306	.9319
1.5	.9332	.9345	.9357	.9370	.9382	.9394	.9406	.9418	.9429	.9441
1.6	.9452	.9463	.9474	.9484	.9495	.9505	.9515	.9525	.9535	.9545
1.7	.9554	.9564	.9573	.9582	.9591	.9599	.9608	.9616	.9625	.9633
1.8	.9641	.9649	.9656	.9664	.9671	.9678	.9686	.9693	.9699	.9706
1.9	.9713	.9719	.9726	.9732	.9738	.9744	.9750	.9756	.9761	.9767
2	.9772	.9778	.9783	.9788	.9793	.9798	.9803	.9808	.9812	.9817
2.1	.9821	.9826	.9830	.9834	.9838	.9842	.9846	.9850	.9854	.9857
2.2	.9861	.9864	.9868	.9871	.9875	.9878	.9881	.9884	.9887	.9890
2.3	.9893	.9896	.9898	.9901	.9904	.9906	.9909	.9911	.9913	.9916
2.4	.9918	.9920	.9922	.9925	.9927	.9929	.9931	.9932	.9934	.9936
2.5	.9938	.9940	.9941	.9943	.9945	.9946	.9948	.9949	.9951	.9952

Note: For example, if $d = .22$, $N(d) = .5871$ (i.e., there is a .5871 probability that a normally distributed variable will be less than .22 standard deviations above the mean).

ANSWERS TO QUIZZES

Chapter 1

1. **(a)** Real; **(b)** executive airplanes; **(c)** brand names; **(d)** financial; **(e)** bonds; **(f)** investment; **(g)** capital budgeting; **(h)** financing.
2. **a.** Financial assets, such as stocks or bank loans, are claims held by investors. Corporations sell financial assets to raise the cash to invest in real assets such as plant and equipment. Some real assets are intangible.
   b. Capital budgeting means investment in real assets. Financing means raising the cash for this investment.
   c. The shares of public corporations are traded on stock exchanges and can be purchased by a wide range of investors. The shares of closely held corporations are not traded and are not generally available to investors.
   d. Unlimited liability: investors are responsible for all the firm's debts. A sole proprietor has unlimited liability. Investors in corporations have limited liability. They can lose their investment, but no more.
   e. A corporation is a separate legal "person" with unlimited life. Its owners hold shares in the business. A partnership is a limited-life agreement to establish and run a business.
3. *c, d, e,* and *g* are real assets. Others are financial.
4. Double taxation and agency costs due to separation of ownership and control. Public organizations also face the higher costs of complying with legal requirements and communicating with dispersed shareholders.
5. *a, c, d.*
6. *c, d.*
7. Principal–agent issues, often amplified by asymmetric information.
8. Conflicts of interest or differences in incentives create principal–agent problems. Agency costs are incurred if value-maximizing decisions are not made and if principals incur costs of monitoring or control.

Chapter 2

1. **(a)** Negative; **(b)** $PV = C_1/(1 + r)$; **(c)** $NPV = C_0 + (C_1/(1 + r))$; **(d)** r is the return foregone by investing in the project rather than the capital market; (e) the return offered by default-free U.S. Treasury securities.
2. $DF_1 = .867$; discount rate $= .154$, or 15.4%.
3. **(a)** .909; **(b)** .833; **(c)** .769.
4. **(a)** Return = profit/investment = $(132 - 100)/100 = .32$, or 32%; **(b)** Negative (if the rate of interest r equals 32%, NPV = 0); **(c)** $PV = 132/1.10 = 120$, or \$120,000; **(d)** $NPV = -100 + 120 = 20$, or \$20,000.
5. Net present value rule: Invest if NPV is positive. Rate of return rule: Invest if the rate of return exceeds the opportunity cost of capital. They give the same answer.
6. The return foregone by investing in a project rather than in securities. The opportunity cost of capital for a risk-free investment is the interest rate on government bonds. For risky investments firms need to estimate the return expected by investors from securities of similar risk.
7. A would lend and consume \$120 next year. G would consume now. Neither would invest at 14%.
8. They will vote for *a* only. The other tasks can be carried out just as efficiently by stockholders.

9. To protect and enhance their reputations; because compensation is tied to earnings and stock price; supervision by the board of directors; the threat of takeover.
10. Investors were concerned that Salomon's damaged reputation would drive away its customers.

Chapter 3

1. \$1.00.
2. $125/139 = .899$.
3. $596 \times .285 = \$170$.
4. $374/(1.09)^9 = \$172$.
5. $\text{PV} = 432/1.15 + 137/(1.15)^2 + 797/(1.15)^3 = 376 + 104 + 524 = 1{,}004$.
6. $100 \times (1.15)^8 = \$305.90$.
7. $\text{NPV} = -1548 + 138/.09 = -\$14.67$.
8. $\text{PV} = 4/(.14 - .04) = \$40$.
9. \$1,006,512.
10. **(a)** $\text{PV} = 1/.10 = \$10$; **(b)** $\text{PV} = (1/.10)/(1.10)^7 = 10/2 = \$5$ (approximately); **(c)** $\text{PV} = 10 - 5 = \$5$ (approximately); **(d)** $\text{PV} = C/(r - g) = 10{,}000/(.10 - .05) = \$200{,}000$.
11. a. From Appendix Table 1, $1/(1.05)^5 = .784$. You therefore need to set aside $10{,}000 \times .784 = \$7{,}840$.
    b. From Appendix Table 3, the present value of \$1 a year for 6 years at 8% is \$4.623. Therefore you need to set aside $12{,}000 \times 4.623 = \$55{,}476$.
    c. From Appendix Table 2, $1.08^6 = 1.587$. Therefore, at the end of 6 years you would have $1.587 \times (60{,}476 - 55{,}476) = \$7{,}935$.
12. $(1.25)/(1.21) - 1 = .033$, or 3.3%.
13. **(a)** $1{,}000e^{.12 \times 5} = 1{,}000e^{.6} = \$1{,}822$; **(b)** $\text{PV} = 5e^{-.12 \times 8} = 5e^{-.96} = \$1.915$ million; **(c)** $\text{PV} = C/r(1 - e^{-rt}) = 2{,}000/.12(1 - e^{-.12 \times 15}) = \$13{,}912$.
14. **(a)** \$12.625 million; **(b)** \$12.705 million; **(c)** \$12.712 million.
15. \$1,133.55. This calculation assumes annual coupon payments and compounding.
16. The yield to maturity is the (single) discount rate that gives a present value equal to a bond's price. It is calculated by trial and error, by computer or calculator, or from bond tables.

Chapter 4

1. **(a)** True; **(b)** true.
2. Investors who buy stocks may get their return from capital gains as well as dividends. But the future stock price always depends on subsequent dividends. There is no inconsistency.
3. $P_0 = (10 + 110)/1.10 = \$109.09$.
4. $r = 5/40 = .125$.
5. $P_0 = 10/(.08 - .05) = \$333.33$.
6. By year 4, earnings will grow to \$18.23 per share. Forecasted price per share at year 4 is $18.23/.08 = \$227.91$.

$$P_0 = \frac{10}{1.08} + \frac{10.50}{(1.08)^2} + \frac{11.03}{(1.08)^3} + \frac{11.58}{(1.08)^4} + \frac{227.91}{(1.08)^4} = 203.05.$$

7. $15/.08 + \text{PVGO} = 333.33$; therefore $\text{PVGO} = \$145.83$.
8. Z's forecasted dividends and prices grow as follows:

	Year 1	Year 2	Year 3
Dividend	10	10.50	11.03
Price	350	367.50	385.88

Calculate the expected rates of return:

$$\text{From year 0 to 1: } \frac{10 + (350 - 333.33)}{333.33} = .08.$$

$$\text{From year 1 to 2: } \frac{10.50 + (367.50 - 350)}{350} = .08.$$

$$\text{From year 2 to 3: } \frac{11.03 + (385.88 - 367.50)}{367.50} = .08$$

Double expects 8% in *each* of the first 2 years. Triple expects 8% in *each* of the first 3 years.

9. **(a)** False; **(b)** true.
10. $\text{PVGO} = 0$, and EPS_1 equals the average future earnings the firm could generate under no-growth policy.
11. Free cash flow equals the net cash flow available to shareholders after paying for all future investments. Free cash flow can be negative if investments are large. Dividends are the cash paid out to stockholders. A company could have negative free cash flow but sell new shares and still pay a dividend.
12. Dividends or free cash flow are forecasted to a horizon, and a horizon value is added. Two-stage models are used when near-term cash flows grow at irregular or unsustainable rates. For example, the company may be recovering from a period of low profits, or profitability and growth may be high for a limited period.
13. The value at the end of a forecast period. It can be estimated by the constant-growth DCF formula or by using price–earnings or market–book ratios for similar companies. If $\text{PVGO} = 0$ at the horizon date H, horizon value equals earnings forecasted at date $H + 1$ divided by r.
14. Earnings forecasted for date $H + 1$ divided by r.

Chapter 5

1. The opportunity cost of capital is the expected rate of return investors could earn in financial markets at the same level of risk as the asset to be valued.
2. **(a)** A = 3 years, B = 2 years, C = 3 years; **(b)** B; **(c)** A, B, and C; **(d)** B and C (NPV_B = $3,378; NPV_C = $2,405); **(e)** false; **(f)** true; **(g)** It will accept no negative-NPV projects but will turn down some with positive NPVs. A project can have positive NPV if all future cash flows are considered but still not meet the stated cutoff period.
3. The ratio of book (accounting) income to book assets. This ratio depends on accounting procedures. It is not calculated from project cash flows. The time value of money is ignored.
4. Given the cash flows $C_0, C_1, \ldots, C_T$, IRR is defined by

$$NPV = C_0 + \frac{C_1}{1 + IRR} + \frac{C_2}{(1 + IRR)^2} + \cdots + \frac{C_T}{(1 + IRR)^T} = 0.$$

It is calculated by trial and error, by financial calculators, or by spreadsheet programs.
5. **(a)** $15,750; $4,250; $0; **(b)** 100%.
6. No (you are effectively "borrowing" at a rate of interest higher than the opportunity cost of capital).
7. **(a)** Two, −50% and +50%; **(b)** yes, NPV = +14.6.
8. The incremental flows from investing in Alpha rather than Beta are −200,000; +110,000; and 121,000. The IRR on the incremental cash flow is 10 percent (i.e., $-200 + 110/1.10 + 121/1.10^2 = 0$). The IRR on Beta exceeds the cost of capital and so does the IRR on the incremental investment in Alpha. Choose Alpha.
9. 1, 2, 4, and 6.
10. Soft rationing means provisional capital constraints imposed by management as an aid to financial control. This doesn't rule out raising more money if necessary. Firms facing hard rationing can't raise money from capital markets. NPV is not ruled out as long as shareholders have access to capital markets.

Chapter 6

1. *a, b, d, g, h.*
2. Real cash flow = 100,000/1.04 = 96,154; real discount rate = 1.08/1.04 − 1 = .0385.

$$PV = \frac{96{,}154}{1.0385} = 92{,}589,$$ four euros short because of rounding error.
3. **(a)** False; **(b)** false; **(c)** false; **(d)** false.
4. The longer the recovery period, the less the present value of depreciation tax shields. This is true regardless of the discount rate. If, say, $r = .10$, then 35% of the 5-year schedule's PV is .271. The same calculation for the 7-year schedule yields .253.
5.

	2000	2001	2002	2003	2004
Working capital	50,000	230,000	305,000	250,000	0
Cash flows	+50,000	+180,000	+75,000	−55,000	−250,000

6. The checklist would include: forecasting cash flows in euros (taking account of French inflation); recognizing French corporate tax rules and rates; and discounting at a euro cost of capital.
7. Comparing present values can be misleading when projects have different economic lives and the projects are part of an ongoing business. For example, a machine that costs $100,000 per year to buy and lasts 5 years is not necessarily more expensive than a machine that costs $75,000 per year to buy but lasts only 3 years. Calculating the machines' equivalent annual costs allows an unbiased comparison.
8. Plan to undertake the project at the future date which yields the highest NPV *today.* (This assumes certainty. We consider timing under uncertainty in Chapter 22.)
9. PV cost = 1.5 + .2 × 14.09 = $4.319 million. Equivalent annual cost = 4.319/14.09 = .306, or $306,000.
10. a. NPV_A = $100,000; NPV_B = $180,000.
    b. Equivalent cash flow of A = 100,000/1.736 = $57,604; equivalent cash flow of B = 180,000/2.487 = $72,376.
    c. Machine B.
11. Replace at end of 5 years ($80,000 > $72,376).

Chapter 7

1. **(a)** About 13%; **(b)** about 9%; **(c)** about 1%; **(d)** about 20% (less in recent years); **(e)** less (diversification reduces risk).
2. Expected payoff is $100 and expected return is zero. Variance is 20,000 (percent squared) and standard deviation is 141%.
3. **(a)** 35.5%; **(b)** 7.1%.
4. Standard deviation of returns, correlated, less, unique, market.
5. Mr. Interchange had a lower average return than the S&P (15.6% versus 19.4%) but also a lower standard deviation (12.0% versus 14.9%).
6. **(a)** False; **(b)** true; **(c)** true; **(d)** true; **(e)** false.
7. *d*
8.

$x_1^2\sigma_1^2$	$x_1x_2\sigma_{12}$	$x_1x_3\sigma_{13}$
$x_1x_2\sigma_{12}$	$x_2^2\sigma_2^2$	$x_2x_3\sigma_{23}$
$x_1x_3\sigma_{13}$	$x_2x_3\sigma_{23}$	$x_3^2\sigma_3^2$

9. **(a)** 26%; **(b)** zero; **(c)** .75; **(d)** less than 1.0 (the portfolio's risk is the same as the market, but some of this risk is unique risk).
10. 1.3 (Diversification does not affect market risk.)
11. A, 1.0; B, 2.0; C, 1.5; D, 0; E, −1.0.
12. False. Corporations can reduce risk by diversifying but so can investors. Therefore they will not be prepared to pay extra for the stocks of diversified companies.

Chapter 8

1. **(a)** 7%; **(b)** 27% with perfect positive correlation; 1% with perfect negative correlation; 19.1% with no correlation; **(c)** See Figure 1; **(d)** No, measure risk by beta, not by standard deviation.
2. **(a)** Portfolio A (higher expected return, same risk); **(b)** Cannot say (depends on investor's attitude toward risk); **(c)** Portfolio F (lower risk, same expected return).
3. **a.** Figure 8.13b: Diversification reduces risk (e.g., a mixture of portfolios A and B would have less risk than the average of A and B).
   b. Those along line *AB* in Figure 8.13a.
   c. See Figure 2.
4. **(a)** See Figure 3; **(b)** A, D, G; **(c)** F; **(d)** 15% in C. **(e)** Put 25/32 of your money in F and lend 7/32 at 12%: Expected return = 7/32 × 12 + 25/32 × 18 = 16.7%; standard deviation = 7/32 × 0 + (25/32) × 32 = 25%. If you could borrow without limit, you would achieve as high an expected return as you'd like, with correspondingly high risk, of course.

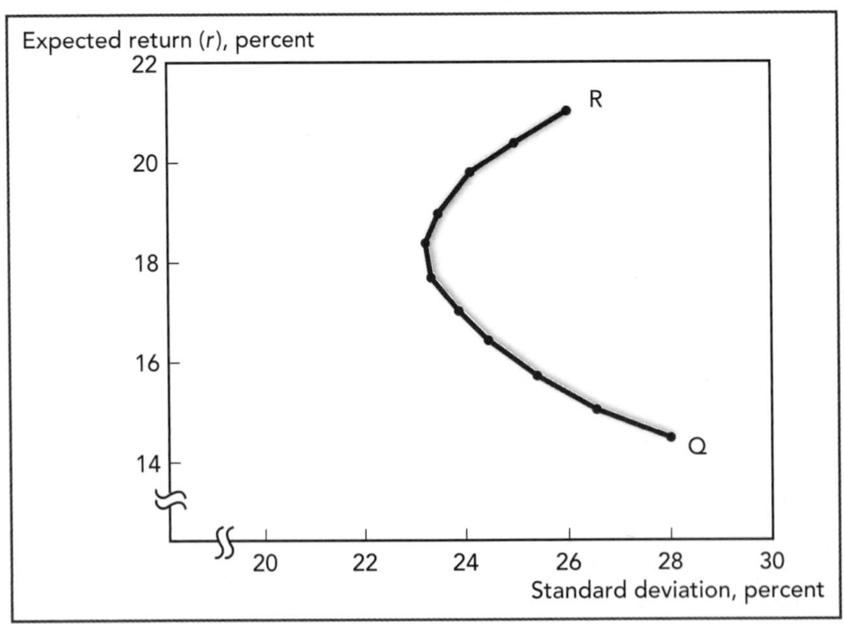

FIGURE 1

Chapter 8, Quiz question 1(c).

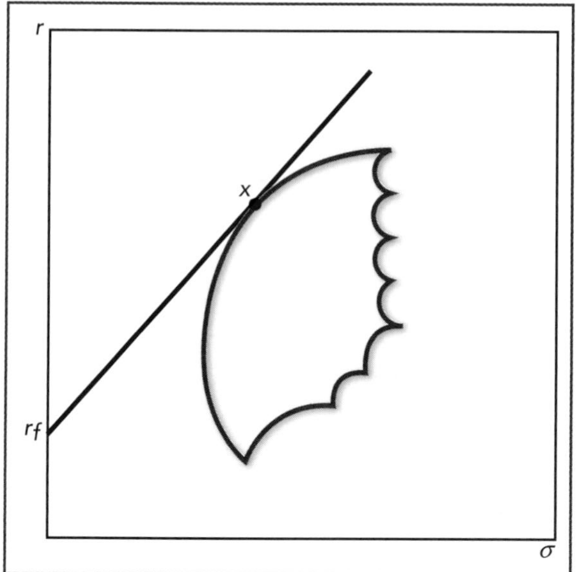

FIGURE 2

Chapter 8, Quiz question 3(*c*).

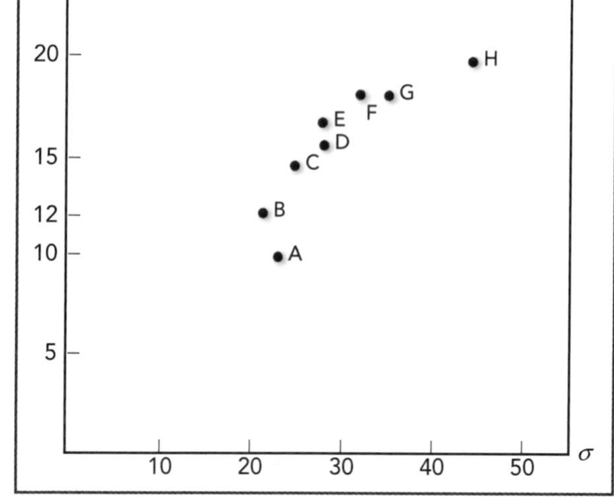

FIGURE 3

Chapter 8, Quiz question 4(*a*).

5. The best portfolio will be a combination of lending or borrowing, plus investment in the stock portfolio with the highest *ratio* of expected risk premium to standard deviation. See Figure 8.6.
6. **(a)** $r = 4 + .68(10 - 4) = 8.08\%$; **(b)** Amazon.com at 23.5%; **(c)** Exxon Mobil at 6.4%; **(d)** lower; **(e)** higher.
7. **(a)** True; **(b)** false (it offers twice the market *risk premium*); **(c)** false.
8. Because beta does not seem to explain average returns. The relationship between beta and average return has been too "flat"—see Figure 8.9. Other factors, such as the book-to-market ratio, seem to explain differences in average returns.
9. $r - r_f = b_1(r_{\text{factor 1}} - r_f) + b_2(r_{\text{factor 2}} - r_f) + \cdots,$

   r = expected return on stock,

   r_f = risk-free interest rate,

   $r_{\text{factor } j}$ = expected return on portfolio of stocks that is exposed only to the jth economic factor,

   b_j = sensitivity of stock to returns on jth factor.
10. **(a)** 7%; **(b)** $7 + 1(5) + 1(-1) + 1(2) = 13\%$; **(c)** $7 + 0(5) + 2(-1) + 0(2) = 5\%$; **(d)** $7 + 1(5) + (-1.5)(-1) + 1(2) = 15.5\%$.
11. Market factor (risk premium), size factor (return on small-firm stocks less return on large-firm stocks), book-to-market factor (return on high book-to-market stocks less return on low book-to-market stocks).

Chapter 9

1. Overestimate.
2. False. Beta depends on returns, not on the levels of stock price or the market index.
3. 27% was explained by market movements, 73% by unique risk. Unique risk shows up as the scatter of points around the fitted line. The standard error is .38, so plus or minus two standard errors gives a range of 1.26 to 2.78.
4. $\beta_{\text{assets}} = 0 \times .40 + .5 \times .60 = .30$, $r = 10 + .30(18 - 10) = 12.4\%$.
5. **a.** $r_f + \beta(r_m - r_f) = 8 + 1.5 \times 9 = 21.5\%$.

   b. $$\beta_{\text{assets}} = \beta_{\text{debt}}\left(\frac{\text{debt}}{\text{debt} + \text{equity}}\right) + \beta_{\text{equity}}\left(\frac{\text{equity}}{\text{debt} + \text{equity}}\right) = 0 \times \frac{4}{4+6} + 1.5 \times \frac{6}{4+6} = .9.$$

   c. $r_f + \beta_{\text{assets}}(r_m - r_f) = 8 + .9 \times 9 = 16.1\%$;

   d. $r = 16.1\%$; **(e)** $r_f + \beta(r_m - r_f) = 8 + 1.2 \times 9 = 18.8\%$.
6. **(a)** .73; **(b)** It would not change at all; **(c)** $r = 5 + .73(6) = 9.4\%$.
7. **(a)** True; **(b)** false; **(c)** true.

8. **(a)** A (higher fixed cost); **(b)** C (more cyclical revenues).
9. Certainty equivalent; $CEQ_t/[(1 + r_f)^t]$; less than; $r_f + \beta(r_m - r_f)$; declines at a constant rate.
10. a.

$$PV = \frac{110}{1 + r_f + \beta(r_m - r_f)} + \frac{121}{[1 + r_f + \beta(r_m - r_f)]^2}$$
$$= \frac{110}{1.10} + \frac{121}{1.10^2} = \$200.$$

b. $CEQ_1/1.05 = 110/1.10$, $CEQ_1 = \$105$; $CEQ_2/1.05^2 = 121/1.10^2$, $CEQ_2 = \$110.25$.
c. $\text{Ratio}_1 = 105/110 = .95$; $\text{Ratio}_2 = 110.25/121 = .91$.

Chapter 10

1. **a.** Analysis of how project profitability and NPV change if different assumptions are made about sales, cost, and other key variables.
   b. Project NPV is recalculated by changing several inputs to new, but consistent values.
   c. Determines the level of future sales at which project profitability or NPV equals zero.
   d. An extension of sensitivity analysis which explores all possible outcomes and weights each by its probability.
   e. A graphical technique for displaying possible future events and decisions taken in response to those events.
   f. Option to modify a project at a future date.
   g. The additional present value created by the option to bail out of a project, and recover part of the initial investment, if the project performs poorly.
   h. The additional present value created by the option to invest more and expand output, if a project performs well.
2. **(a)** False; **(b)** true; **(c)** true; **(d)** true; **(e)** true; **(f)** false.
3. It shows how the project would fare under consistent combinations of input assumptions. Sensitivity analysis changes only one input at a time.
4. Monte Carlo helps reveal what can go wrong (or right) with a project. It helps the manager to obtain an accurate forecast of expected cash flows. It also helps in assessing project risk and determining the appropriate discount rate.
5. **a.** Describe how project cash flow depends on the underlying variables.
   b. Specify probability distributions for forecast errors for these cash flows.
   c. Draw from the probability distributions to simulate the cash flows.
6. Option to expand; option to abandon; option to postpone investment; production options.
7. **(a)** True; **(b)** true; **(c)** false; **(d)** false.
8. If prices of raw materials may change (e.g., price of oil relative to gas), the firm may be able to switch between them. Similarly, if consumer tastes change, the firm may be able to change output quickly and cheaply.

Chapter 11

1. Your best estimate is $1,000 per acre, the actual market value. Why do a discounted-cash-flow analysis to estimate market value when you can observe it directly?
2. **(a)** False; **(b)** true; **(c)** true; **(d)** false.
3. $15
4. Product prices tend to equilibrium levels at which efficient producers see capacity expansion as zero-NPV. Calculating NPV from the point of view of a European competitor allowed estimation of this equilibrium price.
5. First consider whether *renting* the building and opening the Taco Palace is positive NPV. Then consider whether to buy (instead of renting) based on your optimistic view of local real estate.
6. The present value of the future price of gold is equal to today's price. Just multiply production volume by today's gold price.
7. **(a)** 160/1.05 = $152.4 million; **(b)** The expected rate of return is $r_f + \beta(r_m - r_f) = .05 + 1.2(.12 - .05) = .134$, or 13.4%. The expected price is 1,524 × 1.134 = 1,728. The certainty equivalent price is 1,600.
8. The second-hand market value of older planes falls by enough to make up for their higher fuel consumption. Also, the older planes are used on routes where fuel efficiency is relatively less important.
9. *b* and *d* are clear lessons. *c* can be true: reduction in profits from an existing project is a valid concern. But if competitor's new products would harm existing projects in any case, there is no reason to hold back on *your* new product. *a* is wrong: growth or high-tech products do not necessarily mean positive NPV. *e* is wrong: the book value of a plant does not show the opportunity cost of using it.

Chapter 12

1. **(a)** False; **(b)** true; **(c)** true; **(d)** false; **(e)** true (e.g., marketing programs and training); **(f)** false.
2. **a.** Can lead to investment in negative-NPV projects.
   b. Confuses the relative NPVs of projects proposed by different business units.

c. Project interactions may be ignored. Some opportunities, such as the closing or sale of a division, will not be considered. Strategic investments may be missed.
d. Creates a bias in favor of quick payback projects and against long-lived projects that may have large NPVs.

3. A change in the hurdle rate is offset by more or less optimistic forecasts by project sponsors. There's no way out: the financial manager can't avoid careful assessment of cash-flow forecasts.

4. *Agency costs:* value lost when managers do not act to maximize value. This includes costs of monitoring and control.
Private benefits: perks or other advantages enjoyed by managers.
Empire building: investing for size, not NPV.
Free-rider problem: when one shareholder, or group of shareholders, acts to monitor and control management, all shareholders benefit.
Entrenching investment: managers choose or design investment projects which increase the managers' value to the firm.
Delegated monitoring: monitoring on behalf of principals. For example, the board of directors monitors management performance on behalf of stockholders.

5. Monitoring is costly and encounters diminishing returns. Also, completely effective monitoring would require perfect information.

6. **(a)** Dollar amount; **(b)** EVA = Income earned − (cost of capital × investment); **(c)** They are essentially the same; **(d)** EVA makes the cost of capital visible to managers. Compensation based on EVA encourages them to dispose of unnecessary assets and to forego investment unless it earns more than the cost of capital; **(e)** Yes.

7. Return on investment = 1.6/20 = .08 or 8%. EVA = 1.6 − (.115 × 20) = −$.7 million. EVA is negative.

8. **(a)** False: profits may be depressed temporarily, but in a steady state, writing off R&D can increase the book rate of return; **(b)** true—because asset value is understated, the ratio of income to assets is biased upward.

9. Cash flow, economic, less, greater.

10.

	Year 1	Year 2	Year 3
Cash flow	0	78.55	78.55
PV at start of year	100.00	120.00	65.45
PV at end of year	120.00	65.45	0
Change in value during year	+20.00	−54.55	−65.45
Expected economic income	+20.00	+24.00	+13.10

Chapter 13

1. *c*
2. Weak, semistrong, strong, strong, weak.
3. **(a)** False; **(b)** false; **(c)** true; **(d)** false; **(e)** false; **(f)** true.
4. **(a)** Decline to $200; **(b)** less; **(c)** A slight abnormal fall (the split is likely to have led investors to expect an above-average rise in dividends).
5. **(a)** False; **(b)** true; **(c)** false; **(d)** true; **(e)** false; **(f)** true (a small change in price *in the absence of new information* causes a large increase in demand).
6. 6 − (−.2 + 1.45 × 5) = −1.05%.
7. **(a)** True; **(b)** false; **(c)** true; **(d)** true.
8. Decrease. The stock price already reflects an expected 25% increase. The 20% increase conveys bad news relative to expectations.
9. **a.** An investor should not buy or sell shares based on apparent trends or cycles in returns.
   b. A CFO should not speculate on changes in interest rates or foreign exchange rates. There is no reason to think that the CFO has superior information.
   c. A financial manager evaluating the creditworthiness of a large customer could check the customer's stock price and the yield on its debt. A falling stock price or a high yield could indicate trouble ahead.
   d. Don't assume that accounting choices which increase or decrease earnings will have any effect on stock price.
   e. The company should not seek diversification just to reduce risk. Investors can diversify on their own.
   f. Stock issues do not depress price if investors believe the issuer has no private information.

Chapter 14

1.

Internally generated cash	77
Financial deficit	23
Net share issues	−14
Debt issues	38

2. **(a)** False; **(b)** true; **(c)** true; **(d)** false.

3. **(a)** 40,000/.50 = 80,000 shares; **(b)** 78,000 shares; **(c)** 2,000 shares are held as Treasury stock; **(d)** 20,000 shares.

	(e)	(f)
Common stock	$ 45,000	$40,000
Additional paid-in capital	25,000	10,000
Retained earnings	30,000	30,000
Common equity	100,000	80,000
Treasury stock	5,000	30,000
Net common equity	$ 95,000	$50,000

4. **(a)** 80 votes; **(b)** 10 × 80 = 800 votes.
5. *Similarities with debt:* **(a)** Fixed income; **(b)** preferred stockholders have limited voting rights.
   Similarities with equity: **(a)** Dividend is within discretion of directors; **(b)** no final repayment date; **(c)** dividend is not an allowable deduction from taxable profits.
6. **(a)** subordinated; **(b)** floating rate; **(c)** convertible; **(d)** warrant; **(e)** common stock; preferred stock.
7. **(a)** False; **(b)** true; **(c)** false.
8. A debt issue sold in international markets.
9. Support of the payment mechanism, facilitating borrowing and lending, pooling risk.

Chapter 15

1. **(a)** Further sale of an already publicly traded stock; **(b)** U.S. bond issue by foreign corporation; **(c)** Bond issue by industrial company; **(d)** Bond issue by large industrial company.
2. **(a)** B; **(b)** A; **(c)** D; **(d)** C.
3. **a.** Financing of startup companies.
   b. First sale of a security to public investors.
   c. Trading of a security after it is issued.
   d. Description of a security offering filed with the SEC.
   e. Winning bidders for a new issue tend to overpay.
   f. One or a few underwriters buy an entire issue.
4. **(a)** A large issue; **(b)** a bond issue; **(c)** subsequent issue of stock; **(d)** a small private placement of bonds.
5. **(a)** False; **(b)** true; **(c)** true.
6. **(a)** 135,000 shares; **(b)** primary: 500,000 shares; secondary: 400,000 shares; **(c)** $25 or 31%, which is higher than the average underpricing.

   (d)

	Millions
Underwriting cost	$ 5.04
Administrative cost	.82
Underpricing	22.5
Total	$28.36

   Note: Calculation ignores cost of shares sold under greenshoe option.

7. **a.** Net proceeds of public issue = 10,000,000 − 150,000 − 80,000 = $9,770,000; net proceeds of private placement = $9,970,000.
   b. PV of extra interest on private placement = $\sum_{t=1}^{10} \frac{.005 \times 10{,}000{,}000}{1.085^t} = \$328{,}000$, i.e., extra cost of higher interest on private placement more than outweighs saving in issue costs. N.b. We ignore taxes.
   c. Private placement debt can be custom-tailored and the terms more easily renegotiated.
8. An underwriter building a book solicits bids from investors, but the bids are not binding and are used only as a guide to set the issue price.
9. **(a)** Number of new shares, 50,000; **(b)** Amount of new investment, $500,000; **(c)** Total value of company after issue, $4,500,000; **(d)** Total number of shares after issue, 150,000; **(e)** Stock price after issue, $4,500,000/150,000 = $30; **(f)** The opportunity to buy one share is worth $20.

Chapter 16

1. **(a)** A1, B5; A2, B4; A3, B3; A4, B1; A5, B2. **(b)** March 7 = ex-dividend date; **(c)** (.34 × 4)/80.20 = .017, or 1.7%; **(d)** (.34 × 4)/3.20 = .43 or 43%; **(e)** The price would fall to 80.20/1.1 = $72.91.
2. **(a)** .26; **(b)** .36.
3. **(a)** False; **(b)** true.
4. **a.** False. The dividend depends on past dividends and current and forecasted earnings.
   b. True. This target does reflect growth opportunities and capital expenditure requirements.
   c. False. Dividends are adjusted gradually to a target. The target is based on current or forecasted earnings multiplied by the target payout ratio.
   d. True. Dividend changes convey information to investors.
   e. False. Dividends are "smoothed." Managers rarely increase regular dividends temporarily. They may pay a special dividend, however.
   f. False. Dividends are rarely cut when repurchases are being made.

5. **a.** Reinvest 1,000 × \$.50 = \$500 in the stock. If the ex-dividend price is \$150 − \$2.50, this should involve the purchase of 500/147.50, or about 3.4 shares.
   b. Sell shares worth 1,000 × \$3 = \$3,000. If the ex-dividend price is \$200 − \$5, this should involve the sale of 3,000/195, or about 15 shares.
6. **(a)** Raise an additional £2 million by an issue of shares; **(b)** Reduce cash by \$10 million or issue new shares for \$10 million.
7. **a.** Company value is unchanged at 5,000 × 140 = \$700,000. Share price stays at \$140.
   b. The discount rate $r = (\text{DIV}_1/P_0) + g = (20/140) + .05 = .193$. The price at which shares are repurchased in year 1 is 140 × (1 + r) = 140 × 1.193 = \$167. Therefore the firm repurchases 50,000/167 = 299 shares. Total dividend payments in year 1 fall to 5,000 × 10 = \$50,000, which is equivalent to 50,000/(5000 − 299) = \$10.64 a share. Similarly, in year 2 the firm repurchases 281 shares at \$186.52 and the dividend per share increases by 11.7% to \$11.88. In each subsequent year total dividends increase by 5%, the number of shares declines by 6% and therefore dividends per share increase by 11.7%. The constant growth model gives PV share = 10.64/(.193 − .117) = \$140.
8. **a.** \$127.25.
   b. Nothing; the stock price will stay at \$130. 846,154 shares will be repurchased.
   c. The with-dividend price stays at \$130. Ex-dividend it drops to \$124.50; 883,534 shares will be issued.
9. *Current tax law:* **(a)** shouldn't care; **(b)** prefers Lo; **(c)** prefers Hi; **(d)** shouldn't care; **(e)** shouldn't care. *Same rate of tax:* An individual now shouldn't care. Otherwise preferences do not change.

Chapter 17

1. **(a)** .10*P*; **(b)** Buy 10% of B's debt + 10% of B's equity; **(c)** .10(*P* − 100); **(d)** Borrow an amount equal to 10% of B's debt and buy 10% of A's equity.
2. Note the market value of Copperhead is far in excess of its book value:

	Market Value
Common stock (8 million shares at \$2)	\$16,000,000
Short-term loans	\$ 2,000,000

   Ms. Kraft owns .625% of the firm, which proposes to increase common stock to \$17 million and cut short-term debt. Ms. Kraft can offset this by (*a*) borrowing .00625 × 1,000,000 = \$6,250, and (*b*) buying that much more Copperhead stock.
3. Expected return on assets is $r_A = .08 \times 30/80 + .16 \times 50/80 = .13$. The new return on equity will be $r_E = .13 + 20/60(.13 - .08) = .147$. If stockholders pass on more of the firm's risk to debtholders, expected return on equity will be *less* than 14.7%.
4. **a.** (i) $\beta_A = \left(\frac{D}{D+E} \times \beta_D\right) + \left(\frac{E}{D+E} \times \beta_E\right)$
   $1.0 = (.5 \times 0) + (.5 \times \beta_E)$
   $\beta_E = 2.0.$
   (ii) $\beta_D = 0$; (iii) $\beta_A = 1.0$.
   b. (i) .10.
   (ii) $r_A = \left(\frac{D}{D+E} \times r_D\right) + \left(\frac{E}{D+E} \times r_E\right)$
   $.10 = (.5 \times .05) + (.5 \times r_E)$
   $r_E = .15.$
   (iii) $r_D = .05$; (iv) $r_A = .10$.
   c. (i) 50%; (ii) 6.7 (i.e., the P/E ratio falls to offset the increase in EPS).
5. **a.**

Operating income (\$)	500	1,000	1,500	2,000
Interest (\$)	250	250	250	250
Equity earnings (\$)	250	750	1,250	1,750
Earnings per share	.33	1.00	1.67	2.33
Return on shares (%)	3.3	10	16.7	23.3

   b. $\beta_A = \left(\frac{D}{D+E} \times \beta_D\right) + \left(\frac{E}{D+E} \times \beta_E\right)$
   $.8 = (.25 \times 0) + (.75 \times \beta_E)$
   $\beta_E = 1.07$
6. **a.** True, so long as the market value of "old" debt does not change.
   b. False. MM's Proposition I says only that overall firm value ($V = D + E$) does not depend on capital structure.

c. False. Borrowing increases equity risk even if debt is default-risk-free.
d. False. Limited liability affects the relative values of debt and equity, not their sum.
e. True. Limited liability protects shareholders if the firm defaults.
f. True—but the required rate of return on equity and the firm's assets are the same only if the firm holds risk-free assets. In this case r_A, r_D, and r_E all equal the risk-free rate of interest.
g. False. The shareholders could make the same debt issue on their own account.
h. True. To put it more precisely, it assumes that the expected rate of return to equity goes up, but stockholders' required rate of return goes up proportionately. Therefore, stock price is unchanged.
i. False. The formula $r_E = r_A + (D/E)(r_A - r_D)$ does not require r_D = a constant.
j. False. The clientele has to be willing to pay extra for the debt, which it will not do if plenty of corporate debt issues are already available.

7. See Figure 17.5.
8. **(a)** $r_A = .15, r_E = .175$; **(b)** $\beta_A = .6$ (unchanged), $\beta_D = .3, \beta_E = .9$; **(c)** 18.3%.
9. **(a)** 10%; **(b)** 13.3%.
10. **(a)** Not affected; **(b)** 16 million; **(c)** $250 million; **(d)** $D/V = 160/250 = .64$; **(e)** No one.
11. **(a)** It rises by $2 per share or $30 million; **(b)** 5 million; **(c)** $250 million (unchanged); **(d)** $130/250 = .52$ (using market values); **(e)** Shareholders gain, investors in old debt lose.

Chapter 18

1. a. PV tax shield $= \dfrac{T_C(r_D D)}{1 + r_D} = \dfrac{.35(.08 \times 1000)}{1.08} = 25.93.$

   b. PV tax shield $= \displaystyle\sum_{t=1}^{5} \frac{.35(.08 \times 1000)}{(1.08)^t} = \$111.80.$

   c. PV tax shield $= T_C D = \$350.$

2. a. PV tax shield $= T_C D = \$16.$

   b. $T_C \times 20 = \$8.$

   c. New PV tax shield $= \displaystyle\sum_{t=1}^{5} \frac{.40(.08 \times 60)}{(1.08)^t} = \$7.67.$

   Therefore, company value $= 168 - 24 + 7.67 = \$151.67.$

3. a. Relative advantage of debt $= \dfrac{1 - T_p}{(1 - T_{pE})(1 - T_C)} = \dfrac{.69}{(1)(.65)} = 1.06.$

   b. Relative advantage $= .69/(.69)(.65) = 1.54.$

4. a. Direct costs of financial distress are the legal and administrative costs of bankruptcy. Indirect costs include possible delays in liquidation (Eastern Airlines) or poor investment or operating decisions while bankruptcy is being resolved. Also the *threat* of bankruptcy can lead to costs.
   b. If financial distress increases odds of default, managers' and shareholders' incentives change. This can lead to poor investment or financing decisions.
   c. See the answer to 4(*b*). Examples are the "games" described in Section 18.3.

5. Not necessarily. Announcement of bankruptcy can send a message of poor profits and prospects. Part of the share price drop can be attributed to anticipated bankruptcy costs, however.

6. A firm with no taxable income saves no taxes by borrowing and paying interest. The interest payments would simply add to its tax-loss carry-forwards. Such a firm would have little tax incentive to borrow.

7. a. Stockholders win. Bond value falls, since the value of assets securing the bond has fallen.
   b. Bondholder wins if we assume the cash is left invested in Treasury bills. The bondholder is sure to get $26 plus interest. Stock value is zero, because there is no chance that firm value can rise above $50.
   c. The bondholders lose. The firm adds assets worth $10 and debt worth $10. This would increase Circular's debt ratio, leaving the old bondholders more exposed. The old bondholders' loss is the stockholders' gain.
   d. Both bondholders and stockholders win. They share the (net) increase in firm value. The bondholders' position is not eroded by the issue of a junior security. (We assume that the preferred does not lead to still more game playing and that the new investment does not make the firm's *assets* safer or riskier.)
   e. Bondholders lose because they are at risk for longer. Stockholders win.

8. Specialized, intangible assets such as growth opportunities are most likely to lose value in financial distress. Safe, tangible assets with good secondhand markets are least likely to lose value. Costs of financial distress are thus likely to be less for, say, real estate firms or trucking companies than for advertising firms or high-tech growth companies.

9. More profitable firms have more taxable income to shield and are less likely to incur the costs of distress. Therefore the trade-off theory predicts high (book) debt ratios. In practice the more profitable companies borrow least.

10. Firms have a pecking order for new financing. Internal finance is preferred, followed by debt and

then by external equity. Each firm's observed debt ratio reflects its cumulative requirements for external finance. The more profitable companies borrow least because they have sufficient internal finance.

11. When a company issues securities, outside investors worry that management may have unfavorable information. If so the securities can be overpriced. This worry is much less with debt than equity. Debt securities are safer than equity, and their price is less affected if unfavorable news comes out later.

    A company that can borrow (without incurring substantial costs of financial distress) usually does so. An issue of equity would be read as "bad news" by investors, and the new stock could be sold only at a discount to the previous market price.

12. Financial slack is most valuable to growth companies with good but uncertain investment opportunities. Slack means that financing can be raised quickly for positive-NPV investments. But too much financial slack can tempt mature companies to overinvest. Increased borrowing can force such firms to pay out cash to investors.

Chapter 19

1. Market values of debt and equity are $D = .9 \times 75 = \$67.5$ million and $E = 42 \times 2.5 = \$105$ million. $D/V = .39$.

$\text{WACC} = .09(1 - .35).39 + .18(.61) = .1325$, or 13.25%.

   The key assumptions: stable capital structure (D/V constant); Federated will pay taxes at 35% marginal rate in all relevant future years; use WACC as discount rate for projects with same risk as average of firm's assets.

2. Step 1: $r = .09(.39) + .18(.61) = .145$.

   Step 2: $r_D = .086$, $r_E = .145 + (.145 - .086)(15/85) = .155$.

   Step 3: $\text{WACC} = .086(1 - .35).15 + .155(.85) = .14$.

3. **(a)** False; **(b)** true; **(c)** true.

4. The method values the equity of a company by discounting cash flows to stockholders at the cost of equity. See Section 4.5 for more details. The method assumes that the debt-to-equity ratio will remain constant.

5. **(a)** True; **(b)** false, if interest tax shields are valued separately; **(c)** true; **(d)** true.

6. Rule 1 assumes that debt supported by a project is paid off on a fixed schedule regardless of project performance. Rule 2 assumes that debt is rebalanced to keep the ratio of debt to project value constant.

7. Acceptance of a project triggers financing costs or benefits. Examples: interest tax shields, issue costs, subsidized financing tied to the project. Other side effects are encountered in international investment.

8. APV = base-case NPV ± PV financing side effects

   (a) $\text{APV} = 0 - .15(500{,}000) = -75{,}000$; **(b)** $\text{APV} = 0 + 175{,}000 = +175{,}000$; **(c)** $\text{APV} = 0 + 76{,}000 = +76{,}000$

9. **a.** 12%, of course.

   b. $r_E = .12 + (.12 - .075)(30/70) = .139$,

$\text{WACC} = .075(1 - .35)(.30) + .139(.70) = .112$, or 11.2%.

10. PV tax shield $= (.10/.35)576{,}000 = \$164{,}600$; $\text{APV} = 170{,}000 + 164{,}600 = \$334{,}600$.

11. **a.** Base-case $\text{NPV} = -1{,}000 + 1200/1.20 = 0$.

    b. PV tax shield $= (.35 \times .1 \times .3(1000))/1.1 = 9.55$. $\text{APV} = 0 + 9.55 = \$9.55$.

12. No. The more debt you use, the higher rate of return equity investors will require. (Lenders may demand more also.) Thus there is a hidden cost of the "cheap" debt: It makes equity more expensive.

13. The after-tax borrowing or lending rate. This assumes that the company can lend or borrow at a safe after-tax rate.

14. $\text{PV} = 16(1 - .35)/(1 + .055(1 - .35)) = \$10.04$ million.

Chapter 20

1. Call; exercise; put; European; call; assets; bondholders (lenders); assets; promised payment to bondholders.

2. Figure 20.13*a* represents a call seller; Figure 20.13*b* represents a call buyer.

3. **a.** The exercise price of the put option (i.e., you'd sell stock for the exercise price);

   b. The value of the stock (i.e., you would throw away the put and keep the stock).

4. Value of call + PV(exercise price) = value of put + value of asset (e.g., share).

   See table below.

At Maturity:	Share Price Exceeds Exercise Price		Share Price Below Exercise Price	
	Action	Value	Action	Value
Call + PV(EX)	Exercise call	Stock price	Don't exercise call	Exercise price
Put + share	Don't exercise put	Stock price	Exercise put	Exercise price

Relationship holds only for European options with same exercise price.

5. Buy a call and lend the present value of the exercise price.

6. a. Keep gold stocks and buy 6-month puts with an exercise price equal to 83.3% of the current price.

   b. Sell gold stocks, invest £485,000 for 6 months at 6%. The remaining £115,000 can be used to buy calls on the gold stocks with the same exercise price.

7. **(a)** See Figure 4; **(b)** stock price − PV(EX) = 100 − 100/1.1 = $9.09.

8.

At Maturity:	Asset Value Exceeds Loan		Asset Value Below Loan	
	Action	**Value**	**Action**	**Value**
Call on assets with exercise price = amount of loan	Exercise call	Assets − amount of loan	Don't exercise call	Zero
Common stock	Repay loan	Assets − amount of loan	Default	Zero

9. Stockholders have the option to walk away from their debts, in which case lender takes over assets. Default put is important for firms in distress (i.e., asset value low relative to amount of loan).

10. The lower bound is the option's value if it expired immediately: either zero or the stock price less the exercise price, whichever is larger. If an (American) call option's price were less than the lower bound, you could exercise immediately and make a sure profit. The upper bound is the stock price.

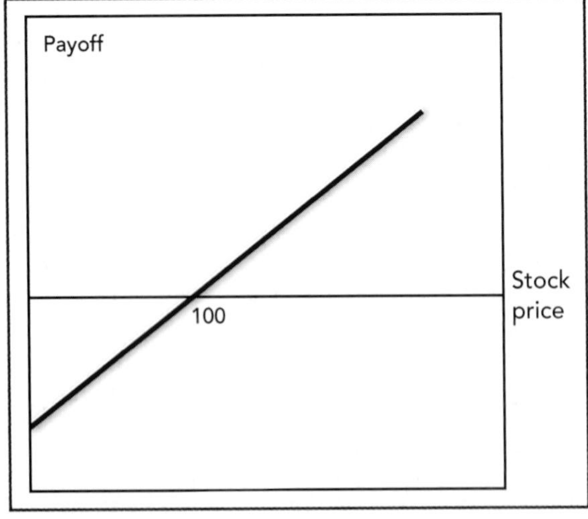

FIGURE 4

Chapter 20, Quiz question 7.

11. Figure 20.13(b) doesn't show the cost of purchasing the call. The profit from call purchase would be negative for all stock prices less than exercise price plus cost of call. Figure 20.13(a) doesn't record the proceeds from selling the call.

12. **(a)** Zero; **(b)** Stock price less the present value of the exercise price.

13. The call price **(a)** increases; **(b)** decreases; **(c)** increases; **(d)** increases; **(e)** decreases; **(f)** decreases.

14. a. All investors, however risk-averse, should value more highly an option on a volatile stock. For both Exxon Mobil and AOL the option is valueless if stock price is below the exercise price, but the option on AOL has more upside potential.

    b. Other things equal, stockholders lose and debtholders gain if the company shifts to safer assets. When the assets are risky, the default put is more valuable. Debtholders bear much of the losses if asset value declines, but shareholders get the gains if asset value increases.

Chapter 21

1. a. Using risk-neutral method, $(p \times 20) + (1 - p)(-16.7) = 1, p = .48$.

$$\text{Value of call} = \frac{(.48 \times 8) + (.52 \times 0)}{1.01} = 3.8.$$

   b. $$\text{Delta} = \frac{\text{spread of option prices}}{\text{spread of stock prices}} = \frac{8}{14.7} = .544.$$

c.

	Current Cash Flow	Possible Future Cash Flows	
Buy call	−3.8	0	+8.0
equals			
Buy .544 shares	−21.8	−18.2	+26.2
Borrow 18.0	+18.0	−18.2	−18.2
	−3.8	0	+8.0

d. Possible stock prices with call option prices in parentheses:

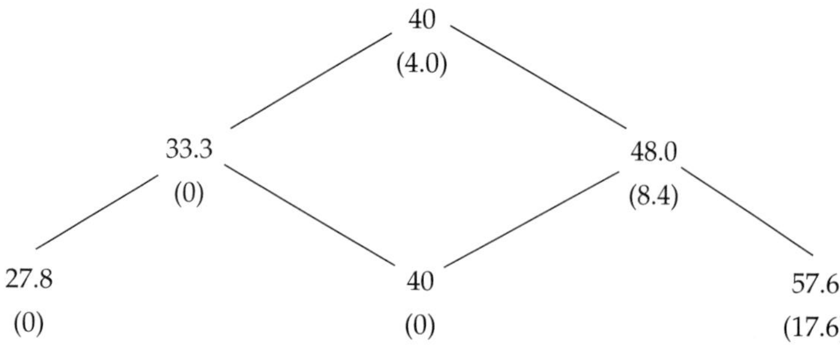

Option prices were calculated as follows:

$$\textit{Month 1:}\ \text{(i)}\ \frac{(.48 \times 0) + (.52 \times 0)}{1.01} = 0,$$

$$\text{(ii)}\ \frac{(.48 \times 17.6) + (.52 \times 0)}{1.01} = 8.4.$$

$$\textit{Month 0:}\ \frac{(.48 \times 8.4) + (.52 \times 0)}{1.01} = 4.0.$$

e. $\text{Delta} = \dfrac{\text{spread of option prices}}{\text{spread of stock prices}} = \dfrac{8.4}{14.7} = .57.$

2. The period to expiration is subdivided into an indefinitely large number of subperiods (and when there is no incentive to early exercise).

3. **(a)** No. The maximum delta is 1.0 when the ratio of stock price to exercise price is very high. **(b)** No. **(c)** Delta increases. **(d)** Delta increases.

4. Because option risk changes as time passes and the stock price changes.

5. Using the replicating portfolio method, delta = 13.33/(73.33 − 41.25) = .416.

	Current Cash Flow	Possible Future Cash Flows	
Buy call	−6.05	0	+13.33
equals			
Buy .416 shares	−22.86	+17.14	+30.48
Borrow 16.81	+16.81	−17.14	−17.14
	−6.05	0	+13.33

Using the risk-neutral method, $(p \times 33.3) + (1 - p)(-25) = 2$, $p = .463$.

$$\text{Value of call} = \frac{(.463 \times 13.33) + (.537 \times 0)}{1.02} = 6.05.$$

The put price is 9.87.

6. Using the replicating portfolio method, delta = 13.75/(68.75 − 44) = .556.

	Current Cash Flow	Possible Future Cash Flows	
Buy call	−6.59	0	+13.75
equals			
Buy .556 shares	−30.56	+24.44	+38.19
Borrow 23.97	+23.97	−24.44	−24.44
	−6.59	0	+13.75

Using the risk-neutral method, $(p \times 25) + (1 - p)(-20) = 2, p = .489$.

$$\text{Value of call} = \frac{(.489 \times 13.75) + (.511 \times 0)}{1.02} = 6.59.$$

Lower risk means less upside for the call option. Thus option value falls.

7. **a.** Delta = 100/(200 − 50) = .667.

b.

	Current Cash Flow	Possible Future Cash Flows	
Buy call	−36.36	0	+100
equals			
Buy .667 shares	−66.67	+33.33	+133.33
Borrow 30.30	+30.30	−33.33	−33.33
	−36.36	0	+100

c. $(p \times 100) + (1 - p)(-50) = 10, p = .4.$

d. $$\text{Value of call} = \frac{(.4 \times 100) + (.6 \times 0)}{1.10} = 36.36.$$

e. No. The true probability of a price rise is almost certainly higher than the risk-neutral probability, but it does not help to value the option.

8. **a.** Call value = $3.44.
   b. Put value = call value + PV(exercise price) − stock price = $1.67.

9. True; as the stock price rises, the risk of the option falls.

10. **a.** You would exercise early if the stock price was sufficiently low. There may be little opportunity for further gains in the option value and it would be better to invest the exercise price to earn interest.
    b. Don't exercise early. The interest savings from delaying payment of the exercise price is larger than the dividend foregone.
    c. If the stock price and dividend are sufficiently high, it may pay to exercise early to capture the dividend.

Chapter 22

1. Expansion option; abandonment option; timing option (i.e., option to postpone investment); flexible production (i.e., option to exchange one asset for another).

2. **a.** Increase value (unless the cash flows from the Mark II needed to be discounted at a higher rate).
   b. Increase value.
   c. Reduce value.

3. **a.** Call (i.e., expansion option); **(b)** option to exchange one asset for another; **(c)** call on oil price; **(d)** timing option (Forest has an in-the-money call); **(e)** call (option to make subsequent investment in China); **(f)** put (i.e., abandonment option); **(g)** timing option (owner has an in-the-money call).

4. **a.** You can't use *any* single discount rate for option payoffs. The risk of an option changes as asset price changes and time passes.
   b. The risky *asset* may be worth less as a result, but option owner can capitalize from up moves while not losing from down moves.
   c. Option value depends on value of underlying asset. DCF is needed to get this value.

5. **a.** You learn more about land prices and best use of the land.
   b. By developing immediately, you capture rents immediately.

Chapter 23

1. **a.** (i) 0; (ii) 0; (iii) 0; (iv) \$10; (v) \$20.
   b.

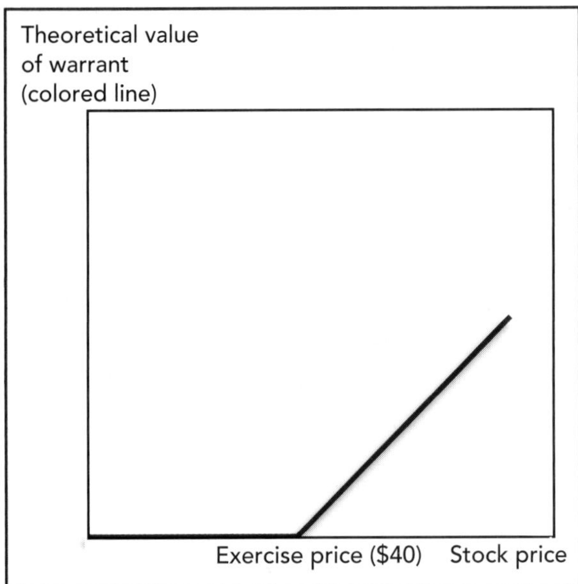

   c. Buy the warrant and exercise, then sell the stock.

   Net gain $= -5 - 40 + 60 = +\$15$.

2. **(a)** No; **(b)** no; **(c)** $1/3 \times 70 = \$23.33$; **(d)** no, worse off; **(e)** zero; **(f)** more; **(g)** (i) less, (ii) less, (iii) more, (iv) more, (v) more; **(h)** when the dividends on the stock outweigh the interest on the exercise price; **(i)** more.
3. **(a)** \$15,000; **(b)** \$29,000.
4. **(a)** $1{,}000/47 = 21.28$; **(b)** $1{,}000/50 = \$20.00$; **(c)** $21.28 \times 41.50 = \$883.12$, or 88.31%; **(d)** $650/21.28 = \$30.55$; **(e)** no (not if the investor is free to convert immediately); **(f)** \$12.22, i.e., $(910 - 650)/21.28$; **(g)** $(47/41.50) - 1 = .13$, or 13%; **(h)** when the price reaches 102.75% of par.
5. **(a)** \$7.00; **(b)** \$7.05.
6. **(a)** False; **(b)** true; **(c)** false; **(d)** false; **(e)** true; **(f)** true.

Chapter 24

1 **a.** Figure 5 shows that an increase in the demand for capital increases investment and savings. The rate of interest also rises.
  b. Figure 6 shows that an increase in the supply of capital also increases investment and savings. The rate of interest falls.

2. There are 20 coupon payments of 6.9375 plus a principal payment of 100. With a discount rate of $8.04/2 = 4.02\%$, PV is

$$\frac{6.9375}{1.0402} + \frac{6.9375}{1.0402^2} + \cdots + \frac{106.9375}{1.0402^{20}} = 139.57$$

3. **a** The Norwegian bond has the highest yield (5.6%) and the Finnish bond has the lowest (4.5%).
   b. The Finnish bond has the longest duration (7.9 years) and the Norwegian has the shortest (7.1 years).

4. **a.** $\text{PV} = \dfrac{50}{1 + r_1} + \dfrac{1{,}050}{(1 + r_2)^2}$
   b. $\text{PV} = \dfrac{50}{1 + y} + \dfrac{1{,}050}{(1 + y)^2}$
   c. Less (it is between the 1-year and 2-year spot rates).
   d. Yield to maturity; spot rate.

5. **a.** Fall (e.g., 1-year 10% bond is worth $110/1.1 = 100$ if $r = 10\%$ and is worth $110/1.15 = 95.65$ if $r = 15\%$).
   b. Less (e.g., see 5(*a*)).
   c. Less (e.g., with $r = 5\%$, 1-year 10% bond is worth $110/1.05 = 104.76$).
   d. Higher (e.g., if $r = 10\%$, 1-year 10% bond is worth $110/1.1 = 100$, while 1-year 8% bond is worth $108/1.1 = 98.18$).
   e. No, low-coupon bonds have longer durations (unless there is only one period to maturity) and are therefore more volatile (e.g., if r falls from 10% to 5%, the value of a 2-year 10% bond rises from 100 to 109.3 (a rise of 9.3%). The value of a 2-year 5% bond rises from 91.3 to 100 (a rise of 9.5%).

6. **a.** $(100/90.826)^{(1/2)} - 1 = .0493$, or 4.93%;
   $(100/73.565)^{(1/7)} - 1 = .0448$, or 4.48%;
   $(100/70.201)^{(1/8)} - 1 = .0452$, or 4.52%;
   $(100/67.787)^{(1/9)} - 1 = .0441$, or 4.41%;
   $(100/29.334)^{(1/30)} - 1 = .0417$, or 4.17%.
   b. Downward.
   c. Higher (the yield is a complicated average of the different spot rates).
   d. $73.565/70.201 - 1 = .0479$, or 4.79%; $70.201/67.787 - 1 = .0356$, or 3.56%.

7. **a.** Price today is 108.425; price after 1 year is 106.930.
   b. Return $= (106.930 + 8)/108.425 - 1 = .06$, or 6%.
   c. If a bond's yield to maturity is unchanged, the return to the bondholder is equal to the yield.

8. **a.** False. Duration depends on the coupon as well as the maturity.
   b. False. Given the yield to maturity, volatility is proportional to duration.
   c. True. A lower coupon rate means longer duration and therefore higher volatility.
   d. False. A higher interest rate reduces the relative present value of (distant) principal repayments.

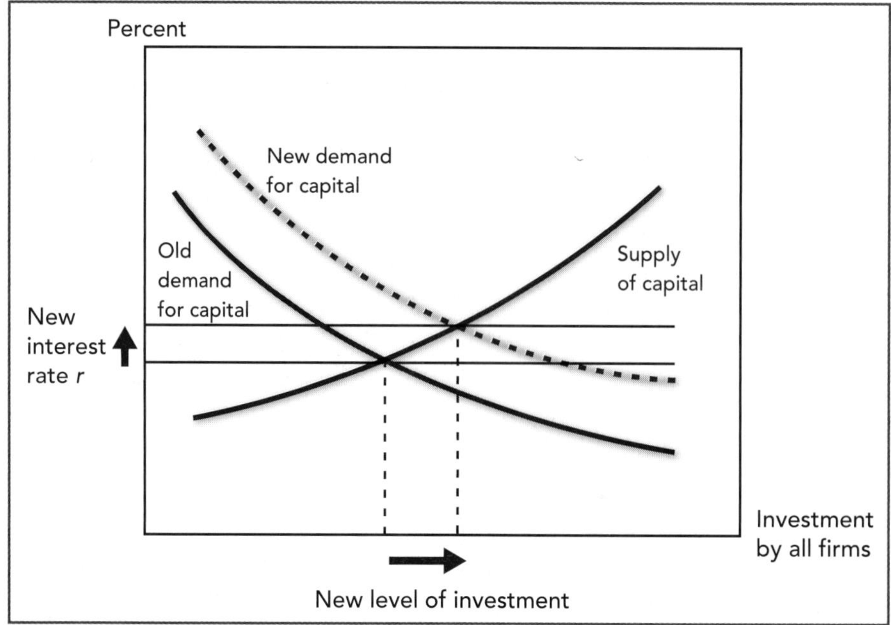

FIGURE 5

Chapter 24, Quiz question 1(*a*).

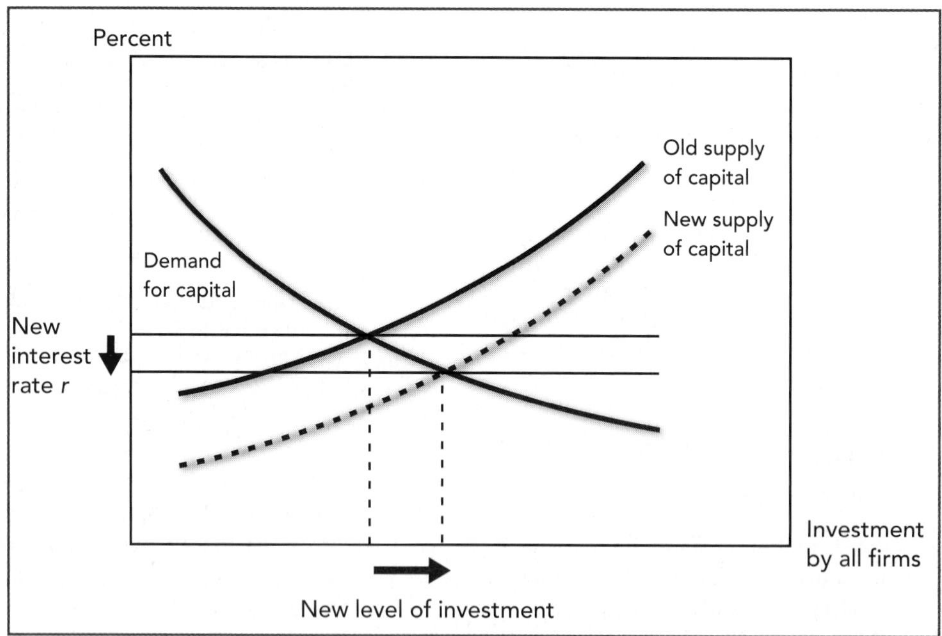

FIGURE 6

Chapter 24, Quiz question 1(*b*).

9.

	Year	C_t		$PV(C_t)$	Proportion of Total Value		Proportion × Time
Security A	1	40		37.04	.359		.359
	2	40		34.29	.333		.666
	3	40		31.75	.308		.924
		V	=	103.08	1.0	Duration =	1.949 years
Security B	1	20		18.52	.141		.141
	2	20		17.15	.131		.262
	3	120		95.26	.728		2.184
		V	=	130.93	1.0	Duration =	2.587 years
Security C	1	10		9.26	.088		.088
	2	10		8.57	.082		.164
	3	110		87.32	.830		2.490
		V	=	105.15	1.0	Duration =	2.742 years

Volatilities: A, 1.80; B, 2.40; C, 2.49.

10. **a.** $(1 + r_2)^2 = (1 + r_1)(1 + f_2)$
$1.03^2 = 1.01 \times (1 + f_2)$
$f_2 = .05$, or 5%.
b. The expected 1-year spot rate at time 1 equals the forward rate f_2.
c. Against (unless one believes that investors have generally expected interest rates to rise).
d. The forward rate equals the expected spot rate *plus* a liquidity premium.
e. Long-term bonds.
f. Short-term bonds.

11. **a.** Aaa, Aa, A, and Baa
b. (i) Increase; (ii) increase; (iii) increase; (iv) increase.

12. Option to put (i.e., sell) company assets to the bondholders for the face value of the debt.

13. Value an option to put (i.e., sell) the company's assets to the government for the amount of the loan.

Chapter 25

1. **(a)** High-grade utility bonds; **(b)** industrial holding companies; **(c)** industrial bonds; **(d)** railroads; **(e)** asset-backed security.

2.
   - Indenture or trust deeds—agreement between the borrower and a trust company representing bondholders.
   - Debentures—long-term unsecured bonds.
   - Mortgage bonds—debt secured by property.
   - Call provision—company has right to call and pay off debt.
   - Sinking fund—provision for repayment of part or most of principal prior to maturity.
   - Foreign bond—bond sold in another country's market.
   - Negative pledge clause—if secured debt is issued, existing debt will also become secured.

3. **(a)** Decreases; **(b)** impossible to say; **(c)** impossible to say. For example, if the bond has a high coupon and is sold at a premium at issue, the prospect of drawings at par could decrease value. For an original-issue discount bond, the effect could be reversed.

4. **a.** You would like an issue of junior debt.
b. You prefer it not to do so (unless it is also junior debt). The existing property may not be sufficient to pay off your debt.

5. **(a)** First Boston, Goldman Sachs, Shearson Lehman, Stifel Nicholaus; **(b)** Continental Bank; **(c)** \$967.25; **(d)** registered; **(e)** 104.26 (percent of par); **(f)** no.

6. **a.** Issue price + approximately 1 month's interest = 976.00+ 95/12 = \$983.92.
b. December 1, 1986; \$47.50.
c. 2016. The sinking fund was designed to pay off all but \$8.64 million of principal by that date. The company must pay off the remaining \$8.64 million.
d. 2002.

7. The 7.8 percent rate is actually 3.9 percent semiannually. The effective annual rate is $1.039^2 - 1 = .0795$, slightly higher than the London quote. International bonds pay interest annually.

8. Private placements: typically have simpler loan agreements—which may nevertheless contain "custom" features; have more stringent covenants; are more easily renegotiated.

9. **a.** False. Lenders usually retain some recourse; e.g., they may demand a completion guarantee.
b. True, but some new securities (e.g., zero-coupon bonds) survive even when the original motive for issuing them disappears.

c. False. The borrower has the option.
d. True. But debt issues with weak covenants suffered in such takeovers.
e. True. The costs of renegotiation are less for private placements.

10. Chapter 7 usually leads to liquidation. Chapter 11 "protects" the firm from its creditors while a reorganization plan is developed.
11. **(a)** False; **(b)** true; **(c)** true, except for costs incurred by the bankruptcy court or trustee; **(d)** true; **(e)** false. Tax-loss carry-forwards do not survive liquidation.
12. There is always a chance that the company can recover, allowing creditors to be paid off and leaving something for shareholders. Also, shareholders may retain some claims on the firm after reorganization in Chapter 11.

Chapter 26

1. *A*, *c*; *B*, *d* or *i*; *C*, *b* or *e*; *D*, *f*; *E*, *a*; *F*, *h*; *G*, *g*.
2. *a*, *b*, *d*, *f*, and *h* (though there may be other ways to reduce AMT).
3. **a.** The lessor must charge enough to cover the present value of the costs of owning and operating the asset over its expected economic life. In a competitive leasing market the present value of rentals cannot exceed the present value of costs. The competitive rental payment ends up equal to the lessor's equivalent annual cost.
   b. The user's equivalent annual cost is the annual cost to the user of owning and operating the asset. If the operating lease rate is less than this cost, it pays to lease.
4. **(a)** True; **(b)** true; **(c)** true, but compare after-tax rates; **(d)** true; **(e)** true; **(f)** true; **(g)** true.
5. The present value of depreciation tax shields on the \$3,000 desk, using the 5-year schedule from Table 6.4, is

$$\begin{aligned}\text{PV (at 9 percent)} &= .35 \times \text{PV (5-year schedule)} \\ &\quad \times 3{,}000 \\ &= \$832.\end{aligned}$$

   After-tax administrative costs are 400(1 − .35) = \$260 per year for 6 years. If the first costs are incurred immediately, their present value is \$1,271. Thus the present value of all costs is \$3,000 − 832 + 1,271 = \$3,439. The break-even lease rate is about \$703 after tax. In other words, the present value of six payments of \$703, with the first payment due immediately, is about \$3,439. The breakeven rate pretax is \$703/.65 = \$1,082.
6. Administrative costs drop to \$200 per year. Moreover, the lease payments are a fixed commitment of the blue-chip company. The six lease payments are discounted at the after-tax rate at which Acme would lend money; that is, 6(1 − .35) = 3.9%. The break-even lease rate falls to about \$514 after tax. The pretax break-even rate is \$791.
7. **a.** \$59,307; the present value of the lease cash flows from $t = 1$ to $t = 3$, discounted at $r(1 - T_c) = .10(1 - .35) = .065$.
   b. \$62,000 − 59,307 = 2,693.
   c. It should not invest. The lease's value of +2,693 does not offset the machine's negative NPV. It would be happy to sign the same lease on a more attractive asset.

Chapter 27

1. **(a)** True; **(b)** true; **(c)** false (depends on coupon); **(d)** false; **(e)** false; **(f)** false; **(g)** true.
2. Since the futures price has risen, your sale is now showing a loss. Your broker will ask you for money.
3. $$\frac{\text{Value of future}}{1.049} = 95 - 4.$$
   Value of future = 95.46.
4. $$\frac{2{,}408}{1.12} = 2{,}550 + 100 - \text{PV (convenience yield)}.$$
   PV (convenience yield) = \$500.
5. **a.** A shortage of heating oil increases net convenience yield and reduces the futures price relative to spot price.
   b. Spot and futures prices decrease. The futures price rises relative to spot because convenience yield falls and storage costs rise.
6. Storage costs are likely to be high. Other things equal, firms will prefer to hold the future rather than the spot commodity, and net convenience yield will be low.
7. **(a)** Profit; **(b)** If the bank took out a new 4-year swap, it would need to pay an extra \$.25 million a year. At the new interest rate of 6.5%, the extra payment has a present value of \$856,000. This is the amount that the bank should charge to terminate.
8. Basis risk means that the hedging instrument is imperfectly correlated with the risk to be hedged. It is highest in *a*, because Disney stock has considerable nonmarket risk. In *b* basis risk is likely to be small, and in *c* it should disappear.
9. Sell short \$1.2 million of the market portfolio. In practice rather than "sell the market" you would sell futures on \$1.2 million of the market index.
10. **(a)** Sell; **(b)** sell 3-month futures on Italian government bonds.

11. a. The calculations for A and C are given for Quiz question 9, Chapter 24. For B, the calculations change to

Year	C_T	$PV(C_T)$	Proportion	Proportion × Time
1	120	111.11	1.0	1.0
2	0	0	0	0
3	0	0	0	0
		V = 111.11	1.0	Duration = 1.0 years

b. A has a duration of 1.949 years. So does a portfolio with 45.5% invested in B and 54.5% invested in C. To hedge A sell $4.55 million of B and $5.45 million of C.

c. Sell $5.13 million of A, borrow 10 − 5.13 = $4.87 million short-term. Alternatively, sell $3.65 million of C and borrow $6.35 million.

Chapter 28

1. a. 9.139.
   b. 9.1865 pesos = $1.
   c. premium.
   d. Using the 1-year forward rate, (9.924 − 9.139)/9.924 = .0791, or 7.91%.
   e. By interest rate parity $1 + r_{peso} = 1.05 \times 12.36/9.84$; $r_{peso} = .126$, or 12.6%.
   f. 9.307 pesos = $1.
   g. If real exchange rate is constant, expected inflation in Mexico over 3 months must be 9.307/9.139 − 1 = .018, or 1.8%, greater in Mexico than in the USA (equivalent to $1.018^4 - 1 =$ .076, or 7.6%, a year).
2. a. The interest rate differential equals the forward premium or discount, i.e.,

$$\frac{1 + r_x}{1 + r_\$} = \frac{f_{x/\$}}{s_{x/\$}}.$$

   b. The expected change in the spot rate equals the forward premium or discount, i.e.,

$$\frac{f_{x/\$}}{s_{x/\$}} = \frac{E(s_{x/\$})}{s_{x/\$}}$$

   c. Prices of goods in different countries are equal when measured in terms of the same currency. It follows that the expected change in the spot rate equals the expected inflation differential; i.e.,

$$\frac{E(1 + i_x)}{E(1 + i_\$)} = \frac{E(s_{x/\$})}{s_{x/\$}}.$$

   d. Expected real interest rates in different countries are equal; i.e.,

$$\frac{1 + r_x}{1 + r_\$} = \frac{E(1 + i_x)}{E(1 + i_\$)}$$

3. a. 2,419 × 1.3/1.02 = R3,083 = $1.
   b. Real value of rupiah fell by 3,083/8,325 − 1 = .63, or 63%.

4.

	1 Month	3 Months	1 Year
Dollar interest rate, %	3.60	3.70	3.70
Peso interest rate, %	9.55	9.99	11.90
Forward pesos per dollar	53.85	54.40	57.844
Forward premium on peso (% per year)	5.6	−5.7	−6.0

5. *b.*
6. Zero, of course. You don't need to do any calculations.
7. It can borrow the present value of €1 million, sell the euros in the spot market, and invest the proceeds in an 8-year dollar loan.
8. **(a)** $(100/1.03)/(100/1.0365^2) - 1 = .043$, or 4.3%; **(b)** 1.043 × 115/120.7 − 1 = −.006, or −.6%; **(c)** 1.043 × 116.52/120.7 − 1 = .007 or .7%.
9. a. NPV = 6.61 × 1.2 = $7.94 million.

b.

Year	0	1	2	3	4	5
Forward rate	1.2	1.223	1.246	1.269	1.293	1.318
$ million	−96	12.23	24.91	29.19	34.92	32.94

c. It doesn't. The company can always hedge against a fall in the euro.

Chapter 29

1. **(a)** 5,114/(5114 + 6,832) = .43; **(b)** (1,674 + 859)/351 = 7.2; **(c)** 3,288/2,704 = 1.2; **(d)** (115 + 1,247)/2,704 = .5; **(e)** (1,674 − 483)/15,980 = .07; **(f)** ((1,499 + 1,329) ÷ 2)/(12,035 ÷ 365) = 42.9; **(g)** 840/((6,832 + 7,173) ÷ 2) = .120; **(h)** 263/840 = .31.
2. The illogical ratios are *a, b, c, f,* and *i*. The correct definitions are

$$\text{Debt–equity ratio} = \frac{\text{long-term debt + value of leases}}{\text{equity}}$$

$$\text{Return on equity} = \frac{\text{earnings available for common}}{\text{average equity}}$$

$$\text{Payout ratio} = \frac{\text{dividend}}{\text{earnings per share}}$$

$$\text{Current ratio} = \frac{\text{current assets}}{\text{current liabilities}}$$

$$\text{Average collection period} = \frac{\text{average receivables}}{\text{sales} \div 365}$$

3. **(a)** False; **(b)** true; **(c)** false; **(d)** false; **(e)** false—it will tend to increase the price–earnings multiple.
4. **(a)** Shipping company; **(b)** United Foods; **(c)** paper mill; **(d)** mail order company; **(e)** Fledgling Electronics.
5. $365,000; 12.2.
6. **(a)** 12%; **(b)** 16%.
7. .25.
8. 3.65%; .73.
9. **(a)** 1.47; **(b)** Net working capital = 40. Total capitalization = 540. Debt to total capitalization = .52.
10. $10 million.
11. $82 million.
12. The return on equity is higher when the return on assets exceeds the debt interest rate.
13. **a.** False (it is a process of deciding which risks to take).
    b. False (financial planning is concerned with possible surprises as well as expected outcomes).
    c. True (financial planning considers both the investment and financing decisions).
    d. False (a typical horizon for long-term planning is 5 years).
    e. True (perfect accuracy is unlikely to be obtainable, but the firm needs to produce the best possible consistent forecasts).
    f. False (excessive detail distracts attention from the crucial decisions).
14. **(a)** $2,900,000; **(b)** $225,000; **(c)** .25.
15. Archimedes will earn $550 and invest $320 to expand assets. Additional borrowing is $120, so retained earnings is $320 − 120 = $200. The residual dividend is $550 − 200 = $350.
16. **(a)** 8.6%; **(b)** 13.75%.

Chapter 30

1. **a.** Long-term financing, cumulative capital requirements, marketable securities
   b. Cash, cash, cash balance, marketable securities
   c. Trial, error, financial models
2.

Cash	Working Capital
1. $2 million decline	$2 million decline
2. $2,500 increase	Unchanged
3. $5,000 decline	Unchanged
4. Unchanged	$1 million increase
5. Unchanged	Unchanged
6. $5 million increase	Unchanged

3. **(a)** Inventories go up (use). **(b)** Accounts receivable go up (use). **(c)** No change shown on the firm's books. **(d)** Increase in cash (source) and reduction in assets. A loss of $100,000 is deducted from retained earnings. **(e)** Cash declines (use) and equity declines. **(f)** Cash unchanged, although net working capital increases (the debt issue is a source of *funds*).
4. Month 3: 18 + (.5 × 90) + (.3 × 120) + (.2 × 100) − $119,000.

   Month 4: 14 + (.5 × 70) + (.3 × 90) + (.2 × 120) = $100,000.
5. **(a)** 19.2, 16.8, 15, 13.2, 12, 12; **(b)** 19.2, 23.2, 20.6, 18.2, 16.4, 16.

6. **a.** Table 30.2: Bank loans = 3, Cash = 8, Current assets = 68, Current liabilities = 30, Total assets = Total liabilities and net worth = 118. Table 30.4: Repaid short-term bank loan = 2, Increase in cash balance = 4. Tables 30.5 and 30.6 unchanged.
   b. Table 30.2: Long-term debt = 22, Gross investment = 82, Net fixed assets = 62, Cash = 3, Total assets = Total liabilities and net worth = 125. Table 30.4: Issued long-term debt = 17, Total sources = 41, Invested in fixed assets = 26, Total uses = 42, Increases in cash balance = −1. Table 30.5: Fixed and Total assets change as in Table 30.2, as do Long term debt and Total liabilities and net worth. Table 30.6: same changes as in Table 30.4, except Increase in net working capital = 6.
   c. Table 30.3: Operating costs = 289, Pretax income = 56, Net income = 28, Retained earnings = 27. Table 30.2: Net worth = 92, Total liabilities and net worth = Total assets = 131; Inventory = 22.5, Cash = 23.5. Table 30.5: Net worth = 92, Long-term liabilities and net worth = Total assets = 104, Net working capital = 54. Table 30.6: Net income = 28, increase in Net working capital = 24.
   d. Table 30.7: Third quarter, Total collections = 120.1, Ending receivables = 26.6. Fourth quarter, Total collections = 129.5, Ending receivables = 28.1. Table 30.8, Third quarter: Sources minus uses and Cash at end of period increase by 11.6, Cumulative financing required decreases by 11.6. Fourth quarter: Sources minus uses increase by 1.5, Cumulative financing required decreases by 13.1 to −12.6.
   e. Table 30.8: Labor, etc. = 26, Sources minus uses decrease by 4 in each quarter. Cumulative financing required decreases by 4 in first quarter, 8 in second, etc.
   f. Table 30.8: Other sources of cash increase by 10 in the second quarter, increasing Sources minus uses and decreasing Cumulative financing required.
   g. Table 30.8: Minimum operating cash balance = 2, Cumulative financing required decreases by 2 in all quarters.
7. **(a)** True; **(b)** false (borrower has a call); **(c)** true; **(d)** false (100/90 − 1 = .111, or 11.1%); **(e)** true.
8. **(a)** Line of credit; **(b)** commitment fee; **(c)** floating charge; **(d)** collateral; **(e)** warehouse receipt; **(f)** commercial paper; **(g)** medium-term notes.

Chapter 31

1. **a.** Payment float = $25,000. Availability float = $75,000.
   b. It can earn interest on these funds.
   c. Payment float increases. The bank's gross ledger balance and available balance increase by the same amount.
2. **a.** The $.40 per check fee is cheaper at 300 × .40 = $120 per day. The cost of putting up $800,000 of compensating balances is .09 × 800,000 = $72,000 per year, or 72,000/365 = $197 per day.
   b. The lock-box system costs $120 per day, or $43,800 per year. You would need $486,700 additional cash to generate this much interest. Thus, the lock-box system must generate at least this much cash. The cash flow is 300 × 1,500 = $450,000 per day. Thus the lock box must speed up average collection time by 486,700/450,000 = 1.08 days.
3. Payment float; availability float; net float; concentration banking; FEDWIRE; CHIPS; lock-box banking.
4. The formula for optimal order size is

$$Q = \sqrt{(2 \times \text{sales} \times \text{cost per order})/\text{carrying cost}}$$
$$= \sqrt{(2 \times 216 \times 2)/6} = \sqrt{144} = 12 \text{ books.}$$

   Everyman should place 216/12 = 18 orders a year and its average inventory should be 12/2 = 6 books.
5. The formula gives

$$Q = \sqrt{\begin{array}{l}(2 \times \text{annual cash disbursements} \\ \times \text{ cost per sale of securities})/\text{interest rate}\end{array}}$$
$$= \sqrt{(2 \times 20{,}000 \times 2)/.02} = \sqrt{4{,}000{,}000}$$
$$= \$2{,}000.$$

   Everyman should sell securities 20,000/2,000 = 10 times a year and its average cash balance should be 2,000/2 = $1,000.
6. **(a)** Less; **(b)** less; **(c)** invest the same amount; **(d)** more.
7. Price = 100 − (182/360)1.75 = 99.115. Compound annual return $=(100/99.115)^2 - 1 = .0179$, or 1.79%.
8. **(a)** Repurchase agreements; **(b)** commercial paper; **(c)** finance company commercial paper; **(d)** medium-term notes; **(e)** 3-month bills; **(f)** Treasury bills; **(g)** Treasury bills.
9. Only 30% of the floating-rate preferred dividend is taxed versus 100% of bond interest. The fixed-dividend preferred also has this advantage but its price fluctuates more than the floating-rate preferred's.

Chapter 32

1. **a.** 1% of $1,000 = $10.
   b. 1% for 30 days = 12.2% per annum simple interest or 12.9% compound interest.
   c. (i) Shorter; (ii) longer; (iii) shorter.
2. **a.** Due lag decreases, therefore pay lag decreases; **b.** Due lag increases, therefore pay lag increases; **c.** Terms lag increases, therefore pay lag increases.

3. Open account, commercial draft, shipping documents, trade acceptance, the customer's, banker's acceptance, letter of credit, the customer's, his or her own, letter of credit, shipping documents, shipping documents.
4. Reject because PV of Q's order = $(.75 \times 50)/1.10^{1/2} - 40 = -\$4.25$ per iron, or $-\$4,250$ in total.
5. **a.** Expected profit = $p(1{,}200 - 1{,}050) - 1{,}050(1 - p) = 0$

$$p = .875$$

Therefore, grant credit if probability of payment exceeds 87.5%.

b. Expected profit from selling to slow payer:

$.8(150) - .2(1050) = -90$. Break-even point for credit check: $(.05 \times 90 \times \text{units}) - 12 = 0$. Units $= 2.67$.

6. Total expected profit on initial order $= -40 + .8[(p_2 \times 200) - 1{,}000(1 - p_2)]/1.2 = 0$

$$p_2 = .88, \text{ or } 88\%.$$

7. **(a)** False; **(b)** true; **(c)** false; **(d)** false—should be collection agency or attorney; **(e)** true.

Chapter 33

1. **(a)** Horizontal; **(b)** conglomerate; **(c)** vertical; **(d)** conglomerate.
2. *a* and *d*; *c* can also make sense, although merging is not the only way to redeploy excess cash.
3. **(a)** \$5 million (We assume that the \$500,000 saving is an after-tax figure.); **(b)** \$4 million; **(c)** \$7.5 million; **(d)** +\$1 million; **(e)** −\$2.5 million.
4. a, b.
5. **(a)** True; **(b)** false; **(c)** false; **(d)** true; **(e)** false (They may produce gains, but "large" is stretching it.); **(f)** false; **(g)** true.
6. Such companies are tempted to undertake negative-NPV investments. If they do, a bidder may try to take over and force a cutback of investment.
7. **a.** Any premium paid by the bidder over the book value of the target's equity is reflected in the bidder's balance sheet, e.g., it is shown as "goodwill."
   b. The bidder offers to buy the target's stock directly from its shareholders.
   c. The target's stockholders can purchase additional shares at a bargain price.
   d. The target purchases shares held by the bidder; the bidder agrees to go away.
   e. The target frustrates a hostile bidder by agreeing to merge with a friendlier and more compatible suitor.

Chapter 34

1. **a.** Purchase of a business using mostly debt financing. The company goes private. Management is given a substantial equity stake.
   b. An LBO undertaken by management.
   c. A parent company creates a new company with part of its assets and operations. Shares in the new business are distributed to the parent's stockholders.
   d. Like a spin-off, but shares in the new business are sold to investors.
   e. Sale of specific assets rather than entire firm. A company borrows to repurchase a large fraction of its shares. Like an LBO, except that the company remains public.
   f. A government-owned business is sold to private investors.
   g. A company moves to a much higher debt ratio. Proceeds of additional borrowing are paid out to stockholders.
2. **(a)** True; **(b)** false; **(c)** false; **(d)** true; **(e)** true; **(f)** false; **(g)** false.
3. Increased efficiency, broader share ownership, and revenue for the government.
4. **a.** Internal capital markets often misallocate capital. The market values of the conglomerate's divisions can't be observed separately, so it's hard to set incentives and to reward risk-taking.
   b. In a smaller, developing economy, size may give easier access to capital markets and make it easier to attract professional management. It may also give political power. An internal capital market may be helpful when external markets are undeveloped or inefficient.
5. In Germany, banks own large, often controlling stakes in nonfinancial corporations. In the U.S. this is not allowed. In Japan, banks play central roles in keiretsus, groups of companies linked by cross-ownership.
6. Temporary conglomerates, such as LBO funds, purchase businesses in different industries but not to invest and manage for the long run. The objective is to buy, fix, and sell.

GLOSSARY*

A

Abnormal return Part of return that is not due to systematic influences, e.g., marketwide price movements.

Absolute priority Rule in bankruptcy proceedings whereby senior creditors are required to be paid in full before junior creditors receive any payment.

Accelerated depreciation Any *depreciation* method that produces larger deductions for depreciation in the early years of a project's life.

Accounts payable (payables, trade debt) Money owed to suppliers.

Accounts receivable (receivables, trade credit) Money owed by customers.

Accrued interest Interest that has been earned but not yet paid.

ACH *Automated Clearing House.*

Acid-test ratio *Quick ratio.*

Adjusted present value (APV) *Net present value* of an asset if financed solely by equity plus the *present value* of any financing side effects.

ADR *American depository receipt.*

Adverse selection A situation in which a pricing policy causes only the less desirable customers to do business, e.g., a rise in insurance prices that leads only the worst risks to buy insurance.

Agency theory Theory of the relationship between a principal, e.g., a shareholder, and an agent of the principal, e.g., the company's manager.

Aging schedule Record of the length of time that *accounts receivable* have been outstanding.

All-or-none underwriting An arrangement whereby a security issue is canceled if the *underwriter* is unable to resell the entire issue.

American depository receipt (ADR) A security issued in the United States to represent shares of a foreign company.

American option *Option* that can be exercised any time before the final exercise date (cf. *European option*).

Amex American Stock Exchange.

Amortization (1) Repayment of a loan by installments; (2) allowance for *depreciation.*

Annual percentage rate (APR) Annual interest rate calculated using *simple interest.*

Annuity Investment that produces a level stream of cash flows for a limited number of periods.

Annuity due *Annuity* whose payments occur at the start of each period.

Annuity factor *Present value* of $1 paid for each of t periods.

**Italicized* words are listed elsewhere in the glossary.

Anticipation Arrangements whereby customers who pay before the final date may be entitled to deduct a normal rate of interest.

Appraisal rights A right of shareholders in a *merger* to demand the payment of a fair price for their shares, as determined independently.

Appropriation request Formal request for funds for a capital investment project.

APR *Annual percentage rate.*

APT Arbitrage pricing theory.

APV *Adjusted present value.*

Arbitrage Purchase of one security and simultaneous sale of another to give a risk-free profit.

"Arbitrage" or "risk arbitrage" Often used loosely to describe the taking of offsetting positions in related securities, e.g., at the time of a takeover bid.

Articles of incorporation Legal document establishing a corporation and its structure and purpose.

Asian currency units Dollar deposits held in Singapore or other Asian centers.

Asian option *Option* based on the average price of the asset during the life of the option.

Ask price (offer price) Price at which a dealer is willing to sell (cf. *bid price*).

Asset-backed securities Securities issued by a special purpose company that holds a package of low-risk assets whose cash flows are sufficient to service the *bonds.*

Auction-rate preferred A variant of *floating-rate preferred* stock where the dividend is reset every 49 days by auction.

Authorized share capital Maximum number of shares that a company can issue, as specified in the firm's *articles of incorporation.*

Automated Clearing House (ACH) Private electronic system run by banks for high-volume, low-value payments.

Availability float Checks deposited by a company that have not yet been cleared.

Aval Bank guarantee for debt purchased by *forfaiter.*

B

BA *Banker's acceptance.*

Backwardation Condition in which *spot price* of commodity exceeds price of *future* (cf. *contango*).

Balloon payment Large final payment (e.g., when a loan is repaid in installments).

Banker's acceptance (BA) Written demand that has been accepted by a bank to pay a given sum at a future date (cf. *trade acceptance*).

Barrier option *Option* whose existence depends on asset price hitting some specified barrier (cf. *down-and-out option, down-and-in option*).

Basis point (bp) 0.01 percent.

Basis risk Residual risk that results when the two sides of a hedge do not move exactly together.

Bearer security Security for which primary evidence of ownership is possession of the certificate (cf. *registered security*).

Bear market Widespread decline in security prices (cf. *bull market*).

Benchmark maturity Maturity of a newly issued Treasury bond.

Benefit–cost ratio One plus *profitability index.*

Best-efforts underwriting An arrangement whereby *underwriters* do not commit themselves to selling a security issue but promise only to use best efforts.

Beta Measure of *market risk.*

Bid price Price at which a dealer is willing to buy (cf. *ask price*).

Bill of exchange General term for a document demanding payment.

Bill of lading Document establishing ownership of goods in transit.

Blue-chip company Large and creditworthy company.

Blue-sky laws State laws covering the issue and trading of securities.

Boilerplate Standard terms and conditions, e.g., in a debt contract.

Bond Long-term debt.

Bookbuilding The procedure whereby *underwriters* gather nonbinding indications of demand for a new issue.

Book entry System whereby only one global certificate is issued for *bond* and evidence of ownership is receipt showing interest in this certificate.

Book runner The managing *underwriter* for a new issue. The book runner maintains the book of securities sold.

Bought deal Security issue where one or two *underwriters* buy the entire issue.

bp *Basis point.*

Bracket A term signifying the extent of an *underwriter's* commitment in a new issue, e.g., major bracket, minor bracket.

Break-even analysis Analysis of the level of sales at which a project would just break even.

Bridging loan Short-term loan to provide temporary financing until more permanent financing is arranged.

Bull–bear bond *Bond* whose *principal* repayment is linked to the price of another security. The bonds are issued in two *tranches:* In the first the repayment increases with the price of the other security; in the second the repayment decreases with the price of the other security.

Bulldog bond *Foreign bond* issue made in London.

Bullet payment Single final payment, e.g., of a loan (in contrast to payment in installments).

Bull market Widespread rise in security prices (cf. *bear market*).

Buy-back *Repurchase agreement.*

C

Cable The exchange rate between U.S. dollars and sterling.

Call option Option to buy an asset at a specified *exercise price* on or before a specified exercise date (cf. *put option*).

Call premium (1) Difference between the price at which a company can call its *bonds* and their *face value;* (2) price of an *option.*

Call provision Provision that allows an issuer to buy back the *bond* issue at a stated price.

Cap An upper limit on the interest rate on a *floating-rate note.*

Capital budget List of planned investment projects, usually prepared annually.

Capitalization Long-term debt plus *preferred stock* plus *net worth.*

Capital lease *Financial lease.*

Capital market Financial market (particularly the market for long-term securities).

Capital rationing Shortage of funds that forces a company to choose between worthwhile projects.

Capital structure Mix of different securities issued by a firm.

CAPM Capital asset pricing model.

CAR Cumulative *abnormal return.*

CARDs (Certificates for Amortizing Revolving Debt) *Pass-through securities* backed by credit card *receivables.*

CARs (Certificates of Automobile Receivables) *Pass-through securities* backed by automobile *receivables.*

Carve-out Public offering of shares in a subsidiary.

Cascade Rational herding in which each individual deduces that previous decisions by others may have been based on extra information.

Cash and carry Purchase of a security and simultaneous sale of a *future,* with the balance being financed with a loan or *repo.*

Cash budget Forecast of sources and uses of cash.

Cash-deficiency arrangement Arrangement whereby a project's shareholders agree to provide the operating company with sufficient *net working capital.*

CAT bond *Catastrophe bond.*

Catastrophe bond (CAT bond) *Bond* whose payoffs are linked to a measure of catastrophe losses such as insurance claims.

CD *Certificate of deposit.*

Certainty equivalent A certain cash flow that has the same present value as a specified risky cash flow.

Certificate of deposit (CD) A certificate providing evidence of a bank time deposit.

CFTC Commodity Futures Trading Commission.

CFO Chief financial officer.

Chaebol A Korean conglomerate.

CHIPS *Clearing House Interbank Payments System.*

Clean price (flat price) *Bond* price excluding *accrued interest* (cf. *dirty price*).

Clearing House Interbank Payments System (CHIPS) An international wire transfer system operated by a group of major banks for high-value dollar payments.

Closed-end mortgage Mortgage against which no additional debt may be issued (cf. *open-end mortgage*).

CMOs *Collateralized mortgage obligations.*

Collar An upper and lower limit on the interest rate on a *floating-rate note.*

Collateral Assets that are given as security for a loan.

Collateralized mortgage obligations (CMOs) A variation on the mortgage *pass-through security,* in which the cash flows from a pool of mortgages are repackaged into several *tranches* of *bonds* with different maturities.

Collateral trust bonds *Bonds* secured by *common stocks* or other securities that are owned by the borrower.

Collection float Customer-written checks that have not been received, deposited, and added to the company's available balance (cf. *payment float*).

Commercial draft (bill of exchange) Demand for payment.

Commercial paper Unsecured *notes* issued by companies and maturing within nine months.

Commitment fee Fee charged by bank on an unused *line of credit.*

Common stock Security representing ownership of a corporation.

Compensating balance Non-interest-bearing demand deposits to compensate banks for bank loans or services.

Competitive bidding Means by which public utility *holding companies* are required to choose their *underwriter* (cf. *negotiated underwriting*).

Completion bonding Insurance that a construction contract will be successfully completed.

Compound interest Reinvestment of each interest payment on money invested to earn more interest (cf. *simple interest*).

Compound option Option on an *option.*

Concentration banking System whereby customers make payments to a regional collection center. The collection center pays the funds into a regional bank account and surplus money is transferred to the company's principal bank.

Conditional sale Sale in which ownership does not pass to the buyer until payment is completed.

Conglomerate merger *Merger* between two companies in unrelated businesses (cf. *horizontal merger, vertical merger*).

Consol Name of a perpetual *bond* issued by the British government. Sometimes used as a general term for *perpetuity.*

Contango Condition in which *spot price* of a commodity is below that of the *future* (cf. *backwardation*).

Contingent claim Claim whose value depends on the value of another asset.

Contingent project Project that cannot be undertaken unless another project is also undertaken.

Continuous compounding Interest compounded continuously rather than at fixed intervals.

Controller Officer responsible for budgeting, accounting, and auditing in a firm (cf. *treasurer*).

Convenience yield The extra advantage that firms derive from holding the commodity rather than the *future.*

Conversion price *Par value* of a *convertible bond* divided by the number of shares into which it may be exchanged.

Conversion ratio Number of shares for which a *convertible bond* may be exchanged.

Convertible bond *Bond* that may be converted into another security at the holder's option. Similarly convertible *preferred stock.*

Convexity Term often used to describe the fact that the effect of an interest rate change on *bond* prices declines as the interest rate rises.

Correlation coefficient Measure of the closeness of the relationship between two variables.

Cost company arrangement Arrangement whereby the shareholders of a project receive output free of charge but agree to pay all operating and financing charges of the project.

Cost of capital *Opportunity cost of capital.*

Coupon (1) Specifically, an attachment to the certificate of a *bearer security* that must be surrendered to collect interest payment; (2) more generally, interest payment on debt.

Covariance Measure of the comovement between two variables.

Covenant Clause in a loan agreement.

Credit derivative Contract for *hedging* against loan default or changes in credit risk (see *default swap, credit option*).

Credit option Similar to a long-term insurance policy against loan default.

Credit scoring A procedure for assigning scores to borrowers on the basis of the risk of default.

Cross-default clause Clause in a loan agreement stating that the company is in default if it fails to meet its obligation on any other debt issue.

Cum dividend *With dividend.*

Cum rights *With rights.*

Cumulative preferred stock Stock that takes priority over *common stock* in regard to dividend payments. Dividends may not be paid on the common stock until all past *dividends* on the *preferred stock* have been paid.

Cumulative voting Voting system under which a stockholder may cast all of his or her votes for one candidate for the board of directors (cf. *majority voting*).

Current asset Asset that will normally be turned into cash within a year.

Current liability Liability that will normally be repaid within a year.

Current ratio *Current assets* divided by *current liabilities*—a measure of liquidity.

D

DCF *Discounted cash flow.*

Debenture Unsecured *bond.*

Decision tree Method of representing alternative sequential decisions and the possible outcomes from these decisions.

Default swap *Credit derivative* in which one party makes fixed payments while the payments by the other party depend on the occurrence of a loan default.

Defeasance Practice whereby the borrower sets aside cash or *bonds* sufficient to service the borrower's debt. Both the borrower's debt and the offsetting cash or bonds are removed from the balance sheet.

Delta *Hedge ratio.*

Depository transfer check (DTC) Check made out directly by a local bank to a particular company.

Depreciation (1) Reduction in the book or market value of an asset; (2) portion of an investment that can be deducted from taxable income.

Derivative Asset whose value derives from that of some other asset (e.g., a *future* or an *option*).

Diff *Differential swap.*

Differential swap (diff, quanto swap) Swap between two *LIBOR* rates of interest, e.g., yen LIBOR for dollar LIBOR. Payments are in one currency.

Dilution Diminution in the proportion of income to which each share is entitled.

Direct lease *Lease* in which the *lessor* purchases new equipment from the manufacturer and leases it to the *lessee* (cf. *sale and lease-back*).

Direct quote For foreign exchange, the number of U.S. dollars needed to buy one unit of a foreign currency (cf. *indirect quote*).

Dirty price *Bond* price including *accrued interest*, i.e., the price paid by the bond buyer (cf. *clean price*).

Discount bond Debt sold for less than its *principal* value. If a discount bond pays no interest, it is called a "pure" discount, or *zero-coupon*, bond.

Discounted cash flow (DCF) Future cash flows multiplied by *discount factors* to obtain *present value.*

Discount factor *Present value* of $1 received at a stated future date.

Discount rate Rate used to calculate the *present value* of future cash flows.

Discriminatory price auction Auction in which successful bidders pay the price that they bid (cf. *uniform price auction*).

Disintermediation Withdrawal of funds from a financial institution in order to invest them directly (cf. *intermediation*).

Dividend Payment by a company to its stockholders.

Dividend reinvestment plan (DRIP) Plan that allows shareholders to reinvest dividends automatically.

Dividend yield Annual *dividend* divided by share price.

Double-declining-balance depreciation Method of *accelerated depreciation.*

Double-tax agreement Agreement between two countries that taxes paid abroad can be offset against domestic taxes levied on foreign *dividends.*

Down-and-in option *Barrier option* that comes into existence if asset price hits a barrier.

Down-and-out option *Barrier option* that expires if asset price hits a barrier.

DRIP *Dividend reinvestment plan.*

Drop lock An arrangement whereby the interest rate on a *floating-rate note* or *preferred stock* becomes fixed if it falls to a specified level.

DTC *Depository transfer check.*

Dual-currency bond *Bond* with interest paid in one currency and *principal* paid in another.

Duration The average number of years to an asset's *discounted cash flows.*

E

EBIT Earnings before interest and taxes.

Economic exposure Risk that arises from changes in real exchange rates (cf. *transaction exposure, translation exposure*).

Economic income Cash flow plus change in *present value.*

Economic rents Profits in excess of the competitive level.

Economic Value Added (EVA) A measure of *residual income* implemented by the consulting firm Stern Stewart.

Efficient market Market in which security prices reflect information instantaneously.

Efficient portfolio Portfolio that offers the lowest risk (*standard deviation*) for its *expected return* and the highest expected return for its level of risk.

Employee stock ownership plan (ESOP) A company contributes to a trust fund that buys stock on behalf of employees.

EPS Earnings per share.

Equipment trust certificate Form of *secured debt* generally used to finance railroad equipment. The trustee retains ownership of the equipment until the debt is repaid.

Equity (1) *Common stock* and *preferred stock.* Often used to refer to common stock only. (2) *Net worth.*

Equivalent annual cash flow *Annuity* with the same *net present value* as the company's proposed investment.

ESOP *Employee stock ownership plan.*

Euribor *Euro Interbank Offered Rate.*

Euro Interbank Offered Rate (Euribor) The interest rate at which major international banks in Europe lend euros to each other.

Eurobond *Bond* that is marketed internationally.

Eurodollar deposit Dollar deposit with a bank outside the United States.

European option *Option* that can be exercised only on final exercise date (cf. *American option*).

EVA *Economic Value Added.*

Evergreen credit *Revolving credit* without maturity.

Exchange of assets Acquisition of another company by purchase of its assets in exchange for cash or shares.

Exchange of stock Acquisition of another company by purchase of its stock in exchange for cash or shares.

Ex dividend Purchase of shares in which the buyer is not entitled to the forthcoming *dividend* (cf. *with dividend, cum dividend*).

Exercise price (striking price) Price at which a *call option* or *put option* may be exercised.

Expectations hypothesis Theory that *forward interest rate* (*forward exchange rate*) equals expected *spot rate.*

Expected return Average of possible returns weighted by their probabilities.

Ex rights Purchase of shares in which the buyer is not entitled to the rights to buy shares in the company's *rights issue* (cf. *with rights, cum rights, rights on*).

Extendable bond *Bond* whose maturity can be extended at the option of the lender (or issuer).

External finance Finance that is not generated by the firm: new borrowing or an issue of stock (cf. *internal finance*).

Extra dividend *Dividend* that may or may not be repeated (cf. *regular dividend*).

F

Face value *Par value.*

Factoring Arrangement whereby a financial institution buys a company's *accounts receivable* and collects the debt.

Fair price provision *Appraisal* rights.

FASB Financial Accounting Standards Board.

FCIA Foreign Credit Insurance Association.

FDIC Federal Deposit Insurance Corporation.

Federal funds Non-interest-bearing deposits by banks at the Federal Reserve. Excess reserves are lent by banks to each other.

Fedwire A wire transfer system for high-value payments operated by the Federal Reserve System (cf. *CHIPS*).

Field warehouse Warehouse rented by a warehouse company on another firm's premises (cf. *public warehouse*).

Financial assets Claims on *real assets.*

Financial engineering Combining or dividing existing instruments to create new financial products.

Financial lease (capital lease, full-payout lease) Long-term, noncancelable *lease* (cf. *operating lease*).

Financial leverage (gearing) Use of debt to increase the *expected return* on *equity.* Financial leverage is measured by the ratio of debt to debt plus equity (cf. *operating leverage*).

Fiscal agency agreement An alternative to a bond *trust deed.* Unlike the trustee, the fiscal agent acts as an agent of the borrower.

Flat price *Clean price.*

Float *See availability float, payment float.*

Floating lien General *lien* against a company's assets or against a particular class of assets.

Floating-rate note (FRN) *Note* whose interest payment varies with the short-term interest rate.

Floating-rate preferred *Preferred stock* paying dividends that vary with short-term interest rates.

Floor planning Arrangement used to finance inventory. A finance company buys the inventory, which is then held in trust by the user.

Foreign bond A *bond* issued on the domestic *capital market* of another country.

Forex Foreign exchange.

Forfaiter Purchaser of promises to pay (e.g., *bills of exchange* or *promissory notes*) issued by importers.

Forward cover Purchase or sale of forward foreign currency in order to offset a known future cash flow.

Forward exchange rate Exchange rate fixed today for exchanging currency at some future date (cf. *spot exchange rate*).

Forward interest rate Interest rate fixed today on a loan to be made at some future date (cf. *spot interest rate*).

Forward rate agreement (FRA) Agreement to borrow or lend at a specified future date at an interest rate that is fixed today.

FRA *Forward rate agreement.*

Free cash flow Cash not required for operations or for reinvestment.

FRN *Floating-rate note.*

Full-payout lease *Financial lease.*

Full-service lease (rental lease) *Lease* in which the *lessor* promises to maintain and insure the equipment (cf. *net lease*).

Fundamental analysis Security analysis that seeks to detect misvalued securities by an analysis of the firm's business prospects (cf. *technical analysis*).

Funded debt Debt maturing after more than one year (cf. *unfunded debt*).

Future A contract to buy a commodity or security on a future date at a price that is fixed today. Unlike forward contracts, futures are generally traded on organized exchanges and are *marked to market* daily.

G

GAAP Generally accepted accounting principles.

Gearing *Financial leverage.*

General cash offer Issue of securities offered to all investors (cf. *rights issue*).

Golden parachute A large termination payment due to a company's management if they lose their jobs as a result of a merger.

Goodwill The difference between the amount paid for a firm in a *merger* and its book value.

Gray market Purchases and sales of *eurobonds* that occur before the issue price is made.

Greenmail Situation in which a large block of stock is held by an unfriendly company, forcing the target company to repurchase the stock at a substantial premium to prevent a takeover.

Greenshoe option *Option* that allows the *underwriter* for a new issue to buy and resell additional shares.

Growth stock *Common stock* of a company that has an opportunity to invest money to earn more than the *opportunity cost of capital* (cf. *income stock*).

H

Haircut An additional margin of *collateral* for a loan.

Hedge ratio (delta, option delta) The number of shares to buy for each *option* sold in order to create a safe position; more generally, the number of units of an asset that should be bought to hedge one unit of a liability.

Hedging Buying one security and selling another in order to reduce risk. A perfect hedge produces a riskless portfolio.

Hell-or-high-water clause Clause in a *lease* agreement that obligates the *lessee* to make payments regardless of what happens to the *lessor* or the equipment.

Highly leveraged transaction (HLT) Bank loan to a highly leveraged firm (formerly needed to be separately reported to the Federal Reserve Board).

HLT *Highly leveraged transaction.*

Holding company Company whose sole function is to hold stock in other companies or subsidiaries.

Horizontal merger Merger between two companies that manufacture similar products (cf. *vertical merger, conglomerate merger*).

Horizontal spread The simultaneous purchase and sale of two *options* that differ only in their exercise date (cf. *vertical spread*).

Hurdle rate Minimum acceptable rate of return on a project.

I

IBF *International Banking Facility.*

IMM *International Monetary Market.*

Immunization The construction of an asset and a liability that are subject to offsetting changes in value.

Imputation tax system Arrangement by which investors who receive a *dividend* also receive a tax credit for corporate taxes that the firm has paid.

Income bond *Bond* on which interest is payable only if earned.

Income stock *Common stock* with high *dividend yield* and few profitable investment opportunities (cf. *growth stock*).

Indenture Formal agreement, e.g., establishing the terms of a *bond* issue.

Indexed bond *Bond* whose payments are linked to an index, e.g., a consumer price index (see *TIPs*).

Index fund Investment fund designed to match the returns on a stockmarket index.

Indirect quote For foreign exchange, the number of units of a foreign currency needed to buy one U.S. dollar (cf. *direct quote*).

Industrial revenue bond (IRB) Bond issued by local government agencies on behalf of corporations.

Initial public offering (IPO) A company's first public issue of *common stock.*

In-substance defeasance *Defeasance* whereby debt is removed from the balance sheet but not canceled (cf. *novation*).

Intangible asset Nonmaterial asset, such as technical expertise, a trademark, or a patent (cf. *tangible asset*).

Integer programming Variant of *linear programming* whereby the solution values must be integers.

Interest cover *Times interest earned.*

Interest equalization tax Tax on foreign investment by residents of the United States (abolished 1974).

Interest-rate parity Theory that the differential between the *forward exchange rate* and the *spot exchange rate* is equal to the differential between the foreign and domestic interest rates.

Intermediation Investment through a financial institution (cf. *disintermediation*).

Internal finance Finance generated within a firm by *retained earnings* and *depreciation* (cf. *external finance*).

Internal growth rate The maximum rate of firm growth without *external finance* (cf. *sustainable growth rate*).

Internal rate of return (IRR) *Discount rate* at which investment has zero *net present value.*

International Banking Facility (IBF) A branch that an American bank establishes in the United States to do eurocurrency business.

International Monetary Market (IMM) The financial futures market within the Chicago Mercantile Exchange.

Interval measure The number of days that a firm can finance operations without additional cash income.

In-the-money option An *option* that would be worth exercising if it expired immediately (cf. *out-of-the-money option*).

Inverse FRN *Floating-rate note* whose payments rise as the general level of interest rates falls and vice versa.

Investment-grade bond *Bond* rated at least Baa by Moody's or BBB by Standard and Poor's.

Investment tax credit Proportion of new capital investment that can be used to reduce a company's tax bill (abolished 1986).

IPO *Initial public offering.*

IRB *Industrial revenue bond.*

IRR *Internal rate of return.*

IRS Internal Revenue Service.

ISDA International Swap and Derivatives Association.

ISMA International Securities Market Association.

Issued share capital Total amount of shares that are in issue (cf. *outstanding share capital*).

J

Junior debt *Subordinated debt.*

Junk bond Debt that is rated below an *investment-grade bond.*

K

Keiretsu A network of Japanese companies organized around a major bank.

L

LBO *Leveraged buyout.*

Lease Long-term rental agreement.

Legal capital Value at which a company's shares are recorded in its books.

Legal defeasance *Novation.*

Lessee User of a leased asset (cf. *lessor*).

Lessor Owner of a leased asset (cf. *lessee*).

Letter of credit Letter from a bank stating that it has established a credit in the company's favor.

Letter stock Privately placed *common stock,* so-called because the *SEC* requires a letter from the purchaser that the stock is not intended for resale.

Leverage See *financial leverage, operating leverage.*

Leveraged buyout (LBO) Acquisition in which (1) a large part of the purchase price is debt-financed and (2) the remaining *equity* is privately held by a small group of investors.

Leveraged lease *Lease* in which the *lessor* finances part of the cost of the asset by an issue of debt secured by the asset and the lease payments.

Liabilities, total liabilities Total value of financial claims on a firm's assets. Equals (1) total assets or (2) total assets minus *net worth.*

LIBOR *London interbank offered rate.*

Lien Lender's claims on specified assets.

Limited liability Limitation of a shareholder's losses to the amount invested.

Limited partnership *Partnership* in which some partners have *limited liability* and general partners have unlimited liability.

Linear programming (LP) Technique for finding the maximum value of some equation subject to stated linear constraints.

Line of credit Agreement by a bank that a company may borrow at any time up to an established limit.

Liquid asset Asset that is easily and cheaply turned into cash—notably cash itself and short-term securities.

Liquidating dividend *Dividend* that represents a return of capital.

Liquidator Person appointed by unsecured creditors in the United Kingdom to oversee the sale of an insolvent firm's assets and the repayment of debts.

Liquidity premium (1) Additional return for investing in a security that cannot easily be turned into cash; (2) difference between the *forward interest rate* and the expected *spot interest rate.*

Liquid yield option note (LYON) *Zero-coupon,* callable, puttable, *convertible bond.*

Load-to-load Arrangement whereby the customer pays for the last delivery when the next one is received.

Lock-box system Form of *concentration banking.* Customers send payments to a post office box. A local bank collects and processes the checks and transfers surplus funds to the company's principal bank.

London interbank offered rate (LIBOR) The interest rate at which major international banks in London lend to each other. (LIBID is London interbank bid rate; LIMEAN is mean of bid and offered rate.)

Long hedge Purchase of a *hedging* instrument (e.g., a *future*) to hedge a short position in the underlying asset (cf. *short hedge*).

Lookback option *Option* whose payoff depends on the highest asset price recorded over the life of the option.

LP *Linear programming.*

LYON *Liquid yield option note.*

M

MACRS *Modified accelerated cost recovery system.*

Maintenance margin Minimum margin that must be maintained on a *futures* contract.

Majority voting Voting system under which each director is voted upon separately (cf. *cumulative voting*).

Management buyout (MBO) *Leveraged buyout* whereby the acquiring group is led by the firm's management.

Margin Cash or securities set aside by an investor as evidence that he or she can honor a commitment.

Marked-to-market An arrangement whereby the profits or losses on a *futures* contract are settled up each day.

Market capitalization rate *Expected return* on a security.

Market risk (systematic risk) Risk that cannot be diversified away.

Maturity factoring *Factoring* arrangement that provides collection and insurance of *accounts receivable.*

MBO *Management buyout.*

MDA *Multiple-discriminant analysis.*

Medium-term note (MTN) Debt with a typical maturity of 1 to 10 years offered regularly by a company using the same procedure as *commercial paper.*

Merger (1) Acquisition in which all assets and liabilities are absorbed by the buyer (cf. *exchange of assets, exchange of stock*); (2) more generally, any combination of two companies.

MIP (Monthly income preferred security) *Preferred stock* issued by a subsidiary located in a tax haven. The subsidiary relends the money to the parent.

Mismatch bond *Floating-rate note* whose interest rate is reset at more frequent intervals than the rollover period (e.g., a note whose payments are set quarterly on the basis of the one-year interest rate).

Modified accelerated cost recovery system (MACRS) Schedule of *depreciation* deductions allowed for tax purposes.

Money center bank A major U.S. bank that undertakes a wide range of banking activities.

Money market Market for short-term safe investments.

Money-market fund *Mutual fund* that invests solely in short-term safe securities.

Monte Carlo simulation Method for calculating the probability distribution of possible outcomes, e.g., from a project.

Moral hazard The risk that the existence of a contract will change the behavior of one or both parties to the contract; e.g., an insured firm may take fewer fire precautions.

Mortgage bond *Bond* secured against plant and equipment.

MTN *Medium-term note.*

Multiple-discriminant analysis (MDA) Statistical technique for distinguishing between two groups on the basis of their observed characteristics.

Mutual fund Managed investment fund whose shares are sold to investors.

Mutually exclusive projects Two projects that cannot both be undertaken.

N

Naked option *Option* held on its own, i.e., not used for *hedging* a holding in the asset or other options.

NASD National Association of Security Dealers.

Negative pledge clause Clause under which the borrower agrees not to permit an exclusive *lien* on any of its assets.

Negotiated underwriting Method of choosing an *underwriter.* Most firms may choose their *underwriter* by negotiation (cf. *competitive bidding*).

Net lease *Lease* in which the *lessee* promises to maintain and insure the equipment (cf. *full-service lease*).

Net present value (NPV) A project's net contribution to wealth—*present value* minus initial investment.

Net working capital *Current assets* minus *current liabilities.*

Net worth Book value of a company's *common stock,* surplus, and *retained earnings.*

Nominal interest rate Interest rate expressed in money terms (cf. *real interest rate*).

Nonrefundable debt Debt that may not be called in order to replace it with another issue at a lower interest cost.

Normal distribution Symmetric bell-shaped distribution that can be completely defined by its mean and *standard deviation.*

Note Unsecured debt with a maturity of up to 10 years.

Novation (legal defeasance) *Defeasance* whereby the firm's debt is canceled (cf. *in-substance defeasance*).

NPV *Net present value.*

NYSE New York Stock Exchange.

O

Odd lot A trade of less than 100 shares (cf. *round lot*).

Off-balance-sheet financing Financing that is not shown as a liability in a company's balance sheet.

Offer price *Ask price.*

OID debt *Original issue discount debt.*

Old-line factoring *Factoring* arrangement that provides collection, insurance, and finance for *accounts receivable.*

On the run The most recently issued (and, therefore, typically the most liquid) government *bond* in a particular maturity range.

Open account Arrangement whereby sales are made with no formal debt contract. The buyer signs a receipt, and the seller records the sale in the sales ledger.

Open-end mortgage Mortgage against which additional debt may be issued (cf. *closed-end mortgage*).

Open interest The number of currently outstanding *futures* contracts.

Operating lease Short-term, cancelable *lease* (cf. *financial lease*).

Operating leverage Fixed operating costs, so-called because they accentuate variations in profits (cf. *financial leverage*).

Opportunity cost of capital (hurdle rate, cost of capital) *Expected return* that is forgone by investing in a project rather than in comparable financial securities.

Option See *call option, put option.*

Option delta *Hedge ratio.*

Original issue discount debt (OID debt) Debt that is initially offered at a price below *face value.*

OTC *Over-the-counter.*

Out-of-the-money option An *option* that would not be worth exercising if it matured immediately (cf. *in-the-money option*).

Outstanding share capital *Issued share capital* less the *par value* of shares that are held in the company's treasury.

Oversubscription privilege In a *rights issue,* arrangement by which shareholders are given the right to apply for any shares that are not taken up.

Over-the-counter (OTC) Informal market that does not involve a securities exchange. Specifically used to refer to the NASDAQ dealer market for *common stocks.*

P

Partnership Joint ownership of business whereby general partners have unlimited liability.

Par value (face value) Value of a security shown on the certificate.

Pass-through securities *Notes* or *bonds* backed by a package of assets (e.g., mortgage pass-throughs, *CARs, CARDs*).

Path-dependent option *Option* whose value depends on the sequence of prices of the underlying asset rather than just the final price of the asset.

Payables *Accounts payable.*

Payback period Time taken for a project to recover its initial investment.

Pay-in-kind bond (PIK) *Bond* that allows the issuer to choose to make interest payments in the form of additional bonds.

Payment float Company-written checks that have not yet cleared (cf. *availability float*).

Payout ratio *Dividend* as a proportion of earnings per share.

PBGC Pension Benefit Guarantee Corporation.

P/E ratio Share price divided by earnings per share.

PERC (Preferred equity redemption cumulative stock) *Preferred stock* that converts automatically into equity at a stated date. A limit is placed on the value of the shares that the investor receives.

Perpetuity Investment offering a level stream of cash flows in perpetuity (cf. *consol*).

PIK *Pay-in-kind bond.*

PN *Project note.*

Poison pill An issue of securities that is convertible, in the event of a *merger,* into the shares of the acquiring firm or must be repurchased by the acquiring firm.

Poison put A *covenant* allowing the *bond*holder to demand repayment in the event of a hostile *merger.*

Pooling of interest Method of accounting for *mergers* (no longer available in the USA). The consolidated balance sheet of the merged firm is obtained by combining the balance sheets of the separate firms (cf. *purchase accounting*).

Position diagram Diagram showing the possible payoffs from a *derivative* investment.

Postaudit Evaluation of an investment project after it has been undertaken.

Preemptive right Common stockholder's right to anything of value distributed by the company.

Preferred stock Stock that takes priority over common stock in regard to *dividends.* Dividends may not be paid on *common stock* unless the dividend is paid on all preferred stock (cf. *cumulative preferred stock*). The dividend rate on preferred is usually fixed at time of issue.

Prepack *Prepackaged bankruptcy.*

Prepackaged bankruptcy (prepack) Bankruptcy proceedings intended to confirm a reorganization plan that has already been agreed to informally.

Present value Discounted value of future cash flows.

Present value of growth opportunities (PVGO) *Net present value* of investments the firm is expected to make in the future.

PRIDE Similar to a *PERC* except that as the equity price rises beyond a specified point, the investor shares in the stock appreciation.

Primary issue Issue of new securities by a firm (cf. *secondary issue*).

Prime rate Benchmark lending rate set by U.S. banks.

Principal Amount of debt that must be repaid.

Principal–agent problem Problem faced by a principal (e.g., shareholder) in ensuring that an agent (e.g., manager) acts on his or her behalf.

Privileged subscription issue *Rights issue.*

Production payment Loan in the form of advance payment for future delivery of a product.

Profitability index Ratio of a project's *NPV* to the initial investment.

Pro forma Projected.

Project finance Debt that is largely a claim against the cash flows from a particular project rather than against the firm as a whole.

Project note (PN) *Note* issued by public housing or urban renewal agencies.

Promissory note Promise to pay.

Prospectus Summary of the *registration* statement providing information on an issue of securities.

Proxy vote Vote cast by one person on behalf of another.

Public warehouse (terminal warehouse) Warehouse operated by an independent warehouse company on its own premises (cf. *field warehouse*).

Purchase accounting Method of accounting for *mergers.* The assets of the acquired firm are shown at market value on the balance sheet of the acquiror (cf. *pooling of interest*).

Purchase fund Resembles a *sinking fund* except that money is used only to purchase bonds if they are selling below their *par value.*

Put option *Option* to sell an asset at a specified *exercise price* on or before a specified exercise date (cf. *call option*).

PVGO *Present value of growth opportunities.*

Q

q Ratio of the market value of an asset to its replacement cost.

QIBs *Qualified Institutional Buyers.*

Quadratic programming Variant of *linear programming* whereby the equations are quadratic rather than linear.

Qualified Institutional Buyers (QIBs) Institutions that are allowed to trade unregistered stock among themselves.

Quanto swap *Differential swap.*

Quick ratio (acid-test ratio) Measure of liquidity: (*current assets* – inventory) divided by *current liabilities.*

R

Range forward A *forward exchange rate* contract that places upper and lower bounds on the cost of foreign exchange.

Real assets *Tangible assets* and *intangible assets* used to carry on business (cf. *financial assets*).

Real estate investment trust (REIT) Trust company formed to invest in real estate.

Real interest rate Interest rate expressed in terms of real goods, i.e., *nominal interest rate* adjusted for inflation.

Receivables *Accounts receivable.*

Receiver A bankruptcy practitioner appointed by secured creditors in the United Kingdom to oversee the repayment of debts.

Record date Date set by directors when making dividend payment. *Dividends* are sent to stockholders who are registered on the record date.

Recourse Term describing a type of loan. If a loan is with recourse, the lender has a general claim against the parent company if the *collateral* is insufficient to repay the debt.

Red herring Preliminary *prospectus.*

Refunding Replacement of existing debt with a new issue of debt.

Registered security Security whose ownership is recorded by the company's *registrar* (cf. *bearer security*).

Registrar Financial institution appointed to record issue and ownership of company securities.

Registration Process of obtaining *SEC* approval for a public issue of securities.

Regression analysis In statistics, a technique for finding the line of best fit.

Regular dividend *Dividend* that the company expects to maintain in the future.

Regulation A issue Small security issues that are partially exempt from *SEC registration* requirements.

REIT *Real estate investment trust.*

Rental lease *Full-service lease.*

Repo *Repurchase agreement.*

Repurchase agreement (RP, repo, buy-back) Purchase of Treasury securities from a securities dealer with an agreement that the dealer will repurchase them at a specified price.

Residual income After-tax profit less the *opportunity cost of capital* employed by the business (see also *Economic Value Added*).

Residual risk *Unique risk.*

Retained earnings Earnings not paid out as *dividends.*

Return on equity Usually, equity earnings as a proportion of the book value of equity.

Return on investment (ROI) Generally, book income as a proportion of net book value.

Revolving credit Legally assured *line of credit* with a bank.

Rights issue (privileged subscription issue) Issue of securities offered to current stockholders (cf. *general cash offer*).

Rights on *With rights.*

Risk premium Expected additional return for making a risky investment rather than a safe one.

ROI *Return on investment.*

Roll-over CD A package of successive *certificates of deposit.*

Round lot A trade of 100 shares (cf. *odd lot*).

RP *Repurchase agreement.*

R squared (R^2) Square of the *correlation coefficient*—the proportion of the variability in one series that can be explained by the variability of one or more other series.

Rule 144a *SEC* rule allowing *qualified institutional buyers* to buy and trade unregistered securities.

S

Sale and lease-back Sale of an existing asset to a financial institution that then *leases* it back to the user (cf. *direct lease*).

Salvage value Scrap value of plant and equipment.

Samurai bond A yen *bond* issued in Tokyo by a non-Japanese borrower (cf. *bulldog bond, Yankee bond*).

SBIC Small Business Investment Company.

Seasoned issue Issue of a security for which there is an existing market (cf. *unseasoned issue*).

Season datings Extended credit for customers who order goods out of the peak season.

SEC Securities and Exchange Commission.

Secondary issue (1) Procedure for selling blocks of *seasoned issues* of stock; (2) more generally, sale of already issued stock.

Secondary market Market in which one can buy or sell *seasoned issues* of securities.

Secured debt Debt that, in the event of default, has first claim on specified assets.

Securitization Substitution of tradable securities for privately negotiated instruments.

Security market line Line representing the relationship between *expected return* and *market risk.*

Self-liquidating loan Loan to finance *current assets.* The sale of the current assets provides the cash to repay the loan.

Self-selection Consequence of a contract that induces only one group (e.g., low-risk individuals) to participate.

Semistrong-form efficient market Market in which security prices reflect all publicly available information (cf. *weak-form efficient market* and *strong-form efficient market*).

Senior debt Debt that, in the event of bankruptcy, must be repaid before *subordinated debt* receives any payment.

Sensitivity analysis Analysis of the effect on project profitability of possible changes in sales, costs, and so on.

Serial bonds Package of *bonds* that mature in successive years.

Series bond *Bond* that may be issued in several series under the same *indenture.*

Shark repellant Amendment to company charter intended to protect against takeover.

Shelf registration A procedure that allows firms to file one *registration* statement covering several issues of the same security.

Shogun bond Dollar *bond* issued in Japan by a nonresident.

Short hedge Sale of a *hedging* instrument (e.g., a *future*) to *hedge* a long position in the underlying asset (cf. *long hedge*).

Short sale Sale of a security the investor does not own.

Sight draft Demand for immediate payment (cf. *time draft*).

Signal Action that demonstrates an individual's unobservable characteristics (because it would be unduly costly for someone without those characteristics to take the action).

Simple interest Interest calculated only on the initial investment (cf. *compound interest*).

Simulation *Monte Carlo simulation.*

Sinker *Sinking fund.*

Sinking fund (sinker) Fund established by a company to retire debt before maturity.

Skewed distribution Probability distribution in which an unequal number of observations lie below and above the mean.

Special dividend (extra dividend) *Dividend* that is unlikely to be repeated.

Specific risk *Unique risk.*

Spin-off Distribution of shares in a subsidiary to the company's shareholders so that they hold shares separately in the two firms.

Spot exchange rate Exchange rate on currency for immediate delivery (cf. *forward exchange rate*)

Spot interest rate Interest rate fixed today on a loan that is made today (cf. *forward interest rate*).

Spot price Price of asset for immediate delivery (in contrast to forward or futures price).

Spread Difference between the price at which an *underwriter* buys an issue from a firm and the price at which the underwriter sells it to the public.

Standard deviation Square root of the *variance*—a measure of variability.

Standard error In statistics, a measure of the possible error in an estimate.

Standby agreement In a *rights issue,* agreement that the *underwriter* will purchase any stock not purchased by investors.

Step-up bond *Bond* whose *coupon* is stepped up over time (also step-down bond).

Stock dividend *Dividend* in the form of stock rather than cash.

Stock split "Free" issue of shares to existing shareholders.

Straddle The combination of a *put option* and a *call option* with the same *exercise price.*

Straight-line depreciation An equal dollar amount of *depreciation* in each period.

Striking price *Exercise price* of an *option.*

Stripped bond *Bond* that can be subdivided into a series of *zero-coupon bonds.*

Strong-form efficient market Market in which security prices reflect instantaneously *all* information available to investors (cf. *weak-form efficient market* and *semistrong-form efficient market*).

Structured debt Debt that has been customized for the buyer, often by incorporating unusual *options.*

Subordinated debt (junior debt) Debt over which *senior debt* takes priority. In the event of bankruptcy, subordinated debtholders receive payment only after senior debt is paid off in full.

Sum-of-the-years'-digits depreciation Method of *accelerated depreciation.*

Sunk costs Costs that have been incurred and cannot be reversed.

Supermajority Provision in a company's charter requiring a majority of, say, 80 percent of shareholders to approve certain changes, such as a *merger.*

Sushi bond A *eurobond* issued by a Japanese corporation.

Sustainable growth rate Maximum rate of firm growth without increasing financial leverage (cf. *internal growth rate*).

Swap An arrangement whereby two companies lend to each other on different terms, e.g., in different currencies, or one at a fixed rate and the other at a floating rate.

Swaption *Option* on a *swap.*

Swingline facility Bank borrowing facility to provide finance while the firm replaces U.S. *commercial paper* with eurocommercial paper.

Systematic risk *Market risk.*

T

Take-up fee Fee paid to *underwriters* of a *rights issue* on any stock they are obliged to purchase.

Tangible asset Physical asset, such as plant, machinery, and offices (cf. *intangible assets*).

Tax-anticipation bill Short-term bill issued by the U.S. Treasury that can be surrendered at *face value* in payment of taxes.

T-bill *Treasury bill.*

Technical analysis Security analysis that seeks to detect and interpret patterns in past security prices (cf. *fundamental analysis*).

TED spread Difference between *LIBOR* and U.S. *Treasury bill* rate.

Tender offer General offer made directly to a firm's shareholders to buy their stock.

Tenor Maturity of a loan.

Terminal warehouse *Public warehouse.*

Term loan Medium-term, privately placed loan, usually made by a bank.

Term structure of interest rates Relationship between interest rates on loans of different maturities (cf. *yield curve*).

Throughput arrangement Arrangement by which shareholders of a pipeline company agree to make sufficient use of pipeline to enable the pipeline company to service its debt.

Tick Minimum amount the price of a security may change.

Time draft Demand for payment at a stated future date (cf. *sight draft*).

Times interest earned (interest cover) Earnings before interest and tax, divided by interest payments.

TIPS (Treasury Inflation Protected Securities) U.S. Treasury *bonds* whose *coupon* and *principal* payments are linked to the Consumer Price Index.

Tombstone Advertisement listing the *underwriters* to a security issue.

Trade acceptance Written demand that has been accepted by an industrial company to pay a given sum at a future date (cf. *banker's acceptance*).

Trade credit *Accounts receivable.*

Trade debt *Accounts payable.*

Tranche Portion of a new issue sold at a point in time different from the remainder or that has different terms.

Transaction exposure Risk to a firm with known future cash flows in a foreign currency that arises from possible changes in the exchange rate (cf. *economic exposure, translation exposure*).

Transfer agent Individual or institution appointed by a company to look after the transfer of securities.

Translation exposure Risk of adverse effects on a firm's financial statements that may arise from changes in exchange rates (cf. *economic exposure, transaction exposure*).

Treasurer Principal financial manager (cf. *controller*).

Treasury bill (T-bill) Short-term discount debt maturing in less than one year, issued regularly by the government.

Treasury stock *Common stock* that has been repurchased by the company and held in the company's treasury.

Trust deed Agreement between trustee and borrower setting out terms of *bond.*

Trust receipt Receipt for goods that are to be held in trust for the lender.

U

Underpricing Issue of securities below their market value.

Underwriter Firm that buys an issue of securities from a company and resells it to investors.

Unfunded debt Debt maturing within one year (cf. *funded debt*).

Uniform price auction Auction in which all successful bidders pay the same price (cf. *discriminatory price auction*).

Unique risk (residual risk, specific risk, unsystematic risk) Risk that can be eliminated by diversification.

Unseasoned issue Issue of a security for which there is no existing market (cf. *seasoned issue*).

Unsystematic risk *Unique risk.*

V

Value additivity Rule that the value of the whole must equal the sum of the values of the parts.

Value-at-risk model (VAR model) Procedure for estimating the probability of portfolio losses exceeding some specified proportion.

Vanilla issue Issue without unusual features.

Variable-rate demand bond (VRDB) Floating-rate *bond* that can be sold back periodically to the issuer.

Variance Mean squared deviation from the expected value—a measure of variability.

Variation margin The daily gains or losses on a *futures* contract credited to the investor's margin account.

VAR model *Value-at-risk model.*

Venture capital Capital to finance a new firm.

Vertical merger *Merger* between a supplier and its customer (cf. *horizontal merger, conglomerate merger*).

Vertical spread Simultaneous purchase and sale of two options that differ only in their *exercise price* (cf. *horizontal spread*).

VRDB *Variable rate demand bond.*

W

WACC *Weighted-average cost of capital.*

Warehouse receipt Evidence that a firm owns goods stored in a warehouse.

Warrant Long-term *call option* issued by a company.

Weak-form efficient market Market in which security prices instantaneously reflect the information in the history of security prices. In such a market security prices follow a random walk (cf. *semistrong-form efficient market* and *strong-form efficient market*).

Weighted-average cost of capital (WACC) *Expected return* on a portfolio of all the firm's securities. Used as *hurdle rate* for capital investment.

White knight A friendly potential acquirer sought out by a target company threatened by a less welcome suitor.

Wi. When issued.

Winner's curse Problem faced by uninformed bidders. For example, in an *initial public offering* uninformed participants are likely to receive larger allotments of issues that informed participants know are overpriced.

With dividend (cum dividend) Purchase of shares in which the buyer is entitled to the forthcoming *dividend* (cf. *ex dividend*).

Withholding tax Tax levied on *dividends* paid abroad.

With rights (cum rights, rights on) Purchase of shares in which the buyer is entitled to the rights to buy shares in the company's *rights issue* (cf. *ex rights*).

Working capital *Current assets* and *current liabilities.* The term is commonly used as synonymous with *net working capital.*

Workout Informal arrangement between a borrower and creditors.

Writer *Option* seller.

Y

Yankee bond A dollar *bond* issued in the United States by a non-U.S. borrower (cf. *bulldog bond, Samurai bond*).

Yield curve *Term structure of interest rates.*

Yield to maturity *Internal rate of return* on a bond.

Z

Zero-coupon bond *Discount bond* making no *coupon* payments.

Z score Measure of the likelihood of bankruptcy.

GLOBAL INDEX

E

F

G

H

I

J

K

L

M

N

O

P

Q

R

S

INDEX

C

D

E

F

J

K

L

M

N

O

Q

R

S